CASES, MATERIALS AND COMMENTARY ON ADMINISTRATIVE LAW

AUSTRALIA
Law Book Co.
Sydney

CANADA and USA
Carswell
Toronto

HONG KONG
Sweet & Maxwell Asia

NEW ZEALAND
Brookers
Auckland

SINGAPORE and MALAYSIA
Sweet & Maxwell Asia
Singapore and Kuala Lumpur

CONTENTS

Part I
Administrative Institutions, Procedures and Non-judicial Mechanisms of Redress

Part II
Judicial Review

CASES, MATERIALS AND COMMENTARY ON ADMINISTRATIVE LAW

By

S.H. Bailey

FOURTH EDITION

LONDON
SWEET & MAXWELL
2005

First Edition 1977
Second Edition 1992
Third Edition 1997
Fourth Edition 2005

Published in 2005 by
Sweet & Maxwell Ltd, 100 Avenue Road,
Swiss Cottage, London NW3 3PF

(www.sweetandmaxwell.co.uk)

Typeset by
Servis Filmsetting Ltd, Manchester
Printed in England by
MPG Books Ltd, Bodmin, Cornwall

No natural forests were destroyed to make this product:
only farmed timber was used and replanted

A CIP catalogue record for this book is available from the
British Library

ISBN 0421 900 709

Part III
Civil Liability

PREFACE

This is the fourth edition of a work first published in 1977 under the joint authorship of myself, Charles Cross and Jack Garner. The second and third editions were jointly produced by myself, Brian Jones and Alastair Mowbray. Unfortunately, neither Brian nor Alastair was available for this edition, for which I am solely responsible.

The period since the third edition appeared, in 1997, has coincided with the term in office (to date) of a Labour Government that has been committed to reforms (fundamental and otherwise) across the public sector and in the legal system. Much of interest has happened in and out of the courts. This edition has expanded by comparison with its predecessor for a number of reasons. First, the enactment of the Human Rights Act 1998 has introduced a new dimension to the legal system, with new constraints on the decisions and acts of public bodies. This is dealt with in a new separate chapter. Secondly, the opportunity has been taken to expand the coverage by way of commentary and notes, recognised in the change of title. Thirdly, there have been important areas that have seen significant and ongoing developments, including the codes of practice and conduct concerning decision making in the public sector, and the law concerning duties, the scope of review for error of fact, delegation, estoppel, irrationality, unjustified inconsistency (interference with substantive legitimate expectations) and lack of proportionality, bias and interest, appeals, the procedure for judicial review and civil liability. All this has necessitated much restructuring and rewriting.

I am grateful to the University of Nottingham for a year's study leave, following a six year term as a Pro-Vice-Chancellor, to the publishers for their help and support, to Fiona Hayes and Claire Jennings who typed a large amount of material, and to Brian Jones who contributed comments at the proof stage.

The manuscript was submitted in May 2005, and some more recent developments have been noted.

S.H.B.
August 31 2005
Nottingham

ACKNOWLEDGMENTS

Grateful acknowledgment is made to the following authors and publishers for permission to quote from their works:

Cabinet Office: Extract from *Executive Agencies' Background and Development*.

Cabinet Office: Extract from *Ministerial Code: A Code of Ethics and Procedural Guidance for Ministers*.

Cabinet Office: Extract from *The Civil Service Code*.

Commission for Local Administration in England: Extract from Local Government Ombudsmen Annual Report 2003–04.

HMSO: Controller of HMSO for extracts from Crown and Parliamentary copyright material.

HM Treasury: Extract from Budget Report 2005 (2004–05 HC 372).

HM Treasury: Extract from PFI: Meeting the Investment Challenge (July 2003).

M. Harris and M. Partington (eds) *Administrative Justice in the 21st Century* (Oxford, Hart Publishing, 1999)

Lord Hoffmann in E. Ellis (ed) *The Principle of Proportionality in the Laws of Europe* (Oxford, Hart Publishing, 1999)

While every care has been taken to establish and acknowledge copyright, and contact copyright owners, the publishers tender their apologies for any accidental infringement. They would be pleased to come to a suitable arrangement with the rightful owners in each case.

TABLE OF CASES

TABLE OF STATUTES

TABLE OF STATUTORY INSTRUMENTS

TABLE OF REPORTS

ABBREVIATIONS

Allen: Sir Carleton Kemp Allen, *Law and Orders* (3rd ed., 1965, Stevens)

Cane: P. Cane, *An Introduction to Administrative Law* (4th ed., 2004, Oxford University Press)

Craig: P.P. Craig, *Administrative Law* (5th ed., 2003, Thomson Sweet & Maxwell)

Cross: S.H. Bailey, *Cross on Local Government Law* (9th ed., Thomson Sweet & Maxwell)

Daintith and Page: T. Daintith and A. Page, *The Executive in the constitution* (1999, Oxford University Press)

de Smith, Woolf and Jowell: Lord Woolf and J. Jowell, *de Smith, Woolf and Jowell, Judicial Review of Administrative Action* (5th ed., 1995, Thomson Sweet & Maxwell)

de Smith CA: S.A. de Smith and R. Brazier, *Constitutional and Administrative Law* (ed., Penguin)

Emery and Smythe: C.T. Emery and B. Smythe, *Judicial Review: Legal Limits of Official Power* (1986, Sweet & Maxwell)

Harlow and Rawlings: C. Harlow and R. Rawlings, *Law and Administration* (2nd ed., 1997, Butterworths)

Lewis: C. Lewis, *Judicial Remedies in Public Law* (3rd ed., 2004, Thomson Sweet & Maxwell)

Wade and Forsyth: Sir William Wade and C.F. Forsyth, *Administrative Law* (9th ed., 2004, Oxford University Press)

Zamir and Woolf: Lord Woolf and J. Woolf, *Zamir, The Declaratory Judgment* (3rd ed., 2002, Thomson Sweet & Maxwell)

Part I

ADMINISTRATIVE INSTITUTIONS AND PROCEDURES AND NON-JUDICIAL MECHANISMS OF REDRESS

INTRODUCTORY NOTE TO PART I

The purpose of this collection of materials is, first, to provide a selective overview of the institutional framework within which modern public administration operates, in order to facilitate an understanding of the nature of the major bodies governed by administrative law. Many fundamental changes have occurred in the existing system and continue to take place. For example, the appointments processes and membership of Non-Departmental Public Bodies, QUANGOs, have been a matter of serious political controversy, which has been partially resolved by the work of the Committee on Standards in Public Life. Secondly, we examine selected features of some of the most important procedures adopted by public authorities so that we can gain an insight into the ways in which these organisations actually perform their duties. These materials reveal a number of tensions existing in the use of various procedures, *e.g.* over the fairest method of conducting inquiries—a topic hotly debated by Sir Richard Scott and some prominent witnesses at his inquiry into the export of defence equipment to Iraq and in the increasing powers being given to the regulators of public utilities whilst the Government is committed to a crusade of deregulation. Thirdly, we consider the increasing workload of the proliferating statutory ombudsmen, together with the adoption of this model of grievance resolution by many private sector trade associations (*e.g.* the creation of a Funerals Ombudsman).

Within the diverse collection of materials contained in Part I it is possible to discern at least four recurring themes in the policy of the Conservative Government to 1997. First, there was the increasing pace of the restructuring of public organisations. By 1997 nearly 70 per cent of civil servants were working in Executive agencies or departments organised on agency lines, rather than in traditional central government departments. Similarly, local government was reshaped in the form of unitary authorities, which replaced the established two-tier system throughout many parts of England and the whole of Wales. Secondly, there was the subjection of the provision of public services to greater competition. Hence, local authorities were obliged to offer for tender the supply of professional services as well as manual ones. Likewise, an expanding range of central government administration was subjected to "market testing" with competition from private sector companies (*e.g.* computer services). Legislation even provided for competition in the supply of schools inspectors. Consequently, the new structures of public administration became to a great extent purchasers, rather than direct providers, of many public services. Thirdly, the privatisation of all the major public utilities, together with many other former public corporations, resulted in the need for the creation of new regulatory offices with extensive statutory powers to control the pricing and competition policies of the resulting private sector monopolies. Therefore, regulation assumed a central role as a method of contemporary public administration. Finally, aspects of all the above policies intersected in the programme of charterism initiated with the Citizen's Charter. This policy viewed citizens as consumers of public services being guided by a plethora of "league tables" measuring the services provided by individual organisations. Symbolically, charterism also refocused attention on the provision of redress for aggrieved individuals by internal and other non-judicial mechanisms. Overall these developments are aspects of what is termed "New Public Management".

The Labour Government in office from 1997 has remained committed to the modernisation of the processes of government, and many of the changes have tended to be in emphasis rather than radical. While Compulsory Competitive Tendering and requirements for market testing of central government activities have been dropped, a wish to continue to involve the private sector in the delivery of services remains, and the emphasis on a plethora of ever-changing targets has increased. Although most formal aspects of the Citizen's Charter were dropped, many of its principles have lived on in other forms. Most local authorities have been required to adopt a new constitutional structure (executive arrangements) with a split between (1) executive and (2) overview and scrutiny functions. All local authorities have the new role of providing community leadership facilitated by new wide general powers. A distinctive new development has been the devolution of significant powers to the Scottish Executive and Scottish Parliament and to the National Assembly for Wales and the Welsh Assembly Government. Among many other dimensions, this development has begun to lead to some significant policy divergences across England, Wales and Scotland, and differences in the ways in which public functions are discharged which can give rise to instructive comparisons.

Overall, the United Kingdom's system of government is commonly now characterised as involving multi-level governance, with central government functioning as part of a range of national (local authorities; devolved administrations), supranational (EU) and international institutions (*e.g.* the Commonwealth, the World Trade Organization, the United Nations and the Council of Europe); and the fragmentation and diffusion of powers inherent in the NPM reforms. (See A. Le Sueur in D. Feldman (ed.), *English Public Law* (2004), paras 3.10–3.14.)

ADMINISTRATIVE INSTITUTIONS

(A) CENTRAL GOVERNMENT

THE absence of a written constitution makes it more difficult than one would expect to identify with precision what is meant by the terms "central government" or "the executive".[1] It is possible to identify the main institutions of central government: ministers, the Cabinet and its committees, the Privy Council, departments, executive agencies, non-departmental public bodies (NDPBs), the Home Civil Service and the Diplomatic Service, the Head of State and the law officers.[2] But exactly where the line is to be drawn is not necessarily straightforward, as with the National Health Service, which remains the responsibility of the Secretary of State for Health and the Department of Health, but where service delivery is the responsibility of a range of trusts, including now Foundation Trusts which are members' organisations subject to their own legal regime and regulatory structure, but still "part of the NHS".[3]

The ways in which legal powers are conferred upon central government institutions is also not straightforward. Legal powers may be conferred on any person or body by statute. The prerogative powers of the Crown are conferred by the common law, and are, for the most part, by convention exercised on the advice of ministers.[4] It is also claimed that the Crown may exercise any of the powers of a natural person unless restricted by statute, and that ministers may exercise such powers as an agent of the Crown.[5]

Whether the Crown enjoys the powers of a natural person as a corporation sole[6] or corporation aggregate (together with ministers and departments)[7] is not, however, settled.[8] Another way of putting this is that it is not clear whether (aside from statute) ministers and their officials can or do have a legal capacity separate from the Crown. There are general statements in the House of Lords in *Town Investments Ltd v Department of the Environment*[9] that they do not. Here, the question concerned leasehold premises occupied by the Secretary of State for the Environment as the successor to the Minister of Works, who had entered the leases "for and on behalf of

---

[1] The leading analysis is T. Daintith and A. Page, *The Executive in the Constitution* (1999). See also A. Le Sueur, "The Nature, Powers and Accountability of Central Government" in D. Feldman (ed.), *English Public Law* (2004), Ch.3; *Craig*, Ch.4; *Wade and Forsyth*, Ch.3. The position in the UK is contrasted with that under the US Constitution, where "the Executive Power shall be vested in a President of the United States of America (Art.II.1 of the Constitution).

[2] Le Sueur, *op.cit.*, para.3.01.

[3] *ibid.* at para.3.02.

[4] See below, p.265.

[5] The "Ram doctrine", below, p.63.

[6] As stated by *Wade and Forsyth*, p.815.

[7] As suggested by Lord Simon in *Town Investments Ltd v Department of the Environment* [1978] A.C. 359 at 400.

[8] See further M. Sunkin and S. Payne (ed.), *The Nature of the Crown* (1999).

[9] [1978] A.C. 359. See C. Harlow, (1977) 40 M.L.R. 728, criticising the position that the Crown as landlord was exempted from the counter-inflation legislation but was nevertheless entitled to benefit from it. Organic theories of government were potentially dangerous as extending immunities. A distinction could be drawn between public and commercial activities, exemptions not applying to the latter.

Her Majesty", and which were used as offices for civil servants from other government departments. If they were "premises . . . occupied by the tenant . . . for the purposes of a business carried on by him" they were subject to restrictions on rent increases under counter-inflation legislation then in force. The House held (Lord Morris of Borth-y-Gest dissenting) that the tenant was the Crown rather than the Secretary of State for the Environment and that the concept of "a business" included the business of government. The limits on rent increases applied. Lord Diplock said[10] that:

> "[s]ome of the more Athanasian-like features[11] of the debate before your Lordships House could have been eliminated if instead of speaking of 'the Crown' we were to speak of 'the government'—a term appropriate to embrace both collectively and individually all of the Ministers of the Crown and Parliamentary Secretaries under whose direction the administrative work of government is carried on by the civil servants employed in the various government departments. It is through them that the executive powers of Her Majesty's Government in the United Kingdom are exercised, sometimes in the more important administrative matters in Her Majesty's name, but most often under their own official designation. Executive acts of government that are done by any of them are acts done by 'the Crown' in the fictional sense in which that expression is now used in English public law . . . .
>
> In my opinion, the tenant was the government acting through its appropriate member or, expressed in the term of art in public law, the tenant was the Crown."

A general proposition that the Crown is indivisible, coupled with the proposition that the Crown can do no wrong, would effectively exempt the Government from the rule of law, was presumably not intended by the House of Lords in the *Town Investments* case, and has not been accepted. Many cases both before and after *Town Investments* have recognised that individual departments and ministers are amenable to *mandamus*, prohibition and certiorari, now mandatory, prohibiting and quashing orders.[12] The House of Lords in *M v Home Office*[13] held that ministers of the Crown in both their official and personal capacities, but as distinct from the Crown, are amenable to both the award of an injunction (by virtue of s.31 of the Supreme Court Act 1981[14]) and the contempt jurisdiction of the High Court. In a concurring speech, Lord Templeman said:[15]

> ". . . the argument that there is no power to enforce the law by injunction or contempt proceedings against a minister in his civil capacity would, if upheld, establish

---

[10] At 381. Lords Simon, Kilbrondon and Lord Edmund-Davies agreed with Lord Diplock.
[11] [ed.] St Athanasius (c 293–373), a Christian theologian, formulated the doctrine that the Son of God is of the same essence, or substance as the Father, and opposed others, who maintained that the Son was of a different substance from that of the Father and was merely a creature, much more perfect than any other creature, who was used by God in subsequent works of creation (Encarta).
[12] See, *e.g. Padfield v Minister of Agriculture, Fisheries and Food* (below, p.528, *mandamus*) and other cases in Pt II, *passim*. For the argument that the prerogative orders should be held to be available against the Crown itself, see *Craig*, pp.873–874.
[13] [1994] 1 A.C. 377. The main speech was delivered by Lord Woolf. The House of Lords held that the Home Secretary, Mr Kenneth Baker, had been in contempt of court in his official capacity, but not his personal capacity, in failing to comply with an order made by a High Court judge that M, whose claim for asylum had been rejected by the Home Office and who had been taken by Home Office officials to Zaire, be returned from Zaire. Mr Baker had acted in accordance with (erroneous) legal advice that the judge's order had been outside his jurisdiction. In the case of contempt by a minister in his official capacity, however, the finding of contempt should suffice. (Proceedings for enforcement are generally barred by s.25(4) of the Crown Proceedings Act 1947, and writs of execution against the Crown by RSC, Ord.77, r.15(1)).
[14] Below, p.924.
[15] At 395.

the proposition that the executive obey the law as a matter of grace and not as a matter of necessity, a proposition which would reverse the result of the Civil War".

Whether, and if so how, the *Town Investments* principle applies accordingly depends on the context.[16] It might be as a decision on either the interpretation of the Counter-Inflation legislation, or more generally the position as regards tenancies.[17] Other contexts in which a principle of indivisibility has not been applied include the point that one department may not exercise a discretionary power under the dictation of another department;[18] the recognition that different parts of the Civil Service are not to be regarded as having a common employer for the purposes of equal pay legislation;[19] and rejection of the proposition that information known to one Crown official must be deemed to be known to all.[20] Much (but not all) of the difficulty would be avoided if the principle that the Crown could do no wrong were held no longer applicable[21] but that further step has not been taken.

Very many legal powers are conferred by statute. They may be conferred on the Crown, ministers, departments, or officials. The commonest form in practice is for powers to be conferred on "the Secretary of State" which means "one of Her Majesty's Principal Secretaries of State."[22] This device simplifies the process of reorganising departments or the transfer of functions between existing departments.[23] It is also the case that legal powers are effectively exercised by (and their use where necessary defended by) individual departments acting with a considerable degree of authority rather than the Executive as a whole, and not under the legal authority of the Prime Minister, whose significant powers tend to be conventional and political rather than legal.[24]

These functions so exercised by ministers of the Crown[25] may take the form of initiating delegated legislation (by orders in Council or by regulations, orders, directions, etc., made by ministers), of exercising discretionary powers,[26] of determining appeals

---

[16] See, *e.g. Minotaur Data Systems, Re* [1998] 4 All E.R. 500 where the *Town Investments* principle was regarded as authority for the proposition that proceedings brought by the Receiver at the direction of the Secretary of State were brought by the Crown; as, however, the Crown was acting through a servant, the Crown was not a "litigant in person" for the purposes of the award of costs; and *R. v Werner*; *R. v Clarke, The Times*, March 24, 1998 (Crown Prosecution Service can prosecute where the Inland Revenue have decided not to, unless this amounts to an abuse of process).

[17] But *cf. Linden v Department of Health and Social Security* [1986] 1 W.L.R. 164 where Scott J. rejected an argument that legislation in 1954 that expressly referred to a tenancy "held by or on behalf of a government department" was devoid of any effect because of the subsequent decision in *Town Investments*.

[18] The *Lavender* principle, below, p.482.

[19] *DEFRA v Robertson* [2004] I.C.R. 1289.

[20] Below, p.478.

[21] As argued extra-judicially by Sir Stephen Sedley, "The Crown in its own Courts" in C. Forsyth and I. Hare (ed.), *The Golden Metwand and the Crooked Cord* (1998), pp.253–266, noting that this principle has no application in Scotland or various Commonwealth countries.

[22] Interpretation Act 1978, s.5 and Sch.1. See A. J. C. Simcock, "One and Many—The Office of Secretary of State" (1992) 70 *Public Administration* 535–553, noting both that there is in law one office of Secretary of State and that a number of individual secretaries of state are each declared by legislation to be a corporation sole in order to facilitate the transfer of property (see the Ministers of the Crown Act 1975, s.2, enabling orders to be made.)

[23] The last major example of a situation where powers were conferred directly on a "Minister" and not the Secretary of State was the Ministry of Agriculture, Fisheries and Food, which was restructured out of existence in 2002 (see SI 2002/794). Note also that the Deputy Prime Minister, Mr J. Prescott, has had significant executive responsibilities for local government, the regions and planning, and is also the First Secretary of State. Where transfers are necessary they are effected by orders under the Ministers of the Crown Act 1975.

[24] See Daintith and Page, *op.cit.*, pp.29–31.

[25] A decision by a subordinate in the name of the minister will normally be accepted by the courts without proof of express delegation: *Carltona Ltd v Commissioners of Works* below, p.472.

[26] *e.g.* as in *British Oxygen Co. Ltd v Minister of Technology* below, p.488.

from the decisions of other government bodies, such as local authorities, and by carrying on the every day activities of administration. These and other administrative procedures are exercised over a wide field of activity, especially in the fields of social security, town and country planning and the environment generally, immigration and foreign relations, home affairs and the regulation of the economy and industrial relations.

In the exercise of their functions, the decisions of ministers are as subject to judicial review as are the decisions of other public bodies, subject always of course to the terms of any relevant enabling statutes.

(i) Departments and Executive Agencies

Until the late 1980s, almost all of the administrative tasks allocated to ministers had been performed by government departments. These are "branches of the central administration which are staffed by civil servants, paid for out of Exchequer funds and headed by a Minister responsible to Parliament"[27] and tend to have been established under the royal prerogative rather then by statute. In 1988, the following report to the Prime Minister, from a group in the Cabinet Office concerned with efficiency inside the government machine, was published. The report derived from interviews with 150 ministers and officials, together with the evidence collected by earlier investigations into the civil service.

EFFICIENCY UNIT: IMPROVING MANAGEMENT IN GOVERNMENT: THE NEXT STEPS (THE IBBS REPORT)

(HMSO) 1988

10. Seventh, the Civil Service is too big and too diverse to manage as a single entity. With 600,000 employees it is an enormous organisation compared with any private sector company and most public sector organisations. A single organisation of this size which attempts to provide a detailed structure within which to carry out functions as diverse as driver licensing, fisheries protection, the catching of drug smugglers and the processing of Parliamentary Questions is bound to develop in a way which fits no single operation effectively.

11. At present the freedom of an individual manager to manage effectively and responsibly in the Civil Service is severely circumscribed. There are controls not only on resources and objectives, as there should be in any effective system, but also on the way in which resources can be managed. Recruitment, dismissal, choice of staff, promotion, pay, hours of work, accommodation, grading, organisation of work, the use of IT equipment, are all outside the control of most Civil Service managers at any level. . . .

12. In our discussions it was clear that the advantages which a unified Civil Service are intended to bring are seen as outweighed by the practical disadvantages, particularly beyond Whitehall itself. We were told that the advantages of an all-embracing pay structure are breaking down, that the uniformity of grading frequently inhibits effective management and that the concept of a career in a unified Civil Service has little relevance for most civil servants, whose horizons are bounded by their local office or, at most, by their department.

19. We recommend that "agencies" should be established to carry out the executive functions of government within a policy and resources framework

---

[27] A.W. Bradley and K.D. Ewing, *Constitutional and Administrative Law* (13th ed., 2005), p.268.

set by a department. An "agency" of this kind may be part of government and the public service, or it may be more effective outside government. We use the term "agency" not in its technical sense but to describe any executive unit that delivers a service for government. The choice and definition of suitable agencies is primarily for Ministers and senior management in departments to decide. In some instances very large blocks of work comprising virtually a whole department will be suitable to be managed in this way. In other instances, where the scale of activity is too small for an entirely separate organisation, it may be better to have one or even several smaller agencies within departments.

20. These units, large or small, need to be given a well defined framework in which to operate, which sets out the policy, the budget, specific targets and the results to be achieved. It must also specify how politically sensitive issues are to be dealt with and the extent of the delegated authority of management. The management of the agency must be held rigorously to account by their department for the results they achieve.

21. The framework will need to be set and updated as part of a formal annual review with the responsible Minister, based on a long-term plan and an annual report. The main strategic control must lie with the Minister and Permanent Secretary. But once the policy objectives and budgets within the framework are set, the management of the agency should then have as much independence as possible in deciding how those objectives are met. . . .

To strengthen operational effectiveness, there must be freedom to recruit, pay, grade and structure in the most effective way as the framework becomes sufficiently robust and there is confidence in the capacity of management to handle the task.

23. Placing responsibility for performance squarely on the shoulders of the manager of an agency also has implications for the way in which Ministers answer to Parliament on operational issues. Clearly Ministers have to be wholly responsible for policy, but it is unrealistic to suppose that they can actually have knowledge in depth about every operational question. The convention that they do is in part the cause of the overload we observed. We believe it is possible for Parliament, through Ministers, to regard managers as directly responsible for operational matters and that there are precedents for this and precisely defined ways in which it can be handled.

24. The detailed nature of the relationship between a department and an agency will vary with the job to be done or the service to be delivered. The agency structure could be used to cover a substantial proportion of the activities of the Civil Service. It is clear from our discussions with Permanent Secretaries that some departments are already moving towards this concept. What is needed is a substantial acceleration and broadening of this trend through a major initiative. Ultimately some agencies could be in a position where they are no longer inside the Civil Service in the sense they are today. Any decision of this kind should be taken pragmatically—the test must always be adopting the structure which best fits the job to be done.

44. The aim should be to establish a quite different way of conducting the business of government. The central Civil Service should consist of a relatively small core engaged in the function of servicing Ministers and managing departments, who will be the "sponsors" of particular government policies and services. Responding to these departments will be a range of agencies employing their own staff, who may or may not have the status of Crown

servants, and concentrating on the delivery of their particular service, with clearly defined responsibilities between the Secretary of State and the Permanent Secretary on the one hand and the Chairmen or Chief Executives of the agencies on the other. Both departments and their agencies should have a more open and simplified structure.

CABINET OFFICE: EXECUTIVE AGENCIES' BACKGROUND AND DEVELOPMENT

(*www.cabinetoffice.gov.uk*)

6. The first agency, the Vehicle Inspectorate, was launched in August 1988. It was soon followed by a number of others, and over the following 10 years around 150 agencies were launched. Agencies came to be seen as the key vehicle for delivering central government services, and virutally every department had at least one of them.

The Financing and Accountability of Next Steps Agencies[28]

7. This 1989 White Paper described the financing and accountability regime for Next Steps agencies. Ut was published in association with the Government Trading Bill, which proposed powers to create trading funds to finance central governement activities.

8. The white Paper acknowledged that effective management of agencies would demand better, more timely and more comprehensive information on all aspects of performance. It stated the aim of the Next Steps initiative: "to the greatest extent practicable, the executive functions of government, as distinct from policy advice, would be carried out by clearly designated units, referred to as agencies". It set out the requirement for regular review (known as "prior options reviews") and the role of framework documents. It also acknowledged that the nature of the Next Steps initiative meant that its financial and other regimes would need to develop and evolve over time.

The Fraser Report[29]

9. In 1991 the Cabinet Office commissioned Sir Angus Fraser to look at the relationships between agencies and departments. It was not intended to reopen the principles for the establishment of agencies or to provide detailed blueprints for these relationships but rather to identify good practice. The report is mainly remembered for the concept of the "Fraser Figure", who was to be a senior official in a department who would support Ministers in their roles in relation to agencies.

10. Other recommendations included the need for departments and agencies to develop and maintain a clear and shared vision of what an agency is there to do and of what its priorities and objectives should be. They should also continue to give a high priority to improving target-setting (the aim being for each agency to have "a handful" of robust and meaningful top-level output targets). Departments should develop suitable pay and reward packages for

[28] HM Treasury and Privy Council Office, Cm.914.
[29] *Making the Most of Next Steps* (HMSO, 1991).

chief executives that offered 'significant rewards for achieving results and clear and effective penalties for failure'. Departments should also review their changing roles in the light of the agency initiative.

11. The report did have a major impact in Whitehall. A number of changes were make to allow greater delegations to chief executives. However, many of the other recommendations gathered dust or were implemented half-heartedly. Unlike lbbs, the Fraser report was not seen as having strong Prime Ministerial backing. The concept of the "Fraser Figure", while adopted by some departments, was ignored by others and there was no consistency in implementation.

The Trosa Report[30]

12. The Cabinet Office commissioned a French civil servant, Sylvie Trosa, to carry out a study on the relationship and effectiveness of current relationships between Ministers, departments and agencies. Her report, which was published in March 1994, made a number of recommendations on Ministerial Advisory Boards, "Fraser Figures", accountability, target setting and the role of central departments.

13. There was a mixed reaction to the report, with reservations expressed about a number of the recommendations, some of which were viewed as being too dirigiste. However, some of the proposals were welcomed and the Cabinet Office issued a response in October 1994 taking some of Trosa's recommendations forward.

Other reports and developments

14. Andrew Massey's 1995 report, After Next Steps,[31] explored the relationship between chief executives and Ministers and the roles of the sponsor departments and agencies in policy formulation and followed up a number of the Trosa report's recommendations. Its recommendations included the need for chief executives (especially those from the private sector) to be aware of the policy implications of management work in order to inform Ministers of problems at an early stage. It also suggested that future changes to the civil service should be put on a statutory footing to improve clarity and accountability.

15. During the 1990s a number of important developments had a direct impact on agencies. These included the drive to privatise and market-test public service functions and the introduction of the Citizen's Charter. Agencies were often used to test such initiatives.

16. By the mid-1990s, the agency was the principal organisational model for many forms of service delivery, including prison administration, welfare provision, many regulatory functions and much of the logistical, procurement and administrative support to the armed forces. By 1997, other three-quarters of civil servants in the Home Civil Service were working in agencies.

17. In the 1998 Next Steps Report[32] the new Government set out its position. It said that whilst agencies were not a complete answer to delivering better services, the principles they embodied-such as looking outwards to users; focusing on the key tasks to be delivered; and increased transparency and

---

[30] *Next Steps: Moving on* (Office of Public Service, 1994).
[31] Office of Public Service and Science, 1995.
[32] Cm.4273, 1998.

accountability-represented important steps in the right direction. At the same time the Government announced that it did not see the coverage of agencies extending substantially beyond the then 76 per cent figure. Instead of agency creation the main focus would be on using agencies in the most effective way. There were three key elements to this:

- ensuring that targets were sufficiently demanding;
- reporting achievement against targets in a clear and open fashion; and
- encouraging agencies to compare the ways in which they do things with best practice in analogous organisations both within and outside the Civil Service.

18. The Modernising Government White Paper was published in March 1999.[33] Although agencies were the main deliverers of central government services there was very little mention of them in the White Paper. Also, the emphasis on horizontal working seemed to fire a shot across the bows of agencies, which were created to deliver deliver discrete services.

19. A greater emphasis on performance measurement and performance management has characterised recent policy. Following the 2000 Spending Review, the Government published Public Service Agreements (PSAs) covering the period 2001/04, together with new Service Delivery Agreements (SDAs) including key commitments on the management of public services. Some agencies are directly involved with SDAs. In many other cases high-level performance targets are cascaded to agencies to assist their attainment. This is reflected in agencies' key ministerial targets.

The 2001/02 Agency Policy Review

20. In March 2001 the Government announced a review of the arrangements for executive agencies to see what lessons could be drawn from current models, in the context of the Modernising Government White Paper and the Civil Service Reform Programme. The terms of reference of the review and its methodology were set out at Annex E of the final report. Pam Alexander, former Chief Executive of English Heritage, led the review.

21. The final report of the Review, Better Government Services—Executive agencies in the 21st century was published in July 2002.[34] It concluded that the agency model had been a success in improving, and in some cases transforming, services and functions delivered by central Government and had brought customer focus and a performance culture into the civil service. However, it found that agencies had in some cases become detached from Ministers and from Departments' increasing focus on strategic aims; and controls over processes had reduced effectiveness and responsiveness without providing a shard strategic direction. The report made 12 recommendations to achieve and maintain strategic connection and improve service delivery. These included:

- department leadership which valued equally policy and delivery skills and agency management with a clear understanding of ministerial objectives;

---

[33] Cm.4310, 1999.
[34] Office of Public Service Reform, Cabinet Office, 2002.

- simpler governance structures providing strategic direction from Departments and external challenge from non-executive directors on management boards;
- alignment of departmental and agency key targets and a cycle of reviews to achievement of key objectives; and
- maximum use of financial and managerial delegations to support responsive, flexible and effective delivery.

22. Since the report was published, the focus in Government has been on implementing its recommendations:

- new guidance on carrying out reviews has been introduced.
- the Cabinet Office has put a number of programmes in place for developing senior civil servants' skills in delivery; see the Centre for Management and Policy Studies website;
- revised Guidance on Framework Documents setting out clearly and simply the relationship between an agency and its parent department;
- revised guidance on target setting to ensure departmental and agency targets are aligned; and to encourage excellence and continuous improvement, and address poor performance; and revised guidance on reporting outcomes against targets
- continuous improvement and the strengthening of departments' ties with their agencies is also emphasised through the development of Performance Partnership Agreements;
- Spending Review settlements since 2000 have continued to provide agencies with three-year funding agreements to support three-year business plans.

Notes

1. In February 1988, Mrs Thatcher gave her general endorsement to the Ibbs Report. She expressed the view that the new agencies would "generally be within the Civil Service, and their staff will continue to be civil servants".[35] This statement provided the (very limited) formal basis for the development. The House of Commons Select Committee on the Treasury expressed concern about the vagueness of the Report, particularly in relation to the accountability of the new agencies to Parliament, and noted that 20 years earlier the Fulton Committee on the Civil Service had recommended the "hiving off" of discrete responsibilities to autonomous agencies (Cmnd.3638).[36]

2. Between 1990 and 1999 Cabinet Office produced an annual review (from 1998, a report) of the Next Steps Agencies. Before an agency is created and thereafter at regular five-yearly intervals a series of questions (called "prior options") will be asked by government. These include: whether an activity needs to continue, whether government has to be responsible for it (or can it be left to the market), does government have to undertake the activity itself (or can it buy those services from outside providers—see further the programme of "Market Testing" discussed in the Contracting section below, p.72) and is the agency properly structured and focused? Common features of established agencies encompass: (1) clearly defined tasks established in published framework documents, (2) annual performance targets announced

[35] H.C.Deb., Vol.127, cols 1149–1156.
[36] Annexe, *Treasury & Civil Service Select Committee 8th Report 1987–88*, H.C. 494 (1987–1988).

to Parliament by ministers (*e.g.* financial targets), (3) each agency is headed by a chief executive (the majority have been appointed through open competition and over half of these have come from outside the civil service) and (4) staff in agencies remain civil servants and are bound by the same rules of conduct as those employed in departmental headquarters.[37]

According to the 2002 Alexander Review (paras 6–9), as at the end of March 2002, there were 127 UK agencies, of which 92 reported to Whitehall departments, ranging in size from Jobcentre plus (90,000 staff) and the Prison Service (42,000 staff) to the Debt Management Office (40 staff). Forty-nine delivered services to external customers; 45 (nearly all MoD agencies) to government departments; 12 offered mainly research services; and 21 were regulators. Agency staff now accounted for 57 per cent of the Home Civil Service (which had reduced in size by 16 per cent since 1988). Not all executive functions are performed by agencies. Other models include departments (such as the Inland Revenue and Customs & Excise, which are to merge) and directorates within departments (*e.g.* the Home Office's Immigration and Nationality Directorate). These operate on agency lines and employ a further 21 per cent of the Home Civil Service. There are then NDPBs (*e.g.* the Environment Agency) and public corporations (*e.g.* British Nuclear Fuels Ltd) (see further below, pp.15 and 21).

Some executive agencies have trading fund status by order under the Government Trading Funds Act 1973. These have a financial framework outside the usual funding regime, with standing authority to meet outgoing expenditure from receipts, and without detailed advance approval by Parliament of gross income and expenditure. This arrangement is suitable where agencies can charge for their services through a genuine customer-supplier relationship and have a reliable income stream. In 2003, there were 20 such agencies, including the Forensic Science Service and the Patent Office (see *How to classify public bodies* at *www.civilservice.gov.uk/improving_services/agencies_ and_public_ bodies/guidance_for_departments*).

3. M. Freedland questioned whether the *Carltona* principle (see below, p.472) could be applied to the exercise of discretionary powers by agencies' staff in the light of the separate financial accountability of each agency from its parent department: see "The Rule against Delegation and the *Carltona* Doctrine in an Agency Context" [1996] P.L. 19.

4. The level of enthusiasm for the impact of executive agencies expressed in the 2002 Review is not necessarily matched by commentators. For example, C. Talbot, (2004) *Public Money & Management* 104–112, notes the absence of an independent formal evaluation, as distinct from the 2002 internal policy review, notwithstanding the initial undertaking that there would be such an evaluation. It is difficult to judge the effectiveness of the new agency structure given the absence of data about pre-reform performance, and the many other changes in the way services are delivered (*e.g.* the Citizen's Charter and market testing) and in the pattern of government departments. The original concept of a single document, annually agreed and constituting a quasi-contract between ministers and the agency chief executive was never implemented. Instead, there has developed "a complex and cumbersome set of overlapping steering and accountability systems involving multiple 'principals' (parent departments, Ministers, Cabinet Office, the Treasury)" (p.108). While the introduction of agencies' annual reports and the Next Steps reviews created "a revolution in the amount of available information", most reports "make scant attempt to link performance information to resources consumed, making judgment about efficiency almost impossible in most cases" (p.109). While performance against targets had improved, agencies had reduced 50 per cent of targets between 1994 and 1999. Overall, while there were many examples in the reports of performance successes, and most external observers have concluded that agencies have improved performance, "it is difficult to accept

---

[37] *Next Steps Agencies in Government Review 1994*, Cm.2775 (1994).

unconditionally" the claim in the 2002 Review of "dramatic improvement" in all the areas identified in the original Next Steps report (p.110). Furthermore, while agencies had improved the management of their own functions, they had not improved the management of the rest of government, given continuing criticism of the strategic management of departments (p.111). A number of these criticisms are also found in *Improving Service Delivery: The Role of Executive Agencies*, Report by the Controller and Auditor General (2002–03 HC 525).

5. Much concern has been focused on the potential dilution of individual ministerial responsibility for agencies. The direct accountability of agencies has been strengthened by the designation of their chief executives as accounting officers, the provision by chief executives of answers to Parliamentary Questions and in some cases their giving of evidence to Parliamentary committees (see Talbot, *op.cit.*, p.107). However, in some cases responsibility for answering PQs has reverted to ministers (*e.g.* the Prison Service) (*ibid.*). The continuing principle of ministerial responsibility is reaffirmed in the Ministerial Code (below, p.34; *Daintith and Page*, p.45). Ministers certainly accept responsibility for giving an account to Parliament. But concerns remain that the lack of clarity in the arrangements facilitates the transfer of blame away from ministers (see Sir Christopher Foster, *British Government in Crisis* (2005), pp.150–154, noting examples of ministerial interference in operational matters supposedly the responsibility of agencies).

6. For further consideration of Executive Agencies, see *Craig*, pp.104–112; G. Drewry, "The Executive: Towards Accountable Government and Effective Governance?" in J. Jowell and D. Oliver (ed.), *The Changing Constitution* (5th ed, 2004), Ch.11; O. James, *The Executive Agency Revolution in Whitehall* (2003).

(ii) Non-Departmental Public Bodies

During the eighteenth and nineteenth centuries, the Board system was a commonly used form of administrative organisation. The key feature of these organisations (ranging from the Poor Law Commission to the General Board of Health) was that they were not directly accountable to Parliament. However, they were gradually replaced by departments as the dominant form of central government administration. Nevertheless, there remain a number of bodies which perform public functions at the national government level that are not part of the ordinary departmental/Next Steps agencies structure. Administrative lawyers are particularly interested in the legal personality of such NDPBs and the judicial remedies available to control them. But, first it is necessary to consider the general issues of the modern functions performed by NDPBs, together with their accountability to Parliament, ministers and the public generally.

REPORT ON NON-DEPARTMENTAL PUBLIC BODIES (PLIATZKY REPORT)

Cmnd.7797 (1979)

[Soon after the election of the Conservative Government in 1979, this report was prepared with the objectives of, *inter alia*, surveying the existing NDPBs and commenting upon the arrangements for their control and accountability. This report divided NDPBs into three categories, "executive bodies" that carried out a wide range of operational or regulatory functions, various scientific and cultural activities, and some commercial work; "advisory bodies" which provided external advice to ministers; and "tribunals". In this section we shall concentrate upon the first two categories and tribunals will be examined in the next chapter.]

3. Organisations in the executive, etc. group generally employ staff and spend money, in some cases large amounts, on their own account. Advisory

bodies and tribunals are not normally employers of staff or spenders of money themselves, but their expenses and the cost of staff working on their behalf are met by their sponsor Departments, that is, the Government Departments concerned with their affairs. In addition, Departments incur staff costs, in some cases substantial, through their own Departmental functions arising from their sponsorship role in relation to all three types of body.

4. Some non-Departmental organisations cover the whole of Great Britain, and a few cover the whole of the United Kingdom, *i.e.* including Northern Ireland. But in many cases Scotland, Wales and Northern Ireland have separate institutions.

5. At the start of this review there were 489 bodies in the executive group. Between them last year they were the channel for expenditure on capital and current account approaching £5,800 million and had around 217,000 staff. In addition Departments spent about £24 million in their sponsoring capacity for these bodies.

7. At the same date there were 1,561 advisory bodies, involving expenditure of about £13 million by their sponsor Departments. Two-thirds of this total is accounted for by as few as 22 networks of advisory bodies, each of which includes eight or more separate bodies, in some cases as many as 100 or 200, so as to cover all areas.

11. Executive-type bodies are mostly set up under a specific Act of Parliament, though some are set up by administrative action—in some cases by forming a company under the Companies Acts; a Department does not need specific legislation in order to form a company, though it needs Parliamentary approval for any money provided to the company. With advisory bodies the reverse is the case; that is to say, most of them are set up by purely administrative action, but some of them have a statutory basis. Tribunals and other judicial bodies are set up to meet a specific statutory requirement. The feature common to all these cases is that they are in some sense part of the apparatus of government, without being Government Departments or divisions or branches or directorates of Departments, so that they do not come under the day to day direction of Ministers and Permanent Secretaries in charge of Departments; nor are they part of a local authority Department.

12. The case in principle for having an advisory committee with representation from outside the Department (as distinct from the justification in detail for all the committees which exist) is that the Department's own staff cannot provide the necessary advice by themselves, or that it may be desirable to enlist the participation of outside interests in order to formulate publicly acceptable proposals.

14. The case for having bodies of the executive type is more complex. It is that Parliament, or the Government with Parliamentary approval for the money involved, have decided that a certain function should be carried out for reasons of public policy, but that it is best carried out at arm's length from central government. There can be a number of reasons for this—because the work is of an executive character which does not require Ministers to take responsibility for its day to day management; because the work is more effectively carried out by a single-purpose organisation rather than by a Government Department with a wide range of functions; in order to involve people from outside government in the direction of the organisation; or, as a self-denying ordinance on the part of Government and Parliament, in order to place the performance of particular functions outside the party political arena.

15. Some fringe bodies go back a long way. The Development Commission, for instance, was set up in 1909, and the Horserace Totalisator Board—the Tote—goes back in one form or another to 1928. Organisations handling large sums of money, such as the New Town Development Corporations, have been set up by successive Governments since the second world war. A further fillip was given to this trend by the Fulton Committee's Report on the Civil Service in 1968 (Cmnd. 3638) which recommended the creation of accountable units of management within Departments and examination of the possibility of a considerable extension of "hiving off" of autonomous bodies from Departments. Subsequent developments included the hiving off of a large part of the functions of the Department of Employment to the Manpower Services Commission, the Health and Safety Commission and the Advisory, Conciliation and Arbitration Service.

34. What is involved in being on a non-Departmental body differs a great deal from one kind of body to another. Generally speaking it is in the executive group that salaried posts are to be found, and even there a typical board will consist of a full-time or less than full-time chairman with a number of part-time members, though there are full-time members in some cases; a board of this kind tends to have a full-time chief executive or equivalent officer whom it appoints.

35. The arrangements for advisory committees vary a great deal from case to case, as does the amount of work involved. Any remuneration paid usually takes the form of an honorarium or daily fee, but a high proportion of these appointments are unpaid.

38. The feature common to non-Departmental bodies generally is that Ministers appoint the chairman and members (though not the staff of bodies which have their own employees) and are accountable to Parliament for these appointments. In the case of some public appointments, not confined to those covered by this report, the relevant legislation provides for certain bodies, such as local authorities or representative organisations of employers or employees, to be consulted about appointments or to make nominations, or requires that the people appointed must have certain qualifications or experience. Otherwise, and subject to the special arrangements for tribunals, Ministers are free to seek the names of possible candidates from any source.

39. There is a Public Appointments Unit in the Civil Service Department which keeps a central list of potential members of public bodies, and some Departments keep a list of people with special qualifications for appointment to the bodies with which they are concerned. Departmental Ministers can obtain names from these sources but are free to seek suggestions from other sources within and outside government circles.

41. . . . On various major appointments, such as the chairmanship of an executive board, Departmental Ministers naturally seek the Prime Minister's concurrence.

74. Legislation under which fringe bodies are set up, whether they are financed by grants or by other methods, generally gives the Minister concerned powers to give directions of at least a general character. Suitable powers of direction are an appropriate safeguard, though they are no substitute for an effective financial regime and a sensible working relationship.

75. Annual reports and accounts of fringe bodies, whether financed by grant in aid or from other sources, should be as informative as possible, not simply in giving news about their activities but also, in all cases where the nature of

the operation lends itself to this approach, in providing material designed to help in forming a judgment on the cost-effectiveness of the organisation's activities or on the costs and benefits involved, where this is a more relevant concept.

76. Reports and accounts should include enough information about the remuneration and expenses of the chairman and members of the governing body and its employees to obviate any reasonable grounds for concern on this score. The material published about remuneration should go at least as far as that required of companies by the Companies Act . . ..

77. When a new fringe body is set up with a fairly finite mission, the legislation should contain provisions for its winding up when the mission is complete. But in general it would not make for good management and morale and successful recruitment to go beyond this and give it only a short initial lease of life, subject to periodical renewal. On the other hand, fringe bodies should not be allowed to continue indefinitely in set ways without a fresh look being taken from time to time both at the need for their continued existence and at the success or otherwise of their form of organisation and method of operations.

79. As a general rule advisory committees should be set up either with a finite remit, which will automatically lead to the dissolution of the committee when the remit is discharged, or with a finite lease of life, after which the Committee would be disbanded unless a positive decision is taken to give it a new lease of life.

81. Between them these suggestions contain most of the ingredients indicated by experience for making up an alternative to a competitive market régime for those public bodies to which in their nature such a régime cannot apply. Within a framework of this kind the function of securing efficiency and economy must rest with the organisation's own management, while the main responsibility for oversight of its performance lies with its sponsoring Minister and Department.

82. There remains one further important ingredient in a régime of this kind, that is, monitoring by an external body. An important part of this function is discharged by the audit-based scrutinies carried out by the Public Accounts Committee of those bodies whose accounts are audited by the Comptroller and Auditor General, or his audits of Departmental expenditure involving non-Departmental bodies to whose books he has access. For the future, a further important contribution will be made by the 14 new Select Committees of the House of Commons set up in response to recommendations from the Select Committee on Procedure to examine the expenditure, administration and policy of the principal Government Departments and associated public bodies, and similar matters within the responsibilities of the Secretary of State for Northern Ireland.

Notes

1. Following the publication of the Pliatzky Report (above), the Civil Service Department issued a document in 1981 entitled *Non-Departmental Public Bodies: A Guide for Departments*; a second edition of this guide was promulgated during 1985 and a third edition in 1992. Further editions were published in 1985, 1992 and 2000. From 2004, the documents has appeared in sections which can be updated separately (see *www.cabinetoffice.gov.uk*). The Guide has been described as the informal constitution for NDPBs because, whilst primarily addressed to officials, it details both

current government policy towards these bodies and the basic legal/administrative processes for their creation and dissolution. Four types of NDPB are now recognised: executive NDPBs, advisory NDPBs, tribunal NDPBs and Independent Monitoring Boards of Penal Establishments and Immigration Removal Centres (covering the former Boards of Visitors in the prison system). The Guide states (section (b), pp.2–3) that at the initial stages it should be asked (a) whether the service or function needs to be delivered at all; (b) whether contracting out is possible; (c) whether a Public Private Partnership would be the best option; (d) whether the work could be undertaken by a voluntary association; and (e) whether the tasks can be performed within the department or by an existing NDPB or agency, or other public body. An NDPB should only be set up "where it can be demonstrated that this is the most appropriate and cost-effective means of carrying out the given function" (section (c), p.3). Subsequent chapters identify the legal means by which NDPBs may be created (*e.g.* through being granted a Royal Charter or incorporation under the Companies Act); advice on the appointment and conditions of service of members; the forms of public disclosure of information relating to NDPBs (*e.g.* through annual reports and accounts); and the procedures for dissolving such bodies (*e.g.* how to wind up a Royal Commission).

Harden has made a number of criticisms of the Guide. He believes that it fails to provide an accurate demarcation between Government and non-government bodies, and is opaque about the appointments process. Furthermore:

"the constitutional danger is that the publicly visible 'NDPB regime' embodied in the guide, and the limited form of public accountability through Parliament which it endorses, will be outflanked in a number of ways. First, 'ministerial responsibility' may become almost as much of a shield for the real activities of quasi-government as it is for those of government itself. Whilst, secondly, bargaining over public policy with powerful interest groups will be structured through quasi-non-government processes and institutions which remain unacknowledged even as 'public'."

Harden, "A Constitution for Quangos?" [1987] P.L. 27 at 35.

2. The Cabinet Office publishes annual statistics on NDPBs. In 1995, there were 320 executive NDPBs (compared with 492 in 1979), their total staff amounted to 109,200 persons (compared with 217,000 persons in 1979) and their collective expenditure was approximately £21 billion (compared with £6 billion in 1979). The number of advisory NDPBs had been reduced from 1,485 in 1979 to 699 in 1995.[38] As at March 31, 2004, there were 210 executive NDPBs, 407 advisory NDPBs, 34 tribunal NDPBs (counted as tribunal systems) and 152 Independent Monitoring Boards (*www.cabinetoffice.gov.uk*). More than 19,500 people were members; 37.5 per cent of appointments being held by women, 6.5 per cent by people with a minority ethnic background and 4.1 per cent by disabled people.

3. Over the years there has been significant public concern over the powers of patronage exercised by ministers regarding NDPBs (*e.g.* over appointments of members of the governing boards of such bodies) and the ethical principles governing the behaviour of board members and staff of these organisations. Hence, the terms of reference of the Nolan Committee on Standards in Public Life made express reference to members and senior staff of NDPBs. After elaborating the seven principles of public life which should govern the behaviour of all holders of public office (see below, p.32), the Committee made a number of recommendations concerning appointments to and the conduct of members/staff of an NDPB. The committee proposed, *inter alia*, that: (1) appointments of board members should always be on the basis of merit; (2) ministers should continue to make these appointments; however, a new independent Public Appointments Commissioner should be created to regulate, monitor and report on the public appointments process; (3) the Commissioner should take over the

[38] *Public Bodies: 1995* (HMSO, 1995).

Cabinet Office's role in promoting best practice in the appointments process; (4) all appointments processes should involve candidates being approved by an advisory panel with an independent element in its membership; (5) all NDPBs should have codes of conduct governing the behaviour of members and staff and (6) internal and external audit procedures should encompass matters of propriety as well as finance. [39]

The Government accepted the above recommendations. It was anticipated that all appointments to executive NDPBs would involve Advisory Panels containing an independent element (*i.e.* person(s) not having an "operational role within the bodies or Government departments concerned") by July 1996. NHS bodies were also covered. However, advisory NDPBs were not subject to this regime and they were also, initially, outside the formal jurisdiction of the Public Appointments Commissioner.[40] In his first annual report, the Commissioner, Sir Leonard Peach, criticised three chairmen of NDPBs for selecting members through the "old boy network" rather than through open advertisements. He also expressed the wish that more women and members of ethnic minority groups would apply for the 89,000 positions on NDPBs.[41]

In January 1997, the Public Services Minister, Roger Freeman, announced that at least one-third of all departmental appointees to public bodies should be women. This was a minimum "benchmark". Some departments (*e.g.* the Scottish Office and the Home Office) had already appointed women to over 40 per cent of such positions; however, the Ministry of Defence only appointed women to 5 per cent of its positions on public bodies.

The Labour Government extended the remit of the Public Appointments Commissioner with effect from October 1, 1998, to include advisory NDPBs, the nationalised industries and public corporations, and the chairs of regulatory bodies. In 2002, the remit was extended to include the regulation of reappointments to NDPBs. The first major parliamentary review of the system was conducted by the Public Administration Select Committee in 2002–03 (Fourth Report, *Government by Appointment: Opening up the Patronage State*, 2002–03 HC 165). The Government rejected its proposal for a Public Appointments Commission to take over responsibility for making appointments, and an investigation of the feasibility of appointment by lot or, in some circumstances, elections.

In its Tenth Report, *Getting the Balance Right: Implementing Standards of Conduct in Public Life* (Cm.6407, 2005), the Committee of Standards in Public Life reviewed the regulatory system for making public appointments and concluded that it worked relatively well, but had significant weaknesses. Strengths included the successful development of a culture which recognises the importance of appointment or merit. Weakness included a small amount of unregulated ministerial intervention in competitions in England. This posed problems at a time when the Committee's research showed a continuing level of public concern about cronyism. There was also continuing underachievement in widening the social base of candidates for public appointments. There should be a new Board of Public Appointments Commissioners to develop strategic thinking and departments should adopt annual Public Appointments Plans. The process for the small number of appointments where ministers would be involved should be reformed, with minister consulted at the short-listing stage but the decision to appoint delegated to the appointment panel. At the time of writing (April 2005) the Government had not yet responded.

For research on the underrepresentation of women on public bodies, see L. Barnes, [2002] P.L. 606.

4. H.M. Treasury has produced a "Code of Best Practice for Board Members of Public Bodies" which is designed to provide guidance for executive NDPBs and related organisations, analogous to that provided by the Cadbury Report on Corporate

---

[39] *Standards in Public Life*, Cm.2850 (1995).
[40] The Government's Response to the First Report from the Committee on Standards in Public Life, Cm.2931 (1995).
[41] *The Times*, October 17, 1996.

Governance for private sector companies. Although the Code has no legal force, it elaborates the relationship of bodies to their sponsoring Departments and the roles of Board Chairpersons, Board members (*e.g.* "The Chairman and other Board members should declare any personal or business interests which may conflict with their responsibilities as Board members": para.17) and accounting officers.

5. For further consideration of NDPBs, see *Craig*, pp.98–103; I. Harden, N. Lewis and P. Birkinshaw, *Government by Moonlight* (1989); C. Skelcher, *The Appointed State* (1998).

6. Other bodies that can be identified beyond Executive Agencies and NDPBs include cross-departmental bodies, advisory committees mainly comprising civil servants, ad hoc advisory bodies, task forces, working groups and reviews, Health Authorities and NHS Trusts, police authorities, local spending bodies (*e.g.* most further and higher education institutions, registered housing associations and registered social landlords), the PCA and the National Audit Office (see *How to Classify Public Bodies* (*op.cit.*, above, p.14).

(iii) Public Corporations

Public corporations are a particular sub-species of public bodies with the distinguishing feature that they always have a separate corporate personality. Their constituent statutes normally provide them with such sweeping powers that the courts are virtually powerless to exercise any substantial supervision over actions. The major issue that has been litigated concerned the question whether a particular corporation was entitled to Crown immunity from suit or from the application of specific legislation; see *Nottingham No.1 Area Hospital Management Committee v Owen* [1958] 1 Q.B. 50 (National Health Service hospital immune from criminal proceedings for an alleged statutory nuisance caused by smoke emitted from one of its chimneys) and *British Medical Association v Greater Glasgow Health Board* [1989] A.C. 1211 (Scottish health authority not immune from interdict proceedings by virtue of the Crown Proceedings Act 1947). Crown immunity has been removed in a number of particular statutory contexts (*e.g.* the National Health Service and Community Care Act 1990, s.60, providing that health service bodies were no longer to be regarded as Crown servants or agents or as enjoying any status, immunity or privilege of the Crown).

Public corporations have been closely associated with the post-Second World War nationalisation of major industries (*e.g.* steel, coal and the railways). However, a major element in the post-1979 Conservative Government's economic and industrial strategy was to subject these public corporations to various forms of privatisation. This development resulted in relatively little direct litigation. An exception concerned the flotation of the trustee savings banks on the stock market in 1986. Under the Trustee Savings Banks Act 1985, the existing statutory trustee savings banks were abolished and replaced by successor limited liability companies. Depositors in the statutory banks brought actions in which they claimed that they were entitled to the surplus assets of the statutory banks when they were abolished. The House of Lords determined that the depositors' rights were limited to receiving their principal sums invested together with the interest due on those investments. Consequently, the surplus assets of the banks would pass to the successor companies and their new private shareholders: *Ross v Lord Advocate* [1986] 1 W.L.R. 1078. In a later case several local authorities had their claim that the privatisation of public water authorities, by the Water Act 1989, infringed valuable property rights possessed by the council struckout. Sir Nicolas Browne-Wilkinson V.C. (as he then was) concluded that the councils had no legal or equitable interests in the assets of the water authorities which were privatised: *Sheffield City Council v Yorkshire Water Services Ltd* [1991] 2 All E.R. 280.

The privatisation of many former public corporations has placed much more emphasis on the regulation of the pricing, ownership and competition policies of the now private sector public utility companies: see below, the section on Regulation at p.44.

Remaining public corporations include the British Coal Corporation, British Nuclear Fuels Ltd, the BBC, the Bank of England, some universities and the Research Councils, and bodies with regulatory functions such as the Civil Aviation Authority, the Health and Safety Executive, the Gaming Board and the Office of Communications and the utility regulators. The Post Office was originally a government department, became a public corporation under the Post Office Act 1969 and then became a public limited company (Royal Mail Group Plc), with all its shares owned by the Crown, under the Postal Services Act 2000, s.62.

For readings on public corporations see: *Wade and Forsyth*, Ch.5, T. Prosser, *Nationalised Industries and Public Control* (1988). Readings on privatisation include: D. March, "Privatisation under Mrs. Thatcher: A Review of the Literature" (1991) 61 *Public Administration* 459; C. Graham and T. Prosser, *Privatising Public Enterprises, Constitutions, the State and Regulation in Comparative Perspective* (1991); C. Foster, *Privatisation, Public Ownership and the Regulation of Natural Monopoly* (1992) and Daintith and Sah, "Privatisation and the Economic Neutrality of the Constitution" [1993] P.L. 465.

(B) LOCAL GOVERNMENT

In this section we will deal with the special position of local authorities, the relationship between members and officers *inter se* and in relation to other persons. Many of the problems that arise in connection with local authorities, in particular in relation to judicial control over their discretionary powers, are similar to those that arise in connection with agencies of central government and public corporations, and are considered elsewhere in this book.

Particular aspects of local government law illustrated elsewhere in this book include: the application of the *ultra vires* principle to local authorities (below pp.396 *et seq.*); delegation (pp.480 *et seq.*); assurances given by officers to members of the public (pp.515 *et seq.*), the fiduciary duty owed by local authorities to their rate/ council taxpayers (pp.552 *et seq.*); appeals against local authority decisions (pp.795 *et seq.*); and the liability of local authorities in tort and contract (Ch.15). Significant changes to the model summarised in the Widdicombe report have been introduced by the Labour Government (see pp.25–30).

THE CONDUCT OF LOCAL AUTHORITY BUSINESS

Cmnd.9797 (1986)

Committee of Inquiry chaired by David Widdicombe Q.C.

The constitutional position of local government

3.3 In Great Britain Parliament is sovereign. Although local government has origins pre-dating the sovereignty of Parliament, all current local authorities are the statutory creations of Parliament and have no independent status or right to exist. The whole system of local government could lawfully be abolished by Act of Parliament. Central government is not itself sovereign, and indeed its powers are—or may be—circumscribed by Parliament just as much as those of local

---

[41a] For general reading see *Wade and Forsyth*, Ch.4; *Craig*, Ch.3; M. Loughlin, *Local Government in the Modern State* (1987) and *Legality and Locality* (1996); I. Leigh, *Law, Politics and Local Democracy* (2000); D. Oliver, *Constitute Reform in the UK* (2003) Ch.16. Detailed consideration of the law relating to local government can be found in the *Encyclopedia of Local Government Law*, and *Cross*.

government. In practice, however, central government is drawn from the political party with a majority in Parliament and its de facto political strength is accordingly much greater than that of local government.

The legislative form of local government

3.7 The principal characteristics of modern local authorities in Great Britain can be traced to the origins of elected local government in the 19th century. There have however been important changes, particularly in the functions they undertake and in their size. The system has never been a static one. Major re-organisations took place in 1974 and, in Scotland 1975, following the reports of the Redcliffe-Maud[42] and Wheatley[43] Commissions. Although a further re-organisation took place in London and the metropolitan counties on April 1, 1986 the characteristics of the great majority of local authorities were determined by those re-organisations, and can be summarised as follows:

(a) they are directly elected by popular franchise;
(b) they are multi-purpose: in most areas responsibilities are divided between two tiers of multi-purpose authorities;
(c) they cover large areas as measured in population (about 120,000 people on average for lower tier authorities);
(d) they have substantial responsibilities for the delivery of services. Indeed this is one of the reasons why it has been felt necessary to create such large authorities. The extent of autonomy from central government in the delivery of services varies between services;
(e) they may only act within the specific powers set by Parliament. It would be possible for Parliament to grant local government a "general competence" to act for the good of its area. Instead they rely primarily on specific powers granted service by service;
(f) they may raise their own revenue. About 60 per cent of national local government expenditure is currently financed from locally determined and collected rates* and rents, from other charges for services and from borrowing. The balance is financed from central government grant;
(g) they are corporate bodies. The powers of local authorities are vested corporately in their councillors as a whole. They are not vested in the majority party, nor in individual councillors, nor in officers. They rely on full-time professional officers, however, for the day-to-day discharge of their functions.

THE VALUE OF LOCAL GOVERNMENT

3.11 The value of local government stems from its three attributes of:

(a) pluralism, through which it contributes to the national political system;
(b) participation, through which it contributes to local democracy;

[42] Report of the Royal Commission on Local Government in England, 1969. Cmnd.4040.
[43] Report of the Royal Commission on Local Government in Scotland, 1969. Cmnd.4150.
* [ed.] Subsequently replaced by the Community Charge (Poll Tax) in relation to domestic dwellings in England and Wales (Local Government Finance Act 1988) and now by the Council Tax (Local Government Finance Act 1992). The percentage determined locally is now much reduced (to 19% in 2001–02).

(c) responsiveness, through which it contributes to the provision of local needs through the delivery of services.

Pluralism

3.13 The case for pluralism is that power should not be concentrated in one organ of state but should be dispersed, thereby providing political checks and balances, and a restraint on arbitrary government and absolutism. This is not an argument for fragmentation of the state, nor for divided sovereignty, but rather for increasing the cohesiveness and stability of the state by making it less brittle and allowing within it some safety valve for the expression of contrary views.

Participation

3.18 Arguments about participation are less concerned with local government's position in the wider political system and more concerned with the quality of democracy within local government. As such they are relatively modern arguments, originating with the introduction of a popular franchise and remain in a continuing state of development as the nature of democracy itself continues to develop.

3.20 Local government offers two kinds of participation; participation in the expression of community views and participation in the actual delivery of services. It does so both through the process of electing representatives as councillors and through the opportunity to influence local government more directly through consultation, co-option, and local lobbying. These factors have led to much recent debate as to the quality of local democracy and how it might best be promoted.

Responsiveness

3.26 Proponents of local government argue that it is an **effective** means of delivering services because it has the ability, unlike a non-elected system of local administration, to be responsive to local needs. There is an important distinction between efficiency and effectiveness. Efficiency is concerned solely with output, effectiveness is concerned also with the meeting of needs. It is a distinction which applies in industry as much as it does in government. Efficiency in the production of manufactured goods is of little value if there is no market for those goods. A successful private industry needs to be responsive to its customers. Similarly those delivering local services need to be responsive to the local community, and it is argued that local government alone possesses that ability.

Notes
1. For an analysis of this report in its political context see P. McAuslan, "The Widdicombe Report: Local Government Business or Politics?" [1987] P.L. 154. Professor McAuslan described central-local government relations thus, "the government's overriding aim which it has pursued with a fair degree of consistency since 1979 is to reduce the role, status, powers, financial independence, functions and, in some cases, the very existence of local government" (p.162).
2. The views of councillors and other academics on the Widdicombe Report can be found in a special edition of the journal *Local Government Studies*, Vol.12, No.6 (1986).

3. Part II of the Local Government Act 1992 established a Local Government Commission for England (replacing the Local Government Boundary Commission for England), whose remit includes the task of examining the structure of local government in England outside London with a view to moving, where appropriate, to single-tier authorities. Central government favours the creation of single-tier unitary authorities, and in 1993, the Secretary of State for the Environment issued statutory policy guidance to the Local Government Commission stating, *inter alia*, that: "Unitary authorities can reduce bureaucracy and costs and improve the coordination and quality of services . . . In some areas the Commission may wish to recommend a continuation of the existing two-tiered structure. But the Government expects that to be the exception, and that the result will be a substantial increase in the number of unitary authorities in both urban and rural areas". Two local authorities brought judicial review actions against the Secretary to challenge this guidance. The High Court held that the final sentence of the guidance quoted above was unlawful as it undermined the statutory criteria, laid down in s.13 of the 1992 Act, which Parliament had elaborated to govern the working of the Commission (see *R. v Secretary of State for the Environment Ex p. Lancashire CC/Derbyshire CC* [1994] 4 All E.R. 165). Revised guidance was subsequently issued and the Commission completed its programme of work. Unitary authorities were established for a number of major cities leaving the two-tier structure of a county council and district councils in place for the rest of the county (*e.g.* Derby and Derbyshire, Nottingham and Nottinghamshire). In some cases a county was divided into a number of unitary authorities (Avon, Berkshire, Cleveland, Humberside). See further *Cross*, Ch.3.

4. The Local Government (Wales) Act 1994, created a new structure for local government in the principality. Twenty-one new unitary authorities ("principal councils") were created. Elections for the new authorities took place in May 1995 and they formally assumed responsibility for the provision of local services in April 1996.

WHITE PAPER, MODERNISING LOCAL GOVERNMENT: IN TOUCH WITH THE PEOPLE

(Cm.4014, 1998)

A brief outline of this White Paper

1. This White Paper sets out a strategy for the reform and modernisation of local government in England. It is an agenda for change stretching for ten years or more—well in to 21st century.

Chapter One—the need for change

2. Modern council should be in touch with the people, provide high quality services and give vision and leadership for local communities. Modern local government plays a vital role in improving the quality of people's lives.

3. Change is needed so that councils everywhere can fulfil this potential. The old culture of paternalism and inwardness needs to be swept away. The framework in which councils operate needs to be renewed.

Chapter Two—bringing about change

4. The Government will introduce legislation to establish this new framework which will provide opportunities and incentives for councils to modernise.

The Government will motivate manage the process of change in partnership with local government. Councils can do much today to reform, and many councils have begun to modernise themselves already.

5. The Government will establish a scheme to select beacon councils to serve as pace-setters and centres of excellence. Councils will be able to seek beacon status for particular services, or for the council as a whole. Those councils which are in touch with local people, have strong and effective links with business, have modern management structures and deliver best value will become beacon councils. Councils with beacon status will get increased scope to act for the benefit of their local community.

Chapter Three—new political structures

6. Councils must have political management structures which are effective and command respect. The current committee system is confusing and inefficient, with significant decisions usually taken elsewhere. Many councillors have little influence over council decisions, yet spend a great deal of their time at council meetings. The result is that people do not know who is running their council.

7. The Government will provide new models of political management for councils. Each model separates the executive role from the backbench role and will provide important and clear roles for all councillors. These models will cover:

- a directly elected executive may or with a cabinet. The mayor will be elected by local people and will appoint a cabinet from among the councillors.
- a cabinet with leader. The leader will be elected by the council, and the cabinet will be made up of councillors either appointed by the leader or elected by the council.
- a directly elected mayor with a council manager. The mayor will be elected by local people, with a full time manager appointed by the council.

8. Councils wanting a directly elected mayor will need to obtain popular endorsement through a local referendum. In addition people will be able to petition locally to have a referendum on having a directly elected mayor.

9. Councils will be under a duty to review their political management arrangements and draw up a plan, with a timetable, to introduce one of the new models. The Government will have a reserve power to require councils who drag their feet to hold a referendum on one of the new models. If people reject the proposal, the council will be able to continue with its existing arrangements or propose an alternative model.

Chapter Four—improving local democracy

10. More frequent local elections will strengthen direct accountability to local people by ensuring that voters in every area have greater opportunity to pass judgement on their local representatives. Councils will have a duty to consult local people about plans and services, and will have a power to hold local referendums.

11. The arrangements for local elections are well over 100 years old and need reform to reflect the modern world. There will be new guidance on maximising registration and turnout. Local government will try out ways of making it easier to vote—such as electronic voting, increased postal voting, mobile polling stations and voting on different days.

Chapter Five—improving local financial accountability

12. Strong local financial accountability is important. Crude and universal council tax capping will be ended. Local people will control the spending and taxation decisions of their councils. Councils will be responsible for meeting the council tax benefit costs of high council tax increases. To protect local people, the Government will have a reserve power to control excessive council tax increases.

13. The Government is determined to provide greater stability in council funding. It is therefore announcing the aggregate grant provision for councils for the next three years. The formula for distributing government grant will be stable for the next three years, and there will be a review of the grant allocation system.

Chapter Six—a new ethical framework

14. There will be a new framework to govern the conduct of councillors and council employees. Councils will be required to adopt a Code of Conduct, based on a national model, which councillors will be under a duty to observe. There will also be a new code of conduct for council employees, built into their conditions of employment.

15. Councils will have Standards Committees, with at least one independent member, responsible for drawing up the Code of Conduct and advising the council on its implementation and operation.

16. There will be an independent Standards Board to deal with complaints that councillors have failed to observe the Code of Conduct, with powers to suspend or disqualify councillors. Surcharge will be ended, but there will be powers to recover losses where a councillor or council employee has gained personally at the taxpayer's expense.

Chapter Seven - improving local services through best value

17. Good local services are vital to people's quality of life. Councils will have a duty to secure best value in the provision of services. The current Compulsory Competitive Tendering (CCT) regime will be abolished.

18. There will be new national performance indicators for efficiency, cost and quality. Some standards and targets will be set nationally, but in other areas councils will set and publish their own local targets against these indicators.

19. Councils will be required to undertake fundamental performance reviews of all their services over a five year period, starting with the worst performing. The reviews will:

- challenge why and how service is being provided;
- compare the service with performance that others are achieving;

- consult with local taxpayers, service users and the wider business community on how the service can be improved; and
- embrace fair competition as a means of securing efficient and effective services.

20. Councils will prepare annual performance plans, bringing together the outcomes of the fundamental reviews, setting new targets and subsequently reporting back on performance.

21. There will be new audit and inspection arrangements. External auditors will ensure that local performance plans are accurate and realistic. A new Best Value Inspectorate, working with other Inspectorates, will oversee an objective and independent process of regular inspection of all local services. The Government will act swiftly should councils fail to tackle serious or persistent performance failures.

Chapter Eight—promoting the well-being of communities

22. Effective local leadership is at the heart of modern local government. Councils will have a duty to promote the economic, social and environmental well-being of their area. They will work with other public, private and voluntary organisations and with local people to do this councils powers to work in partnership to tackle cross cutting issues and promote social inclusion will be strengthened.

23. There will be a new legal framework to enable successful councils to do more for their communities and to enable new approaches to public service to be tested through pilots.

Chapter Nine—Capital finance

24. The Government is providing extra resources for capital investment in the basic infrastructure of public services. New investment will be for modernisation. The local government capital finance system will be simplified. There will be incentives for councils to make better use of their capital resources and assets.

25. There will be a single capital "pot" so that councils can use resources more flexibly and plan for the long term. Councils will be expected to draw up a comprehensive capital investment strategy. The requirement to set aside for debt repayment receipts from the sales of assets (other than council houses) will be abolished.

Chapter Ten—business rates

26. Councils and local businesses will need to build partnerships to involve business in the council's local tax and spending decisions. The national business rate will be retained. The Government proposes that councils will, within defined limits, be able to set a supplementary local rate, or to give a rebate on the national rate. Beacon councils would be able to vary the rate by a higher percentage, again with an overall limit.

27. Business would not be able to block the setting of a local rate supplement, but the use of any income raised would need to be agreed between the council and local business.

Notes

1. The main features of this White Paper were implemented in the Local Government Acts 2000 and 2003 and a large body of associated delegated legislation. Of the three models of executive arrangements, the elected mayor and council manager model has been adopted by one council; the elected mayor and cabinet model has been adopted in 10 (Lewisham, Hackney and Newham LBCs, North Tyneside and Doncaster MDCs, Middlesbrough and Hartlepool (unitary councils) and Bedford, Watford and Mansfield DCs), with the leader and cabinet model adopted by the large majority (81 per cent). Fifty-nine smaller district councils (15 per cent) have exercised their right to adopt "alternative arrangements" nearer to the old ways of working. Research on the operation of the new arrangements summarised in F. Gains *et al.*, *A Summary of Research Evidence on New Council Constitutions in Local Government* (ELG Evaluation Team, ODPM, July 2004) shows that a variety of arrangements have been adopted by different councils. Four typical working patterns for cabinets involve, respectively: a dominant role for the leader or mayor; "multi-actor executives", cabinet members with delegated decision-making powers acting in considerable autonomy from each other and the leader; "team executives" operating with collective decision making; and "disengaged executives" struggling to operate coherently and looking to the full council to approve a large number of plans. While the number of formal meetings has been reduced, executive members and officers spend an equivalent or more time than that in informal meetings. Over half of councillors and officers agreed that decision-making was quicker, with an increase in delegation to officers. Councillors in mayoral authorities are more positive about the workings of their new constitution than in either of the other forms. Non-executive councillors are the most negative about the new system; most executive councillors, officers and stakeholders are more positive about the system. Arrangements for overview and scrutiny are taking longer to establish themselves; for most overview and scrutiny functions the majority of members and officers are unable to agree that the system in their authority had been successful. On the other hand, around 50 per cent of portfolio holders report changing policy as a result of overview and scrutiny activities. Overall, the envisioned reduction in non-executive time commitments has not occurred. But the "dire warnings of chaos" from some who opposed the 2000 Act have not come to fruition.

2. In 2002–03, the Standards Board for England received 2,948 allegations of breach of a council's code of conduct; 43 per cent came from fellow councillors and 15 per cent from an authority employee. Fifty-five per cent concerned parish/town council members (a category comprising 80 per cent of all members). Of the completed cases, there was no evidence of breach in 23 per cent; 27 per cent (108) were referred to the Adjudication Panel for England and no further action was taken in 50 per cent of cases. The 2003–04 figures were broadly similar (20:20: 8 per cent referred to the monitory officers: 12 per cent referred to the Adjudication Panel) (see *www.standardsboard.co.uk*). For the views of the Committee on Standards of Public Life (Tenth Report, *Getting the Balance Right* (Cm.6407, 2005), see below, p.40.

3. The Local Government Act 2003, *inter alia*, introduced new structures for capital finance and grants, enabled the Secretary of State to prescribe a scheme to allow billing authorities to retain a proportion of the non-domestic rates they collect, reformed aspects of council tax and housing finance and introduced new general powers for best value authorities to charge for discretionary services and for the higher-performing authorities to trade through companies.

4. There has been an increasing emphasis on the exercise of functions at a regional level. A government office has been established for each of nine regions in England as a vehicle for the discharge of central government functions in the regions. Regional development agencies were established by the Regional Development Agencies Act 1998 to further economic development and regeneration and promote business efficiency, investment, competitiveness and employment. Members are appointed by the Secretary of State. Non-statutory, consultative regional assemblies, with members

nominated by local authorities and other stakeholders, have been set up in some regions. A programme of referenda under the Regional Assemblies (Preparations) Act 2003 on proposals to establish elected regional assemblies, with consequential local government reorganisation has, however, been abandoned. The region that had showed most support for such a development in the event (the North East) decisively rejected the proposal at a referendum.

(C) THE NATIONAL ASSEMBLY FOR WALES[44]

The elected National Assembly was established by the Government of Wales Act 1998. It has taken over many powers from the Secretary of State for Wales (and other ministers), including powers to make statutory instruments determine appeals (see the National Assembly for Wales (Transfer of Functions) Orders 1999 (SI 1999/672), 1999 (No.2) (SI 1999/2787) and 2000 (SI 2000/253). Unlike the Scottish Parliament, however, it does not have power to make primary legislation. The Assembly elects a First Minister, who appoints a number of Assembly Secretaries (termed ministers) who together form an executive committee which operates as a cabinet and is referred to as the Welsh Assembly Government. It distributes a block grant from central government. Specified fields for the transfer of functions were agriculture, forestry, fisheries and food; ancient monuments and historic buildings; culture; economic development; education and training; the environment; health and health services; highways; housing; industry; local government; social services; sport and recreation; tourism; town and country planning; transport; water and flood defence; and the Welsh language (1998 Act, Sch.2).

---

[44] See further N. Burrows, *Devolution* (2000); R. Rawlings, *Delineating Wales, Constitutional, Legal and Administrative Aspects of National Devolution* (2002).

Chapter 2

ADMINISTRATIVE PROCEDURES

It is only to be expected that the wide variety of functions discharged by public sector organisations leads to considerable variations in the mechanisms by which decisions are taken, and how those mechanisms are enshrined in law or in well-defined and accepted conventions. To take an obvious example, the same process will not be appropriate in respect of a decision that the country should go to war and one that an individual claim for a welfare benefit should be accepted or rejected.

There are, however, some general themes that run through all proper decision-making processes. In the public sector, there are, furthermore, particular expectations that decisions are made and actions taken which are informed by principles of rationality and fairness (both substantive and procedural). These are reflected for example in an increasing range of codes of conduct and good practice guidance applicable to actors in the public sector (see below, pp.32–44) and, ultimately, in legal standards (see Pt II).

Elements that can generally be observed in good decision-making processes in the public sector include the following. First, there must be clarity as to the purpose of a decision and who is to make it. Secondly, appropriate steps must be taken to acquire the information needed to produce the best decision in terms of achievement of the intended objective. This can be through such means as research, a formal investigation or inquiry, a general public consultation process or a specific process for consulting or seeking representations from individuals or bodies particularly affected. Thirdly, the decision must be timely if it is to achieve the benefits it should and minimise burdens. Fourthly, the resources used to reach it should be proportionate to those benefits and burdens. Fifthly, there must be a stage of deliberation to produce the decision. Sixthly, once made, it must be communicated effectively and acted upon. Then, there must be a process by which the decision-maker can be held accountable. This may include accountability to Parliament or to a local authority meeting, scrutiny by an ombudsman and the possibility of legal scrutiny through appeal or judicial review. Each of these stages may (and often must) be structured in law. Trade-offs will always be necessary. For example, over-elaboration in information gathering or deliberation will waste resources and cause delay, that may in turn reduce benefits or increase burdens. There is always room for debate as to whether the process as designed or operated in practice (which may not be the same) is optimal. Regular generic reviews of how well processes are working in achieving their objectives is standard practice.

In many situations, a key turning point is the reaching of a final decision on the matter in question, in that this is likely to stand unless changed through some mechanism *external* to the decision-making body itself. Indeed, final decisions that have legal effect can only be changed if the decision-maker has express or implied legal power to do so, or through an external review mechanism. Some decision-making processes may include at an earlier stage an announcement that the decision-maker is "minded" to come to a particular decision, providing an opportunity for further focused representations and (possibly) legal challenge.

In practice, a very small number of individuals or bodies affected by decisions in the public sector have recourse to external review mechanisms of any kind (see below, pp.102, 176, 196 and 247, on the case-load of the tribunals, ombudsmen and judicial review). While much attention is rightly paid to external review mechanisms, it is also important to analyse and evaluate *internal* mechanisms for the generation and review of decisions (see T.G. Ison, "Administrative Justice: Is it Such a Good Idea" in M. Harris and M. Partington (ed.), *Administrative Justice in the 21st Century* (1999), Ch.1).

Overall, it is right to take the broad view of administrative justice, expressed by Harris and Partington (*op.cit.*, p.2) as a concept which:

"in effect, embraces the whole range of decision-taking, from an initial decision, to the ultimate level of appeal. Administrative justice would, on this view, include not only issues relating to the determination of legal rights or the making of discretionary decisions, but also issues arising from standards of service delivery. On this analysis, 'administrative justice' should be regarded as a normative basis for the whole of the operations of government, and those private or semi-private agencies which now provide many services to the public. It does not imply that any particular type of procedure should be preferred to any other. Rather that the basis on which decisions are taken is a rational and appropriate one, reached with proper collection of evidence and a sensible evaluation of that evidence".

The materials in this chapter set out some of the general standards for decision-making in the public sector, and some of the particular processes use by public bodies to get things done and mechanisms by which individual disputes may be resolved without recourse to the courts.

(A) STANDARDS OF CONDUCT AND GOOD PRACTICE

The last quarter of the twentieth century saw increasing concerns both as to the standards of conduct of individuals in the public service and the effectiveness of the machinery of government in the making and implementation of policy. One response has been the development of a range of standards of conduct and good practice that provide a context for decision-making in the public sector.

(i) The Seven Principles of Public Life

COMMITTEE ON STANDARDS IN PUBLIC LIFE: THE SEVEN PRINCIPLES OF PUBLIC LIFE

(www.public-standards.gov.uk)

The then Prime Minister, the Rt Hon John Major, announced the setting up of the Committee on Standards in Public Life in the House of Commons on 25 October 1994 with the following terms of reference:

To examine current concerns about standards of conduct of all holders of public offence, including arrangements relating to financial and commercial activities, and make recommendations as to any changes in present arrangements which might be required to ensure the highest standards of propriety in public life.

For these purposes, public office should include: Ministers, civil servants and advisers; Members of Parliament and UK Members of the European Parliament; Members and senior officers of all non-departmental public bodies and of national health service bodies; non-ministerial office holders; members and other senior officers of other bodies discharging publicly-funded functions; and elected members and senior officers of local authorities.

Hansard (HC) 25 October 1994, col 758

On 12 November 1997 the terms of reference were extended by the Prime Minister, the Rt Hon Tony Blair MP: "To review issues in relation to the funding of political parties, and to make recommendations as to any changes in present arrangements". Hansard (HC) 12 November 1997, col 899

The Committee on Standards in Public Life has been constituted as a standing body with its members appointed for up to three years. Sir Alistair Graham succeeded Sir Nigel Wicks as Chair on 26 April 2004. Sir Nigel succeeded Lord Neill as Chairman on 1 March 2001 and Lord Neill succeeded Lord Nolan, the Committee's first Chairman, on 10 November 1997.

The Committee has set out 'Seven Principles of Public Life' which it believes should apply to all in the public service. These are:

Selflessness

Holders of public office should act solely in terms of the public interest. They should not do so in order to gain financial or other benefits for themselves, their family or their friends.

Integrity

Holders of public office should not place themselves under any financial or other obligation to outside individuals or organisations that might seek to influence them in the performance of their official duties.

Objectivity

In carrying out public business, including making public appointments, awarding contracts, or recommending individuals for rewards and benefits, holders of public office should make choices on merit.

Accountability

Holders of public office are accountable for their decisions and actions to the public and must submit themselves to whatever scrutiny is appropriate to their office.

Openness

Holder of public office should be as open as possible about all the decisions and actions that they take. They should give reasons for their decisions and restrict information only when the wider public interest clearly demands.

Honesty

Holder of public office have a duty to declare any private interests relating to their public duties and to take steps to resolve any conflicts arising in a way that protects the public interest.

Leadership

Holders of public office should promote and support these principles by leadership and example.

Notes

1. The Committee's first nine reports (available on the Committee's website) covered virtually all elected and appointed office-holders. Prior to publication of the Ninth Report in April 2003, the Committee made a total of 308 recommendations, over 80 per cent of which had been accepted and implemented. Among the consequences have been: the Seven Principles, which have been incorporated into Codes of Conduct of many organisations; the creation of the Office of Parliamentary Commissioner for Standards to oversee new rules on MPs' interests; the establishment of Codes of Conduct for MPs, Lords and Special Advisers; the establishment of the Office of Commissioner for Public Appointments to ensure the highest standard of propriety in appointments to QUANGOs; the introduction of new arrangements for conduct in local government by Pt 3 of the Local Government Act 2000; and the creation of the Electoral Commission, *inter alia*, to oversee rules on donations to political parties. In its Tenth Report, *Getting the Balance Right: Implementing Standards of Conduct in Public Life*, Cm.6407 (2005), it reviewed the processes in the areas of appointment to public bodies (not the Civil Service), the management and enforcement of Codes of Conduct and whether the Seven Principles were being embedded into local culture. On public appointments it concluded that the system was working relatively well, including the successful development of a culture that recognised the importance of appointment on merit, broad (but not universal) acceptance of the Commissioner's authority as custodian of the Code of Practice on Public Appointments and the commitment of most operating authorities to running proportionate operations as regards to the process and outcomes. However, there were significant weaknesses, including a small amount of unregulated ministerial intervention in England (at a time when there was a continuing level of public concern about cronyism); the absence of the tools necessary for the Commissioner to implement a strategic approach; and continuing under-achievement in widening the social base of candidates. Among recommendations to address these matters were the development of the role of the Commissioner, annual Public Appointment Plans for departments, clarification of ministerial roles including removal of ministerial choice among appointable candidates in the case of senior and strategic appointments and clearer procedure for resolving disputes between the Commissioner and appointing authorities. As regards the embedding of the Seven Principles, three key areas for improvement were training and development, the governance of propriety in managing conflicts of interest (particularly possible conflicts between the public and private interests of non-executives); and developing a culture that encourages the challenge of inappropriate behaviour at all levels.

See generally, P. Leopold, "Standards of Conduct in Public Life" in J. Jowell and D. Oliver (ed.), *The Changing Constitution* (5th ed., 2004), Ch.17.

2. The Seven Principles have been incorporate in many other codes of conduct, including the Ministerial Code.

(ii) Codes of Conduct

CABINET OFFICE: A CODE OF CONDUCT AND GUIDANCE ON PROCEDURES FOR MINISTERS

(JULY 2001, *www.cabinetoffice.gov.uk*)

(1) *Ministers of the Crown*

Ministers of the Crown are expected to behave according to the highest standards of constitutional and personal conduct in the performance of their duties.

This Code provides guidance to Ministers on how they should act and arrange their affairs in order to uphold these standards. It lists the principles which may apply in particular situations drawing on past precedent. It applies to all members of the Government (and covers Parliamentary Private Secretaries in section 4).

Ministers are personally responsible for deciding how to act and conduct themselves in the light of the Code and for justifying their actions and conduct in Parliament. The Code is not a rulebook, and it is not the role of the Secretary of the Cabinet or other officials to enforce it or to investigate Ministers although they may provide Ministers with private advice on matters which it covers.

Ministers only remain in office for so long as they retain the confidence of the Prime Minister. He is the ultimate judge of the standards of behaviour expected of a Minister and the appropriate consequences of a breach of those standards, although he will not expect to comment on every allegation that is brought to his attention.

The Code should be read against the background of the overarching duty on Ministers to comply with the law, including international law and treaty obligations, to uphold the administration of justice and to protect the integrity of public life. They are expected to observe the Seven Principles of Public Life set out in the first report of the Nolan Committee, repeated in annex A, and the following principles of Ministerial conduct:

(i) Ministers must uphold the principle of collective responsibility;

(ii) Ministers have a duty to Parliament to account, and be held to account, for the policies, decisions and actions of their departments and 'next steps' agencies;

(iii) it is of paramount importance that Ministers give accurate and truthful information to Parliament, correcting any inadvertent error at the earliest opportunity. Ministers who knowingly mislead Parliament will be expected to offer their resignation to the Prime Minister;

(iv) Ministers should be as open as possible with Parliament and the public, refusing to provide information only when disclosure would not be in the public interest which should be decided in accordance with the relevant statutes and the Government's Code of Practice on Access to Government Information;

(v) Ministers should similarly require civil servants who give evidence before Parliamentary Committees on their behalf and under their direction to be as helpful as possible in providing accurate, truthful and full information in accordance with the duties and responsibilities of civil servants as set out in the Civil Service Code;

(vi) Ministers must ensure that no conflict arises, or appears to arise, between their public duties and their private interests;

(vii) Ministers should avoid accepting any gift or hospitality which might, or might reasonably appear to, compromise their judgement or place them under an improper obligation;

(viii) Ministers in the House of Commons must keep separate their roles as Minister and constituency Member;

(ix) Ministers must not use government resources for Party political purposes. They must uphold the political impartiality of the Civil Service and not ask civil servants to act in any way which would conflict with the Civil Service Code.

Ministers must also comply at all times with the requirements which Parliament itself has laid down. For Ministers in the Commons, these are set by the Resolution carried on 19 March 1997 (Official Report columns 1046–47), the terms of which are repeated at ii. to v. above. For Ministers in the Lords the Resolution can be found in the Official Report of 20 March 1997 column 1057.

Notes

1. The remainder of the Code deals with ministers and the Government, ministers and Parliament, ministers and their departments, ministers and civil servants, ministers' constituency and party interests, ministers' visits, ministers and the presentation of policy, ministers' private interests and ministers' pensions.
2. Paras 22 to 26 of the Code deal with legal matters:

"The Law Officers
22. The Law Officers must be consulted in good time before the Government is committed to critical decisions involving legal considerations. It will normally be appropriate to consult the Law Officers in cases where:
   a. the legal consequences of action by the Government might have important repercussions in the foreign, European Union or domestic field;
   b. a Departmental Legal Adviser is in doubt concerning:
      i. the legality or constitutional propriety of legislation which Government proposes to introduce; or
      ii. the vires of proposed subordinate legislation; or
      iii. the legality of proposed administrative action, particularly where that action might be subject to challenge in the courts by means of application for judicial review;
   c. Ministers, or their officials, wish to have the advice of Law Officers on questions involving legal consideration, which are likely to come before the Cabinet or Cabinet Committee;
   d. there is a particular legal difficulty which may raise political aspects of policy;
   e. two or more Departments disagree on legal questions and wish to seek the view of the Law Officers.
By convention, written opinions of the Law Officers, unlike other Ministerial papers, are generally made available to succeeding Administrations.
23. When advice from the Law Officers is included in correspondence between Ministers, or in papers for the Cabinet or Ministerial Committees, the conclusions may if necessary be summarised but, if this is done, the complete text of the advice should be attached.
24. The fact and content of opinions or advice given by the Law Officers, including the Scottish Law Officers, either individually or collectively, must not be disclosed outside Government without their authority.
Legal proceedings involving Ministers
25. Ministers occasionally become engaged in legal proceedings primarily in their personal capacities but in circumstances which may have implications for them in their official positions. Defamation is an example of an area where proceedings will invariably raise issues for the Minister's official as well as his private position. In all such cases they should consult the Law Officers before consulting their own solicitors, in order to allow the Law Officers to express a view on the handling of the case so far as the public interest is concerned or, if

necessary, to take charge of the proceedings from the outset, for example, by suggesting that the conduct of the case would best be handled by the Treasury Solicitor.

26. In criminal proceedings the Law Officers act wholly independently of the Government. In civil proceedings a distinction is to be drawn between proceedings in which the Law Officers are involved in a representative capacity on behalf of the Government, and action undertaken by them on behalf of the general community to enforce the law as an end in itself".

Allegations of a breach of paras 22 and 23 have been made by Clare Short MP, in relation to the Attorney-General's advice to the Cabinet as to the legality of military action in Iraq in that the complete text of the advice was not given to Cabinet, only the text of a written answer the Attorney was to give in Parliament (*The Independent*, March 9, 2005, p.8). The following day at Question Time, the Prime Minister maintained that there was no breach of the Code as the Attorney had given his opinion in detail to the Cabinet and there was no difference between that opinion and the statement given to the House. This did not satisfy the critics (*The Independent*, March 10, 2005, p.2). The full text of the Attorney's opinion was subsequently published during the 2005 General Election.

3. The Government (Cm.5963) has not accepted recommendations from the CSPL (Ninth Report, Cm.5775, 2003) that an independent office-holder should take over the role of Permanent Secretaries on advising ministers on possible conflicts of interest, and that a panel of senior individuals be established to investigate alleged breaches.

CABINET OFFICE: THE CIVIL SERVICE CODE

(*www.cabinetoffice.gov.uk*)

The Civil Service Code sets out the constitutional framework within which all civil servants work and the values they are expected to uphold. It is modelled on a draft originally put forward by the House of Commons Treasury and Civil Service Select Committee. It came into force on 1 January 1996, and forms part of the terms and conditions of employment of every civil servant. It was revised on 13 May 1999 to take account of devolution to Scotland and Wales. The full text follows, and hard copies are available from the address at the end of the document.

1. The constitutional and practical role of the Civil Service is, with integrity, honesty, impartiality and objectivity, to assist the duly constituted Government of the United Kingdom, the Scottish Executive or the National Assembly for Wales constituted in accordance with the Scotland and Government of Wales Acts 1998, whatever their political complexion, in formulating their policies, carrying out decisions and in administering public services for which they are responsible.

2. Civil servants are servants of the Crown. Constitutionally, all the Administrations form part of the Crown and, subject to the provisions of this Code, civil servants owe their loyalty to the Administrations[1] in which they serve.

---

[1] In the rest of this Code, we use the term Administration to mean Her Majesty's Government of the United Kingdom, the Scottish Executive or the National Assembly for Wales as appropriate.

3. This Code should be seen in the context of the duties and responsibilities set out for UK Ministers in the Ministerial Code, or in equivalent documents drawn up for Ministers of the Scottish Executive or for the National Assembly for Wales, which include:

- accountability to Parliament[2] or, for Assembly Secretaries, to the National Assembly;
- the duty to give Parliament or the Assembly and the public as full information as possible about their policies, decisions and actions, and not to deceive or knowingly mislead them;
- the duty not to use public resources for party political purposes, to uphold the political impartiality of the Civil Service, and not to ask civil servants to act in any way which would conflict with the Civil Service Code;
- the duty to give fair consideration and due weight to informed and impartial advice from civil servants, as well as to other considerations and advice, in reaching decisions; and
- the duty to comply with the law, including international law and treaty obligations, and to uphold the administration of justice;

together with the duty to familiarise themselves with the contents of this Code.

4. Civil servants should serve their Administration in accordance with the principles set out in this Code and recognising:

- the accountability of civil servants to the Minister[3] or, as the case may be, to the Assembly Secretaries and the National Assembly as a body or to the office holder in charge of their department;
- the duty of all public officers to discharge public functions reasonably and according to the law;
- the duty to comply with the law, including international law and treaty obligations, and to uphold the administration of justice; and
- ethical standards governing particular professions.

5. Civil servants should conduct themselves with integrity, impartiality and honesty. They should give honest and impartial advice to the Minister or, as the case may be, to the Assembly Secretaries and the National Assembly as a body or to the office holder in charge of their department, without fear or favour, and make all information relevant to a decision available to them. They should not deceive or knowingly mislead Ministers, Parliament, the National Assembly or the public.

6. Civil servants should endeavour to deal with the affairs of the public sympathetically, efficiently, promptly and without bias or maladministration.

7. Civil servants should endeavour to ensure the proper, effective and efficient use of public money.

8. Civil servants should not misuse their official position or information acquired in the course of their official duties to further their private interests

---

[2] In the rest of this Code, the term Parliament should be read, as appropriate, to include the Parliament of the United Kingdom and the Scottish Parliament.

[3] In the rest of this Code, Ministers encompasses members of Her Majesty's Government or of the Scottish Executive.

or those of others. They should not receive benefits of any kind from a third party which might reasonably be seen to compromise their personal judgement or integrity.

9. Civil servants should conduct themselves in such a way as to deserve and retain the confidence of Ministers or Assembly Secretaries and the National Assembly as a body, and to be able to establish the same relationship with those whom they may be required to serve in some future Administration. They should comply with restrictions on their political activities. The conduct of civil servants should be such that Ministers, Assembly Secretaries and the National Assembly as a body, and potential future holders of these positions can be sure that confidence can be freely given, and that the Civil Service will conscientiously fulfil its duties and obligations to, and impartially assist, advise and carry out the lawful policies of the duly constituted Administrations.

10. Civil servants should not without authority disclose official information which has been communicated in confidence within the Administration, or received in confidence from others. Nothing in the Code should be taken as overriding existing statutory or common law obligations to keep confidential, or to disclose, certain information. They should not seek to frustrate or influence the policies, decisions or actions of Ministers, Assembly Secretaries or the National Assembly as a body by the unauthorised, improper or premature disclosure outside the Administration of any information to which they have had access as civil servants.

11. Where a civil servant believes he or she is being required to act in a way which:

- is illegal, improper, or unethical;
- is in breach of constitutional convention or a professional code;
- may involve possible maladministration; or
- is otherwise inconsistent with this Code;

he or she should report the matter in accordance with procedures laid down in the appropriate guidance or rules of conduct for their department or Administration. A civil servant should also report to the appropriate authorities evidence of criminal or unlawful activity by others and may also report in accordance with the relevant procedures if he or she becomes aware of other breaches of this Code or is required to act in a way which, for him or her, raises a fundamental issue of conscience.

12. Where a civil servant has reported a matter covered in paragraph 11 in accordance with the relevant procedures and believes that the response does not represent a reasonable response to the grounds of his or her concern, he or she may report the matter in writing to the Office of the Civil Service Commissioners.

13. Civil servants should not seek to frustrate the policies, decisions or actions of the Administrations by declining to take, or abstaining from, action which flows from decisions by Ministers, Assembly Secretaries or the National Assembly as a body. Where a matter cannot be resolved by the procedures set out in paragraphs 11 and 12 above, on a basis which the civil servant concerned is able to accept, he or she should either carry out his or her instructions, or resign from the Civil Service. Civil servants should continue to observe their duties of confidentiality after they have left Crown employment.

Notes

1. The principles that civil servants are politically neutral and impartial, and are recruited and promoted on merit through open competition rather than through ministerial patronage were established in the 1850s as part of the Northcote-Trevelyan reforms. It was suggested then by Northcote and Trevelyan that this should be enshrined in legislation, but that was never done, the civil service being managed under the Royal Prerogative. It now seems to be generally accepted that there should be such legislation, with differences over the detail and the urgency for reform. Such a development has the support of the Conservatives and Liberal Democrats and the Public Administration Select Committee (First Report, 2003–04 HC 128, *A Draft Civil Service Bill: Completing the Reform*). The Government published a draft Bill as well as a Consultation Document expressing some scepticism as to the necessity. PASC has strongly affirmed its views (Third Report, 2004–05 HC 336), noting a new consensus that saw the need for early legislation to give the special values of the Civil Service greater force "as part of a growing perception than the Service's value are under threat". Elements of this perception include allegations of ministerial influence in the early 1990s on senior appointments in the Home Office, and signs of the increasing exclusion of civil servants by ministers and special advisers from crucial stages of the policy formulation and analysis (para.7). The Government's draft Bill (Cm.6373, November 2004) would put the Civil Service Commissioners (who oversee appointments) on a statutory footing; confer statutory powers to manage the Civil Service on the Minister of the Civil Service, (except the diplomatic service, where powers are conferred on the Secretary of State), excluding power to recruit, appoint, discipline or dismiss and other powers for day-to-day management; put the Civil Service Code, the diplomatic Service Code of Ethics, and the special advisers Code on a statutory footing, to be laid before each House; confirm the principle of appointment on merit through open competition; and provide for the investigation by the Civil Service Commission of complaints by a civil servant that a person other than the complainant has acted or intends to act in breach of these codes. PASC would go further, and give the Commission power to conduct inquiries into the operation of the codes; further clarify the role of special advisers; require Parliamentary approval for their total number; make the codes subject to the possibility of either House requiring a code to be withdrawn and a substitute prepared; and require management orders to be made by statutory instrument. The government, however, indicated in 2005 that it does not intend to proceed with this proposal.

2. Other Codes of Conduct of importance are the *Guide to the Rules relating to the Conduct of MPs* (Select Committee on Standards and Privileges, (1995–96 HC 688)), replaced by *The Code of Conduct for Members of Parliament and Guide to the Rules* (2001–02 HC 763). This is implemented by the Parliamentary Commissioner for Standards, the Select Committee and the House itself (see Leopold, *op.cit.*, pp.420–427). There is a separate Code of Conduct for the House of Lords (*www.publications.parliament.uk*). See the *Working Group Report on Standards of Conduct in the House of Lords* chaired by Lord Williams of Mostyn QC (2000–01 HL 68). Both incorporate the Nolan Principles.

3. New arrangements for local government were introduced by Pt 3 of the Local Government Act 2000. This requires each local authority to adopt a code of conduct that conforms to the principles of a model code made by the Secretary of State. Complaints of breaches are investigated in England by ethical standards officers overseen by the Standards Board for England, and in Wales by the Local Government Ombudsman. Formal proceedings are heard by case tribunals appointed by the Adjudication Panels for England and Wales. A variety of sanctions may be imposed. Provision has from 2003 been made enabling hearings in appropriate cases to be heard locally with appeal to a tribunal comprising not less than three members of the Adjudication Panel. See generally *Cross*, paras 4–73 to 4–106. The CSPL (*Tenth Report, op.cit.*, pp.3–5) regarded this as a significant improvement on the previous situation, and confirmed that despite incidences of corruption and

misbehaviour, the vast majority of councillors and officers observe high standards of conduct. However, the highly centralised model adopted (contrary to the CSPL's own recommendation in its *Third Report*, Cm.3702, 1997) had proved dispropor-tionate. The system had "generated a large number of apparently minor, vexatious and politically motivated complaints" but had created significant backlog of national investigations. There were serious operational difficulties at the Standards Board. Local standards committee were underused. There should be a move to a more locally based system from January 2007, with most complaints investigated locally.

(iii) Good Practice Guidance

There has been a marked increase in the development of documents that give guidance as to good practice in the design and operation of key public sector processes.

Notes

1. The *Code of Practice on Consultation* was first launched in November 2000 and a revised version came into effect from April 1, 2004 (*www.cabinetoffice.gov.uk*). The guidance is based on six consultation criteria:

"(1) Consult widely throughout the process, allowing a minimum of 12 weeks for written consultation at least once during the development of the policy.
(2) Be clear about what your proposals are, who may be affected, what questions are being asked and the timescale for responses.
(3) Ensure that your consultation is clear, concise and widely accessible.
(4) Give feedback regarding the responses received and how the consultation process influenced the policy.
(5) Monitor your department's effectiveness at consultation, including through the use of a designated consultation co-ordinator.
(6) Ensure your consultation follows better regulation best practice including carrying out a Regulatory Impact Assessment if appropriate.
These criteria must be reproduced within all consultation documents".

The code does not have legal force and cannot prevail over statutory or mandatory external requirements, but "should otherwise generally be regarded as binding on UK department and their agencies, unless Ministers conclude that exceptional cir-cumstances require a departure from it". The code notes that written consultation (Code Introduction) is not the only or even always the most effective means of con-sultation, other forms including stakeholder meetings, public meetings, Web forums, public surveys, focus groups, regional events and targeted leaflet campaigns. A report is made annually on compliance with the Code. The most recent (covering 2003 and April 2003 to March 2004) reported a rise to 76 per cent in compliance with the minimum 12-week written consultation period between 2002 and 2003–04.

2. Very detailed non-statutory guidance has been developed concerning good prac-tice in policy-making (see *www.policyhub.gov.uk*) and regulation (see below, p.44). Guidance on a range of topics has been developed by the Local Government Ombudsman (see below, p.188). The Citizens Charter (below, p.202) set out a series of *Principles of Public Service*, reflected in subsequent statements of standards to be expected in the delivery of public services.

3. These generic guidance codes can be contrasted with the large number of specific codes of guidance, some made under statute, that deal with particular programmes or functions. In general, as a matter of law statutory guidance must be followed unless there is good reason to depart from it (see below, p.462).

(B) ACCESS TO INFORMATION

Notes

1. *Background*. That there should in principle be a presumption of openness in public sector decision-making has long been accepted. It is self-evidently a necessary feature if democratic accountability is to work. At the same time, it is also recognised that this cannot be an absolute; there are a variety of legitimate reasons why in particular circumstances some public sector information should not be disclosed, at least for the time being, or should only be disclosed to particular people for specified purposes. Whether the balance between the two pressures is drawn appropriately perennially causes difficulty and controversy. It can be difficult in particular cases to disentangle good reasons for secrecy from bad reasons that are to do with the protection of individual decision-makers from embarrassment or criticism rather than the public interest.

In the last 25 years or so, there have been three major developments. First has been the increased recognition in non-statutory codes of the importance of openness (*e.g.* the Citizens Charter, below, p.202) and public rights of access to information (the Code of Practice on Access to Government Information first introduced in 1994, below, p.175). Complaints of non-compliance were made to the PCA, who in 2004 noted that it seemed to have been relatively little used by members of the public as distinct from the media and politicians. Secondly, the catch-all provisons (s.2) of the Official Secrets Act 1911 which criminalised all unauthorised disclosures of official information have been repealed and replaced by narrower provisions applying criminal sanctions in respect of the unauthorised (and, except in the case of members of the security intelligence service, damaging) disclosure of information in the particular contexts of security and intelligence, defence, international relations, crime and special investigation powers, and confidential information (Official Secrets Act 1989). Thirdly, a series of statutes has created legal rights of access to specified clauses of official information, most notably the Local Government (Access to Information) Act 1985, Access to Personal Files Act 1987, Access to Medical Records Act 1988, Environment and Safety Information Act 1990, Access to Medical Reports Act 1990 and Data Protection Act 1998.

2. *The Freedom of Information Act 2000*. Most importantly, the Freedom of Information Act 2000, fully in force from January 1, 2005, creates a general right of access to information held by a very large number of public authorities (ss.3–7, Sch.1). In general, a person making a request for information recorded in any form to a public authority is entitled to be informed in writing whether it holds information of the description specified in the request (the "duty to confirm or deny") and, if that is the case, to have that information communicated to him (s.1(1)(a), (b), (6)). There are, however, extensive exceptions and limitations. An exemption may apply to either the duty to communicate alone or both that duty and the duty to confirm or deny, and may be absolute or require the balancing of interests. Accordingly, questions may arise, as the case may be, whether the public interest in maintaining the exclusion of the duty to confirm or deny outweighs the public interest in disclosing whether the public authority holds the information, and whether the public interest in maintaining the exemption outweighs the public interest in disclosing the information (s.2).

The 23 categories of exemption cover information accessible by other means (s.21, an absolute exemption); information intended for future publication (s.22); bodies dealing with security matters (s.23, absolute); information not falling within s.23(1) required for the purpose of safeguarding national security (s.24); defence (s.26); international relations (s.27); relations between any UK administration (s.28); the economy (s.29); investigations and civil and criminal proceedings conducted by public authorities (s.30); law enforcement (s.31); court records (s.32, absolute); audit functions (s.33); parliamentary privilege (s.34, absolute); formulation of government policy, ministerial communications, Law Officers' advice, and the operation of any ministerial private office (s.35); information whose disclosure in the reasonable opinion of a qualified person (usually a minister or a public authority or officer or employee authorised by a minister) would or would be likely to prejudice collective ministerial responsibility, or inhibit the free and frank provision of advice or exchange of views, or otherwise prejudice the effective conduct of public affairs (s.36, absolute in relation to information held by either House); communications with the Queen or other members of the Royal Family or the conferment of honours (s.37); health and safety (s.38); environmental information covered by regulations (s.39); personal information (s.40, the regime under the Data Protection Act 1998 applies instead; in part an absolute exemption); information provided in confidence (s.41, absolute); information protected by legal professional privilege (s.42); commercial interests (s.43); where disclosure otherwise than under the Act is prohibited by an enactment, is incompatible with a Community obligation or would be a contempt of court (s.44, absolute).

Complaints that a request for information has not been dealt with in accordance with Pt 1 of the 2000 Act can be referred to the Information Commissioner for determination. The Commissioner must make a decision unless it appears to him that the complainant has not exhausted any complaints procedure provided by the authority in conformity with a code of practice under s.48 of the Act, there has been undue delay in making the application, or the application is frivolous or vexatious or has been withdrawn or abandoned. A decision notice is to be served on the complainant and the authority, specifying any steps which must be taken for compliance. The Commissioner may obtain information about a public authority's practice by serving an information notice (s.51). If he or she is satisfied (*i.e.* other than on a complaint) that there has been non-compliance with any requirement of Pt 1 of the Act, he or she may serve an enforcement notice, similar in effect to a decision notice (s.52). A decision or enforcement notice ceases to have effect if there is a certificate from an "accountable person" (usually a Cabinet minister) that he or she has on reasonable grounds formed the opinion that, in respect of the request concerned, there was no failure to comply with the duty to communicate information under s.1(1) (b) of the Act (s.53). However, this only applies in respect of the application of the public interest balancing test; the question whether information falls within an exempt category is for the Commissioner or, on appeal, the Information Tribunal or the courts. Non-compliance with a notice can be certified by the Commissioner to the High Court to be dealt with as a contempt of court (s.54). The Act confers no right of action in civil proceedings (s.56). The complainant or the authority may appeal against a decision notice to the Information Tribunal; an authority may appeal against an information or enforcement notice on the grounds that the notice is not in accordance with the law or (to the extent that the notice involved an exercise of discretion by the Commissioner) that he or she ought to have exercised the discretion differently. A further appeal on a point of law lies to the High Court (ss.56–59).

Other points are that each public authority must adopt and maintain a publication scheme approved by or in accordance with a model approved by the Commissioner and publish information in accordance with it (ss.19, 20). A request for information must be made in writing. A fee may be charged, set in accordance with regulations. The information must be communicated promptly and in any event not later than the 20th working day following receipt of the request, although where a public interest exception may apply, the authority need not comply with the request until such time as is reasonable in the circumstances (ss.8–10).

It is of course too early to judge the impact of the Act. The requirement for publication schemes certainly is helpful for those who wish to know what information is held and in what form. The earliest use seems to have been made by political parties and the media, echoing the position under the previous Code of Practice, which the 2000 Act replaces. The existence of the Commissioner, with significant investigatory powers, will be particularly helpful in ensuring an appropriate balance between individual complainants and public authorities. There seems, understandably, to be much greater awareness (and fear) of FOI Act requirements than there was of the previous Code of Practice.

As to the Commissioner's approach in dealing with his responsibilities, see *Regulation under the Freedom of Information Act 2000 and the Environmental Information Regulations 2004* at *www.informationcommissioner.gov.uk*. See generally, P. Birkinshaw, *Freedom of Information* (2001); J. Macdonald and C. Jones, *The Law of Freedom of Information* (2002); T. Straker and P. Coppel, *Information Rights: Law and Practice* (2004).

3. Other legal rights of access to information continue to co-exist with the 2000 Act. See, for example, the Environmental Information Regulations 2004 (SI 2004/3391), implementing Council Directive 2003/4; Pt 5A (ss.100A–100K) of the Local Government Act 1972 (in relation to local authorities generally); and the Local Authorities (Executive Arrangements) (Access to Information) (England) Regulations 2000 (SI 2000/3272) and similar regulations for Wales (SI 2001/2290) (in relation to the operation of executive arrangements (see above, p.29).

4. Information may also be obtained through an ombudsman's investigation (see Ch.3). As to the limited obligation regarding disclosure of documents in judicial review proceedings, see below, p.970. This naturally adds to the importance of the use of other means of access to information, but the tight time scales for judicial review may cause problems in practice.

(C) Getting Things Done

Here, we consider a number of processes by which government can achieve its objectives.

(i) Regulation

The following document gives a good overview of the principles that should be applied in regulation.

BETTER REGULATION TASK FORCE: PRINCIPLES OF GOOD REGULATION

(2003)

Introduction

Regulation may widely be defined as any government measure or intervention that seeks to change the behaviour of individuals or groups. It can both give people rights (e.g. equal opportunities), restrict their behaviour (e.g. compulsory use of seat belts).

Government interventions have an impact on us all, both at home and in the workplace. In prosperous societies there are constant demands for more regulation to protect the environment, workers or consumers. But where regulation is poorly designed or overly complicated it can impose excessive costs and inhibit productivity. The job of government is to get the balance right, providing proper protection and making sure that the impact on those being regulated is proportionate.

Politicians differ about the appropriate level of intervention, but all governments should ensure that regulations are necessary, fair, effective, affordable and enjoy a broad degree of public confidence. To achieve this, any policy intervention, and its enforcement, should meet the following five principles which the Better Regulation Task Force devised in 1997:

- Proportionality
- Accountability
- Consistency
- Transparency
- Targeting

The Principles are a useful toolkit for measuring and improving the quality of regulation and its enforcement, setting the context for dialogue between stakeholders and government. They should be applied to the full range of alternatives for achieving policy objectives, when dealing with both domestic and European legislation. Government Departments and independent regulators alike should use them when considering new proposals and evaluating existing regulations. The Principles should also be used to avoid unnecessary bureaucratic burdens being imposed on the public sector.

The Government has endorsed the give Principles, and integrated them into its Guide to Regulatory Impact Assessment. The European Commission has also taken steps to give the Principles like through its recent Action Plan on Better Regulation.

This leaflet references other documents that will be of use when developing or enforcing regulation.

Achieving Policy Objectives

Policy makers have a wide range of options available for implementing policy objectives. The Task Force urges them to consider them all, rather than automatically assume prescriptive regulation is required. The options chosen will have implications for the incentives facing stakeholders; the burdens imposed on them; levels of compliance; and ultimately the success of a policy. The unintended consequences need to be taken into account, as well as the desired outcomes. Solutions that give stakeholders the flexibility to solve problems themselves are often preferable to imposing rules on them.

Below are some of the alternatives available:

Do nothing

Government consistently faces demands from interest groups and the media to take action, often in response to one-off incidents or tragedies. In many cases the most appropriate response is to do nothing, as government action may be unnecessary, or worse, have costly unintended consequences.

Advertising campaigns and education

Government can influence the behaviour of individuals and firms through information, advice and persuasion—perhaps reinforced by other incentives or penalties. This approach was used to good effect in the campaign against drink driving.

Using the market

Government can remove problems preventing markets from working effectively or can introduce a market where none exists.

Often markets do not function effectively if participants do not have all the information necessary to make an informed decision. Industries can adopt codes of practice, regulating the provision of information themselves or Government can require producers of goods or services to provide relevant information or provide the information itself.

Many industries causing pollution do not meet the financial cost of its impact on the environment and people's lives. Many countries are now using or developing tradable permit schemes to address this problem, effectively creating a market in pollution and incentives to reduce it.

Financial incentives

Financial incentives may take the form of taxes, charges and levies; tax breaks and subsidies; and price caps in non-competitive industries. These create incentives to achieve the outcomes government wishes to secure (e.g. increased innovation or reduced pollution), and have the advantage of leaving managers to manage.

Self-regulation and voluntary codes of practice

Self-regulation and voluntary codes of practice have the advantage of involving stakeholders themselves in the process of regulation, and may be cheaper and more flexible to use than government enforced rules. There are many forms of self-regulation and the level of government intervention will vary, according to the risk posed by the activity being regulated.

Prescriptive regulation

Government can prescribe the behaviour it expects from business and individuals by setting rules or standards (e.g. proposals that part-time workers must be treated no less favourably than full-time workers). There are areas where this is the best means of achieving a policy objective. However, prescriptive regulation, like many other means of government intervention, may have unintended consequences (e.g. employers might avoid employing part-time workers), and without enforcement compliance may be limited. It will often be less flexible and less sympathetic to the way markets work than other tools.

Policy-maker's checklist

This table sets out, against each of the five Principles of Good Regulation, what regulators should bear in mind when devising, implementing, enforcing and reviewing regulations.

Proportionality	*Regulators should only intervene when necessary. Remedies should be appropriate to the risk posed, and costs identified and minimised.*
	• Policy solutions must be proportionate to the perceived problem or risk and justify the compliance costs imposed—don't use a sledgehammer to crack a nut.

	• All the options for achieving policy objectives must be considered—not just prescriptive regulation. Alternatives may be more effective and cheaper to apply. • "Think small first". Regulation can have a disproportionate impact on small business, which account for 99.8% of UK business. • EC Directives should be transposed without gold plating. • Enforcement regimes should be proportionate to the risk posed. • Enforcers should consider an educational, rather than a punitive approach where possible.
Accountability	*Regulators must be able to justify decisions, and be subject to public scrutiny.* • Proposals should be published and all those affected consulted before decisions are taken. • Regulators should clearly explain how and why final decisions have been reached. • Regulators and enforcers should establish clear standards and criteria against which they can be judged. • There should be well-publicised, accessible, fair and effective complaints and appeals procedures. • Regulators and enforces should have clear lines of accountability to Ministers; Parliaments and assemblies; and the public.
Consistency	*Government rules and standards must be joined up and implemented fairly.* • Regulators should be consistent with each other, and work together in a joined-up way. • New regulations should take account of other existing or proposed regulations, whether of domestic, EU or international origin. • Regulation should be predictable in order to give stability and certainty to those being regulated. • Enforcement agencies should apply regulations consistently across the country.
Transparency	*Regulators should be open, and keep regulations simple and user-friendly.* • Policy objectives, including the need for regulation, should be clearly defined and effectively communicated to all interested parties. • Effective consultation must take place before proposals are developed, to ensure that stakeholders' views and expertise are taken into account.

	• Stakeholders should be given at least 12 weeks, and sufficient information, to respond to consultation documents. • Regulations should be clear and simple, and guidance, in plain language, should be issued 12 weeks before the regulations take effect. • Those being regulated should be made aware of their obligations, with law and best practice clearly distinguished. • Those being regulated should be given the time and support to comply. It may be helpful to supply examples of methods of compliance. • The consequences of non-compliance should be made clear.
Targeting	*Regulation should be focused on the problem, and minimise side effects.* • Regulations should focus on the problem, and avoid a scattergun approach. • Where appropriate, regulators should adopt a "goals-based" approach, with enforcers and those being regulated given flexibility in deciding how to meet clear, unambiguous targets. • Guidance and support should be adapted to the needs of different groups. • Enforcers should focus primarily on those whose activities give rise to the most serious risks. • Regulations should be systematically reviewed to test whether they are still necessary and effective. If not, they should be modified or eliminated.

Policy makers and enforcers may also find the following publications useful:

• Better policy making: a guide to regulatory impact assessment (http://www.cabinet-office.gov.uk/regulation/scrutiny/betterpolicy.htm)
• Code of Practice on Written Consultation (http://www.cabinet-office.gov.uk/servicefirst/2000/consult/code/ConsultationCode.htm)
• Guidance on implementation periods (http://www.sbs.gov.uk/content/pdf/implementationguidelines.pdf)
• Enforcement concordat (http://www.cabinet-office.gov.uk/regulation/PublicSector/enforcement/Enforcement.htm)
• Cabinet Office guidance on policy-making (www.policyhub.gov.uk)

Tests of good regulation, and pitfalls to be avoided

These tests build on our give Principles of Good Regulation. They should be applied to the full range of policy tools, not just prescriptive regulation.

Regulations must:

Be balanced and avoid knee-jerk reactions
Ministers can come under pressure to react immediately
profile public concerns. This can lead to ineffective or di
lation being introduced.

- Gun control measures introduced following the tragedy at Dunbla. School appear to have largely been ineffective in tackling gun crime.
- The UK Government resisted pressures for a knee-jerk reaction in the wake of the financial scandals surrounding Enron and Worldcom.

Seek to reconcile contradictory policy objectives
Clear assessments of the likely impact of regulations are essential for identifying and reconciling contradictory objectives.

- Environmental protection must be balanced against economic need when taking planning decisions.
- Chemicals legislation needs to protect workers, the public and the environment without reducing the competitiveness of chemical industries.
- Regulatory Impact Assessments help policy makers to think through the full impact of proposals and to identify alternative options for the desired outcome.

Balance risks, costs and benefits
It is neither practical nor desirable for regulators to seek to remove all risk. Trade-offs between the costs and benefits of regulation need to be assessed, and citizens allowed, within reason, to make their own judgements about the risks in question.

- Rehabilitating criminals into society carries some risk that they will re-offend, but this must be assessed against the potential benefits.
- When government delivers its policies through intermediate agencies, it has a duty to ensure that taxpayers' money is spent appropriately. But excessive audit and reporting requirements hinder front-line staff.
- The accountability burden in the higher education sector is out of proportion to the risk of financial or academic mismanagement.
- The risks to children of using mobile phones have been managed through making information available to parents and letting them decide for themselves, not by imposing restrictions.

Avoid unintended consequences
By regulating in one area, regulators may unintentionally create problems elsewhere.

- Rules requiring single occupancy rooms in care homes prejudiced the therapeutic needs of those being treated for drug and alcohol addiction.
- Requirements to recycle fridges created a "fridge mountain" in the UK, which was ill-prepared to process them.
- Enhanced employment rights could lead to indirect discrimination against those the regulations are trying to help.

Complex regulation often places small firms and voluntary sector groups at a disadvantage against large organisations.

Be easy to understand

People know that they must pay a TV licence fee or are entitled to a minimum wage because the legislation is straightforward. But the complexity of some regulations can underline their effectiveness.

- The Working Time regulations are complex and difficult to administer, reducing their effectiveness.
- The complexity of the Housing Benefit system has made it difficult for claimants to make the transition into work.
- The Fire Safety regulations—which were the subject of 120 Acts and a similar number of subordinate regulations—are being consolidated into a single risk-based regime.

Have broad public support

Broad public support for a policy or regulation is a good indicator that the public sees it as necessary. Where such support is absent, compliance is likely to be low.

- The ban on 'beef on the bone' was widely considered to be excessive, with people preferring to judge the risks themselves.
- Compulsory use of seatbelts in the rear of vehicles is widely supported, as people understand why it is necessary.

However the public's view can change over time, resulting in better compliance or in a gradual disregard for previously accepted regulations.

- Drink-driving laws, which were ineffective for many years are now working well.
- Sunday trading restrictions, on the other hand, which had been well respected for over a century; suddenly lost credibility and were substantially reduced.

Be enforceable

To be effective regulation must also be practical to enforce.

- The Criminal Records Bureau was unable to cope with the demands of conducting checks on all new teachers.

Self-regulation, on the other hand, can provide very effective enforcement mechanisms.

- The Advertising Standards Authority, through its influence in the printed media, can ensure that an advertiser cannot find a medium to publish adverts it has not approved.

Identify accountability

When things go wrong there must be clear accountability without resorting to unfair retribution.

- There is a risk of blurred accountability for the regulation of the rail industry between Ministers and a number of independent regulators.
- Self-regulation can ensure that industries themselves are held accountable for their actions and how they are regulated (e.g. the Banking Code).

Be relevant to current conditions
Regulations should be reviewed on a regular basis to ensure that they remain necessary and relevant.

- Prescriptive regulation quickly becomes outdated in areas where market conditions or technologies change rapidly, and may inhibit innovation.
- Licensing legislation limited opening hours was widely seen as an outdated response to public order concerns, and is being reformed.
- Writing "sunset" clauses into legislation can be a useful tool for keeping regulation up to date.

Notes
1. The Better Regulation Task Force was established in 1997. It is an independent body, sponsored by the Cabinet Office, that advises the government on action to ensure that regulation accords with the Five Principles of Good Regulation.
2. Government control over an activity by means of regulation is a very well established administrative procedure, whose origins can be traced back to the times of the Tudors and Stuarts.

"Almost all areas of industry and trade were at that time subject to very detailed legislative controls, although some were governed by what we would now call 'self-regulation', since guilds were given monopoly rights of supply with powers to regulate the methods of production" (A.I. Ogus, *Regulation: Legal Form and Economic Theory* (1994), p.6).

The mechanisms of regulation are many and various, including the regulation of the development of land (building, engineering and other operations on land and material changes in the use of land) under the Town and Country Planning Act 1990; and the licensing by local authorities of a myriad of activities, including now the liquor licensing under the Licensing Act 2003 (see *Cross on Local Government Law*, Ch.29 and App.D; and cases below on the licensing of hackney carriages (p.697), gaming (p.707), sex shops (p.471) and airlines (p.461). As to the application of natural justice requirements to licensing decisions, see *McInnes v Onslow Fane*, below, p.683.
3. Other very significant areas of regulation are competition law, enforced originally by the Director-General of Fair Trading appointed under the Fair Trading Act 1973, whose legal responsibilities passed to the Office of Fair Trading by virtue of the Enterprise Act 2002; and the various regulators established in respect of privatised public utilities and some other enterprises. The main examples were the Director-General of Telecommunications and the Office of Telecommunications (Oftel); the Gas and Electricity Market Authority and the Office of Gas and Electricity Markets (Ofgem, established by the Utilities Act 2000 in succession to Ofgas and Offer), the Director-General and the Office of Water Services (Ofwat), the Rail Regulator and the Office of the Rail Regulator (ORR) and (in respect of a public sector enterprise) the Postal Services Commission (POSTCOMM). The purposes of regulation have included (with varying emphases in the different sectors) the prevention of the profit maximisation of national monopolies from distorting the efficient distribution of goods and problems that arise when the unregulated price of a good does not fully

reflect its true cost to society; the protection of the public interest (such as the maintenance of standards in broadcasting by Ofcom and the Governors of the BBC); the promotion of competition in particular market sectors where regulatory intervention was needed for the creation of a "level playing field"; and the protection of consumers and vulnerable groups (see T. Prosser in J. Jowell and D. Oliver (ed.), *The Changing Constitution* (5th ed., 2004), pp.352–354)).

The mechanisms used by regulators have included the enforcement of conditions in licences or authorisations granted by ministers (or in some cases by the regulator), and the setting of price limits following Periodic Reviews, usually by reference to a percentage increase below the Retail Price Index (RPI—x) but also where necessary by reference to approved plans for investment to ensure compliance with environmental standards set by UK and EC law (as in the case of water and sewerage undertakers). The Competition and Service (Utilities) Act 1992 enabled the regulators to establish performance standards for licensed undertakers, approve mandatory complaints handling procedures and to resolve disputes. Provision has been made by regulations for set levels of compensation to be payable where particular standards are breached. From the Utilities Act 2000 (in respect of gas and electricity) onwards, the regulators have been restructured to confer legal responsibilities on an office or commission rather than an individual Director-General. This pattern has been followed for the Office of Fair Trading and for postal services (Postal Services Act 2000), communications (Office of Communications Act 2002; Communications Act 2003), railways, (Railways and Transport Safety Act 2003) and water and sewerage (Water Act 2003). The legislation has also in most cases put independent consumer representative bodies on a stronger statutory footing.

When the regulators were first established there were concerns that the lack of accountability through ministers to Parliament and the point that they were not applying clear rules approved by Parliament would lead to highly personalised decision-making. In practice, however, individual regulators "have been, by the standards of British public bodies, exceptionally open in reaching their decisions" with the adoption of very full and open consultation processes (especially by Oftel) (see Prosser, *op. cit.*, pp.364–366). The legislation from 2000 onwards has increased the range of procedural obligations imposed by law on the regulators.

Arrangements for appeals and judicial review vary according to the context (see Prosser, *op.cit.*, pp.367–371). Appeals on the merits lie to the Competition Appeal Tribunal, with a further appeal on a point of law to the Court of Appeal, in the case of telecommunications licensing decisions (Communications Act 2003, ss.192–196) and specified decisions of the regulators and the OFT under the Competition Act 1998 (ss.46–49, as amended by the Enterprise Act 2002, s.17). In the case of financial penalties imposed by a regulator, there is a right of appeal to the High Court on grounds similar to judicial review (*e.g.* Utilities Act 2000, ss.59 and 95). The same applies in respect of challenges to decisions of the OFT concerning mergers under Pt 3 of the Enterprise Act 2002 (s.120; see *Office of Fair Trading v IBA Healthcare Ltd* [2004] EWCA Civ 142; [2004] 4 All E.R. 1103, dismissing an appeal against the CAT's decision to quash the OFT's decision not to refer a proposed merger to the Competition Commission; the Court of Appeal held that the OFT had applied the wrong legal test).

Where judicial review proceedings have been brought where there is no appeal, the courts have "in general intervened in matters of procedure while not double-guessing regulators on matters of substance" (Prosser, *op.cit.*, p.368. See *e.g. R. v Director-General of Gas Supply Ex p. Smith*, unreported, July 31, 1989, QBD (DG's refusal to reconnect gas supply quashed for breach of natural justice where applicants were given no opportunity to comment on meter reader's evidence of meter tampering). Challenges based on grounds of irrationality have, however, failed (see *e.g. R. v Independent Television Commission Ex p. TSW Broadcasting Ltd* [1996] E.M.L.R. 291, HL (challenges to ITC's rejection of TSW's application for Channel 3 licence failed in the absence of any error of law); *R. v Independent Television Commission*

Ex p. Virgin Television Ltd [1996] E.M.L.R. 318, QBD (V's challenge to decision to grant Channel 5 licence to C5B rejected; this was an exercise of judgment by an expert body); *R. v Director-General of Telecommunications Ex p. Cellcom Ltd* [1999] E.C.C. 314 (modification of licences for mobile telephone networks not irrational)).

4. While these forms of regulation have remained and been developed, there has at the same time from the 1980s onwards been a continuing emphasis by both Conservative and Labour governments on the need where possible to reduce burdens on business. This consideration is reflected in the Principles of Good Regulation (above, p.44). Special procedures have been developed to enable measures of deregulation to be effected by delegated legislation (under the Deregulation and Contracting Out Act 1994 and the Regulatory Reform Act 2001; see below p.229). The point was emphasised again in *Budget 2005, Investing for Our Future* (2004–05 HC 372), Ch.3 "Meeting the Productivity Challenge," setting out further steps to deliver better regulatory outcomes while driving down compliance costs for business. New regulatory proposals will be subject to more rigorous review by the Prime Minister's Panel for Regulatory Accountability (PRA) whose establishment had previously been announced in Budget 2004. The Government has accepted a recommendation of the Better Regulation Task Force that a new approach to regulation be adopted which forces departments to prioritise between new regulations and remove unnecessary regulations. Options for removing unnecessary and outdated regulations will always be explored as part of the Regulatory Impact Assessment process required for all new regulatory proposals. The government will always respond, in detail and within 90 days, to suggestions from business for regulatory simplifications. Appropriate objectives on better regulation and reducing bureaucracy will be included in the personal objectives of civil servants (p.48). EU laws will be implemented in the clearest and least burdensome way possible, so that they can be administered in accordance with the principles of good regulatory practice set out in the Hampton Review, *Reducing Administrative Burdens: Effective Inspection and Enforcement* (March 2005), p.49, see further, below, p.56. A new Better Regulation Executive will be established in the Cabinet Office, taking on the work of the existing Regulatory Impact Unit, to bring greater weight to the delivery of regulatory policy across government (p.53). The BTRF will be transformed into a new Better Regulation Commission to provide independent advice to government from business and other stakeholders about new regulatory proposals and about the government's own regulatory performance. The NAO also will take on an enhanced role in overseeing the technical evaluation of departments and regulators in reducing the burden to business of administering regulation (p.54). See further R. Baldwin, "*Is Better Regulation Smarter Regulation?*" [2005] P.L. 485.

(ii) The provision of public services

Notes

1. Apart from regulation, a further major purpose of government is to provide (or, increasingly, secure the provision of) public services. The efficient, effective and economical delivery of public services such as health, education and the provision of welfare support has been seen by all political parties as carrying a high priority with the electorate. There have been successive exercises seeking to set out the basic principles which should govern their provision, beginning with the Citizens' Charter (see below, p.202).

The main documents setting out the Labour Government's approach to the delivery of public services have been the immediate successor to the Citizen's Charter, Service First (Cabinet Office, *Service First: The New Charter Programme* (1998)); the *Modernising Government* White Paper (Cm.4310, 1999) and the paper, *Reforming Our Public Services*, published by the Prime Minister's Office of Public Services Reform in 2002. This last is pitched at a high level of generality, but states at p.10 that:

"to achieve customer-focused public services, four principles are paramount:
- It is the Government's job to set national standards that really matter to the public, within a framework of clear accountability, designed to ensure that citizens have the right to high quality services wherever they live.
- These standards can only be delivered effectively by devolution and delegation to the front line, giving local leaders responsibility and accountability for delivery, and the opportunity to design and develop services around the needs of local people.
- More flexibility is required for public service organisations and their staff to achieve the diversity of service provision needed to respond to the wide range of customer aspirations. This means challenging restrictive practices and reducing red tape; greater and more flexible incentives and rewards for good performance; strong leadership and management; and high quality training and development.
- Public services need to offer expanding choice for the customer. Giving people a choice about the service they can have and who provides it helps ensure that services are designed around their customers. An element of contestability between alternative suppliers can also drive up standards and empower customers locked into a poor service from their traditional supplier.
These four principles underpin the entire programme of reform".

Typical features of the current approach to service delivery accordingly include the setting of standards or performance targets by central government; processes of audit or inspection to monitor and assess performance, including the extent to which targets are met; the publication of performance information and the production of league tables comparing performance where different units (such as local authorities, schools and police forces) are involved in service delivery; the naming and shaming of weak performers; and the joining up of different services operating in the same area (such as health and social care). These arrangements have been applied across the public sector to both central and local government. A recent development has been a new emphasis on the promotion of choice (*Reforming Our Public Services*, Ch.6), illustrated by decisions requiring Primary Care Trusts to purchase a fixed percentage of secondary health care from the private sector, and the M6 Toll Road. Much of this is controversial, both among the political parties and within the services themselves. A recurrent theme is whether the setting of particular targets on which institutions are publicly judged has the effect of distorting delivery in ways that may operate against the needs of those served, or even leading to the falsification of records (a much discussed example being the target that 96 per cent (rising to 98 per cent) of patients attending an Accident and Emergency department are dealt with within 24 hours (see BMA, *Survey of Accident and Emergency Waiting Times* (March, 2005), reporting that only 26 per cent of departments surveyed said that the figures returned were an accurate reflection of their performance, and 82 per cent reported threats to patient safety from pressures to meet the four-hour target).

2. For overviews of the impact of New Public Management, see D. Oliver, *Constitutional Reform in the UK* (2003), Ch.12. For a sceptical view in the light of the operations of the Child Support Agency, see C. Harlow, "Accountability, New Public Management, and the Problems of the Child Support Agency" (1999) 26 J.L.S. 150.

(iii) Inspection

Notes

1. Inspection, involving the direct examination of an activity or object by an officially appointed person, has been a familiar governmental technique for some centuries. It may be used by central government to ensure appropriate standards are being achieved by public sector institutions (*e.g.* HM Inspectors of Constabulary and Schools, the Healthcare Commission) or by central or local government for similar purposes in the

private sector (*e.g.* factory inspectors, now the inspectors of the Health and Safety Executive; inspectors appointed by local authorities to enforce building regulations and consumer protection legislation in such areas as weight and measures, trade descriptions and food safety). Some are appointed by the Crown (*e.g.* the Chief Inspector of Prisons, the Chief Inspectors of Schools for England and for Wales); others by agencies or local authorities. In some areas, such as schools, inspections are normally carried out by individuals or organisations from the private sector registered and engaged by the Chief Inspector of Schools (see *Cross*, paras 20–128 to 20–133). In the case of planning inspectors (see below, pp.127 *et seq.*), inspection is in fact only an incidental function.

Inspection can serve a number of purposes. The inspection of private sector organisations is commonly a means of regulation, involving both ensuring compliance with the law through the spectrum of advice, warnings, the service of statutory notices or prosecution (see below, p.57) and promoting good practice, again through the giving of advice. The inspection of public sector organisations is somewhat similar, involving the twin purposes of reporting on compliance with centrally imposed standards (*cf.* above, pp.44 *et seq.*) and promoting good practice. In each case, there is an obvious tension between the two main purposes which the inspectorate must do its best to resolve.

2. A review of public sector inspectorates was carried out by the Office of Public Services Reform in the Cabinet Office in 2002–03. Its report, *Inspecting for Improvement: Developing a Customer Focused Approach* (2003) recommended that the government should set an overall policy for inspection, that ministers and departments should make sure inspectorates were working in real co-operation and could eliminate any duplication or unnecessary review; that inspectors should be encouraged to adopt certain best practice principles; and that everyone concerned should be expected to make high-quality service delivery the focus of inspection, with service improvement the primary aim. There was a strong case for change. It usefully proposed (at p.5) as a definition:

"Inspection of public services is a review, conducted by external bodies, that should
  • be independent of the service providers;
  • provide assurance, to Ministers and the public, about the safe and proper delivery of those services;
  • contribute to improvement of those services;
  • report in public; and
  • deliver value for money".

Some of the evidence of the effectiveness of inspection was critical. A 2000 survey of local authorities showed 74 per cent of respondents supporting the principle of external inspection as a catalyst for improvement, but only 45 per cent considered that inspections led to improved services for users, and only 27 per cent thought it led to innovation (p.24). The Review recommended 10 *Principles of Inspection and External Review*:

"The principles of inspection in this policy statement place the following expectations on inspection providers and on the departments sponsoring them:
  (1) The **purpose of improvement**. There should be an explicit concern on the part of inspectors to contribute to the improvement of the service being inspected. This should guide the focus, method, reporting and follow-up of inspection. In framing recommendations, an inspector should recognise good performance and address any failure appropriately. Inspection should aim to generate data and intelligence that enable departments more quickly to calibrate the progress of reform in their sectors and make appropriate adjustments.
  (2) A **focus on outcomes**, which means considering service delivery to the end users of the services rather than concentrating on internal management arrangements.
  (3) A **user perspective**. Inspection should be delivered with a clear focus on the experience of those for whom the service is provided, as well as on internal

management arrangements. Inspection should encourage innovation and diversity and not be solely compliance-based.

(4) **Proportionate to risk.** Over time, inspectors should modify the extent of future inspection according to the quality of performance by the service provider. For example, good performers should undergo less inspection, so that resources are concentrated on areas of greatest risk.

(5) Inspectors should encourage rigorous **self-assessment** by managers. Inspectors should challenge the outcomes of managers' self-assessments, take them into account in the inspection process, and provide a comparative benchmark.

(6) Inspectors should use **impartial evidence.** Evidence, whether quantitative or qualitative, should be validated and credible.

(7) Inspectors should disclose the **criteria** they use to form judgements.

(8) Inspectors should be **open** about their processes, willing to take any complaints seriously, and able to demonstrate a robust quality assurance process.

(9) Inspectors should have regard to **value for money,** their own included:
  • Inspection looks to see that there are arrangements in place to deliver the service efficiently and effectively.
  • Inspection itself should be able to demonstrate it delivers benefits commensurate with its cost, including the cost to those inspected.
  • Inspectorates should ensure that they have the capacity to work together on cross-cutting issues, in the interests of greater cost effectiveness and reducing the burden on those inspected.

(10) Inspectors should **continually learn** from experience, in order to become increasingly effective. This can be done by assessing their own impact on the service provider's ability to improve and by sharing best practice with other inspectors".

3. The recommendations of a review of the burden on business of regulatory inspection and enforcement was conducted by Philip Hampton. His final report (*Reducing Administrative Burden: Effective Inspection and Enforcement* (March 2005)) have been accepted by the Government (Budget Report 2005, 2004–05 HC 372, p.53). They were summarised as follows (p.52).

"The final report of the Hampton Review finds that the administrative burden upon business from regulatory inspection and enforcement is significant. The 63 national regulators within the scope of the Review perform at least 600,000 inspections and send out 2½ million forms to businesses each year. In addition, local authorities conduct at least 2½ million inspections.

The final report outlines a balanced package of reforms that will reduce the costs to businesses of complying with regulations. It sets out a number of common principles that it recommends all regulators should follow and which, once implemented, will result in a step change in their culture and management:
  • regulators should take a risk-based approach across all of their enforcement activities, so there should be no inspection of businesses without a reason, and regulators' resources and inspection activity should consequently be strengthened in the areas where the risks are greatest;
  • information requirements should also be based on risk based assessment to reduce the number of forms and requests for information. The number of forms that businesses have to fill in should be reduced, through greater sharing of data between regulators;
  • all new forms sent to businesses by regulatory bodies should have US-style 'time to complete' statements on them, and business reference groups should vet all forms for their business-friendliness before they are introduced;
  • the penalty regime should be based on managing the risk of re-offending, and the impact of the offence, but there will be tougher penalties for 'rogue businesses' that persistently break the rules;

- there should be a greater focus upon giving advice and support to businesses on how to comply with regulations and regulators should provide advice on regulatory compliance to any business that asks for it;
- all regulators should set out standards for service delivery, and publish an annual report setting out their performance against them; and
- new policies should be made with a view to using, wherever possible, existing regulators' inspections, forms and enforcement mechanisms.

The Hampton Review identified a total of 674 different bodies at local and national level that administer regulations upon business. This current structure is fragmented and diffuse with little co-ordination between different bodies, causing overlap and duplication in many areas. The review believes that a confusing and complex regulatory structure imposes potentially avoidable administrative burdens on business, and that a more joined-up approach would improve regulatory outcomes overall. It therefore recommends a significant consolidation of existing regulatory bodies, with 31 existing national regulators being absorbed into seven thematic bodies over the next four years. The Review also recommends reforms to improve the co-ordination of local and national regulatory services to deliver greater consistency for businesses.

The Hampton Review's recommendations represent a far-reaching programme through which regulatory burdens upon businesses will be reduced. To manage the implementation of its advocated reforms, and to ensure a consistency of approach across the public sector, the review recommends that a stronger, and more accountable regulatory framework is needed at the heart of government."

4. For studies of the operation of the two kinds of inspectorate, see P. Wusteman, *Her Majesty's Inspectors of Factories* 1833–1983 (1983); K. Hawkins, *Environment and Enforcement* (1984); B. Hutter, (1986) 26 B.J. Crim. 114; C. Hood *et al.*, *Regulation Inside Government* (1999); K. Walshe, *Regulating Healthcare: A Prescription for Improvement* (2003).

(iv) Prosecution

Prosecution for a criminal offence is frequently available as a mechanism for regulation. The Cabinet Office and the Local Government Association have agreed a document setting out *Principles of Good Enforcement*, which has been widely adopted.

CABINET OFFICE, LOCAL GOVERNMENT ASSOCIATION ENFORCEMENT CONCORDAT

(March 1998)

The Principles of Good Enforcement: Policy and Procedures

This document sets out what business and others being regulated can expect from enforcement officers. It commits us to good enforcement policies and procedures. It may be supplemented by additional statements of enforcement policy.

The primary function of central and local government enforcement work is to protect the public, the environment and groups such as consumers and workers. At the same time, carrying out enforcement functions in an equitable, practical and consistent manner helps to promote a thriving national and local economy. We are committed to these aims and to maintaining a fair and safe trading environment.

The effectiveness of legislation in protecting consumers or sectors in society depends crucially on the compliance of those regulated. We recognise that most businesses want to comply with the law. We will, therefore, take care to help business and others meet their legal obligations without unnecessary expense, while taking firm action, including prosecution where appropriate, against those who flout the law or act irresponsibly. All citizens will reap the benefits of this policy through better information, choice and safety.

We have therefore adopted the central and local government Concordat on Good Enforcement. Included in the term 'enforcement' are advisory visits and assisting with compliance as well as licensing and formal enforcement action. By adopting the concordat we commit ourselves to the following policies and procedures, which contribute to best value, and will provide information to show that we are observing them.

Principles of Good Enforcement: Policy

Standards

In consultation with business and other relevant interested parties, including technical experts where appropriate, we will draw up clear standards setting out the level of service and performance the public and business people can expect to receive. We will publish these standards and our annual performance against them. The standards will be made available to businesses and others who are regulated.

Openness

We will provide information and advice in plain language on the rules that we apply and will disseminate this as widely as possible. We will be open about how we set about our work, including any changes that we set, consulting business, voluntary organisations, charities, consumers and workforce representatives. We will discuss general issues, specific compliance failures or problems with anyone experiencing difficulties.

Helpfulness

We believe that prevention is better than cure and that our role therefore involves actively working with business, especially small and medium sized businesses, to advise on and assist with compliance. We will provide a courteous and efficient service and our staff will identify themselves by name. We will provide a contact point and telephone number for further dealings with us and we will encourage business to seek advice/information from us. Applications for approval of establishments, licences, registrations, etc, will be dealt with efficiently and promptly. We will ensure that, wherever practicable, our enforcement services are effectively co-ordinated to minimise unnecessary overlaps and time delays.

Complaints about Service

We will provide well publicised, effective and timely complaints procedures easily accessible to business, the public, employees and consumer groups. In cases where disputes cannot be resolved, any right of complaint or appeal will be explained, with details of the process and the likely time-scales involved.

Proportionality

We will minimise the costs of compliance for business by ensuring that any action we require is proportionate to the risks. As far as the law allows, we will take account of the circumstances of the case and the attitude of the operator when considering action.

We will take particular care to work with small businesses and voluntary and community organizations so that they can meet their legal obligations without unnecessary expense, where practicable.

Consistency

We will carry out our duties in a fair, equitable and consistent manner. While inspectors are expected to exercise judgement in individual cases, we will have arrangements in place to promote consistency, including effective arrangements for liaison with other authorities and enforcement bodies through schemes such as those operated by the Local Authorities Co-Ordinating Body on Food and Trading Standards (LACOTS) and the Local Authority National Type Approval Confederation (LANTAC).

Principles of Good Enforcement: Procedures

Advice from an officer will be put clearly and simply and will be confirmed in writing, on request, explaining why any remedial work is necessary and over what time-scale, and making sure that the legal requirements are clearly distinguished from best practice advice.

Before formal enforcement action is taken, officers will provide an opportunity to discuss the circumstances of the case and, if possible, resolve points of difference, unless immediate action is required (for example, in the interests of health and safety or environmental protection or to prevent evidence being destroyed).

Where immediate action is considered necessary, an explanation of why such action was required will be given at the time and confirmed in writing in most cases within 5 working days and, in all cases, within 10 working days.

Where there are rights of appeal against formal action, advice on the appeal mechanism will be clearly set out in writing at the time the action is taken (whenever possible this advice will be issued with the enforcement notice).

Notes

1. Offences which may lead to prosecutions by administrative authorities include the following:

   (1) failure to obtain a licence before commencing or continuing an activity, or acting in breach of licence conditions (*e.g.* breaches of planning control: Town and Country Planning Act 1990);
   (2) failing to observe prescribed standards (*e.g.* in relation to food hygiene, trading standards, pollution levels or health and safety at work);
   (3) false claims for rights and privileges, such as social security benefits;

(4) tax evasion;
(5) obstruction of public officials when exercising statutory functions (*e.g. Stroud v Bradbury* [1952] 2 All E.R. 76).

2. A major official study concluded that prosecutions by central and local government bodies, excluding the police (and now, of course, the Crown Prosecution Service), amounted to almost one-fifth of non-traffic criminal cases. These agencies included the following in descending order of their use of the courts: the Post Office (television licence prosecutions), the British Transport Police (rail-fare "dodgers"), the Department of the Environment (vehicle excise tax cases), local authorities (numerous types of criminal behaviour) and the revenue departments (tax fraud, etc.). See K.W. Lidstone *et al.*, *Royal Commission on Criminal Procedure: Prosecutions by Private Individuals and Non-Police Agencies*, Research Study No.10 (HMSO, 1980). There is now much greater openness as to the prosecution policies of administrative authorities exemplified by the Enforcement Concordat (see also dti, *Enforcement Concordat: Good Practice Guide for England and Wales* (June 2003). Good practice in enforcement is part of the wider agenda for good practice in regulation (above, p.444). The Concordat has been adopted by 96 per cent of central and local government bodies with an enforcement function (*www.cabinetoffice.gov.uk/regulation/pst/enforcecon.asp*).

3. Research indicates that the administrative bodies may for a variety of reasons prefer to use other enforcement strategies, such as advice, negotiation and warning, rather than prosecution. See, *e.g.* B. Hutter, *The Reasonable Arm of the Law* (1988) (environmental health officers); K. Hawkins, *Environment and Enforcement* (1984). Another example is the use by the Commissioners of Customs and Excise of their statutory power to compound proceedings (*i.e.* refrain from prosecuting an alleged offender in return for a monetary penalty being paid) in thousands of petty smuggling cases per year. Such alternatives to prosecution raise important legal questions concerning the basic rights of individuals, including the procedure by which such offers are made, the legal status of these agreements and the forms of redress available to aggrieved individuals. For a detailed study see A.R. Mowbray, "The Compounding of Proceedings by the Customs and Excise: Calculating the Legal Implications" (1988) B.T.R. 290.

4. A procedure similar to compounding is used by the Inland Revenue. This is the *Hansard* procedure based on statements to the House of Commons by successive Chancellors of the Exchequer. Under the version set out by John Major MP on October 18, 1990, where a taxpayer made a full confession of fraud and had given full facilities for investigation, the Inland Revenue might accept (but was not bound to accept) a money settlement instead of instituting criminal proceedings. A tax inspector also has statutory power to require a person to provide information that in the inspector's reasonable opinion may contain information relevant to any tax liability; non-compliance is an offence (Taxes Management Act 1970, ss.20(1), 98(1)). The House of Lords has held that obtaining of information in response to a section 20(1) notice does not infringe the right not to incriminate oneself as part of the right to a fair trial under Art.6(1), ECHR (*R. v Dimsey; R. v Allen* [2001] UKHL 45; [2002] 1 A.C. 509). An argument that information provided though the *Hansard* procedure breached that right because of the inducement offered failed. The information provided was false and used as part of the evidence on charges of cheating the public revenue, the reverse of the use as evidence of its truth of a confession obtained by an inducement. Lord Hutton noted (at [35]):

"If, in response to the *Hansard* statement the appellant had given true and accurate information which disclosed that he had earlier cheated the revenue and had then been prosecuted for that earlier dishonesty, he would have had a strong argument that the criminal proceedings were unfair and an even stronger argument that the Crown should not rely on evidence of his admission, but that is the reverse of what actually occurred".

In the light of this, a revised *Hansard* statement was made to on November 7, 2002:

"Further to the statement made on 18th October 1990 at column 882 by the then Chancellor, the Rt. Hon. John Major, the practice of the Board of Inland Revenue in cases of suspected serious tax fraud is as follows:

The Board reserves complete discretion to pursue prosecutions in the circumstances it considers appropriate.

Where serious tax fraud has been committed, the Board may accept a money settlement instead of pursuing a criminal prosecution.

The Board will accept a money settlement and will not pursue a criminal prosecution, if the taxpayer, in response to being given a copy of this Statement by an authorised officer, makes a full and complete confession of all tax irregularities".

See further *www.inlandrevenue.gov.uk/hansard/changes*; Inland Revenue Code of Practice 9; and D.C. Ormerod, [2001] B.T.R. 194 on the pre-2002 position.

The Inland Revenue's general prosecution policy is set out at *www.inlandrevenue. gov.uk/prosecutions/prosecution-policy*.

5. Sir Richard Scott examined the role of the Customs and Excise department prosecuting authority in his Report on defence exports to Iraq (see below, at p.112). He stated that:

"it is an important constitutional principle that a prosecuting authority should be independent, free from political interference and free from direction by Government. Both the Crown Prosecution Service under the Director of Public Prosecutions and the Serious Fraud Office are independent prosecuting authorities in the sense I have mentioned. Both are subject to the superintendence of the Attorney General but it is recognised that, in that capacity, the Attorney General exercise a quasi-judicial role and does not act as a Cabinet Minister. . . . Many Government Departments have statutory prosecution functions [*e.g.* the Department of Trade and Industry, Department of Transport and the Post Office]. . . . Departments cannot, in my opinion, when exercising their statutory prosecution functions be regarded as independent of the executive in quite the sense that the CPS and the SFO are independent. They are, no doubt, independent in the sense of being free from political interference; but their prosecuting function will usually involve the enforcement of laws in respect of which there will be some departmental policy and prosecutions can often legitimately be regarded as a means of enforcing departmental policy in the area in question. Customs, in relation to offences in connection with its revenue functions, has more in common with a departmental prosecuting authority than with the CPS or the SFO. . . . Customs is entitled, in deciding what prosecutions to bring, to take some account of departmental policy relating to the collection of the revenue in question. In relation to export control offences, however, Customs has no departmental responsibility save that of enforcer of the law. In its investigation of these offences, it has a similar function to that of the police in respect of ordinary crime; in prosecuting these offences Customs' role is analogous to that of the CPS or the SFO. Customs should, in my opinion, in takings its decisions on whether to investigate or prosecute export control offences, be as independent as are the police when investigating crime and as are the CPS and the SFO when taking prosecution decisions. These decisions should not be based on what is believed by Customs to be Government policy on export controls. It is, in my opinion, fundamentally unsatisfactory for Customs to regard its function in enforcing export control law as being the enforcement of Government policy" (1995–96 HC 115, paras.K4.6–4.9).

Sir Richard recommended, *inter alia*, that the Attorney-General should supervise the bringing of export control prosecutions by the Commissioners of Customs and Excise. This would involve regular reporting by Customs officials to the Law Officers and the Attorney-General becoming answerable to Parliament for the conduct of such prosecutions (*ibid.*, para.K4.11). More generally on Sir Richard's Report, see R. Austin (ed.), *Iraqgate: The Constitutional Implications of the Matrix-Churchill Affair* (1996).

A further review by John Gower QC and Sir Anthony Hammond in 2001, following the failure of a Customs and Excise prosecution relating to the importation of cocaine valued at £30m, concluded that the Customs and Excise Solicitor's Office should retain its prosecution function but the Solicitor for HM Customs and Excise should become accountable to the Attorney-General in relation to the whole of his prosecution function. Decisions to prosecute would be made by a Customs lawyer after consultation, where appropriate, with an administrator on matters of policy and public interest. The Government accepted these recommendations, with effect from April 2002. This placed lawyers in the Solicitor's Office on the same footing as lawyers in the CPS and the SFO.

Following a further review by Butterfield J. following the high-profile failure of another prosecution, and the merger of the Inland Revenue and HM Customs and Excise, a new fully independent Revenue and Customs Prosecutions Office (RCPO) is to be established (see HM Customs and Excise Annual Report and Accounts 2003–04, 2004–05 HC 119, pp.14, 165). The Butterfield review concluded that the earlier changes had not gone far enough.

6. Two distinct problems arising out of the prosecution powers of such organisations are (1) the extent to which they should be permitted to conduct both investigative and prosecutorial functions, in contrast to the separation of three functions for mainstream functions between the police and the Crown Prosecution Service; and (2) the maintenance of consistent standards in the prosecution policies themselves (see further S.H. Bailey, J. Ching, M.J. Gunn and D.C. Ormerod, *Smith, Bailey and Gunn on the Modern English Legal System* (4th ed., 2002), pp.900–903).

(v) Contracting

There are many dimensions to government contracting. A broad distinction can carefully be drawn between contract "as a medium of exchange" and contract "as a technique of government or regulation" (*Cane*, Ch.12). As to the former, government bodies of all kinds need to enter contracts for the provision to them of the goods and services they require to perform their functions. The suppliers may themselves be from the public or the private sector. A variety of legal issues may arise. There may be purely private law issues involving the application of the law of contract. There may be public law issues arising from such questions as

  (a) whether the public body has legal power to enter the contract in question, the Crown appearing to have much broader powers than other public bodies in this regard;
  (b) whether, and if so, how the general judicial review principles controlling the fettering of discretion and abuse of power apply to the contracting process;
  (c) the application of specific legislative rules that constrain the contracting process.

These issues have long been familiar. See further below, pp.495–509, 956–966 and 1037–1039. The use of contract as a technique of government or regulation is a much more recent phenomenon. It has played a key role in the transformation of the ways in which public services are provided. Significant developments have included:

  (a) the use of contractual powers to achieve particular collateral goals of social or economic policy;
  (b) the wholesale privatisation (or re-privatisation) of particular public services (gas, water, electricity, telecommunications, railways; not as yet postal services); the market testing and contracting out of particular aspects of public services for which central government retains overall responsibility;

(c) the privatisation of many local government services under the Conservative Government's Compulsory Competitive Tendering regime (Local Government Act 1988), continuing under the Best Value regime which replaced CCT by virtue of the Local Government Act 1999;

(d) the facilitation of contracting-out across the public sector by Pt II (ss. 69–79) of the Deregulation and Contracting Out Act 1994;

(e) the entering of new forms of arrangement between public bodies and the private sector through the Private Finance Initiative;

(f) the use of contractual (or contractual-type) models for constructing the relationship between government departments and executive agencies (above, p.8); or between different public bodies engaged together in the delivery of a service (*e.g.* agreements for payment by Primary Care Trusts to Acute Hospital Trusts for the provision of hospital services; agreements between PCTs and NHS Foundation Trusts take the form of legally binding contracts).

Overall, "in a broad sense, government by contract has become the dominant paradigm for the provision of public services" (M. Freedland, "Government by Contract and Public Law" [1994] P.L. 86 and "Government by Contract—Re-examined—Some Functional Issues" in P. Craig and R. Rawlings, *Law and Administration in Europe* (2003), Ch.7, p.124). This should be understood as covering not only the process of government procurement, but also "the creation and operation of the institutional structure within which contractual or contract-like arrangements for the provision of public services may take place" (*ibid.* p.125).

These changes have raised issues as to the relative efficiency and effectiveness of different modes of provisions, whether their adoption leads to an inappropriate dilution of the standards of accountability that previously applied and that should continue to apply, and more generally, the lack of an adequate legislative basis for some of these developments.

(a) *The inherent contractual powers of the Crown*

The Crown has increasingly placed overt reliance on a doctrine that it has an inherent power to take any action, including the entering of contracts, that a natural person might take, unless prohibited expressly or impliedly by legislation. The doctrine is articulated in the following memorandum.

TEXT OF MEMORANDUM FROM GRANVILLE RAM, FIRST PARLIAMENTARY COUNSEL,

(2 NOVEMBER 1945)

"The Ram Doctrine" Ministers of the Crown (Transfer of Functions)

Memorandum by Parliamentary Counsel

I have been asked to write a memorandum upon the question how far legislation is necessary to authorise any extension of the existing powers of a Government Department. It is necessary at the outset to draw a sharp distinction between what is legally possible and what is permissible having regard to established practice, and I therefore deal with each of these aspects of the question in turn.

Legal Position

A Minister of the Crown is not in the same position as a statutory corporation. A statutory corporation (whether constituted by a special statute as, for instance, a railway company is, or constituted under Companies Acts as in the case of an ordinary company) is entirely a creature of Statute and has no powers expect those conferred upon it by under statute, but a Minister of the Crown, even though there may have been a statute authorising his appointment, is not a creature of statute and may, as an agent of the Crown, exercise any powers which the Crown has power exercise, except so far as he is precluded from doing so by statute. In other words, in the case of a Government Department, one must look at the statutes to see what it may not do, not as in the case of a company to see what it may do. There are, of course, innumerable instances in which statutory powers have been conferred on Ministers and there are frequently questions whether an express statutory provision conferring particular power does not by implication have a restrictive effect in the field in which those powers have been granted. Whether or not such an implication ought to be drawn in any particular case must always be a question of construction to be determined on the wording of the relevant statutes, but the governing principle is that express statutory provision is not necessary to enable a Minister to exercise functions.

For reasons explained below in paragraphs 3 to 7 of this Memorandum, this question has become bound up with that of expenditure and it is sometimes thought a Minister's functions are limited to those for which he has been expressly authorised by statute to incur expenditure. This is an inversion of the true position which is that although a Minister may do anything which he is not precluded from doing, he will only be able to pay for what he does if Parliament votes him the money. Nevertheless in statutes conferring statutory power on a Minister it is common to find provisions to the effect that the expenses incurred by him in exercising them shall be defrayed out of moneys provided by Parliament. Such provisions are inserted for two reasons. First, for the purpose of making plain the intention that such expenses shall be paid out of voted money and not out of the Consolidated Fund and secondly, for the purpose of showing that what is contemplated is a permanent annual charge. Moreover, it is also convenient to insert such words in a Bill so that they may be italicised in order to show what portions of the Bill are required to be supported by a Money Resolution. It is, however, important to appreciate that such provisions as these do not form the statutory is, however, important to appreciate that such provisions as these do not form the statutory authority for the payment of the expenditure concerned and that legally they amount to no more than an expression of intention, because no Parliament is able to bind its successors, or even to bind itself, to vote money in future years. Statutory authority for the payment of expenditure out of moneys provided by Parliament must be, and can only be, given year by year by means of the Votes and the Appropriation Act.

Established Practice

During the period 1920–1930 cases occurred in which Departments obtained money by means of the Votes and the Appropriation Act for expenditure which had not been foreshadowed by and previous legislation, and even, in a few instances, for expenditure in excess of limits which had clearly been contemplated by such legislation. Attention was drawn to these points by the Public Accounts Committee in 1930, 1931 and 1932, and on the last mentioned of these occasions the Report of the Committee, after referring to the practice of the Ministry of Labour of obtaining money by votes for the training and resettlement of the unemployed, which was outside certain powers conferred on the Ministry by statute, went on to say—

"Your Committee consider also, as a matter of general principle, that, where it is desired that continuing functions should be exercised by a Government Department, particularly where such functions may involve financial liabilities extending beyond a given financial year, it is proper, subject to certain recognised exceptions, that the power and duties to be exercised should be defined by specific statute."

To this the Treasury replied as follows:

"There have been in the past many instances where continuing services which have never been dealt with by statute—some of them of considerable importance—have been provided for with no more permanent authority than that given by an Appropriation Act, and some of those services continue today, without the propriety of the means of providing for them having been called in question. Moreover there may arise, particularly in circumstances such as the present, emergencies which the Government will prefer to provide for ad hoc through the Appropriation Act in the hope that the need for such provision will not be repeated in future years. In such cases My Lords doubt whether any advantage would result from the enactment of specific legislative authority, and it does not appear to Them that in such cases resort to the authority of the Appropriation Act should necessarily be regarded as contrary to orthodox finance. Nevertheless, while They think that the Executive Government must continue to be allowed a certain measure of discretion in asking Parliament to exercise a power which undoubtedly belongs to it, They agree that practice should normally accord with the view expressed by the Committee that, where it is desired that continuing functions should be exercised by a Government Department (particularly where such functions involve financial liabilities extending beyond a given year) it is proper that the powers and duties to be exercised should be defined by specific statute. Their Lordships will, for their part, continue to aim at the observance of this principle".

Again in 1933, the Public Accounts Committee drew attention to the "general principle" enunciated by the Committee of the previous year and referred to "certain further examples of continuing expenditure not covered by specific legislative sanction" and in particular to the fact that the annual Exchequer grant towards police expenditure had "no statutory basis whatever". They went on to say—

"It has been represented that a number of other important services of a continuing nature are supported solely by the authority of the annual Appropriation Act, but in the opinion of Your Committee this circumstance does not furnish adequate ground for the abandonment of attempts to place such expenditure on a constitutional basis".

With all due respects to the Public Accounts Committee it is submitted they were inaccurate both in saying that grants which were authorised only by the Appropriation Act "had no statutory basis whatever" and in describing the changes of practice they desired as "attempts to place such expenditure on a constitutional basis", because for the reasons explained in paragraph 2 above, the Appropriation Act is in law the only possible "statutory basis" for any voted expenditure and the use of the Appropriation Act without previous general legislation however objectionable it may be is not illegal and therefore not unconstitutional. The Treasury, however, did not reply in this sense partly no doubt because to have done so would have seemed like a legal quibble and partly because they were in agreement with the Public Accounts Committee upon the substance of the points they raised. The reply given was contained in Treasury Minute dated 26th January, 1934, of which the relevant extract is as follows:

> "My Lords note that the Committee accept generally the assurance which have been given them as regards expenditure which is not covered by the statutory powers of Government Departments.
>
> They are aware that there are many items of expenditure, often on a large scale, appearing on Votes from year to year for which is not other authority exists than the successive Appropriation Acts.
>
> It is of course clearly within the right of Parliament to provide even continuing grants on the authority of the Appropriation Acts, but Lords concur in the view of the Committee that the power should be used within reasonable limits and They will endeavour to comply with the wish of the Committee that, when it has been exercised to authorise continuing grants, opportunity should be taken to insert regularising clauses in any appropriate legislation which may be in contemplation".

These interchanges between the Public Accounts Committee and the Treasury formed the basis of the practice which has now come to be regarded a established, but it will be noted that on each occasion the Treasury reply was such as to maintain the legal principle intact.

Conclusion

Form what I have written above it will be seen that the answer to the question put to me may be summarised as follows:
a. Legislation is not legally necessary to authorise an extension of the existing powers of a Government Department except where such an extension is precluded by a previous statute either expressly or by necessary implication.
b. If the extended powers involve an annual charge extended over a period of years legislation though not required by law, is required by established practice formally records in the transactions between the Public Accounts Committee and the Treasury.

It may be added that where the creation of a new office—such, for instance as a new Parliamentary Secretaryship—is involved legislation is not legally necessary unless it is required that the new office holder should sit in the House of Commons, in which case a Bill must be passed unless, of course, there is still in force emergency legislation covering the point.

Notes

1. This memorandum was published as recently as 2003 (see HL Deb, Vol.643, col.WA98, January 22, 2003) in response to a Parliamentary Question from Lord Lester of Herne Hill QC. Lord Lester and M.Weait analyse the doctrine at [2003] P.L. 415, and argue that "the position is unsatisfactory and cries out for reforming legislation placing ministers and civil servants under Parliament rather than the Crown". Their note refers to further written answers by Baroness Scotland (HC Deb Vol.645, col.WA 12, February 25, 2003; Vol.646, col.WA 59, March 24, 2003; Vol.647, col.WA 38, April 9, 2003). The first of these claimed that "ministers and departments have common law powers which derive from the Crown's status as a corporation sole" distinct from their prerogative powers. Whether legislation is needed depends on the circumstances. Sometimes, it is clear that legislation is needed, as where the proposed action might substantially interfere with human rights, in which case a clear and reasonably accessible legal framework is required in order to comply with human rights law. In other cases, a political as well as a legal judgment has to be made as to whether legislation is desirable, taking account of such factors as whether the proposed action is a priority and whether authorising that action by legislating represents a good use of Parliamentary time. In the past five years, common law powers had often been relied on as the legal basis for such government actions as entering contracts, employing staff, conveying property and other management functions not provided for by statute. The second answer added that legislation (or a change in the common law) was always necessary for an extension of ministerial power, and that legislation was also necessary for the imposition of legal obligations, the creation of offences or the raising of taxes.

> "If, however, it is proposed that Ministers exercise powers that are already available at common law to private individuals, or to the Crown by virtue of the prerogative, there is no legal requirement for legislation."

This echoes the assertion by the Cabinet Office's Performance and Information Unit (*Privacy and Data-sharing: The Way Forward for Public Services* (2002) that the Ram doctrine was that "a department can do anything that a natural person can, provided it is not forbidden from doing so".

It will be observed that the Ram doctrine is essentially set out in the 1945 memorandum by way of assertion. The memorandum invokes neither "the status of the Crown as a corporation sole" nor the proposition that the Crown can exercise the all powers of a natural person unless forbidden by statute (see Lester and Weait, *op.cit.* pp.420, 421). Nevertheless, Ram's "Conclusion a" does not seem any narrower in outcome than either of these propositions. The qualifications set out in the recent written answers are accordingly welcome. Furthermore it must be remembered that the general freedom of action of "natural persons", whether or not public officers, does not include power to interfere with the rights of others unless such power is specifically conferred, expressly or by necessary implication, by statute or the common law (the common law, in the case of the Crown, including the prerogative). This proposition is reflected as regards the interpretation of statutes in the principle of legality (*Pierson*, below, p.251), and, as regards the common law, by the decision of the Court of Common Pleas in *Entick v Carrington* (1765) 19 State Tr.1029 rejecting the existence of any general conception of state necessity as the justification for such powers (see S.H. Bailey, D.J. Harris and D.C. Ormerod, *Bailey, Harris and Jones, Civil Liberties: Cases and Materials* (5th ed., 2001), pp.84–86).

It would obviously be unacceptable for the Ram doctrine to be regarded as enabling these principles to be evaded, and it does not seem that the government claims that it does. Given that, it seems to be of less significance whether the ability of the Crown to enter contracts, employ staff, convey property and carry out other management functions without requiring parliamentary authority is a matter of "common law powers derived from the Crown's status as a corporation sole" as claimed, or is, as Lester and Weait argue:

> "part and parcel of the freedom given by Parliament and the common law to everyone, including the Crown (as corporation sole) and other public authorities to make contracts, convey property and manage their affairs" (p.419).

(It is not clear what are the other "public authorities" referred to here. The powers of local authorities, for example, are all conferred expressly or by implication by statute.) Moving on to the question of whether legislation is desirable (as distinct from necessary) there is a strong case (also made by Lester and Weait) for both these powers (however characterised) and the reorganised prerogative powers to be placed on a statutory footing, so as to facilitate appropriate standards of parliamentary and judicial scrutiny. It is remarkable and anomalous that very significant changes in the structure of the civil service and the development of "government by contract" have not been founded on specific legal powers (see above, p.8).

2. The principles of the Ram memorandum are reflected in the Treasury's document, *Government Accounting*, Pts 1.2 and 2. On the Concordat, see T. Daintith, "The Legal Effects of the Appropriation Act" [1998] P.L.552.

3. The proposition that the Crown has the powers of a natural person was confirmed by the Court of Appeal in *R. v Secretary of State for Health Ex p. C* [2000] 1 F.C.R. 627, in holding that a private citizen (and therefore the Crown) was entitled to maintain an index of persons about whom there were doubts about their suitability to work with children. Neither the Crown nor a private individual could exercise their freedoms in such a way as to interfere with the rights of others. The maintenance of the DH's Consultancy Service Index did not involve such interference as decisions whether to employ a person were made by the employer. The position would have been different if inclusion in the Index deprived an applicant of a qualification or licence essential for the lawful conduct of the occupation in question. In addition, the operation of the Index did not involve an unreasonable exercise of discretion in the balancing of competing interests. The position was not affected by the fact that the Index was to be placed on a statutory footing by the Protection of Children Act 1999. The question of the existence and extent of the "common law powers of the Crown" was left open by the House of Lords in *R.(on the application of Hooper) v Secretary of State for Work and Pensions* [2005] UKHL 29 (below, p.318). See further, M. Sunkin and S. Payne (ed.), *The Nature of the Crown* (1999); J. McLean, "The Crown in Contract and Administrative Law" (2004) 24 O.J.L.S. 129 (contrasting the approach of administrative law that disaggregates the state into named officials with the position that contract law constructs the government actor, the Crown, as a common law corporation); and M. Cohn, "Medieval Chains, Invisible Inks: On Non-Statutory Powers of the Executive" (2005) 25 O.J.L.S. 97. Cohn notes that that it is doubtful whether one should seek one theory to be equally applicable to powers, immunities and capacities, and that the lack of a statutory basis for exercises of power "threatens three basic values of proper administrative practice—participation, clarity and accountability" (pp.102–103) and yet does not lead to heightened judicial scrutiny. The current position fails to provide a proper balance between legality and need.

(b) *The use of contractual powers to achieve collateral, social or economic policies*

Notes

1. At the central government level, the possibility of using contracting in this way is facilitated by the apparent general competence of the Crown (above, p.63) and the proposition that "whatever the Crown may lawfully do it may do by means of

contract" (C. Turpin, *Government Procurement and Contracts* (1989), p.84).
Examples of such activity include the express contractual terms in government contracts required by successive Fair Wages Resolutions of the House of Commons
between 1891 and 1983. These aimed to ensure that employees of government
contractors enjoyed wages and working conditions no less favourable than those
generally applicable to similar employment, and freedom to join trade unions, but
there was, "a lack of zeal in its implementation" and it was dropped by the
Conservative Government (see *Turpin, op.cit.*, p.79.) Another is the use of blacklisting by the Labour Government to enforce its policy of limiting maximum pay
increases under its anti-inflation policy. This was analysed by T.C. Daintith
("Regulation by Contract, the New Prerogative" (1979) 32 C.L.P. 41), who noted (at
pp.41–42) that the government:

> "has discovered means of using its increasing economic strength *vis-à-vis* private
> industry so as to promote certain policies in a style, and with results, which for a
> long time we have assumed must be the hallmark of Parliamentary legislation: that
> is to say, officially promulgated rules backed by effective general compulsion. This
> means the power to rule without parliamentary consent, which is the hallmark of
> prerogative . . .".

In the pre-contractual phase, in selecting contractual partners and deciding the terms
offered, the Government enjoyed almost unfettered freedom and total immunity from
judicial review or parliamentary scrutiny; the full potential of constraints under EC
law had not then been adequately appreciated. It would be "sad, but not surprising, if
Parliament . . . were to sit quietly by while Government sanctioned for itself a new prerogative" (p.59). See further T.C. Daintith, "The Techniques of Government" in
J. Jowell and D. Oliver, *The Changing Constitution* (3rd ed., 1994), Ch.8, classifying
the power of government contracting as an element of "dominium" (the ability of
Government to secure its policy objectives through the use of public wealth).

There has since then been no exercise of power exactly similar to the anti-inflation
policy of the late 1970s. Nevertheless, the lack of a legislative basis for such major
developments as the Next Steps and Private Finance Initiatives generates similar concerns. The manner of the exercise of contractual powers is in many cases regulated by
EU procurement law, which has developed significantly since the 1970s (see below,
p.1038).

2. By contrast with the Crown, the contractual powers of local authorities are more
severely constrained by the *ultra vires* doctrine. Attempts to use particular powers to
secure collateral objectives have been constrained by judicial review proceedings (see,
e.g. below, pp.543, 544). Furthermore, s.17 of the Local Government Act 1988 provides that it is the duty of every public authority (as defined in Sch.2, and including all
local authorities), in exercising specified functions in relation to its public supply or
public works contracts, to do so without reference to matters which are non-commercial matters for the purposes of the section. The functions include drawing up lists
of approved tenderers, the inclusion or exclusion of persons from a group invited to
tender for a particular contract, the selection of the person with whom to enter a contract, the nomination (or approval of nomination) of sub-contractors, or termination
of a contract. The specified non-commercial matters are:

> "(a) the terms and conditions of employment by contractors of their workers or the
> composition of, the arrangements for the promotion, transfer or training of or the
> other opportunities afforded to, their workforces;
>
> (b) whether the terms on which contractors contract with their sub-contractors
> constitute, in the case of contracts with individuals, contracts for the provi
> sion by them as self-employed persons of their services only;
>
> (c) any involvement of the business activities or interests of contractors with
> irrelevant fields of Government policy;

(d) the conduct of contractors or workers in industrial disputes between them or any involvement of the business activities of contractors in industrial disputes between other persons;

(e) the country or territory of origin of supplies to, or the location in any country or territory of the business activities or interests of, contractors;

(f) any political, industrial or sectarian affiliations or interests of contractors or their directors, partners or employees;

(g) financial support or lack of financial support by contractors for any institution to or from which the authority gives or withholds support;

(h) use or non-use by contractors of technical or professional services provided by the authority under the Building Act 1984 or the Building (Scotland) Act 1959.

(6) The matters specified in subsection (5) above include matters which have occurred in the past as well as matters which subsist when the function in question falls to be exercised" (s.17(5), (6)) (See DoE Circular 8/1988).

The Conservative Government gave as a reason for s.17 that "political discrimination in the award of contracts is an offensive and growing practice; increasing numbers of councils subjugate the interests of their ratepayers and business men to futile political gesturing" (Secretary of State for the Environment, *Hansard*, HC Vol.119, col.91). Breach of s.17 does not amount to a criminal offence, but is actionable by any person who in consequence suffers loss or damage. Furthermore, potential or former contractors are given standing for the purposes of bringing judicial review proceedings (s.19(7)).

Section.18 of the 1988 Act, as amended by the Race Relations (Amendment) Act 2000, Sch.2, para.20, enables public authorities to ask approved questions and included in a draft contract or tender provisions relating to workforce matters where reasonably necessary to secure compliance with s.71(1) of or any order under s.71(2) of the Race Relations Act 1976. Section 71(1) (substituted by s.2 of the 2000 Act) provides that it is the duty of every local authority to make appropriate arrangements to secure that its functions are carried out with due regard to the need (a) to eliminate unlawful racial discrimination; and (b) to promote equality of opportunity, and good relations between persons of different racial groups. Six questions were approved by the Secretary of State after consultation with the Commission for Racial Equality (Circular 8/88, Annex B).

More recently, the balance has shifted away from an (almost) exclusive concentration on commercial considerations. The matters specified in (a) and (d) cease to be non-commercial matters to the extent that a Best Value authority considers it necessary or expedient, in order to permit or facilitate compliance with the requirement of Pt 1 of the Local Government Act 1999 (Best Value), to exercise functions with reference to them, or in relation to a transfer of staff under the Transfer of Undertakings (Protection of Employment) Regulations 1981 (Local Government Best Value (Exclusion of Non-Commercial Considerations) Order 2001 (SI 2001/909)).

Guidance on the handling of workforce matters in contracting is now contained in Annex C to ODPM Circular 03/2003, substituted by a letter from ODPM dated December 2, 2003, and local authorities must have regard to this guidance (Local Government Act 1999, s.19 (4). This notes (*inter alia*) that good quality services depend on an appropriately skilled and motivated workforce, and that neglecting relevant workforce matters in order to drive down costs can have adverse effects on the desired quality and value for money of the service; the relevance of equal opportunities to the delivery of contracts; and the importance of handling TUPE well, so as to allay workforce reservations about transferring to new employers (para.9). As regards racial equality issues, Best Value authorities are no longer restricted to the six approved questions, but may ask further questions where relevant to the contract and for the purposes of achieving best value (para.43, referring to a CRE Guide, *Race Equality and Procurement in Local Government*).

The ODPM has also (in the same letter) given non-statutory guidance as to the use of social clauses:

"Individual local authorities may wish to use local labour clauses in contracts particularly in the interest of wider regeneration objectives. However, this needs to be done within the scope of the EC Treaty and the European Public Procurement legislation. The European Commission has recently provided clarification on the possibilities that Community law offers public purchasers who wish to take account of relevant social considerations in public procurement procedures. This clarification takes the form of an Interpretative Communication that explains how social concerns may be taken into account at each separate stage of the contract award procedure.

The Interpretative Communication goes some way to clarifying these complex issues, but difficulties may remain about the boundaries of what is admissible. There is limited case law in this area. A contracting authority must make its own judgement about the use of social clauses in procurement based on its own legal advice. Each case will be different and must be judged on its merits.

Where the EC procurement directives apply, award criteria must be relevant to the subject of the contract and provide a benefit to the contracting authority. Even where the directives do not apply, award criteria must be consistent with the fundamental principles of the EC Treaty, particularly non-discrimination.

The Interpretative Communication makes it clear that relevant social and employment issues can be included as contract conditions provided that they are non-discriminatory and included in the contract notice or contract documents. A statement from a tenderer that they are presently and will in the future, be unable to comply, could rule them out of the competition.

If the subject matter of the contract (the supply or service in question) requires specific knowhow in the "social" field, specific experience or ability in this field may be relevant to the assessment of the technical capability of tenderers.

It remains the responsibility of individual local authorities to make their own judgement about the use of social considerations in procurement, consistent with domestic law, including the duty of best value, and the EC legal framework".

(c) *Contracting-out*

Notes

1. Another major theme in the Conservative Government's approach to the exercise of contractual powers by public bodies was the desire to subject the provision of public services to competition from the private sector. Part I of the Local Government Act 1988 empowered the Secretary of State to require local authorities to offer private contractors the opportunity to compete for contracts to provide basic services on behalf of the authorities. Initially the services subject to competitive tendering requirements were manual operations (*e.g.* refuse collection and the cleaning of public buildings); however, professional services (*e.g.* the provision of legal work) subsequently became subject to these requirements.

Research for the Local Government Research Unit into the second exercise of CCT for blue-collar services showed (*inter alia*) that the authorities' own Direct Service Organisations still won a majority of contracts (although the rate of success had fallen from 78 per cent to 71 per cent since the first round); over 80 per cent of the sample authorities reported cost savings, primarily driven by the CCT regime; 58 per cent of DSO managers reported reductions in their workforce; over 80 per cent reported greater efficiency and effectiveness, commonly with reduced conditions for the workforce; authorities generally accepted competition, but strongly disliked compulsion (DTLR, Local Government Research Unit, *CCT and Local Authority Blue Collar Services* by Austin Mayhead and Co. Ltd (1997)).

2. Central government departments and their associated agencies experienced similar competitive pressures through the Government's introduction of a "market-testing" programme in 1991 (see *Competing for Quality*, Cm.730 (1991)). This initiative sought to subject discrete government activities to competition from the private sector by requiring the existing public sector providers to bid against private contractors for the right to undertake these activities in the future. Contracts were won by companies to undertake a wide range of activities from servicing RAF aeroplanes to providing building management services. One of the largest contracts valued at over £1 billion was awarded to an American company (Electronic Data Services) to provide computer facilities for the Inland Revenue over a 10-year period. By 1996, the Government was claiming savings of £720 million a year, with staff cuts of around 30,000; the process was attacked by the opposition and civil service unions as bureaucratic and expensive, with adverse effects on morale (R. Pyper in Jones *et al.* (ed.), *Politics UK* (5th ed., 2004), pp.528–529).

3. The 1997 Labour Government introduced changes at both local and national level. CCT was replaced by the Best Value regime under the Local Government Act 1999. Best value authorities (which include all local authorities) are under a duty to "make arrangements to secure continuous improvement in the way in which functions are exercised, having regard to a combination of economy, efficiency and effectiveness" (1999 Act, s.3). It applies to all functions. National regulations and guidance issued by the Secretary of State provide a framework within which authorities monitor their own performance, which performance is also externally assessed against national standards. (see generally *Cross*, Ch.7). Each authority must undertake a rolling programme of reviews of all its functions (1999 Act, s.5). Fair and open competition must be used wherever necessary as a means of securing efficient and effective services (ODPM Circular 03/2003, para.42.2). Research commissioned by the ODPM reported that a very large majority of respondents cited the regime as a key driver of improvement in their authorities; there was, however, as yet little hard evidence of statistically significant relationships between the regime and changes within authorities. There was widespread dissatisfaction with Best Value inspection (ODPM, Local and Regional Government Research Programme, *Research Summary: Evaluation of the Long-term Impact of the Best Value Regime: First Interim Report*, by the Centre for Local and Regional Government Research at Cardiff University (2004)).

At the national level, the Labour Government's Better Quality Services initiative required departments to review their services and functions over a five-year period starting in 1999, with the aim of identifying the "best supplier" for each service. There was no compulsion to set up a tendering process. From 2001, BQS was no longer co-ordinated from the centre (Pyper, *op.cit.* pp.528–529).

4. Part II of the Deregulation and Contracting Out Act 1994, allows ministers to make orders enabling themselves or "office-holders" (*i.e.* persons holding an office created by a public general Act: 79) to authorise any person (*e.g.* commercial organisations) to undertake a specified statutory or common law functions on behalf of the minister/office-holder. These powers are designed to widen the range of central government activities that could be subjected to market testing. See further; M. Freedland, "Privatising *Carltona*: Part II of the Deregulation and Contracting Out Act 1994" [1995] P.L. 21.

(d) *The Private Finance Initiative (PFI)*

HM TREASURY, PFI: MEETING THE INVESTMENT CHALLENGE

(JULY 2003)

Background

3.1 The Government uses PFI where it is appropriate and where it expects it to deliver value for money. In assessing when PFI is appropriate, the Government's approach is based on its commitment to efficiency, equity and accountability and on the Prime Minister's principles of public service reform. The Government seeks to ensure that there is no inherent bias in favour of one procurement route or another. It explains the benefits PFI can offer when used appropriately and certain key aspects of the PFI programme, such as the Government's approach to partnership, risk sharing, flexibility and the public sector safeguards incorporated in PFI contracts to ensure that key services continue to be delivered even when PFI contractors fall into financial difficulty.

Modernising Public Services

3.2 As outlined in Chapter 2, the Government has significantly increased total investment in public services. To ensure that this increase in investment will have maximum impact on the public services delivered to users, it must be accompanied by reform, and delivered in a way that provides value for money.

The Prime Minister's principles of public service reform

3.3 The Prime Minister has set out the Government's four principles of public service reform[1]:

- national standards, which means working with hospitals, schools, police forces, and local government to agree tough targets, with performance independently monitored so that people can see how their local services compare;
- devolution, whereby central government has to give successful frontline professionals the freedom to deliver;
- flexibility, which means removing artificial bureaucratic barriers which prevent staff improving local services; and
- choice, acknowledging that customers should increasingly be given the kind of options that they take for granted in other walks of life.

The Role of PFI

3.4 There are a number of ways the Government is delivering increased investment. When it comes to procurement, Office of Government Commerce

---

[1] Reforming our Public Services, March 2002.

(OGC) and HM Treasury set out in May 2000 three recommended approaches for improving delivery:

- prime contracting, where a single party acts as the sole point of responsibility between the public sector client and the supply chain, bringing together all of the parties necessary to meet public sector requirements effectively;
- design and build, where a supplier is responsible for both the design and construction of a facility to meet the public sector's output specifications; and
- PFI, where the public sector contracts to purchase quality services, with defined outputs, from the private sector on a long-term basis, and including maintaining or constructing the necessary infrastructure so as to take advantage of private sector management skills incentivised by having private finance at risk.

3.5 For each project or programme of new investment, the Government seeks to identify which of these options will deliver the best value for money. Specifically, in modernising the infrastructure needed for public services such as hospitals, schools and other facilities the Government seeks to avoid the weaknesses of past procurement (see Box 3.1) and ensure its procurement choice will deliver:

- buildings of high quality, maintained to a high standard throughout their life;
- effectively-managed services for the public, while protecting staff; and
- new investment which is completed on time and within budget, so that facilities are available when the public sector needs them, and for the expected price.

3.6 Each of the procurement options set out in paragraph 3.4 have been designed to improve value for money and avoid past difficulties with conventional procurement. Each will offer best value for money in different circumstances. The key for public sector procurement professionals is to judge which project suits which procurement option.

3.7 PFI is characterised by a long-term, whole-of-life commitment by the private sector to deliver and maintain new public infrastructure. This approach will only be suitable for certain types of investment, naturally limiting the use of PFI as laid out below. These constraints have limited the use of PFI to around 11 per cent, or £4.6 billion, of total investment in public services this year (see paragraph 2.9). Historically PFI has not exceeded 15 per cent of total investment for any year since 1997.

3.8 The analysis set out in Chapter 4 of this report suggests that PFI can offer significant advantages for certain major capital projects—such as the construction and maintenance of hospitals or schools, or the provision of major capital assets for defence or transport infrastructure—but has not offered the same advantages in information technology (IT) or for small capital projects. (See paragraphs 4.3 to 4.12 and 4.27 to 4.56.)

3.9 The PFI model is only likely to be applicable where:

- the private sector has the expertise to deliver and there is good reason to think it will offer value for money;

- the structure of the service is appropriate, allowing the public sector to define its needs as service outputs that can be adequately contracted for in a way that ensures effective, equitable and accountable delivery of public services into the long term;
- it can be demonstrated that PFI offers greater value for money for the public sector compared with other forms of procurement; and
- the nature of the assets and services identified as part of the PFI scheme are capable of being costed on a whole of life, long-term basis. Investment with a time horizon of 5–10 years is unlikely to benefit from the PFI approach.

3.10 For example, the use of PFI would be inappropriate where:

- the pre-conditions of equity and accountability in public service delivery could not be met, as in most forms of frontline service delivery;
- the transaction costs of pursuing PFI were disproportionate compared to the value of the investment a project was delivering, impairing its value for money . . .; or
- the fast pace of technological change in a particular sector made it too difficult to establish requirements in the long term, or high levels of integration make enforcing systems risk allocation difficult . . .

How PFI Works

Overview

3.22 In PFI, the public and private sectors enter a contract which shares between them the risk of undertaking an investment project, typically to provide a major capital asset for the public services such as a school or a hospital and related support services like repairs and maintenance. The public sector retains some of the risks it would bear in a conventionally procured project, like demand risk or the risk that it has not adequately assessed its requirements, but transfers the remainder to the private sector. Furthermore, the public sector underwrites the public service, but not the private sector service provider, ensuring that safeguards are in place in event of failures in the private sector. The private sector takes on those risks it is best able to manage, like design, construction and maintenance risks, so that it is better incentivised to perform. The financial cap to the risk assumed by the private sector is the full value of the debt and equity it provides to a project.

PFI Contracts

Specification of Outputs

3.23 The centre of any PFI project is a concession contract within which the public sector specifies the outputs it requires from a public service facility, and the basis for payment for those outputs. The level of outputs required by the public sector is typically drawn up in close consultation with the public sector workers—doctors, teachers, firemen or policemen—who will be using the asset and support services provided through the PFI contract. This contract is the key document that sets out the risk-sharing arrangements between public and private sectors in a PFI project and is the subject of extensive guidance.

3.24 Public service requirements would normally be framed not as precise input specifications and designs for a particular asset, but as an output specification defining the service required; for example, supported hospital beds for a certain number of patients, or prison accommodation for a specific category of inmates. This approach helps utilise the private sector's ability to provide innovative solutions to meet these requirements. Once the public sector has determined the level of outputs it requires to run the public services, the private sector is then invited to submit proposals which meet the desired output objectives using best private sector expertise and know-how to deliver the service.

3.25 When the private sector has submitted bids to fulfil the public sector's requirements, the public sector evaluates these proposals, selecting the option which represents the best value for money. In making this evaluation the public sector should take advantage of the empirical evidence available, both qualitative and quantitative, and exercise objective judgement in selecting the best option, using appraisal and evaluation criteria, and a PSC to determine whether the PFI option offers better value than conventional procurement. It is vital that the public sector is equipped with the skills to do so. Chapter 5 discusses steps the Government has taken to ensure these skills are in place, and Chapter 8 lays out further measures to improve the quality and effectiveness of public sector clients. Chapter 7 discusses reform of the appraisal process to further ensure that all the relevant benefits and disbenefits of PFI procurement are taken into account at the earliest appropriate stage and throughout a procurement.

Performance Regimes

3.26 Also contained within the PFI contract is a payment mechanism and performance regime which outlines how service delivery levels against the public sector's desired outputs—supported hospital beds, pupil places or prison accommodation—is measured. The public sector undertakes to make a unitary charge payment, covering both the availability of the asset and the support services provided along with it. Deductions are then made from this unitary charge to penalise poor performance by the private sector or lack of availability. While Chapter 4 contains some preliminary indications of the operational performance of PFI projects in practice, it is not possible to assess PFI's operational performance as a whole at this early stage in the life of projects.

3.27 This process of setting performance measurement and penalty mechanisms in the PFI contract ensures that the private sector delivers the specific outputs the public sector intends to purchase. It also means the public sector only pays if those services are delivered. For example:

- if an operating theatre in a PFI hospital were unavailable, a deduction would be made from the unitary charge paid to the private sector until that theatre was again in full working order;
- if the pipes in a school burst, flooding it and causing damage to its fabric, the private sector would be responsible for fixing the pipes and returning the school to its proper condition, and in the meantime it would not be paid unitary charges for those parts of the school that were unavailable; or

- if there is an electrical fault in an office's lighting, and the conditions in the office therefore fail to meet the project's output requirements, then the private sector—and in this case typically a specialised facilities management firm that was a part of the private sector consortium—would have a set time period to remedy the fault. If it failed to do so, it would incur a financial penalty until the fault was remedied.

3.28 Once public service requirements have been set, the contract goes out to tender and companies in the private sector compete to fulfil those requirements. In order to produce the most competitive bid, the private sector must:

- build a consortium which is best qualified to meet the specified requirements. This would typically involve an experienced construction contractor forming a joint venture with a facilities management company capable of running and maintaining the asset and with other contractors best qualified to deliver other outputs to be specified in the contract. Increasingly, the consortium would also include specialised investors, who ensure appropriate subcontract structures and perform a 'due diligence' role, evaluating the project's assumptions and exploring its risks; and
- produce a bid which takes into account the whole-of-life cost of the asset, incorporates the proper level of repairs and maintenance, and reflects the cost of the services provided and the cost of third party finance. Competitive tension between bidding consortia helps ensure value for money, while consortia would also have no incentive to place artificially cheap bids. Such bids, which compromised on design or construction quality, or underestimated required maintenance, would seriously damage the profitability of the consortium and place its equity at risk because any failure to deliver in the future would mean unitary charge performance deductions. Equally, the third-party lenders to the consortium would eliminate any such optimism bias in the bids to ensure the safety of their investment.

Risk Sharing

3.29 The appropriate sharing of risks is the key to ensuring value for money benefits in PFI projects are realised. The benefits described above all flow from ensuring that the many different types of risks inherent in a major investment programme, for example construction risk or the risk associated with the design of the building and its appropriateness for providing the required service, are borne by the party who is best placed to manage them. . . .

Notes

1. An excellent account of the PFI is provided by G. Allen, *The Private Finance Initiative* (HC Research Paper 03/79, October 21, 2003). The PFI was announced by the then Chancellor of the Exchequer, Norman Lamont MP, in the 1992 Autumn Statement, as a way of increasing the scope for private financing of capital projects. In future, any privately financed project which could operate profitably would be allowed to proceed, joint ventures would actively be encouraged and greater use of leasing would be allowed; where it could be showed that the risk stayed with the private sector, public organisations would be able to enter operating lease agreements, with only the lease payments counting as public expenditure and without their capital budgets being

cut (HC Deb. Vol. 213, col.998 (November 12, 1992)). The impact of the policy was limited and steps were taken to encourage the use of PFI schemes. Further steps to streamline and improve delivery of PFI projects were taken by the Labour Government from 1997, in the light of a series of reviews. PFI schemes were now seen as part of a broader programme for the making of Public-Private Partnerships of varying kinds, with much more emphasis on the ongoing relationships between private and public sector organisations. A rule that all public sector capital projects should be PFI tested was dropped, but a significant programme continued, being seen as "a small but important part of the Government's strategy for delivery high quality public service" (*www.treasury.gov.uk*). Almost all new hospitals are, for example, provided under PFI schemes. The term PPP applies to any alliance between public bodies and private companies, typically involving the joint ownership of a special purpose vehicle established under company law; PFI schemes are more formal and generally involve the provision of a capital asset and services related to that asset (see *www.pppforum.com*).

The Government Resource and Accounts Act 2000, ss.16–20, authorised the Treasury to incur expenditure in respect of the establishment of and investment in a body for the purpose of carrying on public-private partnership (PPP) business. This means participation in such partnerships whether as investor, consultant or otherwise, and include the provision of advisory or financial services in connection with specific PPPs or PPPs generally. Partnerships UK was accordingly established in 2000 to work with public bodies on specific PPP transactions to improve the process of planning, negotiating and completing projects (see *www.partnershipsuk.org.uk*). In 2001, it became a PPP in its own right, with a 51 per cent stake sold to private investors and 49 per cent retained by the public sector. The Public Private Partnerships Programme (4Ps) has also been established to provide advice, guidance to local government on all forms of partnership working, including PFI schemes.

PFI schemes have generated controversy. The extent to which PFI capital spending is additional to the public sector capital expenditure that would have happened anyway is difficult to demonstrate (Allen, *op.cit.*, p.19). The fact that the capital expenditure is "off-balance sheet" for the public body (on the ground that relevant risks have been transferred to the private sector, which has raised the finance) makes it more difficult to determine the extent of spending commitments for the future (*ibid.*, pp.20–22). It is also difficult to assess the extent to which the transfer of risk under PFI schemes can be deemed optimal (*ibid.*, p.29). The theory is that "where risks are transferred, it is to create the correct discipline and incentives on the private sector to achieve a better outcome" (H.M. Treasury, *PFI: Meeting the Investment Challenge* (July 2003), p.35). The public sector retains responsibility for risks concerning the need for the facility on the date given and the adequacy of its overall size to meet public service needs; the possibility of a change in public sector requirements in the future; whether the standards of delivery set by the public sector sufficiently meet public needs; in most cases, the extent to which the facility is used or not over the contract's life; and general inflation. The risks transferred typically involve: meeting required standards of delivery; cost overrun during construction; timely completion of the facility; underlying costs to the operator of service delivery and the future costs associated with the asset; and the risk of industrial action or physical damage to the asset (*ibid.*, pp.35–36).

The extent to which PFI projects provide value for money is also disputed. It seems that while road and prison projects have achieved reasonable efficiency gains, projects in other sectors such as schools and hospitals have shown minimal gains (Allen, *op. cit.*, pp.30–33).

The Government reaffirmed its commitment to PFI schemes in the light of the 2003 review (*op. cit.*). The main changes following the review were increasing the funding options for private sector contractors; reform of the Public Sector Comparator to ensure an economically rigorous appraisal of a project's outline business case; the end of the use of PFI for low capital value and IT projects; and expanding the scale and scope of PFI into other sectors, including social housing, urban regeneration, waste and recycling and the existing prisons estate (Allen, *op. cit.*, pp.48–52).

The issues that have tended to catch the attention of the media include concerns over the standard of provision by private contractors and the extent of their profits. There remains much uncertainty as to the extent to which these long-term schemes will prove inflexible and costly to the public sector given the likelihood of presently unforeseeable changes in both requirements for public services and the ways in which they are to be delivered.

2. For Freedland ("Public and Private Finance—Placing the Private Finance Initiative in a Public Law Frame" [1998] P.L. 288), the PFI "is at the heart of the 'government by contract' set of concerns" (p.289). The legal and constitutional basis for the PFI is difficult to identify, but seem to be predominantly broad, inherent non-statutory powers for the management of the financial business of the state, but in conjunction with some statutory frameworks (such as that of the NHS) and powers (such as the power to make statutory orders granting concessions for toll roads and crossings under Pt 1 of the New Roads and Street Works Act 1991). There is a relatively elaborate normative structure or discourse based on documents and guides issued by HM Treasury (p.294). Very full information has been made available publicly and while judicial review is not figured significantly as a control mechanism, the PFI generally and particular projects have been extensively scrutinised by the National Audit Office, the Public Accounts Committee and the Treasury Select Committee (p.296). It is less clear that the PFI is "substantively accountable in the sense that it is in its nature coherent and transparent" (p.297), there being a tension in the normative discourse between the regulation of PFI projects and their encouragement, and over time the emphasis has shifted from the former to the latter (pp.297–304). There is also the dilemma for the public sector that the greater the emphasis on risk transfers as part of the justification for a project, the higher the premium rates that will be charged by the private sector to cover that risk (p.305). Much depends on whether it is indeed possible to establish who is best placed to manage difficult sorts of risk; there are doubts as to whether this can be done sufficiently so as to justify arrangements "which present real worries in terms of public policy" (p.307).

Further difficulties may arise out of the long-term nature of relationships between public and private sector organisations given that there are real risks of substantial changes on both sides as public sector bodies are restructured (possibly out of existence) and private sector bodies are taken over or fail (see M. Freedland, "Government by Contract Re-examined—Some Functional Issues" in P. Craig and R. Rawlings, *Law and Administration in Europe* (2003), Ch.7, pp.129–130). Government may assume a key role in both contractual changes and institutional restructuring to ensure the continued functioning of public-private arrangements thus assuming "the role of the makers and maintainers" of a "new kind of mixed public and private market institutions for the provision of public services" (*ibid.*, pp.131–132, citing the ongoing restructuring of the railways). This adds further to the tension with the government's regulatory role (*ibid.*) In response, there is a need not so much for the development of public law, but for delineating "a field of public/private enterprise law in the larger terrain of English law both public and private and including the input from EC law," drawing on both principles of public law and legal techniques from contract, tort and restraint of trade (*ibid.*, pp.132–136).

3. A PFI project is likely to be subject to the EC procurement regime (see below, p.1038). The competitive negotiated procedure, as distinct from the open and restricted procedures, is normally regarded as the only suitable route for such a project. See *R. (on the application of Kathro) v Rhondda Cynon Taff County Borough Council* [2001] EWHC Admin 527; [2002] J.P.L. 304, where Richards J. rejected a claim for judicial review of the use of the negotiated procedure for a major development project. While the council had not properly addressed the question whether this was a works contract or a service contract (the former making the negotiated procedure available in a narrower range of circumstances than the latter), the judge was satisfied that it was the latter, and that even if it had been a works contract, the council would have been entitled to use the negotiated procedure. Furthermore, the claimants (unlike

tenderers or would-be tenderers) were not themselves affected by the choice of tendering procedure and had seized on the point as a fall-back way of trying to stop the project. Accordingly, they lacked a sufficient interest.

(e) *Internal markets*

Note

An illustration of the use of contract-like arrangements for the provision of public services has been the move since 1989 to separate the funders of NHS care from its providers. A succession of models has been adopted, involving the purchase of services by, under the Conservatives, health authorities and GPs with fundholding status, and, under the Labour Government, Primary Care Groups, which have evolved into Primary Care Trusts. PCTs purchase services from NHS Trusts (for acute hospitals, ambulance services and mental health services) through annually negotiated agreements in each Healthcare Community. Agreements with Foundation Trusts (established as members' organisations under Pt 1 of the Health and Social Care (Community Health and Standards) Act 2003; they are part of the NHS, and not answerable to health authorities and subject to regulation by an office known as Monitor) take the form of legally binding contracts. Whether disputes arising out of such contracts will be resolved through litigation remains to be seen; given the complex ongoing relationships between the parties there are grounds to expect that this will very much be the exception. A move is now under way to amalgamate PCTs and confer more purchasing functions on GP practices.

The use of contract-like arrangements within government is considered by A.C.L. Davies, *Accountability: A Public Law Analysis of Government by Contract* (2001), reviewed by P. Vincent-Jones, (2002) 65 M.L.R. 611. Davies argues that the law has failed to protect the public interest in participation and involvement in these arrangements and that the quality of decision-making would be improved if internal contracts were governed by a public law framework embodying natural justice norms, with an internal enforcement and dispute resolution forum. Vincent-Jones (*op.cit.*, pp.616–617) argues, on the other hand, that the adoption of a relatively narrow and exclusive accountability perspective may tend to obscure the dimensions of internal relationships within public services that "the parties belong to the same organisation and share a common purpose in improving public services and rectifying problems, for which they are often jointly responsible". He was also sceptical as to the advantages of establishment of a more effective enforcement process, noting evidence from other studies that existing formal processes for arbitration were relatively little used, given in particular its "unsuitability for resolving intractable disputes over resources with implications beyond individual contracts" (*ibid.* pp.619–620, citing D. Hughes *et al.* in R. Flynn and G. Williams (ed.), *Contracting for Health: Quasi-Markets and the National Health Service* (1997).

(vi) Administrative Rule-making

Following the pioneering writings of the American commentator Professor K.C. Davis (particularly in his book *Discretionary Justice: A Preliminary Inquiry* (1969)), recent years have witnessed a growing interest by British academics in the important process of administrative rule-making. Despite the lack of publicity surrounding many of these provisions it is now generally recognised that the creation of non-statutory rules by central government departments, together with other public bodies, has significant influence on the actual operation of numerous administrative programmes and, consequently, raises many fundamental legal questions about the creation, status and enforcement of such norms. Craig suggests that there are at least four explanations for the creation of administrative rules:

(1) the organisational needs of bureaucratic agencies when faced with the obligation to exercise discretionary powers;

(2) the ability to use non-technical language in such provisions (*e.g.* in the Highway Code);
(3) the flexibility of these provisions compared with formal delegated legislation;
(4) the assertion that such provisions are not legally binding (but see below).

The Citizen's Charter programme (see below, p.202) combined with the Government's Code of Practice on Access to Government Information, which entered into effect in April 1994, began to encourage central government departments and agencies to publish their more important internal administrative guidance. For example, the Inland Revenue published all its major internal guidance manuals (explaining its interpretations and policies towards the collection of relevant taxes) and the Benefits Agency published over 50 of its internal codes and manuals (which perform similar functions in relation to the administration of benefits). A great deal of this information is now available on the internet.

General readings: *Craig*, pp.398–406, *Wade and Forsyth*, pp.867–874; G. Ganz, *Quasi-Legislation: Recent Developments in Secondary Legislation* (1987) and R. Baldwin, *and Government* (1995).

THE PARLIAMENTARY COMMISSIONER AND ADMINISTRATIVE GUIDANCE

ALASTAIR R. MOWBRAY, [1987] P.L. 570[1]

Study of the PCA's reports soon discloses that there is a myriad of individual pieces of administrative guidance being used by departments, not necessarily under this name.[2] Consequently it is necessary to devise a method of classifying these provisions which allows the aggregation of similar forms of guidance into distinct classes. For the purpose of the present study, a threefold functional classification, which is part was derived from United States law,[3] has been adopted. This classification distinguishes between forms of administrative guidance which relate to (a) policy, (b) produce and (c) interpretation. The first class, *policy* guidance, specifies the formal objectives of a departmental programme, such as the designation of approved company auditors, and provides the detailed criteria by which officials are to determine the cases of individuals affected by the programme. The source of this guidance is to be found in the political value judgments espoused by ministers.[4] Secondly, *procedural* guidance informs subordinate officials and/or persons outside the department of the form to be followed in the relevant decision-making process.[5] This guidance is derived from the organisational expertise possessed

---

[1] [ed.] some footnotes have been omitted.
[2] Thus the Scottish Office terms these provisions "guidelines" C126/77, H.C.126 (1977–1978) p.268; the Inland Revenue calls them "departmental instructions" C87/82, H.C.8(1982–1983), p.92; and the Home Office refers to them as "standing orders" C264/G, H.C.290 (1972–1973) p.119.
[3] See administrative Procedure Act, s.553 and more generally the discussion of American rule-making in K.C. Davis, Preliminary Inquiry; R. Baldwin and K. Hawkins, "Discretionary Justice: Davis Reconsidered" [1984] P.L. 570; M. Asimow, "Delegated Legislation U.S. and U.K." (1983) 3 O.J.L.S.253.
[4] See the P.C.A.'s explanation of why the rules governing the sale of surplus government land were changed in 1980, C384/81 H.C.132 (1981–1982, p.8.
[5] *e.g.* the procedure to the observed by war pension medical boards, C260/77, H.C.126 (19787–1978), p.108. Also see A.D. Jergesen, "The Enforcement of Administrative Procedures in G.B. and the U.S." (1982) 30 Am.J. Comp.L. 267 and P. Birkinshaw, "Departments of State, Citizens and the Internal Resolution of Grievances" (1985) C.J.Q. 15.

by departments, supplemented occasionally by legal norms. Finally, *interpretative* guidance seeks to explain the departmental view of what Parliament or any other legislator (in the case of delegated legislation) meant by enacting a particular provision.[6] Inevitably this class of guidance relies upon legal knowledge derived from lawyers. . . .

(a) *Policy guidance*

Provisions falling within this class of guidance are utilised by virtually all the departments subject to the scrutiny of the P.C.A. Examples extend from the Ministry of Overseas Development's rules stating eligibility for foreign income supplements to the DHSS's criteria entitling disabled persons to financial help towards the costs of running a private car. The bulk of policy guidance encountered was concerned with the departments' aims towards the public at large who came within their responsibilities. These aims encompassed all the major functions of the modern state, including regulating conduct, providing benefits (in kind or in cash), and taxing. Such guidance regulated all types of discretionary powers, with 21 instances governing statutory and prerogative powers, 10 applying to extra-statutory discretions (mainly in the field of taxation), and the remaining two sets of provisions having no direct link with any statutory scheme. . . .

(b) *Procedural guidance*

The overwhelming majority of pieces of procedural guidance discovered by the P.C.A. regulated civil servants' conduct towards members of the public, with the remainder governing the form of relations between departments and other public authorities. The largest number of cases dealing with procedural guidance affecting the public elaborated the practices to be followed for the allocation of public largesse (such as the process of determining eligibility for war pensions), although a significant minority of cases concerned procedural guidance controlling the actions of officials in the revenue departments.

(c) *Interpretative guidance*

Unsurprisingly, six of the eight cases revealing interpretative guidance contained interpretations of primary legislation, which ranged in subject-matter from the Purchase Tax Act 1963 to the Countryside Act 1968. However, this category of guidance differed from the two previous categories in the almost all the individual pieces of interpretative guidance had been published. One explanation for this distinction may have been the departments' desire to persuade affected citizens of the accuracy and legitimacy of their interpretations, which could be achieved only via a public promulgation of the interpretations. . . .

CONCLUSIONS

From the reports of the P.C.A. that were surveyed for the purposes of the present article, valuable insight may be gained into the significant role played

---

[6] *e.g.* the Public Notices issued by the Customers and Excise on the scope of the legislation administered by their department, C316/68, H.C.129 (1968–1969), p.20.

by administrative guidance in decision-making across the whole spectrum of central government departments. The reports have disclosed, *inter alia*, policy guidance detailing when the former Ministry of Transport would refuse to appoint garages as approved vehicle testing stations; procedural guidance specifying the method by which capital grants for farmers could be obtained from the Ministry of Agriculture, Fisheries and Food; and interpretative guidance issued by the Department of the Environment elaborating the duties of councils of the status of such provisions in contemporary public law. Definitive answers have yet to be established regarding the circumstances in which departments should be able to create and use these provisions, the situations in which departments ought to be bound by the terms of their guidance, and the grounds upon which affected individuals can challenge the content and application of guidance. The broader constitutional issues include the extent to which departments should be under a legal duty to consult the public about the creation of individual pieces of administrative guidance (particularly policy guidance), and to publish (or at least make available to the public the final version of their internally promulgated guidance.[7]

From the perspective of the P.C.A., the adaptable concept of maladministration has been used to examine the departmental application of all three classes of guidance. Successive Commissioners have scrutinised officials' decision-making to ensure that relevant guidance has been applied with regard to all the material facts of the case. Furthermore, the P.C.A. now demands that officials should not deviate from the requirements of their procedural guidance without good reason. Departments have also had the substance of their procedural, and in exceptional circumstances their interpretative, guidance subjected to critical evaluation by the P.C.A. In developing these responses towards administrative guidance, the P.C.A. has demonstrated a marked tendency towards consistency in assessing whether departmental utilisation of guidance violates the concept of maladiminstration. Yet this consistency has been obtained without the explicit reference to previous cases that one expects in a formal system of presidential decision-making.

By undertaking the above investigations, the P.C.A. has helped to protect the vital rights, interests and duties of citizens [8] from some of the adverse effects of the creation and application of administrative guidance by departments. His role has been particularly valuable in cases where the relevant guidance had not been published and consequently it would have been virtually impossible for the citizen to seek a judicial remedy. Furthermore, the P.C.A.'s responses towards administrative guidance are in many ways more advanced than the newly emerging judicial cognisance of these provisions. For example, since the earliest post-Sachesenhausen days, the P.C.A. has operated on the basis of the presumption that departments should apply their policy guidance to determine all individual cases coming within its scope, unless there are exceptional circumstances; whereas the courts have only recognised a similar legal presumption since 1984. Nevertheless, there is a great potential for the cross-fertilisation of ideas between the P.C.A. and the courts, in their respective assessments of the

---

[7] On the issue of publication see Donald C. Rowat (ed.), *Administrative Secrecy in Developed Countries* (1979).

[8] Including, their right to legal advice in quasi-criminal proceedings (C486/81); their interest in securing lawful consideration of their parole applications (C264/G); their duty to pay the correct amount of tax (C316/68).

limits placed upon the departmental creation and utilisation of guidance by the standards of maladministration and illegality (*e.g.* the acceptability of particular pieces of procedural guidance when assessed against the criteria of "good administrative practice" and procedural fairness/impropriety). It may be concluded that the Parliamentary Commissioner deserves a central place in lawyers' understanding of the mechanisms that currently provide a check on the administration's use of administrative guidance in its decision-making.

Notes

1. A landmark decision in the judicial scrutiny of the way in which public authorities utilise administrative rules was delivered by the House of Lords in *British Oxygen Co. Ltd v Minister of Technology* [1971] A.C. 610 (see below, p.488). In *R. v Secretary of State for the Home Department Ex p. Khan* [1984] 1 W.L.R. 1337, the Court of Appeal reached an equally significant decision by upholding a claim that the Home Secretary was legally obliged to observe the requirements of his own administrative rules which he had published. Hence, English law was beginning to accord legal weight to the contents of such provisions (see A.R. Mowbray, "Administrative Guidance and Judicial Review" [1985] P.L. 558 and below, pp.591–621). After a wide-ranging study of the use and legal characteristics of administrative rules R. Baldwin and J. Houghton concluded:

> "the seeds of a more rational approach do exist, but a disinclination to deal with the effects of informal rules has rendered rule-makers unaccountable and exposed a useful device to exploitation. Questionable decisions have been taken to use informal rules in areas where fundamental liberties and issues of central political contention have been involved (e.g. picketing, policing, immigration, prisons). More than anything, such executive activity should prompt the courts to take action".

"Circular Arguments: The Status and Legitimacy of Administrative Rules" [1986] P.L. 239.

2. Professor Ganz has produced an alternative agenda to regulate the creation and use of administrative rules. She proposes the development of a Code of Practice to control the procedures followed by administrative bodies when making such rules (and see below, n.4). In addition she advocates the establishment of a permanent agency:

> "to advise on the creation of quasi-legal or voluntary rules instead of legal rules and evolve criteria for their use. At present they seem to come into existence largely on an ad hoc basis, often as an afterthought, in response to conflicting pressures to do nothing or to legislate. If the rules are to be observed, rather than be political window dressing, they must be adopted for better reasons than political expediency".

(*Quasi-Legislation: Recent Developments in Secondary Legislation*, p.108)

3. Administrative rules may also come within the purview of particular administrative tribunals. In a study of Value Added Tax Tribunals, it was discovered that the tribunals' response to such rules depended on (a) the breadth of the jurisdiction granted to the tribunals by Parliament and (b) the legal form of the specific administrative rule at issue. Generally, VAT tribunals asserted their independence from the executive by proclaiming their unwillingness to be bound by the Customs and Excise's interpretations of legislative provisions contained in administrative rules. See A.R. Mowbray, "Customs and Excise Public Notices: The Tribunal Response" (1987) B.T.R. 381.

4. There are also many hybrid forms of guidance created by public authorities which have a statutory basis, but are not subordinate legislation.[9] One particular form of

---

[9] See S.H. Bailey and M.J Gunn, *Smith and Bailey on The Modern English Legal System* (4th ed., 2002), pp.349–352.

such guidance is the statutory code of practice. There are now over 40 different statutory provisions relating to codes of practice, most of which have been enacted since 1974. Because of the increasing practical importance of these codes, Parliament expressed its concern that not all the codes were subjects to parliamentary proceedings.[10] The Government responded by producing a document entitled "Guidance on Codes of Practice and Legislaton",[11] directed at officials and parliamentary draftsmen contemplating the proposing of new statutory provisions empowering the issuing of codes of practice. The document states that " a code of practice is an authoritative statement of practice to be followed in some field"(para. 2:1). Codes differ from legislation because, (1) they offer guidance rather than imposing obligations; (2) their provisions are not directly enforceable in legal proceedings and (3) they often contain explanatory materials and argument. The document asserts that codes should not be used to impose specific legal obligations (para. 4:1); their contents should clearly distinguish between prescriptive and explanatory text (para. 9:3); and where their contents have indirect legal effects (either civil or criminal) they ought to be subject to parliamentary proceedings (*e.g.* affirmative or negative resolutions) (para.10:1).

See further: Lord Campbell, "Codes of Practice and Alternative to Legislation" [1985] Stat.L.R. 127; A. Samuels, "Codes of Practice and Legislation" [1986] Stat.L.R. 29; C. McCrudden, "Codes in a Cold Climate: Administrative Rule-Making by the Commission for Racial Equality" (1988) 51 M.L.R. 409.

5. In a theoretical and empirical study (involving the work of the Factory Inspectorate) Baldwin has divided the rules made by Government into secondary legislation and "tertiary rules" (*e.g.* administrative guidance and codes of practice). He argues that the use of such provisions should be evaluated according to five "legitimacy claims": (1) the achieving of legislative objectives, (2) accountability to representative bodies, (3) respect for due process values in the operation of governmental programmes, (4) the facilitation of expert judgments in the administration of such programmes and (5) efficiency in the provision of public services. He concludes that:

"In applying such rationales to the body of secondary and tertiary rules encountered in British government it is remarkable how weak many potential claims to legitimacy are. Secondary legislation, for example, often lacks clear authorization, it is subject to weak systems of accountability and control, and the participatory rights of affected parties are often ill protected. These problems are all the more severe in relation to tertiary rules and where secondary or tertiary rules are employed to implement European Community Directives, or tertiary rules are employed to implement European Community Directives, or in pursuance of policies emanating from the European Union, or within the contractual frameworks of government, special problems of legitimation are encountered. On the positive side, however, secondary and tertiary rules have an important role to play in defining and clarifying statutory mandates and in producing expertise and efficiency gains. The conclusion to be drawn is that, if such rules are to be used, all possible steps should be taken to improve the legitimacy claims to be made on behalf of them—notably by increasing obligations to disclose rules; by linking tertiary and secondary rules more clearly to statutory provisions , and by making the status and force of such rules more clear" (*Rules and Government* (1995), pp.300–301).

(D) DISPUTE RESOLUTION

A range of mechanisms is available through which disputes between public bodies and private citizens or institutions, or between public bodies, may be resolved. It is

---

[10] Debate in the House of Lords, January 15, 1986: *Hansard*, Vol.469, cols 1075–1104.

[11] Produced in December 1987 by H.M. Government: the full text of the document is reproduced in 10 Stat.L.R. 214 (1989).

obviously desirable for potential disputes arising out of the action or inaction of a public body to be identified early and addressed quickly by the institution itself before resort is had to external mechanisms. The external mechanism of litigation, whether founded on public or private law, should be the last resort given the expense and delay involved and the confrontational atmosphere normally engendered. Nevertheless, litigation may prove to be the only route through which justice can be achieved. This section deals with some of the mechanisms that may be available aside from litigation in the courts, dealt with in Part II and ombudsmen, dealt with in the following chapter. A landmark in this area is the publication in July 2004 by the Labour Government of a White Paper, *Transforming Public Services: Complaints, Redress and Tribunals* (Cm.6243, 2004). This includes an overview of existing mechanisms, which in turn provides the context for proposals for reform of the tribunals system (for both administrative and employment tribunals) that will be most significant since the Franks Report of 1956–57.

WHITE PAPER, TRANSFORMING PUBLIC SERVICES: COMPLAINTS, REDRESS AND TRIBUNALS

(Cm.6243, 2004).

1. *Introduction*

1.1 This White Paper is about improving public services and improving access to justice—administrative justice and justice in the workplace.

Administrative justice

1.2 A modern democratic state affects the lives of individuals in many ways. It intervenes to protect the vulnerable and to regulate markets. And there are areas where it has to deal directly with the rights and obligations of individuals and businesses, areas which can affect any of us, such as taxation, benefits and immigration status.

1.3 In a democracy the framework within which we all live is set by democratic institutions acting the public interest. But where State institutions do not just set a framework but make decisions about the rights and obligations of individuals, the State also has an important duty towards that individual. Central, devolved and local government make millions of such decisions every year. What if government gets it wrong? What if the individual feels aggrieved by the decision? What if the individual does not realise that government has got it wrong? Each of us has the right to expect that State institutions will make the right decisions about out individual circumstances.

1.4 The overwhelming majority of these decisions are taken by public officials, these decisions are taken by public officials, usually operating as part of a government department or State agency. Their job is to get those decisions about individuals right. The job of those who organize and lead departments and agencies is to establish, maintain and constantly improve the systems which will enable the individual decision-markers to get the decisions right.

1.5 No system will ever be perfect. There will always be errors and complaints. There will always be uncertainties about how the law should be applied to the circumstances of individuals. There will often be gaps in knowledge and understanding about an individual's circumstances. We are all entitled to receive correct decisions on our personal circumstances; where a mistake occurs we are entitled to complain and to have the mistake put right with the minimum of difficulty; where there is uncertainty we are entitled to expect a quick resolution of the issue; and we are entitled to expect a quick resolution of the issue; and we are entitled to expect that where things have gone wrong the system will learn form the problem and will do better in the future.

1.6 This is the sphere of administrative justice. It embraces not just courts and tribunals but the millions of decisions taken by thousands of civil servants and other officials. So, While much of this Whit Paper is about institutions which provide redress to individuals who seek to reverse a decision, from the point of view of a user or potential user the context is much broader.

1.7 A good service delivery organisation must be designed with these legitimate needs of the users in mind. To make this a reality the system has to have the following features:

- the decision-making system must be designed to minimise errors and uncertainty:
- the individual must be able to detect when something has gone wrong;
- the process for putting things right or removing uncertainty must be proportionate—that is, there should be no disproportionate barriers to user should be identified and rooted out quickly;
- those with the power to correct a decision get things right; and
- changes feed back into the decision making system so that there is less error and uncertainty in the future;

1.8 Despite significant improvements in a range of tribunals and departments the Government does not believe that set against these standards the existing systems for redress provided by central government are as successful as they could or should be. This is further explored on Chapters 3 to 5. We believe that as part of public sector reform the public is entitled to a better service.

Justice in the workplace

1.9 In the modern world of work, employees are entitled to fair and decent standards in the workplace. They are entitled to protection against unfair dismissal and discrimination. Their rights to minimum wage, to maternity leave and to join a trade union have to be protected. It is the duty of the State to put in place machinery to enforce these rights and to provide ways in which employees and employers can resolve any disputes about them.

1.10 Many of these disputes can be successfully resolved in the workplace, through formal and informal means. This is by far the best way of resolving these disputes. Where this is not successful there can be assistance form mediation services and the Advisory Conciliation and Arbitration Service (Acas) who successfully conciliate some 70% of employment tribunal claims. But ultimately there may have to be a judicial determination. This is the role of the employment tribunal system which needs to be:

- even-handed and responsive to the needs of its user;
- accessible and understandable;
- as fast as reasonably practicable;
- reliable, consistent and dependable; and
- properly resourced and organised in an accountable fashion.

1.11 disputes over justice in the workplace differ form administrative justice disputes because they are party vs party rather than individual or business vs State. Their separate requirements are considered at more length in Chapter 8. But there is a common aim: justice.

The Leggatt Review and beyond

1.12 In May 2000 the then Lord Chancellor, Lord Irvine of Lairg, appointed Sir Andrew Leggatt to undertake a review of one part of the justice landscape, the web of tribunals which has grown up over the years primarily to provide a right of appeal against certain decisions by State agencies but also to deal with employment issues and some other disputes. His report—*Tribunals for Users— One System, One Service*—was published in August 2001 and gave a picture of an incoherent and inefficient set of institutions which, despite the efforts of the thousands of people who work in tribunals, provided a service to the public which was well short of what people are entitled to expect and what can be achieved. Sir Andrew set out a convincing case of change and this White Paper acts as a response to his report. But we do not believe that tribunal reform can or should stand alone. What matters to people is the quality and responsiveness of the system as a whole. So this White Paper is also about improving the whole end to end process for administrative justice. This has important implications for the unified tribunal system which he recommended, and our vision for that system is therefore different from, but, we believe, compatible with his.

1.13 The Department for Constitutional Affairs' five year strategy is organized around four key elements:

- developing **policies that help empower citizens** and communities to manage their own problems, protecting them form crime and anti-social behaviour, and narrowing the justice gap;
- moving out of courts and tribunals disputes that could be resolved elsewhere through better use of **education, information, advice** and **proportionate dispute resolution;**
- **changing radically the way we deliver services** so that the courts, tribunals, legal services and constitutional arrangements are fit for purpose and cost effective; and
- **re-shaping the DCA's organization and infrastructure** so that it is aligned structurally to meet the needs of the public and works well with the rest of government.

1.14 This White Paper illustrates the application of this strategy and the principles of public service reform to administrative justice and to justice in the workplace. All strands are represented. It is not just about organisation. We accept Sir Andrew Leggatt's key recommendation that tribunals provided by central government should be brought together into a unified system within what is now the Department for Constitutional Affairs. We believe that this will be more effective and efficient, and will firmly embed the principle of independence. But we see this new body as much more than federation of existing tribunals. This is a new organisation and a new type of organisation. It will have two central pillars: administrative justice appeals, and employment cases. Its task, together with a transformed Council on Tribunals, will not be just to process cases according to law. Its mission will be to help to prevent and resolve disputes, using any appropriate method and working with its partners in and out of government, and to help to improve administrative justice and justice in the workplace, so that the need for disputes is reduced. . . .

2. *Proportionate Dispute Resolution*

2.1 The proposals set out in this White Paper are a major early step in the wider strategy we are developing to transform civil and administrative justice and the way that people deal with legal problems and disputes.

2.2 Our strategy turns on its head the Department's traditional emphasis first on courts, judges and court procedure, and second on legal aid to pay mainly of litigation lawyers. It starts instead with the real world problems people face. The aim is to develop a range of policies and services that, so far so possible, will help people to avoid problems and legal disputes in the first place; and where they cannot, provides tailored solutions to resolve the dispute as quickly and cost-effectively as possible. It can be summed up as '**Proportionate Dispute Resolution**'.

2.3 We want to:

- minimise the risk of people facing legal problems by ensuring that the framework of law defining people's rights and responsibilities is as fair, simple and clear as possible, and that State agencies, administering systems like tax and benefits, make better decisions and give clearer explanations;
- improve people's understanding of their rights and responsibilities, and the information available to them about what they can do and where they can go for help when problems do arise. This will help people to decide how to deal with the problems themselves if they can, and ensure they get the advice and other services they need if they cannot;
- ensure that people have ready access to early and appropriate advice and assistance when they need it, so that problems can be solved and potential disputes nipped in the bud long before they escalate into formal legal proceedings;
- promote the development of range of tailored dispute resolution services, so that different types of dispute can be resolved fairly, quickly, efficiently and effectively, without recourse to the expense and formality of courts and tribunals where this is not necessary;
- but also deliver cost-effective court and tribunal services, that are better targeted on those cases where a hearing is the best option for resolving the dispute or enforcing the outcome.

2.4 'Civil and administrative justice' covers a very wide and varied range of issues and problems. And at the core of our vision is the idea that policies and services must be tailored to the particular needs of people in different contexts, moving away form the limited flexibility of the existing court and legal aid systems. Much of this White Paper is about realising that vision in the field of administrative justice. But other major areas will each in turn need to be the subject of detailed analysis and research in order to develop specific proposals. We are currently considering the areas of debt and domestic violence and hope to publish consultation papers later this year. And the Law Commission will be looking at housing adjudication issues in a similar way.

2.5 All these analyses will start by considering:

- the types of problems and disputes people face, and what outcomes they want to achieve;
- the effectiveness of different dispute resolution options in addressing peoples' needs, particularly identifying any gaps in their provision.

What do people want?

2.6 The outcome that people are looking for will vary considerably from case to case and person to person. A key question will be the extent to which people are looking (just) for a legal remedy, like an award of a disability benefit. Or whether they might really be seeking something else, like an apology or a clear explanation.

2.7 It is also important to consider what people want in terms of the processes they go through. This may well involve striking a balance between competing factors. Most people seem likely to want the process to be quick, cheap, simple and stress-free, but they may also want it to be rigorous, authoritative and final. Some may prefer an informal process where the dispute is resolved consensually. For some, an important consideration may be that the proceedings remain private.

What dispute resolution options are there?

2.8 The existing landscape of dispute resolution options is confused and confusing, with many variations in name, style and technique. A clear and simple analytical framework is and essential starting point. Again, it is helpful to distinguish outcome and process.

2.9 At the simplest level, there are just two possible outcomes. A dispute resolution process separate from the original decision-maker may produce a decision that is binding on the parties whether they like it or not or one to which they must first consent. (As a variant, some ombudsmen make decisions that are binding on the service provider but not the complainant). A second important distinction is whether both parties must agree to take part, or whether if one party chooses to use a particular option, the other is required to take part.

Participation

		Participation	
		Compulsory	Not Compulsory
Decisions	Binding	Courts/Tribunals	Arbitration
	Not Binding	Assisted Settlement	

2.10 Within each category, there can then be a wide range of second-order differences in the process. So, **courts and tribunals** do essentially the same things in that they make binding, final decisions (subject to appeal) on people who are required to participate. This necessarily means they are limited to offering legal remedies. Some formality or process is required, although hearings in a large proportion of small claims are relatively informal. **Tribunals** tend to aspire to a more inquisitorial and less formal approach than courts, reducing the need for the parties to be legally represented. Tribunals have specialist jurisdictions and most sit in panels, often with non-lawyer (expert or lay) members; they do not have their own enforcement powers. Most tribunals do not charge fees or routinely order the losing parties to pay winners' cost.

2.11 There are a number of alternative dispute resolution (ADR) processes:

- **adjudication** involves an impartial, independent third party hearing the claims of both sides and issuing a decision to resolve the dispute. The outcome is determined by the adjudicator, not by the parties. Determinations are usually made on the basis of fairness, and the process used and means of decision-making are not bound by law. It can involve a hearing or be based on documents only;
- **arbitration** involves an impartial, independent third party hearing the claims of both sides and issuing binding decision to resolve the dispute. The outcome is determined by the arbitrator, is final and legally binding, with limited grounds for appeal. It requires both parties' willing and informed consent to participate. It can involve a hearing or be based on documents. Only;
- **conciliation** involves an impartial third party helping the parties to resolve their dispute by hearing both sides and offering an opinion on settlement. It requires both parties' willing and informed consent to participate. The parties determine the outcome, usually with advice from the conciliator. An example Acas conciliation;
- **early neutral evaluation** involves an independent person assessing the claims made by each side and giving an opinion on (a) the likely outcome in court or tribunal, (b) a fair outcome, and/or (c) a technical or legal point. It is non-binding, and the parties decide how to use the opinion in their negotiations. It requires both parties' willing and informed to help moderate a party's unrealistic claims;
- **mediation** involves an independent third party helping parties to reach a voluntary, mutually agreed resolution. A key principle is that the parties, not the mediator, decide the outcome. It requires both parties' willing and informed consent to participate. It requires mediating skills, and it has a structured format;
- **negotiation** involves dealing directly with the person or the organization in dispute. It is non-binding and can be done by the person in dispute or by a representative ('assisted negotiation'). The negotiator is not impartial but instead represents a party's interests. An example of negotiation is settlement discussions between solicitors; and
- **ombudsmen** are impartial independent 'referees' who consider, investigate and resolve complaints about public and private organizations. Their decisions are made on the basis of what is fair and reasonable. They also have a role in influencing good practice in complaints handling.

2.12 In practice, participation in mediation and other non-binding options is usually voluntary. But there is no reason in principle why, even if it is not compulsory, it should not be strongly encouraged in appropriate circumstances. For example, under the Civil Procedure Rules in England and Wales, courts are under a duty to encourage the use of alternative dispute resolution (often mediation) in appropriate cases, and may take account of whether the parties considered this when making case management decisions and ordering cists. A pilot at Central London County Court is automatically referring some civil cases to mediation, and the parties have to give the court their reasons if they do not want to participate. And in most Employment Tribunal cases, there is stage in the process in which Acas seeks to find an agreed solution before a hearing in the tribunal is held. . . .

Note
Chapter 3 of the White Paper surveys the current Administrative Justice Landscape, noting the huge numbers of decisions made by public officials, including millions of decisions in such areas as direct tax, VAT and benefits. Routes to redress include making a complaint to the department or agency, an independent complaint handler, an MP or an ombudsman, court proceedings or a tribunal appeal.

(i) Internal review

Notes
1. Each public body is expected to have in place and to publish its complaints procedure (see below, p.202). Such procedures commonly provide for one or more reviews of a complaint within the public body concerned, before the matter is taken externally.

2. In some cases, provision for a formal internal review is made by legislation. For example, applicants claiming to be owed duties by the local housing authority under Pt VII of the Housing Act 1996 concerning homelessness have the right to request a review of adverse decisions on key elements of the statutory regime (*e.g.* whether they are "homeless", "eligible", in "priority need" and became homeless "intentionally") (Housing Act 1996, s.202(1), as amended by the Homelessness Act 2002, s.8(2); Allocation of Housing and Homelessness (Review Procedures) Regulations 1999 (SI 1999/71). Where a review of an original decision made by an officer is also to be made by an officer, that officer must be someone who was not involved in the original decision and who is senior to the officer who made the original decisions (reg.2). The applicant is entitled to make representations in writing, which must be considered (regs 6, 8). If the applicant remains dissatisfied, he or she may appeal to the county court on a point of law (Housing Act 1996, s.204), as amended by the Homelessness Act 2002, s.11 and Sch.1). While an internal review is not an independent and impartial tribunal for the purposes of Art.6(1) ECHR, the right of appeal serves compliance overall (*Runa Begum v Tower Hamlets LBC* [2003] UKHL 5; [2003] 2 A.C. 430). See below, p.384.

3. Provisions in social security law that required there to be an internal re-assessment before there could be an appeal to a tribunal were repealed by the Social Security Act 1998, which enables the decision-maker to revise a decision on his or her own initiative and gave the applicant the right to request that a decision be revised (see ss.9 (specified benefits), 34 (housing benefit; council tax benefit), 40 (child support)). The provisions repealed had been criticised as illegitimate in principle and undesirable in practice, as constituting the first stage of an appeal without compliance with the Franks standards of independence and impartiality, and creating the risk that claimants unsuccessful on an internal review would be deterred from pursuing an appeal (R. Sainsbury, "Internal Reviews and the Weakening of Social Security Claimants' Rights of Appeal" in G. Richardson and H. Genn, *Administrative Law and Government Action* (1994), pp.287–307). For a defence of such arrangements see M. Harris, "The Place of Formal and Informal Review in the Administrative Justice System" in Harris and Partington (ed.), *Administrative Justice in the 21st Century*

(1999), Ch.2). Harris argues that making a formal review a formal prerequisite of an appeal did not alter its essential character (p.46) that there was not clear evidence of drop-out rates (pp.49–51), and that it would have been better for there to be empirical evidence of the operation of formal review before it was dropped (p.53). The greater use of such a mechanism in principle posed no threat to appeals and would have reinforced the idea of the administrative process itself forming part of an overall system of administrative justice.

(ii) Alternative Dispute Resolution

DEPARTMENT FOR CONSTITUTIONAL AFFAIRS, MONITORING THE EFFECTIVENESS OF THE GOVERNMENT'S COMMITMENT TO USING ALTERNATIVE DISPUTE RESOLUTION (ADR)

REPORT FOR THE PERIOD APRIL 2002 TO MARCH 2003 (AUGUST 2003)

The Pledge

Settlement of Government Disputes Through Alternative Dispute Resolution

Government Departments and agencies make these commitments on the resolution of disputes involving them:

- Alternative Dispute Resolution (ADR) will be considered and used in *all* suitable cases wherever the other party accepts it.
- In future, Departments will provide appropriate clauses in their standard procurement contracts on the use of ADR techniques to settle their disputes. The precise method of settlement would be tailored to the details of individual cases.
- Central Government will produce procurement guidance on the different options available for ADR in Government disputes and how they might be best deployed in different circumstances. This will spread best practice and ensure consistency across Government.
- Departments will improve flexibility in reaching agreement on financial compensation, including using an independent assessment of a possible settlement figure.

There may be cases that are not suitable for settlement through ADR, for example cases involving intentional wrongdoing, abuse of power, public law, Human Rights and vexatious litigants. There will also be disputes where, for example, a legal precedent is needed to clarify the law, or where it would be contrary to the public interest to settle. Government Departments will put in place performance measures to monitor the effectiveness of this undertaking.

The Pledge was announced by the then Lord Chancellor in March 2001.

Activity under the Pledge

Departments, their Agencies and the National Health Service Litigation Authority monitor their use of ADR, sending statistical information to the Lord Chancellor's Department (now the Department for Constitutional

Affairs) which collates this report. Information received in the Department shows that the number of Government disputes in the financial year 2002–2003 where a method of ADR has been used or attempted, is 617—an increase of over 1200% on the previous financial year.

Of the 617 offers of ADR made, 27% were accepted and of those cases where ADR was used, 89% had settled without recourse to a hearing.

This information provides evidence of a significant increase in the level of ADR activity in Government Departments and demonstrates the Government's growing commitment to a culture of settlement rather than a culture of litigation.

Departments have estimated savings of over £6m, attributable to their use of ADR over the period of the report. That said, it has not been possible to quantify potential savings in every instance.

In line with the Pledge and with guidance issued by the Office of Government Commerce, Departments have included ADR clauses in standard procurement contracts.

It should be noted that very many disputes are settled by informal negotiation processes which do not strictly fall within the definition of ADR. For instance, settlement meetings between clients and their legal representatives are used as a means of resolving disputes—especially in personal injury and commercial matters. The headline figures do not reflect, therefore, the very substantial number of disputes which are resolved outside of a formal ADR process and without recourse to litigation.

Notes

1. The Pledge was set out in LCD Press Notice 117, 01, March 23, 2001. The Report proceeded to give examples of the use of ADR, which included the use of mediation in the settlement of contract claims in relation to Foot-and-Mouth Disease, the Alder Hey organ retention group litigation and a complex dispute involving a Home Office NDPB. A range of awareness courses and training events had been held. The use of mediation has also been encouraged as a part of the Inquiries Procedure for major infrastructure projects (Town and Country Planning (Major Infrastructure Project Inquiries Procedure) (England) Rules 2002 (SI 2002/1223), r.11) (see below, p.144) and in the New Circular on Compulsory Purchase Orders (ODPM Circular 02/2003, para.23).

2. The promotion of ADR in resolving public sector disputes is part of a wider objective for the DCA to reduce the proportion of civil disputes resolved by resort to the court (SR 2002, for the Spending Review period 2003/04 to 2005/06, PSA Target 3 within Objective II: To ensure a fair and effective system of civil and administrative law: DCA, *Annual Performance Review 2004*, p.5). For SR 2004, this is to become part of PSA Target 5:

"To achieve earlier and more proportionate resolution of legal problems and disputes by:
   • increasing advice and assistance to help people resolve their disputes earlier and more effectively;
   • Increasing the opportunities for people involved in court cases to settle their disputes out of court; and
   • Reducing delays in resolving those disputes that need to be decided by the courts" (*ibid.*, p.36).

Further information on the work of the Better Dispute Resolution Team within the DCA is given at *www.dca.gov.uk/civil/ads*.

3. A helpful analysis of the extent to which ADR may (or may not) be suitable for dealing with different kinds of disputes involving public bodies is provided by the Advice Services Alliance (ADRnow, *www.adrnow.org.uk*). The use of ombudsmen is

recommended for individual complaints about actions (or inactions) by government bodies; for contractual disputes, mediation "is emerging as the primary ADR option". More specific examples are that ADR is not frequently used in disputes over benefits as most schemes cannot overturn DWP benefit decisions (except the Independent Review Service which can overturn a Social Fund decision). Complaints about the way decisions are made can be taken to an ombudsman (*e.g.* housing benefit cases dealt with by the Local Government Ombudsman). All local education authorities are required to provide independent disagreement resolution services (usually mediation) in respect of disputes concerning special educational needs. Mediation is increasingly being offered as an option for disputes over school exclusions or potential exclusions, but is not readily available in respect of admissions decisions. The Disability Conciliation Service provides free, independent conciliation of disputes under Pts III or IV of the Disability Discrimination Act 1995.

4. The use of ADR instead of proceedings for judicial review is also encouraged by the courts: see below, p.967. However, the courts cannot force unwilling parties to mediate; such compulsion will constitute an unacceptable constraint on the right of access to the court, contrary to Art.6(1), ECHR (*Halsey v Milton Keynes General NHS Trust*; *Steel v Joy* [2004] EWCA Civ 576; [2004] 1 W.L.R. 3002). The unreasonable refusal of ADR may, however, be taken into account in decisions as to the award of costs, although the burden is on the unsuccessful party to demonstrate why costs should not follow the event (*ibid*). See further, M. Smith, [2002] J.R. 152; V. Bundy, [2004] J.R. 306.

(iii) Tribunals

Tribunals are now a familiar and established part of the legal system, determining a wide variety of disputes that arise between the citizen and the state (as a part of the system of administrative justice), and some classes of dispute between citizen and citizen (of which the best example is the contribution of Employment Tribunals and the Employment Appeal Tribunal to justice in the workplace). There have been two major landmarks in the history of tribunals. The first was the Report of the Franks Committee in 1957. Many, although not all, of its recommendations were accepted, the main ones being included in the Tribunals and Inquiries Act 1958 (consolidated in the Act of 1992). The 1958 Act saw the establishment of the Council on Tribunals, changed with the oversight of most tribunals and land use inquiries (see below, p.127). The second is the Leggatt Review in 2001 (see above) which has led to a White Paper published in July 2004 and which will be the basis of further legislation.

REPORT OF THE COMMITTEE ON ADMINISTRATIVE TRIBUNALS AND ENQUIRIES

(HMSO, Cmnd.218, JULY 1957)

CHAIRMAN: Sir Oliver Franks.
[The Committee's terms of reference were:

"To consider and make recommendations on:
  (a) The constitution and working of tribunals other than the ordinary courts of law, constituted under any Act of Parliament by a Minister of the Crown or for the purposes of a Minister's functions.
  (b) The working of such administrative procedures as include the holding of an enquiry or hearing by or on behalf of a Minister on an appeal or as the result of objections or representations, and in particular the procedure for the compulsory purchase of land."]

5. Our terms of reference involve the consideration of an important part of the relationship between the individual and authority. At different times in the history of this country it has been necessary to adjust this relationship and to seek a new balance between private right and public advantage, between fair play for the individual and efficiency of administration. The balance found has varied with different governmental systems and different social patterns. Since the war the British electorate has chosen governments which accepted general responsibilities for the provision of extended social services and for the broad management of the economy. It has consequently become desirable to consider afresh the procedures by which the rights of individual citizens can be harmonised with wider public interests.

6. The problem is not confined to this country. In recent years most other Western governments have been called upon to govern more extensively and more intensively, and finding a right relationship between authority and the individual has consequently become a matter of concern on both sides of the Atlantic.

Disputes between the individual and authority

7. How do disputes between the individual and authority arise in this country at the present time? In general the starting point is the enactment of legislation by Parliament. Many statutes apply detailed schemes to the whole or to large classes of the community (for example national insurance) or lay on a Minister and other authorities a general duty to provide a service (for example education or health). Such legislation is rarely sufficient in itself to achieve all its objects, and a series of decisions by administrative bodies, such as government departments and local authorities is often required. For example, in a national insurance scheme decisions have to be given on claims to benefit, and in providing an educational service decisions have to be taken on the siting of new schools. Many of these decisions affect the rights of individual citizens, who may then object.

8. Once objection has been raised, a further decision becomes inevitable. This further decision is of a different kind: whether to confirm, cancel or vary the original decision. In reaching it account must be taken not only of the original decision but also of the objection.

The resolution of these disputes

9. These further decisions are made in various ways. Some are made in courts of law and therefore by the procedure of a court of law. For example, an order made by a local authority for the demolition of an insanitary house may be appealed against to the county court. Frequently the statutes lay down that these further decisions are to be made by a special tribunal or a Minister. For example, a contested claim to national insurance benefit has to be determined by a special tribunal, and the decision whether or not to confirm an opposed scheme for the compulsory acquisition of land by a local authority must be made by the Minister concerned. In these cases the procedure to be

followed in dealing with objections to the first decision and in arriving at the further decision is laid down in the statute or in regulations made thereunder.

10. But over most of the field of public administration no formal procedure is provided for objecting or deciding on objections. For example, when foreign currency or a scarce commodity such as petrol or coal is rationed or allocated, there is no other body to which an individual applicant can appeal if the responsible administrative authority decides to allow him less than he has requested. Of course the aggrieved individual can always complain to the appropriate administrative authority, to his Member of Parliament, to a representative organisation or to the Press. But there is no formal procedure on which he can insist.

11. There are therefore two broad distinctions to be made among these further decisions which we have been discussing. The first is between those decisions which follow a statutory procedure and those which do not. The second distinction is within the group of decisions subject to a statutory procedure. Some of these decisions are taken in the ordinary courts and some are taken by tribunals or by Ministers after a special procedure.

12. These two distinctions are essential for understanding our terms of reference. We are not instructed to consider those many cases in which no formal procedure has been prescribed. Nor are we instructed to consider decisions made in the ordinary courts. What we are instructed to consider are the cases in which the decision on objections, the further decision as we have called it, is taken by a tribunal or by a Minister after a special procedure has been followed. . . .

CHAPTER 3: THE TWO PARTS OF THE TERMS OF REFERENCE

20. It is noteworthy that Parliament, having decided that the decisions with which we are concerned should not be remitted to the ordinary courts, should also have decided that they should not be left to be reached in the normal course of administration. Parliament has considered it essential to lay down special procedures for them.

Good administration

21. This must have been to promote good administration. Administration must not only be efficient in the sense that the objectives of policy are securely attained without delay. It must also satisfy the general body of citizens that it is proceeding with reasonable regard to the balance between the public interest which it promotes and the private interest which it disturbs. Parliament has, we infer, intended in relation to the subject-matter of our terms of reference that the further decisions or, as they may rightly be termed in this context, adjudications must be acceptable as having been properly made.

22. It is natural that Parliament should have taken this view of what constitutes good administration. In this country government rests fundamentally upon the consent of the governed. The general acceptability of these adjudications is one of the vital elements in sustaining that consent.

Openness, fairness and impartiality

23. When we regard our subject in this light, it is clear that there are certain general and closely linked characteristics which should mark these

special procedures. We call these characteristics openness, fairness and impartiality.

24. Here we need only give brief examples of their application. Take openness. If these procedures were wholly secret, the basis of confidence and acceptability would be lacking. Next take fairness. If the objector were not allowed to state his case, there would be nothing to stop oppression. Thirdly, there is impartiality. How can the citizen be satisfied unless he feels that those who decide his case come to their decision with open minds?

25. To assert that openness, fairness and impartiality are essential characteristics of our subject-matter is not to say that they must be present in the same way and to the same extent in all its parts. Difference in the nature of the issue for adjudication may give good reason for difference in the degree to which the three general characteristics should be developed and applied. Again, the method by which a Minister arrives at a decision after a hearing or inquiry cannot be the same as that by which a tribunal arrives at a decision. This difference is brought out later in the Report. For the moment it is sufficient to point out that when Parliament sets up a tribunal to decide cases, the adjudication is placed outside the department concerned. The members of the tribunal are neutral and impartial in relation to the policy of the Minister, except in so far as that policy is contained in the rules which the tribunal has been set up to apply. But the Minister, deciding in the cases under the second part of our terms of reference, is committed to a policy which he has been charged by Parliament to carry out. In this sense he is not, and cannot be, impartial.

The allocation of decisions to tribunals and Ministers

26. At this stage another question naturally arises. On what principle has it been decided that some adjudications should be made by tribunals and some by Ministers? If from a study of the history of the subject we could discover such a principle, we should have a criterion which would be a guide for any future allocation of these decisions between tribunals and Ministers.

27. The search for this principle has usually involved the application of one or both of two notions, each with its antithesis. Both notions are famous and have long histories. They are the notion of what is judicial, its antithesis being what is administrative, and the notion of what is according to the rule of law, its antithesis being what is arbitrary.

28. What is judicial has been worked out and given expression by generations of judges. Its distinction from what is administrative recalls great constitutional victories and marks the essential difference in the nature of the decisions of the judiciary and of the executive.

29. The rule of law stands for the view that decisions should be made by the application of known principles or laws. In general such decisions will be predictable, and the citizen will know where he is. On the other hand there is what is arbitrary. A decision may be made without principle, without any rules. It is therefore unpredictable, the antithesis of a decision taken in accordance with the rule of law.

30. Nothing that we say diminishes the importance of these pairs of antitheses. But it must be confessed that neither pair yields a valid principle on which one can decide whether the duty of making a certain decision should be laid upon a tribunal or upon a Minister or whether the existing allocation of

decisions between tribunals and Ministers is appropriate. But even if there is no such principle and we cannot explain the facts, we can at least start with them. An empirical approach may be the most useful.

31. Starting with the facts, we observe that the methods of adjudication by tribunals are in general not the same as those of adjudication by Ministers. All or nearly all tribunals apply rules. No ministerial decisions of the kind denoted by the second part of our terms of reference is reached in this way. Many matters remitted to tribunals and Ministers appear to have, as it were, a natural affinity with one or other method of adjudication. Sometimes the policy of the legislation can be embodied in a system of detailed regulations. Particular decisions cannot, single case by single case, alter the Minister's policy. Where this is so, it is natural to entrust the decisions to a tribunal, if not to the courts. On the other hand it is sometimes desirable to preserve flexibility of decision in the pursuance of public policy. Then a wise expediency is the proper basis of right adjudication, and the decision must be left with a Minister.

32. But in other instances there seems to be no such natural affinity. For example, there seems to be no natural affinity which makes it clearly appropriate for appeals in goods vehicle licence cases to be decided by the Transport Tribunal when appeals in a number of road passenger cases are decided by the Minister.

33. We shall therefore respect this factual difference between tribunals and Ministers and deal separately with the two parts of the subject. When considering tribunals we shall see how far the three characteristics of openness, fairness and impartiality can be developed and applied in general and how far their development and application must be adapted to the circumstances of particular tribunals. We shall then proceed to the decisions of Ministers after a hearing or inquiry and consider how far the difference in method of adjudication requires a different development and application of the three characteristics. . . .

PART II: TRIBUNALS IN GENERAL

CHAPTER 4: INTRODUCTORY

The choice between tribunals and courts of law

38. We agree with the Donoughmore Committee [the Committee on Ministers' Powers (Cmd.4060 1932)] that tribunals have certain characteristics which often give them advantages over the courts. These are cheapness, accessibility, freedom from technicality, expedition and expert knowledge of their particular subject. It is no doubt because of these advantages that Parliament, once it has decided that certain decisions ought not to be made by normal executive or departmental processes, often entrusts them to tribunals rather than to the ordinary courts. But as a matter of general principle we are firmly of the opinion that a decision should be entrusted to a court rather than to a tribunal in the absence of special considerations which make a tribunal more suitable.

39. Moreover, if all decisions arising from new legislation were automatically vested in the ordinary courts the judiciary would by now have been

grossly overburdened. We agree that any wholesale transfer to the courts of the work of tribunals would be undesirable. We have not excluded from consideration whether the jurisdiction of any existing tribunal should be transferred to the ordinary courts, though we make no such recommendation. We therefore proceed to consider what improvements and safeguards, including appeals to the courts, should be introduced into the present structure.

Tribunals as machinery for adjudication

40. Tribunals are not ordinary courts, but neither are they appendages of government departments. Much of the official evidence, including that of the Joint Permanent Secretary to the Treasury, appeared to reflect the view that tribunals should properly be regarded as part of the machinery of administration, for which the Government must retain a close and continuing responsibility. Thus, for example, tribunals in the social service field would be regarded as adjuncts to the administration of the services themselves. We do not accept this view. We consider that tribunals should properly be regarded as machinery provided by Parliament for adjudication rather than as part of the machinery of administration. The essential point is that in all these cases Parliament has deliberately provided for a decision outside and independent of the department concerned, either at first instance (for example in the case of Rent Tribunals and the Licensing Authorities for Public Service and Goods Vehicles) or on appeal from a decision of a Minister or of an official in a special statutory position (for example a valuation officer or an insurance officer). Although the relevant statutes do not in all cases expressly enact that tribunals are to consist entirely of persons outside the government service, the use of the term "tribunal" in legislation undoubtedly bears this connotation, and the intention of Parliament to provide for the independence of tribunals is clear and unmistakable.

The application of the principles of openness, fairness and impartiality

41. We have already expressed our belief, in Part I, that Parliament in deciding that certain decisions should be reached only after a special procedure must have intended that they should manifest three basic characteristics: openness, fairness and impartiality. The choice of a tribunal rather than a Minister as the deciding authority is itself a considerable step towards the realisation of these objectives, particularly the third. But in some cases the statutory provisions and the regulations thereunder fall short of what is required to secure these objectives. Our main task in this Part and in Part III will be to assess the extent to which the three objectives are capable of attainment in the field of tribunals and to suggest appropriate measures.

42. In the field of tribunals openness appears to us to require the publicity of proceedings and knowledge of the essential reasoning underlying the decisions; fairness to require the adoption of a clear procedure which enables parties to know their rights, to present their case fully and to know the case which they have to meet; and impartiality to require the freedom of tribunals from the influence, real or apparent, of departments concerned with the subject-matter of their decisions.

WHITE PAPER, TRANSFORMING PUBLIC SERVICES: COMPLAINTS, REDRESS AND TRIBUNALS

(Cm.6243, JULY 2004).

Tribunals

3.24 With legislation creating rights to State services (e.g. to benefits if certain conditions are met) and obligations (such as to pay tax) came specialist statutory tribunals to give binding rulings in the event of disputes. Initially many were seen both by users and administrators more as part of the administration than as wholly independent judicial bodies. They had the effect of diverting responsibility for individual decisions away from Ministers. But with the Franks Report they become more firmly established as part of the judicial system, but separate from the courts, which were not thought able to cope with litigation arising out of statutory rights and benefits.

3.25 Of the tribunals still operating today, the first were the General and Special Commissioners of Income Tax who gradually shed their original administrative responsibilities and became purely judicial bodies. Among the earliest purely judicial tribunals were the 'courts of referees' and 'umpire', established by the National Insurance Act 1911 to handle appeals relating to unemployment benefit and from whom the present-day Appeals Service tribunals and the Social Security Commissioners are descended. They were followed by the Pensions Appeal Tribunals, created after the First World War to make independent decisions about entitlement to war pensions. Many other tribunals followed. When in 1971 Parliament created a new right not to be unfairly dismissed from employment the jurisdiction to decide disputes was given to a tribunal, which formed the basis of the present day Employment Tribunals and Employment Appeal Tribunal. Over the years different tribunals have increased or declined in importance, with social change and the rise and fall of different rights and obligations. The tribunals responsible for setting rents, for instance, have declined with changing regulation of the rented housing sector; conversely, increased migration has generated extra work for the immigration appellate authorities.

3.26 Tribunals were designed to be less formal alternatives to the courts, combining fairness and independence with accessibility and expertise. But whereas they may be fair and expert, to the user they may not always be very clearly distinct from the department whose decisions they review. Many of them continue to be sponsored by those departments, even if their chairmen and members are appointed by the Lord Chancellor and they have a degree of administrative autonomy and a very strong independent ethos. We accept that, for cases which proceed to a full hearing before a tribunal, users are in the main treated fairly and that decisions are accepted. But there is a prior issue. Can people who have a legitimate case overcome the barriers to getting it resolved? Do they even know that they may have a case? Here the picture is much more mixed. There are indications from a number of studies that there may well be significant numbers of individuals who, for a variety of reasons, do not seek redress when they could. Studies in a number of jurisdictions have been summarised in a recent report to the Council on Tribunals by Professor

Michael Adler and Jackie Gulland of the University of Edinburgh.[12] There is evidence in a more general context that people with legal problems feel themselves unable to resolve them, at least using whatever formal means are available to them. The recent publication from the Legal Services Research Centre—*Causes of Action: Civil Law and Social Justice*—revealed that over the 3½ year period of the research:

- more than one in three adults experienced a civil law problem: and,
- one in five took no action to solve their problem.

It was estimated that around one million problems go unsolved each year because people don't understand their basic rights or know how to seek help.[13]

3.27 Compared to most other forms of independent redress tribunals handle large volumes. Workloads of individual tribunals can be volatile but in general about a million people a year have cases dealt with by all types of tribunals. Not all cases are simple and straightforward, with only minor issues or modest sums of money at stake. On the contrary, some tribunals deal with cases involving hundreds of millions of pounds, with high quality legal and expert representation; others deal with hugely complex discrimination cases, or with difficult points of law which have profound importance for both the individual in the case and the community as a whole.

	Received
Appeals Service[14]	235,657
Mental Health Review Tribunals[15]	20,408
CICAP[16]	4,434
SENDIST[17]	3,638
General & Special Commissioners of Income Tax[18]	29,498
VAT & Duties Tribunal[19]	2,496
Social Security and Child Support Commissioners[20]	6,364
Pensions Appeals[21]	3,372
Immigration Adjudicators[22]	91,945
Immigration Appeal Tribunal[23]	41,889

[12] *Tribunal Users Experiences, Perceptions and Expectations: a Literature Review,* available on the Council on Tribunals website *www.council-on-tribunals.gov.uk*
[13] See also *Paths to Justice* by Hazel Genn (Hart: Oxford, 1999)
[14] 1/4/03–31/3/04
[15] Does note include Welsh figures
[16] 1/4/03–31/3/04
[17] 1/4/03–31/3/04 (does not include Welsh figures)
[18] 1/1/03–31/12/03
[19] 1/1/03–31/12/03
[20] 1/4/03–31/3/04
[21] 1/1/02–31/12/02 (decided figure includes withdrawn cases)
[22] 1/4/02–31/3/03
[23] 1/4/02–31/3/03

3.28 The following table shows the number of appeals to the largest tribunals administered by central government.

3.29 The extent to which tribunals succeed in serving the public is considered in Chapter 5.

3.30 So the main response of government to the need to have independent review of decisions about rights and obligations has been to establish a tribunal. There are now some 70 tribunals in existence, some with very large workloads but many moribund or with insignificant workloads. All have some features in common, usually those derived from the courts—but there are also variations and differences between them, many explicable only in historical terms. Governments have proved unimaginative in devising new methods of reviewing their own decisions. There is little by way of alternative dispute resolution methods available to supplement formal tribunal hearings. The only exceptions are:

- the role of Acas in setting employment disputes;
- in cases which may go the Special Educational Needs and Disability Tribunal (SENDIST) local authorities are obliged to set up conciliation arrangements.

3.31 Both the public and private sectors need to create and maintain suitable and cost effective means of redress. In the next chapter we look in more detail at the role of ombudsmen in both the public and the private sectors and the lessons which may be learnt from the way they handle complaints.

[Chapter 4 reviewed the different public sector and private sector ombudsman services (see below, Ch.3). It concluded:]

Lessons from the development of ombudsman services

4.20 The key aim of ombudsmen is to improve service delivery and to promote better administration by learning the lessons from effective complaints handling. Of course the encouraging experience of the ombudsman systems cannot be automatically carried over unchanged into tribunals. Unlike a contractual dispute, decisions arising out of many public sector services, such as entitlement to benefit, cannot be settled with a compromise, splitting the difference between two positions. But the fact that the nature of the decision ultimately to be made is different doest not mean that there is only one way to reach that decision. On the contrary, we believe that the government has much to learn from the success of ombudsman schemes. Our purpose is to reclaim the idea of flexible dispute resolution for a new era and a different scale of operation, so that the public receive a service tailored to their needs.

4.21 Can the changes we want to see brought about happen with the existing institutional structure? We do not believe that they can. Administrative justice can be described as a system but it was not created as a system and no coherent design or design principle has ever been applied systematically to it. It is a patchwork. One option would be to create a new institution of some kind with the job of improving decision-making and resolving disputes informally. But even with such a new institution there would be a need for an authoritative body, with the powers of the court, to have the final word on rights and obligations. We believe the field is too cluttered already with administrative justice institutions. What we need to do is to create the unified tribunal system recommended by Sir Andrew Leggatt but transform it into a new type of organisation which will not only provide formal hearings and authoritative rulings where these are needed but will have as well a mission to resolve disputes fairly and informally either by itself or in partnership with the decision-making department, other institutions and the advice sector.

4.22 In the next chapter we explore in more depth the weaknesses of the present system and in the following chapter we set out how a new body would look and what is would need to do to fulfil the mission we have set for it.

Notes

1. Chapter 5 of the White Paper noted a series of problems with the effectiveness of tribunals today:

(a) Independence. The fact that most central government tribunals are sponsored by the responsible department means that they are not seen to be manifestly independent of those whose decisions they are reviewing.

(b) Waiting times. "In general the delays endured by some tribunal appellants give a picture of an under-performing public service" (para.5.5).

(c) Informal Resolution. In some areas tribunal hearings could be avoided "if there had been a suitable trigger for dispute resolution by the department" (para.5.7).

(d) Accessibility to hearing centres. Almost 40 per cent of users surveyed needed to travel for more than an hour to reach the hearing, and 36 per cent of users said they did not feel "comfortable" in the tribunal building.

(e) Accessibility of process. User representatives argued that clients are often confused by decisions giving rise to appeals or information about appeal rights. Almost 40 per cent of appellants said they received little or no information from the tribunal advising them on what would happen.

Overall the Government accepted Sir Andrew Leggatt's assessment of the present system as incoherent and inefficient (para.5.14). Reforms were needed to deliver an improved service and, apart from that, there was a financial case for reform, with the more efficient and better targeted use of resources (paras 5.16–5.23). The system needed an estates strategy to co-ordinate the provision of (more suitable) accommodation and an overall IT strategy.

2. Chapter 6 of the White Paper states that the new unified tribunal system already proposed by the Lord Chancellor (on March 11, 2003) with at its core the top 10 non-devolved central government tribunals, will become "a new type of organisation, not just a federation of existing tribunals".

Its mission will be "to resolve disputes the best way possible and to stimulate improved decision-making so that disputes do not happen as a result of poor decision-making" (para.6.4). Its key features "need to be independence, professionalism, accessibility and efficiency". The DCA, which already has responsibility for a number of tribunals will also between 2006 and 2008 take over from the current sponsoring department responsibility for the Appeals Service (social security), the Employment Tribunals Service, the Special Educational Needs and Disability Tribunal Panel and the Mental Health Review Tribunal for England. Other tribunals will be transferred as agreed with sponsoring departments. All new tribunals (unless devolved) will become part of the new organisation.

The change will ensure that the largest tribunals in administrative justice are manifestly independent, and are seen to be independent, from those who decision they are reviewing (para.6.14). It will deliver a network of hearing centres with a better geographical spread than any individual tribunal can offer. The DCA will develop a common estate, firmly based on research into consumer wishes and needs, and consultation with user groups, that supports both courts and tribunals, enabling advantage to be taken of the potential for sharing (paras 6.15–6.19). The new organisation will review the way in which services are provided and develop new ways of operating, considering possible alternatives to formal hearings. A number of proportionate dispute resolution pilot projects will be launched to test if alternatives are effective and affordable. Back-office functions will also need to be rationalised. The essential unity of the new organisation will be reinforced by the development of standardised ways of dealing with customers (*e.g.* common terminology, common pathways through the process (where feasible) and common terms for administrative positions) (paras 6.20–6.29). Work will start immediately on a project to provide better information about the tribunal and appeals process (para.6.30). The existing duty of tribunals to hold hearings and right to alter departments' decisions will remain, but be supplemented by power to comment on the way in which a person was treated (although not to conduct in depth investigation in the way that an ombudsman or independent complaints handler can). If a decision is not implemented promptly the appellant will have the right to bring the matter back to the new organisation to get action (para.6.31). The new organisation will be under a duty to provide its views and analysis of departmental decision-making (paras 6.32–6.34). It will not have the formal divisional structure proposed by the Leggatt Review, but will itself determine the degree of autonomy of individual jurisdictions within the structure by reference to what is best for the users; however, employment tribunals and the EAT will continue to maintain a strong degree of administrative separation (paras 6.36–6.38). A single judicial office will be created for those sitting in first-tier tribunals and another for those sitting in the appellate tribunal (Tribunal judges and Tribunal Appellate judges respectively). On appointment new members will be assigned to a jurisdiction or jurisdictions where there is an operational need provided the recruitment board has assessed them as qualified for that jurisdiction. Recommendations for appointment will be made to the Secretary of State for Constitutional Affairs by the Judicial Appointments Commission. Once appointed, it will be possible for judges with the necessary skills and expertise to be assigned to other jurisdictions by the senior Tribunal judiciary. A new office of Senior President of Tribunals will be established, with standing equivalent to a Lord Justice of Appeal. (Carnwath L.J. has been appointed as the Senior President Designate). Individual jurisdictions will continue to have presidents, which positions will be filled by High Court judges or through open competition. The role of non-legal members will be reviewed (paras 6.39–6.67). Provisions will be made for developing training and appraisal systems (paras 6.71–6.81). The tribunals judiciary will be supported by a separate executive agency within the DCA, provisionally known as the Tribunals Service (paras 6.82–6.90).

Tribunal rules will be overhauled, and are to be made by a tribunals procedure committee subject of the approval of the Secretary of State for Constitutional Affairs. The Secretary of State for Trade and Industry will, however, retain responsibility for employment tribunal rules (paras 7.2–7.7). Case management techniques will be extended and developed across the system (paras 7.8–7.31).

Further specific proposals are made for employment tribunals and the EAT (Ch.8) and Tax appeals (with a single, two-tier, structure for the four existing tax appeal bodies (Ch.9).

3. The key area of supporting the user is addressed in Ch.10, which recognises that some people will always need a lot of help, and other some degree of help until services are successfully made more responsive. However, full-scale legal representation to the taxpayer's expense in every administrative dispute or tribunal case would be disproportionate and unreasonable. The extent to which needs should be met at public expense depends on the nature and complexity of the task to be undertaken, the individual's own capabilities and the seriousness of the issues (para.10.3). Investment in helping people make the best possible case at the outset so that the department can get things right first time "may well pay dividends for everyone" (para.10.5). While departments should provide clear and full information about decisions and departments and tribunals jointly information about the options and procedures for

obtaining redress, many users want advice from an independent source about what they should do in relation to their case.

Accordingly, it may be more appropriate for government to support external providers, particularly the voluntary and charitable sector, in providing diagnostic tools and advice. There is a continuing role for public funding in tribunals where the right to asylum and the right to liberty are involved and in the EAT. Within the available resources, pilot innovative schemes will be developed in conjunction with the Legal Services Commission and the voluntary and charitable sector for the provision of enhanced advice (providing assistance in, for example, gathering information and evidence, filling in paperwork and advising on merits and presentation) (paras 10.6–10.10). The extent to which publicly funded advocacy is necessary remains a matter of debate. Tribunals bear many similarities to courts but the hearings are intended to be less formal and adversarial in nature which ought in time to reduce the need for representation. The relevant law may also be more similar than in many court cases, and there will rarely be a need for a party to concern themselves with technical evidential issues or deploy the traditional lawyer skill of cross-examination of witnesses. The Government thought that the current arrangements for legal support from the Community Legal Service was about right, and rejected the Law Society's proposal for the extension of legal aid to social security and employment tribunals. The need for support will any event change as the processes are changed (paras 10.11–10.15).

4. The proposals in the White Paper seem generally sensible, and complement appropriately the changes to the civil justice system through the Woolf reforms. The existing pattern of tribunals is anomalous and the product of history. There is considerable scope for rationalisation. Acceptance of the need for independence from sponsoring departments and confirmation of the place of tribunals as part of the legal system is welcome, and provides a stronger basis for development of their role in providing generic feedback to departments and agencies on the quality of decision-making. Indeed, money spent effectively on improving the quality of initial decision-making (through such steps as clarification and simplification of the rules to be applied, better training and management of the staff who make the decisions and improved IT systems) should prove to be the best investment of all.

There are, however, areas of concern. The organisation will be a large, complex and geographically spread bureaucracy. It will be established on a tight time-scale (the indicative time table (para.12.1) shows royal assent to the Courts and Tribunals Bill in December 2005; new Tribunals Service to start in running informally in April 2005 and formally from April 2006). Structural reorganisation will be accompanied by a large programme of review and reform of processes with a need for new IT systems. There is an obvious risk that the demands on those charged with the responsibilities may be unsustainable. Secondly, innovative methods of resolving disputes will need to be properly evidence-based and closely scrutinised to ensure that they are indeed a fair and effective substitute for the traditional oral hearing.

Thirdly, the stated aim

"to create a situation where individuals in dispute with the State or might be taking a case to a tribunal, or defending one, will be able to have their case resolved, with little or no support or assistance" (para.10.1)

is implausibly ambitious. The arguments that legal representation should not normally be needed (albeit supported by the Leggatt Review: see para.10.12) are unconvincing and are not supported by previous research, which generally demonstrates that legal representation increases the chance of success.

It is difficult to accept that in many cases the law applied by tribunals is any simpler than that applied to courts (consider, for example, the complexities of social security, tax and immigration law). The system will continue to depend on the considerable investment of time and effort by untrained individuals in preparing their own cases, probably greater than would be needed by experts, whether trained lay advisers or lawyers. To that extent the system requires many victims of mistakes by government agencies to pay (at least in time and effort) for their rectification, with little or no support from public funds.

Successive governments have struggled to contain the growing costs of existing publicly funded legal services. They are understandably reluctant to countenance extensions to such services but also reluctant to acknowledge that without such funding the standards of justice are compromised.

5. Note the comments of Professor Hazel Genn, drawing on her extensive empirical research into the workings of tribunals, believes that their decision-making and procedures can be daunting for unrepresented individuals.

"In practice, however, from the perspective of tribunal applicants, the conditions that operate in many tribunals are far from perfect. Despite their conventional characterization as informal, accessible, and non-technical, frequently tribunals are not particularly quick, there is considerable variation in the degree of informality, and the issues dealt with are highly complex in terms of both the regulations to be applied and the factual situations of applicants. This study of tribunal processes and decision-making has highlighted the complexity of many areas of law with which tribunals must deal and the impact of this complexity on decision-making. Although tribunal procedures are generally more flexible and straightforward than court hearings, the nature of tribunal adjudication means that those who appear before tribunals without representation are often at a disadvantage. The short-comings of tribunals as effective checks on administrative decisions are the result of misdescription of procedures as informal and misconceptions about simple decision-making and the scope for unrepresented applicants to prepare, present and advocate convincing cases."

H. Genn, "Tribunal Review of Administrative Decision-Making", Ch.11, p.285 in G. Richardson and H. Genn (ed.), *Administrative Law and Government Action* (1994).

6. For further consideration of tribunals, see G. Richardson in Feldman (ed.) *English Public Law*, Ch.20; *Smith, Bailey and Gunn on the Modern English Legal System* (4th ed. 2002), Chs 2, 13, 16; J.A. Farmer, *Tribunals and Government* (1974); J. Baldwin, N. Wikeley and R. Young, *Judging Social Security* (1992); M. Harris and M. Partington (ed.), *Administrative Justice in the 21st Century* (1999), esp. Pts 4, 6 and 7.

TRIBUNALS AND INQUIRIES ACT 1992

(An Act to consolidate the Tribunals and Inquiries Act 1971 and certain other enactments relating to tribunals and inquiries.)

Procedural rules for tribunals

8.—(1) The power of a Minister, the Lord President of the Court of Session, the Commissioners of Inland Revenue or the Foreign Compensation Commission to make, approve, confirm or concur in procedural rules for any tribunal specified in Schedule 1 shall be exercisable only after consultation with the Council. . . .

(4) In this section "procedural rules" includes any statutory provision relating to the procedure of the tribunal in question.

Procedure in connection with statutory inquiries

9.—(1) The Lord Chancellor, after consultation with the Council, may make rules regulating the procedure to be followed in connection with statutory inquiries held by or on behalf of Ministers; and different provision may be made by any such rules in relation to different classes of such inquiries.

(2) Any rules made by the Lord Chancellor under this section shall have effect, in relation to any statutory inquiry, subject to the provisions of the enactment under which the inquiry is held, and of any rules or regulations made under that enactment.

(3) Subject to subsection (2), rules made under this section may regulate procedure in connection with matters preparatory to such statutory inquiries as are mentioned in subsection (1), and in connection with matters subsequent to such inquiries, as well as in connection with the conduct of proceedings at such inquiries. . . .

Judicial control of tribunals etc.

Reasons to be given for decisions of tribunals and Ministers

10.—(1) Subject to the provisions of this section and of section 14, where—

(a) any tribunal specified in Schedule 1 gives any decision, or
(b) any Minister notifies any decision taken by him—
    (i) after a statutory inquiry has been held by him or on his behalf, or
    (ii) in a case in which a person concerned could (whether by objecting or otherwise) have required a statutory inquiry to be so held,

it shall be the duty of the tribunal or Minister to furnish a statement, either written or oral, of the reasons for the decision if requested, on or before the giving or notification of the decision, to state the reasons.

(2) The statement referred to in subsection (1) may be refused, or the specification of the reasons restricted, on grounds of national security.

(3) A tribunal or Minister may refuse to furnish a statement under subsection (1) to a person not primarily concerned with the decision if of the opinion that to furnish it would be contrary to the interests of any person primarily concerned.

(4) Subsection (1) does not apply to any decision taken by a Minister after the holding by him or on his behalf of an inquiry or hearing which is a statutory inquiry by virtue only of an order made under section 16(2) unless the order contains a direction that this section is to apply in relation to any inquiry or hearing to which the order applies.

(5) Subsection (1) does not apply—

(a) to decisions in respect of which any statutory provision has effect, apart from this section, as to the giving of reasons,
(b) to decisions of a Minister in connection with the preparation, making, approval, confirmation, or concurrence in regulations, rules or byelaws, or orders or schemes of a legislative and not executive character [. . .]

(6) Any statement of the reasons for a decision referred to in paragraph (a) or (b) of subsection (1), whether given in pursuance of that subsection or of any other statutory provision, shall be taken to form part of the decision and accordingly to be incorporated in the record.

(7) If, after consultation with the Council, it appears to the Lord Chancellor and the [Secretary of State] that it is expedient that—

(a) decisions of any particular tribunal or any description of such decisions, or
(b) any description of decisions of a Minister,

should be excluded from the operation of subsection (1) on the ground that the subject-matter of such decisions, or the circumstances in which they are made, make the giving of reasons unnecessary or impracticable, the Lord Chancellor and the [Secretary of State] may by order direct that subsection (1) shall not apply to such decisions.

(8) Where an order relating to any decisions has been made under subsection (7), the Lord Chancellor and the [Secretary of State] may, by a subsequent order made after consultation with the Council, revoke or vary the earlier order so that subsection (1) applies to any of those decisions.

Supervisory functions of superior courts not excluded by Acts passed before August 1, 1958

12.—(1) As respects England and Wales—

(a) any provision in an Act passed before August 1, 1958 that any order or determination shall not be called into question in any court, or
(b) any provision in such an Act which by similar words excludes any of the powers of the High Court,

shall not have effect so as to prevent the removal of the proceedings into the High Court by order of certiorari or to prejudice the powers of the High Court to make orders of mandamus. . . .

(3) Nothing in this section shall apply—

(a) to any order or determination of a court of law, or
(b) where an Act makes special provision for application to the High Court or the Court of Session within a time limited by the Act. . . .

Restricted application of Act in relation to certain tribunals

14.—(1) References in this Act to the working or a decision of, or procedural rules, for,—

(a) any tribunals specified in paragraph 14(a), 20, 33, 34, 39(a) or (b), 40, . . . of Schedule 1,[24]
(b) the [Office of Fair Trading] referred to in paragraph 17 of Schedule 1, or
(c) the Controller of Plant Variety Rights referred to in paragraph 36(a) of Schedule 1,

do not include references to their working, decisions or procedure in the exercise of executive functions. . . .

---

[24] *i.e.* the Information Commissioner, the Foreign Compensation Commission, PCTs and other health bodies, the Comptroller-General of Patents, Designs and Trade Marks, the General and Special Income Tax Commissioners, and Traffic Commissioners and Adjudicators.

(3) For the purposes of this Act, the functions of the Civil Aviation Authority referred to in paragraph 3 of Schedule 1 are to be taken to be confined to those prescribed for the purposes of section 7(2) of the Civil Aviation Act 1982.

Rules and orders

15. Any power of the Lord Chancellor and the Lord Advocate or either of them to make rules or orders under this Act shall be exercisable by statutory instrument subject to annulment in pursuance of a resolution of either House of Parliament.

Interpretation

16.—(1) In this Act, except where the context otherwise requires—

"decision", "procedural rules" and "working", in relation to a tribunal, shall be construed subject to section 14,
"Council" means the Council on Tribunals, "Minister" includes [the National Assembly for Wales and] any Board presided over by a Minister,
"Scottish Committee" means the Scottish Committee of the Council on Tribunals, "statutory inquiry" means—
  (a) an inquiry or hearing held or to be held in pursuance of a duty imposed by any statutory provision, or
  (b) an inquiry or hearing, or an inquiry or hearing of a class, designated for the purposes of this section by an order under subsection (2), and
"statutory provision" means a provision contained in, or having effect under, any enactment.

(2) The Lord Chancellor and the [Secretary of State] may by order designate for the purposes of this section any inquiry or hearing held or to be held in pursuance of a power conferred by any statutory provision specified or described in the order, or any class of such inquiries or hearings.
(3) References in this Act to members of tribunals include references to the person constituting a tribunal consisting of one person. . . .

Notes
1. Sections 1 to 4 of the 1992 Act prescribe the constitution and functions of the Council on Tribunals originally established by the 1958 Act (see below, p.148). Section 5 provides that the Council may make to the appropriate minister general recommendations as to the making of appointments to membership of any of the tribunals listed in Sch.1, and the minister must have regard to the recommendations. The appropriate minister is the minister making the appointments or, otherwise, the minister in charge of the department concerned with the tribunal in question.

The chairmen of specified tribunals are to be selected by the relevant minister from a panel appointed by the Lord Chancellor or in the case of tribunals under s.50 of the Mines and Quarries Act 1954, appointed by him (s.6). In the case of the tribunals specified in Sch.1 (subject to exceptions), the power of a minister, other than the Lord Chancellor, to terminate a person's membership of a tribunal or tribunal panel, is exercisable only with the consent of the Lord Chancellor (if the tribunal does not sit outside England and Wales) and/or the Lord President of the Court of Session and the Lord Chief Justice of Northern Ireland where tribunals sit in those jurisdictions (s.7). In the case of specified tribunals, an appeal lies on a point of law to the High Court (s.11). These are Independent Schools Tribunals; Employment Tribunals; Industrial Training Levy Exemptions Referees; the Insolvency Practitioners Tribunal; Mines and Quarries Tribunals; the Family Health Service Appeal Authority; the Sea Fish Licence Tribunal; and SENDIST.

Section 13 enables the Lord Chancellor and (for Scotland) the Secretary of State to amend Pt I or Pt II of Sch.1 "by adding to that Part any such tribunals, other than any of the ordinary courts of law, as may be provided by the order"; to amend s.6 so as to apply any of its provisions to a specified tribunal or to provide for the appointment by the Lord Chancellor of the Chairman and of any person to be appointed to act as chairman; to apply s.11 to a specified tribunal; and to repeal or amend specified provisions of the Act.

Schedule 1, Pt I sets out tribunals under the general supervision of the Council on Tribunals, and Sch.1, Pt II tribunals under the supervision of the Scottish Committee.

The workload of all these tribunals is summarised in the Annual Reports of the Council on Tribunals (as to which see below, p.148). The workload varies widely (see above, p.102). Of the 81 tribunals in the current list, 26 received no cases in 2003/04.

2. Tribunals not under the supervision of the Council include the tribunals established under s.65 of the Regulation of Investigatory Powers Act 2000 to hear (*inter alia*) complaints concerning the security and intelligence services, the Employment Appeal Tribunal, the Special Immigration Appeal Commission, the Registered Design Appeal Tribunal and Trade Marks appointed persons. In most cases these tribunals are comprised of one or judges.

3. For an evaluation of the original Act of 1958, see J.A.G. Griffith, (1959) 22 M.L.R. 145.

(iv) Inquiries

Notes

1. Public inquiries are held for many different purposes. The most formal ones are those constituted under the Tribunals of Inquiry (Evidence) Act 1921, to inquire into matters of "urgent public importance". However, only 18 such bodies had been created up to 1978 (*e.g.* to examine the Aberfan landslide disaster: (1967–1968 HC 33)), with the result that one commentator criticised successive governments for their reluctance to invoke this power of investigation (see Z. Segal, "Tribunals of Inquiry: A British Invention Ignored in Britain" [1984] P.L. 207). According to R.E. Wraith and G.B. Lamb, *Public Inquiries as an Instrument of Government* (1971), other functions performed by inquiries include (1) "post-mortems" into public scandals or major disasters (*e.g.* the inquiry chaired by Desmond Fennell Q.C. into the King's Cross Underground Fire: (1987–1988 HC 499)); (2) considering objections to administrative decisions (*e.g.* the public local inquiry held to investigate objections to the draft M40 motorway extension which featured in *Bushell v Secretary of State for the Environment* [1981] A.C. 75, below, p.731); and (3), most frequently, hearing appeals against administrative decisions (particularly in the field of town and country planning applications).

2. For further reading see *Wade and Forsyth*, Ch.24; *Craig*, Ch.4; JUSTICE—All Souls Review of Administrative Law, *Administrative Justice: Some Necessary Reforms*, Ch.11; D.G.T. Williams, "Public Local Inquiries—Formal Administrative Adjudication" (1980) 29 I.C.L.Q. 701; W. Le-Las, *Playing the Public Inquiry Game* (1987); M. Purdue in D. Feldman (ed.), *English Public Law* (2004), Ch.22; I. Steele, [2004 P.L. 738. Sir Jack Beatson, "Should Judges Conduct Public Inquiries?" (2005) 121 L.Q.R. 221.

3. For a detailed study of the longest public inquiry held in the United Kingdom (the Sizewell B pressurised water nuclear power station inquiry chaired by Sir Frank Layfield Q.C., which opened in January 1983, closed in March 1985, with the report being presented to the Secretary of State for Energy in December 1986) see T. O'Riordan, R. Kemp and M. Purdue, *Sizewell B: An Anatomy of the Inquiry* (1988).

4. A well-known example of an inquiry falling into Wraith and Lamb's "post-mortems" category is the inquiry conducted by Sir Richard Scott V.C. (*Report of the Inquiry into the Export of Defence Equipment and Dual-Use Goods to Iraq and Related Prosecutions*, (1995–96 HC 115). Several witnesses at the inquiry, including Lord Howe and Douglas Hurd (both former Foreign Secretaries) were critical of the procedure followed by Sir Richard. Lord Howe was especially critical of the inability of witnesses to have lawyers represent their views before the inquiry and conduct cross-examination of other persons giving evidence: "When I first complained that this was to be an inquiry at which—as never before in modern times—'defence lawyers may be seen but not heard', I had scarcely believed myself. But Sir Richard had indeed explicitly discarded almost every one of the established principles". He concluded, "The risk is that [the Scott Inquiry] may, in Dennis Healy's phrase, have done for public or judicial inquiries what the Boston Strangler did for door-step selling. And that would be—for me and for many others—a serious loss from the British constitutional armoury". Lord Howe of Aberavon, "Procedure at the Scott Inquiry" [1996] P.L. at 446–447 and 460. However, Sir Richard sought to distinguish the appropriate procedures for inquiries from those used in ordinary court proceedings. "There is, however, a significant and fundamental difference between litigation and Inquiries that makes procedural comparisons unsafe. Litigation in this country, whether civil or criminal, is adversarial in character. The nature of an Inquiry on the other hand is, with very rare exceptions, investigative or inquisitorial." He then went on to examine whether the six principles articulated in Lord Justice Salmon's report (Report of the Royal Commission on Tribunals of Inquiry, Cmnd.3121 (1966) were truly applicable to inquiries such as his. Sir Richard concluded: "The overall problem, in my view, with the six Salmon 'cardinal principles' is that they are too heavily based on procedural requirements of fairness in an adversarial system. . . . Fairness does not, in my opinion, require that adversarial procedures such as the right to cross-examine other witnesses, the right to have an examination-in-chief or a re-examination conducted orally by a party's lawyer . . . should always be incorporated into the procedure at inquisitorial Inquiries. The golden rule . . . is that there should be procedural flexibility, with procedures to achieve fairness tailored to suit the circumstances of each Inquiry". Sir Richard Scott, "Procedures at Inquiries—The Duty to be Fair" (1995) 111 L.Q.R. 596 at pp.597, 610 and 616. For criticism of the procedure adopted by General Sir John Learmount in his inquiry into "The Review of Prison Service Security in England and Wales and the Escape from Parkhurst Prison on Tuesday January 3, 1995" (Cm.3020), see Sir Louis Blom-Cooper, "Witnesses before Public Inquiries: An Example of Unfairness" [1996] P.L. 11. The Autumn 1996 edition of *Public Law* was devoted to a series of articles on the Scott Inquiry.

Since the Scott Inquiry there have been further important and in some cases controversial inquiries of a similar kind. Some have been convened under the 1921 Act (North Wales Child Abuse Inquiry (Sir R.Waterhouse); the shootings at Dunblane Primary School (Lord Cullen); the ongoing (1998 to date) Bloody Sunday Inquiry (Lord Saville of Newdigate); and the Shipman Inquiry (Dame Janet Smith)). Some have been non-statutory (*e.g.* BSE (Lord Phillip of Worth Matravers); the Hinduja affair (concerning Peter Mandelson MP) (Sir Anthony Hammond); Foot and Mouth Disease 2001 (Dr Ian Anderson); the Investigation into the circumstances surrounding the death of Dr David Kelly (Lord Hutton); and matters concerning David Blunkett MP (Sir Alan Budd)). Yet others have been held under specific statutory provisions (*e.g.* inquiries under the National Health Service Act 1977, s.84 into Bristol Royal Infirmary (Professor Sir Ian Kennedy) and Alder Hey (Michael Redfern Q.C.) and under the Merchant Shipping Act 1995 concerning the Marchioness (Clarke L.J.).

4. The holding of inquiries of this kind have been fully investigated by the Select Committee on Public Administration (*Government by Inquiry*, 2004–05 HC 51) at a time when the Government was taking a new Inquiries Bill through Parliament. The Inquiries Act 2005 (below, p.113) received Royal Assent immediately before the 2005 General Election. It followed a DCA Consultation Paper, *Effective Inquiries* (May 2004), and was the subject of comments by the House of Lords Select Committee

on the Constitution (First Report, 2004–05 HL 21), regretting that the Bill, which was of constitutional importance, had not been the subject of pre-legislative scrutiny. The Government's view was that the Bill was very much a consolidation measure and not one of substantial constitutional significance. The view of the chairman's of the Select Committee was that this was not a tenable position, in particular as the Bill repealed the Tribunals of Inquiry (Evidence) Act 1921 (and other specific provisions for the holding of inquiries). The 1921 Act required there to be a resolution of each House for a Tribunal of Inquiry to be appointed under the Act.

5. It has become increasingly common for persons who object to a decision not be hold an inquiry at all, or to hold an inquiry in private rather than in public, to challenge that decision by way of judicial review. In *R. (on the application of Wagstaff) v Secretary of State for Health* [2001] 1 W.L.R. 292, the Secretary of State's decision to set up an inquiry to be held in private to examine the issues raised by the deaths of many patients of Dr Harold Shipman was quashed. The Divisional Court held that where an inquiry purported to be a public inquiry, as opposed to an internal domestic inquiry, "there is now in law what really amounts to a presumption that it will proceed in public unless there are persuasive reasons for taking some other course" (p.321). The Secretary of State's decision based on considerations of speed, candour, and the proposition that a private hearing "will not be any the less exacting or vigorous" was not (as he argued) "policy-laden" and was irrational. In response, the Secretary of State arranged for the Shipman Inquiry to be conducted by Dame Janet Smith under the Tribunals of Inquiry (Evidence) Act 1921. *Wagstaff* was distinguished in *R. (on the application of Persey) v Secretary of State for Environment, Food and Rural Affairs* [2002] EWHC (Admin) 371; [2003] Q.B. 794, where the Divisional Court rejected challenges to the decision to hold three separate and (mostly) private inquires into the handling of the widespread outbreak of foot and mouth disease in 2001. Simon Brown L.J. (at [28]–[42]) doubted the jurisprudential basis for any legal presumption of openness with regards to all forms of public inquiry. Inquiries into alleged misconduct should indeed normally be held in public, but here the suggestion was that there were mistakes, not that those in charge lacked integrity or honesty. *Wagstaff* was, however, correct on its own facts given that on its facts the court there could see nothing in favour of a closed inquiry and everything to be said for opening it up (Simon Brown L.J. at [45]). The present case was different: the terms of reference were narrower; an open inquiry would last much longer; Art.10 ECHR was not engaged by a decision to hold a closed inquiry.

Litigation of this kind is normally unsuccessful. See also *Crampton v Secretary of State for Health*, unreported, July 9, 1993, CA; *Little, Re* [2002] EWHC (Admin) 3001 (decision not to hold inquiry into objection to a wind power electricity generating station not arguably irrational); *R. (on the application of Howard) v Secretary of State for Health* [2002] EWHC (Admin) 396; [2003] Q.B 830.

6. Article 2 ECHR requires that Member States provide an effective independent official investigation (although not necessarily a public local inquiry) when individuals have been killed by the use of force (*Edwards v UK* (2002) 35 E.H.R.R. 19); *R. (on the application of Amin) v Secretary of State for the Home Department* [2003] UKHL 51).

INQUIRIES ACT 2005

Constitution of inquiry

1. Power to establish inquiry

(1) A Minister may cause an inquiry to be held under this Act in relation to a case where it appears to him that—

(a) particular events have caused, or are capable of causing, public concern, or

(b) there is public concern that particular events may have occurred

(2) In this Act "Minister" means—

(a) a United Kingdom Minister;
(b) the Scottish Ministers;
(c) a Northern Ireland Minister;

and references to a Minister also include references to the National Assembly for Wales.

(3) References in this Act to an inquiry, expect where the context requires otherwise, are to an inquiry under this Act.

2. No determination of liability

(1) An inquiry panel is not to rule on, and has no power to determine, any person's civil or criminal liability.

(2) But an inquiry panel is not to be inhibited in the discharge of its functions by any likelihood of liability being inferred from facts that it determines or recommendations that it makes.

3. The inquiry panel

(1) An inquiry is to be undertaken either—

(a) by a chairman alone, or
(b) by a chairman with one or more other members.

(2) References in this Act ot an inquiry panel are to the chairman and any other member or members.

4. Appointment of inquiry panel

(1) Each member of an inquiry panel is to be appointed by the Minister by an instrument in writing.

(2) The instrument appointing the chairman must state that the inquiry is to be held under this Act.

(3) Before appointing a member to the inquiry panel (otherwise than as chairman) the Minister must consult the person he has appointed, or proposes to appoint, as chairman.

5. Setting-up date and terms of reference

(1) In the instrument under section 4 appointing the chairman, or by a notice given to him within a reasonable time afterwards, the Minister must—

(a) specify the date that is to be the setting-up date for the proposes of this Act; and
(b) before that date—
  (i) set out the terms of reference of the inquiry;
  (ii) state whether or not the Minister proposes to appoint other members to the inquiry panel and if so how many.

(2) An inquiry must not begin considering evidence before the setting-up date.

(3) The Minister may at any time after setting out the terms of reference under this section amend them if he considers that the public interest so requires.

(4) Before setting out or amending the terms of reference the Minister must consult the person he proposes to appoint, or has appointed, as chairman.

(5) Functions conferred by this Act on an inquiry panel or a member of an inquiry panel, are exercisable only within the inquiry's terms of reference.

(6) In this Act "terms of reference", in relation to an inquiry under this Act, means—

(a) the matters to which the inquiry relates;
(b) any particular matters as to which the inquiry panel is to determine the facts;
(c) whether the inquiry panel is to make recommendations;
(d) any other matters relating to the scope of the inquiry that the Minister may specify.

6. Minister's duty to inform Parliament or Assembly

(1) A minister who proposes to cause an inquiry to be held, or who has already done so without making a statement under this section, must a soon as is reasonably practicable make a statement to the effect to the relevant Parliament or Assembly.

(2) A statement under subsection (1) must state—

(a) who is to be, or has been, appointed as chairman of the appoint,
(b) whether the Minister has appointed or proposes to appoint, any other members to the inquiry panel, and if so how many;
(c) what are to be, or are, the inquiry's terms of reference.

(3) Where the terms of reference of an inquiry are amended under section 5(3), the Minister must, as soon as is reasonably practicable, make a statement to the relevant Parliament or Assembly setting out the amended terms of reference.

(4) A statement under this section may be oral or written.

8. Suitability of inquiry panel

(1) In appointing a member of the inquiry panel, the Minister must have regard—

(a) to the need to ensure that the inquiry panel (considered as a whole)has the necessary expertise to undertake the inquiry;
(b) in the case of an inquiry panel consisting of a chairman and one or more other members, to the need for balance (considered against the background of the terms of reference) in the composition of the panel.

(2) For the proposes of subsection (1) (a) the Minister may have regard to the assistance that may be provided to the inquiry panel by any assessor whom the Minister proposes to appoint, or has appointed, under section 11.

9. Requirement of impartiality

(1) The Minister must not appoint a person as a member of the inquiry panel if it appears to the Minister that the person has—

(a) a direct interest in the matters to which the inquiry relates, or
(b) a close association with an interested party,

unless, despite the person's interest or association, his appointment could not reasonably be regarded as a affecting the impartiality of the inquiry panel.

(2) Before a person is appointed as a member of an inquiry panel he must notify the Minister of any matters that, having regard to subsection (1), could affect his eligibility for appointment.

(3) If at any time (whether before the setting-up date or during the course of the inquiry) a member of the inquiry panel becomes aware that he has an interest or association falling within paragraph (a) or (b) of subsection (1), he must notify the Minister.

(4) A member of the inquiry panel must not, during the course of the inquiry, undertake any activity that could reasonably be regarded as affecting his suitability to serve as such.

10. Appointment of judge as panel member

(1) If the Minister proposes to appoint as a member of an inquiry panel a particular person who is a judge of a description specified in the first column of the following table, he must first consult the person specified in the second column.

Description of judge	Person to be consulted
Lord of Appeal in Ordinary	The senior Lord of Appeal in ordinary
Judge of the Supreme Court of England and Wales, or Circuit judge	The Lord Chief Justice of England and Wales.

11. Assessors

(1) One or more persons may be appointed to act as assessors to assist the inquiry panel.

(2) The power to appoint assessors is exercisable—

(a) before the setting-up date, by the Minister;
(b) during the course of the inquiry, by the chairman (whether or not the Minister has appointed assessors).

(3) Before exercising his powers under subsection (2)(a) the Minister must consult the person he proposes to appoint, or has appointed, as chairman.

(4) A person may be appointed as an assessor only if it appears to the Minister or the chairman (as the case requires) that he has expertise that makes him a suitable person to provide assistance to the inquiry panel.

(5) The chairman may at any time terminate the appointment of an assessor, but only with the consent of the Minister in the case of an assessor appointed by the Minister.

14. End of inquiry

(1) For the purposes of this Act an inquiry comes to an end—

(a) on the date, after the delivery of the report of the inquiry, on which the chairman notifies the Minister that the inquiry has fulfilled its terms of reference, or
(b) on any earlier date specified in a notice given to the chairman by the Minister.

(2) The date specified in a notice under subsection (1)(b) may not be earlier than the date on which the notice is sent.
(3) Before exercising his power under subsection(1)(b) the Minister must consult the chairman.
(4) Where the Minister gives a notice under subsection(1)(b) he must—

(a) set out in the notice his reasons for bringing the inquiry to an end;
(b) lay a copy of the notice, as soon as is reasonably practicable, before the releant Parliament or Assembly.

Conversion of inquiries

15. Power to convert other inquiry into inquiry under this Act

(1) Where—

(a) an inquiry ("the original inquiry") is being held, or is due to be held, by one or more persons appointed otherwise than under this Act,
(b) a Minister gives a notice under this section to those persons, and
(c) the person who caused the original inquiry to be held consents,

the original inquiry becomes an inquiry under this Act as from the date of the notice or such later date as may specified in the notice (the "date of conversion").
(2) The power conferred by this section is exercisable only if the original inquiry relates to a case where it appears to the Minister that—

(a) particular events have caused, or capable of causing, public concern, or
(b) there is public concern that particular event may have occurred.

(3) Before exercising that power the Minister must consult the chairman.
(4) A notice under this section must—

(a) state that, as from the date of conversion, the inquiry is to be held under this Act;
(b) in the case of an inquiry panel consisting of more than one member, identify who is to be chairman of the panel;
(c) set out what are to be the terms of reference of the inquiry.

(5) The terms of reference set out under subsection (4) may be different from those of the original inquiry.

(6) The Minister may at nay time after setting out the terms of reference under this section amend them if he considers that the public interest so requires.

(7) The Minister must consult the chairman before—

(a) setting out terms of reference that are different from those of the original inquiry, or
(b) amending the terms of reference under subsection (6).

(8) Section 6 applies, with any necessary modifications, in relation to—

(a) converting an inquiry under this section, or
(b) amending an inquiry's terms of reference under subsection (6),

as it applies in relation to causing an inquiry to be held, or amending an inquiry's terms reference under section5(3).

16. Inquires converted under section 15

(1) This section applies where an inquiry (the "original inquiry") is converted under section 15 into an inquiry under this Act.

(2) The appointment of a person who at the date of conversion is—

(a) one of the persons holding, or due to hold, the original inquiry (an "original member"),
(b) a assessor, counsel or solicitor to the inquiry, or
(c) a person engaged to provide assistance to the inquiry,

continues as if made under this Act, and for the purposes of section 12(5) is treated as made by the Minister on the date of conversion.

(3) Any obligation arising under an order of the original inquiry, or otherwise in connection with that inquiry, is enforceable only as it would be if the original inquiry has not been converted.

(4) No rights or obligations arise under or by virtue of this Act before the date of conversion.

Inquiry proceedings

17. Evidence and procedure

(1) Subject to any provision of this Act or of rules under section 41, procedure and conduct of an inquiry are to be such as the chairman of the inquiry may direct.

(2) In particular, the chairman may take evidence on oath, and for that purpose may administer oaths.

(3) In making any decision as to the procedure or conduct of an inquiry, the chairman must act with fairness and with regard also to the need to avoid any unnecessary cost (whether to public funds or to witnesses or others).

18. Public access to inquiry proceeding and information

(1) Subject to any restrictions imposed by a notice or order under section 19, the chairman must take such steps as he considers reasonable to secure that members of the public (including reporters) are able—

(a) to attend the inquiry or to see and hear a simultaneous transmission of proceedings at the inquiry;

(b) to obtain or to view a record of evidence and documents given, produced or provided to the inquiry or inquiry panel.

(2) No recording or broadcast of proceedings at an inquiry may be made except—

(a) at the request of the chairman, or

(b) with the permission of the chairman and in accordance with any terms on which permission is given.

Any such request or permission must be framed so as not to enable a person to see or hear by means of a recording or broadcast anything that he is prohibited by a notice under section 19 from seeing or hearing.

(3) Section 32(2) of the Freedom of Information Act 2000 (c. 36) (certain inquiry records etc exempt form obligations under that Act) does not apply in relation to information contained in documents that, in pursuance of rules under section 41(1)(b) below, have been passed to and are held by a public authority. . . .

19. Restrictions on public access etc

(1) Restrictions may, in accordance with this section, be imposed on—

(a) attendance at an inquiry, or at any particular part of an inquiry;

(b) disclosure or publication of any evidence or documents given, produced or provided to an inquiry.

(2) Restrictions may be imposed in either or both of the following ways—

(a) by being specified in a notice (a "restriction notice") given by the Minister to the chairman at any time before the end of the inquiry;

(b) by being specified in an order (a "restriction order") made by the chairman during the course of the inquiry.

(3) A restriction notice or restriction order must specify only such restrictions—

(a) as are required by any statutory provision, enforceable Community obligation or rule of law, or

(b) as the Minister or chairman considers to be conductive to the inquiry fulfilling its terms of reference or to be necessary in the public interest, having regard in particular to the matters mentioned in subsection (4).

(4) Those matters are—

(a) the extent to which any restriction on attendance, disclosure or publication might inhibit the allaying of public concern;
(b) any risk of harm or damage that could be avoided or reduced by any such restriction;
(c) any conditions as to confidentiality subject to which a person acquired information that he is to give, or has given, to the inquiry;
(d) the extent to which not imposing any particular restriction would be likely—
   (i) to cause delay or to impair the efficiency or effectiveness of the inquiry, or
   (ii) otherwise to result in additional cost (whether to public funds or to witnesses or others).

(5) In subsection (4)(b) "harm or damage" includes in particular—

(a) death or injury;
(b) damage to national security or international relations;
(c) damage to the economic interests of the United Kingdom or of any part of the United Kingdom;
(d) damage caused by disclosure of commercially sensitive information.

20. Further provisions about restriction notice and orders

(1) Restrictions specified in a restriction notice have effect in addition to any already specified, whether in an earlier restriction notice or in a restriction order.

(2) Restrictions specified in a restriction order have effect in addition to any already specified, whether in a earlier restriction order or in a restriction notice.

(3) The Minister may vary or revoke a restriction notice by giving a further notice to the chairman at nay time before end of the inquiry.

(4) The chairman may vary or revoke a restriction order by making a further order during the course of the inquiry.

(5) Restrictions imposed under section 19 on disclosure or publication of evidence or documents ("disclosure restrictions") continue in force indefinitely, unless—

(a) under the terms of the relevant notice or order the restrictions expire at the end to of the inquiry, or at some other time, or
(b) the relevant notice or order is varied or revoked under subsection (3), (4) or (7).

This is subject to subsection (6).

(6) After the end of the inquiry, disclosure restrictions do not apply to a public authority, or a Scottish public authority, in relation to information held by the authority otherwise than as result of the breach of any such restrictions.

(7) After the end of an inquiry the Minister may, by a notice published in a way that he considers suitable—

(a) revoke a restriction order or restriction notice containing disclosure restrictions that are still in force, or
(b) vary it so as to remove or relax any of the restrictions.

(9) In this section "restriction notice" and "restriction order" have the meaning given by section 19(2).

21. Powers of chairman to require production of evidence etc

(1) The chairman of an inquiry may by notice require a person to attend at a time and place stated in the notice—

(a) to give evidence;
(b) to provide any documents in his custody or under his control that relate to a matter in question at the inquiry;
(c) to produce any other thing in his custody or under his control for inspection, examination or testing by or on behalf of the inquiry panel.

(2) The chairman may by notice require a person, within such period as appears to the inquiry panel to be reasonable—

(a) to provide evidence to the inquiry panel in the form of a written statement;
(b) to provide any documents in his custody or under his control that relate to a matter in question at the inquiry;
(c) to produce any other thing in his custody or under his control for inspection examination or testing by or on behalf of the inquiry panel.

(3) A notice under subsection (1) or (2) must—

(a) explain the possible consequences of not complying with the notice;
(b) indicate what the recipient of the notice should do if he wishes to make a claim within subsection (4)

(4) A claim by a person that—

(a) he is unable to comply with a notice under this section, or
(b) it is not reasonable in all the circumstances to require him to comply with such a notice,

is to be determined by the chairman of the inquiry, who may revoke or vary the notice on that ground.

(5) In deciding whether to revoke or vary a notice on the ground mentioned in subsection (4)(b), the chairman must consider the public interest in the information in question being obtained by the inquiry, having regard to the likely importance of the information.

(6) For the purposes of this section a thing is under a person's control if it is in his possession or if he has a right to possession of it.

22. Privileged information etc

(1) A person may not under section 21 be required to give, produce or provide any evidence or document if—

(a) he could not be required to do so if the proceedings of the inquiry were civil proceedings in a court in the relevant part of the United Kingdom, or
(b) the requirement would be incompatible with a Community obligation.

(2) The rules of law under which evidence or documents are permitted or required to be withheld on grounds of public interest immunity apply in relation to an inquiry as they apply in relation to civil proceedings in a court in the elegant part of the United Kingdom.

23. Risk damage to the economy

(1) This section applies where it is submitted to an inquiry panel on behalf of the Crown, the Financial Services Authority or the Bank of England, that there is information held by any person which, in order to avoid a risk of damage to the economy, ought not to be revealed.

(2) The panel must not permit or require the information to be revealed, or cause it to be revealed, unless satisfied that the public interest in the information being revealed outweighs the public interest in avoiding a risk of damage to the economy.

(3) In making a decision under this section the panel must take account of any restriction notice given under section 19 or any restriction order that the chairman has made or proposes to make under that section.

(4) In this section—

"damage to the economy" means damage to the economic interests of the United kingdom or of any part of the United Kingdom;
"revealed" means revealed to anyone who is not a member of the inquiry panel.

(5) This section does not prevent the inquiry panel from communicating any information in confidence to the Minister.

(6) This section does not affect the rules of law referred to in section 22(2).

Inquiry reports

24. Submission of reports

(1) The chairman of an inquiry must deliver a report to the Minister setting out—

(a) the facts determined by the inquiry panel;
(b) the recommendations of the panel (where the terms of reference required it to make recommendations).

The report may also contain anything else that the panel considers to be relevant to the terms of reference (including any recommendation the panel sees fit to make despite not being required to do so by the terms of reference).

(2) In relation to an inquiry that is brought to an end under section 14(1)(b), the duty imposed by subsection (1) to deliver a report is to be read as a power to do so.

(3) Before making a report under subsection (1) the chairman may deliver to the Minister a report under this subsection (an "interim report") containing anything that a report under subsection (1) may contain.

(4) A report of an inquiry must be signed by each member of the inquiry panel.

(5) If the inquiry panel is unable to produce a unanimous report, the report must reasonably reflect the points of disagreement.

(6) In subsections (4) and (5) "report" includes an interim report.

25. Publication of reports

(1) It is the duty of the Minister, or the chairman if subsection (2) applies, to arrange for reports of an inquiry to be published.

(2) This subsection applies if—

(a) the Minister notifies the chairman before the setting-up date that the chairman is to have responsibility for arranging publication, or

(b) at any time after that date the chairman, on being invited to do so by the Minister, accepts responsibility for arranging publication.

(3) Subject to subsection (4), a report of an inquiry must be published in full.

(4) The person whose duty it is to arrange for a report to be published may withhold material in the report from publication to such extent—

(a) as is required by any statutory provision, enforceable Community obligation or rule of law, or

(b) as the person considers to be necessary in the public interest, having regard in particular to the matters mentioned in subsection (5).

(5) Those matters are—

(a) the extent to which withholding material might inhibit the allaying of public concern;

(b) any risk of harm or damage that could be avoided or reduced by withholding any material;

(c) any conditions as to confidentiality subject to which a person acquired information that he has given to the inquiry.

(6) In subsection (5)(b) "harm or damage" includes in particular—

(a) death or injury;

(b) damage to national security or international relations;

(c) damage to the economic interests of the United Kingldom or of any part of the United Kingdom;

(d) damage caused by disclosure of commercially sensitive information.

(7) Subsection (4)(b) dose not affect any obligation of the Minister, or any other public authority or Scottish public authority, that may arise under the Freedom of Information Act 200 (c. 36) or the Freedom of Information (Scotland) Act 2002 (asp 13).

(8) In this section "report" includes an interim report.

26. Laying of reports before Parliament or Assembly

Whatever is required to be published under section 25 must be laid by the Minister, either at the time of publication or as soon afterwards as is reasonably practicable, before the relevant Parliament or Assembly.

36. Enforcement by High Court or Court of Section

(1) Where a person—

(a) fails to comply with, or acts in breach of, a notice under section 19 or 21 order made by an inquiry, or
(b) threatens to do so,

the chairman of the enquiry, or after the end of the inquiry the Minister, may certify the matter to the appropriate court.

(2) The court, after hearing any evidence or representations on a matter certified to it under subsection (1), may make such order by way of enforcement or otherwise as it could make if the matter had arisen in proceedings before the court.

(3) In this section "the appropriate court" means the High Court or, in the case of an inquiry in relation to which the relevant part of the United Kingdom is Scotland, the Court of Session.

37. Immunity from suit

(1) No action lies against—

(a) a member of an inquiry panel,
(b) an assessor, counsel or solicitor to an inquiry, or
(c) a person engaged to provide assistance to an inquiry,

in respect of any act done or commission made in the execution of his duty as such, or any act done or omission made in good faith in the purported execution of his duty as such.

(2) Subsection (1) applies only to acts done or omissions made during the course of the inquiry, otherwise than during any period of suspension (within the meaning of section 13).

(3) For the purposes of the law of defamation, the same privilege attaches to—

(a) any statement made in or for the purposes of proceedings before an inquiry(including the report and any interim report of the inquiry), and
(b) reports of proceedings before an inquiry,

as would be the case if those proceedings were proceedings before a court in the relevant part of the United Kingdom.

38. Time limit for applying for judicial review

(1) An application for judicial review of a decision made—

(a) by the Minister in relation to an inquiry, or
(b) by a member of an inquiry panel,

must be brought within 14 days after the day on which the applicant became aware of the decision, unless that time limit is extended by the court.

(2) Subsection (1) does not apply where an earlier time limit applies by virtue of Civil Procedure Rules or rules made under section 55 of the Judicature (Northern Ireland) Act 1978 (c. 23).

(3) Subsection (1) does not apply to—

(a) a decision as to the contents of the report of the inquiry;
(b) a decision of which the applicant could not have became aware until the publication of the report.

In this subsection "report" includes any interim report.
(4) This section does not extend to Scotland.

40. Expenses of witnesses etc

(1) The chairman may award reasonable amounts to a person—

(a) by way of compensation of loss of time, or
(b) in respect of expenses properly incurred, or to be incurred, in attending, or otherwise in relation to, the inquiry.

(2) The power to make an award under this section includes power, where the chairman considers it appropriate, to award amounts in respect of legal representation.
(3) A person is eligible for an award under this section only if he is—

(a) a person attending the inquiry to give evidence to produce any document or other thing, or
(b) a person who, in the opinion of the chairman, has such a particular interest in the proceedings or outcome of the inquiry as to justify such an award.

(4) The power to make an award under this section is subject to such conditions or qualifications as may be determined by the Minister and notified by him to the chairman.

43. Interpretation

(1) In this Act—

"assessor" means an assessor appointed under section 11;
"chairman", in relation to an inquiry, means the chairman of the inquiry;
"the course of the inquiry" and similar expressions are to be read in accordance with subsection (2);
"date of conversion" has the meaning given by section 15(1);
"document" includes information recorded in any form (and see subsection (3));
"event", except in sections 13 and 46, includes any conduct or omission;
"inquiry", except where the context requires otherwise, means an inquiry under this Act;
"inquiry panel" is to be read in accordance with section 3(2);
"interested party", in relation to an inquiry, means a person with a particularly significant interest in the proceedings or outcome of the inquiry;
"interim report" means a report under section 24(3);
"joint inquiry" has the meaning given by section 32(2);

"member", in relation to an inquiry panel, includes the chairman;

"Minister" is to be read in accordance with section 1(2) (and see subsection (4)below);

"Northern Ireland Minister" includes the First Minister and the deputy First Minister acting jointly;

"public authority" has the same meaning as in the Freedom of Information Act 2000;

"the relevant Parliament or Assembly" means whichever of the following is or are applicable-

(a) in the case of an inquiry for which the Treasury is responsible, the House of Commons;

(b) in the case of an inquiry for which any other United Kingdom Minister is responsible, or one for which the Secretary of State exercising functions by virtue of section 45(2) is responsible, the House of Parliament of which that minister is a member;

(c) in the case of an inquiry for which the Scottish Ministers are responsible, the Scottish Parliament;

(d) in the case of an inquiry for which the National Assembly for Wales is responsible, that Assembly;

(e) in the case of an inquiry for which a Northern Ireland Minister is responsible, the Northern Ireland Assembly;

"the relevant part of the United Kingdom", in relation to an inquiry, means the part specified under section 31(1);

"report" means a report under section 24(1);

"responsible", in relation to an inquiry, is to be read in accordance with subsection (5);

"Scottish public authority" has the same meaning as in the Freedom of Information (Scotland) Act 2002 (asp 13);

"setting-up date" means the date specified under section 5(1)(a);

"statutory provision" means a provision contained in, or having effect under, any enactment, Act of the Scottish Parliament or Northern Ireland legislation;

"terms of reference", in relation to an inquiry under this Act, has the meaning given by section 5(6);

"United Kingdom Minister"—

(a) means the hold of a ministerial office specified in Part 1, 2 or 3 of Schedule 1 to the Ministerial and other Salaries Act 1975 (c. 27) or a Parlimentary Secretary;

(b) also includes the Treasury.

But a reference to a United Kingdom Minister doe not include a reference to the Secretary of State discharging functions by virtue of section 45(2).

(2) References in this Act to the course of an inquiry are to the period beginning with the setting-up date, or (in the case of an inquiry converted under section 15) the date of conversion, and ending with the date on which the inquiry comes to an end (which is given by section 14).

(3) References in this Act to producing or providing a document, in relation to information recorded otherwise than in legible form, are to be read as references to producing or providing a copy of the information in legible form.

(4) Reference in this Act to "the Minister", in relation to an inquiry, are to the Minister or Ministers responsible for the inquiry.

(5) For the purposes of this Act a Minister is "responsible" for an inquiry if he is the Minister, or one of the Ministers, by whom it was caused to be held under section 1 or converted under section 15.

This is subject to section 34(2)(a).

Notes

1. Other provisions to note include the minister's power to appoint a panel member to fill a vacancy (including a vacancy as chairman) or increase the numbers of members (s.7); the right of a member to resign by giving notice to the minister (s.12(2)); the minister's power to terminate a member's appointment on grounds of incapacity, non-compliance with a duty imposed by the Act, a direct interest in the matters to which the inquiry relates or a close association with an interested party such as his membership of the inquiry panel could reasonably be regarded as affecting its impartiality, or misconduct (s.12(3)–(7)); the minister's power to suspend an inquiry to allow the completion of any other investigation relating to any of the matters to which the inquiry relates or the determination of civil and criminal proceedings (including proceedings before a disciplinary tribunal) arising out of any of these matters (s.13). Separate provision is made in respect of inquiries from which Scottish ministers, the National Assembly for Wales or a Northern Ireland minister is responsible, and for joint inquiries (ss. 27–34). Various offences are created (s.35). The minister may pay inquiry expenses (s.39). There are general rule-making powers (s.41). One area of uncertainty will be the extent to which there will continue to be non-statutory inquiries (see the provisions governing conversion: ss.14, 15). The Act came into force on June 7, 2005.

2. The provision of a standard structure for statutory inquiries is helpful, although there were some areas of controversy. The Public Administration Select Committee in *Government by Inquiry* (above, p.112) welcomed many of the provisions of the Inquiries Bill, but expressed concern at the wide powers for members to restrict access to inquiries, and the long-term diminution in Parliament's role in the process of public inquiries, seen for example with the repeal of the Tribunal of Inquiry (Evidence) Act 1921. It recommended that the Lord Chief Justice or the Senior Law Lord should be equally involved with ministers in all decisions about the use of judges in inquiries (but compare s.10); and that there should be a new mechanism which would enable Parliament to initiate an inquiry in cases where ministers may be unwilling to do so, including the establishment of a Parliamentary Commission of Inquiry.

TOWN AND COUNTRY PLANNING (INQUIRIES PROCEDURE) (ENGLAND) RULES 2000

(SI 2000/1624)

Citation, commencement, and extent

1. (1) These Rules may be cited as the Town and Country Planning (Inquiries Procedure) (England) Rules 2000.

(2) These Rules shall come into force on 1st August 2000.

(3) These Rules extend to England only.

Interpretation

2. In these Rules—

"applicant" in the case of an appeal, means the appellant;
"assessor" means a person appointed by the Secretary of State to sit with an inspector at an inquiry or re-opened inquiry to advise the inspector on such matters arising as the Secretary of State many specify;

"the Commission" means the Historic Buildings and Monuments Commission for England;

"conservation area consent" has the meaning given in section 74(1) of the Listed Buildings Act;

"development order" has the meaning given in section 59 of the Planning Act;

"document" includes a photograph, map or plan;

"inquiry" means a local inquiry in relation to which these Rules apply;

"inspector" means a person appointed by the Secretary of State to hold an inquiry or a re-opened inquiry;

"land" means the land or building to which an inquiry relates;

"the Listed Buildings Act" means the Planning (Listed Buildings and Conservation Areas) Act 1990;

"listed building consent" has the meaning given in section 8(7) of the Listed Buildings Act;

"local Planning authority" means in relation to

    (i) a referred application, the body who would otherwise have dealt with the application;

    (ii) an appeal, the body who were responsible for dealing with the application occasioning the appeal;

"outline statement" means a written statement of the principal submissions which a person proposes to put forward at an inquiry;

"the Planning Act" means the Town and Country Planning Act 1990[30];

"pre-inquiry meeting" means a meeting held before an inquiry to consider what may be done with a view to securing that the inquiry is conducted efficiently and expeditiously, and where two or more such meetings are held references to the conclusion of a pre-inquiry meeting are references to the conclusion of the final meeting;

"questionnaire" means a document in the form supplied by the Secretary of State to local Planning authorities for the purpose of proceedings under these Rules;

"referred application" means an application of any description mentioned in rule 3(1) which is referred to the Secretary of State for determination;

"relevant notice" means the Secretary of State's written notice informing the applicant and the local planning authority that an inquiry is to be held;

"the 1992 Rules" means the town and Country Planning (Inquiries Procedure) Rules 1992

"starting date" means the date of the—

    (a) Secretary of State's written notice to the applicant and the local planning authority that he has received all the documents required to enable him to entertain the application or appeal; or

    (b) relevant notice,

whichever is the later;

"statement of case" means, and is comprised of, a written statement which contains full particulars of the case which a person proposes to put forward at an inquiry and a list of any documents which that person intends to refer to or put in evidence;

"statement of common ground" means a written statement prepared jointly by the local planning authority and the applicant, which contains agreed factual information about the proposal, which is the subject of the application or appeal;

"statutory party' means—

    (a) a person mentioned in paragraph (1)(b)(i) of article 19 of the Town and Country Planning (General Development Procedure) Order 1995 whose representations the Secretary of State is required by paragraph (3) of that article to take into account in determining the referred application or appeal to which an inquiry relates; and, in the case of an appeal, such a person whose representations the local planning authority were required by paragraph (1) of that article to take into account in determining the application occasioning the appeals; and

    (b) a person whose representations the Secretary of State is required by paragraphs (3)(b) and (5) or regulation 6 of the Planning (Listed Buildings and Conservation Areas) Regulations 1990 to take into account in determining the referred application or appeal to which an inquiry relates; and, in the case of an appeal, a person whose representations the local planning authority were required by paragraph (3)(b) of the regulation to take into account in determining the application occasioning the appeal.

Application of Rules

3.—(1) These Rules apply in relation to any local inquiry caused by the Secretary of State to be held in England before he determines—

    (a) an application for planning permission referred to him under section 77, or an appeal to him under section 78, of the Planning Act;

    (b) an application for listed building consent referred to him under section 12, or for variation or discharge of conditions referred to him under that section as applied by section 19, or appeal to him under section 20, of the Listed Buildings Act;

    (c) an application for conservation area consent referred to him under section 12 (including an application to which that section is applied by section 19), or an appeal to him under section 20, of the Listed Buildings Act as those sections are applied by section 74(3) of that Act,

but do not apply to any local inquiry by reason of the application of any provision mentioned in this paragraph by any other enactment.

(2) Where these Rules apply in relation to an appeal which at some time fell to be disposed of in accordance with the Town and Country Planning Appeals (Determination by Inspectors) (Inquiries Procedure) (England) Rules 2000 or Rules superseded by those Rules any step taken or things done under those Rules which could have been done under any corresponding provision of these Rules shall have effect as if it had been taken or done under that corresponding provision.

Preliminary information to be supplied by local planning authority

4.—(1) The local planning authority shall, on receipt of the relevant notice, forthwith inform the Secretary of State and the applicant in writing of the name and Address of any statutory party who has made representations to them; and the Secretary of State shall, as soon as practicable thereafter, inform the applicant and the local planning authority in writing of the name and address of any statutory party who has made representations to him.

(2) This paragraph applies where—

(a) the Secretary of State has given to the local planning authority a direction restricting the grant of planning permission for which application was made; or

(b) in a case relating to listed building consent, the Commission has given a direction to the local planning authority pursuant to serction14(2) of the Listed Buildings Act as to how the application is to be determined; or

(c) the Secretary of State or any other Minister of the Crown or any government department, or any body falling within rule 11(1)(c), has expressed in writing to the local planning authority the view that the application should not be granted either wholly or in part, or should be granted only subject to conditions; or

(d) any person consulted in pursuance of a development order has made representations to the local planning authority about the application.

(3) Where paragraph (2) applies, the local planning authority shall forthwith after the starting date inform the person concerned of the inquiry and, unless they have already done so, that person shall thereupon give the local planning authority a written statement of the reasons for making the direction, expressing the view or making the representations, as the case may be.

(4) Subject to paragraph (5), the local planning authority shall ensure that within 2 weeks of the starting date—

(a) the Secretary of State and the applicant have received a completed questionnaire and a copy of each of the documents referred to in it;

(b) any—
　　(i) statutory party; and
　　(ii) other person who made representations to the local planning authority about the application occasioning the appeal,
has been notified that an appeal has been made and of the address to which and of the period within which they may make representations to the Secretary of State.

(5) The requirements of the previous paragraph do not apply in respect of referred applications.

Procedure where Secretary of State causes pre-inquiry meeting to be held

5.—(1) The Secretary of State shall hold a pre-inquiry meeting—

(a) if the expects an inquiry to last for 8 days or more, unless he considers it is unnecessary;

(b) in respect of shorter inquiries, if it appears to him necessary.

(2) Where the Secretary of State decides to hold a pre-inquiry meeting the following provisions shall apply—

(a) the Secretary of State shall send with the relevant notice—
  (i) notice of his intention to hold a pre-inquiry meeting;
  (ii) a statement of the matters about which he particularly wishes to be informed for the purposes of his consideration of the application or appeal in question and where another Minister of the Crown or a government department has expressed in writing to the Secretary of State a view which is mentioned in rule 4(2)(c), the Secretary of State shall set this out in his statement;
(b) the Secretary of State shall send a copy of the statement described in the previous paragraph to the Minister or government department concerned;
(c) the local planning authority shall publish in a newspaper circulating in the locality in which the land is situated a notice of the Secretary of State's intention to hold a pre-inquiry meeting and of the statement sent in accordance with paragraph (2)(a)(ii) above; and
(d) the applicant and the local planning authority shall ensure that within 8 weeks of the starting date 2 copies of their outline statement have been received by the Secretary of State.

(3) The Secretary of State shall, as soon as practicable after receipt, send a copy of the local planning authority's outline statement to the applicant and a copy of the applicant's outline statement to the local planning authority.

(4) Where rule 4(2) applies, the local planning authority shall—

(a) include in their outline statement—
  (i) the terms of any direction given together with a statement of the reasons for it; and
  (ii) any view expressed or representation made on which they intend to rely in their submissions at the inquiry; and
(b) within the period mentioned in paragraph (2)(d) send a copy of their outline statement to the person concerned.

(5) The Secretary of State may in writing require any other person who has notified him of an intention or a wish to appear at the inquiry to send an outline statement to him, the applicant and the local planning authority and the person shall ensure that they are received by the Secretary of State, the applicant and the local planning authority within 4 weeks of the date of the Secretary of State's written requirement.

(6) The pre-inquiry meeting (or, where there is more than one, the first pre-inquiry meeting) shall be held within 16 weeks of the starting date.

(7) The Secretary of State shall give not less than 3 weeks written notice of the pre-inquiry meeting to—

(a) the applicant;
(b) the local planning authority;
(c) any person known at the date of the notice to be entitled to appear at the inquiry; and
(d) any other person whose presence at the pre-inquiry meeting appears to him to be desirable,

and he may require the local planning authority to take, in relation to notification of the pre-inquiry meeting, one or more of the steps which he may under rule 10(6) require them to take in relation to notification of the inquiry.

(8) The inspector—

   (a) shall preside at the pre-inquiry meeting;
   (b) shall determine the matter to be discussed and the procedure to be followed;
   (c) may require any person present at the pre-inquiry meeting who, in his opinion, is behaving in a disruptive manner to leave; and
   (d) may refuse to permit that person to return or to attend any further pre-inquiry meeting, or may permit him to return or attend only on such conditions as he may specify.

(9) Where a pre-inquiry meeting has been held pursuant to paragraph (1), the inspector may hold a further pre-inquiry meeting and he shall arrange for such notice to be given of a further pre-inquiry meeting as appears to him necessary and ;paragraph (8) shall apply to such a pre-inquiry meeting.

(10) If the Secretary of State requests any further information from the application or the local planning authority at the pre-inquiry meeting, they shall ensure that 2 copies of it have been received by him and a copy has been received by any statutory party within 4 weeks of the conclusion of the pre-inquiry meeting and the Secretary of State shall, as soon as practicable after receipt, send a copy of the further information received from the applicant to the local planning authority and a copy of the further information received from the local planning authority to the applicant.

Receipt of statements of case etc.

6.—(1) the local planning authority shall ensure that within—

   (a) 6 weeks of the starting date, or
   (b) where a pre-inquiry meeting is held pursuant to rule 5, 4 weeks of the conclusion of the that pre-inquiry meeting,

2 copies of their statement of case have been received by the Secretary of State and a copy of their statement of case has been received by any statutory party.

(2) The local planning authority shall—

   (a) include in their statement of case—
      (i) details of the time and place where the opportunity to inspect and take copies described in paragraph (13) below shall be afforded; and
      (ii) where rule 4(2) applies, the matters mentioned in rule 5(4)(a)(ii), unless they have already included these in an outline statement, and
   (b) where rule 4(2) applies, within the period specified in paragraph (1) send a copy of their statement of case to the person concerned.

(3) The applicant shall ensure that within—

(a) in the case of an appeal or are referred application where no pre-inquiry meeting is held pursuant to rule 5, 6 weeks of the starting date, or

(b) in any case where a pre-inquiry meeting is held pursuant to rule 5, 4 weeks of the conclusion of that pre-inquiry meeting,

2 copies of their statement of case have been received by the Secretary of State and a copy of their statement of case has been received by any statutory party.

(4) The Secretary of State shall, as soon as practicable after receipt, send a copy of the local planning authority's statement of case to the applicant and a copy of the applicant's statement of case to the local planning authority.

(5) The applicant and the local planning authority may in writing each require the other to send them a copy of any document, or of the relevant part of any document, referred to in the list of document comprised in the party's statement of case; and any such document, or relevant party, shall be sent, as soon as practicable, to the party who required it.

(6) The Secretary of State may in writing require any other person, who has notified him of an intention or wish to appear at an inquiry, to send—

(a) 3 copies of their statement of case to him within 4 weeks of beings so required; and

(b) a copy of their statement of case to any statutory party,

and the Secretary of State shall, as soon as practicable after receipt, send a copy of each such statement of case to the local planning authority and to the applicant.

(7) The Secretary of State shall as soon as practicable—

(a) send to a person from whom he requires a statement of a case in accordance with paragraph (6) a copy of the statements of case of the applicant and the local planning authority; and

(b) inform that person of the name and address of every person to whom his statement of case is required to be sent.

(8) The Secretary of State or the inspector may in writing require any person, who has sent to him a statement of case in accordance with this rule, to provide such further information about the matters contained in the statement of case as he any specify and may specify the time within which the information shall be received by him.

(9) A local planning authority or applicant required to provide further information, shall ensure that—

(a) 2 copies of that information in writing have been received by the Secretary of State, or as the case may be the inspector, within the specified time; and

(b) a copy has been received by any statutory party within the specified time,

and the Secretary of State, or as the case may be the inspector, shall, as soon as practicable after receipt, send a copy of the further information received from the local planning authority to the applicant and a copy of the further information received from the applicant to the local planning authority.

(10) Any other person required to provide further information shall ensure that—

(a) 3 copies of that information in writing have been received by the Secretary of State, or as the case may be the inspector, within the specified time; and

(b) a copy has been received by any statutory party within the specified time,

and the Secretary of State, or as the case may be the inspector, shall, as soon as practicable after receipt, send a copy of the further information to the local planning authority and the applicant.

(11) Any person other than the applicant who sends a statement of case to the Secretary of State shall send with it a copy of—

(a) any document; or

(b) the relevant part of any document,

referred to in the list comprised in that statement, unless a copy of the document or part of the document in question is already available for inspection pursuant to paragraph (13)

(12) Unless he has already done so, the Secretary of State shall within 12 weeks of the starting date send a written statement of the matters referred to in rule 5(2)(a)(ii) to—

(a) the applicant;

(b) the local planning authority;

(c) any statutory party; and

(d) any person from whom he has required a statement of case.

(13) The local planning authority shall afford to any person who so requests a reasonable opportunity to inspect and, where practicable, take copies of—

(a) any statement of case, written comments, information or other documents a copy of which has been sent to the local planning authority in accordance with this rule; and

(b) the local planning authority's completed questionnaire and statement of case together with a copy of any document, or of the relevant party of any document, referred to in the list comprised in that statement, and any written comments, information or other documents sent by the local planning authority pursuant to this rule.

(14) If the local planning authority or the applicant wish to comment on another person's statement of case they shall ensure that within 9 weeks of the starting date—

(a) 2 copies of their written comments have been received by the Secretary of State; and

(b) a copy of their written comments has been received by any statutory party, and the Secretary of State shall, as soon as practicable after receipt, send a copy of the written comments received from the applicant to the local planning authority and a copy of the written comments received from the local planning authority to the applicant.

(15) Any person, who sends a statement of case to the Secretary of State under this rule and who wishes to comment on another person's statement of case, shall ensure that not less than 4 weeks before the date fixed for the holding of the inquiry—

(a) 3 copies of their written comments have been received by the Secretary of State; and
(b) a copy of their written comments has been received by any statutory party,

and the Secretary of State shall, as soon as practicable after receipt, send a copy of the written comments to the local planning authority and the applicant.

(16) The Secretary of State shall, as soon as practicable after receipt, send to the inspector any statement of case, document or further information or written comments sent to him in accordance with this rule and received by him within the relevant period, if any, specified in this rule.

Further power of inspector to hold pre-inquiry meetings

7.—(1) Where no pre-inquiry meeting is held pursuant to rule 5, an inspector may hold one if he thinks it necessary.

(2) An inspector shall give not less than 2 weeks written notice of a pre-inquiry meeting he proposes to hold under paragraph (1) to—

(a) the applicant;
(b) the local planning authority;
(c) any person known at the date of the notice to be entitled to appear at the inquiry; and
(d) any other person whose presence at the pre-inquiry meeting appears to him to be desirable.

(3) Rule 5(8) shall apply to a pre-inquiry meeting held under this rule.

Inquiry timetable

8.—(1) The inspector shall arrange a timetable for the proceedings at, or at part of, an inquiry where—

(a) a pre-inquiry meeting is held pursuant to rule 5; or
(b) it appears to the Secretary of State likely that an inquiry will last for 8 days or more.

(2) The inspector may arrange a timetable for the proceedings at, or at part of, any other inquiry.

(3) The inspector may, at any time, vary the timetable arranged under the preceding paragraphs.

(4) The inspector may specify in a timetable arranged pursuant to this rule a date by which any proof of evidence and summary sent in accordance with rule 13(1) shall be received by the Secretary of State.

Notification of appointment of assessor

(9) Where the Secretary of State appoints an assessor, he shall notify every person entitled to appear at the inquiry of the name of the assessor and of the matters on which he is to advise the inspector.

Date and notification of inquiry

10.—(1) The date fixed by the Secretary of State for the holding of an inquiry shall be, unless he considers such a date impracticable, not later than —

(a) Subject to paragraph (b), 22 weeks after starting date; or
(b) in a case where a pre-inquiry meeting is held pursuant to rule 5, 8 weeks after the conclusion of the meeting.

(2) Where the Secretary of State considers it impracticable to fix a date in accordance with paragraph (1), the date fixed shall be the earliest date after the end of the relevant period mentioned in that paragraph which he considers to be practicable.

(3) Unless the Secretary of State agrees a lesser period of notice with the applicant and the local planning authority, he hall give not less than 4 weeks written notice or the date, time and place fixed by him for the holding of an inquiry to every persons entitled to appear at the inquiry.

(4) The Secretary of State may vary the date fixed for the holding of an inquiry, whether or not the date as varied is within the relevant period mentioned in paragraph (1); and paragraph (3) shall apply to a variation of a date as it applied to the date originally fixed.

(5) The Secretary of State may vary the time or place for the holding of an inquiry and shall give such notice of any variation as appears to him to be reasonable.

(6) The Secretary of State may in writing require the local planning authority to take one or more of the following steps—

(a) not less than 2 weeks before the date fixed for the holding of an inquiry, to publish a notice of inquiry in one or more newspapers circulating in the locality in which the land is situated;
(b) to send a notice of inquiry to such persons or classes of persons as he may specify, within such period as he may specify; or
(c) to post a notice of the inquiry in a conspicuous place near to the land, within such period as he may specify.

(7) Where the land is under the control of the applicant he shall—

(a) if so required in writing by the Secretary of State, affix a notice of the inquiry firmly to the land or to some object on or near the land, in such manner as to be readily visible to and legible by members of the public; and

(b) not remove the notice, or cause or permit it to be removed, for such period before the inquiry as the Secretary of State may specify.

(8) Every notice of inquiry published, sent or posted pursuant to paragraph (6), or affixed pursuant to paragraph (7), shall contain-

(a) a clear statement of the date, time and place of the inquiry and of the power enabling the Secretary of State to determine the application or appeal in question;
(b) a written description of the land sufficient to identify approximately its location;
(c) a brief description of the subject matter of the application or appeal; and
(d) details of where and when copies of the local planning authority's completed questionnaire and any documents sent by and copied to the authority pursuant to rule 6 may be inspected.

Appearances at inquiry

11.—(1) The persons entitled to appear at an inquiry are—

(a) the applicant;
(b) the local planning authority;
(c) any of the following bodies if the land is situated in their area and they are not the local planning authority—
    (i) a country or district council;
    (ii) an enterprise zone authority designated under Schedule 32 to the Local Government, Planning and Land Act 1980;
    (iii) the Broads Authority, within the meaning of the Norfolk and Suffolk Broads Act 1988;
    (iv) a housing action trust specified in an order made under section 67(1) of the Housing Act 1988;
(d) where the land is in an area previously designated as a new town, the Commission for the New Towns;
(e) any statutory party;
(f) the council of the parish in which the land is situated, if that council made representations to the local planning authority in respect of the application in pursuance of a provision of a development order;
(g) where the application was required to be notified to the Commission under section 14 of the Listed Buildings Act, the Commission;
(h) any other person who has sent a statement of case in accordance with rule 6(6) or who has sent an outline statement in accordance with rule 5(5).

(2) Nothing in paragraph (1) shall prevent the inspector from permitting any other person to appear at an inquiry, and such permission shall not be unreasonably withheld.

(3) Any person entitled or permitted to appear may do so on his own behalf or be represented by any other person.

Representatives of government departments and other authorities at inquiry

12.—(1) where—

(a) the Secretary of State or the Commission has given a direction described in rule 4(2)(a) or (b); or

(b) the Secretary of State or any other Minister of the Crown or any gov-
     ernment department, or any body falling within rule 11(1)(c), has
     expressed a view described in rule 4(2)(c) and the local planning author-
     ity have included the terms of the expression of view in a statement sent
     in accordance with rule 5(2) or 6(1);or
(c) another Minister of the Crown any government department has
     expressed a view described in rule 4(2)(c) and the Secretary of State
     has included its terms in a statement sent in accordance with rule 5(2)
     or 6(12),

the applicant, the local planning authority or a person entitled to appear
may, not later than 4 weeks before the date of an inquiry, apply in writing to
the Secretary of State for a representative of the Secretary of State or of the
other Minister, department or body concerned to be made available at the
inquiry.

(2) Where an application is made in accordance with paragraph (1), the
Secretary of State shall make a representative available to attend the inquiry
or, as the case may be send the application to the other Minister, department
or body concerned, who shall make a representative available to attend the
inquiry.

(3) Any person attending an inquiry as representative in pursuance of the
rule shall state the reasons for the direction or expressed view and shall give
evidence and be subject to cross-examination to the same extent as any other
witness.

(4) Nothing in paragraph (3) shall requires a representative of a Minister or
a government department to answer any question which in the opinion of the
inspector is directed to the merits of government policy.

Proofs of evidence

13.—(1) Any person entitled to appear at an inquiry, who proposes to give,
or to call another person to give evidence at the inquiry by reading a proof of
evidence, shall—

(a) send 2 copies, in the case of the local planning authority and the appli-
     cant, or 3 copies in the case of any other person, of the proof of evi-
     dence together with any written summary, to the Secretary of State; and
(b) simultaneously send copies of these to any statutory party,

and the Secretary of State shall, as soon as practicable after receipt, send a copy
of each proof of evidence together with any summary to the local planning
authority and the applicant.

(2) No written summary shall be required where the proof of evidence proposed to be read contains no more than 1500 words.

(3) The proof of evidence and any summary shall be received by the
Secretary of State no later than—

(a) 4 weeks before the date fixed for the holding of the inquiry, or
(b) where a timetable has been arranged pursuant to rule 8 which specifies
     a date by which the proof of evidence and any summary shall be
     received by the Secretary of State, the date.

(4) The Secretary of State shall send to the inspector, as soon as practicable after receipt, any proof of evidence together with any summary sent to him in accordance with this rule and received by him within the relevant period, if any specified in this rule.

(5) Where a written summary is provided in accordance with paragraph (1), only that summary shall be read at the inquiry, unless the inspector permits or requires otherwise.

(6) Any person, required by this rule to send copies of a proof of evidence to the Secretary of State, shall send with them the same number of copies of the whole, or the relevant part, of any document referred to in the proof of evidence, unless a copy of the document or part of the document in question is already available for inspection pursuant to rule 6(13).

(7) The local planning authority shall afford to any person who so requests a reasonable opportunity to inspect and, where practicable, take copies of any document sent to or by them in accordance with this rule.

Statement of common ground

14.—(1) The local planning authority and the applicant shall—

(a) together prepare an agreed statement of common ground; and
(b) ensure that the Secretary of State receives it and that any statutory party receives a copy of it not less than 4 weeks before the date fixed for the holding of the inquiry.

(2) The local planning authority shall afford to any person who so requests, a reasonable opportunity to inspect, and where practicable, take copies of the statement of common ground sent to the Secretary of State.

Procedure at inquiry

15.—(1) Except as otherwise provided in these Rules, the inspector shall determine the procedure at an inquiry.

(2) At the start of the inquiry the inspector shall identify what are, in his opinion, the main issues to be considered at inquiry and any matters on which he requires further explanation from the persons entitled or permitted to appear.

(3) Nothing in paragraph (2) shall preclude any person entitled or permitted to appear from referring to issues which they consider relevant to the consideration of the application or appeal but which were not issues identified by the inspector pursuant to that paragraph.

(4) Unless in any particular case the inspector otherwise determines, the local planning authority shall begin and the applicant shall have the right of final reply; and the other persons entitled or permitted to appear shall be heard in such order as the inspector may determine.

(5) A person entitled to appear at an inquiry shall be entitled to call evidence and the applicant, the local planning authority and any statutory party shall be entitled to cross-examine persons giving evidence, but, subject to the foregoing and paragraphs (6) and (7), the calling of evidence and the cross-examination of persons giving evidence shall otherwise be at the discretion of the inspector.

(6) The inspector may refuse to permit the—

    (a) giving or production evidence;
    (b) cross-examination of persons giving evidence ; or
    (c) presentation of any other matter,

which he considers to be irrelevant or repetitious; but where he refuses to permit the giving of oral evidence, the person wishing to give the evidence may submit to him any evidence or other matter in writing before the close of the inquiry.

(7) Where a person gives evidence at an inquiry by reading a summary of his proof of evidence in accordance with rule 13(5)—

    (a) the proof of evidence referred to in rule 13(1) shall be treated as tendered in evidence, unless the person required to provide the summary notifies the inspector that he now wishes to rely on the contents of that summary alone; and
    (b) the person whose evidence the proof of evidence contains shall then be subject to cross-examination on it to the same extent as if it were evidence he had given orally.

(8) The inspector may direct that facilities shall be afforded to any person appearing at an inquiry to take or obtain copies of documentary evidence open to public inspection.

(9) The inspector may—

    (a) require any person appearing or present at an inquiry who, in his opinion, is behaving in a disruptive manner to leave; and
    (b) refuse to permit that person to return; or
    (c) permit him to return only on such conditions as he may specify,

but any such person may submit to him any evidence or other matter in writing before the close of the inquiry.

(10) The inspector may allow any person to alter or add to a statement of case received by the Secretary of State or him under rule 6 so far as may be necessary for the purposes of the inquiry; but he shall (if necessary by adjourning the inquiry) give every other person entitled to appear who is appearing at the inquiry an adequate opportunity of considering any fresh matter or document.

(11) The inspector may proceed with an inquiry in the absence of any person entitled to appear at it.

(12) The inspector may take into account any written representation or evidence or any other document received by him from any person before an inquiry opens or during the inquiry provided that he discloses it at the inquiry.

(13) The inspector may from time to time adjourn an inquiry and, if the date, time and place of the adjourned inquiry are announced at the inquiry before the adjournment, no further notice shall be required.

(14) In respect of any inquiry that the Secretary of State expects to last for 8 or more days, any person, who appears at the inquiry and makes closing submissions, shall by the close of the inquiry provide the inspector with a copy of their closing submission in writing.

Site inspections

16.—(1) The inspector may make an unaccompanied inspection of the land before or during an inquiry without giving notice of his intention to the persons entitled to appear at the inquiry.

(2) During an inquiry or after its close, the inspector—

(a) may inspect the land in the company of the applicant, the local planning authority and my statutory party; and

(b) shall make such an inspection if so requested by the applicant or the local planning authority before or during an inquiry.

(3) In all cases where the inspector intends to make an accompanied site inspection he shall announce during the inquiry the date and time at which he process to make it.

(4) The inspector shall not be bound to defer an inspection of the kind refereed to in paragraph (2) where any person mentioned in that paragraph is not present at the time appointed.

Procedure after inquiry

17.—(1) After the close of an inquiry, the inspector shall make a report in writing to the Secretary of State which shall include his conclusions and his recommendations or his reasons for not making any recommendations.

(2) Where an assessor has been appointed, he may, after the close of the inquiry, make a report in writing to the inspector in respect of the matters on which he was appointed to advise.

(3) Where an assessor makes a report in accordance with paragraph (2), the inspector shall append to his own report and shall state in his own report how far he agrees or disagrees with the assessor's report and, where he disagrees with the assessor his reasons for that disagreement.

(4) When making his decision the Secretary of State may disregard any written representation, evidence or any other document received after the close of the inquiry.

(5) If, after the close of an inquiry, the Secretary of State—

(a) differs from the inspector on any matter of fact mentioned in, or appearing to him to be material to, a conclusion reached by the inspector; or

(b) takes into consideration any new evidence or new matter of fact (not being a matter of government policy),

and is for that reason disposed to disagree with a recommendation make by the inspector, he shall not come to a decision which is at variance with that recommendation without first notifying the persons entitled to appear at the inquiry who appeared at it of his disagreement and the reasons for it; and affording them an opportunity of making written representations to him or (if the Secretary of State has taken into consideration any new evidence or new matter of fact, not being a matter of government policy) of asking of the re-opening of the inquiry.

(6) Those persons making written representations or requesting the inquiry to be re-opened under paragraph (5), shall ensure that such representations or

requests are received by the Secretary of State within 3 weeks of the date of the Secretary of State's notification under that paragraph.

(7) The Secretary of State may, as he thinks fit, cause an inquiry to be re-opened, and he shall do so if asked by the applicant or the local planning authority in the circumstances mentioned in paragraph (5) and within the period mentioned in paragraph (6); and where an inquiry is re-opened (whether by the same or a different inspector)—

(a) the Secretary of State shall send to the persons entitled to appear at the inquiry who appeared at it a written statement of the matters with respect to which further evidence is invited; and

(b) paragraphs (3) to (8) of rule 10 shall apply as if references to an inquiry were references to a re-opened inquiry.

Notification of decision

18.—(1) The Secretary of State shall, as soon as practicable, notify his decision on an application or appeal and his reasons for it in writing to—

(a) all persons entitled to appear at the inquiry who did appear, and

(b) any other person who, having appeared at the inquiry, has asked to be notified of the decision.

(2) Where a copy of the inspector's report is not sent with the notification of the decision, the notification shall be accompanied by a statement of his conclusion and of any recommendations make by him, and if a person entitled to be notified to the decision has not received a copy of that report, he shall be supplied with a copy of it on written application to the Secretary of State.

(3) In this rule "report" includes any assessor's report appended to the inspector's report but does no include any other documents so appended; but any person who has received a copy of the report may apply to the Secretary of State in writing within 6 weeks of the date of the Secretary of State's decision, for an opportunity inspecting any such documents and the Secretary of State shall afford him that opportunity.

(4) Any person applying to the Secretary of State under paragraph (2) shall ensure that his application is received by the Secretary of State within 4 weeks of the Secretary of State's determination.

Procedure following quashing of decision

19.—(1) Where a decision of the Secretary of State on an application or appeal in respect of which an inquiry has been held is quashed in proceedings before any court, the Secretary of State—

(a) shall send to the persons entitled to appear at the inquiry who appeared at it a written statement of the matters with respect to which further representations are invited for the purposes of his further consideration of the application or appeal;

(b) shall afford to those persons the opportunity of making written representations to him in respect of those matters or of asking of the re-opening of the inquiry; and

(c) may, as he thinks fit, cause the inquiry to be re-opened (whether by the same or a different inspector) and if he does so paragraphs (3) to (8) of the rule 10 shall apply as if the references to an inquiry were references to a re-opened inquiry.

(3) Those persons making representation or asking for the inquiry to be re-opened under paragraph (1)(b) shall ensure that such representations or requests are received by the Secretary of State within 3 weeks of the date of the written statement sent under paragraph (1)(a).

Allowing further time

20. The secretary of State may at any time in any particular case allow further time for the taking of any step which is required or enabled to be taken by virtue of these Rules, and reference sin these Rules to a day by which, or a period within which, any step is required or enabled to be taken shall be construed accordingly.

Additional copies

21.—(1) The Secretary of State may at any time before the close of an inquiry request from any person entitled to appear additional copies of the following—

(a) an outline statement sent in accordance with rule 5;
(b) a statement of case or comments sent in accordance with rule 6;
(c) a proof of evidence sent in accordance with rule 13; or
(d) any other document or information sent to the Secretary of State before or during an inquiry,

and may specify the time within which such copies should be received by him.

(2) Any person so requested shall ensure that the copies are received by the Secretary of State within period specified.

Notices by post

22. Notices or documents required or authorized to be sent under these Rules may be sent by post.

Notes

1. The 2000 Rules, which apply to cases determined by the Secretary of State following a report to an inspector (the "Secretary of State Rules" replaced SI 1992/2038, which in turn replaced SI 1988/944. Modifications are made with each revision. The main changes made in the latest version include a stronger requirement for pre-inquiry meetings (r.5); the requirement for the inspector to set a time-table for inquiries which the Secretary of State expects to last more than eight days (r.8); the provision for a statement of common ground (r.14); the inspector's statement of the main issues and the requirement that the local planning authority presents its case first (r.15); and the right of the Secretary of State to disregard representations received after the close of the inquiry (r.17(4)).

See DETR Circular 05/2000, *Planning Appeals Procedure Including Called-in Planning Application Inquiries*

The equivalent for Wales is SI 2003/1266.

2. As to the duty to give reasons under r.18, see below, p.851.

3. Planning inquiries into major infrastructure projects are heard in accordance with a separate set of rules, the Town and Country Planning (Major Infrastructure Project Inquiries Procedure) (England) Rules 2002 (SI 2002/1223), replacing with effect from June 7, 2002, a non-statutory code contained originally in Joint Circular 10/88, Annex 1, and subsequently in DETR Circular 05/2000, Annex 4. See DETR Circular 02/2002, *Planning Inquiries into Major Infrastructure Projects: Procedures*. The new procedures were part of a series of measures to streamline the processing of such projects through the planning system. They apply to projects that involve economic, environmental or other issues of regional or sub-regional importance, whether of national or major regional or sub-regional projects. The main changes to inquiry procedures were

(1) that round-table sessions and joint date groups can be held as for non-adversarial discussions with a view to agree facts and narrow the extent of disagreements;
(2) stricter time-tabling;
(3) the possibility of appointing independent technical advisers;
(4) the possibility of mediation;
(5) a power for the inspector to limit cross-examination where the inquiry time-table is put at risk; and
(6) announcements at the end of the inquiry of a date of delivery of the inspector's report.

There were separate proposals, also originally announced by the Secretary of State for Transport, Local Government and the Regions on July 20, 2001 for new procedures to give Parliament the opportunity to approve projects in principle, including the right for people to object before Parliament debates the issues, confining subsequent public inquiries to the consideration of detailed issues. These proposals, which would limit the rights at the inquiry of the owners of land affected by project proposals (and others), were strongly opposed (*e.g.* by the Council on Tribunals) and have not been taken forward.

4. Conversely, many planning inquiries are determined by the inspector rather than the Secretary of State under the Town and Country Planning Appeals (Determination by Inspectors) (Inquiries Procedure) (England) Rules 2000 (SI 2000/1625), as amended by SI 2003/956, Sch.3 (the equivalent for Wales is SI 2003/1267). Furthermore, there is provision for the parties to agree for there to be an informal hearing rather than a formal inquiry, or for the appeal to be determined by written representations. See, respectively, the Town and Country Planning (Hearings Procedure) (England) Rules 2000 (SI 2003/1271); and the Town and Country Planning (Appeals) (Written Representations Procedure) (England) Regulations (SI 2000/1628) (the equivalent for Wales is SI 2003/390).

5. Other important sets of inquiry rules include the Highways (Inquiries Procedure) Rules 1994 (SI 1994/3263). Highways inquiries were particularly controversial in the 1970s, when a number were disrupted by objectors (see J. Tyme, *Motorways versus Democracy* (1978): Mr Tyme was one of the best-known objectors; F. Sharman, [1977] J.P.L. 293; D.G.T. Williams, (1980) 29 I.C.L.Q. 701 at pp.708–709). Steps were taken to improve the amount of information made available to objectors (see the *Report on the Review of Highway Inquiry Procedures*, Cmnd.7133 (1978). Note, however, P. McAuslan's view that, notwithstanding these developments, and, more generally, the changes brought about by the Franks Report, "the overriding purpose of the public local inquiry . . . was and is to advance the administration's version of the public interest" (*The Ideologies of Planning Law* (1980), p.73; road inquiries are considered at pp.55–73).

6. A significant development in the 1970s and 1980s was the desire of certain pressure groups (particularly environmental groups) to question matters of national government policy before specific inquiries. The judiciary sought to limit the legal

obligations on inspectors to hear such challenges (*Bushell v Secretary of State for the Environment*, below, p.731) and reach conclusions on them (*R. v Secretary of State for Transport Ex p. Gwent CC* [1988] Q.B. 429 and see A.R. Mowbray, "Public Inquiries and Government Policy" (1987) 137 N.L.J. 418). Furthermore, studies have demonstrated the weaknesses in this use of inquiries. "Where Government policy is fundamental to the issues which are the subject-matter of an inquiry, a Government witness provides a useful function in explaining and elaborating this policy. . . . However, if Government policies are unclear or in a state of flux, the witness will be put in a difficult position. In the case of the Sizewell B Inquiry this tendency has been increased by the length of the inquiry. As a result, we would argue that it would be unwise to look to public inquiries as a formal mechanism for any definitive assessment of Government policy, especially in those areas which are either unclear or prone to substantial policy flux" M. Purdue *et al.*, "The Government at the Sizewell B Inquiry" [1985] P.L. 475 at pp.488–489.

7. The planning appeal structure overall complies with Art. 6(1) ECHR (see *Alconbury*, below, p.374).

(v) Default Powers

A number of statutes give powers to ministers to act in default of proper action taken by local authorities (*e.g.* the Public Health Act 1936 and the Education Act. See, for example, *Wade and Forsyth*, pp.740–743. Whilst these powers are not formally invoked frequently, their use may be threatened against recalcitrant authorities and Ministers have had resort to them in periods of intense central-local government conflict (see, *e.g. Asher v Secretary of State for the Environment* [1974] 1 Ch. 208). Local authorities also have default powers to take action where individuals fail to comply with statutory notices (*e.g.* to repair unfit houses under the Housing Act 1985). Another respect in which the existence of a default power may be significant is where a person aggrieved by administrative action is refused a remedy in the courts as a result. A request to the authority with power to act in default, or to give instructions to the recalcitrant authority is regarded as the proper course of action; see *Watt v Kesteven County Council* [1955] 1 Q.B. 408.

R. v SECRETARY OF STATE FOR THE ENVIRONMENT EX p. NORWICH CITY COUNCIL

[1982] 1 Q.B. 808; [1982] 1 All E.R. 737; 80 L.G.R. 498 (COURT OF APPEAL)

The Housing Act 1980 provided local authority tenants with the right to buy their homes. Under s.10(1) the landlord council had "as soon as practicable" to serve on a tenant, with an established right to buy, a notice stating what, in the council's opinion, was to be the price for the conveyance and what provisions should be contained therein. Section 11 enabled the tenant to have the value determined by the district valuer. By s.23(1),

> "where it appears to the Secretary of State that tenants of a particular landlord . . . have or may have difficulty in exercising the right to buy effectively and expeditiously, he may, after giving the landlord . . . notice in writing of his intention to do so . . . use his powers under the . . . section".

Subsection (3) empowers the Secretary of State to "do all such things as appear to him necessary or expedient" to enable the tenant to exercise the right to buy.

Within the first month Norwich Council had received 452 applications to buy, but after seven months no sales had been completed. Tenants began to complain about the time taken by the council to complete sales and meetings were held between officials of both the department and the council. These were followed by meetings between ministers and councillors.

In December 1981, the Secretary of State made an order under s.23 of the Act and wrote to the leader of Norwich Council in the following terms:

> "in my view the conduct of your council with respect to the notices required to be served on your council's secure tenants under section 10 of the Housing Act 1980 could well amount to non-compliance with the statutory requirements of Chapter 1 of Part 1 of that Act. But whether or not this is the case I would still conclude that secure tenants of your council have or may have difficulty in exercising the right to buy effectively and expeditiously . . . I cannot however ignore the further delays and difficulties referred to above".

On the same day the council applied to the High Court for an order of certiorari to quash the decision of the Secretary of State. The Divisional Court dismissed the application and the council appealed to the Court of Appeal.

LORD DENNING M.R. . . .

"Default power"

. . . Our present statute, the Housing Act 1980, in section 23 goes as far as anything that I have seen hitherto. It enables the Minister to take over the function himself—to do it all himself by his own civil servants—and to charge the cost to the local authority. . . .

This "default power" enables the central government to interfere with a high hand over local authorities. Local self-government is such an important part of our constitution that, to my mind, the courts should be vigilant to see that this power of the central government is not exceeded or misused. Wherever the wording of the statute permits, the courts should read into it a provision that the "default power" should not be exercised except in accordance with the rules of natural justice. That follows from such cases as *Board of Education v. Rice* [1911] A.C. 179 and *Ridge v. Baldwin* [1964] A.C. 40. After all, the Minister is dismissing the local authority for default in carrying out their duty. He is replacing them by his own civil servants. He is making them pay all the costs and depriving them of the interest they would have received. Simple fairness requires that this should not be done unless they are told what is alleged against them and they have had an opportunity of answering it.

Apart from this, the very decision of the Minister himself is open to judicial review. If the Minister does not act in good faith, or if he acts on extraneous considerations which ought not to influence him, or if he misdirects himself in fact or in law, the court will in a proper case intervene and set his order aside. That follows from such cases as *Padfield v. Minister of Agriculture, Fisheries and Food* [1968] A.C. 997 and *Secretary of State for Employment v. ASLEF (No. 2)* [1972] 2 Q.B. 455, 493, approved by Lord Wilberforce in *Secretary of State for Education and Science v. Tameside Metropolitan Borough Council* [1977] A.C. 1014, 1047. Also if the Minister assumes to interfere with a decision of the local authority to which they came quite reasonably and sensibly, the court may intervene to stop the Minister. . . .

The district valuer

It is quite clear that many local councils, in order to state the price under section 10(1) at which they were ready to sell, consulted the district valuer at the outset. He made the initial valuation on which that price was fixed. That saved the council time and money. Instead of their own staff making the initial valuation in the council's time—and instead of putting out the work to private valuers—the council got the district valuer to do it at no expense to the council at all. This speeded up valuations greatly in many of the other councils. . . .

Pointing to section 11, the Norwich City Council said that the district valuer was like an appeal body. He should not be employed to make the initial valuation where he would sit on appeal from it to make the final valuation. That point impressed me much for some time. It seemed contrary to the accepted principle that "justice should not only be done, but should manifestly and undoubtedly be seen to be done": see *per* Lord Hewart C.J. in *R. v. Sussex Justices, ex p. McCarthy* [1924] 1 K.B. 256, 259 and *F.G.C. Metropolitan Properties Co. Ltd v. Lannon* [1969] 1 Q.B. 577, 599. But this principle—like that of natural justice—must not be carried too far. It is flexible and must be adapted as the case may require. . . .

[After detailing the method of calculation of rateable values.] A similar system is applied in these valuations under the Housing Act 1980. The initial valuation under section 10(1) (on which the local council fixes the price) is made by one of the clerks in the office. If the tenant takes objection and refers the matter to the district valuer under section 11, then the decision is made by the valuation officer himself or his deputy. This system works perfectly well. That is shown by the fact that in 50 per cent of the cases the valuation is reduced: and also by the even more striking fact that no tenant has ever taken any objection to the system. The only person to take objection has been the Norwich City Council.

So justice is *in fact* done by reason of the final valuation being done by a senior officer quite distinct from the one who made the initial valuation. It is *seen* to be done by reason of the fact that no tenant has ever complained of it.

Application to this case

. . . the concern of this court, as always, is to protect the individual from the misuse or abuse of power by those in authority. The individual here is the tenant. He has been given by Parliament the right to buy the house in which he lives. Yet in the exercise of that right he has met with intolerable delay. The responsibility for that delay is, beyond doubt, the responsibility of the Norwich City Council. They acted—or failed to act—in complete good faith. But they were misguided. And they must answer for it. They were badly advised on many matters; such as to insist on scale 1:500 when scale 1:1250 would do. They were badly advised to refuse to employ the district valuer, when it would have speeded things up greatly. No one can excuse himself for his own mistakes by saying that he did it on bad advice: see *Federal Commerce & Navigation Co. Ltd v. Molena Alpha Inc.* [1978] Q.B. 927, 979. The council here showed too little concern for the rights of the tenants. They should have given them higher priority. They were unreasonable not to do so.

What is the remedy? What recourse have the tenants for redress? None by coming to the courts. Nothing could be done effectively by mandamus.

The statute has provided a remedy. It has enabled the Secretary of State to make a "default order". It is a very great power to be used only after careful consideration. The Secretary of State here did give it careful consideration. He gave the council every opportunity to mend their ways. He gave them ample notice of what was alleged against them. He heard all that they had to say before he made his order. He gave them clear warning of the consequences. His order, strong as it was, was within his statutory powers. It cannot be upset in this court.

We were told that, pending these proceedings, the Secretary of State had allowed the Norwich City Council to carry on with the selling of the houses, and had not taken them out of their hands. This holds out hope for a solution. Surely the City Council will agree now to use the district valuer to make the initial valuations. Surely they will speed up the procedure so as to avoid any further complaints. If they do this, there may be no need for the Secretary of State to act upon his order. But that his order was good, I have no doubt. I would dismiss this appeal.

KERR and MAY L.JJ. gave separate judgments dismissing the appeal.

Note
Following the Court of Appeal's decision, Norwich Council co-operated with the Secretary of State by providing an office for his representatives, taking on more staff to process tenants' applications and using the district valuer for first valuations of properties. The Secretary of State withdrew his section 23 notice after three-and-a-half years in May 1985. Two academic commentators assessed the outcome of the Environment Secretary's actions in the following terms:

"in the aftermath of the service of notice of intervention Norwich had held on to administration and co-operated in the best interests of tenants and ratepayers. Although defeat in the courts was unfortunate and the notice had remained in operation longer than had been hoped Norwich can reasonably be regarded to have coped satisfactorily with the circumstances. For central government the outcome was more favourable. Success in the courts had strengthened their hand in relations with other authorities, closeness to detailed day-to-day administration had informed them of problems and issues and again strengthened their position through increasing knowledge".

R. Forrest and A. Murie, *An Unreasonable Act? Central-Local Government Conflict and the Housing Act 1980* (1985), pp.129–130. See also the case commentary by S.H. Bailey, [1983] P.L. 8.

(E) AN ADMINISTRATIVE JUSTICE COUNCIL

WHITE PAPER, TRANSFORMING PUBLIC SERVICES: COMPLAINTS, REDRESS AND TRIBUNALS

(Cm.6243, 2004)

11 An Administrative Justice Council

11.1 For the past 46 years tribunals have been subject to the supervision of the Council on Tribunals. Over that time its powers and remit have changed little. We are now embarking on what is probably the most radical set of changes to tribunals ever, and we believe that the Council needs to change too- to become an Administrative Justice Council, focused on the needs of the public and users. This chapter deals with how we propose to move the Council into that new role.

The Council at Present

11.2 The Council's statutory duties are:

- to keep under review the constitution and working of the tribunals under its supervision;
- to consider and report (to the Lord Chancellor) on such particular matters as may be referred to the Council under the Act. In practice this has involved making mainly general recommendations on procedures and composition of tribunals;
- to be consulted on proposed secondary legislation (rules and regulations) relating to tribunals (but there is no duty to consult the Council on primary legislation);
- to consider and report on matters referred to it concerning statutory inquiries; and
- to make an Annual Report to the Lord Chancellor (to be laid before Parliament).

11.3 Sir Andrew Leggatt made it clear that he saw the Council as having a key role in his proposed tribunal reforms. However, while praising the Council's achievements, he noted a number of deficiencies in the way in which it is obliged to carry out its work. He added that "in focusing on the need for detailed comment on specific issues [the Council] has given insufficient emphasis to strategic thinking about administrative justice generally or about tribunals in particular".[25]

11.4 His recommendations were aimed at developing an enhanced role for the Council. Sir Andrew envisaged a more proactive body, which would champion the needs of users within the Tribunals Service. In pursuit of this aim, it would provide more conferences, more detailed tribunal information more special reports, and more guidance on standards and best practice.

Strengthening the Council's role

11.5 Sir Andrew's main criticisms of the Councils as presently constituted were that it lacked a truly authoritative voice. He observed that "because departments were under no obligation to respond to its criticisms, the Council must have felt that any good it did had to be done by stealth, rather than by conformation, lest departments take offence and withdraws their collaboration. With unresponsive departments, and no Select Committee to report to, it has not been giving such an account of itself as meets the demands of the twenty-first century."[26]

---

[25] para. 7.47 p.96
[26] para. 7.48 p.96.

11.6 We agree that the Council's views should carry greater weight within government, especially where the Council has identified shortcomings in the operation of particular systems. To ensure that the Council can play its full part in assisting the transition to the new tribunal structure and beyond:

- we will introduce a code of practice dealing with consultation with the Council on all forms legislation affecting tribunals;
- in tandem we will give the Council authority to publish its comments on legislation, should it think it appropriate. Not all legislation is published in draft form and so some consultation might have to be on a confidential basis with publication of comments where appropriate following publication of the legislation;
- the Code of Practice will also commit sponsoring government departments to publish its response to the Council's comments as part of the process of publishing primary or subordinate legislation; and
- the Council's reports will be drawn to the attention of the appropriate Select Committee of the House of Commons.

11.7 Much of the above may be achieved without legislation and, coupled with the wider dissemination of the Council's reports will serve to raise its profile across the tribunals world. We will implement these changes as soon as possible.

Supporting the creation of the new dispute resolution system

11.8 The Council has strongly supported the reform and unification of the tribunal system and will have an important role to play in facilitating the establishment of the new system by, for example;

- collaborating with the Chief Executive of the new agency and other tribunals to identify common performance measures, to promote effective alignment of data collection and more effective benchmarking of performance;
- scrutinizing and if necessary challenging the way in which the new organization is being established;
- in collaboration with the JSB, advising the Senior President on an appropriate initial training policy and co-ordinated training programme for the unified tribunals judiciary;
- obtaining the views of users and the advice sector on issues arising from the unification process, formulating advice to DCA on user priorities and concerns, and promoting ongoing dialogue between the unified tribunals and the user community; and
- recommending which tribunals should be brought into the Tribunals Service after the initial big 10.

Judicial Training and Appraisal

11.9 The present productive partnership between the Judicial Studies Board (JSB) and the Council will continue under our reform proposals;

- the Council will continue to promote effective judicial training, performance management and appraisal for tribunals in accordance with its framework of standards;

- the Council will be actively engaged in identifying training needs and priorities, seeking advice from the JSB on how effectively training is being organized and delivered and providing advice and feedback to the JSB on training issues; and
- the JSB will undertake evaluation and quality assurance of the training actually provided within tribunals, ensuring that training is delivered to agreed national standards. This builds on the recent work of the JSB and the Council on Tribunals in developing a common and consistent approach.

Research

11.10 Sir Andrew recommended that the Council should be enabled to commission research into the operation of administrative justice both in the UK and abroad. While we recognize the importance of soundly based research in developing tribunals policy, the creation of a separate Council on Tribunals research arm would be over-ambitious and unnecessary. The Council does however have a number of advantages when it comes conduct of research. It will therefore make recommendations on the priorities for DCA research activity in areas of the Council's interest, as well as playing a major role in dissemination, and lending authority to, any research findings.

An Administrative Justice Council

11.11 With the establishment of the new system the need for the Council's current and proposed activities will change. The establishment of a procedure committee for the tribunals, with judicial, professional and user members, will mean that the Council's current role in commenting on secondary legislation will need to be reviewed. One option may be that the Council might retain a statutory right to be consulted on secondary legislation, but exercise that right through representation on the Procedure Committee. That should mean a better dialogue between the Council and the other interests in the system. Likewise, the creation of a unified system for central government tribunals with a strong and vigorous Senior President and Chief Executive in charge should mean less involvement by the Council in the work of those tribunals. What is needed for the future is a Council which can focus on improvements for the user across the whole administrative justice field, so that the new organisation, and tribunals outside the new organisation, developed and operate under the strategic oversight of an independent and authoritative body with a very wide perspective.

11.12 We therefore propose that the Council should in the longer term, while retaining its supervisory role over all types of tribunal, evolve into an advisory body for the whole administrative justice sector—an Administrative Justice Council. It would report to the Secretary of State for Constitutional Affairs who would have a parallel remit within government to take the lead on redress policy generally. We would, for instance, except an Administrative Justice Council to make suggestions for departmental review, for proportionate dispute resolution and for the balance between the different components of the system. The Council would therefore be concerned to ensure that the relationships between the courts, tribunals, ombudsmen and other ADR routes satisfactorily reflect the needs of users. We envisage a broad-based, mixed membership under an independent Chair, bringing together user representatives and non-executive members with office holder, able to generate ideas for the future that reflect the needs of the various "constituencies" but small enough to function as collective and active body. The Parliamentary Ombudsman is already ex officio a member of the Council on Tribunals: other officer-holder members could include the Senior President and a senior civil servant from the Cabinet Office or a major decision-making department.

11.13 Thus in discharging its statutory function in relation to tribunals, on this model the Council would also be changed with taking full account of the broader landscape of administrative justice, and be empowered to make recommendations about it. The new Administrative Justice Council would in addition to be Council on Tribunals current duties therefore:

- keep under review the performance of the administrative justice system as a whole drawing attention to matters of particular importance or concern;
- review the relationships between the various components of the system (in particular ombudsmen, tribunals and the courts) to ensure that these are clear, complementary and flexible;
- identify priorities for, and encourage the conduct of, research; and
- provide advice and make recommendations to government on changes to legislation, practice and procedure which will improve the workings of the administrative justice system.

11.14 The Council at present has a remit covering England, Wales and (through a statutory committee) Scotland, but not Northern Ireland. With the devolved administrations we will consider whether a new structure and be desirable for the new Council.

11.15 Any legislation necessary to facilitate the new role of Council on Tribunals, as outlined above, will be framed so that it can turn into an Administrative Justice Council when the time is right.

Note

1. These proposals build on the very useful work that has been undertaken for over 45 years by the Council on Tribunals, but appropriately recognise the need for its role to be broadened and strengthened. Suggestions for similar developments have been made for many years (see, *e.g. Special Report: The Functions of the Council on Tribunals* (Cmd.7805, 1980). Much will turn on the financial resources allocated to the strengthened Council.

2. For consideration of the work of the Council on Tribunals, see J.F. Garner, [1965] P.L. 321 and D.G.T. Williams, [1984] P.L. 73. Its Annual Reports and periodic Special Reports are a valuable source of information. Other important contributions include the *Guide to Drafting Procedural Rules* published in 2003, replacing the *Model Rules of Procedure for Tribunals* originally published in 1991; *Guidance on Making Tribunals Accessible to Disabled People* developed jointly with the Disability Rights Commission and the *Framework of Standards for Tribunals* both published in November 2002.

3. The Council's role in opposing (with others) proposals for the exclusion of judicial review in respect of most decisions of the new Asylum and Immigration Tribunal is documented in its Annual Report for 2003–04 (2003–04 HL 750), Ch.5. See further below, p.918.

4. The Council has conducted reviews of particular tribunals. See *Mental Health Review Tribunals* (Cm.4740, 2000) and *School Admission and Exclusion Appeal Panels* (Cm.5788, 2003). It is, regrettably, an illustration of the status of the Council

as currently perceived by government departments that its many concerns and sensible recommendations concerning the latter panels, which echo many issues seen in the past, and addressed, in relation to other tribunals, were relatively summarily rejected by the dfes (letter of October 16, 2003, reproduced on the Council of Tribunals website). The key recommendations were that exclusion appeals should be heard by SENDIST, with legally qualified chairs and a national structure, and admissions appeals as an interim measure and be organised on a regional rather than local basis. Both were rejected: the former on the ground that SENDIST would be less accessible and the latter on the ground that such panels would be expensive and less accessible. The fall-back recommendation for exclusion appeal panels that they should have a legally qualified chair or clerk were rejected, the department trotting out the long-discredited argument that this "would tend to make proceedings more formal, which could alienate or intimidate some parents". (Compare research-based criticisms of Supplementary Benefit Appeal Tribunals that lacked lawyer chairmen.) These appeals, as local rather than central government matters, will not fall within the scope of the new Tribunals Service.

CHAPTER 3

OMBUDSMEN AND OTHER COMPLAINTS MECHANISMS

(A) INTRODUCTION

The idea of an "Ombudsman", or inquirer into the complaints of grievances suffered by citizens at the hands of some organ of the administration, is of Scandinavian origin, where it was conceived as a check on corrupt officials. Imported from Sweden into Denmark in 1954 where he or she is almost an inspector of the administration, the Ombudsman acts on his or her own motion, and relies on publicity and public opinion to achieve the redress of grievances. The idea was familiarised in this country chiefly by the activities of JUSTICE. A Parliamentary Commissioner was Act of 1967, and this was followed by the establishment of the establishment of the Health Service Commissioners for Scotland (National Health Service Reorganisation Act 1972), and for England and Wales (National Health Service Reorganisation Act 1973), and by the Commissions for Local Administration (Local Government Act 1974). Meanwhile, the Parliamentary Commissioner (Northern Ireland) Act was passed in 1969, and also that jurisdiction established a separate local government commissioner, by the Commissioner for Complaints (Northern Ireland) Act 1969.

In the United Kingdom, the Parliamentary Commissioner for Administration (hereafter the PCA.) was initially limited to investigating complaints (referred by Members of Parliament) of "maladministration" causing injustice created by central government departments. However, the Commissioner's jurisdiction was extended by the Parliamentary and Health Service Commission Act 1987 to encompass over 50 Non-Departmental Public Bodies (e.g. the Sports Council), "Next Steps" (executive) agencies fall within the PCA's jurisdiction as they take action on behalf of government departments included in Sch.2 to the Act.

During the 1960s and the 1970s, the Ombudsman idea spread across many legal systems (e.g. the New Zealand Ombudsman was created in 1962 and the French Mediateur in 1973). The 1980s witnessed the emergence of private sector Ombudsmen in the United Kingdom (initially to deal with consumer complaints in the financial services industries—see below, p.199). The 1990s saw the establishment of the Legal Services Ombudsman under the Courts and Legal Services Act 1990 followed by the Pensions Ombudsman (Pensions Schemes Act 1993, s.145).

Further landmark developments have been the establishment of a Financial Ombudsmen Scheme in respect of disputes between "authorised persons" under the Financial Services and Markets Act 2000 and their customers (Pt 16, ss.225–237 of and Sch.17 to the 2000 Act) and structural changes in consequence of devolution. In Scotland, s.91 of the Scotland Act 1998 authorised Parliament to make provision for the investigation of complaints concerning a range of Scottish and cross-border bodies, but required there to be such provision for complaints of a kind that could be investigated under the 1967 Act, concerning (a) members of the Scottish Executive in the exercise of functions conferred on the Scottish Ministers or (b) any other office-holder in the Scottish Administration. Between 1999 and 2002, the PCA was appointed separately to the new position of Scottish Parliamentary Commissioner for Administration by virtue of the Scotland Act 1998 (Transitory and Transitional Provisions) (Complaints of Maladministration) Order 1999 (SI 1999/1451). This office disappeared in 2002, and the jurisdiction (together with those of the Health

Service Commissioner for Scotland, a post previously held by the person also appointed as PCA, the Scottish Local Government Ombudsman, and the Housing Association Ombudsmen for Scotland) passed to the new Scottish Public Services Ombudsman, established by the Scottish Public Services Ombudsmen Act 2002 (asp 11). The PCA retains jurisdiction in relation to reserved matters. (See further, M. Seneviratne, *Ombudsmen: Public Services and Administrative Justice* (2002), pp.255–270).

In Wales, the Government of Wales Act 1998 (s.111 and Sch.9) established a Welsh Administration Ombudsmen with jurisdiction to investigate administrative action taken by the National Assembly for Wales and certain other public bodies in Wales. The PCA was also appointed to this post in the first instance but the opportunity was subsequently taken to appoint the same person to this post, and as Health Service Commissioner in Wales and Local Commissioner for Wales. The Public Services Ombudsmen (Wales) Act 2005 provides a unified legislative structure.

The Parliamentary, Health Services and Local Commissioners in practice use respectively the titles of Parliamentary Ombudsman, Health Service Ombudsman and Local Government Ombudsmen (although these do not (as yet) appear in the legislation).

As can be seen by the steady proliferation in their numbers, ombudsmen have been widely regarded as making a distinctive and effective contribution to the resolution of complaints, both inside and outside the public sector. Of particular advantage to complainants are the ombudsman's investigatory powers and expertise in dealing with the bodies concerned, and the fact that his or her services are free.

As regards public sector ombudsmen, the rationalisation of jurisdiction has taken place in Scotland, and will take place in for Wales. The delay in finding legislative time for this for England is disappointing. There is, moreover, a case for the legislation to be updated so as better to reflect and support the activities as they are undertaken now and as they could sensibly be developed.

Notes

1. There are now a large number of public and sector ombudsmen (see the website of the British and Irish Ombudsmen Association, *www.bioa.org.uk*) There are significant variations in organisation and responsibility both between and within the two sectors. There are many variables, including:

(1) Whether the ombudsman is established by statute (this is so for most public sector and some private sector ombudsmen).

(2) Whether complainants have direct access to the ombudsman (this is so generally, with the notable exception of the PCA, where complaints have to be channelled through an MP).

(3) Whether the ombudsman has legal powers (through statute or contract) to require the provision of information.

(4) Whether the main focus is as a means of the alternative dispute resolution of individual grievances (a *redress* model); or a process of investigating and influencing administrative behaviour at a more general level with the purpose of increasing the quality of the decision-making process and increasing its acceptability in the eyes of the citizen (a *control* model, albeit using "control" in a special sense that does not include power to give a legally binding decision); or some balance between the two.

The distinction between redress and control models is put forward and helpfully analysed by K. Heede, *European Ombudsmen: redress and control at Union Level* (2000), Ch.4. Most UK ombudsmen conform to the redress model, although the public sector ombudsmen have also sought to influence general behaviour through the formulation of standards of good practice and have investigated the operation of general programmes and not just individual decisions.

(5) Whether the standards applied by the ombudsmen are also enforced by the courts, the ombudsman thereby facilitating more quickly and cheaply the resolution of disputes that could be determined by a court, or are extra-legal. While the standards applied by UK ombudsmen (usually in the case of public sector and sometimes in the case of private sector ombudsmen through the concept of "maladministration") include the extra-legal, addressing such matters as rudeness, delay and poor advice, they are not and should not (and indeed could not) be so confined.

(6) Whether the standards applied address the process by which the decision has been taken, or can also reach the substantive merits of that decision. The usual emphasis is on process. Unusually, the Pensions Ombudsman, apart from a jurisdiction concerning maladministration, also has a jurisdiction to determine questions of law and fact, a function normally allocated to a tribunal. One consequence of the Human Rights Act 1998 has been that the Pension Ombudsman is now readier to hold oral hearings than was formerly the case; there are still suggestions that these matters would more appropriately be dealt with by a tribunal, with a greater formality of process (see Lightman J, "The Pensions Ombudsman and the Courts" (2001), *www.dca.gov.uk/judicial/ speeches*).

(7) Whether the ombudsman's decision is legally binding. The normal position is that decisions take the form of recommendations, which are usually in practice accepted. Again, the Pensions Ombudsman is an exception.

2. The establishment of ombudsmen by many (albeit not all) EU Members States formed the background to the creation by the Treaty on European Union (the Maastricht Treaty) of the office of European Ombudsman. Every citizen of the Union may apply to the ombudsman established by Art. 195 EC (ex 138e EC) (Art. 21 EC, ex 8d EC). The ombudsman is appointed by the European Parliament to receive complaints from any citizen of the Union or any natural or legal person residing or having its headquarters in a Member State concerning instances of maladministration in the activities of the Community institutions or bodies, with the exception of the Court of Justice and the Court of First Instance acting in their judicial role. The ombudsman may also conduct inquiries on his own initiative on the basis of complaints submitted to him direct or through an MEP (art. 195 EC). The European Ombudsman has in practice stressed the "redress" side of his role; it has been suggested (K. Heede, *op cit*, Ch. 8) that the needs of the EU would be better addressed by greater emphasis on "control", with increased role in the resolution of legal disputes, and the supervision of joint administration between Community and national authorities and executive rule-making by the Commission. An even more radical development would see a role for the European Ombudsmen in the protection of the rights of Union citizens in relation to national authorities. Treaty amendment would be needed. See further P. Birkinshaw, *European Public Law* (2002), pp.479–596, and *www.euro-ombudsman.eu.int*.

The Treaty on European Union (Maastricht Treaty) created a European Ombudsman who can receive complaints from, *inter alios*, citizens of the Union alleging that they suffered maladministration at the hands of a Community institution (excluding the Court of Justice and the Court of First Instance acting in their judicial roles) as a means of providing such redress at an international level of administration (Art.195 (ex 138e) EC).

3. Today, some 90 countries have created ombudsmen, with a number of "emerging democracies" in Central and Eastern Europe, Latin America and Africa utilising these offices to try and safeguard human rights. Consequently, Professor Gregory has observed:

"looking back over the history of the Ombudsman around the world, what I notice is a combination of three inter-related developments, summed up by the ugly words: *proliferation*—as regards numbers; *diversification*—as regards categories and types; and *mutation and variation*—as regards functions and purpose".[1]

Selected general readings include: *Craig*, pp.233–252; *Wade and Forsyth*, pp.83–108; F. Stacey, *Ombudsmen Compared* (1978); *JUSTICE/All Souls Report*, Ch.5; P. Birkinshaw, *Grievances, Remedies and the State* (2nd ed., 1994), Ch.5; M. Seneviratne, *Ombudsmen in the Public Sector* (1994) and *Ombudsmen: Public Services and Administrative Justice* (2002), R. James, *Private Ombudsmen and Public Law* (1997) and R. Gregory and P. Giddings, *The Ombudsmen, the Citizens and Parliament* (2002)

(B) THE PARLIAMENTARY COMMISSIONER FOR ADMINISTRATION

(i) Constitutional and Jurisdictional Matters

PARLIAMENTARY COMMISSIONER ACT 1967

Appointment and tenure of office

1.—(1) For the purpose of conducting investigations in accordance with the following provisions of this Act there shall be appointed a Commissioner, to be known as the Parliamentary Commissioner for Administration.

(2) Her Majesty may by Letters Patent from time to time appoint a person to be the Commissioner, and any person so appointed shall (subject to [subsections (3) and (3A)] of this section) hold office during good behaviour.

(3) A person appointed to be the Commissioner may be relieved of office by Her Majesty at his own request, or may be removed from office by Her Majesty in consequence of Addresses from both Houses of Parliament, and shall in any case vacate office on completing the year of service in which he attains the age of sixty-five years.

[(3A) Her Majesty may declare the office of Commissioner to have been vacated if satisfied that the person appointed to be the Commissioner is incapable for medical reasons—

(a) of performing duties of his office; and
(b) of requesting to be relieved of it.] . . .[2]

Administrative provisions

3.—(1) The Commissioner may appoint such officers as he may determine with the approval of the Treasury as to numbers and conditions of service.

(2) Any function of the Commissioner under this Act may be performed by any officer of the Commissioner authorised for that purpose by the Commissioner [, by any members of the staff so authorised of the Welsh Administration Ombudsman or of the Health Service Commissioner for

---

[1] R. Gregory, Address to the British and Irish Ombudsman Association: AGM May 16, 1996, para.7; R. Gregory and P. Giddings "The Ombudsman Institution: Growth and Development" in Gregory and Giddings (ed.) *Righting Wrongs: The Ombudsman in Six Continents* (2000).
[2] Subsection (3A) added by the Parliamentary and Health Service Commissioners Act 1987, s.2(1).

Wales or by an officer so authorised of the Health Service Commissioner for England . . .][3]

(3) The expenses of the Commissioner under this Act, to such amount as may be sanctioned by the Treasury, shall be defrayed out of moneys provided by Parliament. . . .

Departments, etc., subject to investigation

[4.—(1) Subject to the provisions of this section and to the notes contained in Schedule 2 to this Act, this Act applies to the government departments, corporations and unincorporated bodies listed in that Schedule; and references in this Act to an authority to which this Act applies are references to any such corporation or body.

(2) Her Majesty may by Order in Council amend Schedule 2 to this Act by the alteration of any entry or note, the removal of any entry or note or the insertion of any additional entry or note.

(3) An Order in Council may only insert an entry if—

  (a) it relates—
      (i) to a government department; or
     (ii) to a corporation or body whose functions are exercised on behalf of the Crown; or
  (b) it relates to a corporation or body—
      (i) which is established by virtue of Her Majesty's prerogative or by an Act of Parliament or on Order in Council or order made under an Act of Parliament or which is established in any other way by a Minister of the Crown in his capacity as a Minister or by a government department;
     (ii) at least half of whose revenues derive directly from money provided by Parliament, a levy authorised by an enactment, a fee or charge of any other description so authorised or more than one of those sources; and
    (iii) which is wholly or partly constituted by appointment made by Her Majesty or a Minister of the Crown or government department.

[(3A) No entry shall be made if the result of making it would be that the Parlimentary commissioner could investigate action which can be investigated by the Welsh administration Ombudsman under Schedule 9 to the Government of Wales Act 1998.][4]

[(3B) No entry shall be made in respect of—

  (a) the Scottish Administration of any part of it;
  (b) any Scottish public authority with mixed functions or no reserved functions within the meaning of the Scotland Act 1998; or
  (c) the Scottish Parliamentary Corporate Body.][5]

---

[3] Substituted by the Government of Wales Act 1998, Sch.12, para.5 and amended by SI 2004/1823, art.5(1), (2).
[4] Inserted by the Government of Wales Act 1998, Sch.12, para.6.
[5] Substituted by SI 1999/1820, Sch.2, Pt I, para.39(1),(2).

(4) No entry shall be made in respect of a corporation or body whose sole activity is, or whose main activities are, included among the activities specified in subsection (5) below.

(5) The activities mentioned in subsection (4) above are—

(a) the provision of education, or the provision of training otherwise than under the Industrial Training Act 1982;
(b) the development of curricula, the conduct of examinations or the validation of educational courses;
(c) the control of entry to any profession or the regulation of the conduct of members of any profession;
(d) the investigation of complaints by members of the public regarding the actions of any person or body, or the supervision or review of such investigations or of steps taken following them.

(6) No entry shall be made in respect of a corporation or body operating in an exclusively or predominantly commercial manner or a corporation carrying on under national ownership an industry or undertaking or part of an industry or undertaking.

(7) Any statutory instrument made by virtue of this section shall be subject to annulment in pursuance of a resolution of either House of Parliament.

(8) In this Act—

(a) any reference to a government department to which this Act applies includes a reference to any of the Ministers or officers of such a department; and
(b) any reference to an authority to which this Act applies includes a reference to any members or officers of such an authority.] [6]

Matters subject to investigation

5.—(1) Subject to the provisions of this section, the Commissioner may investigate an action taken by or on behalf of a government department or other authority to which this Act applies, being action taken in the exercise of administrative functions of that department or authority, in any case where—

(a) a written complaint is duly made to a member of the House of Commons by a member of the public who claims to have sustained injustice in consequence of maladministration in connection with the action so taken; and
(b) the complaint is referred to the Commissioner, with the consent of the person who made it, by a member of that House with a request to conduct an investigation thereon.

[(1A) Subsection (1C) of this section applies if—

(a) a written complaint is duly made to a member of the House of Commons by a member of the public who claims that a person has

[6] Substituted by the Parliamentary and Health Services Commissioners Act 1987, s.1(1).

failed to perform a relevant duty owed by him to the member of the public, and (b) the complaint is referred to the Commissioner, with the consent of the person who made it, by a member of the House of Commons with a request to conduct an investigation into it.

(1B) For the purposes of subsection (1A) of this section a relevant duty is a duty imposed by any of these—

(a) a code of practice issued under section 32 of the Domestic Violence, Crime and Victims Act 2004 (cod of practice for victims), or (b) sections 35 to 44 of that Act (duties of local probation boards in connection with victims of sexual or violent offences).

(1C) If this subsection applies, the Commissioner may investigate the complaint.][7]

(2) Except as hereinafter provided, the Commissioner shall not conduct an investigation under this Act in respect of any of the following matters, that is to say—

(a) any action in respect of which the person aggrieved has or had a right of appeal, reference or review to or before a tribunal constituted by or under any enactment or by virtue of Her Majesty's prerogative;
(b) any action in respect of which the person aggrieved has or had a remedy by way of proceedings in any court of law;

Provided that the Commissioner may conduct an investigation notwithstanding that the person aggrieved has or had such a right or remedy if satisfied that in the particular circumstances it is not reasonable to expect him to resort or have resorted to it.

(3) Without prejudice to subsection (2) of this section, the Commissioner shall not conduct an [investigation under subsection (1) of this section][8] in respect of any such action or matter as is described in Schedule 3 to this Act.

(4) Her Majesty may by Order in Council amend the said Schedule 3 so as to exclude from the provisions of that Schedule such actions or matters as may be described in the Order; and any statutory instrument made by virtue of this subsection shall be subject to annulment in pursuance of a resolution of either House of Parliament.

[(4A) Without prejudice to subsection (2) of this section, the Commissioner shall not conduct an investigation pursuant to a complaint under subsection (1A) of this section in respect of—

(a) action taken by or with the authority of the Secretary of State for the purposes of protecting the security of the State, including action so taken with respect to passports, or (b) any action or matter described in any of paragraphs 1 to 4 and 6A to 11 of Schedule 3 to this Act.

---

[7] Inserted by the Domestic Violence, Crime and Victims Act 2004. Sch.7, paras 1, 2, in force from a day to be appointed.
[8] Inserted by the 2004 Act, Sch.7, paras 1, 2(1), 3, replacing the words "investigation under the Act" from a day to be appointed.

(4B) Her Majesty may by Order in Council amend subsection (4A) of this section so as to exclude from paragraph (a) or (b) of that subsection such actions or matters as may be described in the Order. (4C) Any statutory instrument made by virtue of subsection (4B) of this section shall be subject to annulment in pursuance of a resolution of either House of parliament.][9]

(5) In determining whether to initiate, continue or discontinue an investigation under this Act, the Commissioner shall, subject to the foregoing provisions of this section, act in accordance with his own discretion; and any question whether a complaint is duly made under this Act shall be determined by the Commissioner.

[(5A) For the purposes of this section, administrative functions of a government department to which this Act applies include functions exercised by the department on behalf of the Scottish Ministers by virtue of section 93 of the Scotland Act 1998.

(5B) The Commissioner shall not conduct an investigation under this Act in respect of any action concerning Scotland and not relating to reserved matters which is taken by or on behalf of a cross-border public authority within the meaning of the Scotland Act 1998.][10]

[(6) For the purposes of this section, administrative functions exercisable by any person appointed by the Lord Chancellor as a member of the administrative staff of any court or tribunal shall be taken to be administrative functions of the Lord Chancellor's Department or, in Northern Ireland, of the Northern Ireland Court Service.][11];

[(7) For the purposes of this section, administrative functions exercisable by any person appointed as a member of the administrative staff of a relevant tribunal—

(a) by a government department or authority to which this Act applies; or
(b) with the consent (whether as to remuneration and other terms and conditions of service or otherwise) of such a department or authority,

shall be taken to be administrative functions of that department or authority.

(8) In subsection (7) of this section, "relevant tribunal" means a tribunal listed in Schedule 4 to this Act [constituted under Chapter I of Part I of the Social Security Act 1998].[12]

(9) Her Majesty may by Order in Council amend the said Schedule 4 by the alteration or removal of any entry or the insertion of any additional entry; and any statutory instrument made by virtue of this subsection shall be subject to annulment in pursuance of a resolution of either House of Parliament.][13] . . .

Provisions relating to complaints

6.—(1) A complaint under this Act may be made by any individual, or by any body of persons whether incorporated or not, not being—

---

[9] Inserted by the 2004 Act, Sch.7, paras 1, 2(1), (4) from a day to be appointed.
[10] Inserted by SI 1999/1820, Sch.2, Pt I, para.39(1), (3)(a).
[11] Inserted by the Courts and Legal Services Act 1990, s.110(1).
[12] Substituted for the words "listed in Schedule 4 to this Act" by the Social Security Act 1998, Sch.7, para.3(1), from a day to be appointed.
[13] Inserted by the Parliamentary Commissioner Act 1994, s.1(1).

(a) a local authority or other authority or body constituted for purposes of the public service or of local government or for the purposes of carrying on under national ownership any industry or undertaking or part of an industry or undertaking;

[(b) any other authority or body within subsection (1A) below.

(1A) An authority or body is within this subsection if—

(a) its members are appointed by—
   (i) Her Majesty;
   (ii) any Minister of the Crown;
   (iii) any government department;
   (iv) the Scottish Ministers;
   (v) the First Minister; or
   (vi) the Lord Advocate, or
(b) its revenues consist wholly or mainly of—
   (i) money provided by Parliament; or
   (ii) sums payable out of the Scottish Consolidated Fund (directly or indirectly).][14]

(2) Where the person by whom a complaint might have been made under the foregoing provisions of this Act has died or is for any reason unable to act for himself, the complaint may be made by his personal representative or by a member of his family or other individual suitable to represent him; but except as aforesaid a complaint shall not be entertained under this Act unless made by the person aggrieved himself.

(3) A complaint shall not be entertained under this Act unless it is made to a member of the House of Commons not later than twelve months from the day on which the person aggrieved first had notice of the matters alleged in the complaint; but the Commissioner may conduct an investigation pursuant to a complaint not made within that period if he considers that there are special circumstances which make it proper to do so.

(4) [Except as provided in subsection (5) below] a complaint shall not be entertained under this Act unless the person aggrieved is resident in the United Kingdom (or, if he is dead, was so resident at the time of his death) or the complaint relates to action taken in relation to him while he was present in the United Kingdom or on an installation in a designated area within the meaning of the Continental Shelf Act 1964 or on a ship registered in the United Kingdom or an aircraft so registered, or in relation to rights or obligations which accrued or arose in the United Kingdom or on such an installation, a ship or aircraft.

[(5) A complaint may be entertained under this Act in circumstances not falling within subsection (4) above where—

(a) the complaint relates to action taken in any country or territory outside the United Kingdom by an officer (not being an honorary consular officer) in the exercise of a consular function on behalf of the Government of the United Kingdom; and
(b) the person aggrieved is a citizen of the United Kingdom and Colonies who, under section 2 of the Immigration Act 1971, has the right of abode in the United Kingdom.][15]

[14] Inserted by SI 1999/1820, Sch.2, Pt I, para.39(1), (4).
[15] Added by the Parliamentary Commissioner (Consular Complaints) Act 1981, s.1.

Procedures in respect of investigations

7.—(1) Where the Commissioner proposes to conduct an investigation pursuant to a complaint under [section 5(1) of][16] this Act, he shall afford to the principal officer of the department of authority concerned, and to any person who is alleged in the complaint to have taken or authorised the action complained of, an opportunity to comment on any allegations contained in the complaint.

[(1A) Where the Commissioner proposes to conduct an investigation pursuant to a complaint under section 5(1A) of this Act, he shall give the person to whom the complaint relates an opportunity to comment on any allegations contained in the complaint][17]

(2) Every such [investigation under this Act][18] shall be conducted in private, but except as aforesaid the procedure for conducting an investigation shall be such as the Commissioner considers appropriate in the circumstances of the case; and without prejudice to the generality of the foregoing provision the Commissioner may obtain information from such persons and in such manner, and make such inquiries, as he thinks fit, and may determine whether any person may be represented, by counsel or solicitor or otherwise, in the investigation.

(3) The Commissioner may, if he thinks fit, pay to the person by whom the complaint was made and to any other person who attends or furnishes information for the purposes of an investigation under this Act—

(a) sums in respect of expenses properly incurred by them;
(b) allowances by way of compensation for the loss of their time,

in accordance with such scales and subject to such conditions as may be determined by the Treasury.

(4) The conduct of an investigation under this Act shall not affect any action taken by the department or authority concerned, [or the persons to whom the complaint relates][19], or any power or duty of that department, authority or person to take further action with respect to any matters subject to the investigation; but where the person aggrieved has been removed from the United Kingdom under any Order in force under the Aliens Restriction Acts 1914 and 1919 or under the Commonwealth Immigrants Act 1962, he shall, if the Commissioner so directs, be permitted to re-enter and remain in the United Kingdom, subject to such conditions as the Secretary of State may direct, for the purposes of the investigation.

---

[16] Inserted by the 2004 Act, Sch.7, paras 1, 3, in force from a day to be appointed.
[17] Inserted by *ibid.*, in force from a day to be appointed.
[18] Inserted by *ibid.*, in force from a day to be appointed, replacing the words "such investigation".
[19] Inserted by *ibid.*, in force from a day to be appointed, replacing the words "that department or authority".

Evidence

8.—(1) For the purposes of an investigation under [section 5(1) of][20] this Act the Commissioner may require any Minister, officer or member of the department or authority concerned or any other person who in his opinion is able to furnish information or produce documents relevant to the investigation to furnish any such information or produce any such document.

[(A) For the purposes of an investigation pursuant to a complaint under section 5(1A) of this Act the Commissioner may require any person who in his opinion is able to furnish information or produce documents relevant to the investigation to furnish any such information or produce any such document.][21]

(2) For the purposes of any [investigation under this Act][22] the Commissioner shall have the same powers as the Court in respect of the attendance and examination of witnesses (including the administration of oaths or affirmations and the examination of witnesses abroad) and in respect of the production of documents.

(3) No obligation to maintain secrecy or other restriction upon the disclosure of information obtained by or furnished to persons in Her Majesty's service, whether imposed by any enactment or by any rule of law, shall apply to the disclosure of information for the purposes of an investigation under this Act; and the Crown shall not be entitled in relation to any such investigation to any such privilege in respect of the production of documents or the giving of evidence as is allowed by law in legal proceedings.

(4) No person shall be required or authorised by virtue of this Act to furnish any information or answer any question relating to proceedings of the Cabinet or of any committee of the Cabinet or to produce so much of any document as relates to such proceedings; and for the purposes of this subsection a certificate issued by the Secretary of the Cabinet with the approval of the Prime Minister and certifying that any information, question, document or part of a document so relates shall be conclusive.

(5) Subject to subsection (3) of this section, no person shall be compelled for the purposes of an investigation under this Act to give any evidence or produce any document which he could not be compelled to give or produce in [civil][23] proceedings before the Court.

Obstruction and contempt

9.—(1) If any person without lawful excuse obstructs the Commissioner or any officer of the Commissioner in the performance of his functions under this Act, or is guilty of any act or omission in relation to any investigation under this Act which, if that investigation were a proceeding in the Court, would constitute contempt of court, the Commissioner may certify the offence to the Court.

---

[20] Inserted by the 2004 Act, Sch.7, paras 1, 4, from a day to be appointed.
[21] Inserted by *ibid.*, in force from a day to be appointed.
[22] Inserted by *ibid.*, in force from a day to be appointed, replacing the words "such investigation".
[23] Inserted by the Civil Evidence Act 1968, s.17(1)(b).

(2) Where an offence is certified under this section, the Court may inquire into the matter and, after hearing any witnesses who may be produced against or on behalf of the person charged with the offence, and after hearing any statement that may be offered in defence, deal with him in any manner in which the Court could deal with him if he had committed the like offence in relation to the Court.

(3) Nothing in this section shall be construed as applying to the taking of any such action as is mentioned in subsection (4) of section 7 of this Act.

Reports by Commissioner

10.—(1) In any case where the Commissioner conducts an investigation under [section 5(1) of][24] this Act or decides not to conduct such an investigation, he shall send to the member of the House of Commons by whom the request for investigation was made (or if he is no longer a member of that House, to such member of that House as the Commissioner thinks appropriate) a report of the results of the investigation or, as the case may be, a statement of his reasons for not conducting an investigation.

(2) In any case where the Commissioner conducts an investigation under this Act, he shall also send a report of the results of the investigation to the principal officer of the department or authority concerned and to any other person who is alleged in the relevant complaint to have taken or authorised the action complained of.

[(2A) In any case where the Commissioner conducts an investigation pursuant to a complaint under section 5(1A) of this Act, he shall also send a report of the results of the investigation to the person to whom the complaint relates.][25]

(3) If, after conducting an investigation under [section 5(1) of][26] this Act, it appears to the Commissioner that injustice has been caused to the person aggrieved in consequence of maladministration and that the injustice has not been, or will not be, remedied, he may, if he thinks fit, lay before each House of Parliament a special report upon the case.

[(3A) If, after conducting an investigation pursuant to a complaint under section 5(1A) of this Act, it appears to the Commissioner that—

(a) the person to whom the complaint relates has failed to perform a relevant duty owed by him to the person aggrieved, and
(b) the failure has not been, or will not be, remedied,

the Commissioner may, if he thinks fit, lay before each House of Parliament a special report upon the case.

(3B) For the purpose of subsection (3A) of this section "relevant duty" has the meaning given by section 5(1B) of this Act.][27]

(4) The Commissioner shall annually lay before each House of Parliament a general report on the performance of his functions under this Act and may

---

[24] Inserted by the 2004 Act, Sch.7, para.5, from a day to be appointed.
[25] *Ibid.*
[26] *Ibid.*
[27] *Ibid.*

from time to time lay before each House of Parliament such other reports with respect to those functions as he thinks fit.

(5) For the purposes of the law of defamation, any such publication as is hereinafter mentioned shall be absolutely privileged, that is to say—

    (a) the publication of any matter by the Commissioner in making a report to either House of Parliament for the purposes of this Act;

    (b) the publication of any matter by a member of the House of Commons in communicating with the Commissioner or his officers for those purposes or by the Commissioner or his officers in communicating with such a member for those purposes;

    (c) the publication by such a member to the person by whom a complaint was made under this Act of a report or statement sent to the member in respect of the complaint in pursuance of section (1) of this section;

    (d) the publication by the Commissioner to such a person as is mentioned in subsection (2) [or (2A)][28] of this section of a report to that person in pursuance of that subsection.

Provision for secrecy of information

11.—(1) . . .[29]

(2) Information obtained by the Commissioner or his officers in the course of or for the purposes of an investigation under this Act shall not be disclosed except—

    (a) for the purposes of the investigation and of any report to be made thereon under this Act;

    (b) for the purposes of any proceedings for an offence under [the Official Secrets Act 1911 to 1989][30] alleged to have been committed in respect of information obtained by the Commissioner or any of his officers by virtue of this Act or for an offence of perjury alleged to have been committed in the course of an investigation under this Act or for the purposes of an inquiry with a view to the taking of such proceedings; or

    (c) for the purposes of any proceedings under section 9 of this Act;

and the Commissioner and his officers shall not be called upon to give evidence in any proceedings (other than such proceedings as aforesaid) of matters coming to his or their knowledge in the course of an investigation under this Act.

[(2A) Where the Commissioner also holds office as [Welsh Administration Ombudsmen or][31] a Health Service Commissioner and a person initiates a complaint to him in his capacity as [Welsh Administration Ombudsmen or a Health Service Commissioner][32] which relates partly to a matter with respect to which that person has previously initiated a complaint under this Act,

---

[28] Inserted by the 2004 Act, Sch.7, para.5, from a day to be appointed.
[29] Repealed by the Official Secrets Act 1989, s.16(4), Sch.2.
[30] Substituted by the Official Secrets Act 1989, s.16(3), Sch.1, para.1.
[31] Inserted or substituted by the Government of Wales Act 1998, Sch.12, para.7.
[32] *Ibid.*

or subsequently initiates such a complaint, information obtained by the Commissioner or his officers in the course of or for the purposes of investigating the complaint under this Act may be disclosed for the purposes of his carrying out his functions in relation to the other complaint.][33]

(3) A Minister of the Crown may give notice in writing to the Commissioner, with respect to any document or information specified in the notice, or any class of documents or information so specified, that in the opinion of the Minister the disclosure of that document or information, or of documents or information of that class, would be prejudicial to the safety of the State or otherwise contrary to the public interest; and where such a notice is given nothing in this Act shall be construed as authorising or requiring the Commissioner or any officer of the Commissioner to communicate to any person or for any purpose any document or information specified in the notice, or any document or information of a class so specified.

(4) The references in this section to a Minister of the Crown include references to the Commissioners of Customs and Excise and the Commissioners of Inland Revenue.

[(5) Information obtained from the Information Commissioner by virtue of section 76(1) of the Freedom of Information Act 2000 shall be treated for the purposes of subsection (2) of this section as obtained for the purposes of an investigation under this Act and, in relation to such information, the reference in paragraph (a) of that subsection to the investigation shall have effect as a reference to any investigation.][34]

The Criminal Injuries Compensation Scheme

[**11B**—(1) For the purposes of this Act, administrative functions exercisable by an administrator of the Criminal Injuries Compensation Scheme ("Scheme functions") shall be taken to be administrative functions of a government department to which this Act applies.

(2) For the purposes of this section, the following are administrators of the Scheme—

(a) a claims officer appointed under section 3(4)(b) of the Criminal Injuries Compensation Act 1995;
(b) a person appointed under section 5(3)(c) of that Act;
(c) the Scheme manager, as defined by section 1(4) of that Act, and any person assigned by him to exercise functions in relation to the Scheme.

(3) The principal officer in relation to any complaint made in respect of any action taken in respect of Scheme functions is—

(a) in the case of action taken by a claims officer, such person as may from time to time be designated by the Secretary of State for the purposes of this paragraph;
(b) in the case of action taken by a person appointed under section 5(3)(c) of the Act of 1995, the chairman appointed by the Secretary of State under section 5(3)(b) of that Act; or

---

[33] Inserted by the Parliamentary and Health Service Commissioners Act 1987, s.4(1).
[34] Inserted by the Freedom of Information Act 2000, Sch.7, para.1.

(c) in the case of action taken by the Scheme manager or by any other person mentioned in subsection (2)(c) of this section, the Scheme manager.

(4) The conduct of an investigation under this Act in respect of any action taken in respect of Scheme functions shall not affect—

(a) any action so taken; or
(b) any power or duty of any person to take further action with respect to any matters subject to investigation.] [35]

Interpretation

12.—(1) In this Act the following expressions have the meanings hereby respectively assigned to them, that is to say—

"action" includes failure to act, and other expressions connoting action shall be construed accordingly;
"the Commissioner" means the Parliamentary Commissioner for Administration;
"the Court" means, in relation to England and Wales the High Court, in relation to Scotland the Court of Session, and in relation to Northern Ireland the High Court of Northern Ireland;
"enactment" includes an enactment of the Parliament of Northern Ireland and any instrument made by virtue of an enactment;
"officer" includes employee;
"person aggrieved" means the person who claims or is alleged to have sustained such injustice as is mentioned in section 5(1)(a) of this Act;
["person aggrieved"—

(a) in relation to a complaint under section 5(1) of this Act, means the person who claims or is alleged to have sustained such injustice as is mentioned in section 5(1)(a) of this Act;
(b) in relation to a complaint under section 5(1A) of this Act, means the person to whom the duty referred to in section 5(1A)(a) of this Act is or is alleged to be owed;] [36]

"tribunal" includes the person constituting a tribunal consisting of one person.

(2) References to this Act to any enactment are references to that enactment as amended or extended by or under any other enactment.

(3) It is hereby declared that nothing in this Act authorises or requires the Commissioner to question the merits of a decision taken without maladministration by a government department or other authority in the exercise of a discretion vested in that department or authority. . . .

---

[35] Inserted by the Criminal Injuries Compensation Act 1995, s.10(1).
[36] Substituted for the previous definition by the 2004 Act, Sch.7, paras 1, 6, from a day to be appointed.

SCHEDULE 2

DEPARTMENTS, ETC. SUBJECT TO INVESTIGATION

[Sch.2 as substituted by SI 2005/249 lists 280 bodies. It includes each government department and a wide range of public bodies including ACAS, the Arts Council, the British Council, the British Tourist Authority, the Charity Commission, the Competition Commission, the Disability Rights Commission, the Equal Opportunities Commission, the Commission for Racial Equality, the Electoral Commission, the Environment Agency, the Forestry Commission, the Health and Safety Commission and Executive, the Information Commission, the Land Registry, the Legal Services Commission, the Standards Board for England, the Committee on Standards of Public Life, the Sports Council, urban development corporations and the Urban Regeneration Agency, advisory committees, regulators and national museums and galleries.]

SCHEDULE 3

MATTERS NOT SUBJECT TO INVESTIGATION

1. Action taken in matters certified by a Secretary of State or other Minister of the Crown to affect relations or dealings between the Government of the United Kingdom and any other Government or any international organisation of States or Governments.

2. Action taken, in any country or territory outside the United Kingdom, by or on behalf of any officer representing or acting under the authority of Her Majesty in respect of the United Kingdom, or any other officer of the Government of the United Kingdom other than action which is taken by an officer (not being an honorary consular officer) in the exercise of a consular function on behalf of the Government of the United Kingdom. . . .

3. Action taken in connection with the administration of the government of any country or territory outside the United Kingdom which forms part of Her Majesty's dominions or in which Her Majesty has jurisdiction.

[**4.** Action taken by the Secretary of State under the Extradition Act 2003].

5. Action taken by or with the authority of the Secretary of State for the purposes of investigating crime or of protecting the security of the State, including action so taken with respect to passports.

6. The commencement or conduct of civil or criminal proceedings before any court of law in the United Kingdom, of proceedings at any place under the Naval Discipline Act 1957, the Army Act 1955 or the Air Force Act 1955, or of proceedings before any international court or tribunal.

[**6A.** Action taken by any person appointed by the Lord Chancellor as a member of the administrative staff of any court or tribunal, so far as that action is taken at the direction, or on the authority (whether express or implied), of any person acting in a judicial capacity or in his capacity as a member of the tribunal.

6B.—(1) Action taken by any member of the administrative staff of a relevant tribunal, so far as that action is taken at the direction, or on the authority (whether express or implied), of any person acting in his capacity as a member of the tribunal.

(2) In this paragraph, "relevant tribunal" has the meaning given by section 5(8) of this Act.]

6C. Action taken by any person appointed under section 5(3)(c) of the Criminal Injuries Compensation Act 1995, so far as that action is taken at the direction, or on the authority (whether express or implied), of any person acting in his capacity as an adjudicator appointed under section 5 of that Act to determine appeals.

7. Any exercise of the prerogative of mercy or of the power of a Secretary of State to make a reference in respect of any person to [. . .] the High Court of Justiciary or the Courts-Martial Appeal Court.

8. [(1)] Action taken on behalf of the Minister of Health or the Secretary of State by [a Strategic Health Authority,] [a Health Authority, a Primary Care Trust, a Special Health Authority], [except the Rampton Hospital Review Board] [. . . the Rampton Hospital Board,][the Broadmoor Hospital Board or the Moss Side and Park Lane Hospitals Board,] [. . . a Health Board or the Common Services Agency for the Scottish Health Service] [by the Dental Practice Board or the Scottish Dental Practice Board], or by the Public Health Laboratory Service Board.

[(2) For the purposes of this paragraph, action taken by a [Strategic Health Authority,] Health Authority, Special Health Authority or Primary Care Trust in the exercise of fuctions of the Secretary of State shall be regarded as action taken on his behalf.]

9. Action taken in matters relating to contractual or other commercial trans-actions, whether within the United Kingdom or elsewhere, being transactions of a government department or authority to which this Act applies or of any such authority or body as is mentioned in paragraph (a) or (b) of subsection (1) of section 6 of this Act and not being transactions for or relating to—

(a) the acquisition of land compulsorily or in circumstances in which it could be acquired compulsorily;

(b) the disposal as surplus of land acquired compulsorily or in such circumstances as aforesaid.

10.—(1) Action taken in respect of appointments or removals, pay, discipline, superannuation or other personnel matters, in relation to—

(a) service in any of the armed forces of the Crown, including reserve and auxiliary and cadet forces;

(b) service in any office or employment under the Crown or under any authority [to which this Act applies]; or

(c) service in any office or employment, or under any contract for services, in respect of which power to take action, or to determine or approve the action to be taken, in such matters is vested in Her Majesty, any Minister of the Crown or any such authority as aforesaid.

(2) Sub-paragraph (1)(c) above shall not apply to any action (not otherwise excluded from investigation by this Schedule) which is taken by the Secretary of State in connection with:

(a) the provision of information relating to the terms and conditions of any employment covered by an agreement entered into by him under section 12(1) of the Overseas Development and Cooperation Act 1980 [or pursuant to the exercise of his powers under Part I of the International Development Act 2002].

or

(b) the provision of any allowance, grant or supplement or any benefit (other than those relating to superannuation) arising from the designation of any person in accordance with such an agreement.

11. The grant of honours, awards or privileges within the gift of the Crown, including the grant of Royal Charters.[37]

Notes

1. Other points are that the PCA is paid the same salary as a Permanent Secretary, which is charged to the Consolidated Fund (s.2, as amended by the Parliamentary and other Pensions and Salaries Act 1976, s.6). Provision is made enabling the appointment of an Acting Commissioner where the office becomes vacant (s.3A, inserted by the Parliamentary and Health Service Commissioners Act 1987, s.6(1)); for consultation between the PCA, and the Welsh Administration Ombudsman or Health Service Commissioner (if they are different people) where matters relate to more than one jurisdiction (s.11A, inserted by the 1987 Act. s.4(2), and subsequently amended); and for the disclosure of information to the Information Commissioner for specified purposes under the Data Protection Act 1998 or the Freedom of Information Act 2000 (s.11AA, inserted by the 2000 Act, Sch.7, para.2).

2. At the time of writing (April 2005) there have been eight holders of the office of PCA. The first seven had backgrounds as civil servants or lawyers. The current Parliamentary (and Health Service) Ombudsman, Ann Abrahams, has a very different background, working for 10 years in social housing before becoming, in succession, Chief Executive of the National Association of Citizens Advice Bureaux and Legal Services Ombudsman. She has been described by the chair of the Public Administration Select Committee as "pushing at the boundaries of the office in a way that I think is to be commended: an activist ombudsman" (PASC Minister of Evidence, December 2, 2004).

3. *Exclusions from jurisdiction.* There has been continuing debate over the various exclusions from the PCA's jurisdiction. Local government and the NHS have for many years been covered by separate ombudsmen. The HSC's jurisdiction is not confined to complaints of injustice caused by maladministration and was extended in 1996 to include the questioning of clinical judgments (Health Service Commissioners Act 1993, ss.3, 5, as amended by the Health Service Commissioners (Amendment) Act 1996, s.6; M. Seneviratne, *Ombudsmen: Public Services and Administrative Justice* (2002), Ch.5).

The range of NDPBs included in Sch.2 have expanded significantly, most notably in 1999 when an additional 111 executive and 47 advisory NDPBs were added. Very few executive NDPBs are now excluded (reasons were given in an Annex to 1998–99 HC 817; examples included the Criminal Cases Review Commission, the Police Complaints Authority, the Audit Commission and the Student Loans Company, which were either similar bodies to the PCA or largely concerned with matters excluded from the PCA's jurisdiction). On the other hand, only advisory bodies with significant dealings with the public are included, leaving out such bodies as the Low Pay Commission whose only dealings with the public are as information gatherers to advise government (Fourth Report from the Select Committee on the PCA 1998–99 HC 817, Government Response to the First Report).

The continued exclusion of personnel and contractual matters remains controversial, given that such matters are covered by the European Ombudsman and many ombudsmen abroad, and that they still involve exercises of governmental power; the

---

[37] The legislative origins of the amendments to this Schedule are not included for reasons of space.

arguments offered in favour of the exclusions tend to be assertions that the position of a complainer as an employee or customer is "different" from that as a citizen rather than a fully reasoned justification (see the discussion by Seneviratne, *op. cit.*, pp.105–110; *cf.* below, pp.174, 186).

There is discretion to investigate where the person aggrieved has or had the right to appeal to a tribunal or minister or a remedy by way of proceedings in any court of law (1967 Act, s.5(2)). Where the possible remedy is from a court, the discretion is normally exercised in the complainant's favour, given the delays and expense inherent in such proceedings (see Seneviratne, *op. cit.*, p.113). The same approach is adopted by the LGO (see E. Osmotherley (Chairman of the CLA), "The Local Government Ombudsmen as an Alternative to Judicial Review" (*www.lgo.org.uk*)), noting many examples of investigations into matters that could have been the subject of judicial review proceedings, but also that the LGO will not investigate if the dispute turns on a point of law or statutory interpretation. He also cited the Court of Appeal's strong endorsement of the LGO's decision to investigate matters relating to interest and the fettering of discretion in *R. v Local Commissioner for Administration in North and North East England Ex p. Liverpool City Council* [2001] 1 All E.R. 462, the court emphasising the importance of the LGO's investigatory powers and that the complainants were a group in modest housing unlikely to have the means to pursue judicial review. A narrower approach suggested by Woolf L.J. in *R. v Commissioner for Local Administration Ex p. Croydon LBC* [1989] 1 All E.R. 1033, that such cases should normally be dealt with by judicial review, the LGO only investigating in "particular circumstances" has unsurprisingly not prevailed in the light of the modern emphasis on ADR, Lord Woolf himself expressing extra-judicially a similar view to the *Liverpool* case (see Seneviratne, *op. cit.*, p.57).

There is, however, no jurisdiction to investigate where a judicial remedy has been obtained on the facts (even though different from a remedy obtainable via the ombudsman, here compensation) (*R. v Local Commissioner for Administration Ex p.H (a minor)* (1999) 1 L.G.L.R. 932, in respect of the Local Government Act 1974, s.26(6)(c)); and even where proceedings seeking such a remedy have been commenced (*R.(on the application of Scholarstica Uno) v Commissioner for Local Administration for England* [2003] EWHC (Admin) 3202; [2004] E.L.R. 265).

It is submitted that this is unfortunate, and the matter should be left to the exercise of the ombudsman's discretion, to facilitate the easier, quicker and fairer resolution of relatively small matters without the necessity for judicial review.

4. *Maladministration*: The key concept in delimiting the statutory jurisdiction of the PCA is that of "maladministration". This concept had its origins in the JUSTICE report of 1961,[38] as they believed that this norm of administrative behaviour would prevent the Parliamentary Commissioner from unduly encroaching upon the exercise of discretionary powers by examining if the particular decisions reached were "wrong or unwelcome". During the enactment of the 1967 Act, the Leader of the House of Commons (Richard Crossman) acknowledged that the Government had not been able to define comprehensively the concept of maladministration. Instead, he proposed a non-statutory list containing some of the characteristics of this concept including, "bias, neglect, inattention, delay, incompetence, inaptitude, perversity, turpitude, arbitrariness and so on".[39] Subsequently, this description of maladministration has become known as the "Crossman catalogue".

After several years the PCA's use of maladministration was analysed by Dr G. Marshall. He concluded, "the view (that certainly follows from the Crossman catalogue approach) that maladministration may be inferred from, and can consist in, a complete lack of merits implies that the distinction between merits and maladministration drawn in the 1967 Act is incoherent . . .".[40] Consequently, he favoured

---

[38] *The Citizen and the Administration* (1961).
[39] HC Deb. Vol.754, col.51 (1966).
[40] G. Marshall, "Maladministration" [1973] P.L. 32.

the abandonment of the concept of maladministration with all its ambiguities as the foundation of the PCA's jurisdiction.

In 1977 another report from JUSTICE[41]suggested the replacement of "maladministration", with the PCA being empowered to investigate "unreasonable, unjust, or oppressive action" by government departments. However, this idea was rejected by the Select Committee on the PCA as they did not believe that the new jurisdiction would enable the Parliamentary Commissioner to investigate or criticise anything that did not already come within his authority.[42] The JUSTICE/All Souls report accepted the view of Sir Cecil Clothier (who was PCA during the early 1980s) that "maladministration" was "a wholly adequate basis for his investigations". Therefore, they did not propose any alterations to this concept.[43]

In 1994, the PCA expressed the view that: "to define maladministration is to limit it. Such a limitation could work to the disadvantage of individual complainants with justified grievances which did not fit within a given definition". However, he supplemented the Crossman catalogue with other examples of maladministration including: unwillingness to treat the complainant as a person with rights; refusal to answer reasonable questions; knowingly giving advice which is misleading or inadequate; and showing bias whether because of colour, sex or any other grounds. (Annual Report for 1993–1994, para.7; 1993–94 HC 290).

A practical appreciation of the way in which the concept of maladministration has been invoked by various Parliamentary Commissioners can be ascertained from the extracts below at p.181, examining the casework of the Ombudsman.

The courts have considered the scope of the term "maladministration" in relation to several ombudsman jurisdictions, but have not been in a position to offer a detailed definition. The Court of Appeal in *Eastleigh* (below, p.188, concerning the LGO) held that it concerned the *manner* in which decisions are reached or implemented not the nature, quality and reasonableness of the decision itself (*cf.* Marshall's earlier analysis of PCA decisions, above p.172). This position has been firmly maintained by the courts in a battle with the previous Pensions Ombudsman, Dr Julian Farrand, over the scope of his jurisdiction over complaints of maladministration (see eg. Lightman J. in *R. v Pensions Ombudsmen Ex p. Legal & General Assurance Society Ltd* [2000] 1 W.L.R. 1524, and an extra-judicial lecture, "The Pensions Ombudsman and the Courts" (*www.dca.gov.uk/judicial/speeches*)). See further R. Nobles, [2001] P.L. 308. Beyond this, the courts have not provided guidance. In *R. v Parliamentary Commissioner for Administration Ex p. Balchin (No.1)* [1998] 1 P.L.R. 1, Sedley J. said that:

> "so far as a court of judicial review is concerned the question is not how maladministration should be defined but only whether the Commissioner's decision is within the range of meaning which the English language and the statutory purpose together make possible. For the rest, the question whether any given set of facts amounts to maladministration—or by parity of reasoning, to injustice—is for the Commissioner alone".

The term "maladministration" is not synonymous with illegality. This was confirmed in *R. v Local Commissioner for Administration in North and North East England Ex p. Liverpool City Council* [2001] 1 All E.R. 462, where the Court of Appeal held that the LGO was entitled to find that a failure to declare an interest in breach of the test laid down in the National Code of Local Government Conduct (reasonable suspicion of bias) constituted maladministration even though this differed from what was then the test in law under the *nemo judex* principle (real danger of bias) (see below, p.755).

5. *Injustice.* This concept is not confined to injury redressible in a court of law, but includes the sense of outrage caused by maladministration (Sedley J. in *Balchin (No.1)*

---

[41] *Our Fettered Ombudsman.*
[42] *Review of Access and Jurisdiction* (1977–78 HC 615).
[43] Report, Ch.5.

(above) and the loss of an opportunity (Collins J. in *R. v Commissioner of Local Administration Ex p. S* (1998) 1 L.G.L.R. 633 at 638).

6. In 1993, the Select Committee on the PCA (see below, p.184), published a major report on *The Powers, Work and Jurisdiction of the Ombudsman* (1993–94 HC 33). The Committee recommended, *inter alia*, retention of the MP filter, a new power to investigate a matter raised by the Select Committee, and the conferment of a general jurisdiction over all central government bodies unless specifically excluded. The Government was unwilling to accept the proposal to allow the Select Committee to initiate investigations by the Ombudsman. "While a power to initiate investigations without having received a complaint from a member of the public would allow the Ombudsman to be more proactive, it would also, as he has noted, represent a fundamental change from the concept that his basic role is to investigate and suggest redress for people's grievances" (1993–94 HC 619): para.18). No legislative changes followed.

A Cabinet Office Report in 2000 by Philip Collcutt and Mary Hourihan, *Review of the Public Sector Ombudsmen in England* (2000), set up in response to proposals from the Commission for Local Administration and the PCA, recommended the creation of a new Commission for England, built on the modernisation and consolidation of the existing legislation. There would be a collegiate structure with a number of ombudsmen. Each would have personal jurisdiction across the entire work of the Commission, although specific Local Government and Health Service Ombudsmen roles would be retained. Each could then deal straightforwardly with matters that currently cross the jurisdiction of two or more of the existing offices. The MP filter would be abolished. More complaints could be dealt with more flexibly without increasing resources. Overall there should be no reduction in the Commission's jurisdiction, and separate consideration given to whether there should be any extension. An ombudsman's function should remain grounded in addressing injustice caused to an individual and "own-initiative investigation appears inconsistent with impartiality".

The report made many detailed operational recommendations, encouraging the greater use of informal contacts and processes, and a single "gateway" for complainants. The core concept should be that of the ombudsman seeking resolution, by an agreed settlement if possible, with investigation and the ability to make recommendations as an option. The Review did not endorse suggestions for a "Commission for Public Administration" with a wide role in overseeing the standard of public administration, perhaps conducting research and setting general standards for good administration as this would be a major change in the role of the ombudsman and reduce the focus on the core role (para.6.86). The ombudsman's recommendation should continue not to be binding. A unit in the Cabinet Office should be established to provide strong and vigorous co-ordination of complaints processes across public services (central and local government and the NHS).

The Cabinet Office issued a Consultation Paper in June 2000 (available at the Cabinet Office website), to which the Select Committee on Public Administration (Third Report, 1999–2000 HC 612) unequivocally supported the key recommendations for a single Commission and abolition of the MP filter, but agreed with the view of a witness that the assumption that extra resources would not be needed was "optimistic, not to say naïve" (para.12). It agreed that the legislation should specify bodies outside the jurisdiction rather than those within it. All the current substantive exclusions (such as personnel and contractual matters) and the issues concerning the merit of official decisions should be reviewed. Local government ombudsmen should come under parliamentary oversight, subject to conditions.

Following consultation, the Government expressed itself satisfied that there was "broad support for the review's main recommendations" and that it therefore intended to replace the existing arrangements by a unified and flexible ombudsman body for central and local government and the NHS (excluding NHS pensions). Proposals for the precise arrangements and on whether the jurisdiction should be extended beyond the bodies subject to the existing ombudsmen would be published in due course (Lord Macdonald, HL Deb., October 15, 2001, c.WA 78). All this is very sensible. However, there has subsequently been no apparent progress, apart from the Government's announcement in January 2002 that there would be a further consultation exercise, and the Select Committee has repeated its concerns at the delay and asked for the production of a draft Bill (Third Report, 2002–03 HC 448, paras 1–11). The Government's response merely indicated support for more co-operation across the Ombudsmen community within the existing statutory arrangements (Cm.5890, 2003). Nevertheless, it should only be a matter of time before England follows the path adopted for Scotland and Wales (above, pp.144–145).

On the 2000 Review, see M. Seneviratne, [2000] P.L. 582; B. Thompson, (2001) M.L.R. 459. Thompson welcomed the integrationist approach of the Review but suggested it did not go far enough; there is

> "a need for a body which not only has an overview of the whole field of complaints handling but can use the complaints it processes to inform suggestions for improvement" (p.465).

7. The PCA had an additional, non-statutory role in dealing with complaints that a department or public body had not complied with the (also non-statutory) *Code of Practice on Access to Government Information* introduced in 1994. The PCA could make recommendations and not binding decisions. This has, from January 1, 2005, been replaced by the Freedom of Information Act 2000, under which disputes as to access to information are determined by the Information Commissioner. The Code generated a relative small amount of business for the PCA, but there were unfortunate occasions when departments refused to accept the PCA's interpretation of the Code or respond to the recommendations of the Select Committee. There was increasing evidence of delay and obstruction (see Seneviratne, *op.cit.* pp.152–154). The two most identifiable groups making complaints were the media and MPs, and the original expectation that the Code would used by ordinary members of the public "has only happened to a very limited extent" (Annual Report of the PCA, 2003–04 HC 702, Ch.4). This did not involve a change in primary legislation, but the new responsibility of policing compliance with codes of practice concerning the victims of offences does (s.5(1A) of the 1967 Act). It is not wholly clear why responsibilities in respect of this, among numerous statutory codes of practice, has been allocated to the PCA.

(ii) The Work of the Parliamentary Commissioner

(a) *Workload*

THE PARLIAMENTARY OMBUDSMAN

ANNUAL REPORT 2003–04

[See Table reproduced on the following page]

Notes

1. Further information contained in the 2003–04 Report included the following (Ch.5). The PCA's Customer Service Unit became operational during 2003–04, receiving 6,834 enquiries by telephone, letter or email. The Business Plan provided that for cases clearly outside the jurisdiction the referring MP must be notified within two weeks in 100 per cent of cases. This target was fully met. There were 60 such cases, 55 of which concerned a body and five on subject matter outside jurisdiction. For other complaints, the target was to achieve an appropriate outcome or to put a statement of complaint to the body concerned within an average of five weeks of receipt. This was achieved in only 53 per cent of cases, although for 96 per cent this was done within 13 weeks. The lowest annual workload between 1994 and 2003–04 was 1790 (in 1994) and the highest 2816 (in 1996). An important development has been a steady

CASES RECEIVED, CONSIDERED AND INVESTIGATED 2003–04

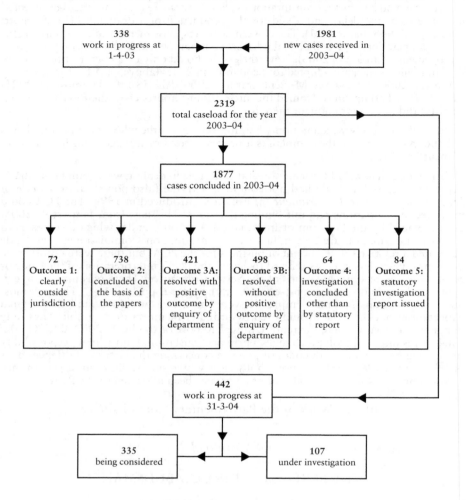

decline in the number of statutory investigations launched since 1997–98 and a corresponding increase in the use of enquiries of the department concerned to resolve complaints. In 2003–04, 84 statutory reports (4.5 per cent of the total workload) were issued compared with 376 (18 per cent) in 1997–98.

2. In 2003–04, the Department of Work and Pensions and its agencies remained the biggest source of complaints (41 per cent) (Annual Report for 2003–04, Ch.2). However, liaison with the Child Support Agency had improved significantly following agreement of a Memorandum of Understanding, and a similar MoU had been agreed with Jobcentre Plus. A useful development was the piloting of an annual letter to the Permanent Secretary providing an overview of work on departmental cases and highlighting general themes and lessons to be learned. General themes were: the need to establish and maintain good practice in dealing with customers; citizens should be able to rely on the accuracy and relevance of the information given them and to plan their affairs accordingly; and agencies need to operate effective complaints processes that focus on resolving complaints as near as possible to the point of service delivery (pp.7–8). These themes also emerged from the PCA's work with most other departments (p.17).

(b) *Casework*

R. v PARLIAMENTARY COMMISSIONER FOR ADMINISTRATION
Ex p. DYER

[1994] 1 W.L.R. 621; [1994] 1 All E.R. 375 (HIGH COURT)

Miss Dyer had complained to her MP (Rt Hon. Roy Hattersley) about a number of matters concerning her claims for various benefits administered by the Department of Social Security. Mr Hattersley had referred her complaints to the PCA who had decided to investigate some of them. In his report the PCA found that Miss Dyer had suffered maladministration and he criticised the local office of the Department for various mistakes in its handling of her claims. The Department apologised and made an *ex gratia* payment of £500. The PCA considered these remedies to be a satisfactory outcome to his investigation. However, Miss Dyer was not satisfied and sought judicial review of the PCA's decision not to reopen his investigation into her complaints. She alleged that the PCA had acted unlawfully by: (1) deciding to investigate some of her original complaints (rather than investigating all of them), (2) giving the Department an opportunity to comment on the factual accuracy of his draft report (whilst denying her such an opportunity) and (3) regarding himself as being precluded from reopening an investigation once he had issued a report.

SIMON BROWN L.J.: . . . This is the first substantive application for judicial review of the Commissioner to come before the courts (an application for leave in an earlier case having been refused). The first question raised for decision upon it concerns the proper ambit of this court's supervisory jurisdiction over the Commissioner, Mr Stephen Richards on his behalf submits to us that, certainly so far as the Commissioner's discretionary powers are concerned, this court has no review jurisdiction whatever over their exercise. In the alternative he submits that the court should intervene only in the most exceptional cases of abuse of discretion, essentially on the same limited basis held by the House of Lords in *R. v. Secretary of State for the Environment Ex p. Nottinghamshire CC* [1986] A.C. 240 and *R. v. Secretary of State for the Environment Ex p. Hammersmith and Fulham LBC* [1991] 1 A.C. 521 to be appropriate in the particular area of decision-making there in question.

The resolution of this initial jurisdictional issue clearly depends essentially on the legislation which created the Commissioner's office and governs the discharge of his functions. . . .

As to his wider proposition—that this court has literally no right to review the Commissioner's exercise of his discretion under the 1967 Act (not even, to give the classic illustration, if he refused to investigate complaints by red-headed complainants)—Mr Richards submits that the legislation is enacted in such terms as to indicate an intention that the Commissioner should be answerable to Parliament alone for the way he performs his functions. The Commissioner is, he suggests, an officer of the House of Commons, and, the argument runs, the parliamentary control provided for by the statute displaces any supervisory control by the courts. Mr Richards relies in particular on these considerations: first, the stipulation under s.5 that a complaint must be referred to the Commissioner by a member of Parliament before even his powers of investigation are engaged; second, the requirement under s.10(1) to report back to the member of Parliament (and, in certain circumstances, to each House of Parliament—see s.10(3)); third, the requirement under s.10(4) annually to lay a general report before Parliament; fourth, the provision under s.1(3) of the Act for the Commissioner's removal from office only in the event of addresses from both Houses of Parliament. Mr Richards points also to the Commissioner being always answerable to the select committee.

Despite these considerations I, for my part, would unhesitatingly reject this argument. Many in government are answerable to Parliament and yet answerable also to the supervisory jurisdiction of this court. I see nothing about the Commissioner's role or the statutory framework within which he operates so singular as to take him wholly outside the purview of judicial review.

I turn next, therefore, to Mr Richards's alternative and narrower submission that, by analogy with [the two House of Lords cases already mentioned], the courts should regard their powers as restricted with regard to reviewing the Commissioner's exercise of the discretions conferred upon him by this legislation.

I need cite one passage only from the speeches in those two cases, this from Lord Bridge's speech in *Ex p. Hammersmith and Fulham LBC* [1991] 1 A.C. 521, 597. [His Lordship cited the paragraph beginning "The restriction . . .", below, p.578.]

Mr Richards concedes that the analogy between the position considered there and that arising here is not a very close one. He submits, however, that the underlying rationale for restricting the scope of judicial review in those cases applies also here. Although, as counsel recognises, the Commissioner's functions are manifestly not political, nevertheless, he submits, the provisions here for parliamentary control afford this case a comparable dimension.

This submission too I would reject. There seems to me no parallel whatever between, on the one hand, decisions regarding the formulation and implementation of national economic policy—decisions "depending essentially on political judgment . . . for politicians to take . . . in the political forum of the House of Commons"—and, on the other hand, decisions of the Commissioner regarding the matters appropriate for investigation and the proper manner of their investigation.

All that said, however, and despite my rejection of both Mr Richards's submissions on the question of jurisdiction, it does not follow that this court will readily be persuaded to interfere with the exercise of the Commissioner's discretion. Quite the contrary. The intended width of these discretions is made strikingly clear by the legislature: under s.5(5), when determining whether to initiate, continue or discontinue an investigation, the commissioner shall "act in accordance with his own discretion"; under s.7(2), "the procedure for conducting an investigation shall be such as the commissioner considers appropriate in the circumstances of the case". Bearing in mind too that the exercise of these particular discretions inevitably involves a high degree of subjective judgment, it follows that it will always be difficult to mount an effective challenge on what may be called the conventional ground of *Wednesbury* unreasonableness (*Associated Provincial Picture Houses Ltd v Wednesbury Corporation* [1948] 1 K.B. 223).

Recognising this, indeed, one may pause to wonder whether in reality the end result is much different from that arrived at by the House of Lords in the two cases referred to, where the decisions in question were held "not open to challenge on the grounds of irrationality short of the extremes of bad faith, improper motive or manifest absurdity". True, in the present case "manifest absurdity" does not have to be shown; but inevitably it will be almost as difficult to demonstrate that the Commissioner has exercised one or other of his discretions unreasonably in the public law sense. . .

Recognising the full width of our jurisdiction but with those considerations in mind I turn to Miss Dyer's grounds of challenge. As to her contention that the Commissioner investigated some only of her original grounds of complaint, that is undoubtedly the case. But is she entitled to criticise the Commissioner for taking that course? More particularly, was the Commissioner acting outside the proper ambit of his discretion under section 5(5) in doing so? . . .

In my judgment, the Commissioner was entitled in the exercise of his discretion to limit the scope of his investigation, to be selective as to just which of Miss Dyer's many detailed complaints he addressed, to identify certain broad categories of complaint (the six main aspects as he called them) and investigate only those. Inevitably such an approach carried the risk that some of the problems which Miss Dyer complained of having experienced with the local office would continue, and that indeed is what Miss Dyer says has occurred. But no investigation should be expected to solve all problems for all time and it cannot in my judgment be said that the approach adopted here by the Commissioner was not one properly open to him.

Turning to Miss Dyer's complaint that the draft report was sent to the department for comment on the facts but not to her, the respondent's evidence indicates that this is a practice which has existed for 25 years, and is known to and acquiesced in by the select committee. The reasons for it are explained as follows. First, that it is the department rather than the complainant who may subsequently be called upon to justify its actions before the select committee and, if it is shown the draft report and does not point out any inaccuracy, it will then be unable to dispute the facts stated in it. Second, the practice affords the department an opportunity to give notice in writing to the Commissioner, as expressly provided for by section 11(3) of the 1967 Act, of any document or information the disclosure of which, in the opinion of the relevant minister, would be prejudicial to the safety of the state or otherwise contrary to the public interest. Third, sight of the draft report gives the department the opportunity to propose the remedy it is prepared to offer in the light of any findings of maladministration and injustice contained in it. The commissioner can then include in his final report what that proposed remedy is and indicate whether he finds that it satisfactorily meets the need.

Miss Dyer recognises, I think, that the same reasons do not exist for sending the draft report to her. Indeed, having regard to section 11(3), it could not be sent to her unless and until it had already been cleared by the department. Therefore, to graft on to the existing practice a need to show the draft report to complainants too would introduce a further stage into the process. Does natural justice require this? I do not think so. As Lord Bridge said in *Lloyd v. McMahon* [1987] A.C. 625 at 702:

> "My Lords, the so-called rules of natural justice are not engraved on tablets of stone. To use the phrase which better expresses the underlying concept, what the requirements of fairness demand when any body, domestic, administrative or judicial, has to make a decision which will affect the rights of individuals depends on the character of the decision-making body, the kind of decision it has to make and the statutory or other framework in which it operates".

Assuming, as I do, and indeed as Mr Richards concedes, that the Commissioner makes "a decision which will affect the rights of" Miss Dyer, it should nevertheless be borne in mind that it is the department and not her who is being investigated and who is liable to face public criticism for its acts. I cannot conclude that fairness here demanded that she too be shown the draft report. Rather it seems to me that the Commissioner, in determining the procedure for conducting his investigation as provided for by section 7(2), was amply entitled to consider it appropriate to follow his long-established practice.

I come finally to Miss Dyer's complaint about the Commissioner's refusal to reopen this investigation. This I can deal with altogether more shortly. It seems to me that the Commissioner is clearly correct in his view that, once his report had been sent to Mr Hattersley and the DSS (as required by section 10(1) and (2)), he was *functus officio* and unable to reopen the investigation without a further referral under section 5(1). Section 5(5), as already indicated, confers a wide discretion indeed; it does not, however, purport to empower the Commissioner to reopen an investigation once his report is submitted. It would seem to me unfair to the department and outside the scheme of this legislation to suppose that the Commissioner could do as Miss Dyer wished. . . .

It follows that, in my judgment, none of Miss Dyer's grounds of challenge can be made good and this application accordingly fails. . . .

Application refused.

Notes

1. Norman S. Marsh, the Chairman of the Committee which proposed the creation of the PCA, criticised Simon Brown L.J.'s reasoning concerning Miss Dyer's allegation that it was unlawful for the PCA to allow departments to comment upon the factual accuracy of his draft reports. Marsh believes there may be factual inaccuracies which relate to complainants' cases and they should be given an opportunity to explain them to the PCA "The impression given by this part of Simon Brown L.J.'s judgment is almost that the underlying purpose of the Parliamentary Commissioner Act is to give government departments a better opportunity to refute accusations of maladministration made against them" (p.349). N.S. Marsh, "The Extent and Depth of Judicial Review of the Decisions of the Parliamentary Commissioner for Administration" [1994] P.L. 347.

2. The courts remain unwilling to strike down decisions whether or not to investigate, or to discontinue an investigation, emphasising the width of the ombudsman's discretion in this regard (see above, p.172). The question whether the PCA should investigate has given rise to particular controversy in the case of a large number of complaints of maladministration in the prudential regulation (*i.e.* supervision of solvency) by the Treasury and the Financial Services Authority of Equitable Life, which had got into severe financial trouble leading to substantial losses to policyholders. In 2003, the PCA reported, following a limited investigation covering 1999–2000, that she found no evidence of maladministration. She agreed with the view of her predecessor that nothing would be gained from an investigation of further complaints concerning earlier years given the PCA's limited remit and that the government had asked a Scottish judge, Lord Penrose, to conduct a full inquiry. However, she would give further consideration to the matter following publication of the Penrose Report (The Parliamentary Ombudsman, *The Prudential Regulation of Equitable Life* (2002–03 HC 809)). This attracted strong criticism from Equitable Life policyholders (see the Equitable Members Action Group website, *www.emag.org.uk*), pressure from MPs and some serious probing from PASC (see PASC Minutes of Evidence, 27 November 2003). In the event, the Penrose Report (*Report of the Equitable Life Inquiry*, 2002–03 HC 290) included serious criticisms of both the regulatory system and operational failures. On reconsideration and after extensive consultation, the PCA decided to conduct a further investigation, in respect of a longer time frame. She applied as the tests whether (1) the body (or bodies) complained about were within the PCA's jurisdiction; (2) there was *prima facie* evidence of maladministration; (3) it appeared that this may have caused an unremedied injustice; and (4) that in investigation may produce a

worthwhile outcome. These tests were satisfied, the Penrose Report having not dealt with the issues of maladministration or redress. (The Parliamentary Ombudsman, *A Further Investigation of the Prudential Regulation of Equitable Life* (2003–04 HC 910)). An important rider was that this decision would be reviewed if her request that the Government Actuary's Department, which had had a key role, be brought within the PCA's jurisdiction (if only for this purpose) were not accepted by the Government. The request was, however, accepted (see Parliamentary Commissioner Order 2004 (SI 2004/2670), making the change in respect of the giving of advice relating to the regulation of insurance companies on or before April 26, 2001. EMAG dropped judicial review proceedings challenging the first report as almost all its concerns had now been met (EMAG website). The investigation is proceeding, and is the last hope of the Equitable Life policyholders. (cf. the absence of a remedy in negligence, below, p.1062.)

3. The first successful action for judicial review of a report issued by the PCA occurred in 1996: *R. v Parliamentary Commissioner for Administration, Ex p. Balchin* (No.1) [1997] J.P.L. 917. The applicants' former home had been seriously affected by planning blight, caused by a proposed nearby road scheme. The Balchins had complained to the PCA about the actions of the Department of Transport in confirming the scheme. In his report the PCA rejected the applicants' complaints. However, Sedley J. held that the PCA had unlawfully failed to have regard to a relevant consideration (whether if the Department had brought a new statutory power for the local highway authority to purchase adjoining land seriously affected by such projects to the attention of the authority the applicants might have received compensation through that route) in reaching his conclusions. Unfortunately, two subsequent reports by the PCA were also quashed. The second report found that there had been no maladministration, concluding that the DoT were aware of the new statutory power and of a circular sent to all local authorities about it, and had no reason to suppose the council would not take account of it. This was quashed by Dyson J. on the ground that the PCA had failed to explain how he had reached the conclusion that the DoT had been aware of the new powers at all material times, and had failed to deal with the question of injustice by outrage or to give adequate reasons on the issue (*R. v Parliamentary Commissioner for Administration Ex p. Balchin (No.2)* (2000) 2 L.G.L.R. 87). The third report made some different findings of fact, concluding that the DoT were not aware of the existence of the power and its availability to the council. There had been maladministration in failing to write to the council expressing ministers' views that the Balchins had a strong claim to favourable consideration by the council when it came to decide whether the new power should be exercised. However, there was ample evidence that the council would have made the same decision, and that ministers' views would not have changed the outcome, and so the maladministration had not caused injustice. This report was quashed on the ground that some of the conclusions were inconsistent with the new findings of fact. The conclusion as to injustice could not, however, be said to be irrational, although it would have to be reconsidered. The matter is being reinvestigated by a third PCA. In the meantime, the Balchins have suffered financial ruin (and the road scheme has not gone ahead). Whatever the ultimate outcome, the situation also provides an illustration of the inadequacy of the statutory code for compensation in respect of such projects. See P. Giddings, [2000] P.L. 205, suggesting that the court here set a very demanding standard for the Ombudsman's findings.

THE BARLOW CLOWES AFFAIR

PCA ANNUAL REPORT FOR 1989: 1989–90 HC 353

64. [This investigation report] was by far the longest and most detailed produced by the Office. It also resulted in the provision of the most substantial financial remedy ever to result from an investigation. I refer to my investigation into the Barlow Clowes affair—which I had decided to conduct following

the publication, in October 1988, of the report[44] on the fact-finding investigation carried out by Sir Godfray Le Quesne Q.C. at the request of the then Secretary of State for Trade and Industry. My own investigation was the subject of a special report[45] which I made to Parliament (under the provisions of section 10(4) of the Parliamentary Commissioner Act) on December 19, 1989. The investigation involved my enquiring into the exercise of licensing duties under the Prevention of Fraud (Investments) Act 1958 by the Department of Trade and Industry over a period of some 14 years. I found that there had been significant maladministration by the Department, in their dealings with Barlow Clowes' partnerships and their successor companies, in five main areas. The businesses concerned had been engaged in the management of client monies running into millions of pounds. They had led the investors to believe that their monies were being put into British Government stocks. Much of the marketing of the businesses' services had been directed to those in retirement and others seeking a risk-free but tax-efficient form of investment, and a substantial part of the attraction to investors had been the use—until it was severely curtailed in 1985—of the tax-avoidance device known as "bond-washing". The volume of the business thus transacted had already grown considerably when, in 1984, the Department sought to bring the operation within the licensing framework having, in 1976 and in the intervening years, allowed it—as described in my report—to continue unlicensed. Partnerships, with identical names but with differing members, had been operating in both the United Kingdom and in Jersey, but the Department had failed to realise that a separate Jersey partnership existed, or to appreciate the need to extend to the Jersey partnership the enquiries they proposed to make into the suitability of the United Kingdom partnership for a licence. I concluded that an examination of the Jersey partnership's affairs would have disclosed that its role was more than that of an investment vehicle for expatriates (as had been represented to DTI), that there had been intermingling between the funds it managed and those of the mainland partnership, and that—at the audit date selected for the examination of the mainland partnership's funds—securities held by the Jersey partnership on behalf of clients fell short of the amount needed to discharge obligations to investors by at least £3.65 million. Had these facts been discovered, the firm's operations would in my view almost certainly have been brought to an end early in 1985. As it was, licences were issued to the United Kingdom business in 1985, 1986 and 1987 (that in 1987 being closely followed by the appointment of Inspectors by the Secretary of State to investigate the company's affairs in the light of serious concerns about its viability and integrity); and, in 1988, the United Kingdom and offshore branches of the business were put into liquidation owing investors many millions of pounds. The final total of the losses had not emerged when my report was issued, but seemed likely to exceed £100 million. Apart from the centrally important errors in relation to the Jersey partnership, I also found that the viability of the schemes offered by Barlow Clowes had not been adequately considered, and that the decision to renew the licence for a third time, in 1987, had involved both excessive delay in responding to worrying information about the company and errors in correctly identifying the options available to the Department.

---

[44] Barlow Clowes Report of Sir Godfray Le Quesne Q.C. to the Secretary of State for Trade and Industry HC 671.
[45] First Report Session 1989–90 HC 76.

65. When I put my findings to the Department they told me, to my disappointment, that the Government disagreed with them and proposed to set out its own views in a separate document to be published at the same time as my report. The Department also said that my report raised a number of important issues about the responsibilities of regulators (on which the document to be published by the Government would also set out the Government's views). They went on to say, however, that the Government recognised that the case had created very great hardship and involved a unique combination of unusual features. In the light of that the Government was, in the exceptional circumstances and without admission of fault or liability, prepared to make a substantial payment to investors who had suffered loss. This payment (the proposed detailed calculation of which the Department explained to me) would be made to investors in both Barlow Clowes Gilt Managers Limited and Barlow Clowes International Limited in return for their assigning to the Secretary of State their rights in the liquidation and against third parties, and giving an undertaking to provide reasonable assistance in the pursuit of those rights. The payments would not distinguish between early and late investors.

66. I concluded that this outcome of the investigation—providing as it would for more than 99 per cent of the investors to receive at least 85 per cent of their capital (and 90 per cent in the case of those with investments of £50,000 or less) and, in addition, payments in lieu of interest lost on that amount since the collapse—was not unsatisfactory. The Government published its observations[46] on my Findings on December 19. However, I saw ground for satisfaction in that the Government—with whatever reservations—was prepared to act as it proposed in providing a fair remedy for what, as I had seen things, had been an injustice suffered by investors as a result of maladministration.

Notes

1. For an analysis of this major investigation, see R. Gregory and G. Drewry, "Barlow Clowes and the Ombudsman" [1991] P.L. 192 and 408.

2. Another major investigation has been the PCA's combined inquiries into a number of complaints about alleged planning blight (*i.e.* the loss of value caused to property near a proposed development) caused by the protracted deliberations over the route for a new high speed rail link from London to the Channel Tunnel. The Ombudsman found maladministration in the way in which the Department of Transport dealt with several claims for compensation for alleged planning blight. However, the Department refused to accept the PCA's findings of maladministration. Therefore, the PCA took the unusual step, for only the second time in the history of the office, of submitting a special report on the matter to Parliament (under s.10(3) of the 1967 Act): *The Channel, Tunnel Rail Link and Blight* (1994–95 HC 193). The Select Committee on the PCA subsequently took evidence from the Permanent Secretary of the Department and the Secretary of State (Dr B. Mawhinney). Later the Committee issued a report recommending that the Department accept the PCA's findings: (1994–95 HC 270). In response the new Transport Secretary (Sir George Young) repeated the Department's position that they were not guilty of maladministration, but "out of respect for the Select Committee and the office of the PCA" he agreed to consider whether compensation should be paid to those suffering extreme and exceptional hardship. For a discussion of these events see, R. James and D. Longley, [1996] P.L. 38. The Equitable Life investigation (above, p.180) will be a major exercise.

3. A.R. Mowbray, "A Right to Official Advice: The Parliamentary Commissioner's Perspective" analyses PCA cases published in 1985–87 concerning failures to give on

---

[46] Observations by the Government on the Report of the Parliamentary Commissioner for Administration on Barlow Clowes, HC 99.

request accurate advice (both fact and opinion) concerning the application of departmental programmes (*e.g.* eligibility for benefit). The provision of incorrect or misleading (*i.e.* partially correct) advice constitutes maladministration, and compensation is commonly recommended where loss results.

The right to advice is merely one of many administrative norms developed by the PCA in his casework (*cf.* his principles governing the use of administrative guidance noted previously in Ch.2 at p. 98). Professor Bradley has analysed this aspect of the PCA's work in the following terms:

> "it was to be expected that 'arbitrary discretion' of the kind which the 1967 Act vested in the British Ombudsman should evolve into a more or less settled body of ascertainable principles which might even harden into rules. . . . Thus, inevitably, the British Ombudsman has developed principles, standards and rules of what he believes to constitute good administration, since otherwise no notion of maladministration could have emerged. As the process of investigation and report continues in every fresh case, so the individual complainant receives the benefit of the Ombudsman's enforcement of the rules and principles which have emerged from the previous case-work. And it may not be pressing this analysis too far to conclude that the individual citizen thus acquires what may properly be called new rights to the maintenance of a certain quality of administration".

"The Role of the Ombudsman in Relation to the Protection of Citizens' Rights" [1980] C.L.J. 304 at 310–311. PCA have not, however, published general guidance documents. The Local Government Ombudsmen have, by contrast, produced a series of guidance documents and the European Ombudsman a *Code on Good Administrative Behaviour*.

4. Because of the MP filter, the relationship between Members of the House of Commons and the Parliamentary Commissioner is crucial to the operation of the scheme. A major survey of MPs' attitudes towards the PCA, conducted in 1993, revealed that 16 per cent of respondents considered his work to be "very satisfactory" and 64 per cent described it as "quite successful". Furthermore, 52 per cent of respondents referred complaints to the PCA "sometimes"; but, rather worryingly, 40 per cent of respondents "seldom" passed on such complaints. See "The Powers, Work and Jurisdiction of the Ombudsman", (1993–94 HC 33). Abolition of the MP filter have been recommended (above, p.174).

5. A positive aspect of the PCA's relationship with the House of Commons has been the support given to him by the Select Committee on the PCA, created in 1967 to monitor his work. Professor Gregory, in a study of the early work of the Committee, discovered that it concentrated upon three tasks. First, seeking to ensure that remedies were provided for complainants where the PCA upheld their claims against departments. If a department was unwilling to provide the redress suggested by the PCA, then the Select Committee would call the Permanent Secretary of the department to give evidence before the Committee explaining his department's actions. Secondly, to examine defects in administrative procedures discovered by the PCA in the course of his investigations. And, thirdly, to keep under review the adequacy of the PCA's powers. Gregory concluded that the Committee had been most successful in performing the first function, because of parliamentary and media concerns with personal "human interest" matters: see R. Gregory, "The Select Committee on the PCA 1967–80" [1982] P.L. 49. The Committee has continued to support the PCA in the, rare, cases where executive bodies have refused to provide redress (*e.g.* the Channel tunnel rail-link cases noted above, p.183). We have also seen how the Committee has continued to periodically review the powers and jurisdiction of the PCA (above, p.174). A new development in the work of the Committee has been its decision to undertake "thematic inquiries" into the matters raised during the course of the PCA's casework. The first such report was published on "Maladministration and Redress", (1994–95 HC 112), and recommended, *inter alia*, criteria for the assessment of redress offered by executive bodies (*e.g.* the person who has suffered injustice as a consequence of maladministration should be put back in the same position as he/she would have been had things gone right in the

first place). From 1997, the Select Committee's responsibilities have been discharged by the Public Administration Select Committee.

(C) THE LOCAL GOVERNMENT OMBUDSMEN

(i) Constitutional and Jurisdictional Matters

Once again it was a report by JUSTICE[47] that advocated the creation of ombudsmen for local government. Because of the large number of local authorities and their responsibility for the provision of many direct services to the public, thereby increasing the likelihood of consumer complaints, it was not considered possible to appoint a single local ombudsman. Instead, the idea of several local commissioners was proposed. When local authorities in England and Wales were restructured during 1974, Parliament took the opportunity to create separate local ombudsman systems for these two parts of the United Kingdom.

Part III of the Local Government Act 1974 creates the Commission for Local Administration in England which currently has three full time Commissioners (commonly called the Local Government Ombudsmen). The Commissioners are appointed by the Queen on the advice of the Secretary of State. Each Commissioner deals with complaints originating from different regions of England. Originally there was a "councillor filter" requirement for complainants, but since 1988[48] the Local Government Ombudsmen can receive complaints directly from members of the public. They may investigate complaints against a number of specified local bodies including, county councils, district councils and urban development corporations.[49] Much of their jurisdiction is modelled on the language of the Parliamentary Commissioner Act 1967. Hence, the Local Government Ombudsmen can investigate complaints that members of the public have "sustained injustice in consequence of maladministration" in connection with the performance of administrative functions by local authorities.[50] However, certain functions are excluded from the Local Government Ombudsmen's remit, *e.g.* contractual/commercial transactions and personnel matters.[51] Their investigations are to be conducted in private and have the backing of the High Court's powers of contempt.[52] When a Local Government Ombudsman has conducted an investigation he or she must send copies of his or her report to, *inter alios*, the complainant and the local authority. As with the Parliamentary Commissioner, the Local Government Ombudsmen have no power to compel the provision of redress by local authorities where they uphold a complaint.

Notes
1. On several occasions, notably in 1978, 1980 and 1984, the English Local Government Ombudsmen formally reviewed their existing jurisdiction. After each review they sought to have their remit extended, but with little support from local authorities or the Secretary of State. Before the Widdicombe Committee examining "The Conduct of Local Government Business", the Local Government Ombudsmen renewed their jurisdictional pleas—in particular for:

(1) direct access by complainants;
(2) contractual/commercial transactions and personnel matters to be open to investigation;

---

[47] *The Citizen and his Council* (1969).
[48] Local Government Act 1988.
[49] 1974 Act, s.25.
[50] *ibid.*, s.26(1).
[51] *ibid.*, Sch.5. *cf.* above, p.171 in relation to the PCA.
[52] *ibid.*, ss.28–29.

(3) the Local Ombudsmen to be given the power to investigate on their own motion without receiving a specific complaint from a member of the public.

The Committee favoured direct access to the Local Government Ombudsmen because:

". . . we believe it is wrong in principle that complainants should be expected to direct their complaints against a council through a member of the executive decision making body for that council".[53]

The Local Government Ombudsmen's desire to investigate commercial transactions was also endorsed:

"we have not been convinced that cases involving commercial and contractual transactions with members of the public are different in kind from cases involving other local authority dealings with the public and that they should therefore as a matter of general principle be excluded from the ombudsman's remit".[54]

But the Committee was only willing to recommend that complaints about appointment procedures used by councils should be within the Ombudsmen's jurisdiction, not general personnel matters. This was due to the Committee's belief that ". . . the primary function of the ombudsmen is in our view to provide support for the consumers of local government services rather than for those who are employed to provide them".[55] The Committee approved a modified power for the Local Government Ombudsmen to initiate investigations, provided they were based upon "good grounds for concern" and directed towards individual injustice.[56]

As indicated above, the Government accepted the desirability of direct public access to the Local Government Ombudsmen and this was enacted in 1988. However, the other proposed changes to the Ombudsmen's jurisdiction were not so well received. Regarding commercial transactions the Government felt:

"Ombudsmen—central and local—are concerned with the inter-action between the executive arm of government and the general public. Actions taken by public bodies in buying and selling goods and services are fundamentally different. The law already provides various safeguards and remedies for the parties involved in such commercial transactions, and there is no case for providing further protection through the local Ombudsman. . . .".[57]

For the same underlying reason the Government did not accept that personnel complaints were appropriate for Local Government Ombudsmen. The idea of self-initiated action by the Ombudsmen was rejected, because the Government felt that it could result in the Ombudsmen losing goodwill if they were perceived as general purpose watchdogs. Instead the Government proposed that the Ombudsmen be given a new power to publish general guidance to local authorities on good administrative practice. This was enacted in s.23 of the Local Government and Housing Act 1989.

2. In 1995 a comprehensive review of the work of the Local Ombudsmen was undertaken by Sir Geoffrey Chipperfield. The first stage of the review would consider, *inter alia*, whether the functions of the Local Ombudsmen were necessary. Sir Geoffrey concluded (*Review of the Commission for Local Administration Stage One* (1995)) that

[53] *The Conduct of Local Government Business*, Cmnd.9797 (1986), para.9.64.
[54] *ibid.*, para.9.73.
[55] *ibid.*, para.9.72.
[56] *ibid.*, para.9.76.
[57] *The Government's Response to the Report of the Widdicombe Committee of Inquiry*, Cm.433 (1988), para.6.27.

the Local Ombudsmen would not be able to handle effectively the increasing number of complaints that he foresaw citizens making. Therefore, he recommended that each local authority should be under a statutory duty to operate its own complaints system (involving both internal and external adjudicators). The role of the Local Ombudsmen would be to monitor these local complaints procedures, but not to investigate individual complaints.

The Local Ombudsmen were concerned that, under Sir Geoffrey's recommendations, the persons investigating citizens' complaints against local government would not be independent of those authorities and that complainants challenging local government would be treated differently from those having access to the Parliamentary Commissioner and Health Service Commissioner. The local authority associations and the National Association of Citizens' Advice Bureaux were also opposed to Sir Geoffrey's proposals.

After considering the Chipperfield report and associated representations, the Government concluded that:

"We recognise the importance of all local authorities having their own effective local complaints systems, although we are not persuaded of the need to seek legislation imposing a new statutory duty on local authorities to establish and maintain such systems. Nor do we believe that the case has been made that there is at present no continued need for the [Local Ombudsmen's] role as a wholly independent body to investigate complaints of maladministration" (*per* Mr David Curry: Minister of State at the Department of the Environment, HC Deb., Vol.271, col.402 (February 12, 1996)).

Therefore, the Department initiated the second stage of the review, to be undertaken by a senior official (Andrew Whetnall), which involved examining the efficiency and effectiveness of the Local Ombudsmen's procedures. That review was concluded in August 1996 and subsequently published (*Report of the Financial Management and Policy Review of the Commission for Local Administration in England: DoE, November 1996*). It recommended, *inter alia*, that the Local Ombudsmen be brought within the jurisdiction of the Select Committee on the Parliamentary Commissioner for Administration (so that the Committee could consider matters of policy, administration and resources concerning the Local Ombudsmen, but not the investigation of individual complaints), and that the relationship between the Local Ombudsmen and the courts should develop in the light of Lord Woolf's report (*Access to Justice: Final Report to the Lord Chancellor on the Civil Justice System in England and Wales: July 1996*). The Government's response was given on November 28, 1996, by Mr Curry:

"On the issues raised by the Review's First Stage, we have concluded that there needs to be a wholly independent body—an Ombudsman—to which citizens who are aggrieved in their dealings with public bodies can turn, if there is to be a guaranteed that complaints of maladministration will be fully and equitably investigated. Accordingly, we confirm our earlier provisional view . . . that the [Local Ombudsmen's] principal role should continue to be as a wholly independent, investigatory body for complaints of maladministration relating to local government in England. . . . The Review's Second Stage concludes that the cost of the [Local Ombudsmen] is a fraction of the cost of resolving a similar number of complaints through legal processes, and makes a range of recommendations for performance improvements covering issues of accountability, jurisdiction, powers, management systems and financial accountability, and quality of service. We believe that overall these recommendations provide a package of measures for significantly modernising and improving the Local Government Ombudsman service in England, and we intend to take them forward. . . ".

The Government did not have any plans to extend the jurisdiction of the Select Committee on the PCA to encompass the Local Ombudsmen. However, it would seek to obtain legislation allowing the appointment of Advisory Commissioners (representing the interests of local authorities and complainants, etc.) who would be able to "introduce a more independent contribution to the [Local Ombudsmen's] thinking". Consideration of the relationship between the LGO and the courts would be postponed because other aspects of the Woolf reforms had priority (*Government Response*, DoE, November 1996).

More recently, the Local Government Ombudsmen have been included within the *Review of Public Sector Ombudsmen in England* and subsequent developments, and are likely to become part of a merged Commission (see above, p.174). Jurisdictional issues await further consideration.

3. The Local Government Ombudsmen have adopted a model than tends towards "redress" rather than "control" (see above, p.155), but have nevertheless been active in developing general guidance. They have an express power to give advice and guidance about good administrative practice (Local Government Act 1974, s.23(12A), (12B), inserted by the Local Government and Housing Act 1989, s.23(1)). They have issued general guidance notes on (1) *Running a Complaints System*; (2) *Good Administrative Practice*; (3) *Council Housing Repairs*; (4) *Members' Interests* (subsequently withdrawn following the introduction of new arrangements for standards of conduct in Pt 3 of the Local Government Act 2000); (5) *Disposal of Land*; and (6) *Remedies*. They have also issued Special Reports on the funding of aftercare under s.117 of the Mental Health Act 1983; arrangements for forwarding housing benefit appeals to the Appeals Service; School Admissions and Appeals; Parking Enforcement by Local Authorities; and Neighbour nuisance and anti-social behaviour (see *www.lso.org.uk*).

4. One area that has always been outside the jurisdiction of the PCA or the LGO has been complaints against the police, which have been dealt with by several successive statutory regimes. The current arrangements are overseen by the Independent Police Complaints Commission, established by the Police Reform Act 2002. The Commission, unlike its predecessors, has power to conduct investigations using its own staff, as well as overseeing investigations conducted by police officers. Notwithstanding the absence of "ombudsmen" from the title, the IPCC is recognised as one by the BIOA (see below, p.200).

(ii) The Courts and the Local Government Ombudsmen

R. v LOCAL COMMISSIONER FOR ADMINISTRATION FOR THE SOUTH, THE WEST, THE WEST MIDLANDS, LEICESTERSHIRE, LINCOLNSHIRE AND CAMBRIDGESHIRE Ex p. EASTLEIGH BC

[1988] 1 Q.B. 855; [1988] 3 All E.R. 151 (COURT OF APPEAL)

A householder complained to the Local Government Ombudsman, for his area of England, that Eastleigh BC had failed properly to inspect the construction of a defective sewer connected to his house as required by the Building Regulations 1976. The Local Ombudsman produced a report (extracts of which appear in the judgment below) in which he stated that the Council had not inspected the sewer at all the relevant stages of its construction and consequently the sewer had not been thoroughly inspected. He went on to find that the householder had sustained injustice as a consequence of the Council's maladministration, but that even if the final inspection of the sewer had been carried out properly he could not be certain that the defect would have been discovered. Therefore, the Ombudsman recommended that Eastleigh BC pay only a part of the costs of remedial work.

The Council sought judicial review of the Local Ombudsman's report on the grounds that (1) it was contrary to s.34(3) of the Local Government Act 1974, in that the Ombudsman had questioned a discretionary decision taken without maladministration by the Council and (2) it was also contrary to s.26(1) of the 1974 Act, in that the Ombudsman had made a report when it was not certain that the householder had suffered injustice in consequence of an act of maladministration by Eastleigh BC In the High Court, Nolan J. upheld the Council's submissions, but refused to grant them a declaration. The Council appealed against the refusal of a remedy and the Local Government Ombudsman cross-appealed against the findings of *ultra vires*.

LORD DONALDSON OF LYMINGTON M.R.: . . . The ombudsman's conclusions are stated in paragraphs 30 and 31 of his report:

"30. In my view good administration dictates that the council should carry out an inspection under the Building Regulations in respect of all stage inspections for which they have received notice from the owner or builder as the case may be. Where inspections have not been made at a particular stage I consider that special attention should be given on the final inspection to remedy the omission. In the case of drains it is a relatively easy matter to carry out a full test, such as a ball test or its equivalent, at the final inspection stage and I consider that a council have a duty to ensure that this is done because a final inspection should mean that, so far as the council are concerned, they have with reasonable diligence and expenditure of officer time found no defect under the Building Regulations. I am satisfied that in this case the private foul sewer in question was not fully or thoroughly inspected. The defects in piping discovered as a result of the soil and vent pipe test should have alerted officers to the possibility of other defects in the pipe work.
31. I find, therefore, that the complainant has sustained injustice as a result of the council's maladministration. However, I cannot say, categorically, whether had the council carried out the final inspection in accordance with the dictates of good administration, the trouble at the centre of this complaint would not have arisen. Equally, I have taken account of the argument that with synthetic piping of the sort employed in this case soil compaction can cause undulation at a later date. I have also considered the fact that the original fault was the builder's and that that (and the council's fault) occurred some years ago. On the other hand the final inspection was, in my view, incomplete and the council could have become aware of the problem at an early stage because of the difficulties experienced by the owner of house 3. Having considered these factors I feel on balance it would be inequitable to ask the council to defray the whole cost of the necessary remedial work. Accordingly, upon the residents' agreement to pay a proportion of the reasonable cost, I consider that the council themselves should take the action which the Assistant Director of Technical Services commended to the residents (see paragraph 29, above)".

The action referred to in paragraph 29 consisted of exposing that part of the sewer which lay between two manholes and adjusting the pipe work to eliminate the undulation.

The ombudsman's cross-appeal

Section 34(3)

This subsection is in the following terms:

> "It is hereby declared that nothing in this Part of this Act authorises or requires a Local Commissioner to question the merits of a decision taken without maladministration by an authority in the exercise of a discretion vested in that authority."

"Maladministration" is not defined in the Act, but its meaning was considered in *R. v Local Commissioner for Administration for the North and East Area of England, ex p. Bradford Metropolitan City Council* [1979] Q.B. 287. All three judges (Lord Denning M.R., at 311, Eveleigh L.J., at 314, and Sir David Cairns, at 319) expressed themselves differently, but in substance each was saying the same thing, namely, that administration and maladministration in the context of the work of a local authority is concerned with the *manner* in which decisions by the authority are reached and the *manner* in which they are or are not implemented. Administration and maladministration have nothing to do with the nature, quality or reasonableness of the decision itself.

The key to this part of the cross-appeal lies in identifying the policy decision of the council in relation to the inspection of drains. This was, as I have stated, to inspect at four of the more important of nine stages in construction. It did not condescend to the nature of the inspections. . . .

Nolan J. read paragraph 30 of the ombudsman's report, which I have set out in full, as questioning the merits of that policy. I do not so read it. I can best illustrate my understanding of that paragraph by adding words which render explicit what, in my judgment, is implicit:

> "In my view good administration dictates that the council should carry out an inspection under the Building Regulations in respect of all stage inspections for which they have received notice from the owner or builder as the case may be. [However I recognise that, on the authority of *Anns'* case [1978] A.C. 728 to which I have referred at length earlier in this report, it was open to the council in the exercise of their discretion and taking account of the competing claims of efficiency and thrift to decide to inspect on fewer occasions. This the council has done and I accept its decisions. That said] Where inspections have not been made at a particular stage I consider that special attention should be given on the final inspection to remedying the omission. [In saying this I am not calling for an expenditure of time and effort which would nullify the council's discretionary decision on the resources to be devoted to building regulation inspections.] In the case of drains it is a relatively easy matter to carry out a full test, such as a ball test or its equivalent, at the final inspection stage. . . . [The choice of test must be a matter for the council's officers and I would not criticise them for not using the ball test, if they had used some equivalent test. However an air pressure test, such as the council's officers used, is not such an equivalent, because it only reveals whether or not the sewer is watertight. It tells the inspector nothing about its gradient or its ability to self-clear and efficiently carry away matter discharged into it as required by regulation N10.]

I consider that [this is of considerable importance and that] a council have a duty to ensure that this is done because a final inspection [if the council decide to make one, as this council did] should mean that, so far as the council are concerned, they have with reasonable diligence and expenditure of officer time found no defect under the Building Regulations. I am satisfied that in this case the private foul sewer in question was not fully or thoroughly inspected [in terms of the council's own 1977 policy. Even if in other circumstances a lesser inspection might have been justified in terms of that policy] the defects in piping discovered as a result of the soil and vent pipe tests should have alerted officers to the possibility of other defects in the pipe work."

So read, and I do so read it, paragraph 30 loyally accepts the council's discretionary decision on the inspection of drains. It simply criticises the way in which that decision was implemented. I do not, therefore, think that this complaint by the council is made out.

Section 26(1)

This subsection is in the following terms:

"Subject to the provisions of this Part of this Act where a written complaint is made by or on behalf of a member of the public who claims to have sustained injustice in consequence of maladministration in connection with action taken by or on behalf of an authority to which this Part of this Act applies, being action taken in the exercise of administrative functions of that authority, a Local Commissioner may investigate that complaint."

. . . [I]t does mean that he cannot report adversely upon an authority unless his investigation reveals not only maladministration, but injustice to the complainant sustained as a consequence of that maladministration.

The mischief at which this subsection is directed is not difficult to detect. Every local authority has living within its boundaries a small cadre of citizens who would like nothing better than to spend their spare time complaining of maladministration. The subsection limits the extent to which they can involve the ombudsman by requiring, as a condition precedent to his involvement, that the complainant shall personally have been adversely affected by the alleged maladministration. If he was not so affected, he did not himself suffer injustice. If he was, he did. . . .

Like Nolan J., I am loath to criticise a busy Local Commissioner on merely semantic grounds, but I think that he laid himself open to criticism by finding maladministration in paragraph 30 and then proceeding, without any explanation, to his conclusion of consequential injustice. . . .

. . . [I]n the end I have come to the conclusion that the ombudsman was intending to say that, whilst there could be no absolute certainty that a proper inspection would have revealed the defects and it was a possibility that the undulation occurred after the date of the inspection, on the balance of probabilities he was satisfied that the defects were present at the time of the inspection, that a proper inspection would have revealed them and that he was therefore satisfied that the complainant had suffered injustice in consequence of the maladministration.

An ombudsman's report is neither a statute nor a judgment. It is a report to the council and to the ratepayers of the area. It has to be written in everyday language and convey a message. This report has been subjected to a microscopic and somewhat legalistic analysis which it was not intended to undergo. Valid criticisms have been made, particularly of paragraph 31, but in my judgment they go to form rather than substance and, notwithstanding occasional dicta to the contrary, judicial review is concerned with substance. I would therefore allow the ombudsman's cross-appeal.

The council's appeal

As Parker and Taylor L.JJ. are minded to dismiss the ombudsman's appeal, it is necessary to consider the council's appeal. I would allow it.

Nolan J. considered that there was no need for any declaration that the ombudsman had exceeded his remit by contravening the limits upon his jurisdiction set by section 34(3). He said that this was a free country and that there was nothing to prevent the council responding to the report with equal publicity. He concluded by saying that, since Parliament had not thought it necessary to create a right of appeal against the findings in the Local Commissioner's report, and in the absence of impropriety, it seemed to him that the courts ought not to provide the equivalent of such a right by judicial review.

I have to say that I profoundly disagree with this approach. Let me start with the fact that Parliament has not created a right of appeal against the findings in a Local Commissioner's report. It is this very fact, coupled with the public law character of the ombudsman's office and powers, which is the foundation of the right to relief by way of judicial review.

Next there is the suggestion that the council should issue a statement disputing the right of the ombudsman to make his findings and that this would provide the council with an adequate remedy. Such an action would wholly undermine the system of ombudsman's reports and would, in effect, provide for an appeal to the media against his findings. The Parliamentary intention was that reports by ombudsmen should be loyally accepted by the local authorities concerned. This is clear from section 30(4) and (5), which require the local authority to make the report available for inspection by the public and to advertise this fact, from section 31(1), which requires the local authority to notify the ombudsman of the action which it has taken and proposes to take in the light of his report and from section 31(2), which entitles the ombudsman to make a further report if the local authority's response is not satisfactory.

Whilst I am very far from encouraging councils to seek judicial review of an ombudsman's report, which, bearing in mind the nature of his office and duties and the qualifications of those who hold that office, is inherently unlikely to succeed, in the absence of a successful application for judicial review and the giving of relief by the court, local authorities should not dispute an ombudsman's report and should carry out their statutory duties in relation to it.

If Nolan J. thought that the publication of his judgment in favour of the council was itself an adequate remedy, he did not say so, and, in any event, I think that he would have been mistaken, because this by itself does not relieve the council of its obligations to respond to the report in accordance with section 31(1) and, assuming that the report should never have been made, it is wrong that the council should be expected to respond.

I would grant a declaration in terms which reflect the decision of this court on the ombudsman's appeal against the decision of Nolan J.

PARKER L.J.: . . . On a fair reading of the whole of paragraph 30 it appears to me that the ombudsman is not concluding that there was maladministration because there was no inspection at all nine stages, but merely that the inspections of the sewer which were called for by the policy of inspecting at the four most important stages were not fully or thoroughly carried out. This conclusion was not dependent upon the view expressed in the opening sentence and indeed it could not have been because the policy did call for drain inspections, indeed two drain inspections. . . .

I conclude therefore that the ombudsman's conclusion in paragraph 30 was valid, but if the council felt it necessary to seek some declaratory relief with regard to the opening words of the paragraph I would be prepared to consider granting it.

I turn to the second question raised on the cross-appeal, namely, whether the conclusion that the complainant had suffered injustice as a result of the maladministration can be sustained. This depends upon paragraph 31 of the report. Had the ombudsman stopped at the first sentence, I should have had no doubt that the decision was sustainable. It seems to me abundantly clear that the complainant had suffered injustice if the failure to inspect properly led to the subsequent expenditure and the ombudsman could in my view easily have determined that it had. It is submitted however that, having stated his conclusion in the opening sentence, he proceeds to negate it and that the paragraph read as a whole really amounts to this: "I cannot say whether the failure to inspect led to the expenditure, but as the council were at fault it would be fair that they should contribute to the cost of remedial measures." For the ombudsman it is submitted that this is not so and that on a fair reading the paragraph says no more than: "I cannot be absolutely sure, but on the balance of probabilities I conclude. . . ."

I regret to say that, unlike Lord Donaldson M.R. I cannot accept this construction. It appears to me that to do so involves applying legal concepts of differing standards of proof in order to uphold a paragraph which, like its predecessor, must be broadly considered. I have, despite its opening words, been able, by a broad reading and the correctness of the ombudsman's directions to himself on the law, to uphold the conclusion in paragraph 30. In the case of paragraph 31 I am unable to do so.

I would therefore dismiss the cross-appeal and allow the appeal.

TAYLOR L.J.: . . . The crucial issue therefore is whether the ombudsman's findings in both paragraphs 30 and 31 of his report can be upheld and his cross-appeal thus allowed. I agree with Nolan J. that both paragraphs contain findings which cannot be justified.

[Regarding paragraph 30.] In my judgment its tenor shows the ombudsman to be trespassing into the field of discretion by laying down what policy as to inspections the dictates of good administration require, and what tests the council ought to ensure are carried out. That is quite different from finding that a test specifically required by the council's policy has not been carried out or has been carried out inefficiently. I therefore agree with Nolan J. that the ombudsman was in breach of section 34(3) of the Local Government Act 1974 in his conclusion that maladministration was established.

As to paragraph 31, I agree with Parker L.J. Only by straining the language used by the ombudsman and attributing to him speculatively considerations as to the burden of proof, could one render his finding on causation sound. I do not think such straining and speculation is justified.

Accordingly I conclude that in respect of both paragraphs 30 and 31 of the report, Nolan J. reached the correct conclusions. I would therefore dismiss the cross-appeal and allow the council's appeal.

Notes

1. M. Jones comments:

"in *Eastleigh*, the court's interpretation of s.34(3) affirms the orthodox view, and the legislature's intent, that the Commissioners ought not to usurp the policy-making discretions of democratically elected local authorities; . . . [nevertheless] the local ombudsmen may continue to find maladministration in the processes by which discretionary decisions are made upon grounds which closely resemble the *Wednesbury* principles of review employed by the courts—relevancy, proper purposes and so on. And there may still be room for a finding of maladministration where a Commissioner considers that the terms of an authority's policy transcend to the bounds of reasonableness, and step into perversity, capriciousness, or what the courts now term 'irrationality'" ("The Local Ombudsman and Judicial Review" [1988] P.L. 608 at pp.615–616.)

Whilst, on the issue of whether the Local Government Ombudsman had found that the complainant's injustice was caused by the Council's maladministration, Mowbray observed:

"the division of opinion on this question by the Court of Appeal again clearly reflected the differing judicial attitudes towards the margin of appreciation to be accorded to the Local Ombudsman in performing his functions. Lord Donaldson was willing to allow the Ombudsman a wide latitude of freedom because, in his opinion, the Ombudsman was not required to produce the kind of reasoned decision expected of a superior court of law. But the majority were unwilling to make similar allowances when scrutinising the Ombudsman's logic. Therefore, if the Local Ombudsman is to avoid such criticisms in the future his reports will have to adopt a more precise and definitive form of reasoning". ("Maladministration and the Local Ombudsmen" (1988) S.J. 1442 at p.1444.)

2. Despite the above opinion of Lord Donaldson that an action for judicial review of a Local Government Ombudsman's report "is inherently unlikely to succeed", the Divisional Court in *R. v Commissioner for Local Administration Ex p. Croydon LBC* [1989] 1 All E.R. 1033 granted declaratory relief in respect of a Commissioner's report concerning the rejection by an education appeal committee of the applicant's appeal concerning which school their daughter should attend, on the ground that there was no foundation on the evidence for a finding of maladministration.

Writing extra-judicially, Sir Harry Woolf (as he then was) suggested that the Ombudsman (whether central or local) should have an express power to refer an issue to the court, whether before, during or after an investigation, "either because there is a point of law of significance involved or because the courts are in a better situation to provide a remedy than he is" (*Protection of the Public—A New Challenge* (1990), pp.90–91). This would "make the best of both systems available to the public" (*ibid.*).

3. It was a matter of concern that in about 6 per cent of cases (by 1995–96) where the Ombudsmen find a local authority guilty of maladministration causing injustice the authority fails to provide a remedy that is acceptable to the Ombudsmen. Consequently, the Local Government Ombudsmen argued before the Widdicombe Committee that, as

in Northern Ireland, where a local authority failed to provide a suitable remedy the complainant should have the right to go to the County Court for a binding judicial order of compensation or remedial action. The Committee endorsed this method of strengthening the remedial powers of the Local Government Ombudsmen (Report, para.9.69).

At about the same time, the Select Committee on the PCA proposed an alternative system for dealing with recalcitrant local authorities, that involved the Select Committee extending its remit to encompass such bodies. The Select Committee suggested that where a council failed to provide a suitable remedy then the leaders of the council could be called to give evidence before the Committee which, as we have already noted, is how reluctant Departments are dealt with (*Local Government Cases: Enforcement of Remedies*, 1985–86 HC 448).

The Government accepted that non-compliance was a problem, "although a rate of compliance of 95 per cent might in other circumstances be considered good for a voluntary system, it is the other 5 per cent of 'failures' which not unnaturally attract attention. There is no doubt that these cases serve to produce a particularly marked sense of grievance on the part of the complainants, as well as undermining the creditibility of the Local Ombudsman system as a whole."[58] However, the Government rejected the solution of judicial enforcement because ". . . local authorities might be less willing to co-operate, and investigations would become increasingly formalised, lengthy, legalistic and costly. Complainants might find the process more intimidating and flexibility would be lost".[59] Moreover, the Select Committee's idea was also dismissed:

"although this has its attractions in that it builds on the existing voluntary principle, it is unlikely to be readily acceptable to local government who do not see themselves as accountable to Parliament—though recognising that they operate within a statutory framework laid down by Parliament".[60]

Instead it was decided to increase the local pressure on councils to comply with Ombudsmen's reports. This approach has now been enacted in Part II of the Local Government and Housing Act 1989. Where a report finding injustice in consequence of maladministration has been made the relevant local authority must consider the report and notify the Local Government Ombudsman of the action they have taken within three months. If the authority does not notify the Ombudsman, or he is not satisfied with the action taken, he may issue a second report. Again, the authority must consider and notify the Ombudsman of its action regarding the second report. If the Ombudsman is still not satisfied with the authority's conduct he may publish an account of his recommendations in two editions of a local newspaper. This lengthy process is clearly less forceful than the Local Government Ombudsmen's desire for judicial enforcement of their reports.

By 1996, the Local Ombudsmen had required the publication of 69 statements in local newspapers where a satisfactory remedy had not been provided. The futility of this process has been noted by the Local Ombudsmen when they commented that the newspaper statements ". . . often costs the council considerably more than the sum the Ombudsman had recommended should be paid in compensation to the complainant in the first place" (Annual Report 1992/1993, p.8.).

During 1995–96 the Local Ombudsmen undertook research into the reasons why local authorities failed to provide the recommended remedies. The major explanation was that the local authority concerned disagreed with the Local Ombudsman's finding of maladministration. The second reason was that authorities disputed the Ombudsmen's findings that complainants had suffered injustice. Consequently, the Ombudsmen have introduced a number of measures to encourage greater compliance

---

[58] *The Government's Response to the Report of the Widdicombe Committee of Inquiry*, para.6.21.
[59] *ibid*., para.6.22.
[60] *ibid*., para.6.23.

with their recommendations. These include: (1) explaining the nature of maladministration and the reasoning behind individual findings of its existence; (2) giving authorities advance notice of potential criticisms which may be included in a final report and
(3) publishing guidance on how the Ombudsmen assess remedies (Annual Report
1995– 1996, p.4). Since then, the position has improved. At March 31, 2004, of the
2,145 reports issued since April 1, 1994, in which injustice was found, there was an
unsatisfactory outcome in 1.8 per cent of cases and a further 2.9 per cent where a settlement was awaited (Annual Report of the English Commission for 2003–04,
App.1(d)). The ombudsmen are not currently pressing for their recommendation to be
made enforceable, as this would make the relationship between them and local authorities adversarial (see Seneviratne, *op.cit.*, pp.217–220).

(iii) The Work of the Local Ombudsmen

LOCAL OMBUDSMAN: ANNUAL REPORT 2003–04

Chapter 4

Analysis of complaints

This chapter provides an analysis of all the complaints we received and determined in the year ended 31 March 2004. The terminology is explained in the
glossary in Appendix 4. More detailed statistics are given in Appendix 1.

Complaints received

We received a total of 18,982 complaints in the year ended 31 March 2004,
compared with 17,610 in the previous year. This is an increase of 8.4 per cent.
   We decided 18,658 complaints. The numbers of complaints received and
complaints determined since 1994/95 are set out in graph 3 below.

COMPLAINTS RECEIVED AND DETERMINED 1994/95–2003/04

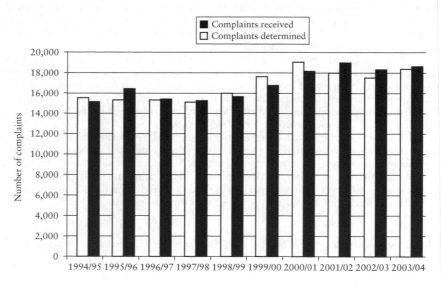

Subjects of complaints

The subjects of complaints are shown in chart 1 opposite.

Outcome of complaints

Table 4 summaries the decisions made on complaints determined. The total number of complaints where redress was obtained was 3,363–29 per cent of all complaints determined (excluding premature complaints and those outside jurisdiction) and three percentage points lower than the previous year.

A breakdown by category of reports issued in the year is given in Appendix 1(c). Unusually planning matters formed the largest percentage of reports issued and housing matters formed the second largest percentage. . . .

Our aim is to obtain redress for people who have suffered an injustice as a result of maladministration. The sooner redress can be achieved, the better. If a council is willing to provide a fair remedy and make any administrative improvements that are necessary, the investigation may be discontinued.

In 2003/04, 3,188 complaints ended in local settlements. Local settlements represented 27.5 per cent of the complaints we determined, excluding premature complaints and those outside our jurisdication; in 2002/03 the percentage was 30.

Local settlements can occur at various stages of the investigation. For example, councils sometimes volunteer settlements in response to our first enquiries about a complaint. Often, however, our staff, having considered the information collected from the council and the complainant, identify what appears to be maladministration and a consequent injustice and propose a settlement. Having considered the views of both sides, we either approve the settlement or continue with the investigation.

COMPLAINTS RECEIVED BY CATEGORY 2003/04

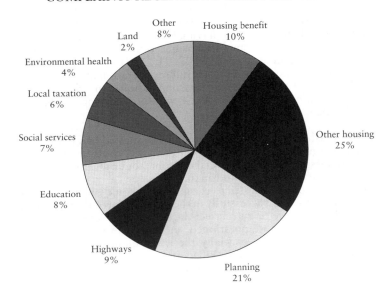

TABLE 4: ANALYSIS OF OUTCOME OF COMPLAINTS DETERMINED 2003/04

	Number of complaints	Percentage of total (excluding premature complaints and those outside jurisdiction)
Local settlement	3,188	27.5
Maladminstration causing injustice (iisued report)	175	1.5
Maladministration, no injustice (issued report)	5	0.1
No maladministration, (issued report)	19	0.2
No or insufficient evidence of maladministration (without report)	5,399	46.5
Ombudsman's discretion not to pursue complaint	2,814	24.2
Premature complaints	4,693	
Outside jurisdiction	2,365	
Total	**18,658**	

Table 5 sets out the numberof local settlements by category of complaint for each of our areas and for the Commission as a whole. It also shows the number of local settlements as a percentage of all complaints determined in each category, excluding premature complaints and those outside our jurisdiction.

Notes

1. In 2003–04, 58.5 per cent of all complaints (excluding prematures) were determined within 13 weeks, 83.9 per cent within 26 and 96.4 per cent within 52. The average cost per complaint was £583 (having fluctuated between £500 and over £550 in the period from 1994–95). Complainants questioned Commissioners' decisions in 7.7 per cent of cases (Annual Report for 2003–04, Ch.3). As with the PCA, most cases are resolved without the need for a formal full investigation and report.

2. A MORI national awareness survey commissioned by the CLA for England jointly with the Parliamentary and Health Service Ombudsman's Office was commissioned in 2003. The principal findings were:

"A quarter of the members of the public questioned had made a complaint to one of the organisations within the Ombudsmen's jurisdiction. Of those, 48 per cent were dissatisfied with the final outcome, but only 2 per cent of those subsequently contacted an Ombudsman.

A further quarter had wanted to complain but could not be bothered, were put off by complaining unsuccessfully in the past, or feared that complaining would make little difference or even affect the standard of service they receive.

More than half of those questioned said they had never heard of any of the Ombudsmen. This was especially the case among young people, black and minority ethnic groups and unskilled and unemployed people. Those who did know about the Ombudsmen's services, however, perceived them to be independent and fair.

TABLE 5: LOCAL SETTLEMENTS BY CATEGORY 2003/04

Subject	Commission		
	Total[61]	LS[62]	%[63]
Council housing management	1,483	372	25.1
Council housing repairs	806	431	53.5
Housing benefit	1,261	784	62.2
Planning	2,567	258	10.1
Education	1,216	296	24.3
Land	193	42	21.8
Highways	979	191	19.5
Environmental health	382	75	19.6
Local taxation	604	244	40.4
Social services	678	173	25.5
Drainage	120	27	22.5
Leisure and recreation	193	53	27.5
Total[64]	**11,600**	**3,188**	**27.5**

Advisory bodies, such as citizens advice bureaux, wanted to be better informed about our services so that they can more effectively advise those who may need to use them".

The Ombudsmen's offices have responded by efforts to promote awareness, especially with advisory bodies and voluntary groups (*ibid.*, p.4; LGO Annual Report 2003–04, p.16).

3. Notwithstanding these disappointing levels of awareness, the work of the Local Government Ombudsmen has been highly regarded (see generally M. Seneviratne, *Ombudsmen: Public Services and Administrative Justice* (2002), Ch.6, esp. pp.236–237, noting the "outcry" when the Chipperfield Report (above, p.186) proposed abolition; N. Lewis, M. Seneviratne and S. Cracknell, *Complaints Procedures in Local Government* (University of Sheffield, 1987) (a major empirical study that reported that the impact of the Local Ombudsmen upon local government had been impressive both in securing redress for complainants and improving procedures). See also C. Crawford, [1988] P.L. 246. (Annual Report of the PCA 2003–04, 2003–04 HC 702, p.3). The Ombudsmen's offices have responded by efforts to promote awareness, especially with advisory bodies and voluntary groups (*ibid.*, p.4; LGO Annual Report 2003–04, p.16).

(D) Private Sector Ombudsmen

The financial services industry took the lead in the creation of ombudsmen to resolve disputes between consumers and commercial organizations. In the 1980s, insurance

---

[61] The total complaints determined in each category, excluding premature complaints and complaints outside the Ombudsmen's jurisdiction.

[62] The total number of local settlements in each category.

[63] The figure in column 2 as a percentage of the figure in column 1.

[64] These figures are not the totals of each column because some categories of complaint are not shown.

companies, the major high street banks and building societies established separate ombudsmen schemes.

They maintained close links and adopted a common conception of their role as impartial decision-makers. They tended to use similar techniques of investigation (notably the reliance on documentary evidence and the utilisation of experts to resolve questions of fact). Complainants were successful in 20–30 per cent of the cases which were subject to formal reports by the various ombudsmen. Although these figures appeared low when compared with the public sector ombudsmen, they could be explained by the need for complainants to have exhausted internal redress before raising the matter with the private sector ombudsmen and the latter's attempts to achieve conciliated settlements.

Overall, the various financial services ombudsmen have evolved without many express references to the heritage of the public sector ombudsmen. But their original methods of investigation could be of relevance to the public sector ombudsmen (especially the PCA) in developing a range of efficient techniques adapted to different types of complaints. See further, A.R. Mowbray, "Ombudsmen: The Private Sector Dimension" in Finnie, Himsworth and Walker (ed.), *Edinburgh Essays in Public Law* (1991); R. James, "The Building Societies Ombudsman Scheme" (1992) 11 C.J.Q. 157; R.W. Hodges, "Ombudsman and other Complaints Procedures in the Financial Services Sector in the U.K." (1992) 21 Anglo-Am.L.R. 1; A. McGee, *The Financial Services Ombudsmen* (1992); P. Rawlings and C. Willett, "Ombudsmen Schemes in the United Kingdom's Financial Sector" (1994) 17 *Journal of Consumer Policy* 307; P.E. Morris, "The Investment Ombudsman—A Critical Review" [1996] J.B.L. 1; and R. James, *Private Ombudsmen and Public Law* (1997).

The Financial Services and Markets Act 2000, Pt XVI (ss.225–234) and Sch.17 provided a statutory framework for what remains a private sector scheme. The Financial Ombudsman Service (*www.financial-ombudsman.org.uk*) replaced a range of former complaints-handling schemes, including the Banking Ombudsmen, Building Societies Ombudsmen, Investment Ombudsmen and the SFA Complaints Bureau. It is administered by a company limited by guarantee and covers complaints about most financial products and services provided in (or from the United Kingdom), covering all retail financial firms regulated by the Financial Services Authority established by the 2000 Act, and some that are not. Complainants must be individuals or a business, charity or trust with (respectively) a yearly turnover, yearly income or net assets of under £1 million. The firm's complaints process must be used first. Complaints are generally settled on the basis of paperwork rather than face-to-face meetings. Complaints under the compulsory jurisdiction (see s.226) are determined by reference to what is, in the opinion of the ombudsmen, fair and reasonable in all the circumstances of the case. In most cases, both sides accept the findings of an adjudicator from the Service but in about 1 in 10 cases either the firm or the consumer asks for a review by the ombudsman; if the consumer accepts an ombudsman's decision within a specified time both the consumer and the firm are bound by the decision. Most complaints are resolved within six months. The service is funded by a combination of a general levy on all firms covered by it, collected by the FSA, and individual case fees.

In 1993 a voluntary organisation, the United Kingdom Ombudsman Association, was created to enable public and private sector ombudsmen (together with other interested persons, *e.g.* academics) to share their experiences, to promote best practices, to define the criteria for using the term "ombudsman" and to accord public recognition to those ombudsmen schemes which met the defined criteria ((1) independence of the ombudsmen from the organisations over which they have jurisdiction, (2) effectiveness, (3) fairness and (4) public accountability). Subsequently, the Association was broadened to cover ombudsmen working in Ireland and renamed the British and Irish Ombudsman Association (see *www.bioa.org*). The Association has, *inter alia*, held conferences to discuss matters affecting ombudsmen, made representations to Government and the European Union, and drafted recommendations for best practice on topics such as the consistency of ombudsmen's decisions and conflicts of interest affecting ombudsmen. In 2005 there were 17 different ombudsmen schemes recognised by the Association in the United Kingdom and four in Ireland. Private sector ombudsmen were still primarily operating in the area of financial services but more recent members included the Estate Agents Ombudsman (dealing with complaints against the large chains of estate agents from private individuals as actual or potential buyers or sellers of residential property in the United Kingdom) and the Funeral Ombudsman (investigating complaints against funeral directors belonging to the major trade associations).

Not all private sector ombudsmen have been successful in providing independent and effective redress for aggrieved individuals. Many of the so called "ombudsmen" created by national newspapers to deal with readers' complaints have been relatively powerless and lacking in credible independence: see A.R. Mowbray, "Newspaper Ombudsmen: The British Experience" (1991) 12 *Journal of Media Law and Practice* 91.

Lord Woolf M.R. has advocated that private sector ombudsmen "should be extended to new fields; that they should remain separate from the courts, but there should be a relationship between them and the courts which enable them to support one another" (The Tom Sargant Memorial Lecture 1996 (1996) 146 N.L.J. 1701 at p.1702). This relationship would involve the ombudsmen being able to refer questions of law to the courts and the civil courts having the power to refer disputed issues of fact for investigation by ombudsmen.

(E) Other Complaints Mechanisms

The various Ombudsmen's offices discussed in this chapter must be seen in the wider context of the formal and informal complaint mechanisms that exist in respect of the multifarious activities of the state, and which have come under increasing scrutiny in recent years. On the role of MPs in handling complaints, see R. Rawlings, "Parliamentary Redress of Grievance" in C. Harlow (ed.), *Public Law and Politics* (1986) and "The MP's Complaints Service" (1990) 53 M.L.R. 22 and 149. On the handling of complaints in local government, see N. Lewis and P. Birkinshaw, "Taking Complaints Seriously: A Study in Local Government Practice" in M. Partington and J. Jowell (eds), *Welfare Law and Social Policy* (1979); N. Lewis, M. Seneviratne and S. Cracknell, *Complaints Procedures in Local Government* (1987), summarised by the latter two authors at (1988) 66 *Public Administration* 181; P. McCarthy *et al.*, *Grievances, Complaints and Local Government* (1992). In 1978, the Local Authorities Association published a Code of Practice, *Complaints Procedures: A Code of Practice for Local Government and Waters Authorities for dealing with queries and complaints* which has been supplemented by a Code of Practice issued by the Local Government Ombudsmen entitled "Devising a Complaints System". More generally, see P. Birkinshaw, *Grievances, Remedies and the State* (2nd ed., 1994), Ch.2.

Birkinshaw (*op. cit.*) has noted the historically "pervasive" practice among government departments of adopting informal or formal but unpublished mechanisms for dealing with complaints, as an aid to discretion or as a means of avoiding "a more rigorous and formal statutory process of hearing grievances or complaints" (Birkinshaw in P. McAuslan and John F. McEldowney (ed.), *Law, Legitimacy and the Constitution* (1985), pp. 164–165). Even today, ". . . in spite of many statutory appeal or complaints procedures, departments make widespread resort to informal methods for the resolution of grievances" (Birkinshaw, *Grievances* (*op. cit.*), p.39). The Council on Tribunals has protested against the introduction of internal review procedures as a substitute for a right of appeal to an independent body: see Annual Reports for 1989–90 (1990–91 HC 64), paras 1.6–1.10, and 1990–91 (1991–92 HC 97), paras 3.25–3.28.

Notes

1. It has been increasingly the norm for the departments and agencies that have most direct dealings with members of the public, and accordingly generate most complaints to establish on a non-statutory basis an independent complaints tier at the top of the internal complaints structure. The persons appointed are commonly senior figures from outside the department or agency; they become part of the department or agency reporting to the ministerial head but are independent of the service providers. They are themselves subject to the jurisdiction of the PCA. They have differing powers and titles. The main examples include the Adjudicator originally appointed for the Inland Revenue and Customs & Excise; the Complaints Adjudicator for Companies House; the Prisons Ombudsman; and the Independent Case Examiner for the Child Support Agency. The Parliamentary Ombudsman has criticised the absence of such an independent tier for Jobcentre Plus; the existence of such a tier would allow the PCA to concentrate on the more complex and intractable cases (Annual Report, 2003–04 HC 702, p.8).

2. The Office of Prisons and Probation Ombudsman (as it now is) was first established in 1994 by the Home Secretary in the exercise of his general powers in respect of prisons and prisoners. He is independent of the Prison and National Probation Services, but not of the Department in that he reports to (and can be removed by) the Home Secretary, who sets the terms of reference. He investigates complaints by prisoners and people on probation and other orders, parole or licence supervised by the NPS, who have gone through internal stages of informal complaint, formal complaint and appeal, without resolution of the matter. From April 1, 2004, he has been asked to investigate all deaths in prisons and deaths of residents of probation hostels and immigration detention accommodation. He also has the discretion to investigate, to the extent appropriate, cases that raise issues about the care provided by a prison. He has inquired into allegations in the *Daily Mirror* of racism and abuse, and into the subsequent fire at Yarl's Wood Removal Centre. There are exclusions from jurisdiction in respect of such matters as policy decisions taken personally by ministers, and the merits of decisions taken by ministers (unless they agree). The original terms of reference were narrowed following a major clash between the ombudsman and the Prison Service over whether a decision to return a mandatory life-sentence prisoner to closed conditions fell within them (see S. Livingstone, T. Owen and A. Macdonald, *Prison Law* (3rd ed., 2003), pp.46–53; *www.ppo.gov.uk*). The department, including the handling of complaints by the PPO, is subject to the jurisdiction of the PCA, but this will end when the Home Office's commitment to put the PPO on a statutory footing is implemented (Annual Report of the PCA, 2003–04 HC 702, p.20).

The Select Committee on the PCA criticised the use of the title "ombudsman" where the department or agency is within the PCA's jurisdiction (1993–94 HC 33, para.28). The Government agreed that it was important to avoid public confusion about the status of different "ombudsmen", but it would be difficult to change the formal titles of existing complaints officers (1993–94 HC 619).

3. The remit of the Adjudicator's Office has been extended to cover complaints about the Customs & Excise and the Contributions Agency (which merged with the IR in 1999) (1995), the Public Guardianship Office (2001) and the Insolvency Service (2003), without institutional reform. The operation of the Adjudicator's Office has been praised for its openness, fairness and effectiveness (see D. Oliver, [1993] P.L. 407; P.E. Morris, [1996] P.L. 309) but the scheme has been said to be flawed in terms of perceived independence and accountability (Morris, *op. cit*, at p.321). On the other hand the existence of an (at least relatively) independent tier nearer to the point of decision than the PCA seems helpful.

4. The importance of complaints procedures received a new emphasis in the Government's *Citizen's Charter*, Cm.1599 (1991). The Charter applied to all public services, including government departments and agencies, local authorities, the NHS, the courts, police and emergency services, and to the key utilities in the private sector. It set out seven Principles of Public Service:

"Every citizen is entitled to expect:

• **Standards**
Explicit standards, published and prominently displayed at the point of delivery. These standards should invariably include courtesy and helpfulness from staff, accuracy in accordance with statutory entitlements, and a commitment to prompt action, which might be expressed in terms of a target response or waiting time. If targets are to be stretched, it may not be possible to guarantee them in every case; minimum, as well as average, standards may be necessary. There should be a clear presumption that standards will be progressively improved as services become more efficient.

• **Openness**
There should be no secrecy about how public services are run, how much they cost, who is in charge, and whether or not they are meeting their standards. Public servants should not be anonymous. Save only where there is a real threat to their safety, all those who deal directly with the public should wear name badges and give their name on the telephone and in letters.

• **Information**
Full, accurate information should be readily available, in plain language, about what services are being provided. Targets should be published, together with full and audited information about the results achieved. Wherever possible, information should be in comparable form, so that there is a pressure to emulate the best.

• **Choice**
The public sector should provide choice wherever practicable. The people affected by services should be consulted. Their views about the services they use should be sought regularly and systematically to inform decisions about what services should be provided.

• **Non-discrimination**
Services should be available regardless of race or sex. Leaflets are being printed in minority languages where there is a need. In Wales public bodies are aware of the needs of Welsh speakers.

• **Accessibility**
Services should be run to suit the convenience of customers, not staff. This means flexible opening hours, and telephone inquiry points that direct callers quickly to someone who can help them.

• **And if things go wrong?**
At the very least, the citizen is entitled to a good explanation, or an apology. He or she should be told **why** the train is late, or **why** the doctor could not keep the appointment. There should be a well-publicised and readily available complaints procedure. If there is a serious problem, it should be put right. And lessons must be learnt so that mistakes are not repeated. Nobody wants to see money diverted from service improvement into large-scale compensation for indifferent services. But the Government intends to introduce new forms of redress where these can be made to stimulate rather than distract from efficiency".

These principles were subsequently reflected in a large number of charters covering key public services at a national level and several thousand covering local service providers. A Charter Mark award scheme recognised excellence and innovation in public service. In 1993, Drewry commented ([1993] P.L. 248 at p.256):

"One's view of the merits of the Citizen's Charter depends on one's views about the political philosophy to which it relates. Disciples of Public Choice will presumably welcome it as a desirable move to redress an imbalance of power between the providers and the consumers of public services; those who do not subscribe to such a philosophy may nevertheless be willing to recognise the Charter as a logical extension of recent policy tendencies—though those who are hostile to those tendencies may see it as a cynical way of squeezing extra productivity out of a rapidly shrinking and over-stretched public sector".

Birkinshaw's assessment of charterism was that "the image is of a government maximising its discretion in government while creating a market for self-interested individuals to complain about other's shortcoming while successfully cocooning themselves from effective censure": *Grievances, Remedies and the State, op. cit.*, p.18. For different views see: W. Waldegrave, *The Reality of Reform and Accountability in Today's Public Service* (1993); A. Barron and C. Scott, "The Citizen's Charter Programme" (1992) M.L.R. 526, and R. Bellamy and J. Greenway, "The New Right Conception of Citizenship and the Citizen's Charter" (1995) 30 *Government and Opposition* 469.

The Labour Government initially revamped and renamed the Charter as "Service First". See C. Scott, [1999] P.L. 595, noting a shift away from the Charter's avowedly consumerist and market ideology. The main elements were then incorporated in the White Paper, *Modernising Government* (Cm.4310, March 1999).

"So the spirit of the original Citizen's Charter lives on—albeit with new nomenclature and as part of a wider agenda of 'modernisation' and 'consumer focus'. . . Charter principles have become absorbed into the bloodstream of public services— and are largely taken for granted by both the producers and users of those services" (G. Drewry, "Whatever Happened to the Citizen's Charter?" [2002] P.L. 9 at p.12).

The Charter Mark scheme remains in operation. One outcome of the Citizen's Charter has been to ensure the existence of complaints schemes across the public service.

(F) Financial Redress

Guidance on the provision of financial redress by departments, agencies and NDPBs in cases where maladministration or (in some situations) the sub-standard quality of the service provided has occurred to the detriment of an individual, company or other body is contained in the Treasury's document, *Government Accounting* (*www.government-accounting.gov.uk*), para.18.7. It applies not only where there is a recommendation by the Parliamentary Ombudsman, but also where the department concludes that there has been maladministration (whether on not there has been a complaint). If the department accepts that maladministration has occurred and financial redress is appropriate, the general principle should be to provide redress which is fair and reasonable in the light of all the facts and circumstances of the case. Where financial loss has been caused or (reasonable) costs incurred, the general approach should be to restore the complainant to the position he or she would have enjoyed had the maladministration not occurred. Payment for non-financial loss can be made in respect of such matters as inconvenience, annoyance, frustration, worry, distress, suffering or anguish, and hardship, but should be exceptional (paras 18.7.5, 18.7.24). Compensation for delays in payments may be appropriate (paras 18.7.17 to 18.7.23).

For comments comparing financial redress recommended by the PCA with tort claims, see M. Amos, [2000] P.L. 21.

DELEGATED LEGISLATION[1]

"PARLIAMENT and government would grind to a halt if there were not built into our constitution an adequate system of Executive legislation" (First Special Report from the Joint Committee on Statutory Instruments 1977–78 (1977–78 HC 169), para.37). In the early part of this century there was considerable debate about the constitutional propriety of the delegation by Parliament, particularly to the government, of powers to legislate. The Committee on Ministers' Powers (Cmd.4060 (1932)) concluded (p.58) that the delegation of legislative powers "is legitimate for certain purposes, within certain limits, and under certain safeguards. It is plain that it is in fact inevitable".

Various reasons were put forward for this conclusion (below, p.206). The committee noted a number of criticisms of delegated legislation that had been voiced, but did not think that the evidence justified "an alarmist view of the constitutional situation" (p.54). What was lacking was coherence and uniformity in operation. There were "real dangers incidental to delegated legislation" and "safeguards" were necessary. The Committee recommended that the existing Rules Publication Act 1893, which required certain categories of delegated legislation to be published, should be replaced by a more comprehensive measure. The many different forms in which an enabling statute might require delegated legislation to be laid before Parliament should be replaced by a standardised procedure. These two matters were addressed by the Statutory Instruments Act 1946 (below, p.211). It was also recommended that each House of Parliament should set up a Standing Committee for the purpose of considering and reporting (a) on every Bill containing a proposal to confer law-making power on a Minister; and (b) on delegated legislation that was subject to a laying requirement. The House of Commons acted on recommendation (b) in 1944. The House of Lords continued to scrutinise delegated legislation that required the approval of the House under arrangements that had commenced in 1925. Following the recommendations of the Joint Committee on Delegated Legislation (The Brooke Committee Report, 1971–1972 HL 184, HC 475), these separate arrangements were replaced by a Joint Committee on Statutory Instruments (below, pp.222–231). Continuing concern as to the adequacy of arrangements for scrutiny of delegated legislation led to further institutional developments, with the establishment by the House of Lords of the Select Committee on the Scrutiny of Delegated Powers.

The establishment of a special procedure for making deregulation orders under Pt I of the Deregulation and Contracting Out Act 1994, which normally may have the effect of modifying primary legislation, saw the introduction of special arrangements for scrutiny by the Lords Committee on Delegated Powers and a new Commons Deregulation Committee.

---

[1] The making of delegated legislation is considered as part of the wider legislative process, including the making of statutes and European legislation, by D.R. Miers and A.C. Page, *Legislation* (2nd ed., 1990); S.H. Bailey, M.J. Gunn, J. Ching and D.C. Ormerod, *Smith, Bailey and Gunn on the Modern English Legal System* (4th ed., 2002), Ch.5. For an unofficial but authoritative review, see *Making the Law: The Report of the Hansard Society Commission on the Legislative Process* (1993). Delegated legislation is also considered in the standard works on administrative law: *Craig*, Ch.7; *Wade and Forsyth*, Ch. 22; and has been the subject of reviews by the House of Commons Select Committee on Procedure: Fourth Report, 1995–96 HC 152, *Delegated Legislation* and First Report, 1999–2000 HC 48, *Delegated Legislation* (see below, p.222).

These were subsequently replaced by regulatory reform orders under broader powers conferred by the Regulatory Reform Act 2001, and the relevant committees of the House of Commons and House of Lords were renamed. A Sifting Committee (the Merits of Statutory Instruments Committee) was established by the House of Lords in 2003. Finally, a further special class of delegated legislation has been created in the form of remedial orders under the Human Rights Act 1998 (below, p.316).

(A) THE NECESSITY FOR DELEGATION

REPORT OF THE COMMITTEE ON MINISTERS' POWERS

(Cmd.4060, 1932, pp.51–52)

Necessity for delegation

11. We have already expressed the view that the system of delegated legislation is both legitimate and constitutionally desirable for certain purposes, within certain limits, and under certain safeguards. We proceed to set out briefly—mostly by way of recapitulation—the reasons which have led us to this conclusion:—

Pressure on Parliamentary time

(1) Pressure upon Parliamentary time is great. The more procedure and subordinate matters can be withdrawn from detailed Parliamentary discussion, the greater will be the time which Parliament can devote to the consideration of essential principles in legislation.

Technicality of subject matter

(2) The subject matter of modern legislation is very often of a technical nature. Apart from the broad principles involved, technical matters are difficult to include in a Bill, since they cannot be effectively discussed in Parliament. . . .

Unforeseen contingencies

(3) If large and complex schemes of reform are to be given technical shape, it is difficult to work out the administrative machinery in time to insert in the Bill all the provisions required; it is impossible to foresee all the contingencies and local conditions for which provision must eventually be made. . . .

Flexibility

(4) The practice, further, is valuable because it provides for a power of constant adaptation to unknown future conditions without the necessity of amending legislation. Flexibility is essential. The method of delegated legislation permits of the rapid utilisation of experience, and enables the results of consultation with interests affected by the operation of new Acts to be translated into practice. In matters, for example, like mechanical road transport, where technical development is rapid, and often unforeseen, delegation is essential to meet the new positions which arise.

Opportunity for experiment

(5) The practice, again, permits of experiment being made and thus affords an opportunity, otherwise difficult to ensure, of utilising the lessons of experience. The advantage of this in matters, for instance, like town planning, is too obvious to require detailed emphasis.

Emergency powers

(6) In a modern State there are many occasions when there is a sudden need of legislative action. For many such needs delegated legislation is the only convenient or even possible remedy. No doubt, where there is time, on legislative issues of great magnitude, it is right that Parliament itself should either decide what the broad outlines of the legislation shall be, or at least indicate the general scope of the delegated powers which it considers are called for by the occasion.

Note
One of the members of the Committee, Miss Ellen Wilkinson, added a note (pp.137–138) which commenced:

"While agreeing generally with this report I would like to add a note regarding the tone of certain passages which rather give the impression that the delegating of legislation is a necessary evil, inevitable in the present state of pressure on parliamentary time, but nevertheless a tendency to be watched with misgiving and carefully safeguarded.

I feel that in the conditions of the modern state, which not only has to undertake immense new social services, but which before long may be responsible for the greater part of the industrial and commercial activities of the country, the practice of Parliament delegating legislation and the power to make regulations, instead of being grudgingly conceded, ought to be widely extended, and new ways devised to facilitate the process".

She went on to argue that Parliament could only deal really effectively with the principle and general plan of proposed legislation. "The details should be left to the experts." In practice, the distinction between "principle" (for primary legislation) and "detail" (for delegated legislation) can be difficult to draw. (See, *e.g.* J.A.G. Griffith, "The Place of Parliament in the Legislative Process" (1951) 14 M.L.R. 279 at p.425). In more recent years the Joint Committee on Statutory Instruments (see below, pp.222, *et seq.*) has expressed concern:

FIRST SPECIAL REPORT FROM THE JOINT COMMITTEE ON STATUTORY INSTRUMENTS 1995–96

REPORT ON PROCEEDINGS 1986–96 (1995–96 HL PAPER 103, HC 582), pp.3–4

General aspects of secondary legislation

Number of statutory instruments

4. In 1973, when the Committee was first established, 2,227 instruments came into force. In 1992 the annual total exceeded 3,000 for the first time and it has remained above 3,000 ever since. In 1995 it reached 3,345. The overall

volume of statutory instruments has increased markedly over this period. In 1988 the total length of all instruments was 6,342 pages; by 1993, the last year for which figures are available, it had grown to 7,944 pages. Instruments registered in 1995 have yet to appear in bound volumes but take up approximately two feet, six inches of bookshelf.

5. The Committee does not consider all of these, local instruments not subject to any kind of parliamentary proceeding being outside its order of reference. It is difficult to compare figures for instruments considered by the Committee as parliamentary sessions vary so much in length. Nevertheless, table 2 below[2] demonstrates clearly that the number of instruments considered by the Committee has grown over the same period. . . .

Scope of instruments

6. It is generally accepted that the nature of statutory instruments has also changed. Instruments have become both more complex and more far-reaching in scope. As the Committee argued in its submission to the Procedure Committee in 1985, "secondary legislation has increasingly been used, not just to implement the 'nuts and bolts' of policies laid down in primary legislation, but actually to *change* policies in ways that were sometimes not envisaged when the enabling primary legislation was passed".

7. Recognition of this concern was one of the factors which led to the establishment of the House of Lords Delegated Powers Scrutiny Committee in Session 1992–1993. That Committee has the responsibility of examining the powers in proposed new primary legislation which will allow the making of statutory instruments in the future. The Committee's work is intended to reduce the risk that instruments change policies in a way that Parliament had not envisaged and to ensure that Parliament has appropriate control over the more wide-ranging powers. We accept that the trend towards the pursuance of measures through secondary rather than primary legislation is probably irreversible but hope that the Delegated Powers Scrutiny Committee will continue to contribute towards more effective scrutiny under these changing circumstances.

(B) The Forms Of Delegated Legislation

REPORT FROM THE JOINT COMMITTEE ON DELEGATED LEGISLATION 1971–72

(1971–72 HL 184, HC 475) pp.X–XII

Delegated legislation:

6. In his memorandum of evidence to Your Committee, Counsel to Mr Speaker (Sir Robert Speed) has defined delegated legislation thus:—

(1) Delegated legislation covers every exercise of a power to legislate conferred by or under an Act of Parliament or which is given the force of

---

[2] Omitted (ed.). In 2003–04 the Joint Committee considered 1,371 instruments and reported 88; the Select Committee considered 74 and reported 1.

law by virtue of an Act of Parliament. It can be expressed in a variety of forms:—

    (a) Measures passed by the General Synod of the Church of England.

    (b) Provisional orders confirmed by a Provisional Order Confirmation Act, including those made under the Private Legislation Procedure (Scotland) Act, 1936.

    (c) Orders in Council and regulations, orders, rules, schemes or other instruments made by a Minister or Government Department or Rule Committee or similar authority.

    (d) Orders, bye-laws or other instruments, made by public or local authorities (in some cases confirmed by the Privy Council, a Minister or a Government Department).

(2) In some cases the power to legislate may be conferred by legislation which is itself a piece of delegated legislation, *e.g.* an Order in Council.

(3) The documents by which a power of delegated legislation is exercised are, in the main, statutory instruments.

(4) The definition of statutory instruments varies according to whether the Act under which the instrument is made was passed before or after January 1, 1948, the date on which the Statutory Instruments Act 1946 [below, pp.211–217] was brought into operation.

(5) In regard to post-1947 Acts, under section 1(1) of the Statutory Instruments Act 1946 every Order in Council made in exercise of a statutory power is a statutory instrument, and every instrument made by a Minister of the Crown in exercise of a statutory power is a statutory instrument if the Act conferring the power expressly so provides.

(6) As regards pre-1948 Acts, broadly speaking, every instrument made under an Act of Parliament—

    (i) by Her Majesty in Council, or

    (ii) by a Minister of the Crown, or

    (iii) relating to any court in the United Kingdom, is a statutory instrument if it is of a legislative and not an executive character.

(7) Measures are not statutory instruments, although in some cases the Measure does apply the Statutory Instruments Act 1946 to the subordinate legislation made thereunder. Also, as a general rule, the instruments referred to in category 1(d) above are not statutory instruments.

(8) Statutory instruments are classified as local or general according to their subject matter. Unless there are special reasons to the contrary, a statutory instrument which is in the nature of a local and personal or private Act is classified as local, and a statutory instrument which is in the nature of a public general Act is classified as general.

(9) The classification is done in the first place by the Minister responsible for the preparation of the Order in Council or the Minister by whom the instrument is made. He, when sending the instrument to the Queen's Printer, certifies it as local or general.

(10) There is a procedure under which a Committee composed of Officers of both Houses, called the Statutory Instruments Reference Committee,

may determine any question referred to them regarding the classification of instruments as general or local. . . .

Notes

1. A number of significant categories of subordinate legislation are not "statutory instruments". These include (1) the byelaws of local authorities, made under powers conferred by the Local Government Act 1972 and other statutes (see *Cross*, Ch. 6) and below, pp.233–238; (2) special procedure orders (see S.H. Bailey, M.J. Gunn, J. Ching and D.C. Ormerod, *Smith Bailey and Gunn on the Modern English Legal System* (4th ed., 2002), p.306); (3) Orders in Council made under the royal prerogative (*ibid.*, p.334). A further special class of statutory instruments are those made by the National Assembly for Wales: see the Government of Wales Act 1998, ss.64–68.

2. Unlike primary legislation, which is almost invariably drafted by parliamentary counsel, statutory instruments made by ministers are normally drafted by departmental lawyers (see Report of the Joint Committee on Delegated Legislation 1971–72 (1971–72 HL 184, HC 475), pp.194 *et seq.*, Memorandum by the Civil Service Department on Departmental Procedures in Producing Delegated Legislation; E.C. Page, *Governing by Numbers* (2001), Ch.6, discussing the relative contributions of lawyers and administrators, the latter commonly being relatively junior). The Joint Committee on Statutory Instruments (First Special Report on Proceedings 1986–96 (1995–96 HL Paper 103, HC 582), pp.5–6), has drawn attention to complaints that regularly arise, including common drafting errors, and observed that "many of these problems could be avoided by closer attention to the guidelines set out in Statutory Instrument Practice" (an internal guidance document used by departments). The Hansard Society Commission rejected a proposal that responsibility for drafting be transferred to Parliamentary Counsel: departmental administrators and lawyers will be much more familiar with practicalities and details regarding the application of legislation; the timing of drafting of SIs is closely related to decisions as to commencement of the statutory provisions, which are departmental responsibilities; the present arrangements would more easily facilitate the increased direct consultation with interested bodies recommended by the Commission (*Making the Law*, p.49).

3. Consultation with other public bodies and outside interest groups is an established feature of the process of making delegated legislation. An example of a statutory advisory body is the Council on Tribunals, which must be consulted before procedural rules are made for a large number of statutory tribunals (Tribunals and Inquiries Act 1992, s.8 and Sch.1) (above, p.107). Another is the Social Security Advisory Committee set up by the Social Security Act 1980 to replace the National Insurance Advisory Committee and the Supplementary Benefits Commission (see N.J. Wikeley, *Ogus, Barendt and Wikeley's, The Law of Social Security* (4th ed., 1995), pp.625–626). One of its functions is to comment on regulations concerning social security benefits other than industrial injuries benefits, war pensions and occupational pensions (for which there are separate bodies). Draft regulations must be sent for it to comment on unless it appears to the Secretary of State "that by reason of the urgency of the matter it is inexpedient so to refer them" or the Committee agrees (Social Security Administration Act 1992, s.173(1)); other exceptions are set out in Sch.7, Pt I, and temporary exceptions are set out in s.173(5). If the Secretary of State subsequently lays the regulations before Parliament, he must lay, in addition, the Committee's report and a statement indicating the extent to which any recommendations have been implemented, and in so far as effect has not been given to them, his reasons why not (1992 Act, s.174). Where draft regulations have not been submitted to the Committee because of urgency, the final regulations must be submitted as soon as practicable, unless the Committee agrees. Moreover, the Secretary of State may, in urgent cases where he has referred drafts to the Committee make the regulations before receiving the Committee's advice (1992 Act, s.173(3)). In these

cases, the Secretary of State must lay the Committee's report before Parliament, with a statement of the extent (if any) to which he proposes to give effect to any recommendations (1992 Act, s.173(4)). See *R. v Secretary of State for Social Services Ex p. Cotton*, *The Times*, December 14, 1985 (sufficient compliance with duty to consult where proposed amendments to regulations were summarised), but *cf. Howker v Secretary of State for Work and Pensions* [2002] EWCA Civ 1623, where a regulation was held to be invalid on the ground of lack of consultation with the SSAC, after committee members had been materially misled by department officials into agreeing that a reference to the SSAC was not necessary; the agreement was not an "informed agreement" and a reference would have been necessary had the true position been understood.

4. Where a statute requires consultation with particular interests, failure to do so will normally render the regulations *ultra vires*, at least as regards the interests not consulted (see below, p.646). In many areas of government decision-making, the courts have been prepared to imply into a statute a requirement of prior consultation with affected interests. This is one aspect of the requirements of "natural justice" and apply to those with a "legitimate expectation" of being consulted (see pp.690 *et seq.*). However, the courts have been unwilling to imply such requirements prior to the making of delegated legislation. See *Bates v Lord Hailsham of St Marylebone* [1972] 1 W.L.R. 1373 (below, p.720).

5. On the operation of the consultation process in respect of delegated legislation, see J.F. Garner, [1964] P.L. 105; A.D. Jergeson [1978] P.L. 290; Page (*op.cit*), Ch.7, noting that the process is dominated by the executive but that interest groups do have an impact, particularly where "their case can be made in a form that fits the conception of what government officials want to achieve" (p.154).

(C) PRINTING, PUBLICATION AND LAYING BEFORE PARLIAMENT

These matters are regulated by the Statutory Instruments Act 1946 and the Statutory Instruments Regulations 1947.

STATUTORY INSTRUMENTS ACT 1946

Definition of "Statutory Instrument"

1.—(1) Where by this Act or any Act passed after the commencement of this Act to make, confirm or approve orders, rules, regulations or other subordinate legislation, is conferred on His Majesty in Council or on any Minister of the Crown then, if the power is expressed—

(a) in the case of a power conferred on His Majesty, to be exercisable by Order in Council;
(b) in the case of a power conferred on a Minister of the Crown, to be exercisable by statutory instrument,

any document by which that power is exercised shall be known as a "statutory instrument" and the provisions of this Act shall apply thereto accordingly.

[(1A) The references in subsection (1) to a Minister of the Crown shall be construed as including references to the National Assembly for Wales.][3]

---

[3] [ed.] Inserted by the Government of Wales Act 1998, Sch.12, para.2.

(2) Where by any Act passed before the commencement of this Act power to make statutory rules within the meaning of the Rules Publication Act 1893, was conferred on any rule-making authority within the meaning of that Act, any document by which that power is exercised after the commencement of this Act shall, save as is otherwise provided by regulations made under this Act, be known as a "statutory instrument" and the provisions of this Act shall apply thereto accordingly.

Numbering, printing, publication and citation

2.—(1) Immediately after the making of any statutory instrument, it shall be sent to the King's printer of Acts of Parliament and numbered in accordance with regulations made under this Act, and except in such cases as may be provided by any Act passed after the commencement of this Act or prescribed by regulations made under this Act, copies thereof shall as soon as possible be printed and sold by [or under the authority of] the King's printer of Acts of Parliament.

(2) Any statutory instrument may, without prejudice to any other mode of citation, be cited by the number given to it in accordance with the provisions of this section, and the calendar year.

Supplementary provisions as to publication

3.—(1) Regulations made for the purposes of this Act shall make provision for the publication by His Majesty's Stationery Office of lists showing the date upon which every statutory instrument printed and sold by [or under the authority of] the King's printer of Acts of Parliament was first issued by [or under the authority of] that office: and in any legal proceedings a copy of any list so published [. . .]shall be received in evidence as a true copy, and an entry therein shall be conclusive evidence of the date on which any statutory instrument was first issued by [or under the authority of] His Majesty's Stationery Office.

(2) In any proceedings against any person for an offence consisting of a contravention of any such statutory instrument, it shall be a defence to prove that the instrument had not been issued by [or under the authority of] His Majesty's Stationery Office at the date of the alleged contravention unless it is proved that at that date reasonable steps had been taken for the purpose of bringing the purport of the instrument to the notice of the public, or of persons likely to be affected by it, or of the person charged.

(3) Save as therein otherwise expressly provided, nothing in this section shall affect any enactment or rules of law relating to the time at which any statutory instrument comes into operation.

Statutory Instruments which are required to be laid before Parliament

4.—(1) Where by this Act or any Act passed after the commencement of this Act any statutory instrument is required to be laid before Parliament after being made, a copy of the instrument shall be laid before each House of Parliament and, subject as hereinafter provided, shall be so laid before the instrument comes into operation:

Provided that if it is essential that any such instrument should come into operation before copies thereof can be so laid as aforesaid, the instrument may be made so as to come into operation before it has been so laid; and where any statutory instrument comes into operation before it is laid before Parliament, notification shall forthwith be sent to the Lord Chancellor and to the Speaker of the House of Commons drawing attention to the fact that copies of the instrument have yet to be laid before Parliament and explaining why such copies were not so laid before the instrument came into operation.

(2) Every copy of any such statutory instrument sold by the King's printer of Acts of Parliament shall bear on the face thereof:

(a) a statement showing the date on which the statutory instrument came or will come into operation; and
(b) either a statement showing the date on which copies thereof were laid before Parliament or a statement that such copies are to be laid before Parliament.

(3) Where any Act passed before the date of the commencement of this Act contains provisions requiring that any Order in Council or other document made in exercise of any power conferred by that or any other Act be laid before Parliament after being made, any statutory instrument made in exercise of that power shall by virtue of this Act be laid before Parliament and the foregoing provisions of this section shall apply thereto accordingly in substitution for any such provisions as aforesaid contained in the Act passed before the said date.

Statutory Instruments which are subject to annulment by resolution of either House of Parliament

5.—(1) Where by this Act or any Act passed after the commencement of this Act, it is provided that any statutory instrument shall be subject to annulment in pursuance of resolution of either House of Parliament, the instrument shall be laid before Parliament after being made and the provisions of the last fore-going section shall apply thereto accordingly, and if either House within the period of forty days beginning with the day on which a copy thereof is laid before it, resolves that an Address be presented to His Majesty praying that the instrument be annulled, no further proceedings shall be taken thereunder after the date of the resolution, and His Majesty may by Order in Council revoke the instrument, so, however, that any such resolution and revocation shall be without prejudice to the validity of anything previously done under the instrument or to the making of a new statutory instrument.

(2) Where any Act passed before the date of the commencement of this Act contains provisions requiring that any Order in Council or other document made in exercise of any power conferred by that or any other Act shall be laid before Parliament after being made and shall cease to be in force or may be annulled, as the case may be, if within a specified period either House presents an address to His Majesty or passes a resolution to that effect, then, subject to the provisions of any Order in Council made under this Act, any statutory instrument made in exercise of the said power shall by virtue of this Act be subject to annulment in pursuance of a resolution of either House of

Parliament and the provisions of the last foregoing subsection shall apply thereto accordingly in substitution for any such provisions as aforesaid contained in the Act passed before the said date.

Statutory Instruments of which drafts are to be laid before Parliament

6.—(1) Where by this Act or any Act passed after the commencement of this Act it is provided that a draft of any statutory instrument shall be laid before Parliament, but the Act does not prohibit the making of the instrument without the approval of Parliament, then, in the case of an Order in Council the draft shall not be submitted to His Majesty in Council, and in any other case the statutory instrument shall not be made, until after the expiration of a period of forty days beginning with the day on which a copy of the draft is laid before each House of Parliament, or, if such copies are laid on different days, with the later of the two days, and if within that period either House resolves that the draft be not submitted to His Majesty or that the statutory instrument be not made, as the case may be, no further proceedings shall be taken thereon, but without prejudice to the laying before Parliament of a new draft.

(2) Where any Act passed before the date of the commencement of this Act contains provisions requiring that a draft of any Order in Council or other document to be made in exercise of any power conferred by that or any other Act shall be laid before Parliament before being submitted to His Majesty, or before being made, as the case may be, and that it shall not be so submitted or made if within a specified period either House presents an address to His Majesty or passes a resolution to that effect, then, subject to the provisions of any Order in Council made under this Act, a draft of any statutory instrument made in exercise of the said power shall by virtue of this Act be laid before Parliament and the provisions of the last foregoing subsection shall apply thereto accordingly in substitution for any such provisions as aforesaid contained in the Act passed before the said date.

Supplementary provisions as to ss.4, 5 and 6

7.—(1) In reckoning for the purposes of either of the last two foregoing sections any period of forty days, no account shall be taken of any time during which Parliament is dissolved or prorogued or during which both Houses are adjourned for more than four days.

(2) In relation to any instrument required by any Act, whether passed before or after the commencement of this Act, to be laid before the House of Commons only, the provisions of the last three foregoing sections shall have effect as if references to that House were therein substituted for references to Parliament and for references to either House and each House thereof.

(3) The provisions of sections four and five of this Act shall not apply to any statutory instrument being an order which is subject to special Parliamentary procedure, or to any other instrument which is required to be laid before Parliament, or before the House of Commons, for any period before it comes into operation. . . .

Interpretation

11.—(1) For the purposes of this Act, any power to make, confirm or approve orders, rules, regulations or other subordinate legislation conferred on the Treasury, . . ., the Board of Trade or any other government department shall be deemed to be conferred on the Minister of the Crown in charge of that department.

(2) If any question arises whether any board, commissioners or other body on whom any such power as aforesaid is conferred are a government department within the meaning of this section, or what Minister of the Crown is in charge of them, that question shall be referred to and determined by [the Minister for the Civil Service].

Notes

1. The words "or under the authority of" were added to ss.2 and 3, and the words "purporting to bear the imprint of the King's printer" deleted from s.3 by the Statutory Instruments (Production and Sale) Act 1996. Indeed, s.1(1) of the 1996 Act provided that the 1946 Act "shall have effect and be taken always to have had effect" with these amendments. However, this "does not affect the operation of section 3(2) of that Act in relation to proceedings commenced before June 21, 1996" (1996 Act, s.1(2)). The changes were made to regularise the fact that the Queen's Printer had in practice contracted out the printing of SIs since at least 1965, failing to note that this did not comply with the statute. (Curiously, there was in fact provision for *statutes* to be printed under the authority of the Queen's Printer.) See HC Deb., Vol.280, cols 984–1009, July 3, 1996; HL Deb., Vol. 574, cols 813–822, 1381–1393, July 16, 24, 1996. In addition to publication in print form, statutory instruments are now published on the internet, together with the Explanatory Memoranda prepared for any SI or draft SI laid before Parliament. These provide information about the SI's policy objective and policy implications.

2. The 1946 Act was of considerable importance in that it brought a measure of order into what had previously been a highly convoluted area, by providing one basic procedure (albeit with some variants) for the making of delegated legislation by central government. On the history of delegation, see C.K. Allen, *Law and Orders* (3rd ed., 1965), Ch.2.

3. The Statutory Instruments Regulations 1947 (SI 1948/1) were made under s.8 of the 1946 Act, which enables the Minister for the Civil Service, with the concurrence of the Lord Chancellor and the Speaker, to make regulations for the purposes of the Act. They were amended by SIs 1977/641 and 1982/1728. Regulation 2(3) provides that s.1(2) of the 1946 Act shall not apply to:

"(a) any document which, although of a legislative character, applies only to a named person or premises and is not required to be laid before or subject to confirmation or approval by Parliament or the House of Commons; or

(b) any Order in Council which, being an Order for which the Lord President of the Council is the responsible authority, confirms or approves subordinate legislation in the nature of a local and personal or private Act; or

(c) any such document as is mentioned in the Schedule to these Regulations".

Regulation 3 requires instruments received by the Queen's Printer to be allocated to the series of the calendar year in which they are made and numbered in that year consecutively as nearly as may be in the order in which they are received. However, instruments subject to the affirmative procedure or special parliamentary procedure are allocated as if made and received on the day they become operative. Regulation 4 provides that instruments are to be classified as local or general. Unless there are special reasons to the contrary, an instrument in the nature of a local or personal or private Act is to be classified as local, and one in the nature of a Public General Act as general. Instruments are to be certified as local or general by the responsible Minister, although the Reference Committee may direct a different classification. Regulations 5 to 8 provide for exemptions from requirements as to printing and sale for (1) local instruments, and general instruments certified by the responsible Minister "to be of a class of document which is or will be otherwise regularly printed as a series and made available to persons affected thereby" (reg.5); (2) temporary instruments (reg.6); (3) a schedule or other document identified by or referred to in an instrument which would otherwise be required to be included in the instrument as printed and sold, where this is "unnecessary or undesirable having regard to the nature of bulk of the document and to any other steps taken or to be taken for bringing its substance to the notice of the public" (reg.7); (4) confidential instruments, where printing and sale of copies before the instrument comes into operation would be "contrary to the public interest" (reg.8). In each case (except that of local instruments) the responsible minister certifies that the exemption applies; in all cases the Reference Committee may direct otherwise. The responsible minister may require the Queen's Printer to comply with s.1(2) in respect of local instruments. Regulation 9 requires HMSO to publish a "Statutory Instruments Issue List" showing the serial number, short title and date of issue of each instrument issued by the office. Regulation 10 requires the publication of an "Annual Edition" comprising copies of all instruments issued (except spent and local instruments), an Annual Numerical and Issue List of Statutory Instruments, a classified list of local instruments, a table showing the effects on existing statutes and statutory instruments, and an index. Regulation 11 establishes a Statutory Instruments Reference Committee, consisting of two or more persons nominated by the Lord Chancellor and the Speaker. Its functions include that of determining any question arising as to numbering, printing or publication of instruments, their classification as general in the nature of a Public General Act or of a local and personal or private Act, and whether a document constitutes a "statutory rule" within the meaning of s.1(2) of the 1946 Act.

4. Section 9(1) of the 1946 Act enables the Queen in Council to apply the provisions of the 1946 Act to powers in pre-1948 statutes to confirm or approve subordinate legislation conferred on a minister of the Crown, where the exercise of such a power would not constitute the making of a statutory rule within the 1893 Act and so would fall outside s.1(2). See the Statutory Instruments (Confirmatory Powers) Order 1947 (SI 1948/2), which applied the Act to certain classes of subordinate legislation authorised by pre-1948 statutes. Most of the classes are no longer important, the legislation in question having since been repealed. One general class that is still provided for is where (1) a minister has power under a pre-1948 statute to confirm or approve subordinate legislation made by an authority which is not a "rule-making authority" under the 1893 Act, (2) the legislation is "of a legislative and not an executive character" and (3) the legislation is required to be laid before Parliament or the House of Commons.

5. Section 1 of the Laying of Documents Before Parliament (Interpretation) Act 1948 provides:

"Meaning of references to laying before Parliament
1.—(1) For the removal of doubt it is hereby declared that a reference in any Act of Parliament or subordinate legislation, whether passed or made before or after the passing of this Act, to the laying of any instrument, report, account or other document before either House of Parliament is, unless the contrary intention appears, to be construed as a reference to the taking, during the existence of a Parliament, of such action as is directed by virtue of any Standing Order, Sessional Order or other direction of that House for the time being in force to constitute the laying of that document before that House, or as is accepted by virtue of the practice of that House

for the time being as constituting such laying, notwithstanding that the action so directed or accepted consists in part or wholly in action capable of being taken otherwise than at or during the time of a sitting of that House; and that a reference in any such Act or subordinate legislation to the laying of any instrument, report, account or other document before Parliament is, unless the contrary intention appears, to be construed accordingly as a reference (construed in accordance with the preceding declaration) to the laying of the document before each House of Parliament.

(2) It is hereby further declared that nothing in section four of the Statutory Instruments Act 1946, is to be taken as indicating an intention that any reference in that section to the laying of copies of certain statutory instruments as therein mentioned is to be construed otherwise than in accordance with the preceding declaration".

By Standing Order No.141, the House of Commons has directed that the delivery of a copy of a statutory instrument to the Votes and Proceedings Office on any day during the existence of a Parliament shall be deemed to be laying before the House. In practice, it is normally then placed in the House of Commons Library. Standing Order No.141 does not, however, apply to instruments required to be laid for any period before it comes into operation. These can only be laid on sitting days. (See *Erskine May's Parliamentary Practice* (21st ed., 1989), pp.543–545).

6. It is unclear whether a requirement that an instrument be laid before Parliament is or is not a pre-condition to the validity of the instrument: see pp.635 *et seq.*). The position appears to be that the matter depends on the exact wording and context of the particular case. There are authorities that suggest that laying requirements are directory: see *Bailey v Williamson* (1873) L.R. 8 Q.B. 118; *Starey v Graham* [1899] 1 Q.B. 406 at 412; *Springer v Doorly* (1950) L.R.B.G. 10 (West Indian Court of Appeal); A.I.L. Campbell [1983] P.L. 43; but see *de Smith, Woolf and Jowell*, p.275, for the argument that they should be mandatory. In *R. v Secretary of State for Social Services, Ex p. Camden LBC*, unreported, February 26, 1986, Macpherson J. held that the requirement in s.33(3)(c) of the Supplementary Benefits Act 1976 that certain social security regulations "shall not be made unless a draft of the regulations has been laid before Parliament and approved by a resolution of each House . . ." was mandatory. Indeed, the words were "clear, strong and mandatory". On appeal, the Court of Appeal assumed this to be so without deciding the point: [1987] 1 W.L.R. 819. The other point that arose for consideration in this case was whether the laying requirement was applicable to a document referred to in the regulations. The regulations in question concerned allowances for board and lodgings and were designed to limit the maximum benefits payable according to areas, and to limit the time for which in any area those benefits would be payable to individual claimants. The regulations provided that in any particular case, the relevant amount was the amount shown as applicable for that area in a booklet entitled *Supplementary Benefit Maximum Amounts, Initial Periods and Board and Lodging Areas*, published by HMSO. The booklet was not laid before Parliament. Macpherson J. held that the booklet did not fall within the laying requirement, as it was not "part of" the statutory instrument, and was not a "document by which the Secretary of State exercises his actual powers" for the purposes of the 1946 Act. See A.I.L. Campbell, [1987] P.L. 328.

R. v SHEER METALCRAFT LTD

[1954] 1 Q.B. 586; [1954] 2 W.L.R. 777; [1954] 1 All E.R. 542
(STREATFEILD J.)

Trial on indictment at Kingston-upon-Thames Assizes. The company, and its managing director were prosecuted for infringement of the Iron and Steel Prices Order 1951

(SI 1951/252). The defendants argued that it was not a valid statutory instrument as its schedules, which set out maximum prices for different commodities of steel, had not been printed with the instrument by the Queen's Printer, as required by s.2(1) of the Statutory Instruments Act 1946 (above, p.212), and the Minister had not certified under reg.7 of the 1947 regulations (above, p.216) that this was unnecessary. Streatfeild J. ruled on this submission.

STREATFEILD J.: . . . [read s.1, 2 and 3 of the 1946 Act (above pp.211–212), and reg.7 of the 1947 Regulations.]

There does not appear to be any definition of what is meant by "issue" [in section 3(1)] but presumably it does mean some act by the Queen's Printer of Acts of Parliament which follows the printing of the instrument. That section, therefore requires that the Queen's Printer shall keep lists showing the date upon which statutory instruments are printed and issued.

It seems to follow from the wording of this subsection that the making of an instrument is one thing and the issue of it is another. If it is made it can be contravened; if it has not been issued then that provides a defence to a person charged with its contravention. It is then upon the Crown to prove that, although it has not been issued, reasonable steps have been taken for the purpose of bringing the instrument to the notice of the public or persons likely to be affected by it.

I do not think that it can be said that to make a valid statutory instrument it is required that all of these stages should be gone through; namely, the making, the laying before Parliament, the printing and the certification of that part of it which it might be unnecessary to have printed. In my judgment the making of an instrument is complete when it is first of all made by the Minister concerned and after it has been laid before Parliament. When that has been done it then becomes a valid statutory instrument, totally made under the provisions of the Act.

The remaining provisions to which my attention has been drawn, in my view, are purely procedure for the issue of an instrument validly made—namely, that in the first instance it must be printed by the Queen's Printer unless it is certified to be unnecessary to print it; it must then be included in a list published by Her Majesty's Stationery Office showing the dates when it is issued and it may be issued by the Queen's Printer of Acts of Parliament. Those matters, in my judgment, are matters of procedure. If they were not and if they were stages in the perfection of a valid statutory instrument, I cannot see that section 3(2) would be necessary, because if each one of those stages were necessary to make a statutory instrument valid, it would follow that there could be no infringement of an unissued instrument and therefore it would be quite unnecessary to provide a defence to a contravention of any such instrument. In my view the very fact that subsection (2) of section 3 refers to a defence that the instrument has not been issued postulates that the instrument must have been validly made in the first place otherwise it could never have been contravened.

In those circumstances I hold that this instrument was validly made and approved and that it was made by or signed on behalf of the Minister on its being laid before Parliament; that so appears on the face of the instrument itself. In my view, the fact that the Minister failed to certify under regulation 7 does not invalidate the instrument as an instrument but lays the burden upon the Crown to prove that at the date of the alleged contraventions reasonable steps had been taken for bringing the instrument to the notice of the public or persons likely to be affected by it. I, therefore, rule that this is admissible.

[When evidence of the steps taken to bring the instrument to the notice of the public and of the contravention of it by the accused had been given. His Lordship summed up and the jury, after a retirement of two minutes, found both the accused guilty on all counts.]

Verdict: Guilty on all counts.

Notes

1. The report at [1954] 1 All E.R. 542 at 545–546, states that evidence was given that the Minister of Supply issued information regarding the deposited schedules to trade journals; that the maximum permitted prices during the relevant months appeared in the *Board of Trade Journal*, the *Metal Bulletin* and the *Ironmonger*; and that the British Iron and Steel Federation sent copies of the schedules to the defendant company when the order of 1951 came into existence.

2. Some support for *Sheer Metalcraft* is provided by *Jones v Robson* [1901] 1 K.B. 673. By s.6 of the Coal Mines Regulation Act 1896:

> "a Secretary of State on being satisfied that any explosive is or is likely to become dangerous, may, by order, of which notice shall be given in such manner as he may direct, prohibit the use thereof in any mine . . . either absolutely or subject to conditions".

The Secretary of State made an Order imposing conditions as to the handling of detonators on and after October 1, 1899. The defendant, the manager of a mine, was prosecuted for breach of the Order. He was aware of the Order, but no notice of it had been published as required by s.6. The Divisional Court held that the defendant could properly be convicted. The Order came into force when it was made by the Secretary of State, and the provisions as to notice were "directory" only.

However, the ruling in *Sheer Metalcraft* that an instrument can come into effect before it is issued is inconsistent with the decision of Bailhache J. in *Johnson v Sargant & Sons* [1918] 1 K.B. 101. The Food Controller made an Order under the Defence of the Realm regulations requisitioning, *inter alia*, imported beans. The Order was dated May 16, 1917, but only became known to the public on May 17. It stated that it did not apply to beans "which have been sold by the original consignees and paid for by the purchasers". On May 16, the plaintiff paid for and took delivery of a cargo of beans from the defendants. They subsequently claimed that the contract had been cancelled by the Order. They referred to the rule that a statute takes effect from the first moment of the day on which it is passed, unless another day is expressly named, in which case it comes into operation immediately on the expiration of the previous day. They argued that, by analogy with the position with statutes, the Order came into operation immediately after midnight on May 15. As the beans were only paid for on May 16, the transaction was caught by the Order. However, Bailhache J. did not regard the analogy as appropriate:

> "there is about statutes a publicity even before they come into operation which is absent in the case of many Orders such as that with which we are now dealing; indeed, if certain Orders are to be effective at all, it is essential that they should not be known until they are actually published. In the absence of authority upon the point I am unable to hold that this Order came into operation before it was known, and, as I have said, it was not known until the morning of May 17."

Accordingly, the transaction fell within the exemption in the Order.

Jones v Robson was not cited in *Johnson v Sargant*, and neither case was cited in *R. v Sheer Metalcraft*.

3. In *Simmonds v Newell* [1953] 1 W.L.R. 826, the Defiant Cycle Co. and two of its directors were prosecuted before justices for selling steel at a price in excess of the maximum permitted by the Iron and Steel Prices Order 1951, as amended. The Order had been made by the Minister of Supply. The maximum prices were set out in schedules. An Assistant Secretary in the Ministry of Supply decided, having regard to reg.7 of the 1947 Regulations (above, p.216), that the printing and sale of the schedules was not necessary. She so decided in view of the bulk of the schedules, because they would be available for inspection at Steel House in London, and because trade associations would be distributing copies of the schedules that were most in demand. The Assistant Secretary wrote to the editor of Statutory Instruments that the schedules had been certified under reg.7 to be exempted from printing and sale, but there was not in fact a certificate to that effect. The Divisional Court held that the letter did not constitute a certificate. The Solicitor-General had accepted that while this did not render the Order invalid, it threw upon the Crown the burden of proving that reasonable steps had been taken to bring the purport of the instrument to the notice of the public, or of persons likely to be affected by it or the person charged (s.3(2) of the 1946 Act). Lord Goddard C.J. commented (at 830):

"That is certainly a very reasonable attitude for the Solicitor-General to take up, because it is not desirable, in criminal matters, that people should be prosecuted for breaches of orders unless the orders can fairly be said to be known to the public".

As no evidence had been given that steps had been taken to publicise the Order, the defendants should have been acquitted. The court left open arguments—

(1) that a contravention of section 2 of the 1946 Act in not causing to be printed an instrument required to be printed would have the effect that the instrument was invalid; and
(2) that the defence in section 3(2) was available even where the instrument was exempt from the printing requirements.

4. In *Lim Chin Aik v The Queen* [1963] A.C. 160, the question before the Privy Council was whether a person could properly be convicted of the offence of remaining in Singapore while the subject of an order prohibiting his entry if he was unaware of the existence of the order. Most of the advice of their Lordships was directed to the issue whether the offence required the proof of *mens rea* (their Lordships held that it did). In addition, they rejected the Crown's argument that once made the Order became part of the law of Singapore and that ignorance of the law is no excuse. *Per* Lord Evershed (at 171):

"In their Lordships' opinion, even if the making of the order by the Minister be regarded as an exercise of the legislative as distinct from the executive or administrative function (as they do not concede), the maxim cannot apply to such a case as the present where it appears that there is in the State of Singapore no provision, corresponding, for example, to that contained in section 3(2) of the English Statutory Instruments Act of 1946, for the publication in any form of an order of the kind made in the present case or any other provision designed to enable a man by appropriate inquiry to find out what 'the law' is".

This appears to suggest that in the context "ignorance of the law" can be an excuse even though (and, indeed, because) there is no express statutory defence.

Lord Evershed noted that the case concerned an order directed at an individual, and that the relevant Ordinance drew a distinction between such orders and an order directed to a class of persons. It expressly provided in the latter case for "publication in the *Gazette* and presentation to the Legislative Assembly" (at 172).

5. These cases raise two questions: (1) can delegated legislation come into effect before it is published?; (2) can a person be properly convicted of an offence created by delegated legislation unless either reasonable steps have been taken to make it public or the defendant is actually aware of it? Justice requires the answer to (2) to be "no" (*cf.* Lord Goddard's remark in *Simmonds v Newell*). That could be achieved by a broad general rule that delegated legislation does not come into force until published. Alternatively, and more narrowly, it could be achieved by a special defence in the criminal law. Such a defence would operate as an exception to the maxim that ignorance of the law is no excuse: the justification is that the maxim would operate harshly if even the best of endeavours would not enable the "law" to be ascertained. Section 3(2) of the 1946 Act provides a defence of that kind. *Lim Chin Aik v The Queen* suggests such a defence might be available even in the absence of a statutory provision. This would make it more acceptable for the answer to question (1) to be "yes". Note that question (2) did not arise in *Jones v Robson*, and that the section 3(2) defence was potentially available in *Simmonds v Newell* and *R. v Sheer Metalcraft*, although not made out on the facts in the second case. *Johnson v Sargant* did not concern a criminal prosecution. Thus in none of these reported cases in this country has a person been convicted of an offence under delegated legislation the details of which had not been published at the time of contravention.

6. Some commentators reconcile *Johnson v Sargant* with the other cases by treating it as authority for the proposition that a piece of delegated legislation *which does not itself state a commencement date* comes into effect on the date of publication and not that on which it was made (see 44 *Halsbury's Laws of England*, 4th ed., para.1003). *Jones v Robson*, *Simmonds v Newell* and *R. v Sheer Metalcraft* all concerned instruments with specified commencement dates. Nothing was, however, made of this point in the cases themselves. Since 1947, all statutory instruments required to be laid before Parliament will show the dates they came into operation (see the 1946 Act, s.4(2)(a) (3), above p.213).

7. D.J. Lanham, ("Delegated Legislation and Publication" (1974) 37 M.L.R. 510) argues strongly that the principle of *Johnson v Sargant* is to be preferred, as a matter of justice, and that the general common law rule is that delegated legislation does not come into force until it is published. The contrary view is expressed by A.I.L. Campbell, [1982] P.L. 569, reply by Professor Lanham, [1983] P.L. 395.

8. Consider s.3(2) of the 1946 Act (above, p.212). To what kinds of statutory instrument does it apply? (see Lanham, *op. cit.*, pp.521–523). This question turns on the meaning of the words "any such statutory instrument". The possibilities are that:

(i) These words refer back to the kinds of statutory instruments specified in s.3(1), i.e. "every statutory instrument printed and sold by the King's printer". This would have the result that the defence would only be available where an instrument *is issued at some time*, but the contravention precedes the date of issue. It would not be available if the instrument is never issued, even where that was in breach of publication requirements. *Simmonds v Newell* and *R. v Sheer Metalcraft* are against this narrow interpretation.

(ii) The words are to be read as referring to "any statutory instrument", no weight being attached to the word "such". The defence would then be available wherever the instrument has not been issued at the date of contravention. This interpretation gives the broadest scope to the section 3(2) defence. Would this be an appropriate occasion for the exercise of the limited power of judges to ignore statutory words to prevent statutory provisions having an absurd result?

(iii) The defence would only be available where the instrument has not been issued at the date of contravention, *and this is in breach of a duty to publish*. This was the situation that arose in *Simmonds v Newell* and *Sheer Metalcraft*. Does the wording of s.3 justify this reading?

9. The defence in s.3(2) appears, with the language but not the substance modified, as clause 50 in the proposed Criminal Code Bill (see *Codification of the Criminal Law: A Report to the Law Commission* (1984–85 HC 270), pp.129–130, 198).

(D) Parliamentary Scrutiny

FIRST REPORT FROM THE SELECT COMMITTEE ON PROCEDURE, 1999–2000 HC 48, DELEGATED LEGISLATION

Introduction

1. In June 1996, the Procedure Committee laid before the House a report on delegated legislation.[4] This concluded that there were defects in the current system for considering such legislation and put forward a package of proposals for remedying them. No Government response to the report has yet appeared. However, in May 1999 the present Leader of the House, the Rt Hon Margaret Beckett MP, acting in her capacity as Chairman of the Select Committee on Modernisation of the House of Commons, requested the Procedure Committee to look again at its 1996 report, and invited the Committee to consider in particular whether any of its recommendations should now be implemented by the House. . . .

4. It will be useful to state at the outset that—with minor modifications, spelled out in paragraphs 36,41 and 57 below—we support the recommendations in the 1996 report, and are strongly desirous of seeing them implemented. We believe that this package of recommendations is a modest and workable attempt to tackle the deficiencies of the existing system. We do not consider that the recommendations, if implemented, will add to the overall workload of the House or necessarily result in longer sitting hours. The recommendations should be seen, we believe, as an integral part of the programme of modernising the work of the House.

The Present System of Scrutiny

5. Parliament does not have time to give comprehensive scrutiny to all legislative proposals. The existence of a system whereby detailed, technical or less significant proposals receive a lower level of scrutiny has long been recognised to be unavoidable. The present system, which has grown up over many years, is founded on the distinction between two categories of statutory instrument: "affirmative instruments", which require a positive Resolution of each House to come into effect, and "negative instruments", which can be annulled by a Resolution of either House if passed within 40 days of their laying.

6. An affirmative instrument stands automatically referred for debate in a Standing Committee on Delegated Legislation ("DL Committee") unless the Government agrees that it be debated on the Floor of the House. Debate in Committee arises on a formal and unamendable motion, "That the Committee has considered the draft XYZ Order 2000", and after a maximum of one and

---

[4] Fourth Report of 1995–96, *Delegated Legislation* (HC 52).

a half hour's debate, the Chairman reports the instrument to the House irrespective of whether or not the motion has been agreed to. A motion to approve the instrument is then put to the House, without further debate. Instruments taken on the Floor are debated for up to an hour and a half, also on an unamendable motion.

7. Negative instruments are not debated unless a motion is tabled seeking ("praying") that the instrument be annulled, and the Government agrees either that the instrument be debated in a DL Committee or, much more rarely, on the Floor of the House. For many years the Government has accepted no obligation so to agree. Proceedings in committee are the same as for an affirmative instrument; however, in the case of negatives referred to committee there are no subsequent proceedings on the Floor (a point of some significance given that negatives can only effectively be annulled by a vote on the Floor).

8. All statutory instruments laid before Parliament are scrutinised by the Joint Committee on Statutory Instruments (JCSI). The committee's task is to consider technical but important issues such as whether the instrument is made within the powers conferred by the parent legislation, and whether its drafting is defective. The committee is precluded from considering the actual merits of instruments or the policy underlying them. It has the assistance of Speaker's Counsel and regularly reports to both Houses. Under House of Lords Public Business Standing Order No.70, no motion for an affirmative resolution of the House of Lords in connection with any instrument may be moved until the JCSI's report on the instrument has been laid before the House. There is no such requirement in Commons standing orders.

9. In the last complete Session, 1998–99, 178 affirmative instruments were laid before the House, of which 150 were considered in committee, 21 were considered on the Floor, and seven were withdrawn. In the same Session, 1,266 negative instruments were laid before the House, of which 28 were considered in committee and one on the Floor.

Criticisms of the Existing System, and the 1996 Report's Recommendations

10. In devising an effective system of scrutiny of delegated legislation, the key question is how best to target Parliament's over-stretched resources of time and expertise. There is widespread agreement that at present those resources are ineffectively targeted. There are three major areas of criticism.

11. *Firstly, it is argued that instruments do not receive scrutiny in proportion to their merits.* The current system, as outlined in paragraphs 5 to 9 above, rests on the assumption that affirmative instruments are intrinsically more significant and debate-worthy than negative ones. This may be true of a majority of instruments, but it is generally acknowledged that there is a significant minority of affirmatives which deal with matters too trivial or technical to merit debate, and negatives which deal with important or sensitive matters where there is demand for a debate. This mismatch between the level of scrutiny provided for in the parent legislation and the level which is actually appropriate may arise from a variety of factors. Ministers may have upgraded procedure from negative to affirmative as a political concession during committee stage of a bill; contrariwise, the conferral of significant powers may have 'slipped through' Parliament without provision for proper scrutiny; whilst in other cases, circumstances may have changed during the years or decades since the passage of the parent legislation, rendering issues once

regarded as important less so, and vice versa. Nonetheless, in the words of the Clerk of the House, "the House is locked into a procedural approach to an instrument by provisions made sometimes many, many years before in the parent act". As a result, the time and expertise of Members is frequently wasted in attendance at I I DL Committees to consider 'trivial affirmatives', often meeting for a few minutes only; whilst significant changes to the law may pass through Parliament unregarded and undebated because contained in negative instruments.

12. Our predecessors in 1996 briefly considered the question of whether the existing distinction between affirmatives and negatives should be retained. They argued that "there would in theory be something to be said for abolishing the distinction, and creating a uniform category of instruments, with a parliamentary mechanism for determining which required positive approval, based on their inherent significance rather than their statutory basis". However, this would require primary legislation, "and possibly wholesale amendment of much of statute law". They therefore did not recommend such an approach, though they added that were their more modest proposals to prove ineffective, serious consideration should be given to the radical proposal of a uniform category and procedure for all delegated legislation. [HC 152, 1995–96, para.8]

13. Our predecessors proposed, as a more realistic and feasible way of tackling the problem, that the House should institute a process of systematic sift of negative instruments within Parliament. The possibility of using the existing Joint Committee on Statutory Instruments (JCSI) for this purpose was considered and ruled out, on the grounds that the sift would involve the application of political judgement and have a direct bearing on the business of the Commons, and was therefore not an appropriate task for a Joint Committee; that it would be a mistake to mix up the politics and the legal *vires* of instruments (the latter being the special concern of the JCSI); and that the sift would require a different set of advisers with different expertise. [*ibid.*, para.29.] Our predecessors also considered the possibility of requiring departmental select committees to examine instruments made by the departments which they shadow. This option was also ruled out, largely on practical grounds (the workload involved would vary dramatically between committee and committee, and from week to week within each committee, whilst the level of enthusiasm for such work on the part of Members might also vary considerably between committees). The Liaison Committee, comprising chairmen of departmental and other select committees, endorsed the Procedure Committee's rejection of this option, whilst urging that departmental select committees should have the opportunity of making an input into the sifting process. [*ibid.*, paras 30–32.]

14. The 1996 report concluded that the most satisfactory way forward would be for the House to establish a single 'Sifting Committee' to consider and assess all SIs laid before Parliament. The committee would have power to call for further information from government departments where necessary. Its key task would be to make recommendations on which negative instruments merited debate. The recommendations would be put to the House by the chairman of the committee in the form of a motion which could be opposed and indeed defeated (thus enabling the Government to retain its ultimate control of the process). [*ibid.*, paras 33–3]. The committee would also have powers to identify affirmative instruments which did *not* merit debate,

and on which the question could be put forthwith unless at least six Members had earlier indicated they wished for a debate. [*ibid.*, paras 38–41]. In order to allow a reasonable time for scrutiny, the report recommended that praying time against negative instruments should be extended from 40 to 60 days (this would require amendment of the Statutory Instruments Act 1946). [*ibid.*, paras 18 and 34] The Sifting Committee would require specialist staff back-up. [*ibid.*, para.34]

15. The 1996 report also recommended that reference of a negative instrument to committee should be permitted to be moved by a Member where a prayer against it had been signed by at least 20 Members, with the ensuing Question being decided on a simple majority; [*ibid.*, para.27] and that minor affirmatives of "broadly similar subject matter" should be grouped together for debate. [*ibid.*, para.40]

16. *A further criticism of the existing system is that debate on instruments in committee is meaningless because it does not take place on a substantive motion.* If a Delegated Legislation Committee votes against the motion, "That the Committee has considered the instrument", the Chairman's report to the House is couched in the same terms as if the motion had been agreed to, and no procedural consequences follow from the Committee's vote.

17. The 1996 report recommended that motions in DL Committee should be substantive and amendable, and that where the Government's motion is defeated there should be up to an hour's further debate on the Floor. It also proposed that aspects of European Standing Committee procedure should be adopted for DL Committees, in particular that proceedings should begin with a Ministerial statement and questions, and that debate should last for up to two and a half hours, rather than one and a half as at present.

18. The 1996 report considered the question of whether statutory instruments themselves should be amendable during their passage. At present instruments cannot be amended unless the parent legislation allows for it, and virtually no legislation currently in force so allows.[5] The Committee concluded that the complications that would ensue from any change in this position would greatly outweigh any likely benefits. [*ibid.*, para.51]

19. The report also looked at the existing differentiation between affirmatives and negatives in terms of the time allocated for debate when taken on the Floor. Under standing orders, affirmatives receive up to an hour and a half's debate without restriction, whilst negatives receive an hour and a half s debate subject to the restriction that debate must be concluded at 11.30 pm, even when it has commenced significantly after 10 pm (as may be the case if divisions have been held at 10 pm). The report concluded that this differentiation was illogical and that standing orders should be amended to repeal the 11.30 pm cut-off on debates on negative instruments. [*ibid.*, para.42]

20. *The existing system of scrutiny has also been criticised for containing no provision for a higher level of scrutiny for a small number of very complex SIs.* The 1996 Committee proposed a new category of "super-affirmatives", whereby proposals for draft Orders would be laid for pre-legislative scrutiny by the relevant departmental select committee. This would be an adaptation of the existing procedure for considering draft Deregulation proposals.

---

[5] Rare exceptions include the Census Act 1920.

21. The 1996 report contained a number of further recommendations. The most important of these was that a standing order should be passed to provide that no decision on a statutory instrument should be made by the House until the instrument had been considered by the Joint Committee on Statutory Instruments. [*ibid.*, para.25] A similar standing order already exists in the House of Lords. The report pointed out tnat it would always be open to the House to override the standing order by resolution if the Government could persuade it that this was justified in a particular case. This recommendation to create a 'scrutiny reserve' has been strongly supported by the Chairman and members of the present JCSI. . . .

Developments since 1996

[The Committee noted that the numbers of statutory instruments and the ratio between those laid under affirmative and negative procedure had not changed significantly; that there had been a major shift from consideration on the Floor to in committee and a reduction in the overall number of negatives debated in either place. These figures reinforced the case for reform, which case was not affected by devolution, or the introduction of parallel sittings of the House in Westminster Hall. The reform proposals had been endorsed by the Royal Commission on the Reform of the House of Lords, *A House for the Future* (Cm.4534, 2000), Ch.7, which favoured sifting by a Joint Committee of both Houses, with a sifting Committee established by the Lords alone as a second-best option (paras 23–41).]

Other procedural developments

42. Since 1996 there have been significant developments in the way the House of Commons operates. The Modernisation Committee has encouraged a greater emphasis on pre-legislative scrutiny of primary legislation, by way of draft bills referred to select or joint committees; and the House has been making greater use of Second Reading Committees and Special Standing Committees to examine bills once introduced.

43. Of equal, perhaps even greater, significance for our present purposes has been the extent to which other, permanent committees both of the Commons and the Lords have been developing techniques of scrutiny in recent years. Several deserve to be highlighted.

44. The *House of Lords Select Committee on Delegated Powers and Deregulation* was set up (as the Select Committee on Delegated Powers) on an experimental basis in 1992–93, and since 1993–94 has been routinely re-appointed on a sessional basis. In 1994 it was given the additional role of scrutinising deregulation proposals. Its job in relation to bills is "to report whether the provisions of any bill inappropriately delegate legislative power, or whether they subject the exercise of legislative power to an inappropriate degree of parliamentary scrutiny". In respect of each bill, the Committee works to a tight timetable, usually publishing a report within three weeks of First Reading. As will have been seen from the order of reference, the Committee's concern is not with the merits of bills but with the justification for and appropriateness of the secondary powers granted by them. In a recent report on its own activities, the Committee commented that it "operates in a non-partisan way" and noted that "we have never needed to divide in the

seven sessions of our existence" [29th Report 1998–99 HL 112, para.9]. added that when it had advised the House that bills should be amended, this advice had "almost always been accepted by the Government and the House". [*ibid.*, para.18]. The Government has undertaken to respond quickly to the Committee's reports, if practicable. [*ibid.*, paras 44–46]

45. In the Commons, the *Deregulation Committee* was first set up in 1994, to consider proposals for orders and draft Orders laid under the Deregulation and Contracting Out Act 1994. In each case the Committee conducts its examination both at the pre-legislative stage (proposals for orders) and, if it is reached, the legislative stage (draft Orders). Within a fixed timetable the Committee can take written or oral evidence, and report to the House its opinion on whether or not the proposal should proceed or the draft Order be approved. What happens to draft Orders in the House depends on the nature of the Committee's report: if it has reported unanimously that the draft Order should be approved, a motion to that effect is put in the House and the Question put forthwith; if it has agreed on Division that the draft Order should be approved, a motion is moved and the Question put after a maximum of one and a half hours' debate; and if it has recommended that the draft Order should not be approved, the Government may move a motion to disagree with the Committee's report on which the Question can be put after a maximum of 3 hours' debate, with the Question on the draft Order put forthwith if that motion is agreed to.

46. Our predecessors in their 1996 report commented on the Deregulation Committee as follows:

"It should be recalled from the outset that Deregulation Orders are peculiar in that they all involve amendment of primary legislation, which would require further primary legislation to amend it, were it not for the terms of the Deregulation and Contracting Out Act 1994 and the parallel establishment of the Deregulation Committee with its special powers. The degree of scrutiny given by the Committee has demanded commitment of substantial resources, which could not conceivably be extended even to all affirmative orders. It is however in our view significant that the Committee has operated smoothly and effectively; that it has used its powers to persuade government to accept nearly all the amendments it has sought; that it and its House of Lords counterpart have effectively killed off one proposal; and that the end result to date is that 17 draft Orders have been agreed to by the House without any debate, but in the full confidence that they are generally acceptable." [1995–96 HC, 152, para.22]

47. The present Chairman of the Deregulation Committee, Mr Peter L. Pike, argued in his written submission that the deregulation procedure has the benefit of allowing public access and giving backbenchers a legislative role, that it is conducted in a bipartisan spirit, and that it need not require much time on the Floor. He urged that "the techniques of the deregulation procedure could and should be extended to other delegated legislation". [*ibid.*, para.36]

[The Committee noted that for European Scrutiny Committee did perform a sifting role in neglect of the further consideration on the Floor or in one of the European Standing Committee of a range of EU Documents (paras 48–50)].

51. The 1996 report commented that "the European Legislation Committee and the Deregulation Committee have demonstrated that scrutiny by committees can work, and can engage Members' attention and commitment." [*ibid.,* para.2] We have taken evidence from the Chairman of both Committees, and are happy to endorse that view. The activities of the European Scrutiny Committee, European Standing Committees, the Deregulation Committee and the House of Lords Delegated Powers and Deregulation Committee have continued to develop during the four years since our predecessors reported, and form a valuable contribution to the effectiveness of Parliament. In Particular, it has been demonstrated that committees working within the Westminster tradition can successfully develop modes of Scrutiny involving the sifting of complex documents, the targeted use of specialist staff resources, the maintenance where appropriate of traditions of non-partisanship, and the holding of Ministers to account in public committee meetings through question-and-answer sessions as well as through debate on amendable and substantive motions. They have also demonstrated the ability of select committees, appropriately resourced, to combine the examination of technical detail which is characteristic of the Joint Committee on Statutory Instruments with the exercise of political judgement. In short, almost every element of the 1996 report's proposed reforms in the field of delegated legislation has been pioneered in one or other of these committees and shown to be eminently workable.

Conclusions

[The Committee concluded that the 1996 package was realistic not Utopian, and that the existing system was urgently in need of reform. They concurred with their predecessors' description of that system as "palpably unsatisfactory" (*ibid.,* para.1). The recommendations did not represent a radical departure from existing procedures but would build on them. Primary legislation would be needed to extend praying time from 40 to 60 days; that would not be necessary for there to be an experiment with a super-affirmative procedure. The proposals should be accepted by the government "as a matter of urgency".]

Notes

1. They were not. The House of Lords set up its own sifting committee in 2003, but a further proposal for the establishment of such a committee for the House of Commons (First Report from the Select Committee on Procedure, 2002–03 HC 501, *Delegated Legislation: Proposals for a Sifting Committee*) was rejected on the ground that this would "lead to greatly increased demands on parliamentary time and on government departments" (see Second Report, 2002–03 HC 684, Annex A). A disappointing and unconvincing response.

Other particular recommendations included in the 1996 package were (1) the passage of a Standing Order to provide that no decision on a statutory instrument should be made by the House until completion of its consideration by the Joint Committee on Statutory Instruments (below); and (2) that debates on negative instruments be arranged within praying time.

2. The House of Lords has changed its practice by indicating that it is prepared to annul an SI laid before it under the negative procedure. It so acted in respect of the Greater London Authority Elections Rules 2000 (SI 2000/208).

3. The Joint Committee on Statutory Instruments considers whether the special attention of the House should be drawn to an instrument on any of the following grounds:

"(i) that it imposes a charge on the public revenues or contains provisions requiring payments to be made to the Exchequer or any government department or to any local or public authority in consideration of any licence or consent or of any services to be rendered, or prescribes the amount of any such charge of payment;

(ii) that it is made in pursuance of any enactment containing specific provisions excluding it from challenge in the courts, either at all times or after the expiration of a specific period;

(iii) that it purports to have retrospective effect where the parent statute confers no express authority so to provide;

(iv) that there appears to have been unjustifiable delay in the publication or in the laying of it before Parliament;

(v) that there appears to have been unjustifiable delay in sending a notification under the proviso to subsection (1) of section four of the Statutory Instruments Act 1946, where an instrument has come into operation before it has been laid before Parliament;

(vi) that there appears to be a doubt whether it is *intra vires* or that it appears to make some unusual or unexpected use of the powers conferred by the statute under which it is made;

(vii) that for any special reason its form or purport call for elucidation;

(viii) that its drafting appears to be defective;

or on any other ground which does not impinge on its merits or on the policy behind it and to report its decision with the reasons thereof in any particular case".

See the Committee's First Special Report on Proceedings 1986–96, 1995–96 HL Paper 103, HC 582, and Annual Reports summarising the returns of Departments on the action taken on instruments drawn to the special attention of the Houses.

4. Regulatory reform orders are made by ministers under the Regulatory Reform Act 2001 in order to amend or repeal legislation which "has the effect of imposing burdens affecting persons in the carrying out of any activity." The Minister must consult widely, lay a proposal for an order before Parliament to allow at least 60 days for Parliamentary consideration and lay a draft order before Parliament and obtain Parliament's approval for it. Scrutiny functions are performed by the Regulatory Reform Committee of the House of Commons (originally the Deregulation Committee and then the Deregulation and Regulatory Reform Committee) and the Delegated Powers and Regulatory Reform Committee of the House of Lords (originally the Select Committee on the Scrutiny of Delegated Powers, and then the Select Committee on Deregulated Powers and Deregulation). The Committees both provide substantive scrutiny and perform the functions of the JCSI, and report to their respective Houses. They operate independently but co-operate closely. The Commons Committee must

"consider in each case whether the proposal:

(a) appears to make an inappropriate use of delegated legislation

(b) removes or reduces a burden or the authorisation or requirement of a burden

(c) continues any necessary protection

(d) has been the subject of, and takes appropriate account of, adequate consultation

(e) imposes a charge on the public revenues or contain provisions requiring payments to be made to the Exchequer or any government department or to any local or public authority in consideration of any licence or consent or of any services to be rendered, or prescribe the amount of any such charge or payment

(f) purports to have retrospective effect

(g) gives rise to doubts whether it is intra vires

(h) requires elucidation, is not written in plain English or appears to be defectively drafted

- (i) appears to be incompatible with an obligation resulting from membership of the European Union
- (j) prevents any person from continuing to exercise any right or freedom which he might reasonably expect to continue to exercise
- (k) satisfies the conditions of proportionality between burdens and benefits set out in sections 1 ["proportionality"] and 3 ["fair balance"] of the Act.
- (l) Satisfies the test of desirability set out in section 3(2)(b) of the Act
- (m) Has been the subject of, and take appropriate account of, estimates of increases or reductions in costs or other benefits which may result from their implementation, and
- (n) Includes provisions to be designated in the draft order as subordinate provisions; and if so, to what Parliamentary procedure any subordinate provisions order should be subject".[6]

Considerably less use of these powers has been made than in targets set for the Cabinet Office, which has in turn made informally a series of proposals which seemed to the Commons Committee to be designed "by widening the scope of RRA and . . . by making the process of preparing and explaining an RRO proposal less onerous, RROs would become a more attractive legislative option for Departments" (First Special Report, 2004–05 HC 273, para.16). The Committee's response was understandably cautious, in the absence of the proposed formal review of the operation of the Act that had been promised for 2004.

Both committees from time to time conduct reviews of their work. See, *e.g.* the First (Special) Report of the Lords Committee, 2003–04 HL 9 (for the Government Response, see the Ninth Report, 2003–04 HL 43); the First Special Report of the Commons Committee, 2002–03 HC 907 (for the Government Response, see 2003–04 HC 256).

5. The Lords' Committee continues to perform its original functions of scrutinising Bills and reporting to the House on the appropriateness of the delegation of legislative powers (see the comments of the Commons Committee, above, p.226). On the work of the Committee as originally established, see C.M.G. Himsworth, [1995] P.L. 34. The Lords' Committee (*inter alia*) pays special attention to "Henry VIII" powers (that enable primary legislation to be amended or repealed by secondary legislation). In a Special Report on *Henry VIII Powers to Make Incidental, Consequential and Similar Provisions* (2002–03 HL 21), it said that it had no doubt that there are occasions when such powers are needed, for example when the number of incidental, etc. amendments would cause a disproportionate increase in the length of a Bill or when, as a matter of practicality, it would be difficult to anticipate the full extent of such amendments during the passage of a Bill. There were good reasons why the wording of such clauses might vary, but the Government should explain why a particular form of wording has been adopted in each case. There should be a presumption in favour of use of the affirmative rather than the negative procedure, and the Government should explain any departure from this in the Explanatory Notes and in the Memorandum to the Committee.

As to the courts' approach to such clauses, see below, p.232.

6. The Lords' Merits of Statutory Instruments Committee was first appointed in December 2003. It is

"required to consider every negative and affirmative statutory instrument (or draft statutory instrument) laid before Parliament with a view to determining whether the special attention of the House should be drawn to it on any of the following grounds:

- that is politically or legally important or gives rise to issues of public policy likely to be of interest to the House;

---

[6] See *www.parliament.uk/parliamentary_committees/regulatory_reform_committee.*

- that it is in appropriate in view of the changed circumstances since the passage of the parent Act;
- that it inappropriately implements EU legislation
- that it imperfectly achieves its policy objectives".

The Committee is assisted in its work by an Explanatory Memorandum which the Government provides with every affirmative and negative instrument. (See *www. Parliament.uk/committees.*)

7. For earlier surveys of arrangements for parliamentary scrutiny, see J.D. Hayhurst and P. Wallington, [1988] P.L. 547 and Hansard Society Commission, *Making the Law* (1993), pp.89–94.

(E) *Vires*

Apart from the procedural matters already considered in this chapter, the validity of a statutory instrument may be challenged on the ground that it is *ultra vires* as a matter of substance.

Notes

1. Examples of challenge on this ground include the following: in *Hotel and Catering Industry Training Board v Automobile Proprietary Ltd* [1969] 1 W.L.R. 697, the House of Lords held that a power to make an order establishing a training board for persons employed "in any activities of industry or commerce" did not enable an order to be made in respect of members' clubs. In *R. v Customs and Excise Commissioners Ex p. Hedges and Butler* [1986] 2 All E.R. 164, a power to demand production of the whole of the records of a business, including records concerning non-dutiable goods, was held not to be "incidental" or "supplementary" to powers concerning the regulation of excise warehouses and dealings in dutiable goods. In *R. v Secretary of State for Social Security Ex p. Joint Council for the Welfare of Immigrants* [1997] 4 W.L.R. 275, the Court of Appeal (Simon Brown and Waite L.JJ., Neill L.J. dissenting) held that regulations, which excluded from social security benefits persons who sought asylum otherwise than immediately on arrival in the United Kingdom and persons whose asylum claims had been rejected and were awaiting appeal, were *ultra vires*. They had the effect of rendering the rights of asylum seekers under the Asylum and Immigration Appeals Act 1993 valueless; the latter would either be deterred from pursuing their claims or be forced to live a life of utter destitution. "Parliamentary legislation alone could . . . achieve that sorry state of affairs" (*per* Simon Brown L.J. at 293). The effect of this decision was subsequently reversed by the Asylum and Immigration Act 1996, although applicants for asylum could seek assistance from local authorities under s.21(1) of the National Assistance Act 1948 (*R. v Westminster City Council Ex p. M* (1997) 1 C.C.L. Rep.85). This possibility was in turn foreclosed for asylum seekers whose need arises solely out of destitution, who may be eligible for support under Pt VI of the Immigration and Asylum Act 1999. This established a national scheme under which support such as the provision of accommodation and other benefits in kind may be provided by the Secretary of State for the Home Department, acting through the National Asylum Support Service. (See M. Symes and P. Jorro, *Asylum Law and Practice* (2003), pp.445–460). Section 55 of the Nationality, Immigration and Asylum Act 2002 enables the Secretary of State to refuse to provide any support, and prohibit local authorities from providing support, where the Secretary of State is not satisfied that an asylum claim has been made as soon as reasonably practicable after the person's arrival in the United Kingdom. Support must, however, be provided where the person has reached such a state of degradation (a concept significantly worse than that of "destitution") that his or her treatment constitutes a breach of Art.3 ECHR (see *R. (on the application of Q) v Secretary of State for the Home Department* [2003] EWCA Civ 364; [2004] Q.B. 36; cf. *R. (on the application of S) v Secretary of State for the Home Department* [2003] EWCA Civ 1285, [2003] U.K.H.R.R. 1321). See further, p.373.

2. The "principle of legality" (below, Ch.5) requires that clear words are needed for the making of subordinate legislation that interferes with fundamental rights. See, *e.g.* *R. v Lord Chancellor Ex p. Witham* [1998] Q.B. 575 (Lord Chancellor's general power to fix court fees cannot be used to set such high levels that would effectively bar the poor from access to the courts), distinguished in *R. v Lord Chancellor Ex p. Lightfoot* [2000] Q.B. 597 (deposit of £250 to be paid by the debtor wishing to petition for bankruptcy did not interfere with the right of access to the court).

The right to appeal to a tribunal or other appellate authority (here the Immigration Appeal Tribunal) was held to be akin to the right of access to the court in *R. v Secretary of State for the Home Department, Ex p. Saleem* [2001] 1 W.L.R. 443. Here a procedural rule that deemed an asylum claimant to have received notice of the determination of a Special Adjudicator two days after it was sent, excluding weekends and bank holidays, regardless of when or whether it was received, was held to be *ultra vires* and unreasonable. Another rule set a non-extendable time limit of five working days for lodging applications for leave to appeal to the IAT, and the effect of challenged rule was in certain circumstances to destroy the very essence of the right of appeal which, if established, attracted the guarantees of Art.6 ECHR (see Hale L.J. at 458). It was not authorised either expressly or by necessary implication.

Clear words are also needed to interfere with rights conferred by other legislation (the *JCWI* case above) or to amend primary legislation (*McKiernan v Chief Adjudication Officer, The Times*, November 1, 1989, (if there is any doubt about the scope of such a power "it should be resolved by a restrictive approach"); *Britnell v Secretary of State for Social Security* [1991] 1 W.L.R. 198; *R. v Secretary of State for Trade and Industry Ex p. Orange Personal Communications Ltd* [2001] Eu.L.R. 165; *cf. R. v Secretary of State for the Environment, Transport and the Regions Ex p. Spath Holme Ltd* [2001] 1 All E.R. 195, *per* Lord Bingham at 202–203 (such an approach only appropriate where there is a genuine doubt about the effect of the statutory provision in question).

The general power under s.2(2) of the European Communities Act 1972 to make regulations for the purposes of implementing Community obligations or enabling any rights to be enjoyed by the United Kingdom under the Treaties, or of dealing with matter arising out of or related to any such obligation or rights, can be used to repeal or disapply provisions of primary legislation, but this must be done explicitly (*Orange*). In *Thoburn v Sunderland CC* [2002] EWHC (Admin) 195; [2003] Q.B. 151, the Divisional Court rejected various arguments that powers to use subordinate legislation to amend primary legislation were subject to general limitations (applicable only to Acts on the statute book when the particular power was checked; to effect only minor of modest changes).

3. A statutory instrument may be *ultra vires* if it conflicts with directly effective Community law (*cf.* (173/99, *R. (on the application of BECTU v Secretary of State for Trade and Industry* [2001] 1 W.L.R. 2313, ECJ (ruling that the Working Time Directive did not permit national legislation to impose a precondition that excluded a category of worker; the offending provision was subsequently revoked by the Working Time (Amendment) Regulations 2001 (SI 2001/3256)); *cf. Oakley Ltd v Animal Ltd* [2005] EWHC 210, ChD (regulations cannot validly be made under s.2(2) of the European Communities Act 1972 to exercise a right to derogate from a Community obligation; s.2(2)(b) cannot be used "to achieve a result not required by a Community obligation, just because its purpose is in some way related to or arises out of that obligation" (*per* Peter Prescott Q.C., sitting as a deputy High Court judge, at [136] not following the approach of Otton L.J. in *R. v Secretary of State for Trade and Industry Ex p. UNISON* [1996] I.C.R. 1003 at 1013; the SI challenged here was, however, saved by severance).

A statutory instrument may also be invalid if it conflicts with a Convention right under the Human Rights Act 1998, see below, Ch.6.

4. On the question whether the invalid part of an instrument can be severed, see *R. v Inland Revenue Commissioners Ex p. Woolwich Equitable Building Society*, below, p.901.

5. It has been unclear whether a statutory instrument, as distinct from a byelaw (see below, pp.234–238) can be challenged for *Wednesbury* unreasonableness or irrationality. A provision in the Immigration Rules (which are not published as statutory instruments) was held to be unreasonable in *R. v Immigration Appeal Tribunal Ex p. Manshoora Begum* [1986] Imm.A.R. 385 (below, p.237). The Court of Appeal has now held that the true position is that delegated legislation, whether or not approved by either or both Houses of Parliament, is indeed subject to challenge on the ground of irrationality, but that in some contexts, such as that of local government finance,

"there is a heavy evidential onus on a claimant for judicial review to establish the irrationality of a decision which may owe much to political, social and economic considerations in the underlying enabling legislation"

(*per* Auld L.J. in *O'Connor v Chief Adjudicating Officer and Secretary of State for Social Security* [1999] E.L.R. 209 at p.221, approved by the Court of Appeal in *R. (on the application of Javed) v Secretary of State for the Home Department* [2002] Q.B. 129 (Secretary of State's inclusion of Pakistan in an Order applying an expedited appeals procedure, as a country in which it appeared to him "that there is in general no serious risk of persecution" was irrational and therefore invalid); *cf. R. (on the application of Tucker) v Secretary of State for Social Security* [2001] EWCA Civ 1646; [2002] H.L.R. 27 (housing benefit regulation held not to be irrational). See to similar effect Mustill L.J. in *R. v Secretary of State for the Environment Ex p. the GLC and ILEA*, unreported, April 3, 1985.

The scope of review may be narrower where an instrument is approved by Parliament but note Auld L.J.'s comments in *O'Connor* (*cf.* below, pp.576–579).

7. A statutory instrument may be challenged on the ground of uncertainty (*R. (on the application of South Wales Sea Fisheries Committee) v National Assembly for Wales* [2001] EWHC Admin 1162, where the challenge on this ground was rejected on its merits).

(F) BYELAWS

Powers for local authorities to make byelaws are found in a large number of Acts of Parliament (see *Cross*, App.E). Such powers may also be conferred on other public bodies. District and London borough councils and unitary councils in England and county and county borough councils in Wales have a general power to

"made byelaws for the good rule and government of the whole or any part of the district [principal area] or borough, as the case may be, and for the prevention and suppression of nuisances therein" (Local Government Act 1972, s.235(1), as amended).

However, this power may not be exercised

"for any purpose as respects any area if provision for that purpose or respects that area is made by, or is or may be made under, any other enactment" (1972 Act, s.235(3)).

The procedure for making any byelaw (unless special provision is otherwise made) is found in s.236 of the 1972 Act. Byelaws have to be conferred by a minister (usually the Secretary of State). At least one month before application for confirmation, notice of intention to apply must be given in "one or more local newspapers circulating in the area to which the byelaws are to apply" and a copy must be deposited at the authority's offices and open to public inspection without payment. The authority must provide a copy of the byelaws (or a part of them) to any person on application, on payment of such sum not exceeding 10p per 100 words as the authority may determine. The confirming authority may confirm or refuse to confirm any byelaw, and may fix the commencement date. If not date is so fixed, the byelaw comes into operation one month after confirmation. After confirmation, byelaws must be printed, deposited at the authority's offices and open to public inspection, and copies must be supplied on application or payment of such sum not exceeding 20p per copy as the authority may determine.

Byelaws are not normally confirmed unless they follow models issued by the relevant Government Department (most commonly the Home Office or the Office of the Deputy Prime Minister).

KRUSE v JOHNSON

[1898] 2 Q.B. 91; 67 L.J.K.B. 782; 78 L.T. 647; 14 T.L.R. 416; 62 J.P. 469; 42 S.J. 509; [1895–1899] All E.R. REP. 105; 46 W.R. 630; 19 Cox C.C. 103 (DIVISIONAL COURT (Q.B.D.))

Kent County Council made a byelaw prohibiting any person from playing music or singing in a public place within 50 yards of any dwelling-house after being required by any constable, or by an inmate of such house to desist. The byelaw was made under s.16 of the Local Government Act 1888 and s.23(1) of the Municipal Corporations Act 1882, which gave power to

> "make such byelaws as to them [the council], seem meet for the good rule and government of the . . . . [county], and for the prevention and suppression of nuisances not already punishable in a summary manner by virtue of any Act. . . ". K was convicted by justices of an offence against this byelaw, in that he had conducted an open-air religious service within 50 yards of a house, after being required to desist by a constable. K appealed by way of case stated to the Divisional Court, contending that the byelaw was *ultra vires* for unreasonableness.

LORD RUSSELL OF KILLOWEN C.J.: . . . . [stated the facts, outlined the relevant legislation, and continued:] We thus find that Parliament has thought fit to delegate to representative public bodies in town and cities, and also in counties, the power of exercising their own judgment as to what are the bye-laws which to them seem proper to be made for good rule and government in their own localities. But that power is accompanied by certain safeguards. There must be antecedent publication of the bye-law with a view, I presume, of eliciting the public opinion of the locality upon it, and such bye-laws shall have no force until after they have been forwarded to the Secretary of State. Further, the Queen, with the advice of her Privy Council, may disallow the bye-law wholly or in part, and may enlarge the suspensory period before it comes into operation. I agree that the presence of these safeguards in no way relieves the Court of the responsibility of inquiring into the validity of bye-laws where they are brought in question, or in any way affects the authority of the Court in the determination of their validity or invalidity. It is to be observed, more-over, that the bye-laws having come into force, they are not like the laws, or what were said to be the laws, of the Medes and Persians— they are not unchangeable. The power is to make bye-laws from time to time as to the authority shall seem meet, and if experience shews that in any respect existing bye-laws work hardly or inconveniently, the local authority, acted upon by the public opinion, as it must necessarily be, of those concerned, has full power to repeal or alter them. It need hardly be added that, should experience warrant that course, the Legislature which has given may modify or take away the powers they have delegated. I have thought it well to deal with these points in some detail, and for this reason—that the great majority of the cases in which the question of bye-laws has been discussed are not cases of bye-laws of bodies of a public representative character entrusted by Parliament with delegated authority, but are for the most part cases of railway companies, dock companies, or other like companies, which carry on their business for their own profit, although incidentally for the advantage of the public. In this class of case it is right that the Courts should jealously watch the exercise of these powers, and guard against their unnecessary or unreasonable exercise to the public disadvantage. But, when the Court is called upon to consider the bye-laws of public representative bodies clothed with the ample authority which I have described, and exercising that authority accompanied by the checks and safeguards which have been mentioned, I think the consideration of such bye-laws ought to be approached from a different stand-point. They ought to be supported if possible. They ought to be, as has been said, "benevolently" interpreted, and credit ought to be given to those who have to administer them that they will be reasonably administered. This involves the introduction of no new canon of construction. But, further, looking to the character of the body legislating under the delegated authority of Parliament, to the subject-matter of such legislation, and to the nature and extent of the authority given to deal with matters which concern them, and in the manner which to them shall seem meet, I think courts of justice ought to be slow to condemn as invalid any bye-law, so made under such conditions, on the ground of supposed unreasonableness. Notwithstanding what Cockburn C.J. said in *Bailey v. Williamson* (1873) L.R. 8 Q.B. 118, 124, an analogous case, I do not mean to say that there may not be cases in which it would be the duty of the Court to condemn bye-laws, made under such authority as these were made, as invalid because unreasonable. But unreasonable in what sense? If, for instance, they were found to be partial and unequal in their operation as between different classes; if they were manifestly unjust; if they disclosed bad faith; if they involved such oppressive or gratuitous interference with the rights of those subject to them as could find no justification in the minds of reasonable men, the Court might well say, "Parliament never intended to give authority to make such rules; they are unreasonable and *ultra vires*." But it is in this sense, and in this sense only, as I conceive, that the question of unreasonableness can properly be regarded. A bye-law is not unreasonable merely because particular judges may think that it goes further than is prudent or necessary or convenient, or because it is not accompanied by a qualification or an exception which some judges may think ought to be there. Surely it is not too much to say that in matters which directly and mainly concern the people of the county, who have the right to choose those whom they think best fitted to represent them in their local government bodies, such representatives may be trusted to understand their own requirements better than judges. Indeed, if the question of the validity of bye-laws were to be determined by the opinion of judges as to what was reasonable in the narrow sense of that word, the cases in the books on this subject are no guide; for they reveal, as indeed one would expect, a wide diversity of judicial opinion, and they lay down no principle or definite standard by which reasonableness or unreasonableness may be tested.

So much for the general considerations which, it seems to me, ought to be borne in mind in considering bye-laws of this class. I now come to the bye-law in question.

It is admitted that the county council of Kent were within their authority in making a bye-law in relation to the subject-matter which is dealt with by the impeached bye-law. In other words, it is conceded, and properly so, that the local authority might make a bye-law imposing conditions under which musical instruments and singing might be permitted or prevented in public places; but it is objected that they had no authority to make a bye-law on that subject in the terms of this bye-law. Further, it is not contended that the bye-law should, in order to be valid, be confined to cases where the playing or singing amounted to a nuisance; but the objections are, as I understand them, that the bye-law is bad—first, because it is not confined to cases where the playing or singing is in fact causing annoyance, and next, because it enables a police constable to bring it into operation by a request on *his* part to the player or singer to desist. As to the first of these objections, if the general principles upon which these bye-laws ought to be dealt with are those which I have already stated, it is clear that the absence of this qualification cannot make the bye-law invalid. But, further, such a qualification in my judgment would render the bye-law ineffective. What is to be the standard of annoyance? What may be a cause of annoyance to one person may be no annoyance, and may even be pleasurable, to another person. Again, who is to be the judge in such case of whether there is or is not an annoyance? Is it to be the resident of the house within 50 yards of the playing or singing; or is it to be the magistrate who hears the charge? It is enough to say that, in my judgment, the absence of the suggested qualification cannot make the bye-law invalid, even if it be admitted that its presence would be an improvement.

As to the second objection—namely, that the policeman has the power of putting the bye-law into operation by requiring the player or singer to desist—I again say that, even if the absence of this power would be an improvement, and would make the bye-law in the apprehension of some more reasonable, it is not, on the principles I have already stated, any ground for declaring the bye-law to be invalid. In support of this objection pictures have in argument, been drawn—more or less highly coloured—of policemen who without rhyme or reason would or might gratuitously interfere with what might be a source of enjoyment to many. In answer, I say a policeman is not an irresponsible person without check or control. If he acts capriciously or vexatiously, he can be checked by his immediate superiors, or he can be taught a lesson by the magistrates should he prefer vexatious charges. If the policeman persisted in saying that the musician should desist when the people in the neighbourhood desired his music, his gratuitous interference would promptly come to an end. Nor is it correct to say, as has been erroneously stated in some of the cases cited, that the magistrate would be bound in every case to convict where the musician did not desist when called upon. It is clear that under s.16 of the Summary Jurisdiction Act 1879, the magistrate, if he thinks the case of so trifling a nature that it is inexpedient to inflict any punishment, may, without proceeding to conviction, dismiss the information. The facts of this case are certainly no illustration of the bye-law having been gratuitously or vexatiously put in force. The case states that, although it was not proved that the occupier of the house within 50 yards had, on the day in question, requested the constable to require the appellant to desist, yet it was proved that the singing was an annoyance to the occupier, and that he had on previous occasions complained to the police of such singing. Indeed, it was stated during the argument that the conviction here appealed from was the second conviction of the appellant for an offence against this bye-law. . . .

In my opinion, judged by the test of reasonableness, even in its narrower sense, this is a reasonable bye-law; but, whether I am right or wrong in this view, I am clearly of opinion that no Court of law can properly say that it is invalid.

SIR F.H. JEUNE P. delivered a concurring judgment. MATHEW J. dissented.

CHITTY L.J., WRIGHT, DARLING AND CHANNELL JJ. concurred with LORD RUSSELL OF KILLOWEN C.J.

Conviction affirmed.

Notes

1. This case has been considered and applied on many occasions. See notes in [1895–1899] All E.R. Rep. 105–106; D.G.T. Williams, *Welsh Studies in Public Law* (ed. by J.A. Andrews, 1970), "The Control of Local Authorities", pp.128 *et seq.*

2. On the validity of byelaws in general, see Alan Wharam, (1973) 36 M.L.R. 611; *Cross*, Ch.6.

3. A byelaw may be *ultra vires* for uncertainty. See *Percy v Hall* [1996] 4 All E.R. 523, where the Court of Appeal held that the correct test was whether "it can be given no meaning or no sensible and ascertainable meaning, and not merely because it is ambiguous or leads to absurd results" (Lord Denning in *Fawcett Properties Ltd v Buckingham County Council* [1961] A.C. 636 at 677–678) and not whether it contains "adequate information as to the duties of those who are to obey" (Mathew J. in *Kruse v Johnson* [1898] 2 Q.B. 91 at 108). While the former test had been established in relation to the validity of planning conditions, Lord Denning expressly equated the position of such conditions and byelaws. This approach had frequently been adopted by the Court of Appeal and House of Lords in relation to planning conditions. The latter test had frequently been applied in byelaw cases, but not above the level of the Divisional Court. Furthermore, it was in itself a test of "great uncertainty" providing "no criteria or principles by which to judge the adequacy of the information, or the degree of certainty, afforded by the byelaws". (See Simon Brown L.J. at pp.531–537.) On the facts, however, the byelaws challenged were not invalid under either test. They prohibited entry on "lands belonging to the Secretary of State" in named parishes, the land being in the vicinity of a military communications installation. The fact that members of the public might have to enquire which lands did belong to the Secretary of State did not render the byelaws uncertain.

4. The tests set out by Lord Russell of Killowen have been applied to test the validity of immigration rules: see *R. v Immigration Appeal Tribunal Ex p. Manshoora Begum* [1986] Imm.A.R. 385 at 393–395, Simon Brown J. (requirement in para.52 of the Immigration Rules that an applicant dependent relative must establish that he has a standard of living substantially below that of his own country held to be "partial and unequal" and "manifestly unjust" in operating adversely against applicants from poorer countries). However, arguments based on *Kruse v Johnson* have failed in subsequent cases (see, *e.g. R. v Immigration Appeal Tribunal Ex p. Fuller* [1993] Imm.A.R. 177; *R. v Secretary of State for the Home Department Ex p. Kwapong* [1994] Imm.A.R. 207 (distinction between husbands and wives in immigration rules not unreasonable under *Kruse v Johnson* given that Parliament had not applied the Sex Discrimination Act 1975 to the rules).

5. The reference to byelaws being unreasonable if "partial and unequal" in their operation has been regarded as illustrating a broader principle of English law requiring equal treatment without unfair discrimination. Acts and decisions that offend this principle may be regarded as irrational or *Wednesbury* unreasonable (see below, p.580; *de Smith, Woolf and Jowell*, pp.576–582; Sedley J. in *R. v Minister of Agriculture, Fisheries and Food Ex p. Hamble (Offshore) Fisheries Ltd* [1995] 2 All E.R. 714 at 722.

6. On the scope of collateral challenge to a byelaw, see *Boddington*, below, p.877.

Part II

JUDICIAL REVIEW

INTRODUCTORY NOTE TO PART II

(A) JUDICIAL REVIEW

The remainder of this book is concerned with the role of the *courts* in relation to the administration of government. A person affected by an act or omission of a public authority may be able to bring the matter before a court in any of the following circumstances:

(i) where the act is *ultra vires* (*i.e.* beyond the powers of the authority or is an unlawful act under the Human Rights Act 1998); or where the authority has omitted to perform a legal duty of a public nature;

Here the normal procedure will be to claim *for judicial review* in the High Court under CPR Pt 54. The various *grounds of challenge* for judicial review will be considered in detail in Chapters 5–10: matters of *procedure and remedy* in claims for judicial review will be dealt with in Chapter 14.

In addition to proceedings for judicial review a matter may be taken to a court:

(ii) where statute provides for a right of *appeal* to a court against a decision taken or a proposed course of action. Such appeal will be to the *kind* of court specified in the statutory provision, and the *grounds of appeal* will be as wide or as narrow as there defined. In this context we shall have occasion to note certain contexts—"statutory applications to quash"—in which although in form the procedure resembles an appeal, in terms of the grounds of challenge the *substance* is more akin to judicial review. These various matters will form the subject-matter of Chapter 11;

(iii) where the act or omission constitutes the commission of a tort or a breach of contract or where a proprietary or restitutionary claim may lie. The liability of public authorities in contract and tort and restitution is considered in Chapter 15. Such claims may either be brought by the ordinary procedures of civil litigation, or may form a part of the remedies sought in an application for judicial review.

In any proceedings, the interpretative duty under s.3 of the Human Rights Act 1998 may come into play (see Ch.6).

Although, understandably, the matter of recourse to the courts is of particular concern to lawyers, it will be apparent from the materials in Part I of this book that this is but one way of seeking redress of a grievance. We have already considered, and stressed the importance of, other non-judicial procedures—for example, appeals to specially created tribunals, opportunities to raise objections at public inquiries, complaints to and investigations by Ombudsmen, intervention of MPs or local councillors to seek to secure resolution of the matter. The collective significance of these matters should be remembered in assessing the subject-matter which follows.

Appreciation that judicial review is but one of a number of means of seeking redress should not, however, lead to its significance being underestimated. The last four decades have witnessed notable developments in the substance, and in the improvement and simplification of the procedures, of judicial review. A period of "judicial activism" dating from the early 1960s developed and refined the various grounds of challenge; and the "new" RSC Ord. 53 introduced, in 1977, rationalised procedures for judicial review challenges. Further important changes were introduced as part of the general reform of civil procedure effected through the Civil Procedure Rules, Pt 54 of which governs judicial review. At the same time there has been a very considerable increase in the number of judicial review claims being brought before the courts, a specialist Bar has emerged. The procedural reforms led to these cases (the Crown Office List) being handled by a nucleus of designated judges with substantial expertise in this area, an arrangement formalised by the establishment of the Administrative Court from October 2, 2000, within the Queen's Bench Division.

Moreover, the significance of judicial review should not be measured simply by the quantity of case-law generated, substantial as this now is. At its heart is the notion of the "rule of law"—that government possesses only those powers which have been bestowed upon it, and, at least in those areas of decision-making governed by statute, must exercise those powers in accordance with certain principles of presumed parliamentary intention. The substance of judicial review is an examination of how the judges have operated this "police" jurisdiction over the administration. The principles of judicial review should, in outline at least, be known to administrators and should influence the exercise of their functions. Concern that this was not sufficiently the case led the Treasury to issue to administrators, in 1987, a brief guide to the grounds of judicial review (*The Judge Over Your Shoulder*—Treasury Solicitor's Department). The purpose of the guide was stated to be to give administrators some basic grounding in the principles of review so that they would be less likely to act in ways which would give rise to a successful challenge. It is significant that on the first page of the document it is stated that "scarcely a day passes without the *Times Law Report* containing one or more cases where someone is challenging the decisions, or actions, of central or local government or a public body". A second edition was issued in 1995 and a third in 2000 (see *www.treasury-solicitor.gov.uk*).

The next chapters will comprise a detailed examination of the various grounds of challenge by way of judicial review. Most of the various grounds of challenge are, at root, aspects of the notion of *ultra vires*. It may be helpful if this notion, and the essence of each of the potential grounds of challenge, is outlined in this Introduction before they are discussed in detail.

(B) The *Ultra Vires* Principle—Grounds of Challenge By Way of Judicial Review

The supervisory, judicial review, jurisdiction inherent in the High Court is intended to ensure that persons or bodies exercising functions under statute (or, exceptionally, the royal prerogative) do not exceed or abuse their *powers*; and also to ensure that such persons or bodies perform such *duties* as have been so imposed upon them. An act or decision which is beyond the powers of the actor/decision-maker is said to be *ultra vires*, and, subject to the matters to be discussed below in Chapters 12 and 13, may be regarded as having no legal validity.

There are a variety of ways in which a body may exceed or abuse its powers. This is reflected in the emergence, in judicial opinions and in the writings of commentators, of a "catalogue" of grounds of challenge.

Each of these grounds is, however, no more than a sub-species of the broader governing notion of *ultra vires*. Some of the grounds "overlap", so that it may sometimes be successfully argued that a decision is tainted on more than one ground—and some decisions of courts expressly taken on the basis of one ground of challenge might equally well have been based on one of the other grounds. Moreover, the various grounds may not, as we shall see, cover the entire field of *ultra vires*—the door remains open for further grounds of challenge to develop.

Nevertheless, the various so-called "grounds of challenge" are of considerable value as a check-list by which to assess the *vires* of an act or decision. The "catalogue" is also of importance for its explanatory power—helping in the demonstration of, and providing constant reminder of, the subtlety and sophistication of the judicial elaboration of the *ultra vires* doctrine. There is no standard, agreed classification of the grounds of review to be found either in the literature or in the case law. A classification set at a very high level of generality was set out by Lord Diplock in *Council of Civil Service Unions v Minister for the Civil Service* [1985] A.C. 374 at 410–411 (below p.694). His Lordship's simple division of challenges into those alleging "illegality", those alleging "irrationality", and those alleging "procedural impropriety" is valuable in drawing important distinctions between the intellectual bases of the various traditional grounds of review. However, most commentators prefer to identify and analyse a series of distinct aspects of Lord Diplock's single category of "illegality" to facilitate understanding of what would otherwise be a mountain of case law.

The traditional catalogue—in outline

(i) "Simple" *Ultra Vires* and "Jurisdictional review"

By "simple" *ultra vires* we mean the situation where a body which has power to do X and Y, in fact does Z. The purported act or decision Z will be *ultra vires*. See below, pp.391–406. The matter will normally turn on the interpretation of the legislation in question in its context. A similar issue arises where it is alleged that a public authority has failed to perform a duty imposed (again normally) by statute. See pp.406–420.

By "jurisdictional control" we mean the situation where a body's power to do X is not conferred "at large", but has been conferred to be exercisable only in certain circumstances defined in the legislation: *i.e.* power to do X where conditions A and/or B prevail. In this situation if the body purports to do X in circumstances where A and/or B do *not* prevail its act or decision will be *ultra vires*.

In each of these situations the task for the reviewing court is to determine the meaning in law of the jurisdictional parameters to the conferment of power, and then to determine whether on the facts the body challenged has acted within or beyond its powers.

For many years the approach of the courts was to consider that a body which has exceeded its powers might have done so either because of an erroneous understanding as regards the circumstances in which its powers were exercisable (error of jurisdictional law) or because of an erroneous appreciation of a prevailing factual precondition to the existence of power (error of jurisdictional fact).

As will be seen below (pp.420–458), the present approach of the courts is to maintain a distinction between errors of fact which "go to jurisdiction" and non-jurisdictional factual errors (see pp.422–435 for cases illustrating this doctrine of "precedent fact"); but they no longer seek to draw a distinction, always an elusive one, between errors of law which should be regarded as going to jurisdiction and other errors of law which would not have such effect. The modern approach, involving a broad power of review simply for "error of law" is evident from the speeches of their Lordships in *Page*. It acknowledges the practical effect of the decision of the House of Lords, two decades earlier, in *Anisminic*: if not the more circumspect statements of principle to be found in the speeches delivered in that earlier decision. In this respect it may be observed that some potential for intellectual confusion would seem to flow from the practice of judges and lawyers of referring to the new-found broad jurisdiction to review for "error of law" as the "*Anisminic* principle".

The abandonment by the courts of their attempt to distinguish between jurisdictional and non-jurisdictional errors of law has rendered redundant a former ground of review in respect of which this distinction had for long not been of significance. Where a decision of a reviewable body displayed what the courts regarded as "error of law on the face of the record" it had since early modern times been accepted that certiorari would lie. With the extension in recent times, by judicial decisions and by legislation, of the concept of "the record" this seemingly slightly archaic ground of challenge for error of law (and not founded upon any notions of *ultra vires*) became a valuable, if unsung, ground of challenge. The recent extension of the scope of review, as confirmed by the speeches in *Page*, extends review to error of law generally, and not just to error of law manifest from review of the "record" of a decision impugned. In the light of these developments the doctrine of error of law on the face of the record no longer seems to warrant detailed treatment. Any who are curious may like to look at Chapter 10 of the second edition of this book. Although detailed treatment no longer seems apposite, it seems appropriate to have alerted readers to its previous existence and significance in order that they may not overestimate the magnitude of the steps taken culminating in *Page*. It might even be thought that that step was scarcely resistible: a matter of "when" rather than "whether".

(ii) Failure to "Retain Discretion" as to Exercise of Discretionary Power

Here the challenger does not dispute that a particular power is, in the circumstances, possessed by the body challenged. The challenge is based, rather, on failure to have complied with an obligation to retain and to exercise a free and unfettered discretion as to the exercise or non-exercise of that power. Such fettering of discretion may occur in various ways, and gives rise to sub-divisions of this ground of challenge. See below, pp.460–463 (acting under dictation), pp.482–495 (over-rigid adherence to self-created policy), pp.495–509 (fettering discretion by contractual or other undertakings affecting exercise of power), pp.523–524 (fettering discretion by unduly narrow construction of scope of discretionary power).

In this section it will be appropriate also to consider the "rule against delegation" of powers. This can be regarded as a want of power in the delegate, or a failure personally to exercise the power by the delegator. See below, pp.463–481. It will be an appropriate place also to consider the issue of estoppel in public law—to what extent may a body's past assertions/assurances as to the scope of its powers, or as to how it will exercise those powers, prevent it from subsequently denying such power, or prevent it from exercising powers so as to defeat expectations which its assurances may have engendered. The House of Lords has recently made it clear that the applicable principle is one of public law concerning the protection of legitimate expectations and not the private law principle of estoppel. See below, pp.509–523.

(iii) Challenge for "Abuse of Discretion"

Such challenges are based on the contention that a power has been exercised by the body in question for a purpose other than one for which the power was conferred—below, pp.525–545; or that in determining how to exercise the power the body took into account considerations which were irrelevant to the proper exercise of the power, or that there was a failure to have taken into account all the considerations which were relevant—below, pp.545–569; or that the decision constituted an unfair interference with a legitimate expectation of the claimant—below, pp.591–621; or that the decision was "unreasonable in the *Wednesbury* sense" (so called after the leading case) or irrational, that is so unreasonable that no reasonable body could have so decided—below, pp.569–591. A further potential ground of challenge is lack of proportionality, established as a ground of challenge in EC law and under the Human Rights Act 1998, but not yet accepted as a ground of general application—below, pp.621–632.

(iv) Challenges on Grounds of Procedural Irregularity

This covers:

(a) failure to have complied with a procedural requirement expressly provided in the legislative grant of power. The task for the reviewing court is to determine whether or not in all the circumstances the failure to comply should make the decision or act invalid. See below, pp.635–651.

(b) failure to comply with natural justice requirements which are implied by the judges, in some contexts, into statutory conferments of power. The rules of natural justice are two:

—that a decision-maker should not decide a matter in respect of which he has a financial interest or an interest as a party or in respect of which there is a real possibility that he is—see below, pp.751–787;

—that no person should be seriously affected by the exercise of power without having first been informed of the intention to exercise the power and having been given an appropriate opportunity to make representations before a final decision is taken—see below, pp.651–751.

(C) The Basis of Judicial Review

The account in the previous section is open to challenge in two ways. First, it may be argued cogently that there are other ways in which the grounds of challenge may properly be classified. This is indeed the case, and a glance at the leading textbooks will at once reveal that each author has his own approach. For example the first systematic analysis of the case law was provided by the late S.A. de Smith in his *Judicial Review of Administrative Action* (1959). The authors of the current (5th) edition have chosen a different structure, modelled on Lord Diplock's threefold classification. These variations in approach makes things a little more complicated for the reader new to the area, but is not of fundamental significance. All the basic grounds of challenge are there, but in a different order. A further point is that the cases do not always fit neatly into any of these structures. The same set of facts may commonly be analysed in different ways, and the terms in which a case is decided by a judge will commonly depend on the way counsel have chosen to present their arguments.

The second and more important issue is that the view of judicial review that sees the *ultra vires* doctrine as its core underlying principle has been strenuously challenged in the literature. The critics have rightly made much of the points (1) that the detailed grounds of judicial review have been developed by the judges with limited reference to the detailed wording of the legislation in question; and (2) that the principles of judicial review are applied to bodies that are not themselves set up by or exercising powers conferred by statute. The judges have only relatively recently begun to address these matters in decided cases, although a number have made important contributions to the literature. We return to these matters below, p.263.

(D) The Human Rights Act 1998

The body of principles of judicial review is now complemented by rights conferred by the Human Rights Act 1998. This raises similar issues to judicial review in terms of such matters as the bodies that are subjects to its requirements, the individuals who are able to assert claims under it, the grounds for intervention and the remedies available. The answers in each case are, however, distinct and the subject of a separate chapter (Ch.6).

(E) THE ROLE OF THE JUDGES

Judicial decision-making in any branch of law is not simply a mechanical process of logical reasoning, with the judges finding the facts and applying precisely formulated legal rules to those facts. In all areas of law it is now well appreciated that the judges possess some degree of freedom as regards the view they may take of the evidence presented, and also as regards their understanding of the relevant legal rules. The way in which individual judges hearing individual cases may behave, within this limited area of freedom of decision-making, will depend upon, and reflect, certain values of a legal, moral and political nature held by individual judges and possessed collectively by judges as a group. This latter aspect is significant. Simply because we may recognise the non-mechanical nature of the task of judging cases, and acknowledge that judges must make choices which will reflect values, we need not subscribe to any extreme view of the significance, case by case, of the presiding judge's personal political, moral or ethical views. An interpretation is possible which recognises that judges may have, in addition to their own personal scheme of values, a view as to what values they should, in their role as judges, allow to have some limited influence on the exercise of their judicial functions. This is perhaps particularly true of decision-making in public law, where many of the "substantive rules" (the grounds for judicial review) are in fact broadly drawn principles, and where the trend is, if anything, for the grounds of review to become less rather than more specific (see for example, the case law on procedural *ultra vires*, on the duty to act fairly and on standing (below, Ch.10 and pp.994–1010)). Moreover, remedies in administrative law are almost invariably discretionary. Thus, in practice, the judges possess considerable leeways of choice, and it becomes important to attempt to discern the values that may influence their decision-making. One difficulty here is that it is unusual for these values to be expressly articulated. Another is that such non-articulated values may change from one period of time to another.

Commentators have identified a variety of themes. J.A.G. Griffith (*The Politics of the Judiciary* (5th ed., 1997)), for example, has noted the homogeneity of the background of the judiciary (almost all male, predominantly public school and Oxbridge) and argues that:

"These judges have by their education and training and the pursuit of their profession as barristers, acquired a strikingly homogenous collection of attitudes, beliefs and principles, which to them represent the public interest. . . . The judicial conception of the public interest, seen in the cases discussed in this book, is threefold. It concerns, first, the interest of the state (including its moral welfare); secondly, the preservation of law and order, broadly interpreted; and, thirdly, the judges' views on social and political issues of one day" (pp.295, 297).

(In earlier editions, the third head was "the promotion of certain political views normally associated with the Conservative Party".)

In his book, Griffith seeks to demonstrate his thesis in relation to a variety of areas of judicial decision-making. One of his chapters (Ch.4) examines and discusses cases on the control of discretionary powers. Griffith's views are strong. Not all would agree that his selection of cases to discuss is representative; nor agree with his analysis of those cases and conclusions. Nevertheless, his discussion is thought-provoking and will repay study. For published critiques of Griffith's views see, *e.g.* Lord Devlin (1978) 41 M.L.R. 501 and S. Lee, *Judging Judges* (1988), Ch.4. Lee comments (p.35):

"Yet Griffith is merely saying that he disagrees with the decisions. One would get the impression that he would almost always decide the opposite way against property, stability, the Conservative Party, etc. But would this be preferable? Would it be more democratic?. . . Does the evidence really show that judges act in this way? Is law really explicable in terms of class interests?"

In his 1997 edition, Griffith continues (Ch.8) to deny the existence of judicial neutrality. This is not a matter of personal political partisanship, but in deciding cases, many of which could be decided either way, they inevitably exercise a political function. Their views follow a political philosophy of conservatism, whether or not it "follows the day-to-day political policies currently associated with the party of that name" (p.341).

A second critique was that of P. McAuslan ("Administrative Law, Collective Consumption and Judicial Policy" (1983) 46 M.L.R. 1). He detected from case law in the 1970s and early 1980s (such as the *Bromley* case (below, p.561)) that the "only coherent jurisprudence of administrative law" that had emerged was "basically antipathetic" to the processes of "collective consumption". This term refers to the services (such as education, health care, social welfare, environmental and cultural facilities, highways, public transport, public housing, land use regulation and urban planning) that are organised, planned and managed on a collective public basis by central or local government or quangos, and are consumed collectively ((1983) 46 M.L.R. at 2). McAuslan also detected a "most significant division of judicial opinions":

"This is between the Divisional Court, staffed for the most part by judges whose whole working life and success has coincided with, and indeed has been in large part formed by, the growth of the processes of collective consumption and the judges in the Court of Appeal and House of Lords, who for the most part either passed their formative and working years in different political milieu, or are generally not oversympathetic to or understanding of the processes of collective consumption. The former judges with their greater understanding of modern administration and politics, and their more recent involvement as lawyers in those processes, are clearly much more reluctant to get drawn into the maelstrom of political and ideological conflicts which masquerade as legal issues justiciable in courts. They appear to be more sensibly aware of the long-term dangers of judges appearing to adopt a partisan political role through their judgments in the courts. In the higher reaches of the judiciary, it seems to be believed that if your judgment is long and full of extracts of statutes and previous decisions, no one will notice that it is a political statement and if anybody does and says so, they can be dismissed as "prejudiced" and in some obscure way "failing to uphold the rule of law" (footnotes omitted; *ibid.* at p.19).

If McAuslan's views about the influence of age and generation are correct what should we expect to find now, two decades later? All our judges have spent their adult lives in post-war Britain. They must understand and be familiar with the "processes of collective consumption". Has this produced the consequences McAuslan foresaw? Can it be contended that the new generation of judges were themselves too old to review "neutrally" the acts and decisions of the Conservative administrations between 1979 and 1997?

A third commentator, D. Feldman ("Public Law Values in the House of Lords" (1990) 106 L.Q.R. 246) suggested that the dominant political theory among law lords in the 1980s was "democratic elitism", which:

"restricts public participation to a periodic take-it-or-leave-it choice between competing political élites, freeing the elected group to do much as it will between elections" (*ibid.* at p.247).

In his discussion Feldman noted the limited applicability of review for irrationality where action has been approved by Parliament (below, pp.576–579) or where the decision-maker is responsible to Parliament (*e.g. R. v Secretary of State for Trade and Industry Ex p. Lonrho Plc*, below, p.535); the marked deference to the political judgment of Ministers where national security is in issue; and a lack of enthusiasm for a more participatory model of democracy (*cf.* the *Bushell* case, below, p.731). Other values identified include deference to the professional expertise of administrators (*cf.* the *Puhlhofer* case, below, p.434) and the limited recognition of individual rights.

"Where rights are recognised they are important: schemes which interfere with rights will be zealously scrutinised; but those dependent on public benefits are not generally seen as having rights, so administrators of schemes conferring benefits are given a freer rein" (*ibid*. at p.259).

Moreover, the European Convention on Human Rights had not been seen as conferring on individuals rights to be protected by English law (*cf.* the *Brind* case, decided more recently than Feldman's article). Finally, Feldman noted that "principled consistency" has tended to give way to pragmatism, usually in the interests of government (*e.g.* the comparison between *Manchester City Council v Greater Manchester CC* and *Westminster City Council, Re* (below, p.394)). In developing this analysis Feldman pointed out that the general picture did conceal heterogeneous approaches, with certain judges giving greater weight (usually in dissent) to rights or to principled consistency.

Feldman's discussion was based on his interpretation of decisions of (only) the House of Lords during an earlier decade. All the themes can still be identified in the courts today, subject to the modification effected by the Human Rights Act 1998.

The role of the judges in deciding cases raising issues under the Human Rights Act 1998 raises similar issues, modified by the fact that the values to be furthered by their decisions are those expressly set out in the Act itself. The techniques to be employed are not entirely a matter for them to develop but are to be founded on the jurisprudence of the European Court of Human Rights. Unlike judicial review, whose development has essentially been undertaken by the judges subject to the toleration of and occasional recognition by Parliament, the democratic legitimacy of judicial intervention is expressly provided by the Act itself. See further Ch.6.

A matter which should not simply be assumed to be constant is the extent to which public authorities have been willing to take action known or suspected to be unlawful. There are well-known cases where Labour local councils have taken steps fairly clearly in defiance of the law (*e.g.* some aspects of "Poplarism" in the 1920s: see below, p.552; the Clay Cross affair (see *Asher v Secretary of State for the Environment* [1974] 1 Ch.208); the proceedings arising out of the wilful misconduct of Liverpool City councillors in delaying making a rate: below, p.722). On the other hand, it has been said that the (Conservative):

"governments since 1979 have become increasingly careless of their obligations to comply with the law in the implementation of their policies. Indeed so general has become this abuse and excess of power, and the taking of actions of doubtful legality that observers would be forgiven for thinking that there was a studied practice of such behaviour".

(P. McAuslan and J.F. McEldowney, "Legitimacy and the Constitution: The Dissonance between Theory and Practice" in McAuslan and McEldowney (ed.), *Law, Legit-imacy and the Constitution* (1985), Ch.1, p.28, giving (at pp.28–31) 12 of the "more noteworthy examples of this casual approach to the use of governmental power" between 1979 and 1985).

Twenty years later, tension between central government and the judiciary in the context of judicial review remains evident, the commonest battleground being the area of asylum and immigration, where the Home Secretary has been publicly critical of particular judicial decisions. See R. Rawlings, (2005) 68 M.L.R. 378.

(F) The Growth of Judicial Review

Research on the statistics of judicial review has been conducted by M. Sunkin (see "What has been Happening to Applications for Judicial Review" (1987) 50 M.L.R. 432 (covering 1981–86); "The Judicial Review Case-Load 1987–1989" [1991] P.L. 490; and by L. Bridges, G. Meszaros and M. Sunkin, *Judicial Review in Perspective*

(1995) and "Regulating the Judicial Review Case-load" (2000) P.L. 651. The research shows that while the overall figures show a substantial growth in applications for judicial review in civil matters (533 applications for leave in 1981; 1,580 in 1989; over 3,200 in 1994), the figures are dominated by applications in particular subject areas, especially immigration and housing. Note the conclusions drawn by Bridges, Meszaros and Sunkin in 1995:

> "In other fields the problem with judicial review is certainly not one of over-use. Growth in the number of applications other than in immigration, homelessness and crime has been relatively modest during the past decade. The limited use of judicial review is demonstrated not only by the relatively small overall number of applications outside of these 'core' areas. It is also shown in the limited extent to which judicial review has penetrated into the practices of solicitors in private practice and into law centres, and in the infrequent appearance of pressure groups directly as applicants. It is further indicated by the surprisingly low rates of use of judicial review to challenge the actions of most central government departments. Outside the fields of immigration and housing, it is used far more readily against local authorities than central government. Although these are early days, our data reveal little evidence that the drive toward privatisation and contracting out of public services has resulted in any significant increase in the use of judicial review against either the new executive agencies or private organisations performing public functions" (*Judicial Review in Perspective*, p.193).

In 2003, the number of applications for permission to apply for judicial review had increased to 5,949 (3,848 (65 per cent) immigration, 245 criminal, 199 homeless and 1,657 others). The incidence of judicial review in homelessness cases has been much reduced by the creation of an appeal to the County Court. However, overall numbers have increased sharply (3,901 in 1996; 4,539 in 1998; 4,247 in 2000; 5,377 in 2002: *Judicial Statistics Annual Reports*).

It would be wrong to judge the efficacy of judicial review solely by reference to the case-load. Harlow and Rawlings (*Law and Administration* (1997), p.530) conclude that "litigant-driven judicial review is indeed sporadic", but emphasise that one court decision may affect "perhaps thousands of similar cases" and that "the mere existence of judicial review and the creation of precedent may influence administrative behaviour" (*ibid.* at p.537).

Research conducted by M. Sunkin and A.P. Le Sueur ("Can Government Control Judicial Review?" (1991) C.L.P. 161) noted the establishment of an official group of high level civil servants to examine the growth in the number of successful applications against government departments, and the consequent steps taken within the civil service. Civil servants were encouraged to reduce the risks of legal challenge by anticipating and planning for challenge throughout their decision-making. Legislation should be expressed in the clearest possible terms; steps should be taken to improve and broaden the quality of legal awareness (note the earlier mentioned circulation of the pamphlet *The Judge Over Your Shoulder*), and there should be developed closer relationships between policy-makers and departmental lawyers. Moreover, the aims seems not to have been entirely negative and defensive. Interviewees told the researchers that, for example, legal awareness training was "aimed at inculcating habits of good administrative conduct" (p.172). The overall impression was:

> "that if the new ethos [was] having an effect it [was] to encourage officials to become more cautious in their work and more aware of the need to explain and justify action" (p.175).

Judicial review was, moreover, only one of many external constraints, which included the PCA, MPs, Select Committees, the media, pressure and interest groups and, increasingly, the European Community and the ECHR. These had all to be set along-side the "internal organisational, policy, financial and other constraints which encroach upon operational practice".

"When decision-makers are constantly forced to balance competing and possibly conflicting constraints, risks of challenge are incurred as an inevitable part of administrative life. The new ethos can do little to change this, save that by obliging decision-takers consciously to address the legal implications of their action, risk-taking may become a more informed, deliberate and explicit process" (*ibid.*).

The point is also made that:

"despite the perceptions of the senior officials that we interviewed, ignorance of the most elementary legal principles (let alone understanding of how they will be applied by the courts) is still likely to be endemic particularly amongst those charged with routine decision-making".

Since then, the involvement of lawyers in administrative decision-making has been accelerated and deepened as the administration calls regularly for legal advice at an early stage (see *Daintith and Page*, pp.336–337). Furthermore, the understanding of legal principles should have been enhanced by the programme of training and provision of guidance surrounding the implementation of the Human Rights Act 1998; the extent of this is, however, difficult to assess. (Note the Audit Commission's finding in 2003 that more than half the public bodies surveyed were not taking it into account in service delivery (*Human Rights: Improving Public Service Delivery* (2003)).)

There is now a significant literature on the impact of judicial review considering a range of contexts across different jurisdictions. See M. Hertogh and S. Halliday (ed.), *Judicial Review and Bureaucratic Impact* (2004). Particular studies include G. Richardson and M. Sunkin, "Judicial Review: Questions of Impact" [1996] P.L. 79; G. Richardson and D. Machin, "Judicial Review and Tribunal Decision Making: A Study of the Mental Health Review Tribunal" [2000] P.L. 494; S. Halliday, "The Influence of Judicial Review on Bureaucratic Decision-Making" [2000] P.L. 110; M. Sunkin and K. Pick, "The Changing Impact of Judicial Review: The Independent Review Service of the Social Fund" [2001] P.L. 736.

CHAPTER 5

THE PRINCIPLE OF LEGALITY

It is relatively unusual for the judges to reflect on fundamental questions as to the basis of and the justifications for the judicial review jurisdiction of the courts. The principles are now well established although still open to further development and refinement. Most cases are determined by the application of existing principles to both familiar and unfamiliar sets of circumstances. There are, however, a number of judicial contributions, mostly at the level of the House of Lords, which seek to address these fundamental questions. Two important speeches were delivered by Lord Diplock in *Council of Civil Service Unions v Minister for the Civil Service* (below, p.690) and *O'Reilly v Mackman* (below, p.976). The former contained an influential classification of the grounds for review; the latter constituted an unfortunate and ultimately unsuccessful attempt to establish a hard principle of procedural exclusivity under which most cases raising judicial review issues would have to be taken through the application for judicial review procedure. Other important contributions have been those of Lord Browne-Wilkinson in *R. v Hull University Visitor Ex p. Page* [1993] A.C. 682 (below, p.450); Lord Steyn and Lord Browne-Wilkinson in *R. v Secretary of State for the Home Department Ex p. Pierson* [1998] A.C. 539 (below); and Lord Steyn in *R. v Secretary of State for the Home Department Ex p. Simms* [2000] 2 A.C. 115 (below, p.261); and *Boddington v British Transport Police* [1999] 2 A.C. 143 (below, p.877).

R. v SECRETARY OF STATE FOR THE HOME DEPARTMENT
Ex p. PIERSON

[1998] A.C. 539; [1997] 3 W.L.R. 492; [1997] 3 All E.R. 577
(HOUSE OF LORDS)

P was convicted of the murder of his parents and given two mandatory life sentences. The trial judge in his report described the crime as horrifying and mystifying. Under the sentencing regime then applicable, the Criminal Justice Act 1967 and then the Criminal Justice Act 1991, the Secretary of State could, if recommended to do so by the Parole Board, release on licence a life sentence prisoner, but only after consultation with the Lord Chief Justice, together with the trial judge, if available. By virtue of a series of policy statements by successive Home Secretaries, a distinction was drawn between the period a prisoner would have to serve to meet the requirements of retribution and deterrence (the "penal element or tariff period") and any remaining period he was required to serve before release (the "risk period"). The former was fixed by the Home Secretary after consultation with the Lord Chief Justice and trial judge (if available). In 1988, the trial judge recommended a tariff of 15 years and the Lord Chief Justice agreed, but the Home Secretary fixed a period of 20 years. P was not told expressly but was able to infer that this was the case from the date fixed for the first review of his case by the Parole Board. In 1993, changes to the regime expressed in a further policy statement provided that the Secretary of State would express an initial view at the beginning of a mandatory life sentence, but could, exceptionally, revise that initial view of the penal element subsequently. This could include a reconsideration of that element to ensure that it was adequate. (Previous statements had provided that the penal element once fixed would not be increased.) P was now told formally that the trial judge had recommended 15 years but that the Home Secretary's view was that 15 years would have been appropriate for a single premeditated offence, but a longer period (20 years) was necessary for a double murder. P was invited to make representations. These were submitted, pointing out that it had never been alleged that P's actions were premeditated and the offences were in practice instantaneous and part of a single incident which took place during a short period of time. In response, the Home Secretary accepted these points but maintained the view that 20 years was appropriate as the penal element. This decision was quashed by certiorari by Turner J. on the ground that the Home Secretary was only entitled to increase the penal element in exceptional circumstances and none existed.

The Court of Appeal held that the Home Secretary did have discretion to increase the penal element initially fixed by his predecessor if he decided it did not meet the requirements of retribution and deterrence. This was reversed by the House of Lords by 3 to 2 (Lords Goff of Chievely, Steyn and Hope of Craighead, Lords Browne-Wilkinson and Lloyd of Berwick dissenting). It was agreed unanimously that the maintenance of the period at 20 years notwithstanding the absence of the two aggravating features was in effect an increase in the penal element.

LORD STEYN: The principal question arising on this appeal is whether the Home Secretary has a general power to increase a tariff which he or a predecessor fixed and communicated to a prisoner. The Court of Appeal answered this question in the affirmative.

It is necessary at the outset to appreciate the width of the power to increase tariffs duly fixed which the Home Secretary now asserts. Counsel argued that the Home Secretary may at any time increase a tariff previously fixed. Counsel said that the Home Secretary may increase a tariff applicable to a prisoner as often as he considers it necessary to do so. And he stated that the Home Secretary may do so across the whole spectrum of mandatory life sentence cases. Counsel said that it is irrelevant in law that a prisoner and his family may have planned their lives on the basis of the tariff communicated to the prisoner and the possibility of release after expiry of the tariff. In the Court of Appeal, at p.560, Sir Thomas Bingham M.R., now the Lord Chief Justice, said that he could well understand the despair of a prisoner serving a very long term of imprisonment as the date of expiry of his penal term recedes before him but he observed that the remedy must lie elsewhere. Recognising the adverse effect of retrospective increases in the tariff on prisoners and their families, counsel for the Home Secretary said that any unfairness is a matter for Parliament. Counsel said that the only qualification to the generality of the power of the Home Secretary to increase tariffs is the need for observing the requirements of procedural fairness by inviting the comments of the prisoner before an increase is made.

The answer to the question before the House is important. It is a difficult question. Professor Neil MacCormick observed that: "there is often a need in hard cases to dig down to the level of constitutional theory in order to solve questions about private rights and public powers:" see "Jurisprudence and the Constitution" (1983) 36 C.L.P. 13, 20. That is so in this case. The structure of the law matters. It is necessary to find the exact location of this case on the map of public law. The starting-point must be an examination of the nature of the power of the Home Secretary to fix a tariff . . . The undeniable fact is that in fixing a tariff in an individual case the Home Secretary is making a decision about the punishment of the convicted man. In any event, a majority holding in *Reg. v. Secretary of State for the Home Department, Ex parte*

Venables [1998] A.C. 407 concludes the matter. Lord Goff of Chieveley, at p.490, held that the Home Secretary is

> "exercising a function which is closely analogous to a sentencing function with the effect that, when so doing, he is under a duty to act within the same constraints as a judge will act when he is exercising the same function."

Lord Hope of Craighead, at p.85G–H, agreed. So did I, at pp.74H–75C. This point is therefore settled by the binding authority of a decision of the House.

That brings me to the question whether any legal consequences flow from the characterisation of the Home Secretary's function as involving a decision on punishment. It is a general principle of the common law that a lawful sentence pronounced by a judge may not retrospectively be increased. In 1971 that principle was put on a statutory basis.

[His Lordship referred to *R. v Menocal* [1980] A.C. 598 and s.11(2) of the Courts Act 1971, which provided that a sentence imposed by the Crown Court may be varied or rescinded within 28 days beginning with the day on which it was imposed; in *Menocal*, the House held that after the 28-day period, the judge had no power to alter the sentence.]

The general principle of our law is therefore that a convicted criminal is entitled to know where he stands so far as his punishment is concerned. He is entitled to legal certainty about his punishment. His rights will be enforced by the courts. Under English law a convicted prisoner, in spite of his imprisonment, retains all civil rights which are not taken away expressly or by necessary implication: *Raymond v. Honey* [1983] 1 A.C. 1, 10H.

The question must now be considered whether the Home Secretary, in making a decision on punishment, is free from the normal constraint applicable to a sentencing power. It is at this stage of the examination of the problem that it becomes necessary to consider where in the structure of public law it fits in. Parliament has not expressly authorised the Home Secretary to increase tariffs retrospectively. If Parliament had done so that would have been the end of the matter. Instead Parliament has by section 35(2) of the Act of 1991 entrusted the power to take decisions about the release of mandatory life sentence prisoners to the Home Secretary. The statutory power is wide enough to authorise the fixing of a tariff. But it does not follow that it is wide enough to permit a power retrospectively to increase the level of punishment.

The wording of section 35(2) of the Act of 1991 is wide and general. It provides that "the Secretary of State may . . . release on licence a life prisoner who is not a discretionary life prisoner." There is no ambiguity in the statutory language. The presumption that in the event of ambiguity legislation is presumed not to invade common law rights is inapplicable. A broader principle applies. Parliament does not legislate in a vacuum. Parliament legislates for a European liberal democracy founded on the principles and traditions of the common law. And the courts may approach legislation on this initial assumption. But this assumption only has prima facie force. It can be displaced by a clear and specific provision to the contrary. These propositions require some explanation.

For at least a century it has been "thought to be in the highest degree improbable that Parliament would depart from the general system of law without expressing its intention with irresistible clearness:" see *Maxwell on Interpretation of Statutes*, 4th ed. (1905), p.121, and 12th ed., p.116. The idea is even older. In 1855 Sir John Romilly M.R. observed:

"the general words of the Act are not to be so construed as to alter the previous policy of the law, unless no sense or meaning can be applied to those words consistently with the intention of preserving the existing policy untouched . . .:" *Minet v. Leman* (1855) 20 Beav. 269, 278.

This observation has been applied in decisions of high authority: *National Assistance Board v. Wilkinson* [1952] 2 Q.B. 648, 659, *per* Lord Goddard C.J. and *Mixnam's Properties Ltd. v. Chertsey Urban District Council* [1964] 1 Q.B. 214, 236, *per* Diplock L.J. In his *Law of the Constitution*, 10th ed. (1959), Dicey explained the context in which Parliament legislates, at p.414:

"By every path we come round to the same conclusion, that Parliamentary sovereignty has favoured the rule of law, and that the supremacy of the law of the land both calls forth the exertion of Parliamentary sovereignty, and leads to its being exercised in a spirit of legality."

But it is to Sir Rupert Cross that I turn for the best modern explanation of "the spirit of legality," or what has been called the principle of legality. (The phrase "the principle of legality" I have taken from *Halsbury's Laws of England*, 4th ed. reissue, vol. 8(2) (1996), p.13, para. 6.) The passage appears in *Cross, Statutory Interpretation*, 3rd ed., pp.165–166, which has been edited by Professor John Bell and Sir George Engle Q.C., formerly first Parliamentary counsel, but it is worth noting that the passage is in all material aspects as drafted by the author: see *Cross, Statutory Interpretation*, 1st ed. (1976), pp.142–143. In the 3rd edition the passage reads:

"Statutes often go into considerable detail, but even so allowance must be made for the fact that they are not enacted in a vacuum. A great deal inevitably remains unsaid. Legislators and drafters assume that the courts will continue to act in accordance with well-recognised rules . . . Long-standing principles of constitutional and administrative law are likewise taken for granted, or assumed by the courts to have been taken for granted, by Parliament. Examples are the principles that discretionary powers conferred in apparently absolute terms must be exercised reasonably, and that administrative tribunals and other such bodies must act in accordance with the principles of natural justice. One function of the word 'presumption' in the context of statutory interpretation is to state the result of this legislative reliance (real or assumed) on firmly established legal principles. There is a 'presumption' that mens rea is required in the case of statutory crimes, and a 'presumption' that statutory powers must be exercised reasonably. These presumptions apply although there is no question of linguistic ambiguity in the statutory wording under construction, and they may be described as 'presumptions of general application'. . . . These presumptions of general application not only supplement the text, they also operate at a higher level as expressions of fundamental principles governing both civil liberties and the relations between Parliament, the executive and the courts. They operate here as constitutional principles which are not easily displaced by a statutory text."

This explanation is the intellectual justification of the often quoted proposition of Byles J. in *Cooper v Wandsworth Board of Works* (1863) 14

C.B.(N.S.) 180 that "although there are no positive words in a statute requiring that a party shall be heard, yet the justice of the common law will supply the omission:" see *Ridge v. Baldwin* [1964] A.C. 40, 69, *per* Lord Reid, and *Bennion, Statutory Interpretation*, pp.726–727.

The operation of the principle of legality can further be illustrated by reference to the decision of the House of Lords in *Reg. v. Secretary of State for the Home Department, Ex parte Doody* [1994] 1 A.C. 531. In that case the House of Lords held that the common law principles of procedural fairness required disclosure to a prisoner of the advice to the Home Secretary of the trial judge and of the Lord Chief Justice in order to enable the prisoner to make effective representations before the Home Secretary fixed the tariff. The premise was that Parliament must be presumed to have intended that the Home Secretary would act in conformity with the common law principle of procedural fairness. And our public law is, of course, replete with other instances of the common law so supplementing statutes on the basis of the principle of legality. A recent and pertinent example is provided by the speeches of the majority in the House of Lords in *Reg. v. Secretary of State for the Home Department, Ex parte Venables* [1998] A.C. 407, so far as a majority decided that in fixing a tariff the Home Secretary may not take into account public protests in aggravation of a particular tariff. That ruling depended on the proposition that the Home Secretary was in substance engaged in a decision on punishment. He was "under a duty to act within the same constraints as a judge:" *per* Lord Goff of Chieveley, at p.490. The assumption was that the Home Secretary would act in conformity with fundamental principles of our law governing the imposition of criminal punishment.

It is to be noted that in *Ex parte Doody* and *Ex parte Venables* the principle of legality served to protect procedural safeguards provided by the common law. But the principle applies with equal force to protect substantive basic or fundamental rights. It is only necessary to refer to the decision of the House of Lords in *Raymond v. Honey* [1983] 1 A.C. 1. The Prison Act 1952 empowered the Home Secretary to make rules "for the regulation and management of prisons:" section 47(1). The Home Secretary made rules which gave prison governors the power to intercept outgoing letters of prisoners. A governor intercepted and failed to send on a letter regarding legal proceedings from a prisoner to his solicitor. The prisoner sought a declaration that the governor's conduct was unlawful. The governor relied on the rules to justify his conduct. The rule-making power was wide and unambiguous and was so regarded by the House. In a speech made with the agreement of three Law Lords Lord Wilberforce referred, at pp.12–13, to a prisoner's right to have unimpeded access to a court and observed that "a section concerned with the regulation and management of prisons . . . is quite insufficient to authorise hindrance or interference with so basic a right." See also *Reg. v. Secretary of State for the Home Department, Ex parte Anderson* [1984] Q.B. 778 and *Reg. v Secretary of State for the Home Department, Ex parte Leech* [1994] Q.B. 198.

A corresponding principle applies in respect of basic standards and safeguards enshrined in legislation. This proposition is hardly radical. Ultimately, common law and statute law coalesce in one legal system. The point can be illustrated by reference to the decision of the House of Lords in *Reg. v Cain* [1985] A.C. 46. In that case a trial court had made a criminal bankruptcy order in circumstances where it had no power to do so. That order could be challenged in judicial review proceedings. But the jurisdictional question arose before the House whether the order could be set aside on appeal. Section 40(1) of the Powers of Criminal Courts Act 1973 provides: "No appeal shall lie against the making of a criminal bankruptcy order." That appeared to rule out any appeal. But the House decided that there was a right of appeal against an order which the court had no power to make. Lord Scarman, with the agreement of the other Law Lords, said, at p.56:

> "In the absence of express indication to the contrary, it would be unthinkable that Parliament could intend to deprive the subject of his right to appeal against a sentence which the court had no power to pass."

The principle of legality applied. These observations are relevant in the present case inasmuch as the common law principle that a sentence may not retrospectively be increased has been put on a statutory basis. But perhaps I have struggled unnecessarily with the point since one could simply say that the statutory enactment of the common law principle a fortiori triggers the principle of legality.

Turning back to the circumstances of the present case, it was easy to conclude that the legislation authorises the policy of fixing a tariff. The wide statutory discretion of the Home Secretary justified that conclusion. But a general power to increase tariffs lawfully fixed is qualitatively in a different category. It contemplates a power unheard of in our criminal justice system until the 1993 policy statement of the Home Secretary (Mr. Michael Howard) (Hansard (H.C. Debates), 27 July 1993, cols. *861–864*: written answer). Such a power is not essential to the efficient working of the system: without a power to increase tariffs the system worked satisfactorily between 1983 and 1993. But I do not rest my judgment on this point. The critical factor is that a general power to increase tariffs duly fixed is in disharmony with the deep rooted principle of not retrospectively increasing lawfully pronounced sentences. In the absence of contrary indications it must be presumed that Parliament entrusted the wide power to make decisions on the release of mandatory life sentence prisoners on the supposition that the Home Secretary would not act contrary to such a fundamental principle of our law. There are no contrary indications. Certainly, there is not a shred of evidence that Parliament would have been prepared to vest a general power in the Home Secretary to increase retrospectively tariffs duly fixed. The evidence is to the contrary. When Parliament enacted section 35(2) of the Act of 1991—the foundation of the Home Secretary's present power—Parliament knew that since 1983 successive Home Secretaries had adopted a policy of fixing in each case a tariff period, following which risk is considered. Parliament also knew that it was the practice that a tariff, once fixed, would not be increased. That was clear from the assurance in the 1983 policy statement (Mr. Leon Brittan (Hansard (H.C. Debates), 30 November 1983, cols. *505–507*: written answer)) that "except where a prisoner has committed an offence for which he has received a further custodial sentence, the formal review date will not be put back." What Parliament did not know in 1991 was that in 1993 a new Home Secretary would assert a general power to increase the punishment of prisoners convicted of murder whenever he considered it right to do so. It would be wrong to assume that Parliament would have been prepared to give to the Home Secretary such an unprecedented power, alien to the principles of our law.

Counsel for the Home Secretary then approached the matter from a different angle. He said that the only possible complaint a mandatory life sentence prisoner could have about the increase of his tariff would be on the basis of the infringement of his legitimate expectations. But, he said, this doctrine has no substantive effect: it merely gives protection against procedural unfairness. This is a controversial question. Counsel is not necessarily right: see *de Smith, Woolf and Jowell, Judicial Review of Administrative Action*, 5th ed. (1995), pp.570–574, paras. 13–029-13–030; P.P. Craig, "Substantive Legitimate Expectations in Domestic and Community Law" [1996] C.L.J. 289. This issue was only briefly mentioned in argument. It is unnecessary to express a view on it. I will assume that counsel for the Home Secretary's proposition about the doctrine of legitimate expectations is correct. But counsel addressed the wrong target. The correct analysis of this case is in terms of the rule of law. The rule of law in its wider sense has procedural and substantive effect. While Dicey's description of the rule of law *(Law of the Constitution*, p.203) is nowadays regarded as neither exhaustive nor entirely accurate even for his own time, there is much of enduring value in the work of this great lawyer. Dicey's famous third meaning of the rule of law is apposite. He said, at p.203:

"The 'rule of law,' lastly, may be used as a formula for expressing the fact that with us the law of constitution, the rules which in foreign countries naturally form part of a constitutional code, are not the source but the consequence of the rights of individuals, as defined and enforced by the courts; that, in short, the principles of private law have with us been by the action of the courts and Parliament so extended as to determine the position of the Crown and its servants; thus the constitution is the result of the ordinary law of the land."

This was the pivot of Dicey's discussion of rights to personal freedom, and to freedom of association and of public meeting, at pp.206–283. It is clear therefore that in the relevant sense Dicey regarded the rule of law as having both procedural and substantive effect. In a valuable essay Professor Jeffrey Jowell has re-examined Dicey's theme: "The Rule of Law Today," in *Jowell and Oliver, The Changing Constitution*, 3rd ed. (1994), pp.74–77. Relying on striking modern illustrations Professor Jowell concluded that the rule of law has substantive content: see *Hall & Co. Ltd v Shoreham-by-Sea Urban District Council* [1964] 1 W.L.R. 240; *Congreve v. Home Office* [1976] Q.B. 629 and *Wheeler v Leicester City Council* [1985] A.C. 1054, *per* Lord Templeman with whom Lord Bridge of Harwich, Lord Brightman and Lord Griffiths agreed. *Wade, Administrative Law*, 7th ed. (1994), pp.24 et seq. and *de Smith and Brazier, Constitutional and Administrative Law*, 7th ed. (1994), p.18, are to the same effect. Unless there is the clearest provision to the contrary, Parliament must be presumed not to legislate contrary to the rule of law. And the rule of law enforces minimum standards of fairness, both substantive and procedural. I therefore approach the problem in the present case on this basis.

It is true that the principle of legality only has prima facie force. But in enacting section 35(2) of the Act of 1991, with its very wide power to release prisoners, Parliament left untouched the fundamental principle that a sentence lawfully passed should not retrospectively be increased. Parliament must therefore be presumed to have enacted legislation wide enough to enable the

Home Secretary to make decisions on punishment on the basis that he would observe the normal constraint governing that function. Instead the Home Secretary has asserted a general power to increase tariffs duly fixed. Parliament did not confer such a power on the Home Secretary.

It follows that the Home Secretary did not have the power to increase a tariff lawfully fixed. But counsel for the Home Secretary argued that in his policy statement of 27 July 1993 (Hansard (H.C. Debates), cols. *861–864*: written answer) the Home Secretary expressly reserved the power to increase the tariff. He emphasised that this supplemental provision is part and parcel of one policy statement. The Home Secretary was entitled to continue a policy of fixing tariffs but he was not entitled to introduce a power to increase tariffs. The only question is whether the entire policy is unlawful or only the reservation of the power to increase tariffs. This resolves itself into a question of remedies. It was suggested that severance would involve "a rewriting" of the policy statement. This is a familiar argument in cases where the circumstances arguably justify a court in saying that the unlawfulness of part of a statement does not infect the whole. The principles of severability in public law are well settled: see *de Smith, Woolf and Jowell, Judicial Review of Administrative Action*, pp.355–357, paras. 6–101–6–102; *Wade, Administrative Law*, pp.329–331. Sometimes severance is not possible, e.g. a licence granted subject to an important but unlawful condition. Sometimes severance is possible, e.g. where a byelaw contains several distinct and independent powers one of which is unlawful. Always the context will be determinative. In the present case the power to increase the tariff is notionally severable and distinct from the power to fix a tariff. Indeed between 1983 and 1993 no power to increase tariffs was even asserted. On the contrary, the 1983 policy statement (Hansard (H.C. Debates), 30 November 1983, cols. 505–507: written answer) made clear that there would be no increase of a tariff duly fixed. It is an obvious case for severance of the good from the bad. To describe this result as a rewriting of the policy statement is to raise an objection to the concept of severance. That is an argument for the blunt remedy of total unlawfulness or total lawfulness. The domain of public law is practical affairs. Sometimes severance is the only sensible course.

It was agreed before your Lordships' House that the Home Secretary's decision letter of 6 May 1994 did communicate a decision to Mr. Pierson to increase the tariff in his case. That decision was in my judgment unlawful and ought to be quashed. My conclusion is based on the proposition that the Home Secretary has no general power to increase a tariff fixed and communicated. That leaves unaffected the question whether in exceptional or special circumstances arising from the facts of a particular case the Home Secretary may have such a power, e.g. where quite plainly the judge and the Home Secretary have been misled. Such qualifications were not explored in argument. I express no view on it. . . .

My Lords, I would allow the appeal and quash the decision of the Home Secretary.

Appeal allowed

Notes

1. Lord Hope of Craighead held (at 603) that the Secretary of State:

"is bound by considerations of substantive fairness to observe the same rules as the judges if the view which he takes about the length of the minimum period is concerned solely with the question of punishment. This means that he cannot increase a minimum period which he or his predecessor has decided upon once that view has been communicated to the prisoner simply because, he now thinks, on further reflection, that the punishment is inadequate".

Lord Goff reached the conclusion that the Secretary of State's decision was unlawful by a different route, holding that the 1993 policy statement did not in any event apply where the penal element had been "fixed" by his predecessor or himself, but only where an "initial view" had been expressed under the new arrangements introduced by the 1993 policy statement. Neither judge commented on Lord Steyn's detailed reasoning based on the principle of legality.

Lord Browne-Wilkinson, who dissented, held:

(1) (at 573) That "Parliament having decided not to confer on the judiciary the duty to fix the appropriate punishment, it would be wrong to subvert that decision by requiring the Home Secretary to perform the executive function as though he were a judge". He was thus not bound by the rules applicable to judges in fixing sentences.

(2) (at 573–574) That there was indeed a general principle of construction that requires the courts, in certain cases, to construe general words contained in a statute as being impliedly limited.

"It is well established that Parliament does not legislate in a vacuum: statutes are drafted on the basis that the ordinary rules and principles of the common law will apply to the express statutory provisions: see *Cross on Statutory Interpretation*, 3rd ed. (1995), pp.165–166; *Bennion, Statutory Interpretation*, 2nd ed. (1992), p.727 and *Maxwell on Interpretation of Statutes*, 12th ed. (1969), p.116. As a result, Parliament is presumed not to have intended to change the common law unless it has clearly indicated such intention either expressly or by necessary implication: *Cross on Statutory Interpretation*, p.166; *Bennion, Statutory Interpretation*, p.718 and *Maxwell on Interpretation of Statutes*, p.116. This presumption has been applied in many different fields including the construction of statutory provisions conferring wide powers on the executive. Where wide powers of decision-making are conferred by statute, it is presumed that Parliament implicitly requires the decision to be made in accordance with the rules of natural justice: *Bennion on Statutory Interpretation*, p.737. However widely the power is expressed in the statute, it does not authorise that power to be exercised otherwise than in accordance with fair procedures. This presumption was the basis on which this House held in *Reg. v. Secretary of State for the Home Department, Ex p Doody* [1994] 1 A.C. 531 that, in fixing the tariff of those subject to mandatory life sentences, the Home Secretary had to inform the prisoner of the gist of the trial judge's advice and give him an opportunity to make representations."

His Lordship referred to *Raymond v Honey* [1983] 1 A.C. 1; *R. v Secretary of State for the Home Department Ex p. Leech* [1994] Q.B. 198.

"The same principles were applied in the recent case of *Reg. v. Lord Chancellor, Ex parte Witham* [1997] 2 All E.R. 779. The Divisional Court held that the statutory power conferred on the Lord Chancellor to 'prescribe the fees to be taken in the Supreme Court' did not authorise the setting of fees at such a level as to preclude access to the courts by would-be litigants. The general words of the statutory provision did not authorise the abrogation of such a basic 'constitutional right' as the right of access to the courts. Although I must not be taken as agreeing with everything said in the judgment in that case (in particular whether basic rights can be overridden by necessary implication as opposed to express provision), I have no doubt that the decision was correct for the principle reasons relied on by Laws J. in his judgment. Such basic rights are not to be overridden by the general words of a statute since the presumption is against the impairment of such basic rights.

From these authorities I think the following proposition is established. A power conferred by Parliament in general terms is not to be taken to authorise the doing of acts by the donee of the power which adversely affect the legal rights of the citizen or the basic principles on which the law of the United Kingdom is based unless the statute conferring the power makes it clear that such was the intention of Parliament."

(3) That there was, however, no general principle of non-aggravation of penalties.
(4) That, contrary to Lord Goff's view, the case did fall within the 1993 policy. Statements of administrative policy should not be construed as if they were a statute or a contract.

Lord Lloyd of Berwick (at 578–584) held (1) that there is no universal principle of justice, fairness or the common law that a sentence of punishment once pronounced may never be increased; and (2) if there were such a principle it would not apply to the tariff announced by the Home Secretary for a mandatory life sentence prisoner. The Home Secretary's policy was not unlawful.

Subsequently, the ECHR in *V v UK* (2000) 30 E.H.R.R. 121 and *Stafford v UK* (2002) 13 B.H.R.C. 260 and the House of Lords in *R. (on the application of Anderson) v Secretary of State for the Home Department* [2002] UKHL 46; [2003] 1 A.C. 837 decided that the involvement of the Home Secretary in determining the length of sentences violated Art.6 ECHR.

2. It will be noted that only Lords Steyn and Browne-Wilkinson, who disagreed as to the outcome, gave any extended attention to what Lord Steyn terms the principle of legality. Lord Steyn referred to this principle again in *R. v Secretary of State for the Home Department Ex p. Simms* [2000] 2 A.C. 115. Here, s.47(1) of the Prison Act 1952 enables the Secretary of State to make rules for, *inter alia*, "the regulation and management of prisons . . . and for the . . . treatment, employment, discipline and control of persons required to be detained therein." Rule 33(1) of the Prison Rules 1964 enabled the Secretary of State:

"with a view to securing discipline and good order or the prevention of crime or the interests of any persons, impose restrictions . . . upon the communications to be permitted between a prisoner and other persons".

Prison Service Standing Order No.5 provided that visits to inmates by journalists in their professional capacity should in general not be allowed; if a journalist visited as a friend or relative, he or she would be required to give a written undertaking that any material obtained at the interview would not be used for professional purposes (para.37) Visits in a professional capacity could take place, exceptionally, with the consent of the governor and the inmate (para.37A). The Home Secretary had, however, adopted a blanket policy excluding all professional visits by journalists to visitors on the ground that to allow any would undermine proper control and discipline. The House of Lords held unanimously that the policy of imposing an indiscriminate ban was unlawful. Any limitations on a prisoner's freedom of expression had to be justified by a pressing social need and as being the minimum interference necessary to achieve the objectives of deprivation of liberty by sentence of the court and discipline and order in prisons. A prisoner had a legitimate interest to enlist the investigative resources of the media in obtaining new evidence to support a reference of the case back to the Court of Appeal; given that it would be administratively workable to allow interviews for such a limited purpose consistently with order and discipline, the blanket rule amounted to an unjustifiable curtailment of the prisoner's right of freedom of expression. The general powers conferred by statute was presumed to have been enacted as subject to fundamental civil liberties, and so paras 37 and 37A could not be construed as conferring the right to impose an indiscriminate ban. While those paragraphs were not *ultra vires*, the indiscriminate ban was. Lord Steyn (at 130) said that

> "there is at stake a fundamental or basic right, namely the right of a prisoner to seek through oral interviews to persuade a journalist to investigate the safety of the prisoner's conviction and to publicise his findings in an effort to gain access to justice for the prisoner. In these circumstances even in the absence of an ambiguity there comes into play a presumption of general application operating as a constitutional principle as Sir Rupert Cross explained in successive editions of his classic work: *Statutory Interpretation*, 3rd ed. (1995), pp.165–166. This is called 'the principle of legality': *Halsbury's Laws of England*, 4th ed. Reissue, vol. 8(2) (1996), pp.13–14, para.6. Ample illustrations of the application of this principle are given in the speech of Lord Browne-Wilkinson, and in my speech, in *Reg. v. Secretary of State for the Home Department, Ex parte Pierson* [1998] A.C. 539, 573G–575D, 587C–590A. Applying this principle I would hold that paragraphs 37 and 37A leave untouched the fundamental and basic rights asserted by the applicants in the present case".

Declarations were granted that the Home Secretary's policy and governors' decisions that applied it were unlawful.

Lords Browne-Wilkinson (at 119) and Hoffmann (at 131) expressly agreed with Lord Steyn's reasons. Lord Hoffmann (at 131–132) added some comments on "the principle of legality". Lord Hobhouse of Woodborough and Lord Millett delivered concurring speeches without express consideration of the principle of legality. Nevertheless, recognition of the principle of legality now has the support of the majority of the House of Lords.

Lord Hoffmann's comments were these:

> "Parliamentary sovereignty means that Parliament can, if it chooses, legislate contrary to fundamental principles of human rights. The Human Rights Act 1998 will not detract from this power. The constraints upon its exercise by Parliament are ultimately political, not legal. But the principle of legality means that Parliament must squarely confront what it is doing and accept the political cost. Fundamental rights cannot be overridden by general or ambiguous words. This is because there is too great a risk that the full implications of their unqualified meaning may have passed unnoticed in the democratic process. In the absence of express language or necessary implication to the contrary, the courts therefore presume that even the most general words were intended to be subject to the basic rights of the individual. In this way the courts of the United Kingdom, though acknowledging the sovereignty of Parliament, apply principles of constitutionality little different from those which exist in countries where the power of the legislature is expressly limited by a constitutional document.
>
> The Human Rights Act 1998 will make three changes to this scheme of things. First, the principles of fundamental human rights which exist at common law will be supplemented by a specific text, namely the European Convention on Human Rights and Fundamental Freedoms. But much of the Convention reflects the common law: see *Derbyshire County Council v. Times Newspapers Ltd.* [1993] A.C. 534, 551. That is why the United Kingdom government felt able in 1950 to accede to the Convention without domestic legislative change. So the adoption of the text as part of domestic law is unlikely to involve radical change in our notions of fundamental human rights. Secondly, the principle of legality will be expressly enacted as a rule of construction in section 3 and will gain further support from the obligation of the minister in charge of a Bill to make a statement of compatibility under section 19. Thirdly, in those unusual cases in which the legislative infringement of fundamental human rights is so clearly expressed as not to yield to the principle of legality, the courts will be able to draw this to the attention of Parliament

by making a declaration of incompatibility. It will then be for the sovereign Parliament to decide whether or not to remove the incompatibility.

What this case decides is that the principle of legality applies to subordinate legislation as much as to Acts of Parliament. Prison regulations expressed in general language are also presumed to be subject to fundamental human rights. The presumption enables them to be valid. But, it also means that properly construed, they do not authorise a blanket restriction which would curtail not merely the prisoner's right of free expression, but its use in a way which could provide him with access to justice".

3. In *R. (on the application of Anufrijeva) v Secretary of State for the Home Department* [2003] UKHL 36; [2004] 1 A.C. 604, the House of Lords held (Lord Bingham dissenting) that the rule that an asylum seeker's entitlement to income support ended on the date on which the claim for asylum was recorded as determined did not apply so that the determination had effect for this purpose before it was communicated to the applicant. The principle that a decision takes effect only upon communication represented elementary fairness, and a fundamental right that could only be overridden by Parliament expressly or by necessary implication. The *Simms* principle applies to fundamental rights beyond the four corners of the ECHR (see Lord Steyn at [27]). The fundamental principle identified was that

"notice of a decision is required before it can have the character of a determination with legal effect because the individual concerned must be in a position to challenge the decision in the courts if he or she wishes to do so. This is not a technical rule. It is simply an application of the right of access to justice" (*per* Lord Steyn at [26]).

Furthermore, the "constitutional principle requiring the rule of law to be observed" requires too

"that a constitutional state must accord to individuals the right to know of a decision before their rights can be adversely affected. The antithesis of such a state was described by Kafka: a state where the rights of individuals are overridden by hole in the corner decisions or knocks on doors in the early hours" (*per* Lord Steyn at [28]).

See J. Jowell, [2004] P.L. 246. The principle of legality was referred to with approval by both majority and minority in *R. (on the application of Roberts) v Parole Board* [2005] UKHL 45.

Similarly, "it is a fundamental requisite of the rule of law that the law should be made known" (*per* Stanley Burnton J. in *Salih v Secretary of State for the Home Department*) [2003] EWHC 2273 at [45]. The Secretary of State's policy not to inform (apparently eligible) failed asylum seekers of a hardcases support scheme available under statutory powers was unlawful.

4. Note that the *Witham* principle (referred to by Lord Browne-Wilkinson in *Pierson* (above, p.260)) does not apply in interpreting the legislation of a colonial legislature (*R. (on the application of Bancoult) v Secretary of State for Foreign and Commonwealth Affairs* [2001] Q.B. 1067, DC, following *Liyanage v The Queen* [1967] 1 A.C. 259, P.C.).

5. Lord Steyn's opinions in *Pierson* and *Boddington v British Transport Police* (below, p.877) address two key points: first, the extent to which the principles of judicial review are applied in statutory contexts as an exercise in statutory interpretation; and, secondly, the approach that is to be adopted in conducting that exercise in protecting fundamental rights. The first point has raised considerable academic controversy, the latter much less. The following note deals with the first; n.7 deals with the second.

6. *The basis of judicial review.* Lord Steyn in *Boddington* endorses the approach of *Wade and Forsyth* that sees the *ultra vires* principle as the "central principle of

administrative law," in the "statute based part of our administrative law." Powers are conferred by Parliament on the assumption that they are to be exercised within the jurisdiction conferred, in accordance with fair procedures and, in a *Wednesbury* sense, reasonably; if they are not, implied limits are exceeded and the decision-maker is acting *ultra vires* his powers and therefore unlawfully (see Lord Browne-Wilkinson in *Page* at 701, cited by Lord Steyn in *Boddington*).

This view has come under sustained attack from a number of commentators, led by Paul Craig (see *Craig*, Ch.1 for a discussion of the issues). It is not possible here to summarise the details of the debate as it has developed and positions of the contributors have (or have not) been modified. The main points made by the critics of the use of the *ultra vires* doctrine to explain and justify judicial review include the following:

(i) An explanation of judicial review is needed that covers its application in both statutory and non-statutory contexts; the *ultra vires* doctrine founded on Parliamentary intention clearly cannot provide that explanation. The proposition that the judges are applying general judge-made principles to control all exercises of power, whether or not founded on statute, can.

(ii) The detailed grounds of judicial review were developed by the judges with little if any foundation in the specifics of Parliamentary intent demonstrated in legislative texts. Reliance on the deemed intention of Parliament that powers are conferred subject to implied limits conceals the truth that these limits are in fact judge-made. This might be convenient for the judges (a "fig-leaf": see Sir John Laws, in M. Supperstone and J. Goudie, *Judicial Review* (2nd ed.,1997), (para.4.15)), but is unreal. The fig-leaf should be discarded and the role of the judges when striking down the decisions of those who exercise power (whether democratically elected or not) recognised for what it truly is, an exercise of judicial power founded on fundamental constitutional principles that lie beyond the (supposed) intentions of Parliament.

Points that can be made the other way include:

(i) Reliance on the *ultra vires* doctrine remains the best explanation for judicial review in statutory contexts; there is no need for a single explanation that holds good in all contexts.

(ii) Reliance on deemed Parliamentary intention has in fact become more plausible over time as the principles that the judges apply through judicial review have been more clearly articulated and frequently applied. It has always been open to Parliament to exclude or modify their operation either in particular cases or generally; it has rarely done the former and never the latter. Indeed, in some cases Parliament has expressly referred to the principles of judicial review and stated that it is those principles that are to be applied on a statutory review, *e.g.* s.179 of the Enterprise Act 2002 provides that any person aggrieved by a decision in connection with a reference or possible reference under Pt 4 of the Act (market investigations) may apply to the Competition Appeal Tribunal for a review of that decision. In determining such an application the Tribunal "shall apply the same principles as would be applied by a court on an application for judicial review" (s.17(4)).

(iii) It is undoubtedly the case that many issues as to the ambit of the powers of a statutory body do turn on the proper interpretation of specific legislative words applying a conventional approach to statutory interpretation, which today normally involves reading the words in their context (which include the purpose of the legislation) and giving them where possible the interpretation that best fulfils the statutory purpose (see generally J. Bell and Sir George Engle, *Cross, Statutory Interpretation* (3rd ed., 1995); *Smith, Bailey and Gunn on the Modern English Legal System* (4th ed., 2002), Ch. 6). The extent to which the issue can be resolved through such an analysis of the statutory text and the identification of a specific parliamentary intent, and how far through the application of principles external to the text (whether characterised as free-standing common law principles or principles incorporated as a matter of deemed parliamentary intent) in fact varies widely, across a wide spectrum of possibilities. While some cases fall clearly at either end of that spectrum, there are cases in the middle that have elements of both approaches. Accordingly, while the *ultra vires* doctrine can provide no explanation for judicial review outside statutory contexts, the view that the principles of judicial review are free-standing principles of the common law does not provide a wholly satisfactory explanation of judicial review in statutory contexts.

(iv) Reliance on the direct assertion of judicial power may facilitate a move to extend that power to include the ability to strike down primary legislation. This has been entertained as a possibility by academic writers and judges writing extra-judicially (*e.g.* Lord Woolf, [1995] P.L. 57, at p.68 (legislation removing or substantially impairing the High Court's powers of judicial review); Sedley, J., [1995] P.L. 386, at p.391 ("obligation of the courts to articulate and uphold the groundrules of ethical social existence which we dignify as fundamental human rights"); Laws, J., [1995] P.L. 72 (protection of fundamental freedoms); criticised by Lord Irvine of Lairg, [1996] P.L. 59. Case law, however, affirms the continued operation of the doctrine of Parliamentary sovereignty (see, *e.g.* Lord Scarman in *Duport Steels Ltd v Sirs* [1980] I.C.R. 161 at p.189–190; *Thoburn v Sunderland City Council* [2002] EWHC (Admin) 195; [2003] 1 Q.B. 151), albeit with modifications by the common law to the extent to which a statutory provision can be repealed by a later statute by implication as distinct from expressly (*Thoburn*). Point (iv) is, however, severable; critics of the *ultra vires* doctrine certainly do not need to espouse an extended power of judicial review to strike down primary legislation as part of their argument.

Overall, there is much in common in the competing analyses. The case-law as regards statutory contexts is clear on the point, and it is difficult to see how the adoption of one approach rather than the other would affect the outcome of any decided case there. There is, however, some uncertainty in the case law as to the basis for judicial review in non-statutory contexts. These include exercises of prerogative power, powers conferred by contract, and, indeed, any other situations in which power is *de facto* exercised by one person or body over another. Prerogative powers are dealt with in n.8, and the applicability of judicial review outside statutory contexts at pp.937–957. Important contributions to the debate on the basis of judicial review are made by D. Oliver, [1987] P.L. 543; P. Craig, [1998] P.L. 63; [1998] P.L. 428; [2003] P.L. 92; and (2004) 24 O.J.L.S. 563; C. Forsyth, [1996] C.L.J. 122; M. Elliott, (1999) 115 L.Q.R. 119; [1999] C.L.J. 129, and *The Constitutional Foundations of Judical Review* (2001); the contributors to C. Forsyth (ed.), *Judicial Review and the Constitution* (2000); P. Craig and N. Bamforth, [2001] P.L. 763; T.R.S. Allan, [2002] C.L.J. 87 (doubting the utility of the debate) and (2003) 23 O.J.L.S. 563.

7. *The protection of fundamental rights.* The general approach to be adopted when interpreting statutes that may affect fundamental rights endorsed by Lords Browne-Wilkinson and Steyn in *Pierson* and Lord Steyn in *Simms* is compelling. The main area of controversy lies in identifying and articulating the precise content of the "fundamental rights" that are to be accorded special protection. The difference of view between Lord Browne-Wilkinson and Lord Steyn in *Pierson* confirms that will not always be easy. Those rights identified in the European Convention on Human Rights are now in any event accorded special protection through the Human Rights Act 1998 (see Ch.6). *Simms* confirms that other "rights" may qualify beyond those. Other possible sources that may provide support for the existence of such a right include the common law, the constitutional texts applicable in other countries and international documents.

Any such right can of course be overridden by an express statutory provision. The point is well illustrated by *R. v Lyons* [2002] UKHL 44; [2003] 1 A.C. 976, where the House of Lords declined to quash the convictions of L and others, directors of Guinness Plc, for offences of dishonest conduct in making a take-over bid for another company, Distillers. This was so notwithstanding the fact that the ECtHR had found that the admission into evidence at trial of answers given by them, under statutory compulsion, to inspectors investigating the affairs of Guinness infringed their right not to incriminate themselves, and so violated their rights under Art.6(1) ECHR. The trial took place before implementation of the Human Rights Act 1998 and it was accepted that L had no remedy under that Act. L argued that the United Kingdom had a duty, binding in international law, to comply with the ECHR as a treaty, including the obligation to abide by judgments of the ECtHR, and that the courts were under a duty to act so far as possible in a manner consistent with the United Kingdom's international obligations. The English court should give full effect to the judgment of the ECtHR. The House of Lords agreed that national courts should, so far as they are free to do so, seek to act in a manner consistent with the obligations of the state binding in international law. However, treaties only took direct effect in domestic law when implemented by statute and, in view of the clear wording of the statutory provision that rendered the evidence admissible (s.434(5) of the Companies Act 1985), it was not open to the courts to quash the convictions. Section 434 had been amended subsequently to take account of Art.6(1), but without retrospective effect.

8. *Prerogative powers and justiciability.* The vast majority of the cases on judicial review concern powers based on statute. However, exercises of power by reference to the Royal Prerogative are also subject to judicial review. The courts have for centuries asserted the power to ensure that a prerogative power which is relied upon does in truth exist (*Case of Proclamations* (1611) 12 Co.Rep. 74; *Burmah Oil Co. v Lord Advocate* [1965] A.C. 75) and has not been superseded by statute (*Att-Gen v De Keyser's Royal Hotel Ltd* [1920] A.C. 508; *R. v Secretary of State for the Home Department Ex p. Northumbria Police Authority* [1989] Q.B. 26).

The House of Lords in *Council of Civil Service Unions v Minister for the Civil Service* [1985] A.C. 374 held that at least delegated powers referable to the prerogative were in principle subject to judicial review for abuse of discretion or procedural impropriety. However, not all the prerogative powers were justiciable; *per* Lord Roskill at 418:

"Prerogative powers such as those relating to the making of treaties, the defence of the realm, the prerogative of mercy, the grant of honours, the dissolution of Parliament and the appointment of ministers as well as others are not, I think, susceptible to judicial review because their nature and subject matter is such as not to be amenable to the judicial process".

Powers that have since been held to be justiciable include the administration of the civil service, other than where action was necessitated by the requirements of national security (the *CCSU* case); the issue or denial or passports (*R. v Secretary of State for Foreign and Commonwealth Affairs Ex p. Everett* [1989] Q.B. 811); the case of a warrant authorising telephone tapping (*R. v Secretary of State for the Home Department Ex p. Ruddock* [1987] 1 W.L.R. 1482, and see now the Interception of Communications Act 1985). Notwithstanding Lord Roskill's general reference to "the prerogative of mercy" in his list of aspects of the prerogative likely not to be susceptible to review, it was held in *R. v Secretary of State for the Home Department Ex p. Bentley* [1994] Q.B. 349, that a decision of the Home Secretary which evidenced a misappreciation of the scope of prerogatival discretion as regards forms of pardon which might be granted, could be reviewed. *cf. Lewis v Att-Gen of Jamaica* [2001] 2 A.C. 50, where the Privy Council held that the exercise of the prerogative of mercy was open to review for procedural irregularity.

The rules of the Criminal Injuries Compensation Scheme set up under the Royal Prerogative (subsequently superseded by a statutory scheme) were held to be open to challenge on the ground of irrationality (*R. v Criminal Injuries Compensation Board Ex p. P* [1995] 1 W.L.R. 845, Evans and Peter Gibson.; Neill L.J. held that the rationality of the scheme was non-justiciable). The Board had previously been held to be subject to judicial review in *Ex p. Lain*, below, p.938.

A claim for judicial review has also been entertained (albeit rejected on the merits) in respect of the rejection of a claim for *ex gratia* compensation to a person whose conviction for conspiracy to cause explosions was quashed *R. (on the application of Mullen) v Secretary of State for the Home Department* [2004] UKHL 18; [2004] 1 W.L.R. 1140. There has been no suggestion that judicial review is limited to delegated prerogative powers.

In a number of areas, including some of those mentioned by Lord Roskill, the courts have reaffirmed that some prerogative decisions are indeed non-justiciable. They have also thrown more light on the concept of non-justiciability and the limits to it. For example, in the context of foreign affairs the House of Lords in *Maclaine Watson & Co. Ltd v Department of Trade and Industry* [1990] 2 A.C. 418 (*per* Lord Oliver at 499–500) confirmed that "the power of the Crown to conclude treaties with other sovereign states is an exercise of the royal prerogative, the validity of which cannot be challenged in municipal law" (citing *Blackburn v Att-Gen* [1971] 1 W.L.R. 1037).

On the other hand, in *R. v Secretary of State for Foreign and Commonwealth Affairs Ex p. Rees-Mogg* [1994] Q.B. 552, the Divisional Court had no difficulty in entertaining (and rejecting on the merits) a claim that the Government would be acting unlawfully in ratifying the Maastricht Treaty by exceeding express or implied statutory limits to the treaty-making power. As to an argument that at common law the Crown was incapable of abandoning or transferring any of its prerogative powers without statutory authority, the court was prepared to assume that the argument was justiciable and that there was such a principle, but held that agreement to Title V of the Treaty establishing a common foreign and security policy among Member States did not in fact involve any such abandonment or transfer. It is submitted that all these matters were indeed justiciable as they concerned the scope of the prerogative power and not the manner of its exercise. Similarly, in *Ex p. Molyneux* [1986] 1 W.L.R. 331, a challenge was made to the validity of an agreement entered into between the Governments of the United Kingdom and the Republic of Ireland. Taylor J. dismissed the action on various grounds, including that "the agreement . . . is in the field of international relations. It is akin to a treaty. It concerns relations between the United Kingdom and another foreign State and it is not the function of the court to inquire into the exercise of the prerogative in entering into such an agreement" (at 336). However, Taylor J. also ruled on (and rejected) arguments that the agreement contravened the Union with Ireland Act 1800 or the common law.

Compare *R. (on the application of Abbasi) v Secretary of State for Foreign and Commonwealth Affairs* [2002] EWCA Civ 1598, where the Court of Appeal held that there was no reason why the decision of the Secretary of State whether to make representations to a foreign state to protect a British citizen suffering or threatened with injury should not be reviewable if it could be shown to be irrational or contrary to legitimate expectation, provided this did not cause the court to "enter the forbidden areas, including decisions affecting foreign policy". It was highly likely that FCO decisions whether to make representations on a diplomatic level would be intimately connected with decisions relating to the United Kingdom's foreign policy, but an obligation to *consider* whether to take action would be unlikely to impinge on a forbidden area (Lord Phillips M.R. at [106]). The court rejected a claim for judicial review by a British national detained without trial by the United States at Guantanemo Bay in which he sought to compel the FCO to make representations on his behalf or take other appropriate action or give an explanation as to why this had not been done. To make such an order would obviously "have an impact on the conduct of foreign policy, and an impact on such policy at a particularly delicate time" (at [107]).

In the context of the *defence of the realm*, the Court of Appeal in *R. (on the application of Thring) v Secretary of State for Defence* (unreported, July 20, 2000) held that it could not consider whether the conduct of bombing operations in Iraq after the first Gulf War was unlawful by virtue of Art.51 of the Geneva Conventions on the ground that incidental loss of civilian life was excessive in relation to the military advantage anticipated. The courts were "not equipped" to consider the policy and nature of the operation of the armed services abroad. Then, in *R. (on the application of the Campaign for Nuclear Disarmament) v Prime Minister of the United Kingdom* [2002] EWHC (Admin) 2777, the Divisional Court declined on various grounds to grant an advisory declaration as to the true meaning of UN Resolution 1441 and more particularly as to whether it authorised states to take military action in the event of non-compliance by Iraq with its terms. Simon Brown L.J. concluded (at [47]):

"(i) The court has no jurisdiction to declare the true interpretation of an international instrument which has not been incorporated into English domestic law and which it is unnecessary to interpret for the purposes of determining a person's rights or duties under domestic law. That is the position here.

(ii) The court will in any event decline to embark upon the determination of an issue if to do so would be damaging to the public interest in the field of international relations, national security or defence. That too is the position here. Whether as a matter of juridicial theory such judicial abstinence is properly to be regarded as a matter of discretion or a matter of jurisdiction seems to me for present purposes immaterial. Either way I regard the substantive question raised by this application to be non-justiciable.

(iii) Even were this claim not barred by either of the above considerations, I would still reject it on the ground that advisory declarations should not be made save for demonstrably good reason. Here there is none. There is no sound basis for believing the government to have been wrongly advised as to the true position in international law. Nor, in any event, could there be any question here of declaring illegal whatever decision or action may hereafter be taken in the light of the United Kingdom's understanding of its position in international law".

Maurice Kay J. (at [49], [50]) was clear that this matter was not justiciable as a matter of principle and not merely the court's discretion. Richards J. (at [60]) noted that while justiciability

"is not a jurisdictional concept, it . . . engages rules of law rather than purely discretionary considerations. They are rules that, in this context at least, the courts have imposed upon themselves in recognition of the limits of judicial expertise and of the proper demarcation between the role of the courts and the responsibilities of the executive under our constitutional settlement".

The "damage to the public interest" here were that "it would adversely affect the conduct of our international relations with regard to the Iraq situation" and "tie the UK's hands if and when it has to re-enter the negotiating chamber" (see Simon Brown L.J. at [41]). The contrary argument that "the only proper course for government to take is to conduct its international relations openly in accordance with whatever advice it has received" and that government "should not . . . dissemble or bluff in its negotiations with other States" was characterised as "a singularly utopian view of international affairs" and rejected (see Simon Brown L.J. at [45]). For the argument that the true challenge here was to legality not rationality and so the non-justiciability rules should not have been applied, see A. Perreau-Saussine, [2003] C.L.J. 538.

Compare Laws L.J.'s comment in *Marchiori v Environment Agency* [2002] EWCA Civ 03; [2002] Eu.L.R. 225, that "the law of England will not contemplate what may be called a merits review of any honest decision of government upon matters of national defence policy" (at [38]). Accordingly, "upon questions of national defence, the courts will recognise that they are in no position to set limits upon the lawful exercise of discretionary power in the name of reasonableness" (at [40]). However, judicial review "remains available to cure the theoretical possibility of actual bad faith on the part of ministers making decisions of high policy" (*ibid*). The context here was an unsuccessful challenge to authorisations permitting the discharge of radioactive waste when decommissioning nuclear weapons part of the Trident programme.

Finally, there are authorities that hold unreviewable the prerogative power of the Attorney-General to give or refuse consent to a relator action (*Gouriet v Union of Post Office Workers* [1978] A.C. 435); and the statutory power of the Attorney-General to institute proceedings (*R. v Solicitor-General Ex p. Taylor* (1995) 8 Admin L.R. 206 (proceedings for contempt of court); *R. v Att-Gen Ex p. Ferrante* [1995] C.O.D. 18 (power to apply for an order that an inquest be held)). Given that analogous powers are reviewable, these authorities should be reconsidered: see *Lewis*, pp.29–30.

It now seems clear that the question of non-justiciability is to be judged by reference not solely to the source of power (*CCSU*) or to the nature of the decision challenged in itself but to the particular ground of challenge put forward to the decision in question (*Marchiori*). A claim of non-justiciability cannot prevent a claim that a decision is contrary to statute (*Rees-Mogg*) and may bar some, but not all grounds of challenge (*Marchiori*). Finally, even if the issue of justiciability involves the application of a rule rather than a discretion (*CND*), it is also clear that the rule is highly fact-sensitive and in practice very close to an exercise of discretion. Is there any good reason why a *class* of decisions should be immune from judicial review? The more sensitive the context the greater the discretionary area of judgment that will be recognised. Hopeless cases can be disposed of summarily.

It is likely that the courts would regard as non-justiciable a challenge to a decision to declare war on the ground of irrationality; what should the position be if it is claimed that the government has acted in bad faith (*cf. Marchiori*)? Whether the legality of the war against Iraq was a justiciable issue was raised in *R. v Jones* [2004] EWCA Crim 1981. The defendants sought to argue that acts of criminal damage at an RAF airbase were done to prevent the unlawful act of the United States and United Kingdom in attacking Iraq, enabling them to rely on defences of duress/necessity, lawful excuse, and the prevention of crime. The Court of Appeal thought there was considerable force in the argument that the *CND* case did not in itself provide the answer to the issue of justiciability here as the matter affected the defendants' rights and duties as a matter of domestic law. However, the legality of the war was legally irrelevant to the defences in question and so the point did not arise.

9. It should be noted that the courts have tended to adopt a broad definition of "prerogative powers" for these purposes rather than Wade's narrower definition of powers that are unique to the sovereign and which also produce legal effects at common law (see H.W.R. Wade, *Constitutional Fundamentals* (1980), pp.46–53 and (1985) 101 L.Q.R. 180). See further *Lewis*, pp.19–21; *Wade and Forsyth*, pp.216–217. On the *CCSU* case, see H.W.R. Wade, (1985) 101 L.Q.R. 153; G.S. Morris, [1985] P.L. 177; S. Lee, [1985] P.L. 186; K. Ewing [1985] C.L.J. 1; C.F. Forsyth, (1985) 36 N.I.L.Q. 25; I.S. Dickinson (1985) 30 J.L.S. 112. On judicial review and the prerogative, see C. Walker, "Review of the Prerogative: The Remaining Issues" [1987] P.L. 62; B. Hough, "Judicial Review where the Attorney-General Refuses to Act: Time for a Change" (1988) 8 L.S. 189; B.V. Harris, "Judicial Review of the Prerogative of Mercy?" [1991] P.L. 386 and "Judicial Review, Justiciability and the Prerogative of Mercy" [2003] C.L.J. 631 (doubting that the courts should ever be concerned to determine whether a class of executive decision-making is potentially justiciable as distinct from whether a particular executive decision is appropriate for the court's supervision).

10. The House of Commons Select Committee on Public Administration (*Taming the Prerogative: Strengthening Ministerial Accountability to Parliament* (Fourth Report, 2003–04 HC 422) recommended that there should be a public consultation exercise on proposals for legislation to provide greater Parliamentary control over all executive powers enjoyed by ministers under the prerogative, including specific proposals for

ensuring full Parliamentary scrutiny of decisions on armed conflict, the conclusion and ratification of treaties and the revocation of passports. The report included a draft Bill prepared by the Committee's adviser, Prof. Rodney Brazier. This persuasive case was rejected by the Government on the basis that existing arrangements for accountability were effective and there was no need for a consultation exercise. It would, however, reflect further on the points concerning treaties.

11. The extent to which judicial review is available in respect of the exercise of powers to enter contracts is considered below, pp.957–966.

12. The courts do not normally have jurisdiction to consider the validity of a statute. As to the extent of their jurisdiction to consider the validity of a statute enacted under the Parliament Acts procedure, see *R. (on the application of Jackson) v Attorney General* [2005] EWCA Civ. 126, [2005] Q.B. 579.

CHAPTER 6

THE HUMAN RIGHTS ACT 1998

The enactment and implementation of the Human Rights Act 1998 is of considerable significance for the structure and operation of English law. It is not, however, as fundamental a change as would be seen with the adoption of a written constitution to which the legislature as well as the executive and the judiciary were subject, and has been seen with the enactment of the European Communities Act 1972. The HRA 1998 introduces a new rule of statutory interpretation that legislation "must be read and given effect in a way which is compatible with Convention rights" (s.3(1)); a power to declare that primary legislation which cannot be so interpreted (or secondary legislation where primary legislation prevents removal of the incompatibility) is incompatible with Convention rights (s.4(1)); and a new rule that it is unlawful for a public authority to act in a way which is incompatible with a Convention right, unless (a) as a result of primary legislation the authority could not have acted differently, or (b) the authority was acting to give effect to provisions of, or made under, incompatible primary legislation (s.6(1), (2)). Accordingly, the courts have no power to disregard or strike down incompatible primary legislation, coercive orders only being available in respect of (most) subordinate legislation, the decisions of public authorities (other than to give effect to incompatible primary legislation) or the common law. The principle of parliamentary sovereignty is to that extent respected. The code of the HRA 1998 is self contained in that it contains its own rules (albeit some that invoke the jurisprudence of the ECtHR) as to the authorities covered, the rights conferred, the remedies available and the persons with standing to obtain them. It is accordingly appropriate to consider them in a separate chapter. Nevertheless, points under the HRA 1998 normally arise alongside points under domestic law or EU law, sometimes adding new additional obligations and new arguments that can be deployed, but sometimes setting standards that are identical to those of domestic law. Given the broad terms in which Convention rights are conferred it would be surprising if there are any areas of state activity into which the HRA 1998 does not reach. The wide range of contexts in which it applies inevitably means that it has effect with significant variations. The extent to which the Act has "horizontal effect" as between citizen and citizen is, moreover, both uncertain and strongly debated.

The Act came fully into effect on October 2, 2000, and generally does not operate retrospectively (although that has been disputed). Considerable efforts were taken to offer guidance and training for decision-makers across the public sector and the Judicial Standards Board organised training for the judiciary. In considering the effects of the Act, a number of dimensions must be taken into account. The number of cases in which the Act has changed outcomes is relatively small, whether in terms of novel interpretations based squarely on s.3, rulings that a decision-maker's view that an interference with a Convention right was justified was disproportionate, or declarations of incompatibility. However, it would be wrong to confine assessments to that. The Act has also had effect in a number of contexts in changing the approach to and analytical bases for public sector decision-making and changing the content of legislation before it is enacted or made. The extent of this is very difficult to measure, but is likely to be more significant than the pattern of decided cases would suggest. The ultimate test may be whether there is any slackening of the number of cases where the United Kingdom is found by the ECtHR to have infringed Convention rights.

The HRA 1998 is different from what has gone before in the common law in that it starts from the viewpoint of the rights of the individual rather than the powers of the State. That is not to say that the rights are absolute; most Convention rights are subject to express qualifications and exceptions and there are uncertainties as to the scope of those that are absolute.[1] Nevertheless, it is for the state to justify its infringement of a Convention right rather than simply for individuals to make good their challenges to the legality of state action (although this conceals subtleties in both under the HRA itself and in public law apart from the HRA). It is also significant that the rights concerned are (to varying extents[2]) recognised by the common law,[3] and are identified and protected in the constitutional arrangements of many other countries. This means that the changes required by the Act are not as radical as would otherwise have been the case. It is also easier for references to the jurisprudence of overseas jurisdictions to help in the resolution of difficult questions.

The main threats to fundamental rights and freedoms in English law have tended to come from legislation rather than the common law. It is accordingly important that, without infringing the ultimate sovereignty of Parliament, the Act provides democratic legitimacy for a strengthened role for the judiciary (*cf.* Lord Bingham in *A v Secretary of State for the Home Department*, below, p.351). Views have always varied as to whether in particular cases or areas the approach of the judges in judicial review excessively interventionist, unduly supine or somewhere in between. The HRA shifts the point of balance, but a similar variety of views continues to be expressed.

Themes that can be identified include the view that the judges in the early years of the operation of the Act have been feeling their way with a caution that should become less necessary or appropriate with time; the understandable concerns of decision-makers who have been challenged successfully in the courts; and the absurd demonisation of the Act by right-wing politicians who are not necessarily in tune with the liberal values inherent in Convention rights, particularly when such rights are relied on by groups who are the object of populist disfavour such as criminal defendants, prisoners, asylum seekers and gypsies. A more fundamental criticism is that Convention rights cannot stop the inexorable drive in the direction of more and more state powers and that in times of crisis the courts do not and will not protect the individual from the state.[4]

Finally, there is an obvious comparison to be made with the European Communities Act 1972. The effects of the 1972 Act are both different in kind and stronger in making a mass of detailed European legislation directly or indirectly part of English law, and requiring the courts from time to time to give effect to Community law rather than primary UK legislation.[5]

The Human Rights Act occupies a middle position in the possible spectrum of constitutional arrangements. Some[6] see it as a step in the direction of the constitutional entrenchment of human rights, and argue the case for such a development. Others[7]

---

[1] C. Gearty, *Principles of Human Rights Adjudication* (2004), pp.8–13.

[2] Compare the common law's long-standing concerns for freedom of expression and fair trials with its inadequacy in the protection of privacy (*Malone v Metropolitan Police Commissioner* [1979] Ch.344).

[3] The background to the development of the ECHR, including the contribution of British lawyers, is examined in A.W.B. Simpson, *Human Rights and the End of Empire* (2001); Lord Lester and D. Pannick, *Human Rights Law and Practice* (2nd ed., 2004), Ch.1.

[4] K. Ewing, "The Futility of the Human Rights Act" [2004] P.L. 829. This preceded the decision in *A v Secretary of State for the Home Department*, below, p.351. See the reply, written after the decision in *A*, by Lord Lester, [2005] P.L. 249, arguing that the HRA has demonstrable utility and praising the record of the judges in deciding cases under the Act.

[5] *R. v Secretary of State for Transport Ex p. Factortame Ltd* [1990] 2 A.C. 85. The proposition that Parliament can no longer legislate contrary to Community law without repealing the 1972 Act was, however, rejected by the Divisional Court in *Thoburn v Sunderland CC* [2002] EWHC (Admin) 195; [2003] Q.B. 151.

[6] *e.g.* Lester, *op cit.*

[7] *e.g.* Gearty, *op cit.*

endorse its structure precisely because of its accommodation of parliamentary sovereignty. Yet others[8] remain sceptical.

In this chapter, we consider the background to the enactment of the HRA 1998, the elements of its structure and the main Convention rights likely to be raised in litigation involving administrative authorities.

(A) BACKGROUND

WHITE PAPER, RIGHTS BROUGHT HOME: THE HUMAN RIGHTS BILL

(CM.3782, 1997)

Chapter 1 – The Case for Change

The European Convention on Human Rights

1.1 The European Convention for the Protection of Human Rights and Fundamental Freedoms is a treaty of the Council of Europe. This institution was established at the end of the Second World War, as part of the Allies' programme to reconstruct durable civilisation on the mainland of Europe. The Council was established before the European Union and, although many nations are members of both, the two bodies are quite separate.

1.2 The United Kingdom played a major part in drafting the Convention, and there was a broad agreement between the major political parties about the need for it (one of its draftsmen later became, as Lord Kilmuir, Lord Chancellor in the Conservative Administration from 1954 to 1962). The United Kingdom was among the first group of countries to sign the Convention. It was the very first country to ratify it, in March 1951. In 1966 the United Kingdom accepted that an individual person, and not merely another State, could bring a case against the United Kingdom in Strasbourg (the home of the European Commission of Human Rights and Court of Human Rights, which were established by the Convention). Successive administrations in the United Kingdom have maintained these arrangements.

1.3 The European Convention is not the only international human rights agreement to which the United Kingdom and other like- minded countries are party, but over the years it has become one of the premier agreements defining standards of behaviour across Europe. It was also for many years unique because of the system which it put in place for people from signatory countries to take complaints to Strasbourg and for those complaints to be judicially determined. These arrangements are by now well tried and tested. The rights and freedoms which are guaranteed under the Convention are ones with which the people of this country are plainly comfortable. They therefore afford an excellent basis for the Human Rights Bill which we are now introducing.

1.4 The constitutional arrangements in most continental European countries have meant that their acceptance of the Convention went hand in hand with its incorporation into their domestic law. In this country it was long

---

[8] *e.g.* Ewing, *op. cit.*

believed that the rights and freedoms guaranteed by the Convention could be delivered under our common law. In the last two decades, however, there has been a growing awareness that it is not sufficient to rely on the common law and that incorporation is necessary.

1.5 The Liberal Democrat Peer, Lord Lester of Herne Hill QC, recently introduced two Bills on incorporation into the House of Lords (in 1994 and 1996). Before that, the then Conservative MP Sir Edward Gardner QC introduced a Private Member's Bill on incorporation into the House of Commons in 1987. At the time of introducing his Bill he commented on the language of the Articles in the Convention, saying: "It is language which echoes right down the corridors of history. It goes deep into our history and as far back as Magna Carta." (Hansard, 6 February 1987, col.1224). In preparing this White Paper the Government has paid close attention to earlier debates and proposals for incorporation.

The Convention rights

1.6 The Convention contains Articles which guarantee a number of basic human rights. They deal with the right to life (Article 2); torture or inhuman or degrading treatment or punishment (Article 3); slavery and forced labour (Article 4); liberty and security of person (Article 5); fair trial (Article 6); retrospective criminal laws (Article 7); respect for private and family life, home and correspondence (Article 8); freedom of thought, conscience and religion (Article 9); freedom of expression (Article 10); freedom of peaceful assembly and freedom of association, including the right to join a trade union (Article 11); the right to marry and to found a family (Article 12); and discrimination in the enjoyment of these rights and freedoms (Article 14).

1.7 The United Kingdom is also a party to the First Protocol to the Convention, which guarantees the right to the peaceful enjoyment of possessions (Article 1), the right to education (Article 2) and the right to free elections (Article 3).

1.8 The rights in the Convention are set out in general terms, and they are subject in the Convention to a number of qualifications which are also of a general character. Some of these qualifications are set out in the substantive Articles themselves (see, for example, Article 10, concerning freedom of expression); others are set out in Articles 16 to 18 of the Convention. Sometimes too the rights guaranteed under the Convention need to be balanced against each other (for example, those guaranteed by Article 8 and Article 10).

Applications under the Convention

1.9 Anyone within the United Kingdom jurisdiction who is aggrieved by an action of the executive or by the effect of the existing law and who believes it is contrary to the European Convention can submit a petition to the European Commission of Human Rights. The Commission will first consider whether the petition is admissible. One of the conditions of admissibility is that the applicant must have gone through all the steps available to him or her at home for challenging the decision which he or she is complaining about. If the Commission decides that a complaint is admissible, and if a friendly settlement cannot be secured, it will send a confidential report to the Committee of

Ministers of the Council of Europe, stating its opinion on whether there has
been a violation. The matter may end there, with a decision by the Committee
(which in practice always adopts the opinion of the Commission), or the case
may be referred on to the European Court of Human Rights[9] for consideration. If the Court finds that there has been a violation it may itself "afford just
satisfaction" to the injured party by an award of damages or an award of costs
and expenses. The court may also find that a formal finding of a violation is
sufficient. There is no appeal from the Court.

Effect of a Court judgment

1.10 A finding by the European Court of Human Rights of a violation of a
Convention right does not have the effect of automatically changing United
Kingdom law and practice: that is a matter for the United Kingdom
Government and Parliament. But the United Kingdom, like all other States
who are parties to the Convention, has agreed to abide by the decisions of the
Court or (where the case has not been referred to the Court) the Committee
of Ministers. It follows that, in cases where a violation has been found, the
State concerned must ensure that any deficiency in its internal laws is rectified
so as to bring them into line with the Convention. The State is responsible for
deciding what changes are needed, but it must satisfy the Committee of
Ministers that the steps taken are sufficient. Successive United Kingdom
administrations have accepted these obligations in full.

Relationship to current law in the United Kingdom

1.11 When the United Kingdom ratified the Convention the view was taken
that the rights and freedoms which the Convention guarantees were already,
in substance, fully protected in British law. It was not considered necessary to
write the Convention itself into British law, or to introduce any new laws in
the United Kingdom in order to be sure of being able to comply with the
Convention.

1.12 From the point of view of the **international** obligation which the United
Kingdom was undertaking when it signed and ratified the Convention, this
was understandable. Moreover, the European Court of Human Rights explicitly confirmed that it was not a necessary part of proper observance of
the Convention that it should be incorporated into the laws of the States
concerned.

1.13 However, since its drafting nearly 50 years ago, almost all the States
which are party to the European Convention on Human Rights have gradually incorporated it into their domestic law in one way or another. Ireland and
Norway have not done so, but Ireland has a Bill of Rights which guarantees
rights similar to those guaranteed by the Convention and Norway is also in
the process of incorporating the Convention. Several other countries with
which we have close links and which share the common law tradition, such as
Canada and New Zealand, have provided similar protection for human rights
in their own legal systems.

[9] Protocol 11 to the Convention, which will come into force on 1 November 1998, will replace the
existing part-time European Commission and Court of Human Rights with a single full-time Court.

The case for incorporation

1.14 The effect of non-incorporation on the British people is a very practical one. The rights, originally developed with major help from the United Kingdom Government, are no longer actually seen as British rights. And enforcing them takes too long and costs too much. It takes on average five years to get an action into the European Court of Human Rights once all domestic remedies have been exhausted; and it costs an average of £30,000. Bringing these rights home will mean that the British people will be able to argue for their rights in the British courts—without this inordinate delay and cost. It will also mean that the rights will be brought much more fully into the jurisprudence of the courts throughout the United Kingdom, and their interpretation will thus be far more subtly and powerfully woven into our law. And there will be another distinct benefit. British judges will be enabled to make a distinctively British contribution to the development of the jurisprudence of human rights in Europe.

1.15 Moreover, in the Government's view, the approach which the United Kingdom has so far adopted towards the Convention does not sufficiently reflect its importance and has not stood the test of time.

1.16 The most obvious proof of this lies in the number of cases in which the European Commission and Court have found that there have been violations of the Convention rights in the United Kingdom. The causes vary. The Government recognises that interpretations of the rights guaranteed under the Convention have developed over the years, reflecting changes in society and attitudes. Sometimes United Kingdom laws have proved to be inherently at odds with the Convention rights. On other occasions, although the law has been satisfactory, something has been done which our courts have held to be lawful by United Kingdom standards but which breaches the Convention. In other cases again, there has simply been no framework within which the compatibility with the Convention rights of an executive act or decision can be tested in the British courts: these courts can of course review the exercise of executive discretion, but they can do so only on the basis of what is lawful or unlawful according to the law in the United Kingdom as it stands. It is plainly unsatisfactory that someone should be the victim of a breach of the Convention standards by the State yet cannot bring any case at all in the British courts, simply because British law does not recognise the right in the same terms as one contained in the Convention.

1.17 For individuals, and for those advising them, the road to Strasbourg is long and hard. Even when they get there, the Convention enforcement machinery is subject to long delays. This might be convenient for a government which was half-hearted about the Convention and the right of individuals to apply under it, since it postpones the moment at which changes in domestic law or practice must be made. But it is not in keeping with the importance which this Government attaches to the observance of basic human rights.

Bringing Rights Home

1.18 We therefore believe that the time has come to enable people to enforce their Convention rights against the State in the British courts, rather than having to incur the delays and expense which are involved in taking a case to the European Human Rights Commission and Court in Strasbourg and which may altogether deter some people from pursuing their rights. Enabling courts in the United Kingdom to rule on the application of the Convention will also help to influence the development of case law on the Convention by the European Court of Human Rights on the basis of familiarity with our laws and customs and of sensitivity to practices and procedures in the United Kingdom. Our courts' decisions will provide the European Court with a useful source of information and reasoning for its own decisions. United Kingdom judges have a very high reputation internationally, but the fact that they do not deal in the same concepts as the European Court of Human Rights limits the extent to which their judgments can be drawn upon and followed. Enabling the Convention rights to be judged by British courts will also lead to closer scrutiny of the human rights implications of new legislation and new policies. If legislation is enacted which is incompatible with the Convention, a ruling by the domestic courts to that effect will be much more direct and immediate than a ruling from the European Court of Human Rights. The Government of the day, and Parliament, will want to minimise the risk of that happening.

1.19 Our aim is a straightforward one. It is to make more directly accessible the rights which the British people already enjoy under the Convention. In other words, to bring those rights home.

Note

The HRA 1998 was one of a series of constitutional measures enacted early in the term of office of the Labour Government elected in 1997, alongside the Scotland Act 1998 and the Government of Wales Act 1998, and the Freedom of Information Act 2000.

(B) THE HUMAN RIGHTS ACT 1998

HUMAN RIGHTS ACT 1998

An Act to give further effect to rights and freedoms guaranteed under the European Convention on Human Rights; to make provision with respect to holders of certain judicial offices who become judges of the European Court of Human Rights; and for connected purposes.

INTRODUCTION

The Convention Rights

1.—(1) In this Act "the Convention rights" means the rights and fundamental freedoms set out in—

    (a) Articles 2 to 12 and 14 of the Convention,
    (b) Articles 1 to 3 of the First Protocol, and
    (c) [Article 1 of the Thirteenth Protocol],[10]

as read with Articles 16 to 18 of the Convention.

(2) Those Articles are to have effect for the purposes of this Act subject to any designated derogation or reservation (as to which see sections 14 and 15).

---

[10] Substituted by SI 2004/1574, art.2(1).

Loan Receipt
Liverpool John Moores University
Library Services

Borrower Name: Reig Alvarez,Laura
Borrower ID: **********0110

Cases, materials and commentary on
administrative law.
31111012125637
Due Date: 08/05/2014 23:59

Total Items: 1
01/05/2014 13:28

Please keep your receipt in case of
dispute.

(3) The Articles are set out in Schedule 1.

(4) The [Secretary of State][11] may by order make such amendments to this Act as he considers appropriate to reflect the effect, in relation to the United Kingdom, of a protocol.

(5) In subsection (4) "protocol" means a protocol to the Convention—

(a) which the United Kingdom has ratified; or
(b) which the United Kingdom has signed with a view to ratification.

(6) No amendment may be made by an order under subsection (4) so as to come into force before the protocol concerned is in force in relation to the United Kingdom.

Interpretation of Convention rights

2.—(1) A court or tribunal determining a question which has arisen in connection with a Convention right must take into account any—

(a) judgment, decision, declaration or advisory opinion of the European Court of Human Rights,
(b) opinion of the Commission given in a report adopted under Article 31 of the Convention,
(c) decision of the Commission in connection with Article 26 or 27(2) of the Convention, or
(d) decision of the Committee of Ministers taken under Article 46 of the Convention,

whenever made or given, so far as, in the opinion of the court or tribunal, it is relevant to the proceedings in which that question has arisen.[12]

(2) Evidence of any judgment, decision, declaration or opinion of which account may have to be taken under this section is to be given in proceedings before any court or tribunal in such manner as may be provided by rules.

(3) In this section "rules" means rules of court or, in the case of proceedings before a tribunal, rules made for the purposes of this section—

(a) by [. . .] the Secretary of State, in relation to any proceedings outside Scotland;
(b) by the Secretary of State, in relation to proceedings in Scotland; or
(c) by a Northern Ireland department, in relation to proceedings before a tribunal in Northern Ireland—

(i) which deals with transferred matters; and
(ii) for which no rules made under paragraph (a) are in force.

---

[11] References to the Secretary of State here and in ss.7, 14–16 were replaced by a reference to the Lord Chancellor, but then restored by SI 2003/1887.

[12] Art.31 provides for a report as to whether the facts found constitute a breach of the Convention; Art.26 provides for decisions of the Commission in connection with the exhaustion of domestic remedies and the requirement that it deal with a matter within six months from the date on which the final decision was taken; Art.27(2) provides for decisions by the Commission that a petition is inadmissible as incompatible with the provisions of the Convention, manifestly ill-founded, or an abuse of the right of petition.

LEGISLATION

Interpretation of legislation

3.—(1) So far as it is possible to do so, primary legislation and subordinate legislation must be read and given effect in a way which is compatible with the Convention rights.

(2) This section—

(a) applies to primary legislation and subordinate legislation whenever enacted;
(b) does not affect the validity, continuing operation or enforcement of any incompatible primary legislation; and
(c) does not affect the validity, continuing operation or enforcement of any incompatible subordinate legislation if (disregarding any possibility of revocation) primary legislation prevents removal of the incompatibility.

Declaration of incompatibility

4.—(1) Subsection (2) applies in any proceedings in which a court determines whether a provision of primary legislation is compatible with a Convention right.

(2) If the court is satisfied that the provision is incompatible with a Convention right, it may make a declaration of that incompatibility.

(3) Subsection (4) applies in any proceedings in which a court determines whether a provision of subordinate legislation, made in the exercise of a power conferred by primary legislation, is compatible with a Convention right.

(4) If the court is satisfied—

(a) that the provision is incompatible with a Convention right, and
(b) that (disregarding any possibility of revocation) the primary legislation concerned prevents removal of the incompatibility,

it may make a declaration of that incompatibility.

(5) In this section "court" means—

(a) the House of Lords;
(b) the Judicial Committee of the Privy Council;
(c) the Courts-Martial Appeal Court;
(d) in Scotland, the High Court of Justiciary sitting otherwise than as a trial court or the Court of Session;
(e) in England and Wales or Northern Ireland, the High Court or the Court of Appeal.

(6) A declaration under this section ("a declaration of incompatibility")—

(a) does not affect the validity, continuing operation or enforcement of the provision in respect of which it is given; and
(b) is not binding on the parties to the proceedings in which it is made.

Right of Crown to intervene

5.—(1) Where a court is considering whether to make a declaration of incompatibility, the Crown is entitled to notice in accordance with rules of court.

(2) In any case to which subsection (1) applies—

(a) a Minister of the Crown (or a person nominated by him),
(b) a member of the Scottish Executive,
(c) a Northern Ireland Minister,
(d) a Northern Ireland department,

is entitled, on giving notice in accordance with rules of court, to be joined as a party to the proceedings.[13]

(3) Notice under subsection (2) may be given at any time during the proceedings.

(4) A person who has been made a party to criminal proceedings (other than in Scotland) as the result of a notice under subsection (2) may, with leave, appeal to the House of Lords against any declaration of incompatibility made in the proceedings.

(5) In subsection (4)—

"criminal proceedings" includes all proceedings before the Courts-Martial Appeal Court; and
"leave" means leave granted by the court making the declaration of incompatibility or by the House of Lords.

PUBLIC AUTHORITIES

Acts of public authorities

6.—(1) It is unlawful for a public authority to act in a way which is incompatible with a Convention right.

(2) Subsection (1) does not apply to an act if—

(a) as the result of one or more provisions of primary legislation, the authority could not have acted differently; or
(b) in the case of one or more provisions of, or made under, primary legislation which cannot be read or given effect in a way which is compatible with the Convention rights, the authority was acting so as to give effect to or enforce those provisions.

(3) In this section "public authority" includes—

(a) a court or tribunal, and
(b) any person certain of whose functions are functions of a public nature,

---

[13] This function is exercised by the National Assembly for Wales concurrently with any minister of the Crown in respect of subordinate legislation made by the National Assembly or for Wales by a minister of the Crown in the exercise of a function exercisable by the National Assembly: National Assembly for Wales (Transfer of Functions) (No.2) Order 2000 (SI 2000/1830), art.2.

but does not include either House of Parliament or a person exercising functions in connection with proceedings in Parliament.

(4) In subsection (3) "Parliament" does not include the House of Lords in its judicial capacity.

(5) In relation to a particular act, a person is not a public authority by virtue only of subsection (3)(b) if the nature of the act is private.

(6) "An act" includes a failure to act but does not include a failure to—

(a) introduce in, or lay before, Parliament a proposal for legislation; or
(b) make any primary legislation or remedial order.

Proceedings

7.—(1) A person who claims that a public authority has acted (or proposes to act) in a way which is made unlawful by section 6(1) may—

(a) bring proceedings against the authority under this Act in the appropriate court or tribunal, or
(b) rely on the Convention right or rights concerned in any legal proceedings,

but only if he is (or would be) a victim of the unlawful act.

(2) In subsection (1)(a) "appropriate court or tribunal" means such court or tribunal as may be determined in accordance with rules; and proceedings against an authority include a counterclaim or similar proceeding.

(3) If the proceedings are brought on an application for judicial review, the applicant is to be taken to have a sufficient interest in relation to the unlawful act only if he is, or would be, a victim of that act.

(4) If the proceedings are made by way of a petition for judicial review in Scotland, the applicant shall be taken to have title and interest to sue in relation to the unlawful act only if he is, or would be, a victim of that act.

(5) Proceedings under subsection (1)(a) must be brought before the end of—

(a) the period of one year beginning with the date on which the act complained of took place; or
(b) such longer period as the court or tribunal considers equitable having regard to all the circumstances,

but that is subject to any rule imposing a stricter time limit in relation to the procedure in question.

(6) In subsection (1)(b) "legal proceedings" includes—

(a) proceedings brought by or at the instigation of a public authority; and
(b) an appeal against the decision of a court or tribunal.

(7) For the purposes of this section, a person is a victim of an unlawful act only if he would be a victim for the purposes of Article 34 of the Convention if proceedings were brought in the European Court of Human Rights in respect of that act.

(8) Nothing in this Act creates a criminal offence.

(9) In this section "rules" means—

(a) in relation to proceedings before a court or tribunal outside Scotland, rules made by the [. . .] Secretary of State for the purposes of this section or rules of court,[14]

(b) in relation to proceedings before a court or tribunal in Scotland, rules made by the Secretary of State for those purposes,

(c) in relation to proceedings before a tribunal in Northern Ireland—
    (i) which deals with transferred matters; and
    (ii) for which no rules made under paragraph (a) are in force,
rules made by a Northern Ireland department for those purposes,

and includes provision made by order under section 1 of the Courts and Legal Services Act 1990.

(10) In making rules, regard must be had to section 9.

(11) The Minister who has power to make rules in relation to a particular tribunal may, to the extent he considers it necessary to ensure that the tribunal can provide an appropriate remedy in relation to an act (or proposed act) of a public authority which is (or would be) unlawful as a result of section 6(1), by order add to—

(a) the relief or remedies which the tribunal may grant; or

(b) the grounds on which it may grant any of them.

(12) An order made under subsection (11) may contain such incidental, supplemental, consequential or transitional provision as the Minister making it considers appropriate.

(13) "The Minister" includes the Northern Ireland department concerned.

Judicial remedies

8.—(1) In relation to any act (or proposed act) of a public authority which the court finds is (or would be) unlawful, it may grant such relief or remedy, or make such order, within its powers as it considers just and appropriate.

(2) But damages may be awarded only by a court which has power to award damages, or to order the payment of compensation, in civil proceedings.

(3) No award of damages is to be made unless, taking account of all the circumstances of the case, including—

(a) any other relief or remedy granted, or order made, in relation to the act in question (by that or any other court), and

(b) the consequences of any decision (of that or any other court) in respect of that act,

the court is satisfied that the award is necessary to afford just satisfaction to the person in whose favour it is made.

---

[14] See the Proscribed Organisations Appeal Commission (Human Rights Act Proceedings) Rules 2001 (SI 2001/127), made under subs.(9)(a) and (b).

(4) In determining—

(a) whether to award damages, or
(b) the amount of an award,

the court must take into account the principles applied by the European Court of Human Rights in relation to the award of compensation under Article 41 of the Convention.

(5) A public authority against which damages are awarded is to be treated—

(a) in Scotland, for the purposes of section 3 of the Law Reform (Miscellaneous Provisions) (Scotland) Act 1940 as if the award were made in an action of damages in which the authority has been found liable in respect of loss or damage to the person to whom the award is made;
(b) for the purposes of the Civil Liability (Contribution) Act 1978 as liable in respect of damage suffered by the person to whom the award is made.

(6) In this section—

"court" includes a tribunal;
"damages" means damages for an unlawful act of a public authority; and
"unlawful" means unlawful under section 6(1).

Judicial acts

9.—(1) Proceedings under section 7(1)(a) in respect of a judicial act may be brought only—

(a) by exercising a right of appeal;
(b) on an application (in Scotland a petition) for judicial review; or
(c) in such other forum as may be prescribed by rules.

(2) That does not affect any rule of law which prevents a court from being the subject of judicial review.

(3) In proceedings under this Act in respect of a judicial act done in good faith, damages may not be awarded otherwise than to compensate a person to the extent required by Article 5(5) of the Convention.

(4) An award of damages permitted by subsection (3) is to be made against the Crown; but no award may be made unless the appropriate person, if not a party to the proceedings, is joined.

(5) In this section—

"appropriate person" means the Minister responsible for the court concerned, or a person or government department nominated by him;
"court" includes a tribunal;
"judge" includes a member of a tribunal, a justice of the peace and a clerk or other officer entitled to exercise the jurisdiction of a court;
"judicial act" means a judicial act of a court and includes an act done on the instructions, or on behalf, of a judge; and
"rules" has the same meaning as in section 7(9).

Power to take remedial action

10.—(1) This section applies if—

(a) a provision of legislation has been declared under section 4 to be incompatible with a Convention right and, if an appeal lies—
   (i) all persons who may appeal have stated in writing that they do not intend to do so;
   (ii) the time for bringing an appeal has expired and no appeal has been brought within that time; or
   (iii) an appeal brought within that time has been determined or abandoned; or
(b) it appears to a Minister of the Crown or Her Majesty in Council that, having regard to a finding of the European Court of Human Rights made after the coming into force of this section in proceedings against the United Kingdom, a provision of legislation is incompatible with an obligation of the United Kingdom arising from the Convention.

(2) If a Minister of the Crown considers that there are compelling reasons for proceeding under this section, he may by order make such amendments to the legislation as he considers necessary to remove the incompatibility.

(3) If, in the case of subordinate legislation, a Minister of the Crown considers—

(a) that it is necessary to amend the primary legislation under which the subordinate legislation in question was made, in order to enable the incompatibility to be removed, and
(b) that there are compelling reasons for proceeding under this section,

he may by order make such amendments to the primary legislation as he considers necessary.

(4) This section also applies where the provision in question is in subordinate legislation and has been quashed, or declared invalid, by reason of incompatibility with a Convention right and the Minister proposes to proceed under paragraph 2(b) of Schedule 2.

(5) If the legislation is an Order in Council, the power conferred by subsection (2) or (3) is exercisable by Her Majesty in Council.

(6) In this section "legislation" does not include a Measure of the Church Assembly or of the General Synod of the Church of England.

(7) Schedule 2 makes further provision about remedial orders.

Safeguard for existing human rights

11. A person's reliance on a Convention right does not restrict—

(a) any other right or freedom conferred on him by or under any law having effect in any part of the United Kingdom; or

(b) his right to make any claim or bring any proceedings which he could make or bring apart from sections 7 to 9.

Freedom of expression

12.—(1) This section applies if a court is considering whether to grant any relief which, if granted, might affect the exercise of the Convention right to freedom of expression.

(2) If the person against whom the application for relief is made ("the respondent") is neither present nor represented, no such relief is to be granted unless the court is satisfied—

(a) that the applicant has taken all practicable steps to notify the respondent; or
(b) that there are compelling reasons why the respondent should not be notified.

(3) No such relief is to be granted so as to restrain publication before trial unless the court is satisfied that the applicant is likely to establish that publication should not be allowed.

(4) The court must have particular regard to the importance of the Convention right to freedom of expression and, where the proceedings relate to material which the respondent claims, or which appears to the court, to be journalistic, literary or artistic material (or to conduct connected with such material), to—

(a) the extent to which—
   (i) the material has, or is about to, become available to the public; or
   (ii) it is, or would be, in the public interest for the material to be published;
(b) any relevant privacy code.

(5) In this section—

"court" includes a tribunal; and
"relief" includes any remedy or order (other than in criminal proceedings).

Freedom of thought, conscience and religion

13.—(1) If a court's determination of any question arising under this Act might affect the exercise by a religious organisation (itself or its members collectively) of the Convention right to freedom of thought, conscience and religion, it must have particular regard to the importance of that right.

(2) In this section "court" includes a tribunal.

DEROGATIONS AND RESERVATIONS

Derogations

14.—(1) In this Act "designated derogation" means—
[. . .]¹⁵
any derogation by the United Kingdom from an Article of the Convention, or of any protocol to the Convention, which is designated for the purposes of this Act in an order made by the [Secretary of State].

(2) [. . .]

(3) If a designated derogation is amended or replaced it ceases to be a designated derogation.

(4) But subsection (3) does not prevent the [Secretary of State] from exercising his power under subsection (1) [. . .] to make a fresh designation order in respect of the Article concerned.

(5) The [Secretary of State] must by order make such amendments to Schedule 3 as he considers appropriate to reflect—

(a) any designation order; or
(b) the effect of subsection (3).

(6) A designation order may be made in anticipation of the making by the United Kingdom of a proposed derogation.

Reservations

15.—(1) In this Act "designated reservation" means—

(a) the United Kingdom's reservation to Article 2 of the First Protocol to the Convention; and
(b) any other reservation by the United Kingdom to an Article of the Convention, or of any protocol to the Convention, which is designated for the purposes of this Act in an order made by the [Secretary of State].

(2) The text of the reservation referred to in subsection (1)(a) is set out in Part II of Schedule 3.

(3) If a designated reservation is withdrawn wholly or in part it ceases to be a designated reservation.

(4) But subsection (3) does not prevent the [Secretary of State] from exercising his power under subsection (1)(b) to make a fresh designation order in respect of the Article concerned.

(5) The [Secretary of State] must by order make such amendments to this Act as he considers appropriate to reflect—

(a) any designation order; or
(b) the effect of subsection (3).

---

¹⁵ Words in ss.14 and 16 repealed by SI 2001/1216, arts 2 and 3 on repeal of the original derogation set out in the Act.

Period for which designated derogations have effect

16.—(1) If it has not already been withdrawn by the United Kingdom, a designated derogation ceases to have effect for the purposes of this Act—

[. . .], at the end of the period of five years beginning with the date on which the order designating it was made.

(2) At any time before the period—

(a) fixed by subsection (1) [. . .], or
(b) extended by an order under this subsection,

comes to an end, the [Secretary of State] may by order extend it by a further period of five years.

(3) An order under section 14(1) [. . .] ceases to have effect at the end of the period for consideration, unless a resolution has been passed by each House approving the order.

(4) Subsection (3) does not affect—

(a) anything done in reliance on the order; or
(b) the power to make a fresh order under section 14(1) [. . .]

(5) In subsection (3) "period for consideration" means the period of forty days beginning with the day on which the order was made.

(6) In calculating the period for consideration, no account is to be taken of any time during which—

(a) Parliament is dissolved or prorogued; or
(b) both Houses are adjourned for more than four days.

(7) If a designated derogation is withdrawn by the United Kingdom, the [Secretary of State] must by order make such amendments to this Act as he considers are required to reflect that withdrawal.

Periodic review of designated reservations

17.—(1) The appropriate Minister must review the designated reservation referred to in section 15(1)(a)—

(a) before the end of the period of five years beginning with the date on which section 1(2) came into force; and
(b) if that designation is still in force, before the end of the period of five years beginning with the date on which the last report relating to it was laid under subsection (3).

(2) The appropriate Minister must review each of the other designated reservations (if any)—

(a) before the end of the period of five years beginning with the date on which the order designating the reservation first came into force; and
(b) if the designation is still in force, before the end of the period of five years beginning with the date on which the last report relating to it was laid under subsection (3).

(3) The Minister conducting a review under this section must prepare a report on the result of the review and lay a copy of it before each House of Parliament. . . .

Statements of compatibility

19.—(1) A Minister of the Crown in charge of a Bill in either House of Parliament must, before Second Reading of the Bill—

(a) make a statement to the effect that in his view the provisions of the Bill are compatible with the Convention rights ("a statement of compatibility"); or
(b) make a statement to the effect that although he is unable to make a statement of compatibility the government nevertheless wishes the House to proceed with the Bill.

(2) The statement must be in writing and be published in such manner as the Minister making it considers appropriate.

Orders etc. under this Act

20.—(1) Any power of a Minister of the Crown to make an order under this Act is exercisable by statutory instrument.

(2) The power of [. . .] the Secretary of State to make rules (other than rules of court) under section 2(3) or 7(9) is exercisable by statutory instrument.

(3) Any statutory instrument made under section 14, 15 or 16(7) must be laid before Parliament.

(4) No order may be made by [. . .] the Secretary of State under section 1(4), 7(11) or 16(2) unless a draft of the order has been laid before, and approved by, each House of Parliament.

(5) Any statutory instrument made under section 18(7) or Schedule 4, or to which subsection (2) applies, shall be subject to annulment in pursuance of a resolution of either House of Parliament.

(6) The power of a Northern Ireland department to make—

(a) rules under section 2(3)(c) or 7(9)(c), or
(b) an order under section 7(11),

is exercisable by statutory rule for the purposes of the Statutory Rules (Northern Ireland) Order 1979.

(7) Any rules made under section 2(3)(c) or 7(9)(c) shall be subject to negative resolution; and section 41(6) of the Interpretation Act Northern Ireland) 1954 (meaning of "subject to negative resolution") shall apply as if the power to make the rules were conferred by an Act of the Northern Ireland Assembly.

(8) No order may be made by a Northern Ireland department under section 7(11) unless a draft of the order has been laid before, and approved by, the Northern Ireland Assembly.

Interpretation, etc

21.—(1) In this Act—

"amend" includes repeal and apply (with or without modifications);

"the appropriate Minister" means the Minister of the Crown having charge of the appropriate authorised government department (within the meaning of the Crown Proceedings Act 1947);

"the Commission" means the European Commission of Human Rights;

"the Convention" means the Convention for the Protection of Human Rights and Fundamental Freedoms, agreed by the Council of Europe at Rome on 4th November 1950 as it has effect for the time being in relation to the United Kingdom;

"declaration of incompatibility" means a declaration under section 4;

"Minister of the Crown" has the same meaning as in the Ministers of the Crown Act 1975;

"Northern Ireland Minister" includes the First Minister and the deputy First Minister in Northern Ireland;

"primary legislation" means any—

    (a) public general Act;

    (b) local and personal Act;

    (c) private Act;

    (d) Measure of the Church Assembly;

    (e) Measure of the General Synod of the Church of England;

    (f) Order in Council—

        (i) made in exercise of Her Majesty's Royal Prerogative;

        (ii) made under section 38(1)(a) of the Northern Ireland Constitution Act 1973 or the corresponding provision of the Northern Ireland Act 1998; or

        (iii) amending an Act of a kind mentioned in paragraph (a), (b) or (c);

and includes an order or other instrument made under primary legislation (otherwise than by the National Assembly for Wales, a member of the Scottish Executive, a Northern Ireland Minister or a Northern Ireland department) to the extent to which it operates to bring one or more provisions of that legislation into force or amends any primary legislation;

"the First Protocol" means the protocol to the Convention agreed at Paris on 20th March 1952;

[. . .]

"the Eleventh Protocol" means the protocol to the Convention (restructuring the control machinery established by the Convention) agreed at Strasbourg on 11th May 1994;

"the Thirteenth Protocol" means the protocol [to the Convention (concerning of the abolition of the death penalty in all circumstances) agreed at Uilnius on 3rd May 2002;][16]

"remedial order" means an order under section 10;

"subordinate legislation" means any—

---

[16] Inserted by SI 2004/1574, art.2(2), which also repealed the definition of the Sixth Protocol, with effect from June 22, 2004.

(a) Order in Council other than one—
(i) made in exercise of Her Majesty's Royal Prerogative;
(ii) made under section 38(1)(a) of the Northern Ireland Constitution Act 1973 or the corresponding provision of the Northern Ireland Act 1998; or
(iii) amending an Act of a kind mentioned in the definition of primary legislation;
(b) Act of the Scottish Parliament;
(c) Act of the Parliament of Northern Ireland;
(d) Measure of the Assembly established under section 1 of the Northern Ireland Assembly Act 1973;
(e) Act of the Northern Ireland Assembly;
(f) order, rules, regulations, scheme, warrant, byelaw or other instrument made under primary legislation (except to the extent to which it operates to bring one or more provisions of that legislation into force or amends any primary legislation);
(g) order, rules, regulations, scheme, warrant, byelaw or other instrument made under legislation mentioned in paragraph (b), (c), (d) or (e) or made under an Order in Council applying only to Northern Ireland;
(h) order, rules, regulations, scheme, warrant, byelaw or other instrument made by a member of the Scottish Executive, a Northern Ireland Minister or a Northern Ireland department in exercise of prerogative or other executive functions of Her Majesty which are exercisable by such a person on behalf of Her Majesty;

"transferred matters" has the same meaning as in the Northern Ireland Act 1998; and

"tribunal" means any tribunal in which legal proceedings may be brought.

(2) The references in paragraphs (b) and (c) of section 2(1) to Articles are to Articles of the Convention as they had effect immediately before the coming into force of the Eleventh Protocol.

(3) The reference in paragraph (d) of section 2(1) to Article 46 includes a reference to Articles 32 and 54 of the Convention as they had effect immediately before the coming into force of the Eleventh Protocol.

(4) The references in section 2(1) to a report or decision of the Commission or a decision of the Committee of Ministers include references to a report or decision made as provided by paragraphs 3, 4 and 6 of Article 5 of the Eleventh Protocol (transitional provisions).

(5) Any liability under the Army Act 1955, the Air Force Act 1955 or the Naval Discipline Act 1957 to suffer death for an offence is replaced by a liability to imprisonment for life or any less punishment authorised by those Acts; and those Acts shall accordingly have effect with the necessary modifications.

Short title, commencement, application and extent

22.—(1) This Act may be cited as the Human Rights Act 1998.
(2) Sections 18, 20 and 21(5) and this section come into force on the passing of this Act.

(3) The other provisions of this Act come into force on such day as the Secretary of State may by order appoint; and different days may be appointed for different purposes.[17]

(4) Paragraph (b) of subsection (1) of section 7 applies to proceedings brought by or at the instigation of a public authority whenever the act in question took place; but otherwise that subsection does not apply to an act taking place before the coming into force of that section.

(5) This Act binds the Crown.

(6) This Act extends to Northern Ireland.

(7) Section 21(5), so far as it relates to any provision contained in the Army Act 1955, the Air Force Act 1955 or the Naval Discipline Act 1957, extends to any place to which that provision extends.

SCHEDULE 1

THE ARTICLES

PART I: THE CONVENTION

RIGHTS AND FREEDOMS

ARTICLE 2: RIGHT TO LIFE

1. Everyone's right to life shall be protected by law. No one shall be deprived of his life intentionally save in the execution of a sentence of a court following his conviction of a crime for which this penalty is provided by law.

2. Deprivation of life shall not be regarded as inflicted in contravention of this Article when it results from the use of force which is no more than absolutely necessary:

(a) in defence of any person from unlawful violence;
(b) in order to effect a lawful arrest or to prevent the escape of a person lawfully detained;
(c) in action lawfully taken for the purpose of quelling a riot or insurrection.

ARTICLE 3: PROHIBITION OF TORTURE

No one shall be subjected to torture or to inhuman or degrading treatment or punishment.

ARTICLE 4: PROHIBITION OF SLAVERY AND FORCED LABOUR

1. No one shall be held in slavery or servitude.

2. No one shall be required to perform forced or compulsory labour.

---

[17] See the Human Rights Act 1998 (Commencement No.1) Order 1998 (SI 1998/2882), bringing s.19 into force on November 24, 1999, and the Human Rights Act 1998 (Commencement No.2) Order 2000 (SI 2000/1851), bringing the rest of the Act into force on October 2, 2000.

3. For the purpose of this Article the term "forced or compulsory labour" shall not include:

(a) any work required to be done in the ordinary course of detention imposed according to the provisions of Article 5 of this Convention or during conditional release from such detention;
(b) any service of a military character or, in case of conscientious objectors in countries where they are recognised, service exacted instead of compulsory military service;
(c) any service exacted in case of an emergency or calamity threatening the life or well-being of the community;
(d) any work or service which forms part of normal civic obligations.

ARTICLE 5: RIGHT TO LIBERTY AND SECURITY

1. Everyone has the right to liberty and security of person. No one shall be deprived of his liberty save in the following cases and in accordance with a procedure prescribed by law:

(a) the lawful detention of a person after conviction by a competent court;
(b) the lawful arrest or detention of a person for non-compliance with the lawful order of a court or in order to secure the fulfilment of any obligation prescribed by law;
(c) the lawful arrest or detention of a person effected for the purpose of bringing him before the competent legal authority on reasonable suspicion of having committed an offence or when it is reasonably considered necessary to prevent his committing an offence or fleeing after having done so;
(d) the detention of a minor by lawful order for the purpose of educational supervision or his lawful detention for the purpose of bringing him before the competent legal authority;
(e) the lawful detention of persons for the prevention of the spreading of infectious diseases, of persons of unsound mind, alcoholics or drug addicts or vagrants;
(f) the lawful arrest or detention of a person to prevent his effecting an unauthorised entry into the country or of a person against whom action is being taken with a view to deportation or extradition.

2. Everyone who is arrested shall be informed promptly, in a language which he understands, of the reasons for his arrest and of any charge against him.
3. Everyone arrested or detained in accordance with the provisions of paragraph 1(c) of this Article shall be brought promptly before a judge or other officer authorised by law to exercise judicial power and shall be entitled to trial within a reasonable time or to release pending trial. Release may be conditioned by guarantees to appear for trial.
4. Everyone who is deprived of his liberty by arrest or detention shall be entitled to take proceedings by which the lawfulness of his detention shall be decided speedily by a court and his release ordered if the detention is not lawful.
5. Everyone who has been the victim of arrest or detention in contravention of the provisions of this Article shall have an enforceable right to compensation.

ARTICLE 6: RIGHT TO A FAIR TRIAL

1. In the determination of his civil rights and obligations or of any criminal charge against him, everyone is entitled to a fair and public hearing within a reasonable time by an independent and impartial tribunal established by law. Judgment shall be pronounced publicly but the press and public may be excluded from all or part of the trial in the interest of morals, public order or national security in a democratic society, where the interests of juveniles or the protection of the private life of the parties so require, or to the extent strictly necessary in the opinion of the court in special circumstances where publicity would prejudice the interests of justice.

2. Everyone charged with a criminal offence shall be presumed innocent until proved guilty according to law.

3. Everyone charged with a criminal offence has the following minimum rights:

   (a) to be informed promptly, in a language which he understands and in detail, of the nature and cause of the accusation against him;
   (b) to have adequate time and facilities for the preparation of his defence;
   (c) to defend himself in person or through legal assistance of his own choosing or, if he has not sufficient means to pay for legal assistance, to be given it free when the interests of justice so require;
   (d) to examine or have examined witnesses against him and to obtain the attendance and examination of witnesses on his behalf under the same conditions as witnesses against him;
   (e) to have the free assistance of an interpreter if he cannot understand or speak the language used in court.

ARTICLE 7: NO PUNISHMENT WITHOUT LAW

1. No one shall be held guilty of any criminal offence on account of any act or omission which did not constitute a criminal offence under national or international law at the time when it was committed. Nor shall a heavier penalty be imposed than the one that was applicable at the time the criminal offence was committed.

2. This Article shall not prejudice the trial and punishment of any person for any act or omission which, at the time when it was committed, was criminal according to the general principles of law recognised by civilised nations.

ARTICLE 8: RIGHT TO RESPECT FOR PRIVATE AND FAMILY LIFE

1. Everyone has the right to respect for his private and family life, his home and his correspondence.

2. There shall be no interference by a public authority with the exercise of this right except such as is in accordance with the law and is necessary in a democratic society in the interests of national security, public safety or the economic well-being of the country, for the prevention of disorder or crime, for the protection of health or morals, or for the protection of the rights and freedoms of others.

ARTICLE 9: FREEDOM OF THOUGHT, CONSCIENCE AND RELIGION

1. Everyone has the right to freedom of thought, conscience and religion; this right includes freedom to change his religion or belief and freedom, either alone or in community with others and in public or private, to manifest his religion or belief, in worship, teaching, practice and observance.

2. Freedom to manifest one's religion or beliefs shall be subject only to such limitations as are prescribed by law and are necessary in a democratic society in the interests of public safety, for the protection of public order, health or morals, or for the protection of the rights and freedoms of others.

ARTICLE 10: FREEDOM OF EXPRESSION

1. Everyone has the right to freedom of expression. This right shall include freedom to hold opinions and to receive and impart information and ideas without interference by public authority and regardless of frontiers. This Article shall not prevent States from requiring the licensing of broadcasting, television or cinema enterprises.

2. The exercise of these freedoms, since it carries with it duties and responsibilities, may be subject to such formalities, conditions, restrictions or penalties as are prescribed by law and are necessary in a democratic society, in the interests of national security, territorial integrity or public safety, for the prevention of disorder or crime, for the protection of health or morals, for the protection of the reputation or rights of others, for preventing the disclosure of information received in confidence, or for maintaining the authority and impartiality of the judiciary.

ARTICLE 11: FREEDOM OF ASSEMBLY AND ASSOCIATION

1. Everyone has the right to freedom of peaceful assembly and to freedom of association with others, including the right to form and to join trade unions for the protection of his interests.

2. No restrictions shall be placed on the exercise of these rights other than such as are prescribed by law and are necessary in a democratic society in the interests of national security or public safety, for the prevention of disorder or crime, for the protection of health or morals or for the protection of the rights and freedoms of others. This Article shall not prevent the imposition of lawful restrictions on the exercise of these rights by members of the armed forces, of the police or of the administration of the State.

ARTICLE 12: RIGHT TO MARRY

Men and women of marriageable age have the right to marry and to found a family, according to the national laws governing the exercise of this right.

ARTICLE 14: PROHIBITION OF DISCRIMINATION

The enjoyment of the rights and freedoms set forth in this Convention shall be secured without discrimination on any ground such as sex, race, colour, language, religion, political or other opinion, national or social origin, association with a national minority, property, birth or other status.

ARTICLE 16: RESTRICTIONS ON POLITICAL ACTIVITY OF ALIENS

Nothing in Articles 10, 11 and 14 shall be regarded as preventing the High Contracting Parties from imposing restrictions on the political activity of aliens.

ARTICLE 17: PROHIBITION OF ABUSE OF RIGHTS

Nothing in this Convention may be interpreted as implying for any State, group or person any right to engage in any activity or perform any act aimed at the destruction of any of the rights and freedoms set forth herein or at their limitation to a greater extent than is provided for in the Convention.

ARTICLE 18: LIMITATION ON USE OF RESTRICTIONS ON RIGHTS

The restrictions permitted under this Convention to the said rights and freedoms shall not be applied for any purpose other than those for which they have been prescribed.

PART II: THE FIRST PROTOCOL

ARTICLE 1: PROTECTION OF PROPERTY

Every natural or legal person is entitled to the peaceful enjoyment of his possessions. No one shall be deprived of his possessions except in the public interest and subject to the conditions provided for by law and by the general principles of international law.

The preceding provisions shall not, however, in any way impair the right of a State to enforce such laws as it deems necessary to control the use of property in accordance with the general interest or to secure the payment of taxes or other contributions or penalties.

ARTICLE 2: RIGHT TO EDUCATION

No person shall be denied the right to education. In the exercise of any functions which it assumes in relation to education and to teaching, the State shall respect the right of parents to ensure such education and teaching in conformity with their own religious and philosophical convictions.

ARTICLE 3: RIGHT TO FREE ELECTIONS

The High Contracting Parties undertake to hold free elections at reasonable intervals by secret ballot, under conditions which will ensure the free expression of the opinion of the people in the choice of the legislature.

PART III: THE THIRTEENTH PROTOCOL

ARTICLE 1: ABOLITION OF THE DEATH PENALTY

The death penalty shall be abolished. No one shall be condemned to such penalty or executed.[18]

SCHEDULE 2

REMEDIAL ORDERS

Orders

1.—(1) A remedial order may—

(a) contain such incidental, supplemental, consequential or transitional provision as the person making it considers appropriate;
(b) be made so as to have effect from a date earlier than that on which it is made;
(c) make provision for the delegation of specific functions;
(d) make different provision for different cases.

(2) The power conferred by sub-paragraph (1)(a) includes—

(a) power to amend primary legislation (including primary legislation other than that which contains the incompatible provision); and
(b) power to amend or revoke subordinate legislation (including subordinate legislation other than that which contains the incompatible provision).

(3) A remedial order may be made so as to have the same extent as the legislation which it affects.
(4) No person is to be guilty of an offence solely as a result of the retrospective effect of a remedial order.

Procedure

2. No remedial order may be made unless—

(a) a draft of the order has been approved by a resolution of each House of Parliament made after the end of the period of 60 days beginning with the day on which the draft was laid; or
(b) it is declared in the order that it appears to the person making it that, because of the urgency of the matter, it is necessary to make the order without a draft being so approved.

Orders laid in draft

3.—(1) No draft may be laid under paragraph 2(a) unless—

---

[18] Substituted by SI 2004/1574, art.2(3), with effect from June 22, 2004.

(a) the person proposing to make the order has laid before Parliament a document which contains a draft of the proposed order and the required information; and

(b) the period of 60 days, beginning with the day on which the document required by this sub-paragraph was laid, has ended.

(2) If representations have been made during that period, the draft laid under paragraph 2(a) must be accompanied by a statement containing—

(a) a summary of the representations; and

(b) if, as a result of the representations, the proposed order has been changed, details of the changes.

Urgent cases

4.—(1) If a remedial order ("the original order") is made without being approved in draft, the person making it must lay it before Parliament, accompanied by the required information, after it is made.

(2) If representations have been made during the period of 60 days beginning with the day on which the original order was made, the person making it must (after the end of that period) lay before Parliament a statement containing—

(a) a summary of the representations; and

(b) if, as a result of the representations, he considers it appropriate to make changes to the original order, details of the changes.

(3) If sub-paragraph (2)(b) applies, the person making the statement must—

(a) make a further remedial order replacing the original order; and

(b) lay the replacement order before Parliament.

(4) If, at the end of the period of 120 days beginning with the day on which the original order was made, a resolution has not been passed by each House approving the original or replacement order, the order ceases to have effect (but without that affecting anything previously done under either order or the power to make a fresh remedial order).

Definitions

5. In this Schedule—

"representations" means representations about a remedial order (or proposed remedial order) made to the person making (or proposing to make) it and includes any relevant Parliamentary report or resolution; and

"required information" means—

(a) an explanation of the incompatibility which the order (or proposed order) seeks to remove, including particulars of the relevant declaration, finding or order; and

(b) a statement of the reasons for proceeding under section 10 and for making an order in those terms.

Calculating periods

6. In calculating any period for the purposes of this Schedule, no account is to be taken of any time during which—

(a) Parliament is dissolved or prorogued; or
(b) both Houses are adjourned for more than four days. . . .

SCHEDULE 3

DEROGATION AND RESERVATION

PART I: DEROGATION

[. . .]¹⁹

PART II: RESERVATION

At the time of signing the present (First) Protocol, I declare that, in view of certain provisions of the Education Acts in the United Kingdom, the principle affirmed in the second sentence of Article 2 is accepted by the United Kingdom only so far as it is compatible with the provision of efficient instruction and training, and the avoidance of unreasonable public expenditure.

Notes

1. *Authority of ECHR jurisprudence.* In the absence of special circumstances, the court should follow any clear and constant jurisprudence of the ECtHR (*per* Lord Slynn of Hadley *obiter* in *Alconbury* [2001] UKHL 23; [2003] 2 A.C. 295, at [26], below, p.376). An indication of what might be a special circumstance was given by Lord Hoffmann in the same case, where he said (at [76]) that had the decisions of the Court "compelled a conclusion so fundamentally at odds with the distribution of powers under the British Constitution, I would have considerable doubts as to whether they should be followed". It has been affirmed in other cases that good reasons are needed not to follow a carefully considered judgment of the ECtHR sitting as a Grand Chamber (Lord Bingham of Cornhill in *R. (on the application of Anderson and Taylor) v Secretary of State for the Home Department* [2003] 1 A.C. 837 at [18] or a clear and consistent line of decisions of the Commission, not inconsistent with those of the ECtHR (*R. (on the application of Carson) v Secretary of State for Work and Pensions* [2002] EWHC Admin 978; [2002] 3 All E.R. 994 at [38]; *cf.* the Court of Appeal, [2003] EWCA 797; [2003] 3 All E.R. 577 at [40], [41]).

An example of a case where a ECtHR decision was not followed was *R. v Spear* [2002] UKHL 31; [2003] 1 A.C. 734 where the House of Lords held that new arrangements for courts martial complied with Art.6(1) and that they had not been properly understood by the ECtHR in *Morris v UK* (2002) 34 E.H.R.R. 52.

¹⁹ A reference to derogation in the Act as originally enacted in respect of powers under terrorism legislation to detain suspects for up to five days was repealed by SI 2001/1216, art.4. A reference to a further derogation in respect of powers of extended detention of aliens under the Anti-terrorism, Crime and Security Act 2001 was inserted by SI 2001/4032, art.2, Sch., and repealed by SI 2005/1071, art.2: see further below, p.371.

See R. Masterman, "Section 2(1) of the Human Rights Act 1998: Binding Domestic Courts to Strasbourg?" [2004] P.L. 725, arguing that by tying domestic cases very closely to Strasbourg authority:

> "UK courts are in danger of . . . fettering themselves to a shifting jurisprudence, and, in doing so, severely curtailing the circumstances in which they will be able to 'give a lead' to the Strasbourg court, counter to the apparent parliamentary intent behind the Act" (p.736).

2. *Primary legislation.* This is defined in s.21(1). An Order in Council made in the exercise of the Royal Prerogative is primary legislation (*Hopkins v Secretary of State for Defence* [2004] All E.R. (D) 362 (Feb)).

3. *Temporal effect.* This has caused some difficulty. The general principle (applicable to all Acts) is that the Act is presumed not to operate with retrospective effect. Section 22(4) constitutes an express exception. This provides that the victim of an unlawful act (by virtue of s.6(1)) may rely (under s.7(1)(b)) on the Convention right(s) concerned in any legal proceedings brought by or at the instigation of a public authority whenever the act in question took place; otherwise, this does not apply to an act taking place before the coming into force of s.7. It is clear that proceedings under s.7(1)(a) can only be brought in respect of post-commencement acts.

One issue is how s.22(4) applies where proceedings are brought pre-commencement and an appeal is brought and heard post-commencement. In *MacDonald v Advocate-General for Scotland* [2003] UKHL 34; [2004] 1 All E.R. 339, the House of Lords held in respect of proceedings for sex discrimination brought against the Advocate-General, representing the Secretary of State for Defence, that appellate proceedings were part of the original proceedings for the purposes of applying s.22(4). Accordingly, M could not rely on the HRA 1998 in a post-commencement appeal brought by the Advocate-General (Lord Nicholls of Birkenhead at [23]). Neither could a different result be reached by arguing that the prosecution of a post-commencement appeal by the public authority constituted an act prohibited by s.6(1) (Lord Nicholls at [24]). It would follow that where civil proceedings are instigated originally by a public authority, the respondent should be able to raise Convention points on a post-commencement appeal, whoever the appellant. This position seemed to be endorsed, *obiter*, by Lord Hope of Craighead in *Wilson v Secretary of State for Trade and Industry* [2003] UKHL 40; [2004] 1 A.C. 816 at [90].

The extent to which s.3(1) can be used with retrospective effect was considered by the House in *Wilson*. The House held that the 1998 Act is not to be held to apply retrospectively so as to interfere with existing rights and duties. A natural reading of the words of ss.6 to 9 was that they were directed to post-Act events; this was powerfully supported by the context: "One would not expect a statute promoting human rights values to render unlawful acts which were lawful when done" (Lord Nicholls at [12]). Section 3 expressly does apply to legislation whenever enacted and so may have the effect of changing the interpretation and effect of legislation already in force. However, this is subject to the general principle that:

> "Parliament is presumed not to have intended to alter the law applicable to past events and transactions in manner which is unfair to those concerned in them, unless a contrary intention appears" (see Lord Nicholls at [19]).

The intention of Parliament must be identified in respect of the particular statutory provision in question, but in general the principle of s.3(1) will not apply to causes of action accruing before it came into force (Lord Nicholls at [20]–[23]). This is, however, a general and not universal principle (Lord Hope at [99]). On the facts of *Wilson*, s.3(1) could not be used to interfere with rights acquired under the Consumer Credit Act 1974.

Another aspect of retrospectivity was considered by the House of Lords in *McKerr, Re* [2004] UKHL 12, where it was held that no remedy was available under the HRA in respect of the state's failure after commencement properly to investigate a death in accordance with its obligations under Art.2 (see below, p.371), where the death in question occurred before commencement. The obligation to investigate was consequential upon the death and the death itself had to be a (post-commencement) death to which s.6 applied. See Lord Nicholls of Birkenhead at [15]–[26].

In criminal cases, however, defendants are not permitted to raise Convention points in post-commencement appeals (*R. v Lambert* [2002] 2 A.C. 545; *R. v Kansal (No.2)* [2002] 2 A.C. 69), by reference to a process of reasoning that has not been applied in civil cases. For strong criticism of *Lambert*, see D. Beyleveld, R. Kirkham and D. Townend, [2002] 22 L.S. 184, arguing that human rights legislation is a necessary exception to the presumption that law should not be applied retrospectively.

4. *Rights under international law.* The rights conferred by the HRA 1998 must be distinguished from the same or similar rights arising under the ECHR itself, other international instruments or general international law. The latter do not have direct effect in English law (*J. H. Rayner (Mincing Lane) Ltd v Department of Trade and Industry* [1990] 2 A.C. 418; *Brind* (below, p.622)). They may influence the development of the common law, but whether the courts are willing to do so so as to provide rights that are co-extensive with them depends on the context. In *McKerr, Re,* [2004] UKHL 12, [2004] 2 All E.R. 409, the House of Lords declined to recognise a common law obligation to hold an investigation into a killing equivalent to that arising under Art.2 ECHR, which would apply in respect of pre-commencement deaths. To do so would be to create a new obligation in an area of the law for which Parliament had long legislated. Lord Hoffmann (at [73]) stated that the very notion of an overarching broad common law principle equivalent to Art.2:

"capable of overriding detailed and statutory and common law rules, is alien to the traditions of the common law. The common law develops from case to case in harmony with statute. Its principles are generalisations from detailed rules, not abstract propositions from which those rules are deduced. Still less does it provide a solvent for any difficulties which may exist in the rules enacted by Parliament. It is in this respect quite different from the general statements which have never been enacted by the 1998 Act . . .".

As to the use of such rights in the general interpretation of statutes, see above p.251.

5. *The effect of the HRA between citizens.* A related question is the extent to which the HRA 1998 has effect (sometimes by analogy with EU law termed "horizontal effect") so as to create or affect rights between private citizens, in addition to its "virtual effect" between individual and state. The strong argument that a court as a "public authority" in a case between private citizens is always obliged to produce a solution that conforms with Convention rights (Sir William Wade, "Horizons of Horizontality" (2000) 116 L.Q.R. 217; *Wade and Forsyth,* pp.181–182) has been resisted (*e.g.* Sir Richard Buxton, "The Human Rights Act and Private Law" (2000) 116 L.Q.R. 48). The two major grounds argued against Wade's position are indications in the terms of the Act and debates on the passage of the Bill through Parliament that this was not the intention, and the point that the Convention rights referred to in the Act are under ECHR jurisprudence rights against the state and not against private individuals. Some of the evidence from the debates is, however, equivocal, and as s.6(1) does clearly apply to *courts,* at least some effect must be given to it. Furthermore, under a number of articles the state more generally is under a duty (under the ECHR and therefore by virtue of s.6(1) of the HRA) to protect a person from violations by other private citizens of his Convention rights (*Lester and Pannick,* para.2.6.3), although a wide margin of appreciation is accorded to states by the ECtHR in such cases (below, p.386). The courts have (perhaps predictably) have been prepared to develop the laws but have done so cautiously, whether considering the common law, or discharging the interpretative obligation under s.3(1), in respect of cases between private citizens. The courts have been ready to develop existing causes of action to secure conformity but

not willing to recognise new causes of action. See Dame Elizabeth Butler-Sloss in *Venables v News Group Newspapers Ltd* [2001] Fam. 430 at [27]; Lord Woolf C.J. in *A v B plc* [2002] EWCA Civ 337; [2003] Q.B. 195 at [4], [ii(vi)] (the court in granting interim injunctions in respect of alleged breach of confidence is able to achieve its obligation under s.6(1) "by absorbing the rights which arts 8 and 10 protect in the long-established action for breach of confidence" giving "a new strength and breadth to the action"; "it is most unlikely that any purpose will be served by a judge seeking to decide whether there exists a new cause of action in tort which protects privacy"). The case for this kind of middle approach was made by M. Hunt, "The 'Horizontal Effect' of the Human Rights Act 1998" [1998] P.L. 423 and N. Bamforth, (2001) 117 L.Q.R. 34. For further arguments in favour of Wade's approach, see J. Morgan, (2002) 22 L.S. 259.

This echoes the approach of the courts to the development of the common law in cases outside the parameters of the HRA. In *Wainwright v Home Office* [2003] UKHL 53; [2004] 2 A.C. 406, where the facts (an unlawful strip search of a visitor to a prison) occurred pre-commencement, the House of Lords rejected the argument that a new general tort of invasion of privacy should be established to secure compliance with Art.8; the real question for the ECtHR in such cases was whether on particular sets of facts English law provided a sufficient remedy and there were different ways in which that could be done (see Lord Hoffmann at [32]–[34]). It was not clear that Art.8 required the creation of a remedy in damages in respect of negligent (as distinct from intentional) invasion of privacy causing only distress, and any gap in remedies against a public authority was now filled by ss.6 and 7 of the HRA (Lord Hoffmann at [51], [52]).

6. *An effective remedy.* Article 13 ECHR provides that:

"Everyone whose rights and freedoms as set forth in this Convention are violated shall have an effective remedy before a national authority notwithstanding that the violation has been committed by persons acting in an official capacity".

Accordingly, where an individual has an arguable claim to be the victim of a violation of an ECHR right, he or she should have a remedy before a national authority (not necessarily judicial) to have the claim decided an, if appropriate , to obtain redress, the aggregate of remedies under domestic law may be sufficient (*Silver v UK* (1983) 5 E.H.R.R. 347.) For examples of breaches, see below, p.1070.

This has not been included in the Convention rights listed in the HRA, on the basis that ss.7–9 of the Act provide an appropriate remedial structure (see Lord Hope of Craighead in *Brown v Stott* [2003] 1 A.C. 681 at 715). Sedley L.J. has also stated that:

"Parliament's intention was that the Human Rights Act itself should constitute the United Kingdom's compliance with Art.13; but this makes it if anything more important that the courts, as part of the state, should satisfy themselves so far as possible that the common law affords adequate control, in conformity with Art.13, of the legality of official measures which interfere with personal autonomy"

(*R. (on the application of K) v Camden and Islington Health Authority* [2002] Q.B. 198 at [54]).

On Art.13, see further *Lester and Pannick*, pp.395–411. Domestic post-HRA judicial review "is probably sufficiently rigorous to comply with Art.13" (para.4.13.14). A declaration of incompatibility, which is not binding on the parties and does not require amending legislation is not (*Hobbs v UK* App. No.63684/00, June 18, 2000) (*ibid.*).

7. *Effect outside the jurisdiction.* The Act does not apply, even in respect of an act of the Secretary of State in right of the UK government (*i.e.* on behalf of the Queen as the Queen's Secretary of State in the United Kingdom) where that act affects a person outside the jurisdiction (*R. (on the application of Quark Fishing Ltd) v Secretary of State for Foreign and Commonwealth Affairs (No.2)* [2004] EWCA Civ 527). Here,

QF sought damages for breach of the First Protocol of Art.1 following the quashing of the refusal to them of a fishing licence (see below, p.534). The Court of Appeal rejected the claim. The ECHR had, but the First Protocol had not, been applied to South Georgia under the ECHR machinery and therefore there had been no breach of Convention rights capable of founding a claim under s.7 of the Act. The Court acknowledged that the First Protocol rights were included in the 1998 Act itself and did not explain why the absence of designation under the ECHR machinery was fatal to a claim under the Act.

8. *The preparation of legislation and ministerial statements under s.19.* The enactment of the HRA, including the section 19 requirement for a statement by the minister in charge of a Bill as to whether its provision are compatible, or if where a statement is not made that the government nevertheless wishes to proceed, has had a demonstrable effect on the preparation of legislation. The Cabinet Office has issued *The Human Rights Act 1998 Guidance for Departments* (2nd ed., 2000) (*www.dca.gov.uk/ hract/guidance*). This is directed at civil servants and emphasises that the Act will have a significant impact on their work and that, wherever they are in a department, an awareness of the Act and the ECHR is necessary (paras 3, 4). Given the minister's obligation to make a statement under s.19, there will need to be a careful examination of the policy and proposed provisions to determine if there are any Convention points: "You will need to consult your legal advisers" and may need to consult other departments to ensure consistency (para.33). A general assessment must be prepared at the policy approval stage. Once a Bill is drafted, a (non-disclosable) document analysing ECHR points must be prepared, probably by departmental lawyers, consulting Law Officers and the FCO as appropriate. This must be cleared with ministers and circulated to the government's Legislation Committee (paras 34, 35).

"If a section 19(1)(a) statement is to be made, a Minister must be clear that, at a minimum, the balance of argument supports the view that the provisions are compatible. A Minister will form his view on the basis of appropriate legal advice. Departmental lawyers will advise, if necessary following consultation with the Law Officers, whether the provisions of the Bill are on balance compatible with the Convention rights. In doing so, they will consider whether it is more likely than not that the provisions of the Bill will stand up to challenge on Convention grounds before the domestic courts and the Strasbourg Court. A Minister should not be advised to make a statement of compatibility where legal advice is that on balance the provisions of the Bill would not survive such a challenge. The fact that there are valid arguments to be advanced against any anticipated challenge is not a sufficient basis on which to advise a Minister that he may make a statement of compatibility where it is thought that these arguments would not ultimately succeed before the courts (para.37)".

The guidance also covers situations outside s.19 where a private member's Bill is a "Government handout" (*i.e.* a Bill that originates in a department) the minister responsible for the policy should express a view on compatibility at Second Reading (para.38). Such a view should also be expressed where a minister invites Parliament to approve delegated legislation, and (in writing) in respect of such legislation which amends primary legislation but is not subject to an affirmative resolution (para.40). The Explanatory Notes with a Government Bill should draw attention to the main Convention issues in the Bill (see *Guidance* that replaced para.39 of the 2000 document requiring fuller information to be given).

The Guidance document also covers the individual Convention rights (paras 41–78); "decision-making and administrative practice (paras 79–90); litigation (paras 91–108); the devolved administration (paras 109–115) the relationship with EC law (paras 116–120) and the Human Rights Committee (para.121).

Part 10 of the *Guide to Legislative Procedures* (*www.cabinetoffice.gov.uk/ legislation*) also contains guidance on the HRA, ECHR and EC legal matters.

Consideration of the impact of legislation on Convention rights "should be an integral part of the policy-making process and not left as a last minute compliance exercise". It adds the point that wherever it is proposed that the Government supports a Private Member's Bill, it should be in a position to make a compatibility statement. The operation of these processes is considered in *Lester and Pannick*, paras 8.02–8.08. The statement is updated for the Second Reading in the second House to consider the Bill. It is not otherwise updated to take account of amendments, but the Joint Committee on Human Rights is able to consider an amendment that raise significant human rights issues and bring it to the attention of each House (*ibid.*, para.8.08).

There have been two occasions when a section 19(1)(b) statement has been made: (1) where the House of Lords amended the Local Government Bill 2000 to prevent the repeal of the prohibition on promoting homosexuality in teaching; and (2) in respect of cl.309 of the Communications Bill 2002–03, which banned political advertising and sponsorship in the broadcast media, notwithstanding an ECtHR decision that a blanket ban violated Art.10 ECHR (*Verein Gegeng Tierfabriken v Switzerland* (2001) 34 E.H.R.R. 159). The relevant provision became s.321(2), (3) of the 2003 Act. The note in *Current Law Statutes* (by T. Gibbons) states that the Government "took a cautious view" and that "it is by no means certain . . . that the provisions of this section would be found incompatible with the Convention".

One example of a provision that can be traced to the section 19 requirements is s.55 of the Nationality, Immigration and Asylum Act 2002 (below, p.373) (see Sir Stephen Sedley, (2005) 32 J.L.S. 3 at pp.14–15).

9. *The Joint Committee on Human Rights.* A very valuable scrutiny role is played by the Joint Committee on Human Rights (see *Lester and Pannick*, paras 8.09–8.43, 8.46); D. Feldman (the Committee's first expert legal adviser), "Parliamentary Scrutiny of Legislation and Human Rights" [2002] P.L. 323. The Committee's remit extends to include compliance with other international instruments and its reports an excellent source of information and analysis for both parliamentarians and commentators.

10. *A Commission for Equality and Human Rights.* In 2004, the Government published proposals for this Commission in *Fairness for All: A New Commission for Equality and Human Rights* (Cm.6185). This would replace the Commission for Racial Equality, the Equal Opportunities Commission and the Disability Rights Commission and its remit would include the promotion of human rights. See F. Klug and C. O' Brien, [2004] P.L. 712.

11. Particularly helpful commentary on the HRA is provided by Lord Lester and D. Pannick, *Human Rights Law and Practice* (2nd ed., 2004); S. Grosz, J. Beatson and P. Duffy, *Human Rights: The 1998 Act and the European Convention* (1999); G. Gearty, *Principles of Human Rights Adjudication* (2004); B. Emerson and J. Simor (ed.), *Human Rights Practice*; A.R. Mowbray, *The Development of Positive Obligations under the European Convention on Human Rights* (2004); D. Feldman (ed.), *English Public Law* (2004).

(C) Interpretation and Declarations of Incompatibility

The approach of the court in considering questions of compatibility is seen by Lord Woolf C.J. (*obiter*, in *Donoghue v Poplar Housing and Regeneration Community Association Ltd* [2001] EWCA Civ 595; [2002] Q. B. 48 at para.[75]) as involving a series of steps. First, the court should ascertain whether, absent s.3, there would be any breach of the Convention as, otherwise, s.3 could be ignored. If there would be a breach, there is then a duty to apply s.3 and to reach a compatible modified meaning through interpretation. If that cannot be done, the court is not entitled to legislate, but has a discretion whether to grant a declaration of incompatibility. There are accordingly two difficult lines to be drawn. The first is between ordinary principles of statutory interpretation and the new rule contained in s.3(1). The second is between cases where compatibility can be secured through s.3(1) and those where it cannot. The second is particularly important. The process of interpretation (whether or not under s.3(1)) produces an answer that will be "the law" and apply both to resolve the instant case and constitute a precedent for other cases. If primary legislation is declared incompatible, the person whose rights have been infringed has no substantive remedy. The existing incompatible legislation may, in the interests of legal certainty, be applied to the claimant pending reform, and this does not necessarily constitute a breach of the Convention (*R. (on the application of Hooper) v Secretary of State for Work and Pensions* [2005] UKHL 29, *per* Lord Hoffmann at [32]–[40]). The claimant is, however, likely to have a remedy in respect of the original breach before the ECtHR. If the law is changed by legislation in response to the declaration of incompatibility this can be applied retrospectively to the claimant and others in his or her position, but may well not be. There are accordingly significant tensions in the relationship between ss.3 and 4.

GHAIDAN v GODIN-MENDOZA

[2004] UKHL 30; [2004] 2 A.C. 557 (HOUSE OF LORDS)

The defendant had, from 1972, lived in a stable and permanent homosexual relationship with the protected tenant of a flat of which the claimant was the freehold owner. The tenant died in 2001. The Rent Act 1977, Sch.1, para.2(1) provided that the surviving spouse of the original tenant, if residing in the dwelling-house immediately before the death of the original tenant, succeeded as statutory tenant. Paragraph 2(2) provided that a person who was living with the original tenant as his or her wife or husband was to be treated as the spouse of the original tenant. The House of Lords, affirming the Court of Appeal ([2002] EWCA Civ 1533; [2003] Ch. 380) held that in its ordinary meaning para.2(2) treated survivors of homosexual partnerships less favourably than survivors of heterosexual partnerships infringed Arts 8 and 14 ECHR, but that para.2(2) could be read as extending to same-sex partners.

LORD NICHOLLS OF BIRKENHEAD: . . . 5. On an ordinary reading of this language paragraph 2(2) draws a distinction between the position of a heterosexual couple living together in a house as husband and wife and a homosexual couple living together in a house. The survivor of a heterosexual couple may become a statutory tenant by succession, the survivor of a homosexual couple cannot. That was decided in *Fitzpatrick's* case. The survivor of a homosexual couple may, in competition with other members of the original tenant's "family", become entitled to an assured tenancy under paragraph 3. But even if he does, as in the present case, this is less advantageous. Notably, so far as the present case is concerned, the rent payable under an assured tenancy is the contractual or market rent, which may be more than the fair rent payable under a statutory tenancy, and an assured tenant may be evicted for non-payment of rent without the court needing to be satisfied, as is essential in the case of a statutory tenancy, that it is reasonable to make a possession order. In these and some other respects the succession rights granted by the statute to the survivor of a homosexual couple in respect of the house where he or she is living are less favourable than the succession rights granted to the survivor of a heterosexual couple.

6. Mr Godin-Mendoza's claim is that this difference in treatment infringes article 14 of the European Convention on Human Rights read in conjunction with article 8. Article 8 does not require the state to provide security of tenure for members of a deceased tenant's family. Article 8 does not in terms give a right to be provided with a home: *Chapman v United Kingdom* (2001) 33

EHRR 399, 427, para.99. It does not "guarantee the right to have one's housing problem solved by the authorities": *Marzari v Italy* (1999) 28 EHRR CD 175, 179. But if the state makes legislative provision it must not be discriminatory. The provision must not draw a distinction on grounds such as sex or sexual orientation without good reason. Unless justified, a distinction founded on such grounds infringes the Convention right embodied in article 14, as read with article 8. Mr Godin-Mendoza submits that the distinction drawn by paragraph 2 of Schedule 1 to the Rent Act 1977 is drawn on the grounds of sexual orientation and that this difference in treatment lacks justification.

7. That is the first step in Mr Godin-Mendoza's claim. That step would not, of itself, improve Mr Godin-Mendoza's status in his flat. The second step in his claim is to pray in aid the court's duty under section 3 of the Human Rights Act 1998 to read and give effect to legislation in a way which is compliant with the Convention rights. Here, it is said, section 3 requires the court to read paragraph 2 so that it embraces couples living together in a close and stable homosexual relationship as much as couples living together in a close and stable heterosexual relationship. So read, paragraph 2 covers Mr Godin-Mendoza's position. Hence he is entitled to a declaration that on the death of Mr Wallwyn-James he succeeded to a statutory tenancy.

Discrimination

8. The first of the two steps in Mr Godin-Mendoza's argument requires him to make good the proposition that, as interpreted in *Fitzpatrick's* case, paragraph 2 of Schedule 1 to the Rent Act 1977 infringes his Convention right under article 14 read in conjunction with article 8. Article 8 guarantees, among other matters, the right to respect for a person's home. Article 14 guarantees that the rights set out in the Convention shall be secured "without discrimination" on any grounds such as those stated in the non-exhaustive list in that article.

9. It goes without saying that article 14 is an important article of the Convention. Discrimination is an insidious practice. Discriminatory law undermines the rule of law because it is the antithesis of fairness. It brings the law into disrepute. It breeds resentment. It fosters an inequality of outlook which is demeaning alike to those unfairly benefited and those unfairly prejudiced. Of course all law, civil and criminal, has to draw distinctions. One type of conduct, or one factual situation, attracts one legal consequence, another type of conduct or situation attracts a different legal consequence. To be acceptable these distinctions should have a rational and fair basis. Like cases should be treated alike, unlike cases should not be treated alike. The circumstances which justify two cases being regarded as unlike, and therefore requiring or susceptible of different treatment, are infinite. In many circumstances opinions can differ on whether a suggested ground of distinction justifies a difference in legal treatment. But there are certain grounds of factual difference which by common accord are not acceptable, without more, as a basis for different legal treatment. Differences of race or sex or religion are obvious examples. Sexual orientation is another. This has been clearly recognised by the European Court of Human Rights: see, for instance, *Fretté v France* [2003] 2 FLR 9, 23, para.32. Unless some good reason can be shown, differences such as these do not justify differences in treatment. Unless good reason exists, differences in legal treatment based on grounds such as these are properly stigmatised as discriminatory.

10. Unlike article 1 of the 12th Protocol, article 14 of the Convention does not confer a free-standing right of non-discrimination. It does not confer a right of non-discrimination in respect of all laws. Article 14 is more limited in its scope. It precludes discrimination in the "enjoyment of the rights and freedoms set forth in this Convention". The court at Strasbourg has said this means that, for article 14 to be applicable, the facts at issue must "fall within the ambit" of one or more of the Convention rights. Article 14 comes into play whenever the subject matter of the disadvantage "constitutes one of the modalities" of the exercise of a right guaranteed or whenever the measures complained of are "linked" to the exercise of a right guaranteed: *Petrovic v Austria* (1998) 33 EHRR 307, 318, 319, paras 22, 28.

11. These expressions are not free from difficulty. In *R (Carson) v Secretary of State for Work and Pensions* [2003] 3 All ER 577, 592–595, paras 32–41, Laws L.J. drew attention to some difficulties existing in this area of the Strasbourg jurisprudence. In the Court of Appeal in the present case Buxton L.J. appeared to adopt the approach, espoused in the leading text book *Grosz, Beatson & Duffy, Human Rights: The 1998 Act and the European Convention* (2000), p.327, para.C14–10, that "even the most tenuous link with another provision in the Convention will suffice for article 14 to enter into play": [2003] Ch. 380, 387, para.9. In your Lordships' House counsel for the First Secretary of State criticised this approach. He drew attention to later authorities questioning its correctness: *R (Erskine) v London Borough of Lambeth* [2003] EWHC 2479 (Admin), paras 21–22, per Mitting J ("it overstates the effect of the Strasbourg case law") and *R (Douglas) v North Tyneside Metropolitan Borough Council* [2004] 1 WLR 2363, paras 53–54, per Scott Baker L.J.

12. This is not a question calling for consideration on this appeal. It is common ground between all parties, and rightly so, that paragraph 2 of Schedule 1 to the Rent Act 1977 is a provision which falls within the "ambit" of the right to respect for a person's home guaranteed by article 8. It is, in other words, common ground that article 14 is engaged in the present case. This being so, and the point not having been fully argued, I prefer to leave open the question whether even the most tenuous link is sufficient to engage article 14.

13. In the present case paragraph 2 of Schedule 1 to the Rent Act 1977 draws a dividing line between married couples and cohabiting heterosexual couples on the one hand and other members of the original tenant's family on the other hand. What is the rationale for this distinction? The rationale seems to be that, for the purposes of security of tenure, the survivor of such couples should be regarded as having a special claim to be treated in much the same way as the original tenant. The two of them made their home together in the house in question, and their security of tenure in the house should not depend upon which of them dies first.

14. The history of the Rent Act legislation is consistent with this appraisal. A widow, living with her husband, was accorded a privileged succession position in 1920. In 1980 a widower was accorded the like protection. In 1988 paragraph 2(2) was added, by which the survivor of a cohabiting heterosexual couple was treated in the same way as a spouse of the original tenant.

15. Miss Carss-Frisk submitted there is a relevant distinction between heterosexual partnerships and same sex partnerships. The aim of the legislation is to provide protection for the traditional family. Same sex partnerships cannot be equated with family in the traditional sense. Same sex partners are

unable to have children with each other, and there is a reduced likelihood of children being a part of such a household.

16. My difficulty with this submission is that there is no reason for believing these factual differences between heterosexual and homosexual couples have any bearing on why succession rights have been conferred on heterosexual couples but not homosexual couples. Protection of the traditional family unit may well be an important and legitimate aim in certain contexts. In certain contexts this may be a cogent reason justifying differential treatment: see *Karner v Austria* [2003] 2 FLR 623, 630, para.40. But it is important to identify the element of the "traditional family" which paragraph 2, as it now stands, is seeking to protect. Marriage is not now a prerequisite to protection under paragraph 2. The line drawn by Parliament is no longer drawn by reference to the status of marriage. Nor is parenthood, or the presence of children in the home, a precondition of security of tenure for the survivor of the original tenant. Nor is procreative potential a prerequisite. The survivor is protected even if, by reasons of age or otherwise, there was never any prospect of either member of the couple having a natural child.

17. What remains, and it is all that remains, as the essential feature under paragraph 2 is the cohabitation of a heterosexual couple. Security of tenure for the survivor of such a couple in the house where they live is, doubtless, an important and legitimate social aim. Such a couple share their lives and make their home together. Parliament may readily take the view that the survivor of them has a special claim to security of tenure even though they are unmarried. But the reason underlying this social policy, whereby the survivor of a cohabiting heterosexual couple has particular protection, is equally applicable to the survivor of a homosexual couple. A homosexual couple, as much as a heterosexual couple, share each other's life and make their home together. They have an equivalent relationship. There is no rational or fair ground for distinguishing the one couple from the other in this context: see the discussion in *Fitzpatrick v Sterling Housing Association Ltd* [2001] 1 AC 27, 44.

18. This being so, one looks in vain to find justification for the difference in treatment of homosexual and heterosexual couples. Such a difference in treatment can be justified only if it pursues a legitimate aim and there is a reasonable relationship of proportionality between the means employed and the aim sought to be realised. Here, the difference in treatment falls at the first hurdle: the absence of a legitimate aim. None has been suggested by the First Secretary of State, and none is apparent. In so far as admissibility decisions such as *S v United Kingdom* (1986) 47 DR 274 and *Roosli v Germany* (1996) 85A DR 149 adopted a different approach from that set out above, they must now be regarded as superseded by the recent decision of the European Court of Human Rights in *Karner v Austria* [2003] 2 FLR 623.

19. For completeness I should add that arguments based on the extent of the discretionary area of judgment accorded to the legislature lead nowhere in this case. As noted in *Wilson v First County Trust Ltd (No.2)* [2004] 1 AC 816, 844, para.70, Parliament is charged with the primary responsibility for deciding the best way of dealing with social problems. The court's role is one of review. The court will reach a different conclusion from the legislature only when it is apparent that the legislature has attached insufficient importance to a person's Convention rights. The readiness of the court to depart from the view of the legislature depends upon the subject matter of the legislation and of the complaint. National housing policy is a field where the court will be less

ready to intervene. Parliament has to hold a fair balance between the competing interests of tenants and landlords, taking into account broad issues of social and economic policy. But, even in such a field, where the alleged violation comprises differential treatment based on grounds such as race or sex or sexual orientation the court will scrutinise with intensity any reasons said to constitute justification. The reasons must be cogent if such differential treatment is to be justified.

20. In the present case the only suggested ground for according different treatment to the survivor of same sex couples and opposite sex couples cannot withstand scrutiny. Rather, the present state of the law as set out in paragraph 2 of Schedule 1 of the Rent Act 1977 may properly be described as continuing adherence to the traditional regard for the position of surviving spouses, adapted in 1988 to take account of the widespread contemporary trend for men and women to cohabit outside marriage but not adapted to recognise the comparable position of cohabiting same sex couples. I appreciate that the primary object of introducing the regime of assured tenancies and assured shorthold tenancies in 1988 was to increase the number of properties available for renting in the private sector. But this policy objective of the Housing Act 1988 can afford no justification for amending paragraph 2 so as to include cohabiting heterosexual partners but not cohabiting homosexual partners. This policy objective of the Act provides no reason for, on the one hand, extending to unmarried cohabiting heterosexual partners the right to succeed to a statutory tenancy but, on the other hand, withholding that right from cohabiting homosexual partners. Paragraph 2 fails to attach sufficient importance to the Convention rights of cohabiting homosexual couples. . . .

24. In my view, therefore, Mr Godin-Mendoza makes good the first step in his argument: paragraph 2 of Schedule 1 to the Rent Act 1977, construed without reference to section 3 of the Human Rights Act, violates his Convention right under article 14 taken together with article 8.

Section 3 of the Human Rights Act 1998

25. I turn next to the question whether section 3 of the Human Rights Act 1998 requires the court to depart from the interpretation of paragraph 2 enunciated in *Fitzpatrick's* case [2001] 1 AC 27.

26. Section 3 is a key section in the Human Rights Act 1998. It is one of the primary means by which Convention rights are brought into the law of this country. Parliament has decreed that all legislation, existing and future, shall be interpreted in a particular way. All legislation must be read and given effect to in a way which is compatible with the Convention rights "so far as it is possible to do so". This is the intention of Parliament, expressed in section 3, and the courts must give effect to this intention.

27. Unfortunately, in making this provision for the interpretation of legislation, section 3 itself is not free from ambiguity. Section 3 is open to more than one interpretation. The difficulty lies in the word "possible". Section 3(1), read in conjunction with section 3(2) and section 4, makes one matter clear: Parliament expressly envisaged that not all legislation would be capable of being made Convention-compliant by application of section 3. Sometimes it would be possible, sometimes not. What is not clear is the test to be applied in separating the sheep from the goats. What is the standard, or the criterion,

by which "possibility" is to be judged? A comprehensive answer to this question is proving elusive. The courts, including your Lordships' House, are still cautiously feeling their way forward as experience in the application of section 3 gradually accumulates.

28. One tenable interpretation of the word "possible" would be that section 3 is confined to requiring courts to resolve ambiguities. Where the words under consideration fairly admit of more than one meaning the Convention-compliant meaning is to prevail. Words should be given the meaning which best accords with the Convention rights.

29. This interpretation of section 3 would give the section a comparatively narrow scope. This is not the view which has prevailed. It is now generally accepted that the application of section 3 does not depend upon the presence of ambiguity in the legislation being interpreted. Even if, construed according to the ordinary principles of interpretation, the meaning of the legislation admits of no doubt, section 3 may none the less require the legislation to be given a different meaning. The decision of your Lordships' House in *R v A (No.2)* [2002] 1 AC 45 is an instance of this. The House read words into section 41 of the Youth Justice and Criminal Evidence Act 1999 so as to make that section compliant with an accused's right to a fair trial under article 6. The House did so even though the statutory language was not ambiguous.

30. From this it follows that the interpretative obligation decreed by section 3 is of an unusual and far-reaching character. Section 3 may require a court to depart from the unambiguous meaning the legislation would otherwise bear. In the ordinary course the interpretation of legislation involves seeking the intention reasonably to be attributed to Parliament in using the language in question. Section 3 may require the court to depart from this legislative intention, that is, depart from the intention of the Parliament which enacted the legislation. The question of difficulty is how far, and in what circumstances, section 3 requires a court to depart from the intention of the enacting Parliament. The answer to this question depends upon the intention reasonably to be attributed to Parliament in enacting section 3.

31. On this the first point to be considered is how far, when enacting section 3, Parliament intended that the actual language of a statute, as distinct from the concept expressed in that language, should be determinative. Since section 3 relates to the "interpretation" of legislation, it is natural to focus attention initially on the language used in the legislative provision being considered. But once it is accepted that section 3 may require legislation to bear a meaning which departs from the unambiguous meaning the legislation would otherwise bear, it becomes impossible to suppose Parliament intended that the operation of section 3 should depend critically upon the particular form of words adopted by the parliamentary draftsman in the statutory provision under consideration. That would make the application of section 3 something of a semantic lottery. If the draftsman chose to express the concept being enacted in one form of words, section 3 would be available to achieve Convention-compliance. If he chose a different form of words, section 3 would be impotent.

32. From this the conclusion which seems inescapable is that the mere fact the language under consideration is inconsistent with a Convention-compliant meaning does not of itself make a Convention-compliant interpretation under section 3 impossible. Section 3 enables language to be interpreted restrictively or expansively. But section 3 goes further than this. It is also apt to require

a court to read in words which change the meaning of the enacted legislation, so as to make it Convention-compliant. In other words, the intention of Parliament in enacting section 3 was that, to an extent bounded only by what is "possible", a court can modify the meaning, and hence the effect, of primary and secondary legislation.

33. Parliament, however, cannot have intended that in the discharge of this extended interpretative function the courts should adopt a meaning inconsistent with a fundamental feature of legislation. That would be to cross the constitutional boundary section 3 seeks to demarcate and preserve. Parliament has retained the right to enact legislation in terms which are not Convention-compliant. The meaning imported by application of section 3 must be compatible with the underlying thrust of the legislation being construed. Words implied must, in the phrase of my noble and learned friend, Lord Rodger of Earlsferry, "go with the grain of the legislation". Nor can Parliament have intended that section 3 should require courts to make decisions for which they are not equipped. There may be several ways of making a provision Convention-compliant, and the choice may involve issues calling for legislative deliberation.

34. Both these features were present in *In re S (Minors) (Care Order: Implementation of Care Plan)* [2002] 2 AC 291. There the proposed "starring system" was inconsistent in an important respect with the scheme of the Children Act 1989, and the proposed system had far-reaching practical ramifications for local authorities. Again, in *R (Anderson) v Secretary of State for the Home Department* [2003] 1 AC 837 section 29 of the Crime (Sentences) Act 1997 could not be read in a Convention-compliant way without giving the section a meaning inconsistent with an important feature expressed clearly in the legislation. In *Bellinger v Bellinger (Lord Chancellor intervening)* [2003] 2 AC 467 recognition of Mrs Bellinger as female for the purposes of section 11(c) of the Matrimonial Causes Act 1973 would have had exceedingly wide ramifications, raising issues ill-suited for determination by the courts or court procedures.

35. In some cases difficult problems may arise. No difficulty arises in the present case. Paragraph 2 of Schedule 1 to the Rent Act 1977 is unambiguous. But the social policy underlying the 1988 extension of security of tenure under paragraph 2 to the survivor of couples living together as husband and wife is equally applicable to the survivor of homosexual couples living together in a close and stable relationship. In this circumstance I see no reason to doubt that application of section 3 to paragraph 2 has the effect that paragraph 2 should be read and given effect to as though the survivor of such a homosexual couple were the surviving spouse of the original tenant. Reading paragraph 2 in this way would have the result that cohabiting heterosexual couples and cohabiting hemosexual couples would be treated alike for the purposes of succession as a statutory tenant. This would eliminate the discriminatory effect of paragraph 2 and would do so consistently with the social policy underlying paragraph 2. The precise form of words read in for this purpose is of no significance. It is their substantive effect which matters.

36. For these reasons I agree with the decision of the Court of Appeal. I would dismiss this appeal.

LORD STEYN

37. My Lords, in my view the Court of Appeal came to the correct conclusion. I agree with the conclusions and reasons of my noble and learned friends,

Lord Nicholls of Birkenhead, Lord Rodger of Earlsferry and Baroness Hale of Richmond. In the light of those opinions, I will not comment on the case generally.

38. I confine my remarks to the question whether it is possible under section 3(1) of the Human Rights Act 1998 to read and give effect to paragraph 2(2) of Schedule 1 to the Rent Act 1977 in a way which is compatible with the European Convention on Human Rights ("ECHR"). In my view the interpretation adopted by the Court of Appeal under section 3(1) was a classic illustration of the permissible use of this provision. But it became clear during oral argument, and from a subsequent study of the case law and academic discussion on the correct interpretation of section 3(1), that the role of that provision in the remedial scheme of the 1998 Act is not always correctly understood. I would therefore wish to examine the position in a general way. . . .

40. My impression is that two factors are contributing to a misunderstanding of the remedial scheme of the 1998 Act. First, there is the constant refrain that a judicial reading down, or reading in, under section 3 would flout the will of Parliament as expressed in the statute under examination. This question cannot sensibly be considered without giving full weight to the countervailing will of Parliament as expressed in the 1998 Act.

41. The second factor may be an excessive concentration on linguistic features of the particular statute. Nowhere in our legal system is a literalistic approach more inappropriate than when considering whether a breach of a Convention right may be removed by interpretation under section 3. Section 3 requires a broad approach concentrating, amongst other things, in a purposive way on the importance of the fundamental right involved.

42. In enacting the 1998 Act Parliament legislated "to bring rights home" from the European Court of Human Rights to be determined in the courts of the United Kingdom. That is what the White Paper said: see Rights Brought Home: The Human Rights Bill (1997) (Cm.3782), para.2.7. That is what Parliament was told. The mischief to be addressed was the fact that Convention rights as set out in the ECHR, which Britain ratified in 1951, could not be vindicated in our courts. Critical to this purpose was the enactment of effective remedial provisions.

43. [His Lordship read ss.3(1), (2) and 4(1), (2)]

If Parliament disagrees with an interpretation by the courts under section 3(1), it is free to override it by amending the legislation and expressly reinstating the incompatibility.

44. It is necessary to state what section 3(1), and in particular the word "possible", does not mean. First, section 3(1) applies even if there is no ambiguity in the language in the sense of it being capable of bearing two *possible* meanings. The word "possible" in section 3(1) is used in a different and much stronger sense. Secondly, section 3(1) imposes a stronger and more radical obligation than to adopt a purposive interpretation in the light of the ECHR. Thirdly, the draftsman of the Act had before him the model of the New Zealand Bill of Rights Act which imposes a requirement that the interpretation to be adopted must be reasonable. Parliament specifically rejected the legislative model of requiring a reasonable interpretation.

45. Instead the draftsman had resort to the analogy of the obligation under the EEC Treaty on national courts, as far as possible, to interpret national legislation in the light of the wording and purpose of Directives. In *Marleasing SA v La Comercial Internacional de Alimentación SA* (Case C-106/89) [1990]

ECR I-4135, 4159 the European Court of Justice defined this obligation as follows:

> "It follows that, in applying national law, whether the provisions in questions were adopted before or after the Directive, the national court called upon to interpret it is required to do so, as far as possible, in light of the wording and the purpose of the Directive in order to achieve the result pursued by the latter and thereby comply with the third paragraph of article 189 of the Treaty."

Given the undoubted strength of this interpretative obligation under EEC law, this is a significant signpost to the meaning of section 3(1) in the 1998 Act.

46. Parliament had before it the mischief and objective sought to be addressed, viz the need "to bring rights home". The linch-pin of the legislative scheme to achieve this purpose was section 3(1). Rights could only be effectively brought home if section 3(1) was the prime remedial measure, and section 4 a measure of last resort. How the system modelled on the EEC interpretative obligation would work was graphically illustrated for Parliament during the progress of the Bill through both Houses. The Lord Chancellor observed that "in 99% of the cases that will arise, there will be no need for judicial declarations of incompatibility" and the Home Secretary said "We expect that, in almost all cases, the courts will be able to interpret the legislation compatibly with the Convention": Hansard (HL Debates), 5 February 1998, col 840 (3rd reading) and Hansard (HC Debates), 16 February 1998, col 778 (2nd reading). It was envisaged that the duty of the court would be to strive to find (if possible) a meaning which would best accord with Convention rights. This is the remedial scheme which Parliament adopted. . ..

[His Lordship considered *R. v A (No.2)* [2002] 1 A.C. 45, *Pickstone v Freemans Plc* [1989] A.C. 66 and *Litster v Forth Dry Dock & Engineering Co. Ltd* [1990] 1 A.C. 546].

49. A study of the case law listed in the appendix to this judgment[20] reveals that there has sometimes been a tendency to approach the interpretative task under section 3(1) in too literal and technical a way. In practice there has been too much emphasis on linguistic features. If the core remedial purpose of section 3(1) is not to be undermined a broader approach is required. That is, of course, not to gainsay the obvious proposition that inherent in the use of the word "possible" in section 3(1) is the idea that there is a Rubicon which courts may not cross. If it is not possible, within the meaning of section 3, to read or give effect to legislation in a way which is compatible with Convention rights, the only alternative is to exercise, where appropriate, the power to make a declaration of incompatibility. Usually, such cases should not be too difficult to identify. An obvious example is *R (Anderson) v Secretary of State for the Home Department* [2003] 1 AC 837. The House held that the Home Secretary was not competent under article 6 of the ECHR to decide on the tariff to be served by mandatory life sentence prisoners. The House found a section 3(1) interpretation not "possible" and made a declaration under section 4. Interpretation could not provide a substitute scheme. *Bellinger* is another obvious example. As Lord Rodger of Earlsferry observed "in relation

---

[20] (ed.) omitted

to the validity of marriage, Parliament regards gender as fixed and immutable": [2003] 2 AC 467, 490, para.83. Section 3(1) of the 1998 Act could not be used.

50. Having had the opportunity to reconsider the matter in some depth, I am not disposed to try to formulate precise rules about where section 3 may not be used. Like the proverbial elephant such a case ought generally to be easily identifiable. What is necessary, however, is to emphasise that interpretation under section 3(1) is the prime remedial remedy and that resort to section 4 must always be an exceptional course. In practical effect there is a strong rebuttable presumption in favour of an interpretation consistent with Convention rights. Perhaps the opinions delivered in the House today will serve to ensure a balanced approach along such lines.

51. I now return to the circumstances of the case before the House. Applying section 3, the Court of Appeal interpreted "as his or her wife or husband" in the statute to mean "*as if they were* his wife or husband". While there has been some controversy about aspects of the reasoning of the Court of Appeal, I would endorse the reasoning of the Court of Appeal on the use of section 3(1) in this case. It was well within the power under this provision.

52. I would also dismiss the appeal.

LORD RODGER OF EARLSFERRY and BARONESS HALE delivered concurring speeches.

LORD MILLETT dissented.

Appeal dismissed

Notes

1. Lord Rodger (at [103]–[110]) noted that the duty under s.3(1) applies not only to the courts but also to everyone else (including public authorities of all kind) who may have to interpret and give effect to legislation. The notions inherent in "read" and "given effect" are distinct; there can be a breach of one of these requirements but not the other. Section 3(1) is not concerned with provisions which, properly interpreted, impose an unavoidable obligation to act in a particular way even if this is in violation of a Convention right (see s.6(2)(a) and (b)). What excludes provisions from the scope of s.3(1) is not a mere matter of their linguistic form, but

"because the entire substance of the provision, what it requires the public authority to do, is incompatible with the Convention. The only cure is to change the provision and that is a matter for Parliament and not for the courts" (at [110]).

Section 3(1)

"does not allow the courts to change the substance of a provision completely, to change a provision from one where Parliament says that x is to happen into one saying that x is not to happen".

In considering what constitutes the substance of the provision(s) under consideration "it is necessary to have regard to their place in the overall scheme of the legislation as enacted by Parliament". Only Parliament can create a "wholly different scheme" (at [110]). Lord Millett dissented. He agreed that the use of s.3(1) was not confined to cases of ambiguity or absurdity in the statute, and went beyond ordinary principles of statutory interpretation. However, the language of para.2(2) and its legislative history showed that "the essential feature of the relationship which Parliament had in contemplation was an open relationship between persons of the opposite sex" (at [78]).

The outcome of the majority view left it unclear as from what date the change in the law had taken place and whether qualifications for the successive tenancy was confined to homosexual relationships that were loving, stable and long lasting. These were essentially questions of social policy which should be left to Parliament (at [99]–[101]). For comment, see A.L. Young, [2005] P.L.23, welcoming the adoption of a midway point between the broad and narrow views of Lords Steyn and Hope, respectively in *R. v A (No.2)* (p.23), and arguing that deference should be limited to cases where the courts are faced with a choice of possible Convention-compatible interpretations or a choice of procedural mechanisms with which to ensure Convention compatibility (p.34).

2. The starting point in a particular case will be the ordinary principles of statutory interpretation, as modified where necessary to take account of the requirements of EU law. Those ordinary principles expect statutory provisions to be interpreted in their context, with the notion of "context" interpreted widely. The courts adopt a purposive approach, apply a presumption that Parliament intend that the United Kingdom complies with its international obligations and have a limited power to add to, alter or ignore statutory words in order to prevent a provision from being totally unreasonable or unworkable (see generally S.H. Bailey *et al.*, *Smith, Bailey and Gunn on the Modern English System* (4th ed., 2002), Ch.6).

3. Lord Steyn's view that its not possible to lay down detailed rules for determining the extent of changes that can properly be made by virtue of s.3(1) is understandable as the question is ultimately one of degree. Some guidance is obviously to be obtained from judicial comments as to the kinds of change that are impermissible, and the outcomes of decided cases. Impermissible changes include those that would:

(a) "remove the very core and essence, the 'pith and substance' of the measure that Parliament enacted" (Lord Rodger in *Ghaidan* at [111], in respect of removal from the Home Secretary of his express statutory power to release prisoners notwithstanding that this infringed Art.6(1), held to be impermissible by the House of Lords in *Anderson*);

(b) the introduction into an Act of something "actually inconsistent with one of its cardinal principles" (Lord Rodger in *Ghaidan* at [114], in respect of the addition by the Court of Appeal to the statutory scheme of the Children Act 1989 concerning final care orders of powers for the courts to supervise the way in which local authorities discharged their parental responsibilities, held to be impermissible by the House of Lords in *S (Minors) (Care Order: Implementation of Care Plan In) Re*);

(c) the adoption of "a meaning which departs substantially from a fundamental feature of an Act of Parliament . . . . This is especially so where the departure has important practical repercussions which the court is not equipped to evaluate" (Lord Nicholls in *S, Re* at [40]; Lord Rodger in *Ghaidan* at [115]);

(d) " 'if the legislation contains provisions which expressly contradict the meaning which the enactment would have to be given to make it compatible' or, indeed, if the legislation contains provisions which do so by necessary implication" (Lord Rodger in *Ghaidan* at [117], citing Lord Hope in *R. v A (No.2)* [2002] 1 A.C. 45 at [108]). See to the same effect Lord Nicholls in *S, Re* at [41] and Lord Steyn in *R. (on the application of Anderson) v Secretary of State for the Home Department* [2003] 1 A.C. 837 at [59];

(e) where to achieve compatibility "would make the statute unintelligible or unworkable" (Lord Hope of Craighead in *R. v Shayler* [2002] UKHL 11; [2003] 1 A.C. 247 at [52]);

(f) "to give the language of statutes a contextual meanings. That would be playing games with words" (Lord Hoffmann in *R. (on the application of Wilkinson) v Inland Revenue Commissioners* [2005] UKHL 30 at [17], holding that the term "widow" could not be taken as referring to the more general concept of "surviving spouse").

Amongst the practical repercussions that should be considered is the fact that the "new" interpretation, which will very commonly not be foreseeable by those who rely on the Act, will operate retrospectively, the courts lacking a power for its rulings to be prospective only.

4. Other examples of reliance on s.3(1) include *R. v Lambert* [2002] 2 A.C. 545 (legal burden of proof placed on defendant incompatible with Art.6 and so to be construed as an evidential burden); *R. (on the application of Sim) v Parole Board* [2003] EWCA Civ 1845; [2004] Q.B. 1288 (provision that Board "shall direct the prisoner's release if satisfied that it is no longer necessary for the protection of the public that he should be confined (but not otherwise)" to be interpreted so that the Board must conclude that it is no longer necessary to detain the recalled prisoner unless the Board is positively satisfied that the interest of the public require that he should be confined, so as to ensure compliance with Art.5(4) ECHR); *R. (on the application of Middleton) v HM Coroner for the Western District of Somerset* [2004] UKHL 10; [2004] 2 A.C. 182 ("how" in the phrase "how, when and where the deceased came by his death" to be read broadly to the circumstances as well as the means of death).

The strength of the interpretative obligation under s.3(1) is such that it may require a court below the level of the House of Lords to disregard a decision of the House. In *R. (on the application of IH) v Secretary of State for the Home Department* [2002] EWCA Civ 646; [2003] Q.B. 320; *R. (on the application of C) v Secretary of State for the Home Department* [2002] EWCA Civ 647, the Court of Appeal held that the powers of a MHRT following an order for conditional discharge of patient were broader than held in *Campbell v Secretary of State for the Home Department* [1988] 1 A.C. 120. This approach was approved by the House of Lords in *IH* [2003] UKHL 59; [2004] 2 A.C. 253. But *cf. Price v Leeds City Council*, below, p.386.

Interpretative techniques that may be permissible according to the circumstances include reading up or down (interpreting words, respectively, broadly or restrictively) or, more unusually, reading particular words in or out of a statute (see D. Feldman, *English Public Law* (2004), paras 7.70–7.80). Examples of all these techniques can also be found in statutory interpretation outside the HRA.

See further A. Kavanagh, "The Elusive Divide between Interpretation and Legislation under the Human Rights Act 1998" (2004) 24 O.J.L.S. 259, arguing that although the former is more limited than the latter, the distinction between them should not to be taken to deny the necessarily creative and evaluative aspect of judicial interpretation, but is an instruction to make law in a cautious manner, within the limits placed on judges (pp.284–285). See also D. Nicol, [2004] P.L. 273 and A. Kavanagh, [2004] P.L. 537.

5. Declarations of incompatibility, not subsequently reversed on appeal, have been made in a small number of cases:

(a) *R. (on the application of H) v Mental Health Review Tribunal* [2002] Q.B. 1. The Court of Appeal found that the reversed burden of proof, in respect of matters justifying the detention of a mental patient, in s.76 of the Mental Health Act 1983 was incompatible with Art.5.

(b) *R. (on the application of International Transport Roth GmbH) v Secretary of State for the Home Department* [2002] EWCA Civ 158; [2003] Q.B. 728. The Court of Appeal held that the penalty regime applicable to lorry drivers and haulage companies as persons responsible for clandestine entrants was incompatible with Art.6 and the First Protocol, Art.1. The penalty imposed was disproportionate to its goal. The statutory regime was replaced by primary legislation.

(c) *R. (on the application of Wilkinson) v Inland Revenue* [2002] EWHC (Admin) 182. Moses J. held that provisions governing a bereavement allowance payable to "widows" constituted unjustified gender discrimination contrary to Art.14 taken with Art.8 or the First Protocol, Art.1. The Court of Appeal ([2003] 1 W.L.R. 2683) dismissed an appeal, holding that the Inland Revenue had no power to pay the equivalent allowance to a widower by way of concession. The House of Lords dismissed a further appeal ([2005] UKHL 30]).

(d) *R. (on the application of Anderson) v Secretary of State for the Home Department* [2002] UKHL 4b; [2003] 1 A.C. 837. The House of Lords held that the involvement of the Home Secretary in fixing the tariff period for a convicted murderer was incompatible with Art.6(1).

(e) *R. (on the application of D) v Secretary of State for the Home Department* [2002] EWHC (Admin) 2805; [2003] 1 W.L.R. 1315. the absence of any power in s.74 of the Mental Health Act 1983 for the release of a prisoner in the circumstances of the claimant was held to be incompatible with Art.5(4).

(f) *Bellinger v Bellinger* [2003] UKHL 21; [2003] 2 A.C. 467. The House of Lords held that those parts of English law which failed to give legal recognition to the acquired gender of transsexual persons were incompatible with Arts 8 and 12. This matter was addressed in the Gender Recognition Act 2004.

(g) *R. (on the application of M) v Secretary of State for Health* [2003] EWHC (Admin) 1904 Maurice Kay J. held that the provision in the Mental Health Act 1983 that prescribed who qualified to be the "nearest relative" of a detained person for the purpose of a number of safeguards in the Act was incompatible with Art.8(1). This was because there was no procedure by which a person unsuitable to discharge the role could be replaced. M's "nearest relative" was her adoptive father, whom she alleged had sexually abused her as a child.

(h) In *R. (on the application of Morris) v Westminster CC (No.3)* [2004] EWHC 2191, Keith J. granted a declaration that a provision that required a housing authority in determining whether a person had a priority need for accommodation to disregard a person from abroad who is not eligible for housing assistance (here, the claimant's daughter) was incompatible with Arts 8 and 14 ECHR. The provision discriminated on the ground of nationality and was unlikely to achieve the legitimate aim of discouraging benefit tourism, give that there was nothing to prevent British citizens bringing dependent children to the United Kingdom simply to render themselves eligible for housing assistance under Pt VII of the 1996 Act.

(i) In *R. (on the application of MH) v Secretary of State for the Home Department* [2004] EWCA Civ 1609; [2005] 1 W.L.R. 1209, the Court of Appeal held that ss.2 and 29(4) of the Mental Health Act 1983 were incompatible with Art.5(4) ECHR.

(j) In *A v Secretary of State for the Home Department* (below, p.351), the House of Lords held that s.23 of the Anti-terrorism, Crime and Security Act 2001 was incompatible with Arts 5 and 14 ECHR.

6. Declarations of incompatibility reversed by a higher court on the ground that there was no breach of a Convention right include those in *Alconbury* (below p.374); *Matthews v Ministry of Defence* (below, p.384); *Wilson v Secretary of State for Trade and Industry* [2004] 1 A.C. 816; *R. (on the application of Uttley) v Secretary of State for the Home Department* [2004] UKHL 38. This can arise from the higher court analysing the terms of the Convention right differently, interpreting the domestic provision(s) in question differently (whether or not through s.3(1)) or finding that a breach can be remedied by other means.

7. A statutory lacuna is not statutory incompatibility. This point arose in *S (Minors) (Care Order: Implementation of Care Plan), Re* [2002] UKHL 10; [2002] 2 A.C. 29. Here the House held that provisions of the Children Act 1989 regulating care orders were compatible with Arts 8 and 6(1) ECHR. As to Art.6(1), there were some conceivable childcare decisions where English law might not satisfy its requirements. These included decisions affecting children with no parent or guardian able and willing to become involved in questioning a care decision by a local authority. However, the absence of provision for access to a court as guaranteed by Art.6(1) did not itself constitute incompatibility (*per* Lord Nicholls at [85], [86]). His Lordship (at [87], [88])

left open the issue whether inconsistency with a basic principle of a statute as distinct from inconsistency with express provision of a statute gives rise to incompatibility for the purpose of s.4. *cf.* the dictum of Elias J. in *R. (on the application of J) v Enfield LBC* [2002] EWHC 432 at [69] that in the case of a failure to take positive steps it may be more appropriate "simply to state that there is a gap in the legal assistance provided which, in certain very limited circumstances, may lead to a breach of a Convention right, without making a formal section 4 declaration".

8. Even where the grounds for making a declaration of incompatibility are established, the court retains a discretion whether to award one. The fact that amending legislation is already before Parliament is not necessarily sufficient reason to refuse a declaration (Maurice Kay J. in *R. (on the application of M) v Secretary of State for Health* (above)).

It seems that a person does not need to be a "victim" (as under s.7) to have standing to be awarded a declaration of incompatibility (*R. (on the application of Rusbridger) v Attorney-General* [2003] UKHL 38; [2004] 1 A.C. 357). However, a declaration will not be granted where the grounds raised do not apply to the party seeking it (*Lancashire CC v Taylor* [2005] EWCA Civ 284).

9. The grant of a declaration of incompatibility where there is to be no appeal is one of the two triggers for the procedure under s.10 and Sch.2 for the making of a remedial order. Two remedial orders have been made to date (April 2005):

  (a) The Mental Health Act 1983 (Remedial) Order 2001 (SI 2001/3712) removed the incompatibility with Art.5(1) and (4) of provision of the 1983 Act that placed a burden on a patient to prove that the criteria justifying his detention no longer existed (see the *H* case, para.5(a) above).

  (b) The Naval Discipline Act 1957 (Remedial) Order 2004 (SI 2004/66) removed the incompatibility with Art.6(1) arising from the position of the judge advocate in naval courts martial. An incompatibility may also be removed by primary legislation (see *e.g.* the Criminal Justice Act 2003, ss.269, 275 (Anderson); and the Gender Recognition Act 2004 (Bellinger)).

If remedial action is not taken, it will of course be open to individuals to pursue proceedings under the ECHR itself.

10. Rights under the ECHR and the HRA may be excluded by derogation under the two regimes. See *A v Secretary of State for the Home Department*, below, p.351.

(D) Unlawful Action

It is unlawful for a public authority to act in a way which is incompatible with a Convention right (s.6(1), above, p.279). This is subject to s.6(2)(a) and (b). This may lead to proceedings under s.7 in which remedies may be awarded as provided for by s.8.

Notes

1. *Public authority*. This concept is considered in *Hampshire CC v Beer* (below, p.938). There has been much criticism of the narrow approach adopted in the *Leonard Cheshire* case discussed in *Hampshire CC v Beer*, which means that most private organisations that contract with public bodies to provide services are not public authorities for the purposes of the HRA. The Joint Committee on Human Rights (Seventh Report, 2003–04 HL 39, HC 382) have recommended that the direct protection of the Act should extend, by interpretation of the Act, to the private sector when it is delivering a "public or governmental programme", a functional rather than institutional approach commended by M. Sunkin, "Pushing Forward the Frontiers of Human Rights Protection" [2004] P.L. 643. *cf.* a more critical comment by D. Oliver, [2004] P.L. 329 at pp.350–351, suggesting that the Committee's approach would give rise to considerable legal uncertainty.

The most extended consideration of this question by the House of Lords was in *Aston Cantlow and Wilmcote with Billesley Parochial Church Council v Wallbank* [2003] UKHL 37; [2004] 1 A.C. 546. Unfortunately, neither *Donoghue* nor *Heather* (discussed in *Hampshire CC v Beer*) was mentioned. The House held that a distinction is to be drawn between a "core" public authority and a "hybrid" public authority. A "core" public authority is one which falls within s.6 of the 1998 Act without reference to the inclusory words of s.6(3). A "hybrid" public authority is one which exercises both public and non-public functions; however, by virtue of s.6(5) it is not a public authority in respect of acts of a private nature. The term "public authority" is "essentially a reference to a body whose nature is governmental in a broad sense of that expression" (*per* Lord Nicholls of Birkenhead at [7], Lord Hope of Craighead at [47], Lord Hobhouse of Woodborough at [87], [88]). Similarly, the distinction between functions of a governmental nature and functions which are not of that nature is a useful guide in drawing the distinction between "public" and "private" for the purpose of s.6(3)(b) and s.6(5) (*per* Lord Nicholls at [10], Lord Hobhouse at [90]). There is no single test of universal application; factors to be taken into account:

"include the extent to which in carrying out the relevant function the body is publicly funded, or is exercising statutory powers, or is taking the place of central government or local authorities, or is providing a public service" (per Lord Nicholls at [12]).

A "non-governmental organisation" for the purposes of Art.34 ECHR ought not to be regarded as a core public authority as this would prevent it being able to claim as a victim under Art.34. The term "governmental organisation" does not refer only to the government or central organs of the state but, where powers are distributed along decentralised lines, it refers to any national authority which exercises public functions: *Ayuntamiento de Mula v Spain*, 68 D.R. 209 (1991) at 215 (where the Commission held that a City Council could not make an application under the former Art.25 (now Art.34) ECHR). The expression "non-governmental organisation" has an autonomous meaning under the ECHR. The decided cases on the amenability of bodies to judicial review are not determinative of whether a body is to be classed as a public authority, whether core or hybrid, but maybe of some assistance. Applying these principles, the House of Lords held that a Parochial Church Council was not a core public authority, and (Lord Scott dissenting) that its act in seeking to enforce the defendants' liability to pay for chancel repairs was an act of a private nature.

For discussion of these cases and *Hampshire CC v Beer* (below, p.938), see D. Oliver, "Functions of a Public Nature under the Human Rights Act" [2004] P.L. 329, who argues that a broad approach is not necessarily desirable and that there are significant differences between what are in fact various tests for amenability to judicial review and the "function of a public nature" concept under the HRA. Attention should be focused on the nature of the function transferred from a (core) public body to a private body, and not on the nature of the relationship between the two. The application of appropriate standards to private bodies taking over services should be addressed not by extending judicial review, but by developing private law principles or by legislation. Otherwise, awkward distinctions will arise between, for example, residents of private care homes paid for by the state and other residents a point made in the *Leonard Cheshire* case. See also Oliver's earlier article, "The Frontiers of the State: Public Authorities and Public Functions under the Human Rights Act" [2000] P.L. 476. For a different view, critical of *Leonard Cheshire*, see P.P. Craig, (2002) 118 L.Q.R. 551.

2. *Failures to act.* The term "act" in s.6(1) includes a failure to act, but not a failure to introduce in or lay before Parliament a proposal for legislation or make any primary legislation or remedial order (s.6(6)). A failure to make regulations subject to the negative resolution procedure does not fall within the exception as laying before Parliament is not a requirement (*R. (on the application of Rose) v Secretary of State for Work and Pensions* [2002] EWHC (Admin) 1593, citing R. Allen and P. Sales, [2000] P.L. 361).

3. *The operation of s.6(2)(a) and (b)*. Section 6(2) helps protect Parliamentary sovereignty by preventing attacks on incompatible primary legislation that cannot be made directly from being made indirectly. As s.6(2)(a) exculpates a public authority that infringes a Convention right it is to be narrowly construed. It accordingly only applies where the provisions of one or more enactments dictate the breach of the right in question and not merely where it is said that the authority has no alternative as the result, for example, of the lack of resources (*R. (on the application of S) v Airedale NHS Trust* [2002] EWHC Admin 1780 (in respect of the seclusion of the claimant under the Mental Health Act 1983; no breach of Art.5 was found on the facts; on appeal a probable breach of Art.8 was found): [2003] EWCA Civ 1036).

A key issue in the application of s.6(2)(b) is to determine when an authority is acting (or failing to act) so as to "give effect to or enforce" incompatible provisions of primary legislation. Section 6(2)(b) applies, for example, in any case where the *exercise* of a power conferred by legislation would necessarily involve incompatibility with a Convention right. It is no answer that compatibility can be achieved by refraining from exercising the power in question (*R. v Kansal (No.2)* [2001] UKHL 62; [2002] 2 A.C. 69, *per* Lord Hope of Craighead at [88]). The power in question may arise from one or more statutory provisions or from the common law (*per* Lord Hope of Craighead in *R. (on the application of Hooper) v Secretary of State for Work and Pensions* [2005] UKHL 29 at [72], [82]–[83]). In *Hooper*, Parliament provided (by ss.36 and 37 of the Social Security Claims and Benefits Act 1992) for certain payments to be made to widows, but not widowers. This constituted unlawful discrimination that was not now claimed to be objectively justified, and new legislation had been put in place with effect from April 9, 2001. The present claims related to the period between the commencement of the HRA and then. The Court of Appeal held that s.6(2)(b) could not be relied upon as the Secretary of State could make the equivalent payments to widowers in the exercise of the Crown's common law powers (see above, p.63; which powers the Secretary of State and the widowers agreed existed) in order to achieve compatibility; refusing to do so was not "necessary" to give effect to the statutory provisions. In the House of Lords, Lord Hoffmann held that s.6(2)(b) applied. This "says nothing about a decision having to be necessary for any particular purpose" (at [48]). The relevant acts and omissions of the Secretary of State were the making of these payments "to widows without making similar payments to widowers" (at [52]):

> "The payments under sections 36 and 37 are essential to any complaint of discrimination. If the Secretary of State had not paid widows, he would have infringed no Convention rights by not paying widowers. If section 6(1) 'does not apply' to the acts of making payments under sections 36 and 37, the argument for unlawful discrimination in domestic law collapses" ([50]).

The incompatibility relied upon therefore only arose because of the provisions of primary legislation. Lord Hope (at [72]–[81]) agreed that s.6(2)(b) applied. If an incompatibility between primary legislation and Convention rights could not be cured by interpretation under s.3(1), then s.6 did not impose a duty to give effect to primary legislation that conflicted with the intention of Parliament. By declining to exercise the common law power to make payments to the widowers, the Secretary of State was simply doing what the legislation told him to do. Lord Brown of Eaton-under-Heywood preferred to base his decision on s.6(2)(a). The Secretary of State was not acting to give effect to the statutory power to make the payments to widows when he declined to make the extra-statutory payments to widowers. However, any such payments would have been unlawful as an abuse of power given the clear intention of Parliament in the matter. Accordingly, the Secretary of State could not have acted differently as a result of the statutory provisions. Lord Scott if forced to a choice would have relied on para.(a), but held that the difference between the two paragraphs was in the circumstances of cases such as the present one immaterial (at [95]). Lord Nicholls of Birkenhead (at [3]–[6]) held that s.6(2) clearly applied and that it was not necessary to choose between paras (a) and (b). Either the common law powers were not available in the light of the statutory provisions, in which case para.(a) applied; or, if they were available, not exercising them to make payments to the widowers was "giving effect to those statutory provisions" and so covered by para.(b). It is submitted, with respect, that the analysis based on para.(a) is more clearly convincing. As to para.(b), if the statutory provisions do not exclude the common law power, it is difficult to see how choosing not to exercise it can be giving effect to them. However, the key issue here is whether the relevant act or omission is correctly identified as the "the refusal to pay the widowers" or as "the payment to widows but not widowers". Lord Hoffmann adopts the latter. But does it *necessarily* follow that because the statutory payments to widows would be protected by s.6(1) that the lack of such payments to widowers should be similarly protected? Similar issues arose in *R. (on the application of Wilkinson) v Inland Revenue Commissioners* [2005] UKHL 30 in relation to widows' bereavement allowance, where the House held that s.6(2)(a) applied as the Commissioners had no power to provide an equivalent allowance to widowers by way of extra-statutory concession.

Section 6(2)(b) does not apply where regulations are incompatible with Convention requirements, unless the incompatibility is a necessary consequence of the legislation which cannot be interpreted so as to be compatible (*R. (on the application of Bono) v Harlow DC* [2002] EWHC Admin 423; [2002] 1 W.L.R. 2475, where there was an enabling provision in very general terms that did not require the regulations to prescribe a constitution for a housing benefit review board that did not conform to the requirements of Art.6 ECHR).

4. *Standing under s.7.* A person who claims that a public authority has acted (or proposes to act) in a way made unlawful by s.6(1) may (a) bring proceedings against the authority or (b) rely on the Convention right(s) in any legal proceedings, but only if he is (or would be) a victim of the unlawful act (s.7(1)). A person is only a "victim" under s.7 if he or she would be a victim for the purposes of Art.34, ECHR, if proceedings were brought in the ECtHR in respect of that Act (s.7(7)). There is significant jurisprudence on the "victim" concept, summarised in Lord Lester and D. Pannick, *Human Rights Law and Practice* (2nd ed., 2004), at para.2.7.2. The concept is narrower than that of a sufficient interest for bringing judicial review proceedings (as to which, see below, pp.994–1010). To be a victim a person need not show that their rights have already been violated by an individual act of implementation, but it is sufficient that they "run the risk of being directly affected by" the measure in question (*Marckx v Belgium* (1979) 2 E.H.R.R. 330 at para.27). A close relative of the person affect may claim to be an indirect victim (*McCann v UK* (1995) 21 E.H.R.R. 97). However, organisations and interest groups do not have standing to bring proceedings on behalf of their members (see *Purcell v Ireland* 70 DR 262 (1991) at 272–273; *Ahmed v UK* (1995) 20 E.H.R.R. CD 72 at 77–78 (admissibility decisions). *Lester and Pannick* (para.2.7.3) argue that it is undesirable to have a narrower test applicable in public law proceedings as "an applicant will be able to raise some grounds of challenges, but not others, and the court will be prevented from considering whether Convention rights are being denied". The fact that the claimant is arguing that someone else's Convention rights have been infringed could presumably be considered by the court in exercising its discretion whether to grant a remedy. In practice, interest groups who wish to bring judicial review proceedings need to join individual victims if HRA points are to be argued. A governmental authority such as a local authority cannot claim to be a victim (see Art.34, which provides that an application to the ECtHR may only be received from "any person, non-governmental organisation or group of individuals claiming to be the victim" of a violation of a Convention right). For an extended discussion of different bases for according standing see J. Miles, "Standing under the Human Rights Act 1998: Theories of Rights Enforcement and the Nature of Public Law Adjudication" [2000] C.L.J. 133. Miles notes (pp.142–143) that it is hard to agree with the Government's apparent position that Convention required the adoption of the victim test; the ECHR provides a floor of protection, not a ceiling. As to the articulated fear that there would be a flood of cases brought by interest groups,

it was difficult to predict litigation patterns, and the selective support for litigation by specialist groups might well save court time. A victim-based rule can put barriers in the way of the vindication of rights (pp.144–146). The adoption of the victim approach "may hamper the emergence of a communitarian philosophy of human rights within the United Kingdom which the Act might otherwise have encouraged" (p.167).

5. *Time-limits.* The one-year time-limit under s.7 may be compared with the (extendable) three-month period for judicial review proceedings (below, pp.1010–1019). The interests of public authorities are, however, protected by the point that remedies are discretionary (see M. Fordham, [2000] J.R. 262).

6. *Remedies.* The remedies available in respect of unlawful acts are set out in s.8. The principles on which awards of damages are to be made were considered by the Court of Appeal in *Anufrijeva v Southwark LBC* [2003] EWCA Civ 1406; [2004] Q.B. 1124 (below).

ANUFRIJEVA v SOUTHWARK LBC; R. (ON THE APPLICATION OF N) v SECRETARY OF STATE FOR THE HOME DEPARTMENT; R. (ON THE APPLICATION OF M) v SECRETARY OF STATE FOR THE HOME DEPARTMENT

[2003] EWCA Civ 1406; [2004] Q.B. 1124; [2004] 2 W.C.R. 603; [2004] 1 All E.R. 833 (COURT OF APPEAL)

The Court of Appeal heard three cases together that raised the question of the principles governing the award of damages under s.8 of the HRA 1998. Each case was based on an alleged infringement of Art.8 ECHR. In *Anufrijeva*, Newman J. dismissed a claim for damages from a family of asylum seekers from Lithuania, who claimed that the council had failed to discharge its duty under s.21 of the National Assistance Act 1948 to provide them with accommodation that met the special needs of one member of the family. They claimed that their quality of family life had been drastically impaired. In *N*, Silber J. allowed a claim for damages by an asylum seeker from Libya who arrived in 2000 and was granted asylum in 2002. His claim was based on the ground that maladministration in the handling of his application had caused delay, and that he had received inadequate financial support during much of that period and had been caused psychiatric injury by the stress of his experience, which infringed Art.8. In *M*, Richards J. had rejected the claim of an asylum seeker from Angola for damages arising out of delay attributable to maladministration in granting permission for his family to join him after he was granted asylum in 2001. The Court of Appeal dismissed appeals in *Anufrijeva* and *M*, and allowed the Home Secretary's appeal in *N*.

The judgment of the court was handed down by LORD WOOLF C.J.: . . .

The nature of article 8 rights

9. Article 8 of the Convention provides: [His Lordship set out Art.8].

10. In *Harrow London Borough Council v Qazi* [2004] 1 AC 983, para.8, Lord Bingham of Cornhill observed that the Convention was an attempt to identify the rights and freedoms most central to the enjoyment of human life in civil society and to give those rights and freedoms an appropriate measure of protection. Article 3 of the Convention provides protection against inhuman and degrading treatment. What is the nature of the right to respect for private and family life, the home and correspondence afforded by article 8? In essence it is the right to live one's personal life without unjustified interference; the right to one's personal integrity. In *Bensaid v United Kingdom* (2001) 33 EHRR 205 the claimant contended that his article 8 rights would

be infringed if he were expelled from this country because of the likely effect that this would have on his mental health. The European Court of Human Rights had this to say, at p.219, para.46, about article 8:

"Not every act or measure which adversely affects moral or physical integrity will interfere with the right to respect to private life guaranteed by article 8. However, the court's case law does not exclude that treatment which does not reach the severity of article 3 treatment may none the less breach article 8 in its private life aspect where there are sufficiently adverse effects on physical and moral integrity."

11. In *Pretty v United Kingdom* (2002) 35 EHRR 1 the issue was whether article 8 required that the claimant should be permitted to enlist the aid of her husband to commit suicide when immobilised in the final stages of motor neurone disease. The Court of Human Rights made the following comment about the ambit of article 8, at pp.35–36, para.61:

"As the court has had previous occasion to remark, the concept of 'private life' is a broad term not susceptible to exhaustive definition. It covers the physical and psychological integrity of a person. It can sometimes embrace aspects of an individual's physical and social identity. Elements such as, for example, gender identification, name and sexual orientation and sexual life fall within the personal sphere protected by article 8. Article 8 also protects a right to personal development, and the right to establish and develop relationships with other human beings and the outside world. Though no previous case has established as such any right to self-determination as being contained in article 8 of the Convention, the court considers that the notion of personal autonomy is an important principle underlying the interpretation of its guarantees."

12. The reference to the right to develop relationships with other human beings demonstrates the link between the right to private life and the right to family life. If members of a family are prevented from sharing family life together, article 8(1) is likely to be infringed.

13. In M the claim is for delay in providing the permission that would enable the sharing of family life to take place. In *Anufrijeva* the claim is for failure to provide the claimants with the facilities that would enable them to enjoy a satisfactory quality of family life. In N there is a claim for subjecting the claimant to stress resulting in psychiatric injury and also for failing to provide the support necessary to achieve a basic quality of personal life. In each case it is possible to understand the basis upon which the claim is contended to fall within the ambit of article 8. Each case involves an allegation that the defendant was at fault in failing to take positive action, which would have averted the adverse consequences of which complaint is made.

When does a duty arise under article 8 to take positive action?

14. We now turn to the issue as to when article 8 can impose an obligation on the state to take positive action to secure enjoyment of the rights that article 8(1) requires should be respected. The jurisprudence of the Court of Human Rights provides some limited assistance with this question.

15. In *Abdulaziz, Cabales and Balkandali v United Kingdom* (1985) 7 EHRR 471 the applicants, who were permanently settled in the United Kingdom, alleged that their right to respect for family life was infringed because their husbands were not permitted to come to live with them in this country. The Court of Human Rights observed, at p.497, para.67:

"The court recalls that, although the essential object of article 8 is to protect the individual against arbitrary interference by the public authorities, there may in addition be positive obligations inherent in an effective 'respect' for family life. However, especially as far as those positive obligations are concerned, the notion of 'respect' is not clear cut: having regard to the diversity of the practices followed and the situations obtaining in the contracting states, the notion's requirements will vary considerably from case to case. Accordingly, this is an area in which the contracting parties enjoy a wide margin of appreciation in determining the steps to be taken to ensure compliance with the Convention with due regard to the needs and resources of the community and of individuals. In particular, in the area now under consideration, the extent of a state's obligation to admit to its territory relatives of settled immigrants will vary according to the particular circumstances of the persons involved. Moreover, the court cannot ignore that the present case is concerned not only with family life but also with immigration and that, as a matter of well-established international law and subject to its treaty obligations, a state has the right to control the entry of non-nationals into its territory."

16. Where the Court of Human Rights identifies a positive obligation on a state in the context of article 8 it often has two aspects: (1) to require the introduction of a legislative or administrative scheme to protect the right to respect for private and family life; and (2) to require the scheme to be operated competently so as to achieve its aim. It is in relation to the latter aspect that maladministration can amount to a breach of article 8, a matter that we shall consider when we come to address the next issue. Thus in *Glaser v United Kingdom* (2000) 33 EHRR 1, 19–20, para.63 the Court of Human Rights stated:

"The essential object of article 8 is to protect the individual against arbitrary interference by public authorities. There may however be positive obligations inherent in an effective 'respect' for family life. These obligations may involve the adoption of measures designed to secure respect for family life even in the sphere of relations between individuals, including both the provision of a regulatory framework of adjudicatory and enforcement machinery protecting individuals' rights and the implementation, where appropriate, of specific steps. In both the negative and positive contexts, regard must be had to the fair balance which has to be struck between the competing interests of the individual and the community, including other concerned third parties, and the state's margin of appreciation."

17. The Court of Human Rights has recognised a wide variety of situations in which states are under a positive obligation to introduce systems to preserve respect for family life: see the list identified by *Clayton & Tomlinson, The Law of Human Rights* (2000), vol 1, para.13.118. In particular, the Court of

Human Rights has recognised the possibility that a state might be under an obligation to admit relatives of settled immigrants in order to develop family life: *Gül v Switzerland* (1996) 22 EHRR 93. Such an obligation was recently established by the Court of Human Rights in *Sen v The Netherlands* (2001) 36 EHRR 81.

18. There are other fields in which the Court of Human Rights has ruled that states are under an obligation to put in place a system which ensures that article 8 rights are respected. Thus article 8 can require a system that gives official recognition to a change of gender upon gender reassignment by a transsexual: see *Bellinger v Bellinger (Lord Chancellor intervening)* [2003] 2 AC 467. In *López Ostra v Spain* (1994) 20 EHRR 277, the Court of Human Rights held that a duty existed to take reasonable and appropriate measures to prevent severe environmental pollution from having an adverse effect on the private and family life of a family living in the vicinity.

19. This last case demonstrates that a deterioration in the quality of life can result in infringement of article 8 and this is particularly true where it impacts upon the claimant's home: see *Marcic v Thames Water Utilities Ltd* [2002] QB 929. There is, however, a difference between protecting the quality of life that a claimant enjoys in his existing home and providing him with a home where he can enjoy a particular quality of life. The Court of Human Rights has always drawn back from imposing on states the obligation to provide a home, or indeed any other form of financial support. In *Chapman v United Kingdom* (2001) 33 EHRR 399 the claimant complained that she had been refused planning permission to live in a caravan on her own land. In rejecting her claim the Court of Human Rights made this observation, at pp.427–428, para.99, which echoed earlier jurisprudence:

"It is important to recall that article 8 does not in terms give a right to be provided with a home. Nor does any of the jurisprudence of the court acknowledge such a right. While it is clearly desirable that every human being has a place where he or she can live in dignity and which he or she can call home, there are unfortunately in the contracting states many persons who have no home. Whether the state provides funds to enable everyone to have a home is a matter for political not judicial decision."

20. *Clayton & Tomlinson*, vol 1, para.13.120, comment that the positive obligations on the state to respect family life will rarely go so far as to require financial or other practical support. Thus in *Andersson and Kullman v Sweden* (1986) 46 DR 251 the Commission held inadmissible an application that Sweden had infringed article 8 by failing to provide a mother with financial assistance that would have allowed her to stay at home to look after her children, rather than placing them in a creche and going out to work. The Commission observed, at p.253:

"the Convention does not as such guarantee the right to public assistance either in the form of financial support to maintain a certain standard of living or in the form of supplying day home care places. Nor does the right under article 8 of the Convention to respect for family life extend so far as to impose on states a general obligation to provide for financial assistance to individuals in order to enable one of two parents to stay at home to take care of children."

21. Whether article 8 imposed a duty on the defendant to provide support to the claimant is an issue in both the *Anufrijeva* and the N appeal. It is thus necessary to give further consideration to this question as a matter of principle.

23. Mr Sales appeared for the defendant in N. He was concerned to rebut the suggestion that a breach of duty in administering this country's statutory scheme of social security would automatically infringe article 8. He submitted that the welfare system provides benefits which go far beyond any positive action required by the Convention. If failure to provide the benefits at all would not infringe the Convention, how could maladministration in the provision of those benefits do so? In support of his submission Mr Sales relied upon the recent decision of the Court of Appeal in *R (Carson) v Secretary of State for Work and Pensions* [2003] 3 All ER 577.

24. We accept Mr Sales's submission on this point. Indeed, as we have noted, its correctness was accepted by Mr Clayton [counsel for A and N] in reply. This leaves unanswered the question of whether the Convention requires this country to provide welfare support in order positively to ensure that those within our borders can enjoy some minimum standard of private and family life, and, if so, what standard has to be achieved. Mr Sales did not assert that there was no such obligation. What he did assert was that the Convention, and the Strasbourg jurisprudence, required all states to adhere to a single uniform standard when giving effect to article 8 obligations. If a state chose to be more generous to its citizens than this, that did not have the effect of establishing a higher standard with which the state had to comply.

25. Strasbourg provides little guidance in this area, for we are not aware of any case where the Court of Human Rights has held a state in breach of the Convention for failure to provide housing to a certain standard, or for failure to provide welfare support. In these circumstances, Mr Sales's uniform minimum standards are not readily identified. . . .

30. It is noteworthy that, so far as we are aware, the Strasbourg court has not yet given a decision that a state has infringed article 3 as a result of failure to provide welfare support, let alone that article 8 has been infringed in such circumstances. The court has, however, recognised the possibility of such an infringement. In *Marzari v Italy* (1999) 28 EHRR CD 175 the applicant suffered from a rare disease that, at times, constrained him to use a wheelchair. He complained that his article 8 rights had been infringed in that he had been evicted and that the alternative accommodation offered to him was not suitable, having regard to his special needs. The court observed, at pp.179–180:

> "The court must first examine whether the applicant's rights under article 8 were violated on account of the decision of the authorities to evict him despite his medical condition. It further has to examine whether the applicant's rights were violated on account of the authorities' alleged failure to provide him with adequate accommodation. The court considers that, although article 8 does not guarantee the right to have one's housing problem solved by the authorities, a refusal of the authorities to provide assistance in this respect to an individual suffering from a severe disease might in certain circumstances raise an issue under article 8 of the Convention because of the impact of such refusal on the private life of the individual. The court recalls in this respect that, while the essential object of article 8 is to protect the individual against arbitrary interference by public authorities, this provision does not merely compel the state to abstain

from such interference: in addition to this negative undertaking, there may be positive obligations inherent in effective respect for private life. A state has obligations of this type where there is a direct and immediate link between the measures sought by an applicant and the latter's private life . . ."

31. The court went on to hold that it was not for it to review the decisions taken by the local authorities as to the adequacy of the accommodation offered to the applicant, observing, at p.180, that they had offered to carry out further works to make the accommodation suitable. In these circumstances the court held that the local authorities could be considered to have "discharged their positive obligations in respect of the applicant's right to respect for his private life".

32. In *O'Rourke v United Kingdom* (Application No 39022/97) (unreported) 26 June 2001, the applicant, who was in poor health, complained of infringement of his article 3 and 8 rights in that he was not provided with suitable accommodation after his discharge from prison. The court referred to *Marzari's* case and observed that "any positive obligation to house the homeless must be limited". In so far as there was any obligation to house the applicant the court considered that this was discharged by advice given to the applicant to attend a night shelter and efforts that were made to find suitable temporary or permanent occupation.

33. Thus, while Strasbourg has recognised the possibility that article 8 may oblige a state to provide positive welfare support, such as housing, in special circumstances, it has equally made it plain that neither article 3 nor article 8 imposes such a requirement as a matter of course. It is not possible to deduce from the Strasbourg jurisprudence any specific criteria for the imposition of such a positive duty.

34. If this is an area of the law where Strasbourg jurisprudence affords little positive guidance, both our domestic legislation and our own jurisprudence provide some assistance. Our complex, and frequently changing, scheme of provision of social security benefits distinguishes between different classes of those who are within our borders. Those who have an established right to live here, including those whose refugee status has been accepted, enjoy more generous rights to support than those who are seeking asylum, but whose claims have yet to be determined. And there is a statutory prohibition on providing any support to asylum seekers where the Secretary of State is not satisfied that they applied for asylum as soon as reasonably practicable after arrival in the United Kingdom. This prohibition is, however, subject to the exercise by the Secretary of State of a power "to the extent necessary for the purpose of avoiding a breach of a person's Convention rights": see section 55 of the Nationality, Immigration and Asylum Act 2002 and its legislative history as set out in paras 6–12 of the judgment of this court in *R (Q) v Secretary of State for the Home Department* [2004] QB 36, 54–57. Thus the statute itself appears to recognise the possibility that the Secretary of State will be required to exercise his power to provide support in order to comply with the Convention.

35. In Q there was discussion in argument as to whether, and in what circumstances, the Convention would impose an obligation to provide support to an asylum seeker and as to whether any such obligation was a positive obligation, or was an aspect of a negative obligation imposed by article 3 not to subject asylum seekers to inhuman or degrading treatment. The Attorney General, for the Secretary of State, argued that failure to provide support could never constitute "treatment" but accepted that, in extreme circumstances, article 3 could impose a positive obligation on the state to provide support for an asylum seeker. He gave by way of example the predicament of a heavily pregnant woman. The court held that the regime imposed on asylum seekers constituted "treatment". Thus it did not have to decide whether, as a matter of general principle, the state is under a positive obligation to provide support in so far as is necessary to prevent persons within this country reaching that condition of degradation which, if resulting from treatment, would infringe article 3. Addressing this point in the present case, we consider that the Attorney General's concession in Q was properly made. There is a stage at which the dictates of humanity require the state to intervene to prevent any person within its territory suffering dire consequences as a result of deprivation of sustenance. If support is necessary to prevent a person in this country reaching the point of article 3 degradation, then that support should be provided. We refer to p.390, paras 59 and 60, of the judgment in Q in relation to the degree of deprivation necessary to establish infringement of article 3.

36. Is there a positive obligation to provide support that is needed to enjoy article 8 rights? In Q this court had this to say, at pp.70–71, para.64, about the effect of the treatment of asylum seekers on their article 8 rights:

"Article 8 provides that 'Everyone has a right to respect for his private and family life, his home and his correspondence'. Similar considerations apply in relation to this right to those that we have discussed in relation to article 3. If the denial of support to an asylum seeker impacts sufficiently on the asylum seeker's private and family life, which extends to the individual's physical and mental integrity and autonomy: see *X and Y v The Netherlands* (1985) 8 EHRR 235, the Secretary of State will be in breach of the negative obligation imposed by article 8, unless he can justify his conduct under article 8(2)–as to which there was little debate before us . . . Certainly article 8 without more does not entitle the claimant to a roof over his head: see *Marzari v Italy* (1999) 28 EHRR CD 175. On the facts of this case, we find it easier to envisage the risk of infringement of article 3 rights than of article 8 rights."

37. While it is possible to identify a degree of degradation which demands welfare support, it is much more difficult to identify some other basic standard of private and family life which article 8 requires the state to maintain by the provision of support. In principle, if such a basic standard exists, it seems to us that it must require intervention by the state, whether the claimant is an asylum seeker who has not sought asylum promptly on entering the country or a citizen entitled to all the benefits of our system of social security. We turn to consider how judges in this jurisdiction have addressed the problem.

[His Lordship considered domestic cases, including *R. (on the application of Bernard) v Enfield LBC* [2003] L.G.R. 423. Here Sullivan J. found a breach of Art.8, but not Art.3, where the council, in breach of its duty under s.21(1)(a) of the National Assistance Act 1948, provided a family of a husband, wife and six children with a small house wholly unsuited to the wife's severe disability, condemning "the claimants to living conditions which made it virtually impossible for them to have any meaningful private or family life".]

Conclusions

43. Neither Mr Sales nor Mr Swirsky, who appeared for the defendant in *Anufrijeva* challenged the decision of Sullivan J in *Bernard's* case, either in principle or on the facts. Our conclusion is that Sullivan J was correct to accept that article 8 is capable of imposing on a state a positive obligation to provide support. We find it hard to conceive, however, of a situation in which the predicament of an individual will be such that article 8 requires him to be provided with welfare support, where his predicament is not sufficiently severe to engage article 3. Article 8 may more readily be engaged where a family unit is involved. Where the welfare of children is at stake, article 8 may require the provision of welfare support in a manner which enables family life to continue. Thus, in *R (J) v Enfield London Borough Council* [2002] EWHC 735 (Admin), where the claimant was homeless and faced separation from her child, it was common ground that, if this occurred, article 8(1) would be infringed. Family life was seriously inhibited by the hideous conditions prevailing in the claimants' home in *Bernard* and we consider that it was open to Sullivan J to find that article 8 was infringed on the facts of that case.

In what circumstances does maladministration constitute breach of article 8?

44. We consider this question in relation to the particular type of maladministration that has taken place in each of the three appeals before us—the failure, in breach of duty, to provide the claimant with some benefit or advantage to which the claimant was entitled under public law. Such failure may have come to an end before the trial. If not, it is likely to be brought to an end as a consequence of a finding of breach of duty made at the trial, so that what is likely to be in issue is the consequences of delay.

45. In so far as article 8 imposes positive obligations, these are not absolute. Before inaction can amount to a lack of respect for private and family life, there must be some ground for criticising the failure to act. There must be an element of culpability. At the very least there must be knowledge that the claimant's private and family life were at risk: see the approach of the Court of Human Rights to the positive obligation in relation to article 2 in *Osman v United Kingdom* (1998) 29 EHRR 245 and the discussion of Silber J in N [2003] EWHC 207 (Admin) at [126]–[148]. Where the domestic law of a state imposes positive obligations in relation to the provision of welfare support, breach of those positive obligations of domestic law may suffice to provide the element of culpability necessary to establish a breach of article 8, provided that the impact on private or family life is sufficiently serious and was foreseeable.

46. Where the complaint is that there has been culpable delay in the administrative processes necessary to determine and to give effect to an article 8 right, the approach of both the Strasbourg court and the commission has been not to find an infringement of article 8 unless substantial prejudice has been caused to the applicant. In cases involving custody of children, procedural delay has been held to amount to a breach of article 8 because of the prejudice such delay can have on the ultimate decision—thus in *H v United Kingdom* (1987) 10 EHRR 95 the court held, at p.112, para.89, article 8 infringed by delay in the conduct of access and adoption proceedings because the proceedings "lay within an area in which procedural delay may lead to a de facto determination of the matter at issue", which was precisely what had occurred.

The Court of Human Rights had adopted similar reasoning in *W v United Kingdom* (1987) 10 EHRR 29. In contrast, in *Askar v United Kingdom* (Application No 26373/95) (unreported) 16 October 1995, the commission held inadmissible a complaint of substantial delay in granting permission for the family of a refugee to join him in this country, observing:

> "The commission recalls that delay in proceedings concerning matters of 'family life' may raise issues under article 8 of the Convention. In *H v United Kingdom* 10 EHRR 95, the court found a violation of article 8 in respect of proceedings concerning the applicant mother's access to her child which lasted two years and seven months. However, the court had regard in reaching that conclusion that the proceedings concerned a fundamental element of family life (whether the mother would be able to see her child again) and that they had a quality of irreversibility, lying within an area in which delay might lead to a de facto determination of the matter, whereas an effective respect for the mother's family life required that the question be determined solely in the light of all relevant considerations and not by mere effluxion of time . . ."

H v United Kingdom 10 EHRR 95, *W v United Kingdom* 10 EHRR 29 and a third case were then cited. The commission continued:

> "The commission finds that the present case is not comparable. The subject matter of the proceedings concerns the granting of permission to enter the United Kingdom for members of the applicant's family, whom the applicant had not seen for at least six years and with some of whom the nature of his ties has not been specified beyond the fact that, pursuant to Somali tradition, the applicant has on the death of his father become head of the extended family group. Further, it is not apparent that the delay in the proceedings has any prejudicial effect on their eventual determination or that the effect of the passage of time is such as to prevent the proper and fair examination of the merits of the case."

47. We consider that there is sound sense in this approach at Strasbourg, particularly in cases where what is in issue is the grant of some form of welfare support. The Strasbourg court has rightly emphasised the need to have regard to resources when considering the obligations imposed on a state by article 8. The demands on resources would be significantly increased if states were to be faced with claims for breaches of article 8 simply on the ground of administrative delays. Maladministration of the type that we are considering will only infringe article 8 where the consequence is serious.

48. Newman J. suggested in *Anufrijeva* that it is likely that the acts of a public authority will have to have so far departed from the performance of its duty as to amount to a denial or contradiction of that duty before article 8 will be infringed. We think that this puts the position somewhat too high, for in considering whether the threshold of article 8 has been reached it is necessary to have regard both to the extent of the culpability of the failure to act and to the severity of the consequence. Clearly, where one is considering whether there has been a lack of respect for article 8 rights, the more glaring the deficiency in the behaviour of the public authority, the easier it will be to establish the necessary want of respect. Isolated acts of even significant carelessness are unlikely to suffice.

When should damages be awarded?

The nature of a claim for damages under the HRA

49. The Law Commission in its helpful and informative report on Damages under the Human Rights Act 1998 (October 2000) (Law Com No. 266) (Cm. 4853) suggests that the obvious analogy to a claim for damages under the HRA is a claim against a public authority in tort (paras 4.14 and 4.15). The Commission adds (para.4.26) that in the majority of situations it will be "possible and appropriate to apply the rules by which damages in tort are usually assessed to claims under the HRA" and that it may be "appropriate to treat those rules as the prima facie measure to be applied" unless they are in conflict with the Strasbourg approach. However, the report also contains timely warnings as to the dangers of drawing the analogy too strictly. As is stated earlier in the report, "the exercise is difficult and the comparisons must be treated with care" (paras 4.12 and 4.13). This is particularly important in cases such as those before us because there is a basic distinction between a claim under the HRA for compensation in respect of the consequences of maladministration and a claim by a member of the public against a public officer for damages for breach of a duty owed in tort. In the former case the claimant is seeking a remedy that would not be available in this jurisdiction for misfeasance prior to the HRA.

50. As we shall see, whereas damages are recoverable as of right in the case of damage caused by a tort, the same is not true in the case of a claim brought under the HRA for breach of the Convention. The language of the HRA and the jurisprudence of the Court of Human Rights make this clear.

The relevant provisions of the HRA

51. [His Lordship set out ss.6 to 8 of HRA 1998].

Reference should also be made to two articles of the Convention that are not included in Schedule 1 to the HRA: see (1953) (Cmd 8969). The first is article 13, which requires everyone whose rights and freedoms are violated to "have an effective remedy". The second is article 41, which is referred to in section 8 of the HRA, and requires the Court of Human Rights to afford "just satisfaction" to an injured party if this is not provided by a domestic court.

Features of a claim for compensation under the HRA

52. The sections of the HRA cited above establish a code governing the award of damages which has to be applied with due regard to the Strasbourg jurisprudence. However, as we shall show, the assistance to be derived from that jurisprudence is limited. The remedy of damages generally plays a less prominent role in actions based on breaches of the articles of the Convention, than in actions based on breaches of private law obligations where, more often than not, the only remedy claimed is damages.

53. Where an infringement of an individual's human rights has occurred, the concern will usually be to bring the infringement to an end and any question of compensation will be of secondary, if any, importance. This is reflected in the fact that, when it is necessary to resort to the courts to uphold and protect human rights, the remedies that are most frequently sought are the orders which are the descendants of the historic prerogative orders or declaratory judgments. The orders enable the court to order a public body to refrain from or to take action, or to quash an offending administrative decision of a public body. Declaratory judgments usually resolve disputes as to what is the correct answer in law to a dispute. This means that it is often procedurally convenient for actions concerning human rights to be heard on an application for judicial review in the Administrative Court. That court does not normally concern itself with issues of disputed fact or with issues as to damages. However, it is well placed to take action expeditiously when this is appropriate.

54. That damages or compensation should play a different role in relation to claims in respect of public law rights from that which it plays in private law proceedings is not confined to the Convention and the HRA. It also true of claims for infringement of Community law (see *Dillenkofer v Federal Republic of Germany* (Joined Cases C-178, 179 and 188–190/94) [1997] QB 259) and, for claims for infringement of human rights, under, for example, the Indian constitution: see *Nilabati Behera v State of Orissa* (1993) 80 AIR 1960, 1966, 1969–1970, paras 10, 16, 17, 22.

55. The code recognises the different role played by damages in human rights litigation and has significant features which distinguish it from the approach to the award of damages in a private law contract or tort action. The following points need to be noted. (a) The award of damages under the HRA is confined to the class of unlawful acts of public authorities identified by section 6(1): see section 8(1) and (6). (b) The court has a discretion as to whether to make an award (it must be "just and appropriate" to do so) by contrast to the position in relation to common law claims where there is a right to damages: see section 8(1). (c) The award must be necessary to achieve "just satisfaction"; language that is distinct from the approach at common law where a claimant is invariably entitled, so far as money can achieve this, to be restored to the position he would have been in if he had not suffered the injury of which complaint is made. The concept of damages being "necessary to afford just satisfaction" provides a link with the approach to compensation of the Court of Human Rights under article 41. (d) The court is required to take into account in determining whether damages are payable and the amount of damages payable the different principles applied by the Court of Human Rights in awarding compensation. (e) Exemplary damages are not awarded.

56. In considering whether to award compensation and, if so, how much, there is a balance to be drawn between the interests of the victim and those of the public as a whole. The requirement to adopt a balanced approach was recognised in the White Paper (Rights Brought Home: The Human Rights Bill (1997) (Cm.3782)) where the following comments were made, at para.2.6, under the heading "Remedies for a failure to comply with the Convention":

> "A public authority which is found to have acted unlawfully by failing to comply with the Convention will not be exposed to criminal penalties. But the court or tribunal will be able to grant the injured person any remedy which is within its normal powers to grant and which it considers appropriate and just in the circumstances. *What remedy is appropriate will of course depend both on the facts of the case and on a proper balance between the rights of the individual and the public interest. In some cases, the right course may be for the decision of the public authority in the particular case to be quashed. In other cases, the only appropriate remedy may be an award of damages.*" (Emphasis added.)

The court has a wide discretion in respect of the award of damages for breach of human rights. *Scorey & Eicke, Human Rights Damages, Principles and Practice*, looseleaf ed, do not view this wide discretion as problematic. Instead, at para.A4–035, they consider it to derive from the nature of the new approach created by the HRA:

> "Given that it is anticipated that the majority of cases in which civil claims will be brought under the HRA will be by way of judicial review which has always been discretionary, it is appropriate that section 8(1) of the HRA also has a broad discretionary nature . . . Also, the language of a 'just and appropriate' remedy is not novel, either to the United Kingdom nor to other human rights instruments."

In their analysis of the phrase "just and appropriate", *Scorey & Eicke* consider the case law in respect of similarly phrased statutes in Canada and South Africa and conclude that it would not be surprising if the English courts took an approach similar to that of those jurisdictions. In essence this involves determining the "appropriate" remedy in the light of the particular circumstances of an individual victim whose rights have been violated, having regard to what would be "just", not only for that individual victim, but also for the wider public who have an interest in the continued funding of a public service: para.A4–036. Damages are not an automatic entitlement but, as I also indicate, a remedy of "last resort": para.A4–040.

The Strasbourg principles

57. Section 8(4) of the HRA requires the court to take into account the principles applied by the Court of Human Rights when deciding whether to award damages and the amount of an award. Both the decisions of that court and the HRA make it plain that when damages are required to vindicate human rights and to achieve just satisfaction, damages should be awarded. Our approach to awarding damages in this jurisdiction should be no less liberal than those applied at Strasbourg or one of the purposes of the HRA will be defeated and claimants will still be put to the expense of having to go to Strasbourg to obtain just satisfaction. The difficulty lies in identifying from the Strasbourg jurisprudence clear and coherent principles governing the award of damages.

58. The Law Commission Report (Law Com No.266) (Cm.4853) states, at para.3.4: "Perhaps the most striking feature of the Strasbourg case law . . . is the lack of clear principles as to when damages should be awarded and how they should be measured." The Law Commission correctly suggests that part of the explanation for this is the absence of a common approach to damages in the different jurisdictions. It also refers to the views of different commentators, including the statement of Karen Reid (*A Practitioner's Guide to the European Convention of Human Rights* (1998), p.398): "The emphasis is not on providing a mechanism for enriching successful applicants but rather on its role in making public and binding findings of applicable human rights standards." *Lester & Pannick, Human Rights Law and Practice* (1999), p.41, note 3 comment: "The case law of the European Court of Human Rights lacks coherence, and advocates and judges are in danger of spending time attempting to identify principles that do not exist."

59. Despite these warnings it is possible to identify some basic principles the Court of Human Rights applies. The fundamental principle underlying the

award of compensation is that the court should achieve what it describes as restitutio in integrum. The applicant should, in so far as this is possible, be placed in the same position as if his Convention rights had not been infringed. Where the breach of a Convention right has clearly caused significant pecuniary loss, this will usually be assessed and awarded. The awards of compensation to homosexuals, discharged from the armed forces, in breach of article 8, for loss of earnings and pension rights in *Lustig-Prean and Beckett v United Kingdom* (2000) 31 EHRR 601 and *Smith and Grady v United Kingdom* (2000) 31 EHRR 620 are good examples of this approach. The problem arises in relation to the consequences of the breach of a Convention right which are not capable of being computed in terms of financial loss.

60. None of the rights in section I of the Convention is of such a nature that its infringement will automatically give rise to damage that can be quantified in financial terms. Infringements can involve a variety of treatment of an individual which is objectionable in itself. The treatment may give rise to distress, anxiety, and, in extreme cases, psychiatric trauma. The primary object of the proceedings will often be to bring the adverse treatment to an end. If this is achieved is this enough to constitute "just satisfaction" or is it necessary to award damages to compensate for the adverse treatment that has occurred? More particularly, should damages be awarded for anxiety and distress that has been occasioned by the breach? It is in relation to these questions that Strasbourg fails to give a consistent or coherent answer.

61. *Clayton & Tomlinson, The Law of Human Rights*, vol 1, have analysed the claims for compensation made to the Court of Human Rights. They set out their results and comment on these as follows:

"21.32. The court does not routinely award compensation to successful applicants. Between 1972 and 1981 the court made awards in seven cases and rejected three such claims. Between 1982 and 1991 applicants sought non-pecuniary damages in 51 cases where the court held that the judgment alone gave just satisfaction. It has been suggested that these cases share certain general characteristics: the court was very divided on the merits; a large majority of cases concerned individuals who were accused of (or were guilty of) criminal offences; and they often involved procedural errors in civil or administrative hearings. The same pattern continued from 1992 until the new court was established in November 1998. The court found its judgment sufficient to meet the moral injury caused in 79 of the cases.

"21.33. Although section 8(4) [of the HRA] requires the court or tribunal to examine Convention principles, analysis of the case law on just satisfaction is likely to be of limited assistance. There are serious concerns about the lack of consistency in the case law (for example, over the treatment of criminal fines as financial loss and the appropriate methodology for valuing property), about the obscure nature of the basis on which the court makes awards of specified amounts of compensation and about the moral judgments the court makes when evaluating different types of applicants (such as the claims of convicted criminals and terrorists to just satisfaction)."

62. The disinclination of the Court of Human Rights to pay compensation for procedural errors is consonant with its disinclination to recognise that maladministration resulting in delay engages article 8 at all, unless this has led to

serious consequences. Such an approach is not, however, open in the case of the very different language of article 5, which deals expressly with delay. [His Lordship set out Art.5.]

63. In *R (KB) v South London and South and West Region Mental Health Review Tribunal* [2004] QB 936 Stanley Burnton J had to consider three cases that he heard together in which damages were claimed by mental health patients whose rights under article 5(4) had been infringed because of inordinate delay in processing their claims to mental health review tribunals. We commend the quality of his judgment. He concluded that article 5(5) did not make an award of damages mandatory in such cases. It was complied with provided that it was possible to make an application for compensation; it did not preclude the contracting states from making the award of compensation conditional upon proof that procedural delay had resulted in damage.

64. Stanley Burnton J gave particular consideration to the question of whether compensation should be awarded where delay has caused frustration and distress. He concluded, at p.957, para.41:

"I conclude that there is no 'clear and constant jurisprudence' of the European court on the recoverability of damages for distress under article 5(5) in the absence of a deprivation of liberty. There are two principles applied by the court: that damages are not recoverable in the absence of a deprivation of liberty, and that damages are recoverable for distress which may be inferred from the facts of the case. It follows that this court must itself determine the principles it is to apply."

65. The principle that he decided should be applied, having due regard for the vulnerability of mental health patients detained by the state, he set out at p.966, para.73:

"Thus, even in the case of mentally ill claimants, not every feeling of frustration and distress will justify an award of damages. The frustration and distress must be significant: 'of such intensity that it would in itself justify an award of compensation for non-pecuniary damage.' In my judgment, an important touchstone of that intensity in cases such as the present will be that the hospital staff considered it to be sufficiently relevant to the mental state of the patient to warrant its mention in the clinical notes."

This principle has no application to the article 8 cases which we are considering, for the consequences of delay must amount to more than distress and frustration before article 8 will even be engaged. This impressive judgment demonstrates, as does the judgment of Sullivan J in *Bernard's* case [2003] LGR 423, that, especially at first instance, courts dealing with claims for damages for maladministration should adopt a broad-brush approach. Where there is no pecuniary loss involved, the question whether the other remedies that have been granted to a successful complainant are sufficient to vindicate the right that has been infringed, taking into account the complainant's own responsibility for what has occurred, should be decided without a close examination of the authorities or an extensive and prolonged examination of the facts. In many cases the seriousness of the maladministration and whether there is a need for damages should be capable of being ascertained by an examination of the correspondence and the witness statements.

66. In determining whether damages should be awarded, in the absence of any clear guidance from Strasbourg, principles clearly laid down by the HRA may give the greatest assistance. The critical message is that the remedy has to be "just and appropriate" and "necessary" to afford "just satisfaction". The approach is an equitable one. The "equitable basis" has been cited by the Court of Human Rights both as a reason for awarding damages and as a basis upon which to calculate them. There have been cases where the seriousness or the manner of the violation has meant that as a matter of fairness, the Court of Human Rights has awarded compensation consisting of "moral damages". The Law Commission stated in its report (Law Com No.266) (Cm.4853), para.4.96, that the Court of Human Rights took account of "a range of factors including the character and conduct of the parties, to an extent which is hitherto unknown in English law".

67. The scale and manner of violation can therefore be taken into account. *Scorey & Eicke, Human Rights Damages, Principles and Practice*, para.A2–041 state that:

> "Where particularly grave violations have been found, the European Court of Human Rights is much more willing to accept that the non-pecuniary damage sustained is also more severe and is also more amenable to accepting the claims for pecuniary loss."

The example cited is *Aksoy v Turkey* (1996) 23 EHRR 553, where the applicant had been detained, tortured and finally released without charge and damages were awarded for pecuniary loss and for non-pecuniary loss (distress to the father of the applicant who continued the case after his son had died).

68. In addition to the violation committed being particularly serious, the manner or way in which the violation took place has in some cases been considered sufficiently serious to lead the Court of Human Rights to award damages.

69. *Halford v United Kingdom* (1997) 24 EHRR 523 can be contrasted with *Kopp v Switzerland* (1998) 27 EHRR 91. In the former, the Court of Human Rights considered the police force's surveillances of the applicant's telephone (to obtain information regarding a sex discrimination claim she was pursuing in the employment tribunal) to be a "serious infringement of her rights" (article 8 and 13), particularly in the light of the improper use to which the police wished to put the material obtained: 24 EHRR 523, 550, para.76. The applicant was awarded £10,000 as non-pecuniary damages (even though they rejected her claims that she suffered a stress-related illness as a result of the breach). In contrast, in the latter case, a lawyer whose home telephone was tapped as part of an investigation by the public prosecutor relating to the possibility that his wife was disclosing confidential information from the Department of Justice where she worked (she was subsequently acquitted) was refused his claim, although the monitoring of his telephone lines had seriously perturbed his relations with his family and the members of his firm. The court did not seem to view the breach as having a serious impact. They described the breach of article 8 as meaning simply that the applicant "did not enjoy the minimum degree of protection required by the rule of law in a democratic society" and without giving more reasoning stated that "the finding of a violation of article 8 constitutes sufficient compensation": p.117, para.75 and p.118, para.83.

70. This factor is similar to that called "degree of loss" by the Law Commission in its report, where it states, at para.3.44, that:

"In a number of cases, the Court [of Human Rights] has held that, although the applicant has clearly suffered some non-pecuniary damage, the loss suffered is insufficient to render an award of damages necessary."

For example, in *Silver v United Kingdom* (1983) 5 EHRR 347, a case on unlawful interference with correspondence by prison authorities, the Court of Human Rights stated, at p.63, para.10:

"It is true that those applicants who were in custody may have experienced some annoyance and sense of frustration as a result of the restrictions that were imposed on particular letters. It does not appear, however, that this was of such intensity that it would in itself justify an award of compensation for non-pecuniary damage."

How should damages be assessed?

71. This question arises in relation to injury which is not quantifiable in financial terms. In this jurisdiction the principles governing awards of "general damages" are well established by case precedent. The same is not true of the Strasbourg jurisprudence. *Clayton & Tomlinson* comment, at vol 1, para.21.41:

"If the court decides to award compensation, then it is guided by the particular circumstances in every case, having regard to what it describes as equitable considerations. The court has given little guidance about how the discretion should be exercised, the relevant factors appear to be the applicant's conduct and the extent of the breach."

72. An infringement of a Convention right may have similar consequences to a tort giving rise to a claim under our domestic law—indeed the same act may constitute both a tort and a breach of a Convention right. An example is the comparison between a breach of article 5(1), the right to liberty, and the tort of false imprisonment. Stanley Burnton J had to give consideration to this example in *R (KB) v South London and South and West Region Mental Health Review Tribunal* [2004] QB 936. Where a breach of article 5(4) results in a patient continuing to be detained in a hospital where he would otherwise have been released, the consequence of the breach bears close comparison with the consequences of the tort of false imprisonment. Should the English court, when awarding damages under the HRA, use the damages awarded for the tort of false imprisonment as a model?

73. In considering this question, Stanley Burnton J. referred to a possible principle suggested by Lord Woolf CJ when writing extrajudicially. He suggested that not only should damages be moderate (an approach which has since been endorsed by decisions in this jurisdiction) but also that damages should be on the low side in comparison to those awarded for torts in our courts. This suggestion was criticised by the Law Commission. It was not followed by Sullivan J in *Bernard's* case [2003] LGR 423 nor by Stanley Burnton J. It should in future be ignored.

74. We have made plain that the discretionary exercise of deciding whether to award compensation under the HRA is not to be compared to the approach adopted where damages are claimed for breach of an obligation under civil law. Where, however, in a claim under the HRA, the court decides that it is appropriate to award damages, the levels of damages awarded in respect of torts as reflected in the guidelines issued by the Judicial Studies Board, the levels of awards made by the Criminal Injuries Compensation Board and by the Parliamentary Ombudsman and the Local Government Ombudsman may all provide some rough guidance where the consequences of the infringement of human rights are similar to that being considered in the comparator selected. In cases of maladministration where the consequences are not of a type which gives rise to any right to compensation under our civil law, the awards of the ombudsman may be the only comparator.

75. We have indicated that a finding of a breach of a positive obligation under article 8 to provide support will be rare, and will be likely to occur only where this impacts severely on family life. Where such a breach does occur, it is unlikely that there will be any ready comparator to assist in the assessment of damages. There are good reasons why, where the breach arises from mal-administration, in those cases where an award of damages is appropriate, the scale of such damages should be modest. The cost of supporting those in need falls on society as a whole. Resources are limited and payments of substantial damages will deplete the resources available for other needs of the public including primary care. If the impression is created that asylum seekers whether genuine or not are profiting from their status, this could bring the HRA into disrepute.

76. Similar considerations apply to delay in processing asylum claims or the procedure for admitting the relatives of refugees. Those admitted are likely, at least initially, to require support. In view of the numbers involved, some delay in the processing of asylum claims is inevitable and, at times, in the interest of the asylum seekers themselves, the process is understandably lengthy. The factors that weigh against recognising administrative delay as engaging article 8 militate equally in favour of either no award or modest awards where article 8 is engaged.

77. In *Bernard's* case [2003] LGR 423 Sullivan J observed that an award of damages should not be minimal as this would undermine the respect for Convention rights but that a restrained or moderate approach to quantum would provide the necessary degree of encouragement to public authorities whilst not unduly depleting welfare funds. He rightly observed that there was no comparable tort. He looked for assistance when assessing damages to three comparators: (1) damages for discomfort, inconvenience and injury to health arising out of breaches of repairing covenants in residential tenancies; (2) awards of the Local Government Ombudsman on behalf of disabled persons deprived of benefits or assistance as a result of administration; (3) Judicial Studies Board guidelines for damages for personal injuries where there has been full recovery and where the damages are principally for pain and suffering. He concluded, at p.448, para.60, that the second was the best com-parable as he was dealing with "in essence, an extreme example of malad-ministration which has deprived the [mother] of much needed social services care (suitably adapted accommodation) for a lengthy period: some 20 months". Sullivan J. assessed damages at £10,000–£8,000 to the mother and £2,000 to the father–the total being right at the top end of the range of

relevant awards made by the ombudsman. Sullivan J's award to the mother was also right at the top end of the range of damages that could properly be awarded for a breach of article 8 on the facts of the case before him.

78. We consider that Sullivan J acted appropriately in turning to the awards made by the ombudsman for guidance on the appropriate compensation, indeed the fact that compensation can be obtained from the ombudsman is an important factor when considering questions of procedure, to which we now turn.

What procedures should be followed to ensure that the costs of obtaining relief are proportionate to that relief?

79. In the course of the hearing of these appeals the court asked the parties to indicate the scale of costs incurred by them in the court below. The reason for the request was misunderstood by some of the media and possibly the parties. The object was not to make any criticism of the lawyers before us. On the contrary, from the way the cases have been presented before us we have every reason to believe that they were appropriately conducted in the court below. However, we were concerned that, even if the proceedings were conducted as economically as possible, the cost of the proceedings would be totally out of proportion to the damages likely to be awarded. This has proved to be the position, even after making generous allowance for lack of experience of the parties and the courts with litigation in relation to damages under the HRA and the fact that initially the relief sought included other remedies in addition to damages. The precise figures are not important. What is important is that in each case the combined costs of both sides were many times greater than the damages that could reasonably have been anticipated. The costs at first instance of each party were totally disproportionate to the amount involved. When the total costs of both sides are looked at, including the appeal, the figures are truly horrendous, and the situation is made even more worrying by the fact that all the parties are funded out of public funds and this court sought, as no doubt did the courts below, to try to save costs by engaging in an intensive reading programme out of court. When we deal with the individual cases we shall set out the costs that have been incurred.

80. The reality is that a claim for damages under the HRA in respect of maladministration, whether brought as a free-standing claim or ancillary to a claim for other substantive relief, if pursued in court by adversarial proceedings, is likely to cost substantially more to try than the amount of any damages that are likely to be awarded. Furthermore, as we have made plain, there will often be no certainty that an entitlement to damages will be established at all.

81. What can be done to avoid a repetition of this situation in future proceedings? Based on the experience available at present we suggest as follows in relation to proceedings which include a claim for damages for maladministration under the HRA.

(i) The courts should look critically at any attempt to recover damages under the HRA for maladministration by any procedure other than judicial review in the Administrative Court.
(ii) A claim for damages alone cannot be brought by judicial review (CPR r 54.3(2)) but in this case the proceedings should still be brought in the Administrative Court by an ordinary claim.

(iii) Before giving permission to apply for judicial review, the Administrative Court judge should require the claimant to explain why it would not be more appropriate to use any available internal complaint procedure or proceed by making a claim to the Parliamentary Commissioner for Administration or Local Government Ombudsman at least in the first instance. The complaint procedures of the Parliamentary Commissioner for Administration and the Local Government Ombudsman are designed to deal economically (the claimant pays no costs and does not require a lawyer) and expeditiously with claims for compensation for maladministration. (From inquiries the court has made it is apparent that the time scale of resolving complaints compares favourably with that of litigation.)

(iv) If there is a legitimate claim for other relief, permission should if appropriate be limited to that relief and consideration given to deferring permission for the damages claim, adjourning or staying that claim until use has been made of alternative dispute resolution, whether by a reference to a mediator or an ombudsman or otherwise, or remitting that claim to a district judge or master if it cannot be dismissed summarily on grounds that in any event an award of damages is not required to achieve just satisfaction.

(v) It is hoped that with the assistance of this judgment, in future claims that have to be determined by the courts can be determined by the appropriate level of judge in a summary manner by the judge reading the relevant evidence. The citing of more than three authorities should be justified and the hearing should be limited to half a day except in exceptional circumstances.

(vi) There are no doubt other ways in which the proportionate resolution of this type of claim for damages can be achieved. We encourage their use and do not intend to be prescriptive. What we want to avoid is any repetition of what has happened in the court below in relation to each of these appeals and before us, when we have been deluged with extensive written and oral arguments and citation from numerous lever arch files crammed to overflowing with authorities. The exercise that has taken place may be justifiable on one occasion but it will be difficult to justify again.

[Newman J.'s decision in *Anufrijeva* that on the facts the council had in fact been assiduous in seeking to accommodate the special needs of one family member was upheld; Silber J.'s decision in *N* was reversed on the ground that on the facts there was no infringement of Art.8. Silber J. had held that the defendant knew or ought to have been aware that N was suffering or at risk of degrading or humiliating treatment of the kind necessary to engage Art.8. The Court of Appeal held that foreseeability that an important adverse decision might cause psychiatric harm if the recipient were particularly vulnerable was not enough. His Lordship continued:]

143. . . . Where the breach of a human right has the incidental effect of causing psychiatric harm, that fact can properly be reflected in an award of damages. That, however, is not this case. Here it is the causing of the psychiatric harm which has itself been held to be the infringement of article 8. Where a public authority commits acts which it knows are likely to cause psychiatric harm to an individual, those acts are capable of constituting an infringement

of article 8. Maladministration will not, however, infringe article 8 simply because it causes stress that leads a particularly susceptible individual to suffer such harm in circumstances where this was not reasonably to be anticipated. No lack of respect for private life is manifested in such circumstances. The eggshell skull principle forms no part of the test of breach of duty under the HRA or the Convention . . .

[Richard J.'s decision in *M* that there was no breach of Art.8 was upheld. There were numerous administrative failings, some but not all the delay was the responsibility of the authorities, but there was also evidence of people trying to move things along, and overall, no lack of respect for the claimant's family life.]

Appeal in N *allowed; appeals in* Anufrijeva *and* M *dismissed.*

Note

1. This case illustrates a conundrum. The levels of damages awards for cases of this kind contemplated by the Court of Appeal are such that expensive High Court procedures are clearly not proportionate where a damages award is the only issue. The recognition that a complaint to an ombudsman is often a more suitable procedure is welcome, and adds weight to the case for the development of a closer and more flexible relationship between the processes of courts and of ombudsmen (see further above, p.172). The question whether the consequences for an individual of the state's inaction are so severe as to constitute a breach of Art.3 or (exceptionally, as in *Bernard*, Art.8(1)) is a very difficult question of fact. One advantage of the ombudsmen's jurisdiction is that they can recommend the award of compensation for maladministration whether or not it has caused an infringement of Convention rights, and so does not depend on a conclusive determination of this difficult question.

2. On the availability of a negligence remedy for maladministration, see below, p.1068. This is available as of right if the ingredients are established but the awards may be limited to proved economic losses or psychiatric damage.

3. Unusually, the Crown as a public authority may incur direct liability for an unlawful act under ss.7 and 8. The Crown is normally can only be held vicariously liable for the tort of an individual Crown servant (see the *Chagos Islanders* case, below, p.1099).

4. For further discussion see D. Fairgrieve, "The Human Rights Act 1998, Damages and Tort Law" [2001] P.L. 695.

(E) THE AREA OF DISCRETIONARY JUDGMENT AND PROPORTIONALITY

The jurisprudence of the ECtHR recognises that in some contexts Member States are accorded a "margin of appreciation." This takes account of the fact that the ECHR machinery is subsidiary to the national systems safeguarding human rights, leaving to those systems in the first instance the task of securing the Convention rights and freedoms, and the point that some of the concepts enshrined in the ECHR articles do not have a uniform European content (*Handyside v UK* (1976) 1 E.H.R.R. 737 at para.48). It is accordingly for state authorities to make the initial assessment of such questions as whether a restriction on freedom of expression is "necessary in a democratic society . . . for the protection of morals" (Art.10(2)), and those authorities are left "a margin of appreciation". Their decisions are then subject to "supervision" by the ECtHR, which must decide whether the reasons given by national authorities to justify measures of "interference" are relevant and sufficient, applying a test of proportionality (*ibid.*, paras 49, 50). The scope of the margin of appreciation varies according to context. So, for example, the concept of "maintaining the authority . . . of the judiciary" (also in Art.10(2)) has a "far more objective notion" than the protection of morals, the domestic law and practice of Member States revealing "a fairly substantial measure of common ground." Here, "a more extensive European supervision corresponds to a less discretionary power of appreciation" (*Sunday Times v UK (No.1)* (1979) 2 E.H.R.R. 245 at para.59). Contexts in which a margin of appreciation has been recognised include the establishment of justifications for interference with protected rights and freedoms under para.2 of Arts 8 to 11; areas where the article in question contains vague expressions (*e.g.* the justifications for a derogation under Art.15: *Lawless v Ireland (No.3)* (1961) 1 E.H.R.R. 15 at para.207)); and areas where the ECtHR has to determine whether a state has failed to comply with a positive obligation to protect a Convention right (*e.g. TP and KM v UK*, below, p.1070).

The margin of appreciation does not as such apply where an English court is reviewing decisions and acts of public authorities under the HRA 1998. It would accordingly be possible in each case where an issue arises whether an interference with a Convention right is proportionate for the court itself to balance the relevant factors and form a primary judgment on that matter. In one sense this is indeed the position, in that whether an interference proportionate is a question of law for the court to determine, the court not being confined to a review of the opinion of the decision-maker (whether human being, public body or Parliament) on the matter. Nevertheless, it is only exceptionally that the court will itself balance the relevant factors while attaching no weight (one way or the other) to the decision-maker's opinion. The courts have accepted that there are areas where the decision-maker enjoys a "discretionary area of judgment" where "the judiciary will defer, on democratic grounds, to the considered opinion of the elected body or person whose act or decision is said to be incompatible with the Convention" (*per* Lord Hope of Craighead in *R. v DPP Ex p. Kebiline* [2000] 2 A.C. 326 at 380–381). The extent of "deference," where it exists, varies according to context. It is impossible sensibly to argue that in no case should the opinion of the decision-maker be accorded any weight at all. There is then room for significant debate as to the principles that should guide the courts in determining how much weight should be accorded to the decision-maker's opinion in particular contexts. It has also been doubted whether the term "deference" correctly captures the essence of the idea.

The main cases in this section are the leading authority on proportionality (*Daly*), and the landmark decision in the *Belmarsh prisoners* case (below p.351).

R. (ON THE APPLICATION OF DALY) v SECRETARY OF STATE FOR THE HOME DEPARTMENT

[2001] UKHL 26; [2001] 2 A.C. 532; [2001] 2 W.L.R. 1622; [2001] 3 All E.R. 433 (HOUSE OF LORDS)

D was a long-term prisoner. He stored in his cell correspondence with his solicitor about his security categorisation reviews and parole. All prisoners were subject to a standard cell searching policy contained in the Security Manual issued by the Secretary of State as an instruction to prison governors. The Secretary of State had power under s.47(1) of the Prison Act 1952 to make rules for the regulation and control of prisoners. The policy was introduced in 1995, implementing the recommendations of a review that followed the escape of six category A prisoners from HM Prison Whitemoor. It required that prisoners be excluded during cell searches to prevent intimidation and to prevent prisoners acquiring a detailed knowledge of search techniques. It provided the officers were to examine, but not read, any legal correspondence in the cell to check that nothing had been written on it by the prisoner, or stored within its leaves, which was likely to endanger prison security. D's application for judicial review of the decision to require examination of prisoners' legally privileged correspondence in their absence was rejected by the Court of Appeal. The House of Lords unanimously allowed an appeal.

The legal background

5. Any custodial order inevitably curtails the enjoyment, by the person confined, of rights enjoyed by other citizens. He cannot move freely and choose his associates as they are entitled to do. It is indeed an important objective of such an order to curtail such rights, whether to punish him or to protect other members of the public or both. But the order does not wholly deprive the person confined of all rights enjoyed by other citizens. Some rights, perhaps in an attenuated or qualified form, survive the making of the order. And it may well be that the importance of such surviving rights is enhanced by the loss or partial loss of other rights. Among the rights which, in part at least, survive are three important rights, closely related but free standing, each of them calling for appropriate legal protection: the right of access to a court; the right of access to legal advice; and the right to communicate confidentially with a legal adviser under the seal of legal professional privilege. Such rights may be curtailed only by clear and express words, and then only to the extent reasonably necessary to meet the ends which justify the curtailment.

6. These propositions rest on a solid base of recent authority.

[His Lordship cited *R. v Board of Visitors of Hull Prison Ex p. St Germain* [1979] Q.B. 425, 455; *Raymond v Honey* [1983] 1 A.C. 1; *R. v Secretary of State for the Home Department Ex p. Anderson* [1984] Q.B. 778; *Campbell v UK* (1992) 15 E.H.R.R. 137; *R. v Secretary of State for the Home Department Ex p. Leech* [1994] Q.B. 198; *Ex p. Simms* (above, p.261); and *Ex p. Pierson*, (see above, p.251).]

15. It is necessary, first, to ask whether the policy infringes in a significant way Mr Daly's common law right that the confidentiality of privileged legal correspondence be maintained. He submits that it does for two related reasons: first, because knowledge that such correspondence may be looked at by prison officers in the absence of the prisoner inhibits the prisoner's willingness to communicate with his legal adviser in terms of unreserved candour; and secondly, because there must be a risk, if the prisoner is not present, that the officers will stray beyond their limited role in examining legal correspondence, particularly if, for instance, they see some name or reference familiar to them, as would be the case if the prisoner were bringing or contemplating bringing proceedings against officers in the prison. For the Home Secretary it is argued that the policy involves no infringement of a prisoner's common law right since his privileged correspondence is not read in his absence but only examined.

16. I have no doubt that the policy infringes Mr Daly's common law right to legal professional privilege. This was the view of two very experienced judges in *R v Secretary of State for the Home Deprtment, Ex p. Simms* [1999] QB 349, against which decision the present appeal is effectively brought. At p.366, Kennedy LJ said:

"In my judgment legal professional privilege does attach to correspondence with legal advisers which is stored by a prisoner in his cell, and accordingly such correspondence is to be protected from any unnecessary interference by prison staff. Even if the correspondence is only inspected to see that it is what it purports to be that is likely to impair the free flow of communication between a convicted or remand prisoner on the one hand and his legal adviser on the other, and therefore it constitutes an impairment of the privilege."

Judge LJ was of the same opinion. At p.373, he said:

> "Prisoners whose cells are searched in their absence will find it difficult to believe that their correspondence has been searched but not read. The governor's order will sometimes be disobeyed. Accordingly I am prepared to accept the potential 'chilling effect' of such searches."

In an imperfect world there will necessarily be occasions when prison officers will do more than merely examine prisoners' legal documents, and apprehension that they may do so is bound to inhibit a prisoner's willingness to communicate freely with his legal adviser.

17. The next question is whether there can be any ground for infringing in any way a prisoner's right to maintain the confidentiality of his privileged legal correspondence. Plainly there can. Some examination may well be necessary to establish that privileged legal correspondence is what it appears to be and is not a hiding place for illicit materials or information prejudicial to security or good order.

18. It is then necessary to ask whether, to the extent that it infringes a prisoner's common law right to privilege, the policy can be justified as a necessary and proper response to the acknowledged need to maintain security, order and discipline in prisons and to prevent crime. Mr Daly's challenge at this point is directed to the blanket nature of the policy, applicable as it is to all prisoners of whatever category in all closed prisons in England and Wales, irrespective of a prisoner's past or present conduct and of any operational emergency or urgent intelligence. The Home Secretary's justification rests firmly on the points already mentioned: the risk of intimidation, the risk that staff may be conditioned by prisoners to relax security and the danger of disclosing searching methods.

19. In considering these justifications, based as they are on the extensive experience of the prison service, it must be recognised that the prison population includes a core of dangerous, disruptive and manipulative prisoners, hostile to authority and ready to exploit for their own advantage any concession granted to them. Any search policy must accommodate this inescapable fact. I cannot however accept that the reasons put forward justify the policy in its present blanket form. Any prisoner who attempts to intimidate or disrupt a search of his cell, or whose past conduct shows that he is likely to do so, may properly be excluded even while his privileged correspondence is examined so as to ensure the efficacy of the search, but no justification is shown for routinely excluding all prisoners, whether intimidatory or disruptive or not, while that part of the search is conducted. Save in the extraordinary conditions prevailing at Whitemoor before September 1994, it is hard to regard the conditioning of staff as a problem which could not be met by employing dedicated search teams. It is not suggested that prison officers when examining legal correspondence employ any sophisticated technique which would be revealed to the prisoner if he were present, although he might no doubt be encouraged to secrete illicit materials among his legal papers if the examination were obviously very cursory. The policy cannot in my opinion be justified in its present blanket form. The infringement of prisoners' rights to maintain the confidentiality of their privileged legal correspondence is greater than is shown to be necessary to serve the legitimate public objectives already identified. I accept Mr Daly's submission on this point.

[His Lordship stated that he was fortified in reaching this conclusion by four considerations: (1) a recommendation by the Prisons Ombudsman that a revised procedure suggested by the Security Group be adopted, whereby legal documents are placed in a sealed tag and only searched in the prisoner's presence; (2) the adoption of such a procedure by HPM Full Sutton which did not appear to give rise to difficulty in practice; (3) the rule for cell searches in Scotland that they be conducted by at least two officers, in the prisoner's presence suggested that generally permitting a prisoner to be present during a search of legal correspondence unless there are good reasons for exclusion was not unworkable in practice; (4) only two items of illicit property had been found among legal documents and the great majority of items found in cell searches could not have been concealed that way.]

21. In *R v Secretary of State for the Home Department, Ex p. Simms* [1999] QB 349 and again in the present case, the Court of Appeal held that the policy represented the minimum intrusion into the rights of prisoners consistent with the need to maintain security, order and discipline in prisons. That is a conclusion which I respect but cannot share. In my opinion the policy provides for a degree of intrusion into the privileged legal correspondence of prisoners which is greater than is justified by the objectives the policy is intended to serve, and so violates the common law rights of prisoners. Section 47(1) of the 1952 Act does not authorise such excessive intrusion, and the Home Secretary accordingly had no power to lay down or implement the policy in its present form. I would accordingly declare paragraphs 17.69 to 17.74 of the Security Manual to be unlawful and void in so far as they provide that prisoners must always be absent when privileged legal correspondence held by them in their cells is examined by prison officers.

22. Although, in response to a request by the House during argument, counsel for Mr Daly proffered a draft rule which might be adopted to govern the searching of privileged legal correspondence, it would be inappropriate for the House to attempt to formulate or approve the terms of such a rule, which would call for careful consideration and consultation before it was finalised. It is enough to indicate that any rule should provide for a general right for prisoners to be present when privileged legal correspondence is examined, and in practice this will probably mean any legal documentation to avoid time-wasting debate about which documents are privileged and which are not. But the rule must provide for the exclusion of the prisoner while the examination takes place if there is or is reasonably believed to be good cause for excluding him to safeguard the efficacy of the search, and the rule must permit the prison authorities to respond to sudden operational emergencies or urgent intelligence.

23. I have reached the conclusions so far expressed on an orthodox application of common law principles derived from the authorities and an orthodox domestic approach to judicial review. But the same result is achieved by reliance on the European Convention. Article 8(1) gives Mr Daly a right to respect for his correspondence. While interference with that right by a public authority may be permitted if in accordance with the law and necessary in a democratic society in the interests of national security, public safety, the prevention of disorder or crime or for protection of the rights and freedoms of others, the policy interferes with Mr Daly's exercise of his right under article 8(1) to an extent much greater than necessity requires. In this instance, therefore, the common law and the Convention yield the same result. But this need not always be so. In *Smith and Grady v United Kingdom* (1999) 29 EHRR

493, the European Court held that the orthodox domestic approach of the English courts had not given the applicants an effective remedy for the breach of their rights under article 8 of the Convention because the threshold of review had been set too high. Now, following the incorporation of the Convention by the Human Rights Act 1998 and the bringing of that Act fully into force, domestic courts must themselves form a judgment whether a Convention right has been breached (conducting such inquiry as is necessary to form that judgment) and, so far as permissible under the Act, grant an effective remedy. On this aspect of the case, I agree with and adopt the observations of my noble and learned friends Lord Steyn and Lord Cooke of Thorndon which I have had the opportunity of reading in draft.

LORD STEYN

24. My Lords, I am in complete agreement with the reasons given by Lord Bingham of Cornhill in his speech. For the reasons he gives I would also allow the appeal. Except on one narrow but important point I have nothing to add.

25. There was written and oral argument on the question whether certain observations of Lord Phillips of Worth Matravers MR in *R (Mahmood) v Secretary of State for the Home Department* [2001] 1 WLR 840 were correct. The context was an immigration case involving a decision of the Secretary of State made before the Human Rights Act 1998 came into effect. The Master of the Rolls nevertheless approached the case as if the Act had been in force when the Secretary of State reached his decision. He explained the new approach to be adopted. The Master of the Rolls concluded, at p.857, para.40:

"When anxiously scrutinising an executive decision that interferes with human rights, the court will ask the question, applying an objective test, whether the decision-maker could reasonably have concluded that the interference was necessary to achieve one or more of the legitimate aims recognised by the Convention. When considering the test of necessity in the relevant context, the court must take into account the European jurisprudence in accordance with section 2 of the 1998 Act."

These observations have been followed by the Court of Appeal in *R (Isiko) v Secretary of State for the Home Department* The Times, 20 February 2001; Court of Appeal (Civil Division) Transcript No 2272 of 2000 and by Thomas J in *R (Samaroo) v Secretary of State for the Home Department* (unreported) 20 December 2000.

26. The explanation of the Master of the Rolls in the first sentence of the cited passage requires clarification. It is couched in language reminiscent of the traditional *Wednesbury* ground of review (*Associated Provincial Picture Houses Ltd v Wednesbury Corpn* [1948] 1 KB 223), and in particular the adaptation of that test in terms of heightened scrutiny in cases involving fundamental rights as formulated in *R v Ministry of Defence, Ex p. Smith* [1996] QB 517, 554E-G per Sir Thomas Bingham MR. There is a material difference between the *Wednesbury* and *Smith* grounds of review and the approach of proportionality applicable in respect of review where Convention rights are at stake.

27. The contours of the principle of proportionality are familiar. In *de Freitas v Permanent Secretary of Ministry of Agriculture, Fisheries, Lands and Housing* [1999] 1 AC 69 the Privy Council adopted a three-stage test. Lord

Clyde observed, at p.80, that in determining whether a limitation (by an act, rule or decision) is arbitrary or excessive the court should ask itself:

> "whether: (i) the legislative objective is sufficiently important to justify limiting a fundamental right; (ii) the measures designed to meet the legislative objective are rationally connected to it; and (iii) the means used to impair the right or freedom are no more than is necessary to accomplish the objective."

Clearly, these criteria are more precise and more sophisticated than the traditional grounds of review. What is the difference for the disposal of concrete cases? Academic public lawyers have in remarkably similar terms elucidated the difference between the traditional grounds of review and the proportionality approach: see Professor Jeffrey Jowell QC, "Beyond the Rule of Law: Towards Constitutional Judicial Review" [2000] PL 671; Professor Paul Craig, *Administrative Law*, 4th ed (1999), pp.561–563; Professor David Feldman, "Proportionality and the Human Rights Act 1998", essay in *The Principle of Proportionality in the Laws of Europe* edited by Evelyn Ellis (1999), pp.117, 127 et seq. The starting point is that there is an overlap between the traditional grounds of review and the approach of proportionality. Most cases would be decided in the same way whichever approach is adopted. But the intensity of review is somewhat greater under the proportionality approach. Making due allowance for important structural differences between various convention rights, which I do not propose to discuss, a few generalisations are perhaps permissible. I would mention three concrete differences without suggesting that my statement is exhaustive. First, the doctrine of proportionality may require the reviewing court to assess the balance which the decision maker has struck, not merely whether it is within the range of rational or reasonable decisions. Secondly, the proportionality test may go further than the traditional grounds of review inasmuch as it may require attention to be directed to the relative weight accorded to interests and considerations. Thirdly, even the heightened scrutiny test developed in *R v Ministry of Defence, Ex p Smith* [1996] QB 517, 554 is not necessarily appropriate to the protection of human rights. It will be recalled that in *Smith* the Court of Appeal reluctantly felt compelled to reject a limitation on homosexuals in the army. The challenge based on article 8 of the Convention for the Protection of Human Rights and Fundamental Freedoms (the right to respect for private and family life) foundered on the threshold required even by the anxious scrutiny test. The European Court of Human Rights came to the opposite conclusion: *Smith and Grady v United Kingdom* (1999) 29 EHRR 493. The court concluded, at p.543, para.138:

> "the threshold at which the High Court and the Court of Appeal could find the Ministry of Defence policy irrational was placed so high that it effectively excluded any consideration by the domestic courts of the question of whether the interference with the applicants' rights answered a pressing social need or was proportionate to the national security and public order aims pursued, principles which lie at the heart of the court's analysis of complaints under article 8 of the Convention."

In other words, the intensity of the review, in similar cases, is guaranteed by the twin requirements that the limitation of the right was necessary in a democratic society, in the sense of meeting a pressing social need, and the question whether the interference was really proportionate to the legitimate aim being pursued.

28. The differences in approach between the traditional grounds of review and the proportionality approach may therefore sometimes yield different results. It is therefore important that cases involving Convention rights must be analysed in the correct way. This does not mean that there has been a shift to merits review. On the contrary, as Professor Jowell [2000] PL 671, 681 has pointed out the respective roles of judges and administrators are fundamentally distinct and will remain so. To this extent the general tenor of the observations in *Mahmood* [2001] 1 WLR 840 are correct. And Laws LJ rightly emphasised in *Mahmood*, at p.847, para.18, "that the intensity of review in a public law case will depend on the subject matter in hand". That is so even in cases involving Convention rights. In law context is everything.

LORD COOKE OF THORNDON

29. My Lords, having had the advantage of reading in draft the speeches of my noble and learned friends, Lord Bingham of Cornhill and Lord Steyn, I am in full agreement with them. I add some brief observations on two matters, less to supplement what they have said than to underline its importance.

30. First, while this case has arisen in a jurisdiction where the European Convention for the Protection of Human Rights and Fundamental Freedoms applies, and while the case is one in which the Convention and the common law produce the same result, it is of great importance, in my opinion, that the common law by itself is being recognised as a sufficient source of the fundamental right to confidential communication with a legal adviser for the purpose of obtaining legal advice. Thus the decision may prove to be in point in common law jurisdictions not affected by the Convention. Rights similar to those in the Convention are of course to be found in constitutional documents and other formal affirmations of rights elsewhere. The truth is, I think, that some rights are inherent and fundamental to democratic civilised society. Conventions, constitutions, bills of rights and the like respond by recognising rather than creating them.

31. To essay any list of these fundamental, perhaps ultimately universal, rights is far beyond anything required for the purpose of deciding the present case. It is enough to take the three identified by Lord Bingham: in his words, access to a court; access to legal advice; and the right to communicate confidentially with a legal adviser under the seal of legal professional privilege. As he says authoritatively from the woolsack, such rights may be curtailed only by clear and express words, and then only to the extent reasonably necessary to meet the ends which justify the curtailment. The point that I am emphasising is that the common law goes so deep.

32. The other matter concerns degrees of judicial review. Lord Steyn illuminates the distinctions between "traditional" (that is to say in terms of English case law, *Wednesbury*) standards of judicial review and higher standards under the European Convention or the common law of human rights. As he indicates, often the results are the same. But the view that the standards are substantially the same appears to have received its quietus in *Smith and Grady v United Kingdom* (1999) 29 EHRR 493 and *Lustig-Prean and Beckett v United Kingdom* (1999) 29 EHRR 548. And I think that the day will come when it will be more widely recognised that *Associated Provincial Picture Houses Ltd v Wednesbury Corpn* [1948] 1 KB 223 was an unfortunately retrogressive decision in English administrative law, in so far as it suggested that there are degrees of unreasonableness and that only a very extreme degree can bring an administrative decision within the legitimate scope of judicial invalidation. The depth of judicial review and the deference due to administrative discretion vary with the subject matter. It may well be, however, that the law can never be satisfied in any administrative field merely by a finding that the decision under review is not capricious or absurd.

33. I, too, would therefore allow the present appeal.

LORDS HUTTON AND SCOTT OF FOSCOTE agreed with LORD BINGHAM, and with LORD STEYN'S observations on *Mahmood*. LORD SCOTT also agreed with LORD COOKE.

Appeal allowed

Notes

1. The *Daly* case is a good illustration of an over-inclusive policy whose unjustifiable interference with fundamental rights could be cured relatively straightforwardly. It was both unlawful at common law and a breach of Art.8(1) ECHR (the applicability of the HRA 1998 itself was not argued).

2. Lord Steyn's opinion on the proper approach to proportionality has been frequently cited. Lord Cooke's can also be seen as a step in the journey that is likely to lead to the formal adoption of proportionality in place of *Wednesbury* unreasonableness or irrationality as a ground of judicial review of general application (see below, p.630).

3. Further consideration of proportionality was given by the Court of Appeal in *R. (on the application of Samaroo) v Secretary of State for the Home Department* [2001] EWCA Civ 1139; [2001] U.K.H.R.R. 1150. Here the Court held that in deciding what proportionality requires in any particular case the issue will normally have to be considered in two stages. The first question is "can the objective of the measure be achieved by means which are less interfering of an individual's rights?" At the second stage, it is assumed that the means employed are necessary in the sense that they are "the least intrusive of Convention rights that can be devised in order to achieve the aim". The question here is "does the measure have an excessive or disproportionate effect on the interests of affected persons?". The *Daly* case illustrated the application of the first question: the blanket policy was unlawful as the legitimate aim of maintaining security in prison would be met by a rule that entitled prisoner officers to examine privileged correspondence of an individual prisoner who was attempting to intimidate or disrupt a search, or whose past conduct had shown that he was likely to do so.

The *Samaroo* case illustrated the application of the second question. It was clear that in general terms the objective of preventing crime and disorder was sufficiently important to justify limiting a fundamental right (here the right to family life) and that the deportation of those convicted of serious criminal offences (especially, as here, drug trafficking offences) was a measure rationally connected to that objective. The only issue here was whether a deportation had a disproportionate effect on the applicant's rights under Art.8(1). The task of the Secretary of State was within his discretionary area of judgement to "strike a fair balance" between the legitimate aim and the affected person's Convention rights. The task of the court in reviewing his decision was supervisory of that discretionary area of judgment. It had to decide:

"whether the Secretary of State has struck the balance fairly between the conflicting interests of [the applicant's] right to respect for his family life on the one hand and the prevention of crime and disorder on the other. In reaching its decision, the court must recognise and allow to the Secretary of State a discretionary area of judgment".

Factors relevant in determining to what extent (if at all) there should be deference to the decision-maker included (based on Lord Lester and D. Pannick (ed.), *Human Rights Law and Practice* (1999), para.3.26):

(a)	the nature of the Convention right; is it absolute or does it require a balance to be struck? The court is less likely to defer to the decision-maker in the former case;
(b)	the extent to which the issues require consideration of social, economic or political factors; the court will usually accord considerable deference in such cases because it is not expert in the realm of policy making, nor should it be because it is not democratically elected or accountable;
(c)	the extent to which the court has special expertise, for example in relation to criminal matters; and
(d)	where the rights claimed are of especial importance (*e.g.* freedom of expression and access to the courts) a "high degree of constitutional protection" will be appropriate.

In the present case, a "significant margin of discretion" to the decision of the Secretary of State was appropriate. The Convention right was not absolute and the court did not have expertise in judging how effective the deportation policy was as a deterrent. It was for the Secretary of State to show that he had struck a fair balance. How much weight he gave to each factor would be the subject of careful scrutiny by the court and the court would interfere with the weight accorded by the decision-maker, "if, despite an allowance for the appropriate margin of discretion, it concludes that the weight accorded was unfair and unreasonable" (at [39]).

On the facts of *Samaroo*, the Secretary of State was entitled to regard Class A drug trafficking offences as very serious; to attach importance to his general policy of deporting those convicted of importation of Class A drugs to protect UK residents and to deter others; and to attach particular weight to the applicant's role as a "crucial part of the organisation". He recognised the serious interference with the applicant's right to family life under Art.8(1). Overall, the Secretary of State's conclusion was a "fair and reasonable conclusion that he was entitled to reach" (at [41]).

Note also Laws L.J.'s formulation of four principles stating how UK courts should approach the issue of deference: *R. (on the application of International Transport Roth GmbH) v Secretary of State for the Home Department* [2003] Q.B. 728 at [83]–[87]. These are that:

(1)	"greater deference is to be paid to an Act of Parliament than a decision of the Executive or subordinate measure;
(2)	there is more scope for deference "where the Convention itself requires a balance to be struck much less where the right is stated in terms which are unqualified;
(3)	greater deference will be due to the democratic powers where the subject-matter in hand is peculiarly within their constitutional responsibility and less when it lies more particularly with the constitutional responsibility of the courts;
(4)	greater or lesser deference will be due according to whether the subject-matter lies more readily with the actual or potential expertise of the democratic powers or the courts".

Laws L.J., dissented on the outcome of the case.

Laws L.J.'s general approach said to be "of great interest" by Lord Walker of Gestingthorpe in *R. (on the application of Prolife Alliance) v BBC* [2003] UKHL 23; [2004] 1 A.C. 185 at [136], but agreed (at [144]) with Lord Hoffmann (at [74]–[76]) that "deference" "(Simply as a matter of the English language) . . . may not be the best word to use if only because it is liable to be misunderstood".

Lord Hoffmann said:

"75. My Lords, although the word 'deference' is now very popular in describing the relationship between the judicial and other branches of government, I do not think that its overtones of servility, or perhaps gracious concession, are appropriate to describe what is happening. In a society based upon the rule of law and the separation of powers, it is necessary to describe which branch of government has in any particular instance the decision-making power and what the legal limits of that power are. That is a question of law and must therefore be decided by the courts.

76. This means that the courts themselves often have to decide the limits of their own decision-making power. That is inevitable. But it does not mean that their allocation of decision-making power to the other branches of government is a matter of courtesy or deference. The principles upon which decision-making powers are allocated are principles of law. The courts are the independent branch of government and the legislature and executive are, directly and indirectly respectively, the elected branches of government. Independence makes the courts more suited to deciding some kinds of questions and being elected makes the legislature or executive more suited to deciding others. The allocation of these decision-making responsibilities is based upon recognised principles. The principle that the independence of the courts is necessary for a proper decision of disputed legal rights or claims of violation of human rights is a legal principle. It is reflected in article 6 of the Convention. On the other hand, the principle that majority approval is necessary for a proper decision on policy or allocation of resources is also a legal principle. Likewise, when a court decides that a decision is within the proper competence of the legislature or executive, it is not showing deference. It is deciding the law. . .".

This approach has been criticized by Lord Steyn, in "Deference: A Tangled Story" [2005] P.L. 346, where he argues that deference is not a matter of law but a "matter of discretion to be exercised in the objective circumstances of the particular case" (p.350). The degree of deference appropriate depends on and varies with the context. The true justification for it is "the relative institutional competence or capacity of the branches of Government" (p.352). There cannot be a legal principle requiring the court to desist from making judgments in cases concerning policy or the allocation of scarce resources (p.357). The courts cannot be required automatically to defer to the views of persons who have been elected (p.358). (Do Lord Hoffmann's views go that far?) Compare Lord Bingham's comments in *A v Secretary of State for the Home Department*, below, p.351.

In the second edition of *Lester and Pannick*, factors relevant in deciding what discretionary area of judgment to accord are set out in para.3.21. Additional factors mentioned to those listed in *Samaroo* are (1) the degree of interference with the rights in question; (2) the constitutional status of the decision-maker; and (3) the existence or non-existence of common ground between the laws of the contracting states.

4. It has subsequently been held that the first *Samaroo* stage will not be appropriate in cases where the interests of parties other than the state have to be balanced: *Lough v First Secretary of State* [2004] EWCA Civ 905; *R. (on the application of Lloyds Housing Co-operative Ltd v Housing Corporation)* [2004] EWCA Civ 1658. In *Lough*, a reasonable balance was to be struck between the claimant's loss of amenity, arising from the implementation of a project the grant of planning permission for which was challenged, and infringing Art.8(1) interests, and the interests of the prospective developing landowner (protected by the First Protocol, Art.1). It is indeed difficult to see how the first *Samaroo* question could appropriately be investigated in these circumstances.

5. Cases where an infringement has been found on the ground of lack of proportionality, and survived an appeal, are rare. Examples include *Daly* (where the decision was unlawful on common law grounds as well); *R. (on the application of Hirst) v Secretary of State for the Home Department* [2002] EWHC Admin 602; [2002]

1 W.L.R. 2929 (policy imposing blanket ban on prisoner having contact with the media held unlawful by Elias J.); and *A v Secretary of State for the Home Department* (below, p.351).

Cases were finding of lack of proportionality have been overturned on appeal include *R. (on the application of Farrakhan) v Secretary of State for the Home Department* [2002] EWCA Civ 606; [2002] 2 Q.B. 1391, when the Court of Appeal upheld the Secretary of State's decision to maintain the exclusion of F from the United Kingdom, following an application to enter for a particular visit. F, the spiritual leader of the Nation of Islam, had made public pronouncements in the United States, in extreme language, accusing wealthy Jews of exploiting black people. Turner J. ([2001] EWHC Admin 781) quashed the decision on the ground that the Secretary of State had not justified the restriction on freedom of expression under Art.10 (2). He had not shown there was more than a "nominal risk" that community relations would be harmed if the visit was permitted (essentially a risk of disorder), and had therefore failed to demonstrate objective justification for the exclusion. The Court of Appeal found that the reason for the exclusion was the risk that F's presence in the United Kingdom "might prove a catalyst for disorder" (at [58]). The court (at [71]–[79]) held that there were factors that made it "appropriate to accord a particular wide margin of discretion to the Secretary of State". These were that the case concerned an immigration decision, the ECtHR attaching considerable weight to the right under international law of a state to control immigration into its territory; the decision in question was the personal decision of the Secretary of State after detailed consideration, involving widespread consultation; the Secretary of State was far better placed to reach an informed decision as to the likely consequences of admitting F to the United Kingdom than the court; the Secretary of State was democratically accountable for this decision. There was force in the submission that these considerations were not reflected in Turner J.'s judgment, "but that he had replaced his own evaluation of the relevant facts for that of the minister". The court noted that the restriction on F's freedom of expression was limited; he was not prevented from communicating his views within the UK by other means. While it would have been better if the minister had been "less diffident about explaining the nature of the information and advice that he had received", and the merits of the appeal were "finely balanced", the court concluded that he had provided sufficient explanation to demonstrate that his decision, made for the purpose of the prevention of disorder, did not involve a disproportionate interference with freedom of expression.

It is submitted that the approach of the Court of Appeal is unsatisfactory, in that in the absence of full information, it was prepared to trust the Home Secretary to have made the correct judgment as to the proportionality of the decision. The court's position would have been stronger if, having been apprised of all the relevant information (subject to any possible claim of public interest immunity), it chose, in coming to its own view in what it agreed was a borderline case, to attach decisive weight to the opinion of the Secretary of State as to the level of risk.

5. In some cases, it has been held that the court must itself conduct the relevant balancing exercise and determine for itself whether the interference with the claimant's Convention rights is proportionate. This may be because there is no "decision" to which there could be "deference" or the decision that there is does not deserve any deference. Examples include an exercise of discretion by the High Court to grant injunctive relief to enforce planning legislation (*South Bucks DC v Porter* [2003] UKHL 26; [2003] 2 A.C. 558). Here the court is exercising an original jurisdiction and is subject to the section 6(1) duty to act compatibly with Convention rights. Furthermore, the factors normally to be considered in the exercise of such a discretion are equivalent to those required by Art.8. (See Lord Bingham of Cornhill at [37]). There is thus no question of any "deference" to the local authority's decision to seek an injunction. Another example is *R. (on the application of Wilkinson) v Broadmoor Special Hospital Authority* [2001] EWCA Civ 1545; [2002] 1 W.L.R. 419, where the Court of Appeal held that where a decision to administer medical treatment to a mental patient without his consent under s.58(3)(6) of the Mental Health Act 1983

was challenged by way of judicial review, the Administrative Court is entitled to reach it own view as to whether the treatment infringed the claimant's human rights, and require the presence of the doctors concerned (the two doctors who certify that the statutory conditions for forcible treatment are met and the claimant's own expert) for cross-examination. The basis for this appears to be that the potential inference with the patient's rights under Arts 3 and 8 is such that, whatever the pre-HRA position, the question whether the statutory conditions to justify treatment without consent were established was one of precedent fact. See also *Huang v Secretary of State of the Home Department* [2005] EWCA Civ 105.

A different reason for denying weight to the opinion of the decision-maker (or "deference") is where the latter has failed to analyse the issues in the manner required by the proportionality test: where a decision is made "without proper consideration . . . of highly relevant proportionality issues" it never reaches "the point of refinement at which the judicial obligation of deference" crystallises (*per* Maurice Kay J. in *R. (on the application of CD) v Secretary of State for the Home Department* [2003] EWHC 155). See also *R. (on the application of Munjaz) v Mersey Care NHS Trust; R. (On the application of S) v Airedale NHS Trust* [2003] EWCA Civ 1036; [2004] Q.B. 395 (seclusion of mental patient in disregard of Code of Practice issued by the Secretary of State violated Art.8(1) and was not justified under Art.8(2)).

6. At the other end of the spectrum from the cases considered in the previous note, there are situations where the appropriate justification for interference with the protected right can be derived from the statutory scheme itself and need not be demonstrated on a case by case basis, provided there is compliance with the scheme (*Wandsworth LBC v Michalak* [2002] EWCA Civ 271; [2003] 1 W.L.R. 617, *per* Brooke L.J. at [46], [47], *cf. Qazi*, below, p.385).

A v SECRETARY OF STATE FOR THE HOME DEPARTMENT; X v SECRETARY OF STATE FOR THE HOME DEPARTMENT

[2004] UKHL 56; [2005] 2 W.L.R. 87; [2005] 3 All E.R.169 (HOUSE OF LORDS)

Following the terrorist attacks in the United States on September 11, 2001, for which the organisation Al-Qaeda was responsible, and in the light of threats made by that organisation specifically directed against the United Kingdom, the Government (1) secured the passage of ss.21 to 32 within Pt 4 of the Anti-terrorism, Crime and Security Act 2001 and (2) made the Human Rights Act 1998 (Designated Derogation) Order 2001 (SI 2001/3644). Section 21(1) empowered the Secretary of State to issue a certificate in respect of a person if he reasonably "(a) believes his presence in the UK is a risk to national security, and (b) suspects that the person is a terrorist". "Terrorist" meant a person who is or has been concerned in the commission, preparation or instigation of acts of international terrorism, or who belonged to or had links with an international terrorist group (s.21(1)). Normally, a non-UK national in respect of whom a deportation order has been made, and who is not charged with a crime, may only be detained for such time as is reasonably necessary for the process of deportation to be carried out (*Ex p. Hardial Singh*, below, p.395). Such detention is authorised by Art.5(1)(f) ECHR (see above, p.291).

However, this does not authorise the long-term detention of a person where his return to his home country would involve a real risk of his being subjected to treatment contrary to Art.3, and there is no other country (where there would not be such a risk) willing to take him. Section 23 disapplied that rule in the case of persons certified as suspected international terrorists, enabling indefinite detention. The point that the application of this would infringe Art.5(1) ECHR was met by a derogation notified under Art.15 ECHR and the derogation order under the 1998 Act, s.14. An appeal against certification lay (only) to the Special Immigration Appeals Commission (s.25), which would also carry out periodic reviews (s.26). SIAC also had exclusive jurisdiction in respect of challenges on derogation matters (s.3)). A number of persons were detained (in Belmarsh) prison by virtue of these provisions. They challenged the validity of the derogation order and the compatibility of the detention provisions with their Convention rights. SIAC ([2002] H.R.L.R. 45) rejected a challenge to the derogation order, but held that s.23 was incompatible with Art.14 as discriminatory on the ground of national origin and disproportionate. The Court of Appeal ([2004] Q.B. 335) allowed the Secretary of State's appeal. The House of Lords allowed a further appeal by the claimants. Seven members of the House (Lords Bingham of Cornhill, Nicholls of Birkenhead, Hope of Craighead, Scott of Foscote, Rodger of Earlsferry and Carswell, and Baroness Hale of Richmond) held (1) that the derogation order could not be challenged on the basis that there neither was nor is a "public emergency threatening the life of the nation" within Art.15(1); but (2) that the order should be quashed, and a declaration granted that s.23 of the 2001 Act was incompatible with Arts 5 and 14 ECHR, on the ground that this was a disproportionate response to the emergency. Notwithstanding that Art.15 ECHR was not incorporated, the Attorney-General was content to argue the case in the footing that the derogation order had to be justified by reference to it (see Lord Scott of Foscote at [149]–[152]). Lord Hoffmann dissented on the "emergency" issue, and expressed no opinion on the proportionality and discrimination issues. Lord Walker of Gestingthorpe agreed on the "emergency" issue and dissented on the proportionality and discrimination issues. The main opinion for the majority was given by LORD BINGHAM OF CORNHILL: . . .

Public emergency

16. The appellants repeated before the House a contention rejected by both SIAC and the Court of Appeal, that there neither was nor is a "public emergency threatening the life of the nation" within the meaning of article 15(1). Thus, they contended, the threshold test for reliance on article 15 has not been satisfied. . . .

[His Lordship referred to the jurisprudence of the ECtHR, which had held that this test referred to "an exceptional situation of crisis or emergency which affects the whole population and constitutes a threat to the organised life of the community of which the state is composed" (*Lawless v Ireland (No.3)* (1961) 1 E.H.R.R. 15 at para.28, a case where "very low-level IRA terrorist activity in Ireland and Northern Ireland between 1954 and 1957" (in Lord Bingham's words) was held to constitute such an emergency). In *The Greek Case* (1969) 12 YBI, the Commission stated (at para.153) that:

> "Such a public emergency may then be seen to have, in particular, the following characteristics: (1) It must be actual or imminent. (2) Its effects must involve the whole nation. (3) The continuance of the organised life of the Community must be threatened. (4) The crisis or danger must be exceptional, in that the normal measures or restrictions, permitted by the Convention for the maintenance of public safety, health and order, are plainly inadequate."

In *Ireland v UK* (1978) 2 E.H.R.R. 25, the Court stated (at para.207) that Art.15(1) left the national authorities a wide margin of appreciation.]
    20. The appellants did not seek to play down the catastrophic nature of what had take place on 11 September 2001 nor the threat posed to western democracies by international terrorism. But they argued that there had been

no public emergency threatening the life of the British nation, for three main reasons: if the emergency was not (as in all decided cases) actual, it must be shown to be imminent, which could not be shown here; the emergency must be of a temporary nature, which again could not be shown here; and the practice of other states, none of which had derogated from the European Convention, strongly suggested that there was no public emergency calling for derogation. . . .

[As to imminence, the appellants pointed to ministerial statements in October 2001 and March 2002: "There is no immediate intelligence pointing to a specific threat to the UK, but we remain alert, domestically as well as internationally;" and "it would be wrong to say that we have evidence of a particular threat." As to temporariness, official spokesmen had declined to suggest when, if ever, the present situation might change. No state other than the United Kingdom had derogated from Art.5, although France, Italy and Germany had all been threatened as well as the United Kingdom. The view of the Joint Committee on Human Rights was that insufficient evidence had been presented to Parliament to make it possible for them to accept that derogation was strictly required.]

25. The Attorney General, representing the Home Secretary, answered these points. He submitted that an emergency could properly be regarded as imminent if an atrocity was credibly threatened by a body such as Al-Qaeda which had demonstrated its capacity and will to carry out such a threat, where the atrocity might be committed without warning at any time. The Government, responsible as it was and is for the safety of the British people, need not wait for disaster to strike before taking necessary steps to prevent it striking. As to the requirement that the emergency be temporary, the Attorney General did not suggest that an emergency could ever become the normal state of affairs, but he did resist the imposition of any artificial temporal limit to an emergency of the present kind, and pointed out that the emergency which had been held to justify derogation in Northern Ireland in 1988 had been accepted as continuing for a considerable number of years: see *Marshall v United Kingdom* (Application No 41571/98), para.18 above. Little help, it was suggested, could be gained by looking at the practice of other states. It was for each national government, as the guardian of its own people's safety, to make its own judgment on the basis of the facts known to it. In so far as any difference of practice as between the United Kingdom and other Council of Europe members called for justification, it could be found in this country's prominent role as an enemy of Al-Qaeda and an ally of the United States. The Attorney General also made two more fundamental submissions. First, he submitted that there was no error of law in SIAC's approach to this issue and accordingly, since an appeal against its decision lay only on a point of law, there was no ground upon which any appellate court was entitled to disturb its conclusion. Secondly, he submitted that the judgment on this question was pre-eminently one within the discretionary area of judgment reserved to the Secretary of State and his colleagues, exercising their judgment with the benefit of official advice, and to Parliament.

26. The appellants have in my opinion raised an important and difficult question, as the continuing anxiety of the Joint Committee on Human Rights, the observations of the Commissioner for Human Rights and the warnings of the UN Human Rights Committee make clear. In the result, however, not without misgiving (fortified by reading the opinion of my noble and learned

friend Lord Hoffmann), I would resolve this issue against the appellants, for three main reasons.

27. First, it is not shown that SIAC or the Court of Appeal misdirected themselves on this issue. SIAC considered a body of closed material, that is, secret material of a sensitive nature not shown to the parties. The Court of Appeal was not asked to read this material. The Attorney General expressly declined to ask the House to read it. From this I infer that while the closed material no doubt substantiates and strengthens the evidence in the public domain, it does not alter its essential character and effect. But this is in my view beside the point. It is not shown that SIAC misdirected itself in law on this issue, and the view which it accepted was one it could reach on the open evidence in the case.

28. My second reason is a legal one. The European Court decisions in *Ireland v United Kingdom* 2 EHRR 25; *Brannigan and McBride v United Kingdom* 17 EHRR 539; *Aksoy v Turkey* 23 EHRR 553 and *Marshall v United Kingdom* (Application No 41571/98) seem to me to be, with respect, clearly right. In each case the member state had actually experienced widespread loss of life caused by an armed body dedicated to destroying the territorial integrity of the state. To hold that the article 15 test was not satisfied in such circumstances, if a response beyond that provided by the ordinary course of law was required, would have been perverse. But these features were not, on the facts found, very clearly present in *Lawless v Ireland (No 3)* 1 EHRR 15. That was a relatively early decision of the European Court, but it has never to my knowledge been disavowed and the House is required by section 2(1) of the 1998 Act to take it into account. The decision may perhaps be explained as showing the breadth of the margin of appreciation accorded by the court to national authorities. It may even have been influenced by the generous opportunity for release given to Mr Lawless and those in his position. If, however, it was open to the Irish Government in *Lawless* to conclude that there was a public emergency threatening the life of the Irish nation, the British Government could scarcely be faulted for reaching that conclusion in the much more dangerous situation which arose after 11 September.

29. Thirdly, I would accept that great weight should be given to the judgment of the Home Secretary, his colleagues and Parliament on this question, because they were called on to exercise a pre-eminently political judgment. It involved making a factual prediction of what various people around the world might or might not do, and when (if at all) they might do it, and what the consequences might be if they did. Any prediction about the future behaviour of human beings (as opposed to the phases of the moon or high water at London Bridge) is necessarily problematical. Reasonable and informed minds may differ, and a judgment is not shown to be wrong or unreasonable because that which is thought likely to happen does not happen. It would have been irresponsible not to err, if at all, on the side of safety. As will become apparent, I do not accept the full breadth of the Attorney General's argument on what is generally called the deference owed by the courts to the political authorities. It is perhaps preferable to approach this question as one of demarcation of functions or what Liberty in its written case called "relative institutional competence". The more purely political (in a broad or narrow sense) a question is, the more appropriate it will be for political resolution and the less likely it is to be an appropriate matter for judicial decision. The smaller, therefore, will be the potential role of the court. It is the function of political and not judicial bodies to resolve political questions. Conversely, the greater the legal content

of any issue, the greater the potential role of the court, because under our constitution and subject to the sovereign power of Parliament it is the function of the courts and not of political bodies to resolve legal questions. The present question seems to me to be very much at the political end of the spectrum: see *Secretary of State for the Home Department v Rehman* [2003] 1 AC 153, para.62, per Lord Hoffmann. The appellants recognised this by acknowledging that the Home Secretary's decision on the present question was less readily open to challenge than his decision (as they argued) on some other questions. This reflects the unintrusive approach of the European court to such a question. I conclude that the appellants have shown no ground strong enough to warrant displacing the Secretary of State's decision on this important threshold question.

Proportionality

30. Article 15 requires that any measures taken by a member state in derogation of its obligations under the Convention should not go beyond what is "strictly required by the exigencies of the situation". Thus the Convention imposes a test of strict necessity or, in Convention terminology, proportionality. The appellants founded on the principle adopted by the Privy Council in *de Freitas v Permanent Secretary of Ministry of Agriculture, Fisheries, Lands and Housing* [1999] 1 AC 69, 80. In determining whether a limitation is arbitrary or excessive, the court must ask itself:

> "whether: (i) the legislative objective is sufficiently important to justify limiting a fundamental right; (ii) the measures designed to meet the legislative objective are rationally connected to it; and (iii) the means used to impair the right or freedom are no more than is necessary to accomplish the objective."

This approach is close to that laid down by the Supreme Court of Canada in *R v Oakes* [1986] 1 SCR 103, paras 69–70, and in *Libman v Attorney General of Quebec* (1997) 3 BHRC 269, para.38. To some extent these questions are, or may be, interrelated. But the appellants directed the main thrust of their argument to the second and third questions. They submitted that even if it were accepted that the legislative objective of protecting the British people against the risk of catastrophic Al-Qaeda terrorism was sufficiently important to justify limiting the fundamental right to personal freedom of those facing no criminal accusation, the 2001 Act was not designed to meet that objective and was not rationally connected to it. Furthermore, the legislative objective could have been achieved by means which did not, or did not so severely, restrict the fundamental right to personal freedom.

31. The appellants' argument under this head can, I hope fairly, be summarised as involving the following steps.

(1) Part 4 of the 2001 Act reversed the effect of the decisions in *Ex p. Hardial Singh* [1984] 1 WLR 704 and *Chahal* 23 EHRR 413 and was apt to address the problems of immigration control caused to the United Kingdom by article 5(1)(f) of the Convention read in the light of those decisions.

(2) The public emergency on which the United Kingdom relied to derogate from the Convention right to personal liberty was the threat to the security of the United Kingdom presented by Al-Qaeda terrorists and their supporters.

(3) While the threat to the security of the United Kingdom derived predominantly and most immediately from foreign nationals, some of whom could not be deported because they would face torture or inhuman or degrading treatment or punishment in their home countries and who could not be deported to any third country willing to receive them, the threat to the United Kingdom did not derive solely from such foreign nationals.

(4) Sections 21 and 23 did not rationally address the threat to the security of the United Kingdom presented by Al-Qaeda terrorists and their supporters because (a) it did not address the threat presented by UK nationals, (b) it permitted foreign nationals suspected of being Al-Qaeda terrorists or their supporters to pursue their activities abroad if there was any country to which they were able to go, and (c) the sections permitted the certification and detention of persons who were not suspected of presenting any threat to the security of the United Kingdom as Al-Qaeda terrorists or supporters.

(5) If the threat presented to the security of the United Kingdom by UK nationals suspected of being Al-Qaeda terrorists or their supporters could be addressed without infringing their right to personal liberty, it is not shown why similar measures could not adequately address the threat presented by foreign nationals.

(6) Since the right to personal liberty is among the most fundamental of the rights protected by the European Convention, any restriction of it must be closely scrutinised by the national court and such scrutiny involves no violation of democratic or constitutional principle.

(7) In the light of such scrutiny, neither the Derogation Order nor sections 21 and 23 of the 2001 Act can be justified.

32. It is unnecessary to linger on the first two steps of this argument, neither of which is controversial and both of which are clearly correct. The third step calls for closer examination. The evidence before SIAC was that the Home Secretary considered "that the serious threats to the nation emanated predominantly (albeit not exclusively) and more immediately from the category of foreign nationals". In para.95 of its judgment SIAC held:

> "But the evidence before us demonstrates beyond argument that the threat is not so confined [to the alien section of the population]. There are many British nationals already identified-mostly in detention abroad-who fall within the definition of 'suspected international terrorists,' and it was clear from the submissions made to us that in the opinion of the [Home Secretary] there are others at liberty in the United Kingdom who could be similarly defined."

This finding has not been challenged, and since SIAC is the responsible fact-finding tribunal it is unnecessary to examine the basis of it. There was however evidence before SIAC that "upwards of a thousand individuals from the UK are estimated on the basis of intelligence to have attended training camps in Afghanistan in the last five years", that some British citizens are said to have planned to return from Afghanistan to the United Kingdom and that "The backgrounds of those detained show the high level of involvement of British citizens and those otherwise connected with the United Kingdom in the terrorist networks". It seems plain that the threat to the United Kingdom did not derive solely from foreign nationals or from foreign nationals whom it was unlawful to deport. Later evidence, not before SIAC or the Court of

Appeal, supports that conclusion. The Newton Committee recorded the Home Office argument that the threat from Al-Qaeda terrorism was predominantly from foreigners but drew attention, at para.193, to

"accumulating evidence that this is not now the case. The British suicide bombers who attacked Tel Aviv in May 2003, Richard Reid ('the Shoe Bomber'), and recent arrests suggest that the threat from UK citizens is real. Almost 30% of Terrorism Act 2000 suspects in the past year have been British. We have been told that, of the people of interest to the authorities because of their suspected involvement in international terrorism, nearly half are British nationals."

33. The fourth step in the appellants' argument is of obvious importance to it. It is plain that sections 21 and 23 of the 2001 Act do not address the threat presented by UK nationals since they do not provide for the certification and detention of UK nationals. It is beside the point that other sections of the 2001 Act and the 2000 Act do apply to UK nationals, since they are not the subject of derogation, are not the subject of complaint and apply equally to foreign nationals. Yet the threat from UK nationals, if quantitatively smaller, is not said to be qualitatively different from that from foreign nationals. It is also plain that sections 21 and 23 do permit a person certified and detained to leave the United Kingdom and go to any other country willing to receive him, as two of the appellants did when they left for Morocco and France respectively. . . . Such freedom to leave is wholly explicable in terms of immigration control: if the British authorities wish to deport a foreign national but cannot deport him to country A because of *Chahal* their purpose is as well served by his voluntary departure for country B. But allowing a suspected international terrorist to leave our shores and depart to another country, perhaps a country as close as France, there to pursue his criminal designs, is hard to reconcile with a belief in his capacity to inflict serious injury to the people and interests of this country. It seems clear from the language of section 21 of the 2001 Act, read with the definition of terrorism in section 1 of the 2000 Act, that section 21 is capable of covering those who have no link at all with Al-Qaeda (they might, for example, be members of the Basque separatist organisation ETA), or who, although supporting the general aims of Al-Qaeda, reject its cult of violence. The Attorney General conceded that sections 21 and 23 could not lawfully be invoked in the case of suspected international terrorists other than those thought to be connected with Al-Qaeda, and undertook that the procedure would not be used in such cases. A restrictive reading of the broad statutory language might in any event be indicated: *Padfield v Minister of Agriculture, Fisheries and Food* [1968] AC 997. The appellants were content to accept the Attorney General's concession and undertaking. It is not however acceptable that interpretation and application of a statutory provision bearing on the liberty of the subject should be governed by implication, concession and undertaking. . . .

35. The fifth step in the appellants' argument permits of little elaboration. But it seems reasonable to assume that those suspected international terrorists who are UK nationals are not simply ignored by the authorities. When G, one of the appellants, was released from prison by SIAC on bail (*G v Secretary of State for the Home Department* (unreported) 20 May 2004) it was on condition (among other things) that he wear an electronic monitoring tag at all

times; that he remain at his premises at all times; that he telephone a named security company five times each day at specified times; that he permit the company to install monitoring equipment at his premises; that he limit entry to his premises to his family, his solicitor, his medical attendants and other approved persons; that he make no contact with any other person; that he have on his premises no computer equipment, mobile telephone or other electronic communications device; that he cancel the existing telephone link to his premises; and that he install a dedicated telephone link permitting contact only with the security company. The appellants suggested that conditions of this kind, strictly enforced, would effectively inhibit terrorist activity. It is hard to see why this would not be so.

36. In urging the fundamental importance of the right to personal freedom, as the sixth step in their proportionality argument, the appellants were able to draw on the long libertarian tradition of English law, dating back to chapter 39 of Magna Carta 1215, given effect in the ancient remedy of habeas corpus, declared in the Petition of Right 1628, upheld in a series of landmark decisions down the centuries and embodied in the substance and procedure of the law to our own day. . . . In its treatment of article 5 of the European Convention, the European Court also has recognised the prime importance of personal freedom. [*Kurt v Turkey* (1998) 27 EHRR 373, para.122; *Garcia Alva v Germany* (2001) 37 EHRR 335, para.39]

37. While the Attorney General challenged and resisted the third, fourth and fifth steps in the appellants' argument, he directed the weight of his submission to challenging the standard of judicial review for which the appellants contended in this sixth step. He submitted that as it was for Parliament and the executive to assess the threat facing the nation, so it was for those bodies and not the courts to judge the response necessary to protect the security of the public. These were matters of a political character calling for an exercise of political and not judicial judgment. Just as the European court allowed a generous margin of appreciation to member states, recognising that they were better placed to understand and address local problems, so should national courts recognise, for the same reason, that matters of the kind in issue here fall within the discretionary area of judgment properly belonging to the democratic organs of the state. It was not for the courts to usurp authority properly belonging elsewhere. The Attorney General drew attention to the dangers identified by Richard Ekins in "Judicial Supremacy and the Rule of Law" (2003) 119 LQR 127. This is an important submission, properly made, and it calls for careful consideration.

38. Those conducting the business of democratic government have to make legislative choices which, notably in some fields, are very much a matter for them, particularly when (as is often the case) the interests of one individual or group have to be balanced against those of another individual or group or the interests of the community as a whole. The European court has recognised this on many occasions: *Chassagnou v France* (1999) 29 EHRR 615, para.113, and *Hatton v United Kingdom* (2003) 37 EHRR 611, paras 97–98, may be cited as recent examples. In para.97 of *Hatton*, a case which concerned aircraft noise at Heathrow, the court said:

"At the same time, the court reiterates the fundamentally subsidiary role of the Convention. The national authorities have direct democratic legitimation and are, as the court has held on many occasions, in principle better placed than an international court to evaluate local needs and conditions. In matters of general policy, on which opinions within a democratic society may reasonably differ widely, the role of the domestic policy maker should be given special weight."

Where the conduct of government is threatened by serious terrorism, difficult choices have to be made and the terrorist dimension cannot be overlooked. This also the European commission and court have recognised in cases such as *Brogan v United Kingdom* (1988) 11 EHRR 117, para.80; *Fox, Campbell & Hartley v United Kingdom* (1990) 13 EHRR 157, paras 32, 34; and *Murray v United Kingdom* (1994) 19 EHRR 193, para.47. The same recognition is found in domestic authority: see, for example, *Secretary of State for the Home Department v Rehman* [2003] 1 AC 153, paras [28], [62].

39. While any decision made by a representative democratic body must of course command respect, the degree of respect will be conditioned by the nature of the decision. As the European court observed in *Fretté v France* (2002) 38 EHRR 438, para.40:

"the contracting states enjoy a margin of appreciation in assessing whether and to what extent differences in otherwise similar situations justify a different treatment in law. The scope of the margin of appreciation will vary according to the circumstances, the subject-matter and its background; in this respect, one of the relevant factors may be the existence or non-existence of common ground between the laws of contracting states."

A similar approach is found in domestic authority. In *R v Director of Public Prosecutions, Ex p. Kebilene* [2000] 2 AC 326, 381, Lord Hope of Craighead said:

"It will be easier for such [a discretionary] area of judgment to be recognised where the Convention itself requires a balance to be struck, much less so where the right is stated in terms which are unqualified. It will be easier for it to be recognised where the issues involve questions of social or economic policy, much less so where the rights are of high constitutional importance or are of a kind where the courts are especially well placed to assess the need for protection."

Another area in which the court was held to be qualified to make its own judgment is the requirement of a fair trial: *R v A (No 2)* [2002] 1 AC 45, para.36. The Supreme Court of Canada took a similar view in *Libman v Attorney General of Quebec* 3 BHRC 269, para.59. In his dissenting judgment (cited with approval in *Libman*) in *RJR-MacDonald Inc v Attorney General of Canada* [1995] 3 SCR 199, para.68, La Forest J, sitting in the same court, said:

"Courts are specialists in the protection of liberty and the interpretation of legislation and are, accordingly, well placed to subject criminal justice legislation to careful scrutiny. However, courts are not specialists in the realm of policy-making, nor should they be."

See also McLachlin J in the same case, para.135. Jackson J, sitting in the Supreme Court of the United States in *West Virginia State Board of Education v Barnette* (1943) 319 US 624, para.3, stated, speaking of course with reference to an entrenched constitution:

> "The very purpose of a Bill of Rights was to withdraw certain subjects from the vicissitudes of political controversy, to place them beyond the reach of majorities and officials and to establish them as legal principles to be applied by the courts . . . We cannot, because of modest estimates of our competence in such specialties as public education, withhold the judgment that history authenticates as the function of this court when liberty is infringed."

40. The Convention regime for the international protection of human rights requires national authorities, including national courts, to exercise their authority to afford effective protection. The European Court made this clear in the early case of *Handyside v United Kingdom* (1976) 1 EHRR 737, para.48:

> "The court points out that the machinery of protection established by the Convention is subsidiary to the national systems safeguarding human rights. The Convention leaves to each contracting state, in the first place, the task of securing the rights and freedoms it enshrines."

Thus the European Commissioner for Human Rights had authority for saying (Opinion 1/2002, para.9):

> "It is furthermore, precisely because the Convention presupposes domestic controls in the form of a preventive parliamentary scrutiny and posterior judicial review that national authorities enjoy a large margin of appreciation in respect of derogations. This is, indeed, the essence of the principle of the subsidiarity of the protection of Convention rights."

In *Smith and Grady v United Kingdom* (1999) 29 EHRR 493 the traditional *Wednesbury* approach to judicial review (see *Associated Provincial Pictures Houses Ltd v Wednesbury Corpn* [1948] 1 KB 223) was held to afford inadequate protection. It is now recognised that "domestic courts must themselves form a judgment whether a Convention right has been breached" and that "the intensity of review is somewhat greater under the proportionality approach": *R (Daly) v Secretary of State for the Home Department* [2001] 2 AC 532, paras 23, 27.

41. Even in a terrorist situation the Convention organs have not been willing to relax their residual supervisory role: *Brogan v United Kingdom* above, para.80; *Fox, Campbell & Hartley v United Kingdom*, above, paras 32–34. In *Aksoy v Turkey* 23 EHRR 553, para.76, the court, clearly referring to national courts as well as the Convention organs, held:

> "The court would stress the importance of article 5 in the Convention system: it enshrines a fundamental human right, namely the protection of the individual against arbitrary interference by the state with his or her right to liberty. Judicial control of interferences by the executive with the individual's right to liberty is an essential feature of the guarantee embodied in article 5(3), which is intended to minimise the risk of arbitrariness and to ensure the rule of law."

In *Korematsu v United States* (1984) 584 F Supp 1406 para.21, Judge Patel observed that the Supreme Court's earlier decision (1944) 323 US 214 "stands as a caution that in times of distress the shield of military necessity and national security must not be used to protect governmental actions from close scrutiny and accountability". Simon Brown LJ observed in *International Transport Roth GmbH v Secretary of State for the Home Department* [2003] QB 728, para.27, that "the court's role under the 1998 Act is as the guardian of human rights. It cannot abdicate this responsibility." He went on to say, in para.54:

> "But judges nowadays have no alternative but to apply the Human Rights Act 1998. Constitutional dangers exist no less in too little judicial activism as in too much. There are limits to the legitimacy of executive or legislative decision-making, just as there are to decision-making by the courts."

42. It follows from this analysis that the appellants are in my opinion entitled to invite the courts to review, on proportionality grounds, the Derogation Order and the compatibility with the Convention of section 23 and the courts are not effectively precluded by any doctrine of deference from scrutinising the issues raised. It also follows that I do not accept the full breadth of the Attorney General's submissions. I do not in particular accept the distinction which he drew between democratic institutions and the courts. It is of course true that the judges in this country are not elected and are not answerable to Parliament. It is also of course true, as pointed out in para.29 above, that Parliament, the executive and the courts have different functions. But the function of independent judges charged to interpret and apply the law is universally recognised as a cardinal feature of the modern democratic state, a cornerstone of the rule of law itself. The Attorney General is fully entitled to insist on the proper limits of judicial authority, but he is wrong to stigmatise judicial decision-making as in some way undemocratic. It is particularly inappropriate in a case such as the present in which Parliament has expressly legislated in section 6 of the 1998 Act to render unlawful any act of a public authority, including a court, incompatible with a Convention right, has required courts (in section 2) to take account of relevant Strasbourg jurisprudence, has (in section 3) required courts, so far as possible, to give effect to Convention rights and has conferred a right of appeal on derogation issues. The effect is not, of course, to override the sovereign legislative authority of the Queen in Parliament, since if primary legislation is declared to be incompatible the validity of the legislation is unaffected (section 4(6)) and the remedy lies with the appropriate minister (section 10), who is answerable to Parliament. The 1998 Act gives the courts a very specific, wholly democratic, mandate. As Professor Jowell has put it "The courts are charged by Parliament with delineating the boundaries of a rights-based democracy" ("Judicial Deference: servility, civility or institutional capacity?" [2003] PL 592, 597). See also Clayton, "Judicial deference and 'democratic dialogue': the legitimacy of judicial intervention under the Human Rights Act 1998" [2004] PL 33.

43. The appellants' proportionality challenge to the Order and section 23 is, in my opinion, sound, for all the reasons they gave and also for those given by the European Commissioner for Human Rights and the Newton Committee. The Attorney General could give no persuasive answer. In a discussion paper "Counter-Terrorism Powers: Reconciling Security and Liberty

in an Open Society" (Cm 6147) (February 2004) the Secretary of State replied to one of the Newton Committee's criticisms in this way:

"32. It can be argued that as suspected international terrorists their departure for another country could amount to exporting terrorism: a point made in the Newton Report at para.195. But that is a natural consequence of the fact that Part 4 powers are immigration powers: detention is permissible only pending deportation and there is no other power available to detain (other than for the purpose of police inquiries) if a foreign national chooses voluntarily to leave the UK. (Detention in those circumstances is limited to 14 days after which the person must be either charged or released.) Deportation has the advantage moreover of disrupting the activities of the suspected terrorist."

This answer, however, reflects the central complaint made by the appellants: that the choice of an immigration measure to address a security problem had the inevitable result of failing adequately to address that problem (by allowing non-UK suspected terrorists to leave the country with impunity and leaving British suspected terrorists at large) while imposing the severe penalty of indefinite detention on persons who, even if reasonably suspected of having links with Al-Qaeda, may harbour no hostile intentions towards the United Kingdom. The conclusion that the Order and section 23 are, in Convention terms, disproportionate is in my opinion irresistible.

44. Since, under section 7 of the Special Immigration Appeals Commission Act 1997 and section 30(5) of the 2001 Act, an appeal from SIAC lies only on a point of law, that is not the end of the matter. It is necessary to examine SIAC's reasons for rejecting this part of the appellants' challenge. They are given in para.51 of SIAC's judgment, and are fourfold.

(1) that there is an advantage to the UK in the removal of a potential terrorist from circulation in the UK because he cannot operate actively in the UK whilst he is either not in the country or not at liberty;

(2) that the removal of potential terrorists from their UK communities disrupts the organisation of terrorist activities;

(3) that the detainee's freedom to leave, far from showing that the measures are irrational, tends to show that they are to this extent properly tailored to the state of emergency; and

(4) that it is difficult to see how a power to detain a foreign national who had not been charged with a criminal offence and wished to leave the UK could readily be defended as tending to prevent him committing acts of terrorism aimed at the UK.

Assuming, as one must, that there is a public emergency threatening the life of the nation, measures which derogate from article 5 are permissible only to the extent strictly required by the exigencies of the situation, and it is for the derogating state to prove that that is so. The reasons given by SIAC do not warrant its conclusion. The first reason does not explain why the measures are directed only to foreign nationals. The second reason no doubt has some validity, but is subject to the same weakness. The third reason does not explain why a terrorist, if a serious threat to the UK, ceases to be so on the French side of the English Channel or elsewhere. The fourth reason is intelligible if the foreign national is not really thought to be a serious threat to the UK, but hard to understand if he is. I do not consider SIAC's conclusion as one to which it could properly come. In dismissing the appellants' appeal, Lord Woolf CJ broadly considered that it was sensible and appropriate for the Secretary of State to use immigration legislation, that deference was owed to his decisions (para.40) and that SIAC's conclusions depended on the evidence before it (para.43). Brooke LJ reached a similar conclusion (para.91), regarding SIAC's findings as unappealable findings of fact. Chadwick LJ also regarded SIAC's finding as one of fact (para.150). I cannot accept this analysis as correct. The European Court does not approach questions of proportionality as questions of pure fact: see, for example, *Smith and Grady v United Kingdom* 29 EHRR 493. Nor should domestic courts do so. The greater intensity of review now required in determining questions of proportionality, and the duty of the courts to protect Convention rights, would in my view be emasculated if a judgment at first instance on such a question were conclusively to preclude any further review. So would excessive deference, in a field involving indefinite detention without charge or trial, to ministerial decision. In my opinion, SIAC erred in law and the Court of Appeal erred in failing to correct its error.

Discrimination

45. As part of their proportionality argument, the appellants attacked section 23 as discriminatory. They contended that, being discriminatory, the section could not be "strictly required" within the meaning of article 15 and so was disproportionate. The courts below found it convenient to address this discrimination issue separately, and I shall do the same.

46. The appellants complained that in providing for the detention of suspected international terrorists who were not UK nationals but not for the detention of suspected international terrorists who were UK nationals, section 23 unlawfully discriminated against them as non-UK nationals in breach of article 14 of the European Convention. That article provides:

> "*Prohibition of discrimination*
> The enjoyment of the rights and freedoms set forth in this Convention shall be secured without discrimination on any ground such as sex, race, colour, language, religion, political or other opinion, national or social origin, association with a national minority, property, birth or other status."

It is well established that the obligation on the state not to discriminate applies only to rights which it is bound to protect under the Convention. The appellants claim that section 23 discriminates against them in their enjoyment of liberty under article 5. Article 14 is of obvious importance. In his influential work "An International Bill of the Rights of Man" (1945), p 115, Professor Hersch Lauterpacht wrote: "The claim to equality before the law is in a substantial sense the most fundamental of the rights of man." Jackson J reflected this belief in his well-known judgment in *Railway Express Agency Inc v New York* (1949) 336 US 106, 112–113, when he said:

> "I regard it as a salutary doctrine that cities, states and the Federal Government must exercise their powers so as not to discriminate between their inhabitants except upon some reasonable differentiation fairly related to the object of regulation. This equality is not merely abstract justice. The framers of the Constitution knew, and we should not forget today, that there

is no more effective practical guaranty against arbitrary and unreasonable government than to require that the principles of law which officials would impose upon a minority must be imposed generally. Conversely, nothing opens the door to arbitrary action so effectively as to allow those officials to pick and choose only a few to whom they will apply legislation and thus to escape the political retribution that might be visited upon them if larger numbers were affected. Courts can take no better measure to assure that laws will be just than to require that laws be equal in operation."

More recently, the Privy Council (per Lord Hoffmann, *Matadeen v Pointu* [1999] 1 AC 98, 109) observed, with reference to the principle of equality:

"Their Lordships do not doubt that such a principle is one of the building blocks of democracy and necessarily permeates any democratic constitution. Indeed, their Lordships would go further and say that treating like cases alike and unlike cases differently is a general axiom of rational behaviour."

47. The United Kingdom did not derogate from article 14 of the European Convention (or from article 26 of the ICCPR, which corresponds to it). The Attorney General did not submit that there had been an implied derogation, an argument advanced to SIAC but not to the Court of Appeal or the House.

48. The foreign nationality of the appellants does not preclude them from claiming the protection of their Convention rights. By article 1 of the Convention (which has not been expressly incorporated) the contracting states undertook to secure the listed Convention rights "to everyone within their jurisdiction". That includes the appellants. The European Court has recognised the Convention rights of non-nationals: see, for a recent example, *Conka v Belgium* (2002) 34 EHRR 1298. This accords with domestic authority. In *R v Secretary of State for the Home Department, Ex p. Khawaja* [1984] 1 AC 74, 111–112:

"Habeas corpus protection is often expressed as limited to 'British subjects'. Is it really limited to British nationals? Suffice it to say that the case law has given an emphatic 'no' to the question. Every person within the jurisdiction enjoys the equal protection of our laws. There is no distinction between British nationals and others. He who is subject to English law is entitled to its protection. This principle has been in the law at least since Lord Mansfield freed 'the black' in *Sommersett's Case* (1772) 20 St Tr 1. There is nothing here to encourage in the case of aliens or non-patrials the implication of words excluding the judicial review our law normally accords to those whose liberty is infringed."

49. It was pointed out that nationality is not included as a forbidden ground of discrimination in article 14. The Strasbourg court has however treated nationality as such. In *Gaygusuz v Austria* (1996) 23 EHRR 364, para.42, it said:

"However, very weighty reasons would have to be put forward before the court could regard a difference of treatment based exclusively on the ground of nationality as compatible with the Convention."

The Attorney General accepted that "or other status" would cover the appellants' immigration status, so nothing turns on this point. Nationality is a forbidden ground of discrimination within section 3(1) of the Race Relations Act 1976 and the Secretary of State is bound by that Act by virtue of section 19B(1). It was not argued that in the present circumstances he was authorised to discriminate by section 19D.

50. The first important issue between the parties was whether, in the present case, the Secretary of State had discriminated against the appellants on the ground of their nationality or immigration status. The court gave guidance on the correct approach in the *Belgian Linguistic Case (No 2) (1968) 1 EHRR 252*, para.10:

"In spite of the very general wording of the French version ('sans distinction aucune'), article 14 does not forbid every difference in treatment in the exercise of the rights and freedoms recognised. This version must be read in the light of the more restrictive text of the English version ('without discrimination'). In addition, and in particular, one would reach absurd results were one to give article 14 an interpretation as wide as that which the French version seems to imply. One would, in effect, be led to judge as contrary to the Convention every one of the many legal or administrative provisions which do not secure to everyone complete equality of treatment in the enjoyment of the rights and freedoms recognised. The competent national authorities are frequently confronted with situations and problems which, on account of differences inherent therein, call for different legal solutions; moreover, certain legal inequalities tend only to correct factual inequalities. The extensive interpretation mentioned above cannot consequently be accepted.

"It is important, then, to look for the criteria which enable a determination to be made as to whether or not a given difference in treatment, concerning of course the exercise of one of the rights and freedoms set forth, contravenes article 14. On this question, the court, following the principles which may be extracted from the legal practice of a large number of democratic states, holds that the principle of equality of treatment is violated if the distinction has no objective and reasonable justification. The existence of such a justification must be assessed in relation to the aim and effects of the measure under consideration, regard being had to the principles which normally prevail in democratic societies. A difference of treatment in the exercise of a right laid down in the Convention must not only pursue a legitimate aim: article 14 is likewise violated when it is clearly established that there is no reasonable relationship of proportionality between the means employed and the aim sought to be realised."

The question is whether persons in an analogous or relevantly similar situation enjoy preferential treatment, without reasonable or objective justification for the distinction, and whether and to what extent differences in otherwise similar situations justify a different treatment in law: *Stubbings v United Kingdom* (1996) 23 EHRR 213, para.70. The parties were agreed that in domestic law, seeking to give effect to the Convention, the correct approach is to pose the questions formulated by *Grosz, Beatson & Duffy, Human Rights: The 1998 Act and the European Convention* (2000), para.C14–08, substantially adopted by Brooke LJ in *Wandsworth London Borough Council v*

Michalak [2003] 1 WLR 617, para.20, and refined in the later cases of *R (Carson) v Secretary of State for Work and Pensions* [2002] 3 All ER 994, para.52; [2003] 3 All ER 577, paras 56–61, *Ghaidan v Godin-Mendoza* [2004] 2 AC 557, paras 133–134 and *R(S) v Chief Constable of the South Yorkshire Police* [2004] 1 WLR 2196. As expressed in para.42 of this last case the questions are:

"(1) Do the facts fall within the ambit of one or more of the Convention rights? (2) Was there a difference in treatment in respect of that right between the complainant and others put forward for comparison? (3) If so, was the difference in treatment on one or more of the proscribed grounds under article 14? (4) Were those others in an analogous situation? (5) Was the difference in treatment objectively justifiable in the sense that it had a legitimate aim and bore a reasonable relationship of proportionality to that aim?"

51. It is plain that the facts fall within the ambit of article 5. That is why the United Kingdom thought it necessary to derogate. The Attorney General reserved the right to argue in another place at another time that it was not necessary to derogate, but he accepted for the purpose of these proceedings that it was. The appellants were treated differently from both suspected international terrorists who were not UK nationals but could be removed and also from suspected international terrorists who were UK-nationals and could not be removed. There can be no doubt but that the difference of treatment was on grounds of nationality or immigration status (one of the proscribed grounds under article 14). The problem has been treated as an immigration problem.

52. The Attorney General submitted that the position of the appellants should be compared with that of non-UK nationals who represented a threat to the security of the UK but who could be removed to their own or to safe third countries. The relevant difference between them and the appellants was that the appellants could not be removed. A difference of treatment of the two groups was accordingly justified and it was reasonable and necessary to detain the appellants. By contrast, the appellants' chosen comparators were suspected international terrorists who were UK nationals. The appellants pointed out that they shared with this group the important characteristics (a) of being suspected international terrorists and (b) of being irremovable from the United Kingdom. Since these were the relevant characteristics for purposes of the comparison, it was unlawfully discriminatory to detain non-UK nationals while leaving UK nationals at large.

53. Were suspected international terrorists who were UK nationals, the appellants' chosen comparators, in a relevantly analogous situation to the appellants? The question, as posed by Laws LJ in *R (Carson) v Secretary of State for Work and Pensions* [2003] 3 All ER 577, para.61, is whether the circumstances of X and Y are so similar as to call (in the mind of a rational and fair-minded person) for a positive justification for the less favourable treatment of Y in comparison with X. The Court of Appeal thought not because (per Lord Woolf CJ, para.56) "the nationals have a right of abode in this jurisdiction but the aliens only have a right not to be removed". This is, however, to accept the correctness of the Secretary of State's choice of immigration control as a means to address the Al-Qaeda security problem, when the

correctness of that choice is the issue to be resolved. In my opinion, the question demands an affirmative answer. Suspected international terrorists who are UK nationals are in a situation analogous with the appellants because, in the present context, they share the most relevant characteristics of the appellants.

54. Following the guidance given in the *Belgian Linguistic Case (No 2)* (see para.50 above) it is then necessary to assess the justification of the differential treatment of non-UK nationals "in relation to the aim and effects of the measure under consideration". The undoubted aim of the relevant measure, section 23 of the 2001 Act, was to protect the UK against the risk of Al-Qaeda terrorism. As noted above (para.32) that risk was thought to be presented mainly by non-UK nationals but also and to a significant extent by UK nationals also. The effect of the measure was to permit the former to be deprived of their liberty but not the latter. The appellants were treated differently because of their nationality or immigration status. The comparison contended for by the Attorney General might be reasonable and justified in an immigration context, but cannot in my opinion be so in a security context, since the threat presented by suspected international terrorists did not depend on their nationality or immigration status. It is noteworthy that in *Ireland v United Kingdom* 2 EHRR 25 the European Court was considering legislative provisions which were, unlike section 23, neutral in their terms, in that they provided for internment of loyalist as well as republican terrorists. Even so, the court was gravely exercised whether the application of the measures had been even handed as between the two groups of terrorists. It seems very unlikely that the measures could have been successfully defended had they only been capable of application to republican terrorists, unless it were shown that they alone presented a threat.

[[55]–[65]. His Lordship proceeded to reject the Attorney-General's argument that the ECHR permits the differential treatment of aliens as compared with nationals. There can be such differential treatment, in the immigration content, arising from the point that nationals have the right of abode and non-nationals do not, but apart from that there was no European or other authority to support the Attorney General's argument. The Joint Committee on Human Rights had consistently expressed its concern that these provisions unjustifiably discriminated on the ground of nationality.]

68. . . . Article 15 requires any derogation measures to go no further than is strictly required by the exigencies of the situation and the prohibition of discrimination on grounds of nationality or immigration status has not been the subject of derogation. Article 14 remains in full force. Any discriminatory measure inevitably affects a smaller rather than a larger group, but cannot be justified on the ground that more people would be adversely affected if the measure were applied generally. What has to be justified is not the measure in issue but the difference in treatment between one person or group and another. What cannot be justified here is the decision to detain one group of suspect international terrorists, defined by nationality or immigration status, and not another. To do so was a violation of article 14. It was also a violation of article 26 of the ICCPR and so inconsistent with the United Kingdom's other obligations under international law within the meaning of article 15 of the European Convention.

[[69]–[70]. His Lordship rejected the Attorney-General's argument that international law sanctioned the detention of aliens in time of war or public emergency.]

73. I would allow the appeals. There will be a quashing order in respect of the Human Rights Act 1998 (Designated Derogation) Order 2001. There will also be a declaration under section 4 of the Human Rights Act 1998 that section 23 of the Anti-terrorism, Crime and Security Act 2001 is incompatible with articles 5 and 14 of the European Convention in so far as it is disproportionate and permits detention of suspected international terrorists in a way that discriminates on the ground of nationality or immigration status. The Secretary of State must pay the appellants' costs in the House and below.

LORD HOFFMANN: . . . This is one of the most important cases which the House has had to decide in recent years. It calls into question the very existence of an ancient liberty of which this country has until now been very proud: freedom from arbitrary arrest and detention. The power which the Home Secretary seeks to uphold is a power to detain people indefinitely without charge or trial. Nothing could be more antithetical to the instincts and traditions of the people of the United Kingdom.

87. At present, the power cannot be exercised against citizens of this country. First, it applies only to foreigners whom the Home Secretary would otherwise be able to deport. But the power to deport foreigners is extremely wide. Secondly, it requires that the Home Secretary should reasonably suspect the foreigners of a variety of activities or attitudes in connection with terrorism, including supporting a group influenced from abroad whom the Home Secretary suspects of being concerned in terrorism. If the finger of suspicion has pointed and the suspect is detained, his detention must be reviewed by the Special Immigration Appeals Commission. They can decide that there were no reasonable grounds for the Home Secretary's suspicion. But the suspect is not entitled to be told the grounds upon which he has been suspected. So he may not find it easy to explain that the suspicion is groundless. In any case, suspicion of being a supporter is one thing and proof of wrongdoing is another. Someone who has never committed any offence and has no intention of doing anything wrong may be reasonably suspected of being a supporter on the basis of some heated remarks overheard in a pub. The question in this case is whether the United Kingdom should be a country in which the police can come to such a person's house and take him away to be detained indefinitely without trial.

88. The technical issue in this appeal is whether such a power can be justified on the ground that there exists a "war or other public emergency threatening the life of the nation" within the meaning of article 15 of the European Convention on Human Rights. But I would not like anyone to think that we are concerned with some special doctrine of European law. Freedom from arbitrary arrest and detention is a quintessentially British liberty, enjoyed by the inhabitants of this country when most of the population of Europe could be thrown into prison at the whim of their rulers. It was incorporated into the European Convention in order to entrench the same liberty in countries which had recently been under Nazi occupation. The United Kingdom subscribed to the Convention because it set out the rights which British subjects enjoyed under the common law.

89. The exceptional power to derogate from those rights also reflected British constitutional history. There have been times of great national emergency in which habeas corpus has been suspended and powers to detain on suspicion conferred on the Government. It happened during the Napoleonic

Wars and during both World Wars in the 20th century. These powers were conferred with great misgiving and, in the sober light of retrospect after the emergency had passed, were often found to have been cruelly and unnecessarily exercised. But the necessity of draconian powers in moments of national crisis is recognised in our constitutional history. Article 15 of the Convention, when it speaks of "war or other public emergency threatening the life of the nation", accurately states the conditions in which such legislation has previously been thought necessary.

90. Until the Human Rights Act 1998, the question of whether the threat to the nation was sufficient to justify suspension of habeas corpus or the introduction of powers of detention could not have been the subject of judicial decision. There could be no basis for questioning an Act of Parliament by court proceedings. Under the 1998 Act, the courts still cannot say that an Act of Parliament is invalid. But they can declare that it is incompatible with the human rights of persons in this country. Parliament may then choose whether to maintain the law or not. The declaration of the court enables Parliament to choose with full knowledge that the law does not accord with our constitutional traditions.

91. What is meant by "threatening the life of the nation"? The "nation" is a social organism, living in its territory (in this case, the United Kingdom) under its own form of government and subject to a system of laws which expresses its own political and moral values. When one speaks of a threat to the "life" of the nation, the word life is being used in a metaphorical sense. The life of the nation is not coterminous with the lives of its people. The nation, its institutions and values, endure through generations. In many important respects, England is the same nation as it was at the time of the first Elizabeth or the Glorious Revolution. The Armada threatened to destroy the life of the nation, not by loss of life in battle, but by subjecting English institutions to the rule of Spain and the Inquisition. The same was true of the threat posed to the United Kingdom by Nazi Germany in the Second World War. This country, more than any other in the world, has an unbroken history of living for centuries under institutions and in accordance with values which show a recognisable continuity.

92. This, I think, is the idea which the European Court of Human Rights was attempting to convey when it said (in *Lawless v Ireland (No 3)* (1961) 1 EHRR 15) that it must be a "threat to the organised life of the community of which the state is composed", although I find this a rather desiccated description. Nor do I find the European cases particularly helpful. All that can be taken from them is that the Strasbourg court allows a wide "margin of appreciation" to the national authorities in deciding "both on the presence of such an emergency and on the nature and scope of derogations necessary to avert it": *Ireland v United Kingdom* (1978) 2 EHRR 25, at para.207. What this means is that we, as a United Kingdom court, have to decide the matter for ourselves.

93. Perhaps it is wise for the Strasbourg court to distance itself from these matters. The institutions of some countries are less firmly based than those of others. Their communities are not equally united in their loyalty to their values and system of government. I think that it was reasonable to say that terrorism in Northern Ireland threatened the life of that part of the nation and the territorial integrity of the United Kingdom as a whole. In a community riven by sectarian passions, such a campaign of violence threatened the fabric of

organised society. The question is whether the threat of terrorism from Muslim extremists similarly threatens the life of the British nation.

94. The Home Secretary has adduced evidence, both open and secret, to show the existence of a threat of serious terrorist outrages. The Attorney General did not invite us to examine the secret evidence, but despite the widespread scepticism which has attached to intelligence assessments since the fiasco over Iraqi weapons of mass destruction, I am willing to accept that credible evidence of such plots exist. The events of 11 September 2001 in New York and Washington and 11 March 2003 in Madrid make it entirely likely that the threat of similar atrocities in the United Kingdom is a real one.

95. But the question is whether such a threat is a threat to the life of the nation. The Attorney General's submissions and the judgment of the Special Immigration Appeals Commission treated a threat of serious physical damage and loss of life as necessarily involving a threat to the life of the nation. But in my opinion this shows a misunderstanding of what is meant by "threatening the life of the nation". Of course the Government has a duty to protect the lives and property of its citizens. But that is a duty which it owes all the time and which it must discharge without destroying our constitutional freedoms. There may be some nations too fragile or fissiparous to withstand a serious act of violence. But that is not the case in the United Kingdom. When Milton urged the government of his day not to censor the press even in time of civil war, he said: "Lords and Commons of England, consider what nation it is whereof ye are, and whereof ye are the governours".

96. This is a nation which has been tested in adversity, which has survived physical destruction and catastrophic loss of life. I do not underestimate the ability of fanatical groups of terrorists to kill and destroy, but they do not threaten the life of the nation. Whether we would survive Hitler hung in the balance, but there is no doubt that we shall survive Al-Qaeda. The Spanish people have not said that what happened in Madrid, hideous crime as it was, threatened the life of their nation. Their legendary pride would not allow it. Terrorist violence, serious as it is, does not threaten our institutions of government or our existence as a civil community.

97. For these reasons I think that the Special Immigration Appeals Commission made an error of law and that the appeal ought to be allowed. Others of your Lordships who are also in favour of allowing the appeal would do so, not because there is no emergency threatening the life of the nation, but on the ground that a power of detention confined to foreigners is irrational and discriminatory. I would prefer not to express a view on this point. I said that the power of detention is at present confined to foreigners and I would not like to give the impression that all that was necessary was to extend the power to United Kingdom citizens as well. In my opinion, such a power in any form is not compatible with our constitution. The real threat to the life of the nation, in the sense of a people living in accordance with its traditional laws and political values, comes not from terrorism but from laws such as these. That is the true measure of what terrorism may achieve. It is for Parliament to decide whether to give the terrorists such a victory.

Notes

1. This decision caused great political difficulty for the Government. It secured, amid much contentious debate, the passage of the Prevention of Terrorism Act 2005, which provided for the making of control orders imposing obligations on individuals

suspected of involvement in terrorist-related activities. Orders are made by the Secretary of State with the prior permission (or in cases of urgency the subsequent confirmation) of the High Court, the court applying principles applicable on an application for judicial review (s.3). An order that would involve derogating from the ECHR can only be made by the court on the application of the Secretary of State (s.4). Sections 21 to 23 of the 2001 Act lapsed on March 14, 2005 when not continued by order under s.29.

The House was not asked to rule on the question whether the detention (or continued detention) of the suspected terrorists was unlawful. They were released after a further period in detention while the legislation was reconsidered by Parliament.

2. The decision is of significance on many points, including the extent of "deference" (or regulation of "relative institutional competence") appropriate in different contexts, the application of the requirement of proportionality and the approach to discrimination under Art.14 (as to which see further above, p.303). As to relative institutional competence, compare the approaches to the derogation and proportionality issues.

Why is a "less intrusive" approach justified on the first issue? Why do the difficulties of predicting human behaviour turn the matter into one of a "pre-eminently political judgment"? Compare the interpretations of Lord Bingham and Lord Hoffmann of "threatening the life of the nation". Although not subsequently doubted by the ECtHR, it is difficult to square the outcome in *Lawless* with either the wording of Art.15(1) ECHR or subsequent comments of the Commission and Court. The HRA 1998 requires English courts to take *Lawless* into account, but does not require it to be accepted as setting the threshold for the purposes of UK law.

If they were really strong evidence of an imminent threat to the life of the nation, should the view on the proportionality and discrimination issue change?

3. Lord Hoffmann's robust approach on the derogation issue places much emphasis on constitutional freedoms protected by the common law and to be protected by an appropriate interpretation of legislative provisions that violate them. The dismissive references to "European law" (and some Europeans), however, seem ungenerous given that it has only been the measure of incorporation of the ECHR by the HRA 1998 that has strengthened the power of the judges in the face of legislation designed to interfere with human rights and fundamental freedoms. The UK and the common law can hardly claim whole credit for the ECHR. It is also to be expected that Lord Hoffmann would adopt a more conventional approach to the style and content of his arguments in a case where he was delivering a major opinion for all or the majority of the House. For further comments, see A. Tomkins, [2005] P.L. 259, welcoming "the beginnings of a much belated judicial awakening to the fact that even in the context of national security the courts have a responsibility to ensure that the rule of law is respected" (p.263). Note also the discussion of the applicability of Art.15 at pp.261–262. See also comments by T. Hickman, S. Tierney, D. Dyzenhaus and J. Herbert, (2005) 68 H.L.R. 654–680.

(F) Convention Rights

This section deals with Convention rights, with fuller detail on those that arise most commonly in respect of the acts and decisions of administrative authorities.

(i) Article 2

The right to life, guaranteed by Art.2, is regarded as "one of the most fundamental provisions in the Convention" and must be "strictly construed" (*McCann v UK* (1995) 21 E.H.R.R. 97 at para.147). Violations may arise from the intentional and unlawful taking of life by the state (including a lack of appropriate care in the control and organisation of an arrest operation that leads to deaths: (*McCann*); a failure to take operational protective measures where the state knows or ought to know of a real and immediate risk to identified individual(s) from the criminal act of a third party (*Osman v UK*, below, p.1069, no violation on the facts; *Edwards v UK* (2002) 35 E.H.R.R. 487 (violation found in respect of killing of prisoners by cellmate); and a failure to undertake effective investigations into all killings whether or not by state agents, involving "some form of independent and public scrutiny capable of leading to a determination of whether the force used was or was not justified" (*Kava v Turkey* (1998) 28 E.H.R.R. 1; *Jordan v UK* (2001) 37 E.H.R.R. 52). As regards the third of these, there may on the facts be inadequacies in the police investigation, the inquest or both. See further *McKerr v UK* (2002) 34 E.H.R.R. 20; *Finucane v UK* (2003) 37 E.H.R.R. 29; *R. (on the application of Amin) v Secretary of State for the Home Department* [2003] UKHL 51; [2003] 3 W.L.R. 1169 (police and private Prison Service investigations into killing of prisoner by cellmate inadequate for compliance in the light (*inter alia*) of a failure to involve the deceased's family); *R. (on the application of Middleton) v West Somerset Coroner* [2004] UKHL 10 (inquest procedure followed not sufficient to meet the requirements of Art.2; the requirement in the Coroners Rules that the jury consider "how . . . the deceased came by his death" to be interpreted as requiring consideration of "by what means and in what circumstances" and not merely "by what means".

(ii) Article 3

1. This provides that "no one shall be subjected to torture or to inhuman or degrading treatment or punishment". It is the subject of no exceptions and cannot be the subject of a derogation. "Inhuman treatment" includes the adoption of a practice of violence by police officers leading to intense suffering and physical injury (*Ireland v UK* (1978) 2 E.H.R.R. 25 at para.174, in respect of interrogation techniques used in Northern Ireland in 1971) and the causing of severe mental distress and anguish (*Kurt v Turkey* (1998) 27 E.H.R.R. 373). "Treatment" in the ECtHR's case law:

> "refers to 'ill-treatment' that attains a minimum level of severity and involves actual bodily injury or intense physical or mental suffering. Where treatment humiliates or debases an individual showing lack of respect for, or diminishing, his or her human dignity or arouses feelings of fear, anguish or inferiority capable of breaking an individual's moral and physical resistance, it may be characterised as degrading and also falls within the prohibition of Art.2. The suffering which flow from naturally occurring illness, physical or mental, may be covered by Art.3, where it is, or risks being, exacerbated by treatment, whether flowing from conditions of detention, expulsion or other measures, for which the authorities can be held responsible"

(*Pretty v UK* [2002] 2 F.C.R. 97 at para.52). "Degrading punishment" includes judicial corporal punishment (*Tyrer v UK* (1978) 2 E.H.R.R. 1).

The assessment of whether the level reaches the minimum necessary for a finding that Art.3 has been violated depends on all the circumstances of the case, such as the nature and content of the treatment, its duration, its physical and mental aspects and, in some circumstances, the sex, age and state of health of the victim (*A v UK* (1998) 27 E.H.R.R. 611 at para.20; see also *Pretty*, above). The ECtHR is imposing increasingly high standards (*Selmoni v France* (2000) 29 E.H.R.R. 652). Apart from liability based on the actions of state officials themselves, the state is obliged by Art.3 to undertake an effective official investigation where an individual raises an arguable claim that he has been seriously ill-treated by state officials in breach of that article (*Jordan v UK* (2001) 37 E.H.R.R. 52 (lack of effective investigation into death of person shot by police officer)). Furthermore the state must take positive steps, including the enactment of appropriate criminal offences to protect persons from being subject to Art.3 mistreatment by other private persons (*A v UK* (caning of child by stepfather sufficiently serious to engage Art.3; criminal law that provided defence of reasonable chastisement to be disproved beyond reasonable doubt held to be inadequate protection)), although there is a wide margin of appreciation. It is a breach of the Art.3 to take action in relation to someone within the jurisdiction which carries the real risk that it will expose that person to infringement of his Art.3 rights outside the jurisdiction (*Soering v UK* (1989) 11 E.H.R.R. 439 (extradition); *Chahal v UK* (1996) 23 E.H.R.R. 413 (deportation; risk of intentional ill treatment in home country)); but not, other than in very exceptional circumstances, simply the absence of sufficient provision of medical care (*N v Secretary of State for the Home Department* [2005] UKHL 31). Furthermore, the principle may apply where the risk is of a flagrant infringement of other articles (*R. (on the application of Ullah v Special Adjudicator* [2004] UKHL 26; [2004] 3 W.L.R. 23; *R. (on the application of Razgar)* [2004] UKHL 27; [2004] 3 W.L.R. 58).

2. In *Z v UK* [2002] 34 E.H.R.R 3, the Court held that the failure of a local authority to take steps to protect four children in its areas from severe neglect, deprivation and abuse at the hands of their parents constituted a breach of Art.3; the authorities had been aware of the serious ill-treatment and neglect suffered by the children for over four years. The Government did not contest the Commissions findings of a breach of Art.3 (see below, p.1070). See also *E v UK* (2003) 36 E.H.R.R. 519 (breach of Art.3 arising from inadequacies of authorities in investigating allegations of child abuse against person cohabiting with children's mother); *cf. DP & JC v UK* (2003) 36 E.H.R.R. 183 (not shown that local authority should have been aware of sexual abuse inflicted on applicants in their home).

3. Section 55 of the Nationality, Immigration and Asylum Act 2002 sought to reduce the annual cost of providing support to asylum seekers by prohibiting the Secretary of State or local authorities from providing support under specified powers to a person where the Secretary of State was not satisfied that the claim was made as soon as reasonably practicable after the person's arrival in the United Kingdom (s.55(1)–(4)). This does not prevent "the exercise of a power by the Secretary of State to the extent necessary for the purpose of a person's Convention rights within the meaning of the Human Rights Act 1998" (s.55(5)). Accordingly, powers had to be exercised so as to avoid a breach of Art.3 (*R. (on the application of Q) v Secretary of State for the Home Department* [2003] EWCA Civ 364; [2004] Q.B. 36). Here the Court of Appeal held that the regime imposed on asylum seekers who are denied support by reason of s.55(1) constituted "treatment" within the meaning of Art.3. There was "something more than passivity on the part of the state" in the imposition of a regime that prohibited asylum seekers from working and the grant, to them, when destitute, of support; this amounted to positive action directed against asylum seekers and not to more inaction (Lord Phillips M.R. at [56], [57]). As to the point at which "treatment" becomes inhuman or degrading this fell significantly below the definition of "destitution" that triggers off the Secretary of State's power to provide support under s.95(1) of the Immigration and Asylum Act 1999.

A person is "destitute" for these purposes if "(a) he does not have adequate accommodation or any means of obtaining it (whether or not his other essential living needs are met); or (b) he has adequate accommodation or the means of obtaining it, but cannot meet his other essential living needs" (s.95(3)). The fact that there is a "real risk" that an asylum seeker would be brought to the level described in *Pretty* (above) was not sufficient. It was also not unlawful for the Secretary of State to decline to provide support unless and until it was clear that charitable support had not been provided and the individual was incapable of fending for himself (Lord Phillips M.R. at [63]). In the landmark case of *R. (on the application of Adam) v Secretary of State for the Home Department* [2004] EWCA Civ 540; [2004] A.C.D. 70, the Court of Appeal (Laws L.J. dissenting) held that the judge in three cases had been entitled to find imminent breaches of Art.3. In two of the cases, it was held that there was such an imminent breach where an asylum seeker showed that he would have to sleep on the streets because his reasonable steps to find accommodation and other support had failed. Laws L.J. held, however, that the state could "wait and see" if the threshold was crossed.

Section 55 of the 2002 Act led to a very large number of cases where interim relief was sought in reliance on Art.3. Sir Stephen Sedley, (2003) 32 J.L.S. 3 at p.15 noted that the judges of the Administrative Court made over 1,000 orders for interim payment of benefit to asylum seekers, the Home Office returned to court to get the order discharged in barely any of these cases. The Home Office abandoned the entire system following the decision in *Adam*. Revised guidance from the Immigration and Nationality Directorate of the Home Office (*www.ind.homeoffice.gov.uk*) confirmed that there was a presumption that a claim made within three days of arrival would generally be regarded as made as soon as reasonably practicable after arrival. Furthermore, support under s.55 would not be refused unless NASS was positively satisfied that the asylum seeker did have some alternative source(s) of support available to him or her. This support should include adequate food, and basic amenities such as washing facilities and right shelter. Asylum seekers would also no longer be required routinely to undergo a detailed interview for the purpose of making a s.55 decision. The Home Office has appealed to the House of Lords.

Similar issues will arise in respect of the withdrawal of support to failed asylum seekers and their families, who refuse to leave voluntarily, by virtue of s.9 of the Asylum and Immigration (Treatment of Claimants, Etc.) Act 2004.

Compare *Smith and Grady v UK* (1999) 29 E.H.R.R. 493 at paras 120–122, where the ECtHR held that the treatment of homosexual service personnel by the Ministry of Defence, although distressing and humiliating, was not so severe as to infringe Art.3.

(iii) Article 4

This has generated little case law of the ECtHR and no English cases in which it has been raised as a substantive issue.

(iv) Article 5

This article has been raised in a large number of cases concerning detention in a range of contents including criminal justice, mental health and immigration (*e.g.* the detention of suspected terrorists considered in *A v Secretary of State for the Home Department*, above p.351). It includes express provision for compensation for detention in violation of Art.5 (*cf.* above, p.333).

(v) Article 6

R. (ON THE APPLICATION OF ALCONBURY DEVELOPMENT LTD) v SECRETARY OF STATE FOR THE ENVIRONMENT, TRANSPORT AND THE REGIONS;

R. (ON THE APPLICATION OF HOLDING AND BARNES PLC) v SECRETARY OF STATE FOR THE ENVIRONMENT, TRANSPORT AND THE REGIONS

SECRETARY OF STATE FOR THE ENVIRONMENT, TRANSPORT AND THE REGIONS v LEGAL AND GENERAL ASSURANCE SOCIETY LTD

[2001] UKHL 23; [2003] 2 A.C. 295; [2001] 2 W.L.R. 1389; [2001] 2 All E.R. 929 (HOUSE OF LORDS)

In the first case a company agreed that, if planning permission was granted, it would develop a disused airfield owned by the Ministry of Defence into a national distribution centre. Applications were made to the district and county councils for relevant planning permissions and to the Secretary of State for the Environment, Transport and the Regions, under the Transport and Works Act 1992, for permission to build a rail connection. When the District Council refused and the County Council failed to determine the applications made to them, the Secretary of State recovered the applications for determination by him under para.3 of Sch.6 to the Town and Country Planning Act 1990. Groups of local objectors claimed that determination by the Secretary of State of the applications under both the 1990 and 1992 Acts was contrary to the right to have civil rights and obligations determined by an independent and impartial tribunal guaranteed by Art.6(1) ECHR. The company applied for judicial review of the Secretary of State's decision to entertain the applications.

In the second case, a company applied for planning permission to use land as a depot for wrecked cars. The Health and Safety Executive objected because the development was near to gas storage facilities. The local planning authorities resolved to grant planning permission, but the Secretary of State called in the application for determination by him pursuant to s.77 of the 1990 Act. The company applied for judicial review of that decision on the grounds of incompatibility with Art.6(1).

In the third case, the Highways Agency, a branch of the Secretary of State's department, proposed an improvement scheme to a major road junction, the construction of which would involve the compulsory purchase of land belonging to a company. The Highways Act 1980 and the Acquisition of Land Act 1981 provided that the Secretary of State was the decision-maker who would approve the scheme and the draft compulsory purchase order. At the invitation of the company the Secretary of State sought a ruling as to the compatibility of the procedure with Art.6(1).

The Divisional Court declared, under s.4 of the Human Rights Act 1998, that all impugned powers of the Secretary of State were incompatible with the provisions of Art.6(1), but that the Secretary of State would not be acting unlawfully in exercising those powers under s.6(1) of that Act because s.6(2) applied.

The House of Lords unanimously allowed an appeal by the Secretary of State.

LORD SLYNN OF HADLEY: . . .

[His Lordship summarised the relevant provisions of the legislation concerning town and country planning, transport and works orders authorising compulsory purchase and the operation of a railway, and highways. A common feature is an inquiry held by an inspector who will either have power to make a decision or will make representations to the Secretary of State. There is no appeal on the merits from the decision of either the inspector or the Secretary of State, but provision for a statutory application to quash, the equivalent of judicial review.]

23. The contention in these proceedings is that the processes which I have set out violate article 6. These are civil rights which are determined without a fair and public hearing by an independent and impartial tribunal established by law.

24. There is really no complaint about the inquiry conducted by an inspector or about the safeguards laid down for evidence to be called and challenged and for representations and objections to be heard. It is not suggested that the inspector himself is not independent and impartial even though he is a member of, *e.g.*, the Planning Inspectorate in the case of planning appeals. The essential complaint is that when a decision is taken, not by such an inspector but by the Secretary of State or one of the Ministers of State or an Under-Secretary on behalf of the Secretary of State there is such an interest in the decision that the person concerned cannot be regarded as an independent and impartial tribunal. The Secretary of State or his department, it is said, lays down policy and directs what he or the department considers to be the most efficient and effective use of land in what he sees to be the public interest. They issue guidance and framework directions which local authorities, inspectors and officials operating the planning system must follow. All of these are bound to affect the mind of the Secretary of State when he takes decisions on called in applications or on appeals which he recovers, it is alleged. Moreover it is said that in the case of Alconbury there is a particular factor in that the land in question is owned by another government department, the Ministry of Defence.

25. Mr Kingston on behalf of HDC also criticised the correspondence and minutes relevant to the Alconbury project. He contends that the role of the officials involved at the Planning and Transport Division in the Government Office for the Region ("GO") was such that there was a real connection not only with planning matters and planning ministers but also with transport ministers and officials and their policies. A site visit by the Parliamentary Under-Secretary for Transport may not have been prejudicial to the determination of the application before the matter was taken over by the Secretary of State. It was quite different once he took over the case for his own decision. As it was put in the case, even leaving aside the fact that the Secretary of State was carrying out his own policy "it is quite clear that the structures in place in relation to cases where the Secretary of State has recovered jurisdiction do not preserve any appearance of independence".

26. Your Lordships have been referred to many decisions of the European Court of Human Rights on article 6 of the Convention. Although the Human Rights Act 1998 does not provide that a national court is bound by these decisions it is obliged to take account of them so far as they are relevant. In the absence of some special circumstances it seems to me that the court should follow any clear and constant jurisprudence of the European Court of Human Rights. If it does not do so there is at least a possibility that the case will go to that court, which is likely in the ordinary case to follow its own constant jurisprudence.

27. It is not necessary to refer to all these cases but some statements of principle by the European Court of Human Rights are important in guiding the House in the present decisions. A preliminary question has arisen as to whether a dispute over administrative law matters of the present kind involved the determination of "civil rights". At first sight to a common lawyer there appears a difference and that difference might seem stronger to a lawyer in a civil law country. In *Ringeisen v Austria (No 1) (1971)* 1 EHRR 455, para.94, however, the court said:

> "For article 6(1) to be applicable to a case ('contestation') it is not necessary that both parties to the proceedings should be private persons, which is the view of the majority of the Commission and of the Government. The wording of article 6(1) is far wider; the French expression 'contestations sur [des] droits et obligations de caractère civil' covers all proceedings the result of which is decisive for private rights and obligations. The English text, 'determination of . . . civil rights and obligations', confirms this interpretation. The character of the legislation which governs how the matter is to be determined (civil, commercial, administrative law, etc) and that of the authority which is invested with jurisdiction in the matter (ordinary court, administrative body, etc) are therefore of little consequence."

See also *Kaplan v United Kingdom* (1980) 4 EHRR 64, 85, *Allan Jacobsson v Sweden* (1989) 12 EHRR 56.

28. In *Fredin v Sweden* (1991) 13 EHRR 784 the court accepted that disputes under planning rules could affect civil rights to build on the applicant's land. Despite the submissions of the Lord Advocate that a decision on a called in application is not a "contestation" on the basis of these and a number of other cases it seems to me plain that this dispute is one which involves the determination of "civil rights" within the meaning of the Convention.

29. The European Court of Human Rights has, however, recognised from the beginning that some administrative law decisions which affect civil rights are taken by ministers answerable to elected bodies. Where there is a two-stage process, *i.e.* there is such an administrative decision which is subject to review by a court, there is a constant line of authority of the European court that regard has to be paid to both stages of the process. Thus even where "jurisdictional organs of professional associations" are set up:

"None the less, in such circumstances the Convention calls at least for one of the two following systems: either the jurisdictional organs themselves comply with the requirements of article 6(1), or they do not so comply but are subject to subsequent control by a judicial body that has full jurisdiction and does provide the guarantees of article 6(1)."

See *Albert and Le Compte v Belgium* (1983) 5 EHRR 533, para.29. See also *Le Compte, Van Leuven and De Meyere v Belgium* (1981) 4 EHRR 1, *Golder v United Kingdom* (1975) 1 EHRR 524.

30. In *Kaplan v United Kingdom* 4 EHRR 64 the Commission noted, at para.150, that

"it is a feature of the administrative law of all the contracting states that in numerous different fields public authorities are empowered by law to take various forms of action impinging on the private rights of citizens."

The Commission referred to its earlier opinion in *Ringeisen v Austria (No 1)* 1 EHRR 455, para.666, where having referred to a number of examples of state regulation the Commission had stated:

"These examples, to which numerous others could be added, seem to indicate that it is a normal feature of contemporary administrative law that the rights and obligations of the citizen, even in matters which relate very closely to his private property or his private activities, are determined by some public authority which does not fulfil the conditions laid down in article 6(1) with respect to independent and impartial tribunals."

31. The Commission continued, at para.159, in relation to judicial review: "It is also a common feature of their administrative law, and indeed almost a corollary of the grant of discretionary powers, that the scope of judicial review of the relevant decisions is limited." And, at para.161:

"An interpretation of article 6(1) under which it was held to provide a right to a full appeal on the merits of every administrative decision affecting private rights would therefore lead to a result which was inconsistent with the existing, and long-standing, legal position in most of the contracting states."

[His Lordship referred to decisions accepting that overall the level of review available on an appeal to a court on a point of law in a statutory application to quash was sufficient for compliance overall with Art.6(1). These were *ISKON v UK* (1994) 18 E.H.R.R. 133 (an appeal on a point of law against an enforcement notice that addressed all the applicant's points); *Bryan v UK* (1995) 21 E.H.R.R. 342 (inspector deciding an appeal against enforcement notice conducted a fair hearing but was not independent and impartial as his appointment could be revoked in a situation where the executive's own policies might be in issue; scope of review by the court, including the point that irrational findings of fact could be set aside, was sufficient for overall compliance, the court emphasising the safeguards attending the procedure before the inspector, including its quasi-judicial nature and the inspector's duty to exercise an independent judgment); *Chapman v UK* (2001) 33 E.H.R.R. 399 (following *Bryan* in respect of an appeal to an inspector against a refusal of planning permission and service of an enforcement notice).]

41. On the basis which I have accepted that the planning, compulsory purchase and other related decisions do affect civil rights even if the procedures and decisions are of an administrative law nature rather than strictly civil law in nature, the first question is, therefore, whether the decision of the Secretary of State which effectively determined these rights in itself constitutes "a fair and public hearing within a reasonable time by an independent and impartial tribunal established by law".

42. "Independent" and "impartial" may import different concepts but there is clearly a link between them and both must be satisfied. It is not suggested that there is actual bias against particular individuals on the part of the Secretary of State or the officials who report to him or who advise him. But it is contended that the Secretary of State is involved in laying down policy and in taking decisions on planning applications in accordance with that policy. He cannot therefore be seen objectively to be independent or impartial. The position is said to be even more critical when roadworks and compulsory purchases are initiated by the Highways Agency or when as in the Alconbury case the land involved belongs to another ministry of the Crown.

43. Before the House the Secretary of State did not contend that in dealing with called in or recovered matters he is acting as an independent tribunal. He accepts that the fact that he makes policy and applies that policy in particular cases is sufficient to prevent him from being an independent tribunal and for the same reasons he is not to be seen as an impartial tribunal for the purposes of article 6 in Part I of Schedule 1 to the 1998 Act.

44. But the many decisions of the European Court of Human Rights make it plain that one does not stop there. A choice was recognised as early as *Albert and Le Compte v Belgium* 5 EHRR 533, para.29 that:

"either the jurisdictional organs themselves comply with the requirements of article 6(1), or they do not so comply but are subject to subsequent control by a judicial body that has full jurisdiction and does provide the guarantees of article 6(1)."

45. These judgments also show that the test whether there is a sufficient juris-dictional control is not a mechanical one. It depends on all the circumstances.

46. On the basis of these decisions it is in my view relevant as a starting point to have regard to such procedural safeguards as do exist in the decision-making process of the Secretary of State even if in the end, because he is apply-ing his policy to which these controls do not apply, he cannot be seen as an impartial and independent tribunal. The fact that an inquiry by an inspector is ordered is important. This gives the applicant and objectors the chance to put forward their views, to call and cross-examine witnesses. The inspector as an experienced professional makes a report, in which he finds the facts and in which he makes his recommendations. He has of course to take account of the policy which has been adopted in, *e.g.*, the development plan but he provides an important filter before the Secretary of State takes his decision and it is sig-nificant that in some 95% of the type of cases with which the House is con-cerned the Secretary of State accepts his recommendation. The Divisional Court had evidence that other steps are taken to ensure that the contentions of the applicant and the objectors are adequately considered. Thus the Divisional Court quoted evidence, in para.62 of their judgment, as to the way in which it is sought to ensure that all material considerations needed to reach an informed, fair, unbiased and reasonable decision could be arrived at as quickly as practicable. Decisions were taken by ministers who so far as pos-sible had no connection with the area from which the case came, and in respect of the decision officer who dealt with the case it was said, in para.63, that he

"works separately from the casework team of which he is nominally a part, does not discuss the merits of the planning decisions before him with an individual either within or without GO East, is not copied into or involved in the preparation of the Regional Planning Guidance ('RPG') or the exer-cise of any of the Secretary of State's powers of intervention under the Town and Country Planning Act, and only has before him the information which the inspector would have had at the inquiry into the particular appeal or called in application, together with any representation made after the close of the inquiries (all relevant parties are given the opportunity to comment on any such representations where they are material or raise new matters)."

47. On the decision-making process I do not suggest that one can make arti-ficial distinctions between different branches of a government department. I refer to what was said by Lord Diplock in *Bushell v Secretary of State for the Environment* [1981] AC 75, 95. But there is nothing unusual or sinister in the methods provided for planning decisions to be taken by the executive in the United Kingdom. The European Court of Human Rights has recognised that in many European countries planning decisions are made by elected or appointed officers with a limited judicial review even though the extent of this may vary from state to state. In *B Johnson & Co (Builders) Ltd v Minister of Health* [1947] 2 All ER 395, 399 Lord Greene MR recognised the importance of the administrative stage of the decision:

"the raising of the objections to the order, the consideration of the matters so raised and the representations of the local authority and the objectors— is merely a stage in the process of arriving at an administrative decision. It is a stage which the courts have always said requires a certain method of approach and method of conduct, but it is not a lis inter partes, and for the simple reason that the local authority and the objectors are not parties to anything that resembles litigation. A moment's thought will show that any such conception of the relationship must be fallacious, because on the substantive matter, viz, whether the order should be confirmed or not, there is a third party who is not present, viz, the public, and it is the function of the minister to consider the rights and the interests of the public . . . It may well be that, on considering the objections, the minister may find that they are reasonable and that the facts alleged in them are true, but, nevertheless, he may decide that he will overrule them. His action in so deciding is a purely administrative action, based on his conceptions as to what public policy demands."

48. The adoption of planning policy and its application to particular facts is quite different from the judicial function. It is for elected Members of Parliament and ministers to decide what are the objectives of planning policy, objectives which may be of national, environmental, social or political significance and for these objectives to be set out in legislation, primary and secondary, in ministerial directions and in planning policy guidelines. Local authorities, inspectors and the Secretary of State are all required to have regard to policy in taking particular planning decisions and it is easy to overstate the difference between the application of a policy in decisions taken by the Secretary of State and his inspector. As to the making of policy, *Wade & Forsyth, Administrative Law*, 8th ed (2000), p 464 says:

"It is self-evident that ministerial or departmental policy cannot be regarded as disqualifying bias. One of the commonest administrative mechanisms is to give a minister power to make or confirm an order after hearing objections to it. The procedure for the hearing of objections is subject to the rules of natural justice in so far as they require a fair hearing and fair procedure generally. But the minister's decision cannot be impugned on the ground that he has advocated the scheme or that he is known to support it as a matter of policy. The whole object of putting the power into his hands is that he may exercise it according to government policy."

As Mr Gregory Jones put it pithily in argument it is not right to say that a policy maker cannot be a decision maker or that the final decision maker cannot be a democratically elected person or body.

49. Accepting this method of proceeding, the question, as the European court has shown, is whether there is a sufficient judicial control to ensure a determination by an independent and impartial tribunal subsequently. The judgments to which I have referred do not require that this should constitute a rehearing on an application by an appeal on the merits. It would be surprising if it had required this in view of the difference of function between the minister exercising his statutory powers, for the policy of which he is answerable to the legislature and ultimately to the electorate, and the court. What is required on the part of the latter is that there should be a sufficient review of the legality of the decisions and of the procedures followed. The common law has developed specific grounds of review of administrative acts and these have been reflected in the statutory provisions for judicial review such as are provided for in the present cases. See as relatively straightforward examples *Ashbridge Investments Ltd v Minister of Housing and Local Government* [1965] 1 WLR 1320 and *Stringer v Minister of Housing and Local Government* [1970] 1 WLR 1281.

50. It has long been established that if the Secretary of State misinterprets the legislation under which he purports to act, or if he takes into account matters irrelevant to his decision or refuses or fails to take account of matters relevant to his decision, or reaches a perverse decision, the court may set his decision aside. Even if he fails to follow necessary procedural steps—failing to give notice of a hearing or to allow an opportunity for evidence to be called or cross-examined, or for representations to be made or to take any step which fairness and natural justice requires—the court may interfere. The legality of the decision and the procedural steps must be subject to sufficient judicial control. But none of the judgments before the European Court of Human Rights requires that the court should have "full jurisdiction" to review policy or the overall merits of a planning decision. This approach is reflected in the powers of the European Court of Justice to review executive acts under article 230 of the EC Treaty:

"It shall for this purpose have jurisdiction in actions brought by a member state, the Council or the Commission on grounds of lack of competence, infringement of an essential procedural requirement, infringement of this Treaty or of any rule of law relating to its application, or misuse of powers."

51. The European Court of Justice does of course apply the principle of proportionality when examining such acts and national judges must apply the same principle when dealing with Community law issues. There is a difference between that principle and the approach of the English courts in *Associated Provincial Picture Houses Ltd v Wednesbury Corpn* [1948] 1 KB 223. But the difference in practice is not as great as is sometimes supposed.

The cautious approach of the European Court of Justice in applying the principle is shown inter alia by the margin of appreciation it accords to the institutions of the Community in making economic assessments. I consider that even without reference to the Human Rights Act 1998 the time has come to recognise that this principle is part of English administrative law, not only when judges are dealing with Community acts but also when they are dealing with acts subject to domestic law. Trying to keep the *Wednesbury* principle and proportionality in separate compartments seems to me to be unnecessary and confusing. Reference to the Human Rights Act 1998 however makes it necessary that the court should ask whether what is done is compatible with Convention rights. That will often require that the question should be asked whether the principle of proportionality has been satisfied: see *R v Secretary of State for the Home Department, Ex p. Turgut* [2001] 1 All ER 719; *R (Mahmood) v Secretary of State for the Home Department* [2000] 1 WLR 840.

52. This principle does not go as far as to provide for a complete rehearing on the merits of the decision. Judicial control does not need to go so far. It should not do so unless Parliament specifically authorises it in particular areas.

53. In *R v Criminal Injuries Compensation Board, Ex p. A* [1999] 2 AC 330, 344–345 I accepted that the court had jurisdiction to quash for a misunderstanding or ignorance of an established and relevant fact. I remain of that

view, which finds support in *Wade & Forsyth, Administrative Law*, 7th ed (1994), pp.316–318. I said:

> "Your Lordships have been asked to say that there is jurisdiction to quash the board's decision because that decision was reached on a material error of fact. Reference has been made to Wade & Forsyth, Administrative Law, 7th ed (1994), pp.316–318 in which it is said: 'Mere factual mistake has become a ground of judicial review, described as "misunderstanding or ignorance of an established and relevant fact" [*Secretary of State for Education and Science v Tameside Metropolitan Borough Council* [1977] AC 1014, 1030] or acting "upon an incorrect basis of fact" . . . This ground of review has long been familiar in French law and it has been adopted by statute in Australia. It is no less needed in this country, since decisions based upon wrong facts are a cause of injustice which the courts should be able to remedy. If a "wrong factual basis" doctrine should become established, it would apparently be a new branch of the ultra vires doctrine, analogous to finding facts based upon no evidence or acting upon a misapprehension of law.' *de Smith, Woolf & Jowell, Judicial Review of Administrative Action*, 5th ed (1995), p.288: 'The taking into account of a mistaken fact can just as easily be absorbed into a traditional legal ground of review by referring to the taking into account of an irrelevant consideration, or the failure to provide reasons that are adequate or intelligible, or the failure to base the decision on any evidence. In this limited context material error of fact has always been a recognised ground for judicial intervention.' "

54. I accordingly hold that, in relation to the judicial review of the Secretary of State's decision in a called in application or a recovered appeal under the planning legislation and to a review of the decisions and orders under the other statutes concerned in the present appeals, there is in principle no violation of article 6 of the European Convention on Human Rights as set out in Part I of Schedule 1 to the Human Rights Act 1998. The scope of review is sufficient to comply with the standards set by the European Court of Human Rights. That is my view even if proportionality and the review of material errors of fact are left out of that account: they do, however, make the case even stronger. It is open to the House to rule on that question of principle at this stage of the procedure in the various cases.

55. I do not consider that the financial interests of the Ministry of Defence automatically precludes a decision on planning grounds by the Secretary of State, or that the communication between government departments and site visits by ministers to which reference has been made in argument in principle vitiate the whole process. If of course specific breaches of the administrative law rules are established, as for example if the financial interests of the government were wrongly taken into account by the Secretary of State, then specific challenges on those grounds may be possible on judicial review.

56. I would accordingly allow the appeals, dismiss the cross-appeals and set aside the declarations of the Divisional Court.

LORDS NOLAN, HOFFMANN, CLYDE and HUTTON delivered concurring opinions.

Appeals allowed

Notes

1. There is a large body of case law on the scope of Art.6(1). Article 6(2) and (3) concern criminal proceedings and are not considered in detail here.

2. *Determination of civil rights and obligations.* Like Lord Slynn, Lords Hoffmann, Clyde and Hutton (at [131]–[135], [145]–[157], [181]–[184]) rejected the argument, raised on the intervention by Scottish ministers, that these planning decisions did not involve the *determination* of civil rights and obligations but were simply the exercise of legal powers which affected, and perhaps changed, such rights and obligations. A "dispute" or "contestation" arose at least from the time when a power was exercised and objection was taken to that exercise (*per* Lord Clyde at [147]. It has subsequently been held that a decision to grant planning permission to X in respect of Y's land is a determination affecting Y's rights (*British Telecommunications plc v Gloucester CC* [2001] EWHC Admin 1001); as is a decision to grant planning permission to X in respect of X's land for a development that will detrimentally affect both the enjoyment by Y of his home and its monetary value (*R. (on the application of Kathro) v Rhondda Cynon Taff LBC* [2001] EWHC Admin 527, distinguished in *R. (on the application of Vetterlein) v Hampshire CC* [2001] EWHC Admin 560; [2002] Env. L.R. 8 (objections to incinerator from persons living 1.63, 1.79 and 2.14 miles from the application site).

A decision by a local authority to take steps required by an enforcement notice in default of compliance by its recipient does not engage Art.6(1); the "civil rights" in question will have already have been determined by a procedure that led to a valid and effective notice (*R. (on the application of M) v Horsham DC* [2003] EWHC 234).

3. For there to be a determination of civil rights and obligations there must be a genuine and serious dispute and that its resolution has a direct effect on a civil right or obligation. "Civil rights" may include entitlements to social insurance and welfare benefits provided by the state (*Feldbrugge v Netherlands* (1986) 8 E.H.R.R. 425) but not situations where benefits may be provided as a matter of discretion (*Machatova v Slovak Republic* (1997) 24 E.H.R.R. D44). Further examples from English law of such determinations include: the determination under regulations whether a person was to be treated as possessing capital of which he had deprived himself for the purpose of decrease the amount that he might be liable to pay for his residential care (*R. (on the application of Beeson) v Dorset CC* [2002] EWCA Civ 1812); the decision of a review panel in respect of the termination of an introductory tenancy (*R. (on the application of McLellan) v Bracknell Forest BC* [2001] EWCA Civ 1510; [2002] Q.B. 1129); and a decision of the Secretary of State to withdraw support from a destitute asylum seeker (*R. (on the application of Husain) v Asylum Support Adjudicator* [2001] EWHC Admin 832) or to refuse support on the ground that he was not satisfied that asylum was claimed as soon as reasonably practicable after arrival in the United Kingdom (*R. (on the application of Q) v Secretary of State for the Home Department* [2003] EWHC 194, Collins J.; on appeal, the applicability of Art. 6 was assumed (but not conceded by the Attorney-General), the court holding that the possibility of judicial review was sufficient to satisfy Art.6); and proceedings on an application (on notice) for an Anti-social Behaviour Order (*R. (on the application of McCann) v Manchester Crown Court* [2003] 1 A.C. 78; as distinct from proceedings without notice for an interim ASBO (*R. (on the application of M) v Secretary of State for Constitutional Affairs* [2003] EWHC 2963; [2004] 1 W.L.R. 2298).

On the other hand, decisions to refuse admission to or expel a pupil from a secondary school does not involve the determination of a civil right (*R. (on the application of B) v Head Teacher and Governing Body of Alperton Community School* [2001] EWHC Admin 2209. Whether the duty of a housing authority, in specified circumstances, to secure accommodation for a homeless person gives rise to a civil right was left open by the House of Lords in *R. (on the application of Rena Begum) v Tower Hamlets LBC* [2003] UKHL 5. [2003] 2 A.C. 430.

4. *Criminal charge.* This term is also given an autonomous meaning, taking account of the type of national law embodying the offence (and how such conduct is dealt with in other jurisdictions), the nature of the conduct prohibited and the severity of the punishment (*Engel v The Netherlands* (1976) 1 E.H.R.R. 647; *Att-Gen's Reference (No.2 of 2001)* [2003] UKHL 68; [2004] 2 A.C. 72). For example, the term covers disciplinary adjudications by prison governors leading to additional days in prison (*Ezeh and Connors v UK* (2002) 35 E.H.R.R. 691; *R. (on the application of Greenfield) v Secretary of State for the Home Department* [2005] UKHL 14); but not ASBO proceedings (*McCann*, above), or school exclusion proceedings (*Alperton*, above).

6. *Fair and public hearing.* This may include a right of effective access to a court (*Golder v UK* (1975) 1 E.H.R.R. 524 (right of access to a court by a prisoner for determination of civil claim)); cf. *Osman v UK*, below, p.1069. For example, the imposition of a fixed penalty regime disproportionate to the object to be achieved was held to infringe the applicant's right to have the appropriate level of penalty determined by an independent tribunal in *R. (on the application of International Transport Roth GmbH) v Secretary of State for the Home Department* [2002] EWCA Civ 158; [2003] Q.B. 728. On the other hand, the six-week time-limit on appeals under s.288 of the Town and Country Planning Act 1990 and the requirement of promptness for a claim for judicial review do not constitute a disproportionate restriction on the right of access (*Matthews v Secretary of State for the Environment, Transport and the Regions* [2001] EWHC Admin 815 (s.288); *Lam v UK* (App. No.41671/98) (judicial review). Limitations set by law to the scope of substantive rights, as distinct from procedural bars, will not normally violate Art.6(1). See *Matthews v Ministry of Defence* [2003] UKHL 4; [2004] 1 A.C. 1163 (bar to tort claim by servicemen, below p.1103); *Wilson v Secretary of State for Trade and Industry* [2003] UKHL 40; [2004] 1 A.C. 816 (provision that a regulated agreement under s.8 of the Consumer Credit Act 1974 is not enforceable unless a document containing all the prescribed terms is signed by the debtor held not to be a procedural bar). See T. Hickman, "The 'Uncertain Shadow': Throwing Light on the Right to a Court under Article 6(1) ECHR" [2004] P.L 122.

The requirement also includes "equality of arms" including adequate disclosure of relevant evidence (*Rowe and Davis v UK* (2000) 30 E.H.R.R. 1) (*cf.* the common law of natural justice, Ch.10 and a requirement for courts to give reasons for their judgments (*Garcia Ruiz v Spain* (2001) 31 E.H.R.R. 22; *English v Emery Reimbold & Strick Ltd* [2002] 1 W.L.R. 2409).

7. *Independent and impartial tribunal.* This element echoes the rule against interest and bias and has led to some modifications to the common law to bring it into line with Art.6(1) (see Ch.10). "Independent" and "impartial" are separate but closely related requirements. An appeal to a court with "full jurisdiction" may overall secure compliance (*Alconbury*, above).

The significance of the distinction between policy and fact drawn in *Alconbury* has, however, been reduced by the decision of the House of Lords in *Runa Begum v Tower Hamlets LBC* [2003] UKHL 5; [2003] 2 A.C. 430. Here, the House held that the possibility of review by the county court of determinations, including decisions on matters of fact, by a local housing authority as to whether it owed a duty under Pt 7 of the Housing Act 1996 to secure accommodation for a homeless person, was sufficient for compliance with Art.6(1). The review mechanism, an appeal under s.204 of the 1996 Act, applied conventional judicial review principles. The House held that there was no necessity for an appeal on the merits on factual issues, although it left open the question whether the county court should apply a greater intensity of review on factual issues. The House, furthermore, indicated that review on conventional judicial review grounds would generally be sufficient in cases of administrative decision-making, as in discharging regulatory functions (such as licensing or granting planning permission) or administering schemes of social welfare (see Lord Hoffmann at [42], [59]. At [41] his Lordship distinguished *Bryan v UK*, above, on the ground that it concerned an appeal against an enforcement notice where the inspector's decision on an appeal would be binding in subsequent criminal proceedings). Accordingly, in a number of situations previously considered by the lower courts the distinction between policy and fact would no longer be significant, judicial review being sufficient in all cases. It should be noted, however, that the decision in *Runa Begum* concerned a matter where it was assumed that a "civil right" was engaged and recognised that a decision that it was so engaged would involve an extension of the Strasbourg jurisprudence. It is submitted that the more clearly a situation falls within the core of the "civil right" concept, the less likely it is where facts are in issue that the right to an independent and impartial tribunal will be satisfied by recourse to a court equipped only with the conventional powers of judicial review. For discussion of *Alconbury* and *Begum*, see P.P. Craig, "The Human Rights Act, Article 6 and Procedural Rights" [2003] P.L. 753.

(vi) Article 7

This applies a non-derogable prohibition on retrospective criminal legislation. This does not prevent the "gradual clarification" of the criminal law through judicial development provided the resulting development is consistent with the essence of the offence and can reasonably be foreseen (*SW and CR v UK* (1995) 21 E.H.R.R. 363, in relation to the removal of the marital rape exemption by the House of Lords in *R. v R* [1992] 1 A.C. 599). A violation arises if a prisoner is subsequently subjected to a heavier penalty than that which *could* have been improved under the law in force at the time he committed the offence (*R. (on the application of Uttley) v Secretary of State for the Home Department* [2004] UKHL 38; [2004] 1 W.L.R. 2278 (no violation therefore arose from an unfavourable change in the release regime for a prisoner sentenced to 12 years' imprisonment for rape as he could have been sentenced to life imprisonment).

(vii) Article 8

Article 8(1) covers much ground, requiring respect for private life, family life, home and correspondence subject to the qualifications in Art.8(2).

Notes

1. *Private Life*. The requirement of respect for private life covers such matters as the collection of secret information concerning individuals (*Leander v Sweden* (1987) 9 E.H.R.R. 433), the disclosure of personal information concerning children (*Re S (a child)* [2004] UKHL 47) and the disclosure to the media of CCTV footage by a local authority of the events following a suicide attempt by a person in a public street (*Peck v UK* (2001) 36 E.H.R.R. 41).

2. *Family Life*. The right to respect for family life is of particular significance in such areas as the decision-making of local authorities concerning children in care (below, p.1070); the policy of the prison service with respect to the length of time babies would be permitted to live with their mothers in prison (*R. (on the application of P) v Secretary of State for the Home Department* [2001] EWCA Civ 1151; [2001] 1 W.L.R. 2002 (below, p.490)); the provision of wholly unsuitable accommodation to a severely disabled claimant (*R. (on the application of Bernard v Enfield LBC* [2002] EWHC 2282; [2003] H.R.L.R. 111 (discussed in *Anufrijeva v Southward LBC*, above, p.336); and immigration decisions affecting family life (*Anufrijeva*).

3. *Home*. The right to respect for a home does not include a right to be provided with a home (*Chapman v UK* (2001) 33 E.H.R.R. 18 at para.99). However, whether a particular habitation is a "home" depends on the existence of sufficient and continuous links and is not confined to a residence legally established in accordance with national law (*Buckley v UK* (1996) 23 E.H.R.R. 101). Enforcement action in respect caravans on land in breach of planning law may accordingly infringe Art.8 (*Buckley*;

no violation found). In a controversial decision, the House of Lords in *Harrow LBC v Qazi* [2003] UKHL 43; [2004] 1 A.C. 983, by a majority (Lords Hope of Craighead, Millett and Scott of Foscote, Lords Bingham of Cornhill and Steyn dissenting), held that while Art.8(1) is "applicable" to or "engaged" by an eviction from a home, the grant of an order for possession to a person or body with an unqualified right to possession, following service of a notice to quit, does not, save in wholly exceptional circumstances, violate the essence of the right to respect for the home (see Lord Hope at [83]) or, in the alternative, that the interference is automatically justified under Art.8(2) as "necessary to protect the rights and freedoms" of the person entitled to possession (see Lord Millett at [100]–[103] and Lord Scott at [149]). The majority noted that Art. 8 essentially protected privacy as distinct from property interests, the latter being protected by the First Protocol, Art.1. Where the decision to evict is made by the authority under a statutory scheme on the basis of the claimant's conduct (the termination here was effected by the acts of the joint tenant not of the local authority), issues of reasonableness and proportionality may be raised on claim for judicial review (see Lord Hope at [79]). Lord Steyn dissenting (at [27]) regarded this decision as contrary to a purposive interpretation of Art.8 and emptying Art.8(1) of any or virtually any meaningful content; it would be surprising if it withstood European scrutiny. For a critical analysis of *Qazi*, see I. Loveland, [2004] P.L. 594.

The ECtHR has held that the summary procedure for the eviction of gypsies in breach of licence conditions at a caravan site run by a local authority violated Art.8 ECHR. These arrangements were not shown to be justified by a pressing social need or proportionate to the legitimate aim pursued (*Connors v UK* (2004) 16 B.H.R.C. 639). Furthermore, the Court of Appeal in *Price v Leeds City Council* [2005] EWCA Civ 289 has held that this decision:

"is unquestionably incompatible with the proposition that the exercise by a public authority of an unqualified proprietary right under domestic law to repossess its land will never constitute an interference with the occupier's right to respect for his home, or will always be justified under Art. 8(2). To that extent *Connors* is incompatible with *Qazi*".

Furthermore, the reasoning in *Connors* cannot be confined to cases concerning gypsies. However, it would not be right for the Court of Appeal to follow the decision in *Connors* in preference to that of the House of Lords in *Qazi* (*per* Lord Phillips M.R. at [26] and [29]). *Qazi* will clearly need further attention from the House of Lords.

The right to respect for a home may be infringed by causing, or allowing others to create, severe environmental pollution (*cf. Hatton v UK* (2002) 34 E.H.R.R. 1 (aircraft noise generated by flights at Heathrow; infringement found)). A person's loss of amenity in his home arising from flooding from public sewers or from the grant of planning permission for a development on neighboring land must accordingly be balanced against the other interests involved, including where relevant those of other landowners and the general public. See, respectively *Marcic v Thames Water Utilities Ltd* [2003] UKHL 66; [2004] 2 A.C. 42 (statutory scheme under the Water Industry Act 1991 held to strike a reasonable balance between the interests of customers whose properties were prone to sewer flooding and the interests of all the other customers of the sewerage undertaker (see Lord Nicholls of Birkenhead at [37]–[46]); *Lough v First Secretary of State* [2004] EWCA Civ 905 (claimants' loss of amenity, comprising as claimed here loss of privacy, overlooking, loss of light, loss of a view and interference with television reception, to be balanced against interests of prospective developing landowner). Article 8 creates not absolute right to amenities currently enjoyed (*per* Pill L.J. in *Lough* at [41]).

4. *Positive obligations.* Overall, states are accorded a wide margin of appreciation by the ECtHR, particularly in respect of arguments that they should take positive steps in support of the rights protected by Art.8(1) (see *Anufrijeva*, above, p.320).

5. *Article 8(2)*. For an interference with rights protected by Art.8(1) to be justified by reference to Art.8(2) it must be (a) "in accordance with the law"; (b) "necessary in a democratic society"; and (c) "for a legitimate aim". To be "in accordance with the law", the interference must have some basis in domestic law (such as primary and delegated legislation but not internal instructions); the law must be "adequately accessible: the citizen must be able to have an indication that is adequate, in the circumstances, of the legal rules applicable to a given case"; and a norm to be regarded as "law" must be "formulated with sufficient precision to enable the citizen to regulate his conduct: he must be able—if need be with appropriate advice—to foresee, to a degree that is reasonable in the circumstances, the consequences which a given action may entail" (*Silver v UK* (1983) 5 E.H.R.R. 347 at paras [85]–[88], applying the principles developed in respect of Art.10 by the Court in *Sunday Times v UK* (1979) 2 E.H.R.R. 245). As regards what is "necessary in a democratic society", it has been stated that:

"(a) The adjective 'necessary' is not synonymous with 'indispensable', neither has it the flexibility of such expressions as 'admissible', 'ordinary', 'useful', 'reasonable or desirable'. . .

(b) The Contracting States enjoy a certain but not unlimited margin of appreciation in the mater of the imposition of restrictions, but it is for the Court to give the final ruling on whether they are compatible with the Convention.

(c) The phrase 'necessary' in a democratic society means that, to be compatible with the Convention, the interference must, *inter alia*, correspond to a 'pressing social need' and be 'proportionate to the legitimate aim pursued'.

(d) Those paragraphs of Articles of the Convention which provide for an exception to a right guaranteed are to be narrowly interpreted. . ." (*ibid.*, para.97).

Justifications under Art.8(2) have been found in a wide variety of circumstances. In some contexts, the court itself is the primary decision-maker, as where it exercises its jurisdiction to grant an injunction under s.187B of the Town and Country Planning Act 1990 (*South Bucks DC v Porter* [2003] UKHL 26; [2003] 2 A.C. 558). Here it must be satisfied that to grant the remedy is necessary and proportionate to the aim to be achieved.

In others, as where it is hearing an appeal against a refusal of planning permission or an application for judicial review of the grant of planning permission, claimed to infringe rights under Art.8(1), its role is to ensure that the appropriate balancing exercise has been carried out by the local planning authority and the inspector, whether or not express reference has been made to the principle of proportionality (*Lough v First Secretary of State* [2004] EWCA Civ 905 (although Pill L.J. did say (at [48]) that

"Article 8 should in my view normally be considered as an integral part of the decision maker's approach to material considerations and not, as happened in this case, in effect as a footnote")).

Similarly, a balancing exercise will have to be conducted in respect of a decision to close a care home (*R. (on the application of Haggerty) v St. Helens Council* [2003] EWHC 803; [2003] H.L.R. 69).

(viii) Article 9

The right to freedom of thought, conscience and religion is subject to qualifications similar to Arts 8(2), 10(2), 11(2). The freedom to hold a belief (whether or not religious) is absolute; the right to manifest a belief is a qualified right. For example, the belief of parents that the use of corporal punishment as a means of discipline is necessary for the proper upbringing of children is capable of being protected by Art.9(1) provided the punishment is of a mild nature; however the prohibition of corporal punishment by teachers in all schools by s.548 of the Education Act 1996 is not disproportionate and is justified under Art.9(2) as being for the protection of children (*R. (on the application of Williamson) v Secretary of State for Education and Employment* [2005] UKHL 15, [2005] 2 W.L.R. 590). A school must consider whether the adoption of a school uniform policy to which there are objections on religious grounds is justified under Art.9(2) (*R. (on the application of SB) v Governors of Denbigh High School* [2005] EWCA Civ. 199, [2005] 2 All E.R. 396).

(ix) Article 10

This protects freedom of expression, a core value of a democratic society that is also enshrined in the common law (*cf.* Lord Styen in *Simms,* below, p.261). The HRA 1998, however, applies a test of proportionality to interference with the freedom (see *Sunday Times v UK* (1979) 2 E.H.R.R. 245; *Reynolds v Times Newspapers* [2001] 1 A.C. 127 (modifying the law of qualified privilege in its application to public figures); but *cf. R. (on the application of ProLife Alliance) v BBC* [2003] UKHL 23; [2004] 1 A.C. 185, where the compatibility of the application of generally standards of taste and decency to party election broadcasts with Art.10 was not challenged).

(x) Article 11

This confers a right to freedom of peaceful assembly and to freedom of association. Both the ban on trade unions at GCHQ and the restrictions on the right of senior local authority officers to engage in political activity have been held to be justified under Art.11(2) (*Council of Civil Service Unions v UK* (App. No.11603/85, 50 DR 228, E Com HR) (see below, p.690); *Ahmed v UK* (1998) 29 E.H.R.R. 1).

(xi) Article 12

Article 12 confers the right to marry and to found a family. A couple's inability to conceive a child does not itself remove the right to marry (*Goodwin v UK* (2002) 35 E.H.R.R. 447). States may, without infringing Art.12, prohibit same-sex marriages; but not marriages between transsexuals following gender reassignment (*ibid.*); see *Bellinger v Bellinger,* above, p.315).

(xii) Article 14

This does not constitute a free-standing prohibition of discrimination on the stated grounds (which are themselves given as examples; other impermissible grounds include sexual orientation). Complaints must be concerned with one or more of the substantive protected rights and freedoms taken in conjunction with Art.14 (*Belgian Linguistic Case (No.2)* (1968) 1 E.H.R.R. 252 at para.9). The principles of Art.14 are considered in *Ghaidan* (above, p.303) and *A v Secretary of State for the Home Department* (above, p.351).

(xiii) First Protocol, Article 1

This in substance guarantees the right to property (*Marckx v Belgium* (1979) 2 E.H.R.R. 330, para.63). The first sentence sets out a general principle, that extends to interferences with property falling short of full deprivation. The second sentence deals with deprivation, and the third sentence provides an exception where the state is seeking to control the use of property for a permitted purpose. The second and third sentences are "particular instances" of interference with the right to the peaceful enjoyment of property and so should be construed in the light of the general principle (*James v UK* (1986) E.H.R.R. 123 at para.37). The court has to determine whether interference is lawful under domestic law and, if so, whether a "fair balance" has been struck between the demands of the general interest of the community and the requirements of the protection of the individual's fundamental rights, applying a proportionality test while recognising a wide margin of appreciation (*Sporrong and Lonnroth v Sweden* (1982) 5 E.H.R.R. 35 at para.69; *Wilson v Secretary of State for Trade and Industry* [2003] UKHL 40; [2004] 1 A.C. 816).

A violation was found where a local authority granted the applicant an option to renew a lease, but when it came to be exercised argued successfully in the courts that the grant of the option was *ultra vires* The ECtHR (*Stretch v UK*, App. No.44277/98, judgment of June 24, 2003) held that this was a disproportionate interference, noting that there was no issue that the local authority had acted against the public interest in the way in which it has disposed of its property or that any third-party interests or the pursuit of any other statutory function would have been prejudiced by giving effect to the option. Express provision for the grant of such options had been made in subsequent legislation.

The Article implicitly requires the payment of compensation (although not necessarily full market value) as a necessary condition for taking of property of anyone within the jurisdiction of a contracting state, on the basis that their taking without such payment would normally be disproportionate (*James v UK*, above).

"Possessions" can be existing possessions or assets, including claims, in respect of which the applicant can argue that he has at least a legitimate expectation of obtaining effective enjoyment of a property right; but not the hope of recognition of the survival of an old property right which it has long been impossible to exercise effectively, or a conditional claim which lapses as a result of non fulfillment of a condition (*Stretch*). The term "possessions" accordingly extends to cover interferences with economic interests arising from such matters as the revocation of a licence needed to run a business (*Tre Traktoorer Aktiebolag v Sweden* (1989) 13 E.H.R.R. 309 (restaurant licence to sell alcohol)), a decision that a grant of planning permission was a nullity (*Pine Valley Developments Ltd v Ireland* (1992) 14 E.H.R.R. 319), and the non-payment of benefits where contributions have been made into the underlying scheme.

The term "possessions" does not apply to non-contributory benefits (*R. (on the application of Reynolds) v Secretary of State for Work and Pensions* [2003] EWCA Civ 797; [2003] 3 All E.R. 577 at [42]–[49]); a failure to uprate the state pension for pensions living abroad (*R. (on the application of Carson) v Secretary of State for Work and Pensions* [2002] EWCA Civ 797; [2003] 3 All E.R. 577 at [17]–[23]); or *ex gratia* payments unenforceable by action under domestic law (*R. (on the application of Association of British Civilian Internees) v Secretary of State for Defence* [2002] EWHC (Admin) 2119).

(xiv) First Protocol, Article 2

Note the United Kingdom's reservation to this provision (above, p.297).

(xv) First Protocol, Article 3

This covers the right to vote at elections to the European Parliament (*Matthews v UK* (1999) 28 E.H.R.R. 361 (United Kingdom held responsible for the lack of such elections in Gibraltar)). The blanket restriction on the right of all convicted prisoners to vote has been held to be disproportionate (*Hirst v UK* (No.2) (App. No.74025/01, judgment of March 30, 2004).

(xv) Thirteenth Protocol

This abolishes the death penalty at any time, and replaced the Sixth Protocol, Arts 1 and 2 which provided for a right not to be sentenced to death save in respect of acts committed in time of war or imminent threat of war.

Chapter 7

ILLEGALITY

In this chapter we deal with cases at the core of the concept of illegality or, in statutory contexts, the *ultra vires* doctrine. Typically, they raise the question whether a public authority has power to perform a particular act that it has performed or wishes to perform (pp.391–406), or is, indeed, under a duty to perform that act (pp.406–420). A more complex variant can arise, commonly but not solely in the context of bodies exercising a judicial rather than administrative function, where power is only exercisable in specified circumstances. Difficult questions can arise as to whether it is for the decision-maker or for the court on a claim for judicial review to decide whether those circumstances exist. These are considered at pp.420–458.

In practice, the issues that arise in these kinds of cases are commonly to be resolved through an exercise in statutory interpretation of the relevant words in their context, rather than the application of general principles external to the text (*cf.* above, p.263).

(A) "Simple" *Ultra Vires*—The Basic Principles

ATTORNEY-GENERAL v FULHAM CORPORATION

[1921] 1 CH. 440; 90 L.J. CH. 281; 125 L.T. 14; 85 J.P. 213; 37 T.L.R. 156 (CHANCERY DIVISION, SARGANT J.)

The defendant, a statutory authority, had power under the Baths and Wash-houses Acts 1846 to 1878 to establish baths, wash-houses and open bathing places. In the exercise of these powers it had for many years operated a wash-house at which persons coming to the wash-house had an opportunity of washing their clothes. The only assistance given, beyond the provision of the facilities, was that an attendant operated the "hydro-extractor" (wringer), and another attendant controlled the "box mangle". In due course, the corporation resolved to "confer a lasting benefit on all classes of the community" by "establishing a system of mechanical washing" in the borough. A public notice was issued, headed—"Household problem solved! A boon to house-wives!!!." The notice continued: "the Council has established a department at the baths and wash-house, for the purpose of relieving Housewives to a great extent of this most laborious work". The new scheme involved the purchase of a bag. This the customer would fill with washing and leave at the wash-house. The laundered washing would later be delivered to the customer, or the customer could collect.

Sargant J.: This is an action by the Attorney-General, at the relation of the ratepayers of Fulham, against the municipal borough of Fulham, to restrain it, to use a short phrase, from carrying on a laundry, or something in the nature of a laundry.

In considering what the corporation may do, and what it may not do, I have to take as my guiding authority the words of Lord Selborne L.C. in *Attorney-General v. Great Eastern Ry Co.* (1880) 5 App.Cas. 473, 478. He says:

"I assume that your Lordships will not now recede from anything that was determined in *Ashbury Ry Co. v. Riche* (1875) L.R. 7 H.L. 653. It appears to me to be important that the doctrine of *ultra vires*, as it was explained in that case, should be maintained. But I agree with James L.J. that this doctrine ought to be reasonably, and not unreasonably, understood and applied, and that whatever may fairly be regarded as incidental to, or consequential upon, those things which the Legislature has authorized, ought not (unless expressly prohibited) to be held, by judicial construction, to be *ultra vires*." That recognizes that in every case it is for a corporation of this kind to show that it has affirmatively an authority to do particular acts; but that in applying that principle, the rule is not to be applied too narrowly, and the corporation is entitled to do not only that which is expressly authorized but that which is reasonably incidental to or consequential upon that which is in terms authorized. And it is, of course, for the defendant corporation to point out the authority under which it has acted in what it has done. [His Lordship stated the facts, as set out above, including the new laundry scheme, and continued:] Now that is the new scheme and the method of carrying it out, and the question I have to consider is this, whether that scheme is authorized by the Baths and Washhouses Act 1846, and the Baths and Wash-houses Act, 1847.

It is quite clear that the new scheme of the corporation is not directly authorized by those Acts, but I have also to see, whether, although it is not authorized in terms by the Acts, it is something which in the language I have cited, "may fairly be regarded as incidental to or consequent upon those things which the Legislature has authorized". For that purpose I have to look at the two Acts. [His Lordship summarised the principal provisions of the Acts, and continued:]

Now what is the effect of that legislation? It appears to me to be quite clear that the whole scheme is to afford facilities for persons who have not such facilities themselves and cannot pay for them, so that they may, so far as the wash-houses are concerned, do their own washing. Throughout there is no sort of suggestion, as far as I can see, that anything is to be provided for those persons except facilities for their doing the work themselves. . . .

Under the new system which has been inaugurated what has been provided for the persons who become customers is, in my judgment, not facilities for doing their own washing, but the washing itself. It seems to me that, in view of the fact that the control of the articles in question is entirely parted with, that the articles are washed up to a certain point absolutely and entirely irrespective of the labours or attention or care of the customers, and that the articles when that process has been gone through are redelivered in their semi-finished state to the customers, it is impossible to say that the council have been doing anything else except the washing of the clothes down to a certain point for the particular customers. Now is that something which may fairly be regarded as incidental to or consequential upon the provision of facilities for washing? In my judgment, it is not . . .

There will therefore be a declaration that the defendant corporation is not entitled to carry on any enterprise which involves the total or partial washing of clothes for others by the defendant corporation, as distinguished from facilities for enabling others to come to the wash-house to wash their clothes; and there will be an injunction to restrain the defendant corporation, its officers, servants and agents, acting in contravention of this declaration. . . .

Notes

1. The decision of the House of Lords in *Ashbury Railway Carriage & Iron Co. Ltd v Riche* (1875) L.R. 7 H.L. 653 established that "a statutory corporation, created by Act of Parliament for a particular purpose, is limited, as to all its powers, by the purposes of its incorporation as defined in that Act" (*per* Lord Selborne at p.693). Accordingly, a company incorporated to make, sell or lend on hire all kinds of railway plant did not have power to enter a contract for the construction of a railway. Glosses on this principle were subsequently provided by Lord Selborne in *Att.-Gen. v Great Eastern Ry Co.* (1880) 5 App. Cas. 473 at 478 (quoted by Sargant J.) and by Lord Watson in *Baroness Wenlock v River Dee Company* (1884–85) 10 App.Cas. 354. Here, the respondent company was empowered by an Act of 1851 to borrow up to £25,000 on mortgage. The company subsequently borrowed on mortgage over £150,000. The House of Lords held that the lender's executors could only recover £25,000. In the course of his speech Lord Watson said (at 362):

> "I am of opinion not only that the objects which the corporation may legitimately pursue must be ascertained from the Act itself, but that the powers which the corporation may lawfully use in furtherance of those objects must be expressly conferred or derived by reasonable implication from its provisions. That appears to me to be the principle recognised by this House in *Ashbury Company v. Riche* . . . and in *Attorney-General v. Great Eastern Railway Company...*".

The principles thus established with respect to the powers of statutory undertakers were held to be applicable to a local authority, as a statutory corporation, in *London CC v Att.-Gen.* [1902] A.C. 165. Here, the House of Lords held *ultra vires* the operation of a separate omnibus service by a local authority authorised to operate tramways. Lord Macnaghten said (at 169):

> "The London County Council are carrying on two businesses—the business of a tramway company and the business of omnibus proprietors. For the one they have the express authority of Parliament; for the other, so far as I can see, they have no authority at all. It is quite true that the two businesses can be worked conveniently together; but the one is not incidental to the other. The business of an omnibus proprietor is no more incidental to the business of a tramway company than the business of steamship owners is incidental to the undertaking of a railway company which has its terminus at a seaport".

Similarly, in *Att.-Gen. v Manchester Corporation* [1906] 1 Ch.643, Farwell J. held that the corporation could not rely on its powers to operate tramways, which included power to convey goods and parcels, to operate a general parcels delivery business within and beyond the area covered by their tramways, and not confined to parcels and goods carried on them. His Lordship said at 656:

> "The question . . . is not whether the business can be conveniently or advantageously conducted with the tramway business, but whether it is by necessary implication incidental or accessory to it, and I think that it is not. To collect and deliver parcels for the tramway is fairly incidental; to collect and deliver parcels outside the radius of the tramway, and without any connection with the tramway, is not incidental to the tramway business, but distinct from it. At the best it could only be said to be incidental to the incidental . . .".

These cases may be compared with the decision in *Att.-Gen. v Smethwick Corp.* [1932] 1 Ch.562, where the establishment of a printing, bookbinding and stationery works was held to be incidental to the performance of its functions.

2. A feature of *Fulham* which seems to have weighed with Sargant J. in reaching his decision that the municipal enterprise of operating the laundry was *ultra vires* was that,

notwithstanding the opinion of the council sub-committee which had recommended the scheme, it appeared that the laundry was to be a substantial loss-making activity. Sargant J. discussed, in this connection, the economics of an aspect of this scheme which involved the establishment of a horse and van delivery service, and concluded:

> "the service is being performed at about half . . . of the cost to the Council. That is an instance I think . . . of the light way in which operations are conducted by persons who have not their own pockets to consider, but who have behind them what they regard as the unlimited or nearly unlimited purse of the ratepayers".

There are echoes here of the controversial notion that local authorities have a quasi-fudiciary duty to local ratepayers or council taxpayers (see below, p.552). Also lying behind the decision seems to be concern that subsidised activities of this kind may constitute unfair competition with local traders. The extent to which local authorities should engage in municipal trading was particularly controversial in the nineteenth and early twentieth century (see M. Loughlin, *Legality and Locality* (1996), pp.46, 209–210; S. Cirell and J. Bennett, *Municipal Trading* (1992)). In the late twentieth century local authorities were required to put most of their services through a process of compulsory competitive tendering which might well lead to their outsourcing (see the Local Government Act 1988). The CCT regime has now been replaced by a Best Value regime under the Local Government 1999 under which the possibilities for outsourcing must be kept under review. The wheel has, however, turned back with the conferment of express powers to trade through a company in function-related activities on the better-performing local authorities (Local Government Act 2003, ss.95, 96; *Cross on Local Government Law*, paras 1–76, 1–77). The *Fulham* case is an example of a relator action (see p.1027).

3. There are of course very many examples of successful challenges of this kind to both central and local government and other statutory bodies across a wide variety of contexts from those where fundamental rights are at stake (as in *R. v Secretary of State for the Home Department Ex p. Pierson* (above, p.251)) to the relatively mundane.

Other examples of successful challenges include the following. In *R. v Manchester City Council Ex p. Fulford* (1982) 81 L.G.R. 292, the schools sub-committee of the education committee resolved that corporal punishment should be abolished in all the city's schools. This resolution was confirmed by the education committee and the council, but was quashed by certiorari on the ground that it concerned the general direction of the conduct of the school rather than its general educational character and was thus for the school governors to determine and not the council, in accordance with the Articles of Government for County Secondary Schools.

In *Westminster City Council, Re* [1986] A.C. 668, the House of Lords held that a proposed grant of £40 million to the Inner London Education Authority by the Greater London Council, approved shortly before the latter's abolition under the Local Government Act 1985, was *ultra vires*. The 1985 Act made complete and comprehensive provision for the financing of the new ILEA, and only a clear express provision in the Act enabling the GLC to make such a grant could have given it power to do so. Moreover, grants to certain "umbrella bodies" for distribution to named voluntary associations after abolition should they not otherwise be funded, and to the revenue reserve for the funding of an arts centre, were also *ultra vires*. These grants offended the principle that local government finance is conducted on an annual basis. (*cf. R. v GLC Ex p. London Residuary Body* (1986) 19 H.L.R. 175.)

A startling and unfortunate example of illegality is provided by *R. (on the application of Bancoult) v Secretary of State for Foreign and Commonwealth Affairs* [2001] Q.B. 1067, where the Divisional Court held that the statutory power to make laws for the "peace, order and good government" of an overseas territory did not authorise delegated legislation made in 1971 (furthering an agreement with the United States made in 1964) providing for the removal of its entire civilian population). The population of the Chagos Archipelago (the British Indian Ocean Territory) had been removed to Mauritius in order to facilitate the establishment of a strategic American military base on the main island, Diego Garcia. The power assumed that the people would be governed, not removed. Some of the internal government documents disclosed were "embarrassing and worse" (*per* Laws L.J. at [63]).

4. Challenges may be made to the *vires* of delegated or subordinate legislation. See above, p.231; and *R. v Secretary of State for Social Security Ex p. Joint Council for the Welfare of Immigrants* [1996] 4 All E.R. 385, C.A. (in order to be valid subordinate legislation must not only be within the powers of the enabling (social security) statute, it must also not conflict with, or render nugatory, statutory rights conferred by other primary legislation (asylum claims)). Essentially the same principle applies where a court is called upon to determine whether a prerogative power has ever existed, or has been superseded by statute (see p.265).

5. As explained in the following note, powers may be conferred by implication and not only expressly. Conversely, in appropriate circumstances, a power may be held to be subject to substantive limits that are themselves implied. In *R. v Governor of Durham Prison Ex p. Hardial Singh* [1984] 1 W.L.R. 704, Woolf J. held that the power to detain an individual under the Immigration Act 1971, Sch.3, para.2(2) pending the making of a deportation order was subject to the implied limitations that the detention could only be for a period which was reasonably necessary for the purpose, and that the Secretary of State should exercise all reasonable expedition to ensure that the steps are taken which will be necessary to ensure the removal of the individual within a reasonable time. This was approved by the Privy Council in *Tan Te Lam v Superintendent of Tai A Chau Detention Centre* [1997] A.C. 97. The effect of *Hardial Singh* was nullified in respect of suspected international terrorists in that by virtue of s.23 of the Anti-terrorism, Crime and Security Act 2001, such persons may be detained despite the fact that his removal or departure from the United Kingdom is prevented (whether temporarily or indefinitely) by (a) a point of law which relates to an international agreement, or (b) a practical consideration. The United Kingdom derogated from Art.5(1), ECHR in respect of this provision (see p.297). Section 23 was subsequently held to be incompatible with Art.5 (*A v Secretary of State for the Home Department*, above, p.351).

6. *Implied and incidental powers.* The operation of the *ultra vires* doctrine is made more flexible by the recognition of the availability of implied and incidental powers. These concepts overlap but are not identical. Implied powers are those "derived by reasonable implication" from the provisions of the statute (*Baroness Wenlock*); incidental powers are those "incidental to, or consequential upon, those things which the legislature has authorised" (*Att.-Gen. v Great Eastern Ry Co.*) and it would seem that such authority can itself be express of implied. On this approach, incidental powers will tend to be of a lesser order of magnitude than implied powers. Another way of putting it would see incidental powers as examples of but not coterminous with implied powers. The relationship between the two concepts has, however, only really been of practical significance in the context of the interpretation of s.111 of the Local Government Act 1972 (below).

The point that powers may be conferred by implication, and not only expressly, is confirmed by *R. (on the application of A) v Hertfordshire CC* [2001] EWHC Admin 211; [2001] B.L.G.R. 435. The Court of Appeal held that a local authority social services department had power to communicate to the education department and school governors the conclusion, after inquiries under s.47 of the Children Act 1989, that a head teacher presents a risk of significant harm to children; this power was available by implication from the authorities' responsibilities for the welfare and protection of children, as distinct from s.111(1) of the Local Government Act 1972 (see below). See also *R. v Broadmoor Special Hospital Ex p. S, H and D* [1998] C.O.D. 199, where the Court of Appeal held that the power to detain patients for treatment under the Mental Health Act 1983, ss.3, 37, included such implied powers for control and discipline for which the hospital could show "a self-evident and pressing need" (Steyn

L.J. in *R. v Secretary of State for the Home Department Ex p. Leech (No.2)* [1994]
Q.B. 198). These include powers to restrain patients; to keep them in seclusion (see *R.
(on the application of Munjaz) v Mersey Care NHS Trust* [2003] EWCA Civ 1036;
[2004] Q.B. 395); to deprive them of their possessions for their own safety; to regulate the frequency and manner of visits to them; to search without cause (*Ex p. S, H
and D*) and to control what clothes they wear (*R. (on the application of E) v Ashworth
Hospital Authority* [2001] EWHC Admin 1089; [2002] A.C.D. 23).

7. *Local Government Act 1972, s.111.* The doctrine of incidental powers is given
statutory force for local authorities by s.111 of the Local Government Act 1972.

"Subsidiary powers of local authorities

111.—(1) Without prejudice to any powers exercisable apart from this section but
subject to the provisions of this Act and any other enactment passed before or after
this Act, a local authority shall have power to do any thing (whether or not involving the expenditure, borrowing or lending of money or the acquisition or disposal
of any property or rights) which is calculated to facilitate, or is conducive or incidental to, the discharge of any of their functions . . .

(3) A local authority shall not by virtue of this section raise money, whether by
means of rates, precepts or borrowing, or lend money except in accordance with the
enactments relating to those matters respectively. . . .".

There are many cases illustrating the scope of s.111 (see the notes to s.111 in the
Encyclopedia of Local Government Law and *Cross on Local Government Law*, paras
1–25 to 1–36).

Section 111 has been held to authorise the release of a member of staff to a joint
committee of trade unions in the interests of good industrial relations (but not the
release of staff in support of a campaign against government policy) (*R. v GLC Ex p.
Westminster City Council*, *The Times*, December 27, 1984); the establishment of a
council working party comprising staff and officers to consider ways of improving the
council's structure and efficiency (*R. v Eden DC Ex p. Moffatt*, *The Times*, November
24, 1988); the release to the media of video recordings made pursuant to a statutory
power to provide CCTV systems (*R. v Brentwood BC Ex p. Peck*, *The Times*,
December 18, 1997); the secondment of an officer to a joint committee (*Islington LBC
v Camp* [2004] B.L.G.R. 48); a registration scheme for doormen (*R. v Liverpool City
Council Ex p. Barry* (2001) 3 L.G.L.R. 832); and the provision of an indemnity for
the costs of libel proceedings brought by council officers (*R. (on the application of
Comninos) v Bedford BC* [2003] EWHC 121).

There are many important cases the other side of line, showing that the principle
cannot be stretched too far.

In *Hazell v Hammersmith and Fulham LBC* [1990] 2 Q.B. 722–723, the House of
Lords held that interest rate swap transactions entered into on behalf of the council
(and also many other local authorities) were *ultra vires*. These were speculative transactions on the money markets, entered into in order to make a profit. Profits were
dependent on interest rates falling, but in fact they increased. The council's auditor
obtained a declaration under s.19 of the Local Government Finance Act 1982 that
these transactions were contrary to law; otherwise, the council stood to lose in excess
of £100m. The transactions were not authorised by Sch.13 to the Local Government
Act 1972, which covered borrowing by local authorities, nor by the, more generally
worded, s.111 of that Act. At first instance Woolf L.J. said:

"What is a function for the purposes of the subsection is not expressly defined
but in our view there can be little doubt that in this context 'functions' refers to the
multiplicity of specific statutory activities the council is expressly or impliedly under
a duty to perform or has power to perform under the other provisions of the Act of
1972 or other relevant legislation. The subsection does not of itself, independently

of any other provision, authorise the performance of any activity. It only confers, as the sidenote to the section indicates, a subsidiary power. A subsidiary power which authorises an activity where some other statutory provision has vested a specific function or functions in the council and the performance of the activity will assist in some way in the discharge of that function or those functions".

This was approved by the Court of Appeal [1990] 2 Q.B. 697 at 785, and the House of Lords [1992] 2 A.C. 1 at 29. In the House of Lords, Lord Templeman accepted that "borrowing" was a "function" for these purposes, but that interest rate swap transactions neither "facilitated" nor were "conducive" or "incidental to" borrowing. A power was not incidental merely because it was convenient or desirable or profitable. See further on *Hazell*: M. Loughlin, "Innovative Financing in Local Government Law: The Limits of Legal Instrumentalism" [1990] P.L. 372, [1991] P.L. 568 and *Legality and Locality* (1996). The *Hazell* case gave rise to substantial litigation as to the extent of the banks' remedies in restitution (see below, pp.1106–1107).

In *R. v Richmond upon Thames LBC Ex p. McCarthy & Stone (Developments) Ltd* [1992] 2 A.C. 48, the House of Lords, reversing the Court of Appeal, held that s.111 did not authorise the levy of a charge on developers in respect of pre-planning application meetings and discussions. The consideration and determining of planning applications *was* a function of the council; the giving of pre-application advice facilitated and was conducive and incidental to that function, but was not *itself* a "function". Charging was thus "incidental to the incidental", which was too remote a relationship (*cf.* Farwell J. in *Att.-Gen. v Manchester Corporation* [1906] 1 Ch.643 at 656). Lord Lowry rejected the Court of Appeal's argument that while no charge could be made without express authority in respect of the performance of a *duty*, a charge could be made in respect of a function which it had *power* to provide.

In *Allsop v North Tyneside MBC* (1992) L.G.R. 462, the Court of Appeal held that s.111 did not authorise payments under a voluntary redundancy scheme in excess of the limits permitted under statutory regulations authorising redundancy payments. These regulations took effect by virtue of the Superannuation Act 1972, which was an "other enactment" for the purposes of s.111.

Also of great significance were the decisions of the Court of Appeal in *Credit Suisse v Allerdale BC* [1997] Q.B. 302 and *Credit Suisse v Waltham Forest LBC* [1997] Q.B. 362 that, where detailed provision was made as to how certain statutory functions were to be carried out, s.111 could not be relied upon to support the existence of wholly additional powers lying outside the statutory code. Accordingly, guarantees in respect of loans to companies specially established for the purposes of a timeshare development (*Allerdale*) and the provision of housing for the homeless (*Waltham Forest*) were *ultra vires* and void; s.111 did not provide an escape route from the limits to borrowing powers enshrined in Sch.13 to the 1972 Act. (Statutory protection in respect of those who contract with local authorities in specified circumstances is now provided by the Local Government (Contracts) Act 1997.)

Whether s.111 may be applied in relation to "implied functions" or only to functions expressly conferred remains unresolved (see *Cross* para. 1–25). The broader view was expressed by Woolf L.J. in *Hazell* (above) and by Nourse L.J. in *R. v Eden DC Ex p. Moffatt* (above); *McCarthy & Stone* seems to support the narrower view, but the point was not argued. So far as local authorities are concerned, the point is rendered academic in view of the broad powers conferred by the Local Government Act 2000 (see below). However, s.111 (or the equivalent) remains particularly important for authorities that do not benefit from those powers, such as parish or community councils and police authorities.

LOCAL GOVERNMENT ACT 2000

Part I
Promotion of Economic, Social or Environmental Well-being etc

Promotion of well-being

2.—(1) Every local authority are to have power to do anything which they consider is likely to achieve any one or more of the following objects—

(a) the promotion or improvement of the economic well-being of their area,
(b) the promotion or improvement of the social well-being of their area, and
(c) the promotion or improvement of the environmental well-being of their area.

(2) The power under subsection (1) may be exercise in relation to or for the benefit of—

(a) the whole or any part of a local authority's area, or
(b) all or any persons resident or present in a local authority's area.

(3) In determining whether or how to exercise the power under subsection (1), a local authority must have regard to their strategy under section 4.
(4) The power under subsection (1) includes power for a local authority to—

(a) incur expenditure,
(b) give financial assistance to any person,
(c) enter into arrangement or agreements with any person,
(d) co-operate with, or facilitate or co-ordinate the activities of, any person,
(e) exercise on behalf of any person any functions of that person, and
(f) provide staff, goods, services or accommodation to any person.

(5) The power under subsection (1) includes power for a local authority to do anything in relation to, or for the benefit of, any person or area situated outside their area if they consider that it is likely to achieve any one or more of the objects in that subsection.
(6) Nothing in subsection (4) or (5) affects the generality of the power under subsection (1).

Limits on power to promote well-being

3.—(1) The power under section 2(1) does not enable a local authority to do anything which they are unable to do by virtue of any prohibition, restriction or limitation on theirs powers which is contained in any enactment (whenever passed or made).
(2) The power under section 2(1) does not enable a local authority to raise money (whether by precepts, borrowing or otherwise).
(3) The Secretary of State may by order make provision preventing local authorities from doing, by virtue of section 2(1), anything which is specified, or is of a description specified, in the order.

(4) Before making an order under subsection (3), the Secretary of State must consult such representatives of local government and such other persons (if any) as he considers appropriate.

(5) Before exercising the power under section 2(1), a local authority must have regard to any guidance for the time being issued by the Secretary of State about the exercise of that power.

(6) Before issuing any guidance under subsection (5), the Secretary of State must consult such representatives of local government and such other persons (if any) as he considers appropriate.

(7) In its application to Wales, this section has effect as if for any reference to the any reference to the Secretary of State there were substituted a reference to the National Assembly for Wales.

(8) In this section "enactment" includes an enactment comprised in subordinate legislation (within the meaning of the Interpretation Act 1978).

Notes

1. These powers are available to county, district and London borough councils, the Common Council of the City of London in its capacity as a local authority and the Council of the Isles of Scilly (in England) and county and county borough councils in Wales (2000 Act, s.1). Section 4 imposes a duty on each of these authorities to prepare a community strategy (*i.e.* a strategy for promoting the economic, social and environmental well-being of their area and contributing to the achievement of sustainable development in the United Kingdom). The Secretary of State has power by order to amend, repeal, revoke or disapply an enactment that prevents or obstructs local authorities from exercising their power under s.2(1) (2000 Act, s.5).

2. These powers are the broadest general powers yet conferred on local authorities, and are part of a package of measures designed to promote a new role of community leadership (see p.28). There have over the years been suggestions that a power of general competence should be conferred on local authorities (*e.g.* by the Maud Committee on the Management of Local Government (HMSO, 1967)) but these had been resisted by central government. A modest power to spend up to the product of a 0.4p rate in the interest of their area or any part of it or all or some of its inhabitants were conferred by the Local Government (Financial Provisions) Act 1963, s.6 (re-enacted in s.137 of the Local Government Act 1972, which raised the limit to 2p). A research report in 2000 found that overall the *ultra vires* doctrine in its application to local authorities "is now generally seen as inhibiting innovation", given the increasingly narrow approach of the courts and its complexity and uncertainty (C. Crawford *et al.*, *Law Relating to Local Government* (DETR, 2000), pp.2–3). The courts have helpfully adopted a broader rather than narrower approach to the interpretation of the new powers: see *R. (on the application of Khan) v Oxfordshire* CC [2004] EWCA Civ 309 (below). However, limits on the financial resources available to local authorities have meant that relatively little use has been made of the new powers (Transport, Local Government and the Regions Committee, *How the Local Government Act 2000 is Working* (14th report, 2001–02 HC 602-I), paras 9–11.

R. (ON THE APPLICATION OF KHAN) v OXFORDSHIRE CC

[2004] EWCA Civ 309; WESTLAW TRANSCRIPT 2004 WL 413046;
[2003] H.L.R. 23 (COURT OF APPEAL)

Mrs Khan, a national of Pakistan, was in 2001 given leave to enter the United Kingdom to join her husband. Shortly thereafter the marriage broke down as a result of his repeated violence towards her. She was kidnapped and escaped, kidnapped again and released by the police. She lived away from her husband. Questions arose as to the extent of her eligibility to be provided residential accommodation under s.21 of the National Assistance Act 1948 and financial support under s.2 of the Local Government Act 2000. The county council determined that she was not eligible, and she sought judicial review of that determination. Moses J. held that the council had erred in law in its approach to s.21 of the 1948 Act, and that the provision of support under s.2 of the 2000 Act was barred by s.21(1A) of the 1948 Act. The Court of Appeal allowed an appeal by the council on the first point and dismissed a cross-appeal on the second point. (Mrs Khan was granted indefinite leave to remain in the United Kingdom in May 2003 and so the issues became academic for her; she was nevertheless given leave to cross-appeal as the issue was one of general importance.)

DYSON L.J.: . . .
   11. Section 21 of the NAA provides:

"Duty of local authorities to provide accommodation
   (1) Subject to and in accordance with the provisions of this Part of this Act, a local authority may with the approval of the Secretary of State, and to such extent as he may direct shall, make arrangements for providing—
        (a) residential accommodation for persons who by reason of age, illness, disability or any other circumstances are in need of care and attention which is not otherwise available to them;
   (1A) A person to whom section 115 of the Immigration and Asylum Act 1999 (exclusion from benefits) applies may not be provided with residential accommodation under subsection 1(a) if his need for care and attention has arisen solely—
        (a) because he is destitute; or
        (b) because of the physical effects, or anticipated physical effects, of his being destitute."
   12. Since the Secretary of State has made directions there is an obligation, and not merely a power, upon the local authority under section 21(1)(a).
   13. Section 21(2) provides:

"In making any such arrangements a local authority shall have regard to the welfare of all persons for whom accommodation is provided, and in particular to the need for providing accommodation of different descriptions suited to different descriptions of such persons as are mentioned in the last foregoing subsection."

   14. Section 21(5) provides:

"References in this Act to accommodation provided under this part thereof shall be construed as references to accommodation provided in accordance with this and the five next following sections, and as including references to board and other services, amenities and requisites provided in connection with the accommodation except where in the opinion of the authority managing the premises their provision is unnecessary."

[His Lordship referred to ss.2 and 3(1) of the Local Government Act 2000.]

The Council's Appeal

[His Lordship held that the council's appeal should be allowed. It had applied the correct test under s.21(1A) in concluding that K's need for care and attention was not to any material extent made more acute by circumstances other than lack of accommodation and funds. The fact that she had suffered abuse was not the cause of any specific need, rather it was merely the reason why she had no funds to provide accommodation for herself. Any further violence could be prevented by informing the police or taking out an appropriate injunction. The council's conclusion was not challenged as *Wednesbury* unreasonable, and was adequately reasoned.]

The Cross Appeal

29. The judge dealt with this issue very briefly at paras 27–33 of his judgment. He had no doubt that the restriction in section 21 (1A) of the NAA falls within the meaning of section 3 of the LGA. Thus it was not open to the Council to provide assistance to the claimant under section 2 of the LGA.

30. It is common ground that there is a distinction between the definition of the scope of a power and the imposition of a prohibition, restriction or limitation on the exercise of a power. This distinction was articulated by Mr Philip Sales and apparently accepted by Elias J. in *R v Enfield LBC* [2002] EWHC 432 (Admin), [2002] LGR 390 at paras 53–57. As Mr Lewis points out in his skeleton argument, status frequently confer power on authorities to do specific acts in respect of specific categories of person. The definition of the scope of a power by reference to particular criteria does not involve the imposition of a prohibition, restriction or limitation on the doing of an act in respect of person outside the scope of the criteria. Rather, the fact that the authority cannot do the act in such circumstances reflects the fact that it has not been given the power to act, and not that it has been prohibited form doing so, or subjected to any limitation or restriction.

31. Conversely, if statute expressly prohibits the use of a power to do a particular thing or prohibits the use of a power in respect of certain persons or in certain situations, that can constitute a prohibition, restriction or limitation within the meaning of section 3(1) of the LGA. But even here, as Elias J. said at para.53:

"... it will be necessary in each case to scrutinise the legislation carefully to see whether, properly analysed, it is intended to provide a bar to its exercise at all, or whether it is merely intended to prevent the power being exercised under the particular legislation in which the restriction is to be found."

32. I find this a helpful analysis, although it is not always easy to distinguish between a provision which defines the scope of a power and a provision which restricts or limits the exercise of a power. Nevertheless, Mr Jay accepts that section 21(1A) is a prohibition on the exercise of the power to make arrangements for providing residential accommodation pursuant to section 21(1)(a).

33. But he submits that:

(i) section 21(1A) only prohibits the provision of residential accommodation under section 21 (1)(a), and not under any other statutory power, so that the power to provide accommodation under section 2(4)(f) is not affected;

    (ii) section 21(1)(a) does not give power to make payments for accommo-
dation, so that section 21(1A) does not prohibit the making of such
payments;

   (iii) section 21(1A) does not prohibit the provision of staff, goods, or services under section 2(4)(f); and

   (iv) even if section 21(1A) prohibits the making of payments, it only prohibits payments for accommodation as defined in section 21(5), and not
other financial assistance pursuant to section 2(4)(b).

34. Mr Jay relies on the fact that (as is common ground) section 2(1) of the
LGA confers broad and general powers on a local authority. Absent any prohibition, limitation or restriction, the power in section 2 can be used to provide
accommodation or financial assistance to any person if the requirements of
section 2 are met. The explanatory notes to the LGA are a legitimate aid to
construction: see per Lord Hope in R v A[2002] UKHL 25, [2002] 1 AC 45,
at 79 (para.82). They explain (at para.15) the broad purpose behind section 2:

> "Together, these sections allow local authorities to undertake a wide range
> of activities for the benefit of their local area and to improve the quality of
> life of local residents, businesses and those who commute to or visit the area.
> This is intended to clear up much of the uncertainty which currently exists
> about what authorities can do. Sections 2 and 3 allow authorities to take
> any action, unless it is subject to statutory prohibitions, restrictions or lim-
> itations specifically set out in legislation. The intention is to broaden the
> scope for local authority action while reducing the scope for challenge on
> the grounds that local authorities lack specific powers."

35. Mr Jay also points to the guidance given by the Office of the Deputy
Prime Minister which explains how innovative actions by local authorities have
been stifled by concerns over the scope of their powers (Chapter.1, para.5); that
the purpose of these provisions in the LGA was to "reverse that traditionally
cautious approach" (Chapter.1, para.6); that the new power is "wide-ranging"
(Chapter.1, para.7); and that "the breadth of the power is such that councils
can regard it as a "power of first resort". Rather than searching for a specific
power elsewhere in statute in order to take a particular action, councils can
instead look to the well-being power in the first instance . . ." (Chapter.1,
para.10).

**Prohibition on the provision of accommodation, or only on provision of
accommodation under s.21(1)(A) of NAA?**

36. The first question, therefore, is whether section 21(1A) only prohibits
the provision of residential accommodation under section 21(1)(a), or whether
it prohibits the provision of residential accommodation under *any* statutory
power (i) to any person who is over the age of 18 and in need of care and attention, and (ii) where the need arises by reason of age, illness disability or any
other circumstances. I shall refer to these as "the section 21(1)(a) conditions".
I leave out of account the condition that the care and attention is not available
otherwise than by the provision of residential accommodation under section
21(1)(a), because the question at issue is whether the provision of accommodation is otherwise available under section 2 of the LGA, notwithstanding the
provisions of section 3.

37. Mr Jay emphasises the phrase "under subsection (1)(a)" in section 21(1A). He submits that this shows that the prohibition in section 21(1)(a) (and no other) in relation to persons who satisfy the section 21(1A) criteria. I should add in parenthesis that the only two statutory provisions under which it has been suggested that the claimant might have been entitled to accommodation are section 21(1)(a) of the NAA and section 2 of the LGA. . . .

39. Mr Jay relies on the linguistic point to which I have referred (viz: "under subsection(1)(a)") and seeks to derive support for his argument from the policy consideration that section 2 should be construed widely (and section 3 correspondingly narrowly) for the reasons already given.

40. In my view, section 3 has the effect of preventing an authority from exercising the power in section 2 of the LGA to do that which is prohibited by section 21(1A). It is true that the phrase "under subsection (1)(a)" in section 21(1A)makes it clear that what is prohibited is the provision of residential accommodation *under* section 21(1)(a) for persons who satisfy the section 21(1)(a) conditions, but who are subject to immigration control, and whose need for care and attention arises solely because of destitution. Thus if (leaving section 2 of the LGA out of account for the moment) there were some other statutory power than section 21(1)(a) by which accommodation could be provided to persons who satisfy the section 21(1)(a) conditions, then the exercise of that power would not be prohibited by section 21(1A). But it is agreed that there is no other such power. Indeed, if there were, the section 21(1)(a) power could not be exercised in any event, since the condition that care and attention is not available otherwise than by the provision of residential accommodation under that particular power would not be satisfied.

41. The effect of section 3(1) is to prohibit the doing of "anything" which a local authority is unable to do by virtue of any prohibition on its powers contained in any enactment. In the present context, the "thing" which is under consideration is the provision of residential accommodation to persons who, but for the prohibition in section 21(1A), would be entitled to accommodation under section 21(1)(a). It is that "thing" which the local authority is prohibited from providing by section 21(1A), and which it cannot provide under any other statutory power, unless it can do so under section 2. But the very reason why section 3(1) was enacted was to prevent section 2 being used to do that which is prohibited by another statute. If Mr Jay were right, it would seem that no statutory prohibition would trump section 2 of the LGA unless it stated expressly that it was a prohibition for the purposes of section 3 of the LGA. An example of such a provision is to be found in para.1(2) to Sch 3 to the Nationality and Asylum Act 2002. This provides that:

"a power or duty under a provision referred to in subparagraph (1) may not be exercised or performed in respect or a person to whom this paragraph applies."

One of the provisions referred to in sub-paragraph (1) is section 2 of the LGA.

42. But as Mr Swift points out, to interpret section 3 in this way is inconsistent with the language of section 3(1) itself which refers to any prohibition etc which is contained in any enactment *whenever* passed.

43. So far as the policy consideration is concerned, I accept that section 2 has a broad purpose. The scope of the powers given by section 2 should not be narrowly construed. The local authority is given a wide discretion to exercise its powers to promote well-being. But the fact that section 2 should be construed broadly does not help in deciding the meaning and scope of a prohibition, restriction or limitation on the exercise of powers which is contained in *another* enactment whenever passed or made. It is clear from section 3 that Parliament did not intend to override legislative schemes that already existed. The prohibition contained in s.21(1A) of the NAA must be given its natural meaning. For the reasons that I gave given, it cannot be circumvented by s.2 of the LGA. If the prohibition in s.21(1A) were trumped by s.2, the prohibition in s 3(1) would be severely emasculated and, at any rate in relation to pre-existing legislative schemes, of no practical effect, since they do not (and could not) refer to the LGA.

44. It follows in my judgment that accommodation cannot be provided under s.2(4)(f) of the LGA to persons to whom it cannot be provided under s.21(1)(a) of the NAA.

Does s.21(1A) prohibit the making of payments for accommodation?

[45]–[50] [His Lordship held that the prohibition in s.21(1A) also applied to the power under s.21(1)(a), as extended in effect by regulations under the Health and Social Care Act 2001, s.57, to make payments for accommodation.]

The Human Rights Act 1998

[51]–[56] . . . [His Lordship held that s.3 of the Human Rights Act 1998 did not require s.21(1A) to be construed narrowly so that in every case it only prohibits the provision of accommodation under s.21(1)(a) and does not affect any of the powers in s.2(4) of the 2000 Act, in order to avoid the possible violation of a person's rights under art. 3 or 8, ECHR. A modified interpretation might, however, be necessary in a particular case to avoid such a violation.]

Financial assistance which is not for accommodation

[57]–[60] . . . [His Lordship held that s.21(1A) did not bar the provision of financial assistance under s.2(4)(b) (other than for accommodation: see paras [45]–[50]) or staff, goods and services under s.2(4)(f). While "accommodation" was widely defined to include "board and other services, amenities and requisites provided in connection with the accommodation" (s.21(5)), this did not extend to all of a person's essential living needs, such as clothes.]

SIR CHRISTOPHER STAUGHTON and WARD L.J. agreed.

Appeal allowed; cross-appeal dismissed

Notes
1. The first judgment on the scope of ss.2 and 3 was given by Elias J. in R. *(on the application of J) v Enfield LBC* [2002] EWHC (Admin) 432; [2002] L.G.R. 390. The question here was whether the local authority had power to provide accommodation or financial assistance that would enable accommodation to be secured to the applicant; she had overstayed her permission to remain in the United Kingdom and was seeking leave to remain but not asylum. She was HIV positive and gave birth to a daughter while awaiting the outcome of her application. She would have been entitled to accommodation as a homeless person under Pt 7 of the Housing Act 1996, apart from her immigration status (s.185 of that Act). Elias J. held that (1) there was power for accommodation to be provided under s.21 of the National Assistance Act 1948 provided the authority was satisfied that the claimant was in imminent need as

the result of her health; (2) s.17 of the Children Act 1989 (general duty to safeguard and promote the welfare of children in their area who are in need and to promote their upbringing by their families by providing services appropriate to their needs) did not confer power to provide financial assistance for accommodation to the claimant's child (and therefore the claimant), except that such a power could be read into the section via s.3 of the Human Rights Act 1998 where necessary to give effect to the claimant's rights under that Act; (3) there was power to provide financial assistance to the claimant and her child under s.2 of the Local Government Act 2000. As to (3), s.2(4)(b) expressly covered the provision of financial assistance and such provision would be capable of promoting the social-well-being of the area by benefiting two persons resident there. There were "restrictions" preventing the provision of accommodation itself, given the claimant's statue as an overstayer (Housing Act 1996, ss.159–161, 185; Immigration and Asylum Act 1999, s.118), but not to the provision of financial assistance (confirmed *obiter* by the Court of Appeal in *R. (on the application of W) v Lambeth LBC* [2002] EWCA Civ 613). Elias J. said (at [57]):

"[Section 2] is drafted in very broad terms which provide a source of power enabling authorities to do many things which they could not hitherto have done. In my view, a 'prohibition, restriction or limitation' is one which will almost always be found in an express legislative provision. I do not discount the possibility that such might arise by necessary implication, but I would have thought that would be very rare. (I note that the Guidance . . . assumes that any restriction, prohibition or limitation must be expressly spelt out in the legislation: see paras.62 and 63. However, Mr Sales did not adopt that position, and I doubt whether it must always do so as a matter of construction of section 3.) Of course, where Parliament has conferred positive power to do X, it will by implication have denied the right for that power to be exercised to do Y, but that is merely saying the Parliament has defined a clear boundary for marking out the scope of the power. In my view it would be inapt to describe the area where no power has been conferred as constituting a prohibition, restriction or limitation on the power which is contained in an enactment".

It had been accepted that providing accommodation for the child by taking her into care in these circumstances would constitute a breach of the claimant's rights under Art.8 ECHR; there was no justification for separating mother (a "good mother") and child. Accordingly,

"If the refusal to exercise the section 2 powers would infringe the rights of the claimant or her daughter under Article 8, then of course the authority would be under an obligation to exercise the power in her favour. To that extent, the broad discretion conferred upon the authority under section 2 will be limited by the obligation imposed upon them properly to give effect to human rights" (at [58]).

The confirmation that a broad approach is to be adopted to s.2 is welcome; it would be unfortunate if the excessively narrow approach adopted in some of the cases on the general application of the *ultra vires* doctrine were simply replaced by an overbroad interpretation of the "prohibition, restriction or limitation" exception.

[It should be noted that the Court of Appeal in *R. (on the application of W) v Lambeth LBC* [2002] EWCA Civ 613; [2002] 2 All E.R. 901, subsequently held that local authorities did have power under s.17 of the Children Act 1989 to provide financial assistance for accommodation, not following its own previous decision in *R. (on the application of A) v Lambeth LBC* [2001] EWCA Civ 1624; [2001] 3 F.C.R. 673, on which Elias J. had relied in determining point (2). (Section 17(6) of the 1989 Act was subsequently amended to confer expressly a power to provide accommodation by s.116(1) of the Adoption and Children Act 2002). See further the decision in *R. (on the application of G) v Barnet LBC* [2003] UKHL 57 (heard with appeals in *W* and *A*), below p.406.

2. Other cases on ss.2 and 3 include *R. (on the application of Theophilus) v Lewisham LBC* [2002] EWHC (Admin) 1371 (s.2 can be used to provide student support in respect of a course outside the United Kingdom, in accordance with the applicant's legitimate expectation arising from information given by the council, notwithstanding that the relevant regulations provided for support only in respect of courses in the United Kingdom); *R. (on the application of A) v East Sussex CC (No.1)* [2002] EWHC (Admin) 2771 (s.2 enables provision of care staff for disabled persons through a user independent trust).

(B) DUTIES

Parliament when conferring statutory functions on public authorities may do so in the form of powers (discretions) or duties. The distinction is obviously crucial. Where a duty is imposed, there is *ex hypothesi* no choice as to whether it is to be performed. A mandatory order may be sought on a claim for judicial review or (exceptionally) a mandatory injunction (see further, pp.1023–1024). A claim for damages for breach of statutory duty may also (but rarely) be available (see p.1041). Where a discretion is imposed, the possibility of judicial review is limited to ensuring that a genuine discretion is exercised and there is no abuse of power (Ch. 8 and 9). Where a duty is imposed, lack of resources is no excuse for non-performance; by contrast it will be difficult to challenge a public authority that has regard to the availability (or otherwise) of resources in exercising a discretion. The point is frequently observed in local government where the continuing pressure on the availability of resources for local authorities make them concentrate more on fulfilling their statutory duties at the expense of the exercise of powers.

For these reasons, determining the exact scope of a statutory duty, through interpretation of the statute in its context, can be of great practical significance. It should be noted that the choice for the court is not simply between "power" and "duty". Different levels of "duty" have been identified in different contexts. Not all duties are owed to and enforceable by specific individuals; duties may instead be held to be "target" duties specifying at a general level what is to be done. These issues arose in the following case, in which a difference of view between the majority and minority is instructive.

R. (ON THE APPLICATION OF G) v BARNET LBC;
R. (ON THE APPLICATION OF W) v LAMBETH LBC;
R. (ON THE APPLICATION OF A) v LAMBETH LBC

[2003] UKHL 57; [2004] 2 A.C. 208; [2003] 3 W.L.R. 1194; [2004] 1 All E.R. 9 (HOUSE OF LORDS)

Two issues arose concerning the nature and extent of the duty imposed on local authorities by s.17 of the Children Act 1989. These were (1) whether it requires a local authority to assess the needs of a child who is in need *and and to meet those needs when they have been assessed*; and (2) whether a local authority may insist on providing accommodation for a child alone, as distinct from a child and his mother, when a child is in need of accommodation and it would cost no more to provide accommodation for both of them. The issues arose in three cases.

In G, the claimant was a Dutch national of Somali origin who entered the United Kingdom on a Dutch passport. She was refused income support and assistance with housing as she did not satisfy the habitual residence test. She had a child, born in 1999, and assistance from Barnet LBC, a social services authority, which assessed the child's need as best served by the return of both mother and child to Holland where they were entitled at once to accommodation and other benefits. It was common ground that it was not in the child's best interests for him to be removed from G's care, but that if

G refused to return to Holland, the child would be placed with foster parents and no accommodation provided for G.

In *A*, a family of a mother and three children was housed in accommodation that was not suitable for the childrens' needs, two of whom were autistic and required constant supervision. The accommodation comprised a ground floor flat very close to the road and had no outside play area; the two disabled children were prone to run out of the front door and climb through the windows.

In *W*, W, who had two children, became homeless intentionally within the meaning of the homelessness legislation and so did not qualify for assistance under that legislation. The council as social services authority refused assistance with accommodation for the family under the 1989 Act, but in an assessment under Pt III of the Act was prepared to provide accommodation for the children alone under s.20 of the 1989 Act.

The decisions challenged were, respectively (1) *G*: Barnet LBC's decision to cease making weekly payments to G for accommodation and subsistence for herself and her child; (2) *A*: Lambeth LBC's refusal to rehouse A and her family in suitable accommodation; and (3) *W*: the assessment made by Lambeth LBC under Pt III of the 1989 Act.

The Court of Appeal held in each case that the local authority had not acted unlawfully in refusing to provide accommodation for both child (or children) and parent (*G*: [2001] EWCA Civ 540; [2001] 2 F.C.R. 193; *A*: [2001] EWCA Civ 1624; [2001] 3 F.C.R. 673; *W*: [2002] EWCA Civ 613; [2002] 2 All E.R. 901.

The House of Lords by 3 to 2 (Lords Hope of Craighead, Millett and Scott of Foscote, Lords Nicholls of Birkenhead and Steyn dissenting) dismissed appeals, holding that s.17 of the 1989 Act imposed duties of a general nature only which were not intended to be enforceable as such by individuals. Lord Nicholls (with whom Lord Steyn agreed) held that s.17(1) did impose a duty which was, however not an absolute duty but one which was duty to do what was appropriate in the circumstances.

LORD NICHOLLS OF BIRKENHEAD (dissenting): . . .
[*R.(G) v Barnet LBC*]

Allocation of resources

10. Behind the legal questions arising in these appeals is the seemingly intractable problem of local authorities` lack of resources. Local authorities discharge a wide range of function, from education to housing, upkeep of roads to disposal of waste. All these activities call for money, of which there is never enough to go round. Often there is also a shortage, sometimes acute, of other resources such as trained staff.

11. The financial resources of local authorities are finite. The scope for local authorities to increase the amount of their revenue is strictly limited. So, year by year, they must decide what priority to give to the multifarious competing demands on their limited resources. They have to decide which needs are the most urgent and pressing. The more money they allocate for one purpose the less they have to spend on another. In principle, this decision on priorities is entrusted to the local authorities themselves. In respect of decisions such as these council members are accountable to the local electorate.

12. The ability of a local authority to decide how its limited resources are best spent in its areas is displaced when the authority is discharging a statutory duty as distinct from exercising a power. A local authority is obliged to comply with a statutory duty regardless of whether, left to itself, it would prefer to spend its money on some other purpose. A power need not be exercised, but a duty must be discharge. That is the nature of a duty. That is the underlying purpose for which duties are imposed on local authorities. They leave the authority with no choice.

13. The extent to which a duty precludes a local authority from ordering its expenditure priorities for itself varies from one duty to another. The governing consideration is the proper interpretation of the statute in question. But identifying precise content of a statutory duty in this respect is not always easy. This is perhaps especially so in the field of social welfare, where local authorities are required to provide services for those who need them. As a general proposition, the more specific and precise the duty the more readily the statute may be interpreted as imposing an obligation of an absolute character. Conversely, the broader and more general the terms of the duty, the more readily the statute may be construed as affording scope for a local authority to take into account matters such as cost when deciding how best to perform the duty in its own area. In such cases the local authority may have a wide measure of freedom over what steps to take in pursuance of its duty.

14. Towards one edge of this spectrum are instances such as section 23(1) of the Children Act 1989. Under this subsection it is the duty of a local authority looking after a child to provide accommodation for him while he is in the authority's care. This is a duty of an absolute character. An example of the opposite edge of the spectrum, taken from the field of education, is the broad duty imposed on local education authority by section 8 of the Education Act 1944, now section 14 of the Education Act 1996, "to secure that there shall be available for their area sufficient school. . . for providing primary education". In *R v Inner London Education Authority, Ex p Ali* (1990) 2 Admin LR 822, 828, Woolf LJ described this as a "target duty".

15. Often the duty is expressed in more specific terms than this, but the terms themselves give the local authority an area of discretion. Paragraph 9 of Schedule 2 of the Children Act 1989 imposes upon every local authority a duty to provide such family centers "as they consider appropriate" in relation to children in need within their area. Another form of words apt to give considerable latitude to a local authority is where the duty is "to take reasonable steps" to achieve a stated object. Paragraph 4 of schedule 2 of the Children Act 1989 is an illustration of this. A local authority is required to take reasonable steps to prevent children within its are suffering ill-treatment or neglect. Again, although not explicitly stated, a statute may implicitly afford a local authority considerable latitude. Section 18(1) of the Children Act 1989 provides that every local authority shall provide such day care for pre-school children in need within its areas "as is appropriate". In deciding what is appropriate the local authority may properly take into account a wide range of matters including cost.

16. The primary question raised by these appeals is the proper interpretation, in this context, of section 17(1) of the Children Act 1989.

Part III of the Children Act 1989

19. I turn to the relevant legislative provision. Section 17 of the Children Act 1989 is the first section in a small group of sections concerning provision of services for children "in need" and their families. A child is taken to be in need if he is disabled or if, without the provision of local authority services, he is unlikely to achieve or maintain "a reasonable standard of health or development" or his health or development is "likely to be significantly impaired": section 17(10). A child without accommodation is a child in need: *R v Northavon District Council, Ex p Smith* [1994] 2 Ac 402, 406, per Lord

Templeman. Section 17(11) defines disability, "development" and "health" in wide terms.

20. Section 17(1) prescribes the general duty of local authorities regarding children in need. The general duty of every local authority is to provide a range and level of services appropriate to the needs of such children:

"It shall be the general duty of every local authority (in addition to the other duties imposed on them by this Part)—
(a) to safeguard and promote the welfare of children within their area who are in need; and
(b) so far as is consistent with that duty, to promote the upbringing of such children by their families,
by providing a range and level of services appropriate to those children's needs."

21. This general duty is augmented by a motley collection of "specific duties and powers" set out in Part I of schedule 2: section 17(2). Local authorities are given these specific duties and powers principally for the purpose of facilitating the discharge of the general duty imposed by section 17(1). Some of these specific duties and powers are general in their impact on children, such as the duty to produce and keep under review plans for the provision of children's services under Part III of the Act (paragraph 1A). Others relate to the circumstances of a particular child. Two examples will suffice, one of a power; the other of a duty. A local authority is empowered to assess the needs of a child in need under the Children Act 1989 at the same time as any assessment of his needs is made under other enactments, such as the Chronically Sick and Disabled Persons Act 1970 (paragraph 3). A local authority is under a duty to take such steps as are reasonably practicable to enable a child who is not living with his family to live with them or promote contact between them if that is necessary to safeguard or promote his welfare (paragraph 10).

22. Two other provisions in section 17 call for mention. Both are enabling powers in respect of any service provided by an authority in the exercise of functions conferred on the authority by section 17. If provided with a view to safeguarding or promoting the child's welfare, the service may be provided for the family of a particular child in need, or any member of his family: section 17(3). The service may include providing accommodation and giving assistance in kind or, in exceptional circumstances, in cash: section 17(6).

The reference to accommodation in this subsection was inserted by section 116 of the Adoption and Children Act 2002 to lay at rest doubts arising from the Court of Appeal decision in *A's* case.

23. Section 17 covers a wide range of services. Section 20 is focused more narrowly. It is concerned specifically with the accommodation needs of children in need. Section 20 obliges every local authority to provide accommodation for children in need who appear to need accommodation:

"(1) Every local authority shall provide accommodation for any child in need within their area who appears to them to require accommodation as a result of—
(a) there being no person who has parental responsibility for him;
(b) his being lost or having been abandoned; or

(c) the person who has been caring for him being prevented (whether or not permanently, and for whatever reason) from providing him with suitable accommodation or care."

24. "Prevented . . . for whatever reason" in paragraph (c) is to be interpreted widely. It includes as case where the person caring for the child is intentionally homeless. A child is not to be visited with the shortcomings of his parents. A similarly wide interpretation was given to the comparable provision in section 1 of the Children Act 1948 the predecessor to section 2(1) of the Child Care Act 1980: see *Attorney General ex rel Tilley v Wandsworth London Borough Council* [1981] 1 WLR 854.

Section 17(1) of the Children Act 1989

25. I turn to the interpretation of section 17(1). Section 17(1) is not just a statement of general principle, important though it is in that regard. Nor does it merely confer a new or enlarged function on local authorities. It imposes a duty. It imposes a duty expressed to be additional to the other duties imposed by Part III of the Children Act 1989. By definition, the additional obligation thus imposed on local authorities is enforceable by the court in appropriate circumstances on the application of a person with sufficient interest. The crucial issue is to identify the content of this additional duty.

26. At first sight section 17(1) does not seem to impose a duty in respect of the particular needs of an individual child. The duty is expressed in general, overall terms regarding the collective needs of children in need in the local authority's area. It is not expressed by reference to the needs of any one child. This generality, however, is not conclusive. The generality of an obligation regarding children in a local authority's area is not of itself inconsistent with the obligation being a duty in relation to the needs of individual children in the area. An obligation in respect of the general may include an obligation in respect of the particular. A duty in respect of an entire class or group as a whole may include a duty in respect of the individual members of the class or group. It all depends upon the language read in its context.

27. So I turn to the language of section 17(1). The starting point is to note the statutory description of the duty as a "general" duty. Read in context, this description is not, of itself, of much value as a pointer on the issue now under consideration. This description is used by way of contrast to the "specific" duties and powers mentioned in section 17(2). The latter duties and powers are specific because they relate to particular, limited aspects of the general duty imposed by section 17(1). The purpose of section 17(1) is wider. The purpose is to set out, at the very forefront of Part III and by way of contrast to the specific duties and powers, a primary additional duty of a more comprehensive character.

28. Next, the nature of the general duty imposed on a local authority by section 17(1): this is twofold. The duty is to safeguard and promote the welfare of children within its area who are in need, and to promote the upbringing of such children by their families. "Safeguard" and "promote" are broad terms; necessarily so, in the context of the welfare of a child. There is nothing in the use of these terms to suggest the duty is not a duty in respect of each child within the local authority's area who is in need. The phrase "children within their area who are in need" refers to all the children in need within the local authority's area. But the duty to promote the welfare and upbringing of all

such children makes little sense unless it is a duty in respect of the welfare and upbringing of each such child. Indeed, if this were not so section 17(1) would be a poor sort of additional general duty. Section 22 is another example of a duty, described as a general duty, to safeguard and promote the welfare of children. A local authority "looking after any child" is obliged "to safeguard and promote his welfare". It cannot be doubted that this duty under section 22(3), although described as a general duty and although expressed in broad terms, is a duty which relates to the individual child and is enforceable as such.

29. Section 17(1) then proceeds to state the means by which this duty is to be discharged: "by providing a rang and level of services appropriate to those children's needs." This, again is the language of generality. But, here also, the language could hardly be otherwise, given the comprehensive nature of the obligation imposed. Section 17(1) deliberately eschews references to particular types of servics. Section 17(1) is intended to be wide in its scope because the needs of children vary widely. So local authorities must provide an appropriate range and level of services, whatever those services may be. Section 17(3) and (6) make clear that the types of services mentioned in those two subsections are among the services a local authority may provide in carrying out its duty under section 17.

30. Thus far I am broadly in agreement with the interpretation urged by the claimants. But I short of the conclusion submitted by them. In my view section 17(1) does not impose an absolute, or near absolute, duty on local authorities to meet the specific needs of every child who is in need, whatever those needs may be. There is no place for absolutes in such a wide-ranging duty regarding the welfare of children. Nor would that be consistent with the qualified nature of some of the specific duties imposed in Part I of schedule 2. The "needs" of a child for services is itself an inherently imprecise concept. "Needs" are open-ended. Some limit can be placed on what are to be regarded as the needs of a child for the purposes of this legislation if the legislation is read, as it should be, as a reference to reasonable needs. Even so, this leaves much scope of differing views. Question of degree will often arise. Likewise, the statutory obligation to provide a range and level of services "appropriate" to the needs of children in need gives a local authority considerable latitude in determining what is "appropriate" in an individual case in all the circumstances. In some cases the type and level of service provided may properly fall short of meeting all the child's needs as assessed. The extent of the latitude in each case depends upon the circumstances, prominent among which are the nature of the service in question and the nature and extent of the needs of the child. Cost is also an element which may properly be taken into account in deciding what is "appropriate" in a particular case. The extent to which cost, and hence the resources of a local authority; may be taken into account depends upon all the circumstances including how basic is the assessed needs, the ease or difficulty with which it may be met, and the consequences of not meeting it. In a word, despite this latitude the council must act reasonably.

31. The degree of latitude thus afforded to a local authority may make it difficult for a claimant to establish a breach of this duty. But this is not a sufficient reason for denying the existence of the duty. Nor are the default powers of the Secretary of State under section 84 of the Children Act 1989 an adequate substitute for the ability to have recourse to the court. These default powers cannot be expected to provide an adequate remedy in individual cases.

32. I am fortified in my view that section 17 imposes a duty respect of the individual child by noting the consequences of the alternative approach. On the local authorities approach, since section 17(1) does not impose a duty in relation to an individual child, it follows that a local authority is not under a duty to assess the needs of child in need under section 17(1). That cannot be right. That would go far to stultify the whole purpose of Part III of the Children Act 1989. The first step towards safeguarding and promoting the welfare of a child in need by providing services for him and his family is to identify the child's need for those services. It is implicit in section 17(1) that a local authority will take reasonable steps to assess, for the purposes of the Act, the needs of any child in its area who appears to be in need. Failure to carry out this duty may attract a mandatory order in an appropriate case, as occurred in *R(on the application of AB and SB) v Nottinghamshire County Council* [2001] EWHC Admin 235 (2001) 4 CCLR 295. Richards J. ordered a local authority to carry out a full assessment of a child's needs in accordance with the guidance given by the Secretary of State in "Framework for the Assessment of Children in Need and their Families" (March 200).

33. Where does such an assessment lead? According to the local authorities, nowhere as a matter of legal obligation, so far as an individual child is concerned beyond, presumably, an obligation on the part of the authority to consider the assessment and decide whether to exercise any of its statutory powers. That would be a surprisingly weak outcome. That would represent a lacuna in the law relating to children in need. I cannot think Parliament intended this should be so. I prefer a different approach. If section 17(1) is apt to impose a duty on a local authority to take reasonable steps to assess the needs of an individual child in need, it is equally apt to impose the duty mentioned about to provide a range and level of services "appropriate" to those needs.

34. In several cases it has been assumed, or conceded, that section 17(1) imposes an obligation in respect of the needs of an individual child; for instance, in *R v Tower Hamlets London Borough Council, Ex p Bradford Council*, (1997) 1 CCLR 294, 301 per Kay J, and *R v Wigan Metropolitan Borough Council, Ex p Tammadge* (1998) 1 CCLR 581, 584, per Forbes J. In other cases, where the point has been argued, the contrary view has been preferred. These cases culminated in the decision of the Court of Appeal in the instant case involving A and her two disabled children: *R (on the application of A) v Lambeth London Borough Council* (2001) 4 CCLR 486. The Court of Appeal held that an assessment of needs under section 17 does not give rise to a duty enforceable at the suit of an individual, although a decision by a local authority not to exercise its powers under section 17 is open to judicial review on ordinary principles. For the reasons I have given I respectfully consider that the responsibilities of local authorities under section 17(1), although far from absolute, are of a higher order than this.

35. I should add a further comment regarding the assessment of needs under section 17. In *R v Gloucestershire County Council, Ex p Barry* [1997] AC 584 a question abut the relevance of cost arose in the context of a duty to make certain arrangements where a local authority is satisfied this is "necessary" in order to meet the "needs" of disabled persons. The majority of the House held that on the proper interpretation of section 2(1) of the Chronically Sick and Disabled Persons Act 1970 the local authority is entitled to have regard to its resources when performing this duty. Whether, under that section, resources should be taken into account when assessing "needs" as distinct from when the authority is deciding whether it is "necessary" to meet those needs, is not a matter which arose in *Barry's* case. In *Barry's* case the local authority had merged the two stages into one by providing services in accordance with elaborate "eligibility criteria". What was in issue was whether the authority could lawfully raise the eligibility criteria because of shortage of money. Later cases, such as *R v Sefton Metropolitan Borough Council, Ex p Help the Aged* (1997) 1 CCLR 57 and *R v East Sussex County Council, Ex p Tandy* [1998] AC 714, show it is desirable to keep these two stages separate. Ordinarily cost, where relevant, will be a matter to be taken into account by a local authority when considering its response to an assessed need rather than at the stage of assessment. That is the position under section 17(1) of the Children Act 1989.

Accommodating a child with his parents

[36]–[58] [His Lordship held that a social services authority would not discharge its duty to the child under s.17(1) of the 1989 Act if, in a case where the child is not old enough to understand what was happening, or, if he is, he would be likely to be significantly upset at being separated from his parent, it refused to exercise its power to accommodate the parent as well as the child, where that was no more expensive. In this type of case, a local authority should not, expressly or tacitly, threaten a parent that the most it will do is to accommodate the child alone. Lambeth LBC's policy thus required reconsideration.]

LORD STEYN agreed with LORD NICHOLLS OF BIRKENHEAD.
LORD HOPE OF CRAIGHEAD: [set out the legislative background and continued:]
76. . . . Does section 17(1) require a local social services authority to meet every need which has been identified by an assessment of the needs of each individual child in need within their area? For the appellants it is maintained that, once there has been an assessment of the needs of each individual child in need, there is a specific duty on the local social services authority under this subsection to provide services to meet the child's assessed needs. It follows that the child has an absolute right to the provision of residential accommodation, if this is the need which has been identified by the assessment. If this approach is right, neither the cost of providing these services nor the availability of resources can play any part in the assessment of the child's need by the local social services authority or in its decision as to whether, and if so how, it should meet that need.
77. My noble and learned friend Lord Nicholls has said that, on the respondents' approach to the construction of section 17(1), it follows that a local authority is not under a duty to assess the needs of a child in need under section 17(1) and that this would go far to stultify the purpose of Part III of the Act. I should make it clear, before I embark on my analysis, that I am unable to agree that this conclusion follows from the respondents' argument. Section 17(2) provides that, for the purpose of facilitating the discharge of the general duty under that section, every local authority shall have the specific duties and powers set out in Part I of Schedule 2. The duty of the local authority to take reasonable steps to identify the extent to which there are children in need in their area is to be found in paragraph 1 of the Schedule. That will involve assessing the needs of each child who is found to be in need in their area as paragraph 3 makes clear.

A v Lambeth: section 17(1)

78. The situation in this case raises the question which these cases have identified under section 17(1) in its most acute form . . .

79. The duty which has been placed on the local social services authority by section 17(1) to provide a range and level of services appropriate to the children's needs is described by the subsection as a "general duty". This duty is said by the opening words of the subsection to be in addition to the other duties imposed on them by Part III of the Act. And section 17(2) provides that, for the purpose principally of facilitating the discharge of their general duties under that section, every local authority shall have the specific duties and powers set out in Part I of Schedule 2. The duty on which the appellant seeks to rely in this case is not one of the other duties imposed on the respondents by Part III of the Act, nor is it one of the specific duties set out in Part I of Schedule 2. Her case rests therefore fairly and squarely on the propositions that the general duties described in section 17(1) are owed to each and every child in need individually, and that they are enforceable against them by or on behalf of each individual child accordingly. The contrary view is that section 17(1) is designed to set out the general principles which the local services authority must apply when providing services to children in need in their area.

80. An examination of the range of duties mentioned elsewhere in Part III of the Act and Part I of Schedule 2 tends to support the view that section 17(1) is concerned with general principles and is not designed to confer absolute rights on individuals. These other duties appear to have been carefully framed so as to confer a discretion on the local services authority as to how it should meet the needs of each individual child in need.

81. Section 18(1), which imposes a duty to provide day care for pre-school children, provides that the local authority shall provide such day care "as is appropriate". Section 20(1), which imposes a duty to provide accommodation for a child for whom no person has parental responsibility, who is lost or abandoned or whose carer has been prevented from providing him with suitable accommodation or care, and section 20(3), which imposes a duty to provide accommodation for children over sixteen, leave important matters to the judgment of the local authority: "appears to them to require accommodation" in section 20(1); "whose welfare the authority consider is likely to be seriously prejudiced" in section 20(3). So too does section 22, which imposes a duty on the local authority (described in the side-note, but not in the section itself, as a "general" duty) before making a decision with respect to a child whom they are looking after to ascertain the wishes and feeling of the child and various other people "so far as is reasonably practicable" and to give "due consideration" to such wishes and feeling as they have been able to ascertain. So too does section 23, which imposes a duty on the local authority to provide accommodation for children whom they are looking after, as section 23(2) sets out a range of options which includes in subsection 2(f)(i) such other arrangements as "seems appropriate to them". The duties in Schedule 2 follow the same pattern. The duties in paragraphs 6 and 7 also leave important matters to the judgment of the local authority: "designed" to "minimise" the effect in paragraph 6; "designed" to "reduce", to "encourage" and to "avoid" in paragraph 7. Those in paragraphs 8 and 9(1) are qualified by the expression "as they consider appropriate", and the duty in paragraph 10 is qualified by the words "take such steps as are reasonably practicable".

82. The discretion which is given by these provisions to the local authority is framed in various ways, but the result is the same in each case. Where a discretion is given, the child in need does not have an absolute right to the provision of any of these services.

83. The use of the expression "general duty" in section 17(1), too, suggests that the purpose of the subsection was to set out duties of a general nature only and that they were not intended to be enforceable as such by individuals. The DHHS *Review of Child Care Law* contained the following recommendations:

"5.7 Local authority powers and duties regarding children living with their families could be regarded as having two main aims: to provide 'family support' to help parents bring up their children; and to seek to prevent admission to care or court proceedings except where this is in the best interests of the child . . . .

5.8 We believe the provisions should be stated clearly in general terms of making services available at an appropriate level to the needs of the area rather than in terms of duties owed to individual children or families, in order to leave local authorities a wide flexibility to decide what is appropriate in particular cases while providing for a reasonable overall level of provision. It is for local authorities to decide on their priorities within the resources available to them."

84. The recommendations of the DHHS Working Part of Child Care Law were taken into account in the White Paper, *The Law on Child Care and Family Services*, which preceded the introduction of the Bill which became the 1989 Act. Chapter Two of the White Paper deals with services to families with children. In paragraph 14 it was explained that the powers and duties of local authorities to provide services to promote the care and upbringing of children and to diminish the need to take them compulsorily into local authority care were to be revised, and that there was to be a new focus on the provision of services in voluntary partnership with parents. In paragraph 18 the proposals for promoting the care and upbringing of children in their families were introduced in this way [emphasis as printed in the White Paper]:

"It is proposed to give local authorities a broad "umbrella" *power* to provide services to promote the care and upbringing of children, and to help prevent the breakdown of family relationship which might eventually lead to a court order committing the child to the local authority's care. Within this power the local authority will be able to provide services to a child at *home*, for example family aide to assist within the *home*; at a *day centre*, for example a day nursery for pre-school children, an after school scheme for school age children or placement with a childminder; or *residential facilities* allowing a child to stay for short or long periods away from home, say with a foster family or in a children's home. The local authority will also be able to offer financial assistance in exceptional circumstances. This is not an exclusive list . . .."

85. This legislative background serves to reinforce the impression which the structure and language of the legislation itself gives, that the so-called "general duty" in section 17(1) is owed to all the children who are in need within their area and not to each child in need individually. It is an overriding duty, a statement of general principle. It provides the broad aims which the local authority is to bear in mind when it is performing the "other duties" set local authority is to bear in mind when it is performing the "other duties" set out in part III

(see the words in parenthesis in section 17(1) and the "specific duties" for facilitating the discharge of those general duties which are set out in Part I of Schedule 2 (see section 17(2)). A child in need within the meaning of section 17(10) is eligible for the provision of those services, but he has no absolute right to them . . . .

91. I think that the correct analysis of section 17(1) is that it sets out duties of a general character which are intended to be for the benefit of children in need in the local social services authority's area in general. The other duties and the specific duties which then follow must be performed in each individual case by reference to the general duties which section 17(1) sets out. What the subsection does is to set out the duties owed to a section of the public in general by which the authority must be guided in the performance of those other duties: see *R v London Borough of Barnet Ex p B* [1994] ELR 357. . . .

As Mr Goudie QC for the respondents accepted, members of that section of the public have a sufficient interest to enforce those general duties by judicial review. But they are not particular duties owed to each member of that section of the public of the kind described by Lord Clyde in *R v Gloucestershire Country Council, Ex p Barry* [1997] AC 584, 610A which give a correlative right to the individual which he can enforce in the event of a failure in its performance.

92. A further point is particularly relevant to this case, as the service which is sought is the provision of residential accommodation. The need which the assessment has identified is not for the provision of temporary accommodation only. As the recommendation at the end of the assessment puts it, what this family needs is to be "re-housed". Section 17 refers to a range and level of services appropriate to the children's needs. It is broadly expressed, with a view to giving the greatest possible scope to the local social services appropriate to the children's needs. It is broadly expressed, with a view to giving the greatest possible scope to the local social services authority as to what it chooses to do in the provision of these services. Although the services which the authority provides may "include" the provision of accommodation (see section 17(6)), the provision of residential accommodation to re-house a child in need so that he can live with his family is not the principal or primary purpose of this legislation. Housing is the function of the local housing authority, for the acquisition and management of whose housing stock detailed provisions are contained in the Housing Acts. Provisions of that kind are entirely absent from this legislation.

93. We were informed that this is far form being an isolated case of its kind, as about 200 such cases involving children in need had been identified by the respondents in their area in the past 5 months. The expenditure of limited resources on the provision of residential accommodation for housing these children with their families would be bound to mean that there was less available for expenditure on other services designed for the performance of the general duty which section 17(1) has identified. A reading of that subsection as imposing a specific duty on the local social services authority to provide residential accommodation to individual children in need who have been assessed to be in need of such accommodation would sit uneasily with the legislation in the Housing Acts. As Mr Goudie pointed out, it could have the effect of turning the social services department of the local authority into another kind of housing department, with a different set of priorities for the provision of housing for the homeless than those which section 59 of the Housing Act 1985 lays down for the local housing authority.

94. There was no failure in this case to assess the needs of the appellant's children: contrast *R (on the application of AB and SB) v Nottinghamshire County Council* [2001] EWHC Admin 235; (2001) 4 CCLR 295. The failure which is alleged is a failure to purchase residential accommodation which is suitable for the children's needs. The order which the appellant seeks is an order that the respondent must provide services pursuant to section 17 to meet their assessed needs and a declaration that the respondent has acted in breach of its statutory duties. Her argument is entirely dependent upon the proposition that the effect of that assessment has been to crystallise the general duty under section 17(1) so that it has become a specific duty owed to A's children as individuals. Troublesome though A's case is in view of the difficulties which the assessment has so carefully identified, I am unable to accept that this approach is consistent with the language of the statue. I would therefore reject the argument which has been advance under section 17(1), in all three cases. . . .

LORD MILLETT and LORD SCOTT OF FOSCOTE delivered concurring opinions also expressly agreeing with LORD HOPE OF CRAIGHEAD'S opinion.

Appeal dismissed

Notes

1. Consider how far the competing interpretations offered here reflect (1) the text of s.17(1) read in context; and (2) concerns about resource issues for social services authorities.

2. The term "target duty" was first used by Woolf L.J. in *R. v Inner London Education Authority Ex p. Ali* (1990) 2 Admin L.R. 822 at 828 in respect of the duty of a local education authority under s.8 of the Education Act 1944 "to secure that there shall be available sufficient schools" for providing primary and secondary education. This arose out a complaint to the Secretary of State under s.99 of the Education Act 1944 that ILEA had breached s.8 by reacting too slowly to an increase in the school-age population in Tower Hamlets leading to a shortfall in school places. The Secretary of State refused to make a direction under s.99 on the ground that ILEA was taking reasonable steps to improve the situation; that decision was not challenged, but the applicants sought a remedy in respect of ILEA's breach of s.8. Woolf L.J. said:

> "In order to arrive at the correct interpretation of section 8, it is important to recognise that the duty which it places upon the local education authority is in very broad and general terms. It is a counterpart of the even wider duty placed upon the Secretary of State by section 1. It is the type of duty which is a common feature of legislation which is designed to benefit the community: see, for example, section 1 of the National Health Service Act 1977.
>
> This type of duty can be described as a 'target duty'. In the language of Mr Goudie there is built into section 8 a 'degree of elasticity'. While there are a number of standards which are required to be achieved by the local education authority, the setting of those standards is, in the first instance, for the local education authority alone to determine as long as those standards are not outside the tolerance provided by the section.
>
> There are going to be situations, some of which can and others which cannot reasonably be anticipated, where the education provided falls below the statutory standard and the standards which the local education authority would set for itself. It is undoubtedly the position that within the area for which ILEA is responsible at the present time, the statutory standards and the standards that it would set for itself are not being met but this does not mean that ILEA are necessarily in breach of their

duty under section 8. The question is whether ILEA has taken the steps which the statute requires to remedy the situation which exists . . . .

However, I would not accept, as Mr Goudie [counsel for ILEA] contends, that it is entirely for the local education authority to decide what steps it should reasonably take. Such an approach would be inconsistent with the fact that the Secretary of State is not only given the power under section 68 to intervene when he is satisfied that the local education authority has acted or is proposing 'to act unreasonably'; he is also given the power to intervene when the local education authority has failed 'to discharge any duty imposed upon him' under section 99. . . .

The duty under section 8 is not absolute. A local education authority which is faced with a situation where, without any fault on its part, it has not complied with the standard which the section sets for a limited period is not automatically in breach of the section. Here I refer to changing situations which could not be anticipated, not questions of resources or priorities.

Furthermore, even where there is a breach of section 8 the Court in their discretion may not intervene if by the time the matter comes before the Court the local education authority is doing all that it reasonably can to remedy the situation. The situation is best left in the hands of the bodies to whom Parliament has entrusted performance of the statutory duty if they are seeking to fulfil that duty".

His Lordship held (1) that the proposition that the section 8 duty was intended to enure for the public in general and not to give the individual litigant a cause of action was fatal to a claim for damages; (2) that the jurisdiction of the court to intervene by way of judicial review was not, however, excluded by the existence of the section 99 default power, although it was relevant to the question whether the application for judicial review would be entertained or a remedy granted in the exercise of the court's discretion. A target duty thus remains a "duty" although it may well be difficult to show non-compliance, and there will in any event be no remedy in damages.

Other duties imposed for the general benefit of the community that have been held to be target duties include the duty of a local education authority to secure the provision of adequate facilities for further education (*R. v Further Education Funding Council Ex p. Parkinson* [1997] E.L.R. 204); the duty of local authority to make arrangements for promoting the welfare of disabled persons (*R. v Islington LBC Ex p. Rixon* [1997] E.L.R. 66) and the duty of a fire authority to "make provision for firefighting purposes" (*Capital Counties plc v Hampshire CC* [1997] Q.B. 1004) (see C. Callaghan, "What is a 'Target Duty'?" [2000] J.R. 184).

3. Examples of duties that are to be interpreted as imposing obligations for the benefit of individuals include the duty under s.21(1)(a) of the National Assistance Act 1948 (as amended), in accordance with a direction by Secretary of State, to provide residential accommodation for persons aged 18 or over who by reason of age, illness, disability or any other circumstances are in need of care and attention which is not otherwise available to them; once a person's needs have been assessed as fulfilling these criteria the authority comes under a continuing duty to provide accommodation while the applicant's needs remain as originally assessed (*R. v Kensington and Chelsea RLBC Ex p. Kujtim* [1999] 4 All E.R. 161). See also *R. v Richmond LBC Ex p. Watson* [2002] 2 A.C. 1127 (duty of health authorities under s.117 of the Mental Health Act 1983 to provide after care services to mental patients following discharge from hospital held to be a specific absolute duty for which they could not charge; it was a free-standing duty not a "gateway provision" imposing a duty to secure provision under other enactments) and the cases discussed in the following note.

4. Once the scope of a duty has been determined, it is clear that a lack of resources is no justification for failing to perform it. However, the availability of resources may, depending on the wording of the duty and its statutory context be relevant in determining the prior question of the scope of the duty. This point is illustrated, for example, by Lord Nicholls' approach in *R. (on the application of G) v Barnet LBC* (above, p.406). It proved particularly controversial, however, in the decision of the

House of Lords in *R. v Gloucestershire CC Ex p. Barry* [1997] A.C. 584. Section 2 of the Chronically Sick and Disabled Person Act 1970 (as amended) provided that where a local authority having functions in respect of disabled persons under s.29 of the National Assistance Act 1948 was satisfied in the case of such person ordinarily resident in its area "that it is necessary in order to meet the needs of that person for that authority to make arrangement for" all or any of a list of specified matters, then "it shall be the duty of that authority to make those arrangements in exercise of their functions under the said section 29". B was elderly and infirm and his needs were twice assessed as "home care . . . for shopping, pension, laundry, cleaning, meals on wheels". Cleaning and laundry services were then withdrawn by the council "because the money allocated to it by central government had been reduced". The House of Lords held by 3 to 2 (Lords Nicholls of Birkenhead, Hoffmann and Clyde, Lords Lloyd of Berwick and Steyn dissenting) that in assessing an applicant's need for a service, the degree of that need and the necessity to make arrangements for it, a local authority had to balance the severity of the disabling condition against the cost of those arrangements and the availability of resources. Lord Clyde said (at 610–611):

> "The words 'necessary' and 'needs' are both relative expression, admitting in each case a considerable range of meaning. They are not defined in the Act and reference to dictionary definitions does not seem to me to advance the construction of the subsection. In deciding whether there is a necessity to meet the needs of the individual some criteria have to be provided. Such criteria are required both to determine whether there is a necessity at all or only, for example, a desirability, and also to assess the degree of necessity. Counsel for Mr Barry suggested that a criterion could be found in the values of a civilised society. But I am not persuaded that that is sufficiently precise to be of any real assistance. It is possible to draw up categories of disabilities, reflecting the variations in the gravity of such disabilities which could be experienced. Such a classification might enable comparisons to be made between persons with differing kinds and degrees of disability. But in determining the question whether in a given case the making of particular arrangements is necessary in order to meet the needs of a given individual it seems to me that a mere list of disabling conditions graded in order of severity will still leave unanswered the question at what level of disability is the stage of necessity reached. The determination of eligibility for the purposes of the statutory provision requires guidance not only on the assessment of the severity of the condition or the seriousness of the need but also on the level at which there is to be satisfaction of the necessity to make arrangements. In the framing of the criteria to be applied it seems to me that the severity of a condition may have to be to be matched against the availability of resources. Such an exercise indeed accords with everyday domestic experience in relation to things which we do not have. If my resources are limited I have to need the thing very much before I am satisfied that it is necessary to purchase it. It may also be observed that the range of the facilities which are listed as being the subject of possible arrangements, 'the service list,' is so extensive as to make it unlikely that Parliament intended that they might all be provided regardless of the cost involved. It is not necessary to hold that cost and resources are always an element in determining the necessity. It is enough for the purposes of the present case to recognise that they may be a proper consideration. I have not been persuaded that they must always and necessarily be excluded from consideration".

While Lord Clyde focussed on the issue of "necessity", Lord Nicholls of Birkenhead held (at 604–605) that a person's needs for services cannot sensibly be assessed without having some regard to the cost of providing them; and the importance of cost must vary both according to both the benefit to be derived from the suggested expenditure and the means of the person called upon to pay. Lord Hoffmann agreed with both Lord Clyde and Lord Nicholls (at 606).

Lord Lloyd of Berwick delivered a powerful dissent, noting (at 597) that it had been right for the Secretary of State to be joined in the appeal "for it is the failure of central government to supply the funds necessary to enable the council to carry out what I regard as their statutory duty which, departing from the fine words contained in the Government White Paper 'Caring for People: Community Care in the Next Decade and Beyond' (1989) (Cm.849), has put the council into what the Divisional Court called an impossible position; truly impossible, because even if the council wished to raise the money themselves to meet the need by increasing council tax, they would be unable to do so by reason of the government-imposed rate-capping".

It was common ground that the duty under s.2 is owed to the disabled person. "Need" is the lack of what is essential for the ordinary business of living. It was for the authority to assess an individual's needs against the standards of civilised society. Such needs could not become less because the authority lacked resources to meet them.

"Simply looking at the language of section 2 of the Act of 1970, against the background of Pt 3 of the Act of 1948, it is clear enough that Parliament did not intend that provision for the needs of the disabled should depend on the availability of resources" (at 601).

By contrast, when determining whether it is necessary to make arrangements to meet the needs, "the council must obviously be allowed a good deal of flexibility as to the arrangements which they make, provided always that the need is met" (at 598). On this approach, lack of resources is no justification for failing meeting an assessed need; availability of resources will be relevant in considering how this is to be done.

The reasons given in dissent seem, with respect, to be the more compelling. The interpretation of the majority turns the duty in effect into a duty to do what is "appropriate" to meet the assessed need. But the section does not say that. This approach has not found favour in other contexts: see *R. v East Sussex CC Ex p. Tandy* [1998] A.C. 714, HL (resources held irrelevant to statutory duty to provide "suitable" education); *R. v Birmingham City Council Ex p. Mohammed* [1999] 1 W.L.R. 33 (local housing authority not entitled to have regard to its financial resources in determining whether to approve an application for a disabled facilities grant within s.23(1) of the Housing Grants, Construction and Regeneration Act 1996); *cf. R. v Sefton MBC Ex p. Help the Aged* [1997] 4 All E.R. 532 (the authority's resources can be relevant in determining whether a person is "in need of care and attention" for the purposes of s.21(1)(a) of the National Assistance Act 1948, but not to the duty to provide accommodation once such a need was assessed).

(C) JURISDICTIONAL REVIEW

Overview: Development of current scope of review

In the cases considered above (pp.391–420) the principal question for the courts has been relatively straightforward: whether the actions of a public body were, or were not, authorised or required (expressly or impliedly) by the terms of legislation.

What is essentially the same question may arise, however, in a different and slightly more complex way. It may be that there is no dispute between the parties that in certain circumstances the body in question may do what it has done. The contention of the applicant is not that what has been done is, in the simple sense considered above, unlawful or beyond the powers of the public body in question. Rather, the challenge will be founded on the contention that power to do what has been done has not been conferred by the legislation to be exercised "at large"—whenever the body in question so pleases—but has been conferred subject to limitations as to the circumstances which must prevail before the power may validly be exercised. To put the matter another way: it is the difference between legislative grant of power to do "X"; and the grant of power to do "X" in (and, implicitly, *only* in) defined circumstances.

What should be the scope of review where power has been conferred in this latter way? It is clear that if it is the role of the High Court to keep grantees of powers within the bounds of the powers conferred, the judges must be willing to review the jurisdictional parameters set by the legislation in question. The notion that such a grantee of power might also be given the right conclusively to determine the existence or non-existence of the circumstances upon which the validity of such power might depend was acknowledged as a legislative possibility (Parliament being sovereign) in the *Income Tax Commissioners* case (below, p.429): but this idea has not been applied in any subsequent decision.

The courts will, in the exercise of the jurisdictional control described above, be confronted with arguments of two principal kinds. On the one hand it may be argued that a public body has come to an incorrect conclusion as regards the circumstances which must exist in order for it to exercise the power in question. This will involve a question of disputed interpretation of the legislative text. Alternatively, it might be that there is simply a dispute about the existence or non-existence of the circumstances which it is agreed must prevail if there is to be a valid exercise of the statutory power. In other words the critical issues may be ones of law or may be ones of fact.

The first cases in the section which follows this overview involve the issue of the willingness of the High Court to review issues of fact upon which, it is argued, the existence of statutory power may depend. It will be seen that there are cases (*White and Collins*; *Khawaja*) where the courts have demonstrated a preparedness to review the existence of facts which are, therefore, said to be "precedent to jurisdiction". In other cases—and the legislative and factual context may here be critical—the courts may be less willing to intervene (*Dowty*; *Puhlhofer*), leaving a measure of judgment here to the executive body.

Issues of jurisdictional *law* have tended to arise in the context of the functioning of adjudicatory (as distinct from purely administrative) bodies, giving rise to more complex issues for the courts as regards the kinds of errors which should, and which should not, found judicial review. It may be helpful to an understanding of the cases which follow (*Anisminic* and its progeny) to explain this point a little more fully.

The law which is relevant to an adjudicatory body in the exercise of its functions will cover a variety of matters. In respect of each matter it will be necessary for the body to come to determinations. The issue to be considered is: in relation to what questions will a wrong decision by an adjudicatory body result in its proceedings or decision being *ultra vires*?

It may help, first, to consider the kinds of legal questions which such a body may have to determine. These may relate to any, or all, of the following matters:

—the *proper composition* of the tribunal,
—the *types of case* which the tribunal has power to hear,
—the *procedural rules* to be followed in hearing and determining cases,
—the *substantive rules* to be applied to the facts in reaching decisions,
—the *order or orders* to be made consequent upon the decision reached.

The question with which we are concerned may be restated: given that tribunals may make errors in respect of each and any of these matters, which errors will give rise to successful judicial review proceedings and which not?

It is not difficult to see how errors in respect of the first, second, third and fifth of the kinds of legal question listed above are likely to qualify for jurisdictional review. Functions are given to tribunals on an assumption that the statutorily designated membership presides over cases; that the body hears, and only hears, the kinds of dispute within its jurisdictional remit; and also restricts itself to making the kinds of orders which statute has authorised.

But what of the "correctness" of the tribunal's actual substantive decisions? This would seem to represent a situation where, unless review and appeal are to become one and the same, it may be necessary for the reviewing court to draw back and consider that a properly constituted tribunal hearing a case within its jurisdiction *has jurisdiction* to make errors of law (and of fact) in coming to its actual decision in that case. Such errors would be remediable only if an appropriately widely defined right to *appeal* exists.

Although this may well be a logical application of the basic principles of jurisdictional review to the decisions of adjudicatory bodies, it does not now represent the general law. The approach now is that, in most although not all situations, any error of law made by decision-making body will cause it to act *ultra vires* or exceed its jurisdiction.

That this is so can perhaps be explained on a number of grounds. In the first place, the notion of "jurisdiction to err" is perhaps not an easy one to explain to disappointed judicial review applicants. The temptation for a judge to intervene if an error of law has been made by a tribunal or other body in reaching a decision is inevitably great; all the more so, given the power (referred to above, pp.242–243) to intervene for *error on the face of the record* (in cases where the error so appears) whether or not that error is in respect of a jurisdictional matter. It is not, therefore, surprising that the courts have held that their power to review decisions of tribunals extends not just to their proper composition and the nature of the cases they hear, but also to their decisions on points of substantive law.

The difficulty for the courts for a number of years, exemplified by the speeches in *Anisminic* (below, p.436), was how to devise a formula so that some errors in the course of coming to decisions would qualify for review, whilst others would not. In this context the courts sometimes stated a distinction between "errors which go to jurisdiction" and "errors which go to the merits" of the particular case. But this, of course, was simply to ask the basic question in a different guise, rather than the provision of any guiding test. The search by the courts for a suitable guiding test proved an elusive one; and also one in respect of which, over the passage of time a number of differing approaches prevailed.

The modern approach, exemplified in the speeches in the House of Lords in *Page* (below, p.450) appears to have made otiose much of the old learning to be found in *Anisminic* and its successor cases. Nevertheless, *Anisminic* remains an important case and is extracted below. Its name seems now indelibly associated with the new broad doctrine of "review for error of law" (see comment above at p.242); and an appreciation of the decision is important to a comprehension of the speeches in *Page*. Moreover, it contains important statements on the matter of the judicial interpretation of statutory provisions purporting to exclude judicial review (on which, see below, Ch.13).

In the light of the discussion above, the materials which follow are organised in the following sequence: (a) Precedent fact review; (b) Review for error of law.

(i) Precedent fact review

Re RIPON (HIGHFIELD) CONFIRMATION ORDER 1938, WHITE & COLLINS v MINISTER OF HEALTH

[1939] 2 K.B. 838; 180 L.J.K.B. 768; 161 L.T. 109; 55 T.L.R. 956; 83 S.J. 622; [1939] 3 All E.R. 548; 103 J.P. 331 (COURT OF APPEAL)

Under Part 5 of the Housing Act 1936, a local authority had power to acquire land compulsorily for the provision of houses for the working classes. By s.75 nothing in the Act was to authorise the compulsory acquisition of land "which at the date of the compulsory purchase forms part of any park, garden or pleasure ground or is otherwise required for the amenity or convenience of any house". Ripon Borough Council made an order for the compulsory purchase of about 23 acres of land, forming part of the grounds of a house at Ripon called "Highfield", which comprised in all about 35 acres. The 23 acres were at the time let for grazing purposes. The owners (the present appellants) objected that the land was part of a park and required for the amenity or convenience of the house, and that the order was therefore contrary to s.75. The Minister, after causing a public inquiry to be held, confirmed the order. The owners applied to the High Court for the order to be quashed. Further evidence was given by affidavit. The only material evidence on the question under s.75 was given on behalf of the applicant by an expert who stated that the land was undoubtedly park land attached to Highfield, it being obvious on inspection that the architect had so placed the house as to benefit by the amenity of the land. Charles J. dismissed the motion on the ground that the question was one of fact, and that it was not open to the court to interfere by rehearing the case and evidence. The owners appealed to the Court of Appeal.

LUXMOORE L.J.: . . . The evidence in the affidavits in support of the application is uncontradicted, and leads only to the conclusion that the land is part of the park. This evidence was not before the Minister, and, although it was before Charles J. when he heard the motion, he does not appear to have considered it, for, in refusing to quash the order of the borough council and its confirmation by the Minister, he based that refusal on the ground that the Minister had decided that the land in question was not part of the park or required for the amenity or convenience of the house, and that, as these were questions of fact, he would not interfere with the findings, as he had no power to retry or to rehear the case.

In my judgment Charles J. was in error in deciding as he did. As I have already pointed out, the proceeding before Charles J. was not by way of appeal from any order made by the borough council or its confirmation by the Minister of Health, but was a new and independent proceeding and not a rehearing or a retrial.

The first and most important matter to bear in mind is that the jurisdiction to make the order is dependent on a finding of fact; for, unless the land can be held not to be part of a park or not to be required for amenity or convenience, there is no jurisdiction in the borough council to make, or in the Minister to confirm, the order. In such a case it seems almost self-evident that the court which has to consider whether there is jurisdiction to make or confirm the order must be entitled to review the vital finding on which the existence of the jurisdiction relied upon depends. If this were not so, the right to apply to the court would be illusory.

There is however ample authority that the court is entitled so to act, for the point has been considered in a number of cases. It is sufficient to refer to the case of *Bunbury v. Fuller* (9 Ex. 111, 140). In that case Coleridge J. delivering the judgment of the Court of Exchequer Chamber said: "it is a general rule, that no court of limited jurisdiction can give itself jurisdiction by a wrong decision on a point collateral to the merits of the case upon which the limit to its jurisdiction depends; and however its decision may be final on all particulars, making up together that subject-matter which, if true, is within its jurisdiction, and however necessary in many cases it may be for it to make a preliminary inquiry, whether some collateral matter be or be not within the limits, yet, upon this preliminary question, its decision must always be open to inquiry in the superior court. Then to take the simplest case—suppose a judge with jurisdiction limited to a particular hundred, and a matter is brought before him as having arisen within it, but the party charged contends that it arose in another hundred, this is clearly a collateral matter independent of the merits; on its being presented, the judge must not immediately forbear to proceed, but must inquire into its truth or falsehood and for the time decide it, and either proceed or not with the principal subject-matter according as he finds on that point; but this decision must be open to question, and if he has improperly either forborne or proceeded on the main matter in consequence of an error, on this the Court of Queen's Bench will issue its mandamus or prohibition to correct his mistake."

As in *Bunbury v. Fuller* and also in *R. v. Bradford* [1908] 1 K.B. 365, so also in the present case, the decision on the question whether the particular land is part of a park or not is preliminary to the exercise of the jurisdiction to make and confirm the order conferred by the Housing Act 1936, s.75, and is therefore open to review in this court. Charles J. in arriving at his decision stated that he agreed with the decision of [. . .] Swift J. in *Bowman's* case [1932] 2 K.B. 621, 627, 634 in support of the view that he had no power to review the decision of the Minister of Health, because the question to be determined was one of fact.

. . . Reliance in this Court was placed on the statement of Swift J. that an aggrieved person "is not entitled to come here and complain that the local authority have made a mistake of fact in making the order. He is not entitled to say that his house is not insanitary or unfit for human habitation and therefore the order should not have been made." If this statement was intended by the learned judge to be of universal application to all cases under section 11(3) of the 1930 Act, and therefore also to all cases under the second clause of the Second Schedule to the 1936 Act, I should have no hesitation in saying that it went too far, for it ignores the rule laid down in *Bunbury v. Fuller* to which reference has already been made: a decision which Swift J. had no power to overrule; indeed no reference appears to have been made to it during the argument of *Bowman's* case. I think the remarks of Swift J. must be read in the light of the facts of the case before him, and especially with regard to the provisions of the Act of 1930, s.1, which appear in express terms to make the local authority the judge whether the houses in question are fit for habitation or not; for the material words of that section are: "Where a local authority upon consideration of an official representation or other information in their possession are satisfied" that the houses in the area are unfit, then an order may be made.

This provision differs materially from the present case; section 75 of the Act of 1936 does not refer in terms to the local authority being satisfied that the land is not part of a park. The making of the order for compulsory purchase is prohibited if the land is part of a park, a matter which can only be proved or disproved by evidence. . . .

In the present case, as I have already stated, I am satisfied that there was no evidence before the inspector sufficient to entitle the local authority or the Minister to come to a conclusion that the land in question was not part of the park of Highfield; I am further satisfied that on the affidavit evidence . . . the only conclusion open to the court is that the land was part of the park of Highfield. . . . In my judgment the appeal must be allowed.

HUMPHREYS J. agreed.

Order quashed.

Notes

1. These proceedings were in the form of a "statutory application to quash"—proceedings which are something of a hybrid between appeal and review. See further on this procedure below, p.805. The statements in the case about the basis and scope of review for error of jurisdictional fact remain authoritative as to the substance of this

ground of judicial review, although in the particular context of statutory applications to quash the modern approach is now as stated by Lord Denning M.R. in *Ashbridge Investments Ltd v Minister of Housing and Local Government*—see further below, p.808.

2. If the question had turned on whether the local authority had been "satisfied" that the land was not part of the park, the decision of the local authority would have still been open to challenge, but on *Wednesbury* grounds (see Ch. 9). It would not have been open to the court to form its own view on the matter.

R. v SECRETARY OF STATE FOR THE HOME DEPARTMENT Ex p. KHAWAJA

[1984] A.C. 74; [1983] 2 W.L.R. 32; [1983] 1 All E.R. 765 (HOUSE OF LORDS)

In this case two separate appeals to the House of Lords raising the same legal issues were heard together. The appellants, Khera and Khawaja, were both persons who, having been admitted to the United Kingdom as immigrants, had later been detained and ordered for removal as "illegal entrants" under the Immigration Act 1971. Argument centred on two questions—(i) the meaning of the term "illegal entrant" and (ii) the scope of review of the exercise of power to remove such persons from the United Kingdom.

These two questions had earlier been considered by the House of Lords in *Zamir v. Secretary of State for the Home Department* [1980] A.C. 930. In that case it had been held that the term "illegal entrant" included one who had obtained permission to enter after having failed positively to disclose some matter which would have led to the refusal of permission to enter had that information been known at the time. This was so even though no request for such information may have been made by any official—in other words, *Zamir* imposed a positive duty to disclose relevant information to immigration officers, even beyond answering truthfully the various questions which might specifically have been asked by the officers. In *Khawaja* the House of Lords over-ruled *Zamir* on this point, holding that a person who had been admitted entry was only an "illegal entrant" where some positive deception had been practised.

Our concern, however, is with the second of the two questions: in proceedings for judicial review is it sufficient for the Secretary of State to satisfy the court that when he exercised his power to order removal he had reasonable grounds to believe the appellant to be an illegal entrant? Or is not the critical issue whether the appellant does, or does not, in fact fall within that statutory category? *Zamir* had decided that the scope of review was of the former extent. The appellants called upon the House of Lords to reconsider the matter.

LORD SCARMAN: . . . [In *Zamir*] . . . [t]he House approved a line of authority (beginning with *R. v. Secretary of State for the Home Department, ex p. Hussain* [1978] 1 W.L.R. 700) which put a gloss on the words of the critical provision in the 1971 Act, *i.e.* Sched. 2, para.9 to the Act. The paragraph declares an illegal entrant to be liable to removal. It provides that where an illegal entrant is not given leave to enter or remain in the United Kingdom an immigration officer may give directions for his removal. Unless he (or the Secretary of State, para.10) gives such directions, no power to detain him arises; for para.16(2) provides a power to detain only in respect of a person who may be so removed. . . .

The gloss which the House in *Zamir's* case put on the words of para.9 was to read them as meaning not "where a person *is* an illegal entrant" but "where the immigration officer *has reasonable grounds for believing a person to be* an illegal entrant" he may be removed if not given leave to enter. If it be sought to justify the gloss as a proper construction of the statutory language, there is a difficulty. The gloss requires the introduction into the paragraph of words that are not there. Must they, then, be implied? This question lies at the heart of the problem.

In *Zamir's* case the House was impressed with the difficulties arising if the implication were not to be made. The House attached importance to three considerations: (1) the line of cases beginning with *Hussain*, in which the Court of Appeal had held it necessary to make the implication; (2) the scheme of the Immigration Act; and, especially, (3) the nature and process of the power of decision conferred by the Act on immigration officers.

These considerations, in the view of the House, made it necessary to reject the appellant's argument based on the well-established principle that, where the exercise of an executive power depends on the precedent establishment of an objective fact, it is for the court, if there be a challenge by way of judicial review, to decide whether the precedent requirement has been satisfied. In *R. v. Governor of Pentonville Prison, ex p. Azam* [1974] A.C. 18, 34 Lord Denning M.R. (in the Court of Appeal) considered the principle applicable in the case of removal of an illegal entrant. The House recognised the existence of the principle, but, following and approving *Hussain's* case, opted for a construction of the legislation which would oust it.

In rejecting the appellant's argument based on the "precedent fact" principle of review Lord Wilberforce said [in *Zamir*] [1980] A.C. 930, 948:

> "My Lords, for the reasons I have given I am of opinion that the whole scheme of the Act is against this argument. It is true that it does not, in relation to the decisions in question, use such words as 'in the opinion of the Secretary of State' or 'the Secretary of State must be satisfied', but it is not necessary for such a formula to be used in order to take the case out of the 'precedent fact' category. The nature and process of decision conferred on immigration officers by existing legislation is incompatible with any requirement for the establishment of precedent objective facts whose existence the court may verify."

He therefore implied into para.9 the words needed to bring it outside the "precedent fact" category of provision. My Lords, in most cases I would defer to a recent decision of your Lordships' House on a question of construction, even if I thought it wrong. I do not do so in this context because for reasons which I shall develop I am convinced that the *Zamir* reasoning gave insufficient weight to the important (I would say fundamental) consideration that we are here concerned with, the scope of judicial review of a power which inevitably infringes the liberty of those subjected to it. This consideration, if it be good, outweighs, in my judgment, any difficulties in the administration of immigration control to which the application of the principle might give rise. The *Zamir* construction of para.9 deprives those subjected to the power of that degree of judicial protection which I think can be shown to have been the policy of our law to afford to persons with whose liberty the executive is seeking to interfere. It does therefore, in my view, tend to obstruct the proper development and application of the safeguards our law provides for the liberty of those within its jurisdiction. . . .

Accordingly, faced with the jealous care our law traditionally devotes to the protection of the liberty of those who are subject to its jurisdiction, I find it impossible to imply into the statute words the effect of which would be to take the provision, para.9 of Sched. 2 to the 1971 Act, "out of the 'precedent fact' category" (see *Zamir* [1980] A.C. 930 at 948, *per* Lord Wilberforce). If Parliament intends to exclude effective judicial review of the exercise of a power in restraint of liberty, it must make its meaning crystal clear.

LORD BRIDGE: . . . [T]he authorities from *R. v. Secretary of State for the Home Department, ex p. Hussain* to *Zamir* have consistently affirmed the principle that the decision of an immigration officer to detain and remove a person as an illegal entrant under these provisions can only be attacked successfully on the ground that there was no evidence on which the immigration officer could reasonably conclude that he was an illegal entrant.

It will be seen at once that this principle gives to an executive officer, subject, no doubt, in reaching his conclusions of fact to a duty to act fairly, a draconian power of arrest and expulsion based on his own decision of fact. . . . It will be further observed that to justify the principle important words have to be read into para.9 of Sched. 2 by implication. That paragraph, on the face of the language used, authorises the removal of a person who is an illegal entrant. The courts have applied it as if it authorised the removal of a person whom an immigration officer on reasonable grounds believes to be an illegal entrant. The all-important question is whether such an implication can be justified. . . .

In *Zamir* [1980] A.C. 930, 948–949 Lord Wilberforce said:

"The nature and process of decision conferred on immigration officers by existing legislation is incompatible with any requirement for the establishment of precedent objective facts whose existence the court may verify.

The immigration officer, whether at the stage of entry or at that of removal, has to consider a complex of statutory rules and non-statutory guidelines. He has to act on documentary evidence and such other evidence as inquiries may provide. Often there will be documents whose genuineness is doubtful, statements which cannot be verified, misunderstandings as to what was said, practices and attitudes in a foreign state which have to be estimated. There is room for appreciation, even for discretion."

He proceeds to contrast the disadvantageous position of the Divisional Court as a fact-finding tribunal in the relevant field. . . .

My Lords, we should, I submit, regard with extreme jealousy any claim by the executive to imprison a citizen without trial and allow it only if it is clearly justified by the statutory language relied on. The fact that, in the case we are considering, detention is preliminary and incidental to expulsion from the country in my view strengthens rather than weakens the case for a robust exercise of the judicial function in safeguarding the citizen's rights.

So far as I know, no case before the decisions under the Act which we are presently considering has held imprisonment without trial by executive order to be justified by anything less than the plainest statutory language, with the sole exception of the majority decision of your Lordships' House in *Liversidge v. Anderson* [1942] A.C. 206. No one needs to be reminded of the now celebrated dissenting speech of Lord Atkin in that case, or of his withering condemnation of the process of writing into the statutory language there under consideration the words which were necessary to sustain the decision of the majority. Lord Atkin's dissent now has the approval of your Lordships'

House in *R. v. Inland Revenue Commissioners, ex p. Rossminster Ltd* [1980] A.C. 952.

A person who has entered the United Kingdom with leave and who is detained under Sched. 2, para.16(2) pending removal as an illegal entrant on the ground that he obtained leave to enter by fraud is entitled to challenge the action taken and proposed to be taken against him both by application for habeas corpus and by application for judicial review. On the view I take, para.9 of Sched. 2 must be construed as meaning no more and no less than it says. There is no room for any implication qualifying the words "illegal entrant". From this it would follow that, while, prima facie, the order for detention under para.16(2) would be a sufficient return to the writ of habeas corpus, proof by the applicant that he had been granted leave to enter would shift the onus back to the immigration officer to prove that the leave had been obtained in contravention of s.26(1)(c) of the Act, in other words by fraud. . . .

LORDS FRASER, WILBERFORCE and TEMPLEMAN delivered concurring speeches.

Notes

1. See N.P. Gravells, (1983) 99 L.Q.R. 363; I.A. Macdonald, and N.J. Blake, *Macdonald's Immigration Law and Practice* (4th ed., 1995), Chs 16, 18; G.L. Peiris, "Judicial Review and Immigration Policy: Emerging Trends" (1988) 8 L.S. 201.

2. In *R. v Secretary of State for the Environment Ex p. Davies* (1990) 61 P. & C.R. 487, the Court of Appeal held that the question whether a person had an "interest in land" to which an enforcement notice related, and so was entitled to appeal to the Secretary of State under the Town and Country Planning Act 1971, s.88 (now the 1990 Act, s.174), was a matter that went to the jurisdiction of the Secretary of State. Neill L.J. said (at 492) that:

> "it is now clear that it is common ground that where the decision-maker had to determine a preliminary question as to his own jurisdiction and this determination involved the inferences to be drawn from correspondence and other documents, the test to be applied by the court on judicial review is not that of perversity or unreason-ableness. It is accepted that the court is entitled to look at the matter afresh and make up its own mind.
>
> The only remaining question between the parties on this first issue is as to the weight, if any, to be attached to the decision of the Secretary of State. . . .
>
> As will become clear, we are concerned in this case with a claim by the appellant that at the material time she was in adverse possession of land and thus, it is said, had an interest in the land for the purposes of section 88(1) of the 1971 Act. It is necessary for her to establish an interest in land in order that she can appeal to the Secretary of State. It seems to me that in such circumstances, where the decision impugned involves a question as to the jurisdiction of the decision-maker and where the primary facts are contained in documents and do not involve any questions of credibility or policy, the court should look at the matter afresh and make up its own mind. That means, however, that the court must look at the matter on the basis of the evidence which was before the Secretary of State at the time when he reached his decision, because it is his decision against which judicial review is sought".

The court concluded on the facts, in agreement with the Secretary of State, that the applicant did not have an interest in the land.

For further illustrations of facts classified as jurisdictional facts in a variety of contexts, see, *e.g. Butler, Camberwell (Wingfield Mews) (No.2) Clearance Order 1936, Re* [1939] 1 K.B. 570 (whether clearance order buildings were "houses"); *Relton and Sons*

(Contracts) Ltd v Whitstable UDC (1967) 201 E.G. 955 (whether street a "new street"); *R. v Agricultural Land Tribunal for Wales and Monmouth Area Ex p. Davies* [1953] 1 W.L.R. 722 (whether conditions existed upon which depended ministerial power to consent to eviction); *R. v Secretary of State for the Environment, Transport and the Regions Ex p. Alliance against the Birmingham Northern Relief Road* [1999] C.O.D. 45 (whether information related to the environment for the purpose of the Environmental Information Regulations 1992 (SI 1992/3240) and if it did whether it fell within any exemption from the requirement of disclosure under the regulations).

Where a court is required to determine a precedent fact it is entitled to look at all the material on which the decision-maker legitimately relied (and any additional material put before it), and is not confined to evidence presented in strictly admissible form (*R. v Secretary of State for the Home Department Ex p. Rahman (Saidur)* [1998] Q.B. 136)

3. The notion that a body which has powers exercisable in certain defined situations or circumstances cannot by its *own* decision determine conclusively that such conditions exist needs qualification, Parliament, may, although arguably only by express words (*cf. R. v Secretary of State for the Home Department Ex p. Pierson*, above, p.251), confer powers on a body, make them exercisable in defined circumstances only, yet also make that body the conclusive judge as to whether those circumstances exist. This possibility, much limiting the review powers of the courts, was adverted to by Lord Esher M.R. in *R. v Income Tax Special Purposes Comrs* (1888) 21 Q.B.D. 313, CA. His Lordship adverted to two types of case. In the first type the jurisdictional facts are fully subject to review. In the second type:

"the legislation may entrust the . . . body with a jurisdiction which includes the jurisdiction to determine whether the preliminary state of facts exists as well as the jurisdiction, on finding that it does exist, to proceed further or do something more".

The second type of case has not, however, arisen in practice. See Lord Wilberforce in the *Anisminic* case, below p.436. Very clear words would be needed for this situation to arise in cases affecting individual liberty: *Tan Le Tan v Superintendent of Tai A Chau Detention Centre* [1996] 4 All E.R. 256 at 268 (Lord Browne-Wilkinson).

4. The normal problem for the courts in this kind of case is to decide in relation to the fact in question whether it is to be determined (1) by the court, as a precedent or jurisdictional fact; or (2) by the original decision-maker, subject to review by the court on *Wednesbury* grounds (*i.e.* usually on the ground that the decision maker has failed to take account of relevant considerations, taken account of irrelevant considerations or come to an irrational decision: see generally Ch.9).

In deciding this question the particular wording of the legislation will, of course, be of critical importance. However, of equal significance are likely to be factors such as the formulation of the jurisdictional yardsticks (*e.g.* are they precise factual matters upon which a court can confidently rule, or less clear-cut matters upon the existence of which reasonable persons might differ); the nature of the decision-making body (*e.g.* is it accountable for its actions in other ways, such as by being an elected body; is it a body whose membership makes it specially qualified to make judgments on these matters?); and the nature of the power ultimately to be exercised (does it interfere with fundamental rights or liberties?). Powerful disincentives to classifying a fact as jurisdictional include (1) a wish not to add unnecessarily to the pressures of the case load in the Administrative Court (*cf. Puhlhofer*, below p.434); and (2) the general disinclination of the Administrative court to investigate questions of fact (*cf.* the general unwillingness to order disclosure of documents or cross-examination on witness statements, below p.970). Compare the cases summarised above with those discussed at pp.430–434 in the light of these considerations. The gap between the two standards of review is reduced in cases where (1) the court decides that a particular fact is *not* a precedent fact; but (2) the situation is one where, for example because of the affect of the case on individual rights, a heightened level of scrutiny is imposed on in applying the *Wednesbury* principles ("super-*Wednesbury*": below pp.581–589). See *R. v*

Collins Ex p. Brady (2000) 58 B.M.L.R. 173, where the decision whether medical treatment (forcefeeding in response to Ian Brady's hunger strike) was given to him "for the mental disorder from which he is suffering" as so authorised by s.63 of the Mental Health Act 1983, was held to be for the Responsible Medical Officer to decide, subject to "super-*Wednesbury*" review rather than a precedent fact for the court. This matter was about the clinical judgment of the RMO. (His view would on the facts have been endorsed in either basis.) But see now the approach in *Wilkinson*, below.

5. Where the existence of a particular fact is necessary to justify interference with a Convention right (see Ch.6) it is likely to be classified as a precedent fact the determination of which may require the cross-examination of witnesses: *R. (on the application of Wilkinson) v The Responsible Medical Officer Broadmoor Hospital* [2001] EWCA Civ 1545; [2002] 1 W.L.R. 419 (preconditions for compulsory medical treatment without consent of detained mental patient).

R. v CITY OF LONDON, ETC., RENT TRIBUNAL Ex p. HONIG

[1951] 1 K.B. 641; [1951] 1 T.L.R. 41; [1951] 1 All E.R. 195; 115 J.P. 42; 49 L.G.R. 252, D.C. (KING'S BENCH DIVISION)

In 1949, the applicant, Emanuel Honig, let two furnished rooms in a house to one Albert Shomade, on a weekly tenancy. In 1950, S was given a week's notice to quit, to expire on a Monday. A month later, having remained in possession, he referred his contract of tenancy to the rent tribunal under the Furnished Houses (Rent Control) Act 1946, in order to secure a reduction of rent. At the rent tribunal hearing, H argued that the notice to quit was valid and that therefore there was no "contract of tenancy" subsisting which could be referred to the tribunal. The tribunal held, however, that as the notice to quit was invalid, the tenancy being from Saturday to Saturday, they had jurisdiction to reduce the rent. H applied for certiorari to quash this reduction, on the ground that the tribunal had no jurisdiction to inquire whether the notice to quit was good or bad.

LORD GODDARD C.J.: The question in the present case is whether the tribunal can, first of all, decide the question of the existence of a tenancy. Unless they can do so, they can only proceed in a case in which both parties agree that a contract is in existence. If they did not so agree, it would, of course, always be open to a landlord to dispute the existence of the tenancy, in which case the parties would first of all be relegated to the county court to have that preliminary matter determined. . . . I cannot think that it was intended that anything of that kind should take place in connection with proceedings under this Act.

It is not necessary, however, to embark upon any inquiry of that kind because the principles upon which these tribunals can act appear to me to be well established by decided cases. The first thing to consider is whether the tribunal, in order to obtain jurisdiction, must find that a certain state of affairs exists which is collateral to the main question. The question whether there is a contract or not seems to me to be collateral, and clearly collateral, to the main question which the tribunal have jurisdiction to decide, namely, what is the fair rent under a contract of tenancy. If there is no contract, they cannot, of course, determine that question. If there is a contract, they can determine it, and therefore they must decide for themselves in the first instance whether or not the contract exists. . . .

I am of opinion that the tribunal in the present case had power to inquire into the collateral fact, namely, whether there was a contract, because it was only if there was a contract that they could exercise the jurisdiction which the Act of Parliament has given them. When they have decided that, it is open to the person who complains of that decision to ask this court to inquire into it by means of certiorari. In many cases—at any rate in some cases—this court has been able to inquire into the matter by means of documents and other information put before it and has come to the conclusion in some cases that the tribunal decided erroneously, and in others that it acted rightly.

In a case like the present, depending as it did on oral statement against oral statement, although it is not impossible for this court to inquire into the matter it appears to me to be quite impossible for us to hold that the tribunal below were wrong. At any rate, the onus of showing that they were wrong is upon the person who applies for certiorari. The matter here depended entirely on oral statements, and the tribunal saw the witnesses and heard them. It is true that they were not cross-examined on oath, because the proceedings before the tribunals are not conducted on oath. That, again, is a matter for the legislature and not for the courts. These tribunals act on all kinds of evidence which no court of law would look at for a minute. That is one of the difficulties which frequently arise in these cases, and very often arguments are addressed to the court on that ground. But this court has nothing to do with that. If Parliament chooses to set up a tribunal to decide disputed questions of fact not on oath, that is a matter for Parliament and not for this court. Where, as in the present instance, the matter depends on oral statements with flat contradictions on one side or the other, the only people who can come to a decision are those who see and hear the witnesses—I use that word in the colloquial sense of people called before a tribunal to depose to certain facts. The tribunal here heard both parties and came to a decision on the question of fact, and there is nothing before us which can satisfy us that they came to a wrong conclusion. Therefore, certiorari cannot issue and the application must be refused.

HILBERY J. and PARKER J. concurred.

Application refused.

Note
This case illustrates that the questions (1) whether a fact is a jurisdictional fact; and (2) whether the court will be willing to come to a different view on the evidence available to it from that of original decision-maker on the existence of the fact are distinct issues. The court will not always be prepared to undertake a full rehearing with oral evidence on the matter.

DOWTY BOULTON PAUL LTD v WOLVERHAMPTON CORPORATION (NO.2)

[1976] CH.13; [1973] 2 W.L.R. 618; [1973] 2 All E.R. 491; 71 L.G.R. 323; 25 P. & C.R. 282 (COURT OF APPEAL)

On August 27, 1935, the plaintiffs entered into an agreement with the defendants. The agreement stated that the Corporation would apply to the Air Council, under the Air Navigation Act 1920, for permission to establish and maintain an aerodrome on land to be acquired by them; that they would lease a site on the western side of the aerodrome to the plaintiffs for the purpose of a factory and that they would allow the plaintiffs to use the aerodrome in connection with their business of manufacturing aircraft.

In 1936 the Corporation conveyed the fee simple of the factory site to the plaintiffs instead of leasing it. By cl.2 of the conveyance, the plaintiffs covenanted to erect a factory and use it for the purpose of manufacturing, etc. aircraft and aeronautical equipment or parts thereof and for the purpose of carrying on a school for the training and teaching of flying. By cl.3, the Corporation covenanted to allow the plaintiffs to use the airport for the purpose of test, delivery and other flights in connection with their business, and for the purpose of flying in connection with the flying school, for 99 years from December 1, 1935, or as long as the Corporation maintained the airport as a municipal aerodrome whichever was longer. The conveyance further provided that, without prejudice to the Corporation's powers to deal with the aerodrome, they should not, in exercise of their powers, unreasonably affect the plaintiff's rights. At the time the Corporation welcomed the establishment of a factory which would be a substantial employer of labour in the area.

By 1957, the plaintiffs were no longer manufacturing aircraft, and thereafter used the factory for making airframes and equipment. They no longer used the aerodrome for test flying, but only for executive flights. They had never operated a flying school. There were only 26 flights by the plaintiffs to or from the aerodrome in 1967, 56 in 1968, 16 in 1969 and none in 1970. The need in the area for land for housing purposes had substantially increased, and in 1971 the Corporation resolved to reappropriate the land forming the aerodrome for planning purposes, namely a comprehensive development for housing, shops and schools, acting under s.163 (1) of the Local Government Act 1933. This provided that:

> "Any land belonging to a local authority and not required for the purposes for which it was acquired or has since been appropriated may be appropriated for any other purpose approved by the Minister for which the local authority are authorised to acquire land. . .".

Once planning permission for the redevelopment was granted, the Corporation would have power under s.127 of the Town and Country Planning Act 1971 (formerly s.81 of the 1962 Act and now s.237 of the 1990 Act) to carry out works which in effect would destroy the plaintiffs' airfield rights, on payment of compensation. By writ dated September 22, 1970, the plaintiffs sought, *inter alia*, declarations that, so long as the plaintiffs used the land in accordance with the conveyance and required the aerodrome for their purposes, the Corporation were under an obligation to maintain it; the plaintiffs were entitled to use it; and, in the event of the Corporation, in breach of contract, failing to maintain it, the plaintiffs were entitled to maintain it. By originating summons taken out in 1971, the plaintiffs sought declarations that on the true construction of (1) s.81 and 87 of the Town and Country Planning Act 1962 and s.163 of the Local Government Act 1933, (2) the conveyance, and (3) the agreement, the Corporation were not entitled to vary the appropriation of the land in breach of convenant so that the aerodrome could be used for a purpose other than that of an aerodrome.

The case came before Pennycuick V.C. in November, 1970 on a motion for interlocutory relief, in anticipation of the Corporation's resolution, which was refused: see [1971] 1 W.L.R. 204, below, p.506. Plowman J. heard the action and summons together, and dismissed them both ([1973] Ch.94). The plaintiffs appealed. They contended that there had not been a valid appropriation for planning purposes on the ground that it could not be said that the airfield site was not required for use as an airfield, having regard to the existence of the rights of the plaintiffs under the 1936 conveyance. They contended that it was for the court to decide whether the factual precondition of a non-requirement existed; that it was not necessary to show that the Corporation had acted *mala fide*, nor that no local authority on the facts could reasonably form the view that land was not required for airfield purposes; that the airfield purpose of the original appropriation or acquisition included flight use by the plaintiffs who still required so to use it, and accordingly the airfield purpose was not spent; that on the evidence the land was required for use as such by the plaintiffs both now and potentially to a greater extent in the future should they revert to manufacture of aircraft requiring flight testing.

The Corporation relied on the decision of Maugham J. in *Att-Gen v Manchester Corp.* [1931] 1 Ch.254 that the question whether the land was not relevantly required was for the decision of the local authority acting bona fide and not for the court.

RUSSELL L.J.: . . . The question whether land is not required for the purpose for which it was acquired has long been posed in statutory enactments relating to corporations and authorities with the ability compulsorily to acquire land. In general the situation was that land not so required had to be disposed of: it was regarded as basically wrong that it should be retained for some other purpose when the authority no longer needed it for the purpose for which is was compulsorily acquired. Subsequently, the statutory system has been to allow a local authority in such a case to appropriate the land to some other purpose for which it has powers of compulsory acquisition, I suppose to avoid the double step of (a) sale and (b) further compulsory acquisition. Section 163 of the Local Government Act 1933 is one example: as originally enacted, the exercise of the power of appropriation required the approval of the Minister, but that requirement was later dropped by amendment. It is a curious fact that no decision directly on this point is to be found, save in that of Maugham J. in *Attorney-General v. Manchester Corporation* [1931] 1 Ch. 254. [Here, Maugham J. held (at 269) in respect of s.175 of the Public Health Act 1875, as amended, which was in terms not relevantly different to the provision now under consideration, that "the local authority, acting in good faith, must be the sole judges of whether the land is no longer required, or is not required for the purpose for which the land was acquired".]

Now that decision, on an indistinguishable section, has we are told been ever since noticed in relevant textbooks without adverse comment. Counsel were unable to find any criticism in any learned articles, over a period in which there has been intensive study and analysis of the powers of the court to disagree with and substitute its own view of the validity of administrative acts for that of, for example, a local authority. Moreover, it is by no means without significance, and is indeed persuasive—though not, of course, conclusive—that the legislature has enacted the same formula in statutes subsequent to that clear decision. Further, for my part, I consider the decision to be correct. It is a function of a local authority to study and keep under review the needs of the inhabitants of the locality and to exercise to the best of its ability its powers with those needs in mind. This must involve the authority in consideration of the relative importance of different needs, not least in connection with the use to which lands of the authority are to be put for the public benefit. I would construe "not required" in the section as meaning "not needed in the public interest of the locality" for the original purpose: and it appears that Maugham J. so construed them. Now that question, it is plain to me, involves matters both of degree and of comparative needs, as to which there can be no question but that the local authority is better qualified than the court to judge, assuming it to be acting bona fide and not upon a view that no reasonable local authority could possibly take. In the present case lack of bona fides is no longer pursued, the abandonment of the site as a municipal airport is in no way criticised, and I can see no ground for holding that the decision of Maugham J., with which I agree, is not directly applicable. Moreover, in so far as the degree of *private* need for use of the airfield as such is said to be relevant, the evidence of likely need to use it for purposes of the plaintiffs' business (other than flight testing of aircraft manufactured at the plaintiffs' factory) is extremely small in extent, and related to convenience rather than need: and the evidence directed to the possibility of future manufacture of aircraft, for which it might fairly be said that there would be a need for the airfield, is purely speculative and on balance of probability unlikely. . . . It was argued for the plaintiffs that authority showed that the court will always inquire into and decide upon the existence of a factual pre-condition of an administrative step; that non-requirement here was such; and that the views of Maugham J. were erroneous. It seems to me that this depends on what is meant by a factual pre-condition, or rather what sort of factual pre-condition is in question. We were referred to *Eleko v. Officer Administering the Government of Nigeria* [1931] A.C. 662, where the administrative or executive step that was challenged could only be taken if the appellant was a native chief in the particular area. That, of course, was a simple factual pre-condition which the court was as competent to decide as anyone else. In *Re Ripon (Highfield) Housing Confirmation Order 1938; White and Collins v. Minister of Health* [1939] 2 K.B. 838 a compulsory order was quashed on the ground that the land formed part of a park, and such land was excluded from the power of compulsory purchase: a similar type of case. . . .

Accordingly, in my judgment, the contention that the appropriate resolution was invalid on the ground that the land was still required for the purpose for which it was originally acquired or appropriated is unsound and the appeal should be dismissed.

BUCKLEY L.J. (*dubitante*) and LAWTON L.J. delivered concurring judgments.

Appeal dismissed.

Notes

1. Section 163 was re-enacted, with modifications, as s.122 of the Local Government Act 1972. The question whether land is no longer required for a particular purpose must be formally considered by the council as a question of fact, although its conclusion on the matter will only be challengeable on *Wednesbury* grounds: *R. v Leeds City Council Ex p. Leeds Industrial Cooperative Society Ltd* (1996) 73 P. & C.R. 70.

2. A similar approach was adopted in *Puhlhofer v Hillingdon LBC* [1986] A.C. 484. Under the Housing (Homeless Persons) Act 1977 (see now Pt 7 of the Housing Act 1996) local authorities had certain duties to secure accommodation for homeless persons. Section 1(1) of the 1977 Act provided that a person was "homeless . . . if he has no accommodation", and set out circumstances in which a person is to be treated as having no accommodation. In *Puhlhofer*, the applicants were a couple with two young children, who were all living in one room in a guest house. The local authority had determined that they therefore were not persons without accommodation and so the duties imposed by the legislation on local authorities did not apply. The issue for the House of Lords was whether the condition of homelessness was fully reviewable by the courts in judicial review proceedings alleging that a determination by a local authority on that issue was wrong either in fact or in law; or, alternatively, whether the legislation should be regarded as conferring on *local authorities* power to determine the ambit of their housing duties by making *them* the proper judges of the meaning and application of the statutory jurisdictional tests. Was this a situation like the *White and Collins* case or was it more like the *Dowty* case? Their Lordships preferred the latter approach and the words of Lord Brightman are instructive: He said:

"I am troubled at the prolific use of judicial review for the purpose of challenging the performance by local authorities of their functions under the 1977 Act. Parliament intended the local authority to be the judge of fact. . . . Where the existence or non-existence of a fact is left to the judgment and discretion of a public body and that fact involves a broad spectrum ranging from the obvious to the debatable to the just conceivable, it is the duty of the court to leave the decision of that fact to the public body to whom Parliament has entrusted the decision-making power save in a case where it is obvious that the public body, consciously or unconsciously, are acting perversely."

In other words, provided the authority makes its determination without disclosing expressly or implicitly a misunderstanding of the legislative words applicable, and provided it does not act for an improper purpose or on the basis of irrelevant considerations, and provided there is no procedural irregularity tainting its decision, then its decision as to homelessness will be unchallengeable even though that decision is not the same decision as the reviewing court might have come to had it regarded itself as qualified to make its own determination of that matter. Note, however, the legislative response to this decision: Housing and Planning Act 1986, amending Housing Act 1985, ss.58 and 69 (persons only to be regarded as "accommodated" if accommodation "reasonable for him to continue to occupy").

3. For more recent examples of the approach exemplified by *Puhlhofer* and *Dowty*, see *R. v Westminster City Council Ex p. Tansey* (1988) 20 H.L.R. 520 (issue whether accommodation "suitable"); *R. v Monopolies and Mergers Commission Ex p. South Yorkshire Transport Ltd* [1992] 1 W.L.R. 291 (whether a reference area specified by the Secretary of State for an investigation by the Commission into a possible merger situation can be characterised as a "substantial part" of the United Kingdom); *R. v Brent LBC Ex p. Grossett* (1994) 28 H.L.R. 9 (issue whether applicant could have "afforded rent payments" a matter for local authority, not an issue of precedent jurisdictional fact for the court); *R. v South Hams DC Ex p. Gibbs* [1995] Q.B. 158 (applicants, status as "gypsies" not a matter of precedent jurisdictional fact: rather a question for the local authority, whose decision unassailable so long as correct legal test applied and decision arrived at not unreasonable); *R. v Secretary of State for the Environment Ex p. Gosforth Allotments and Gardens Association* (1995) 70 P. & C.R. 480 (whether "adequate provision" made under alternative allotment rules); *R. v East Sussex CC Ex p. Tandy* [1997] 3 F.C.R. 525 (whether a local authority has made arrangements for the provision of "suitable education" for a child of compulsory school age); *R. v Kent CC Ex p.* [1998] E.L.R. 108 (whether a school is suitable for the purposes of the local education authority's duty to make arrangements for transport to school); *R. v Secretary of State for the Home Department Ex p. Onibiyo* [1996] Q.B. 768; and *Cakabay v Secretary of State for the Home Department (No.2)* [1999] Imm. A.R. 176 (whether a second claim for asylum is repetitious or a fresh claim); *R. (on the application of Malster) v Ipswich BC* [2002] P.L.C.R. 251 (whether a proposed development falls within the description of development for which an Environmental Impact Assessment must be conducted).

4. It is not uncommon for statutory conferments of power to be couched in terms which limit power or jurisdiction not to the *existence* of defined facts or circumstances, but either (a) to the donee of the power's *belief* in the existence of the statutory requirement; or (b) the donee's *reasonable belief* in that matter. For the scope of review in such circumstances see below, p.536. Compare the power asserted by the courts to review subjectively worded conferments of power with the scope of review exerted in the *Dowty* and *Puhlhofer* cases (see above, pp.431–435).

(ii) Review for error of law

ANISMINIC LTD v THE FOREIGN COMPENSATION COMMISSION

[1969] 2 A.C. 147; [1969] 2 W.L.R. 163; [1969] 1 All E.R. 208
(HOUSE OF LORDS)

Anisminic Ltd was a British company which in 1956 owned a mining property in Egypt, which they claimed was worth over £4 million. On the outbreak of hostilities between Israel and Egypt the property was occupied by Israeli forces and damaged to the extent of some £500,000. On November 1, 1956, property in Egypt belonging to British subjects had been sequestrated by the Egyptian Government. On April 29, 1957, after the Israeli forces had withdrawn, the Egyptian Government authorised a sale of the appellants' property, and it was sold to an Egyptian organisation, TEDO. The appellants' property had included a large quantity of manganese ore, and they took steps to dissuade their customers from buying ore from TEDO. This apparently embarrassed the Egyptian authorities, and on November 23, 1957, an agreement was made between the appellants, TEDO and the Sequestrator General whereby the appellants purported to sell to TEDO, for £500,000, their whole business in Egypt. This was not, however, to include any claim which the appellants might "be entitled to assert against any governmental authority other than the Egyptian Government, as a result of loss suffered by, or of damage to or reduction in the value of" their business or assets during the events of October and November 1956.

In 1959, a Treaty was concluded between the British and Egyptian Governments under which compensation was paid to the British Government in respect of certain properties, including the appellants', listed in Annex E to the Treaty. It was accepted that at that stage the disposal of the sum was in the discretion of the British Government. The distribution of the compensation was entrusted to the Foreign Compensation Commission by the Foreign Compensation (Egypt) (Determination and Registration of Claims) Order 1959 (subsequently amended), made under the Foreign Compensation Act 1950. Article 4 of the 1962 Order provided that:

"(1) The Commission shall treat a claim under this Part of the Order as established if the applicant satisfies them of the following matters:—(a) that his application relates to property in Egypt which is referred to in Annex E; (b) if the property is referred to in paragraph (1)(a) or paragraph (2) of Annex E—(i) that the applicant is the person referred to in paragraph (1)(a) or in paragraph (2), as the case may be, as the owner of the property or is the successor in title of such person; and (ii) that the person referred to as aforesaid and any person who became successor in title of such person on or before February 28, 1959, were British nationals on October 31, 1956, and February 28, 1959; . . .

(2) . . .

(3) For the purposes of sub-paragraphs (b)(ii) and (c)(ii) of paragraph (1) of this article, a British national who died, or in the case of a corporation or association ceased to exist, between October 31, 1956, and February 28, 1959, shall be deemed to have been a British national on the latter date and a person who had not been born, or in the case of a corporation or association had not been constituted, on October 31, 1956, shall be deemed to have been a British national on that date if such person became a British national at birth or when constituted, as the case may be; provided that a converted company shall for the purposes of sub-paragraphs (b)(ii) and (c)(ii) of paragraph (1) of this article be deemed not to have been a British national. . . .".

The appellants submitted a claim for compensation to the Commission. After various proceedings, the Commission made a provisional determination to the effect that Anisminic Ltd had failed to establish entitlement to a claim under the Order, in respect of the sequestrated property, on the ground that TEDO, which had become the successor in title to the appellants, was not at any time a British national. Section 4(4) of the 1950 Act provided that "The determination by the Commission of any application made to them under this Act shall not be called in question in any court of law". Browne J. ([1969] 2 A.C. 223; [1969] C.L.J. 230) made a declaration that the Commission's provisional determination was a nullity, and that the Commission were under a statutory duty to treat the appellants' claim as established. The Court of Appeal ([1968] 2 Q.B. 852) set aside his judgment. Anisminic Ltd appealed to the House of Lords.

The main questions were as follows:

(1) Was the nationality of a "successor-in-title" relevant where the claimant was the original owner of property mentioned in Annex E of the Treaty? Lords Reid, Pearce and Wilberforce held that it was not. In their view, Art.4(1) was defectively drafted. It was meant to convey (1) that if a person claimed as the original owner, he had to show he was a British national on the dates specified, and (2) that if he claimed as the universal successor, for example after the death of an original owner or the liquidation of an original owning company, he had to show that both he and the original owner were British nationals. (See Lord Reid [1969] 2 A.C. 173–175; Lord Pearce at 201–205; Lord Wilberforce at 212–214.) Lord Morris of Borth-y-Gest did not express a final opinion on this point. Lord Pearson (at 219–223) thought the Commission correct in holding that "successor-in-title" meant "successor-in-title" to the claim of the owners against the Egyptian Government, and that this claim had been sold to TEDO as part of the business assets in Egypt.

(2) Did the error cause the Commission to exceed their jurisdiction, or was it an error within jurisdiction? Lords Reid, Pearce and Wilberforce held that there was an excess of jurisdiction. Lord Pearson (at 215) accepted that had they made such an error it would have taken them outside their jurisdiction. Lord Morris was of the opinion that it was a matter within their jurisdiction.

(3) If the determination was made in excess of jurisdiction, was it nevertheless protected by s.4(4)? All five members of the House of Lords were agreed that it was not. (Exclusion of judicial review is considered further in Ch.13.)

[The extracts given here are mainly concerned with the second and third questions.]

LORD REID: . . . The next argument was that, by reason of the provisions of section 4(4) of the 1950 Act, the courts are precluded from considering whether the respondent's determination was a nullity, and therefore it must be treated as valid whether or not inquiry would disclose that it was a nullity. Section 4(4) is in these terms:

"The determination by the commission of any application made to them under this Act shall not be called in question in any court of law."

The respondent maintains that these are plain words only capable of having one meaning. Here is a determination which is apparently valid: there is nothing on the face of the document to cast any doubt on its validity. If it is a nullity, that could only be established by raising some kind of proceedings in court. But that would be calling the determination in question, and that is expressly prohibited by the statute. The appellants maintain that that is not the meaning of the words of this provision. They say that "determination" means a real determination and does not include an apparent or purported determination which in the eyes of the law has no existence because it is a nullity. Or, putting it in another way, if you seek to show that a determination is a nullity you are not questioning the purported determination—you are maintaining that it does not exist as a determination. It is one thing to question a determination which does exist: it is quite another thing to say that there is nothing to be questioned.

Let me illustrate the matter by supposing a simple case. A statute provides that a certain order may be made by a person who holds a specified qualification or appointment, and it contains a provision, similar to section 4(4), that such an order made by such a person shall not be called in question in any court of law. A person aggrieved by an order alleges that it is a forgery or that the person who made the order did not hold that qualification or appointment. Does such a provision require the court to treat that order as a valid order? It is a well established principle that a provision ousting the ordinary jurisdiction of the court must be construed strictly—meaning, I think, that, if such a provision is reasonably capable of having two meanings, that meaning shall be taken which preserves the ordinary jurisdiction of the court.

Statutory provisions which seek to limit the ordinary jurisdiction of the court have a long history. No case has been cited in which any other form of words limiting the jurisdiction of the court has been held to protect a nullity. If the draftsman or Parliament had intended to introduce a new kind of ouster clause so as to prevent any inquiry even as to whether the document relied on was a forgery, I would have expected to find something much more specific than the bald statement that a determination shall not be called in question in any court of law. Undoubtedly such a provision protects every determination which is not a nullity. But I do not think that it is necessary or even reasonable to construe the word "determination" as including everything which purports to be a determination but which is in fact no determination at all. And there are no degrees of nullity. There are a number of reasons why the law will hold a purported decision to be a nullity. I do not see how it could be said that such a provision protects some kinds of nullity but not others: if that were intended it would be easy to say so.

The case which gives most difficulty is *Smith v. East Elloe Rural District Council* [1956] A.C. 736 where the form of ouster clause was similar to that in the present case. But I cannot regard it as a very satisfactory case. The plaintiff was aggrieved by a compulsory purchase order. After two unsuccessful actions she tried again after six years. As this case never reached the stage of a statement of claim we do not know whether her case was that the clerk of the council had fraudulently misled the council and the Ministry, or whether it was that the council and the Ministry were parties to the fraud. The result would be quite different, in my view, for it is only if the authority which made the order had itself acted in mala fide that the order would be a nullity. I think that the case which it was intended to present must have been that the fraud was only the fraud of the clerk because almost the whole of the argument was on the question whether a time limit in the Act applied where fraud was alleged; there was no citation of the authorities on the question whether a clause ousting the jurisdiction of the court applied when nullity was in question, and there was little about this matter in the speeches. I do not therefore regard this case as a binding authority on this question. The other authorities are dealt with in the speeches of my noble and learned friends, and it is unnecessary for me to deal with them in detail. I have come without hesitation to the conclusion that in this case we are not prevented from inquiring whether the order of the commission was a nullity.

It has sometimes been said that it is only where a tribunal acts without jurisdiction that its decision is a nullity. But in such cases the word "jurisdiction" has been used in a very wide sense, and I have come to the conclusion that it is better not to use the term except in the narrow and original sense of the tribunal being entitled to enter on the inquiry in question. But there are many cases where, although the tribunal had jurisdiction to enter on the inquiry, it has done or failed to do something in the course of the inquiry which is of such a nature that its decision is a nullity. It may have given its decision in bad faith. It may have made a decision which it had no power to make. It may have failed in the course of the inquiry to comply with the requirements of natural justice. It may in perfect good faith have misconstrued the provisions giving it power to act so that it failed to deal with the question remitted to it and decided some question which was not remitted to it. It may have refused to take into account something which it was required to take into account. Or it may have based its decision on some matter which, under the provisions setting it up, it had no right to take into account. I do not intend this list to be exhaustive. But if it decides a question remitted to it for decision without committing any of these errors it is as much entitled to decide that question wrongly as it is to decide it rightly. I understand that some confusion has been caused by my having said in *R. v. Governor of Brixton Prison, ex p. Armah* [1968] A.C. 192, 234 that if a tribunal has jurisdiction to go right it has jurisdiction to go wrong. So it has, if one uses "jurisdiction" in the narrow original sense. If it is entitled to enter on the inquiry and does not do any of those things which I have mentioned in the course of the proceedings, then its decision is equally valid whether it is right or wrong subject only to the power of the court in certain circumstances to correct an error of law. I think that, if these views are correct, the only case cited which was plainly wrongly decided is *Davies v. Price* [1958] 1 W.L.R. 434. But in a number of other cases some of the grounds of judgment are questionable.

I can now turn to the provisions of the Order under which the commission acted, and to the way in which the commission reached their decision. It was said in the Court of Appeal that publication of their reasons was unnecessary and perhaps undesirable. Whether or not they could have been required to publish their reasons, I dissent emphatically from the view that publication may have been undesirable. In my view, the commission acted with complete propriety, as one would expect looking to its membership.

The meaning of the important parts of this Order is extremely difficult to discover, and, in my view, a main cause of this is the deplorable modern drafting practice of compressing to the point of obscurity provisions which would not be difficult to understand if written out at rather greater length.

The effect of the Order was to confer legal rights on persons who might previously have hoped or expected that in allocating any sums available discretion would be exercised in their favour. We are concerned in this case with article 4 of the Order and more particularly with para.(1)(b)(ii) of the article. Article 4 is as follows:

[His Lordship read Art.4.]

The task of the commission was to receive claims and to determine the rights of each applicant. It is enacted that they shall treat a claim as established if the applicant satisfies them of certain matters. . . .

The main difficulty in this case springs from the fact that the draftsman did not state separately what conditions have to be satisfied (1) where the applicant is the original owner and (2) where the applicant claims as the successor in title of the original owner. It is clear that where the applicant is the original owner he must prove that he was a British national on the dates stated. And it is equally clear that where the applicant claims as being the original owner's successor in title he must prove that both he and the original owner were British nationals on those dates, subject to later provisions in the article about persons who had died or had been born within the relevant period. What is left in obscurity is whether the provisions with regard to successors in title have any application at all in cases where the applicant is himself the original owner. If this provision had been split up as it should have been, and the conditions, to be satisfied where the original owner is the applicant had been set out, there could have been no such obscurity.

This is the crucial question in this case. It appears from the commission's reasons that they construed this provision as requiring them to inquire, when the applicant is himself the original owner, whether he had a successor in title. So they made that inquiry in this case and held that TEDO was the applicant's successor in title. As TEDO was not a British national they rejected the appellants' claim. But if, on a true construction of the Order, a claimant who is an original owner does not have to prove anything about successors in title, then the commission made an inquiry which the Order did not empower them to make, and they based their decision on a matter which they had no right to take into account. If one uses the word "jurisdiction" in its wider sense, they went beyond their jurisdiction in considering this matter. It was argued that the whole matter of construing the Order was something remitted to the commission for their decision. I cannot accept that argument. I find nothing in the Order to support it. The Order requires the commission to consider whether they are satisfied with regard to the prescribed matters. That is all they have to do. It cannot be for the commission to determine the limits of its powers. Of course if one party submits to a tribunal that its powers are wider than in fact they are, then the tribunal must deal with that submission. But if they reach a wrong conclusion as to the width of their powers, the court must be able to correct that—not because the tribunal has made an error of law, but because as a result of making an error of law they have dealt with and based their decision on a matter with which, on a true construction of their powers, they had no right to deal. If they base their decision on some matter which is not prescribed for their adjudication, they are doing something which they have no right to do and, if the view which I expressed earlier is right, their decision is a nullity. So the question is whether on a true construction of the Order the applicants did or did not have to prove anything with regard to successors in title. If the commission were entitled to enter on the inquiry whether the applicants had a successor in title, then their decision as to whether TEDO was their successor in title would I think be unassailable whether it was right or wrong: it would be a decision on a matter remitted to them for their decision. The question I have to consider is not whether they made a wrong decision but whether they inquired into and decided a matter which they had no right to consider.

. . . In themselves the words "successor in title" are, in my opinion, inappropriate in the circumstances of this Order to denote any person while the original owner is still in existence, and I think it most improbable that they were ever intended to denote any such person. There is no necessity to stretch them to cover any such person. I would therefore hold that the words "and any person who became successor in title to such person" in Article 4(1)(b)(ii) have no application to a case where the applicant is the original owner.

It follows that the commission rejected the appellants' claim on a ground which they had no right to take into account and that their decision was a nullity. I would allow this appeal.

LORD MORRIS OF BORTH-Y-GEST: [dissenting: stated the facts and continued:] This is not a case in which there has been any sort of suggestion of irregularity either of conduct or procedure on the part of the commission. It has not been said that anything took place which disqualified the commission from making a determination. No occasion arises, therefore, to refer to decisions which have pointed to the consequences of failing to obey or of defying the rules of natural justice: nor to decisions relating to bias in a tribunal: nor to decisions in cases where bad faith has been alleged: nor to decisions in cases where a tribunal has not been properly constituted. If a case arose where bad faith was alleged the difficult case of *Smith v. East Elloe Rural District Council* [1956] A.C. 736 would need consideration: but the present case can, in my view, be approached without any examination of or reliance upon that case.

The provisions of section 4(4) of the Act do not, in my view, operate to debar any inquiry that may be necessary to decide whether the commission has acted within its authority or jurisdiction. The provisions do operate to debar contentions that the commission while acting within its jurisdiction has come to wrong or erroneous conclusions. There would be no difficulty in pursuing, and in adducing evidence in support of, an allegation such as an allegation that those who heard a claim had never been appointed or that those who had been appointed had by some irregular conduct disqualified themselves from adjudicating or continuing to adjudicate. There would be no difficulty in raising any matter that goes to the right or power of the commission to adjudicate (see *R. v. Bolton* (1841) 1 Q.B. 66). What is forbidden is to question the correctness of a decision or determination which it was within the area of their jurisdiction to make.

It is, of course, clear that no appeal is given from a determination of the commission. When Parliament sets up a tribunal and refers matters to it, it becomes a question of policy as to whether to provide for an appeal. Sometimes that is thought to be appropriate. Thus, where (by the Indemnity Act 1920), provision was made for the assessment by the War Compensation Court of certain claims for compensation for acts done in pursuance of prerogative powers it was enacted that though the decision of the tribunal (presided over by a judge) was to be final there could be an appeal by a party aggrieved by a direction or determination of the tribunal on any point of law. Sometimes, on the other hand, it is not thought appropriate to provide for an appeal. In reference to the Foreign Compensation Tribunal it was presumably thought that the advantages of securing finality of decision outweighed any disadvantages that might possibly result from having no appeal procedure. It was presumably thought that there was every prospect that right determinations would be reached if those appointed to reach them were persons in whom there could be every confidence.

I return, then, to the question as to how the appellants can justify the calling in question by them of the determination of the commission. The answer is that they boldly say that what looks like a determination was in fact no determination but was a mere nullity. That which, they say, should be disregarded as being null and void, is a determination explained in a carefully reasoned document nearly 10 pages in length which is signed by the chairman of the commission. There is no question here of a sham or spurious or merely purported determination. Why, then, is it said to be null and void? The answer given is that it contains errors in law which have caused the commission to exceed their jurisdiction. When analysed this really means that it is contended that when the commission considered the meaning of certain words in Article 4 of the Order in Council they gave them a wrong construction with the consequence that they had no jurisdiction to disallow the claim of the applicants.

It is not suggested that the commission were not acting within their jurisdiction when they entertained the application of the appellants and gave it their consideration nor when they heard argument and submissions for four days in regard to it. The moment when it is said that they strayed outside their allotted jurisdiction must, therefore, have been at the moment when they gave their "determination".

The control which is exercised by the High Court over inferior tribunals (a categorising but not a derogatory description) is of a supervisory but not of an appellate nature. It enables the High Court to correct errors of law if they are revealed on the face of the record. The control cannot, however, be exercised if there is some provision (such as a "no certiorari" clause) which prohibits removal to the High Court. But it is well settled that even such a clause is of no avail if the inferior tribunal acts without jurisdiction or exceeds the limit of its jurisdiction.

In all cases similar to the present one it becomes necessary, therefore, to ascertain what was the question submitted for the determination of a tribunal. What were its terms of reference? What was its remit? What were the questions left to it or sent to it for its decision? What were the limits of its duties and powers? Were there any conditions precedent which had to be satisfied before its functions began? If there were, was it or was it not left to the tribunal itself to decide whether or not the conditions precedent were satisfied? If Parliament has enacted that provided a certain situation exists then a tribunal may have certain powers, it is clear that the tribunal will not have those powers unless the situation exists. The decided cases illustrate the infinite variety of the situations which may exist and the variations of statutory wording which have called for consideration. Most of the cases depend, therefore, upon an examination of their own particular facts and of particular sets of words. It is, however, abundantly clear that questions of law as well as of fact can be remitted for the determination of a tribunal.

If a tribunal while acting within its jurisdiction makes an error of law which it reveals on the face of its recorded determination, then the court, in the exercise of its supervisory function, may correct the error unless there is some provision preventing a review by a court of law. If a particular issue is left to a tribunal to decide, then even where it is shown (in cases where it is possible to show) that in deciding the issue left to it the tribunal has come to a wrong conclusion, that does not involve that the tribunal has gone outside its jurisdiction. It follows that if any errors of law are made in deciding matters which are left to a tribunal for its decision such errors will be errors within jurisdiction. If issues of law as well as of fact are referred to a tribunal for its determination, then its determination cannot be asserted to be wrong if Parliament has enacted that the determination is not to be called in question in any court of law.

[His Lordship cited passages from the judgments in *R. v Governor of Brixton Prison Ex p. Armah* [1968] A.C. 192 at 234 (Lord Reid); *R. v*

Northumberland C.A.T. Ex p. Shaw [1952] 1 K.B. 338 at 346 (Denning L.J.); *R. v Nat Bell Liquors Ltd* [1922] 2 A.C. 128 at 156 (Lord Sumner).]

If, therefore, a tribunal while within the area of its jurisdiction committed some error of law and if such error was made apparent in the determination itself (or, as it is often expressed, on the face of the record) then the superior court could correct that error unless it was forbidden to do so. It would be so forbidden if the determination was "not to be called in question in any court of law". If so forbidden it could not then even hear argument which suggested that error of law had been made. It could, however, still consider whether the determination was within "the area of the inferior jurisdiction".

So the question is raised whether in the present case the commission went out of bounds. Did it wander outside its designated area? Did it outstep the confines of the territory of its inquiry? Did it digress away from its allotted task? Was there some preliminary inquiry upon the correct determination of which its later jurisdiction was dependent?

For the reasons which I will endeavour to explain it seems to me that at no time did the commission stray from the direct path which it was required to tread. Under Article 4 of the Order in Council the commission was under a positive duty to treat a claim under Part III as established if the applicant satisfied them of certain matters. If they had stated that they were satisfied of those matters but had then declined to treat a claim as established, there would have been a situation very different from that now under consideration and one in which the court could clearly act. So also if they had stated that they were not satisfied of the matters but had nevertheless treated the claim as established. They would have had no right to treat the claim as established unless they were satisfied of the matters. The present is a case in which, faithfully following the wording of Article 4, they stated that they were not satisfied of the matters and, therefore, did not treat the claim as established. In stating why they were not satisfied of the matters they have set out the processes of their reasoning. The more that reasoning is examined the more apparent does it, in my view, become that the members of the commission applied their minds very carefully to a consideration of the matters about which the applicant had to satisfy "them". To no one else were the matters remitted but to "them". It was for them to be satisfied and not for anyone else. The words of Article 4 state their terms of reference. In those terms were certain words and certain phrases. The commission could not possibly discharge their duty without considering those words and phrases and without reaching a decision as to their meaning. The commission could not burke that task. It seems to me that the words which stated that it was for the commission to be satisfied of certain matters, and defined those matters, inevitably involved that any necessary interpretation of words within the compass of those matters was for the commission. They could not come to a conclusion as to whether they were satisfied as to the specified matters unless and until they gave meaning to the words which they had to follow. Unless such a phrase as "successor in title" was defined in the Order—and it was not—it was an inescapable duty of the commission to consider and to decide what the phrase signified. Doubtless they heard ample argument before forming a view. The same applies in regard to many other words and sequences of words in Article 4. But the forming of views as to these matters lay in the direct path of the commission's duties. They were duties that could not be shirked. They were central to the exercise of their jurisdiction. When their fully reasoned statement of their conclusions (which in this case can be regarded as a part of their "determination") is studied it becomes possible for someone to contend that an alternative construction of Article 4 should be preferred to that which was thought correct by the commission. But this calling in question cannot, in my view, take place in any court of law. Parliament has forbidden it. . . .

In this case there has been much concentration on the question whether the commission correctly decided that the phrase "successor in title" included an assignee. But this was but one of very many matters which might receive determination by the commission. A perusal of the Orders in Council shows that they bristle with words and phrases needing construction. For my part I cannot accept that if, in regard to any one of the many points in respect of which interpretation and construction became necessary a view can be formed that the commission made an error, the consequence follows that their determination became a nullity as being made in excess of jurisdiction. . . .

The claim of the applicants had to be determined by the commission and the applicants were under the obligation of satisfying the commission as to certain stated matters. They could not decide whether or not they were satisfied until they had construed the relevant parts of the Order in Council. When they were hearing argument as to the meaning of those relevant parts they were not acting without jurisdiction. They were at the very heart of their duty, their task and their jurisdiction. It cannot be that their necessary duty of deciding as to the meaning would be or could be followed by the result that if they took one view they would be within jurisdiction and if they took another view that they would be without. If at the moment of decision they were inevitably within their jurisdiction because they were doing what they had to do, I cannot think that a later view of someone else, if it differed from theirs, could involve that they trespassed from within their jurisdiction at the moment of decision.

It is sometimes the case that the jurisdiction of a tribunal is made dependent upon or subject to some condition. Parliament may enact that if a certain state of affairs exists then there will be jurisdiction. If in such case it appears that the state of affairs did not exist, then it follows that there would be no jurisdiction. Sometimes, however, a tribunal might undertake the task of considering whether the state of affairs existed. If it made error in that task such error would be in regard to a matter preliminary to the existence of jurisdiction. It would not be an error within the limited jurisdiction intended to be conferred. An illustration of this appeared in 1853 in *Bunbury v. Fuller* (1853) 9 Ex. 111. . . . [T]here is here no room for any suggestion that the commission failed to satisfy any condition precedent or failed to state the existence of any matter essential to their jurisdiction. . . .

In the submissions on behalf of the appellants a phrase much used was that the commission had asked themselves wrong questions. The phrase can be employed when consideration is being given to a question whether a tribunal has correctly decided some point of construction. If, however, the point of construction is fairly and squarely within the jurisdiction of the tribunal for them to decide, then a suggestion that a wrong question has been posed is no more than a means of deploying an argument: and if construction has been left to the tribunal the argument is unavailing. The phrase is, however, valuable and relevent in cases where it can be suggested that some condition precedent has not been satisfied or where jurisdiction is related to the existence of some state of affairs. . . . So in some cases a tribunal may reveal that by asking some wrong question it fails to bring itself within the area of the demarcation of its jurisdiction. In *Maradana Mosque Trustees v. Mahmud* [1967] 1 A.C. 13, P.C., one part of the decision was that the rules of natural justice had been violated. The other part of the decision, relevant for present purposes, was that where statutory authority was given to a Minister to act if he was satisfied that a school *is* being administered in a certain way he was not given authority to act because he was satisfied that the school *had been* administered in that way. It could be said that the Minister had asked himself the wrong question: so he had, but the relevant result was that he never brought himself within the area of his jurisdiction. . . .

I would dismiss the appeal.

LORD PEARCE: My Lords, the courts have a general jurisdiction over the administration of justice in this country. From time to time Parliament sets up special tribunals to deal with special matters and gives them jurisdiction to decide these matters without any appeal to the courts. When this happens the courts cannot hear appeals from such a tribunal or substitute their own views on any matters which have been specifically committed by Parliament to the tribunal.

Such tribunals must, however, confine themselves within the powers specially committed to them on a true construction of the relevant Acts of Parliament. It would lead to an absurd situation if a tribunal, having been given a circum-scribed area of inquiry, carved out from the general jurisdiction of the courts, were entitled of its own motion to extend that area by misconstruing the limits of its mandate to inquire and decide as set out in the Act of Parliament.

If, for instance, Parliament were to carve out an area of inquiry within which an inferior domestic tribunal could give certain relief to wives against their husbands, it would not lie within the power of that tribunal to extend the area of inquiry and decision, that is, jurisdiction, thus committed to it by constru-ing "wives" as including all women who have, without marriage, cohabitated with a man for a substantial period, or by misconstruing the limits of that into which they were to inquire. It would equally not be within the power of that tribunal to reduce the area committed to it by construing "wives" as exclud-ing all those who, though married, have not been recently co-habiting with their husbands. Again, if it is instructed to give relief wherever on inquiry it finds that two stated conditions are satisfied, it cannot alter or restrict its juris-diction by adding a third condition which has to be satisfied before it will give relief. It is, therefore, for the courts to decide the true construction of the statute which defines the area of a tribunal's jurisdiction. This is the only logical way of dealing with the situation and it is the way in which the courts have acted in a supervisory capacity.

Lack of jurisdiction may arise in various ways. There may be an absence of those formalities or things which are conditions precedent to the tribunal having any jurisdiction to embark on an inquiry. Or the tribunal may at the end make an order that it has no jurisdiction to make. Or in the intervening stage, while engaged on a proper inquiry, the tribunal may depart from the rules of natural justice; or it may ask itself the wrong questions; or it may take into account matters which it was not directed to take into account. Thereby it would step outside its jurisdiction. It would turn its inquiry into something not directed by Parliament and fail to make the inquiry which Parliament did direct. Any of these things would cause its purported decision to be a nullity.

Further, it is assumed, unless special provisions provide otherwise, that the tribunal will make its inquiry and decision according to the law of the land. For that reason the courts will intervene when it is manifest from the record that the tribunal, though keeping within its mandated area of jurisdiction, comes to an erroneous decision through an error of law. In such a case the courts have intervened to correct the error.

The courts have, however, always been careful to distinguish their intervention whether on excess of jurisdiction or error of law from an appellate function. Their jurisdiction over inferior tribunals is supervision, not review:

> "That supervision goes to two points: one is the area of the inferior jurisdiction and the qualifications and conditions of its exercise; the other is the observance of the law in the course of its exercise" (*R. v Nat Bell Liquors Ltd* [1922] 2 A.C. 128 at 156).

It is simply an enforcement of Parliament's mandate to the tribunal. If the tribunal is intended on a true construction of the Act to inquire into and finally decide questions within a certain area, the courts' supervisory duty is to see that it makes the authorised inquiry according to natural justice and arrives at a decision whether right or wrong. They will intervene if the tribunal asks itself the wrong questions (that is, questions other than those which Parliament directed it to ask itself). But if it directs itself to the right inquiry, asking the right questions, they will not intervene merely because it has or may have come to the wrong answer, provided that this is an answer that lies within its jurisdiction.

It is convenient to set out the matter in broad outline because there has been evolution over the centuries and there have been many technicalities. There have also been many border-line cases. And the courts have at times taken a more robust line to see that the law is carried out and justice administered by inferior tribunals, and at times taken a more cautious and reluctant line in their anxiety not to seem to encroach or to assume an appellate function which they have not got. . . .

[His Lordship held that s.4(4) did not protect a purported determination made without jurisdiction.]

In my opinion, the subsequent case of *Smith v. East Elloe Rural District Council* [1956] A.C. 736 does not compel your Lordships to decide otherwise. If it seemed to do so, I would think it necessary to reconsider the case in the light of the powerful dissenting opinions of my noble and learned friends, Lord Reid and Lord Somervell. It might possibly be said that it related to an administrative or executive decision, not a judicial decision, and somewhat different considerations might have applied; certainly none of the authorities relating to absence or excess of jurisdiction were cited to the House. I agree with Browne J. that it is not a compelling authority in the present case. Again, the fact that this commission was expressly exempted from the provisions of section 11 of the Tribunals and Inquiries Act passed in 1958, though no doubt a tribute to the high standard of the commission and the fact that its chairman was a lawyer of distinction, cannot have any bearing on the construction of the Foreign Compensation Act, 1950.

If, therefore, the commission by misconstruing the Order in Council which gave them their jurisdiction and laid down the precise limit of their duty to inquire and determine, exceeded or departed from their mandate, their determination was without jurisdiction and Brown J. was right in making the order appealed from.

Pursuant to the Foreign Compensation Act 1950 the Order in Council which deals with the present claim gave a wide power to determine the amount of compensation. But with regard to the establishment of the claims under Article 4 it gave narrow powers. It gave no general discretion at all. If the applicant satisfies them of certain listed matters, the commission shall treat the claim as established. The only listed matters so far as relevant to the present claim were, the appellants argue, (1) the fact that the property referred to in Annex E was in Egypt; (2) the identity of the claimant as referred to in Annex E; and (3) the nationality of the claimant on certain dates. There is no dispute that on these matters they satisfied the commission. Therefore, on the appellants' argument, the commission had a mandatory duty to treat their claim as established. If their construction of Article 4 is correct, the appellants are right in this contention. There was no discretion in the commission, no jurisdiction to put further hurdles, other than those listed, in the path of the appellants' claim or to embark on inquiries other than those which the Order in Council directed. The commission, on the other hand, construed the Order as giving them jurisdiction to inquire and be satisfied on two further points; since they were not satisfied on these they rejected the claim. If *their* construction is correct, they were entitled to do so and have not exceeded their jurisdiction.

[His Lordship held that the commission's construction was erroneous.]

Lord WILBERFORCE: . . . In every case, whatever the character of a tribunal, however wide the range of questions remitted to it, however great the permissible margin of mistake, the essential point remains that the tribunal has a derived authority, derived, that is, from statute: at some point, and to be found from a consideration of the legislation, the field within which it operates is marked out and limited. There is always an area, narrow or wide, which is the tribunal's area; a residual area, wide or narrow, in which the legislature has previously expressed its will and into which the tribunal may not enter. Equally, though this is not something that arises in the present case, there are certain fundamental assumptions, which without explicit restatement in every case, necessarily underlie the remission of power to decide such as (I do not attempt more than a general reference, since the strength and shade of these matters will depend upon the nature of the tribunal and the kind of question it has to decide) the requirement that a decision must be made in accordance with principles of natural justice and good faith. The principle that failure to fulfil these assumptions may be equivalent to a departure from the remitted area must be taken to follow from the decision of this House in *Ridge v. Baldwin* [1964] A.C. 40. Although, in theory perhaps, it may be possible for Parliament to set up a tribunal which has full and autonomous powers to fix its own area of operation, that has, so far, not been done in this country. The question, what is the tribunal's proper area, is one which it has always been permissible to ask and to answer, and it must follow that examination of its extent is not precluded by a clause conferring conclusiveness, finality, or unquestionability upon its decisions. These clauses in their nature can only relate to decisions given within the field of operation entrusted to the tribunal. They may, according to the width and emphasis of their formulation, help to ascertain the extent of that field, to narrow it or to enlarge it, but unless one is to deny the statutory origin of the tribunal and of its powers, they cannot preclude examination of that extent. . . .

The courts, when they decide that a "decision" is a "nullity", are not disregarding the preclusive clause. For, just as it is their duty to attribute autonomy of decision of action to the tribunal within the designated area, so, as the counterpart of this autonomy, they must ensure that the limits of that area which have been laid down are observed (see the formulation of Lord Sumner in *R. v. Nat Bell Liquors Ltd* [1922] 2 A.C. 128, 156). In each task they are carrying out the intention of the legislature, and it would be misdescription to state it in terms of a struggle between the courts and the executive. What would be the purpose of defining by statute the limit of a tribunal's powers if, by means of a clause inserted in the instrument of definition, those limits could safely be passed?. . .

[His Lordship cited *R. v Commissioners for Special Purposes of the Income Tax* (1888) 21 Q.B.D. 313 at 319 (Lord Esher M.R.); *R. v Shoreditch Assessment Committee, Ex p. Morgan* [1910] 2 K.B. 859 at 880 (Farwell L.J.); and *R. v Northumberland C.A.T. Ex p. Shaw* [1952] 1 K.B. 338 at 346 (Denning L.J.).]

These passages at least answer one of the respondents' main arguments, to some extent accepted by the members of the Court of Appeal, which is that *because* the commission has (admittedly) been given power, indeed required, to decide some questions of law, arising out of the construction of the relevant Order in Council, it must necessarily have power to decide those questions which relate to the delimitation of its powers; or conversely that if the court has power to review the latter, it must also have power to review the former. But the one does not follow from the other: there is no reason why the Order in Council should not (as a matter of construction to be decided by the court) limit the tribunal's powers and at the same time (by the same process of construction) confer upon the tribunal power, in the exercise of its permitted task, to decide other questions of law, including questions of construction of the Order. I shall endeavour to show that this is what the Order has done.

The extent of the interpretatory power conferred upon the tribunal may sometimes be difficult to ascertain and argument may be possible whether this or that question of construction has been left to the tribunal, that is, is within the tribunal's field, or whether, because it pertains to the delimitation of the tribunal's area by the legislature, it is reserved for decision by the courts. Sometimes it will be possible to form a conclusion from the form and subject-matter of the legislation. In one case it may be seen that the legislature, while stating general objectives, is prepared to concede a wide area to the authority it establishes: this will often be the case where the decision involves a degree of policy-making rather than fact-finding, especially if the authority is a department of government or the Minister at its head. I think that we have reached a stage in our administrative law when we can view this question quite objectively, without any necessary predisposition towards one that questions of law, or questions of construction, are necessarily for the courts. In the kind of case I have mentioned there is no need to make this assumption. In another type of case it may be apparent that Parliament is itself directly and closely concerned with the definition and delimitation of certain matters of comparative detail and has marked by its language the intention that these shall accurately be observed. If *R. v. Minister of Health* [1939] 1 K.B. 232 was rightly decided, it must be because it was a case of the former type. The dispute related to a superannuation allowance and the statute provided that "any dispute" should be determined by the Minister. The basis of the decision is not very clearly expressed but can, I think, be taken to be that, as the context and subject-matter showed, the Minister had a field of decision extending to the construction of the super-annuation provisions of the Act. The present case, by contrast, as examination of the relevant Order in Council will show, is clearly of the latter category.

I do not think it desirable to discuss further in detail the many decisions in the reports in this field. But two points may perhaps be made. First, the cases in which a tribunal has been held to have passed outside its proper limits are not limited to those in which it had no power to enter upon its inquiry or its jurisdiction, or has not satisfied a condition precedent. Certainly such cases exist (for example *ex p. Bradlaugh* (1878) 3 Q.B.D. 509) but they do not exhaust the principle. A tribunal may quite properly validly enter upon its task and in the course of carrying it out may make a decision which is invalid—not merely erroneous. This may be described as "asking the wrong question" or "applying the wrong test"—expressions not wholly satisfactory since they do not, in themselves, distinguish between doing something which is not in the tribunal's area and doing something wrong within that area—a crucial distinction which the court has to make. Cases held to be of the former kind (whether, on their facts, correctly or not does not affect the principle) are *Estate and Trust Agencies (1927) Ltd v. Singapore Improvement Trust* [1937] A.C. 898, 915–917; *Seereelall Jhuggroo v. Central Arbitration and Control Board* [1953] A.C. 151, 161 ("whether [the board] took into consideration matters outside the ambit of its jurisdiction and beyond the matters which it was entitled to consider"); *R. v. Fulham, Hammersmith and Kensington Rent Tribunal, ex p. Hierowski* [1953] 2 Q.B. 147. The present case, in my opinion, and it is at this point that I respectfully differ from the Court of Appeal, is of this kind. Secondly, I find myself obliged to state that I cannot regard *Smith v. East Elloe Rural District Council* [1956] A.C. 736 as a reliable solvent of this appeal, or of any case where similar questions arise. The preclusive clause was indeed very similar to the present but, however inevitable the particular decision may have been, it was given on too narrow a basis to assist us here. I agree with my noble and learned friends, Lord Reid and Lord Pearce, on this matter.

LORD PEARSON dissented.

Appeal allowed.

Notes
1. This was for several years the most significant modern case on jurisdictional control, and it generated a series of important articles; see H.W.R. Wade, (1969) 85 L.Q.R. 198; S.A. de Smith, [1969] C.L.J. 161; B.C. Gould, [1970] P.L. 358; J.A. Smillie, (1969) 47 Can. Bar Rev. 623; D. Gordon (1971) 34 M.L.R. 1. See also D.G.T. Williams [1969] A.S.C.L. 125–126, 129–130; Cooke J., [1975] N.Z.L.J. 529; Sykes and Maher, (1970) 7 Melbourne U.L.R. 385; J.K. Bentil (1976) U. of W.A.L.R. 543.

The judgments of Browne J. (at first instance) and of Diplock L.J. (in the Court of Appeal) also contain valuable analyses of the issues and of the case law.

3. The sequel to *Anisminic* was summarised by S.A. de Smith [1969] C.L.J. at 164–166. See the Foreign Compensation Act 1969, s.3. Points of interest in s.3 include the express power of the Commission "to determine any question as to the construction or interpretation of any provision of an Order in Council under section 3 of the 1950 Act with respect to claims failing to be determined by them" (1969 Act, s.3(1)); the provision of an appeal by way of case stated on a point of law to the Court of Appeal (s.3(4)–(7)); and the provision that a "determination" (which includes a "provisional

determination" and "anything which purports to be a determination" (s.3(3))) is not to be called in question in any court of law (s.3(9)) except on the ground of breach of natural justice (s.3(10)).

4. The question whether *all* errors of law (or just some: and if so, which) should be regarded as going to jurisdiction was considered in a somewhat troublesome line of decisions in the years following *Anisminic*. In 1979, Lord Denning M.R. in *Pearlman v Keepers and Governors of Harrow School* [1979] Q.B. 56 expressed the view that the search for a test by which to distinguish errors of law which were jurisdictional from those which were not should be abandoned: and that thenceforth all errors of law upon which a decision-maker's decision depended should be regarded as jurisdictional. The other judges of the Court of Appeal expressed more limited opinions. Both Eveleigh and Lane LL.J. approached the matter on the basis that the distinction remained significant. The former regarded the error in question as going to jurisdiction; the latter viewed the error as non-jurisdictional.

Then in *Racal Communications, Re* [1981] A.C. 374, Lord Diplock offered further comments on the scope of review for error of law. His Lordship drew a distinction for purposes of the scope of such review between different kinds of body subject to review. In his opinion the decision on a point of law of a county court judge (as in *Pearlman*) was reviewable only where the error was such as to go to jurisdiction in the traditional (albeit somewhat unclear sense). *Pearlman* should therefore be regarded as wrongly decided, and the approach of Lane L.J. (regarding the alleged error of law as non-jurisdictional) was supported. Lord Diplock drew a distinction, however, between such cases and the more usual situation where the body under challenge was an "administrative tribunal" or "administrative authority". In such cases the distinction between jurisdictional and non-jurisdictional errors of law should be regarded as redundant. The decision in *Anisminic* should, it was argued, be regarded as an instance of the application of this wider power of review for error of law *simpliciter*: the Foreign Compensation Commission being a statutory tribunal. Having so explained this leading case, His Lordship proceeded, in language which has found much favour since, to describe this undifferentiated power of review as the "*Anisminic* principle".

Lord Diplock returned to this matter in his opinion in *O'Reilly v Mackman* [1983] 2 A.C. 237, below, p.976. In order to clarify the position as regards the scope of review of certain inferior courts of law (but not disturbing the approach towards the county court) his Lordship revised his formulation of the bodies subject to the "*Anisminic* principle" so as now to comprise "inferior courts, administrative and statutory tribunals and administrative authorities".

R. v LORD PRESIDENT OF THE PRIVY COUNCIL Ex p. PAGE

[1993] A.C. 682; [1993] 3 W.L.R. 1112; [1993] 1 All E.R. 97 (HOUSE OF LORDS)

In 1988, Mr Page, who had held a lectureship at the University of Hull since 1966, was given three months' written notice terminating his employment on the ground of redundancy. His appointment was subject to the terms of his letter of appointment and also the statutes of the University.

Mr Page commenced an action in the High Court for wrongful dismissal. This was struck out on the grounds that Mr Page's complaint lay within the exclusive jurisdiction of the visitor of the university, Her Majesty the Queen. Mr Page petitioned the visitor for a declaration that his purported dismissal was contrary to the statutes of the university, was *ultra vires* and of no effect.

The Lord President of the Council took advice from Lord Jauncey of Tullichettle (a Lord of Appeal in Ordinary) as regards the proper construction of the statutes. The advice tendered was that on the true construction of the statutes the dismissal was valid and *intra vires*. The visitor therefore dismissed the petition.

Mr Page then commenced proceedings by way judicial review to seek to quash the visitor's decision. Two issues were raised: (i) did the High Court have jurisdiction to review decisions of the university visitor; and (ii) if it did, had the visitor rejected the petition on the basis of a misconstruction of the statutes?

The Divisional Court answered both questions in the affirmative. The Court of Appeal recognised jurisdiction in the High Court to review abuse of power by visitors (including misconstruction of statutes), but held that there had been no such misconstruction in this case. Mr Page appealed to the House of Lords on the point of construction: the visitor and the university appealed on the issue of the power of judicial review in respect of visitors.

Their Lordships were unanimous that the visitor had made no error in the interpretation of the statutes. On the issue of the power to review decisions of visitors a majority of their Lordships (Lords Browne-Wilkinson, Griffiths and Keith) held that visitors were not subject to review for misconstruction of the statutes laying down the domestic law of their charitable foundation. A visitor would be subject to review, however, should he or she act outside jurisdiction in the sense of embarking upon a dispute where this was beyond the visitor's functions laid down in the governing statutes. Equally, a visitor was subject to review for breach of natural justice. The minority (Lords Mustill and Slynn) considered that visitors' decisions should be reviewable also for error of law.

LORD BROWNE-WILKINSON: . . . Under the modern law, certiorari normally lies to quash a decision for error of law. Therefore, the narrow issue in this case is whether, as Mr Page contends and the courts below have held, certiorari lies against the visitor to quash his decision as being erroneous in point of law notwithstanding that the question of law arises under the domestic law of the university which the visitor has "exclusive" jurisdiction to decide. . . .

The decision of Holt C.J. in *Philips v. Bury* is the locus classicus of the law of visitors. It has been repeatedly applied for the last 300 years, most recently in *Thomas v. University of Bradford*. For present purposes it is important for three reasons. (1) It shows that the court can and will inquire whether the visitor has jurisdiction to determine the question, *i.e.* to enter into the matter.

(2) If the visitor has such jurisdiction, the court has no power to ignore it or review it by way of mandamus or in any other way. (3) The reason for such lack of jurisdiction to review in the court is that an eleemosynary corporation is governed by a system of private law which is not of "the common known laws of the kingdom" but the particular laws and constitutions assigned by the founder. . . .

In my judgment this review of the authorities demonstrates that for over 300 years the law has been clearly established that the visitor of an eleemosynary charity has an exclusive jurisdiction to determine what are the internal laws of the charity and the proper application of those laws to those within his jurisdiction. The court's inability to determine those matters is not limited to the period pending the visitor's determination but extends so as to prohibit any subsequent review by the court of the correctness of a decision made by the visitor acting within his jurisdiction and in accordance with the rules of natural justice. This inability of the court to intervene is founded on the fact that the applicable law is not the common law of England but a peculiar or domestic law of which the visitor is the sole judge. This special status of a visitor springs from the common law recognising the right of the founder to lay down such a special law subject to adjudication only by a special judge, the visitor.

How then is it contended that the courts have power to review the visitor's decision as to the effect of the domestic law of the university in this case? The Divisional Court and the Court of Appeal did not consider in any detail the old authorities to which I have referred. They started from the position, in my judgment incorrectly, that the references in *Thomas*'s case to the visitor's jurisdiction being exclusive meant simply that the court did not have concurrent jurisdiction with him. Then, since this House in *Thomas*'s case had accepted that judicial review by way of certiorari did lie to the visitor at least to restrain an abusive process, they held that there was jurisdiction to correct errors of law since "illegality" is one of the accepted heads of judicial review.

Before your Lordships, Mr Burke Q.C. refined this argument. He relied upon the great development that has recently taken place in the law of judicial review whereby the courts have asserted a general jurisdiction to review the decisions of tribunals and inferior courts. He points to the way in which the law has developed from a maze of individual sets of circumstances in which one or other of the prerogative writs would lie to a general principle under which courts will review decisions on the three grounds of illegality, irrationality and procedural impropriety: see *Council of Civil Service Unions v. Minister for the Civil Service* [1985] A.C. 374 at 410 *per* Lord Diplock. Mr Burke submits that, if judicial review lies at all, then it is not possible to pick and choose between Lord Diplock's three categories: it must lie on all three grounds or not at all. As to illegalilty, recent developments in the law have shown that any relevant error of law made by the decision-maker, whether as to his powers or as to the law he is to apply, may lead to his decision being quashed. In the present case, since the decision in *Thomas*'s case shows that judicial review does lie against the visitor, so his decision is capable of being reviewed on any one of Lord Diplock's three grounds, including illegality. If, therefore, the visitor has made an error in construing the statutes of the university, his decision can be quashed on judicial review.

I accept much of Mr Burke's submissions. Over the last 40 years the courts have developed general principles of judicial review. The fundamental principle is that the courts will intervene to ensure that the powers of public decision-making bodies are exercised lawfully. In all cases, save possibly one, this intervention by way of prohibition or certiorari is based on the proposition that such powers have been conferred on the decision-maker on the underlying assumption that the powers are to be exercised only within the jurisdiction conferred, in accordance with fair procedures and, in a *Wednesbury* sense (see *Associated Provincial Picture Houses Ltd v. Wednesbury Corp* [1948] 1 K.B. 223), reasonably. If the decision-maker exercises his powers outside the jurisdiction conferred, in a manner which is procedurally irregular or is *Wednesbury* unreasonable, he is acting *ultra vires* his powers and therefore unlawfully: see Wade, *Administrative Law* (6th ed., 1988), p.39 *et seq*. The one possible exception to this general rule used to be the jurisdiction of the court to quash a decision taken within the jurisdiction of the decision-taker where an error of law appeared on the face of the record: *R. v. Northumberland Compensation Appeal Tribunal, ex p. Shaw* [1952] 1 K.B. 338.

In my judgment the decision in *Anisminic Ltd v. Foreign Compensation Commission* [1969] 2 A.C. 147 rendered obsolete the distinction between errors of law on the face of the record and other errors of law by extending the doctrine of *ultra vires*. Thenceforward it was to be taken that Parliament had only conferred the decision-making power on the basis that it was to be exercised on the correct legal basis: a misdirection in law in making the decision therefore rendered the decision *ultra vires*. Professor Wade considers that the true effect of the *Anisminic* case is still in doubt: see *Wade*, pp.299 *et seq*. But in my judgment the decision of this House in *O'Reilly v. Mackman* [1983] 2 A.C. 237 establishes the law in the sense that I have stated. Lord Diplock, with whose speech all the other members of the committee agreed, said that the decision in the *Anisminic* case—

> "has liberated English public law from the fetters that the courts had theretofore imposed upon themselves so far as determinations of inferior courts and statutory tribunals were concerned, by drawing esoteric distinctions between errors of law committed by such tribunals that went to their jurisdiction, and errors of law committed by them within their jurisdiction. The breakthrough that *Anisminic* made was the recognition by the majority of this House that if a tribunal whose jurisdiction was limited by statute or subordinate legislation mistook the law applicable to the facts as it had found them, it must have asked itself the wrong question, *i.e.* one into which it was not empowered to inquire and so had no jurisdiction to determine. Its purported 'determination', not being 'a determination' within the meaning of the empowering legislation, was accordingly a nullity." (See [1983] 2 A.C. 237 at 278.)

Therefore, I agree with Mr Burke that in general any error of law made by an administrative tribunal or inferior court in reaching its decision can be quashed for error of law. . . .

Although the general rule is that decisions affected by errors of law made by tribunals or inferior courts can be quashed, in my judgment there are two reasons why that rule does not apply in the case of visitors. First, as I have sought to explain, the constitutional basis of the courts' power to quash is that the decision of the inferior tribunal is unlawful on the grounds that it is *ultra vires*. In the ordinary case, the law applicable to a decision made by such a body is the general law of the land. Therefore, a tribunal or inferior court acts *ultra vires* if it reaches its conclusion on a basis erroneous under the general law. But the position of decisions made by a visitor is different. As the authorities which I have cited demonstrate, the visitor is applying not the general law of the land but a peculiar, domestic law of which he is the sole arbiter and of which the courts have no cognisance. If the visitor has power under the regulating documents to enter into the adjudication of the dispute (*i.e.* is acting within his jurisdiction in the narrow sense) he cannot err in law in reaching this decision since the general law is not the applicable law. Therefore he cannot be acting *ultra vires* and unlawfully by applying his view of the domestic law in reaching his decision. The court has no jurisdiction either to say that he erred in his application of the general law (since the general law is not applicable to the decision) or to reach a contrary view as to the effect of the domestic law (since the visitor is the sole judge of such domestic law).

The second reason is closely allied to the first. In *Pearlman v. Keepers and Governors of Harrow School* [1979] Q.B. 56 a statute provided that the decision of the county court as to whether works constituted an "improvement" within the meaning of the Act should be "final and conclusive". A tenant claimed that the installation of a central heating system constituted an "improvement". The county court judge ruled that it did not. The tenant then applied to the Divisional Court by way of judicial review to quash the judge's decision. The majority of the Court of Appeal held that it had jurisdiction to quash the judge's order. However, Geoffrey Lane L.J. dissented. He held that the judge had done nothing which went outside the proper area of his inquiry. The question was not whether the judge had made a wrong decision but whether he had inquired into and decided a matter which he had no right to consider. Therefore he held that the court had no jurisdiction to review the decision of the county court judge for error of law.

This dissenting judgment of Geoffrey Lane L.J. has been approved by the Privy Council in *South East Asia Fire Bricks Sdn Bhd v. Non-Metallic Mineral Products Manufacturing Employees Union* [1981] A.C. 363 at 370 and by a majority in this House in *Re Racal Communications Ltd* [1981] A.C. 374 at 384, 390–391. In the latter case, Lord Diplock pointed out that the decision in *Anisminic* applied to decisions of administrative tribunals or other administrative bodies made under statutory powers: in those cases there was a presumption that the statute conferring the power did not intend the administrative body to be the final arbiter of questions of law. He then contrasted that position with the case where a decision-making power had been conferred on a court of law. In that case no such presumption could exist; on the contrary where Parliament had provided that the decision of an inferior court was final and conclusive the High Court should not be astute to find that the inferior court's decision on a question of law had not been made final and conclusive, thereby excluding the jurisdiction to review it.

In my judgment, therefore, if there were a statutory provision that the decision of a visitor on the law applicable to internal disputes of a charity was to be "final and conclusive", courts would have no jurisdiction to review the visitor's decision on the grounds of error of law made by the visitor within his jurisdiction (in the narrow sense). For myself, I can see no relevant distinction between a case where a statute has conferred such final and conclusive jurisdiction and the case where the common law has for 300 years recognised that the visitor's decision on questions of fact and law are final and conclusive and are not to be reviewed by the courts. Accordingly, unless this House is prepared to sweep away long-established law, there is no jurisdiction in the court to review a visitor's decision for error of law committed within his jurisdiction.

Mr Burke urged that the position of a visitor would be anomalous if he were immune from review on the grounds of error of law. He submitted that the concept of a peculiar domestic law differing from the general law of the land was artificial since in practice the charter and statutes of a university are expressed in ordinary legal language and applied in accordance with the same principles as those applicable under the general law. He pointed to the important public role occupied by universities and submitted that it was wrong that they should be immune from the general law of the land: "There must be no Alsatia in England where the King's writ does not run": see *Czarnikow v. Roth Schmidt & Co.* [1922] 2 K.B. 478 at 488; *per* Scrutton L.J. He further suggested that to permit review of a visitor's decision for error of law would not impair the effectiveness of the visitor's domestic jurisdiction.

I accept that the position of the visitor is anomalous, indeed unique. I further accept that where the visitor is, or is advised by, a lawyer the distinction between the peculiar domestic law he applies and the general law is artificial. But I do not regard these factors as justifying sweeping away the law which for so long has regulated the conduct of charitable corporations. There are internal disputes which are resolved by a visitor who is not a lawyer himself and has not taken legal advice. It is not only modern universities which have visitors: there are a substantial number of other long-established educational, ecclesiastical and eleemosynary bodies which have visitors. The advantages of having an informal system which produces a speedy, cheap and final answer to internal disputes has been repeatedly emphasised in the authorities, most recently by this House in the *Thomas v. University of Bradford* [1987] A.C. 795 at 825 *per* Lord Griffiths; see also *Patel v. University of Bradford Senate* [1978] 1 W.L.R. 1488 at 1499–1500. If it were to be held that judicial review for error of law lay against the visitor I fear that, as in the present case, finality would be lost not only in cases raising pure questions of law but also in cases where it would be urged in accordance with the *Wednesbury* principle that the visitor had failed to take into account relevant matters or taken into account irrelevant matters or had reached an irrational conclusion. Although the visitor's position is anomalous, it provides a valuable machinery for resolving internal disputes which should not be lost.

I have therefore reached the conclusion that judicial review does not lie to impeach the decisions of a visitor taken within his jurisdiction (in the narrow sense) on questions of either fact or law. Judicial review does lie to the visitor in cases where he has acted outside his jurisdiction (in the narrow sense) or abused his powers or acted in breach of the rules of natural justice. Accordingly, in my judgment the Divisional Court had no jurisdiction to entertain the application for judicial review of the visitor's decision in this case. . . .

Notes

1. Notwithstanding the positive comments by Lord Browne-Wilkinson on the role of the visitor in those universities subject to a visitorial jurisdiction, there have been concerns at the delay involved in reference to a visitor and a growing view that different arrangements are needed that are applicable to all universities. It is also arguable that the visitorial jurisdiction does not comply with Art.6(1) ECHR: see Collins J. in *R. (on the application of Varma v HRH The Duke of Kent* [2004] EWHC 1705 at [26]. An Office for Student Complaints has been established and the visitorial jurisdiction is in due course to be abolished. The *Page* approach has been held applicable to the exercise of a visitorial jurisdiction by the Charity Commissioners in respect of a decision of charity trustees to set aside the applicant's appointment as an alms person (*R. v Charity Commissioners for England and Wales Ex p. Baldwin* (2000) 33 H.L.R. 538).

2. The outcome of *Page* was helpfully summarised by Lord Cooke of Thorndon in the House of Lords in *Williams v Bedwellty Justices* [1996] 3 All E.R. 737 at 742, 743:

"In approaching the appeal I will avoid as far as reasonably practicable that which the certified question successfully avoids, namely the use of the term 'jurisdiction'. It is a term used in a number of different senses, and possibly its popularity and convenience are partly due to its very ambiguity. For instance one can say, without any distortion of ordinary language, (i) that a superior court of general jurisdiction, such as the High Court of Justice, has jurisdiction to determine, subject to any provisions for appeal, the limits of its own jurisdiction; (ii) that the authorities now establish that the Queen's Bench Division of the High Court has normally in judicial review proceedings jurisdiction to quash a decision of an inferior court, tribunal or other statutory body for error of law, even though the error is neither apparent on the face of the record nor so serious as to deprive the body of jurisdiction in the original and narrow sense of powers to enter on the inquiry and to make against persons subject to its jurisdiction the kind of decision in question; and (iii) that the second proposition may often be otherwise expressed by saying that the body acts outside its jurisdiction if it asks itself the wrong question. Such familiar propositions illustrate some (but not all) of the diverse shades of meaning which the term can bear.

Perhaps it is indeed the versatility rather than the precision of the term that has lent persuasiveness to some leading judgments of the past. A sufficient illustration is the judgment of Lord Sumner in the Privy Council case of *R. v. Nat Bell Liquors Ltd* [1922] 2 A.C. 128 at 151–152, with its statement:

> 'A justice who convicts without evidence is doing something that he ought not to do, but he is doing it as a judge, and if his jurisdiction to entertain the charge is not open to impeachment, his subsequent error, however grave, is a wrong exercise of a jurisdiction which he has, and not a usurpation of a jurisdiction which he has not. How a magistrate, who has acted within his jurisdiction up to the point at which the missing evidence should have been, but was not, given, can, thereafter, be said by a kind of relation back to have had no jurisdiction over the charge at all, it is hard to see.'

To convict or commit for trial without any admissible evidence of guilt is to fall into an error of law. As to the availability of certiorari to quash a committal for such an error, I understood at the end of the arguments that all your Lordships were satisfied that in principle the remedy is available and that the only issue presenting any difficulty relates to the exercise of the court's discretion. This conclusion about principle reflects the position now reached in the development of the modern law of judicial review in England through a sequence of cases beginning with [*Shaw*] and extending by way most notably of [*Anisminic*] to (at present) [*Page.*] It is enough to take *Page*'s case as stating the developed law.

In *Page*'s case the five members of the Appellate Committee (Lord Keith of Kinkel, Lord Griffiths, Lord Browne-Wilkinson, Lord Mustill and Lord Slynn of Hadley) were unanimous that usually any error of law made by an administrative tribunal or inferior court in reaching its decision can be quashed by certiorari for error of law. There were, however, observations to the effect that as regards an inferior court of law a statutory provision that its decision is to be 'final and conclusive' or the like will confine the remedy to cases of abuse of power, acting outside jurisdiction in the narrow sense, or breach of natural justice. Moreover, there was a division of opinion on whether the university visitor was applying a peculiar domestic law of which, historically and for reasons of policy, he was to be treated as the sole arbiter".

3. *Racal* confirms that the decisions of the superior courts, including the High Court (as a court of unlimited jurisdiction), are not subject to judicial review. A decision of a High Court judge sitting in that capacity cannot be challenged for lack of jurisdiction, and only by way of appeal. While there are no orders of such a court that can simply be ignored because they are void (see Ch.2),

> "there is a category of orders of such a court which a person affected by the order is entitled to apply to have set aside *ex debito justitiae* in the exercise of the inherent jurisdiction of the court without his needing to have recourse to the rules that deal expressly with proceedings to set aside orders for irregularity and give to the judge a discretion as to the order he will make" (*per* Lord Diplock in *Isaacs v Robertson* [1985] A.C. 97, PC at 102–103).

This was cited in *St George's NHS Trust v S* [1999] Fam. 26 where the Court of Appeal held that declaration that had been granted on an *ex parte* application, in proceedings not instituted by the issue of a summons, without the respondent's knowledge or even any attempt to inform her or her solicitor of the application and without any evidence, oral or by affidavit, was such an order. S was a pregnant woman who was diagnosed with pre-eclampsia but who rejected medical advice that she needed to be admitted to hospital for an induced delivery. She was admitted to a mental hospital for assessment under s.2 of the Mental Health Act 1983. The hospital obtained *ex parte* a declaration dispensing with her consent to treatment and a Caesarian section was performed. The Court of Appeal allowed an appeal, set aside the declaration and held that it provided no defence to a claim for damages for trespass.

4. If all errors of law go to jurisdiction the scope of the concept "error of law" becomes critical, and itself becomes the vehicle by which the courts may extend or limit their scope of review. See further, below, pp.816–854. Note that a mistake of fact causing unfairness is now recognised as a separate discrete example of error of law (pp.828–841).

5. In *Page*, reference is made to the notion of review for "lack of jurisdiction in the narrow sense". This ground of review remains applicable as regards bodies not subject to review for error of law in the sense described in *Page* (*e.g.* those exercising visitorial jurisdictions, the county court as in *Pearlman*). It has similarly been held that the decision of an adjudicator under the special regime for dealing with construction contract disputes under s.108 of the Housing Grants, Construction and Regeneration Act 1996 is enforceable by summary judgment unless the adjudicator lacks jurisdiction in the narrow sense or breaches natural justice (*London & Amsterdam Properties Ltd v Waterman Partnerships Ltd* [2003] EWHC 3059 (TCC); [2004] Build.L.R. 179).

What is meant by "lack of jurisdiction in the narrow sense"? In addition to the illumination of the concept given in the extract above, the following points seem established by the case law. The proper composition of a tribunal is usually a jurisdictional matter. For example, in *Howard v. Borneman (No.2)* [1976] A.C. 301, the House of Lords had to decide whether a provision (the Finance Act 1960, s.28(7)) that a tribunal shall consist of a chairman "and two or more persons appointed by the Lord Chancellor as having special knowledge of and experience in financial or commercial matters" meant that the tribunal was only validly constituted for a particular case if all the appointed members took part. The House decided that the tribunal was validly constituted provided that the chairman and not less than two of the appointed members took part. See also, *R. v. Merseyside Coroner, Ex p. Carr* [1993] 4 All E.R. 65 (improperly summoned jury); *cf. Tameside MBC v Grant* [2002] Fam. 194 (proceedings of family proceedings court held not to be vitiated by presence of one justice who was not a member of the family panel). A tribunal or court not properly constituted may, according to the circumstances, not be "established by law" for the purposes of compliance with Art.6 ECHR (see *Grant* and above, p.384).

It is, however, quite common for Parliament to provide that the acts of a tribunal or other body shall be valid notwithstanding a defect in the appointment of a person purporting to be a member. An example is para.20(2) of Sch.IX to the Agriculture Act 1947, which was held by the Court of Appeal to cure the defective appointments of two members of an agricultural land tribunal in *Woollett v Minister of Agriculture* [1955] 1 Q.B. 103. (The defects were that they were appointed neither by the Minister as specified by para.15 of Sch.IX, nor by a properly authorised civil servant.) Denning L.J. said at 121:

"I cannot help remarking that it would be most unfortunate if we came to any other conclusion. The members of the land tribunals in the eastern province have been appointed in this way for several years. They have made decisions in a great many disputes and people have acted on the faith of their decisions. Indeed, we have had cases in this court where these tribunals have given consent to notices to quit by landlords to tenants; and many landlords have recovered their lands on the basis that the decisions are valid: see *Martin-Smith v. Smale* [1954] 1 W.L.R. 247. If all the decisions were now invalidated by a technical defect, it would produce great confusion and injustice. It is just the thing which paragraph 20(2) was made to avoid".

Other similar statutory provisions include section 82 of the Local Government Act 1972 (members of local authorities).

Illegality

Questions of the composition of a trubinal, are also raised by allegations of bias against a tribunal member, on which see below, pp.751–787, below, and by the general rule that no person ought to participate in the deliberations of a judicial or quasi-judicial body unless he is a member of it (see *Ward v Bradford Corporation* (1971) 70 L.G.R. 27). See further: P. Jackson, (1974) 90 L.Q.R. 158 and (1975) 91 L.Q.R. 469. Similarly, an argument that a University Visitor has improperly delegated his decision-making function can be raised on an application for judicial review: see *R. (on the application of Varma) v HRH The Duke of Kent* [2004] EWHC 1705, where it was held that the appointment of a Circuit judge to report on the case to the Visitor was not an improper delegation.

The geographical competence of a tribunal is usually regarded as a jurisdictional question. For example, each panel of General Commissioners for Income Tax exercises jurisdiction in respect of a particular geographical area or "division". The allocation of the various kinds of proceedings which may come before the General Commissioners, to the appropriate panel, is governed by s.44 and Sch.3 to the Taxes Management Act 1970. These rules may include the determination of such questions as where trade is "carried on", or where the appellant "ordinarily resides". See *Lack v Doggett* (1970) 46 T.C. 497, CA and *R. v Inland Revenue Commissioners Ex p. Knight* [1973] 3 All E.R. 721, CA.

A tribunal may lack jurisdiction where proceedings before it are not properly instituted. cf. *Campbell v Wallsend Slipway & Engineering Co. Ltd* [1978] I.C.R. 1015 where the Divisional Court held that justices did have jurisdiction to proceed with certain informations laid by an inspector of the Health and Safety Executive. The justices had dismissed the informations on the ground that the inspector was not competent to prosecute. The court held (1) that the presumption *omnia praesumuntur rite esse acta* applied in favour of the validity of the appointment of the Executive, and of the inspector, which presumption could only be rebutted by evidence; and (2) that provisions of the Health and Safety at Work etc. Act 1974, requiring certain formalities on the appointment of the Executive, were directory only.

CHAPTER 8

RETENTION OF DISCRETION

In this and the following chapter we shall be considering judicial review in relation to the exercise of discretionary powers. By "discretionary power" we mean the situation where a body has a power of choice, in the circumstances, to do "X" or not to do "X"; or to do "X" and/or "Y" or do neither. We shall be concerned to see what principles of review are applied by the courts in supervising such discretionary powers. We are not here concerned with the situation where a body has had a "duty" imposed upon it to act in a designated way in defined circumstances, involving no exercise of discretion on the part of that body.

In the cases which follow there is usually no argument as to whether the body challenged has, in the circumstances, the discretionary power in question. In this way the cases differ from those which have formed the subject-matter of Chapter 7. In the cases which follow the challenge is made on the ground that a body on which the statutory power in question has been conferred *either*:

(i) has failed properly to retain that degree of free and unfettered power of judgment as to whether, and, if so how, it should exercise its discretionary powers, which (in statutory contexts) Parliament is assumed by the courts to have intended that donees of such powers should have retained. Such a failure may arise in a number of ways, and we shall look at the decisions under the following sub-headings—"acting under dictation", "failure to retain discretion by unauthorised delegation of power", "over-rigid adherence to self-created rules of policy", "fettering discretion by contractual or similar undertakings" and "fettering discretion by estoppel". These matters are considered in this Chapter.

(ii) has exercised its powers in a way which the reviewing court may categorise as an "abuse of power". The courts have consistently stated that powers must be exercised for "proper purposes," must be exercised on the basis of the consideration of "relevant" matters and the exclusion from consideration of "irrelevant" matters, and the exercise of power must not in substance be "unreasonable" or "irrational"—must not be a manner of exercising the power which no reasonable person/body could have chosen. To these well-established grounds of challenge the courts have recently added the proposition that an exercise of power that interferes with a legitimate expectation may, in a relatively limited range of circumstances, be challenged on the ground that there has been "substantive unfairness." Lack of "proportionality" is established as a ground of challenge under EU law or the Human Rights Acts 1998, but not yet outside these categories. These grounds of challenge for abuse of power are dealt with in Ch.9. Finally it should be noted that unfairness arising from a mistake of fact has been recognised by the Court of Appeal as a discrete category of error of law (see pp.828–841).

A general consideration that must be borne in mind is that the identification of categories for the fettering or abuse of discretion is ultimately one of convenience. The categories are themselves fluid and they may to a significant extent overlap in their application to particular factual situations.

(A) ACTING UNDER DICTATION

A public body (X) upon which a discretion has been conferred may not exercise that discretion in accordance with the dictation (whether real or imagined) of another body (Y), unless that other body has a power to give directions. Body X will have fettered its discretion; if body Y has actually sought to exercise a power to give directions that it does not have, it will too have acted unlawfully. There are many examples of powers to give directions or guidance, and the extent to which "guidance" must be followed will depend on the statutory context.

R. v. THE MAYOR, ALDERMEN AND COUNCILLORS OF STEPNEY

[1902] 1 K.B. 317; 71 L.J.K.B. 238; 86 L.T. 21; 18 T.L.R. 98; 66 J.P. 183; 46 S.J. 106; 50 W.R. 412, D.C. (KING'S BENCH DIVISION)

Mr Jutsum was clerk to the vestry of Mile End Old Town from 1872 to 1901. In 1901, this parish was included in the new Metropolitan Borough of Stepney. The existing parish officers were transferred to the borough council. Under the London Government Act 1899, s.30(1), the council had power to abolish the office of any officer transferred to them, whose office they deemed unnecessary. They accordingly abolished J's office. He was now entitled to compensation calculated in accordance with the Local Government Act 1888, s.120. This stated that regard should be had, *inter alia*, to the conditions on which his appointment was made, to the nature of his office or employment, to the duration of his service "and to all the other circumstances of the case, and the compensation shall not exceed the amount which, under the Acts and Rules relating to Her Majesty's Civil Service, is paid to a person on abolition of office".

J held his post on a part-time basis, as he was also a solicitor in private practice. The town clerk of Stepney wrote to the Treasury asking what their rule was as to the amount of compensation paid to a person in the civil service on abolition of an office, held part time. The reply was that the Treasury's practice was to calculate the compensation allowance as if the office was full time, but to deduct a quarter of the amount so arrived at. The council acted on this letter and assessed the compensation accordingly.

J applied for *mandamus* to compel the council to deal with his claim properly.

CHANNELL J.: . . . I think that the mandamus ought to go because the local authority have not in fact exercised their discretion upon this matter. They have, by a mistake, thought that they were bound by a practice of the Treasury as though it were a rule, and consequently they exercised no discretion in the matter. In my opinion, if they had said "We quite know that we are not bound by this absolutely, but we think it right to follow the Treasury practice", and had so followed it, they would have exercised their discretion and would have been right; but they thought that they were bound when they were not bound, and consequently it is a case for a mandamus calling upon them to exercise their discretion in the matter . . .

LORD ALVERSTONE C.J. and DARLING J. delivered concurring judgments.

Notes
1. In *Roncarelli v Duplessis* (1959) 16 D.L.R. (2d) 689, it was found that D, the Prime Minister and Attorney-General of Quebec, ordered the Quebec Licensing Commission to revoke R's liquor permit, in response to R's activities in acting in over 380 cases as surety for Jehovah's Witnesses charged with distributing literature (some of which was

thought to be seditious) without a licence. The discretion to revoke was legally the Commission's, but there was "ample evidence to sustain the finding of the trial judge that the cancellation . . . was the result of instructions given by the respondent to the Managers of the Commission" (Martland J. at 737). D stated in a press interview:

"It was I, as Attorney-General of the Province charged with the protection of good order, who gave the order to annul [R's] permit. By so doing not only have we exercised a right but we have fulfilled an imperious duty. The permit was cancelled not temporarily but definitely and for always".

This was held to be unlawful on the ground that the Commission acted under dictation, and also because "it was a gross abuse of legal power expressly intended to punish [R] for an act wholly irrelevant to the statute . . ." (Rand J. at 706).

2. Parliament, in conferring grants of power, commonly imposes an obligation to consult with specified or unspecified persons or bodies prior to exercising the power. As will be seen, when we consider review for failure to comply with procedural requirements, this obligation to consult is one which the courts have regarded as of being of a "mandatory" nature. See below, pp.646–651. Even beyond instances where an express statutory obligation to consult may exist, the process of consultation prior to coming to a decision may be regarded as part of the required process by which, as we shall see (below, p.551), a decision-maker must seek to inform himself of *all relevant circumstances* in relation to the decision he is to take. More generally still, the process of consultation has been regarded as part and parcel of the process of "good administration"—as providing a mechanism, by which decision-makers may take account of, and benefit from, a broad range of expertise and opinion in coming to their eventual decisions.

This present ground of challenge shows that those exercising statutory powers must steer a proper course between the process, voluntary or mandatory, of consultation and the requirement that the ultimate power of decision must remain in their hands. A context in which consultation is, perhaps, most likely to drift into dictation is where there is consultation of one organ of government by another. See, *e.g. Lavender v Minister of Housing and Local Government* (below, p.482) where it could be said that the respondent Minister had acted under the dictation of the Minister of Agriculture.

3. *Power to give guidance.* In some instances legislation may expressly empower one body to issue "guidance" to another as to the exercise of the latter's powers. In *Laker Airways v Department of Trade* [1977] Q.B. 643, the Court of Appeal considered the provisions of the Civil Aviation Act 1971 under which the Secretary of State was empowered to give "guidance" to the Civil Aviation Authority as to the exercise of its functions, and the CAA was, in turn, obliged to "perform those functions in such manner as it considers is in accordance with" such guidance (1971 Act, s.3(2)). Construing the scope of this power to issue guidance, the Court of Appeal held that it did not cover guidance which contradicted the general policy objectives which were expressly stated in the 1971 Act itself. The power to issue guidance was restricted to power to explain, amplify or supplement those objectives. As regards the CAA's duty to follow guidance given under the Act, Lord Denning M.R. explained (at 699):

"So long as the 'guidance' given by the Secretary of State keeps within the due bounds of guidance, the Authority is under a duty to follow his guidance. Even so, the Authority is allowed some degree of flexibility. It is to perform its functions 'in such manner as it considers is in accordance with the guidance'. So, whilst it is obliged to follow the guidance, the manner of doing so is for the Authority itself. . . ."

Note that a power, in the 1971 Act, under which the Secretary of State could give "directions" to the CAA was interpreted as denoting power to give orders which had to be obeyed by the CAA and which could, unlike the guidance, be contrary to the Act's general objectives.

In determining the extent to which a body is obliged to follow statutory guidance the particular terms of the legislation must be considered. For example, in *R. v Police Complaints Board Ex p. Madden* [1983] 1 W.L.R. 447, the Police Complaints Board was required by the Police Act 1976 to "have regard to" certain guidance given to it by the Secretary of State. The Board adopted a policy of following the guidance given. McNeill J. held that the Board had thereby failed properly to exercise its own discretion as to the exercise of its powers. It had erred in regarding its obligation to "have regard to" the guidance as an obligation to "comply with" the guidance. Rather the Board, "as an independent body, ought to [have been] asserting its independence" (at 470). Certainly it was obliged to take the guidance into account in reaching its own decisions. It fell into error in regarding the legislation as conferring a power of dictation on the Minister. See also *R. v Secretary of State for the Environment Ex p. Lancashire CC* [1994] 4 All E.R. 165.

The extent to which a decision-maker is constrained by guidance to which he or she must "have regard" was summarised by Laws L.J. for the Court of Appeal in *R. (on the application of Khatun) v Newham LBC* [2004] EWCA Civ 55; [2004] 3 W.L.R. 417 at [47] in the proposition that "respondents to such a circular must (a) take it into account and (b) if they decide to depart from it, give clear reasons for doing so". Here, a procedural obligation arises (to give reasons) but the decision will only otherwise be challengeable if the decision-maker fails to take account of the guidance (a "relevant consideration") or, if it is taken into account, if the decision is *Wednesbury* unreasonable or irrational. (See further Ch.9.)

An apparently stronger obligation arises from s.7(1) of the Local Authority Social Services Act 1970, which provides that:

> "local authorities shall, in the exercise of their social services functions, including the exercise of any discretion conferred by any relevant enactment, act under the general guidance of the Secretary of State."

(s.7A (inserted by the National Health Service and Community Care Act 1990, s.50) gives an express power for the Secretary of State to give directions and provide that local authorities shall exercise their social services functions in accordance with any such directions.) Section 7(1) has been interpreted as requiring local authorities:

> "to follow the path charted by the Secretary of State's guidance, with liberty to deviate from it where the local authority judges on admissible grounds that there is good reason to do so, but without freedom to take a substantially different course"

(*per* Sedley J. in *R. v Islington LBC Ex p. Rixon* (1998) 1 C.C.L.R. 119 at p.123). Accordingly, a decision may be quashed for failure, without good reason, to follow guidance (*R. v Lambeth LBC Ex p. K* (2000) 3 C.C.L.R. 141).

A weak form of words may be interpreted in their context as imposing a strong level of obligation. This is well illustrated by *R. (on the application of Munjaz) v Mersey Care NHS Trust* [2003] EWCA Civ 1036; [2004] Q.B. 395, where the Court of Appeal held that the Mental Health Act 1983, Revised Code of Practice issued by the Secretary of State under s.118 of the Mental Health Act 1983 "for the guidance of" medical practitioners, hospitals and others, in relation to the admission of patients to hospitals under the Act and their medical treatment "should be observed by all hospitals unless they have a good reason for departing from it in relation to an individual patient . . . [T]hey cannot depart from it as a matter of policy" (see Hale L.J. at [71]–[76]). In relation to those matters where a patient's human rights were or might be engaged, the arguments for according the Code the greater status were compelling; indeed publication of a code which agents of the State would be required to follow on this basis would enable the state to discharge its obligations under Art.3, and meet the requirements of legality under Arts 5 and 8(1) ECHR (*ibid., at.* [74]).

It is now common practice for the Secretary of State to indicate whether a guidance document (or particular provisions of such a document) are to be treated as "statutory guidance" for the purposes of particular statutory provision. In *Rixon*, Sedley J. held that practice guidance not issued under s.7(1), although not of the same status, was nevertheless a relevant consideration conscientiously to be taken into account. See further, K. Markus and M. Westgate, [1997] J.R. 154.

4. A local education authority may not use its power to dismiss school governors as a means of imposing its views on educational matters on the governors; it is the policy of the Education Act 1944 that the governors and the authority should have different spheres of responsibility: *R. v Inner London Education Authority Ex p. Brunyate* [1989] 1 W.L.R. 542, H.L.; *R. v Trustee of the Roman Catholic Diocese of Westminster Ex p. Andrews, The Times*, August 18, 1989. On the other hand, a decision that all council-appointed governors should face reappointment and replacement in order to ensure that the number of governors appointed by each political party continued to be in proportion with party representation on the council was held to be lawful in *R. v Warwickshire County Council Ex p. Dill-Russell* (1990) 89 L.G.R. 640, DC and CA.

5. The extent to which a decision by a councillor to vote in accordance with the "party line" can fall foul of the rule against the fettering of discretion was considered in the following case. In *R. v Waltham Forest LBC Ex p. Baxter* [1988] Q.B. 419, members of the majority group on the council held a private, party meeting where they discussed what the policy of the group would be as to the setting of the rate at the forthcoming council meeting. After discussion, the group agreed to support a rate increase of 62 per cent for the domestic rate and 56.6 per cent for the non-domestic rate. The group's standing orders provided that members were required to refrain from voting in opposition to group decisions, the sanction being withdrawal of the party whip. A number of members who voted against this level of increase at the group meeting voted in favour at the council meeting, at which a resolution to increase the rate by the previously agreed amounts was passed by 31 votes to 26. A number of ratepayers sought judicial review on a variety of grounds. The Divisional Court rejected arguments to the effect (i) that the councillors had fettered their discretion by regarding themselves as bound by the terms of their election manifesto to undertake expenditure which rendered such a rate inevitable: (ii) that the resolution was "irrational" or "*Wednesbury* unreasonable"; (iii) that there was no genuine or adequate consultation with representatives of commerce and industry; and (iv) that six or seven councillors had voted contrary to their personal views. The Court of Appeal dismissed an appeal confined to issue (iv). The court held that had the councillors in question voted for the resolution not because they were in favour of it but because their discretion had been fettered by the vote at the group meeting, then the councillors would have been in breach of their duty to make up their own minds as to what rate was appropriate. However, that was not established on the facts. The councillors were entitled to take account of party loyalty and party policy as relevant considerations provided that this did not dominate so as to exclude other considerations. The court noted that the sanction was only withdrawal of the party whip: there was nothing to prevent a councillor who voted against the party line continuing as an independent member. Furthermore, these procedures were widely adopted by political groups throughout the country and had not been regarded by the Widdicombe Committee on the Conduct of Local Authority Business, Cmnd. 9797 (1986), as a matter for concern.

(B) Unauthorised Delegation of Power

This ground of challenge reflects a presumption of statutory interpretation known as the principle *delegatus non potest delegare*—the principle that where a function has been entrusted by statute to body "X", the function should be performed by "X" and not delegated by "X" for performance by body "Y". The theory is that the legislature has delegated power to "X" and that a delegate does not itself have power further to delegate such power.

It is convenient to consider this ground of challenge here. Body "X" may be said in these circumstances to have failed properly to exercise its discretion by having delegated its power of decision to another body. Alternatively, we could have considered this topic in the context of "want of jurisdiction" (see above, pp.420 *et seq.*). The purported exercise of power by the body to whom there has been an unlawful delegation is challengeable as an act beyond the powers of that body.

This principle, taken to an extreme, could operate as a severe restraint on administrative decision-making. The materials which follow demonstrate not only the operation of the principle, but also important legislative and case-law limits. Thus we shall note that:

(i)   the principle does not prevent the exercise by civil servants of powers entrusted by legislation to the ministerial head of a Department or entrusted to the Department itself—the *Carltona* principle, and that this principle may extend more broadly (below, pp.471–479);

(ii) Parliament may provide express authority to a body, on whom it has conferred powers, to delegate, and even for that delegate to subdelegate, those powers. The maxim delegatus non potest delegare is a presumption of interpretation which must give way to clear contrary legislative intention. Where a power of delegation does exist, the courts may still, of course, be called upon to consider whether the delegate has acted within or beyond the scope of the powers delegated. An important legislative provision of this kind, permitting wide powers of delegation in the context of the exercise of functions conferred on local authorities, is the Local Government Act 1972, s.101 (below, p.480);

(iii) The rule against delegation has been interpreted as requiring that the ultimate power of decision as to the whether and how a discretionary power is to be exercised should be retained by the designated statutory body. It does not preclude that body from delegating to another body some preliminary tasks leading up to that final decision. In so doing the appointed body is adopting a procedure by which it seeks assistance in reaching what can still be regarded as its own decision on the matter. Thus a body may delegate certain fact-finding tasks to, and even seek recommendations from, another body (or its own sub-committee). It must, however, retain to itself the power of final decision—it must not allow itself to be dictated to by the delegate, not can it confer power to make any binding decision (as distinct from non-binding recommendation) on the delegate. In truth this is no exception to the principle stated above—it is simply a situation where a court may hold that no delegation of the power of decision has in fact occurred. As we shall see the courts have been more tolerant of such decision-making arrangements in relation to the exercise of administrative functions than in relation to the exercise of judicial powers. See, generally, below, pp.466–471.

Note

On delegation, see generally J. Willis, "Delegatus Non Potest Delegare" (1943) 21 Can. Bar Rev. 257; *Allen*, pp.177–195; P.H. Thorp, (1972) 2 Auck.U.L.J. 85.

HUTH v CLARKE

(1890) 25 Q.B.D. 391; 59 L.J.Q.B. 559; 63 L.T. 348; 6 T.L.R. 373; 55 J.P. 86; [1886–1890] All E.R. REP. 542 (QUEEN'S BENCH DIVISION)

By Sch.6 to the Contagious Diseases (Animals) Act 1878 a county council had power to appoint an executive committee with all the council's powers under the Act. In turn, the executive committee could appoint a sub-committee and delegate all or any of the committee's powers to it. A delegation could be revoked or altered from time to time. In 1889, West Sussex County Council appointed an executive committee. On October 9, 1889, the executive committee appointed local sub-committees, and authorised them to exercise certain powers, including power under the Rabies Order 1887, to make regulations for the muzzling of dogs. No such regulations were in fact made by the local sub-committee, but on March 21, 1890, the executive committee made an order under the Rabies Order that no dog should be at large within the district of Chichester local sub-committee unless it was effectively muzzled or kept under proper control. The appellant was summoned for a breach of this order. He argued in his defence that the order was *ultra vires*, on the ground that it could only be made by the Chichester sub-committee. The justices stated a case for the opinion of the High Court.

LORD COLERIDGE C.J.: . . . [W]e . . . have a regulation in force in the district made by the proper authority and dealing with a subject-matter with which they were competent to deal. It is suggested, however, that, because there was another authority which might (had it chosen) have violated good sense by making an inconsistent order, the executive committee had no power to make the regulation in question. But delegation does not imply a denudation of power and authority; the 6th schedule of the Act provides that the delegation may be revoked or altered and the powers resumed by the executive committee. The word "delegation" implies that powers are committed to another person or body which are as a rule always subject to resumption by the power delegating, and many examples of this might be given. Unless, therefore, it is controlled by statute, the delegating power can at any time resume its authority. Here the executive committee has exercised the power which the sub-committee might have exercised—but did not—and no question of conflict of jurisdiction arises. I think, therefore, that the justices came to a perfectly right conclusion, and the conviction must be upheld.

WILLS J: I am of the same opinion. The case really turns on the meaning of the word "delegate," a word which has appeared on the statute-book for the last thirty years, occurring, as it does, at least as far back as 24 & 25 Vict. c. 133, sched., part 2(6). Delegation, as the word is generally used, does not imply a parting with powers by the person who grants the delegation, but points rather to the conferring of an authority to do things which otherwise that person would have to do himself. The best illustration of the use of the word is afforded by the maxim, Delegatus non potest delegare, as to the meaning of which it is significant that it is dealt with in Broom's Legal Maxims under the law of contracts: it is never used by legal writers, so far as I am aware, as implying that the delegating person parts with his power in such a manner as to denude himself of his rights. If it is correct to use the word in the way in which it is used in the maxim, as generally understood, the word "delegate" implies that the executive committee parted with their own authority is misconceived.

Notes

1. Is there any difference of substance between Lord Coleridge C.J. and Wills J., given that the former accepts that power may be "resumed" simply by exercising it, without any express revocation of the delegation to the committee? In holding that delegation does not mean parting with authority altogether, this case conflicts with

Blackpool Corporation v Locker [1948] 1 K.B. 349. It is suggested that *Huth v Clarke* is correct on this point (see *de Smith*, pp.361–363) and that *Black-pool Corporation v Locker* must be read in the light of its special facts. (See generally on this case *Allen*, pp.187 *et seq.*; C.K. Allen, *Law and Disorders*, p.87; "Squaring the Circular", 11 M.L.R. 338; 12 M.L.R. 37; 64 L.Q.R. 306; 66 L.Q.R. 14.) The approach in *Locker* was treated as binding by the Employment Appeal Tribunal in *DEFRA v Robertson* [2004] I.C.R. 1289, but the better view is that the observation in question (1) related to the powers to requisition property at issue in that case (or similar powers) and (2) were *obiter*. See further, S.H.Bailey, [2005] J.R. 84. The point was not considered on appeal in *Robertson*, [2005] I.C.R. 750.

2. A principal may at any time revoke authority which it has given to a delegate. The revocation of authority will, however, be of prospective effect only—it will not affect the validity of any acts already done under delegated authority: see *Battelley v Finsbury BC* (1958) 56 L.G.R. 165. Note also, that acts of an *unauthorised* body may be ratified or adopted by a body which *has* authority in the matter. This adoption will, however, be of prospective effect only—it does not give retrospective validity to the acts of the unauthorised body: see *Firth v Staines* [1897] 2 Q.B. 70; *Warwick RDC v Miller-Mead* [1962] Ch. 441; *Stoke-on-Trent City Council v B&Q Retail Ltd* [1984] Ch. 1, discussed in *Cross*, paras 4–75 to 4–84; *Webb v Ipswich BC* (1989) 21 H.L.R. 325; *R. v Rochester upon Medway City Council Ex p. Hobday* (1989) 58 P. & C.R. 424. And see D. Lanham, (1981) 5 Otago L.R. 35.

BARNARD v NATIONAL DOCK LABOUR BOARD

[1953] 2 Q.B. 18; [1953] 2 W.L.R. 995; 97 S.J. 331; [1953] 1 All E.R. 1113; [1953] 1 LLOYD'S REP. 371 (COURT OF APPEAL)

The Dock Workers (Regulation of Employment) Order 1947 set up a scheme to ensure greater regularity of employment for dock workers, and to secure an adequate number of dock workers available for the efficient performance of dock work. The National Dock Labour Board was established by the Order to administer the scheme. It was required by the Order to delegate to local boards all appropriate functions. These included the operation of a disciplinary code. Under cl.16, the local board could suspend for seven days a registered dock worker who failed to comply with any of the provisions of the scheme. One of the local boards, the London Dock Labour Board, passed a resolution which had the effect of leaving the power of suspension to the London port manager, Mr Hogger. As the result of a dispute, Mr Hogger suspended the plaintiffs. They exercised their rights of appeal to an appeal tribunal set up under the Order, which only had power to revise penalties imposed by the local board. Their appeals were dismissed. Further industrial action followed. Eventually the plaintiffs applied to the High Court for declarations that their suspensions had been wrongful in the light of the facts of the dispute. At the discovery of documents stage, the plaintiffs learned for the first time that they had been suspended, not by the local board, but by the port manager. They amended their pleadings and claimed a further declaration that the original notices of suspension were *ultra vires* and invalid. Counsel for the Board argued that the disciplining of dock workers was an administrative function, which could be delegated.

McNair J. held that the local board had power to delegate its disciplinary functions to the port manager.

The Court of Appeal reversed McNair J. on this point.

DENNING L.J.: . . . It was urged on us that the local board had power to delegate their functions to the port manager on the ground that the power of suspension was an administrative and not a judicial function. It was suggested that the action of the local board in suspending a man was similar in character to the action of an employer in dismissing him. I do not accept this view. Under the provisions of the scheme, so far from the board being in the position of an employer, the board are put in a judicial position between the men and the employers; they are to receive reports from the employers and investigate them; they have to inquire whether the man has been guilty of misconduct, such as failing to comply with a lawful order, or failing to comply with the provisions of the scheme; and if they find against him they can suspend him without pay, or can even dismiss him summarily. In those circumstances they are exercising a judicial function just as much as the tribunals which were considered by this court in the corn-porters' case, *Abbott v Sullivan* [1952] 1 K.B. 189 and in *Lee v Showmen's Guild of Great Britain* [1952] 2 Q.B. 329 the only difference being that those were domestic tribunals, and this is a statutory one. The board, by their procedure, recognize that before they suspend a man they must give him notice of the charge and an opportunity of making an explanation. That is entirely consonant with the view that they exercise a judicial function and not an administrative one, and we should, I think, so hold.

While an administrative function can often be delegated, a judicial function rarely can be. No judicial tribunal can delegate its functions unless it is enabled to do so expressly or by necessary implication. In *Local Government Board v Arlidge* [1915] A.C. 120 the power to delegate was given by necessary implication; but there is nothing in this scheme authorizing the board to delegate this function, and it cannot be implied. It was suggested that it would be impracticable for the board to sit as a board to decide all these cases; but I see nothing impracticable at all; they have only to fix their quorum at two members and arrange for two members, one from each side, employers and workers, to be responsible for a week at a time: probably each pair would only have to sit on one day during their week.

Next, it was suggested that even if the board could not delegate their functions, at any rate they could ratify the actions of the port manager; but if the board have no power to delegate their functions to the port manager, they can have no power to ratify what he has done. The effect of ratification is to make it equal to a prior command; but just as a prior command, in the shape of a delegation, would be useless, so also is a ratification. . . .

We have to consider here two decisions: first, the decision to suspend the men; second, the decision of the appeal tribunal. So far as the decision to suspend is concerned, as I see it, . . . we are asked to interfere with the position of a usurper. The port manager (if he will forgive my saying so) is a usurper, or, at any rate, is in the position of a usurper. I do not mean this unkindly, because I know that he acted in good faith on the authority of the board; nevertheless, he has assumed a mantle which was not his, but that of another. This is not a case of a tribunal which has a lawful jurisdiction and exercises it; it is a case of a man acting as a tribunal when he has no right to do so. These courts have always had jurisdiction to deal with such a case. . . . We can declare that the suspension ordered by the port manager was unlawful and void. We can declare it to be the nullity which in law it was.

So far as the decision of the appeal tribunal is concerned, it seems to me that, once the port manager's order is found to be a nullity it follows that the order of the appeal tribunal is also a nullity. The appeal tribunal has no original jurisdiction of its own; it cannot itself make a suspension order; it can only affirm or disaffirm a suspension order which has already been made. If none has been made because it is a nullity, the tribunal can do nothing. It cannot make something out of nothing any more than anybody else can: see *Toronto Railway Co. v Corporation of the City of Toronto* [1904] A.C. 809, 815. . . .

SINGLETON and ROMER L.JJ. delivered concurring judgments.

Notes

1. See case notes at 69 L.Q.R. 451; 16 M.L.R. 506.
2. As regards the issue of the power to delegate administrative, as distinct from judicial, functions compare the statements of Denning L.J. in *Barnard* with the decision of the House of Lords in *Vine v National Dock Labour Board* [1957] A.C. 488, where the facts were similar. The plaintiff, a registered dockworker, was dismissed by a disciplinary committee appointed by the South Coast Local Dock Labour Board. Ormerod J. awarded him £250 damages and granted a declaration that the purported dismissal was *ultra vires*. His judgment was upheld in the House of Lords. Their Lordships were agreed that delegation was not permissible in the circumstances—the matter was "too important to delegate" (Lord Kilmuir L.C. at 499), and "of a judicial character" (Lord Morton at 502). Lord Cohen (at 505) doubted "whether the mere fact that it was an administrative act would be conclusive of the matter", but did not explore the point as he was satisfied that the local board was acting "in a judicial capacity". Lord Somervell (at 512) said:

"In deciding whether a 'person' has power to delegate one has to consider the nature of the duty and the character of the person. Judicial authority normally cannot, of course, be delegated, though no one doubted in *Arlidge's* case that the Local Government Board, which consisted of the President, the Lord President of the Council, the Secretaries of State, the Lord Privy Seal and the Chancellor of the Ex-chequer (Local Government Board Act 1871), could act by officials duly deputed for the purpose, whether or not the act to be done had judicial ingredients. There are, on the other hand, many administrative duties which cannot be delegated. Appointment to an office or position is plainly an administrative act. If under a statute a duty to appoint is placed on the holder of an office, whether under the Crown or not, he would, normally, have no authority to delegate. He could take advice, of course, but he could not by a minute authorize someone else to make the appointment without further reference to him. I do not, therefore, find it necessary to consider what judicial requirements might be held implicit in the local board's proceedings under clause 16. I am, however, clear that the disciplinary powers, whether 'judicial' or not, cannot be delegated. The non-entitlement to pay, the suspension, the notice or the dismissal must be a step taken by the board and not by a delegate. The penalties, in some cases, may be slight but, in some cases, very great. A man who has worked all his life in the docks may find himself precluded altogether from doing so. Today it may be easy for him to get other work, but that has not always been so. The constitution of the board also supports the conclusion. It is clearly constituted so as to inspire confidence and weigh fairly the interests of employers and employed. The purported delegation in the present case was to a representative of each side, but it is impossible to imply a limited right of delegation. *Osgood v Nelson* (1872) L.R. 5 H.L. 636 [below, p.469] decides that in somewhat similar circumstances the appointment of a committee to take evidence and report is not in itself a delegation of authority. If there are administrative difficulties, this may be an answer to them".

See note by E.C.S. Wade, [1957] C.L.J. 6.
3. Denning L.J. held that the board's decision could not retrospectively validate the decision of the unauthorised port manager. Compare the approach of the courts to the "curative" effect of appeal proceedings where the decision appealed from is tainted by failure to have complied with the principles of natural justice. See below, p.740.

4. In *Osgood v Nelson* (1872) L.R. 5 H.L. 636, the House of Lords held that there was no delegation where the Common Council of the City of London referred allegations against the plaintiff, an officer, of neglect in the performance of his duties to their "Officers and Clerks' Committee". The plaintiff appeared before the Committee, had access to relevant documents, and was permitted to adduce evidence and cross-examine witnesses. The Committee reported that in their opinion irregularities had occurred such as seriously interfered with the proper conduct of public business. The matter was then considered by the full council, at a meeting at which the plaintiff was present, represented by counsel. The Council had before it the committee's report and a transcript of the notes of evidence. Its decision to dismiss the plaintiff was held to be lawful. Fairness did not required there to be a completely new trial before the Council.

Compare *Jeffs v New Zealand Dairy Production and Marketing Board* [1967] 1 A.C. 551, where the Board had power to define zones from which particular factories could get cream and milk. The Board set up a committee of three of its members to investigate the question of supply to two factory-owning dairy companies. The committee, acting on its own initiative, held a public hearing at which farmers and other interested parties gave evidence and made oral and written submissions. The farmers opposed zoning. The committee made a written report, and recommended certain zonings, which were accepted by the Board without alteration. The report did not record, even in a summary form, the evidence given at the hearing, but did state the submissions that had been made. The Board conceded that it was under a duty to act judicially in determining zoning questions affecting the rights of individuals. The Privy Council held that the Board acted in breach of natural justice in failing to hear the interested parties, but that they would have complied with natural justice had the evidence and submissions been fully summarised. The appointment of a person or persons to hear evidence and submissions was appropriate where the credibility of witnesses was not involved. See K.J. Keith (1968) 31 M.L.R. 87.

Similarly, in *R. v Derbyshire Police Authority Ex p. Wilson*, *The Times*, August 8, 1989, the Court of Appeal quashed the authority's decision to refuse to exercise their power indemnifying two police officers for their legal costs of appearing before the district auditor; the authority had delegated the power to hear submissions and report to a panel of five members, but then acted on the bare recommendation in the panel's report where the report did not summarise the applicants' submissions.

2. In *R. v Race Relations Board Ex p. Selvarajan* [1975] 1 W.L.R. 1686, CA, S's complaint of unlawful discrimination was investigated by a conciliation committee appointed under s.15(2)(a) of the Race Relations Act 1968, and then reinvestigated by the Board under s.15(5). The Board had power under s. 14(4) to act by a group of members selected by the chairman, and the reinvestigation was undertaken by the Board's employment committee of seven. Each committee member was given a copy of the conciliation committee's report of over 100 pages and some other notes. Further information was collected by one of the Board's conciliation officers. When the employment committee met to consider the matter only three of the members had seen the full papers. The other four only had the officer's summary of the results of her inquiries. The committee decided that there had been no unlawful discrimination. Lord Denning M.R. inferred that the four "were not in a position to form an opinion of their own. They must have gone by the opinion of the other three. . . . If this had been a judicial body, I do not think this would be right. Every member of a judicial body must have access to all the evidence and papers in the case, he must have heard all the arguments, and he must come to his own conclusion. The maxim *delegatus non potest delegare* applies strictly to judicial functions. But it is different with a body which is exercising administrative functions or which is making an investigation or conducting preliminary inquiries, especially when it is a numerous body" ([1975] 1 W.L.R. 1686 at 1695). Lord Denning distinguished *Jeffs v New Zealand Dairy Board* on the ground that the Dairy Board, unlike the Race Relations Board, had no power to delegate its functions.

For contrasting decisions applying these principles see *R. v Hertsmere BC Ex p. Woolgar* (1995) 160 L.G.R. 261 and *R. v West Dorset DC Ex p. Gerrard* (1994) 27 H.L.R. 150.

3. For modern illustrations of judicial reticence as regards the delegation of judicial functions see, for example, *R. v Gateshead Justices Ex p. Tesco Stores Ltd* [1981] Q.B. 470 (held to be an unlawful delegation of a judicial function for magistrates to have delegated to their clerks certain decision-making functions in respect of the issuance of summonses; *R. v D.P.P. Ex p. First Division Association* [1988] NLJLR 158, *The Times*, May 24, 1988 (successful challenge to policy under which the initial screening of prosecutions had been delegated by the DPP not to legally qualified Crown Prosecutors, as expressly permitted by the legislation, but to non-legally qualified civil servants. The decisions delegated involved evaluation of evidence and the exercise of judgment as to whether the public interest required a prosecution to take place); *R. v Manchester Stipendiary Magistrate Ex p. Hill* [1983] 1 A.C. 328.

For decisions that confirm that recognition of a strict approach as regards judicial-type functions does not mean that the courts will not also apply the principle in relation to the exercise of administrative functions, see *Allingham v Minister of Agriculture and Fisheries* [1948] 1 All E.R. 780; *R. v Liverpool City Council Ex p. Professional Association of Teachers* (1984) 82 L.G.R. 648.

4. In *Mills v London CC* [1925] 1 K.B. 213, the LCC had granted a licence to Mills, a cinema proprietor, subject to the following condition:

"That no film . . . which has not been passed for universal exhibition by the British Board of Film Censors shall be exhibited in the premises without the express consent of the Council during the time that any child under . . . the age of 16 is therein".

Mills contended that the condition was *ultra vires* because it involved delegation by the Council of that body's functions under the Cinematograph Act 1909 to another body, the BBFC. The Divisional Court upheld the condition. Lord Hewart C.J. said (at 220–221):

"It is said, first of all, that this condition is bad, because it means that the London County Council have delegated, or transferred, to the British Board of Film Censors no small part of the duties of the London County Council under the Act, and reference is made to *Ellis v Dubowski* [1921] 3 K.B. 621. In that case the condition which was attached to the licence was in these terms: 'That no film be shewn . . . which has not been certified for public exhibition by the British Board of Film Cen-sors.' It was held with some doubt that that condition was unreasonable and *ultra vires*. . . . But one thing was made very plain by that Court, both in the course of the argument and also in the judgment, that different considerations would have applied if the condition had been so framed as to make the certificate or the decision of the British Board of Film Censors not final, but subject to review. . . . In the present case that mischief is avoided. This condition with which we are now concerned provides an exception where the express consent of the Council is given. In other words, there is an appeal in the matter from the decision of the British Board of Film Censors to the Council itself. In my opinion, therefore, the first objection fails. . . .".

In *R. v Greater London Council Ex p. Blackburn* [1976] 1 W.L.R. 550, the Court of Appeal unanimously upheld the decision in *Mills*. Lord Denning M.R. explained (at 554–555):

"I do not think the county councils can delegate the whole of their responsibilities to the board . . .; but they can treat the board as an advisory body whose views they can accept or reject, provided that the final decision—aye or nay—rests with the county council. If the exhibitor—or any member of the public—brings the film up before the county council, they ought themselves to review the decision of the British

Board of Film Censors and exercise their own judgment on it. That is, I think, the right way to interpret *Mills v London County Council*. When the board issues a certificate permitting the exhibition of a film—and the county council take no objection to it—that is equivalent to a permission by the county council themselves. When the board refuses a certificate, the exhibitor can appeal to the county council. The county council can then give their consent to the exhibition, and from their decision there is no appeal.

The upshot of it all is this. The county council are in law the body which has the power to censor films for exhibition in cinemas, but in practice it is the board which carries out the censorship, subject to review by the county council".

5. In *R. v Chester BC Ex p. Quietlynn Ltd* (1985) 83 L.G.R. 308, the Court of Appeal considered the practice of the local authority in handling applications for licences to operate sex shops, under the Local Government (Miscellaneous Provisions) Act 1982. The local authority had delegated its power to grant or refuse such licences to its Environmental Services Committee. There was clear statutory authority for this delegation (Local Government Act 1972, s.101, below, p.480). That committee set up a licensing panel to consider applications and to make recommendations to the committee. The panel consisted of five of the members of the committee. The panel held a hearing at which the applicants appeared, and then made a recommendation to the Environmental Services Committee that the application be refused. Refusal was on grounds relating to the character of the locality, the uses to which premises in the vicinity were being put, and that it considered that the appropriate number of sex establishments in the area should be nil. This recommendation was put before a meeting of the committee, at which 13 members (including the five panel members) were present. At this meeting some detailed discussion first took place in connection with another application, that application eventually being granted. When the applicants' application came up for consideration there was no report made and no discussion—simply a vote taken, which refused the application. The applicants argued that there had been a failure to comply with the statutory obligation, under the 1982 Act, that the committee or sub-committee should afford a hearing to an applicant before refusing a licence; and that this obligation had not, in the circumstances, been satisfied by the hearing before the panel. The local authority argued that as the members of the panel had been present at the committee meeting and therefore were available to have given any information about the hearing had any such information been requested by the other members; and because the panel decision, based on "character of locality", was based on information within the knowledge of all the members, it was not necessary for there to have been anything by way of full report to the committee. The Court of Appeal upheld the applicants' contentions. Stephen Brown L.J. noted (at 316) that

> "no report of any kind was made to the decision-making committee. It may be that a report could have been a very short report indeed, but . . . it is a requisite of the [legislation] that the applicants' representations should be considered by the committee making the decision".

The decision of the authority was therefore quashed.

R. (ON THE APPLICATION OF CHIEF CONSTABLE OF THE WEST MIDLANDS) v BIRMINGHAM JUSTICES

[2002] EWHC (ADMIN 1087); Westlaw Transcript 2002 WL 820118 (DIVISIONAL COURT)

Section 1 of the Crime and Disorder Act 1998 enables a chief officer of police after consulting the local authority for the area to apply to a magistrates' court for an

Anti-social Behaviour Order prohibiting the defendant from doing anything described in the order. The Chief Constable of the West Midlands issued an internal memorandum authorising "all OCU [Operational Command Unit] Commanders, their Operation and Crime Managers, Operational Departmental Heads and their Deputies to apply for "ASBOs" and to exercise all ancillary powers in connection with those applications until such authority is terminated by me". In the present case, an application was made by Superintendent Ellis; such consultation as had occurred was done by Sergeant Higgins. The District Judge held that the person consulting must at the very least be a person no lower than the rank of superintendent and held that the proceedings were null and void. The Divisional Court (Sedley L.J. and Poole J.) allowed a claim for judicial review by the Chief Constable.

SEDLEY L.J.: . . .

7. I therefore turn the issue of delegation. Although the Chief Constable's power to delegate his functions under section 1 off the Crime and Disorder Act 1998 is not contested it is important to see why he has this power, for to do so sheds light on the extent of the power.

8. The reason why a power of delegation may be spelt out of legislation conferring functions on a public official in virtue of his or her office were classically described by Lord Greene MR in *Carltona Ltd v Commissioners of Works* [1943] 2 All ER 560. A power to requisition property was given by the Defence Regulations to any "competent authority", an expression which included the Commissioners of Works. By statue, the post of First Commissioner of Works was held by the Minister of Works. The Minister's power had been exercised in the case before the court by an assistant secretary. Lord Greene considered that there was no substance in the argument that the decision was therefore not, as in law it had to be, the decision of The First Commissioner.

"In the administration of government in this country the functions which are given to misters . . . are functions so multifarious that no minister could ever attend to them. To take the example of the present case no doubt there have been thousands of requisitions in this country by individual ministries. It cannot be supposed that this regulation meant that, in each case, the minister in person should direct his mind to the matter. The duties imposed on ministers and the powers given to ministers are normally exercised under the authority of the ministers by responsible officials of the department. Public business could not be carried on if that were not the case. Constitutionally, a decision of such an official is, of course, the decision of the minister. The minister is responsible. It is he who must answer before Parliament for anything that his officials have done under his authority, and, if for an important matter he selected an official of such junior standing that he could not be expected competently to perform the work, the minister would have to answer to Parliament."

9. Although the *Carltona* case is frequently cited as a source of the "alter ego" doctrine, it can be seen that Lord Greene's reasoning is not predicated on this. It is predicated on the proposition that the departmental head is responsible for things done under his authority. The relevance of the "alter ego" doctrine is that Crown servants were at that time taken in law to hold their positions by grace and not by contract, so that the minister was first among equals, not an employer with servants or a principal with agents. His implied power to delegate functions depended, therefore, on two things: the conferment of a power in

terms which implicitly permitted their delegation and the existence of persons to whom he could delegate them without parting with ultimate responsibility.

10. A Chief Constable similarly is not the employer of the officers under his or her command but is legally answerable for them. The *Carltona* principle appears to apply readily in such a situation, with two well-established qualifications. One is that some functions are such that they cannot, consistently with the statutory purpose, be delegated at all: see *R v. Chief Constable of Greater Manchester, Lainton* (C.A. 28 March 2000, unreported), paragraph 28. The other is that delegation has to be to somebody suitable. As *Carltona* demonstrates, who is suitable is primarily for the office-holder to decide. Today, however, it is clear that an improper delegation will be a matter for the courts, at least where the discharge of a statutory office is in issue.

11. Mr Beer, for the Chief Constable, has been hesitant to rely squarely on *Carltona* because of the decision of this court in *Nelms v Roe* [1970] 1 WLR 4. Here the information against a driver had been signed on behalf of the Metropolitan Police Commissioner, in whom the statutory power vested, by a police inspector on the authority of his superintendent. There had been no express delegation of power to either. The Divisional Court held that there was an implied delegation and sub-delegation of authority, preferring this route to the *Carltona* route which had also been argued. Lord Parker CJ said:

> "in the present case Mr Farquharson urged that exactly the same principles ought to be applied to the Commissioner of Metropolitan Police as apply in the case of Ministers. It has always been a principle in this country that, a Minister being responsible to Parliament for the acts of officers of his department and having to act through others, an act done by the proper officer of his department is the act of the Minister; the proper responsible officials are the alter ago of the minister. And accordingly no question of delegation arises. That principle is very well known; the case which is always quoted in connection with that is *Carltona v Works Commissioners* [1943] 2 All ER 560. . . .
>
> I feel grave difficulties in extending that well-known principle to a case such as this, to the Commissioner or the Metropolitan Police. It is not, I think sufficient to say that it is a principle which it applicable when ever it is difficult or impractical for a person to act for himself, in other words when ever he has to act through others the principle applies. I see grave difficulties in going that far, and, as it seems to me, superintendent Williams was, by reason of his position, not the alter ego of the Commissioner but merely had implied delegated authority, by reason of his position, from the Commissioner."

Lord Parker went on to deal with and to reject the consequent argument, that the further delegation from superintendent to inspector was contrary to legal principle, holding that the commissioner had impliedly delegated not only the power but a power to delegate it.

12. With all possible respect, I do not consider that we are required to adopt this reasoning. As has been seen, the *Carltona* principle, which binds this court, does not depend upon on the peculiar status of civil servants as the alter ego of their minister. It is sufficiently ample to a Chief Constable to discharge functions of the kind we are concerned with through an officer for whom he or she is answerable. To fall back instead on implied delegation and sub-delegation is capable of appearing to be a ratification by the court of an accomplished fact and to beg the question of power to delegate.

13. There are other functions imposed upon individuals in virtue of their office which may not be delegable at all: for example the function of a health and safety inspector under section 38 of the Health and Safety at Work Act 1974. In *R(WH Smith Ltd) v Croydon Justices* DC, 6 November 2000, unreported, Elias J said at paragraph 15:

"...where the power to take certain steps is given to an officer appointed pursuant to statute then it is only going to be in a very exceptional case that the courts will imply a power to delegate in the absence of any express provision."

He cited in support, as other courts have done, this passage from De Smith, Woolf and Jowell, *Judicial Review of Administrative Action* (5th edition)p.66:

"Where the exercise of a discretionary power is entrusted to a named officer—e.g. a chief officer of police, a medical officer of health or an inspector—another officer cannot exercise his powers in his stead unless express statutory provision has been made for the appointment of a deputy or unless in the circumstances the administrative convenience of allowing a deputy or other subordinate to act as an authorised agent very clearly outweighs the desirability of maintaining the principle that the officer designated by statue should act personally."

The *Carltona* decision is not cited in this section of the work. It is separately treated (at page 369 ff) in an exposition of the alter ego principle.

14. For my part I can see good reason to differentiate, where Parliament has conferred powers on the holder of a named office, between those officers which are the apex of an organisation itself composed of office-holders or otherwise hierarchically structured, and those offices designated by Parliament because of the personal qualifications of the individual holder. Thus, of the three examples given by De Smith, Woolf and Jowell, one can readily infer that when Parliament confers functions on a chief officer of police, all but the most important are likely to be delegable; whereas the likelihood is that powers conferred on a medical officer of health or on a statutory inspector, each professionally qualified as an individual, are to be exercised by the office-holder alone. This, with respect, seems to me a better legal test than overriding administrative convenience, although it may produce similar outcomes.

15. Such being the basis on which the Chief Constable is able lawfully to delegate, is his exercise of the power constricted to the extent held by District Judge Cadbury? He concluded:

"Having considered the principle of delegation and the practicalities involved I am firmly of the view that the Commander of the particular OCU where the anti-social behaviour order is sought is the proper and appropriate agent for the Chief Constable in relation to section 1 Crime and Disorder Act, or his operations and crime managers, or operational department head of at least the rank of superintendent."

To this Mr Howat is prepared, in deference to the inclusion of "deputies" in the memorandum, to add officers acting up in the rank of superintendent, but no more.

16. No doubt an officer of the rank or status described in the memorandum is a proper and appropriate agent; but to hold that such an officer is the proper and appropriate agent is not to interpret but to legislate. The question for a court is not how it considers that the Chief Constable should be exercising his power of delegation; it is whether the Chief Constable has exercised it within permissible limits. For my part I can see nothing in the legislation which enables the court to set a limit of such specificity as that set by the District Judge. Mr Howat is of course right when he points out that both consulting about ASBOs and deciding whether to apply for them, when they may be directed at any person from the age of 10 upwards, is a problematical and sensitive task. But it is for the Chief Constable to decide who is best suited to do it on his behalf; and it is not for the court to second-guess him unless his choice is irrational or otherwise beyond his powers.

17. The District Judge went on to hold:

"By reference to the principles of delegation, the practicalities involved (including the number of anti-social behaviour order applications) and the clear wording of section 1 Crime and Disorder Act, 1 conclude that it must be a person of the same rank who carries out the duties under section 1(2) as section 1(1) and it must be the commander of the OCU or at the very least a person no lower than the rank of superintendent."

The last part of this holding follows from the District Judge's previous conclusion. Its nub, however, is that the functions of consultation and application must be carried out at the same level of the police hierarchy.

18. Here too, I regret that I can see no foundation for such a decision. It is not and could not be contended that the same individual must do both things; and there are many reasons—resources, availability, skills, contacts, experience, knowledge and so forth—which may result in the choice of one officer rather than another for one of the statutory tasks. Once it is clear that the chief constable is not constrained as to the rank to which he may delegate either task, there is no logical reason why they cannot be properly carried out at different levels.

19. . . . .[I]t was therefore open to the Chief Constable to delegate or devolve to any officer or officers judged suitable by him the respective functions set out in subsections (1) and (2). . . .

[His Lordship noted that it might be open to the defendant to argue that, if no consultation had taken place or it had been conducted by someone who lacked due authority on behalf of the Chief Constable, the resulting process would still be challengeable. However, it was not clear on the evidence whether Sergeant Higgins had been authorised to consult on behalf of the Chief Constable.]

[Poole J. agreed.]

Decision quashed

Notes

1. In *Local Government Board v Arlidge* [1915] A.C. 120, Arlidge sought certiorari to quash an order made by the Board. The Board's order had rejected A's appeal against his local authority's decision not to terminate a closure order it had made in respect of his house, which it considered to be unfit for human habitation. One of the grounds on which certiorari was sought was that neither the Board, nor anyone lawfully

authorised to act for them, had in fact determined the appeal. The matter had been investigated by one of the Board's housing inspectors, who had held an inquiry at which A had been represented. The inspector had submitted his report to the Board, together with a shorthand note of the speeches. The order of the Board did not indicate which officer of the Board had taken the final decision on the matter. In the House of Lords, Viscount Haldane L.C. said (at 133):

> "The Minister at the head of the Board is directly responsible to Parliament like other Ministers. He is responsible not only for what he himself does but for all that is done in his department. The volume of work entrusted to him is very great and he cannot do the great bulk of it himself. He is expected to obtain his materials vicariously through his officials, and he has discharged his duty if he sees that they obtain these materials for him properly. To try to extend his duty beyond this and to insist that he and other members of the Board should do everything personally would be to impair his efficiency. Unlike a judge in a court he is not only at liberty but is compelled to rely on the assistance of his staff. When, therefore, the Board is directed to dispose of an appeal that does not mean that any particular official of the Board is to dispose of it".

Lord Shaw of Dunfermline said (at 136):

> ". . . My Lords, how can the judiciary be blind to the well-known facts applicable not only to the constitution but to the working of such branches of the Executive? The department is represented in Parliament by its responsible head. On the one hand he manages its affairs with such assistance as the Treasury sanctions, and on the other he becomes answerable in Parliament for every departmental act. His Board—that is, all the members of it together—may never meet, or they may only be convened on some question of policy; but a determination, signed and sealed and issued in correct form, stands as the deliverance of the Board as such, for which determination the President becomes answerable to Parliament. This is the general rule, acknowledged and familiar, of departmental action and responsibility. . . .".

2. The *Arlidge* and *Carltona* cases were each decided in wartime. They illustrate a degree of judicial self-restraint which is, perhaps, not surprising in such circumstances. Compare *Liversidge v Sir John Anderson* [1942] A.C. 206, and below, p.536, note 8. The English courts have not, however, in the years since the decision in *Carltona* seemed anxious to impose limits to the scope of that decision.

Thus, in *R. v Skinner* [1968] 2 Q.B. 700, the Court of Appeal held that approval of the "Alcotest" breath-testing device by the Home Secretary required by s.7(1) of the Road Safety Act 1967 (which was a necessary precondition to a conviction for an offence under the breathalyser legislation), could be expressed by an assistant secretary in the police department of the Home Office, acting in the name of the Home Secretary. The court applied the *Carltona* case, and dicta in *Lewisham BC v Roberts* [1949] 2 K.B. 608. The personal approval of the Home Secretary was not necessary even though this was an isolated matter unlike the thousands of requisitioning cases that arose during the war which no Minister could have considered personally. Widgery L.J. emphasised (at 707) that: "It is not strictly a matter of delegation; it is that the official acts as the Minister himself and the official's decision is the Minister's decision".

Then, in *Golden Chemical Products Ltd, Re* [1976] Ch. 300, Brightman J. considered the exercise of powers contained in s.35 of the Companies Act 1967. This section empowered the Secretary of State to present a petition to the High Court for the winding-up of a company where "it appears [to the Secretary of State] . . . that it is expedient in the public interest that the body be wound up. . .". His Lordship held that the functions of the Secretary of State under s.35 need not be exercised by the Secretary of State personally. His Lordship rejected the argument of counsel for the company, that unless a statute conferring a power on a minister to do an act if it appears to him expedient provided otherwise, the initial decision-making process could be performed by someone other than the minister only if it led to no serious invasion of the freedom or property rights of the subject. This argument ran counter to the *Carltona*, *Lewisham* and *Skinner* cases, and would result in a distinction which would be "impossibly vague" (*per* Brightman J. at 310). His Lordship accepted that the relationship between the Minister and his official was not one of delegation.

By way of contrast, a willingness by the courts to review the exercise by a Minister of his *Carltona* power to devolve decision-making was indicated by the courts in *R. v Secretary of State for the Home Department Ex p. Oladehinde* [1991] 1 A.C. 254. This concerned the lawfulness of a practice by which the Home Secretary had "delegated" to immigration inspectors (officials in the civil service equivalent in grade to senior executive officers, and who have considerable experience in immigration matters) his powers under the Immigration Act 1971 to authorise service of notices of intention to deport persons from the United Kingdom. The inspectors reached their decisions in the light of reports compiled by immigration officers. Following the service of such notices a right of appeal in certain cases might lie to an independent immigration adjudicator or to the Immigration Appeal Tribunal. However, such appeals, by "overstayers" served with notices of intention to deport, were severely restricted by the Immigration Act 1988. Following an unsuccessful appeal, or in the absence of an appeal, the deportation department at the Home Office reviewed each case before a final decision as to the making of a deportation order was made by the Secretary of State, acting on the advice of his department and his Minister of State.

In the Divisional Court ([1991] 1 A.C. 254 at 258) certiorari was granted to quash decisions of immigration inspectors. Woolf L.J. referred to the *Carltona* principle and stated that the principle should be "regarded as an implication which is read into a statute in the absence of any clear contrary indication by Parliament that the implication is not to apply" (at 264–265). Such implications might be express (see, *e.g.* 1971 Act, ss.13(5), 14(3), and 15(3) and (4)—requiring certain decisions to be taken by the Secretary of State personally) or implied. In determining whether the principle was impliedly excluded, a number of matters were of relevance. Woolf L.J. noted that the scheme of the legislation was, somewhat unusually, to divide responsibilities and to assign specific functions to the Secretary of State and to particular categories of official. In such circumstances an implication was appropriate that the Secretary of State could not, under the *Carltona* principle, devolve to those officials the powers which had been conferred on himself. In addition to the "structure" of the legislative allocation of power, Woolf L.J. paid regard to the nature of the power devolved, noting the serious consequences for the individuals affected which might follow from the making of a deportation order. Pill J. analysed the *Carltona* principle in similar terms and agreed that "Parliament did not intend the relevant powers given to the Secretary of State with respect to deportation to be exercised on his behalf by members of the immigration service" (at 270).

In the Court of Appeal ([1991] 1 A.C. at 278), Lord Donaldson M.R., giving the judgment of the court, stated (at 282) that the *Carltona* power to devolve decision-making was a "common law constitutional power, but one which is capable of being negatived or confined by . . . clearly necessary implication". In this connection his Lordship said that such challenge would normally be on the basis that the decision to devolve was *Wednesbury* unreasonable, *i.e.* not an arrangement for the exercise of the function which any reasonable minister could have chosen to adopt. The Court of Appeal differed, however, from the Divisional Court in its view as to whether in this case these limitations to the *Carltona* power to devolve applied. It stressed that in its view:

"there are clear advantages and no unfairness in the (provisional) decision to deport, which does not of itself affect the status of the immigrant . . ., being taken by civil servants who are readily available and have considerable experience and expertise in immigration matters".

The House of Lords affirmed the decision of the Court of Appeal. On the issue of the ambit of the *Carltona* principle, Lord Griffiths noted that the 1971 Act contained three explicit limitations on the Secretary of State's power to devolve—see sections referred to above. In these circumstances a court should be "very slow to read into the statute a further implicit limitation". His Lordship continued (at 303):

> "The immigration service is comprised of Home Office civil servants for whom the Home Secretary is responsible and I can see no reason why he should not authorise members of that service to take decisions under the Carltona principle *providing they do not conflict with or embarrass them in the discharge of their specific statutory duties under the Act and that the decisions are suitable to their grading and experience*" (emphasis added).

By way of example of a situation which would fall within the conflict/embarrassment limitation Lord Griffiths said (at 303): "it would not be right to authorise an inspector to take a decision . . . in any case in which he had been engaged as an immigration officer, for to do so would be too much like asking a prosecutor to be judge in the same cause". Lords Keith, Templeman, Brandon and Ackner concurred with Lord Griffiths.

3. The *Carltona* principle remains applicable to the relationship between the responsible minister and an officer of an Executive Agency of the department, here the Benefits Agency of the DSS (*R. v Secretary of State for Social Security Ex p. Sherwin* (1996) 32 B.M.L.R. 1, QBD; leave to appeal refused by the CA, July 22, 1996. Note Craig's argument (*Craig*, pp.527–528) that the arrangements for executive agencies which provide for operational autonomy lead to "difficulties in accepting that a decision taken by an official in such a case as this can really be regarded as a decision taken on behalf of the Secretary of State". Given that the minister will remain legally and politically accountable, how great is the problem here? The position may vary according to the agency in question, given the variations in the ways they are set up (see Sedley L.J. in *R. (on the application of National Association of Health Stores) v Secretary of State for Health* [2005] EWCA Civ 154, at [40] and [41]).

4. The *West Midlands* case opens the way for a much broader application of *Carltona* than originally assumed. Given the emphasis in *Arlidge* and *Carltona* on the accountability of a minister to Parliament, is it necessarily appropriate to apply *Carltona* outside that context? Note the criticisms expressed by *Wade and Forsyth*, p.322. There still seems, however, to be a difference between the position of ministers and civil servants, where "the authority of officials derives from a general rule of law and not any particular act of delegation" (*Wade and Forsyth*, p.320; a proposition not controverted by *West Midlands*), and other areas, where actual authority must be established (as in the case of Sergeant Higgins). That there need be no evidence of a decision by the Secretary of State to delegate his power to his officers is confirmed by the Court of Appeal in *Odishu v Secretary of State for the Home Department* [1994] Imm. A.R. 475.

5. The *Carltona* principle is not recognised as applicable to the workings of foreign governments: see *Barry v Government of Portugal*, unreported, March 28, 2000, DC, where a request for extradition to Portugal was required by s.26(1) of the Extradition Act 1989 to be made by a "Minister of State" and the court held that a request made by the Attorney-General, who was not a Minister of State in Portugal, was insufficient, notwithstanding that powers had been delegated to him.

6. Issues may arise as to the application of the *Carltona* principle to the provision of information to and disclosure of information by a government department.

First, it is clear that where there is an obligation to disclose a fact to a government department, this will be interpreted as requiring disclosure to the officers who were the relevant decision-maker, and not just to any officer of the department (or any officer of the Crown). In *Hinchy v Secretary of State for Work and Pensions* [2003] EWCA Civ 138, the Court of Appeal held that there was no failure by H to disclose a material fact where the DWP's Disability Living Allowance Office was aware that she was no longer entitled to DLA but failed to notify the DWP's Income Support Office, given that it was reasonable to believe that that information would reach the relevant decision-makers. A further point was that, in any event, "the Secretary of State cannot disclaim knowledge of his own decisions" (*per* Carnwath L.J., with whom Henry L.J. agreed). However, this was reversed by the House of Lords (Lord Scott of Foscote dissenting) as H had been expressly instructed to disclose to the local social security office. Carnwath L.J.'s proposition was rejected as an application of "theoretical constitutional principles" that had consistently been rejected by the Social Security Commissioners, whose expert views designed to give effect to the legislative scheme for overpayments were entitled to great respect (see Lord Hoffman at [28]–[30]).

Where the question is whether information required to be taken into account by a minister taking a decision personally as a relevant consideration has so been taken into account, it is not sufficient that it is available to officials involved in advising him but has not been shown to have been considered personally (*R. (on the application of National Association of Health Stores) v Secretary of State for Health* [2005] EWCA Civ 154). The proposition that "ministers need know nothing before reaching a decision so long as those advising them know the facts" would be "the law according to Sir Humphrey Appleby" (per Sedley L.J. at [37]). It had previously been held that *Carltona* imputes to a minister knowledge only of those employees with a responsibility for the receipt, consideration and transmission to a minister of that information and not merely postroom staff (*Best v Secretary of State for the Environment* [1997] E.G.C.S. 39).

Secondly, it is a corollary of the *Carltona* principle that, while it is expected that affidavit evidence will be given to explain a departmental decision challenged in the courts, a minister is not generally obliged to disclose separately the contents of internal advice (as distinct from external advice) on which he relies, unless there is some new point on which the parties have had no opportunity to make representations (*R. v Secretary of State for Education Ex p. S* [1995] E.L.R. 71; *R. (on the application of Burgess) v Secretary of State for the Home Department*, unreported, November 3, 2000. See further *Bushell v Secretary of State for the Environment*, below, p.73. Furthermore, a departmental official may give affidavit evidence explaining a departmental decision even where it has been taken or approved ultimately by the minister personally; there is no need for an affidavit from the minister. The minister's decision would be reached in her capacity as head of department and the official would be entitled to give evidence about the formation of the department's decision since it represented the state of mind of those, including the Secretary of State, by whose authority he gave the decision. The position would be different if there was any question of the minister having been activated by private motives of her own, but that was not alleged. *R. v Secretary of State for Health Ex p. Hackney LBC*, unreported, April 22, 1994.

7. Express provision is made by Pt II of the Deregulation and Contracting Out Act 1994 (ss.69–79) for the contracting-out of functions. This applies by virtue of s.69 to any function of a minister or office-holder conferred by or under any enactment, and which, by virtue of any enactment or rule of law (which would include *Carltona*) may be exercised by an officer of his, and not excluded by s.71. Provisions can be made ministerial order for such a function to be exercised by, or by employees of, a person authorised by the office-holder or minister whose function it is. Similar rules apply in respect of local authority functions (s.70). With some exceptions, anything done or omitted to be done by the authorised person is treated as done or omitted to be done by or in relation to the minister, office-holder or local authority (s.72). The transfer of statutory powers to private persons or bodies has been significant and dubious development (see *Craig*, pp.528-530; M. Freedland, [1996] P.L. 21). Relatively limited use of the powers have been made.

8. See generally on the *Carltona* principle, D. Lanham, "Delegation and the *Alter Ego* Principle" (1984) 100 L.Q.R. 587, and M. Freedland, [1996] P. L. 1.6.

LOCAL GOVERNMENT ACT 1972

PART VI

DISCHARGE OF FUNCTIONS

Arrangements for discharge of functions by local authorities

101.—(1) Subject to any express provision contained in this Act or any Act passed after this Act, a local authority may arrange for the discharge of any of their functions—

(a) by a committee, a sub-committee or an officer of the authority; or
(b) by any other local authority. . . .

(2) Where by virtue of this section any functions of a local authority may be discharged by a committee of theirs, then, unless the local authority otherwise direct, the committee may arrange for the discharge of any of those functions by a sub-committee or an officer of the authority and where by virtue of this section any functions of a local authority may be discharged by a sub-committee of the authority, then, unless the local authority or the committee otherwise direct, the sub-committee may arrange for the discharge of any of those functions by an officer of the authority.

(3) Where arrangements are in force under this section for the discharge of any functions of a local authority by another local authority, then, subject to the terms of the arrangements, that other authority may arrange for the discharge of those functions by a committee, sub-committee or officer of theirs and subsection (2) above shall apply in relation to those functions as it applies in relation to the functions of that other authority.

(4) Any arrangements made by a local authority or committee under this section for the discharge of any functions by a committee, sub-committee, officer or local authority shall not prevent the authority or committee by whom the arrangements are made from exercising those functions.

(5) Two or more local authorities may discharge any of their functions jointly and, where arrangements are in force for them to do so,—

(a) they may also arrange for the discharge of those functions by a joint committee of theirs or by an officer of one of them and subsection (2) above shall apply in relation to those functions as it applies in relation to the functions of the individual authorities; and
(b) any enactment relating to those functions or the authorities by whom or the areas in respect of which they are to be discharged shall have effect subject to all necessary modifications in its application in relation to those functions and the authorities by whom and the areas in respect of which (whether in pursuance of the arrangements or otherwise) they are to be discharged. . . .

(6) A local authority's functions with respect to levying, or issuing a precept for, a rate [. . .] shall be discharged only by the authority . . .

Notes

1. This section gives very wide powers of delegation to local authorities without using the term "delegation". The general power of delegation to officers was new in the 1972 Act. Section 101(1) does not authorise the delegation of functions to a single member: *R. v Secretary of State for Education and Science Ex p. Birmingham DC* (1984) 83 L.G.R. 79, where it was held that a proposal by a local education authority to close a school had not been lawfully made where the date of closure had been fixed not by the authority but by its chairman. This view was confirmed by Woolf J. and the Court of Appeal in *R. v Secretary of State for the Environment Ex p. Hillingdon LBC* [1986] 1 W.L.R. 192 and 867, in respect of the issue of enforcement notices. The word "committee" in the 1972 Act did not extend to a committee of one. Woolf J. recognised, however, that the difficulties could be circumvented by delegating a power to an officer acting *in consultation* with a member. This would enable urgent action to be taken between meetings of the relevant committee or sub-committee. Where it is arranged for decisions to be made by an officer in consultation with a councillor the ultimate decision must be the officer's: if the dominant role is taken by the councillor, the decision will be *ultra vires*: *R. v Port Talbot BC Ex p. Jones* [1988] 2 All E.R. 207. On the other hand, there is no objection to standing orders requiring the officer to obtain the approval of a member of the council, such as a committee chairman, before exercising the delegated power: *Fraser v Secretary of State for the Environment* (1987) 56 P. & C.R. 386. The difference appears to be that, in the former case, the officer would not have made the positive decision in question had it not been for the intervention of the councillor. In the latter, the officer made a provisional decision independently, but was then required to obtain approval from a committee chairman before it could be made effective. The former situation was unlawful, the latter arrangement was lawful.

2. Whether power has been lawfully delegated may turn on the proper interpretation of the relevant resolution (see *Liverpool City Council v Rosemary Chavasse Ltd* [1999] N.P.C. 115; *R. (on the application of Calton-Conway) v Harrow LBC* [2002] EWCA Civ 927; [2002] J.P.L. 1216 (resolution to delegate to planning officer power to grant planning permission "except where the proposals do not conflict with agreed policies, standards and guidelines" held not to cover the present case, where the issues and policies were complex); *R (on the application of Springhall) v Richmond Upon Thames LBC* [2005] EWHC 52 (Admin)).

3. Separate statutory powers of delegation are conferred in respect of the discharge of functions by local authorities (the vast majority of authorities other than parish and community councils) that have adopted executive arrangements under Pt 2 of the Local Government Act 2000: see ss.14–20 and the regulations made thereunder. Section 101 of the 1972 Act does not generally apply here: see s.101(1A)–(1C), (5A), (5B), inserted by SI 2001/1517, arts 2, 3(a) (England) and SI 2002/803, arts 2, 3(a) (Wales). Under these arrangements, functions may be discharged by, *inter alia*, elected mayors and individual councillors who are members of a local authority executive.

4. For indications that something analogous to the *Carltona* principle may have some operation in the context of *local* government decision-making, see *Provident Mutual Life Assurance Association v Derby City Council* (1981) 79 L.G.R. 297, HL (enabling "administrative matters" in connection with rate collection to be dealt with by members of the treasurer's staff where power had been delegated to the treasurer), applied in *Cheshire CC v Secretary of State for the Environment* [1988] J.P.L. 30; *Fitzpatrick v Secretary of State for the Environment*, (1990) 154 L.G. Rev. 72; *R. (on the application of Pryterch) v Conwy BC* [2001] EWHC Admin 869 and *Younger Homes (Northern) Ltd v First Secretary of State* [2003] EWHC (Admin) 3058. In *Fitzpatrick*, however, the member of the district secretary's staff was merely implementing an instruction by the council to the district secretary to issue an enforcement notice; as neither the member of staff nor the district secretary was exercising any independent discretion the problem of the delegation of power did not strictly arise. See also *R. v Southwark LBC Ex p. Bannerman* (1990) 22 H.L.R. 459 (possession proceedings

instituted on the recommendation of a member of the Borough Valuer's staff, acting in the name of the Borough Valuer; proceedings held to be validly instituted).

(C) OVER-RIGID ADHERENCE TO SELF-CREATED RULES OF POLICY

The cases which follow demonstrate the balance which has been struck by the courts between:

    (i) applying the presumption, often stated, that statutes conferring discretionary powers should be interpreted as intending that decisions as to whether and how that power is to be exercised should be taken in the light of individual consideration of the merits of each particular case; and,

  (ii) appreciation that such individualised, case-by-case, decision-making may be less conducive to good and fair administration than an approach under which discretionary decisions are taken in the light of, though not unduly constrained by, previously determined (and perhaps promulgated) rules or principles of policy.

Individual justice is important. But decision-makers should also have regard to the "administrative justice" which is associated with consistency and predictability in decision-making. See further, below, pp.591–621, on "inconsistency" as a ground of challenge.

In any case where a decision has been taken in accordance with a self-created rule of policy the following matters must be considered:

    (i) is the policy intrinsically flawed? For example, does it require the decision-maker to take into account irrelevant considerations? Does it seek to utilise the powers for an improper purpose? Is the policy *Wednesbury* "unreasonable" or irrational? These grounds of challenge are considered in the next chapter;

  (ii) assuming that there is nothing intrinsically objectionable about the policy, has the policy been applied over-rigidly and to the exclusion of the genuine exercise of discretion in the particular case? The tests applied by the courts in determining this question appear from the cases which follow.

Note
See generally H.L. Molot, (1972) 18 McGill L.J. 310; D.J. Galligan, [1976] P.L. 332; C. Hillson, [2002] P.L. 111.

LAVENDER (H.) & SON LTD v MINISTER OF HOUSING AND LOCAL GOVERNMENT

[1970] 1 W.L.R. 1231; 114 S.J. 636; [1970] 3 All E.R. 871; (1969) 68 L.G.R. 408

The company applied for planning permission to extract sand, gravel and ballast from part of Rivernook Farm, Walton-on-Thames. Most of the site was within an area of high quality agricultural land reserved for that purpose in accordance with the Waters Report on Sand and Gravel, 1948–1953. The planning authority refused planning permission, and the company appealed to the Minister. The only substantial objection to the development came from the Ministry of Agriculture, which wished to see the land maintained as agricultural land. There was evidence that the company would be able to restore the land to a high standard of fertility after excavation. The inspector who conducted the public inquiry could find no reason to refuse planning permission apart from the objection of the Ministry of Agriculture. The Minister dismissed the appeal. His decision letter included the two sentences:

"It is the Minister's present policy that land in the reservations should not be released for mineral working unless the Minister of Agriculture, Fisheries and Food is not opposed to working. In the present case the agricultural objection has not been waived, and the Minister has therefore decided not to grant planning permission for the working of the appeal site".

The company applied to the High Court under s.179 of the Town and Country Planning Act 1962 (now s.288 of the 1990 Act) for the Minister's decision to be quashed.

WILLIS J.: . . . It is those last two sentences in the decision letter which lie at the heart of the matter in issue; and it is submitted, first of all, by counsel for the applicants, that they show, in this case, that the Minister had so fettered his own discretion to decide the appeal by the policy which he had adopted that the decisive matter was not the exercise of his own discretion on a consideration of the report and other material considerations, but the sustained objection of the Minister of Agriculture. In effect, he says that the decision was not that of the Minister of Housing and Local Government, the tribunal entrusted with the duty to decide, but the Minister of Agriculture, who had no status save perhaps in a consultative capacity and certainly no status to make the effective decision. . . .

. . . In general support of his main submission, counsel for the applicants has referred me to Professor de Smith's well-known work, *Judicial Review of Administrative Action* ((2nd ed., 1968), pp.292–297) and to certain of the cases cited therein. He really puts his argument in two ways: (1) that the Minister has fettered his discretion by a self-created rule of policy; and (2) that the Minister, who has a duty to exercise his own discretion in determining an appeal, has in this case delegated that duty to the Minister of Agriculture, who has no such duty and is, statutorily, a stranger to any decision. It is, of course, common ground that the Minister is entitled to have a policy and to decide an appeal in the context of that policy. He can also differ from the inspector on any question of fact, and disagree with the inspector's conclusion and recommendations. He can, and no doubt should, reject any recommendation of an inspector which runs counter to his policy, since, as counsel for the Minister points out, it is of the very essence of the duties laid on the Minister by section 1 of the Minister of Town and Country Planning Act 1943 that he should secure consistency and continuity in the framing and execution of a national policy with respect to the use and development of land.

The courts have no authority to interfere with the way in which the Minister carries out his planning policy (see *per* Lord Denning M.R., *Lord Luke of Pavenham v Minister of Housing and Local Government* [1968] 1 Q.B. 172 at 192). There is also no question but that the Minister, before making a decision whether or not to allow an appeal, may obtain the views of other government departments (see *Darlassis v Minister of Education* (1954) 52 L.G.R. 304 at 318, *per* Barry J.). The duties of the Minister and their extent in relation to a matter such as the appeal in the present case, comprising in a hybrid form both administrative and quasi-judicial functions, were enunciated by Lord Greene M.R. in a well-known passage in *B. Johnson & Co. (Builders) Ltd v Minister of Health* [1947] 2 All E.R. 395, at 397 and 399:

"The duty placed on the Minister with regard to objections is to consider them before confirming the order. He is also to consider the report of the person who held the inquiry. Having done that, his functions are laid down by the last words of the paragraph (i.e. para.4 of Sch. 1 to the Housing Act 1936), viz., 'and may then confirm the order either with or without modification'. Those words are important, because they make it clear that it is to the Minister that Parliament has committed the decision whether he will or will not confirm the order after he has done all that the statute requires him to do. There is nothing in that paragraph, or anywhere else in the Act, which imposes on the Minister any obligation with regard to the objections, save the obligation to consider them. He is not bound to base his decision on any conclusion that he comes to with regard to the objections, and that must be so when one gives a moment's thought to the situation. The decision whether to confirm or not must be made in relation to questions of policy, and the Minister, in deciding whether to confirm or not, will, like every Minister entrusted with administrative duties, weigh up the considerations which are to affect his mind, the preponderating factor in many, if not all, cases being that of public policy, having regard to all the facts of the case. . . . That decision must be an administrative decision, because it is not to be based purely on the view that he forms of the objections, *vis-à-vis* the desires of the local authority, but is to be guided by his view as to the policy which in the circumstances he ought to pursue."

Can there, nevertheless, come a point in this hybrid process when the court can interfere with a Ministerial decision which, *ex facie*, proceeds on a consideration of the inspector's report and concludes by applying Ministerial policy?

Counsel for the applicants submits that such a point can be reached and has been reached in this case. It is reached, he says, adopting the words of Professor de Smith (see p.294), if a tribunal, entrusted with a discretion as the Minister was in the present case, disables itself from exercising that discretion in a particular case by the prior adoption of a general policy. In *R. v. Port of London Authority, ex p. Kynoch Ltd*, Bankes L.J. said, at p.184:[1]

"In the present case there is another matter to be borne in mind. There are on the one hand cases where a tribunal in the honest exercise of its discretion has adopted a policy, and, without refusing to her an applicant, intimates to him what its policy is, that, after hearing him, it will in accordance with its policy decide against him, unless there is something exceptional in his case. . . . On the other hand there are cases where a tribunal has passed a rule, or come to a determination not to hear an application of a particular character by whomsoever made."

---

[1] (ed) Bankes L.J.'s dictum in full reads: "In the present case there is another matter to be borne in mind. There are on the one hand cases where a tribunal in the honest exercise of its discretion has adopted a policy, and, without refusing to her an applicant, intimates to him what its policy is, and that, after hearing him, it will in accordance with its policy decide against him, unless there is something exceptional in his case. I think counsel for the applicants would admit that, if the policy has been adopted for reasons which the tribunal may legitimately entertain, no objection could be taken to such a course. On the other hand there are cases where a tribunal has passed a rule, or come to a determination, not to hear an application of a particular character by whomsoever made. There is a wide disinction to be drawn between these two classes . . .."

In another licensing case. *Reg. v. Flintshire County Council Licensing (Stage Plays) Committee, Ex parte Barrett* [1957] 1 Q.B. 350, where the decision was given in the interests of consistency, Jenkins L.J. said, at pp.367, 368:

> "Then they went on . . . to conclude . . . that the Queen's Theatre licence must follow the fate of the Pavilion Theatre licence, because it was essential that the same rule should be applied in all cases or, in other words, that the committee should be consistent. I cannot think that that method fulfils the requirement that the matter should be heard and determined according to law . . . . It seems to me that it wrongly pursues consistency at the expense of the merit of individual cases."

I have referred to those two cases since they were relied on by Mr Frank, but I am inclined to agree with Mr Slynn that the considerations applicable to licensing cases are not of much assistance when considering the scope of a Minister's duties within a statutory framework. . . .

It is, of course, clear that if the Minister has prejudged any genuine consideration of the matter before him, or has failed to give genuine consideration to (*inter alia*) the inspector's report, he has failed to carry out his statutory duties properly (see *Franklin v Minister of Town and Country Planning* [1948] A.C. 87 [below, p.774]).

In the present case counsel for the applicants does not shrink from submitting that the decision letter shows that no genuine consideration was given to the question whether planning permission could, in the circumstances, be granted. I have carefully considered the authorities cited by counsel, but I have not found any clear guide to what my decision should be in this case. I have said enough to make it clear that I recognise that in the field of policy, and in relation to Ministerial decisions coloured or dictated by policy, the courts will interfere only within a strictly circumscribed field (see *per* Lord Greene M.R. in *Associated Provincial Picture Houses Ltd v Wednesbury Corp.* [see below, p.570]). It is also clear, and is conceded by counsel for the Minister, that where a Minister is entrusted by Parliament with the decision of any particular case he must keep that actual decision in the last resort in his own hands (see *R. v Minister of Transport, Grey Coaches* (1933) 77 S.J. 301). I return, therefore, to the words used by the Minister. It seems to me that he has said in language which admits of no doubt that his decision to refuse permission was solely in pursuance of a policy not to permit minerals in the Waters agricultural reserves to be worked unless the Minister of Agriculture was not opposed to their working. Counsel for the Minister submits that, read as a whole, the decision letter should be taken as implying some such words as

> "I have gone through the exercise of taking all material considerations into account, but you have not persuaded me that this is such an exceptional case as would justify me in relaxing my policy; therefore I stick to it and apply it."

If that were the right construction perhaps counsel for the Minister would be justified in saying that there was no error in law. But in my judgment the language used is not open to any such such implication. There is no indication that this might be an exceptional case such as would or could induce the

Minister to change his policy. It is common ground that the Minister must be open to persuasion that the land should not remain in the Waters reservation. How can his mind be open to persuasion, how can an applicant establish an "exceptional case" in the case of an inflexible attitude by the Minister of Agriculture? That attitude was well known before the inquiry, it was maintained during the inquiry, and presumably thereafter. The inquiry was no doubt, in a sense, into the Minister of Agriculture's objection, since, apart from that objection, it might well have been that no inquiry would have been necessary, but I do not think that the Minister, after the inquiry, can be said in any real sense to have given genuine consideration to whether, on planning (including agricultural) grounds, this land could be worked. It seems to me that by adopting and applying his stated policy he has in effect inhibited himself from exercising a proper discretion (which would of course be guided by policy considerations) in any case where the Minister of Agriculture has made and maintained an objection to mineral working in an agricultural reservation. Everything else might point to the desirability of granting permission, but by applying and acting on his stated policy I think that the Minister has fettered himself in such a way that in this case it was not he who made the decision for which Parliament made him responsible. It was the decision of the Minister of Agriculture not to waive his objection which was decisive in this case, and while that might properly prove to be the decisive factor for the Minister when taking into account all material considerations, it seems to me quite wrong for a policy to be applied which in reality eliminates all the material considerations save only the consideration, when that is the case, that the Minister of Agriculture objects. That means, as I think, that the Minister has by his stated policy delegated to the Minister of Agriculture the effective decision on any appeal within the agricultural reservations where the latter objects to the working . . .

If the Minister was intending to follow his stated policy, I think that it was very undesirable that it should not have been made known in advance. It is possible to imagine great hardship falling on appellants who, all unawares, embark on an expensive appeal foredoomed to failure by reason of a strict though unannounced policy. However, I agree with counsel for the Minister that the failure to publicise the policy is not a ground for questioning the decision. . .

On the main ground on which this case has been argued, however, I am satisfied that the applicants should succeed. I think that the Minister failed to exercise a proper or indeed any discretion by reason of the fetter which he imposed on his exercise in acting solely in accordance with his stated policy; and further that on the true construction of the Minister's letter the decision to dismiss the appeal, while purporting to be that of the Minister, was in fact, and improperly, that of the Minister of Agriculture.

Questions

1. Was *Ex p. Kynoch* applied in this case, or was some different rule adopted? See Galligan, *op. cit.*, pp.348–350.

2. When may it be desirable for a decision-maker to evaluate "the weight of at least some factors that may be relevant to an exercise of discretion *in the future*"? (Galligan, *op. cit.*, p.350, emphasis added). Compare Lord Browne-Wilkinson's statement in *R. v Secretary of State for the Home Department Ex p. Venables* [1997] 3 All E.R. 97 at 120 that "the person on whom . . . power has been conferred cannot fetter the way he

will use that power by ruling out of considerations on the future exercise of that power factors which may then be relevant to such exercise".

Notes

1. See case note by D.G.T. Williams, [1971] C.L.J. 6. Note that it was rightly not suggested that the Crown was indivisible for these purposes (*cf.* above, p.6). Other cases in which there has been successful challenge on this ground include: *R. v Windsor Licensing Justices Ex p. Hodes* [1983] 1 W.L.R. 685 (justices failed to consider merits of particular application for liquor licence applying their "store within store" super-market policy over-rigidly); *R. v Hampshire Education Authority Ex p. J* (1985) 84 L.G.R. 547 (over-rigid policy in respect of exercise of discretion to pay independent school fees); *R. v Canterbury City Council Ex p. Gillespie* (1986) 19 H.L.R. 7 (over-rigid application of statutorily required general policy as to allocation of council accommodation); *R. v Secretary of State for Transport Ex p. Sherriff and Sons Ltd*, *The Times*, December 18, 1986 (revocation of discretionary grant based on over-rigid wording of Ministry's Memorandum of Explanation as to the availability of grants; see A.W. Bradley [1987] P.L. 141 and [1989] P.L. 197); *R. v Bexley LBC Ex p. Jones* [1994] C.O.D. 393 (local authority policy as regards award of dicretionary student grants held legitimate so long as authority prepared to consider exceptional cases: however, no reference in application form to the policy; nor, consequently, any oppor-tunity to plead special circumstances); *R v North West Lancashire HA Ex p. A* [2001] 1 W.L.R. 977 (quashing HA's refusal to fund gender reassignment surgery; while the HA's policy not to fund such surgery referred to the possibility of exceptions based on overriding clinical need, on the evidence the HA did not in fact treat transsexualism as an illness. Its stance was not a genuine application of a policy subject to individually determined exceptions).

The question whether discretion has been fettered is ultimately a question of fact. Relevant evidence may include both *statements* by decision-makers that indicate an over-rigid approach (*cf.* the *N.W. Lancashire* case, above, and *Sagnata Ltd v Norwich Corporation*, below, pp.491–493) and their actions. As to the former, more weight may be attached to contemporary correspondence than to affidavits sworn for the purpose of the litigation (see *R. v Bolton MBC Ex p. Lloyd* (Unreported, April 2, 1987)). As to the latter, see *R. v Warwickshire CC Ex p. Collymore* [1995] E.L.R. 217, as explained in *R. v Buckinghamshire CC Ex p. Sharma* [1998] C.O.D. 182 (no unlaw-ful fetter on the facts; the true *ratio* of *Collymore* was that the court in that case inferred from the absence of any successful student application for a discretionary grant over a three-year period that the council, no matter what the form, was in sub-stance applying a blanket policy).

Lavender was distinguished in *R. v Tandridge DC Ex p. Al Fayed* (1999) 79 P. & C.R. 227, where Carnwath J. held that the planning authority had been entitled to attach great weight to the view of the Health and Safety Executive that there were no reasons on health and safety grounds why the erection of a radio telephone base station tower should not be given planning permission, but had not regarded itself as bound by that view. The Court of Appeal (2000) 80 P. & C.R. 90) dismissed an appeal, this point not being raised.

2. *Stringer v Minister of Housing and Local Government* [1970] 1 W.L.R. 1281 con-cerned (*inter alia*) the long-standing policy of the Ministry to discourage development which would interfere with the efficient operation of the Jodrell Bank radio telescope. Cooke J. held that the Minister was entitled to rely on this policy in refusing an appeal on application for planning permission, stating at 1298:

"It seems to me that the general effect of the many relevant authorities is that a Minister charged with the duty of making individual administrative decisions in a fair and impartial manner may nevertheless have a general policy in regard to mat-ters which are relevant to those decisions, provided that the existence of that general policy does not preclude him from fairly judging all the issues which are relevant to each individual case as it comes up for decision.

I think that in this case the Minister was entitled to have a policy in regard to Jodrell Bank, and I think that his policy is not such as to preclude him from fairly considering a planning appeal on its merits. I do not think that it precluded him from fairly considering Mr Stringer's appeal. I do not think that the Minister has prejudged the case, or tied his own hands, or abdicated any of his functions".

Further aspects of *Stringer* are considered below, p.504.

BRITISH OXYGEN CO. LTD v MINISTER OF TECHNOLOGY

[1971] A.C. 610; [1970] 3 W.L.R. 488; [1970] T.R. 143; 114 S.J. 682; [1970] 3 All E.R. 165 (HOUSE OF LORDS)

The company manufactured, sold and delivered industrial and medical gases, which had to be kept in special containers of various kinds. One general class of container included individual cylinders of different sizes. The company bought a large number of these over three years, their total expenditure exceeding £4 million. They cost, on average, £20 each. The Board of Trade had a discretion to award investment grants under the Industrial Development Act 1966 in respect of new "plant". They had a rule of practice not to approve for grant, expenditure on items which cost individually less than £25, however great the number of such individual items purchased at any one time. The company applied for a declaration that the Board of Trade was not entitled to decline to make a grant on the sole ground that each cylinder cost less than £25. Buckley J. ([1969] 1 Ch. 57) granted the declaration, saying that this "would not be an exercise of the discretion but an abrogation of it . . . every genuine and reasonable application . . . must be considered on its merits. Refusals to consider an application merely on the ground of the low cost of the individual equipment provided involves ignoring whatever characteristics the application has meriting approval". The Court of Appeal allowed an appeal ([1969] 2 Ch. 174, *sub nom. British Oxygen Co. Ltd v Board of Trade*). There was a further appeal to the House of Lords.

LORD REID: . . . [I]t is necessary to consider what is the duty of the respondent in administering the Act and what rights, if any, the Act confers on those eligible for grants.

Section 1 of the Act provides that the Board of Trade "may" make grants.. . . . But how were the Board intended to operate that discretion? Does the Act read as a whole indicate any policy which the Board is to follow or even give any guidance to the Board? If it does then the Board must exercise its discretion in accordance with such policy or guidance (*Padfield v Minister of Agriculture, Fisheries and Food* [below, p.528]). One generally expects to find that Parliament has given some indication as to how public money is to be distributed. In this Act Parliament has clearly laid down the conditions for eligibility for grants and it has clearly given to the Board a discretion so that the Board is not bound to pay to every person who is eligible to receive a grant. But I can find nothing to guide the Board as to the circumstances in which they should pay or the circumstances in which they should not pay grants to such persons.

[His Lordship referred to the long title, s.1(6) and s.2 to 8 of the 1966 Act.]

Sections 11 and 12 are perhaps more relevant. Section 11 provides for the appointment of committees to advise the Board on the administration of the Act and it could be taken as an indication that otherwise the Board's discretion is unlimited. Section 12 provides for an annual report to Parliament so that Parliament can ex *post facto* consider the way in which this discretion has been exercised. . . .

I cannot find that these provisions give any right to any person to get a grant. It was argued that the object of the Act is to promote the modernisation of machinery and plant and that the Board were bound to pay grants to all who are eligible unless, in their view, particular eligible expenditure would not promote that object. That might be good advice for an advisory committee to give but I find nothing in the Act to require the Board to act in that way. If the Minister who now administers the Act, acting on behalf of the Government, should decide not to give grants in respect of certain kinds of expenditure, I can find nothing to prevent him. . . .[I]f the Minister thinks that policy or good administration requires the operation of some limiting rule, I find nothing to stop him.

[His Lordship cited *R. v Port of London Authority Ex p. Kynoch*, in particular the passage from the judgment of Bankes L.J. beginning—"There are on the one hand . . .", and ending—"between these two classes".]

I see nothing wrong with that. But the circumstances in which discretions are exercised vary enormously and that passage cannot be applied literally in every case. The general rule is that anyone who has to exercise a statutory discretion must not "shut his ears to an application" (to adapt from Bankes L.J.). I do not think there is any great difference between a policy and a rule. There may be cases where an officer or authority ought to listen to a substantial argument reasonably presented urging a change of policy. What the authority must not do is to refuse to listen at all. But a Ministry or large authority may have had to deal already with a multitude of similar applications and then they will almost certainly have evolved a policy so precise that it could well be called a rule. There can be no objection to that, provided the authority is always willing to listen to anyone with something new to say—of course I do not mean to say that there need be an oral hearing. In the present case the respondent's officers have carefully considered all that the appellants have had to say and I have no doubt that they will continue to do so. . . .

VISCOUNT DILHORNE: . . . [His Lordship read the passage from *Ex p. Kynoch* quoted by Lord Reid above.]

Bankes L.J. clearly meant that in the latter case there is a refusal to exercise the discretion entrusted to the authority or tribunal but the distinction between a policy decision and a rule may not be easy to draw. In this case it was not challenged that it was within the power of the Board to adopt a policy not to make a grant in respect of such an item. That policy might equally well be described as a rule. It was both reasonable and right that the Board should make known to those interested the policy it was going to follow. By doing so fruitless applications involving expense and expenditure of time might be avoided. The Board says that it has not refused to consider any application. It considered the appellants'. In these circumstances it is not necessary to decide in this case whether, if it had refused to consider an application on the ground that it related to an item costing less than £25, it would have acted wrongly.

I must confess that I feel some doubt whether the words used by Bankes L.J. in the passage cited above are really applicable to a case of this kind. It seems somewhat pointless and a waste of time that the Board should have to consider applications which are bound as a result of its policy decision to fail. Representations could of course be made that the policy should be changed.

I cannot see any ground on which it could be said that it was *ultra vires* of the Board to decide not to make grants on items costing less that £25 . . . In my opinion, this appeal should be dismissed.

LORD MORRIS OF BORTH-Y-GEST, LORD WILBERFORCE and LORD DIPLOCK concurred with LORD REID.

Notes
1. To what extent does the *British Oxygen* case modify the position in *Ex p. Kynoch*? In *R. (on the application of P) v Secretary of State for the Home Department; R. (on the application of Q) v Secretary of State for the Home Department* [2001] EWHC Admin 357; [2001] 2 F.L.R. 383, Lord Woolf C.J. said (at [51]) that the important words in Lord Reid's speech in *British Oxygen* "are that the authority must always be willing to 'listen to anyone with something new to say.' Policies must not be over rigid and they must not be unreasonable." Here the Prison Service's policy that enabled a mother in prison to have her baby with her up to the age of 18 months was held to be valid. It was not necessary for the policy "to be reduced to the most general of guidelines, indeed guidelines to be departed from whenever they do not produce the ideal result for a particular child". While the Prison Service did not have to deal with a vast number of mothers with very young children, the number was nevertheless such to make such an approach very difficult if not impossible to operate in practice (*per* Lord Woolf C.J. at [54]). The Prison Service was, however, obliged to consider making an exception to the policy where there were exceptional circumstances. On the facts here, there was nothing unusual about the two babies concerned in the proceedings. On this approach, it would seem that the key variable is the extent to which the court will require individualised decision-making. The House of Lords in *British Oxygen* and the Divisional Court in *P and Q* brought that there was only a limited requirement for such decision-making in the circumstances of those cases.

The point is thrown into relief by the decision of the Court of Appeal in *P and Q* ([2001] EWCA Civ 1151; [2001] 1 W.L.R. 2002) that a more individualised approach was necessary because of the human rights context. The court held that the Prison Service had to have a more flexible policy under which the interference with the child's family life had to be considered to be proportionate to the legitimate aims of the Prison Service, taking account of the necessary limitations on the mother's rights and freedoms brought about by her imprisonment; the extent to which relaxation of the policy would cause problems within the prison or the Prison Service generally; and the welfare of the individual child. This balancing had to be undertaken in respect of each child.

> "The Prison Service policy itself emphasises the need for individual consideration, so there can be no insuperable objection to a discretionary element in these decisions. In the great majority of cases, almost all those considerations would point to separating mother and child at or before the age of 18 months. . . But there may be very rare exceptions where the interests of mother and child coincide and outweigh any other considerations. The mother must be given a fair opportunity to argue that that is so" (*per* Hale L.J. at para.[106].)

It is, however, for the Secretary of State to conduct that balancing exercised, subject to review by the court on *Daly* principles (see p.340); it is not for the court to decide on the merits what is in the best interests of the child (*CF v Secretary of State for the Home Department* [2004] EWHC 111; [2004] 2 F.L.R. 517).
2. The approach of the majority of the Court of Appeal in *Sagnata Investments Ltd*

v Norwich Corporation [1971] 2 Q.B. 614 to the policy fetter issue has attracted some criticism. Here, the corporation by a majority of 41 to 1 took a policy decision not to grant permits for amusements with prizes so as to allow there to be any amusement arcade in Norwich. Sagnata applied for a permit. The committee to which power to determine applications had been delegated afforded Sagnata a full hearing at which it was represented by a solicitor, but rejected the application, applying the policy decision. The reasons given were:

"(a) The use of these premises as an amusement place would be likely to have undesirable social effects on the young people expected to frequent them; (b) the making available of gaming facilities in Norwich which could be used by children was something which the committee are not prepared to permit."

(A third reason was not subsequently relied upon.) On an appeal to quarter sessions (by way of a rehearing: see below, p.795) the recorder (Michael Havers Q.C.) held that the committee had so fettered its discretion in following the Council's policy that no application could succeed, and that the committee had failed to exercise its discretion. This decision was upheld by the majority of the Court of Appeal (Edmund Davies and Phillimore L.JJ.). Lord Denning M.R. dissented. He held that the committee had conducted a hearing with the "utmost fairness and discretion". The authorities (including *Stringer* and *British Oxygen*) established that an authority was entitled to have and apply a general policy provided that it did not shut its ears to an application. Here, "the licensing committee did not regard [the council's] policy as inflexible or as binding on them" and "listened to everything that the applicant had to say" (p.627). The recorder had misdirected himself in holding that the committee had fettered its discretion. Edmund Davies L.J. (at 632–633) noted that the recorder had rightly concluded that the council was entitled to adopt the general policy of refusing such applications,

"provided that no inflexible, unvarying attitude was adopted and that the local authority was prepared to depart from it where the justice of a particular case so required. But he continued:

'I am forced to the conclusion that in this case, where the application met with all the ordinary requirements as to suitability of site, premises and management, the general policy must have applied. In other words, no application to the local authority, however suitable, would succeed'.

Directing himself that, this being an appeal to quarter sessions, he was required to approach the matter *de novo* and 'with a complete and unfettered discretion', he proceeded to consider the available material. While confessing that he personally sympathised with the approach exemplified in grounds (a) and (b) of those stated by the local authority, he continued:

"Parliament has not seen fit to impose any safeguards in respect of young people; it could have been done, as it has done in the Licensing Acts, and I would require some evidence not only that such a place would be used to a considerable extent by young people, but also that such use would be socially undesirable".

While expressly stating that he did *not* overlook that the local authority had by a 41 to 1 majority voted against amusement arcades in Norwich, he expressed himself as compelled to hold that the appeal be allowed and the permit granted. He said:

"In my view (and Mr. Marriage virtually conceded this), the licensing committee have decided that they will not grant a permit for *any* amusement place with prizes in the City of Norwich, and the reasons they give for *this* refusal would apply to *any* application".

"(The italics are my own.) This virtual concession of counsel for the local authority is far from surprising, having regard to the evidence given at quarter sessions by
none other than the chairman of the committee, . . ."

His Lordship concluded that the recorder had not erred in law. Phillimore L.J. said
(at 638–639):

> "Now there is no need for authority for the proposition that a council and its com-
> mittees are entitled to agree on a policy provided that they do not impose it inflex-
> ibly. In this case, however, we were told that the chairman of the committee—a
> former Mayor of Norwich—gave evidence before the recorder to the effect that they
> had rejected the application solely on the basis of the policy decision taken by the
> General Purposes Committee.. . ."[His Lordship cited the first passage quoted by
> Edmund Davies L.J. above]:
>
> "In other words the council had *not* exercised any form of discretion. They had
> simply dismissed this application after going through the necessary motions without
> regard to its individual merits or demerits. I take this to be a finding of fact with
> which this court is in no position to interfere.
>
> Incidentally, I cannot see that the recorder could avoid this decision. Apparently
> no evidence was called to support either ground (a) or ground (b). Nobody came
> forward to say that this sort of arcade had resulted in disastrous damage to the
> morality of the young in Great Yarmouth or any other seaside place or was likely
> to prove particularly harmful to the young of Norwich. . .".

A number of points can be made. First, there is clearly a difference between Lord
Denning M.R. and his colleagues on the question of fact whether the committee had
fettered its discretion. The evidence that it had seems strong. It is not clear whether
Lord Denning's view that it had not rests solely only the fact that it had held a full
hearing, or on an overall assessment of the facts. If it is the former, then it is submitted that where, as here, there is evidence that a blanket policy has been applied, the
authority should not necessarily be able to escape that conclusion merely by showing
that it held a hearing. On the other hand, the approach of Edmund Davies and
Phillimore L.JJ. has been criticised as requiring too much of the authority. See D.
Galligan, [1976] P.L. 332, 340–343, 352–354, *Craig*, pp.532–533:

> "To insist on the type of factual 'back-up' which the majority demanded . . . is
> excessive . . . It should be borne in mind that the test should be not what evidence
> a social scientist with full research grant and expertise, etc., could produce, but what
> evidence would be available to the Corporation, apart from the general feeling that
> such places were a bad influence on the young".

Whether this criticism is justified turns on the nature of the "evidence" before the
recorder. The committee's chairman, an experienced councillor, had given evidence,
expressing his fears as to the extent to which the arcade would be used by children
and whether that would be socially undesirable. The recorder found that this did
not amount to anything more than the expression of a realistic and honest opinion.
There were also the views of the council as expressed through its policy; the recorder
indicated that he was not prepared to act on "unproved general principles of social
undesirability and potential danger to young people" but wanted evidence. The
recorder and the Court of Appeal majority did indicate the matter on which they
would have wished to see additional evidence but did not give details of the extent or
kind of evidence needed. If the council's resolution had been based on anything more
than "general feelings", then that could have been produced; but it is noteworthy that
it was not. It should also be remembered that the absence of this additional evidence
was potentially relevant to support conclusions on two distinct matters: (1) that the
authority had in law fettered its discretion; and (2) that the recorder had been
entitled (on a rehearing) to take a different view from that of the authority, and had

not failed to give adequate weight to its views. As to the latter, given that Parliament had chosen to create an appeal on the merits to a court, it was really for the recorder to evaluate the evidence before him, with the Court of Appeal on an appeal on a point of law able to intervene only if he had gone wrong in principle. While it is fair to say that "a policy represents a choice of social goals and values, for which reasons may be given, but which often cannot be reduced to questions of fact for objective determination" (Galligan, *op. cit.* p.342), a policy supported *in no respect* by *any* objective evidence is likely to be suspect, and even if not challengeable as irrational, a factor to which the recorder would be entitled to attach relatively little weight. *Sagnata* certainly does not stand for a broad principle that policies can only be lawful if supported by objective evidence (*cf.* Galligan's discussion at pp.342–343). Overall, the criticisms directed at the majority (including those of Lord Denning M.R. in dissent) seem harsh.

4. In *R. v Secretary of State for the Environment Ex p. Brent LBC* [1982] Q.B. 593, the Secretary of State had exercised powers to reduce the rate support grant payable to the applicant local authority. In so doing the Secretary of State had acted in accordance with a policy earlier formulated to deal with "overspending" authorities. He had refused to meet representatives of the local authority to discuss any alteration or amendment of the policy, regarding his policy on the matter as "settled". In the words of Ackner L.J. (at 644): ". . . the Secretary . . . clearly decided to turn a deaf ear to any and all representations to change the policy . . .". In so acting the Secretary of State was held by the Court of Appeal to have erred. Again in the words of Ackner L.J. (*ibid.*): "In our judgment [he] was obliged to listen to any objector who showed that he might have something new to say; putting it negatively, he was obliged not to declare his unwillingness to listen. . . . We accept that to be entitled to be heard it was for the objector to show that he had, or might have, something new to say. . .". The Secretary of State's decision was, accordingly, quashed. The court rejected the Secretary of State's argument that the "fettering" principle applied only to cases where a discretionary power conferred was of a general nature, to be exercised on more than one occasion and in relation to applications for the grant of some right which the person holding the power can confer, such as a permission or licence: see [1982] Q.B. at 640–642. See S.H. Bailey, [1983] P.L. 8.

5. Note how this ground of challenge overlaps with others. To fail to give proper consideration to the merits of an individual matter may at one and the same time be to apply a policy over-rigidly and to fail to take into account a relevant consideration (see below, p.545). Equally, to defend successfully a decision taken in accordance with a policy it may be necessary to show that one has "acted fairly" in the sense of having given notice of the policy which was to be followed, and having indicated that representations that an exception should be made or that the policy should be changed would be considered (see further on the "duty to act fairly," below, pp.652 *et seq.*). The application of a rigid policy may amount to the "predetermination" of the issue and so offend the rule against bias (see pp.751–787). The need to make the policy known to those who may be affected by it would seem to follow from the obligation to be receptive to representations. This obligation is only of substance if those affected are aware of the policy in respect of which they may raise arguments.

Note also that *failure* to have followed a published guideline or policy without good reason may give rise to successful challenge. See, for example, *R. v Director of Public Prosecutions Ex p. C* (1994) 159 J.P. 227 (failure of Crown Prosecution Service to have followed its Code for Prosecutors); *Morbaine v Secretary of State for the Environment* (1993) 68 P. & C.R. 525 (all facts pointed to one decision, following an announced policy; different decision was reached and the court was willing to infer absence of valid reason); *R. v Leeds CC Ex p. Hendy* (1994) 6 Admin. L.R. 439; *R. v Secretary of State for the Environment Ex p. West Oxfordshire DC* (1993) 26 H.L.R. 417.

6. Hillson ([2002] P.L. 111) regards the non-fetter principle as an unsatisfactory compromise between the advantages of rule-based decision-making (clarity, consistency and efficiency) and individualised decision-making (just to individuals; more accurate fulfilment of relevant aims). However, the advantages of the principle in

producing a fine-tuned approach to fairness in exceptional cases must be set against the disadvantages that in particular cases (1) a rigid policy is necessary to achieve officially determined aims; or (2) wholly individualised decision-making is necessary (see pp.112–114). Accordingly, the court should in each situation examine the nature of the relevant discretion and its desired aims and then decide on the most appropriate form of legal control. Some situations will be as in (1) and (2) above, leaving the traditional non-fetter between these extremes (p.129). It is submitted with respect, that Hillson rightly distinguishes between the traditional principle and situation (2), citing the *P&Q* case (above). However, the extent to which situation (1) properly exists is more questionable. One example given here (at p.112) is that where:

"a local authority believes that amusement arcades pose a threat to children and its aim is to protect them, then a rule prohibiting amusement arcades is the only way in which this aim will be achieved. Allowing discretionary exceptions would compromise the aim".

This is presumably a reference to *Sagnata* (above, p.491), which Hillson regards as a wrong decision (p.129). However, here Parliament gave local authorities power to license arcades not prohibit them. It is well established that a power to "regulate" may not be used to "prohibit". The local authority is not entitled to adopt the aim that only a rigid policy or rule will deliver. On the other hand, it is always open to Parliament expressly (see n.7) or by necessary implication to enable an authority in a particular situation to adopt a rule which permits of no exceptions. This is illustrated by *Smith v Inner London Education Authority* [1978] 1 All E.R. 411, where the Court of Appeal held that ILEA was entitled to adopt, and had not acted *Wednesbury* unreasonably in adopting, a policy in determining the character of local secondary schools that all should be comprehensive and not selective (see Lord Denning M.R. at 418, Brown L.J. at 422 and Geoffrey Lane L.J. at 425). On the facts, a challenge to ILEA's particular decision to close Marylebone Grammar School failed. However, it should be noted that it had already been accepted that the school should end selective admissions and the decision to close was based on a reduced need for secondary school places in the area. Lord Denning M.R. did say (at 418) that the *British Oxygen* principle did apply when the ILEA was considered whether to close an individual school, the ILEA being obliged to listen to objections. However, the significance of this is much reduced by his acknowledgment that the parents who objected had not even put forward the argument that the school should be retained on a selective basis "because it was known that it would not be acceptable". The background policy was thus accepted as a binding one.

7. In certain situations, local authorities have express statutory power to pass "blanket" resolutions that would otherwise be impermissible under the rule against the fettering of discretion. A local authority is empowered by the Gaming Act 1968, Sch. 9, para.3, to resolve not to grant or renew permits under Pt III in respect of "a class of premises specified in the resolution". However, the power cannot apply to premises used or to be used wholly or mainly for the provision of amusements by means of machines to which Pt III applies (para.4), thus requiring applications in respect of amusement centres, arcades and the like to be considered on their merits. The policy behind this power was:

"parliament's view that local consideration should be given considerable weight in determining in which types of premises amusements with prizes generally, and machines in particular, should be available to the general public for gaming. A particular factor which influenced parliament . . . was the availability of such machines to persons under the age of 18" (Smith and Monkcom, *op.cit.*, p.325).

It is uncertain whether a local authority's resolution not to grant or renew permits in respect of *all* premises in its area other than those exempted by para.4 would be *intra vires* (see Smith and Monkcom, *op.cit.*, pp.326–328, noting the view of Woolf J. in

Westminster City Council v Lunepalm Ltd, The Times, December 10, 1985, that it would be, but dicta to the contrary in *Walker v Leeds City Council* [1978] A.C. 403 at 421 422, *per* Lords Simon and Kilbrandon). In *R. v Barnet LBC Ex p. Ellina* (QBD, March 31, 1992), Otton J. agreed with Woolf J.'s approach and held that such a resolution was *intra vires* and not *Wednesbury* unreasonable.

Similarly, the Lotteries and Amusements Act 1976, Sch.3, para.2 enables a local authority to pass a resolution that it will not grant, or will neither grant nor renew, any permits for the commercial provision of amusements with prizes in respect of premises of a class specified in the resolution. By para.3, such a resolution may not be passed in respect of premises used or to be used wholly or mainly for the purposes of a pleasure fair consisting wholly or mainly of amusements. These provisions, which formerly appeared in the Betting, Gaming and Lotteries Act 1963, Sch.6 (as amended), were considered in *R.v Herrod Ex p. Leeds City Council* [1976] Q.B. 540, CA; affirmed, *sub nom. Walker v Leeds City Council* [1978] A.C. 403, HL. The Court of Appeal emphasised that the courts should construe the power to pass "blanket" resolutions strictly, as the refusal or non-renewal of a licence without a hearing seemed contrary to natural justice and a non-renewal might cause serious economic loss (see Lord Denning M.R. at 560, James L.J. at 566 and Shaw L.J. at 570–571). Accordingly, the term "pleasure fair" in the para.3 exemption was to be given a wide meaning as including premises used for the purposes of playing prize bingo. An appeal to the House of Lords was dismissed. Lord Wilberforce stated at 417 that if the term "pleasure fair" was to be interpreted restrictively as meaning "fun fair," bingo hall owners in areas where the appropriate "blanket" resolutions were passed would

"unable be even to present a case on the merits to the local authorities. They are automatically resolved out of business. This, in relation to a comparatively innocuous form of activity, seems rather draconian, and at least justifies the courts looking to see whether there is a possible alternative".

(D) Fettering Discretion by Contract or Undertaking

A distinction is to be drawn between a contract or other binding undertaking made by a public authority as a valid exercise of a discretionary power and one which is (or would be if permitted) an invalid fetter on the exercise of a discretionary power. The distinction can be difficult to draw. The law must, (for example) balance the public interest in ensuring that a public authority performs properly its statutory and other functions, against the interest of the other party to an agreement (with the authority) in keeping the authority to its word. Indeed, keeping an authority to its word may aid it in the performance of its functions, for example by encouraging private contractors to do business with it. The cases set out below show that the question whether a particular undertaking is (or would be) an invalid fetter on the exercise of discretion may arise in a variety of ways. There are many variables:

(1) the undertaking may be express or implied: *e.g.* an *express* contract (*Henry Leetham*), agreement (*Birkdale; Stringer*) or restrictive covenant (*Ayr Harbour Trustees; Stourcliffe; Dowty Boulton Paul*); or an implied undertaking not to exercise a power (*Amphitrite; Cory*), an implied covenant of quiet enjoyment (*Page*), or an implied grant of a right of way (*Westmorland*)

(2) the undertaking may be relied on in litigation by the public authority (*Ayr Harbour Trustees*) or the other party to it (most of the other cases) or used as the basis for a legal challenge by a third party to a decision influenced by it (*Stringer*).

(3) In some cases the other party is seeking to enforce the undertaking (*Birkdale, Henry Leetham, Stourcliffe, Dowty Boulton Paul*); in others the other party will want compensation for non-compliance (*Cory*) or to resist an obligation

to pay rent (*Page*); in yet others the legality of the undertaking is directly challenged (*Ayr Harbour Trustees*; where this governed the amount payable in compensation).

(4) In some cases it is clear that the undertaking is binding but there is an issue as to the proper interpretation of an express power to override it (*Thames*).

(5) The issue may arise in respect of different kinds of public authority, including the Crown, local authorities, public corporations, and other public bodies.

The key principle applied in deciding whether there is (or would be) an invalid fetter on discretion seems to be whether the undertaking is *incompatible with the proper performance of the (usually) statutory purposes of the public authority in question*. There are, however, a number of uncertainties. First, while there are many cases that apply the incompatibility principle, there is not always sufficient clarity about exactly what it is against which compatibility is to be tested. It is, however, clear that it is not sufficient simply to show that there is (or would be) an *inconsistency* between the undertaking and the exercise of a statutory power. In some cases undertakings have been held not to be incompatible even though the exercise of some ancillary power is thereby excluded (see *Stourcliffe*; *Westmorland*). This must be right otherwise no public authority could enter binding contracts and other agreements without express power when doing so to override inconsistent statutory powers. Accordingly, it will only be undertakings with a more fundamental disabling effect that are invalid (see, *e.g.* the formulations in *Westmorland*). Secondly, there are some suggestions that the incompatibility principle applies differently to different kinds of public authority (see Lord Sumner in *Birkdale* and Lord Radcliffe in *Westmorland*). It is submitted that this would add an unnecessary complication and that it is better to concentrate on the relationship between the statutory purposes in question and the undertaking. Thirdly, there are suggestions that the *Ayr Harbour Trustees* case applies a stricter test than one of incompatibility; there is no good reason why it should and the better view is that it does not. Fourthly, there is a question as to when incompatibility is to be judged. *Westmorland* suggests that this is to be done at the time issue of compatibility is determined at trial and that a test of reasonable foreseeability is to be applied.

The courts in practice are rightly reluctant to allow public authorities to escape from *express* contractual or proprietary obligations that they have deliberately entered. They are similarly rightly reluctant to accept that a public authority can *impliedly* undertake not to exercise statutory powers.

Note
See generally J.D.B. Mitchell, *The Contracts of Public Authorities* (1954), Ch.2, esp. pp.57–65; C. Turpin, *Government Contracts* (1972), pp.19–25; P.W. Hogg, (1970) 44 A.L.J. 154; E. Campbell, (1971) 45 A.L.J. 338; P. Rogerson, [1971] P.L. 288.

BIRKDALE DISTRICT ELECTRIC SUPPLY CO. LTD v SOUTHPORT CORPORATION

[1926] A.C. 355; 95 L.J.Ch. 587; 134 L.T. 673; 42 T.L.R. 303; 90 J.P. 77; 24 L.G.R. 157 (HOUSE OF LORDS)

In 1901, the appellants, an electricity company, took over, under an Electric Lighting Order (made under the Electric Lighting Acts), the local electricity supply undertaking from Birkdale UDC. Under a Supplemental Deed to the Main Deed of Transfer, it was agreed that the prices to be charged by the appellants to private consumers should not exceed those charged in the adjoining borough of Southport by Southport Corporation, which also operated an electricity supply undertaking. In 1911, Southport Corporation "took over" Birkdale UDC. The appellants continued to supply the Birkdale area. In 1923, the Corporation applied for an injunction to restrain the appellants from charging prices in excess of the Southport prices (as had been done since 1921). The appellants argued that the 1901 agreement was an *ultra vires* fetter on their own power to fix the price (subject to statutory maxima) of electricity supplied by them. In the future they might be faced with a difficult situation, and need to raise their prices above those in Southport. The Corporation argued that the 1901 agreement was a business agreement which was not incompatible with the proper performance by the appellants of their statutory functions. The question of incompatibility had to be judged at the date of the agreement. The fact that the agreement might be improvident, and lead to lower profits, was a matter between the appellant company and their shareholders, but did not render the agreement *ultra vires*. Astbury J. dismissed the action ([1925] 1 Ch. 63), but was reversed by the Court of Appeal ([1925] 1 Ch. 794). The company appealed to the House of Lords.

LORD SUMNER: . . . Are . . . [the agreements] void at common law as being *ultra vires* the appellants, a trading company, incorporated to exercise statutory powers vested in them in the public interest under the authority of the Legislature? This is a doctrine, which it may be unwise to circumscribe within the limits of an inelastic definition. We have, however, a long series of decisions, extending over nearly a century, and at any rate illustrating the cases to which the rule has been understood to extend. With the exception of *York Corporation v Henry Leetham & Sons* [1924] 1 Ch. 557 no case has been cited, in which a contract by a trading company to compound with a customer without limit of time for the price to be paid for services rendered to him, has been declared to be *ultra vires*, and we were told that the diligence of counsel had failed to find any other case. Certainly I have been able to go no further.

Hitherto the question has mainly arisen, where servitudes have been claimed over the property, which the alleged servient owner acquired under statutory authority and for the purposes of a public undertaking. In *R. v Inhabitants of Leake* (1833) 5 B. & Ad. 469 a public right of way was alleged to exist over the bank of a drain constructed by statutory Commissioners and reparable as such by the inhabitants of Leake. In *Staffordshire and Worcestershire Canal Navigation v Birmingham Canal Navigations* (1866) L.R. 1 H.L. 254 a right was claimed to have water discharged from the respondents' canal into the canal of the appellants at the bottom of a flight of locks connecting the two navigations. . . . The right in these cases . . . was rested on prescription and not on express grant, but the argument, which prevailed, was that the theory of dedication to the public use rests on an implied grant but none could be implied, since even an express grant would have been void as being *ultra vires*.

Parallel with these decisions there is a line of cases, in which the servitude claimed has been upheld on the ground that a dedication would not under the circumstances have been incompatible with full observance of the terms and full attainment of the purposes for which the statutory powers had been granted. This principle is stated as early as *R. v Inhabitants of Leake*, in which the dedication was upheld, and was acted on in *Grand Junction Canal Co. v Petty* (1888) 21 Q.B.D. 273, a case of a public right of walking on a towpath, and in *Greenwich Board of Works v. Maudslay* (1870) L.R. 5 Q.B. 397, a case of a footpath along a sea wall. . . . Parke J. says, in the *Leake* case, that, if the bank was vested in the Commissioners by statute, so that they were thereby bound to use it for some special purpose, incompatible with a public right of walking along it, they must be deemed to have been incapable in law of thus dedicating their property; otherwise they were in that regard in the same position as other landowners. . . . In the *Grand Junction* case Lindley L.J. says, that such incompatibility is a matter of evidence, and, in practice, evidence has regularly been given and considered for the purpose of testing the question.

My Lords, I do not think that these cases assist the appellants in any way, but in most respects are against them, for they show that, in default of proof of incompatibility in the present case, some other consideration of a cogent kind must be found. The incompetence of the company is only an incompetence *sub modo*, beyond which the powers necessary to its operation may be freely exercised.

Ayr Harbour Trustees v Oswald (1883) 8 App.Cas. 323 introduces a new matter and is nearer to the present case. Harbour trustees, whose statutory power and duty were to acquire land, to be used as need might arise for the construction of works on the coast line of the harbour, sought to save money in respect of severance on the compulsory acquisition of a particular owner's land by offering him a perpetual covenant not to construct their works on the land acquired, so as to cut him off from access to the waters of the harbour, or otherwise to affect him injuriously in respect of land not taken but from which the acquired land was severed. It was held that such a covenant was *ultra vires*. Lord Blackburn's words should be quoted. "I think", he says, "that where the legislature confer powers on any body to take land compulsorily for a particular purpose, it is on the ground that the using of that land for that purpose will be for the public good. Whether that body be one which is seeking to make a profit for shareholders, or, as in the present case, a body of trustees acting solely for the public good . . . a contract, purporting to bind them and their successors not to use those powers, is void."

Founding on this case, Russell J. held in *York Corporation v Henry Leetham & Sons* [1924] 1 Ch. 557 that a contract, terminable only by the customer, to carry his traffic at a fixed annual sum was equally *ultra vires*. Just as the covenant in the *Ayr Harbour* case tied the hands of the successors to the then trustees, and prevented them from constructing works on the land acquired, however necessary they might have become for the proper management of the undertaking, so he held that the corresponding contracts with Leetham fettered the free management of the canal in perpetuity, no matter how urgent it might be to increase the revenues of the undertaking.

My Lords, I do not think that there is a true analogy between these cases. On examining the facts in the *Ayr Harbour* case it is plain that, in effect, the trustees did not merely propose to covenant in a manner that committed the business of the harbour to restricted lines in the future; they were to forbear, once and for all, to acquire all that the statute intended them to acquire, for, though technically they acquired the whole of the land, they were to sterilize part of their acquisition, so far as the statutory purpose of their undertaking was concerned. This is some distance from a mere contract entered into with regard to trading profits. The land itself was affected in favour of the former owner in the *Ayr* case just as a towpath is affected in favour of the owner of a dominant tenement, if he is given a personal right of walking along it. If the Ayr trustees had reduced the acquisition price by covenanting with the respondent for a perpetual right to moor his barges, free of tolls, at any wharf they might construct on the water front of the land acquired, the decision might, and I think would, have been different.

There is, however, another aspect of the *Ayr Harbour* case which ought to be loyally recognized. It is certainly some ground for saying that there may be cases where the question of competence to contract does not depend on a proved incompatibility between the statutory purposes and the user, which is granted or renounced, but is established by the very nature of the grants or the contract itself. It was not proved in the *Ayr* case that there was any actual incompatibility between the general purposes of the undertaking and the arrangement by which the particular proprietor was to be spared a particular interference with the amenities or the advantages of his back land. I think the case was supposed to speak for itself and that, in effect, the trustees were held to have renounced a part of their statutory birthright. The appellants, however, contend, and Russell J. appears to have thought, that your Lordships' House extended other principles, namely, those applicable to servitudes over land acquired, to mere contracts restricting the undertakers' future freedom of action in respect to the business management of their undertaking. This point of view ought therefore to be examined.

The appellants, as I understand them, say that the doctrine is not confined to the creation of servitudes or other derogations by grant from plenary ownership, but extends also to such covenants in perpetuity as may, in events not actually impossible, starve their undertaking and spell its ruin. Southport, they say, now standing in the shoes of the Birkdale Council as well as in its own (if I may somewhat distort their metaphor), has behind it the pockets of the ratepayers of both areas, and though these may be no more inexhaustible than their patience, at least they may prove deeper and more enduring than the paid-up or uncalled capital of the appellant company, or its shareholders' willingness to subscribe to new issues of debentures or of preference stock. The thing speaks for itself. The covenant is fraught with potential suicide for the covenantors, and so is *ultra vires*.

My Lords, this hypothesis is conceivable, though neither from the evidence nor the argument have I gathered why these machinations should be attributed to the respondents or be tolerated by their outraged ratepayers. Municipal finance is capable of much curious development, but I think that among ordinary ratepayers a passion to supply current below cost price to private consumers is purely academic. If it exists at Southport, I think it should be proved by testimony.

The argument must be either that it is one of the direct statutory objects of the Electric Lighting Order that the undertakers should make a profit or at least not suffer any loss, or else that this is an indirect statutory object, since, if the undertakers make no profit, they will either pursue the undertaking without zeal or will drop it, so soon as this imaginary rate-war exhausts their resources.

My Lords, I am afraid this is beyond me. It may be the policy of the Electric Lighting Acts to get trading companies to take up and work Electric Lighting Orders in hope of gain, but I cannot see that it is any part of the direct purposes of the Order, that money should be made or dividends distributed. The primary object of the Electric Lighting Order was to get a supply of electric energy for the area in question, a thing only feasible at the time by getting a trading company to undertake the business. It was not to secure that certain charges should be made or that certain results should be shown upon a profit and loss account. As for the indirect effect, which will follow if no money is made or enough money is lost, the Order itself imposes a maximum price for the current and conceivably, therefore, might itself lead to the exhaustion of the company's funds. How, then, can it be part of the legal objects of the grant of these powers, that they should never result in financial disaster? The Order is really as little concerned with the company's ultimate ability to continue the undertaking as with its earning of a profit. The latter is the company's own affair; the former will simply lead to the revocation of the Order and the grant of a more favourable one to someone else. If this is so, there is a wide and more than sufficient difference between the contract of the Ayr Harbour Trustees not to acquire all that they were intended to acquire, and that of the appellants to obtain the transfer of the Order by convenanting among other considerations for something, which obviously is not and may never be, incompatible with the fulfilment of all the purposes of the Order and most of the purposes of the company's trading as well.

In *York Corporation v Henry Leetham & Sons* there were two navigations, both vested in the Corporation of York, which appear to have differed somewhat in their incidents, the Ouse Navigation and the Foss Navigation. The original Act of 1726, which authorized the former, empowered trustees to levy tolls on craft using the navigation when completed, and, for the purpose of constructing the navigation, authorized them to mortgage these prospective tolls and so to raise the necessary capital. The resources of the trustees were therefore of a character wholly different from those of a limited liability company. A later Act, that of 1732, fixed a schedule of rates and provided that all commodities carried "shall" bear them, and that it should be lawful for the trustees to take the rates "by this Act directed and no others", though, if the full revenue derived from these rates proved to be more than was required to maintain the undertaking, there was power to moderate them. The Act, which authorized the latter navigation, provided for the incorporation of a company having a capital of 25,400*l.* in 100*l.* shares and borrowing powers up to 10,000*l.* No distinction appears, from the judgment of Russell J., to have been drawn in argument between these two undertakings, but it is possible that the agreement in dispute, by which the undertakers compounded the rate with a particular customer, might be regarded as a direct breach of the mandatory charging clause of the Ouse Act of 1732, and consequently *ultra vires*. The same view could not arise on the Foss Act. The *ratio decidendi* of the judgment, however, proceeds entirely on the analogy of the *Ayr Harbour* case.

My Lords, with all respect to the learned judge, I am unable to adopt this reasoning. As I have said, it is no part of the intention of the Legislature that the appellants should make a profit or avoid a loss. If, again, the agreement is to be *ultra vires* at all, it must be *ultra vires* all through. In cases like the *Ayr Harbour* case the land acquired under statutory powers was fettered in the undertakers' hands from the time the agreement was made. In the present case the company's activities have not yet been and may never be impaired by the agreement at all. So far it may have been and probably has been safe and beneficial. How then, can it have been *ultra vires* hitherto? There is further, in my opinion, a wide distinction between the position of the appellants and of such undertakers as the Ayr Harbour Trustees. The scheme here is that a limited liability company, not deprived of its right, as such, to go into voluntary liquidation or otherwise to terminate its enterprise, obtained the Order with the Board of Trade's consent and with the like consent may part with it. In other words, the Board of Trade is here the constituted authority, by whose discretionary intervention the supply of electricity may be secured in the interest of the locality. This is a very different scheme from a constitution of undertakers, which under the same statute establishes their existence, confers their powers, and defines their purposes.

It appears to me that no line can be drawn between the agreement now in question and any ordinary trading contract, if the appellants are right in testing the validity of the contract by its ultimate and theoretic possibility of bringing upon them a crippling loss. I do not think that a speculation as to the possible effect of what they have done is a legitimate ground for relieving them from their bargain, and it seems to me that the appeal should be dismissed.

THE EARL OF BIRKENHEAD, LORD ATKINSON, LORD WRENBURY and LORD CARSON concurred.

Notes

1. The Earl of Birkenhead (at 364) formulated the basic principle as:

"a well established principle of law, that if a person or public body is entrusted by the Legislature with certain powers and duties expressly or impliedly for public purposes, those persons or bodies cannot divest themselves of these powers and duties. They cannot enter into any contract or take any action incompatible with the due exercise of their powers or the discharge of their duties".

2. The *Ayr Harbour Trustees* case, where an unlawful fetter was found, has been difficult to interpret. Lord Sumner appears to suggest that it applied a different test from the incompatibility test. In *British Transport Commission v Westmorland CC* [1958] A.C. 126, Lord Cohen stated (at 163) that Lord Sumner was simply applying the *res ipsa loquitur maxim* ("the thing speaks for itself") and so there was no need for *proved* incompatibility. Viscount Simonds (at 143) said that *Ayr Harbour Trustees* "was. . . an example of incompatibility, not a decision to the effect that incompatibility does not supply a test". It would also be too wide a reading of *Ayr Harbour Trustees* to say that it was authority for the proposition that any inconsistency with any statutory powers would be sufficient: see Lord Radcliffe below in *Westmorland*.

3. The leading modern case on the implied dedication of rights of way by statutory corporations is *British Transport Commission v Westmorland CC* [1958] A.C. 126. The House of Lords emphasised that the validity of express or implied dedications depends on the question of fact whether such dedication is incompatible with (as variously put by their Lordships) the statutory purpose for which the land was acquired (see Viscount Simonds at 145); "the statutory objects of the company" or "the adequate and efficient discharge of the undertaker's statutory duties" (*per* Lord Morton of Henryton at 147, 148); or "the object prescribed by the statute appointing commissioners or creating the statutory company as the case might be" (*per* Lord Cohen at 164 or "with the running of the railway" (*per* Lord Keith of Avonholm at 166). Their Lordships rejected the Commission's argument that there could only be

compatibility if it could be proved that in no conceivable circumstances could the proposed user at any future time and in any way possibly interfere with the statutory
purpose for which the land was acquired. *Per* Viscount Simonds at 144:

> "to give to incompatibility such an extended meaning is in effect to reduce the prin-
> ciple to a nullity. For a jury, invited to say that in no conceivable circumstances and
> at no distance of time could an event possibly happen, could only fold their hands
> and reply that it was not for them to prophesy what an inscrutable Providence might
> in all the years to come disclose. I do not disguise from myself that it is difficult to
> formulate with precision what direction should be given to a jury. But, after all, we
> live in a world in which our actions are constantly guided by a consideration of rea-
> sonable probabilities of risks that can reasonably be foreseen and guarded against,
> and by a disregard of events of which, even if we think of them as possible, we can
> fairly say that they are not at all likely to happen. And it is, in my opinion, by such
> considerations as these, imprecise though they may be, that a tribunal of fact must
> be guided in determining whether a proposed user of land will interfere with the
> statutory purpose for which it was acquired".

Lord Radcliffe (at 155–156) referred to Lord Sumner's description of the *Ayr*
case as an example of an attempt to renounce a part of the "statutory
birthright" of the trustees:

"Striking as the phrase is, it does not seem to me to offer much help in deciding
which are the cases in which the principle of *Paterson's* case (1880–1881) 6
App.Cas. 833 and *Oswald's* case is to be applied, where, as he says, 'the very nature
of the grants or the contract itself' provides the answer, and which are those many
other cases in which the test to be applied is the humbler one of incompatibility
proved by evidence. The birthright of a statutory corporation includes all those
powers and rights with which it is thought proper to invest it at its creation: and I
do not think it easy for a court of law to decide merely by the nature of the thing
which of those powers are inalienably entailed and which can be disentailed and disposed of by ordinary grant.

In my opinion, we are bound to recognize that the principle of these two cases
cannot be applied in all circumstances and on all occasions to all statutory corporations and public bodies. That, indeed, has already been recognized by the decision
of this House in the *Birkdale* case, in which the electric supply company had certainly made a contract which deprived themselves and their successors of power at
any future time to raise the charges for their supply beyond a fixed limit, however
much the needs of their undertaking might require it. It is of some importance to
remember, when searching for a dividing line, that the two cases which 'spoke for
themselves' were both concerned with defined areas of land of no great extent, and
the possible consequence of renouncing powers over such areas could be stated as
a matter of practical observation. But nothing like the same observation can be
brought to bear when the factors of the problem are, on the one hand, all the general
powers derived by a railway company from the Railway Clauses Consolidation Act,
1845, and, on the other hand, many miles of railway lines covering great varieties
of setting. In such cases what I have called the pragmatic test is, I think, to be
preferred. . . .".

The House of Lords held that a right of way had been impliedly dedicated over an
accommodation bridge that connected land severed by the construction of the railway.
This was so notwithstanding that this might in the future hinder the exercise of an
express power to discontinue bridges. The House disapproved a statement by Sir
George Jessel M.R. in *Mulliner v Midland Reg. Co.* (1879) 11 Ch.D. at 623 that a right

of way could never be impliedly dedicated by a railway company. Viscount Radcliffe noted (at 153) that there had never (with one possible exception) been a finding that a right of way had been dedicated over railway lines at the level of the lines.

4. In *Stourcliffe Estates Co. Ltd v Bournemouth Corporation* [1910] 2 Ch. 12, CA, the defendant corporation purchased some land from the plaintiff to be used as a public park, and entered into a covenant not to erect any building except "such structures as summer houses a band stand or shelters". The corporation had power under the Bournemouth Improvement Act 1892 to build public conveniences on any of their public parks. The plaintiff was granted an injunction to restrain the corporation from erecting public conveniences on the land they had sold. The corporation's argument that the covenant was *ultra vires* was rejected. *Per* Cozens-Hardy M.R. at 18–19:

> "That . . . is a proposition which seems to me to be startling. If the deed is wholly *ultra vires* I can understand it, but to suppose that the corporation could be allowed to retain the land and to repudiate the consideration or part of the consideration for it is a proposition to which certainly I could not give my adhesion".

His Lordship distinguished the *Ayr* case on the ground that in that case:

> "the Act of Parliament, for public purposes and in the public interest, declared that certain land should be purchased by the undertakers, who were given compulsory powers for the purpose. That land included Mr Oswald's land. Not only were they to make the harbour and a quay, but they had power—it was obviously part of the essence of the undertaking—to make over any part of the land so purchased, certain warehouses facing a certain road. . . . Here the corporation have general powers to purchase land for, *inter alia*, the purposes of a public park. They may go anywhere they like and may make a contract with anybody who is willing to enter into a contract with them for these purposes, and to say that a vendor under those circumstances cannot rely upon a restrictive covenant entered into by the purchaser would really be to render it practically impossible for a municipal corporation ever to enter into a contract with a landowner for purposes of this kind".

Buckley L.J. pointed out (at 22) that the corporation

> "must acquire not for all and every purpose for which they can acquire land anywhere, but for some definite purpose, some one of the purposes in respect of which they are entitled to acquire land . . .".

His Lordship saw no reason why the corporation should not take the land while binding themselves not to put a urinal there:

> "It is said that that is divesting themselves of some power, because under s.85 of their Act of 1892 they could have put a urinal there. That section means that it is not an improper expenditure of money by the corporation to, amongst other things, erect urinals in proper places, but it is not necessary that the corporation should with every piece of land which they buy acquire also the right to put a urinal there".

5. In *William Cory & Son Ltd v London Corporation* [1951] 2 K.B. 476; [1951] 2 All E.R. 85, CA, the corporation as sanitary authority entered a contract with Cory's for the removal by Cory's barges of refuse from the City of London. Subsequently, the corporation as port health authority made new byelaws with requirements as to coamings and coverings that were more stringent than the terms of the contract. Compliance with the byelaws would have been onerous, requiring expenditure of over £400 per barge, and preventing the use of the barges for carrying coal on the return journey. The company purported to treat the making of the byelaws as repudiation by anticipatory breach, to accept the repudiation, and to claim rescission. They claimed that there was

an implied term in the contract to the effect that the corporation should not use their powers to make byelaws to impose more onerous burdens than those provided by the contract. The Court of Appeal, affirming Lord Goddard C.J. ([1951] 1 K.B. 8 held that in general an implied term might be read into a contract that one party should not act so as to prevent the other from being able to perform its obligations. However, the court held that, given the statutory responsibilities of the sanitary authority, there was in this case no such implied term, and therefore no repudiation. In the words of Lord Asquith of Bishopstone at 484–485:

> "I consider that such a term, whether implied or even express, could not be valid. The language of section 84(1)(a) of the Public Health (London) Act, 1936, is mandatory. The provision is as follows: '(1) Every sanitary authority shall make by-laws (a) for the prevention of nuisances arising from snow, ice, salt, dust, ashes, rubbish, offal, carrion, fish or filth or other matter or thing in any street.' If the suggested term were express, it would have to take some such form as this: 'True we are charged by Parliament with the duty of making such by-laws with reference to refuse as may be called for from time to time by considerations of public health. But even if these considerations call, and call peremptorily, for a provision not less stringent than that made by the 1948 by-laws, even if a second plague of London is likely to occur, unless such provision is made, we undertake in such an event to neglect or violate our statutory duty so far as the requirement of such a by-law may exceed the requirements imposed by cl. 1 of our contract with the claimants.' Such a contractual provision would seem to be plainly invalid. . . .".

His Lordship relied on the point that the corporation was not "a body trading for profit", unlike the body executing statutory duties in *Southport Corporation v Birkdale District Electric Supply Co.*, and like the trustees in the *Ayr* case. Thus "the considerations which were thought relevant in the *Southport* case (so far as that decision threw doubt in [*sic*] the *York* case) have no application here".

It was accepted, however, that the contract had been frustrated from the date the byelaws came into effect.

6. In March 1967, Cheshire County Council and Congleton Rural District Council entered into an agreement with Manchester University, whereby the councils undertook to discourage development "within the limits of their powers" in a zone within the rural district. The aim was to protect the Jodrell Bank radio telescope, which was operated by a department of the University. The rural district council dealt with applications for planning permission as agents for the county council (the local planning authority).

In *Stringer v Minister of Housing and Local Government* [1970] 1 W.L.R. 1281, Cooke J. held that this agreement was *ultra vires* as inconsistent with the proper performance of the duties of a planning authority under the Town and Country Planning Act 1962, s.17(1). This required the authority to have regard to the provisions of the development plan, and to any other material considerations. It was admitted that after the agreement was signed the local planning authority did not override the Jodrell Bank objections to development, and the judge held that the intention of the agreement was to bind the authority to disregard considerations to which, under s.17(1), they were required to have regard. The judge held, further, that in refusing S's application for planning permission for 23 houses, the rural district council had intended to honour this agreement, it being immaterial whether or not it was legally binding, and so had failed to comply with s.17(1). The Rural District Council's determination was therefore void.

Nevertheless, Cooke J. ultimately decided against S. S had appealed to the Minister against the Rural District Council's determination. The Minister had dismissed the appeal on the ground that the development would give rise to a very serious danger to the continued operation of the telescope. S was now applying under s.179(1) of the 1962 Act for an order to quash the Minister's decision on the ground that it was not within the powers of the Act (see now s.288 of the 1990 Act and below, pp.805–816). Cooke J. held that as the Minister had power to deal with appeals *de novo* (under s.23(4) of the 1962 Act; now, s.79(1) of the 1990 Act), he could entertain an appeal in this case even though the Rural District Council's determination was void. On the facts, the Minister had not been influenced by the 1967 agreement, and had not applied rigidly his policy to protect the telescope (see above, p.488). S's application was dismissed.

7. An undertaking that a public authority will act in a particular way may give rise to a legitimate expectation protected (in various ways) by public law. The authority will not be bound by it as such and so the no-fettering principle does not come into play. See further below: pp.515–520, 591–621, 690–701.

8. A number or cases apply a no-fettering principle to the Crown, although it is not clear whether it is the same in all respects as that applicable to other public authorities. In *Rederiaktiebolaget Amphitrite v The King* [1921] 3 K.B. 500, a Swedish shipowning company sued the Crown by petition of right for damages for breach of contract. During the First World War, the British Government unequivocally undertook that if the petitioner's ship, the *SS Amphitrite*, proceeded to the UK with at least 60 per cent approved goods, it would be given clearance to leave. In the event clearance was refused. Rowlatt J. held that there was no enforceable contract. He said (at 503-504):

> "No doubt the Government can bind itself through its officers by a commercial contract, and if it does so it must perform it like anybody else or pay damages for the breach. But this was not a commercial contract; it was an arrangement whereby the Government purported to give a assurance as to what its executive action would be in the future in relation to a particular ship in the event of her coming to this country with a particular kind of cargo. And that is, to my mind, not a contract for the breach of which damages can be sued for in a Court of law. It was merely an expression of intention to act in a particular way in a certain event. My main reason for so thinking is that it is not competent for the Government in fetter its future executive action, which must necessarily be determined by the needs of the community when the question arises. It cannot by contract hamper its freedom of action in matters which concern the welfare of the State. Thus in the case of the employment of public servants, which is a less strong case than the present, it has been laid down that, except under an Act of Parliament, no one acting on behalf of the Crown has authority to employ any person except upon the terms that he is dismissible at the Crown's pleasure; the reason being that it is in the interests of the community that the ministers for the time being advising the Crown should be able to dispense with the services of its employees if they think it desirable. Again suppose that a man accepts an office which he is perfectly at liberty to refuse, and does so on the express terms that he is to have certain leave of absence, and that when the time arrives the leave is refused in circumstances of the greatest hardship to his family or business, as the case may be. Can it be conceived that a petition of right would lie for damages? I should think not. I am of opinion that this petition must fail and there must be judgement for the Crown".

This brief judgment is the source of the so-called "doctrine of executive necessity" under which the Crown may apparently plead executive necessity as a defence to an action for breach of contract. It was cited by Devlin L.J. in *Commissioners of Crown Lands v Page* [1960] 2 Q.B. 274 at 291, along with *Ayr Harbour Trustees* (p.498) and *Cory* (p.503) as authority for the proposition that

> "When the Crown, or any other person, is entrusted, whether by virtue of the prerogative or by statute, with discretionary powers to be exercised for the public good, it does not, when making a private contract in general terms, undertake (and it may be that it could not even with the use of specific language validly undertake) to fetter itself in the use of those powers, and in the exercise of its discretion".

In *Page*, the Court of Appeal held an implied covenant of quiet enjoyment in a lease of premises denied by the Crown as Commissioners of Crown Lands could not be construed so as to fetter the discretion of the Crown (through the Minister of Works) to requisition the premises under statutory powers. The premises had been let in 1937, requisitioned in 1945, and de-requisitioned in 1955. The lessee had been compensated for the requisition and in these proceedings was held liable to the Commissioners for arrears of rent. Devlin L.J. also indicated, *obiter*, (at 292, 293) that the position would have been the same if there had been an express covenant of quiet enjoyment:

> "When the Crown, in dealing with one of its subjects, is dealing as if it too were a private person, and is granting leases or buying and selling as ordinary persons do, it is absurd to suppose that it is making any promise about the way in which it will conduct the affairs of the nation. No one can imagine, for example, that when the Crown makes a contract which could not be fulfilled in time of war, it is pledging itself not to declare war for so long as the contract lasts. Even if, therefore, there was an express promise by the Crown that it would not do any act which might hinder the other party to the contract in the performance of his obligations, the covenant or promise must by necessary implication be read to exclude those measures affecting the nation as a whole which the Crown takes for the public good. . . .
> I need not examine the question whether, if the Crown sought to fetter its future action in express and specific terms, it could effectively do so. It is most unlikely that in a contract with the subject, it would ever make the attempt. For the purpose of this case it is unnecessary to go further than to say that in making a lease or other contract with its subjects, the Crown does not (at least in the absence of specific words) promise to refrain from exercising its general powers under a statute or under the prerogative, or to exercise them in any particular way".

On the *Amphitrite* principle, see P.W. Hogg, Liability of the Crown (2nd ed., 1989), pp.169–172; J.D.B. Mitchell, *The Contracts of Public Authorities*, pp.27–32, 52–57 and Ch.V; C. Turpin, *Government Contracts* (1972), pp.19–25. Does it (and *Page*) suggest that the Crown is always entitled to override a contract by the exercise of one of its statutory or prerogative powers? Or must the power be one with some significant public interest (as those in *Amphitrite* and *Page* were). Does the Crown need the protection of the *Amphitrite* principle? An injunction, or an order for specific performance cannot be awarded against the Crown (see s.21 of the Crown Proceedings Act 1947), and so the Crown in relying on this principle would merely be avoiding the payment of damages. See Hogg, *op.cit.*, p.171,who suggests that the *Amphitrite* was wrongly decided, and Mitchell, *op.cit.*, who accepts the statements of Rowlatt J. "as containing a sound general principle of law" (p.222) but argues that compensation should be payable wherever contractual obligations are overridden in the public interest. Consider also the impact of the First Protocol, Art.1 ECHR (pp.388–389).

DOWTY BOULTON PAUL LTD v WOLVERHAMPTON CORPORATION

[1971] 1 W.L.R. 204; (1970) 115 S.J. 76; [1971] 2 All E.R. 277; 69 L.G.R. 192 (CHANCERY DIVISION, PENNYCUICK V.C.)

[The facts are stated above at pp.431–433 in relation to the sequel to this application.] By notice of motion dated September 23, 1970, the company sought an interlocutory injunction that the corporation should ". . . do nothing which would cause the Board of Trade [later the Department of Trade and Industry] to determine the existing licence enabling Pendeford Aerodrome, Wrottesley, Wolverhampton to be used as a licensed airfield and shall do nothing to prevent the company from using the airfield for their lawful purposes".

PENNYCUICK V.C.: . . . The first issue which has arisen upon the hearing of this motion is whether under the terms of the 1936 conveyance or under the general law the corporation is entitled to override the rights conferred upon the company under the 1936 conveyance. If it is so entitled that would be the end of the matter: the corporation will do no wrong to the company if it does nullify those rights by developing the airfield as a housing estate and the company will have no remedy whether by way of injunction or damages or otherwise.

Mr Bagnall for the company was content to rely on the plain terms of the 1936 conveyance. . . .

Mr Newsom's [main] contention . . . was that, under the general law regarding the exercise of statutory powers, the corporation is at any time entitled to override this licence, if it requires to use the airfield for any of its statutory purposes. These, of course, include its powers as a housing authority. Mr Newsom accepted that the grant of the licence under the 1936 conveyance was within the powers of the corporation. . . .

Mr Newsom based his contention on the principle that a body entrusted with statutory powers cannot by contract fetter the exercise of those powers. He referred to a number of cases which establish beyond all doubt that principle. I refer shortly to three of those authorities.

[His Lordship referred to the *Ayr* case, *York Corporation v H. Leetham* and *Southend-on-Sea Corporation v Hodgson* [1962] 1 Q.B. 416 at 424.]

. . . That seems to me, however, a principle wholly inapplicable to the present case. What has happened here is that the corporation has made what is admittedly a valid disposition in respect of its land for a term of years. What is, in effect, contended by Mr Newsom is that such a disposition—and, indeed, any other possible disposition of property by a corporation for a term of years, for example, an ordinary lease—must be read as subject to an implied condition enabling the corporation to determine it should it see fit to put the property to some other use in the exercise of any of its statutory powers. Nothing in the cases cited supports this startling proposition. The cases are concerned with attempts to fetter in advance the future exercise of statutory powers otherwise than by the valid exercise of a statutory power. The cases are not concerned with the position which arises after a statutory power has been validly exercised. Obviously, where a power is exercised in such a manner as to create a right extending over a term of years, the existence of that right *pro tanto* excludes the exercise of other statutory powers in respect of the same subject-matter, but there is no authority and I can see no principle upon which that sort of exercise could be held to be invalid as a fetter upon the future exercise of powers. . . .

[His Lordship referred to *Stourcliffe Ltd v Bournemouth Corporation* (above, p.503) which had not been cited by counsel.]

I conclude for the purpose of this motion that the company has made out a *prima facie* case that it is entitled to this right and that the corporation is not entitled to override that right either under the terms of the 1936 conveyance or in exercise of its statutory power.

I turn now to consider the remedy available to the company should the corporation persevere in its intention to appropriate this land for housing. It seems to me that the remedy of the company must lie in damages only and that the company is not now entitled, and will not be entitled at the hearing of the action, if it is then otherwise successful, to any relief by way of injunction or mandatory order.

The right vested in the company necessarily involves the maintenance of the airfield as a going concern. That involves continuing acts of management, including the upkeep of runways and buildings, the employment of staff, compliance with the Civil Aviation Act 1949 and so forth, _i.e._ in effect the carrying on of a business. That is nonetheless so by reason that so far the corporation has elected to engage Don Everall Aviation Ltd to manage the airfield on its behalf. It is very well established that the court will not order specific performance of an obligation to carry on a business or, indeed, any comparable series of activities: see in this connection _Halsbury's Laws of England_ (3rd ed., 1961), Vol. 36, pp.267 to 269:

"The court does not enforce the performance of contracts which involve continuous acts and require the watching and supervision of the court."

. . . The principle is established, I should have thought, beyond argument. For this purpose there is no difference between an order for specific performance of the contract and a mandatory injunction to perform the party's obligation under the contract. In the present case the notice of motion is expressed as one for a negative injunction, but one has only to look at it to see that it does involve a mandatory order upon the corporation to maintain the airfield. In order that the corporation could continue to allow the company to use the airfield, it is essential that the corporation should maintain the airfield. It would be quite impossible for the company to use the airfield if the corporation did not maintain it. So an injunction in the terms asked would put upon the corporation a duty, to be observed for something over 60 years, to maintain the airfield.

I conclude therefore in the first place, always so far as this interlocutory motion is concerned, that the company has made out a _prima facie_ case that it is entitled to the right conferred by the 1936 conveyance, and the corporation will do an actionable wrong if it prevents the company from exercising that right. I conclude further that the remedy and the only remedy of the company lies in damages, with the consequence that I must make no order on this motion.

Notes

1. Could the corporation's liability to pay damages for breach of covenant properly be regarded as a fetter on the exercise of their statutory housing powers? Are those powers among the primary powers of the local authority (_cf._ the _Stourcliffe_ case, above, p.503)?

2. If the corporation had covenanted not to build dwelling-houses on the airport site, and such a covenant would have been binding on a private covenantor, should an injunction have been granted?

3. Given that any contract which a public authority has purported to make must be one which is itself within the scope of its legal powers, the issue for the courts may be regarded as one of determining the extent to which an authority's exercise of _one_ of its powers may legitimately inhibit its freedom as regards its exercise of _other_ powers. When looked at in this way it is, perhaps, understandable why a none-too-strict approach should be adopted by the courts.

The point was well illustrated in _R. v Hammersmith and Fulham LBC Ex p. Beddowes_ [1987] Q.B. 1050. Here the Court of Appeal upheld a council resolution which purported to dispose of part of a run-down housing estate to a private developer and to accept a restrictive covenant over retained parts of the estate as to the types of lettings it would grant in those retained parts. The Court of Appeal acknowledged that:

> "if a statutory power is lawfully exercised so as to create legal rights and obligations between the council and third parties, the result will be that the council will for the time being be bound, even though that hinders or prevents the exercise of other statutory powers" (*per* Fox L.J.).

In other words, the mere fact that the exercise of one power may fetter the exercise of another should not suffice to constitute a ground of challenge, provided that the decision so to exercise the former power was taken properly: that is, for proper purposes, on the basis of consideration of all relevant matters (including the extent to which it might fetter the exercise of other powers) and not unreasonably.

4. The scope of an express power to override a covenant was considered in *Thames Water Utilities v Oxford City Council* [1999] 1 E.G.L.R. 1998. Here, Thames Water transferred land to the Council and the council covenanted not to use it or permit it to be used other than for highway, recreational or ancillary purposes. Three years later the council appropriated land, including this land, to planning purposes and agreed the use of powers under s.237 of the Town and Country Planning Act 1990 to override the covenant. It subsequently granted a lease of the land to Oxford United F.C. Thames Water obtained a declaration that that this was in breach of covenant. " Recreational activities" did not include the commercial exploitation of football. Also, s.237 was to be construed narrowly rather than broadly. It enabled the council to override a restrictive covenant to enable "the erection construction or carrying out or maintenance of any building or work on land". This was held by Judge Rich Q.C., sitting as a High Court judge, to apply only to covenants restraining the execution of works and not covenants, such as the one here, restricting the user of the land. The judge was influenced by the consideration that the compensation available by virtue of s.237 through s.10 of the Compulsory Purchase Act 1965 would only cover injurious affection to land retained by Thames Water caused by the execution of works and not their use. This decision would preserve Thames Water's ability to obtain a higher sum on being bought out by agreement of its rights under the covenant. The judge noted the general position that where land is purchased compulsorily or by agreement by a public authority, the acquisition will override any restrictive covenants that would be inconsistent with the statutory purpose for which the land is purchased, leaving the person with the benefit of the covenant to a claim for compensation under the applicable provisions of the 1965 Act. See *Kirby v School Board for Harrogate* [1896] 1 Ch. 437, CA; *Manchester, Sheffield and Lincolnshire Ry v Anderson* [1898] 2 Ch. 294; *Long Eaton Recreation Grounds Co. v Midland Railway Co.* [1902] 2 K.B. 574; *Brown v Heathlands Mental Health NHS Trust* [1996] 1 All E.R. 133; *6, 8, 10 and 12 Elm Avenue, New Milton, Re* [1984] 1 W.L.R. 1398. However a covenant will not be overridden by the exercise of a statutory power ancillary to the essential purpose of the acquisition; the right to obtain an injunction remains (*Stourcliffe*, above, p.503).

(E) FETTERING DISCRETION BY ESTOPPEL

"Estoppel" is a private law principle which prevents a person who has led another to believe in a particular state of affairs from going back on the words or conduct which lead to that belief when it would be unjust or unequitable (unconscionable) for him to do so; the first person is "estopped" (*i.e.* stopped) from going back on the statement, promise or assurance he has made (*Halsbury's Laws of England*: Estoppel, para.951). This principle exists in a number of forms of which the main ones are common law estoppel by representation, promissory estoppel and proprietary estoppel. *Halsbury* (Estoppel, paras 957-959) defines these as follows (footnotes omitted):

(i) common law estoppel by representation

"Where a person has by words or conduct made to another a clear and unequivocal representation of fact, either with knowledge of its falsehood or with the intention that it should be acted upon, or has so conducted himself that another would, as a reasonable person, understand that a certain representation of fact was intended to be acted upon, and the other person has acted upon such representation and thereby altered his position, an estoppel arises against the party who made the representation, and he is not allowed to aver that the fact is otherwise than he represented it to be."

(ii) promissory estoppel

"Promissory estoppel is an extension by equity of common law estoppel by representation. The principle of promissory estoppel is that, when one party has, by his words or conduct, made to the other a clear and unequivocal promise or assurance which was intended to affect the legal relations between them and to be acted on accordingly, then, once the other party has taken him at his word and acted on it, the one who gave the promise or assurance cannot afterwards be allowed to revert to their previous legal relations as if no such promise or assurance had been made by him, but must accept their legal relations subject to the qualification which he himself has so introduced."

(iii) proprietary estoppel

". . . [P]roprietary estoppel has been described as follows. The owner of land, A, in some way leads or allows the claimant, B, to believe that he has or can expect some kind of right or interest over A's land. To A's knowledge, B acts to his detriment in that belief. A then refuses B the anticipated right or interest in circumstances that make the refusal unconscionable. In those circumstances, an equity arises in B's favour. This gives B the right to go to court and seek relief. The court has a very wide discretion as to how it will give effect to this equity."

With the exception of proprietary estoppel, where a promise of an interest in land has been made and relied on, estoppel cannot constitute a cause of action in itself.

These principles are potentially applicable to public authorities as they are to private persons or bodies. However, the statutory context in which a public authority operates may prevent an estoppel applying to it that would otherwise have applied. The cases in this section illustrate different ways in which this may happen. Accordingly (i) the legal (usually statutory) powers of a public body cannot be extended by the creation of an estoppel: the *Rhyl* case, below, p.511, (ii) a body cannot be estoppel from performing a legal (usually statutory) duty; the *Maritime Electric* case, below, p.514; (iii) a discretion conferred upon a public body (usually a statute) cannot be fettered by the creation of an estoppel. Where no such problem arises then a public authority may indeed by bound by an estoppel, illustrated by a number of cases on proprietary estoppel (see below, p.523).

A recurring problem has arisen, however, where a public authority, or someone speaking or apparently speaking on its behalf, has made a statement or given a promise or assurance as to the view it takes or will take on a particular matter arising in the course of performing its functions. Where the authority itself has made a final decision on a matter within its powers, then it will indeed normally be bound by that unless it has express or implied power to revoke that decision. This is sometimes seen as the application of an associated principle, estoppel by record or estoppel *per rem judicatam* (see further below, pp.522–523), but is a distinct principle (*Wade and Forsyth*, pp.243–244). In other situations where the authority has not made a final decision, but a statement is made by itself or an officer, the courts have for many years sought to identify an appropriate way of reconciling two competing considerations. These are first, that a public authority should not be hindered from the proper exercise of its statutory functions by the creation of an estoppel; and secondly, that a strict application of that principle may well be unfair to an individual who relied detrimentally on the statement made by or on behalf of the public authority. Concern to protect the interests of such individuals led Lord Denning to favour the development and application of estoppel principles in public law. In *Howell v Falmouth Boat Construction Co.* [1951] 2 K.B. 16, Denning L.J. *obiter* (at 26) stated that:

"wherever government officers, in their dealings with a subject, take on themselves to assume authority in a matter with which he is concerned, the subject is entitled to rely on their having the authority which they assume. He does not know and cannot be expected to know the limits of their authority, and he ought not to suffer if they exceed it".

In the House of Lords [1951] A.C. 827, Lord Simonds stated (also *obiter*) (at 845): "I know of no such principle in our law nor was any authority for it cited". Notwithstanding this firm rebuttal, Lord Denning M.R. (as he had become), without citing *Howell* stated in *Lever (Finance) Ltd v Westminster Corp.* [1971] 1 Q.B.222 (at 230) that:

"If an officer, acting within the scope of his ostensible authority, makes a representation on which another acts, then a public authority may be bound by it, just as much as a private concern would be".

Here, the Court of Appeal held that the local authority was bound by a statement made by an officer that a change in a developer's plans was not a material change requiring fresh planning permission. The Court of Appeal subsequently held in *Western Fish Products Ltd v Penwith DC* [1981] 2 All E.R. 204 (below, p.519) that the estoppel principle applied to public authorities only within narrow limits.

More recently, other grounds for judicial review have been developed to afford better protection to the legitimate expectations of private individuals and bodies arising from representations made by or on behalf of a public authority. In particular, a decision to resile from a representation that gives rise to a legitimate exception in a way that is as a matter of substance unfair is now open to challenge as an abuse of discretion (see. pp.591–621). In the light of this there has been a clear statement in the House of Lords in *R. (on the application of Reprotech (Pebsham) Ltd v East Sussex CC* that the doctrine of estoppel will have a limited role to play in public law (below, p.515).

Note
See generally J.A. Andrews, "Estoppels against Statutes" (1966) 29 M.L.R. 1; G. Ganz, [1965] P.L. 237; M.A. Fazal, [1972] P.L. 43; P.P. Craig, (1977) 93 L.Q.R. 398 and *Craig*, Ch.16; A.W. Bradley, "Administrative Justice and the Binding Effect of Official Acts" (1981) C.L.P. 1.

(i) No Enlargement of Powers by Estoppel

RHYL URBAN DISTRICT COUNCIL v RHYL AMUSEMENTS LTD

[1959] 1 W.L.R. 465, [1959] 1 All E.R. 257, 57 L.G.R. 19 (HARMAN J.)

Rhyl Urban District Council sought a declaration that a 31-year lease which they had in 1932 granted to the defendant company was void. The only power under which the lease might have been granted was contained in s.177 of the Public Health Act 1875. This required the consent of the Minister of Health to have been obtained. No such consent had been obtained.

HARMAN J.: It was . . . argued by the defendants, and so pleaded, that the plaintiffs are now estopped from denying the validity of the lease. The plea is based on the fact that the relations of the parties have been regulated by it ever since 1932 and that in that year the defendants changed their position by surrendering their 1921 lease on a promise to grant the new one. The representation so acted on must have been that the plaintiffs had power to grant a valid new lease. If the plaintiffs were private people this would be a strong plea, but in my judgment a plea of estoppel cannot prevail as an answer to a claim that something done by a statutory body is *ultra vires*: see *Minister of Agriculture and Fisheries v Hulkin* (1948), an unreported case alluded to by Cassels J. in *Minister of Agriculture and Fisheries v. Matthews* [1950] 1 K.B. 148, where he said (at 153):

> "If, therefore, the Minister does something which is an *ultra vires* act, it is not the act of the Minister at all. In the unreported case of *Minister of Agriculture and Fisheries v Hulkin* the present plaintiff was suing for the possession of a cottage and garden which was in the possession of the defendant. The action was brought in the county court and the county court judge took the view that under the relevant defence regulations it was competent for the County Agricultural Committee, acting under the authority of the Minister, and as the delegate of the Minister's own powers, to create a relationship of landlord and tenant between the Minister and the defendant.
>
> The case went to the Court of Appeal and the appeal of the plaintiff was allowed. The first point which called for consideration was the finding of the county court judge that under the regulation the Minister had power to create a tenancy and that, by the document relied on in that case, he had in fact done so. In the Court of Appeal the defendant's counsel disclaimed any intention of attempting to support the county court judge's judgment on that point. He contended, however, that the Minister having done what he had done in that case was estopped from denying that the document, under which the defendant was in possession, created a tenancy.
>
> In dealing with that contention, Lord Greene M.R. said: 'He (the defendant's counsel) suggested, first of all, that even assuming, as he conceded, that the regulations gave no power to the Minister to create a tenancy, nevertheless the Minister was estopped from denying that the document in question did create a tenancy and, accordingly, the relationship must be regarded as one of landlord and tenant. There is, I think, a very short answer to that. Accepting the view which Mr Bailleu (the defendant's counsel) accepts, that the Minister had no power under the regulations to grant a tenancy, it is perfectly manifest to my mind that he could not by estoppel give himself such power. The power given to an authority under a statute is limited to the four corners of the power given. It would entirely destroy the whole doctrine of *ultra vires* if it was possible for the donee of a statutory power to extend his power by creating an estoppel. That point, I think, can be shortly disposed of.' "

If I may say so with respect, this seems as good sense as it is good law.

It was ingeniously argued that the present was not a case of the plaintiff council having no power, but that they had a power if they obtained the necessary consent and that the doctrine does not apply except where no power exists, so that the plaintiffs might be estopped from denying that they obtained consent. If this be not, as I suspect, a quibble, a like answer could be made that it would destroy the necessity of ever obtaining consent if a statutory body omitting to obtain it could thereafter be held estopped. Such a body could by these means confer on itself a power which it had not got, and the *ultra vires* doctrine would be reduced to a nullity.

Declaration granted.

Notes

1. The same principle applies where a contract is void having been entered into *ultra vires*; the other party cannot rely on any representation that the contract was valid to support an argument that it was so valid (Clarke J. in *South Tyneside MBC v Svenska International Plc* [1995] 1 All E.R. 545). However, this does not bar a contractual claim for reliance losses for misrepresentation and negligent misstatement as the claimant is not thereby seeking to give validity to the void agreement (*Salmon Harvester Proprieties Ltd v Metropolitan Police Authority* [2004] EWHC 1159 (QB) (refusal to strike out)).

2. In *Vestry of the Parish of St Mary, Islington v Hornsey Urban District Council* [1900] 1 Ch.695, CA, the plaintiffs allowed certain Hornsey landowners to use the plaintiffs' sewer. These "rights" were acquired by the defendants, and the plaintiffs allowed the defendants to use the sewer for over 30 years. By 1900, heavy use of the sewer by the defendants caused a serious nuisance in Islington. The Court of Appeal held, first, that the plaintiffs could not grant anything more than a revocable licence. A contract, or the grant of an easement, for the discharge of sewage through the plaintiffs' sewer would have been *ultra vires* as the Metropolis Management Acts only authorised persons within the metropolitan district to use metropolitan sewers. Islington was within, and Hornsey outside the metropolitan district. Secondly, the court held that the plaintiffs were not estopped or debarred by laches or acquiescence from revoking the licence. The only concession to the defendants' argument that disconnection would cause a public nuisance in Hornsey was that they were given 12 months to make alternative arrangements, with the plaintiffs given leave to apply for an injunction at the end of that time.

3. In *Yabbicom v King* [1899] 1 Q.B. 444, DC, Mr King deposited plans for a house with the urban district council which revealed that when built it would not comply with byelaws made by the council under the Public Health Act 1875, s.157. The plans were nevertheless approved by the council. This approval was held to be no defence to a prosecution subsequently brought for breach of the byelaws by the council's successor, Bristol Corporation. *Per* Day J. at 488: "The district council could not control the law, and byelaws properly made have the effect of laws; a public body cannot any more than private persons dispense with laws . . . they have no dispensing power whatever".

4. In *R. v Lambeth BC Ex p. Clayhope Properties Ltd* (1986) 18 H.L.R. 541, a local authority was held not to be estopped from asserting the invalidity of notices it had served under what is now the Housing Act 1985. As the notices were invalid the local authority was entitled to resist claims to, otherwise mandatory, repair grants.

(ii) No Release of Duty by Estoppel

MARITIME ELECTRIC CO. LTD v GENERAL DAIRIES LTD

[1937] A.C. 610; 53 T.L.R. 391; [1937] 1 All E.R. 748 (PRIVY COUNCIL: LORDS ATKIN, THANKERTON, RUSSELL OF KILLOWEN, ALNESS AND MAUGHAM)

The plaintiffs, although a private electricity supply company, were under a statutory duty to furnish reasonably adequate service and facilities, and were strictly limited as to the charges they could make, which had to be in exact accordance with filed schedules open to public inspection. To determine the amount of electricity supplied it was necessary to multiply the meter dial reading by 10. Through the plaintiffs' error this was not done over 28 months in relation to the defendants, a dairy company, who as a result, were charged for only one-tenth of the electricity supplied in this period. The plaintiffs sought to recover the balance of nine-tenths. The defendants had relied on the accuracy of the sums actually charged them for electricity in fixing the amounts they paid to the farmers who supplied them, and in fixing the prices they charged their customers.

LORD MAUGHAM: . . . The sections of the Public Utilities Act which are here in question are sections enacted for the benefit of a section of the public, that is, on grounds of public policy in a general sense. In such a case—and their Lordships do not propose to express any opinion as to statutes which are not within this category—where, as here, the statute imposes a duty of a positive kind, not avoidable by the performance of any formality, for the doing of the very act which the plaintiff seeks to do, it is not open to the defendant to set up an estoppel to prevent it. This conclusion must follow from the circumstance that an estoppel is only a rule of evidence which under certain special circumstances can be invoked by a party to an action; it cannot therefore avail in such a case to release the plaintiff from an obligation to obey such a statute, nor can it enable the defendant to escape from a statutory obligation of such a kind on his part. It is immaterial whether the obligation is onerous or otherwise to the party suing. The duty of each part is to obey the law. . . .

A similar conclusion will be reached if the question put by the learned judge is looked at from a somewhat different angle. It cannot be doubted that if the appellants, with every possible formality, had purported to release their right to sue for the sums remaining due according to the schedules, such a release would be null and void. A contract to do a thing which cannot be done without a violation of the law is clearly void. It may be asked with force why, if a voluntary release will not put an end to the obligation of the respondents, an inadvertent mistake by the appellants acted upon by the respondents can have the result of absolving the appellants from their duty of collecting and receiving payment in accordance with the law. . . . Their Lordships are unable to see how the Court can admit an estoppel which would have the effect *pro tanto* and in the particular case of repealing the statute.

(iii) Estoppel and Discretion

R. (ON THE APPLICATION OF REPROTECH (PEBSHAM) LTD) v EAST SUSSEX CC

[2003] 1 W.L.R. 348; [2002] 4 All E.R. 58 (HOUSE OF LORDS)

A waste treatment plant was vested in a company owned by the county council. A potential purchaser of the site wanted to generate electricity by using waste and was told by the county planning officer that this would not amount to a material change of use requiring planning permission. However, no formal application for a determination under s.64 of the Town and Country Planning Act 1990 was made. This enabled a person who proposed to carry out any operations on land or make any change in the use of land to apply for a determination by the local planning authority whether (i) this would involve development of the land, and (ii) if so, whether an application for planning permission was required. Delegated legislation provided for a formal procedure for such applications, including requirements of publicity similar to those applicable to applications for planning permission.

There was a condition in the existing planning permission that generally prohibited the use of power-driven machinery at night. Commercial electricity generation would require 24-hour operation. Accordingly, the potential purchaser applied under s.73 of the 1990 Act for the condition to be relaxed. The relevant council sub-committee was advised by the planning officer that no material change of use was involved. It resolved, subject to a satisfactory noise alteration scheme being agreed with the county planning officer, to authorise him to vary the planning condition so as to exclude power generation equipment, this was not taken further.

R Ltd subsequently purchased the site, with full knowledge of the resolution. Some years later it wished to pursue the matter of electricity generation. The council deemed that it was not bound by the planning officer's opinion that no material change of use was involved and that a formal application for a certificate of lawful use under s.192 of the 1990 Act was necessary. (This had, by amendments effected by the Planning and Compensation Act 1991, replaced s.64 in different terms).

R Ltd sought declarations (i) that the views expressed by the planning officer in 1991 constituted a section 64 determination that no planning permission was required for electricity generation; (ii) that the resolution constituted such a determination; and (iii) that the use of the land for this purpose did not require planning permission. Tucker J. ([2000] Env. 381) granted all three. Declaration (i) was not pursued in the Court of Appeal [2001] Env L.R. 263, which upheld the other two, following *Wells v Minister of Housing and Local Government* [1967] 1 W.L.R. 1000. The House of Lords unanimously allowed the council's appeal.

26. LORD HOFFMAN. . . My Lords, I think that there is room of argument on the question of construction. The resolution has to be read against the general background of the way the planning system work. Although the planning officer described the question of whether electricity generation required planning permission as a "key issue", the committee did not in fact have to decide it. It was not invited to make a determination. In my pinion it is not enough to say that varying condition 10 in the way they did was pointless except on the assumption that electricity generation was permitted. The committee my have thought that ESEL (and anyone buying from ESEL) was content to rely in its own views or the informal advice of the planning officer without going though the formalities of seeking a determination on the question. If they were right, well and good. If they were wrong, they could apply

for planning permission and rely upon the variation of condition 10 as an argument against any objection based on the need of continuous working. As Schiemann LJ said in the Court of Appeal, developers often prefer to take things in stages. So I would not necessarily infer that the committee was intending to make any statement on the question.

27. Be that as it may, the important question, as Aldous LJ recognised, is whether the resolution counted as a determination under section 64. Such a determination is a juridical act, giving rise to legal consequences by virtue of the provisions of the statue. The nature of the required act must therefore be ascertained from the terms of the statue, including any requirements pre-scribed by subordinate legislation such as the General Development Order. Whatever might be the meaning of the resolution, if it was not a determina-tion within the meaning of the Act, it did not have the statutory consequences. If I may quote what I said in the *Mannai* case [1997] AC 749, 776B: "If the clause had said that the notice had to be on blue paper, it would have been no good serving a notice on pink paper, however clear it might have been that the tenant wanted to terminate the lease."

28. A reading of the legislation discloses the following features of a deter-mination. First, it is made in response to an application which provides the planning authority with details of the proposed use and existing use of the land. Secondly, it is entered in the planning register to give the public the opportunity to make representations to the planning authority or the Secretary of State. Thirdly, it requires the district authority to be given the opportunity to make representations. Fourthly, it requires that the Secretary of State have the opportunity to call in the application for his own determination. Fifthly, the determination must be communicated to he applicant in writing and noti-fied to the district authority.

29. It is, I think, clear from this brief summary that a determination is not simply a matter between the applicant and the planning authority in which they are free to agree on whatever procedure they please. It is also a matter which concerns the general public interest and which requires other planning authorities. the Secretary of State on behalf of the national interest and the public itself to be able to participate.

30. My Lords, it is now ten years since section 64 was repealed and I do not think there is much point in deciding which elements of the section 64 proce-dure might have been omitted without depriving it of the character of a statu-tory determination. In the *Wells* case [1967] 1 WLR 1000, to which Aldous LJ referred, a majority of the Court of Appeal decided that an express appli-cation was not needed. In that case, the plaintiff had applied for planning per-mission and received a reply saying that their application would not be considered because the General Development Order had already given per-mission for the proposed development . Lord Denning MR said that the reply was determination notwithstanding that it had not been formally requested. It is not necessary to decide whether this case was correctly decided, although, like Megaw LJ in the later case of *Western Fish Product Ltd v Penwith District Council* [1981 2 All ER 204, 223, I respectfully think that the dissenting judg-ement of Russell LJ is very powerful. in my opinion, however, the present case cannot be brought within the principle applied by the majority in the *Wells* case.

31. In the *Wells* case [1967] 1 WLR 1000 the majority considered that the planning authority's letter was intended to be decision having immediate legal

consequences. It was a refusal of planning permission on the ground that, in the opinion of authority, planning permission already existed. But the resolution of 27 February 1991 was a conditional authorisation of the planning officer to issue a new planning permission. Reprotech accepts that it did not operate as a planning permission. So far as its express terms are concerned, it has never had any legal effect. For my part, I find it impossible to see how a conditional resolution to grant planning permission which does not bind the planning authority can impliedly constitute a binding determination under section 64. In my opinion the resolution as such was not intended to have any legal effect at all. Whether a grant of planning permission would also have amounted to an implied determination need not be considered.

32. Mr Porten, who appeared for Reprotech, submitted that even if the resolution was not a determination under section 64, the county council are estopped by representation or convention from denying that electricity can be generated on the site without further planning permission. I think that even if the council was a private party, there is no material upon which an estoppel can be founded. The opinion of the county planning officer could not reasonably have been taken as binding representation that no planning permission was required. Planning officers are generally helpful in offering opinions on such matters but everyone knows that if a binding determination is required, a formal application must be made under what is now section 191 or 192. Nor was the committee resolution such a representation. If, as I consider, it was not a determination, it cannot have been a representation that it was. And there is no basis of finding any agreed assumption on the basis of which the parties acted. The position at the time when Reprotech bought the site and upon which the parties proceeded was that the resolution had been passed: no more and no less.

33. In any case, I think that it is unhelpful to introduce private law concepts of estoppel into planning law. As Lord Scarman pointed out in *Newbury District Council v Secretary of State for the Environment* [1981] AC 578, 616, estoppels bind individuals on the ground that it would be unconscionable for them to deny what they have represented or agreed. But these concepts of private law should not be extended into "the public law of planning control, which binds everyone". (*See also Dyson J in R v Leicester City Council, Ex p Powergen UK Ltd* [2000] JPL 629, 637.)

34. There is of course an analogy between a private law estoppel and the public law concept of a legitimate expectation created by a public authority, the denial of which may amount to an abuse of power: see *R v North and East Devon Health Authority. Ex p Coughlan* [2001] QB 213. But it is no more than an analogy because remedies against public authorities also have to take into account the interests of the general public which the authority exists to promote. Public law can also take into account the hierarchy of individual rights which exist under the Human Rights Act 1998, so that, for example, the individual's right to a home is accorded a high degree of protection (see *Coughlan's* case, at pp 254–255) while ordinary property rights are in general far more limited by considerations of public interest: see *R (Alconbury Developments Ltd) v Secretary of State for the Environment, Transport and the Regions* [2001] 2 WLR 1389.

35. It is true that in early cases such as the *Wells* case [1967] 1 WLR 1001 and *Lever Finance Ltd v Westminster (City) London Borough Council* [1971] 1 QB 222, Lord Denning MR used the language of estoppel in relation to planning law. At that time the public law concepts of abuse of power and legitimate expectation were very undeveloped and no doubt the analogy of estoppel seemed useful. In the *Western Fish* case [1981] 2 All ER 204 the Court of Appeal tried its best to reconcile these invocations of estoppel with general principle that a public authority cannot be estopped from exercising a statutory discretion or performing a public duty. But the result did not give universal satisfaction: see the comments of Dyson J in the *Powergen* case [2001] JPL 629, 638. It seems to me that in this area, public law has already absorbed whatever is useful from the moral values which underlie the private law concept of estoppel and the time has come for it to stand upon its own two feet.

[His Lordship doubted that the judge had jurisdiction to grant declaration (iii) but held that in any event it had no point and should not be made.]

LORDS NICHOLLS of BIRKENHEAD, MACKAY of CLASHFERN, HOPE of CRAIGHEAD and SCOTT of FOSCOTE agreed with LORD HOFFMANN.

Appeal allowed

Notes

1. The extent to which an authority can be bound by statements (i) made by itself, which will in practice normally be conveyed through an officer) (as in *Wells*) (ii) or made by an officer (as in *Lever Finance* and *Western Fish*) gave rise to a significant and difficult body of case law. There is an important distinction between the two situations.

Where an authority has itself gone through an appropriate decision-making process and what appears to be its final decision is communicated to the person affected, two kinds of case may arise: first whether it does indeed have legal effect as a final decision; and, secondly, the extent to which, if at all, there is power to revoke or modify it. As to the first, the court will need to analyse the precise legal context and the facts closely in order to determine whether what was done was sufficient to constitute a final decision. This process is illustrated by *56 Denton Road, Re,* (below, n.6), where the judge had little difficulty in finding the relevant letter to be a final determination; the *Wells* case, where the Court of Appeal found there to have been a final determination that planning permission was not required even though the prescribed procedure for obtaining such a determination had not been followed; and *Reprotech* where the House held that there had clearly been no final determination. In principle, the fact that there has been some informality in the process should not be fatal provided that overall the decision-making has been done with sufficient attention to relevant considerations and those who have the right to be heard (*cf.* cases on "directory" procedural requirements and the equivalent (below, pp.635–651)). The principle that applies here is similar to that of estoppel by record or *per rem judicatam*, although it should be noted that the latter is regarded by some as a separate principle falling outside the doctrine of estoppel.

The second question, whether there is an express or implied power to revoke, again depends heavily on the statutory context. In planning law, for example, there is express power to revoke or modify a planning permission, but compensation may be payable (Town and Country Planning Act 1990, ss.97–100, 107–113). See further n.6 below.

On the other hand, the application of estoppel to hold an authority bound by a statement made by an officer that he has not been specifically authorised by the authority to make is much more doubtful. Various problems may arise. Clearly, an authority cannot be bound by a statement if that would involve an extension of its powers (*cf. Rhyl*, above, p.511) or prevent the performance of a statutory duty (*cf. Maritime Electric*, above, p.514). In other situations, to hold the authority bound may offend the rule against delegation (*e.g.* where at the time there was no power for a local authority to delegate power to an officer: *cf. Southend-on-Sea Corp. v Hodgson* [1962] 1 Q.B. 416). Or it might mean that a decision is made without full consideration of the appropriate matters or following proper processes designed to protect the interests of others (see Lord Hoffmann's speech in *Reprotech*). Accordingly, the approach of Lord Denning M.R. in *Lever Finance* (see above, p.511 and below, n.2) attached excessive weight to the interests of those who rely on statements by officials.

2. In *Lever (Finance) Ltd v Westminster LBC* [1971] 1 Q.B. 222, developers obtained planning permission for a housing development. Their architects had a telephone conversation with the authority's planning officer in which the latter said that a proposed change whereby one house would be 23ft away from existing house rather than 40ft would not be a material change and that no further planning consent was therefore necessary. The developers proceeded with the revised plan. The Court of Appeal (Lord Denning M.R. and Megaw L.J.) held that there was an established practice whereby officers told applicants whether variations were material, that the statement was within the officer's ostensible authority and bound the authority, which accordingly had no power to issue an enforcement notice. (Sachs L.J. came to the same conclusion on the basis that there had been an implied delegation of power to the officer to make a determination under s.43 of the Town and Country Planning Act 1962, the forerunner of s.64 of the 1990 Act, discussed in *Reprotech*; this reasoning was disapproved in *Western Fish*.)

The Court of Appeal in *Western Fish Products Ltd v Penwith DL* [1981] 2 All E.R. 204 agreed that a statutory body could not be estopped from performing its statutory duties but was bound by existing case law to recognise two exceptions. The first was based on *Lever Finance*. However, this was to be interpreted narrowly, and regarded as an application of the principle that a decision once made cannot be revoked (a principle akin to *res judicata*). It was not authority for the proposition that every representation made by a planning authority within his ostensible authority binds the authority:

"for an estoppel to arise there must be some evidence justifying the persons dealing with the planning officer for thinking that what the officer said would bind the planning authority. Holding an office, however senior, cannot .. be enough by itself" (*per* Megaw L.J. at 220).

The second exception, based on *Wells*, was that a planning authority could be estopped from relying on a lack of formality that it had waived. Neither exception applied on the facts of *Western Fish*. The Court also drew attention to the real danger on the facts of *Lever Finance* of injustice to the neighbours who had not been able to be heard on the question whether the modifications were material. Is *Lever Finance* to be regarded as overruled by *Reprotech*? How would the modern principle concerning substantive legitimate expectations (below, pp.591–621) apply on the facts of *Lever Finance*?

3. In *R. (on the application of Wandsworth LBC) v Secretary of State for Transport, Local Government and the Regions* [2003] EWHC 622, Sullivan J. held that the "first exception" in *Western Fish* had not survived the decision in *Reprotech*, in which

"the House of Lords could not have made it more plain that estoppel no longer has any place in planning law. . . . If a matter is *res judicata* there is no need for an estoppel, if it is not there is no longer any scope for estoppels which are akin to *res judicata*" (at [21]).

Here, the decision of a planning inspector before *Reprotech* applying the principle of estoppel by representation to a planning authority was quashed. It is submitted that Sullivan J.'s statement should not be interpreted as calling into question the applicability of the *Denton Road, Re*, or estoppel *per rem judicatam* principles in public law, but only the highly strained justification on this basis for *Lever Finance* put forward in *Western Fish*.

The scope of *Reprotech* was also considered in *Stancliffe Stone Co. Ltd v Peak District National Park Authority* [2004] EWHC 1475, [2005] Env.L.R. 4, where the question was whether four quarries owned by the claimant were to be treated as one mineral site (as they argued) or as separate sites (two of which were dormant—the view of the authority). Moore-Bick J. upheld the authority's view, but rejected one of its arguments, namely that the *claimants* were estopped from arguing that they were to be treated as one site through an application of the principle of estoppel by convention. (This is closely related to estoppel by representation and applies where the parties to a transaction proceed on the basis of an underlying assumption on which they have conducted the dealings between them.) Moore-Bick J. held (1) that Lord Hoffmann's statements concerning the role of estoppel in public law were *obiter*, but "are . . . of the highest persuasive authority and are not restricted in their application to one kind of estoppel only" (at. [35]); and (2) that he did not think "that the doctrine of estoppel can operate in favour of an authority against an applicant any more than it can operate against an authority in favour of an applicant" (at [35]). Furthermore, in the case of estoppel by convention there was the added difficulty that if the authority could not be held to the common understanding it was unlikely to be fair or just to hold the applicant to it (*ibid*).

5. There were a number of cases decided before *Reprotech* in which the courts held that a particular representation was insufficiently clear and unambiguous to give rise to an estoppel, or that a representation made by an officer did not fall within the ostensible authority of the officer. Notwithstanding *Reprotech* these may still be helpful in deciding whether a particular representation given rise to a legitimate expectation. See further, pp.621–615.

6. The questions whether a decision is final and conclusive and, if so, whether there is power subsequently to revoke or modify it have been considered in a number of cases. In *56 Denton Road, Twickenham, Re* [1953] Ch. 51, the plaintiff's house was partly demolished by enemy action, and the local authority subsequently pulled down what was left. The War Damage Act 1943 provided that compensation was payable to cover the cost of works in repairing damage, unless the damage involved total loss in which case a "value payment" was payable, unless the War Damage Commission exercised its power to make a cost of works payment instead. For the plaintiff, a "value payment" would be much lower than "cost of works payment". The Commission initially made a "preliminary classification" of total loss, then told the plaintiff by letter dated November 12, 1945, that it had been "reclassified" as not a total loss, with a cost of works payment accordingly becoming payable. The Commission purported subsequently to change its mind again and revert to the original classification. Vaisey J. granted a declaration that the November 1945 letter constituted a final determination that the damage was one for which a cost of works payment ought to be awarded. His Lordship accepted the following proposition of the plaintiff's counsel:

> "that where Parliament confers upon a body such as the War Damage Commission the duty of deciding or determining any question, the deciding or determining of which affects the rights of the subject, such decision or determination made and communicated in terms which are not expressly preliminary or provision is final and conclusive, and cannot in the absence of express statutory power or the consent of the person or persons affected be altered or withdrawn by that body. I accept that proposition as well-founded, and applicable to the present case. It is, I think, supported by *Livingstone v Westminster Corporation* [1904] 2 K.B. 109 and *Robertson v Minister of Pensions* [1949] 1 K.B. 227.
>
> I think that the letter of November 12, 1945, was one upon which the plaintiff was invited to rely and was and is entitled to rely. It is, I think, admitted that if she had altered her position in reliance upon it, a case of estoppel would have been raised against the defendants. But I really cannot see that it ought to be denied its proper force and effect, quite apart from such a case.
>
> I think that the contrary view would introduce a lamentable measure of uncertainty, and so much disturbance in the minds of those unfortunate persons who have

suffered war damage that the Act cannot have contemplated the possibility of such vacillations as are claimed to be permissible in such a case as the present".

See case notes at 214 L.T. 291; 69 L.Q.R. 13 (R.E.M.).

Compare this case with *R. v Special Adjudicator Ex p. Bashir*, unreported, December 6, 1999 where Harrison J. held that an oral statement by the adjudicator at the end of an appeal hearing that he was allowing the appeal was not a final determination; he could, accordingly change his mind and reflect a different conclusion in the written notice of a determination required by the Asylum Appeals (Procedure) Rules 1996. The rules required this to contain a concise statement of the decision on the substantial issues raised, findings of fact and the reasons for it. This was "a substantive task going to the heart of the decision upon which any appeal . . . will be based", and not some-thing done by the adjudicator if he were *functus officio* following the oral decision. There were other cases under other statutory provisions that pointed the other way but the position here depended on the statutory framework in question.

The position is even clearer where what appears to be a final determination is com-municated in error. In *R. v Secretary of State for Education and Science Ex p. Hardy*, *The Times*, July 28, 1988, proposals for the reorganisation of Ilkeston School were placed before the Parliamentary Under-Secretary for approval under s.12(6) of the Education Act 1980. He gave approval by ticking the word "Approve". Following a misunderstanding, an officer in the department informed the authority in confidence that the proposals had been approved. The Secretary of State subsequently decided that the proposals should be rejected. McNeill J. held that compliance with s.12(6) only occurred when there was a formal, precise and published decision. The initial approval was accordingly not an irrevocable decision, and could not be made so by a leak from the Minister's private office. Similarly, the principle in *Denton Road*, does not apply to bind an authority where a final decision is incorrectly communicated: *R. v Birmingham City Council Ex p. L* [2000] E.L.R. 543.

7. It has been held that the *Denton Road* principle does not apply in respect of exer-cises of discretion. In *Rootkin v Kent CC* [1981] 1 W.L.R. 1186, the council measured the travelling distance between the plaintiff's house and her daughter's school at over three miles; on this basis it was in effect by virtue of the Education Act 1944, ss.39(2)(c) and 55(1) under a duty either to provide transport or to reimburse travel-ling expenses; it chose to provide a free bus pass (a yearly season ticket). It subse-quently made a more precise measurement, found the distance to be under three miles and withdrew the pass. The Court of Appeal held that the council was entitled to do so. It accepted that:

"if a citizen is entitled to payment in certain circumstances and a local authority is given the duty of deciding whether the circumstances exist and if they do exist of making the payment, then there is a determination which the local authority cannot rescind. That was established in *Livingston v Westminster Corp.* [1904] 2 K.B. 109. But that line of authority does not apply to a case where the citizen has no right to a determination on certain facts being established, but only to the benefit of the exer-cise of discretion by the local authority" (*per* Lawton L.J. at 1195).

Eveleigh L.J. (at 1197) said that:

"generally speaking . . . a discretionary power may be exercised from time to time unless a contrary intention appears. I can see nothing in the [Education Act 1944] to prevent the education authority from reversing its decision from time to time, when the decision is under s.55(2)".

Sir Stanley Rees agreed with both judgments.

(The court also held that the council could not be prevented from exercising its statu-tory discretion by estoppel (*Southend-on-Sea Corporation v Hodgson (Wickford) Ltd*

[1961] 1 Q.B. 416 applied); the *Western Fish* exception did not apply, and the plaintiff had not altered her position in reliance on the decision: see Lawton L.J. at 1197).

It is submitted that this cannot be taken too far. First, it should be noted that if the distance had been more than three miles, the council's discretion would have been very limited: either to provide transport or reimburse travelling expenses (see Sir Stanley Rees at 1198). Eveleigh L.J.'s reference to the general discretion to reimburse travelling expenses under s.55(2) seems beside the point. Accordingly, there would have been a strong argument that the issue of the bus pass *for that year* would have fallen within the *Denton Road* principle. This did not arise on the facts as (1) the council did not purport to withdraw the pass with retrospective effect; and (2) the plaintiff actually refused to hand it over and her daughter continued to use it, presumably for the year. What the plaintiff wanted was to hold the council bound to continue providing free passes through her daughter's time at this school. That would be to stretch *Denton Road* too far. It was entirely appropriate to interpret the legislation to enable the factual pre-condition for free transport to be revisited; this might for example, have been necessary if a new road providing a more direct route to school had been constructed. It cannot be the law that any decision made in exercise of a discretionary power can be revised at will (or even, necessarily because there has been some mistake) and *Rootkin* should not be so interpreted; *cf. Wade and Forsyth*, p.229, drawing a distinction between "powers of a continuing character and powers which, once exercised, are finally expended so far as concerns the particular case".

8. Vaisey J. accepted in *56 Denton Road, Re,* that a final decision could be reconsidered with the consent of the person affected. In *R. v Hertfordshire CC Ex p. Cheung, The Times*, April 4, 1986, the council in 1978 had refused C a student grant on the ground that he was not "ordinarily resident" in the United Kingdom. The test applied was shown to be erroneous by the House of Lords in *R. v Barnet LBC Ex p. Shah* [1982] 2 A.C. 309. Leave to challenge the 1978 decision was refused. The council refused C's request to reconsider the matter. McNeill J. at first instance held that the council did have power to reconsider the matter in the light of C's request; the Court of Appeal simply asserted that there was a discretion to reconsider. (The Court of Appeal held that C's case should have been reconsidered for the 1978–79 academic year so as to be consistent with one of the students in the *Shah* case.) See C. Lewis [1987] P.L. 21, noting that the Court of Appeal had offered no guidance on the extent of the implied discretion to reconsider.

9. In appropriate cases, the courts may interpret a statute as providing a power of revocation by implication, but only for specific purposes; *cf. R. v Hillington LBC Ex p. London Regional Transport* [1999] B.L.G.R. 543 . Here the Court of Appeal held that the provisions in s.104(1) of the London Passenger Transport Act 1934 that enable LRT to erect and maintain bus shelters, except that it could not use for the purpose any part of the highway without the consent of the council, was not to be interpreted as enabling the council to revoke its consent for reasons unconnected with highway and safety considerations. The council had purported to revoke the consents given by its predecessors so that it could use its powers to provide bus shelters under s.4 of the Local Government (Miscellaneous Provisions) Act 1953, and thereby obtain the benefit of the associated advertising revenue. The court did not need to reach the question whether there was indeed an implied power to revoke for heath and safety reasons, but presumably there would be. At first instance Hidden J. (*The Times*, January 20, 1999) had held (1) that there had to be a continuing consent under s.104; (2) alternatively that there was an implied power to revoke, not restricted to health and safety reasons; and (3) that the question of additional benefits to the council for advertising revenue were not legally irrelevant considerations. *Rootkin* was to be distinguished from *Denton Road* "on the ground that *Rootkin* was dealing with a continuing state of affairs whereby *56 Denton Road* was dealing with a one off payment".

10. The principle of estoppel by record or estoppel *per rem judicatam* can apply in the public law context. This includes (1) cause of action estoppel (where a legal claim has been judicially determined in a final manner between the parties by a tribunal

having jurisdiction in the matter and the same issue comes directly in question in subsequent proceedings between the same parties); and (2) issue estoppel (where an issue has been judicially determined as a necessary step in reaching a judgment and the issue arises in subsequent proceedings between the same parties) (definitions taken from H.L.E., Estoppel, para.953). This is "more properly regarded as part of the law of evidence" than as part of the law of estoppel (*ibid.*, p.951). If not essentially the same principle, this and the *Denton Road* principle are clearly related. Both promote legal certainty; neither depends on any reliance by the parties. A decision on a planning appeal may give rise to issue estoppel binding on the local planning authority (*Thrasyvoulou v Secretary of State of the Environment* [1990] 2 A.C. 273; C. Crawford (1990) 53 M.L.R. 814). However, it seems that the decision of an officer within one government department cannot give rise to an issue estoppel binding on another department. This was so held in *R. (on the application of Nahar) v Social Security Commissioners* [2001] EWHC Admin 1049; [2002] 1 F.L.R. 670, where Munby J. held that the decision of two immigration adjudicators that the claimant was married to a British citizen could not give rise to an issue estoppel binding on the Secretary of State for Work and Pensions, whose department had decided that she was not so married in rejecting her claim for a widow's pension. There were "neither identity of parties nor any sufficient privity of interest" between the two departments. On appeal, the Court of Appeal ([2002] EWCA Civ 927; [2002] A.C.D. 105) held that reliance on issue estoppel was in any event misconceived as the relevant adjudicator's decision was that of the second adjudicator, which came after that of the Social Security Appeal Tribunal that rejected N's claim to a pension. It expressed no view on Munby J's conclusion on the law, save to note that they seemed to be in line with *Spencer Bower, Turner and Handley, Res Judicata*, pp.116–117.

The Court of Appeal in *R. (on the application of Munjaz) v Mersey Care NHS Trust* [2003] EWCA Civ 1036; [2004] Q.B. 395 has indeed doubted whether issue estoppel (a "doctrine appropriate to proceedings in private law") can ever apply in judicial review proceedings, where "there is always a third party who is not present: the wider public or public interests," which should not be prejudiced by the failure of a public authority to place all the relevant material and arguments before the court on the first occasion (*per* Hale L.J. at [79]). Accordingly, the Trust was entitled (albeit unsuccessfully) to defend a revised policy on the seclusion of mental patients where its original policy had been declared unlawful. Nevertheless, the court did not rule out the possibility that in certain circumstances it would be an abuse of process "to permit a public authority which has acted in disregard of a declaration or order made in judicial review proceedings to seek to reopen debate about whether its actions were justified" (*ibid.*)

11. For examples of cases where a public authority has been held bound by a proprietary estoppel, see *Crabb v Arun DC* [1976] Ch. 179; *Salvation Army Trustee Co. Ltd v West Yorkshire CC* (1980) 41 P. & C.R. 179; *Att-Gen (Ex rel Scotland) v Barrett Manchester Ltd* (1991) 63 P. & C.R. 179

12. See generally on the issues of *res judicata* and revocability, G. Ganz [1965] P.L. 237, M.B. Akehurst, [1982] P.L. 613, D.C. Stanley (1983) 32 U.N.B. Law Journal 221; *Wade and Forsyth*, pp.229–232, 243–249.

(F) Error of Law in Construing the Scope of a Discretion

R. v VESTRY OF ST PANCRAS

(1890) 24 Q.B.D. 371 (COURT OF APPEAL)

Mr R. Westbrook was appointed to the office of Collector of Rates for the parish of St Pancras in 1858. In 1888, he wished to retire on health grounds, "upon such superannuation allowance as the vestry are empowered to grant for long services". The Superannuation (Metropolis) Act 1866, s.1, provided that the vestry might "at their discretion, grant . . . an annual allowance, not exceeding in any case two-thirds of his then salary, regard being had to the scale of allowances hereinafter contained. . . .". The scale indicated that a man with W's length of service would receive £230 per annum. The vestry thought that they only had discretion as to whether the full allowance suggested by the statute should or should not be paid, and as they did not think W should have so large an allowance, they resolved to pay nothing. W sought *mandamus* to compel the vestry to consider his application in accordance with the statute.

LORD ESHER M.R.: . . . I have no doubt that the vestry should take his application into their fair consideration, and do what they think fair to the man under the circumstances, and if they do this, I have equally no doubt that the legislature has entrusted the sole discretion to them, and that no mandamus could go to them to alter their decision. But they must fairly consider the application and exercise their discretion on it fairly, and not take into account any reason for their decision which is not a legal one. If people who have to exercise a public duty by exercising their discretion take into account matters which the Courts consider not to be proper for the guidance of their discretion, then in the eye of the law they have not exercised their discretion. . . .

[T]he vestry of any parish and certain other bodies may in their discretion grant to any officer who satisfies the conditions an annual allowance. If the matter had stopped there, and in a subsequent part of the statute there had been found a fixed amount which was to be given, I should have thought that the discretion was limited to the question whether there should be an allowance or not. But the section goes on, "an annual allowance not exceeding two-thirds of his then salary". This by necessary implication involves that they may give less than the two-thirds. . . . Then there are the words in section 1, "regard being had to the scale of allowance hereinafter contained". That scale is set out in section 4, and is a rising scale according to the number of years' service. They are, therefore, to look at the scale to see the number of years' service, but that does not affect the power given by section 1 or the necessary implication from the words, "not exceeding", used in that section. It seems to me, therefore, that they have a discretion as to the amount though they cannot go beyond that set out in the scale. This interpretation takes away all difficulty in considering the meaning of section 4, for the word "shall" only applies to the use of the scale to ascertain the maximum, and not otherwise to the question of amount; and further it gives a reasonable, fair and sufficiently elastic power to the vestry, instead of a hard and fast rule which may work injustice in some cases. . . .

The result in this case seems to me to be that . . . the vestry did not bring their minds to the question which they had to decide, and took into account circum-stances which they ought not to have taken into account, and so did not properly exercise their discretion. . . .

FRY L.J. delivered a concurring judgment.

Note
For an example of modern application of this ground of review, see, *e.g. R. v Secretary of State for the Environment Ex p. Dudley BC, The Times,* June 14, 1989.

CHAPTER 9

ABUSE OF DISCRETION

In this chapter we shall consider various grounds upon which it may be alleged that the manner of exercise of an admitted discretionary power amounts to an abuse of power. In this context the courts have consistently stated that their function is not to act as a "court of appeal" on the merits of the discretionary decision—their function is to intervene only if one or more of the established grounds of review, considered below, has been infringed. Consider, in reading the cases which follow, whether this distinction between "merits" and "legality" is tenable, and whether in all of the cases the courts have indeed been influenced only by the latter and not the former consideration.

The material which follows is divided into the following sections:

(A) Use of powers for an improper purpose;
(B) Taking into account irrelevant considerations; failure to have taken into account relevant considerations;
(C) Unreasonableness;
(D) Inconsistency (unfair interference with a substantive legitimate expectation);
(E) Proportionality.

This last ground is (at the time of writing) only formally a ground of challenge in the context of EC law and under the Human Rights Act 1998.

(A) Use of Powers for an Improper Purpose

A statutory power must only be used for the purposes expressed in, or to be implied from, the relevant statute. The *Municipal Council of Sydney* case (below) provides an example of successful challenge where the statute expressly stated the purpose(s) for which the power had been conferred.

Where purposes are not explicitly stated, the courts look to the legislation as a whole and determine the legislative purpose that is to be furthered. See *Padfield* (below, p.528) and *Congreve* (below, p.543).

In some cases it may appear that a decision has been motivated by a *mixture* of legitimate and illegitimate purposes. This issue will be treated after review for "relevant/irrelevant considerations" has been considered (see pp.563–569).

MUNICIPAL COUNCIL OF SYDNEY v CAMPBELL

[1925] A.C. 338; 94 L.J.P.C. 65; 133 L.T. 63
(PRIVY COUNCIL: VISCOUNT CAVE, LORD BLANESBOROUGH,
DUFF J., SIR ADRIAN KNOX)

(Appeal from the Supreme Court of New South Wales)

By s.16 of the Sydney Corporation Amendment Act 1905, the council was empowered to purchase compulsorily any land required for "carrying out improvements in or remodelling any portion of the city". The council resolved that certain land including the property of the respondents should be purchased. Their object was to get the benefit of the increase in the value of this land which would result from the proposed extension of a highway by the council. No plan for improvement or remodelling was at any time proposed to, or considered by, the council. The Chief Judge in Equity granted injunctions restraining the council from acting on their resolution (24 S.R. (N.S.W.) 179). The council appealed to the Privy Council. The opinion of their Lordships was delivered by Duff J.

DUFF J.: . . . Their Lordships think it not reasonably disputable that at the time of the passing of the resolution in June, the council conceived it to be within its powers to resume lands not needed for the extension itself, but solely for the purpose of appropriating the betterments arising from the extension; and that, as Street C.J.E. found, the council had not at that time applied itself to the consideration of any other object in connection with the resumption of the residual lands. . . .

The legal principles governing the execution of such powers as that conferred by section 16, in so far as presently relevant, are not at all in controversy. A body such as the Municipal Council of Sydney, authorized to take land compulsorily for specified purposes, will not be permitted to exercise its powers for different purposes, and if it attempts to do so, the courts will interfere. As Lord Loreburn said, in *Marquess of Clanricarde v. Congested Districts Board* (1914) 79 J.P. 481: "Whether it does so or not is a question of fact." Where the proceedings of the council are attacked upon this ground, the party impeaching those proceedings must, of course, prove that the council, though professing to exercise its powers for the statutory purpose, is in fact employing them in furtherance of some ulterior object.

Their Lordships think that the conclusion of the learned Chief Judge in Equity upon this question of fact is fully sustained by the evidence.

Notes

1. The principles were stated more fully by the House of Lords in *Marquess of Clanricarde v Congested Districts Board for Ireland* (1914) 79 J.P. 481. The Marquess claimed that the Board were exercising their powers of compulsory purchase (*inter alia*) for the reinstatement of evicted tenants, and not for the lawful purpose of the amalgamation or enlargement of smallholdings. The House held that there was no evidence to support the plaintiff's claims.

Per Earl Loreburn at 481:

"In form their [i.e. the Board's] proceedings were regular, but in substance, so the appellant contended, they were proceeding *ultra vires*. . . .. I believe the law is as follows. When an administrative body is authorised by statute to take land compulsorily for specified purposes, the court will interfere if it uses those powers for different purposes. Whether it does or not is a question of fact. The administrative body must really intend to act for a statutory purpose, and the land they seek to take must be land which is capable of being made use of for a statutory purpose, by which I mean that, looking at the land as a whole, a man might in reason think the purchase could be utilised for any of the statutory purposes. That also is a question of fact. But anyone who objects to what is done on either of these grounds must prove his objection. In the one case he must prove that there was not such a purpose, and in the other case he must prove that the land was quite incapable of being so used. And the court will not interfere with the discretion or revise the opinion of the administrative body if there was anything on which it could in reason come to the conclusion it reached. Of course fraud or dishonesty stands on quite a different footing. A court will always defeat that under any shape, and quite regardless of all form. But when a board is set up with such compulsory powers as are possessed by the Congested Districts Boards, it is not intended that courts of law shall do what we have been invited to do, namely, dog its footsteps and peer into its minutes as if they were to be suspected of meaning more than they say, or trip it up upon the ground that it has not acted judiciously or has not kept proper minutes, or upon any other ground, dishonesty apart, than that it has in fact exceeded its powers".

In these cases, the purposes for which the power could be used were specified. Compare *Padfield* (below) where the legislative purpose had to be inferred by the court.

2. In some situations, Parliament may confer more than one power that can be used to achieve a particular result and a question may arise whether the authority is at all constrained in its choice of which power to use. In *Westminster Bank v Beverley BC* [1971] A.C. 509, the House of Lords held that the council as local planning authority could refuse planning permission for an extension to a bank on the ground that it "might prejudice the future widening" of the street, even though as highways authority the council could have prescribed an improvement line under the Highways Act 1959 to preserve a strip of land for the scheme. The improvement line procedure did, but refusal of planning permission did not, involve payment of compensation. It was held that it was not an "excess of power" to refuse planning permission on this ground. Section 118(1) of the Town and Country Planning Act 1947 provided "that the provisions of this Act . . . apply . . . in relation to any land notwithstanding that provision is made by any enactment in force at the passing of this Act . . . for . . . regulating any development of the land". The relevant Highways Act provisions were re-enacted from pre-1947 legislation. On the question as to whether there was an "abuse of power" in choosing the procedure where no compensation was payable:

Per Lord Reid (at 530):

"Parliament has chosen to set up two different ways of preventing development which would interfere with schemes for street widening. It must have been aware that one involved paying compensation but the other did not. Nevertheless it expressed no preference, and imposed no limit on the use of either. No doubt there might be special circumstances which make it unreasonable or an abuse of power to use one of these methods but here there were none. Even if the appellants' view of the facts is right, the authority had to choose whether to leave the appellants without compensation or to impose a burden on its ratepayers. One may think that it would be most equitable that the burden should be shared. But the Minister of Transport had made it clear in a circular sent to local authorities in 1954 that there would be no grant if a local authority proceeded in such a way that compensation would be payable, and there is nothing to indicate any disapproval of this policy by Parliament and nothing in any of the legislation to indicate that Parliament disapproved of depriving the subject of compensation. I cannot in these circumstances find any abuse of power in the local authority deciding that the appellants and not its rate-payers should bear the burden . . .".

cf. Asher v Secretary of State for the Environment [1974] 1 Ch. 208; *Hoveringham Gravels Ltd v Secretary of State for the Environment* [1975] Q.B. 754; *R. v Exeter City Council Ex p. J.L. Thomas & Co. Ltd* [1991] 1 Q.B. 471.

PADFIELD v MINISTER OF AGRICULTURE, FISHERIES AND FOOD

[1968] A.C. 997; [1968] 2 W.L.R. 924; 112 S.J. 171; [1968] 1 ALL E.R.
694 (HOUSE OF LORDS)

The Agricultural Marketing Act 1958 contained (*inter alia*) provisions relating to the
milk marketing scheme. By s.19:

"(3) A committee of investigation shall— . . . (b) be charged with the duty, if the
Minister in any case so directs, of considering, and reporting to the Minister on,
any . . . complaint made to the Minister as to the operation of any scheme which, in
the opinion of the Minister, could not be considered by a consumers' committee. . .
(6) If a committee of investigation report to the Minister that any provision of a
scheme or any act or omission of a board administering a scheme is contrary to the
interests of consumers of the regulated product, or is contrary to the interests of
any persons affected by the scheme and is not in the public interest, the Minister,
if he thinks fit to do so after considering the report—(a) may by order make such
amendments in the scheme as he considers necessary or expedient for the purpose
of rectifying the matter; (b) may by order revoke the scheme; (c) in the event of the
matter being one which it is within the power of the board to rectify, may by order
direct the board to take such steps to rectify the matter as may be specified in the
order . . .".

Under the scheme, producers had to sell their milk to the Milk Marketing Board, which
fixed the different prices paid to the producers for milk in each of the 11 regions into
which England and Wales were divided. The differentials reflected (*inter alia*) the
varying costs of transporting milk from the producers to the consumers.

Had there been no controls, the profits of the south-eastern producers would have
been the largest, as they were near to a very large market, and their transport costs
would have been the lowest in the country. Under the scheme, transport costs were
borne by the Board. Had a fixed price been paid to all producers, those in the south-
east would have been treated unfairly. The current differentials had been fixed
several years previously, when transport costs were much lower. For about 10 years,
the south-eastern producers had unsuccessfully been urging the Board to increase
the differentials. The differential between the south-east region and the far west
(where the lowest price was paid) was 1.19d per gallon, and the south-eastern producers wanted this increased to 3.5d. Since the total sum available to the Board to
pay for milk bought in all regions was fixed each year, giving effect to this claim
would mean that the south-eastern producers and perhaps those in some other
regions would get higher prices, but producers in the far west and several other
regions would get less.

The Board was constituted in such a way that the south-eastern producers could not
hope to get a majority for their proposals. The present appellants, who were office
bearers of the south-east regional committee, asked the Minister to appoint a committee of investigation under s.19. On May 1, 1964, they had been informed by letter
that:

"3. In considering how to exercise his discretion the Minister would, amongst other
things, address his mind to the possibility that if a complaint were so referred and
the committee were to uphold it, he in turn would be expected to make a statutory
order to give effect to the committee's recommendations. It is this consideration,
rather than the formal eligibility of the complaint as a subject for investigation, that
the Minister would have in mind in determining whether your particular complaint
is a suitable one for reference to the committee. We were unable to hold out any
prospect that the Minister would be prepared to regard it as suitable.

4. The reasons which led us to this conclusion were explained to you as follows: (a) The guarantee given to milk producers under the Agriculture Acts is a guarantee given to the board on behalf of all producers. The Minister owes no duty to producers in any particular region, and this is a principle that would be seriously called into question by the making of an Order concerned with a regional price; (b) Such action would also bring into question the status of the Milk Marketing Scheme as an instrument for the self-government of the industry and such doubt would also, by extension, affect the other Marketing Schemes as well; and (c) It is by no means clear that the Minister could make an Order pertaining to the price of milk in the south-east without determining at least one of the major factors governing prices in the other regions, and he would therefore be assuming an inappropriate degree of responsibility for determining the structure of regional prices through England and Wales".

On March 23, 1965, the private secretary to the Minister wrote to inform the appellants that the Minister had decided not to refer the matter to the committee. The following reasons were given:

"The Minister's main duty in considering this complaint has been to decide its suitability for investigation by means of a particular procedure. He has come to the conclusion that it would not be suitable. The complaint is of course one that raises wide issues going beyond the immediate concern of your clients, which is presumably the prices they themselves receive. It would also affect the interests of other regions and involve the regional price structure as a whole. In any event the Minister considers that the issue is of a kind which properly falls to be resolved through the arrangements available to producers and the board within the framework of the scheme itself".

The appellants' solicitor by a letter of November 4, 1965, asked the Minister if he had excluded from his mind the considerations set out in the 1964 letter. The Minister did not give a direct answer to this question, merely stating: "I considered that the issue . . . was one which in all the circumstances should be dealt with by the board rather than the committee of investigation".

In 1966, the Divisional Court granted an order of *mandamus* commanding the Minister (1) to refer the complaint to the committee or (2) to deal effectively with the complaints on relevant considerations only to the exclusion of irrelevant considerations (*The Times*, February 4, 1966). The Minister appealed successfully to the Court of Appeal (Diplock and Russell L.JJ., Lord Denning M.R. dissenting: [1968] A.C. 1003E–1015). The applicants appealed to the House of Lords.

LORD REID: . . . The respondent contends that his only duty is to consider a complaint fairly and that he is given an unfettered discretion with regard to every complaint either to refer it or not to refer it to the committee as he may think fit. The appellants contend that it is his duty to refer every genuine and substantial complaint, or alternatively that his discretion is not unfettered and that in this case he failed to exercise his discretion according to law because his refusal was caused or influenced by his having misdirected himself in law or by his having taken into account extraneous or irrelevant considerations.

In my view, the appellants' first contention goes too far. There are a number of reasons which would justify the Minister in refusing to refer a complaint. For example, he might consider it more suitable for arbitration, or he might consider that in an earlier case the committee of investigation had already rejected a substantially similar complaint, or he might think the complaint to be frivolous or vexatious. So he must have at least some measure of discretion. But is it unfettered?

It is implicit in the argument for the Minister that there are only two possible interpretations of this provision—either he must refer every complaint or he has an unfettered discretion to refuse to refer in any case. I do not think that is right. Parliament must have conferred the discretion with the intention that it should be used to promote the policy and objects of the Act; the policy and objects of the Act must be determined by construing the Act as a whole and construction is always a matter of law for the court. In a matter of this kind it is not possible to draw a hard and fast line, but if the Minister, by reason of his having misconstrued the Act or for any other reason, so uses his discretion as to thwart or run counter to the policy and objects of the Act, then our law would be very defective if persons aggrieved were not entitled to the protection of the court. So it is necessary first to construe the Act.

When these provisions were first enacted in 1931 it was unusual for Parliament to compel people to sell their commodities in a way to which they objected and it was easily foreseeable that any such scheme would cause loss to some producers. Moreover, if the operation of the scheme was put in the hands of the majority of the producers, it was obvious that they might use their power to the detriment of consumers, distributors or a minority of the producers. So it is not surprising that Parliament enacted safeguards.

The approval of Parliament shows that this scheme was thought to be in the public interest, and in so far as it necessarily involved detriment to some persons, it must have been thought to be in the public interest that they should suffer it. But in sections 19 and 20 Parliament drew a line. They provide machinery for investigating and determining whether the scheme is operating or the board is acting in a manner contrary to the public interest.

The effect of these sections is that if, but only if, the Minister and the committee of investigation concur in the view that something is being done contrary to the public interest the Minister can step in. Section 20 enables the Minister to take the initiative. Section 19 deals with complaints by individuals who are aggrieved. I need not deal with the provisions which apply to consumers. We are concerned with other persons who may be distributors or producers. If the Minister directs that a complaint by any of them shall be referred to the committee of investigation, that committee will make a report which must be published. If they report that any provision of this scheme or any act or omission of the board is contrary to the interests of the complainers *and* is not in the public interest, then the Minister is empowered to take action, but not otherwise. He may disagree with the view of the committee as to public interest, and, if he thinks that there are other public interests which out-weigh the public interest that justice should be done to the complainers, he would be not only entitled but bound to refuse to take action. Whether he takes action or not, he may be criticised and held accountable in Parliament but the court cannot interfere.

I must now examine the Minister's reasons for refusing to refer the appellants' complaint to the committee. I have already set out the letters of March 23 and May 3, 1965. I think it is right also to refer to a letter sent from the Ministry on May 1, 1964, because in his affidavit the Minister says he has read this letter and there is no indication that he disagrees with any part of it. It is as follows: [His Lordship read the letter and continued:]

The first reason which the Minister gave in his letter of March 23, 1965, was that this complaint was unsuitable for investigation because it raised wide issues. Here it appears to me that the Minister has clearly misdirected himself.

Section 19(6) contemplates the raising of issues so wide that it may be neces-s-ary for the Minister to amend a scheme or even to revoke it. Narrower issues may be suitable for arbitration but section 19 affords the only method of investigating wide issues. In my view it is plainly the intention of the Act that even the widest issues should be investigated if the complaint is genuine and substantial, as this complaint certainly is.

Then it is said that this issue should be "resolved through the arrangements available to producers and the board within the framework of the scheme itself". This restates in a condensed form the reasons given in paragraph 4 of the letter of May 1, 1964, where it is said "the Minister owes no duty to producers in any particular region", and reference is made to the "status of the Milk Marketing Scheme as an instrument for the self-government of the industry", and to the Minister "assuming an inappropriate degree of responsibility". But, as I have already pointed out, the Act imposes on the Minister a responsibility whenever there is a relevant and substantial complaint that the board are acting in a manner inconsistent with the public interest, and that has been relevantly alleged in this case. I can find nothing in the Act to limit this responsibility or to justify the statement that the Minister owes no duty to producers in a particular region. The Minister is, I think, correct in saying that the board is an instrument for the self-government of the industry. So long as it does not act contrary to the public interest the Minister cannot interfere. But if it does act contrary to what both the committee of investigation and the Minister hold to be the public interest the Minister has a duty to act. And if a complaint relevantly alleges that the board has so acted, as this complaint does, then it appears to me that the Act does impose a duty on the Minister to have it investigated. If he does not do that he is rendering nugatory a safeguard provided by the Act and depriving complainers of a remedy which I am satisfied that Parliament intended them to have.

Paragraph 3 of the letter of May 1, 1964, refers to the possibility that, if the complaint were referred and the committee were to uphold it, the Minister "would be expected to make a statutory Order to give effect to the committee's recommendations". If this means that he is entitled to refuse to refer a complaint because, if he did so, he might later find himself in an embarrassing situation, that would plainly be a bad reason. I can see an argument to the effect that if, on receipt of a complaint, the Minister can satisfy himself from information in his possession as to the merits of the complaint, and he then chooses to say that, whatever the committee might recommend, he would hold it to be contrary to the public interest to take any action, it would be a waste of time and money to refer the complaint to the committee. I do not intend to express any opinion about that because that is not this case. In the first place it appears that the Minister has come to no decision as to the merits of the appellants' case and, secondly, the Minister has carefully avoided saying what he would do if the committee were to uphold the complaint.

It was argued that the Minister is not bound to give any reasons for refusing to refer a complaint to the committee, that if he gives no reasons his decision cannot be questioned, and that it would be very unfortunate if giving reasons were to put him in a worse position. But I do not agree that a decision cannot be questioned if no reasons are given. If it is the Minister's duty not to act so as to frustrate the policy and objects of the Act, and if it were to appear from all the circumstances of the case that that has been the effect of the Minister's refusal, then it appears to me that the court must be entitled to act. . . .

I have found no authority to support the unreasonable proposition that it must be all or nothing—either no discretion at all or an unfettered discretion. Here the words "if the Minister in any case so directs" are sufficient to show that he has some discretion but they give no guide as to its nature or extent. That must be inferred from a construction of the Act read as a whole, and for the reasons I have given I would infer that the discretion is not unlimited, and that it has been used by the Minister in a manner which is not in accord with the intention of the statute which conferred it.

As the Minister's discretion has never been properly exercised according to law, I would allow this appeal.

LORD HODSON: . . . The reasons disclosed are not, in my opinion, good reasons for refusing to refer the complaint seeing that they leave out of account altogether the merits of the complaint itself. The complaint is, as the Lord Chief Justice pointed out, made by persons affected by the scheme and is not one for the consumer committee as opposed to the committee of investigation and it was eligible for reference to the latter. It has never been suggested that the complaint was not a genuine one. It is no objection to the exercise of the discretion to refer that wide issues will be raised and the interests of other regions and the regional price structure as a whole would be affected. It is likely that the removal of a grievance will, in any event, have a wide effect and the Minister cannot lawfully say in advance that he will not refer the matter to the committee to ascertain the facts because, as he says in effect, although not in so many words, "I would not regard it as right to give effect to the report if it were favourable to the appellants."

It has been suggested that the reasons given by the Minister need not and should not be examined closely for he need give no reason at all in the exercise of his discretion. True it is that the Minister is not bound to give his reasons for refusing to exercise his discretion in a particular manner, but when, as here, the circumstances indicate a genuine complaint for which the appropriate remedy is provided, if the Minister in the case in question so directs, he would not escape from the possibility of control by mandamus through adopting a negative attitude without explanation. As the guardian of the public interest he has a duty to protect the interests of those who claim to have been treated contrary to the public interest.

I would allow the appeal accordingly. . . .

LORD PEARCE: . . . It is quite clear from the Act in question that the Minister is intended to have *some* duty in the matter. It is conceded that he must properly consider the complaint. He cannot throw it unread into the waste-paper basket. He cannot simply say (albeit honestly) "I think that in general the investigation of complaints has a disruptive effect on the scheme and leads to more trouble than (on balance) it is worth; I shall therefore never refer anything to the committee of investigation." To allow him to do so would be to give him power to set aside for his period as Minister the obvious intention of Parliament, namely, that an independent committee set up for the purpose should investigate grievances and that their report should be available to Parliament. This was clearly never intended by the Act. Nor was it intended that he could silently thwart its intention by failing to carry out its purposes. I do not regard a Minister's failure or refusal to give any reasons as a sufficient exclusion of the court's surveillance. If all the *prima facie* reasons seem to point in favour of his taking a certain course to carry out the intentions of Parliament in respect of a power which it has given him in that regard, and he gives no reason whatever for taking a contrary course, the court may infer that he has no good reason and that he is not using the power given by Parliament to carry out its intentions. In the present case, however, the Minister has given reasons which show that he was not exercising his discretion in accordance with the intentions of the Act. . . .

LORD UPJOHN: . . . My Lords, I would only add this: that without throwing any doubt upon what are well known as the club expulsion cases, where the absence of reasons has not proved fatal to the decision of expulsion by a club committee, a decision of the Minister stands on quite a different basis; he is a public officer charged by Parliament with the discharge of a public discretion affecting Her Majesty's subjects; if he does not give any reason for his decision it may be, if circumstances warrant it, that a court may be at liberty to come to the conclusion that he had no good reason for reaching that conclusion and order a prerogative writ to issue accordingly.

The Minister in my opinion has not given a single valid reason for refusing to order an inquiry into the legitimate complaint (be it well founded or not) of the South-Eastern Region; all his disclosed reasons for refusing to do so are bad in law.

LORD MORRIS OF BORTH-Y-GEST dissented.

Appeal allowed.

The House of Lords ordered that the cause be remitted to the Divisional Court of the Queen's Bench Division to require the respondent, the Minister of Agriculture, Fisheries and Food, to consider the complaint of the appellants according to law.

Notes
1. After the House of Lords' decision, the Minister "decided to refer the complaint to the Committee of Investigation".[1] The Committee reported on January 7, 1969, "that the acts and/or omissions of the Board in prescribing the terms on, and the prices at which, milk should be sold to the Board were contrary to the reasonable interests of the complainants and were not in the public interest".[2] The Minister (Mr Cledwyn Hughes having by then succeeded Mr Fred Peart) announced his decision in a written answer in the House of Commons[3]:

". . . I have carefully considered the Committee's findings. I am satisfied that even if its recommendations were implemented within the framework of the regional pricing structure of the Milk Marketing Scheme, they would have a profound effect on incomes of milk producers in different parts of the country. Many of them, particularly those in the West of the country, would suffer significant losses. Moreover, if the principle that each and every producer should be paid according to his proximity to a liquid market were pursued to its logical conclusion, it would bring to an end the present system for the organised marketing of milk which has been so successful.

[1] Report on Agricultural Marketing Schemes for 1966–67, p.10 (1967–68 HCP 423).
[2] Report for 1967–68, p.12 (1968–69 HCP 445).
[3] 780 HC Deb., cols 46–47 (March 31, 1969).

The Committee recognised that the wider questions of agricultural, economic and social policy involved in this matter were beyond the scope of its inquiry. These must, however, in my view be given full weight. After considering with great care all the issues involved, and the very wide implications of the Committee's recommendations, I have concluded that it would not be in the public interest for me to direct the Board to implement the Committee's conclusions".

The Minister's decision was welcomed by dairy farmers in other parts of Britain, and by *The Times*, which pointed out in a leading article (April 1, 1969) that implementation of the Committee's recommendations could "easily reduce large tracts of the country, now relatively prosperous, to a condition where they were farmed on the 'dog-and-stick' methods of the inter-war years".

2. See case notes by J.F. Garner, (1968) 31 M.L.R. 446; H.W.R. Wade, (1968) 84 L.Q.R. 166; J.A. Farmer (and P.J. Evans), [1970] N.Z.L.J. 184. Note also the criticisms expressed by R.C. Austin, (1975) C.L.P. 150 at pp.167–173.

3. This case can be regarded as an example of the Minister taking irrelevant considerations into account (see following section) as well as a failure to exercise a power in accordance with the purpose for which the power was given.

4. *cf. British Oxygen Co. Ltd v Minister of Technology* (above, p.488) where it was held that Parliament had not given any guidance as to how the Ministry's power to give grants to eligible applicants was to be exercised.

5. In *Secretary of State for Employment v ASLEF (No.2)* [1972] 2 Q.B. 443, CA, the Secretary of State could apply to the NIRC for a secret ballot order where it appeared to him (*inter alia*) that there were "reasons for doubting" whether workers would be taking part in industrial action in accordance with their wishes, and whether they had had an adequate opportunity of indicating their wishes. The Minister gave no reasons for his decision to apply for such an order. Lord Denning M.R. stated at 493–494:

"We have been referred to several recent cases, of which *Padfield v. Minister of Agriculture, Fisheries and Food* [1968] A.C. 997 is the best example, in which the courts have stressed that in the ordinary way a Minister should give reasons, and if he gives none the court may infer that he had no good reasons. Whilst I would apply that proposition completely in most cases, and particularly in cases which affect life, liberty or property, I do not think that it applies in all cases. Here we are concerned with a ballot to ascertain the wishes of 170,000 men. The executive committees of the unions consist, we are told, of 60 men. These 60 are, no doubt, fully convinced that the whole 170,000 will support them. It is the honourable tradition of the men to support their leaders. There are many messages and telegrams which have told of support from the branches. Yet there are times when even their leaders, in touch as they are, may be mistaken.

The Solicitor-General suggested to us some reasons for doubting whether the wishes of the individual men were behind this. The Minister, he suggested, might think that, as the dispute has been discussed and debated, before a chairman agreed by both sides, many of the workers would wish to accept his award rather than take part in industrial action. The Minister also had asked the leaders of the unions earnestly to consider holding a ballot of the workers so as to ascertain their wishes. The leaders were quite sure, and are quite sure, that the men are wholly in support of this industrial action. If so, there would seem to be no good reason why they should in any way not be content for a ballot to be held. I do not say that those reasons are right, but they are such as a reasonable Minister might entertain; and, if they are such—if the Minister could on reasonable grounds form the view and opinion that he did—as I read the law and the statute this court has no jurisdiction or power to interfere with his decision".

Per Roskill L.J. at 511:

> "It has often been said that there must be a strong case before the court will inter-fere. The court will, I apprehend, interfere in a case where there could in the nature of things be no evidence upon which a reasonable Secretary of State could have formed the reasons for the doubt claimed to exist and to justify an application. In my judgment, this point was effectively answered by the Solicitor-General yesterday after-noon. He was not giving the Secretary of State's actual reasons. Whether or not the Secretary of State gives those reasons is, as Buckley L.J. said, a matter of policy for him. It may be wise in some cases to give them, it may be unwise not to give them. That is not a matter with which this court is concerned. The Solicitor-General put forward, not as the Secretary of State's actual reasons, but as evidence before the court which was also available to the Secretary of State, evidence on which a reason-able Secretary of State could have formed the view that there were reasons to doubt whether the workers who were taking, or who were expected to take, part were or would be taking part in accordance with their wishes".

6. The *Padfield* dicta concerning the inferring of bad reasons from silence have only applied in a few cases. In *R. v Penwith DC Ex p. May*, unreported, November 22, 1985. From about 1981, the Penzance and District Campaign for Nuclear Disarmament sold and distributed literature, badges and similar material in a pedestrian precinct in Penzance. The District Council resolved that as from April 1, 1984, Sch.4 to the Local Government (Miscellaneous Provisions) Act 1982 would be applied in respect of this precinct and other streets. Accordingly, CND's activities in selling material now required street trading consent. The council refused consent, without giving reasons. (Schedule 4 did not impose a requirement to give reasons.) There had been no objections to CND's activities over the years, no objections to their application for consent and the Environmental Services Committee had recommended that consent be given. Taylor J. held, applying the *Padfield* dicta, that he was prepared to infer that the council had no good reasons for refusal and granted certiorari to quash the refusal of consent.

A variant of this situation was identified by Laws L.J. in *R. (on the application of Quark Fishing Ltd) v Secretary of State for Foreign and Commonwealth Affairs* [2002] EWCA Civ 1409 where (with the agreement of Aldous and Jonathan Parker L.JJ.) he cited Lord Upjohn's dictum in *Padfield* (above, p.533), and stated (at [62]) that the same applies "where the minister has given conflicting, or apparently conflicting, reasons". Here, different explanations were given at different times by civil servants of the basis on which two of four existing holders of licences to fish for Patagonian Toothfish in the territorial waters of South Georgia and the South Sandwich Islands were selected to be awarded licences for the 2001 season. In the circumstances, he was "not prepared to assume, or find as a fact in these proceedings that the decision was taken on rational grounds having regard only to relevant considerations". The court was also critical of the fact that some relevant documents had only been disclosed on the last day of the appeal hearing (see [49]–[55]).

7. A limited view of the inferring of bad reasons from silence was taken by the House of Lords in *R. v Secretary of State for Trade and Industry Ex p. Lonhro Plc* [1989] 1 W.L.R. 525. In 1985, House of Fraser Plc was taken over by a company controlled by the Al Fayed brothers, over the strong opposition of Lonhro Plc, led by "Tiny" Rowland. The Secretary of State decided not to refer the proposed acquisition to the Monopolies and Mergers Commission (MMC). In 1987, he appointed inspectors to inquire into the affairs of the company, in particular in relation to the acquisition of House of Fraser. Their report was submitted in 1988. The Secretary of State referred it to the Serious Fraud Office (SFO) and to the Director-General of Fair Trading. He subsequently decided (1) that the report would not be published while the SFO was considering it; and (2) on the Director's advice, not to exercise the power, where it appeared to him that there were new material facts about the merger, to refer the merger to the MMC.

The Divisional Court held that both decisions were *ultra vires*, but was reversed by the Court of Appeal. The House of Lords dismissed a further appeal. As to the first, the Secretary of State was entitled to take the view that early publication might be prejudicial to the SFO and a fair trial; his decision was neither perverse nor irrational. As to the second, the Divisional Court had been wrong to regard it as the policy of the Act that there should be a reference to the MMC on the ground that "when a merger situation is complicated by factors which are best understood by men rich in experience of the business world, their powers of investigation should be enlisted and their advice invited." This approach converted the Secretary of State's discretion into a duty and ignored the expertise of the Office of Fair Trading. The legislation considered in *Padfield* was distinguishable. Lonrho also relied on the *Padfield* dicta that bad reasons could be inferred from silence. Lord Keith of Kinkel commented (at 539–540).

> ". . . it was not submitted to you Lordships that there was any general duty to give reasons for a decision in all cases, nor was it submitted that this Act imposed a particular duty on the Secretary of State to give reasons for his refusal to make a reference to the MMC; and it is not the practice of the Secretary of State to give reasons when he decides not to make a reference to the MMC.
>
> The absence of reasons for a decision where there is no duty to give them cannot of itself provide any support for the suggested irrationally of the decision. The only significance of the absence of reasons is that if all other known facts and circumstances appear to point overwhelmingly in favour of a different decision, the decision-maker who has given no reasons cannot complain if the court draws the inference that he had no rational reason for his decision."

Here, no competition or consumer issues were involved. If there had been fraud in the take-over, then criminal proceedings or proceedings under the Company Directors Disqualification Act 1986 could be taken. The Secretary of State's powers following an MMC finding that a merger was contrary to the public interest were designed to prevent or correct damage to the economy as a consequence of an undesirable merger rather than as punitive measures against individuals. The Secretary of State's decision not to refer the merger had not been shown to be irrational.

It is submitted that this is an unduly restrictive interpretation of the *Padfield* dicta, which would indeed empty them of any significance. Compare the approach in *Quark Fishing*, above, where it would not be said that the facts pointed "overwhelmingly" to a different decision.

See further below, pp.743–751, on the development of obligations to give reasons.

8. In some cases decided during or shortly after the Second World War, it was suggested that powers conferred on a minister in subjective terms (*e.g.* to act if he was "satisfied" that a state of affairs existed or that it was "necessary" or "expedient" to act) gave an unlimited discretion provided he acted in good faith (Lord Atkin in *Liversidge v Anderson* [1942] A.C. 206 at 233; Somervell L.J. in *Robinson v Minister of Town and Country Planning* [1947] A.C. 702 at 721). These statements "do not apply today" (*Secretary of State for Education and Science v Tameside MBC* [1977] A.C. 1014 at 1024–1025 (Lord Denning M.R.), 1030–1031 (Scarman L.J.), 1047 (Lord Wilberforce). The whole range of grounds for review for abuse of discretion are potentially applicable. The wording of a provision in subjective terms would, however, suggest that the matter is not one of precedent or jurisdictional fact (above, p.429).

PORTER v MAGILL; WEEKS v MAGILL

[2001] UKHL 67; [2002] 2 A.C. 357; [2002] 2 W.L.R. 37; [2002] 1 All E.R. 465 (HOUSE OF LORDS)

In May 1986, the Conservative Party retained control of Westminster City Council with a majority reduced from 26 to 4. The Conservative leader of the council (P) and deputy leader (W) played key roles in the development of a policy to increase the number of Conservative voters in eight marginal wards by increasing the designated sales of council dwellings in those wards to owner-occupiers, who were believed to be more likely to vote Conservative. ("Designated sales" were sales of dwellings, when vacant, otherwise than under existing right-to-buy arrangements.) These sales were associated with a programme of capital grants for the purchase of dwellings. In 1987, the chairmen's group (a party group rather than a council committee, chaired by P and comprising the chairmen of committees) decided to adopt a target of 250 designated sales per annum in the marginal wards. Counsel advised that the council could not lawfully sell 250 properties per annum in the marginal wards alone, and that properties had to be designated for proper reasons across the whole of the city. The chairmen's group increased the total number of planned sales to 500 across the city, still enabling 250 sales to be achieved in the marginal wards. The housing committee, of which neither P nor W was a member, was presented with three options, of which the plan for 500 sales was the Conservative Party's preferred option. This was adopted by the committee and subsequently approved by the council. The auditor subsequently found that the council had adopted the policy with the predominant purpose of achieving electoral advantage for the Conservative Party, that P and W were party to its adoption and implementation in the knowledge that it was unlawful and that the policy had caused financial loss to the council. Accordingly, he certified under s.20 of the Local Government Finance Act 1982 that some £31 million was due to the council as a result of the wilful misconduct of P, W and others.

The Divisional Court ((1996) 96 L.G.R. 157) allowed appeals by the chairman of the housing committee, the director of housing and the managing director of the council, but dismissed appeals by P and W, accepting the auditor's findings in relation to them. The Court of Appeal ([2002] 2 A.C. 357 at 360) (Kennedy and Schliemann L.JJ., Robert Walker L.J. dissenting) allowed appeals by P and W holding that since they had acted on what they believed to be legal advice they had not been guilty of wilful misconduct; that the Divisional Court had acted inconsistently in allowing some appeals and not others; and that since other members of the housing committee had not voted for improper reasons, any improper motive or purpose attributed to P and W did not render the committee's decision unlawful and was not causative of the council's loss. A further appeal to the House of Lords was allowed.

The extracts here deal with the unlawfulness of the council's conduct. Issues concerning the independence of and the fairness of the procedures adopted by the auditor are dealt with below (p.771).

LORD BINGHAM OF CORNHILL: . . .

The underlying legal principles

19. The legal principles which underlie the auditor's findings against Dame Shirley Porter and Mr. Weeks are not in the main controversial, but since they are the bedrock of his decision they should be briefly summarised.

(1) *Powers conferred on a local authority may be exercised for the public purpose for which the powers were conferred and not otherwise* A very clear statement of this principle is to be found in *Wade & Forsyth Administrative Law.* 8th ed (2000). pp.356–357. The corresponding passage in an earlier edition of that work was expressly approved by Lord Bridge of Harwich in *R. v Tower Hamlets London Borough Council Ex p. Chetnik Developments Ltd* [1988] A.C. 858, 872:

"Statutory power conferred for public purposes is conferred as it were upon trust, not absolutely—that is to say, it can validly be used only in the right and proper way which Parliament when conferring it is presumed to have intended."

The principle is routinely applied, as by Neill LJ in *Crédit Successes Allerdale Borough Council* [1997] QB 306, 333 who described it as "a general principle of public law".

(2) *Such powers are exercised by or on the delegation of councillors. It is misconduct in a councillor to exercise or be party to the exercise of such powers otherwise than for the public purpose for which the powers were conferred.* Where public powers are conferred on a council, it is the body of elected councillors who must exercise those powers save to the extent that such exercise is lawfully delegated to groups of councillors or to officers. All will act in the name or on behalf of the council. It follows from the proposition that public powers are conferred as if upon trust that those who exercise powers in a manner inconsistent with the public purpose for which the powers were conferred betray that trust and so misconduct themselves. This is an old and very important principle. It was clearly expressed by the Lord Chancellor of Ireland in *Attorney General v Belfast Corpn* (1855) 4 Ir Ch R 119, 160–161:

> "Municipal corporations would cease to be tangible bodies for any purpose of redress on account of a breach of trust, if the individuals who constitute its executive, and by whom the injury has been committed, cannot be made responsible. They are a collection of persons doing acts that, when done are the acts of the corporation but which are induced by the individuals who recommend and support them, and this court holds that persons who withdraw themselves from the duties of their office may be rendered equally answerable for the acts of those whom they allow, by their absence, to have exclusive definition over the corporate property. As the trustees of the corporate estate, nominated by the legislature, and appointed by their fellow-citizens, it is their duty to attend to the interests of the corporation, conduct themselves honestly and uprightly, and to see that every one acts for the interests of the trust over which he and they are placed."

(3) *If the councillors misconduct themselves knowingly or recklessly it is regarded by the law as wilful misconduct.* The auditor's power to surcharge councillors under section 20(1)(b) of the 1982 Act is dependent on a finding of wilful misconduct. That expression was defined by Webster J. in *Graham v Teesdale* (1981) 81 LGR 117, 123 to mean "deliberately doing something which is wrong knowing it to be wrong or with reckless indifference as to whether it is wrong or not". That definition was approved by the Court of Appeal was adopted by the Divisional Court in the present case 96 LGR 157, 167–168. It was also accepted by the Court of Appeal: ante, pp.3851–386A. There was no challenge to this definition before the House and I would accept it as representing the intention of Parliament when using this expression.

(4) *If the wilful misconduct of a councillors is found to have caused loss to a local authority the councillor is liable to make good such loss to the council.* This is the rule now laid down in section 20(1) of the 1982 Act. But it is not a new rule. A similar provision was expressed in section 247(7) of the Public Health Act 1875 (38 & 39 Vict, c.55). Section 228(1)(d) of the Local Government Act 1933 and in section 161(4) of the Local Government Act

1972 (although in the two earlier sections the reference was to "negligence or misconduct" and not to "wilful misconduct"). Even before these statutory provisions the law had been declared I clear terms. One such statement may be found in *Attorney General v Wilson* (1840) Cr. & Ph.1. 23–27 where Lord Cottenham LC said:

"The true way of viewing this is to consider the members of the governing body of the corporation as its agents, bound to exercise its functions for the purposes for which they were given, and to protect its interests and property; and if such agents exercise those functions for the purposes of injuring its interests and alienating its property, shall the corporation be estopped in this court from complaining because the act done was ostensibly an act of the corporation? . . . As members of the governing body, it was their duty as the corporation, whose trustees and agents they, in that respect, were, to preserve and protect the property confided to them; instead of which, having previously, as they supposed, placed the property, by the deeds of the 30 May 1835, in a convenient position for that purpose, they take measures for alienating that property, with the avowed design of depriving the corporation of it; and, with this view, they procure trusts to be declared, and transfers of part of the property to be made to the several other defendants in this cause, for purposes in no manner connected with the purposes to which the funds were devoted, and for which it was their duty to protect and preserve them. This was not only a breach of trust and a violation of duty towards the corporation, whose agents and trustees they were but an act of spoliation against all the inhabitants of Leeds liable to the borough rate, every individual of whom had an interest in the fund, for has exoneration, pro tanto, from the borough rate. If any other agent or trustee had so dealt with property over which the owner had given him control, can there be any doubt but that such agent or trustee would in this court, be made responsible for so much of the alienated property as could not be recovered in specie. But if Lord Hardwicke was right in the *Charitable Corpn* case, and I am right in this case, in considering the authors of the wrong as agents or trustees of the corporation, then the two cases are identical. I cannot doubt, therefore, that the plaintiffs are entitled to redress against the three trustees and those members of the governing body who were instrumental in carrying into effect the acts complained of and it is proved that the five defendants fall under that description."

(5) *Powers conferred on a local authority may not lawfully be exercised to promote the electoral advantage of a political party.* Support for this principle may be found in *R. v Board of Education* [1910] KB 165, 181 where Farwell LJ said:

"If this means that the Board were hampered by political considerations. I can only say that such considerations are pre-eminently extraneous, and that no political consequence can justify the Board in allowing their judgment and discretion to be influenced thereby."

This passage was accepted by Lord Upjohn in *Padfield v Minister of Agriculture. Fisheries and Food* [1968] AC 997, 1058, 1061. In *R. v Port Talbot Borough Council. Ex p. Jones* [1988] 2 All ER 207, 214 where council accommodation had been allocated to an applicant in order that she should be the better able to fight an election, Nolan J regarded that decision as based on irrelevant considerations.

20. Counsel for Dame Shirley Porter and Mr Weeks urged upon the House what were said to be the realities of party politics. Councillors elected as members of a political party and forming part of that party group on the council could not be expected to be oblivious to considerations of party political advantage. So long as they had reasons for taking action other than purely partisan political reasons their conduct could not be impugned. Reliance was placed on observations of Kennedy L.J. in the Court of Appeal, ante, p.386D-1.

"Some of the submissions advanced on behalf of the auditor have been framed in such a way as to suggest that any councillor who allows the possibility of electoral advantage even to cross his mind before he decides upon a course of action is guilty of misconduct. That seems to me to be unreal. In local, as in national, politics many if not most decisions carry an electoral price tag, and all politicians are aware of it. In most case they cannot seriously be expected to disregard it, but they know that if the action which they take is to withstand scrutiny (to be 'judge-proof') there must be sound local government reasons, not just excuses, on which they can rely."

Schiemann I. J., ante, pp.390C–D. 391C–D. spoke to similar effect:

"Whether or not the decision of the housing committee was unlawful depends, in the circumstances of this case, on the motivation of the committee at the time of the vote. If its motive was purely to secure electoral advantage for the Conservative Party then the decision was unlawful. If purely Housing Act considerations were its motivation then its decision would be lawful . . . There is a complication. Frequently individual persons act from mixed motives. Further, group decisions may have multiple motivations—in part because there are many votes cast and in part because each voter may himself have several motivations . . . It is legitimate for councillors to desire that their party should win the next election. Our political system works on the basis that they desire that because they think that the policies to which their party is wedded are in the public interest and will require years to be achieved. There is nothing disgraceful or unlawful in councillors having that desire. For this court to hold otherwise would depart from our theory of democracy and current reality."

21. Whatever the difficulties of application which may arise in a borderline case, I do not consider the overriding principle to be in doubt. Elected politicians of course wish to act in a manner which will commend them and their party (when, as is now usual, they belong to one) to the electorate. Such an ambition is the life blood of democracy and a potent spur to responsible decision-taking and administration. Councillors do not act improperly or unlawfully if, exercising public powers for a public purpose for which such powers were conferred, they hope that such exercise will earn the gratitude and support of the electorate and thus strengthen their electoral position. The law would indeed part company with the realities of party politics if it were to hold otherwise. But a public power is not exercised lawfully if it is exercised not for a public purpose for which the power was conferred but in order to

promote the electoral advantage of a political party. The power at issue in the present case is section 32 of the Housing Act 1985, which conferred power on local authorities to dispose of land held by them subject to conditions specified in the Act. Thus a local authority could dispose of its property, subject to the provisions of the Act, to promote any public purpose for which such power was conferred, but could not lawfully do so for the purpose of promoting the electoral advantage of any party represented on the council.

22. The House was referred to a number of cases in which the part which political allegiance may properly play in local government has been explored: *R. v Sheffield City Council. Ex p. Chadwick* (1985) 84 LGR 563: *R. v Waltham Forest London Borough Council. Ex p. Baxter* [1988] QB 419: *Jones v Swansea City Council* [1990] 1 WLR 54: *R. v Bradford City Metropolitan Council. Ex p. Wilson* [1990] 2 QB 375; *R. v Local Comr for Administration in North and North-East England. Ex p. Liverpool City Council* [2001] 1 All ER 462. These cases show that while councillors may lawfully support a policy adopted by their party they must not abdicate their responsibility and duty of exercising personal judgment. There is nothing in these cases to suggest that a councillor may support a policy not for valid local government reasons but with the object of obtaining an electoral advantage.

The findings made against Dame Shirley Porter and Mr Weeks

[His Lordship held that the auditor and the Divisional Court had been entitled to find the following: (1) That the council had adopted a policy the object of which was to achieve a specified annual level of sales of properties owned by the council in the eight marginal wards with the intention that the properties thus vacated should be sold to new residents who, as owner-occupiers, might reasonably be expected to vote Conservative and so increase the electoral strength of the Conservative Party in those wards in the 1990 council elections. "It follows from the legal principles already summarised that the council's policy was unlawful because directed to the pursuit of electoral advantage and not the achievement of proper housing objectives" (at [25]).

(2) That P and W were both party to the adoption and implementation of this unlawful policy

(3) That P and W both knew the designated sales policy targeted on marginal wards to be unlawful. They accepted in their respective printed cases for the appeal that they knew the council could not use its powers for electoral advantage. It followed that in adopting and implementing the designated sales policy both acted in a way they knew to be unlawful. The Court of Appeal had not been entitled to overturn the finding of the Divisional Court that they had not acted in accordance with what they believed to be legal advice given to the council.

(4) That the designated sales policy promoted and implemented by P and W caused financial loss to the council. Without the support of P and W there would have been no proposal put to the housing committee for an increased programme of designated sales targeted on marginal wards.

As to the argument based on inconsistency it might very well be that the other three were fortunate to be exonerated from findings of wilful misconduct, but the findings against P and W were very strong and they were respectively "the prime architect and midwife of this policy" (at [45]). No injustice was done to P and W by upholding the findings against them. As to causation, once the policy had been adopted by the majority party, "it was to all intents and purposes bound to be approved by the committee" (at. [46]). If it were appropriate to inquire into the motivation of the seven Conservative members of the housing committee, the Chairman (Mr Hartley) and one other were aware of the objective to increase the Conservative Party's voting strength in marginal wards; other members were not in a position to exercise an informed independent judgment because they were never given a clear picture of why the policy had been adopted. There was therefore "no informed exercise of independent judgment by members of the committee such as could break the chain of causation between the conduct of [P and W] and the consequences which followed (at [47]).]

The liability of Dame Shirley Porter and Mr Weeks

48. The Divisional Court's findings adverse to Dame Shirley Porter and Mr Weeks, reached on a mass of evidence, were fully justified, if not inevitable. The Court of Appeal majority erred in departing from them. The passage of time and the familiarity of the accusations made against Dame Shirley Porter and Mr Weeks cannot and should not obscure the unpalatable truth that this was a deliberate, blatant and dishonest misuse of public power. It was a misuse of power by both of them not for the purpose of financial gain but for that of electoral advantage. In that sense it was corrupt. The auditor may have been strictly wrong to describe their conduct as gerrymandering, but it was certainly unlawful and he was right to stigmatise it as disgraceful.

LORDS STEYN, HOPE OF CRAIGHEAD HOBHOUSE OF WOODBOROUGH AND SCOTT OF FOSCOTE agreed with LORD BINGHAM. LORD SCOTT delivered a concurring speech.

Notes
1. The council's loss was held to be the difference between the full market value of the properties sold and the discounted price received, and came to some £26.5 million. It was not open to P and W to argue that if the properties had been sold under a lawful policy then they would have been sold at equally discounted prices. Proceedings were taken to recover from P and W (1) the sums certified as due by the auditor; and (2) damages for breach of trust, as trustees of the council's assets, in committing the acts of wilful misconduct. Under the first head, interest was payable 14 days after the final resolution of the appeals by the House of Lords in 2001; under the second head, interest could be awarded from the date of the certificates in 1996. Hart J. ([2003] Ch. 346) held (1) that the right of a corporation to sue its own members where they "fraudulently and illegally used the power of the corporation for the purposes of depriving it of property to which it was by law entitled" (*Att-Gen v Wilson* (1840) Cr. & Ph. 1, *per* Lord Cottenham at 23–24), had not been excluded by the statutory machinery of audit and certification; it was however wrong to characterise the members as trustees of the council's assets; (2) that it was not necessary for the council to elect between the two remedies, although the cumulative entitlement did not entitle the council to recover anything more than the higher of the two sums. P subsequently paid £12 million to the council in settlement of the claim against her (*BBC News*, Monday July 5, 2004).

Note that the power of the auditor to certify that a person has failed to bring into account a sum that ought to have been brought to account or that a loss has been incurred or a deficiency has been caused by wilful misconduct has been repealed (so far for England and for police authorities in Wales) by the Local Government Act 2000, s.90. The liability based on *Att-Gen v Wilson* is unaffected by this change.

Furthermore, the new express powers of local authorities to give indemnities to members and officers (Local Government Act 2000, ss.101, 105; Local Authorities (Indemnities for Members and Officers) Order 2004 (SI 2004/3082) cannot be exercised in respect of action or inaction which is the result of fraud, or other deliberate wrongdoing or recklessness.

2. The evidence in *Porter v Magill* justified the conclusion that the predominant purpose of the policy adopted by the council had been unlawful. The analysis is more difficult where the evidence is that electoral advantage is one (but not the dominant) consideration alongside lawful considerations that support the same result. There was some discussion of this in the Court of Appeal in *Porter v Magill*. Kennedy L.J. ((1999) 1 L.G.L.R. 523 at 544) said:

"In local, as in national politics, many if not most decisions carry an electoral price tag, and all politicians are aware of it. In most cases, they cannot seriously be expected to disregard it, but they know that if the action which they take is to withstand scrutiny (to be 'judge-proof') there must be sound local government reasons, not just excuses on which they can rely".

Schiemann L.J. stated (at 548) that "It is legitimate for councillors to desire that the party should win the next election . . . There is nothing disgraceful or unlawful in having that desire". This would be an illegitimate motive for a committee or the council itself, but on the facts there was no evidence of their motivation. As regards individual voting councillors, designating properties city wide did not "become unlawful merely because it achieved [P]'s objective of 250 in marginal wards". Accordingly, the fact that councillors have electoral advantage in mind cannot sensibly be fatal to the legality of what they do. Clearly there is no difficulty if electoral advantage is simply the additional consequence of the adoption of a substantive policy judgment made in the public interest that is not itself open to challenge on public law principles (*cf.* Lord Bingham, above p.540). What is left unclear is the extent to which it may be a "motivating factor" with any greater weight than that (*cf.* the cases on mixed purpose or considerations: below, pp.563–569).

3. Compare *Wheeler v Leicester City Council* [1985] A.C. 1054, where the council purported to terminate the use which Leicester [Rugby] Football Club made of a recreation ground owned by the council. The club had refused to put pressure on three of its players not to take part in rugby tour to South Africa. Lord Templeman stated (at 1081) that:

"this use by the council of its statutory powers was a misuse of power. The council could not properly seek to use its statutory powers of management or any other statutory powers for the purposes of punishing the club when the club had done no wrong".

Lord Roskill also found the council to have acted unfairly procedurally and was disposed to find that they had acted unreasonably on *Wednesbury* principles (see p.1079). For comments on *Wheeler*, see C. Turpin, [1985] C.L.J. 333; T.R.S. Allan, (1985) 48 M.L.R. 448 (on the Court of Appeal decision) and (1986) 49 M.L.R. 121 (expressing a preference for the judgment of Browne-Wilkinson L.J. in the Court of Appeal).

4. In *Congreve v. The Home Office* [1976] 1 Q.B. 629, Mr Congreve was one of over 20,000 people who took out a second colour television licence before the expiry of an existing one, in anticipation of an increase in the licence fee, from £12 to £18, as from April 1, 1975. By s.1(2) of the Wireless Telegraphy Act 1949, "A licence . . . may be issued subject to such terms, provisions and limitations as the [Minister] may think fit". Section 1(4) provided that a licence "may be revoked . . . by a notice in writing served on the holder . . .". There were no other limitations expressed in the statute. The Home Office feared that a substantial part of the anticipated revenue from the issue of licences would be lost in view of the large estimated number of "overlappers". They initially

demanded an extra £6 from each "overlapper" under threat of revocation, and subsequently modified their policy to one of revocation after eight months (£12 worth at an annual rate of £18). The Court of Appeal granted a declaration that the purported revocation of the plaintiff's licence was unlawful, invalid and of no effect. Lord Denning's somewhat extravagant reasoning, including the passage cited by Lord Templeman in *Wheeler*, was not echoed by the other judges in *Congreve*. Geoffrey Lane L.J., for example, put the matter more simply (at 662):

> ". . . The licence was a valid one at the time of its issue. At that time the new regulation increasing the fee to £18 had not come into operation and therefore did not in law exist. There was no power to demand the extra £6 nor to receive it. . . . [The revocation] is illegal for two reasons. First, it is coupled with an illegal demand which taints the revocation and makes that illegal too. Secondly, or possibly putting the same matter in a different way, it is an improper exercise of a discretionary power to use a threat to exercise that power as a means of extracting money which Parliament has given the executive no mandate to demand: see *Attorney-General v. Wilts United Dairies* (1922) 91 L.J.K.B. 897 . . .".

The Parliamentary Commissioner for Administration concluded that many members of the public had been caused needless distress and confusion through maladministration by the Home Office and their agents, the Television Licence Records Office, mainly in failing to make their policy officially and openly clear to the public (see his conclusions at para.38 of his Report: the Seventh Report of the PCA for Session 1974–75 HCP 680). However, on the assumption that it was lawful, he "found no ground for questioning the principle behind the arrangements" (para.42).

The decision of the Court of Appeal was celebrated by Mr Bernard Levin in *The Times*, December 5, 1975 ("Blow the Loud Trumpets of Victory for Us over Them in the T.V. Licence War"). It was also welcomed by H.W.R. Wade, (1976) 92 L.Q.R. 331. G. Ganz, however, was unenthusiastic ([1976] P.L. 14–15):

> "To elevate tax avoidance into a liberty of the subject protected by the Bill of Rights is a complete inversion of moral values. . . . The case epitomises the dangers of allowing the courts more scope to impose their values in this area of law as advocated by Scarman L.J. in *English Law—The New Dimension*. Their values have become fossilised so that they still see the individual battling against a hostile Executive once embodied in an autocratic King. They do not see the issue as one between the plaintiff and other taxpayers who will pay more whilst he pays less and that their judgment leads to an unequal sharing of burdens by the many for the benefit of a few".

5. In *R. v Derbyshire CC Ex p. The Times Supplements Ltd* (1990) 3 Admin. L.R. 241, the council resolved to remove all its advertising from newspapers owned by Mr Rupert Murdoch. Shortly before, *The Sunday Times* had published articles about the council which had led to the institution of libel proceedings by Councillor Bookbinder, the council leader. The decision involved switching advertising for teaching posts from *The Times Educational Supplement* to *The Guardian* notwithstanding that the cost was greater and the likely readership among teachers much smaller. The Divisional Court granted certiorari to quash the decision. The court was satisfied on the evidence (some councillors were cross-examined on their affidavits) that there was no educational ground for the decision (contrary to the claims of councillors) and that the majority Labour group on the council had been activated by bad faith or vindictiveness. The decision was "an abuse of power contrary to the public good" (Watkins L.J. at 253). Had it been necessary to do so his Lordship was sure that the decision would have been held to be perverse, as having no sensible or justifiable basis (*ibid.*): *cf. R. v Ealing LBC Ex p. Times Newspapers* (1986) 85 L.G.R. 316 (successful challenge to decision of three councils to ban certain newspapers from public libraries; decisions taken to demonstrate support for former employees of those newspapers'

publishers in a long, bitter and unresolved dispute were not taken with a view to fulfilling obligations to provide a "comprehensive . . . library service".

(B) Taking into Account Irrelevant Considerations; Failure to Have Regard to Relevant Considerations

Logically, this ground of challenge is wide enough to cover situations where powers are exercised for an improper purpose, given that desire to achieve that purpose will inevitably constitute the taking into consideration of an irrelevant consideration. However, the case law shows that a distinction between these grounds of challenge can be drawn.

As with "purposes", statutes sometimes are explicit as to the matters which are to be taken into consideration in coming to a decision as to the exercise of a power; more usually, it is for the courts to determine what are impliedly relevant or irrelevant considerations that must (or must not) be taken into account. Even where a statute states certain matters which must be taken into consideration, it will be a matter of construction for the courts as to whether these are exhaustive of relevant considerations. Furthermore, outside any analysis that a statute expressly or impliedly *requires* particular considerations to be taken (or not to be taken) into account it will be for the decision-maker to determine (subject to control for *Wednesbury* unreasonableness or irrationality) what considerations are to be taken into account.

Finally, difficult questions may arise where a decision is motivated by a plurality of purposes or considerations, some lawful others unlawful.

(i) Relevant and irrelevant considerations

R. v SOMERSET CC Ex p. FEWINGS

[1995] 1 W.L.R. 1037; [1995] 3 All E.R. 20 (COURT OF APPEAL)

In 1921, the county council acquired land known as the Quantock Lodge Estate. Most of it was then let to the Forestry Commission or tenant farmers. Another part was a strip of land, the Over Stowey Customs Common, which bisected the territory over which red deer had for many years been hunted by staghounds. On August 4, 1993, the council resolved by a vote of 26 to 22 that "This council, as landowners, with immediate effect, resolves to ban the hunting of deer with hounds on the county council owned land at Over Stowey Customs Common". On an application for judicial review by representatives of the Quantock Staghounds, Laws J. ([1995] 1 All E.R. 513) held that the majority who supported the ban were moved to do so by their belief that hunting involved unacceptable and unnecessary cruelty to the red deer who were the victims of the chase. It was common ground between the parties that the land had been appropriated in 1974 under s.122 of the Local Government Act 1972 for the purposes specified in s.120(1)(b) of that Act, which provides that:

"(1) for the purposes of . . . (b) the benefit, improvement or development of their area, a principal council may acquire by agreement any land, whether situated inside or outside their area".

Laws J. held (at 525–526) that a prohibition on hunting might be justified by reference to the preservation or betterment of the area's amenities (*e.g.* the protection of rare flora damaged by the hunt, or the survival of the animals hunted if their numbers were low, or the protection of the enjoyment by others of the land's amenities). Furthermore, there were some statutory powers where a moral element was part and parcel of the purposes for which the power was conferred (*e.g.* powers to make byelaws for the preservation of public decency or to control Sunday trading). However, here the decision was not based on the preservation or betterment of amenities. While the conservation of the area's wildlife was a relevant consideration under s.120(1)(b) this did not extend beyond matters of good management of the deer herd, and the decision was not based on such matters either.

Section 120(1)(b) did not:

"permit the council to take a decision about activities carried out on its land which is based upon freestanding moral perceptions as opposed to an objective judgment about what will conduce to the better management of the herd".

An alternative ground was that, even if the law on this part had been otherwise, the ban would have been unlawful on the ground that the council had not considered how the herd would be managed and conserved in the future if hunting were banned.

An appeal to the Court of Appeal was dismissed (Simon Brown L.J. dissenting).

SIR THOMAS BINGHAM M.R: . . . .. The point is often made that unelected unrepresentative judges have no business to be deciding questions of potentially far-reaching social concern which are more properly the preserve of elected representatives at national or local level. In some cases the making of such decisions may be inescapable, but in general the point is well made. In the present case it certainly is. The court has no role whatever as an arbiter between those who condemn hunting as barbaric and cruel and those who support it as a traditional country sport more humane in its treatment of deer or foxes (as the case may be) than other methods of destruction such as shooting, snaring, poisoning or trapping. This is of course a question on which most people hold views one way or the other. But our personal views are wholly irrelevant to the drier and more technical question which the court is obliged to answer. That is whether the county council acted lawfully in making the decision it did on the grounds it did. In other words, were members entitled in reaching their decision to give effect to their acceptance of the cruelty argument?

In seeking to answer that question it is, as the judge very clearly explained, at pp.523–525, critical to distinguish between the legal position of the private landowner and that of a land-owning local authority. To the famous question asked by the owner of the vineyard ("Is it not lawful for me to do what I will with mine own?" St. Matthew, chapter 20, verse 15) the modern answer would be clear: "Yes, subject to such regulatory and other constraints as the law imposes." But if the same question were posed by a local authority the answer would be different. It would be: "No, it is not lawful for you to do anything save what the law expressly or impliedly authorises. You enjoy no unfettered discretions. There are legal limits to every power you have." As Laws J. put it, at p.524, the rule for local authorities is that any action to be taken must be justified by positive law. . . .

Mr. Supperstone, for the county council, submitted that the judge had construed section 120(1)(b) too narrowly. It was, he reminded us, common ground that "the benefit . . . of their area" included wildlife benefit: see [1995] 1 All E.R. 513, 523. Those who accepted the cruelty argument were, he said, entitled to give effect to their view that the use of the county council's land for hunting was not for the benefit of the area, and the judge was wrong to treat that expression as applying to the management of the herd alone. He argued that on an issue of this kind county councillors were bound, and if not bound entitled, to have regard to the ethical arguments for and against hunting and the judge had been wrong to treat such considerations as irrelevant. Where power had been entrusted to a popular assembly, the court should be slow to interfere with the exercise of that power.

For the hunt, Mr. Beloff supported the judge's reasoning. The issue was a short point of statutory construction and the judge had construed the section correctly. Acceptance of the cruelty argument had nothing to do with the benefit of the area. The resolution was an impermissible attempt by those who accepted the cruelty argument to outlaw an activity very recently regulated by Parliament in the Deer Act 1991. In resolving as it did the county council acted as if it enjoyed the free discretion of a private landowner and without regard to the constraints which bound a local authority.

I accept the county council's basic contention that the judge put too narrow a construction on the words "the benefit . . . of their area." The draftsman would have been pressed to find broader or less specific language. I would not accept the judge's view that the cruelty argument, or the contrary argument that hunting is a less cruel means of controlling the herd than available alternatives (also, in the judge's terms, a moral argument), is necessarily irrelevant to consideration of what is for the benefit of the area. That is in my opinion to place an unwarranted restriction on the broad language the draftsman has used.

There is, however, as I think, a categorical difference between saying "I strongly disapprove of X" and saying "It is for the benefit of the area that X should be prohibited." The first is the expression of a purely personal opinion which may (but need not) take account of any wider, countervailing argument. There are, for example, those so deeply opposed to the capital penalty on moral grounds that no counter-argument (however cogent) could shake their conviction. The second statement is also the expression of a personal opinion, but involves a judgement on wider, community-based grounds of what is for the benefit of the area.

Both statements may of course lead to the same conclusion, but they need not. There is nothing illogical in saying "I strongly disapprove of X, but I am not persuaded that it is for the benefit of the area that X should be prohibited." Thus a person might be deeply opposed to the capital penalty but conclude that it would not be for the benefit of the community to prohibit it so long as its availability appeared to deter the commission of murder.

The question therefore arises whether, in resolving as it did on 4 August 1993, the county council exercised its power to further the object prescribed by the statute, the benefit of the county council area. I conclude that it did not, for these reasons.

(1) At no point, before or during the debate, was the attention of the council drawn to what is now agreed to be the governing statutory provision. The minds of councillors were never drawn too the question they should have been addressing. As the judge observed [1995] 1 All E.R. 513, 523F: "It follows that if the ban was lawful, it was so more by good luck than judgment."

(2) A paper circulated to county councillors with the agenda concluded:

"In the final analysis people go hunting primarily because they find it a sport they enjoy. The county council must come to a decision, as the National Trust report said, 'largely on the grounds of ethics, animal welfare and social considerations . . .' which are matters for members to decide."

I accept that animal welfare and social considerations were relevant matters to take into account, and I have accepted that ethical considerations could be. But this statement does not express or exhaust the statutory test, and could well be read as an invitation to councillors to give free rein to their personal views.

(3) The reference in the resolution to the county council "as landowners," and the statement in the letter (quoted ante, p.1042C-D), written after the resolution, that it was for every landowner to decide what activities he wished to allow on his land, appear to equip a rate the positions of private and local authority landowners. This in my view reflected a failure to appreciate the overriding statutory constraint.

(4) The lack of reference to the governing statutory test was not in my view a purely formal omission, for if councillors had been referred to it they would have had to attempt to define what benefit a ban would confer on the area and conversely what detriment the absence of a ban would cause. It may be that they could have done so, but as it was they did not need to try. The note certainly suggests that the debate ranged widely, and reference was made to "economic grounds" and "social damage" as well as to the cruelty argument and the contrary moral argument. But the note also suggests that expressions of purely personal opinion loomed large: "rituals unwholesome instincts," "systematically torture," "barbaric and amusement," "uniquely abhorrent," "pleasure torturing animals." In the absence of legal guidance, it was not, I think, appreciated that personal views, however strongly held, had to be related to the benefit of the area.

I accordingly agree, although on much narrower grounds, that the county council were not entitled to make the decision they did on the grounds they relied on. I leave open, but express no view on, the possibility that the same decision could have been reached on proper grounds. In reaching this conclusion I gain no assistance from authorities such as *Slattery v Naylor* (1888) 13 App. Cas. 446 and *Kruse v Johnson* [1898] 2 Q.B. 91 on judicial review of byelaws made by popular assemblies. The present case involves no issue of reasonableness. The question is whether a statutory power was exercised to promote the purpose for which the power was conferred. I conclude that it was not.

The judge ruled [1995] 1 All E.R. 513, 532, that he would, had it been necessary, have quashed the county council's decision on an alternative ground. This was that the county council failed to take account of a relevant consideration in reaching their decision, namely the effect which a ban would have on the management of the herd and how the deer were to be conserved in the light of it. If I am wrong in the main conclusion I have expressed, I do not share the judge's view that the decision is vulnerable on this alternative ground. The note shows that frequent references were made in the debate to the use of marksmen to cull deer and dispatch casualties. But in any event the question of management and conservation did not require an immediate solution. On the assumption that the ban would take effect at once, it remained to be seen what effect it would have (since it only applied to the common) on the herd as a whole. There was time to explore alternative measures later. And if alternative measures proved impracticable the ban could be revoked. I would dismiss this ground of challenge. . . .

SIMON BROWN L.J.: . . . . I agree with Sir Thomas Bingham M.R. that the judge construed too narrowly the statutory power here in question and erred in regarding the cruelty argument as necessarily irrelevant to the council's decision. I, for my part, indeed, would go further than the Master of the Rolls and conclude that the cruelty argument, as well indeed as the countervailing ethical considerations, were necessarily relevant to the decision. Had they been ignored I believe that the council would have been open to criticism.

There is a passage in the judgment below, at p.525C, in which the judge speaks of "a decision-maker who fails to take account of all and only those considerations material to his task." It is important to bear in mind, however, as Mr. Supperstone contended and Mr. Beloff accepted, that there are in fact three categories of consideration. First, those clearly (whether expressly or impliedly) identified by the statute as considerations to which regard must be had. Second, those clearly identified by the statute as consideration to which regard must not be had. Third, those to which the decision-maker may have regard if in his judgment and discretion he thinks it right to do so. There is, in short, a margin of appreciation within which the decision-maker may decide just what considerations should play a part in his reasoning process. On Wednesbury challenges (see *Associated Provincial Picture Houses Ltd. v Wednesbury Corporation* [1948] 1 K.B. 223) it is often salutary to bear in mind this short passage from Cooke J.'s judgment in *CREEDNZ. Inc. v Governor-General* [1981] 1N.Z.L.R. 172, 183:

> "What has to be emphasised is that it is only when the statute expressly or impliedly identifies considerations required to be taken into account by the authority as a matter of legal obligation that the court holds a decision invalid on the ground now invoked. It is not enough that a consideration is one that may properly be taken into account, nor even that it is one which many people, including the court itself, would have taken into account if they had to make the decision."

Even had I not thought the cruelty argument a category one consideration, I should certainly have regarded it as falling into category three. But in either event, of course, it does not follow that those councillors espousing the cruelty argument were bound to regard it as decisive. They could have concluded that it was preferable to allow hunting to continue until Parliament addressed the issue on a national level. Or they might have felt that their own personal views did not properly represent those of the majority of their community so that it would be wrong to give effect to them.

Provided only and always, however, that those councillors espousing the cruelty argument had regard to such other considerations as were necessarily in play, they were clearly entitled to regard it as decisive: its weight in the overall balance was exclusively a matter for them.

I pass, therefore, to the second question: can the council's decision be impugned on the conventional Wednesbury basis that those voting for the the ban failed to have regard to certain matters that they were bound to consider?

The judge found the decision flawed on this ground too: he criticised the council for failing to have regard to the future management of the deer in the event of a ban. In common with Sir Thomas Bingham M.R. and for the reasons he gives—essentially that it was not necessary for the council to fix upon a contemporaneous solution to whatever problem might result from the ban—I disagree.

What then of other relevant considerations? On this question I reluctantly find myself in respectful disagreement with Sir Thomas Bingham M.R. I would not for my part conclude that the council failed to have regard to the true nature of the question before it. I recognise, of course, that the councillors had not been advised as to the actual terms of their statutory power. But, as I have indicated, that power I believe merely to mirror the common law constraints that must in any event invariably rule council decision making.

I recognise too that both in its resolution, and in Mr. Temperley's subsequent letter, the council was emphasising the significance of its ownership of the common. But I would not think it right to infer from this that the councillors lost sight of their duty to act in the public interest and for the benefit of their area. The fact of ownership surely was of some significance. Given, as Mr. Temperley's letter postulated (although as the applicants reserve the right to contest), that there exists no right to hunt under the provisions of section 193(1) of the Law of Property Act 1925 (quoted [1995] 1 All E.R. 513, 552), the council's licence is required. The fact that it could not ban hunting on other land in its area (and may well not have been entitled under section 120(1)(b) to acquire other land in its area with a view to banning hunting over it, or for that matter with a view to allowing hunting over it—questions I think it unnecessary to decide) does not mean that it must allow hunting on its own land, and it seems to me harsh to construe that letter as a bald assertion that the councillors felt entitled merely to indulge their personal wishes in the matter. Given, moreover, that the hunt required the council's continuing licence, it seems to me inappropriate to speak of the prohibition as "manifestly interfer-[ing] with the lawful freedom of those who take part in the sport:" see [1995] 1 All E.R. 513, 529. It would be otherwise if section 193(1) conferred the right to hunt; then I accept it would be inappropriate for the council to attach weight to their status as owners of the common and I would be inclined to concur in quashing the ban and dismissing the appeal on that basis.

As it is, however, I find no sufficient reason for holding that those councillors in favour of the ban gave effect to unlawful considerations or failed to address what ultimately was the true question before them: what to do in the public interest and for the benefit of their area. Of course, combing through the note of the debate, one can always find arguments recorded in terms suggesting an improper approach to the question at issue. That, however, is not a sound basis for impeaching a decision of this nature: see *Rex v London County Council, Ex parte London and Provincial Electric Theatre Ltd.* [1915] 2 K.B. 466, 490–491.

In short, I conclude that the majority of the council here genuinely regarded huntig over the common as a cruel and socially undesirable activity inimical to the best interests of their area. It is not, of course, for me to say whether I think that a sound and sensible view. But that being a view which I believe the council was entitled to reach and reached, it follows that I for my part would have found the decision lawful and would accordingly have allowed this appeal.

SWINTON THOMAS L.J.:... In my judgment the Council passed a resolution without any consideration of the statutory restraints imposed on it, albeit in wide terms, by section 120(1)(b). It is certainly not fanciful to think that had they done so, some councillors might have taken a different view. Accordingly, the council never considered the powers under which they were acting, or applied them, and for that reason I would uphold the decision of the judge.

[On the broader issue whether the views of the majority of councillors that hunting was morally repulsive was a proper basis under s.120(1)(b) for imposing a ban, his Lordship agreed with Laws. J. that it was not. He also agreed with Sir Thomas Bingham M.R. and Simon Brown L.J. that Laws J's decision on the alternative ground should not be upheld.]

Appeal dismissed.

Notes

1. This case illustrates a number of dimensions of the "considerations" ground of challenge. What are or are not legally relevant considerations are questions of law to be determined by the courts by an interpretation of the relevant provisions in their context. Note here the broader views of Sir Thomas Bingham M.R. and Simon Brown L.J. that moral considerations (respectively) could be or were legally relevant. Whether all the right considerations have been taken into account is a question of fact to be resolved (usually) by examining the record of the decision making process. The outcome here was determined crucially by the view of Sir Thomas Bingham M.R. and Swinton Thomas L.J. that the council had not considered the statutory context provided by s.120(1)(b) of the 1972 Act.

An irrelevant consideration may be taken into account or a relevant consideration ignored as the result of a mistake of law (*cf. Anisminic*, above, p.436) or a mistake of fact (see Lord Wilberforce in *Secretary of State for Education v Tameside MBC* [1977] 1 A.C. 1014 at 1047, below, p.591, and further on mistake of fact as error of law, pp.828–841.

2. Note also the recognition given by Simon Brown L.J., by reference to the *CREEDNZ* case from New Zealand, that there is a middle category of considerations where it is for the authority, guided by the policy and objects of the statute, to determine the relevance, subject to control for *Wednesbury* unreasonableness. This proposition has been accepted as good law in other cases. See Lord Scarman in *Findlay Re* [1985] A.C. 319 at pp.333–334; Laws L.J. in *R. (on the application of S (a child) v North Warwickshire BC* [2001] EWC Civ 315; [2001] P.L.C.R. 31 at [20], and in *R. (on the application of Khatun) v Newham LBC* [2004] EWCA Civ 55.

It is, conversely, not the law that unless a decision-maker is expressly required to take into account some matter, he is only "impliedly" required by law to do so if it is one which no reasonable decision-maker would fail to take into account: *per* Hodgson J. in *R. v Secretary of State for the Environment Ex p. Boston MBC* [1991] J.P.L. 32.

Related to the *CREEDNZ* proposition is the point that the court may in appropriate circumstances require a decision-making authority "to take reasonable steps to acquaint [itself] with the relevant information" (*per* Lord Diplock in *Secretary of State for Education and Science v Tameside MBC* [1997] A.C. 1014 at 1064–1065 (see below, p.591). This has been applied to such matters as the discretion of the Secretary of State to confirm a compulsory purchase order (*Prest v Secretary of State for Wales* (1982) 81 L.G.R. 193, *per* Watkins L.J. at 207, 208) and the discretion of a local authority to make a removal direction under the Criminal Justice and Public Order Act 1994 (*R. v Wealden DC Ex p Wales* (1995) 8 Admin. L.R. 529 at 543); but not the more general discretion of a local authority whether to grant planning permission (*R. v Tendring DC Ex p. Leonard* (1998) 76 P. & C.R. 567).

3. For examples of statutes specifying considerations that must be taken into account, see s.604(1) of the Housing Act 1985 listing matters to which regard shall be had in determining whether a house is unfit for human habitation; and s.71 of the Race Relations Act 1976, providing that it is the duty of every local authority to secure that their functions are carried out with due regard to the needs (a) to eliminate unlawful racial discrimination, and (b) to promote equality of opportunity, and good relations, between persons of different racial groups. On the latter, see *R. v Lewisham LBC Ex p. Shell UK Ltd*, below, p.569. Local authorities and other public bodies are frequently required to have regard to guidance issued by the Secretary of State or a central government agency, and give it its proper weight without regarding it as a binding direction (above, pp.461–463).

4. There are many other examples of situations where the relevant or irrelevant considerations are identified by the courts. There is, for example, a large body of case law on the question what are material planning considerations (see *Encyclopedia of Planning Law and Practice*, notes to the Town and Country Planning Act 1990, s.70). The Court of Appeal in *Bristol DC v Clark* [1975] 1 W.L.R. 1443 identified a number of factors which were relevant to decisions to evict council tenants. The affordability of

a proposed exercise of a *discretionary* power is likely to be a highly relevant considera-tion (*per* Stanley Burnton J. in *R. (on the application of Birmingham Care Consortium) v Birmingham City Council* [2002] EWHC (Admin) 2118 at [17]. A notable example is *R. v Cambridge DHA Ex p. B* [1995] 1 W.L.R. 898 where the Court of Appeal rejected a challenge to the authority's refusal to allocate some £75,000 for proposed non-stan-dard treatment with a small prospect of success for a girl suffering from acute myeloid leukaemia who was thought by doctors to have six to eight weeks to live. The judge, Laws J., held that the authority had to "do more than toll the bell of tight resources" and explain adequately their finding priorities. Sir Thomas Bingham M.R. said (at 906) that the authority could not be criticised on either basis. "Difficult and agonising judg-ments have to be made as to how a limited budget is best allocated to the maximum advantage of the maximum number of patients. This is not a judgment which the court can make". It would be "totally unrealistic to require the authority to come to court with its accounts and seek to demonstrate that if this treatment were provided to B then there would be a patient, C, who would have to go without treatment. No major author-ity could run its financial affairs in a way which would permit such a demonstration".

See also *R. v Chief Constable of Sussex Ex p. Trader's Ferry Ltd* [1999] 2 A.C. 418, where the House of Lords held that the duty of the police to uphold the law was subject to a discretion on the part of the chief constable as to the policing to be provided, here in respect of ongoing protests to the export of live animals through the port of Shoreham. He was entitled to take into account, *inter alia*, the number of men avail-able to him and his financial resources to provide police officers. (See Lord Slynn at 431.) The chief constable's decision to provide no policing save (with certain exclu-sions) on two consecutive days a week or on four days consecutively a fortnight, was held not to be *Wednesbury* unreasonable.

Lack of resources can, but is much less likely to, be held to be relevant to perform-ance of a duty (see pp.418–420).

5. The requirements of procedural fairness may require that the views of a person affected by a decision be taken into account (see Ch.10). On the relationship between this and the "considerations" grounds, see Laws L.J. in *R. (on the application of Khatun) v Newham LBC* [2004] EWCA Civ 55; [2004] 3 W.L.R. 417 at [23]–[24], [33]–[40].

6. The following case deals with what can be seen as a special consideration to be taken into account by local authorities in making decisions that involve expenditure, its supposed "fiduciary duty" owed to ratepayers.

(ii) The "fiduciary duty"

ROBERTS v HOPWOOD

[1925] A.C. 578; 94 L.J.K.B. 542; 133 L.T. 289; 41 T.L.R. 436; 89 J.P. 105; 69 S.J. 475; [1925] All E.R.REP. 24; 23 L.G.R. 337 (HOUSE OF LORDS)

Poplar Borough Council had power under s.62 of the Metropolis Management Act 1855 to pay to their employees "such salaries and wages as . . . [the council] may think fit". In 1914, the minimum wage for the lowest grade of worker was 30s per week for men, and 22s 6d for women, these being in line with wages paid by the other metropolitan councils. By 1920, these figures had risen to 64s and 49s 9d respectively. When auditing the 1920–21 accounts the district auditor, Mr Carson Roberts, noted an increase to 80s as the minimum for both men and women from May 1, 1920. He did not then raise any objection as the cost of living had greatly increased since 1914. In 1923, the auditor found that the rate of 80s per week was still being maintained, although the cost of living had materially reduced. Indeed, he found that the total of the wage payments made by the council in 1921–22 exceeded by about £17,000 the total amount that would have been paid if the trade union rates had been applicable; that wage increases since 1914 exceeded cost-of-living increases by between 85 per cent and 200 per cent depending upon the grade of worker; that working hours were considerably shorter in 1922 than in 1914; and that in the lower grades the new minimum rate varied from nearly three times to over four times the rate paid per hour in 1914.

The auditor heard representations from the Socialist councillors who controlled the council, led by George Lansbury, to the effect that they regarded themselves as bound to maintain these wage levels by a "mandate of the electors". He decided that the council had not paid due regard to the interests of the ratepayers, and had made payments far in excess of those necessary to obtain the service required and to maintain a high standard of efficiency, which were thus in reality gifts to their employees in addition to remuneration for their services. He was under a duty under s.247(7) of the Public Health Act 1875 to "disallow every item of account contrary to law, and surcharge the same on the person making or authorising the making of the illegal payment". Acting under this section he disallowed £5,000 and surcharged it on the councillors concerned.

The councillors applied for certiorari under the Public Health Act to quash the disallowance and surcharge. Section 247(8) enabled a person aggrieved to apply for a writ of certiorari to remove the disallowance to the King's Bench Division. As interpreted in earlier cases, *e.g. R. v Roberts* [1908] 1 K.B. 407, this was regarded as giving in effect a right to appeal on fact and/or law. The Divisional Court (Lord Hewart C.J., Sankey and Salter JJ.) rejected their application ([1924] 1 K.B. 514: *sub nom. R. v Roberts, Ex p. Scurr*). The councillors appealed successfully to the Court of Appeal ([1924] 2 K.B. 695). The House of Lords unanimously allowed the auditor's appeal.

LORD BUCKMASTER: . . . [T]he general rule applicable is that the council shall pay such wages as they may think fit, the discretion as to the reasonable nature of the wages being with them. The discretion thus imposed is a very wide one, and I agree with the principle enunciated by Lord Russell in the case of *Kruse v. Johnson* [1899] 2 Q.B. 91, 99 [below, p.234], that when such a discretion is conferred upon a local authority the court ought to show great reluctance before they attempt to determine how, in their opinion, the discretion ought to be exercised.

Turning to what the borough council have done, the reason for their action is to be found in the affidavit sworn by Mr Scurr, Mr Key, Mr Lansbury and Mr Sumner. In para.6 of that affidavit they make the following statement: "The council and its predecessors the district board of works have always paid such a minimum wage to its employees as they have believed to be fair and reasonable without being bound by any particular external method of fixing wages, whether ascertainable by Trade Union rate, cost of living, payments by other local or national authorities or otherwise." And if the matter ended there it would be my opinion that a decision so reached could not be impeached until it were shown that it was not *bona fide*, and absence of *bona fides* is not alleged in the present proceedings. Para.9, however, of the same affidavit puts the matter in a different form. It is there said: "9. . . . The Council did not and does not take the view that wages paid should be exclusively related to the cost of living. They have from time to time carefully considered the question of the wages and are of the opinion, as a matter of policy, that a public authority should be a model employer and that a minimum rate of 4*l.* is the least wage which ought to be paid to an adult having regard to the efficiency of their workpeople, the duty of a public authority both to the rate-payers and to its employees, the purchasing power of the wages and other considerations which are relevant to their decisions as to wages."

Now it appears that on August 31, 1921, a resolution was passed by the borough council to the effect that no reduction of wage or bonus should be made during the ensuing four months, and this was acted upon for the following 12 months. It was, I think, well within their power to fix wages for a reasonable time in advance, and there are cogent reasons why this should be done, but that decision should be made in relation to existing facts, which they appear to have ignored. In August 1921, the cost of living had been continuously fall since November of the previous year, and it continued to fall, so that it is difficult to understand how, if the cost of living was taken into account in fixing the wages for adult workers at a minimum basis of 4*l*., the sharp decline in this important factor should have been wholly disregarded by the borough council. But the affidavit contains another statement, which I think is most serious for the council's case. It states that 4*l*. a week was to be the minimum wage for adult labour, that is without the least regard to what that labour might be. It standardised men and women not according to the duties they performed, but according to the fact that they were adults. It is this that leads me to think that their action cannot be supported, and that in fact they have not determined the payment as wages, for they have eliminated the consideration both of the work to be done and of the purchasing power of the sums paid, which they themselves appear to regard as a relevant though not the dominant factor. Had they stated that they determined as a borough council to pay the same wage for the same work without regard to the sex or condition of the person who performed it, I should have found it difficult to say that that was not a proper exercise of their discretion. It was indeed argued that that is what they did, but I find it impossible to extract that from the statement contained in the affidavit. It appears to me, for the reasons I have given, that they cannot have brought into account the considerations which they say influenced them, and that they did not base their decision upon the ground that the reward for work is the value of the work reasonably and even generously measured, but that they took an arbitrary principle and fixed an arbitrary sum, which was not a real exercise of the discretion imposed upon them by the statute.

It is for these reasons that I think the appeal should succeed.

LORD ATKINSON: . . . It is but right and natural that the rate of wages should rise if the cost of living rises, because this tends directly to keep the purchasing power of the labourer's wage at what it was before the cost of living increased. The principle apparently adopted by the council, however, is that wages should rise if the cost of living rises, but should never go down if the cost of living goes down. . . .

In the sixth paragraph of Mr Scurr's affidavit he states that "the Council have always paid such a minimum wage as they have believed to be fair and reasonable without being bound by any particular external method of fixing wages, whether by trade union rates, cost of living, payments of other local or national authorities or otherwise". Nobody has contended that the council should be bound by any of these things, but it is only what justice and common sense demand that, when dealing with funds contributed by the whole body of the ratepayers, they should take each and every one of these enumerated things into consideration in order to help them to determine what was a fair, just and reasonable wage to pay their employees for the services the latter rendered. The council would, in my view, fail in their duty if, in administering funds which did not belong to their members alone, they put aside all these aids to the ascertainment of what was just and reasonable remuneration to give for the services rendered to them, and allowed themselves to be guided in preference by some eccentric principles of socialist philanthropy, or by a feminist ambition to secure the equality of the sexes in the matter of wages in the world of labour.

In para.9 of Mr Scurr's affidavit he is good enough to disclose what the council did take into consideration in fixing the minimum rate of wages to be paid to their employees. . . .

This system of procedure might possibly be admirably philanthropic, if the funds of the council at the time that they were thus administered belonged to the existing members of that body. These members would then be generous at their own expense. . . . A body charged with the administration for definite purposes of funds contributed in whole or in part by persons other than the members of that body, owes, in my view, a duty to those latter persons to conduct the administration in a fairly businesslike manner with reasonable care, skill and caution, and with a due and alert regard to the interest of those contributors who are not members of the body. Towards these latter persons the body stands somewhat in the position of trustees or managers of the property of others.

This duty is, I think, a legal duty as well as a moral one, and acts done in flagrant violation of it should, in my view, be properly held to have been done "contrary to law" within the meaning of section 247(7) of the Public Health Act of 1875. . . . It was strongly pressed in argument that the auditor believed the council acted *bona fide*; but what in this connection do the words "*bona fide*" mean? Do they mean, as apparently this gentleman thought, that no matter how excessive or illegal their scale of wages might be, they were bound to put it into force because their constituents gave them a mandate so to do, or again, do the words mean that as the payment of wages was a subject with which they had legally power to deal, the amount of their funds which they devoted to that purpose was their own concern which no auditor had jurisdiction to revise, or in reference to which he could surcharge anything? The whole system of audit to which the Legislature has subjected every municipal corporation or council is a most emphatic protest against such opinions as these. . . .

[A]s wages are remuneration for services, the words "think fit" must, I think, be construed to mean "as the employer shall think fitting and proper" for the services rendered. It cannot, in my view, mean that the employer, especially an employer dealing with moneys not entirely his own, may pay to his employee wages of any amount he pleases. Still less does it mean that he can pay gratuities or gifts to his employees disguised under the name of wages. . . .

What is a reasonable wage at any time must depend, of course, on the circumstances which then exist in the labour market. I do not say there must be any cheeseparing or that the datum line, as I have called it, must never be exceeded to any extent, or that employees may not be generously treated. But it does not appear to me that there is any rational proportion between the rates of wages at which the labour of these women is paid and the rates at which they would be reasonably remunerated for their services to the council.

I concur with the auditor in thinking that what has been given to the women as wages is really to a great extent gifts and gratuities disguised as wages, and is therefore illegal. The council have evidently been betrayed into the course they have followed by taking into consideration the several matters mentioned in Mr Scurr's affidavit, which they ought not properly to have taken into their consideration at all, and consequently did not properly exercise the discretion placed in them, but acted contrary to law: see *R. v. Adamson* (1875) 1 Q.B.D. 201; *R. v. St Pancras Vestry*, 24 Q.B.D. 371 [above, p.523]; *R. v. Board of Education* [1910] 2 K.B. 165 at 179.

I think the appeal succeeds.

LORD SUMNER: . . . The respondents conceded that for wages fixed *mala fide* no exemption from review could be claimed and that the mere magnitude of the wages paid, relatively to the wages for which the same service was procurable, might be enough in itself to establish bad faith. This admission, I am sure, was rightly made, but it leads to two conclusions. First, the final words of the section are not absolute, but are subject to an implied qualification of good faith—"as the board may *bona fide* think fit". Is the implication of good faith all? That is a qualification drawn from the general legal doctrine, that persons who hold public office have a legal responsibility towards those whom they represent—not merely towards those who vote for them—to the discharge of which they must honestly apply their minds. *Bona fide* here cannot simply mean that they are not making a profit out of their office or acting in it from private spite, nor is *bona fide* a short way of saying that the council has acted within the ambit of its powers and therefore not contrary to law. It must mean that they are giving their minds to the comprehension and their wills to the discharge of their duty towards that public, whose money and local business they administer.

The purpose, however, of the whole audit is to ensure wise and prudent administration and to recover for the council's funds money that should not have been taken out of them. If, having examined the expenditure and found clear proof of bad faith, which admittedly would open the account, the auditor further found that the councillors' evil minds had missed their mark, and the expenditure itself was right, then the expenditure itself would not be "contrary to law" and could not be disallowed. Bad faith admittedly vitiates the council's purported exercise of its discretion, but the auditor is not confined to asking, if the discretion, such as it may be, has been honestly exercised. He has to restrain expenditure within proper limits. His mission is to inquire if there is any excess over what is reasonable. I do not find any words limiting his functions merely to the case of bad faith, or obliging him to leave the ratepayers unprotected from the effects on their pockets of honest stupidity or unpractical idealism. The breach in the words "as they may think fit", which the admitted implication as to bad faith makes, is wide enough to make the necessary implication one both of honesty and of reasonableness. It might be otherwise if the express words were to be read as absolute and unqualified, but if they are to be read as subject to some qualification, I think that qualification must be derived from the purpose of the statutory audit, which is the protection of the ratepayers' pockets and not the immunity of spend-thrift administration. Next, in the case and for the purpose assumed, the auditor, when he reviews the accounts, is entitled and bound to use his own judgment as to the wages that would be reasonable under the circumstances. He must do so, in order to measure from that datum the excess of the wages paid, and to decide if the excess is so great as to evidence *mala fides*. So it will be also with the courts of law on appeal. If in the case of bad faith the auditor is capable of finding a reasonable amount and is bound to proceed to do so, I find no words in the section which, on a sound construction, preclude him from doing the same thing when good faith is present, and I think that in both cases the reasonableness of the amounts is a subject for his review. . . . I can find nothing in the Acts empowering bodies to which the Metropolis Management Act 1855 applies which authorizes them to be guided by their personal opinions on political, economic or social questions in administering the funds which they derive from levying rates.

Much was said at the Bar about the wide discretion conferred by the Local Government Acts on local authorities. In a sense this is true, but the meaning of the term needs careful examination. What has been said in cases which lie outside the provisions as to audit altogether is not necessarily applicable to matters which are concerned with the expenditure of public money. There are many matters which the courts are indisposed to question. Though they are the ultimate judges of what is lawful and what is unlawful to borough councils, they often accept the decisions of the local authority simply because they are themselves ill equipped to weigh the merits of one solution of a practical question as against another. This, however, is not a recognition of the absolute character of the local authority's discretion, but of the limits within which it is practicable to question it. There is nothing about a borough council that corresponds to autonomy. It has great responsibilities, but the limits of its powers and of its independence are such as the law, mostly statutory, may have laid down, and there is no presumption against the accountability of the authority. Everything depends on the construction of the sections applicable. In the present case, I think that the auditor was entitled to inquire into all the items of expenditure in question, to ask whether in incurring them the council had been guided by aims and objects not open to them or had disregarded considerations by which they should have been guided, and to the extent to which they had in consequence exceeded a reasonable expenditure, it was his duty to disallow the items.

LORD WRENBURY: . . . The cardinal word upon which emphasis is principally to be laid is the word "wages". Wages are the pecuniary return for services rendered. To determine the proper or true amount which in a given state of facts has been paid or is payable for services rendered is far from easy. It can never be determined with exactness. It is impossible to name in any particular case an amount which if diminished by 1s. a week would be too small, and if increased by 1s. a week would be too large. But it is possible to name an amount which would certainly be too large—as, for instance, if a charwoman were paid 2l. a day. Using my best endeavour to state the matter in general terms, I express it thus:

Wages in a particular service are such sum as a reasonable person, guiding himself by an investigation of the current rate in fact found to be paid in the particular industry, and acting upon the principle that efficient service is better commanded by paying an efficient wage, would find to be the proper sum. The figure to be sought is not the lowest figure at which the service could be obtained, nor is it the highest figure which a generous employer might, upon grounds of philanthropy or generosity, pay out of his own pocket. It is a figure which is not to be based upon or increased by motives of philanthropy nor even of generosity stripped of commercial considerations. It is such figure as is the reasonable pecuniary equivalent of the service rendered. Anything beyond this is not wages. It is an addition to wages, and is a gratuity. The authority is to pay not such sum but such wages as they think fit.

I pass from the word "wages" to the words "as [they] may think fit". We have heard argument upon the question whether these words are or are not to be understood as if the word "reasonable" or "reasonably" were inserted, so that the sentence would run "as they reasonably think fit" or "such reasonable wages as they may think fit". Is the verb "think" equivalent to "reasonably think"? My Lords, to my mind there is no difference in the meaning, whether the word "reasonably" or "reasonable" is in or out. . ... I rest my opinion upon higher grounds. A person in whom is vested a discretion must exercise his discretion upon reasonable grounds. A discretion does not empower a man to do what he likes merely because he is minded to do so—he must in the exercise of his discretion do not what he likes but what he ought. In other words, he must, by the use of his reason, ascertain and follow the course which reason directs. He must act reasonably.

Thirdly, and lastly, I point to the word "fit". That word means, I think, "fitting" or "suitable". The words "as they think fit" do not mean "as they choose". The measure is not the volition of the person vested with the discretion, it is the suitability or adequacy or fitness of the amount in the reasonable judgment of the person vested with the discretion.

[LORD CARSON delivered a short speech, concurring with some hesitancy. He held that it was "open to the auditor, upon coming to the conclusions as stated in his affidavit, to draw the inference that the council were not engaged in merely fixing a rate of wages, but were affected by considerations which could not be held to come within the ambit of the discretion entrusted to them".]

Appeal allowed.

Notes

1. One of the problems of interpretation considered by the House was that while the power under s. 62 of the 1855 Act was a general power to employ officers and servants and to pay "such salaries and wages" as the authority "may think fit", other statutes which conferred on local authorities powers to employ persons for the purposes of the relevant statute often gave power to pay "reasonable" wages. Lord Buckmaster (at 588) regarded s.62 as the dominant section. Lord Atkinson thought that "in each and every case the payment of all salaries and wages must be 'reasonable'. I see no difficulty in so construing the words of section 62" (at 599). Lord Wrenbury thought that "there is no difference in the meaning, whether the word 'reasonably' or 'reasonable' is in or out" (at 613). Nevertheless his Lordship did not rely on the presence of "reasonable" in some statutes—it was not obvious which provisions should give way. Lord Sumner and Lord Carson did not deal with the problem.

2. *Roberts v Hopwood* also settled that the district auditor's power to disallow an "item" contrary to law was not limited to the situation where a complete item of account was *ultra vires* (as it would have been, for example, if the council had had no power to employ and pay any servants at all), but could be used in relation to *excessive* expenditure on an otherwise lawful item—the excess only being *ultra vires*. The powers of disallowance and surcharge (subsequently re-enacted in ss.17 and 18 of the Audit Commission Act 1998), were repealed (so far as for England and for police authorities in Wales) by the Local Government Act 2000, s.90.

3. Note the attitude of the majority in the Court of Appeal ([1924] 2 K.B. 695) who were willing to defer to the views of elected representatives of the people in such a matter as this, except in a clear case. Is the decision of the House of Lords correct, leaving aside the purple passages? Would the case have been decided differently had there been no stress on the quasi-fiduciary duty owed by local authorities to ratepayers? Can any general propositions of law concerning "reasonableness" in the exercise of discretions be derived from this case?

4. The leaders of Poplar Borough Council had recently been in conflict with central government on another issue: the payment of outdoor relief to the able-bodied poor. The story of "Poplarism" is told by B. Keith-Lucas [1962] P.L. 52, and further background information is given by G.W. Jones, "Herbert Morrison and Poplarism" [1973] P.L. 11 and N. Branson, *Poplarism* (1979). See also *Roberts v Cunningham* (1925) 42 T.L.R. 162 and *Woolwich Corp. v Roberts* (1927) 96 L.J.K.B. 757, where two other councils which paid "model" wages took their cases to the House of Lords. At one stage in the events at Poplar, the councillors were imprisoned for their contempt of court in disobeying a writ of mandamus issued by the King's Bench Divisional Court. Some marched off to prison headed by the town band (at the cost of £10 which was subsequently disallowed by the District Auditor). Their imprisonment was a considerable political embarrassment for the Minister of Health.

5. In *Prescott v Birmingham Corp.* [1955] 1 Ch. 210, the corporation, which had power to charge "such fares as they may think fit" on their public transport services resolved to introduce a scheme for free bus travel for old people. The corporation sought the consent of the traffic commissioners as required by the Road Traffic Act 1930. Consent was given, subject to the payment of £90,000 from the general rate fund to the account of the transport undertaking. A ratepayer brought an action for a declaration that the scheme was *ultra vires*. Vaisey J. and the Court of Appeal granted the declaration. Jenkins L.J. stated at 235–238 that if a trustee running a bus service allowed a class of persons whom he considered badly off to travel free or at reduced fares:

"it may be that passengers charged the full fare could not object on that account. But we apprehend that the *cestuis que trustent* certainly could. . . .

Local authorities are not, of course, trustees for their ratepayers, but they do, we think, owe an analogous fiduciary duty to their ratepayers in relation to the application of funds contributed by the latter. Thus local authorities running an omnibus undertaking at the risk of their ratepayers, in the sense that any deficiencies must be met by an addition to the rates are not, in our view, entitled, merely on the strength of a general power, to charge different fares to different passengers or classes of passengers, to make a gift to a particular class of persons of rights of free travel on their vehicles, simply because the local authority concerned are of opinion that the favoured class of persons ought, on benevolent or philanthropic grounds, to be accorded that benefit. In other words, they are not, in our view, entitled to use their discriminatory power as proprietors of the transport undertaking in order to confer out of rates a special benefit on some particular class of inhabitants whom they, as the local authority for the town or district in question, may think deserving of such assistance. In the absence of clear statutory authority, for such a proceeding (which to our mind a mere general power to charge differential fares certainly is not) we would, for our part, regard it as illegal, on the ground that, to put the matter bluntly, it would amount simply to the making of a gift or present in money's worth to a particular section of the local community at the expense of the general body of ratepayers. . . .

We are not persuaded by Mr Rowe's argument to the effect that the relevant legislation would allow the defendants to charge no fares at all to anyone and to finance their transport undertaking entirely out of the rates. We think it is clearly implicit in the legislation, that while it was left to the defendants to decide what fares should be charged within any prescribed statutory maxima for the time being in force, the undertaking was to be run as a business venture, or, in other words, that fares fixed by the defendants at their discretion, in accordance with ordinary business principles, were to be charged. That is not to say that in operating their transport undertaking the defendants should be guided by considerations of profit to the exclusion of all other considerations. They should, no doubt, aim at providing an efficient service of omnibuses at reasonable cost, and it may be that this objective is impossible of attainment without some degree of loss. But it by no means follows that they should go out of their way to make losses by giving away rights of free travel.

As to the instances of legitimate discrimination given by Mr Rowe, the concession in favour of workmen is enjoined by statute, and therefore does not advance his argument. The concessions in favour of children (who travel free or at half-fares according to age) are of a kind commonly, if not universally, accorded by transport undertakings, and, we should have thought, readily justifiable on business principles. The practice of allowing free travel to blind and disabled persons may, or may not, be strictly justifiable, but may perhaps be classed as a minor act of elementary charity to which no reasonable ratepayer would be likely to object.

In our opinion the scheme now in question goes beyond anything which can reasonably be regarded as authorized by the discretionary power of fixing fares and differentiation in the fares charged to different passengers or classes of passengers possessed by the defendants under the relevant legislation, and is, accordingly, *ultra vires* the defendants.

. . . [T]he scheme fares no better if its adoption is considered as a purported exercise by the defendants of their discretion in a matter not, on the face of it, necessarily outside the general ambit of the discretionary power of differentiation of fares conferred on them by the relevant legislation. . . . If we are right in thinking that, after all allowance is made for their special position as a local authority, the defendants owe a duty to their ratepayers to operate their transport undertaking substantially on business lines, we think it must necessarily follow that, in adopting the scheme, the defendants misapprehended the nature and scope of the discretion conferred on them, and mistakenly supposed that it enabled them to confer benefits, in the shape of rights of free travel, on any class or classes of the local inhabitants appearing to them to be deserving of such benefits by reason of their advanced age and limited means. Accordingly, if the case is to be regarded as turning upon the question whether the decision to adopt the scheme was a proper exercise of a discretion conferred on the defendants with respect to the differential treatment of passengers in the matter of fares, the answer, in our opinion, must be that it was not a proper exercise of such discretion. We think some support for this view is to be derived from the speeches in the House of Lords in *Roberts v Hopwood* [1925] A.C. 578". [See above, pp.552–558.]

See case notes at 72 L.Q.R. 237; 18 M.L.R. 159; [1955] C.L.J. 135. Parliament intervened to validate existing concessions by the Public Service Vehicles (Travel Concessions) Act 1955, and to give general powers to make such concessions by the Travel Concessions Act 1964. See now the Transport Act 1985, ss.93–105.

6. Consider the implications of Lord Sumner's suggestion that where bad faith is proved but the amount of expenditure is reasonable, the courts cannot interfere. See *Walker's Decision, Re* [1944] K.B. 644; *Robins v Minister of Health* [1939] 1 K.B. 520 at 537–538.

7. A modern analysis of *Roberts v Hopwood* is provided by P. Fennell, "Roberts v Hopwood: The Rule against Socialism" (1986) 13 J.L.S. 401. He comments (at 419):

"In Roberts v. Hopwood the conduct of the councillors was stigmatised as unreasonable, irrational, arbitrary and eccentric. In subsequent cases the courts have ruled that to policies which require expenditure of the rates is attached the requirement that the interests of the ratepayers must be considered at every turn. The connection between socialism and irresponsibility is never made as explicitly as it was in Lord Atkinson's judgment, because it is neither politic nor necessary to do so. A party elected on a policy of reducing rates and charging for services is already doing its legal duty; a party elected on a policy of increasing welfare services has it yet to do".

See also A. Bradney, "Facade: The Poplar Case" (1983) 43 N.I.L.Q. 1, who examines the political background of the judges who heard the case.

8. *Roberts v Hopwood* was distinguished by the Divisional Court in *Pickwell v Camden LBC* [1983] 1 Q.B. 962, which held that the council had been entitled to

make a pay settlement with staff higher than a national settlement. It had not ignored any relevant consideration or acted unreasonably in the *Wednesbury* sense. Note Forbes J.'s rationalisation of *Roberts v Hopwood*:

"The case seems to me to decide no more than this, that where the inevitable inference which must be drawn is that an obviously excessive wage payment was agreed to be paid without any regard to any commercial consideration and solely on some extraneous principle, as, for instance, philanthropy, such a payment can only be regarded as a gift and is not covered by a statutory power to pay reasonable wages. Looking back, as we do, over 60 years of progress in the field of social reform and industrial relations some of their Lordships' observations may, with the benefit of this hindsight, appear unsympathetic. But what has changed over those years is our attitudes to what should be regarded as pure philanthropy; the basic principle, that a payment is illegal which cannot be justified by reference to the objects for which a statutory power is granted, still remains".

9. The notion of a "fiduciary duty" owed to ratepayers (now also council tax-payers) was one of a number of grounds upon which the House of Lords ruled against the Greater London Council's introduction of its new "Fares Fair" public transport subsidy policy in 1981: *Bromley LBC v Greater London Council* [1982] 1 A.C. 768. Here, the GLC resolved to implement one of the election manifesto commitments of the controlling Labour group to cut fares on London Transport buses and tubes by an average of 25 per cent. A supplementary precept was issued requiring rating authorities in London to increase the rates. The money would be paid by the GLC to the London Transport Executive to cover the deficit that LTE would incur as a result, in the exercise of GLC's power to make grants to the LTE "for any purpose" under s.3 of the Transport (London) Act 1969. The GLC was aware that its fare reduction policy would result in the loss of some £50 million of rate support grant from the Government. The House of Lords granted an application by one of the rating authorities, Bromley LBC, for certiorari to quash the supplementary precept, on a variety of grounds. The legislation was interpreted as requiring the LTE to run its transport undertaking on "ordinary business principles", ensuring, so far as practicable, that outgoings were met by revenue. The GLC's power to make grants could not be used to achieve some object of social policy in total disregard of the LTE's objections. Furthermore,

(1) there was a breach of the fiduciary duty owed to ratepayers (*Prescott*, above, p.559), the GLC having failed to balance that duty against the duty to transport users (see Lord Wilberforce at 815, 819–820; Lord Diplock at 829–830; Lord Scarman at 838–839, 882).
(2) The decision to implement the policy in the knowledge that the originally contemplated cost to the ratepayers would be nearly doubled by loss of RSG was not a decision which the council, directing itself properly in law, could reasonably have made (see Lord Brandon at 853; *cf.* Lord Wilberforce at 820 and Lord Diplock at 930, who regarded this as a factor in establishing a breach of the fiduciary duty);
(3) The majority group on the GLC had misdirected itself by regarding the GLC as univocally committed by the election manifesto to carry out the policy (see Lord Diplock at 830–831 and Lord Brandon at 853).

The decision was highly controversial both politically and with commentators (*cf.* J. Dignan, (1983) 99 L.Q.R. 605; M. Loughlin, *Local Government and the Modern State* (1986), pp.70–75 and *Legality and Locality* (1996), pp.231–247).

"By ignoring such obvious signposts to interpretation as the legislative history and by utilizing an anachronistic concept [the fiduciary duty] as their guide, the Law Lords effectively succeeded in turning sense into nonsense." (Loughlin, *op. cit.*, at p.234)

It is significant that *Bromley* was subsequently distinguished in a number of cases in the Divisional Court. In *R. v Merseyside City Council Ex p. Great Universal Stores* (1982) 80 L.G.R. 639, Woolf J. rejected a challenge to the validity of the council's policy of subsidising bus fares from the rates; the legislation here was differently worded, there was no question of the automatic loss of rate support grant (there was no more to lose) and the proposal had been considered afresh after the elections. In *R. v London Transport Executive Ex p. GLC* [1983] Q.B. 484, the Court upheld the validity of a revised plan to subsidise LT fares from the rates. The GLC was held to be entitled to make grants to LTE to cover continuing losses provided there was no breach of the *Wednesbury* and *Prescott* principles (in reality a more persuasive interpretation of the relevant legislation; the court, however, loyally stated that *Bromley* had been widely misinterpreted). Furthermore the courts were unwilling to allow the fiduciary duty to be used by those who sought to challenge the spending decision of local author-ities as anything more than a consideration that had to be taken into account; the inter-ests of ratepayers were not to be over-emphasised and over-protected (see *R. v GLC Ex p. Kensington and Chelsea RLBC, The Times*, April 7, 1982; *R. v Ealing LBC Ex p. Dunstan*, unreported, June 15, 1987; *R. v Waltham Forest LBC Ex p. Waltham Borough Ratepayers Action Group*, unreported, July 29, 1987, discussed by Loughlin, *op. cit.*, pp.250–255). On *Bromley*, see also J.A.G. Griffith, "Judicial Decision-making in Public Law" [1985] P.L. 564 at 575–579. The opinion of counsel for Bromley, Harry Sales, is reproduced at [1991] P.L. 499. The impact of *Bromley* on local authorities was the subject of an interdisciplinary study: L. Bridges *et al.*, *Legality and Local Politics* (1987).

Compare the attitude of Lord Diplock and Lord Brandon on the significance to be attached to election manifesto commitments with that of the House of Lords in the *Tameside* case, below, p.591.

10. It is unusual for separate reliance in argument in litigation concerning local authorities to be placed on the fiduciary duty. However, in *R. (on the application of Molinaro) v Kensington and Chelsea RLBC* [2001] EWHC Admin 896, Elias J. said (at [40]) that:

"the doctrine of fiduciary duties can sometimes be used to enable the court to con-sider the weight afforded to the relevant factors and to ensure that the fiduciary obligation is given proper significance".

However, where the effect of a challenged policy on the local taxpayer is limited "then the doctrine is not in truth engaged in any significant way" and does not really add anything to the doctrine of irrationality (*ibid.* at [42]–[44]). In some cases the facts support findings both of *Wednesbury* unreasonableness and a breach of fiduciary duty (cf. *R. (on the application of Structadene Ltd) v Hackney LBC* (2001) 3 L.G.L.R. 19 (council's decision to sell industrial units to the tenants for £100,000 less than another offer).

It is not obvious that the interests of local taxpayers (who contribute a small proportion of the income of local authorities) deserve any special protection, in which case the fiduciary duty might sensibly be quickly forgotten. If a different view were taken on this point, could the fiduciary duty in the sense described by Elias J. survive the introduction of proportionality as a general ground of challenge in administrative law?

(iii) Mixed purposes or considerations

WESTMINSTER CORP. v LONDON AND NORTHWESTERN RAILWAY CO.

[1905] A.C. 426; 74 L.J. Ch. 629; 93 L.T. 143; 69 J.P. 425; 3 L.G.R. 1120 (HOUSE OF LORDS)

The Corporation, a sanitary authority, constructed public lavatories underground in the middle of Parliament Street. In the words of Lord Macnaghten:

> "The plan of the construction is this: On each aside of the roadway there is an entrance, five feet nine inches wide, protected by railings and leading by a staircase of the same width to a passage or subway, ten feet wide and eight feet high, which runs the whole way across on a level with the underground conveniences. Out of this subway there are openings—two for men and one for women—into spacious chambers, where the usual accommodation (politely described as lavatories and cloak-rooms) is provided on a large and liberal scale. All the arrangements seem to have been designed and carried out with due regard to decency, and with every possible consideration for the comfort of wayfarers in need of such accommodation".

The Railway Company owned a large block of buildings on the east side of Parliament Street. They objected to the sanitary works, and sought to have them removed, basing their claim alternatively on trespass, or obstruction to the highway causing special damage. The Corporation relied on their powers under the Public Health (London) Act 1891 to provide, make and maintain public lavatories and sanitary conveniences. The Company pointed out that both the Corporation and its predecessor, the Vestry of St Margaret's, Westminster, had exhibited a wish to have a subway constructed at that site. In September 1900, the Vestry's surveyor wrote to the Company referring to the construction of a "subway", and making no mention of the construction of the convenience. In December the acting town clerk of Westminster wrote that

> "the intention is the construction of a subway to facilitate pedestrians crossing . . . a thoroughfare of great width and very considerable traffic. . . . Admission to the conveniences, which will be accessible from the subways, could otherwise have been provided from refuges above them".

The railway company claimed an injunction to prevent the corporation from continuing to trespass on their premises and to obstruct the footway opposite the premises and damages. When the parties came to trial, it was found that owing to some mistake, the corporation's works had encroached upon the footway. The trial judge, Joyce J. ([1902] 1 Ch. 269), ordered the corporation to remove the encroachment. On appeal, the Court of Appeal (Vaughan Williams, Stirling and Cozens-Hardy L.JJ. [1904] 1 Ch. 759) ordered the corporation to

> "pull down and remove the whole of the staircase, railings, and other works placed by the defendants upon the lands of the plaintiffs other than the conveniences in the pleadings mentioned, and such further portion of the construction as the court [might], upon application, sanction as a proper approach to the said conveniences."

The order was suspended pending an appeal to the House of Lords. On appeal the corporation acquiesced in the order of Joyce J. but contended that the order of the Court of Appeal was wrong.

EARL OF HALSBURY L.C.: . . . [I]f the power to make one kind of building was fraudulently used for the purpose of making another kind of building, the power given by the Legislature for one purpose could not be used for another; but I have endeavoured to show that the Legislature did contemplate making subterranean works under the roadway and also access to them. Under these circumstances, I think it is a question of degree, and if there be the express provision, as I think there is, to make a tunnel under the street for the purpose of these conveniences, then I think the question of its extent or cost is a matter with which neither a Court of law or equity has any concern, since the thing contemplated by the statute has been done, and done in the way which the statute contemplated it might be done. That the public may use it for a purpose beyond what the statue contemplated is nothing to the purpose.

LORD MACNAGHTEN: . . . There can be no question as to the law applicable to the case. It is well settled that a public body invested with statutory powers such as those conferred upon the corporation must take care not to exceed or abuse its powers. It must keep within the limits of the authority committed to it. It must act in good faith. And it must act reasonably. The last proposition is involved in the second, if not in the first. But in the present case I think it will be convenient to take it separately.

Now, looking merely at what has been done—at the work as designed and actually constructed—it seems to me that, apart from the encroachment on the footway, it is impossible to contend that the work is in excess of what was authorized by the Act of 1891. The conveniences themselves, extensive as the accommodation is, have not been condemned by the Court of Appeal or even attacked in the evidence.

[His Lordship then held that the entrance from the roadway was not excessively wide.]

Then I come to the question of want of good faith. That is a very serious charge. It is not enough to shew that the corporation contemplated that the public might use the subway as a means of crossing the street. That was an obvious possibility. It cannot be otherwise if you have an entrance on each side and the communication is not interrupted by a wall or a barrier of some sort. In order to make out a case of bad faith it must be shewn that the corporation constructed this subway as a means of crossing the street under colour and pretence of providing public conveniences which were not really wanted at that particular place. That was the view of their conduct taken by the Court of Appeal. "In my judgment," says Vaughan Williams L.J., "it is not true to say that the corporation have taken this land which they have taken with the object of using it for the purposes authorized by the Legislature." "You are acting *mala fide*," he added, "if you are seeking to acquire and acquiring lands for a purpose not authorized by the Act of Parliament." So you are; there can be no doubt of that. The other learned Lord Justices seem to take the same view of the conduct of the corporation. Now this, as I have said, is a very serious charge. A gross breach of public duty, and all for a mere fad! The learned judge who tried the case had before him the chairman of the works committee. That gentleman declared that his committee considered with very great care for a couple of years or more the question of these conveniences in Parliament Street. He asserted on oath that "the primary object of the committee was to provide these conveniences". Why is this gentleman not to be believed? The learned judge who saw and heard him believed his statement.

The learned judges of the Court of Appeal have discredited his testimony, mainly, if not entirely, on the ground of two letters about which he was not asked a single question . . .. The letter of the surveyor was a foolish letter, which the writer seems to have thought clever. The letter of the temporary representative of the acting town clerk, if you compare the two letters, seems to have derived its inspiration from the same source. I cannot conceive why the solemn statement of the chairman of the committee should be discredited on such a ground. I do not think there is anything in the minutes tending to disprove his testimony. I entirely agree with Joyce J. that the primary object of the council was the construction of the conveniences with the requisite and proper means of approach thereto and exit therefrom . . ..

LORD JAMES (dissenting): . . . [T]he question to be solved seems to be thus formulated: Was the so-called tunnel an approach to the conveniences only, or was it something more? (1) Was it a subway distinct from the approach, or
(2) was it a subway in combination with the approach used for two distinct purposes?

In my judgment the construction in question comes within one or other of the two latter alternatives. Possibly within the first, certainly within the second.

If this finding on the facts is correct, the works, so far as they constitute the subway, are constructed without legal authority. The Legislature has not thought it right to confer on local bodies the power to compulsorily take land or impose rates for the purpose of constructing subways. In this case some land has been taken which would not have been required if the approach had not been enlarged into a subway, and an unauthorized burthen has been imposed upon the ratepayers in consequence of this enlargement.

Thus it is, in my opinion, that the appellants have acted beyond their powers and without justification.

LORD LINDLEY delivered a speech in favour of allowing the appeal, concurring with LORD MACNAGHTEN on the bad faith argument.

Appeal allowed. Order of Joyce J. restored.

Notes and questions

1. What is the principle of law applied in this case? Note that the speeches consider separately (1) the question whether the works were in excess of what were authorised by the statute permitting the construction of public conveniences and the means of access thereto; and (2) the motivation of the council.

On the assumptions that (1) the works are no more than what is permitted by the sanitary legislation, and (2) that they would not in fact have been constructed had it not been for the council's desire to see the two sides of the street connected by a subway, what should the answer be in the light of the principles applied in the following cases?

2. The terminology used by Lord Macnaghten in considering whether the council had used its powers for an improper purpose was to ask whether it had acted in "bad faith". This label today should be reserved for cases of the dishonest misuse of powers: see *Cannock Chase DC v Kelly* [1978] 1 W.L.R. 1 at 6 (Megaw L.J.) and 11 (Sir David Cairns).

3. The subway and conveniences at issue in this case are still in use for the purposes intended by the council.

R. v INNER LONDON EDUCATION AUTHORITY Ex p. WESTMINSTER CITY COUNCIL

[1986] 1 W.L.R. 28; [1986] 1 All E.R. 19 (GLIDEWELL J.)

The ILEA, being opposed to central government public expenditure limitation policies, commenced a programme by which they sought to raise public awareness of those policies and of their implications. Under s.142(2) of the Local Government Act 1972, the ILEA had power to incur expenditure on publishing within its area "information on matters relating to local government". In July 1984, a sub-committee of the ILEA resolved to retain an advertising agency to mount a media and poster campaign, at a cost of some £651,000. The ILEA acknowledged that the purpose of the campaign was both to "inform" the public about government proposals and their effects (a lawful purpose) and to "persuade" the public to support the ILEA's stance on this matter (an unlawful purpose). The applicant council argued that the resolution was *ultra vires* the power in s.142(2), *inter alia*, because of the unlawful purpose and because the ILEA had taken into account an irrelevant consideration—its desire to persuade the public to oppose government policy.

GLIDEWELL J. [outlined the facts, reviewed the terms of s.142(2), and continued:] . . . [T]he decision of July 23, 1984, was made with the two purposes of informing and persuading.

Two purposes

This brings me to what I regard as being the most difficult point in the case, namely: if a local authority resolves to expend its ratepayers' money in order to achieve two purposes, one of which it is authorised to achieve by statute but for the other of which it has no authority, is that decision invalid?

I was referred to the following authorities.

(i) *Westminster Corp. v London and North Western Ry Co.* [1905] A.C. 426 . . ..

[His Lordship summarised this decision and concluded:] . . . this suggests that a test for answering the question is, if the authorised purpose is the primary purpose, the resolution is within the power.

(ii) *Sydney Municipal Council v Campbell* [1925] A.C. 338. This . . . decision of the Privy Council . . . does not really deal with the question that confronts me of a resolution passed with two purposes in mind.

(iii) More recently in *Hanks v Minister of Housing and Local Government* [1963] 1 Q.B. 999, Megaw J. did have to deal with a case in which it was alleged that a compulsory purchase order had been made for two purposes, one of which did not fall within the empowering Act. At 1019, he quoted part of the dissenting judgment of Denning L.J. in *Earl Fitzwilliam's Wentworth Estates Co. Ltd v Minister of Town and Country Planning* [1951] 2 K.B. 284, 307:

"If Parliament grants to a government department a power to be used for an authorised purpose, then the power is only validly exercised when it is used by the department genuinely for that purpose as its dominant purpose. If that purpose is not the main purpose, but is subordinated to some other purpose which is not authorised by law, then the department exceeds its powers and the action is invalid."

It had been submitted to Megaw J. that, although Denning L.J. had dissented from the decision of the majority, this passage in his judgment did not differ from the view of the majority.

Megaw J. went on ([1963] 1 Q.B. 999, 1020):

"I confess that I think confusion can arise from the multiplicity of words which have been used in this case as suggested criteria for the testing of the validity of the exercise of a statutory power. The words used have included 'objects', 'purposes', 'motives', 'motivation', 'reasons', 'grounds' and 'considerations'. In the end, it seems to me, the simplest and clearest way to state the matter is by reference to 'considerations'. A 'consideration', I apprehend, is something which one takes into account as a factor in arriving at a decision. I am prepared to assume, for the purposes of this case, that, if it be shown that an authority exercising a power has taken into account as a relevant factor something which it could not properly take into account in deciding whether or not to exercise the power, then the exercise of the power, normally at least, is bad. Similarly, if the authority fails to take into account as a relevant factor something which is relevant, and which is or ought to be known to it, and which it ought to have taken into account, the exercise of the power is normally bad. I say 'normally', because I can conceive that there may be cases where the factor wrongly taken into account, or omitted, is insignificant, or where the wrong taking-into-account, or omission, actually operated in favour of the person who later claims to be aggrieved by the decision. . . ."

I have considered also the views of the learned authors of textbooks on this. Professor Wade in *Administrative Law* (5th ed., 1982), p.388 under the heading "Duality of Purpose" says:

"Sometimes an act may serve two or more purposes, some authorised and some not, and it may be a question whether the public authority may kill two birds with one stone. The general rule is that its action will be lawful provided the permitted purpose is the true and dominant purpose behind the act, even though some secondary or incidental advantage may be gained for some purpose which is outside the authority's powers."

Professor Evans, in *de Smith's Judicial Review of Administrative Action* (4th ed., 1980), pp.329–332, comforts me by describing the general problem of plurality of purpose as "a legal porcupine which bristles with difficulties as soon as it is touched". He distils from the decisions of the courts five different tests on which reliance has been placed at one time or another, including—

"(1) What was the true purpose for which the power was exercised? If the actor has in truth used his power for the purposes for which it was conferred, it is immaterial that he was thus enabled to achieve a subsidiary object . . .. (5) Was any of the purposes pursued an unauthorised purpose? If so, and if the unauthorised purpose has materially influenced the actor's conduct, the power had been invalidly exercised because irrelevant considerations have been taken into account."

These two tests, and Professor Evans' comment on them, seem to me to achieve much the same result and to be similar to that put forward by Megaw J. in *Hanks v Minister of Housing and Local Government* [1963] 1 Q.B. 999 in the first paragraph of the passage I have quoted from his judgment. That is the part that includes the sentence: "In the end, it seems to me, the simplest and clearest way to state the matter is by reference to 'considerations'." I gratefully adopt the guidance of Megaw J., and the two tests I have referred to from *de Smith*.

It thus becomes a question of fact for me to decide, on the material before me, whether, in reaching its decision of July 23, 1984, the staff and general sub-committee of I.L.E.A. was pursuing an unauthorised purpose, namely that of persuasion, which has materially influenced the making of its decision. I have already said that I find that one of the sub-committee's purposes was the giving of information. But I also find that it had the purpose of seeking to persuade members of the public to a view identical with that of the authority itself, and indeed I believe that this was a, if not the, major purpose of the decision . . . .

Adopting the test referred to above, I thus hold that I.L.E.A.'s sub-committee did, when making its decision of July 23, 1984, take into account an irrelevant consideration, and thus that decision was not validly reached.

Declaration granted.

Notes

1. The approach of Megaw J. in *Hanks* was also followed by Forbes J. in *R. v Rochdale MBC Ex p. Cromer Ring Mill Ltd* [1982] 3 All E.R. 761, who interpreted it as establishing that

> "the exercise of a power is bad if it is shown that an authority exercising that power has taken an irrelevant factor into account, as long as that irrelevant factor is not insignificant or insubstantial" (p.770).

Here, the council "may well have been substantially influenced" by advice from an officer that an unfettered discretion to refund overpaid rates should only be used to alleviate gross unfairness and not where there were simply differences of opinion over value. A further gloss was placed on this by May L.J. in *R. v Broadcasting Complaints Commission Ex p. Owen* [1985] Q.B. 1153, where the Divisional Court rejected a challenge by Dr David Owen, Leader of the Social Democratic Party, to the decision of the BCC in the exercise of its discretion not to entertain a complaint that the SDP/Liberal Alliance was the subject of "unjust or unfair treatment" in radio and television programmes. The essence of the complaint was that the broadcasting organisations were giving considerably more attention to the views of the Labour Party which while obtaining many more seats in the 1983 general election had only 2 per cent more of the votes than the SDP and Liberals.

The BCC gave a number of reasons held by the court to be good (*e.g.* the BCC would have to express a view about a fundamental issue of British politics, the desirability of proportional representation, on which strongly different views from those of the Alliance were held by both the Conservative and Labour parties). One reason was bad (that the BCC's task of investigating the complaint would be burdensome and require perhaps the employment of additional staff). May L.J. said (at 1177) that the material law was as stated by Forbes J. in *Cromer Ring Mill*,

> "but with one qualification .. . . [W]here the reasons given by a statutory body for taking or not taking a particular course of action are not mixed and can clearly be disentangled, but where the court is quite satisfied that even though one reason may be bad in law, nevertheless the statutory body would have reached precisely the same decision on the other valid reasons, then this court will not interfere by way of judicial review. In such a case, looked at realistically and with justice, such a decision of such a body ought not to be disturbed".

Here, he was "quite satisfied" that the BCC would have reached the same conclusion if they had never thought about the bad reason. An alternative approach would be that the court in the exercise of its discretion would decline to grant a remedy in these circumstances.

May L.J.'s approach was adopted by the Divisional Court in *R. v Lewisham LBC, Ex p. Shell U.K. Ltd* [1988] 1 All E.R. 938, where the council passed a resolution to boycott Shell products. The Divisional Court found that it had two purposes: (1) a lawful purpose to promote good race relations in the borough in accordance with its duty under s.71 of the Race Relations Act 1976; and (2) an unlawful purpose to put pressure on Shell to withdraw from South Africa. The court held that where two reasons or purposes could not be disentangled, and one was bad, or, where they could be disentangled the bad reason demonstrably exerted the substantial influence, the court could interfere to quash the decision. Here, the two purposes were inextricably mixed up and the unlawful purpose had the effect of vitiating the decision as a whole. See T.R.S. Allan, [1988] C.L.J. 334.

2. On this approach it is necessary to determine whether the irrelevant consideration has "materially" (or "significantly" or "substantially") influenced the outcome. Clearly this will be the case if the decision would not have been made but for that consideration (*Thompson v Randwick Corp.* (1950) 81 C.L.R. 87, 106, cited by *Wade and Forsyth*, pp.415–416; *Owen*, above). Whether something less that this may still constitute "material" influence remains open. In any event, in so far as there is a burden of proof on this issue it should rest with the authority to adduce clear evidence from the contemporary record that the same result would have been reached. (It should be noted that the courts are rightly distrustful of what may be *ex post facto* rationalisation of doubtful decision-making exercises: see below, p.850).

3. In some contexts, the courts have shown a disinclination to apply the considerations test. For example, it has been suggested that where the amount of expenditure by a local authority on a particular item is not unreasonable, the fact that irrelevant considerations may have been taken into account may not render the expenditure unlawful (*per* Lord Sumner in *Roberts v Hopwood*, above, p.556; *Walker's Decision, Re* [1944] 1 K.B. 644). In *Pickwell v Camden LBC* [1983] 1 Q.B. 962, Ormrod L.J. held that a failure to take into account relevant matters, or the taking into account of irrelevant matters were in effect only evidence that the authority might have acted *ultra vires* (*cf.* the approach of Forbes J. who simply held that a breach of the *Wednesbury* principles was not established on the evidence).

A suggestion of the Court of Appeal that the full *Wednesbury* principles might not apply in relation to purely administrative decisions not affecting rights (*R. v Barnet and Camden Rent Tribunal Ex p. Frey Investments Ltd* [1972] 2 Q.B. 342) has not found favour (see *Wade and Forsyth*). In *R. v Commission for Racial Equality Ex p. Hillingdon LBC*, Griffiths L.J. in the Court of Appeal ([1982] Q.B. 276 at 298–300) and Lord Diplock in the House of Lords ([1982] A.C. 779 at pp.397–792) expressly affirmed that the *Wednesbury* principles apply to administrative functions.

It may be that suggestions that the considerations test does not apply in a particular context are simply a reflection of the point that there is no breach of the test where an authority considers but is not influenced by a particular legally irrelevant matter, or the same decision would have been reached by reference to other considerations (*Ex p. Owen*, above).

(C) Unreasonableness

The grounds of challenge considered in sections A and B, above, require evidence and proof of the purpose(s) of the body challenged, or the considerations which were or were not taken into account. In other words attention focuses in such cases on the "thought-processes" of the challenged body in exercising its discretionary power. Evidence of this may appear from any reasons, or explanation, it may give (or may be required to give) for its decision; or from sworn statements (or, in exceptional cases, cross-examination) in the course of the legal challenge itself.

Challenge on the ground of "unreasonableness" proceeds on a rather different footing. It invites the court to hold that notwithstanding that there may be no firm evidence of improper purpose or concerning relevant/irrelevant considerations, nevertheless the court should intervene on the basis that the decision as to the exercise of power is in substance one which no reasonable body could have come to. This test was articulated by Lord Greene M.R. in the *Wednesbury* case (below) in what has probably been the most cited judgment in public law.

The courts have consistently stated that in considering challenges on this ground they must preserve the distinction between review on the "merits" (is this the decision I would have come to?) and review of "legality" (is this a decision which a reasonable person could have come to?). The former is only appropriate where statute provides for an appeal on the merits; it is beyond the proper remit of the judges in proceedings for judicial review. "Unreasonableness" can be justified as a ground of review of legality on the basis that although Parliament may have intended to authorise a variety of ways in which a power might be exercised, and have intended to leave such choice to the body in question rather than to the judges, it can be assumed that Parliament had not intended its grant of that power to cover an exercise of it that is "unreasonable" in this narrow sense. Lord Greene M.R. in *Wednesbury* regarded such decisions as in excess of the powers granted by Parliament. It is of course also argued that the principle is really a free-standing principle of the common law that such an abuse of power is unlawful; see above, p.263. Furthermore, Lord Diplock in *CCSU* case (below, p.690) regarded legality and irrationality as discrete grounds of challenge.

(i) *Wednesbury* Unreasonableness

ASSOCIATED PROVINCIAL PICTURE HOUSES LTD v WEDNESBURY CORP.

[1948] 1 K.B. 223; 177 L.T. 641; 63 T.L.R. 623; 112 J.P. 55; 92 S.J. 26; [1947] 2 All E.R. 680; 45 L.G.R. 635; [1948] L.J.R. 190 (COURT OF APPEAL)

The plaintiff company, the owners and licensees of the Gaumont Cinema, Wednesbury, Staffordshire, were granted by the defendants who were the licensing authority for that borough under the Cinematograph Act 1909, a licence to give performances on Sundays under s.1(1) of the Sunday Entertainments Act 1932; but the licence was granted subject to a condition that "no children under the age of 15 years shall be admitted to any entertainment whether accompanied by an adult or not". In these circumstances the plaintiffs brought an action for a declaration that the condition was *ultra vires* and unreasonable.

Henn Collins J. ([1947] L.J.R. 678) dismissed the action, and the plaintiffs appealed to the Court of Appeal. Section 1(1) of the 1932 Act provided that the authority might attach to a licence "such conditions as the authority think fit to impose . . .".

LORD GREENE M.R.: . . . Mr Gallop, for the plaintiffs, argued that it was not competent for the Wednesbury Corporation to impose any such condition and he said that if they were entitled to impose a condition prohibiting the admission of children, they should at least have limited it to cases where the children were not accompanied by their parents or a guardian or some adult. His argument was that the imposition of that condition was unreasonable and that in consequence it was *ultra vires* the corporation. The plaintiffs' contention is based, in my opinion, on a misconception as to the effect of this Act in granting this discretionary power to local authorities. The courts must always,

I think, remember this: first, we are dealing with not a judicial act, but an executive act; secondly, the conditions which, under the exercise of that executive act, may be imposed are in terms, so far as language goes, put within the discretion of the local authority without limitation. Thirdly, the statute provides no appeal from the decision of the local authority.

What, then, is the power of the courts? They can only interfere with an act of executive authority if it be shown that the authority has contravened the law. It is for those who assert that the local authority has contravened the law to establish that proposition. On the face of it, a condition of the kind imposed in this case is perfectly lawful. It is not to be assumed prima facie that responsible bodies, like the local authority in this case will exceed their powers; but the court, whenever it is alleged that the local authority have contravened the law, must not substitute itself for that authority. It is only concerned with seeing whether or not the proposition is made good. When an executive discretion is entrusted by Parliament to a body such as the local authority in this case, what appears to be an exercise of that discretion can only be challenged in the courts in a strictly limited class of case. As I have said, it must always be remembered that the court is not a court of appeal. When discretion of this kind is granted the law recognizes certain principles upon which that discretion must be exercised, but within the four corners of those principles the discretion, in my opinion, is an absolute one and cannot be questioned in any court of law. What then are those principles? They are well understood. They are principles which the court looks to in considering any question of discretion of this kind. The exercise of such a discretion must be a real exercise of discretion. If, in the statute conferring the discretion, there is to be found expressly or by implication matters which the authority exercising the discretion ought to have regard to, then in exercising the discretion it must have regard to those matters. Conversely, if the nature of the subject-matter and the general interpretation of the Act make it clear that certain matters would not be germane to the matter in question, the authority must disregard those irrelevant collateral matters. There have been in the cases expressions used relating to the sort of thing that authorities must not do, not merely in cases under the Cinematograph Act but, generally speaking, under the other cases where the powers of local authorities came to be considered. I am not sure myself whether the permissible grounds of attack cannot be defined under a single head. It has been perhaps a little bit confusing to find a series of grounds set out. Bad faith, dishonesty—those of course, stand by themselves—unreasonableness, attention given to extraneous circumstances, disregard of public policy and things like that have all been referred to, according to the facts of individual cases, as being matters which are relevant to the question. If they cannot all be confined under one head, they at any rate, I think, overlap to a very great extent. For instance, we have heard in this case a great deal about the meaning of the word "unreasonable".

It is true the discretion must be exercised reasonably. Now what does that mean? Lawyers familiar with the phraseology commonly used in relation to exercise of statutory discretions often use the word "unreasonable" in a rather comprehensive sense. It has frequently been used and is frequently used as a general description of the things that must not be done. For instance, a person entrusted with a discretion must, so to speak, direct himself properly in law. He must call his own attention to the matters which he is bound to consider. He must exclude from his consideration matters which are irrelevant to what he has to consider. If he does not obey those rules, he may truly be said, and often is said, to be acting "unreasonably". Similarly, there may be something so absurd that no sensible person could ever dream that it lay within the powers of the authority. Warrington L.J. in *Short v Poole Corporation* [1926] Ch.66, 90, 91, gave the example of the red-haired teacher, dismissed because she had red hair. That is unreasonable in one sense. In another sense it is taking into consideration extraneous matters. It is so unreasonable that it might almost be described as being done in bad faith; and, in fact, all these things run into one another.

In the present case, it is said by Mr Gallop that the authority acted unreasonably in imposing this condition. It appears to me quite clear that the matter dealt with by this condition was a matter which a reasonable authority would be justified in considering when they were making up their mind what condition should be attached to the grant of this licence. Nobody, at this time of day, could say that the well-being and the physical and moral health of children is not a matter which a local authority, in exercising their powers, can properly have in mind when those questions are germane to what they have to consider. Here Mr Gallop did not, I think, suggest that the council were directing their mind to a purely extraneous and irrelevant matter, but he based his argument on the word "unreasonable", which he treated as an independent ground for attacking the decision of the authority; but once it is conceded, as it must be conceded in this case, that the particular subject-matter dealt with by this condition was one which it was competent for the authority to consider, there, in my opinion, is an end of the case. Once that is granted, Mr Gallop is bound to say that the decision of the authority is wrong because it is unreasonable, and in saying that he is really saying that the ultimate arbiter of what is and is not reasonable is the court and not the local authority. It is just there, it seems to me, that the argument breaks down. It is clear that the local authority are entrusted by Parliament with the decision on a matter which the knowledge and experience of that authority can best be trusted to deal with. The subject-matter with which the condition deals is one relevant for its consideration. They have considered it and come to a decision upon it. It is true to say that, if a decision on a competent matter is so unreasonable that no reasonable authority could ever have come to it, then the courts can interfere. That I think, is quite right; but to prove a case of that kind would require something overwhelming, and, in this case, the facts do not come anywhere near anything of that kind. I think Mr Gallop in the end agreed that his proposition that the decision of the local authority can be upset if it is proved to be unreasonable, really meant that it must be proved to be unreasonable in the sense that the court considers it to be a decision that no reasonable body could have come to. It is not what the court considers unreasonable, a different thing altogether. If it is what the court considers unreasonable, the court may very well have different views to that of a local authority on matters of high public policy of this kind. Some courts might think that no children ought to be admitted on Sundays at all, some courts might think the reverse, and all over the country I have no doubt on a thing of that sort honest and sincere people hold different views. The effect of the legislation is not to set up the court as an arbiter of the correctness of one view over another. It is the local authority that are set in that position and, provided they act, as they have acted, within the four corners of their jurisdiction, this court, in my opinion, cannot interfere.

This case, in my opinion, does not really require reference to authority when once the simple and well known principles are understood on which alone a court can interfere with something prima facie within the powers of the executive authority, but reference has been made to a number of cases. . . . [His Lordship referred to *Harman v Butt* [1944] K.B. 491; *R. v. Burnley JJ.*, 85 L.J. (K.B.) 1565; and *Ellis v Dubowski* [1921] 3 K.B. 621, the latter two being cases of unlawful delegation of powers.] Another case on which Mr Gallop relied is *Roberts v Hopwood* [1925] A.C. 578, [above, p.552]. That was a totally different class of case. The district auditor had surcharged the members of a council who had made payments of a minimum wage of 4*l.* a week to their lowest grade of workers. That particular sum had been fixed by the local authority not by reference to any of the factors which go to determine a scale of wages, but by reference to some other principle altogether, and the substance of the decision was that they had not fixed 4*l.* a week as wages at all and that they had acted unreasonably. When the case is examined, the word "unreasonable" is found to be used rather in the sense that I mentioned a short while ago, namely, that in fixing 4*l.* they had fixed it by reference to a matter which they ought not to have taken into account and to the exclusion of those elements which they ought to have taken into consideration in fixing a sum which could fairly be called a wage. That is no authority whatsoever to support the proposition that the court has power, a sort of overriding power, to decide what is reasonable and what is unreasonable. The court has nothing of the kind. . . .

In the result, this appeal must be dismissed. I do not wish to repeat myself but I will summarize once again the principle applicable. The court is entitled to investigate the action of the local authority with a view to seeing whether they have taken into account matters which they ought not to take into account, or, conversely, have refused to take into account or neglected to take into account matters which they ought to take into account. Once that question is answered in favour of the local authority, it may still be possible to say that, although the local authority have kept within the four corners of the matters which they ought to consider, they have nevertheless come to a conclusion so unreasonable that no reasonable authority could ever have come to it. In such a case, again, I think the court can interfere. The power of the court to interfere in each case is not as an appellate authority to override a decision of the local authority, but as a judicial authority which is concerned, and concerned only, to see whether the local authority have contravened the law by acting in excess of the powers which Parliament has confided in them. The appeal must be dismissed with costs.

SOMERVELL L.J. and SINGLETON L.J. agreed.

Appeal dismissed.

Notes

1. In addition to the regularly quoted words of Lord Greene M.R. a number of other formulations of this test of "unreasonableness" have been suggested. In each case, the courts have been concerned to stress the distinction between review on this ground and reconsideration on the merits.

Thus, in *R. v Greenwich LBC Ex p. Cedar Holdings* [1983] R.A. 173, Griffiths L.J. warned that a court might "all to easily [be] lure[d] . . . into substituting its own view of the way in which the . . . council should have exercised its discretion for that of the council itself". This temptation was, at all costs, to be avoided: "Only in a case where the decision of the council had been so outrageous that no right thinking person could support it would it be right to interfere. . . .". In *Council of Civil Service Unions v Minister for the Civil Service* [1985] A.C. 374, 410, Lord Diplock, having described the basis of this challenge as challenge for "irrationality", commented: "It applies to a decision which is so outrageous in its defiance of logic or of accepted moral standards that no sensible person who had applied his mind to the question to be decided could have arrived at it". See further on this case, above, p.242 and below, pp.690–697. In *Nottinghamshire CC v Secretary of State for the Environment* [1986] A.C. 240 at 247, Lord Scarman explained that for this ground of challenge to succeed a decision must be so absurd that the decision-maker "must have taken leave of his senses".

Concern that the principle might, if stated in overly extreme terms, prove "awkward" for courts to apply even in appropriate cases led Lord Donaldson to express a preference for the expression *Wednesbury unreasonable* rather than the term *irrational*. In a situation where a usually reliable body has in a particular instance taken an unjustifiable decision, His Lordship felt that courts would feel more willing to intervene, and would cast less in the way of unnecessary aspersion, applying the former label than the latter: see *R. v Devon CC Ex p. G* [1989] A.C. 573 at 577.

Lord Greene's formulation of the test for unreasonableness has been criticised as follows by Lord Cooke of Thorndon in *R. v Chief Constable of Sussex Ex p. International Trader's Federation* [1999] 2 A.C. 418 at 452 (see above, p.552):

". . . I agree with the proposition of Lord Lester of Herne Hill that on the particular facts of this case the European concepts of proportionality and margin of appreciation produce the same result as what are commonly called *Wednesbury* principles. Indeed in many cases that is likely to be so. It seems to me unfortunate that *Wednesbury* and some *Wednesbury* phrases have become established incantations in the courts of the United Kingdom and beyond. *Associated Provincial Picture Houses Ltd. v Wednesbury Corporation* [1948] 1 K.B. 223, an apparently briefly-considered case, might well not be decided the same way today, and the judgment of Lord Greene M.R. twice uses (at pp.230 and 234) the tautologous formula 'so unreasonable that no reasonable authority could ever have come to it.' Yet judges are entirely accustomed to respecting the proper scope of administrative discretions. In my respectful opinion they do not need to be warned off the course by admonitory circumlocutions. When, in *Secretary of State for Education and Science v Tameside Metropolitan Borough Council* [1977] A.C. 1014, the precise meaning of 'unreasonably' in an administrative context was crucial to the decision, the five speeches in the House of Lords, the three judgments in the Court of Appeal and the two judgments in the Divisional Court all succeeded in avoiding needless complexity. The simple test used throughout was whether the decision in question was one which a reasonable authority could reach. The converse was described by Lord Diplock, at p.1064, as 'conduct which no sensible authority acting with due appreciation of its responsibilities would have decided to adopt.' These unexaggerated criteria give the administrator ample and rightful rein, consistently with the constitutional separation of powers".

This ground of challenge has been argued, and referred to by the courts, on many occasions. Usually the courts hold that on the facts the test has not been satisfied.

2. Notwithstanding the frequency with which the courts have noted this ground of challenge only to hold that, on the facts, the challenge did not succeed, there have been a number cases where this principle *has* formed the basis (sometimes together with other grounds) of successful challenge. Thus, in *Backhouse v Lambeth LBC, The Times*, October 14, 1972, the Labour-controlled council resolved to increase the rent of a three-bedroomed council house (unoccupied since May 1972 because of deficiencies in the damp course) from some £7 to the massive £18,000 per week.

Section 62(1) of the Housing Finance Act 1972 provided that: "Every local authority shall . . . make the increases [*i.e.* towards fair rents] required by sections 63 and 64 . . . ". Section 63(1) provided that such increases should not be made "If the authority made a general rent increase in the first half of 1972–73 which produces £26 or more per dwelling in 1972–73 . . .". The council hoped to avoid a general rent increase of 55p per week by putting all the increase contemplated by s.63(1) on one house. Any tenant would get an "enormous" rebate. B, the leader of the council tenants, sought a declaration that the resolution was valid. Melford Stevenson J., however, held that it was *ultra vires*. His Lordship held that this was a resolution at which no reasonable local authority could have arrived. It was admittedly designed and only designed to avoid or evade obligations cast on the council by the 1972 Act. Counsel for the Secretary of State for the Environment, who defended the case instead of the council, also submitted that the council had obviously ignored all relevant considerations.

In *West Glamorgan City Council v Rafferty* [1987] 1 W.L.R. 457, the Court of Appeal held that the council had acted unreasonably in the *Wednesbury* sense in seeking an order for possession against gypsies occupying a council-owned site and causing a nuisance. The council had for over 10 years been in breach of its duty under s.6 of the Caravan Sites Act 1968 to provide adequate accommodation for gypsies in its area, and had not on this occasion made any arrangements for alternative accommodation. Ralph Gibson L.J. said (at 477):

"The court is not, as I understand the law, precluded from finding a decision to be void for unreasonableness merely because there are admissible factors on both sides of the question. If the weight of the factors against eviction must be recognised by a reasonable council, properly aware of its duties and its powers, to be overwhelming, then a decision the other way cannot be upheld if challenged. The decision upon eviction was a decision which required the weighing of the factors according to the personal judgment of the councillors but the law does not permit complete freedom of choice or assessment because legal duty must be given proper weight".

Given that there were "admissible factors on both sides of the question" in *Rafferty*, can it be said that the council "must have taken leave of its senses" in coming to its decision? If not, the case suggests that the test for unreasonableness is not in practice as extreme as the dicta cited in note 1 suggests. For comments on *Rafferty*, see R. Ward, [1987] C.L.J. 374.

For further examples of successful challenge on the ground of *Wednesbury* unreasonableness, see, *e.g. Niarchos (London) Ltd v Secretary of State for the Environment and Westminster City Council (No.2)* (1981) 79 L.G.R. 264, *R.v. Norfolk CC Ex p. M* [1989] 2 All E.R. 359 (decision of child abuse case conference to register M as a known/suspected abuser after a brief, one-sided investigation held to be *Wednesbury* unreasonable); *R. v Barnet LBC Ex p. Johnson* (1990) 89 L.G.R. 581 (conditions on use of pleasure ground by Community Festival banning political activity and the participation of any political party or group held to have such a variety of possible meanings as to be in effect meaningless and to be *Wednesbury* unreasonable); *R. v Lewisham LBC Ex p. P* [1991] 3 All E.R. 529 (disclosure of name of foster parent alleged to have abused child to other persons who had care of the child held to be *Wednesbury* unreasonable where the council had failed to carry out an exercise balancing the need to protect the child by such disclosure against the grave consequences of naming to the individual and his family); *R. v Newham LBC Ex p. Gentle* (1993) 26 H.L.R. 466 (policy requiring person to move into offered accommodation before being able to appeal on the ground that it was unsuitable both inflexible and "tainted with irrationality"); *R. v Secretary of State for the Home Department Ex p. Zakrocki* (1998) 1 C.C.L.R. 374 (decision to refuse leave to remain to a married couple who were providing constant care for the wife's brother, a British citizen, held to be *Wednesbury* unreasonable; there was no evidence for the Secretary of State's assertion that adequate alternative arrangements would be made); *R. v Secretary of State for the*

Home Department Ex p. Bostanci [1999] Imm. A.R. 411 (decision to bar B, an interpreter, from immigration interviews on the ground of her father's political affiliation
held to be *Wednesbury* unreasonable in the absence of evidence of any political authority by her); *R. (on the application of R and L) v Manchester CC* [2001] EWHC Admin
707 (policy to pay short-term foster carers who were friends or relatives of child at a
very significantly lower rate held to be irrational); *R. (on the application of Essex CC,
Medway Council and Mead) v Secretary of State for Transport, Local Government and
the Regions* [2002] EWHC Admin 2516 (decision to exclude possible expansion at
Gatwick from review of development of air transport in the South-East which would
consider possible expansion at Heathrow and Stansted and a possible new airport at
Cliffe in Kent held to be irrational); *R. (on the application of Ann Summers Ltd) v
Jobcentre Plus* [2003] EWHC (Admin) 1416 (policy to prevent company that sold lin-
gerie and sex toys from advertising job vacancies at jobcentres held to be irrational)
R. v Norfolk CC Ex p. M [1989] 2 All E.R. 359. The ground was also a part of the
reasoning in the speeches of Lord Brandon in the *Bromley* case (above, p.561) and of
Lord Roskill in the *Wheeler* case (above, p.543).

3. Note that the *Wednesbury* formula is also used by the courts for certain other
purposes in the context of judicial review and appeals. See, *e.g.* the "no evidence" rule
(below, p.826), and the scope of review of decisions of fact on an appeal on a point of
law (below, p.817).

4. "Unreasonableness" constitutes a ground upon which the validity of byelaws may
be challenged—see *Kruse v Johnson* [1898] 2 Q.B. 91 (above, p.234).

5. It has been held that "irrationality" is not fully available as a ground of challenge
where the decision has been approved by one or both Houses of Parliament. This point
has arisen in cases where the Secretary of State for the Environment has sought to
"cap" the expenditure of designated local authorities. The most recent decision is *R. v
Secretary of State for the Environment Ex p. Hammersmith and Fulham LBC* [1991]
1 A.C. 521, where the House of Lords rejected challenges by 19 of 21 designated
authorities to the Secretary of State's decisions under the Local Government Finance
Act 1988, s.100, to impose maximum budgets. (This would in turn require each
authority to set a lower level of community charge.) Lord Bridge, having rejected arguments based on illegality, continued (at 594–597):

"The remaining grounds of challenge fall under the heads of irrationality or procedural impropriety. Before turning to these grounds it is appropriate to consider
whether any limitations upon the scope of judicial review are imposed by the
subject-matter of the legislation. In this we are not without authoritative guidance.
    In *R. v. Secretary of State for the Environment, Ex p. Nottinghamshire County
Council* [1986] A.C. 240, the House had to consider an earlier challenge to the
action of the Secretary of State under the Local Government, Planning and Land Act
1980 which had this in common with the action here in question that the 'expenditure guidance' which the Secretary of State had there issued to local authorities and
which the authorities sought to challenge had a directly restraining effect on the
authorities' conduct of their financial affairs but before it could take effect required
the approval by resolution of the House of Commons. The appellant authorities in
that case had challenged the Secretary of State's statutory expenditure guidance on
the ground, *inter alia*, that it was unreasonable as contravening the principles
expounded in the judgment of Lord Greene M.R. in *Associated Provincial Picture
Houses Ltd v. Wednesbury Corporation* [1948] 1 K.B. 223, 229, which is the classic
statement of the basis for a challenge to an administrative decision on the ground
of irrationality. Adverting to this challenge in the *Nottinghamshire* case [1986] A.C.
240, 247, Lord Scarman said:

    'The submission raises an important question as to the limits of judicial review.
    We are in the field of public financial administration and we are being asked to
    review the exercise by the Secretary of State of an administrative discretion which

inevitably requires a political judgment on his part and which cannot lead to action by him against a local authority unless that action is first approved by the House of Commons. . . . I cannot accept that it is constitutionally appropriate, save in very exceptional circumstances, for the courts to intervene on the ground of "unreasonableness" to quash guidance framed by the Secretary of State and by necessary implication approved by the House of Commons, the guidance being concerned with the limits of public expenditure by local authorities and the incidence of the tax burden as between taxpayers and ratepayers. Unless and until a statute provides otherwise, or it is established that the Secretary of State has abused his power, these are matters of political judgment for him and for the House of Commons. They are not for the judges or your Lordships' House in its judicial capacity. For myself, I refuse in this case to examine the detail of the guidance or its consequences. My reasons are these. Such an examination by a court would be justified only if a prima facie case were to be shown for holding that the Secretary of State had acted in bad faith, or for an improper motive, or that the consequences of his guidance were so absurd that he must have taken leave of his senses.'

Later he added, at 250–251:

'To sum it up, the levels of public expenditure and the incidence and distribution of taxation are matters for Parliament, and, within Parliament, especially for the House of Commons. If Parliament legislates, the courts have their interpretative role: they must, if called upon to do so, construe the statute. If a minister exercises a power conferred on him by the legislation, the courts can investigate whether he has abused his power. But if, as in this case, effect cannot be given to the Secretary of State's determination without the consent of the House of Commons and the House of Commons has consented, it is not open to the courts to intervene unless the minister and the House must have misconstrued the statute or the minister has—to put it bluntly—deceived the House. The courts can properly rule that a minister has acted unlawfully if he has erred in law as to the limits of his power even when his action has the approval of the House of Commons, itself acting not legislatively but within the limits set by a statute. But, if a statute, as in this case, requires the House of Commons to approve a minister's decision before he can lawfully enforce it, and if the action proposed complies with the terms of the statute (as your Lordships, I understand, are convinced that it does in the present case), it is not for the judges to say that the action has such unreasonable consequences that the guidance upon which the action is based and of which the House of Commons had notice was perverse and must be set aside. For that is a question of policy for the minister and the Commons, unless there has been bad faith or misconduct by the minister. Where Parliament has legislated that the action to be taken by the Secretary of State must, before it is taken, be approved by the House of Commons, it is no part of the judges' role to declare that the action proposed is unfair, unless it constitutes an abuse of power in the sense which I have explained; for Parliament has enacted that one of its Houses is responsible. Judicial review is a great weapon in the hands of the judges: but the judges must observe the constitutional limits set by our parliamentary system upon the exercise of this beneficent power.'

Lord Scarman's speech commanded the agreement of all members of the Appellate Committee participating in the decision, of whom I was one. I regard the opinions expressed in the passages quoted as an accurate formulation of an important restriction on the scope of judicial review which is precisely in point in the instant case. There is here no suggestion that the Secretary of State acted in bad faith or for an improper motive or that his decisions to designate the appellant authorities or the maximum amounts to which he decided to limit their budgets were so absurd that he must have taken leave of his senses. Short of such an extreme challenge, and provided always that the Secretary of State has acted within the four corners of the Act, I do not believe there is any room for an attack on the rationality of the Secretary of State's exercise of his powers under Part VII of the Act.

This accords with the view expressed by the Divisional Court, though they went on to examine on their merits and to reject the grounds relied on by the applicant authorities including those challenging the rationality of the Secretary of State's decisions and orders. The Court of Appeal expressed a somewhat different view. Referring to irrationality as a ground for judicial review of the exercise of a statutory discretion they said, *ante*, 935D–E:

'This head is relevant if it is alleged that the decision taker has had regard to matters which are legally irrelevant or has failed to have regard to matters which are legally relevant or that his decision would frustrate the policy of the Act upon which he relies for his authority: see *Padfield v. Minister of Agriculture, Fisheries and Food* [1968] A.C. 997. There is nothing in the judgments in the *Nottinghamshire* case [1986] A.C. 240 to suggest that this aspect of the jurisdictional head of "irrationality" has no application to decisions concerning public financial administration, whether or not they are also subject to review by one or both Houses of Parliament and no principle dictates that this should be the case.'

I think there is a danger of confusion in terminology here. If the court concludes, as the House did in the *Padfield* case [1986] A.C. 997, that a minister's exercise of a statutory discretion has been such as to frustrate the policy of the statute, that conclusion rests upon the view taken by the court of the true construction of the statute which the exercise of the discretion in question is then held to have contravened. The administrative action or inaction is then condemned on the ground of illegality. Similarly, if there are matters which, on the true construction of the statute conferring discretion, the person exercising the discretion must take into account and others which he may not take into account, disregard of those legally relevant matters or regard of those legally irrelevant matters will lay the decision open to review on the ground of illegality.

The restriction which the *Nottinghamshire* case [1986] A.C. 240 imposes on the scope of judicial review operates only when the court has first determined that the ministerial action in question does not contravene the requirements of the statute, whether express or implied, and only then declares that, since the statute has conferred a power on the Secretary of State which involves the formulation and the implementation of national economic policy and which can only take effect with the approval of the House of Commons, it is not open to challenge on the grounds of irrationality short of the extremes of bad faith, improper motive or manifest absurdity. Both the constitutional propriety and the good sense of this restriction seem to me to be clear enough. The formulation and the implementation of national economic policy are matters depending essentially on political judgment. The decisions which shape them are for politicians to take and it is in the political forum of the House of Commons that they are properly to be debated and approved or disapproved on their merits. If the decisions have been taken in good faith within the four corners of the Act, the merits of the policy underlying the decisions are not susceptible to review by the courts and the courts would be exceeding their proper function if they presumed to condemn the policy as unreasonable".

[His Lordship concluded that an argument that the determination was *Wednesbury* unreasonable, which he rejected on its merits (in agreement with the Court of Appeal) was in any event "inadmissible".]

This restriction has been the subject of academic criticism: see C.M.G. Himsworth, 1985 S.L.T. 369 and [1986] P.L. 139; and A.I.L. Campbell, 1986 S.L.T. 101 (on the similar approach of the Court of Session in the context of statutory instruments in *City of Edinburgh DC v Secretary of State for Scotland* 1985 S.L.T. 551; Himsworth, [1986] P.L. 347; R. Ward, (1986) 49 M.L.R. 645 (on the *Nottinghamshire* decision) and [1991] P.L. 76 (on the *Hammersmith* decision). On the other hand, the point can be made that it is difficult to see what grounds of challenge are actually excluded by the terms of Lord Bridge's speech, given that a challenge to the *merits* of a "capping" decision would not in any event fall within the *ultra vires* doctrine. A possible explanation is that while in an ordinary case *Wednesbury* unreasonableness is not confined to the extent suggested by the dicta summarised in note 1 above, but that where an act has been approved by Parliament, it is so confined. However, the better view, following the decision in *Ex p. Smith* is that there is simply a sliding scale under which deference to the decision-maker is, according to the context, more or less appropriate, the situation in *Nottinghamshire* being at or towards the former end of the scale. This approach was followed by the Court of Appeal in *R. (on the application of Javed) v Secretary of State for the Home Department* [2001] EWCA Civ 789; [2002] Q.B. 129, in holding that the *Nottinghamshire* principle "cannot be treated as a proposition of law applicable to any order subject to affirmative resolution" (*per* Lord Phillips M.R. at [49]). The subject-matter of the *Hammersmith* and *Nottinghamshire* cases "was at an extreme end of the spectrum". The validity of the order here, certifying that Pakistan was a country where there was in general no severe risk of persecution and so appropriate for the application of an expedited procedure for asylum cases, was to be tested on ordinary *Wednesbury* grounds, albeit without the heightened scrutiny appropriate in cases affecting fundamental rights. The certification of Pakistan was held to be irrational in the light of evidence concerning the position of women and the authorities' attitude towards Ahmadis.

A different perspective is provided by Lord Irvine of Lairg Q.C. ("Judges and Decision-makers: The Theory and Practice of *Wednesbury* Review" [1996] P.L. 59 at p.66):

"The danger with Lord Bridge's judgment is that it suggests that there is a level of 'irrationality' short of manifest absurdity which may found judicial review in the ordinary case. This encourages applications on a false basis".

Lord Diplock's formulation of *Wednesbury* unreasonableness in the *CCSU* case (below, p.695): "leaves no scope for 'super-*Wednesbury* irrationality'" (at 66–67) (the term coined by Simon Brown L.J. in *R. v Ministry of Defence Ex p. Smith* [1995] 4 All E.R. 427 at 441, 445). This position is, however, against the weight of the case law.

The *Nottinghamshire* principle was held not to be applicable to the scope of review of social security regulations which were held to be *ultra vires* because they rendered nugatory rights of asylum-seekers provided under separate, asylum, legislation: *R. v Secretary of State for Social Security Ex p. Joint Council for the Welfare of Immigrants* [1997] 1 W.L.R. 2. It was also held not to be applicable in *Ex p. Smith*, below, p.581.

6. J. Jowell and A. Lester ("Beyond *Wednesbury*: Substantive Principles of Administrative Law" [1987] P.L. 368) argue persuasively that as a concept "*Wednesbury* unreasonableness" is unsatisfactory (at 372–374). It is "inadequate", providing insufficient justification for judicial intervention:

"Intellectual honesty requires a further and better explanation as to *why* the act is unreasonable. The reluctance to articulate a principled justification naturally encourages suspicion that prejudice or policy considerations may be hiding underneath *Wednesbury*'s ample cloak".

It is "unrealistic", the courts in practice being "willing to impugn decisions that are far from absurd and are indeed often coldly rational". It is "confusing, because it is tautologous". Instead, the courts should develop substantive principles of review, that prohibit decisions that are " 'irrational' in the accepted sense of that term" or arbitrary; that violate accepted standards of administrative probity (*e.g.* fraudulent decisions or decisions in bad faith) or good administrative practice (*e.g.* decisions that are unjustifiably inconsistent or disproportionate); or that violate fundamental rights and freedoms.

Further examples of "principled justifications" for a finding of *Wednesbury* unreasonableness include:

(1) uncertainty: see *R. v Barnet LBC Ex p. Johnson* (above);
(2) oppression: see *Wheeler* (above, p.543); *de Smith, Woolf and Jowell*, paras 13–046 to 13–054; *R. (on the application of Khatun) v Newham LBC* [2004] EWCA Civ 55; [2005] 1 Q.B. 34, *per* Laws L.J. at [41] noting under the heading of "oppression" that
> ". . . a public body may choose to deploy powers it enjoys under statute in so draconian a fashion that the hardship suffered by affected individuals in consequence will justify the court in condemning the exercise as irrational or perverse. That is of course the language of *Wednesbury* . . .".

(No oppression was found on the facts: see below, pp.675, 689).
(3) unjustifiable inconsistency of treatment: this can give rise to a finding of irrationality, but has also developed as an independent head of challenge where there is an unfair interference with a substantive legitimate expectation; see below, pp.591–621;
(4) unjustified unequal treatment: see, *eg. R & L* (above); *R. (on the application of Middlebrook Mushrooms Ltd) v Agricultural Wages Board of England and Wales* [2004] EWHC 1447.
(5) unjustified interference with fundamental rights: see *Ex p. Smith*, below.

A number of these were foreshadowed in Lord Russell of Killowen C.J.'s judgment in *Kruse v Johnson*, above, p.234. As to the lack of proportionality, see below, pp.621–634.

See further on *Wednesbury*, Sir John Laws' essay in *The Golden Metwand and the Crooked Cord* (Forsyth and Hare ed., 1998), pp.185–201), and A. Le Sueur, "The Rise and Ruin of Unreasonableness" [2005] J.R. 32 (arguing that unreasonableness is struggling to survive as a coherent and useful ground of review; further clarification is needed on the different levels of intensity of review).

7. In *R. (on the application of Association of British Civilian Internees (Far-East Region) v Secretary of State for Defence* [2003] EWCA Civ 473; [2003] Q.B. 1397 at [83]–[86], the Court of Appeal left open the question whether there is a free-standing principle of equality in English domestic law. Lord Hoffmann in *Matadeen v Poitu* [1999] 1 A.C. 98 at 109, said:

> "As a formulation of the principle of equality, the [Supreme Court of Mauritius] cited Rault J. in *Police v. Rose* [1976] M.R. 79, 81: 'Equality before the law requires that persons should be uniformly treated, unless there is some valid reason to treat them differently'. Their Lordships do not doubt that such a principle is one of the building blocks of democracy and necessarily permeates any democratic constitution. Indeed, their Lordships would go further and say that treating like cases alike and unlike cases differently is a general axiom of rational behaviour. It is, for example, frequently invoked by the courts in proceedings for judicial review as a ground for holding some administrative act to have been irrational: see Professor Jeffrey Jowell Q.C., 'Is Equality a Constitutional Principle?' (1994) 47 C.L.P. 1, 12–14 and *de Smith, Woolf and Jowell, Judicial Review of Administrative Action*, 5th ed. (1995), pp.576–582, paras. 13–036 to 13–045".

Whether the reason for unequal treatment is valid was, however, not always justiciable.

In the *Internees* case, the court held (at [85]) that Lord Hoffmann was not propounding a free-standing principle of equality, but "discussing how the *Wednesbury* test should be accommodated in cases of alleged unjustified discrimination".

In many cases equality issues can be raised under Art.14 ECHR (above, p.388). Here, any common law principle of equality would not add much if anything: *R. (on the application of Montana) v Secretary of State for the Home Department* [2001] 1 W.L.R. 552, at [12]–[15].

R. v MINISTRY OF DEFENCE Ex p. SMITH

[1996] Q.B. 517; [1996] 2 W.L.R. 305; [1996] 1 All E.R. 257; (COURT OF APPEAL)

The four appellants, a lesbian and three homosexual men, were administratively discharged from service in the armed forces pursuant to a Ministry of Defence policy. The policy related to sexual orientation. It mandated discharge even without there being any evidence of overt sexual conduct; nor any evidence of an individual's ability to discharge responsibilities having been impaired. In fact all four servicemen were accepted to have exemplary service records. The appellants sought judicial review of the Ministry of Defence policy. The Divisional Court held the Ministry policy to be lawful. The appellants appealed to the Court of Appeal.

SIR THOMAS BINGHAM M.R.: . . . The applicants challenge the lawfulness of their discharge and thus, indirectly, of the policy which required them to be discharged. They say that the policy is irrational, and in breach of the European Convention for the Protection of Human Rights and Fundamental Freedoms, and contrary to Council Directive (76/207/E.E.C.) (the Equal Treatment Directive). They accept without reservation that any member of the armed services who acts inappropriately towards any other member, or who is guilty of any harassment, or who commits any offence or breach of service discipline, may be discharged administratively, if not on disciplinary grounds. So too if a member's sexual orientation undermines the member's efficiency as a member of the service or is shown to cause demonstrable damage to the service. They claim no right or liberty to commit homosexual acts or to make homosexual advances on the mess-deck or in the barrack-room or in any other service setting. They accept that membership of disciplined fighting force involves a curtailment of freedoms enjoyed by others in civilian employments, and recognise that the exigencies of service life may properly justify restrictions on homosexual activity and manifestations of homosexual orientation. Their challenge is, and is only, to the blanket, non-discretionary, unspecific nature of the existing policy.

The applicants' challenge was rejected by the Queen's Bench Divisional Court (Simon Brown L.J. and Curtis J.) on 7 June 1995: see, ante, pp.523A et seq. But the court urged the Ministry of Defence to re-examine its policy in the light of changing attitudes and circumstances, and of all available evidence, and we are told that such a review is now in progress. Meanwhile, the applicants contend that the Divisional Court were wrong to reject their challenge.

Background

There can be no doubt that public attitudes to homosexuality have in the past varied widely from country to country, and within the same country at different times, and among different social groups in the same country. Almost any generalisation can be faulted. But there has in this country been a discernible trend, over the last half century or so, towards greater understanding and greater tolerance of homosexuals by heterosexuals, and towards greater openness and honesty by homosexuals. In part this trend has prompted, in part it may have been a result of, legislative change.

Section 1(1) of the Sexual Offences Act 1967 decriminalised homosexual acts between consenting adults in private. It applied to males, since homosexual acts between women were not criminal anyway. This legislative change, now nearly 30 years ago, followed and gave effect to the Report of the Committee on Homosexual Offences and Prostitution, 1957 (Cmnd. 247, chaired by Sir John Wolfenden). At that time very few European countries took cognisance of homosexual behaviour between consenting parties in private: see paragraph 59 and Appendix III of the Report. It does not appear that that committee addressed the issues with specific reference to the armed forces. But it is important to note that section 1(1) of the Act did not, by virtue of section 1(5), prevent a homosexual act being an offence (other than a civil offence) under the statues governing the three services. Any person subject to those statutes remained liable to punishment for homosexual acts. So, by section 2 of the Act of 1967, did the crew of British merchant ships. Plainly, the view was then taken that to permit homosexual acts by or between members of the armed services, or in the special conditions pertaining aboard ship, would be subversive of discipline, efficiency and good order.

The routine quinquennial review of the statutes governing the armed forces has the effect that issues such as the treatment of homosexuals are reconsidered periodically. In 1986 a Select Committee of the House of Commons, despite argument that service law should be brought into line with civilian law, concluded that the law should remain as it then stood. But opinion did not stand still. In 1991 another House of Commons Select Committee returned to the subject. Submissions were then made that service law should be brought into line with civilian law and that homosexual orientation *alone should* not be a bar to membership of the armed forces. The select committee accepted the first of these submissions, seeing "no reason why service personnel should be liable to prosecution under service law for homosexual activity which would be legal in civilian law." But they rejected the second submission, concluding that there was "considerable force to the M.O.D.'s argument that the presence of people known to be homosexual can cause tension in a group of people required to live and work sometimes under great strees and physically at very close quarters, and thus damage its cohesion and fighting effectiveness." The select committee were not persuaded in 1991 that the time had yet come to permit the armed forces to accept homosexuals or homosexual activity.

In 1992 the responsible minister announced that in future individuals who engaged in homosexual activity that was legal in civilian law would not be prosecuted under service law. For want of parliamentary time, legislative effect was not given to this change until 1994, when section 146(1) of the Criminal Justice and Pubic Order Act 1994 was enacted. But section 146(4) provided that this change should not prevent a homosexual act (with or without other acts or circumstances) from constituting a ground for discharging a member of the armed forces.

In upholding the existing policy that homosexual activity or orientation should be an absolute bar to membership of the armed forces in 1991 select committee undoubtedly reflected the overwhelming consensus of service and official opinion in this country. It does not appear that the select committee required or received any evidence of actual harm done by sexual orientation alone or by private homosexual activity outside the context of service life. Nor does the select committee appear to have considered whether the objectives of the existing policy could be met by a rule less absolute in its effect than that which was then applied.

In other areas of national life opinion has shifted. In July 1991 the Prime Minister announced that neither homosexual orientation nor private homosexual activity should henceforth preclude appointment even to sensitive posts in the home civil service and the diplomatic service. The Lord Chancellor has made similar announcements in relation to judicial office. In July 1994 the Royal Fleet Auxiliary introduced an equal opportunities policy stating that it did not discriminate on grounds of homosexuality. A majority of police forces now follow the same policy.

Outside the United Kingdom also, opinion has not stood still. Very few N.A.T.O. countries bar homosexuals from their armed forces. This practice does not appear to have precluded the closest co-operation between such forces and our own. In the course of 1992–93 Australia, New Zealand and Canada relaxed their ban on homosexuals in their armed services but, importantly, introduced codes of conduct which defined the forms of homosexual conduct which were judged to be unacceptable In the United States, on the other hand, as an authoritative report in 1993 made plain, military opinion remained overwhelmingly against allowing homosexuals to serve. The lawfulness of the legislative compromise adopted in that country is in doubt: see *Able v. United States* (1995) 44 F.3d 128. In arguing that case the U.S. Government "recognised that a policy mandating discharge of homosexuals merely because they have a homosexual orientation or status could not withstand judicial scrutiny."

I regard the progressive development and refinement of public and professional opinion at home and abroad, have very briefly described, as an important feature of this case. A belief which represented unquestioned orthodoxy in year X may have become questionable by year Y and unsustainable by year Z. Public and professional opinion are a continuum. The four applicants were discharged towards the end of 1994. The lawfulness of their discharge falls to be judged as of that date.

Irrationality

(a) *The test*

Mr. David Pannick, who represented three of the applicants, and whose arguments were adopted by the fourth, submitted that the court should adopt the following approach to the issue of irrationality:

> "The court may not interfere with the exercise of an administrative discretion on substantive grounds save where the court is satisfied that the decision is unreasonable in the sense that it is beyond the range of responses open to a reasonable decision-maker. But in judging whether the decision-maker has exceeded this margin of appreciation the human rights context is important. The more substantial the interference with human rights, the more the court will require by way of justification before it is satisfied that the decision is reasonable in the sense outlined above."

This submission is in my judgment an accurate distillation of the principles laid down by the House of Lords in *Reg. v. Secretary of State for the Home*

Department, Ex parte, Bugdaycay [1987] A.C. 514 and *Reg. v. Secretary of State for the Home Department, Ex parte, Brind* [1991] A.C. 696. In the first of these cases Lord Bridge of Harwich said, at p.531:

"I approach the question raised by the challenge to the Secretary of State's decision on the basis of the law stated earlier in this opinion, viz. that the resolution of any issue of fact and the exercise of any discretion in relation to an application for asylum as a refugee lie exclusively within the jurisdiction of the Secretary of State subject only to the court's power of review. The limitations on the scope of that power are well known and need not be restated here. Within those limitations the court must, I think, be entitled to subject an administrative decision to the more rigorous examination, to ensure that it is in no way flawed, according to the gravity of the issue which the decision determines. The most fundamental of all human rights is the individual's right to life and when an administrative decision under challenge is said to be one which may put the applicant's life at risk, the basis of the decision must surely call for the most anxious scrutiny."

Lord Templeman, at p.537H, spoke to similar effect. In the second case, having concluded that it was not open to an English court to apply the European Convention on Human Rights, Lord Bridge said [1991] 1 A.C. 696, 748–749:

"But I do not accept that this conclusion means that the courts are powerless to prevent the exercise by the executive of administrative discretions, even when conferred, as in the instant case, in terms which are on their face unlimited, in a way which infringes fundamental human rights. Most of the rights spelled out in terms in the Convention, including the right to freedom of expression, are less than absolute and must in some cases yield to the claims of competing public interests. Thus, article 10(2) of the Convention spells out and categorises the competing public interests by reference to which the right to freedom of expression may have to be curtailed. In exercising the power of judicial review we have neither the advantages nor the disadvantages of any comparable code to which we may refer or by which we are bound. But again, this surely does not mean that in deciding whether the Secretary of State, in the exercise of his discretion, could reasonably impose the restriction he has imposed on the broadcasting organisations, we are not perfectly entitled to start from the premise that any restriction of the right to freedom of expression requires to be justified and that nothing less than an important competing public interest will be sufficient to justify it. The primary judgment as to whether the particular competing public interest justifies the particular restriction imposed falls to be made by the Secretary of State to whom Parliament has entrusted the discretion. But we are entitled to exercise a secondary judgment by asking whether a reasonable Secretary of State, on the material before him, could reasonably make that primary judgment."

Again, Lord Templeman spoke to similar effect, at p.751:

"It seems to me that the courts cannot escape from asking themselves whether a reasonable Secretary of State, on the material before him, could reasonably conclude that the interference with freedom of expression which he determined to impose was justifiable."

It is important to note that, in considering whether English law satisfies the requirement in article 13 of the European Convention that there should be a national remedy to enforce the substance of the Convention rights and freedoms, the European Court of Human Rights has held that it does, attaching very considerable weight to the power of the English courts to review administrative decisions by way of judicial review: see *Vilvarajah v. United Kingdom* (1991) 14 E.H.R.R. 248, 291, 292.

It was argued for the ministry in reliance on *Reg. v. Secretary of State for the Environment, Ex parte Nottinghamshire County Council* [1986 A.C. 240 and *Reg. v. Secretary of State for the Environment, Ex parte Hammersmith and Fulham London Borough Council* [1991] 1 A.C. 521 that a test more exacting than *Wednesbury (Associated Provincial Picture Houses Ltd. v Wednesbury Corporation* [1948] 1 K.B. 223) was appropriate in this case. The Divisional Court rejected this argument and so do I. The greater the policy content of a decision, and the more remote the subject matter of a decision from ordinary judicial experience, the more hesitant the court must necessarily be in holding a decision to be irrational. That is good law and, like most good law, common sense. Where decisions of a policy-laden, esoteric or security-based nature are in issue even greater caution than normal must be shown in applying the test, but the test itself is sufficiently flexible to cover all situations.

The present cases do not affect the lives or liberty of those involved. But they do concern innate qualities of a very personal kind and the decisions of which the applicants complain have had a profound effect on their careers and prospects. The applicants' rights as human beings are very much in issue. It is now accepted that this issue is justifiable. This does not of course mean that the court is thrust into the position of the primary decision-maker. It is not the constitutional role of the court to regulate the conditions of service in the armed forces of the Crown, nor has it the expertise to do so. But it has the constitutional role and duty of ensuring that the rights of citizens are not abused by the unlawful exercise of executive power. While the court must properly defer to the expertise or responsible decision-makers, it must not shrink from its fundamental duty to "do right to all manner of people. . . ."

(b) *The facts*

The reasons underlying the present policy were given in an affidavit sworn by Air Chief Marshal Sir John Willis K.C.B., C.B.E., the Vice-Chief of the Defence Staff, an officer of great seniority and experience. The relevant paragraphs of his affidavit have been recited in full by Simon Brown L.J. in his judgment in the Divisional Court, ante, pp.316F–318A, and it is unnecessary to duplicate that recital. Sir John advanced three reasons. The first related to morale and unit effectiveness, the second to the role of the services as guardian of recruits under the age of 18 and the third to the requirement of communal living in many service situations. Sir John described the ministry's policy as based not on a moral judgment but on a practical assessment of the implications of homosexual orientation on military life. By "a practical assessment" Sir John may have meant an assessment of past experience in practice, or he may have meant an assessment of what would be likely to happen in practice if the present policy were varied. His affidavit makes no reference to any specific past experience, despite the fact that over the years very many homosexuals

must have served in the armed forces. He does, however, make clear the apprehension of senior service authorities as to what could happen if the existing
policy were revoked or varied, and the grounds upon which he relies were the
subject of consideration by the House of Commons select committees to which
reference has already been made.

The first factor relied on by Sir John, morale and unit effectiveness, was the
subject of searing criticism by Mr. Pannick. He submitted that the effect of a
homosexual member of any military unity would depend on the character,
ability and personality of the member involved. He pointed out that many
homosexuals had successfully served in the services over the years. He drew
attention to the experience of other disciplined forces such as the police. He
submitted that inappropriate behaviour by homosexual members of the armed
forces could be effectively regulated. He submitted that the ministry should
not be deterred from doing what fairness and good sense demanded by appre-
hensions of irrational and prejudiced behaviour on the part of others.

Mr. Pannick also criticised the second factor relied on by Sir John. He
pointed out that any service member behaving inappropriately towards an
under-age member of the service could be disciplined and punished in the
same way as in society at large. He rejected the suggestion that homosexuals were less able to control their sexual impulses than heterosexuals.
Again he suggested that the policy of the ministry was pandering to ignorant
prejudice.

Mr. Pannick accepted, of course, that members of the services could in many
situations find themselves living together in conditions of very close.
Proximity, although he pointed out that one of the applicants (by reason of his
seniority) and another of the applicants (by reason of her particular occupation) were in no foreseeable situation likely to share accommodation with
anyone. The lack of privacy in service life was, he suggested, a reason for
imposing strict rules and discipline, but not a reason for banning the membership of any homosexual. He drew the attention to the experience of other
disciplined services. He pointed out that each of the applicants had worked in
the armed forces for a number of years without any concern being expressed
or complaints made about inappropriate behaviour. Each of them had earned
very favourable reports. The same, it was said, was true of many other homosexual members of the services.

Above all, Mr. Pannick criticised the blanket nature of the existing rule. He
placed great emphasis on the practice of other nations whose rules were
framed so as to counter the particular mischiefs to which homosexual orientation or activity might give rise. He pointed out that other personal problems
such as addiction to alcohol, or compulsive gambling, or marital infidelity
were dealt with by the service authorities on a case by case basis and not on
the basis of a rule which permitted no account to be taken of the peculiar features of the case under consideration.

The arguments advanced by Mr. Pannick are in my opinion of very considerable cogency. They call to be considered in depth, with particular reference
to specific evidence of past experience in this country, to the developing experience of other countries and to the potential effectiveness or otherwise of a
detailed prescriptive code along the lines adopted elsewhere in place of the
present blanket ban. Such a reassessment of the existing policy is already, as
I have noted, in train, and I note that the next Select Committee quinquennial
review of the policy is to receive a departmental paper of evidence covering all

the matters canvassed on this appeal. What the outcome of the review will be, I do not know.

The existing policy cannot in my judgment be stigmatised as irrational at the time when these applicants were discharged. It was supported by both Houses of Parliament and by those to whom the ministry properly looked for professional advice. There was, to my knowledge, no evidence before the ministry which plainly invalidated that advice. Changes made by other countries were in some cases very recent. The Australian, New Zealand and Canadian codes had been adopted too recently to yield much valuable experience. The ministry did not have the opportunity to consider the full range of arguments developed before us. Major policy changes should be the product of mature reflection, not instant reaction. The threshold of irrationality is a high one. It was not crossed in this case.

The European Convention

[His Lordship read Art.8 ECHR.]

It is, inevitably, common ground that the United Kingdom's obligation, binding in international law, to respect and secure compliance with this article is not one that is enforceable by domestic courts. The relevance of the Convention in the present context is as background to the compliant of irrationality. The fact that a decision-maker failed to take account of Convention obligations when exercising an administrative discretion is not of itself a ground for impugning that exercise of discretion. . . .

I could dismiss these appeals.

HENRY L.J. and THORPE L.J. delivered concurring judgments.

Notes

1. See case note by M. Norris [1996] P.L. 590. The issue raised in this case was subsequently taken to the European Court of Human Rights, which found relatively little difficulty in holding that the ban infringed Art.8 ECHR: *Smith and Grady v UK* (1999) 29 E.H.R.R. 493 and *Lustig-Prean and Beckett v UK* (1999) 29 E.H.R.R. 548. The investigation process was exceptionally intrusive, the administrative discharge had a profound effect on the applicants' careers and prospects (they had "exemplary records") and the policy was absolute and general in character. While the interferences arising from both the intrusive investigations that were conducted and the administrative discharges were in accordance with the law (the policy had been endorsed by s.146 of the 1994 Act), and pursued the legitimate aims of the interests of national security and the prevention of disorder (by maintaining the morale of service personnel, thus promoting operational effectiveness), they were not shown to be necessary in a democratic society. The Government had not offered convincing and weighty reasons justifying the policy. There was a lack of concrete evidence to substantiate the alleged damage (as noted by Thorpe L.J. in the Court of Appeal (at [99]); and negative attitudes found in a survey could not amount to sufficient justification to the extent that they merely represented a "predisposed bias on the part of a heterosexual majority against a homosexual minority" (at [97]); the Court was not satisfied that any difficulties to be anticipated as a result of a change in the policy could not be covered by a strict code of conduct. Following this decision, the policy was changed (see A.R. Mowbray, *Cases and Materials on the European Convention on Human Rights* (2001), pp.355–356).

2. The case is of particular interest in its exploration of the applicability of *Wednesbury* principles in the context of the protection of human rights. Note (1) the

recognition that the appellants' human rights were "very much in issue"; (2) the proposition that the "more substantial the interference with human rights, the more the court
will require by way of justification before it is satisfied that the decison is reasonable";
and (3) the rejection of the Ministry's attempt to invoke the so-called "super-
Wednesbury" standard of even greater deference to the decision-maker than the norm
(based on the *Nottinghamshire* and *Hammersmith* cases, above, pp.576–579). In the
course of dealing with the third of these points, Sir Thomas Bingham M.R. stated that

> "The greater the policy content of a decision, and the more remote the subject
> matter of a decision from ordinary judicial experience, the more hesitant the court
> must necessarily be in holding the decison to be irrational".

Is this in fact reconcilable with proposition (2)? Does proposition (2) in reality involve
"lowering the threshold of unreasonableness", a step rejected as impermissible by
Neill L.J. in *R. v Secretary of State for the Environment Ex p. NALGO* (1992) 5
Admin. L.R. 785 at 798 and criticised by Lord Irvine of Lairg, in "Judges and
Decision-makers: The Theory and Practice of *Wednesbury* Review" [1996] P.L. 59 at
pp.63–65 (see discussion by Norris [1996] P.L. 590 at pp.593–597).
   (Note that, very confusingly, the label "super-*Wednesbury*" is sometimes used to
denote the "heightened scrutiny" approach of *Smith* rather than the *Nottinghamshire*
test: see cf *R. v Collins Ex p. Brady* (2000) 58 B.M.L.R. 173.)
   3. The formulation of the *Wednesbury* test of David Pannick Q.C., approved by the
Court of Appeal, is whether the decision was "unreasonable in the sense that it is
beyond the range of responses open to a reasonable decision-maker". This does not
seem to be intended to be a different test from Lord Greene's formulation in
Wednesbury, but is rather a more felicitous wording of the same test. What is important is the rider that the more substantial the interference with human rights, the more
the court will require by way of justification before it is satisfied that the decision is
reasonable. This can be compared with the formulation of Simon Brown L.J. in the
Divisional Court (at 538) based on the Court of Appeal in *R. v Secretary of State for
the Environment Ex p. NALGO* (1992) 5 Admin. L.R. 785 at 797–798:

> ". . . [E]ven where fundamental human rights are being restricted, 'the threshold of
> unreasonableness' is not lowered. On the other hand, the minister on judicial review
> will need to show that there is an important competing public interest which he
> could reasonably judge sufficient to justify the restriction and he must expect his
> reasons to be closely scrutinised. Even that approach, therefore, involves a more
> intensive review process and a greater readiness to intervene than could ordinarily
> characterise a judicial review challenge".

This was endorsed in argument by counsel for the Secretary of State in *Smith*, who
characterised it as the conventional *Wednesbury* approach adapted to a human rights
context (at 549).
   Is there any material difference between the approaches of Simon Brown L.J. in the
Divisional Court of and Sir Thomas Bingham M.R. in the Court of Appeal? In *R. v Lord
Saville of Newdigate Ex p. A* [1999] 4 All E.R. 860, the Court of Appeal at [37] expressly
agreed with the second sentence of the passage quoted from Simon Brown L.J.
   For the argument that it is problematic to see the heightened scrutiny in cases concerning rights as *simply* a variant of *Wednesbury*, see *Craig*, pp.614–615. For examples of the application of the heightened scrutiny approach to strike down a decision,
see *R. v Secretary of State for the Home Department Ex p. M* [1999] Imm. A.R. 548
(SSHD's view that to return a terminally ill AIDS sufferer to Uganda would not subject
him to acute physical and mental suffering (in terms of para.2.1 of the exceptional
leave to remain policy) held to be unreasonable); *R. v Lord Saville of Newdigate Ex p.
A* [2000] 1 W.L.R. 1855 (decision to refuse anonymity at the Saville Inquiry into the
Bloody Sunday shootings to military witnesses who had fired shots held not to be open

to the tribunal); *R. (on the application of Wagstaff v Secretary of State for Health* [2001] 1 W.L.R. 292 (Secretary of State's decision that an inquiry into issues following the conviction of Dr. Harold Shipman on multiple counts of murder should be in private held to be irrational).

4. The difference in outcome between the English courts and the ECtHR in *Ex p. Smith*, can be explained by the point that the latter applied the test of proportionality which was not open to the former. The proportionality test is seen as providing for a greater intensity of review than *Wednesbury* unreasonableness or irrationality, even with the "heightened scrutiny" accepted to be appropriate in cases concerning rights. The gap between the two is, however, difficult to characterise. See further, pp.629–630. How convincing do you find the application of heightened scrutiny by the Court of Appeal on the facts of *Smith*? One possible analysis is that the claimants had done enough to show that continuation of the policy was indeed beyond the range of reasonable responses open to the decision-maker. The gap between the heightened scrutiny approach (properly applied) and proportionality may be small. See further the discussion in *Daly*, above, p.340.

The practical significance of the "heightened scrutiny" *Wednesbury* approach is of course reduced by the enactment of the Human Rights Act 1998 (see Ch.6). It remains of significance where that Act does not apply, for example, where there are fundamental rights not covered by the Act, and transitionally to the extent that the Act is not retrospective in effect (see pp.298–299).

5. It has been emphasised in subsequent cases that it would be wrong to conclude that there are two tests at play in two distinct categories of case, heightened scrutiny in cases concerning fundamental rights and traditional *Wednesbury* unreasonableness elsewhere. The better view is that there is a sliding scale of review. As Laws L.J. put it in *R. v Secretary of State for Education and Employment Ex p. Begbie* [2000] 1 W.L.R. 1111, at 1130:

> "Fairness and reasonableness (and their contraries) are objective concepts; otherwise there would be no public law, or if there were it would be palm tree justice. But each is a spectrum, not a single point, and they shade into one another. It is now well established that the Wednesbury principle itself constitutes a sliding scale of review, more or less intrusive according to the nature and gravity of what is at stake: see for example, in the field of human rights, the observations of Sir Thomas Bingham MR as he then was in *Ex p. Smith* . . .".

(ii) Express Requirements of Reasonableness

In some instances a grant of discretionary power may expressly provide that the power is only to be exercisable "reasonably," or is only to be exercisable where the body in question has "reasonable" grounds to consider that certain defined circumstances exist. In such cases the courts may consider whether the positive requirement of reasonableness has been satisfied. They will not be restricted to a consideration of whether the decision on the relevant issue is "so unreasonable . . .". The extent to which a reviewing court will be willing to substitute its own judgment of reasonableness for that of the statutorily designated body may, however depend on context. Compare the decisions in *Nak-kuda Ali* and *Luby v Newcastle-under-Lyme Corp.* [1965] 1 Q.B. 214 (requirement that rents be "reasonable": *per* Diplock L.J., "a matter with which the knowledge and experience of [the local] authority can best be trusted to deal": "reasonable" interpreted as "not unreasonable").

NAKKUDA ALI v M.F. de S. JAYARATNE

[1951] A.C. 66; 66 T.L.R. (PT 2) 214; 94 S.J. 516 *SUB NOM.*
ALI v JAYARATNE

(Privy Council on appeal from the Supreme Court of Ceylon)

The respondent, the Controller of Textiles in Ceylon, exercised his power to cancel a textile dealer's licence "where the Controller has reasonable grounds to believe that any dealer is unfit to be allowed to continue as a dealer". The appellant sought a mandate in the nature of certiorari to quash the cancellation on the ground of breach of natural justice. The Privy Council held that there had been no breach, but that in any event certiorari would not lie as the Controller was not acting judicially but taking executive action to withdraw a privilege. This general aspect of the case is discussed by Lord Reid in *Ridge v Baldwin* (below, p.658). One specific point dealt with by the Privy Council was whether the requirement that the Controller have "reasonable grounds" indicated that he was acting judicially, which was the view of the Supreme Court.

LORD RADCLIFFE delivered the opinion of the Privy Council (LORDS PORTER, OAKSEY and RADCLIFFE, SIR JOHN BEAUMONT and SIR LIONEL LEACH): . . . It would be impossible to consider the significance of such words as "Where the Controller has reasonable grounds to believe . . ." without taking account of the decision of the House of Lords in *Liversidge v. Sir John Anderson* [1942] A.C. 206. That decision related to a claim for damages for false imprisonment, the imprisonment having been brought about by an order made by the Home Secretary under the Defence (General) Regulations, 1939, reg. 18B, of the United Kingdom. It was not a case that had any direct bearing on the court's power to issue a writ of certiorari to the Home Secretary in respect of action taken under that regulation: but it did directly involve a question as to the meaning of the words "If the Secretary of State has reasonable cause to believe any person to be of hostile origin or associations . . ." which appeared at the opening of the regulation in question. And the decision of the majority of the House did lay down that those words in that context meant no more than that the Secretary of State had honestly to suppose that he had reasonable cause to believe the required thing. On that basis, granted good faith, the maker of the order appears to be the only possible judge of the conditions of his own jurisdiction.

Their Lordships do not adopt a similar construction of the words in reg. 62 which are now before them. Indeed, it would be a very unfortunate thing if the decision of *Liversidge's* case came to be regarded as laying down any general rule as to the construction of such phrases when they appear in statutory enactments. It is an authority for the proposition that the words "if A.B. has reasonable cause to believe" are capable of meaning "if A.B. honestly thinks that he has reasonable cause to believe" and that in the context and attendant circumstances of Defence Regulation 18B they did in fact mean just that. But the elaborate consideration which the majority of the House gave to the context and circumstances before adopting that construction itself shows that there is no general principle that such words are to be so understood; and the dissenting speech of Lord Atkin at least serves as a reminder of the many occasions when they have been treated as meaning "if there is in fact reasonable cause for A.B. so to believe". After all, words such as these are commonly found when a legislature or law-making authority confers powers on a minister or official. However read, they must be intended to serve in some sense as a condition limiting the exercise of an otherwise arbitrary power. But if the question whether the condition has been satisfied is to be conclusively decided by the man who yields the power the value of the intended restraint is in effect nothing. No doubt he must not exercise the power in bad faith: but the field in which this kind of question arises is such that the reservation for the case of bad faith is hardly more than a formality. Their Lordships therefore treat the words in reg. 62, "where the Controller has reasonable grounds to believe that any dealer is unfit to be allowed to continue as a dealer" as imposing a condition that there must in fact exist such reasonable grounds, known to the Controller, before he can validly exercise the power of cancellation. . . .

Notes

1. This aspect of *Nakkuda Ali v Jayaratne* is generally accepted as correct. See Lord Reid in *Ridge v Baldwin*, below, p.666, and *IRC v Rossminster Ltd* [1980] A.C. 952—concession by IRC on this point. *Liversidge v Anderson* was not relied upon by the Solicitor-General in *Secretary of State for Employment v ASLEF (No.2)* [1972] 2 Q.B. 443.

2. *Liversidge v Anderson* [1942] A.C. 206 is a notorious case, but highly exceptional. For discussion, see R.F.V. Heuston, *Essays in Constitutional Law*, pp.171–177; *Allen*, pp.256, 297 and Appendix 1; R.F.V. Heuston, "*Liversidge v Anderson* in Retrospect" (1970) 86 L.Q.R. 33, and "*Liversidge v Anderson*, Two Footnotes" (1971) 87 L.Q.R. 161.

3. The power of the Secretary of State under s.68 of the Education Act 1944 to give directions, *inter alia*, where he was "satisfied . . . that any local education authority . . . have acted or are proposing to act unreasonably with respect to the exercise of any power conferred or the performance of any duty imposed by or under this Act" was interpreted narrowly by the House of Lords in *Secretary of State for Education and Science v Tameside MBC* [1977] A.C. 1014. The House held that the Secretary of State was only entitled to interfere if no reasonable authority could have so acted (or proposed to act). Here, following an election, the now Conservative local authority withdrew plans to introduce comprehensive schools. The Secretary of State intervened on the basis that to change the plans when they were "designed to come into effect three months later must in his opinion give rise to considerable difficulties". The House of Lords held that either (1) he had applied the wrong legal test for unreasonableness; or (2) assuming the right test was applied, there was no evidence to support his conclusion. Comments on the scope of review for error of fact were subsequently taken further by the Court of Appeal in *E v Secretary of State for the Home Department*, below, p.828.

(D) Inconsistency

In the previous chapter we noted the unwillingness of the courts to utilise notions of estoppel in favour of applicants for review who claim to have been misled by a public body as to the scope of its powers, or by an official or a committee as to the extent of his or its authority. See above, pp.515–523. The concern of the courts in these cases has been an unwillingness to allow the concept of estoppel to result in the enlargement of the powers actually conferred by the terms of the legislation, or of the powers actually delegable, or delegated, by the respondent body.

Furthermore, the courts have recognised that the private law principle of estoppel focuses on the relationship between the public authority and the person claiming to have been misled, and takes insufficient account of the wider public interest.

The courts have instead developed a principle that an authority may be held to have abused its discretion by unfairly interfering with a person's legitimate expectations. It was already well established that a legitimate expectation could give rise to procedural obligations (see the *CCSU* case, p.690). Furthermore, the existence of such an expectation might constitute a consideration that had to be taken into account, and disregard of it might be held in the circumstances to be *Wednesbury* unreasonable or irrational. However, the Court of Appeal in *R. v North and East Devon HA Ex p. Coughlan* [2001] Q.B. 213 held that this did not exhaust the substantive effects to which a legitimate expectation could give rise.

R. v NORTH AND EAST DEVON HEALTH AUTHORITY
Ex p. COUGHLAN

[2001] Q.B. 213; [2000] 2 W.L.R. 622; [2000] 3 All E.R. 850
(COURT OF APPEAL)

C was severely injured in a road accident in 1971. She was tetraplegic, doubly incontinent and partially paralysed in the respiratory tract and was subject to recurrent headaches. In 1993, she and seven comparably disabled patients were moved with their agreement from a hospital, which it was desired to close, to a purpose-built facility, Mardon House. They were assured that this would be their home by the health authority's predecessor, Exeter HA, for life. In 1996, the Department of Health issued guidance that "specialist" nursing services should be provided by the NHS but that "general" nursing care should be purchased by local authorities. The health authority concluded that C and the other Mardon House residents did not meet these criteria and in 1998, after public consultation, decided to close Mardon House. The closure decision was quashed by Hidden J. An appeal to the Court of Appeal was dismissed.

The judgment of the court (LORD WOOLF M.R, MUMMERY and SEDLEY L.JJ.) was delivered by LORD WOOLF M.R.: . . .

[The court held, first, that the decision was unlawful on the ground that the health authority had misinterpreted the legislation setting out its responsibilities. The Secretary of State was under a "duty to continue the promotion in England and Wales of a comprehensive health service . . . and for that purpose to provide or secure the effective provision of services in accordance with this Act" (National Health Service Act 1977, s.1(1)); and a "duty to provide . . . to such extent as he considers necessary to meet all reasonable requirements" a series of services, including hospital accommodation, other accommodation for the purpose of any service provided under the Act, nursing services, and such facilities for the care of persons suffering from illness and the after-care of persons who have suffered from illness as he considers are appropriate as part of the health service (1977 Act, s.3(1)). Under s.21(1) of the National Assistance Act 1948, as amended, a local authority had power (and could be directed) to make arrangements for providing residential accommodation for persons aged 18 or over who by reason of age, illness, disability or any other circumstances are in need of care and attention which is not otherwise available to them. Unlike the provision of NHS services these would be subject to means-testing. However, nothing in s.21 could authorise or require a local authority to make any provision authorised or required to be provided under the 1977 Act (1948 Act, s.21(8)). The court held that the Secretary of State could take into account available resources and conclude that it was not necessary to provide some nursing services through the NHS; however, the local authority could only provide nursing services that could legitimately be regarded as being provided in connection with accommodation provided under s.21 of the 1948 Act, as part of a social services care package. The distinction between nursing services which were and those which were not capable of being included in such a package was one of degree which would depend in a borderline case on a careful appraisal of the facts of the individual case and not on a broad distinction between "specialist" and "general" services. As a very general indication it could be said that if the nursing services were (i) merely incidental or ancillary to the provision of accommodation under s.21 and (ii) of a nature which it could be expected that an authority whose primary responsibility to provide social services could be expected to provide, then they could be provided under s.21. On this basis, the needs of C and her fellow occupants were primarily health needs for which the Health Authority was as a matter of law responsible. The eligibility criteria drawn up by the health authority purported to place a responsibility on the local authority which went beyond the terms of s.21. The misinterpretation had been a factor contributing to the closure of Mardon House.

His Lordship then turned to the health authority's specific legal obligations owed to C.]

C. The promise of a home for life

50. The health authority appeals on the ground that the judge wrongly held that it had failed to established that there was an overriding public interest which entitled it to break the "home for life" promise. In particular, the judge erred in concluding that the health authority had applied the wrong legal test in deciding whether the promise could or should be broken and that it had wrongly diluted the promise and treated it as merely a promise to provide care. It contends that it applied the correct legal test and that the promise had, in the decision-making process, been plainly and accurately expressed and given appropriate prominence.

51. It is also contended that the judge failed to address the overwhelming evidence on the urgent need to remedy the deficiencies of the reablement service and of the serious and acute risks to the reablement service if the status quo at Mardon House were maintained. If he had addressed that issue he would and should have concluded that the health authority was entitled to decide that such consideration pointed inexorably to the closure decision.

52. It has been common ground throughout these proceedings that in public law the health authority could break its promise to Miss Coughlan that Mardon House would be her home for life if, and only if, an overriding public interest required it. Both Mr Goudie and Mr Gordon adopted the position that, while the initial judgment on his question has to be made by the health authority, it can be impugned if improperly reached. We consider that it is for the court to decide in an arguable case whether such a judgment albeit properly arrived at, strikes a proper balance between the public and the private interest. . . .

Legitimate expectation—the court's role

55. In considering the correctness of this part of the judge's decision it is necessary to begin by examining the court's role where what is in issue is a promise as to how it would behave in the future made by a public body when exercising a statutory function. In the past it would have been argued that the

promise was to be ignored since it could not have nay effect on how the public body exercised its judgment in what it thought was the public interest. Today such an argument would have no prospect of success, as Mr Goudie and Mr Gordon accept.

56. What is still the subject of some controversy is the court's roe when a member of the public, as a result of a promise or other conduct, has a legitimate expectation that he will be treated in one way and the public body wishes to treat him or her in different way. Here the starting point has to be to ask what in the circumstances the member of the public could legitimately expect. In the words of Lord Scarman in *In re Findlay* [1985] AC 318, 338, "But what was their *legitimate* expectation?" Where there is a dispute as to this, the dispute has to be determined by the court, as happened in *In re Findlay*. This can involve a detailed examination of the precise terms of the promise or representation made, the circumstances in which the promise was made and the nature of the statutory or other discretion.

57. There are at least three possible outcomes. (a) The court may decide that the public authority is only required to bear in mind its previous policy or other representation, giving it the weight it thinks right, but no more, before deciding whether to change course. Here the court is confined to reviewing the decision on *Wednesbury* grounds (*Associated Provincial Picture Houses Ltd v Wednesbury Corpn* [1948] 1 KB 223). This has been held to be effect of changes of policy in cases involving the early release of prisoners: see *In re Findlay* [1985] AC 318; *R v Secretary of State for the Home Department, Ex p. Hargreaves* [1997] 1 WLR 906. (b) On the other hand the court may decide that the promise or practice induces a legitimate expectation of, for example, being consulted before a particular decision is taken. Here it is uncontentious that the court itself will require *the opportunity for consultation* to be given unless there is an overriding reason to resile from it (see *Attorney General of Hong Kong v Ng Yuen Shiu* [1983] 2 AC 629) in which case the court will itself judge the adequacy of the reason advanced for the change of has policy, taking into account what fairness requires. (c) Where the court considers that a lawful promise or practice has induced a legitimate expectation of a *benefit which is substantive*, not simply procedural, authority now establishes that here too the curt will in a proper case decide whether to frustrate the expectation is so unfair that to take a new and different course will amount to an abuse of power. Here, once the legitimacy of the expectation is established, the court will have the task of weighing the requirements of fairness against any overriding interest relied upon for the change of policy.

58. The court having decided which of the categories is appropriate, the court's role in the case of the second and third categories is different from that in the first. In the case of the first, the court is restricted to reviewing the decision on conventional grounds. The test will be rationality and whether the public body has given proper weight to the implications of not fulfilling the promise. In the case of the second category the court's task is the conventional one of determining whether the decision was procedurally fair. In the case of the second category the court's task is the conventional one of determining whether the decision was procedurally fair. In the case of the third, the court has when necessary to determine whether there is a sufficient overriding interest to justify a departure from what has been previously promised.

59. In many cases the difficult task will be decide into which category the decision should be allotted. In what is sill a developing field of law, attention

will have to be given to what it is in the first category of case which limits the applicant's legitimate expectation (in Lord Scarman's words in *In re Findlay* [1985] AC 318 to an expectation that whatever policy is in force at the time will be applied to him. As to the second and third categories, the difficulty of segregating the procedural from the substantive is illustrated by the line of cases arising out of decisions of justices not to commit a defendant to the Crown Court for sentence, or assurances given to a defendant by the court: here to resile from such a decision or assurance may involve the breach of legitimate expectation: see *R v Grice* (1977) 66 Cr App R 167; cf *R v Reilly* [1982] QB 1208, *R v Dover Magistrates' Court, Ex p Pamment* (1994) 15 Cr App R(S) 778, 782. No attempt is made in those cases, rightly in our view, to draw the distinction. Nevertheless, most cases of an enforceable expectation of substantive benefit (the third category) are likely in the nature of things to be cases where the expectation is confined to one person or a few people, giving the promise or representation the character of a contract. We recognise that the courts' role in relation to the third category is still controversial; but, as we hope to show, it is now clarified by authority.

60. We consider that Mr Goudie and Mr Gordon are correct, as was the judge, in regarding the facts of this case as coming into the third category. (Even if this were not correct because of the nature of the promise, and even if the case fell within the second category, the health authority in exercising its discretion and in due course the court would have to take into account that only an overriding public interest would justify resiling from the promise.) Our reasons are as follows, first, the importance of what was promised to Miss Coughlan (as we will explain later, this is a matter underlined by the Human Rights Act 1998); second, the fact that promise was limited to a few individuals, and the fact that the consequences to the health authority of requiring it to honour its promise are likely to be financial only.

The authorities

61. Whether to frustrate a legitimate expectation can amount to an abuse of power is the question which was posed by the House of Lords in *R v Inland Revenue Comrs, Ex p Preston* [1985] AC 835 and addressed more recently by this court in *R v Inland Revenue Comrs, Ex p Unilever plc* [1996] STC 681. In each case it was in relation to a decision by a public authority (the Crown) to resile from a representation about how it would treat a member of the public (the taxpayer). It cannot be suggested that special principles of public law apply to the Inland Revenue or to taxpayers. Yet this is an area of law which has been a site of recent controversy, because while *Ex p Preston* has been followed in tax cases, using the vocabulary of abuse of power, in other fields of public law analogous challenges, couched in the language of legitimate expectation, have not all been approached in the same way.

62. There has never been any question that the propriety of a breach by a public authority of a legitimate expectation of the second category, of a *procedural* benefit—typically a promise of being heard or consulted—is a matter for full review by the court. The court has, in other words, to examine the relevant circumstances and to decide for itself whether what happened was fair. This is of a piece with the historic jurisdiction of the courts over issues of procedural justice. But in relation to a legitimate expectation of a substantive benefit (such as a promise of a home for life) doubt has been cast upon whether

the same standard of review applies. Instead it is suggested that the proper standard is the so-called *Wednesbury* standard which is applied to the generality executive decisions. This touches the intrinsic quality of the decision, as opposed to the means by which it has been reached, only where the decision is irrational or (per Lord Diplock in *Council of Civil Service Unions v Minister for the Civil Service* [1985] AC 374, 410) immoral.

63. This is not a live issue in the common law of the European Union, where a uniform standard of full review for fairness is well established; see *Schwarze, European Administrative Law* (1992), pp.1134–1135 and the European Court of Justice cases reviewed in *R v Ministry of Agriculture, Fishers and Food Ex p Hamble (offshore) Fisheries Ltd* [1995] 2 All ER 714, 726–728. It is, however, something on which the Human Right Act 1998, when it comes into force, may have a bearing.

64. It is axiomatic that a public authority which derives its existence and its powers from statute cannot validly act outside those powers. This is the familiar ultra vires doctrine adopted by public law from company law (*Colman v Eastern Countries Railway Co* (1846) 10 Beav 1). Since such powers will ordinarily include anything fairly incidental to the express remit, a statutory body may lawfully adopt and follow policies (*British Oxygen Co Ltd v Board of Trade* [1971] AC 610) and enter into formal undertakings. But since it cannot abdicate its general remit, not only must it remain free to change policy; its undertakings are correspondingly open to modification or abandonment. The recurrent question is when and where and how the courts are to intervene to protect the public from unwarranted harm in this process. The problem can readily be seen to go wider than the exercise of statutory powers. It may equally arise in relation to the exercise of the prerogative power, which at least since *R v Criminal Injuries Compensation Board, Ex p Lain* [1967] 2 QB 864, has been subject to judicial review, and in relation to private monopoly powers: *R v Panel on Take-over and Mergers, Ex p Datafin plc* [1987] QB 815.

65. The court's task in all these cases is not to impede executive activity but to reconcile its continuing need to initiate or respond to change with the legitimate interests or expectations of citizens or strangers who have relied, and have been justified in relying, on a current policy or an extant promise. The critical question is by what standard the court is to resolve such conflicts. It is when one examines the implications for a case like the present of the proposition that, so long as the decision-making process has been lawful, the court's only ground of intervention is the intrinsic rationality of the decision, that the problem becomes apparent. Rationality, as it has developed in modern public law, has two faces: one is the barely known decision which simply defies comprehension; the other is a decision which can be seen to the proceeded by flawed logic (though this can often be equally well allocated to the intrusion of an irrelevant factor). The present decision may well pass rationality test; the health authority knew of the promise and its seriousness; it was aware of its new policies and may not easily be challenged as irrational. As Lord Diplock said in *Secretary of State for Education and Science v Tameside metropolitan Borough Council* [1977] AC 1014,1064:

"The very concept of administrative discretion involves a right to choose between more than one possible course of action up which there is room for reasonable people to hold differing opinions as to which is to the preferred."

But to limit the court's power of supervision to this is to exclude from consideration another aspect of the decision which is equally the concern of the law.

66. In the ordinary case there is no space for intervention on grounds of abuse of power once a rational decision directed to a proper purpose has been reached by lawful process. The present class of case is visibly different. It involves not one but two lawful exercises of power (the promise and the policy change) by the same public authority, with consequences for individuals trapped between the two. The policy decision may well, and often does, make as many exceptions as are proper and feasible to protect individual expectations. The departmental decision in *Ex p Hamble (Offshore) Fisheries Ltd* [1995] 2 All ER 714 is a good example. If it does not, as in *Ex p Unilever plc* [1996] STC 681, the court is there to ensure that the power to make and alter policy has not been abused by unfairly frustrating legitimate individual expectations. In such a situation a bare rationality test would constitute the public authority judge in its own cause, for a decision to priorities a policy change over legitimate expectations will almost always be rational form where the authority stands, even if objectively it is arbitrary or unfair. It is in response to this dilemma that two distinct but related approaches have developed in the modern cases.

67. One approach is to ask not whether the decision is ultra vires in the restricted *Wednesbury* sense but whether, for example through unfairness or arbitrariness, it amounts to an abuse of power. The leading case on the existence of this principle is *Ex p Preston* [1985] AC 835. It concerned an allegation, not in the event made out, that the Inland Revenue Commissioners had gone back impermissibly on their promise not to reinvestigate certain aspects of an individual taxpayer's affairs. Lord Scarman, expressing his agreement with the single fully reasoned speech (that of Lord Templeman) advanced a number of important general propositions. First, he said, at p.851:

". . . I must make clear my view that the principle of fairness has an important place in the law of judicial review: and that in an appropriate case it is a ground upon which the court can intervene to quash a decision made by a public officer or authority in purported exercise of power conferred by law."

Second, Lord Scarman reiterated, citing the decision of the House of Lords in *R v Inland Revenue Comrs, Ex p National Federation of Self-Employed and Small Businesses Ltd* [1982] AC 617, that a claim for judicial review may arise where the Commissioners have failed to discharge their statutory duty to an individual or "have abused their powers or acted outside them". Third, that "unfairness in the purported exercise of a power can be such that it is an abuse or excess of power".

68. It is evident from these passages and from Lord Scarman's further explanation of them that, in his view at least, it is unimportant whether the unfairness is analytically within or beyond the power conferred by law: on either view public law today reaches it. The same approach was taken by Lord Templeman, at p.862:

"Judicial review is available where a decision-making authority exceeds its powers, commits an error of law, commits a breach of natural justice, reaches a decision which no reasonable tribunal could have reached, or abuses its powers."

69. Abuses of power may take many forms. One, not considered in the *Wednesbury* case [1948] 1 KB 223 (even though it was arguably what the case was about), was the use of a power for a collateral purpose. Another, as cases like *Ex p Preston* [1985] AC 835 now make clear, is reneging without adequate justification, by an otherwise lawful decision, on a lawful promise or practice adopted towards a limited number of individual. There is no suggestion in *Ex p Preston* or elsewhere that the final arbiter of justification, rationality apart, is the decision-maker rather than the court. Lord Templeman, at pp.864–866, reviewed the law in extenso, including the classic decisions in *Laker Airways Ltd v Department of Trade* [1977] QB 643; *Padfield v Minister of Agriculture, Fisheries and Food* [1968] AC 997; *Congreve v Home Office* [1976] QB 629 and *HTV Ltd v Price Commission* [1976] ICR 170 ("It is a commonplace of modern law that such bodies must act fairly . . . And that the courts have power to redress unfairness": Scarman LJ at p.189.) He reached this conclusion, at pp.866–867:

> "In principle I see no reason why the [taxpayer] should not be entitled to judicial review of a decision taken by the commissioners if that decision is unfair to the [taxpayer] because the conduct of the commissioners is equivalent to a breach of contract or a breach of representation. Such a decision falls within the ambit of an abuse of power for which in the present case judicial review is the sole remedy and an appropriate remedy. There may be cases in which conduct which savours of breach of [contract] or breach of representation does not constitute an abuse of power; there may be circumstances in which the court in its discretion might not grant relief by judicial review notwithstanding conduct which savours of breach of contract or breach of representation. In the present case, however, I consider that the [taxpayer] is entitled to relief by way of judicial review for 'unfairness' amounting to abuse of power if the commissioners have been guilty of conduct equivalent to breach of contract or breach of representations on their part."

The entire passage, too long to set out here, merits close attention. It may be observed that Lord Templeman's final formulation, taken by itself, would allow no room for a test of overriding public of overriding public interest. This, it is clear, is because of the facts then before the House. In a case such as the present the question posed in the *HTV* case [1976] ICR 170 remains live.

70. This approach, in our view, embraces all the principles of public law which we have been considering. It recognizes the primacy of the public authority both in administration and in policy development but is insists, where these functions come into tension, upon the adjudicative role of the court to ensure fairness to the individual. It does not overlook the passage in the speech of Lord Browne-Wilkinson in *R v Hull University Visitor, Ex p Page* [1993] AC 682, 701, that the basis of the "fundamental principle . . . that the courts will intervene to ensure that the powers of public decision-making bodies are exercised lawfully" is the *wednesbury* limit on the exercise of powers; but it follows the authority not only of *Ex p Preston* [1985] AC 835 but of Lord Scarman's speech in *R v Secretary of State for the Environment, Ex p. Nottinghamshire County Council* [1986] AC 240, 249, in treating a power which is abused as a power which has not been lawfully exercised.

71. Fairness in such a situation, if it sis to mean anything, must for the reasons we have considered include fairness of outcome. This in turn is why the doctrine of legitimate expectation has emerged as a distinct application of the concept of abuse of power in relation to substantive as well as procedural benefits, representing a second approach to the same problem. If this is the position in the case of the third category, why is it not also the position in relation to the first category? May it be (though this was not considered in *In re Findlay* [1985] AC 318 *Ex p Hargreaves* [1991] 1 WLR 906) that, when a promise is made to a category of individuals who have the same interest, it is more likely to be considered to have binding effect than a promise which is made generally or to a diverse class, when the interests of those to whom the promise is made may differ or, indeed, may be in conflict? Legitimate expectation may play different parts in different aspects of public law. The limits to its role have yet to be finally determined by the courts. Its application is still being developed on a case by case basis. Even where it reflects procedural expectations, for example concerning consultation, it may be affected by an overriding public interest. It may operate as an aspect of good administration, qualifying the intrinsic rationality of policy choices. And without injury to the *Wednesbury* doctrine it may furnish a proper basis for the application of the now established concept of abuse of power.

72. A full century ago in the seminal case of *Kruse v Johnson* [1898] QB 91 Lord Russell of Killowen CJ set the limits of the courts' benevolence towards local government byelaws at those which were manifestly unjust, partial, made in bad faith or so gratuitous and oppressive that no reasonable person could think them justified. While it is the latter two classes which reappear in the decision of this court in the *Wednesbury* case [1948] 1 KB 223, the first two are equally part of the law. Thus in *R v Inland Revenue Comrs, Ex p MFK Underwriting Agents Ltd* [1990] 1 WLR 1545 a Divisional Court (Bingham LJ Judge J) rejected on the facts a claim for the enforcement of a legitimate expectation in the face of a change of practice by the Ireland Revenue. But having set out the need for certainty of representation, Bingham LJ went on, at pp.1569–1570.

"In so stating these requirements I do not, I hope, diminish or emasculate the valuable, developing doctrine of legitimate expectation. If public authority so conducts itself as to create a legitimate expectation that a certain course will be followed it would often be unfair if the authority were permitted to follow a different course to the detriment of one who entertained the expectation, particularly if he acted on it. If in private law a body would be in breach of contract in so acting or estopped from so acting a public authority should generally be in better position. The doctrine of legitimate expectation is rooted in fairness."

73. This approach, which makes no formal distinction between procedural and substantive unfairness, was expanded by reference to the extant body of authority by Simon Brown LJ in *R v Devon County Council, Ex p Baker* [1995] 1 All ER 73, 88–89. He identified two categories of *substantive* legitimate expectation recognized by modern authority;

"(1) Sometimes the phrase is used to demote a substantive right: an entitlement that the claimant asserts cannot be denied him. It was used in this sense and the assertion upheld in cases such as *R v Secretary of State for the Home Department, Ex p Asif Mahmood Khan* [1984] 1 WLR 1337 and

R v Secretary of State for the Home Department, Ex p Ruddock [1987] 1 WLR 1482. It was used in the same sense but unsuccessfully in, for instance, *R v Inland Revenue Comrs, Ex p MFK Underwriting Agents Ltd* [1990] 1 WLR 1545 and *R v Jockey Club, Ex p RAM Racecourses Ltd* [1993] 2 All ER 225. These various authorities show that the claimant's right will only be found established when there is a clear and unambiguous representation upon which it was reasonable for him to rely. Then the administrator or other public body will be held bound in fairness by the representation made unless only its promise or undertaking as to how its power would be exercised is inconsistent with the statutory duties imposed upon it. The doctrine employed in this sense is akin to an estoppel. In so far as the public body's representation is communicated by way of a stated policy, this type of legitimate expectation falls into two distinct sub-categories: cases in which the authority are held entitled to change their policy even so as to affect the claimant, and those in which they are not. An illustration of the former is *R v Torbay Borough Council, Ex p Cleasby* [1991] COD 142, of the latter *Ex p Asif Mahmood Khan*. (2) Perhaps more conventionally the concept of legitimate expectation is used to refer to the claimant's interest in some ultimate benefit which he hopes to retain (or, some would argue, attain). Here, therefore, it is the interest itself rather than the benefit that is the substance of the expectation. In other words the expectation arises not because the claimant asserts any specific right to a benefit but rather because his interest in it is one that the law holds protected by the requirements of procedural fairness; the law recognizes that the interest cannot properly be withdrawn (or denied) without the claimant being given an opportunity to comment and without the authority communicating rational grounds for any adverse decision. Of the various authorities drawn to our attention, *Schmidt v Secretary of State for Home Affairs* [1969] 2 Ch 149, *O'Reilly v Mackman* [1983] 2 AC 237 and the recent decision of Roch J in *R v Rochdale Metropolitan Borough Council, Ex p Schemet* [1993] 1 FCR 306 are clear examples of this head of legitimate expectation."

Simon Brown LJ has not in that passage referred expressly to the situation where the individual can claim no higher expectation than to have his individual circumstances considered by the decision-maker in the light of the policy then in force. This is not surprising because this entitlement, which can also be said to be rooted in fairness, adds little to the standard requirements of any exercise of discretion: namely that the decision will take into account all relevant matters which here will include the promise or other conduct giving rise to the expectation and that if the decision-maker does so the courts will not interfere except on the basis that the decision is wholly unreasonable. It is the classic *Wednesbury* situation, not because the expectation is substantive but because it lacks legitimacy.

74. Nowhere in this body of authority, nor in *Ex p Preston* [1985] AC 835, nor in *In re Findlay* [1985] AC 318, is there any suggestion that judicial review of a decision which frustrates a substantive legitimate expectation is confined to the rationality of the decision. But in *Ex p Hargreaves* [1997] 1 WLR 906, 921,925 Hirst LJ (with whom Peter Gibson LJ agreed) was persuaded to reject the notion of scrutiny for fairness as heretical, and Pill LJ to reject it as "wrong in principle".

75. *Ex p Hargreaves* concerned prisoners whose expectations of home leave and early release were not to be fulfilled by reason of a change of policy. Following *In re Findlay* [1985] AC 318 this court held that such prisoners' only legitimate expectation was that their applications would be considered individually in the light of whatever policy was in force at the time: in other words the case came into the first category. This conclusion was dispositive of the case. What Hirst LJ went on to say, at p.919, under the head of "The proper approach for the court to the Secretary for State's decision" was therefore obiter. However Hirst LJ accepted in terms the submission of leading counsel for the Home Secretary that, beyond review on *Wednesbury* gounds, the law recognised to enforceable legitimate expectation of a substantive benefit. In relation to the decision in *Ex p Hamble (Offshore) Fisheries Ltd* [1995] 2 All ER 714, he said [1997] 1 WLR 906,921:

"Mr Beloff characterised Sedley J's approach as heresy, and in my judgment he was right to do so. On matters of substance (as contrasted with procedure) Wednesbury provides the correct test."

A number of leaned commentators have questioned this conclusion (see *e.g.* P P Craig. "Substantive legtimate expectations and the principles of judicial review" in *English Public Law and the Common Law of Europe*, ed. M Andenas (1998); T R S Allan, "Procedure and substance in judicial review" [1997] CLJ 246; Steve Foster, "Legitimate expectations and prisoners' rights" (1997) 60 MLR 727).

76. *Ex p Hargreaves* [1997] 1WLR 906 can, in any event, be distinguished from the present cse. Mr Gordon has sought to distinguish it on the ground that the present case involves an abuse of power. On one view all cases where proper effect is not given to a legitimate expectation involve an abuse of power. Abuse of power can be said to be out another name for acting contrary to law. But the real distinctin between *Ex p Hargreaves* and this case is that in this case it is contended that fairness in the statutory context required more of the decision-maker than *Ex p Hargreaves* where the sole legitimate expectation possessed by the prisoners had been met. It required the health authority, as a matter of fairness, not to resile from their promise unless there was an overriding justification for doing so Another way of expressing the same thing is to talk of the unwarranted frustration of a legitimate expectation and thus an abuse of power or a failure of substantive fairness. Again the labels are not important except that they all distinguish the issue here from that in *Ex p. Hargreaves*. They identify a different task for the court from that where what is in issue is a conventional application of policy or exercise of discretion. Here the decision can only be justified if there is an overriding public interest. Whether there is an overriding public interest is a question for the court.

77. The cases decided in the European Court of Justice cited in *Ex p. Hargreaves(Offshore) Fisheries Ltd* [1995] 2 All ER 714 all concern policies or practices conferring substantive benefits from which member states were not allowed to resile when the policy or practice was altered. In this country *R v Secretary of State for the home Department, Ex p Ruddock* [1987] 1 WLR 1482 and *R v Secretary of State for the Home Department, Ex p. Asif Mahmood Khan* [1984] 1 WLR 1337 were cited as instances of substantive legitimate expectations to which the courts were if appropriate prepared to give effect. Reliance was also placed, as we would place it, on Lord Diplock's

carefully worded summary in *Council of Civil Service Unions v Minister for the Civil Service* [1985] AC 374, 408–409 of the contemporary heads of judicial review. They included benefits or advantages which the application can legitimately expect to be permitted to continue to enjoy. Not only did Lord Diplock not limit these to procedural benefits or advantage; he referred expressly to *In re Findlay* [1985] AC 318 (a decision in which he had participated) as an example of a case concerning a claim to a legitimate expectation— plainly a substantive one, albeit that the claim failed. One can readily were why: Lord Scarman's speech in *In re Findlay* is predicated on the assumption that the court will protect a substantive legitimate expectation if one is established; and Taylor J so interpreted it in *Ex p Ruddock* [1987] 1 WLR 1482. None of these case suggests that the standard of review is always limited to bare rationality, though none developed it as the revenue cases have done.

78. It is from the revenue cases that, in relation to the third category, the proper test emerges. Thus in *Ex p Unilever plc* [1996] STC 681 this court concluded that for the Crown to enforce a time limit which for years it had not insisted upon would be so unfair as to amount to an abuse of power. As in other tax cases, there was no question of the court's deferring to the Inland Revenue's view of what was fair. The court also concluded that the Inland Revenue's conduct passed the "notoriously high" threshold of irrationality; but the finding of abuse through unfairness was not dependent on this.

79. It is worth observing that this was how the leading text book writers by the mid-1990s saw the law developing. In the (still current) seventh edition of *Wade Forsyth's Administrative Law* (1994) the authors reviewed a series of modern cases and commented, at p.419:

> "These are revealing decisions. They show that the courts now expect government departments to honour their statements of policy or intention or else to treat the citizen with the fullest personal consideration. Unfairness in the form of unreasonableness is clearly allied to unfairness by violation of natural justice. It was in the latter context that the doctrine of legitimate expectation was invented, but it is now proving to be source of substantive as well as of procedural rights. Lord Scarman [in Ex p Preston [1985] AC 835] has stated emphatically that unfairness in the purpoted exercise of power can amount to an abuse or excess of power, and this may become an important general doctrine."

To similar effect is *de Smith, Woolf & Jowell, Judicial Review of Administrative Action*, 5th ed. (1995), pp.575–576, para.13–035. *Craig, Administrative Law*, 3rd ed. (1994), pp.672–675, links the issue, as Schwarze does (*European Administrative Law* (1992)), to the fundamental principle of legal certainty.

80. In *Ex p Unilever plc* [1996] STC 681, 695 Simon Brown LJ proposed a valuable reconciliation of the existing strands of public law:

> " 'Unfairness amounting to an abuse of power' a . . . In Preston and the other revenue cases in unlawful not because it involves conduct such as would offend some equivalent private law principle, not principally indeed because it breaches a legitimate expectation that some different substantive decision will be taken, but rather because it is illogical or immoral or both for a public authority to act with conspicuous unfairness and in the sense abuse its power. As Lord Donaldson MR said in *R v Independent Television*

Commission, Ex p TSW Broadcasting Ltd, The Times, 7 February 1992: 'The test in public law is fairness, not an adaptation of the law of contract or estoppel.' In short, I regard the *MFK* category of legitimate expectation as essentially but a head of *Wednesbury* unreasonableness, not necessarily exhaustive of the grounds upon which a successful substantive unfairness challenge may be based."

81. For our part, in relation to this category of legitimate expectation, we do not consider it necessary to explain the modern doctrine in *Wednesbury* terms, helpful though this is in terms of received jurisprudence (cf Dunn LJ in *R v Secretary of State for the Home Department, Ex p Asif Mahmood Khan* [1984] 1 WLR 1337, 1352: "an unfair action can seldom be a reasonable one"). We would prefer to regard the *Wednesbury* categories themselves as the major instance (not necessarily the sole ones: see *Council of Civil Service Unions v Minister for the Civil Service* [1985] AC 374, 410, per Lord Diplock) of how public power may be misused. Once it is recognised that conduct which is an abuse of power is contrary to law its existence must be for the court to determine.

82. The fact that the court will only give effect to a legitimate expectation within the statutory context in which it has arisen should avoid jeopardising the important principle that the executive's policy-making powers should not be trammeled by the courts: see *Hughes v Department of Health and Social Security* [1985] AC 766, 788, per Lord Diplock. Policy being (within the law) for the public authority alone, both it and the reasons for adopting or changing it will be accepted by the courts as part of the factual data—in other words, as not ordinarily open to judicial review. The court's task—and this is not always understood—is then limited to asking whether the application of the policy to an individual who has been led to expect something different is a just exercise of power. In many cases the authority will already have considered this and made appropriate exceptions (as was envisaged in *British Oxygen Co Ltd v Board of Trade* [1971] AC 610 and as had happened in *Ex p Hamble (Offshore) Fisheries Ltd* [1995] 2 All ER 714), or resolved to pay compensation where money alone will suffice. But where no such accommodation is made, it is for the court to say whether the consequent frustration of the individual's expectation is so unfair as to be a misuse of the authority's power.

Fairness and the decision to close

83. How are fairness and the overriding public interest in this particular context to be judged? The question arises concretely in the present case. Mr Goudie argued, with detailed references, that all the indicators, apart from the promise itself, pointed to an overriding public interest, so that the court ought to endorse the health authority's decision. Mr Gordon contended, likewise with detailed references, that the data before the health authority were far from uniform. But this is not what matters. What matters is that, having taken it all into account, the health authority voted for closure in spite of the promise. The propriety of such an exercise of power should be tested by asking whether the need which the health authority judged to exist to move Miss Coughlan to a local authority facility was such as to outweigh its promise that Mardon House would be her home for life.

84. That a promise was made is confirmed by the evidence of the health authority that:

> "the applicant and her fellow residents were justified in treating certain statements made by the health authority's predecessor, coupled with the way in which the authority's predecessor conducted itself at the time of the residents' move from Newcourt Hospital, as amounting to an assurance that, having moved to Mardon House, Mardon House would be a permanent home for them."

And the letter of 7 June 1994 sent to the resident by Mr Peter Jackson, the then general manager of the predecessor of the health authority, following the withdrawal of John Grooms stated:

> "During the course of a meeting yesterday with Rose Bentley's father, it was suggested that each of the former Newcourt residents now living at Mardon House would appreciate a further letter of reassurance from me. I am writing to confirm therefore, that the health authority has made it clear to the community trust that it expects the trust to continue to provide good quality care for you at Mardon House for as long as you chose to live there. I hope that this will dispel any anxieties you may have arising from the forthcoming change in management arrangements, about which I wrote to you recently."

As has been pointed out by the health authority, the letter did not actually use the expression "home for life."

85. The health authority had, according to its evidence, formed the view that it should give considerable weight to the assurances given to Miss Coughlan; that those assurances had given rise to expectations which should not in the ordinary course of things, be disappointed; but that it should not treat those assurances as giving rise to an absolute and unqualified entitlement on the part of the Miss Coughlan and her co-residents since that would be unreasonable and unrealistic; and that:

> "if there were compelling reasons which indicated overwhelmingly that closure was the reasonable and—other things being equal—the right course to take, provided that steps could be taken to meet the applicant's (and her fellow residents') expectations to the greatest degree possible following closure, it was open to the authority, weighing up all these matters with care and sensitivity, to decide in favour of the option of closure."

Although the first consultation paper made no reference to the "home for life" promise, it was referred to in the second consultation paper as set out above.

86. It is denied in the health authority's evidence that there was any misrepresentation at the meeting of the board on 7 October 1998 of the terms of the "home for life" promise. It is asserted that the board had taken the promise into account; that members of the board had previously seen a copy of Mr Jackson's letter of 7 June 1994, which, they were reminded, had not used the word "home", and that every board member was well aware that, in terms of its fresh decision-making, the starting point was that the Newcourt patients had moved to Mardon on the strength of an assurance that Mardon would be their home as long as they chose to live there. This was an express promise or representation made on a number of occasions in precise terms. It was made to a small group of severely disabled individuals who had been housed and cared for over a substantial period in the health authority's predecessor's premises at Newcourt. It specifically related to identified premises which it was represented would be their home for as long as they chose. It was in unqualified terms. It was repeated and confirmed to reassure the residents. It was made by the health authority's predecessor for its own purposes, namely to encourage Miss Coughlan and her fellow residents to move out of Newcourt and into Mardon House, a specially built substitute home in which they would continue to receive nursing care. The promise was relied on by Miss Coughlan. Strong reasons are required to justify resiling from a promise given in those circumstances. This is not a case where the heath authority would, in keeping the promise, be acting inconsistently with it statutory or other public law duties. A decision not to honour it would be equivalent to a breach of contract in private law.

87. The health authority treated the promise as the "starting point" from which the consultation process and the deliberations proceeded. It was a factor which should be given "considerable weight", but it could be outweighed by "compelling reasons which indicated overwhelmingly that closure was the reasonable and the right course to take". The health authority, though "mindful of the history behind the residents' move to Madron House and their understandable expectation that it would be their permanent home", formed the view that there were "overriding reasons" why closure should nonetheless proceed. The health authority wanted to improve the provision of reablement services and considered that the mix of a long stay residential service and a reablement service at Mardon House was inappropriate and detrimental to the interests of both users of the service. The acute reablement service could not be supported there without an uneconomic investment which would have produced a second class reablement service. It was argued that there was a compelling public interest which justified the health authority's prioritization of the reablement service.

88. It is, however, clear from the health authority's evidence and submissions that it did not consider that it had a legal responsibility or commitment to provide a *home*, as distinct from care or finding of care, for the applicant and her fellow residents. It considered that, following the withdrawal of the John Grooms Association, the provision of care services to the current residents had become "excessively expensive," having regard to the needs of the majority of disabled the authority's area and the "insuperable problems" involved in the mix of long-term residential care and reablement services at Mardon House. Mardon House had, contrary to earlier expectations, become:

"a prohibitively expensive white elephant. The unit was not financially viable. Its continued operation was dependent upon the authority supporting it at an excessively high cost. This did not represent value for money and left fewer resources for other services."

The health authority's attitude was that

"It was because of our appreciation of the residents' expectation that they would remain at Mardon House for the rest of their lives that the board agreed that the authority should accept a continuing commitment to finance the care of the residents of Mardon for whom it was responsible."

But the cheaper option favoured by the health authority misses the essential point of the promise which had been given. The fact is that the health authority has not offered to the applicant an equivalent facility to replace what was promised to her. The health authority's undertaking to fund her care for the remainder of her life is substantially different in nature and effect from the earlier promise that care for her would be provided *at Mardor House*. That place would be her home for as long as she chose to live there.

89. We have no hesitation in concluding that the decision to move Miss Coughlan against her will and in breach of the health authority's own promise was tin the circumstances unfair. It was unfair because it frustrated her legitimate expectation of having a home for life in Mardon House. There was no overriding public interest which justified it. In drawing the balance of conflicting interests the court will not only accept the policy change without demur but will pay the closest attention to the assessment made by the public body itself. Here, however, as we have already indicated, the health authority failed to weigh the conflicting interests correctly. Furthermore, we do not know (for reasons we will explain later) the quality of the alternative accommodation and services which will be offered to Miss Coughlan. We cannot prejudge what would be the result if there was on offer accommodation which could be said to be reasonably equivalent to Mardon House and the health authority made a properly considered decision in favour of closure in the light of that offer. However, absent such an offer, here there was unfairness amounting to an abuse of power by the health authority.

D. Human rights

90. One further element must be considered by the court. Mardon House is Miss Coughlan's home, and by article 8(1) of the European Convention for the Protection of Human Rights and Fundamental Freedoms (1953) (Cmd 8969): "Everyone has the right to respect for . . . his home . . . "Once the Human Rights Act 1998 is in force it will be the obligation of the court as a public authority to give effect to this value, except to the extent that statutory provision makes this impossible. In the interim between the enactment and the coming into force of the Act it is right that the courts should pay particular attention to them. Article 8(2) provides:

"There shall be no interference by a public authority with the exercise of the right except such as is in accordance with the law and is necessary in a democratic society in the interests of . . . the economic well-being of the country. . ."

91. Not one but two policy decisions were in play. The first, which we have considered separately, was to let Miss Coughaln's nursing care be providing by the local social services authority. The second was to evict Miss Coughlan from the home which had been promised to her for life in order to maker better and more economic use of the premises. For reasons which we have given we do not consider that the kind of nursing care needed by Miss Coughaln could lawfully be provided by the local authority under section 21 of the 1948 Act;

but this need not have affected the second decision, since the health authority has in any case been prepared to pay for Miss Coughlan's future nursing care wherever she is located. So the health authority's decision to move Miss Coughlan from Mardon House falls to be matched, irrespective of the larger health care provision issue, against its promise that this would not happen. To consider this properly the health authority needed to be in a position, which it was not, to compare what Mardon House offered with what the alternative accommodation would offer Miss Coughlan.

92. The extent to which the public cost was going to be reduced by moving Miss Coughlan to local authority care was not dramatic. The local authority and the health authority between them would still be paying for the whole of her care—for we have no doubt that the undertaking to pay was rightly given. The saving would be in terms of economic and logistical efficiency in the use respectively of Mardon House and the local authority home. The price of this saving was to be not only the breach of a plain promise made to Miss Coughlan but, perhaps more importantly, the loss of her only home and of a purpose-built environment which had come to mean even more to her that a home does to most people. It was know to the health authority, as it is known to this court, that Miss Coughlan views the possible loss of her accommodation in Mardon House as life-threatening. While this may be putting the reality too high, we can readily see why it seems so to her; and we accept, on what is effectively uncontested evidence, that an enforced move of this kind will be emotionally devastating and seriously anti-therapeutic.

93. The judge was entitled to treat this as a case where the health authority's conduct was in breach of article 8 and was not justified by the provisions of article 8(2). Mardon House is, in the circumstances described, Miss Coughlan's home. It has been that since 1993. It was promised to be just that for the rest of her life. It is not suggested that it is not her home or that she ahs a home elsewhere or that she has done anything to justify depriving her other home at Mardon House. By closure of Mardon House the health authority will interfere with what will soon be her right to her home. For the reasons explained, the health authority would not be justified in law in doing so without providing accommodation which meets her needs. As Sir Thomas Bingham MR said in *R v Ministry of Defence, Ex p Smith* [1996] QB 517, 554: "The more substantial the interference with human rights, the more the court will reaquire by way of justification before it is satisfied that the decision is reasonable . . ." Or, we would add, in a case such as the present, fair. . . .

F. Consultation

108. It is common ground that, whether or not consultation of interested parties and the public is a legal requirement, if it is embarked upon it must be carried out properly. To be proper, consultation must be undertaken at a time when proposals are still at a formative stage; it must include sufficient reasons for particular proposals to allow those consulted to give intelligent consideration and an intelligent response; adequate time must be given for this purpose; and the product to consultation must be conscientiously taken into account when the ultimate decision is take: *R v Brent London Borough Council, Ex p Gunning* (1985) 84 LGR 168.

109. We have dealt separately with the impact of the "home for life" promise and with the assessments made of the applicant. These had a bearing,

of course, on the content of the consultation process, but we are concerned here with the machinery of consultation. Central to Miss Coughlan's successful critique of it was the report of Dr Clark, which is summarised in paragraph 16 above. Hidden J held:

"the decision process ended with the board considering the ethical decision-making paper which said that 'Professionals advise that leaving the residents isolated will do particular harm to two residents.' Next to that sentence was the further information that 'professionals advise that not moving the acute service will do harm to other disabled people.' Such a combination of arguments in favour of the decision to close Mardon House . . . were unseen by the applicant and therefore not something upon which she could comment or which she could refute. They are far from the stuff of which true consultation is made. The same is true of the report of Dr Clark which was commissioned by the stuff of which true consultation is made. The same is true of the report of Dr. Clark which was commissioned by the health authority and seen by the board who drew comfort from it but not seen by the applicant and the other consultees who would have wished to refute it."

110. Hidden J was also impressed by the letter from the health authority commissioning Dr Clark's report. It anticipated a judicial review hearing following the "final decision", suggesting an anticipation that the decision would be in favour of closure. He rejected the health authority's reason—lack of time—for the non-disclosure of Dr Clark's repot; and he went on to deduce from it that the consultation process had been too hurried to meet the *Gunning* standard. He concluded that none of the four *Gunning* criteria was met.

111. Although the notice of appeal does not contest every one of the judge's findings about consultation, Mr Goudie attacks his conclusion in relation to three critical issues: Dr Clark's report, the length of the consultation period and the question of prejudgment.

112. Miss Coughlan's solicitor received Dr Clark's report only two working days before the board met on 7 October, a date well after the end of the consultation period, which had run only on 24 September 1998. Although Mr Goudie's skeleton argument focuses upon the substance of Miss Coughlan's opportunity to respond, he has taken in oral argument a point which seems to us to be sound and to bypass this debate: there was, he submits, no need to consult on Dr·Clark's report, which was external advice on the opinions of local clinicians and was therefore itself a response to the consultation, albeit one solicited by the health authority. It has to be remembered that consultation is not litigation: the consulting authority is not required to publicise every submission it receives or (absent some statutory obligation) to disclose all its advice. Its obligation is to let those who have a potential interest in the subject matter know in clear terms what the proposal is and exactly why it is under positive consideration, telling them enough (which may be a good deal) to enable them to make an intelligent response. The obligation, although it may be quite onerous, goes no further than this .

113. We accept, too, Mr Goudie's submission that the letter went from an officer of the authority and not from any of its decision-makers. It did undoubtedly reveal an anticipated outcome, but the mind was not that of a decision-maker. It may well be, as Mr Gordon suggests, that Dr Clark would

have had little difficulty in deducing which way Mrs Jeffries, who wrote the letter to him, would prefer his advice to go; but this is a long way from a case of prejudgment in either the authority or the adviser.

114. The formal consultation period lasted just over three weeks, from 2 to 24 September 1998. It had, however, been preceded by an eight-week consultation period in the first months of the year, leading to the first closure decision which was quashed by consent. Among the effects of the shortage of time identified by Mr Gordon is the loss of a proper opportunity of comment on Dr Clark's report. Mr Goudie relies not only on the prehistory of consultation but on the fact that the consultation paper itself had an input from the applicant and her advisers: they had had it in draft some weeks before the beginning of the consultation period, and had made their view known, there seems to us to be strength in the health authority's position in this regard.

115. Mr Gordon, however, defends Hidden J's conclusion by reference to a number of other aspects of the consultation. It turned out when the consultation was over that the health authority had had before it a paper on ethical decision-making which Miss Coughlan and her adviser would have wanted an opportunity to comment on. The paper, it seems to us, is of the same character as Dr Clark's report. It was not a part of the proposal and not necessary to explain the proposal. The risk an authority takes by not disclosing such documents is not that the consultation process will be insufficient but that it may turn out to have taken into account incorrect or irrelevant matters which, had there been an opportunity to comment, could have been corrected. That however, is not this case.

116. There is, it is true, a further list of flaws with which Mr Gordon submits the consultation process was riddled. Without reciting these, we consider that all are points which within the admittedly modest time available were fully capable of being pointed out to the health authority before it met to take its decision. To draw attention to them now is not to the point.

117. We conclude therefore that although there are criticisms to be leveled at the consultation process, and although it ran certain risks, it was not flawed by any significant non-compliance with the *Gunning* criteria.

Conclusions

It follows that, although we disagree with some of the reasoning of the judge. Miss Coughlan was entitled to succeed and we dismiss the appeal.

Our conclusions may be summarized as follows.

(a) The NHS does not have sole responsibility for all nursing care. Nursing care for a chronically sick patient may in appropriate cases be provided by a local authority as a social service and the patient may be liable to meet the cost of that care according to the patient's means. The provisions of the 1977 Act and the 1948 Act do not, therefore, make it necessarily unlawful for the health authority to decide to transfer responsibility for the general nursing care of Miss Coughlan to the local authority' social services. Whether it was unlawful depends, generally, on whether the nursing services are merely (i) incidental or ancillary to the provision of the accommodation which a local authority is under a duty to provide and (ii) of a nature which it can be expected that an authority whose primary responsibility is to provide social services can be expected to provide Miss Coughlan needs services of a wholly different category.

(b) The consultation process adopted by the health authority preceding the decision to close Mardon House is open to criticism, but was not unlawful

(c) The decision to close Mardon House was, however, unlawful on the ground that: (i) the health authority reached a decision which depended on a misinterpretation of its statutory responsibilities under the 1977 Act, (ii) the eligibility criteria adopted and applied by the health authority for long-term NHS health care were unlawful and depended on an approach to the services which a local authority was under a duty to provide which was not lawful; and (iii) the decision was an unjustified breach of a clear promise given by the health authority's predecessor to Miss Coughlan that she should have a home for life at Mardon House. This constituted unfairness amounting to an abuse of power by the health authority. It would be a breach of article 8 of the European Convention of Human Rights.

(d) In these circumstances assessments of Miss Coughlan and other patients on the basis of the eligibility criteria were also similarly flawed.

Appeal dismissed with costs.

Notes

1. Following the court's decision on the first point, revised guidance was issued by the Department of Health: Health Service Circular HSC 2001/015; Local Authority Circular LAC (2001) 18, *Continuing Care: NHS and Local Councils' responsibilities*. The decision mean that both the Secretary of State and the Royal College of Nursing (who had intervened to challenge the distinction between "general" and "specialist" nursing) could claim a measure of victory (see A. Loux, S. Kerrison, A.M. Pollock, *BMJ* 2000; 320: 5–6. Fresh provision for the boundary between social care and NHS provision was made by s.49 of the Health and Social Care Act 2001, which provided that nothing in the enactments relating to the provision of community care services shall authorise or require a local authority to provide or arrange for the provision of nursing care by a registered nurse.

2. As to the second point, the case establishes that the validity of an interference with a legitimate expectation is in an appropriate case to be judged by reference to a criterion of fairness as distinct from *Wednesbury* unreasonableness or irrationality. This would suggest that the grounds of judical review have been enlarged. Is it legitimate for the judges to take such a step? (Note the criticisms expressed by M. Elliott, [2000] J.R. 27) Compare the courts' refusal to introduce proportionality as a general ground of challenge in judicial review (below, pp.630–631). On the other hand it also seems from the discussion of Art.8 ECHR that the decision was probably in any extent open to challenge as irrational under the heightened scrutiny approach of *Smith* (see above, p.581), in which case the apparent extension of judicial review would not seem to have affected the outcome on the facts. It is clear that the fairness approach of *Coughlan* is intended to be more intrusive than "bare *Wednesbury* irrationality". However, it is not at all clear that it is intended to be more intrusive than the heightened scrutiny approach under *Wednesbury* where fundamental rights are at stake, and such a position would make no sense (*cf.* Elliott, *op. cit.*, at p.32). In *R. (on the application of Zequiri v Secretary of State for the Home Department* [2001] EWCA Civ 342; [2002] Imm. A.R. 42, the court in quashing a decision of the Home Secretary for breach of a legitimate expectation held (at [70]) that the outcome on the facts was the same whether one applied the unfairness test of *Coughlan* or the heightened scrutiny test of *Smith*. (On appeal, the House of Lords held that no legitimate expectation arose on the facts without adverting to this question: [2002] UKHL 3; [2002] Imm. A.R. 296.) In the light of this, a more straightforward approach would have been to hold that a legitimate expectation may in appropriate circumstances be of sufficient weight,

even where fundamental rights are not at stake, to justify "heightened scrutiny" by the court on the lines of *Smith*. Assuming a similar intensity of scrutiny, when a judge says that the outcome of the authority's balancing of a legitimate expectation against the public interest is "unfair" is this really any different from saying that it is "unreasonable" or "irrational"? On this basis could any decision be "substantively unfair but *Wednesbury* reasonable", or "substantively fair but *Wednesbury* unreasonable"?

3. A further question is whether a sharp distinction can in fact be drawn between *Coughlan* categories 1 and 3. The only plausible view is there cannot, as explained by Laws L.J. in *R. v Secretary of State for Education and Employment Ex p. Begbie* [2000] 1 W.L.R. 1115, where he said (at 1030–1031):

"As it seems to me the first and third categories explained in the *Coughlan* case are not hermetically sealed. The facts of the case, viewed always in their statutory context, will steer the court to a more or less intrusive quality of review. In some cases a change of tack by a public authority, though unfair from the applicant's stance, may involve questions of general policy affecting the public at large or a significant section of it (including interests not represented before the court); here the judges may well be in no position to adjudicate save at most on a bare Wednesbury basis, without themselves donning the garb of policy-maker, which they cannot wear. The local government finance cases, such as *R v Secretary of State for the Environment, ex parte Hammersmith and Fulham LBC* [1991] 1 AC 521 exemplify this. As Wade and Forsyth observe (Administrative Law, 7th edn p.404):

'Ministers' decisions on important matters of policy are not on that account sacrosanct against the unreasonableness doctrine, though the court must take special care, for constitutional reasons, not to pass judgment on action which is essentially political'.

In other cases the act or omission complained of may take place on a much smaller stage, with far fewer players. Here, with respect, lies the importance of the fact in the *Coughlan* case that few individuals were affected by the promise in question. The case's facts may be discrete and limited, having no implications for an innominate class of persons. There may be no wide-ranging issues of general policy, or none with multi-layered effects, upon whose merits the court is asked to embark. The court may be able to envisage clearly and with sufficient certainty what the full consequences will be of any order it makes. In such a case the court's condemnation of what is done as an abuse of power, justifiable (or rather, falling to be relieved of its character as abusive) only if an overriding public interest is shown of which the court is the judge, offers no offence to the claims of democratic power.

There will of course be a multitude of cases falling within these extremes, or sharing the characteristics of one or other. The more the decision challenged lies in what may inelegantly be called the macro-political field, the less intrusive will be the court's supervision. More than this: in that field, true abuse of power is less likely to be found, since within it changes of policy, fuelled by broad conceptions of the public interest, may more readily be accepted as taking precedence over the interests of groups which enjoyed expectations generated by an earlier policy".

Would the extended ground recognised in *Coughlan* be needed if proportionality were accepted as a general ground of challenge?

What is clear in any event is that either the *Coughlan* approach or heightened scrutiny under *Wednesbury* is a more appropriate way of reconciling the competing interests than the private law of estoppel (see the *Reprotech* case, above, p.515).

Note that the legitimate expectation doctrine does not apply where the issue is whether a finding on the facts by a tribunal in one set of judicial proceedings is binding in subsequent proceedings between the parties before another tribunal; the relevant doctrines here are its estoppel *per rem judicatam* and abuse of process (*R. (on the application of Nahar) v Social Security Commissioner* [2001] EWHC Admin 1049; [2002] 1 F.L.R. 670, above p.523).

4. There is now a very large body of case law on the legitimate expectation doctrine. Cases that consider how far such expectations give rise to procedural obligations are considered in Ch.10 (see the *CCSU* case, below, p.690). We concentrate here on cases that fall into categories 1 and 3 of the *Coughlan* typology. In *R. (on the application of Bibi) v Newham LBC* [2002] 1 W.L.R. 237, Schiemann L.J. at [19] stated that in all legitimate expectation cases, whether substantive or procedural,

> "three practical questions arise. The first question is to what has the public author- ity, whether by practice or promise, committed itself; the second is whether the authority has acted or proposes to act unlawfully in relation to its commitment; the third is what the court should do".

In determining the first question it will be normally necessary to consider whether the promise or practice was both of an appropriate kind and sufficiently unequivocal to give rise to a commitment, and whether such a commitment would be within the lawful powers of the authority. In determining, the second question, it will be necessary to identify the consequences that flow from the commitment in terms of the *Coughlan* typology.

5. To what, if anything, is the authority committed?

(a) Many cases turn on whether the representation or conduct is sufficiently clear and unequivocal to give rise to a legitimate expectation. Close attention will be paid to the exact terms of any representations. For example, what is normally required if statements by the Inland Revenue are to give rise to a legitimate expectation was dis- cussed by Bingham L.J. in *R. v Inland Revenue Commissioners Ex p. MFK Underwriting Agents Ltd* [1990] 1 W.L.R. 1545 at 1569–1570:

> "I am of opinion that in assessing the meaning, weight and effect reasonably to be given to statements of the Revenue the factual context, including the position of the Revenue itself, is all important. Every ordinarily sophisicated taxpayer knows that the Revenue is a tax-collecting agency, not a tax-imposing authority. The taxpayers' only legitimate expectation is, prima facie, that he will be taxed according to statute, not concession or a wrong view of the law (see *R. v. Attorney-General, ex p. Imperial Chemical Industries plc* (1986) 60 T.C. 1, 64 *per* Lord Oliver). Such taxpayers would appreciate, if they could not so pithily express, the truth of the aphorism of "One should be taxed by law, and not be untaxed by concession". See *Vestey v. Inland Revenue Commissioners, per* Walton J. [1979] Ch. 177, 197. No doubt a statement formally published by the Revenue to the world might safely be regarded as binding, subject to its terms, in any case falling clearly within them. But where the approach to the Revenue is of a less formal nature a more detailed inquiry is, in my view, necessary. If it is to be successfully said that as a result of such an approach the Revenue has agreed to forgo, or has represented that it will forgo, tax which might arguably be payable on a proper construction of the relevant legislation it would in my judgment, be ordinarily necessary for the taxpayer to show that certain condi- tions had been fulfilled. I say "ordinarily" to allow for the exceptional case where different rules might be appopriate, but the necessity in my view exists here. First, it is necessary that the taxpayer should have put all his cards face upwards on the table. This means that he must give full details of the specific transaction on which he seeks the Revenue's ruling, unless it is the same as an earlier transaction on which a ruling has already been given. It means that he must indicate to the Revenue the ruling sought. It is one thing to ask an official of the Revenue whether he shares the tax- payer's view of a legislative provision, quite another to ask whether the Revenue will forgo any claim to tax on any other basis. It means that the taxpayer must make plain that a fully considered ruling is sought. It means, I think, that the taxpayer should indicate the use he intends to make of any ruling given. This is not because the

Revenue would wish to favour one class of taxpayers at the expense of another but because knowledge that a ruling is to be publicised in a large and important market could affect the person by whom and the level at which a problem is considered and, indeed, whether it is appropriate to give a ruling at all. Second, it is necessary that the ruling or statement relied on should be clear, unambiguous and devoid of relevant qualification.

In so stating these requirements I do not, I hope, diminish or emasculate the valuable developing doctrine of legitimate expectation. If a public authority so conducts itself as to create a legitimate expectation that a certain course will be followed it would often be unfair if the authority were permitted to follow a different course to the detriment of one who entertained the expectation, particularly if he acted on it. If in private law a body would be in breach of contract in so acting or estopped from so acting a public authority should generally be in no better position. The doctrine of legitimate expectation is rooted in fairness. But fairness is not a one-way street. It imports the notion of equitableness, of fair and open dealing, to which the authority is as much entitled as the citizen. The Revenue's discretion, while it exists, is limited. Fairness requires that its exercise should be on a basis of full disclosure. Counsel for the applicants accepted that it would not be reasonable for a representee to rely on an unclear or equivocal representation. Nor, I think, on facts such as the present, would it be fair to hold the Revenue bound by anything less than a clear, unambiguous and unqualified representation".

On the facts, expressions of view that the index-linked element payable on the redemption of a certain kind of security would be taxed only as capital gains and not income were held to be tentative rather than precise and unambiguous representations expressing a concluded view. The Revenue accepted that they were bound by some specific assurances concerning particular issues of this kind of security, but there had been no general assurance. A number of the statements had been given wider circulation by their recipients than the Revenue had anticipated. It was common practice for taxpayers and their advisers to seek comfort from discussions with Revenue officials concerning tax issues. Bingham L.J. noted (at 1570) that:

"they faced a familiar problem: while any favourable expression of opinion by the Revenue was of value, any request for a commitment by the Revenue in more general or explicit terms risked a blank refusal, which would be unhelpful".

Clearly, therefore, if the court had set less stringent conditions for a legitimate expectation to arise, then the Revenue would have had to become less helpful in giving preliminary indications of view. See further A.R. Mowbray, (1990) 106 L.Q.R. 568; S. Tidball, [1991] B.T.R. 48 and W. Hinds, [1991] B.T.R. 191. This may be compared with the decision in *R. (on the application of Greenwich Property Ltd) v Customs and Excise Commissioners* [2001] EWHC Admin 230; [2001] S.T.C. 618, where matters had reached the later stage of a formal concession, on which the applicant was held to have a legitimate expectation of being able to rely; the issue here turned on its proper interpretation.

Representations that may give rise to a legitimate expectations may arise in a variety of ways, including documents published containing criteria for the exercise of particular powers and correspondence with individuals. However, a legitimate expectation cannot be based purely on what is said in Parliament as that would be to infringe the Bill of Rights 1689 (*per* Laws L.J. in *Thoburn v Sunderland CC* [2002] EWHC Admin 195; [2003] Q.B. 151, at [76]).

(b) That a legitimate expectation may arise from *conduct* and not merely a *representation* was confirmed by the Court of Appeal in *R. v IRC Ex p. Unilever Plc* [1996] S.T.C. 681. Here, tax computations by the applicants had been accepted by the Revenue notwithstanding that relief in respect of trading losses was not expressly sought; such an express claim was required by s.393 of the Income and Corporation Taxes Act 1988 as the computations were submitted more than two years after the accounting period to which they related. The Court of Appeal held that on these "unique facts" the Revenue's actions in rejecting the claims in reliance on the two-year time-limit, without clear and general advance notice, were so unfair as to amount to an abuse of power. The old arrangement had fully met the need of both the Revenue and the applicants and enforcement of the two-year rule was demonstrably pointless. (The Revenue's actions were also held to be *Wednesbury* unreasonable or irrational, Simon Brown L.J. (inconsistently with the subsequent conclusion in *Coughlan*) regarding the *MFK* category of legitimate expectation as essentially but a head of *Wednesbury* unreasonableness" (p.695)).

(c) Other cases turn not on the content of a representation or of conduct, but on whether a person making a representation has actual or ostensible authority to make it on behalf of the public authority concerned. For example, in *South Buckinghamshire DC v Flanagan* [2002] EWCA Civ 690; [2002] 1 W.L.R. 2601, it was held that a solicitor appearing on behalf of a local authority in criminal proceedings for breach of enforcement notices had authority to withdraw the prosecution but had no actual or ostensible authority to withdraw the underlying notices. In *R. (on the application of Bloggs 61) v Secretary of State for the Home Department* [2002] EWCA Civ 686; [2003] 1 W.L.R. 2724, it was held that the police could not bind the prison service to treat the claimant, an informant, as a protected witness while in prison in the absence of actual or ostensible authority to do so. Even if a public authority holds out a person as having authority sufficient to establish ostensible authority as a matter of the private law of estoppel, that may not necessarily be sufficient for the establishment of a legitimate expectation (see Auld L.J. in *Bloggs 61* at [39]; his Lordship seems to state here that ostensible authority can never give rise to a legitimate expectation but it is submitted that this overstates the position and is inconsistent with the approach of Keene L.J. in *Flanagan*, above, at [18], and cited with apparent approval by Auld L.J. in *Bloggs 61* at [41]). A similar point could presumably arise as to whether the *conduct* of an officer could be attributed to his or her authority. A variant of the ostensible authority point is that a legitimate expectation cannot be founded on the pre-election statement of prominent opposition politicians whose party wins the ensuing general election; at the time the statements are made they are not made on behalf of a public authority (*per* Peter Gibson L.J. in *R. v Secretary of State for Education and Employment Ex p. Begbie* [2000] 1 W.L.R. 1115 at 1125).

(d) Apart from the matters considered in (a) to (c) above, there are other factors which may be held to mean that even unambiguous representations or conduct will not give rise to a *legitimate* expectation. Given that an opposition party will not know all the ramifications of election promises until it achieves office, the consequences of failure to keep them "should be political and not legal" (per Peter Gibson L.J. in *Begbie* at 1126). In most of the cases where a substantive legitimate expectation is found to have arisen, the matter is essentially one between the individual and the public body. It is much less likely that such an expectation will be established in cases where the interests of third parties or the public are also involved. This point was made by Laws L.J. in *Begbie* (above, p.611) and by the Court of Appeal in *Henry Boot Homes Ltd v Bassetlaw DC* [2002] EWCA Civ 983; [2003] P. & C.R. 372. Here the court held that developers could not base a legitimate expectation on the opinion of the local planning authority that works on a site carried out in breach of condition constituted the lawful commencement of development. The opinion was wrong in law and the developers, a substantial house-building company, had access to legal advice had it wished to take it. Any expectation was not legitimate and there was no abuse of power. Keene L.J. said (at [24]):

"It is possible that circumstances might arise where it was clear that there was no third party or public interest in the matter and a court might take the view that a legitimate expectation could then arise from the local planning authority's conduct or representations. But . . . one suspects that such cases will be very rare. The situation which normally arises in a planning context is very different from that which maintains in cases such as Unilever, where the issue is essentially one as between the individual and the public body, in that case the Inland Revenue. Legitimate expectation has a far greater role to play in such circumstances".

6. *Ultra vires representations.* Overall,

"if the public body has done nothing and said nothing which can legitimately have generated the expectation that is advanced to the court, the case ends there"

(*per* Schiemann L.J. in *R. (on the application of Bibi) v Newham LBC* [2002] 1 W.L.R. 237 at [21]). Furthermore, "it seems likely that a representation made without lawful power will be in this class" (*ibid.*).

This last point was confirmed by the Court of Appeal in *R. v Department of Education and Employment Ex p. Begbie* [2000] 1 W.L.R. 1116, where it was held that there could be no legitimate expectation that the applicant's education at an independent school would continue to be funded to the end of the secondary stage, following the ending of the Conservative Government's Assisted Places Scheme by the incoming Labour Government in 1997. The applicant relied on various statements by ministers in newspapers and correspondence which were held to be insufficiently clear and unambiguous to cover the applicant's position; and on one statement which did clearly so apply, but which was made by mistake and the mistake corrected without being relied upon by the applicant to her detriment. The central reason why effect could not have been given to any such legitimate expectation was, however, that that would have been inconsistent with the express arrangements under the Education Act 1997, which provided for continued funding on a transitional basis for a number of categories of pupils currently within the APS, but not the applicant's.

The point was also considered by the Court of Appeal in *Rowland v Environment Agency* [2003] EWCA Civ 1885; [2004] 3 W.L.R. 249. Here, the claimant and her late husband purchased property including a stretch of the River Thames (Hedsor Water) in the belief that there were no public rights of navigation over that stretch. The same belief was shared by successive navigation authorities for the Thames, predecessors of the Environment Agency (EA), who had acted on that footing for at least 80 years. In 2001, the EA took the (legally correct) view that public rights of navigation had never been extinguished. The court held (1) that there was the necessary representation or practice to found a legitimate expectation; but (2) that EA had conducted a balancing exercise and its conclusion that it should assert PRNs was not so unfair as to amount to an abuse of power. It was common ground that there could only be a legitimate expectation founded on a *lawful* representation or practice and so her claim to a legitimate expectation that she would continue to be entitled to enjoy Hedsor Water as private was bound to fail as a matter of English domestic law (see Peter Gibson L.J. at [73], [79] and [80]). The expectation as to the privacy of Hedsor Water was a "possession" protected by the First Protocol, Art.1 ECHR, even though it arose from an act unlawful under domestic law (see *Pine Valley Developments Ltd v Ireland* (1991) 14 E.H.R.R. 319 and *Stretch v UK* (2003) 38 E.H.R.R. 196). However, the decision to interfere with that possession was lawful, in that it was in accordance with English law, pursued the legitimate aim of safeguarding the legal rights of the public over Hedsor Water and was proportionate (*ibid.* at [92]–[96]). The only effect given to the legitimate expectation was a declaration that the EA was obliged to take into account in the exercise of its statutory functions the common assumption prior to November 2000 of the Rowlands and the EA to the effect that Hedsor Water was private (see Mance L.J. at [153]–[155], [163]). May L.J. agreed, but argued *obiter* that the position in orthodox English domestic law that "does not allow the individual to retain the benefit which is the subject of the legitimate expectation, however strong, if creating or maintaining that benefit is beyond the power of the public body" (at [102])

was unjust. There was much to be said for a balancing approach proposed by Craig (citing Craig's *Administrative Law* (4th ed., 1999), pp.635–650 and 907; see now *Craig*, pp.671–680). Under this approach, the courts would balance the injustice to the individual against the public interest even in cases based on *ultra vires* representations. However, it was not open to the Court of Appeal to implement this approach:

"At this level, it would amount to legislation. I say nothing about whether the House of Lords could or would consider implementing it" (at [120]).

This last point is, with respect, a little obscure. The view could be taken that the introduction of such a principle would be so radical a step as to require legislation rather than introduction by case law at any level. If that is not the case then only binding precedent should properly be taken inhibiting the Court of Appeal from developing the law as it thinks appropriate. Furthermore, there are other examples of judicial modifications to the *ultra vires* doctrine, including the points that non-compliance with statutory procedural requirements does not necessarily cause the decision-maker to act *ultra vires* (see pp.635–651), and that the court retains a discretion whether to grant a remedy (pp.1010–1022).

7. *Treaties not incorporated into English law*. It has been said, *obiter*, that the ratification of a treaty by the United Kingdom, not incorporated into English law, can give rise to a legitimate expectation that the government will act in accordance with its terms (Lord Woolf M.R. and Hobhouse L.J. in *R. v Secretary of State for the Home Department Ex p. Ahmed* [1998] I.N.L.R. 570 at 583–584, 591–592). This was applied by the Divisional Court in *R. v Uxbridge Magistrates' Court Ex p. Adimi* [2001] Q.B. 667 in respect of Art.31 of the Refugee Convention 1951, but sits uneasily with the established proposition that unincorporated treaties cannot confer rights in domestic law (see Lord Oliver of Aylmerton in *J.H. Rayner (Mincing Lane) Ltd v Department of Trade and Industry* [1990] 2 A.C. 418 at 500). The principle cannot apply where Parliament chooses to enact legislation in different terms to those of the treaty (*R. (on the application of Pepushi) v Crown Prosecution Service* [2004] EWHC 798 (referring to s.31 of the Immigration and Asylum Act 1999, which is narrower in scope than Art.31 of the 1951 Convention); or where the Secretary of State clearly adopts a policy by executive act which is different in terms from the treaty or the terms of the treaty are not intended to confer rights or entitlements to individuals (*per* Lord Phillips M.R. in *R. (on the application of Zeqiri) v Secretary of State for the Home Department* [2002] Imm. A.R. 42 at [49]; *per* Latham L.J. in *R. (on the application of Lika) v Secretary of State for the Home Department* [2002] EWCA Civ 1855 at [26]). In any event the principle stated in *Ahmed* has itself been strongly criticised as inconsistent with decisions to the contrary of the Court of Appeal in *Chundawadra v Immigration Appeal Tribunal* [1988] Imm. A.R. 161 (ECHR) and *Behluli v Secretary of State for the Home Department* [1998] Imm. A.R. 407 (the Dublin Convention 1997) (see Laws L.J. in *R. (on the application of European Roma Rights Centre) v Immigration Officer, Prague Airport* [2003] EWCA Civ 666; [2004] Q.B. 811 at [95]–[101]; *cf.* Simon Brown L.J. at [51]). This point did not arise on appeal: [2004] UKHL 55; [2005] 2 W.L.R. 1.

8. *Is the authority acting unlawfully in relation to the commitment?* The starting point here is that an authority is very unlikely to be held to have acted unlawfully simply by deciding to change its policy or to introduce an exception to it. It is well established that "estoppel cannot be allowed to hinder the formation of government policy" (*per* Lawton L.J. in *Laker Airways Ltd v Department of Trade* [1977] Q.B. 643 at 728). Accordingly, the incoming Labour Government could not be prevented by estoppel from reversing its predecessor's policy and deciding that only one UK airline should be licensed for any given long-haul route, notwithstanding that this

would involve ending Laker Airways' cheap passenger service to New York that they had been encouraged by the previous Conservative Government to develop. (Nevertheless, the court held that the means chosen to implement this change of policy were unlawful (see above, p.401)). Similarly, there can be no legitimate expectation that would prevent a change of policy altogether. In *Findlay, Re* [1985] A.C. 318, the Secretary of State for the Home Department announced changes in parole policy that meant that a certain life sentence prisoners would now be able to expect release much later than under the previous policy. Lord Scarman commented (at 338):

"The doctrine of legitimate expectation has an important place in the developing law of judicial review. It is however, not necessary to explore the doctrine in this case, it is enough merely to note that a legitimate expectation can provide a sufficient interest to enable one who cannot point to the existence of a substantive right to obtain the leave of the court to apply for judicial review. These two appellants obtained leave. But their submission goes further. It is said that the refusal to except them from the new policy was an unlawful act on the part of the Secretary of State in that his decision frustrated their expectation. But what was their legitimate expectation? Given the substance and purpose of the legislative provisions governing parole, the most that a convicted prisoner can legitimately expect is that his case will be examined individually in the light of whatever policy the Secretary of State sees fit to adopt provided always that the adopted policy is a lawful exercise of the discretion conferred upon him by the statute. Any other view would entail the conclusion that the unfettered discretion conferred by the statute upon the minister can in some cases be restricted so as to hamper, or even prevent, changes of policy. Bearing in mind the complexity of the issues which the Secretary of State has to consider and the importance of the public interest in the administration of parole I cannot think that Parliament intended the discretion to be restricted in this way".

Again, it will be difficult to establish a legitimate expectation that would prevent a minister making any exception to an existing policy. In *R. (on the application of Mullen) v Secretary of State for the Home Department* [2003] Q.B. 993, the Divisional Court rejected an argument that the Home Secretary could never make any exception to his general policy concerning the payment of *ex gratia* compensation to persons whose convictions are quashed (see Simon Brown L.J. at [31]–[32]).

Conversely, it will be straightforward to hold that an authority has acted unlawfully where the evidence is that it has not even taken an established legitimate expectation into account (see *R. v Camden LBC Ex p. Bodimeade* [2001] EWHC Admin 271 (promise of "home for life" to residents of old peoples' home not considered in coming to decision to close the home; *R. (on the application of Bibi) v Newham LBC*, below, n.9).

This leaves cases where the question is whether it was irrational (*Coughlan* category 1) or unfair (*Coughlan* category 3) for the authority to override the legitimate expectation. The line between the two categories is not hard and fast (see above, n.2). Indeed, the courts do not always decide or need to decide which category applies; for example, if a decision is not unfair applying the more stringent category 3 approach then it cannot be found to be irrational under the category 1 approach.

Thus in *Mullen*, the Home Secretary's decision not to pay *ex gratia* compensation to a person whose conviction for conspiracy to cause explosions was quashed on the ground that the method by which he was returned to the United Kingdom from abroad was an abuse of power, was held to be neither irrational nor unfair (see Simon Brown L.J. at [33]–[36], approved by Lord Steyn in the House of Lords, [2004] UKHL 18; [2004] 1 W.L.R. 1140 at [58]–[62] (referring only to irrationality)).

It should be remembered that in cases where there can be no *substantive* legitimate expectation that a policy will not be changed, there can still commonly be room for a *procedural* legitimate expectation as to the manner in which the change is introduced, such as a right to notice to make representations against the change or in favour of an exception to the new policy. For example, in *R. (on the application of Nurse*

Prescribers Ltd v Secretary of State for Health [2004] EWHC 403, Mitting J. held (1) that the DH had not promised the claimant that they would never change their policy that limited nurse prescribers to prescribing generic rather than branded products (salines); but (2) that it should have notified him of the change given that it was aware that he planned to supply such generic products and was likely to incur some expense. However, no remedy was granted.

9. Cases since *Coughlan* in which it has been found that it has been *Wednesbury* irrational or unreasonable (*Coughlan* category 1) or unfair (*Coughlan* category 3) to defeat a substantive legitimate expectation have been few and far between. One that comes near is the decision of Turner J in *R. (on the application of Bibi) v Newham LBC,* unreported, July 28, 2000. His Lordship found that a longstanding express promise to provide accommodation with security of tenure gave rise to a legitimate expectation. This was so notwithstanding that it was based on the council's mistaken belief that they were under a legal *duty* to do so, given that they had *power* to provide such accommodation. He granted a declaration that the council was bound to treat their duties originally owed to the applicants as homeless persons as not discharged until they were provided with suitable accommodation on a secure tenancy. As Schiemann L.J. noted in the Court of Appeal ([2002] 1 W.L.R. 237 at [61]),

> "it seems implicit in his declaration that there can not be factors which inhibit fulfilment of the legitimate expectations, even where the authority has never so concluded".

This was going too far. The Court of Appeal agreed that a legitimate expectation had arisen. However, the council had not acknowledged that their promises were a relevant consideration and this was itself an error of law (at [49]). Accordingly the court did not need to reach the question whether a final decision to go back on the promise (for example in the light of the position of other applicants for accommodation) would be substantively unfair, on the lines of the decision in *Coughlan.* The court instead granted a declaration that the council was under a duty to consider the applicants' application for suitable housing on the basis that they had a legitimate expectation that they would be provided with suitable accommodation on a secure tenancy. In subsequent litigation, the High Court held that the council's statutory duty to offer suitable accommodation had been discharged by the allocation of temporary accommodation in 1991. (*R. (on the application of Bibi) v Newham LBC* [2003] EWHC 1860). When that litigation was commenced, it was expected that major issues would be (1) whether the council's allocation scheme could properly have given effect to Mrs Bibi's legitimate expectation, but this was dropped following the adoption of a revised scheme; and (2) whether a refusal of a tenancy (apparently a secure tenancy) in 1998 was unreasonable, but the council changed its position on this point. Had these remained live issues, council was prepared to argue that the legitimate expectation had necessarily been outweighed by policy considerations (thus supporting the interpretation that *Bibi* does fall into *Coughlan's* category 3).

Compare *Rowland v Environment Agency* [2003] EWCA Civ 1885, [2004] 3 W.L.R. 249, discussed in n.6. A further point illustrated by this decision is that the question is not simply whether a legitimate expectation exists, but also what is its nature, scope and strength (see Mance L.J. at [151]–[162], who concluded that the expectation here only justified the limited declaration granted in favour of the claimants (see n.6)).

10. *Detrimental reliance.* This is a normal but not a necessary requirement if the authority is to be held to have acted unlawfully. This was considered by the Court of Appeal in *Bibi* (above). Schiemann L.J. said:

> "28. As indicated in *R v Secretary of State for Education and Employment, ex parte Begbie* [2000] 1 W.L.R. 1115 reliance, though potentially relevant in most cases, is not essential. In that case a letter sent to the parents of one child affected

by legislative and policy change concerning assisted school places came to the knowledge of another child's parent, who relied on it in judicial review proceedings. Peter Gibson L.J., giving the leading judgment, said at pages 1123–1124:

'Mr. Beloff submits . . . (v) it is not necessary for a person to have changed his position as a result of such representations for an obligation to fulfil a legitimate expectation to subsist; the principle of good administration prima facie requires adherence by public authorities to their promises. He cites authority in support of all these submissions and for my part I am prepared to accept them as correct, so far as they go. I would however add a few words by way of comment on his fifth proposition, as in my judgment it would be wrong to understate the significance of reliance in this area of the law. It is very much the exception, rather than the rule, that detrimental reliance will not be present when the court finds unfairness in the defeating of a legitimate expectation.'

29. In the light of this, we respectfully adopt what Professor Craig has proposed in this regard in *Craig, Administrative Law*, 4th ed, at p.619:

'Detrimental reliance will normally be required in order for the claimant to show that it would be unlawful to go back on a representation. This is in accord with the policy, since if the individual has suffered no hardship there is no reason based on legal certainty to hold the agency to its representation. It should not, however, be necessary to show any monetary loss, or anything equivalent thereto.'

30. But he gives the following instance of a case where reliance is not essential:

'Where an agency seeks to depart from an established policy in relation to a particular person detrimental reliance should not be required. Consistency of treatment and equality are at stake in such cases, and these values should be protected irrespective of whether there has been any reliance as such.'

31. In our judgment the significance of reliance and of consequent detriment is factual, not legal. In *Begbie's* case both aspects were in the event critical: there had been no true reliance on the misrepresentation of policy and therefore no detriment suffered specifically in consequence of it. In a strong case, no doubt, there will be both reliance and detriment; but it does not follow that reliance (that is, credence) without measurable detriment cannot render it unfair to thwart a legitimate expectation".

As to the submission that neither applicant had changed his or her position on the strength of the expectation, Schiemann L.J. commented:

"52. It was submitted that neither applicant has changed his or her position on the strength of the expectation and therefore no weight ought to be given to the fact that the promises have not been fulfilled. We have already said that this factor does not rank as a legal inhibition on giving effect to the legitimate expectation. But what weight ought to be given to the lack of change of position?
53. The fact that someone has not changed his position after a promise has been made to him does not mean that he has not relied on the promise. An actor in a play where another actor points a gun at him may refrain from changing his position just because he has been given a promise that the gun only contains blanks.
54. A refugee such as Mr Al-Nashed [one of the applicants] might, had he been told the true situation, have gone to one of the bodies which assist refugees for advice as to where in England and Wales he might have better prospects; or have tried to find the deposit on an assured tenancy, with the possibility thereafter of housing benefit to help with the rent.
55. The present case is one of reliance without concrete detriment. We use this phrase because there is moral detriment, which should not be dismissed lightly, in the prolonged disappointment which has ensued; and potential detriment in the

deflection of the possibility, for a refugee family, of seeking at the start to settle some-where in the United Kingdom where secure housing was less hard to come by. In our view these things matter in public law, even though they might not found an estoppel or actionable misrepresentation in private law, because they go to fairness and through fairness to possible abuse of power. To disregard the legitimate expec-tation because no concrete detriment can be shown would be to place the weakest in society at a particular disadvantage. It would mean that those who have a choice and the means to exercise it in reliance on some official practice or promise would gain a legal toehold inaccessible to those who, lacking any means of escape, are com-pelled simply to place their trust in what has been represented to them".

It should, however, be noted that these comments were made in the context of case where the court ultimately decided that the matter should be reconsidered by the local authority.

While reliance is therefore not necessary in all cases, it may on a particular set of facts make the crucial difference justifying a finding that there has been an abuse of power (see Laws L.J., *obiter*, in *Begbie* at 1131).

11. *Compensation.* In many cases the just outcome where an individual's legitimate expectation is overridden by a change of policy in the public interest is an award of compensation. However, English law does not easily provide such a remedy. There may in principle be liability under *Hedley Byrne* where there is an assumption of responsi-bility financial loss is caused by a negligent misstatement or a negligent failure to speak where there is a duty to take care to do so; but this is difficult to establish. There is no general tort of causing financial loss through maladministation (see p.1068), although the Ombudsman may recommend payments in such cases (see p.204). In *R. (on the application of Nurse Prescribers Ltd) v Secretary of State for Health* [2004] EWHC 403 (n.8, above), the claimant entered a long-term contract for the supply of saline solution as a generic product on the assumption that the DH would not change its policy on restricting nurse prescribers to generic products. He sought, *inter alia*, an order for monetary compensation or a declaration that his legitimate expectation had been disappointed and an invitation to the DH to consider making compensation to the claimant. Mitting J. found that there was a procedural legitimate expectation, but held (1) that there was no obligation to reimburse risk capital expended as the result of the claimant's commercial decision before the legitimate expectation arose. No claim was justified in respect of the order given that the claimant had not told the DH of his intention to enter such a commitment. There was overall no reliable or just measure of compensation the department might properly consider itself obliged to pay. The direct claim for compensation was in any event not available directly in judicial review proceedings (see Mitting J. at [80]–[82]). (It should be noted that a claim under *Hedley Byrne*, in the unlikely event of its being available, could properly be joined to a claim for judicial review.)

If an authority seeks to correct a mistake and offers compensation for any financial loss, this may in any event make the court less inclined to find that there has been an abuse of power (*cf.* Latham J. in *R. v Birmingham City Council Ex p. L* [2000] Ed.C.R. 484 at 490).

12. The legitimate expectation concept, in both its procedural and substantive aspects, has given rise to a considerable literature. See G. Ganz, "Legitimate Expectation: A Confusion of Concepts" in *Public Law and Politics* (Harlow ed., 1986), Ch.8; R. Baldwin and D. Horne, "Expectations in a Joyless Landscape" (1986) 4 M.L.R. 685; P. Elias, "Legitimate Expectation and Judicial Review" in *New Directions in Judicial Review* (Jowell and Oliver ed., 1988), pp.37–50; C.F. Forsyth, "The Provenance and Protection of Legitimate Expectations" [1988] C.L.J. 238; P.P. Craig, "Legitimate Expectations: A Conceptual Analysis" (1992) 108 L.Q.R. 79 and "Substantive Legitimate Expectations in Domestic and Community Law" [1996] C.L.J. 289; P.P. Craig and S. Schonberg, "Substantive legitimate expectations after *Coughlan*" [2000] P.L. 684; S. Schonberg, *Legitimate Expectations in Administrative Law* (2000);

P. Sales and K. Steyn, "Legitimate Expectations in English Public Law: An Analysis" [2004] P.L. 564. Some commentators have been sceptical of the soundness of the substantive dimension to the concept, arguing that it can lead to conflict with the rule against the fettering of discretion (*e.g.* Ganz); others have welcomed the development (*e.g.* Forsyth, Craig).

(E) PROPORTIONALITY

Proportionality is well established as a ground of challenge in the jurisprudence of civil law countries, and has thereby become a regularly used tool of legal reasoning in the Court of Justice of the European Communities and the European Court of Human Rights. The principle has been summarised as consisting of

> "three sub-principles, namely (1) suitability: an administrative or legal power must be exercised in a way which is suitable to achieve the purpose intended and for which the power was conferred; (2) *necessity*: the exercise of the power must be necessary to achieve the relevant purpose; and (3) *proportionality in the narrower sense*: the exercise of the power must not impose burdens or cause harm to other legitimate interests which are disproportionate to the importance of the object to be achieved".

(Lord Hoffmann in *The Principle of Proportionality in the Laws of Europe* (Ellis ed., 1999), p.107, citing essays in the same volume by F.G. Jacobs and W. Van Gerven). It should be noted, however, that in some contexts, the Court of Justice adopts two-stage formulation under which the issues of necessity and proportionality are not regarded as distinct. The conventional view is that this ground of challenge provides a more intrusive criterion for review than *Wednesbury* unreasonableness (see, *e.g.* Laws J. in *First City Trading* (below, p.632) or irrationality and Lord Steyn in *Daly* (above, p.340)).

Lord Diplock in the *CCSU* case (below, p.690) treated it as distinct from irrationality and a principle that might in due course be adopted in English domestic law. In *Brind* (below), however, the House of Lords declined to take general step, as has the Court of Appeal subsequently. In the meantime it has become firmly established as a full part of English law in the particular context of EU law and the ECHR, by virtue of statutes that require the approaches of the ECJ and the ECtHR to be followed by English courts (European Communities Act 1972; Human Rights Act 1998). There are furthermore, cases where it is said that a decision quashed as disproportionate would probably not be quashed as *Wednesbury* unreasonable, as in *B v Secretary of State for the Home Department* [2000] Imm. A.R. 478, *per* Sedley L.J. at 486, where the Court of Appeal allowed an appeal against the IAT's decision (on appeal from the Home Secretary) that B, an Italian national, should be deported notwithstanding near a life-long residence in the United Kingdom, following convictions for child abuse. The decision was disproportionate under EC law in the absence of evidence of a propensity to reoffend.

The question whether the step declined in *Brind* should now be taken has generated much debate. It is increasingly clear that proportionality is nearer to the established grounds of challenge in English law than previously thought; some take the view that there are no real differences in terms of the outcomes of cases that flow from the way in which the competing tests are formulated. Note Lord Slynn's comment in the *International Trader's Ferry* case (above, p.552) ([1999] 2 A.C. 418 at 439):

> "In [*Brind*] the House treated *Wednesbury* reasonableness and proportionality as being different. So in some ways they are though the distinction between the two tests in practice is in any event much less than is sometimes suggested. The cautious way in which the European Court usually applies this test, recognising the importance of respecting the national authority's margin of appreciation, may mean

that whichever test is adopted, and even allowing for a difference in onus, the result is the same".

If this is right the balance of argument in favour of making the change becomes over-whelming (see further, below, pp.629–631).

R. v SECRETARY OF STATE FOR THE HOME DEPARTMENT
Ex p. BRIND

[1991] 1 A.C. 696; [1991] 2 W.L.R. 588; [1991] 1 All E.R. 721
(HOUSE OF LORDS)

In October 1988 the Home Secretary, exercising powers under the Broadcasting Act 1981 (in respect of independent broadcasting) and the BBC's licence and agreement (in respect of that body), issued a directive prohibiting the broadcasting of "words spoken" by any person representing or purporting to represent certain organisations. The organisations were those proscribed under the Northern Ireland (Emergency Provisions) Act 1978, the Prevention of Terrorism (Temporary Provisions) Act 1984, and Sinn Féin, Republican Sinn Féin and the Ulster Defence Association.

The powers under the 1981 Act and the licence/agreement authorised the Home Secretary to require the broadcasting authorities to "refrain from broadcasting any matter or classes of matter specified in the notice".

The applicants, who were journalists, sought judicial review of the Home Secretary's decision. They were unsuccessful in the Divisional Court and the Court of Appeal ([1990] 1 A.C. 700). On appeal to the House of Lords:

LORD BRIDGE OF HARWICH: My Lords, this appeal has been argued prima-rily on the basis that the power of the Secretary of State . . . to impose restric-tions . . . may only be lawfully exercised in accordance with art. 10 of the European Convention on Human Rights. . . . Any exercise by the Secretary of State of the power in question necessarily imposes some restriction on freedom of expression. The obligations of the United Kingdom, as a party to the con-vention, are to secure to every one within its jurisdiction the rights which the convention defines, including both the right to freedom of expression under art. 10 and the right under art. 13 to "an effective remedy before a national authority" for any violation of the other rights secured by the convention. It is accepted, of course, by the appellants that, like any other treaty obligations which have not been embodied in the law by statute, the convention is not part of the domestic law, that the courts accordingly have no power to enforce convention rights directly and that, if domestic legislation conflicts with the convention, the courts must nevertheless enforce it. But it is already well settled that, in construing any provision in domestic legislation which is ambiguous in the sense that it is capable of a meaning which either conforms to or conflicts with the convention, the courts will presume that Parliament intended to legislate in conformity with the convention, not in conflict with it. Hence, it is submitted, when a statute confers upon an administrative author-ity a discretion capable of being exercised in a way which infringes any basic human right protected by the convention, it may similarly be presumed that the legislative intention was that the discretion should be exercised within the limitations which the convention imposes. I confess that I found considerable persuasive force in this submission. But in the end I have been convinced that the logic of it is flawed. When confronted with a simple choice between two possible interpretations of some specific statutory provision, the presumption whereby the courts prefer that which avoids conflict between our domestic legislation and our international treaty obligations is a mere canon of construction which involves no importation of international law into the domestic field. But where Parliament has conferred on the executive an administrative discretion without indicating the precise limits within which it must be exercised, to presume that it must be exercised within convention limits would be to go far beyond the resolution of an ambiguity. It would be to impute to Parliament an intention not only that the executive should exercise the discretion in conformity with the convention, but also that the domestic courts should enforce that conformity by the importation into domestic administrative law of the text of the convention and the jurisprudence of the European Court of Human Rights in the interpretation and application of it. If such a presumption is to apply to the statutory discretion exercised by the Secretary of State . . . in the instant case, it must also apply to any other statutory discretion exercised by the executive which is capable of involving an infringement of convention rights. When Parliament has been content for so long to leave those who complain that their convention rights have been infringed to seek their remedy in Strasbourg, it would be surprising suddenly to find that the judiciary had, without Parliament's aid, the means to incorporate the convention into such an important area of domestic law and I cannot escape the conclusion that this would be a judicial usurpation of the legislative function.

But I do not accept that this conclusion means that the courts are powerless to prevent the exercise by the executive of administrative discretions, even when conferred, as in the instant case, in terms which are on their face unlimited, in a way which infringes fundamental human rights. Most of the rights spelled out in terms in the convention, including the right to freedom of expression, are less than absolute and must in some cases yield to the claims of competing public interests. Thus, art. 10(2) of the convention spells out and categorises the competing public interests by reference to which the right to freedom of expression may have to be curtailed. In exercising the power of judicial review we have neither the advantages nor the disadvantages of any comparable code to which we may refer or by which we are bound. But again, this surely does not mean that in deciding whether the Secretary of State, in the exercise of his discretion, could reasonably impose the restriction he has imposed on the broadcasting organisations, we are not perfectly entitled to start from the premise that any restriction of the right to freedom of expression requires to be justified and that nothing less than an important competing public interest will be sufficient to justify it. The primary judgment as to whether the particular competing public interest justifies the particular restriction imposed falls to be made by the Secretary of State to whom Parliament has entrusted the discretion. But we are entitled to exercise a secondary judgment by asking whether a reasonable Secretary of State, on the material before him, could reasonably make that primary judgment.

Applying these principles to the circumstances of the case. . . . I find it impossible to say that the Secretary of State exceeded the limits of his discretion. In any civilised and law-abiding society the defeat of the terrorist is a public interest of the first importance. That some restriction on the freedom of the terrorist and his supporters to propagate his cause may well be justified in support of that public interest is a proposition which I apprehend the appellants hardly dispute. Their real case is that they, in the exercise of their editorial judgment, may and must be trusted to ensure that the broadcasting media are not used in such a way as will afford any encouragement or support to terrorism and that any interference with that editorial judgment is necessarily an unjustifiable restriction on the right to freedom of expression. Accepting, as I do, their complete good faith, I nevertheless cannot accept this proposition. The Secretary of State, for the reasons he made so clear in Parliament, decided that it was necessary to deny to the terrorist and his supporters the opportunity to speak directly to the public through the most influential of all the media of communication and that this justified some interference with editorial freedom. I do not see how this judgment can be categorised as unreasonable. What is perhaps surprising is that the restriction imposed is of such limited scope. There is no restriction at all on the matter which may be broadcast, only on the manner of its presentation. The viewer may see the terrorist's face and hear his words provided only that they are not spoken in his own voice. I well understand the broadcast journalist's complaint that to put him to the trouble of dubbing the voice of the speaker he has interviewed before the television camera is an irritant which the difference in effect between the speaker's voice and the actor's voice hardly justifies. I well understand the political complaint that the restriction may be counter-productive in the sense that the adverse criticism it provokes outweighs any benefit it achieves. But these complaints fall very far short of demonstrating that a reasonable Secretary of State could not reasonably conclude that the restriction was justified by the important public interest of combating terrorism. I should add that I do not see how reliance on the doctrine of "proportionality" can here advance the appellants' case. But I agree with what my noble and learned friend, Lord Roskill, says in his speech about the possible future development of the law in that respect.

I would dismiss the appeal.

LORD TEMPLEMAN: . . . The English courts must, in conformity with the *Wednesbury* principles . . . consider whether the Home Secretary has taken into account all relevant matters and has ignored irrelevant matters. These conditions are satisfied by the evidence in this case, including evidence by the Home Secretary that he took the convention into account. If these conditions are satisfied, then it is said on *Wednesbury* principles the court can only interfere by way of judicial review if the decision of the Home Secretary is "irrational" or "perverse".

The subject-matter and date of the *Wednesbury* principles cannot in my opinion make it either necessary or appropriate for the courts to judge the validity of an interference with human rights by asking themselves whether the Home Secretary has acted irrationally or perversely. It seems to me that the courts cannot escape from asking themselves only whether a reasonable Secretary of State, on the material before him, could reasonably conclude that the interference with freedom of expression which he determined to impose was justifiable. In terms of the convention, as construed by the European Court of Human Rights, the interference with freedom of expression must be necessary and proportionate to the damage which the restriction is designed to prevent.

My Lords, applying these principles I do not consider that the court can conclude that the Home Secretary has abused or exceeded his powers. The broadcasting authorities and journalists are naturally resentful of any limitation on their right to present a programme in such manner as they think fit. But the interference with freedom of expression is minimal and the reasons given by the Home Secretary are compelling.

I, too, would dismiss this appeal.

LORD ACKNER: . . . The Secretary of State's reasons for taking the action complained of are set out in the Hansard Reports of those debates and were before your Lordships. The four matters which influenced the Secretary of State were . . . (1) offence had been caused to viewers and listeners by the appearance of the apologists for terrorism, particularly after a terrorist outrage; (2) such appearances had afforded terrorists undeserved publicity which was contrary to the public interest; (3) these appearances had tended to increase the standing of terrorist organisations and to create a false impression that support for terrorism is itself a legitimate political opinion; (4) broadcast statements were intended to have, and did in some cases have, the effect of intimidating some of those at whom they were directed.

The challenge

I now turn to the bases upon which it is contended that the Secretary of State exceeded his statutory powers.

(1) . . .

(2) The directives were unlawful on "*Wednesbury*" grounds save only in one respect, namely the European Convention for the Protection of Human Rights and Fundamental Freedoms . . . which is the subject-matter of a later heading, it is not suggested that the minister failed to call his attention to matters which he was bound to consider, nor that he included in his considerations matters which were irrelevant. In neither of those senses can it be said that the minister acted unreasonably. The failure to mount such a challenge in this appeal is important. In a field which concerns a fundamental human right, namely that of free speech, close scrutiny must be given to the reasons provided as justification for interference with that right. Your Lordships' attention was drawn to *R. v. Secretary of State for Transport, ex p. de Rothschild* [1989] 1 All E.R. 933, a case which concerned compulsory purchase and therefore involved, albeit somewhat indirectly, another fundamental human right—the peaceful enjoyment of one's possessions: see art. 1 of the First Protocol to the Convention. In that case Slade L.J. said, at 939:

"Given the obvious importance and value to land owners of their property rights, the abrogation of those rights in the exercise of his discretionary power to confirm a compulsory purchase order would, in the absence of what he perceived to be a sufficient justification on the merits, be a course which surely no reasonable Secretary of State would take."

Slade L.J. was in no sense increasing the severity of the *Wednesbury* test. . . . He was applying that part of it which requires the decision-maker to call his attention to matters that he is obliged to consider. He was emphasising the Secretary of State's obligation to identify the factors which had motivated his decision so as to ensure that he had overlooked none which a reasonable Secretary of State should have considered.

There remains however the potential criticism under the *Wednesbury* grounds . . . that the conclusion was "so unreasonable that no reasonable authority could ever have come to it". This standard of unreasonableness, often referred to as "the irrationality test", has been criticised as being too high. But it has to be expressed in terms that confine the jurisdiction exercised by the judiciary to a supervisory, as opposed to an appellate, jurisdiction. Where Parliament has given to a minister or other person or body a discretion, the court's jurisdiction is limited, in the absence of a statutory right of appeal, to the supervision of the exercise of that discretionary power, so as to ensure that it has been exercised lawfully. It would be a wrongful usurpation of power by the judiciary to substitute its view, the judicial view, on the merits and on that basis to quash the decision. If no reasonable minister properly directing himself would have reached the impugned decision, the minister has exceeded his powers and thus acted unlawfully and the court, in the exercise of its super-visory role, will quash that decision. Such a decision is correctly, though unat-tractively, described as a "perverse" decision. To seek the court's intervention on the basis that the correct or objectively reasonable decision is other than the decision which the minister has made, is to invite the court to adjudicate as if Parliament had provided a right of appeal against the decision, that is to invite an abuse of power by the judiciary.

So far as the facts of this case are concerned it is only necessary to read the speeches in the Houses of Parliament, . . . to reach the conclusion, that whether the Secretary of State was right or wrong to decide to issue the directives, there was clearly material which would justify a reasonable minister making the same decision. In the words of Lord Diplock in *Secretary of State for Education and Science v. Tameside Metropolitan Borough* [1977] A.C. 1014, 1064:

"The very concept of administrative discretion involves a right to choose between more than one possible course of action on which there is room for reasonable people to hold differing opinions as to which is to be preferred."

. . . I entirely agree with McCowan L.J. [in the Court of Appeal] when he said that he found it quite impossible to hold that the Secretary of State's political judgment that the appearance of terrorists on programmes increases their standing and lends them political legitimacy is one that no reasonable Home Secretary could hold. . . .

Mr Lester has contended that in issuing these directives the Secretary of State has used a sledgehammer to crack a nut. Of course that is a picturesque way of describing the *Wednesbury* "irrational" test. The Secretary of State has in my judgment used no sledgehammer. Quite the contrary is the case.

I agree with Lord Donaldson M.R. who, when commenting on how limited the restrictions were, said in his judgment . . .:

"They have no application in the circumstances mentioned in para.3 (pro-ceedings in the United Kingdom Parliament and elections) and, by allowing reported speech either verbatim or in paraphrase, in effect put those affected in no worse a position than they would be if they had access to newspaper publicity with a circulation equal to the listening and viewing audiences of the programmes concerned. Furthermore, on the applicants' own evidence, if the directives had been in force during the previous 12 months, the effect would have been minimal in terms of air time. Thus, [ITN] say that 8 minutes 20 seconds (including repeats) out of 1,200 hours, or 0.01%, of air time would have been affected. Furthermore, it would not have been necessary to omit these items. They could have been recast into a form which complied with the directives."

Thus the extent of the interference with the right to freedom of speech is a very modest one. . ..

(3)*The minister failed to have proper regard to the European Convention for the Protection of Human Rights and Fundamental Freedoms and in particular art. 10*

[His Lordship read Art.10(1) ECHR: see above, p.293]

[His Lordship noted that the Convention is a treaty to which the United Kingdom is a party but which has not been incorporated by legislation into English domestic law. He also noted that the terms of a treaty may be used to resolve an ambiguity in an Act, but held that there was no such ambiguity in the terms of the 1981 Act. He then referred to a further argument of counsel for the applicants, and continued:]

. . . Mr Lester . . . claims that the Secretary of State before issuing his directives should have considered not only the convention (it is accepted that he in fact did so) but that he should have properly construed it and correctly taken it into consideration. It was therefore a relevant, indeed a vital, factor to which he was obliged to have proper regard pursuant to the *Wednesbury* doctrine, with the result that his failure to do so rendered his decision unlawful. The fallacy of this submission is, however, plain. If the Secretary of State was obliged to have proper regard to the convention, *i.e.* to conform with art.10, this inevitably would result in incorporating the convention into English domestic law by the back door. It would oblige the courts to police the operation of the convention and to ask itself in each case, where there was a challenge, whether the restrictions were "necessary in a democratic society . . ." applying the principles enunciated in the decisions of the European Court of Human Rights. The treaty, not having been incorporated in English law, cannot be a source of rights and obligations and the question—did the Secretary of State act in breach of art. 10?—does not therefore arise. . . .

(4) *The Secretary of State has acted ultra vires because he has acted "in a disproportionate manner"*

This attack is not a repetition of the *Wednesbury* "irrational" test under another guise. Clearly a decision by a minister which suffers from a total lack of proportionality will qualify for the "*Wednesbury* unreasonable" epithet. It is, ex hypothesi, a decision which no reasonable minister could make. This is, however, a different and severer test.

Mr Lester is asking your Lordships to adopt a different principle: the principle of "proportionality" which is recognised in the administrative law of several members of the European Economic Community. What is urged is a further development in English administrative law, which Lord Diplock viewed as a possibility in *Council of Civil Service Unions v. Minister for the Civil Service* [1985] A.C. 374, 410.

In his written submissions, Mr Lester was at pains to record "that there is a clear distinction between an appeal on the merits and a review based on whether the principle of proportionality has been satisfied". He was prepared to accept that to stray into the realms of appellate jurisdiction involves the courts in a wrongful usurpation of power. Yet in order to invest the proportionality test with a higher status than the *Wednesbury* test, an inquiry into and a decision upon the merits cannot be avoided. Mr Pannick's (Mr Lester's junior) formulation—could the minister reasonably conclude that his direction was necessary?—must involve balancing the reasons, pro and con, for his decision, albeit allowing him "a margin of appreciation" to use the European concept of the tolerance accorded to the decision-maker in whom a discretion has been vested. The European test of "whether the 'interference' complained of corresponds to a 'pressing social need' " (*The Sunday Times v. United Kingdom* (1979) 2 E.H.R.R. 245 at 277) must ultimately result in the question—is the particular decision acceptable?—and this must involve a review of the merits of the decision. Unless and until Parliament incorporates the convention into domestic law, a course which it is well known has a strong body of support, there appears to me to be at present no basis upon which the proportionality doctrine applied by the European Court can be followed by the courts of this country.

I would accordingly dismiss this appeal. . . .

Appeal dismissed.

Notes

1. Lord Roskill agreed with the reasons given by Lord Bridge. On the issue of proportionality he referred to Lord Diplock's statement in the *Council of Civil Service Unions* case about the "possible adoption in future" of this principle of review, and noted Lord Diplock's view that any such development would be on a case by case basis. Lord Roskill continued (at 750):

"I am clearly of the view that the present is not a case in which the first step can be taken for the reason that to apply the principle in the present case would be for the court to substitute its own judgment of what was needed to achieve a particular objective for the judgment of the Secretary of State upon whom that duty has been laid by Parliament. But so to hold in the present case is not to exclude the possible future development of the law in this respect . . .".

Lord Lowry agreed with Lord Ackner. On the issue of "proportionality" as a ground of challenge, he said (at 766–767):

"In my opinion proportionality and the other phrases are simply intended to move the focus of discussion away from the hitherto accepted criteria for deciding whether the decision-maker has abused his power and into an area in which the court will feel more at liberty to interfere.

The first observation I would make is that there is *no* authority for saying that proportionality in the sense in which the appellants have used it is part of the English common law and a great deal of authority the other way. This, so far as I am concerned, is not a cause for regret for several reasons. (1) The decision-makers, very often elected, are those to whom Parliament has entrusted the discretion and to interfere with that discretion beyond the limits as hitherto defined would itself be an abuse of the judges' supervisory jurisdiction. (2) The judges are not, generally speaking, equipped by training or experience, or furnished with the requisite knowledge and advice, to decide the answer to an administrative problem where the scales are evenly balanced, but they have a much better chance of reaching the right answer where the question is put in a *Wednesbury* form. The same applies if the judges' decision is appealed. (3) Stability and relative certainty would be jeopardised if the new doctrine held sway, because there is nearly always something to be said against any administrative decision and parties who felt aggrieved would be even more likely than at present to try their luck with a judicial review application both at first instance and on appeal. (4) The increase in applications for judicial review of administrative action (inevitable if the threshold of unreasonableness is lowered) will lead to the expenditure of time and money by litigants, not to speak of the prolongation of uncertainty for all concerned with the decisions in question, and the taking up of court time which could otherwise be devoted to other matters. The losers in this respect will be members of the public, for whom the courts provide a service.

1(1) *Halsbury's Laws of England* (4th ed., vol. 1(1) reissue, 1989) recognises proportionality in the context of administrative law as follows:

> '78. Proportionality. The courts will quash exercise of discretionary powers in which there is not a reasonable relationship between the objective which is sought to be achieved and the means used to that end, or where punishments imposed by administrative bodies or inferior courts are wholly out of proportion to the relevant misconduct. The principle of proportionality is well established in European law, and will be applied by English courts where European law is enforceable in the domestic courts. The principle of proportionality is still at a stage of development in English law; lack of proportionality is not usually treated as a separate ground of review in English law, but is regarded as one indication of manifest unreasonableness.'

(The High Court's decision in the instant case (see *The Times*, May 30, 1989) is cited in the copious footnotes to this paragraph as the authority for the concluding statement.)

It finally occurs to me that there can be very little room for judges to operate an independent judicial review proportionality doctrine in the space which is left between the conventional judicial review doctrine and the admittedly forbidden appellate approach. To introduce an intermediate area of deliberation for the court seems scarcely a practical idea, quite apart from the other disadvantages by which, in my opinion, such a course would be attended".

2. See comments by C. Lewis, [1991] C.L.J. 211; B. Thompson, [1989] P.L. 527 (on *Brind* in the Divisional Court) and [1991] P.L. 346; J. Jowell, [1990] P.L. 149 (on *Brind* in the Court of Appeal); and M. Halliwell, (1991) 42 N.I.L.Q. 246.

3. Since *Brind* there have been a number of significant developments. First, the Human Rights Act 1998 has required the courts to apply a proportionality test in cases arising under that Act and there is now a body of case law exploring the limits of that principle (see above, pp.339–371). This demonstrates that the proportionality test provides a more detailed and coherent structure for analysis than *Wednesbury* unreasonableness and does not involve the unpermitted substitution of the judge's view of the merits. Secondly, the propositions in *Brind* about the application of *Wednesbury* unreasonableness have been taken forward in subsequent cases, most notably *R. v Ministry of Defence Ex p. Smith* (above, p.581). It is now firmly established that the intensity of review under the *Wednesbury* unreasonableness/irrationality principle varies according to the context, with heightened scrutiny in cases concerning fundamental rights. Thirdly, a very similar approach has been adopted in developing the principle of substantive unfairness in the context of the protection of legitimate expectations (above, pp.591–621). Fourthly, it is better understood that the proportionality principle both provides for both an intensity of review and a discretionary area of judgment for the decision-maker that vary according to context. The arguments in favour of the development are strong. See the discussion in *Craig*, pp.630–632, noting that it would be advantageous for the same approach to be applicable in all cases, both inside and outside the reach of EU law and the Human Rights Act 1998; that proportionality provides a structured form of inquiry and facilitates a reasoned inquiry of a kind often lacking under the traditional *Wednesbury* approach; and that EU law shows that the concept can be applied with varying degrees of intensity.

The main differences between the two approaches seem to be these. First, the proportionality principle requires the respondent to adduce evidence and not merely argument enshrined in the submissions of counsel to justify its position (but *cf.* the approach of the court *R. v Ministry of Defence, Ex p. Smith*, above, p.581). Secondly, the proportionality principle in some (but not all) contexts requires the respondent to demonstrate *necessity* (i.e. that the least restrictive option has been adopted). (But should not rational decision-makers in such contexts do that anyway?) Thirdly, it may be speculated that there is a psychological effect on the judge. Even if the circumstances of a case could justify more intensive scrutiny and a decision to strike down under the rubric of *Wednesbury* unreasonableness, the proportionality approach provides the judge with a firmer foundation and thus greater confidence for intervening.

A further important point is that the *wording* of these grounds for review provides only part of the picture. Both the various formulations of *Wednesbury* unreasonableness and the proportionality principle (including the variable elements of the discretionary area of judgment) are broadly worded principles not detailed "brightline" tests. They are applied in a wide range of contexts. In trying to make sense of the tests it is essential to see how they are applied in practice by the judges and to look at outcomes.

If there are particular outcomes that suggest that the judge has come too near to substituting his or her view on the merits, or has been unduly deferential, the problem is unlikely plausibly to be traced to the wording of the tests in question, but would lie in differences of view between the judge and the critic as to the proper evaluation of the facts of the case. There must be many cases on the borderline where the judge could not be criticised for a decision either way; and the general nature of the tests to be applied means that this borderline is not a narrow one. All this means that is dangerous to make generalisations about whether one test is in practice stricter than another. Only one thing seems absolutely clear, that the proportionality test is more intrusive than a test where the judge only considers whether the decision-maker has taken leave of his or her senses (see above, p.574). Whether *Wednesbury* unreasonableness was ever, properly understood, limited to that is debateable, but it is clearly now not so confined. Overall, it is better to regard *Wednesbury* unreasonableness and proportionality as co-existing "as complementary notions on a single continuum" (see M. Elliott, "The HRA 1998 and the Standard of Substantive Review" [2002] J.R. 97 at p.108), the question whether proportionality should *replace Wednesbury* unreasonableness thus not arising. Note also Elliott's point that it is necessary to keep separate (1) the desirability of the adoption of a structured and transparent approach to analysis, as found with the proportionality principle and (2) the standard of review ultimately to be applied to the decision under challenge. A structured approach to analysis is not inconsistent with leaving where appropriate significant latitude to the decision-maker.

For further discussions of the proportionality principle see M. Fordham and T. de la Mare, "Identifying the Principles of Proportionality" in *Understanding Public Law Principles* (Jowell and Cooper ed., 2001); M. Fordham, [2002] J.R. 110; R. Clayton Q.C, [2002] J.R. 124.

4. There have been dicta in a number of cases in favour of the move to recognise proportionality as a ground of challenges in English domestic law. In the *Alconbury* case, (above, p.381), Lord Slynn said *obiter* ([2003] 2 A.C. 295 at para.[51]:

"I consider that even without reference to the Human Rights Act 1998 the time has come to recognise that this principle is part of English administrative law, not only when judges are dealing with Community acts but also when they are dealing with acts subject to domestic law. Trying to keep the *Wednesbury* principle and proportionality in separate compartments seems to be unnecessary and confusing".

This point was left open by other judges (Lord Nolan at para.[62], Lord Clyde at para.[169]) or not mentioned (Lords Hoffmann and Hutton). Lord Slynn's dictum has, however, been applied by the Court of Appeal in *R. (on the application of Tucker) v*

Secretary of State for Social Security [2001] EWCA Civ 1646; [2002] H.R.L.R. 27, where it considered (and rejected on the merits) a common law proportionality based challenge to the validity of an amendment to the Housing Benefits (General) Regulations 1987 (SI 1987/1971) under which a person in the position of the claimant, who was responsible for the child of the landlord, had to be treated as not liable to make payments in respect of the dwelling. A proportionality challenge arising in the context of an alleged breach of Art.14 in conjunction with Art.8 was also rejected. Nevertheless, in *R. (on the application of Association of British Civilian Internees "Far East Region") v Secretary of State for Defence* [2003] EWCA Civ 473; [2003] Q.B. 1397, the Court of Appeal held that although trying to keep the *Wednesbury* principle and proportionality in separate compartments was unnecessary and confusing, the criteria of proportionality being more precise and sophisticated and there being no justification for retaining the *Wednesbury* principle, it was not for the Court of Appeal "to perform its burial rites" (*per* Dyson L.J. at [34]). The continued existence of the *Wednesbury* principle had been recognised by the House of Lords (*Brind; International Trader's Ferry*) and it was for the House to effect any change.

5. *Proportionality in EC law.* Proportionality as a ground of challenge in EU law has been the subject of much detailed analysis. See, the essays by Jacobs, van Gerven, Tridimas and Ellis in *The Principle of Proportionality in the Laws of Europe* (Ellis ed., 1999), and T. Tridimas, *The General Principles of EC law* (1999), Chs 3 and 4. There are significant variations in how the proportionality principle is both formulated and applied by the Court of Justice in different contexts, and this has remained so notwithstanding its express inclusion by amendment in the EC Treaty (Art.5 (ex 3b) EC): "Any action by the Community shall not go beyond what is necessary to achieve the objectives of the Treaty".

At least some of the factors that influence an approach that is more, or less, intrusive tend to echo similar arguments found in the English domestic law of judicial review. See the overview of factors in Tridimas, *op.cit*, pp.122–123. For example, a less intrusive approach tends to be adopted in respect of legislative measures of economic policy and measures the adoption of which requires complex economic and technical evaluations. In the context of the Common Agricultural Policy, it was stated in Case 331/88, *Fedesa* [1990] E.C.R. I–4023 that "the legality of a measure adopted in that sphere can be affected only if the measure is manifestly inappropriate having regard to the objective which the competent institution is seeking to pursue" (para.14). A similar approach was adopted in respect of the United Kingdom's challenge to the Working Time Directive (Council Directive 93/104), which involved the legislature (here the Council) "in making social policy choices" and required it "to carry out complex assessments" (Case C–84/94, *United Kingdom v Council* [1996] E.C.R I–5755). Particular weight may be attached to the need to protect international or national security (see the cases discussed by Jacobs in Ellis (ed.), *op.cit.*, at pp.13–16).

On the other hand, the greater the interference by a Community measure with individual private interests the stricter the approach likely to be adopted (see, *e.g.* cases on the imposition as protective measures of levies on importers and exporters: Case C–24/90, *Hauptzollamt Hamburg-Jonas v Werner Faust OHG* [1991] E.C.R I–4905 and Case C–25/90, *Hauptzollamt Hamburg-Jonas v Wunsche Handelsgesellschaft mbH and Co. K.G.* [1991] E.C.R. I–4939, (levy on imports over quota of preserved mushrooms at 150 per cent of the cost price of top-quality mushrooms held to be disproportionate). A stricter approach is also adopted in cases concerning the legality of national measures that give effect to Community legislation or interfere with a fundamental freedoms enshrined in EC law (see Tridemas, Ch.4). There is room for argument that in particular contexts the Court's approach is unduly deferential (see Ellis's discussion of discrimination cases in Ellis (ed.), *op.cit.*).

6. An English court may be required to identify and apply the appropriate EC law approach to proportionality in determining the legality of a national measure. See, e.g. *R. v Secretary of State for Health Ex p. Eastside Cheese Co.*(1999) 2 L.G.L.R. 41 at 62–66, where an emergency control order prohibiting the carrying out of any

commercial operation in relation to cheese from a particular producer, following one
case of E-coli poisoning from one batch of the producer's cheese, was held by the
Court of Appeal not to be disproportionate. The judge had applied the right test of
proportionality but wrongly concluded that the Secretary of State had taken account
of irrelevant considerations of administrative convenience. Lord Bingham C.J. at 65
commended the discussion of the relationship between proportionality and
Wednesbury unreasonableness by Laws J. in *R. v Ministry of Agriculture, Fisheries
and Food Ex p. First City Trading* [1997] 1 C.M.L.R. 250 at 278–279. Here, Laws
J. rejected a challenge to the legality of a scheme of emergency aid for the operators
of slaughterhouses and cutting premises who were seriously affected by the worldwide ban on exports of beef from the United Kingdom following the identification of
risks to human health from consuming beef from cattle affected by BSE. The applicants, beef exporters who did not own slaughterhouses or cutting premises, failed in
arguments that their exclusion from the scheme was either *Wednesbury* unreasonable
or discriminatory under EC law. Laws J. cited Case 138/79, *Roquette Freres v Council*
[1980] E.C.R. 3333, where the Court of Justice, in considering whether there was
unjustified discrimination between manufacturers of sugar and isoglucose, said at
para.25:

> "When the implementation by the Council of the agricultural policy involves the
> need to evaluate a complex economic situation, the discretion which it has does not
> apply exclusively to the nature and scope of the measures to be taken but also to
> some extent to the finding of the basic facts inasmuch as, in particular, it is open to
> the Council to rely on general findings. In reviewing the exercise of such a power
> the Court must confine itself to examining whether it contains a manifest error or
> constitutes a misuse of power or whether the authority in question did not clearly
> exceed the bounds of its discretion".

His Lordship continued:

> "Unsurprisingly Mr Parker fixes on this passage to found a submission that in rela-
> tion to the principle of equal treatment the Court of Justice accords the decision-
> maker—in the language of Strasbourg—a 'margin of appreciation', at least where
> the subject-matter is in economic terms complex and a decision had to be reached
> speedily. His argument, I think, amounted to a claim that in such circumstances
> (which/he would say/plainly apply to this case) the Court's jurisprudence in reality
> applies a test closely akin to *Wednesbury*.
>
> But *Wednesbury* is not the test. By our domestic law, if a public decision-maker
> were to treat apparently identical cases differently there would no doubt be a prima
> facie *Wednesbury* case against him, since on the face of it such an approach bears
> the hallmark of irrationality. To that extent the rule is akin to the European princi-
> ple. The court would look for an explanation of the difference; but the justification
> offered would in the ordinary way only be rejected on grounds of perversity. That,
> I think, marks the divide. The Community rule requires the decision-maker to
> demonstrate a substantive justification for a discriminatory decision, although there
> is a nice question how far a 'margin of appreciation' is allowed to the decision-
> maker. In case after case concerned with its fundamental principles the Court of
> Justice has proceeded on the footing that the facts must be examined by the review-
> ing court and reached a view as to whether the decision taken measures up to the
> substantive standards which it has set. Mr Green correctly submitted in reply that
> *Roquette* was a special case on its facts. He cited *Miro* [1985] ECR 3731 and
> *Stoke & Norwich* [1993] 1 CMLR 426: see per the Advocate General at 457. I need
> not set them out. He was correct also to submit that:
>
>> 'the fact that proportionality is an integral part of the principle of equality also
>> serves to curtail any otherwise broad discretion, since the measure in dispute

must itself be finely attuned (proportionate) to the objective justification advanced for it'.

There must, however, remain a difference between the approach of the court in arriving at a judicial decision on the question whether a measure is objectively justified and that of the primary decision-maker himself in deciding upon the measure in the first place. Within the diverse contexts in which the principle of equality may be called in question, there will no doubt always be a range of options factually open to the decision-maker. It is not the court's task to decide what it would have done had it been the decision-maker, who (certainly in the case of elected government) enjoys a political authority, and carries a political responsibility, with which the court is not endowed. The court's task is to decide whether the measure in fact adopted falls within the range of options legally open to the decision-maker. In the nature of things it is highly unlikely that only one of the choices available to him will pass the test of objective justification; and the court has no business to give effect to any preference for one possible measure over another when both lie within proper legal limits. In this sense it may be said that the decision-maker indeed enjoys a margin of appreciation.

The difference between *Wednesbury* and European review is that in the former case the legal limits lie further back. I think there are two factors. First, the limits of domestic review are not, as the law presently stands, constrained by the doctrine of proportionality. Secondly, at least as regards a requirement such as that of objective justification in an equal treatment case, the European rule requires the decision-maker to provide a fully reasoned case. It is not enough merely to set out the problem, and assert that within his discretion the Minister chose this or that solution, constrained only by the requirement that his decision must have been one which a reasonable Minister might make. Rather the court will test the solution arrived at, and pass it only if substantial factual considerations are put forward in its justification: considerations which are relevant, reasonable, and proportionate to the aim in view. But as I understand the jurisprudence the court is not concerned to agree or disagree with the decision; that would be to travel beyond the boundaries of proper judicial authority and usurp the primary decision-maker's function. Thus *Wednesbury* and European review are different models—one looser, one tighter— of the same juridical concept, which is the imposition of compulsory standards on decision-makers so as to secure the repudiation of arbitrary power".

Laws J. also considered the line to be drawn between those situations to which general principles of Community law were and were not applicable. He held that they only applied to national measures "taken pursuant to Community law: either as implementing a Community provision, or because in promulgating it the government would have been in breach of Community law but for a permission or derogation granted by Community legislation" (p.271). Accordingly, they did not apply to the emergency aid scheme. It was not sufficient that the scheme was made in consequence of the ban imposed under EC law; or operated in the same field as other Community measures (not relied on in bringing forward the scheme); or had been notified to the Commission as a State aid.

For other examples of English courts applying a proportionality test under EC law, see *R. v International Stock Exchange of the UK and the Republic of Ireland Ltd Ex p. Else* [1993] Q.B. 534; *R. v Chief Constable of Sussex, Ex p. International Trader's Ferry Ltd* [1999] 2 A.C. 418, HL; *R. (on the application of Hoverspeed Ltd) v Customs and Excise Commissioners* [2002] EWCA Civ 1804; [2003] Q.B. 1041.

7. *Proportionality and the principle of legality*. In appropriate contexts, the principle of *legality* may lead a court to conclude that a particular power may only lawfully be exercised where the interference with fundamental rights would be proportionate: see the decision in *Simms*, above, p.261. In such a case, a decision will certainly be unlawful where the decision-maker on the evidence has not addressed his

or her mind to the question whether that is the case (*R. v (1) A Local Authority in the Midlands and (2) A Police Authority in the Midlands Ex p. LM* (1999) 2 L.G.L.R. 1043 (the respondents had failed to consider whether there was a pressing social need for the disclosure of uncorroborated allegations against the application of sexual assault to potential employers). See further M. Fordham and T. de la Mare in *Understanding Human Rights Principles* (Jowell and Cooper ed., 2001), pp.72–77.

CHAPTER 10

ERRORS OF PROCEDURE

(A) FAILURE TO OBSERVE STATUTORY REQUIREMENTS

Action taken by a public authority may be void if it offends against procedural conditions laid down, expressly or by necessary implication, in the enabling statute. This principle may be applied in a variety of situations, including the procedure by which a decision is taken, the timing of the decision and the identity of the persons taking the decision. In the latter instance, there may be a breach of the rule against delegation (*delegatus non potest delegare*) (above, pp.463–481) or an authority may be found to have been improperly constituted (above, pp.457–458).

A distinction has traditionally been drawn in the case law between procedural requirements which are *mandatory*, breach of which renders the ultimate decision *ultra vires*, and those which are *directory*. In the latter case, the requirements should be observed, but if they are not there is at most a mere *intra vires* error. "[I]n each case you must look to the subject matter; consider the importance of the provision that has been disregarded, and the relation of that provision to the general object intended to be secured by the Act . . ." (*per* Lord Penzance in *Howard v Bodington* (1877) 2 P.D. 203 at 211). *de Smith, Woolf and Jowell* consider that the terms mandatory and directory:

> ". . . often cause more problems than they solve. The law relating to the effect of failure to comply with statutory requirements thus resembles an inextricable tangle of loose ends and judges have often stressed the impracticability of specifying exact rules for the assignment of a provision to the appropriate category" (p.266).

In recent times the judges have been adopting a more flexible approach.

R. v SECRETARY OF STATE FOR THE HOME DEPARTMENT Ex p. JEYEANTHAN; RAVICHANDRAN v SECRETARY OF STATE FOR THE HOME DEPARTMENT

[2000] 1 W.L.R. 354; [1999] 3 All E.R. 231 (COURT OF APPEAL)

In each case, an asylum seeker appealed successfully to a special adjudicator against a refusal of asylum by the Secretary of State. The Secretary of State applied for leave to appeal against that decision by letter rather than by using the form prescribed for such applications by r. 13(3) of the Asylum Appeals (Procedure) Rules 1993. The reason for this was that the prescribed form contained elements that made it more suitable for use by an asylum seeker than the Secretary of State. The letter contained all the relevant information required by the prescribed form, except for a declaration of truth, as there was nothing to which such a declaration could sensibly relate. In the *Jeyeanthan* case, the Immigration Appeal Tribunal held that the application for leave was not a nullity, allowed the appeal and remitted the matter to the special adjudicator. This was in turn quashed by the Sedley J. on an application for judicial review on the ground that the IAT's decision was a nullity.

Without the declaration of truth, there had not been "substantial compliance" with the requirements; it was important there should be equality of treatment between the immigrant and the minister. His Lordship declined to follow the decision of Latham J. in *R. v Immigration Appeal Tribunal Ex p. Nichalapillai* [1998] Imm. A.R. 232 that a form without the declaration was "substantially to the like effect".

In the *Ravichandran* case, the validity of the application for leave was not questioned before the IAT, which allowed the appeal and quashed the decision of the special adjudicator. The Secretary of State in the first case and Ravichandran in the second case appealed to the Court of Appeal.

LORD WOOLF C.J.: . . .

What should be the approach to procedural irregularities?

The issue is of general importance and has implications for the failure to observe procedural requirements outside the field of immigration. The conventional approach when there has been noncompliance with a procedural requirement laid down by a statute or regulation is to consider whether the requirement which was not complied with should be categorised as directory or mandatory. If it is categorized as directory it is usually assumed it can be safely ignored. If it is categorized as mandatory then it is usually assumed the defect cannot be remedied and has the effect of rendering subsequent events dependent on the requirement a nullity or void or as being made without jurisdiction and of no effect. The position is more complex than this and this approach distracts attention from the important question of what the legislator should be judged to have intended should be the consequence of the non-compliance. This has to be assessed on a consideration of the language of the legislation against the factual circumstances of the non-compliance. In the majority of cases it provides limited, if any, assistance to inquire whether the requirement is mandatory or directory. The requirement is never intended to be optional if a work such as "shall" or "must" is used.

A requirement to use a form is more likely to be treated as a mandatory requirement where the form contains a notice designed to ensure that a member of the public is informed of his or her rights, such as a notice of a right to appeal. In the case of a right to appeal, if, notwithstanding the absence of the notice, the member of the public exercises his or her right of appeal, the failure to use the form usually ceases to be of any significance irrespective of the outcome of the appeal. This can confidently be said to accord with the intention of the author of the requirement.

There are cases where it has been held that even if there has been no prejudice to the recipient because, for example, the recipient was aware of the right of appeal but did not do so, the non-compliance is still fatal. The explanation for these decisions is that the draconian consequence is imposed as a deterrent against not observing the requirement. However even where this is the situation the consequences may differ if this would not be in the interests of the person who was to be informed of his rights.

Because of what can be the very undesirable consequences of a procedural requirement which is made so fundamental that any departure from the requirement makes everything that happens thereafter irreversibly a nullity it is to be hoped that provisions intended to have this effect will be few and far between. In the majority of cases, whether the requirement is categorised as directory or mandatory, the tribunal before whom the defect is properly raised has the task of determining what are to be the consequences of failing to comply with the requirement in the context of all the facts and circumstances of the case in which the issue arises. In such a situation that tribunal's task will be to seek to do what is just in all the circumstances: see *Brayhead (Ascot)Ltd. v Berkshire County Council* [1964] 2 Q.B. 303, applied by the House of Lords in *London & Clydeside Estates Ltd. v Aberdeen District Council* [1980] 1 W.L.R. 182.

By contrast, a requirement may be clearly directory because it lays down a time limit but a tribunal is given an express power to extend the time for compliance. If the tribunal grants or refuses an extension of time the position is clear. If the time limit is extended the requirement is of no significance. If an extension is refused the requirement becomes critical. It may, for example, deprive a member of the public of a right to appeal which if exercised in time would have been bound to succeed. In the latter situation a directory requirement has consequences which are as significant as any mandatory requirement.

A far from straightforward situation is where there is a need for permission to appeal to a tribunal but this is not appreciated at the time. The requirement is mandatory in the sense that the tribunal or the party against whom the appeal was being brought would have been entitled to object to the appeal proceeding without the permission and if they had done so the appeal would not have been accepted. However, what is the position if because they were unaware of the existence of the requirement no objection is made and the appeal is heard and allowed? Is the appellant, when the mistake is learnt of, to be deprived of the benefits of the appeal? If the answer is yes the result could be very unjust. This would be especially so, if in fact the tribunal in error had told the appellant that permission is not needed and he would have been in time to make the application if he had not been misinformed. Could it have been the intention of the author of the requirement that the requirement should have the effect of depriving the appellant, of the benefit of his appeal? Clearly not. In such a situation the non-compliance would almost inevitably be regarded as being without significance. It must be remembered that procedural requirements are designed to further the interests of justice and any consequence which would achieve a result contrary to those interests should be treated with considerable reservation.

These comments are relevant to Ravichandran's case. Ravichandran was unaware of there being anything which was inappropriate about the Secretary of State's successful application for leave to appeal to the tribunal. Ravichandran took a full part in the hearing. He exercised his statutory right to appeal from the decision of the tribunal to the Court of Appeal. He then agreed the outcome of that appeal with the Secretary of State. At the last moment, having learnt of Sedley J.'s decision, he contends he is entitled to treat the decision of the tribunal and everything that followed as being a nullity. As a matter of principle this should not be the position. In his case, if he were entitled to succeed the only consequence would be that he is entitled to asylum notwithstanding that if the issue had been properly determined, this might not have been the result. However, if the position has been the other way around and he had obtained form the tribunal a decision which was more favourable to him than that of the special adjudicator, it would be most unfortunate if he could be deprived of the benefit of that decision because of the non-compliance with a procedural requirement.

An examination of the relevant authorities, the leading textbooks and the numerous authorities to which they refer confirm the limitations of applying a solely mandatory/directory classification: see *Wade and Forsyth, Administrative Law*, 7th ed. (1994), p.225, *Supperstone and Goudie, Judicial Review*, 2nd ed.

(1997), chapter 4 and *de Smith, Woolf and Jowell, Judicial Review of Administrative Action,* 5th ed. (1995), pp.265–271. Frequently the investigation involves doing no more than deciding the sense in which the word "shall" has been used as part of a particular procedural requirement. As the word "shall" is normally inserted to show that something is required to be done, the exercise tends to be an unrewarding one. Much more important is to focus on the consequences of non-compliance. Here the authorities show no constant pattern. This is the result of courts in those cases focusing on the issue of whether or not a requirement is mandatory and ignoring or failing to pay sufficient attention to the issue of the consequences of non-compliance with, in particular, a mandatory requirement. Here it is desirable to remember the wise words of Lord Hailsham of St. Marylebone L.C. in his speech in *London and Clydeside Estates Ltd. v Aberdeen District Council* [1980] 1 W.L.R. 182, 188–190. They are so important that it is desirable to set out the passage verbatim:

"The contention was that in the categorisation of statutory requirements into 'mandatory' and 'directory,' there was a subdivision of the category 'directory' into two class composed (i) of those directory requirements 'substantial compliance' with which satisfied the requirement to the point at which a minor defect of trivial irregularity could be ignored by the court and (ii) those requirements so purely regulatory in character that failure to comply could in no circumstances affect the validity of what was done. The contention of the respondents was that, even on the assumption against themselves that the requirement of the Order that the certificate should include a notification of the appellants' rights to appeal to the Secretary of State, the rest of the certificate was so exactly in accordance with the provisions of the Order that the remaining defect could be safely ignored.

I do not consider that this argument assists the respondents in the present appeal. I have already held that the requirement relating to notification of the appellants' rights of appeal was mandatory and not directory in either sense contended for by the respondents. But on the assumption that I am wrong about this, a total failure to comply with a significant part of a requirement cannot in any circumstances be regarded as 'substantial compliance' with the total requirement in such a way as to bring the respondents' contention into effect.

Nevertheless I wish to examine the contention itself. In this appeal we are in the field of the rapidly developing jurisprudence of administrative law, and we are considering the effect of non-compliance by a statutory authority with the statutory requirements affecting the discharge of one of its functions. In the reported decisions there is much language presupposing the existence of stark categories such as 'mandatory' and 'directory,' 'void' and 'voidable,' a 'nullity,' and 'purely regulatory.'

Such language is useful; indeed, in the course of this opinion I have used some of it myself. But I wish to say that I am not at all clear that the language itself may not be misleading in so far as it may be supposed to present a court with the necessity of fitting a particular case into one or other of mutually exclusive and starkly contrasted compartments, compartments which in some cases (e.g. 'void' and 'voidable') are borrowed from the language of contract or status, and are not easily fitted to the requirements of administrative law.

When Parliament lays down a statutory requirement for the exercise of legal authority it expects its authority to be obeyed down to the minutest detail. But what the courts have to decide in a particular case is the legal consequence of non-compliance on the rights of the subject viewed in the light of a concrete state of facts and a continuing chain of events. It may be that what the courts are faced with is not so much a stark choice of alternatives but a spectrum of possibilities in which one compartment or description fades gradually into another. At one end of this spectrum there may be cases in which a fundamental obligation may have been so outrageously and flagrantly ignored or defied that the subject may safely ignore what has been done and treat it as having no legal consequences upon himself. In such a case if the defaulting authority seeks to rely on its action it may be that the subject is entitled to use the defect in procedure simply as a shield or defence without having taken any positive action of his own. At the other end of the spectrum the defect in procedure may be so nugatory or trivial that the authority can safely proceed without remedial action, confident that, if the subject is so misguided as to rely on the fault, the courts will decline to listen to his complaint. But in a very great number of cases, it may be in a majority of them, it may be necessary for a subject, in order to safeguard himself, to go to the court for declaration of his rights, the grant of which may well be discretionary, and by the like token it may be wise for an authority (as it certainly would have been here) to do everything in its power to remedy the fault in its procedure so as not to deprive the subject of his due or themselves of their power to act. In such cases, though language like 'mandatory,' 'directory,' 'void,' 'voidable,' 'nullity' and so forth may be helpful in argument, it may be misleading in effect if relied on to show that the courts, in deciding the consequences of a defect in the exercise of power, are necessarily bound to fit the facts of a particular case and a developing chain of events into rigid legal categories or to stretch or cramp them on a bed of Procrustes invented by lawyers for the purposes of convenient exposition. As I have said, the case does not really arise here, since we are in the presence of total non-compliance with a requirement which I have held to be mandatory. Nevertheless I do not wish to be understood in the field of administrative law and in the domain where the courts apply a supervisory jurisdiction over the acts of subordinate authority purporting to exercise statutory powers, to encourage the use of rigid legal classifications. The jurisdiction is inherently discretionary and the court is frequently in the presence of differences of degree which merge almost imperceptibly into differences of kind."

These comments of Lord Hailsham L.C. were made in case where a mandatory requirement was not complied with and this resulted in a document being set aside. It was not, however, held to be a nullity in the sense that it was not capable of being the foundation of valid proceedings. This was the position even though the requirement involved informing the subject of his right to question a decision. Lord Keith of Kinkel considered a different result "totally unrealistic:" p.202H.

Bearing in mind Lord Hailsham L.C.'s helpful guidance I suggest that the right approach is to regard the question of whether a requirement is directory or mandatory as only at most a first step. In the majority of cases there are other questions which have to be asked which are more likely to be of greater assistance than the application of the mandatory/directory test. The questions which are likely to arise are as follows.

1. Is the statutory requirement fulfilled if there has been substantial compliance with the requirement and, if so, has there been substantial compliance in the case in issue even though there has not been strict compliance? (The substantial compliance question.)

2. Is the non-compliance capable of being waived, and if so, has it, or can it and should it be waived in this particular case? (The discretionary question.) I treat the grant of an extension of time for compliance as a waiver.

3. If it is not capable of being waived or is not waived then what is the consequence of the non-compliance? (The consequences question.)

Which questions arise will depend upon the facts of the case and the nature of the particular requirement. The advantage of focusing on these questions is that they should avoid the unjust and unintended consequences which can flow from an approach solely dependant on dividing requirements into mandatory ones, which oust jurisdiction, or directory, which do not. If the result of non-compliance goes to jurisdiction it will be said jurisdiction cannot be conferred where it does not otherwise exist by consent or waiver.

The Rules

[His Lordship considered r.13 of the 1993 Rules, noting that applications for leave to appeal had to be made not later than five days after the appellant received notice of the determination. The courts had adopted a strict approach to the time requirements for applying for leave, rejecting any implied power to extend the five-day period. This approach was "readily understandable because there are obvious administrative reasons why it is important that asylum claims are finally determined as soon as practical".]

Mr Pleming submits that as the time limits in rule 13 are applied strictly, so the other requirements should be applied in the same way. However there are no policy or other reasons why it should be assumed that a requirement of rule 13(3) not dealing with time limits but the form of the notice of the application for leave is to be given a particularly restrictive interpretation. The application is served on the tribunal and not on the proposed respondent to the appeal. If leave is granted it becomes the notice of appeal but there is still no express requirement in the Rules of 1993 that it should be served on the respondent though in practice it is served. It may "as such a notice of appeal" be amended under rule 14 of the Rules of 1993. It is also relevant to refer to rule 45 of the Immigration Appeals (Procedure) Rules 1984 which by rule 22 of the Rules of 1993 are to apply to Part V (headed "General Procedure") of the Rules of 1993. Rule 45 of the Rules of 1984 states: "The forms set out in the Schedule to these Rules or forms substantially to the like effect may be used with such variations as the circumstances may require." It is accepted that this provision applies to the requirement to use Form A2 contained in rule 13(4) of the Rules of 1993. It imports a degree of flexibility as to the use of Form A2. In addition rule 38 of the Rules of 1984 is applied to the Rules of 1993 by rule 22. Rule 38 deals with irregularities. It provides:

"Any irregularity resulting from failure to comply with these Rules before an appellate authority has reached its decision shall not by itself render the proceedings void, but the appellate authority may, and shall if it considers that any person may have been prejudiced, take such steps as it thinks fit before reaching its decision to cure the irregularity, whether by amendment of any document, the giving of any notice or otherwise."

The purpose of this rule is to prevent technical points interfering with the jurisdiction of the tribunal. There is therefore ample reason for saying that unlike the provisions as to time the requirement to use Form A2 is not be regarded as a strict requirement. . . .

Conclusions

As to the substantial compliance question, I have no doubt that the decision of Sedley J. is correct. I would however express my reasons somewhat differently. In this context landlord and tenant cases concerning the requirements on landlords for the protection of tenants only provide marginal assistance. I regard a form with a declaration of truth and a form without such a declaration as being very different documents. Most importantly the answer to the question must be the same for the asylum seeker and the Secretary of State. If the document is substantially to the like effect then it fulfils the requirements of rule 13 of the Rules of 1993. I consider it is inconceivable that the asylum seeker and thus equally the Secretary fo State was intended to be able to dispense with the declaration even if this was required by the tribunal. Yet this would be the effect of answering this question in favour of the Secretary of State. *Ex parte Nichalapillai*[1998] Imm. A.R. 232 is wrongly decided.

This is however by no means the end of this appeal. It does not follow that the application, although it does not have the required declaration, is a nullity. It is still necessary to answer the second and third questions I have identified.

It is convenient to deal with the discretion and consequences questions together in this appeal. The absence of the declaration does not contaminate the leave to appeal which was given, so depriving the tribunal of jurisdiction to hear the appeal. This could not be the position having regard to the express discretion granted to the tribunal to vary the notice of application when it becomes a notice of appeal after leave to appeal has been given. An application for leave was made. The tribunal could have required the application to be varied to include the declaration either before or after it was considered, but they could not refuse to consider the application, at any rate, once it was accepted. Jeyeanthan was perfectly entitled to raise the absence of a declaration but it would not be a proper exercise of the tribunal's powers to do more than give the Secretary of State time, possibly a very short amount of time, to rectify his default. Although it appears the tribunal was not happy about the Secretary of State's practice they were under protest accepting it and thus waiving the requirement. The waiver was on their part and not on the part of Jeyeanthan, but his position would be fully protected by his being able to raise the matter before the tribunal. He did so, but took the point on jurisdiction and did not require a declaration to be completed. This was probably because he appreciated that the completion of a declaration would be of no benefit to him.

Ravichandran's position is different. By taking part in the hearing of the appeal he had effectively impliedly waived the requirement. His position to that extent is less strong than that of Jeyeanthan.

I turn to the power contained in rule 38 of the Rules of 1984. The existence of this power to deal with irregularities confirms that the tribunal is not intended to allow technicalities to interfere with its responsibility to determine the merits of appeals. Because of a lack of familiarity with English and the procedures of tribunals in this country, asylum applicants are likely to make many procedural errors. If they are not to be caused injustice rule 38 should be given a wide interpretation. I do not accept Mr Pleming's submission that a stricter approach should be adopted than was adopted to the wide power contained in R.S.C., Ord. 2, r1: see *Golden Ocean Assurance Ltd v Martin* [1990] 2 Lloyd's Rep. 215. The procedures of tribunals should normally be less and not more strict than the procedures of the High Court. The absence of a declaration would be an irregularity which could if necessary be dealt with under rule 38.

If in these appeals you concentrate on what the Rules intend should be the just *consequence* of non-compliance with the statutory requirements as to the contents of an application for leave to appeal I would suggest the answer to these appeals is obvious. Neither Jeyeanthan nor Ravichandran have in any way been affected by the omission. It was as far as they were concerned a pure technicality. Other than to discipline the Secretary of State there could be no reason well after the event to treat his successful applications for leave as a nullity. Both the discretion and consequences questions should be answered in the Secretary of State's favour. I agree with Judge L.J.'s judgment which I have seen in draft and I would dismiss Ravichandran's appeal, allow the Secretary of State's appeal and, in those circumstances make the agreed orders.

JUDGE L.J. I agree with Lord Woolf M.R.'s illuminating analysis of the dangers of over rigidly seeking to pigeon hole requirements of the kind under consideration in these appeals by the application of a single descriptive and apparently all embracing word, whether "mandatory" or "directory" or "regulatory," to them. I nevertheless venture to express the hope that counsel will not seek in argument hereafter to reanalyse his analysis, or restate the principles using slightly different language, with the unlooked for consequence that the argument itself will become laboured and over elaborate. The true focus for attention, assisted by Lord Woolf M.R.'s analysis, remains the relevant statutory framework considered as a whole. . . .

MAY L.J. agreed

> *Secretary of State's appeal allowed;*
> *Ravichandran's appeal dismissed.*

Notes

1. The traditional approach to determining the consequences of a failure to comply with a procedural requirement expressly imposed by primary or delegated legislation has been to identify two categories of requirement, mandatory (or imperative) and directory. Non-observance of a mandatory requirement renders the ultimate decision *ultra vires* and unlawful; non-observance of a directory requirement does not have that effect. This tends to generate the false belief that the case law supports a generic analysis of different kinds of requirement as falling into one or other of these categories, and that the task of the judge in a particular case is to decide into which category the requirement in question falls. Some generalisations are indeed possible. The courts have been likely, for example, to hold to be mandatory requirements that provide an important safeguard to individual interests, such as a requirement to give prior notice of a decision or to hold a hearing (*Bradbury v Enfield LBC* [1967] 1 W.L.R. 1311); or

to give notice of rights of appeal (*Rayner v Stepney Corp.* [1911] 2 Ch. 312; the *Clydeside* case); or rights to make objections (*R. v Lambeth LBC Ex p. Sharp* (1988) 55 P. & C.R. 232); or to give the prescribed period of notice of the implementation of a licensing scheme by a council resolution (*R. v Birmingham Ex p. Quietlynn Ltd* (1985) 83 L.G.R. 461 at 471–479, 512–514); or to consult appropriate bodies (the *Aylesbury Mushrooms* case, below).

The *Jeyeanthan* case is helpful in its emphasis that the effect of disregard of a procedural requirement should not be judged solely by an analysis of the *requirement*, without regard to the *legal and factual context* in which the breach takes place. The labels "mandatory" and "directory" are statements of the conclusion the court reaches rather than part of a test as to what the right conclusion should be. It is unlikely that the adoption of the *Jeyeanthan* approach would lead to different outcomes in those cases.

Lord Woolf's general approach was endorsed by the House of Lords in *Att-Gen's Reference (No.3) of 1999* [2001] 2 A.C. 91, in holding DNA evidence admissible notwithstanding that the investigation had made use of a sample that should have been destroyed in accordance with the Police and Criminal Evidence Act 1984, s.64(3B). However, the paragraph beginning "A far from straightforward situation" was held to be broadly expressed, *obiter*, and inapplicable in a situation where there was a want of jurisdiction in *Rydqvist v Secretary of State for Work and Pensions* [2002] EWCA Civ 947; I.C.R. 1383.

2. In *Wang v Commissioner of Inland Revenue* [1994] 1 W.L.R. 1286, the Privy Council held that in cases where a question arises as to the consequences of a failure to comply with a time provision (here a requirement that tax assessments against to which there is an objection be confirmed by the Commissioner "within a reasonable time")

Lord Slynn said (at 1296):

". . . their Lordships consider that when a question like the present one arises—an alleged failure to comply with a time provision—it is simpler and better to avoid these two words mandatory and directory and to ask two questions. The first is whether the legislature intended the person making the determination to comply with the time provision, whether a fixed time or a reasonable time. Secondly, if so, did the legislature intend that a failure to comply with such a time provision would deprive the decisionmaker of jurisdiction and render any decision which he purported to make null and void?

In the present case the legislature did intend that the commissioner should make his determination within a reasonable time. At the same time it is no less plain that the legislation imposed on the Revenue authorities, including the commissioner, the duty of assessing and collecting profits tax from 'every person carrying on a trade, profession or business in Hong Kong:' section 14. If the commissioner failed to act within a reasonable time he could be compelled to act by an order of mandamus. It does not follow that his jurisdiction to make a determination disappears the moment a reasonable time has elapsed. If the court establishes the time by which a reasonable time is to be taken as having expired, which will depend on all the circumstances, including factors affecting not only the taxpayer but also the Inland Revenue, it would be surprising if the result was that the commissioner had jurisdiction to make the determination just before but not just after that time. Their Lordships do not consider that that is the effect of a failure to comply with the obligation to act within a reasonable time in the present legislation. Such a result would not only deprive the government of revenue, it would also be unfair to other taxpayers who need to shoulder the burden of government expenditure; the alternative result (that the commissioner continues to have jurisdiction) does not necessarily involve any real prejudice for the taxpayer in question by reason of the delay.

Their Lordships accordingly consider that in the context of this legislation a failure to act within a reasonable time (had it occurred) would not have deprived the commissioner of jurisdiction or made any determination by him null and void".

It is submitted that asking what Parliament intends merely restates the problem without providing a solution. Note, however the factors relied on to support the Privy Council's conclusion. This approach was endorsed by Lord Bingham in *Robinson v Secretary of State for Northern Ireland* [2002] UKHL 32; [2002] N.I. 390 at [13].

3. In a number of cases in the Court of Appeal decided before *Jeyeanthan*, the more flexible approach articulated by Lord Hailsham in the *London & Clydeside* case was commended. For example, in *Main v Swansea City Council* (1984) 49 P. & C.R. 26, the Court of Appeal held that in principle the grant of outline planning permission for the residential development of certain land was vitiated as an (unidentified) owner of a small part of it had not been notified, and the Secretary of State should also have been notified as the land was within 67 metres of the middle of a highway. Parker L.J. said (at 37) that the most helpful observation of Lord Hailsham's speech was that the court must consider the consequences in the light of a concrete state of facts and a continuing chain of events.

> "This recognises that the court looks not only at the nature of the failure but also at such matters as the identity of the applicant for relief, the lapse of time, the effect on other parties and on the public and so on".

The court, however, declined to quash the permission, in the exercise of its discretion. The outline permission had been granted in 1977; reserved matters were approved in 1980 and during this period no objections had been made to the outline permission; the actual development would not take place on the land owned by the unidentified person; the Secretary of State had for a very long time been aware of the position and had not sought relief.

In *R. v Lambeth LBC Ex p. Sharp* (1986) 55 P. & C.R. 232, notice of a proposed development published in a local newspaper failed to specify the period during which objections should be made, and failed to state that objections should be in writing. The Court of Appeal upheld the trial judge's decision to quash the subsequent grant of planning permission. Stephen Brown L.J. said (at p.238):

> "It seems to me that it is not necessary to consider whether these requirements are 'mandatory' or 'directory', or whether they go to powers or duties. One has to look at the terms of the regulations, and a breach of them, in my judgment, clearly provides a basis upon which the court can be seized of an application for judicial review. It is of course material to consider the nature of such a breach—that is to say, its gravity and relevance—when considering whether relief shall be granted. For my part, I am satisfied that the breach in question, which I find the judge was right to hold established, was fundamental, bearing in mind that it is a provision which requires notification of proposed development to members of the public. This was in a conservation area and is obviously a matter of general local public interest. Public notification of the proposed grant of planning permission must accordingly be of fundamental public importance. I would hold that this is not a mere procedural technicality but rather it is a requirement fundamental to the operation of this particular planning procedure".

His Lordship also rejected an argument that the court should decline to quash the permission on the basis that there had been substantial compliance with the requirement of the regulation as a whole, and that no one had been prejudiced. This was a fundamental flaw; it was impossible to say that the applicant had not been prejudiced (he had not seen the site notice); and it was a matter of intense public interest in the locality.

Woolf L.J. said (at 239–240):

> "The regulations are but an example of the numerous different statutory regulations which lay down procedures which have to be followed by public authorities in carrying out their functions. When the provisions of such regulations are contravened,

almost invariably it is unhelpful to consider what are the consequences of non-compliance with the regulations by classifying them as containing mandatory or directory provisions, or as containing a condition precedent, or as containing a provision which renders a decision void or voidable, or by considering whether they contain a provision which goes to jurisdiction. What has to be considered is: what is the particular provision designed to achieve? If, as here, it is designed to give the public an opportunity to make objections to what is proposed, then the court is bound to attach considerable importance to any failure to comply with the requirements.

However, the breach of the requirements cannot be considered alone. It has to be considered in the context of the particular circumstances in relation to which the matter comes before the court".

(His Lordship stated that he adopted the approach of Parker L.J. in *Main v Swansea City Council*, which in turn was based upon Lord Hailsham's speech in the *London Clydeside* case.)

"In adopting that approach to the circumstances in this case, I would come to the same conclusion as the learned judge and my Lord, Stephen Brown L.J. I appreciate that it may be said that this approach introduces an element of uncertainty as to what will be the consequences of a breach of regulations of this nature. However, while accepting that this may be the position, I observe that the attempts which have been made in the past to categorise breaches, and therefore their consequences, have not in fact achieved any degree of continuity and, indeed, have in themselves been a source of considerable litigation as to the particular category in relation to which a particular breach could be said to fall".

Sir John Donaldson M.R. agreed with both judgments.

These cases were considered by Sedley J. in *R. v Tower Hamlets LBC Ex p. Tower Hamlets Combined Traders Association* [1994] C.O.D. 325. His Lordship held that the council's failure to give street traders notice of a designated statutory period of time in which they could make representations concerning a proposed large increase in fees was a breach of a fundamental aspect of the statutory scheme rendering the inquiry decision to increase fees by 90 per cent a nullity. His Lordship held that the *ratio decidendi* of the *London & Clydeside* case was to be found in the speech of Lord Keith, and included the proposition that the question whether non-compliance with a procedural requirement rendered a decision invalid was a question of judgment according to legal criteria and not of discretion, and depended on the general significance of the requirement and not the effect of its omission on the particular applicant. It was also clear that the court retained a discretion to refuse to grant a remedy even in respect of a breach of a requirement of fundamental importance. His Lordship had difficulty with Lord Hailsham's speech in so far as it could be interpreted as conflating these separate points. Furthermore, the adoption of Lord Hailsham's remarks by the Court of Appeal in *Main* and *Sharp* was to be regarded as relating to the exercise of discretion whether to grant a remedy and not to the prior question of the legal effect of the failure to comply with a procedural requirement. See further, below, p.875. This is, with respect, a wholly persuasive analysis and, while it was not cited in *Jeyeanthan*, the Court of Appeal's approach is not inconsistent with that position.

4. Notwithstanding the strictures in *London & Clydeside*, *Wang* and *Jeyeanthan*, use of the terms "mandatory" and "directory" is still frequently found, particularly in case law concerning the procedures of the civil and criminal courts.

5. There are authorities that hold that non-compliance with a directory requirement is only excused if there is substantial compliance. In *Cullimore v Lyme Regis Corporation* [1962] 1 Q.B. 718, the council had power to levy charges in respect of coast protection works on the owners of land benefited, and was to determine these matters within six months of completion of the works. The council did so almost two years after completion. The charges were held by Edmund Davies J. to be *ultra vires*

and void, on the grounds that either (1) the six-month period was mandatory; or (2) even if it were a directory requirement, there had been nothing approaching substantial compliance. What is sufficient for substantial compliance will of course depend on the circumstances. In the *London & Clydeside* case, Lord Hailsham L.C. stated *obiter* (at pp.189–190) that "a total failure to comply with a significant part of a requirement cannot in any circumstances be regarded as 'substantial compliance' with the total requirement . . .": *cf.* the comments on this issue in *Jeyeanthan* (where the legislation imported a "substantial compliance" principle).

A similar outcome to *Cullimore* was reached applying the *Jeyeanthan* approach in *R. (on the application of Dawkins) v Standards Committee of Bolsolver DC* [2004] All ER (D) 168 (Dec), where Hughes J. held that the time requirement that a standards committee hold a hearing into an allegation that a councillor had failed to comply with the council's code of conduct, within three months of receipt of a report by the monitoring officer, was satisfied if there was substantial compliance. Unforeseen events, such as illness, could justify delay, but not ordinary operational reasons. There had not been such compliance where hearing that should have been held by November 20 2003, was held on April 6, 2004 and the decision on April 20.

6. The extent of any prejudice to the applicant and others is potentially relevant at both stages of the analysis, the exercise of judgment as to the legal effect of non-compliance and the exercise of discretion as to the grant of a remedy. Presumably at the first stage the arguments should be more generic, for example as to the extent to which particular requirements are imposed for the benefit of a class of persons and to which non-compliance is likely to prejudice them. It is clear that in an appropriate case (involving breach of a mandatory requirement) an act or decision may be quashed even though the applicant has not been prejudiced (*per* Lord Hailsham L.C. in the *London & Clydeside* case, [1982] 1 W.L.R. 182 at 183; *R. v Birmingham City Council Ex p. Quietlynn* (1985) 83 L.G.R. 461 at 471–479). Compare the position in respect of a failure to comply with natural justice (below, p.863) and under statutory applications to quash (below, p.811).

In other situations, however, the court simply focuses on the question whether procedural defects have caused substantial prejudice (see *Haringey LBC v Awartife* (1999) 32 H.L.R. 517, followed in *Godwin v Rossendale BC* [2002] EWCA Civ 726).

7. The following case deals with one particularly important procedural requirement, the obligation to consult. Statutory duties to give reasons are considered below, pp.841–853.

AGRICULTURAL, HORTICULTURAL AND FORESTRY INDUSTRY TRAINING BOARD v AYLESBURY MUSHROOMS LTD

[1972] 1 W.L.R. 190; (1971) 116 S.J. 57; [1972] 1 All E.R. 280; [1972] I.T.R. 16 (DONALDSON J.)

The Industrial Training Act 1964 provided for the establishment by Order of industrial training boards. Each board arranged training for those employed in the industries concerned, and was supported by levies imposed on the employers in those industries. Section 1(4) of the Act provided:

"Before making an industrial training order the Minister shall consult any organisation or association of organisations appearing to him to be representative of substantial numbers of employers engaging in the activities concerned and any organisation or association of organisations appearing to him to be representative of substantial numbers of persons employed in those activities; and if those activities are carried on to a substantial extent by a body established for the purpose of carrying on under national ownership any industry or part of an industry or undertaking, shall consult that body".

In 1965, the Ministry of Labour was minded to set up the plaintiff board. Consultations were held between Ministry officials and the largest representative body concerned, the National Farmers' Union. By April 1966 a draft Order had been prepared. An advance copy of the schedule to the Order, which defined the industry to which the order related, was sent to the National Farmers' Union on April 15, 1966. On April 26, 1966, copies of this document were circulated to a large number of addresses, including the Mushroom Growers' Association, inviting comments. Simultaneously there was a press notice summarising the activities which it was proposed should be covered by the new board and advising any organisation which considered that it had an interest in the draft schedule and which had not received a copy to apply to the Ministry of Labour. No comments were received from the Mushroom Growers' Association and no application was made by them for a copy of the schedule.

The Order was made on August 2, 1966, laid before Parliament on August 11, and came into operation on August 15. The Mushroom Growers' Association applied in May 1968 for complete exemption from the Order on various grounds. They had never received a copy of the draft schedule, and had no knowledge of the consultations between the Ministry and the National Farmers' Union, or of the press notice. The Mushroom Growers' Association was a specialist branch of the National Farmers' Union, although largely autonomous. It represented about 85 per cent of all mushroom growers in England and Wales, who were responsible for about 80 per cent of mushroom production.

The Board sought a determination as to whether the Minister had complied with his duty of consultation, and if not, what were the consequences. The real defendants were the Mushroom Growers' Association, but as that was an unincorporated association, it was thought more convenient that the nominal defendants should be Aylesbury Mushrooms Ltd, who were representative of the Mushroom Growers' Association membership.

DONALDSON J.: . . . Both parties are agreed that under the terms of section 1(4) of the Act, some consultation by the Minister is mandatory and that in the absence of any particular consultation which is so required, the persons who should have been but were not consulted are not bound by the Order, although the Order remains effective in relation to all others who were in fact consulted or whom there was no need to consult. Both parties are further agreed that if consultation with the Mushroom Growers' Association was mandatory and there was no sufficient consultation the Order takes effect according to its terms subject to a rider that it does not apply to the growing of mushrooms or to persons engaged in this activity solely by reason of their being so engaged. They may, of course, come within the scope of the Order in some other capacity.

Both parties are also agreed that the organisations required to be consulted are those which appear to the Minister, or to his alter ago who in this case was a Mr Devey, to be representative of substantial numbers of employers engaging in the activities concerned or persons employed therein and nationalised industries which engage in those activities to a substantial extent. Thus whether any particular organisation has to be consulted depends upon a subjective test, subject always to *bona fides* and reasonableness which are not in question.

Against this background Mr Bradburn, for the association, submits that the court must see what organisations appeared to the Minister to fall into the specified categories, and that the Minister clearly sought to consult the Mushroom Growers' Association thereby showing that he regarded it as being within the class of organisation which had to be consulted. It follows, as he submits, that neither the board nor the Minister can now turn round and say that consultation with the National Farmers' Union constituted a sufficient discharge of his duties. Mr Bradburn goes on to submit that there can be no consultation without at least unilateral communication and that no such communication occurred.

Mr Gettleson for the board submitted that "any" in the phrase "the Minister shall consult any organisation" imposed a duty to consult not more than one organisation, that posting the letter of April 26, 1966, constituted consultation with the Mushroom Growers' Association despite the fact that it was never received, that the Mushroom Growers' Association was not an organisation which had to be consulted and that consultation with the National Farmers' Union involved consultation with all its branches including the Mushroom Growers' Association.

I have no doubt that Mr Gettleson's first point is without foundation. "Any" must mean "every" in the context of section 1(4). There is a little more to be said for his submission that the mere sending of the letter of April 26, 1966, constituted consultation in that the Shorter Oxford English Dictionary gives as one definition of the verb "to consult" "to ask advice of, seek counsel from; to have recourse to for instruction or professional advice". However, in truth the mere sending of a letter constitutes but an attempt to consult and this does not suffice. The essence of consultation is the communication of a genuine invitation, extended with a receptive mind, to give advice: see *per* Bucknill L.J. approving a dictum of Morris J. in *Rollo v Minister of Town and Country Planning* [1948] 1 All E.R. 13, 17. If the invitation is once received, it matters not that it is not accepted and no advice is proffered. Were it otherwise organisations with a right to be consulted could, in effect, veto the making of any order by simply failing to respond to the invitation. But without communication and the consequent opportunity of responding, there can be no consultation.

This leaves only the related questions of whether the Mushroom Growers' Association did in fact appear to the Minister to be an organisation falling within the categories set out in section 1(4) with the consequence that he was under an obligation to consult them and whether in any event his consultations with the National Farmers' Union constituted consultation with the Mushroom Growers' Association as a branch of the N.F.U. This is the heart of the problem.

Mr Devey has deposed in paragraph 5 of his affidavit:

"In accordance with practice the circulation of the draft schedule was not restricted to organisations that appeared to me to be representative of substantial numbers of employers engaging in activities specified in the draft schedule. This will appear sufficiently from a persual of the document. In particular the Mushroom Growers' Association was listed, although it was, and remains, a specialist branch of the National Farmer's Union. The listed address of the association is the same as that of the union which is Agriculture House, Knightsbridge, London, S.W.1."

In each case he sent a covering letter in one of three forms. The addresses on the first list, such as the National Farmers' Union, the Trades Union Congress, the Confederation of British Industry, and major government departments received special letters from Mr Devey. Those on the second list received letters which were in standard form but were sent personally to named officials of the organisation concerned. These included the Local Government Examinations Board which clearly is an organisation which should have been consulted, but not one which in the terms of the Act had to be consulted. Those on the third list, including the Mushroom Growers' Association, received or should have received letters in standard form addressed to the organisation impersonally. I can find no clue in the form of the covering letter to whether any particular addressee appeared to the Minister to be a section 1(4) organisation and examples can be found in each list of organisations which plainly fall outside this category. I am thus thrown back on Mr Devey's affidavit coupled with a letter dated January 20, 1969, signed by a Mr Thomson of the Department of Employment and Productivity which states that a copy of the draft schedule was sent to the National Farmers' Union of which it is understood that the Mushroom Growers' Association is a specialist branch "and also as a matter of courtesy to that association". Bearing in mind the importance which attaches to consultation in the scheme of the Industrial Training Act 1964, which seems to be based upon the healthy principle of "no taxation without consultation", and the fact that Mr Devey has not in terms said that the association did not appear to him to fall within the scope of section 1(4), I feel obliged to conclude that it was an organisation which had to be consulted, although its small membership in the context of the number of persons employed in agriculture, horticulture and forestry, and the specialised nature of their activities could well have led the Minister to take a different view.

This only leaves the question of whether it was consulted vicariously, and it may be accidentally, by means of the consultations with the National Farmers' Union. This is a nice point. *Prima facie* consultation with the parent body undoubtedly constitutes consultation with its constituent parts, but I think that this general rule is subject to an exception where, as here, the Minister has also attempted and intended direct consultation with a branch. The association's complaint has very little merit, because it seems to have been completely blind to all that was going on around it. Nevertheless it is important that statutory powers which involve taxation shall strictly construed and, so construed, I consider that the association should have been consulted and was not consulted.

I therefore answer the questions in the originating summons as follows: "Whether before making an order establishing a training board for the agricultural, horticultural and forestry industry, the Minister was under a duty to consult the Mushroom Growers' Association"—yes.

"Whether the consultations held by the Minister with the National Farmers' Union constituted a sufficient consultation with an organisation or association of organisations representative of those engaged in the activity of horticulture"—no.

"If it be held that the Minister was under a duty to consult the Mushroom Growers' Association, whether on the facts such consultation took place"—no.

"If it be held that the Minister was under a duty to consult the Mushroom Growers' Association and failed to do so, what effect such failure had upon the provisions of the Industrial Training (Agricultural, Horticultural and Forestry Board) Order 1966 (S.I. 1966 No. 969)"—the Order has no application to mushroom growers as such.

Order accordingly.

Notes

1. See case note by D. Foulkes, (1972) 35 M.L.R. 647.

2. A statutory duty to consult interested parties has been consistently regarded as mandatory. Questions more commonly arise as to who should be consulted and what constitutes sufficient for compliance with the duty. A formulation frequently cited is the submission of Stephen Sedley Q.C. adopted by Hodgson J. in *R. v Brent LBC Ex p. Gunning* (1985) 84 L.G.R. 168 at 189, and endorsed by the Court of Appeal in *Coughlan* (above, p.607). This is applicable whether consultation is a statutory requirement or is based on a legitimate expectation (below pp.699–700).

3. The question of consultation was raised in *R. v Secretary of State for the Environment, Ex p. Association of Metropolitan Authorities* [1986] 1 W.L.R. 1. The Secretary had power under the Housing Benefits Act 1982 to make regulations constituting the housing benefit scheme. Section 36(1) of the Act provided that before making regulations (including amending regulations) "the Secretary of State shall consult with organisations appearing to him to be representative of the authorities concerned" (*i.e.* local authorities). The Secretary of State habitually consulted the local authority associations, including the AMA, before making regulations, and it was common ground that the AMA was one of the organisations contemplated by s.36(1). On November 16, 1984, the DHSS wrote to the AMA requesting their views on proposals to make certain amendments to the regulations designed to close a "loophole". The letter was received on November 22 and a response was sought by November 30. The AMA requested an extension of time but no answer was forthcoming. Further proposed amendments were summarised in a letter of December 4, which sought a response by December 12. No draft of the proposed amendments was enclosed, and no mention was made of a material feature (which would require local authorities to investigate the background to the creation of joint tenancies by claimants so as to satisfy themselves that the tenancies had not been contrived to take advantage of the housing benefit scheme). The AMA replied on December 13 with brief comments. The amending regulations were made on December 17 and became law on December 19. Webster J. granted a declaration that the Secretary of State had failed to comply with s.36(1), but refused, in the exercise of his discretion, to quash the regulations. Webster J. said (at 4–5):

> "There is no general principle to be extracted from the case law as to what kind or amount of consultation is required before delegated legislation, of which consultation is a precondition, can validly be made. But in any context the essence of consultation is the communication of a genuine invitation to give advice and a genuine receipt of that advice. In my view it must go without saying that to achieve consultation sufficient information must be supplied by the consulting to the consulted party to enable it to tender helpful advice. Sufficient time must be given by the consulting to the consulted party to enable it do to that, and sufficient time must be available for such advice to be considered by the consulting party. Sufficient, in that context, does not mean ample, but at least enough to enable the relevant purpose to be fulfilled. By helpful advice, in this context, I mean sufficiently informed and considered information or advice about aspects of the form or substance of the proposals, or their implications for the consulted party, being aspects material to the implementation of the proposal as to which the Secretary of State might not be fully informed or advised and as to which the party consulted might have relevant information or advice to offer.
>
> These propositions, as it seems to me, can partly be derived from, and are wholly consistent with, the decisions and various dicta, which I need not enumerate, in *Rollo v Minister of Town and Country Planning* [1948] 1 All E.R. 13 and *Port Louis Corporation v Attorney-General of Mauritius* [1965] A.C. 1111".

Webster J. noted that as the day-to-day administration of the scheme was in the hands of local authorities, who bore 10 per cent of the scheme's cost, the obligation to consult was mandatory and not directory. In considering whether the consultation required by s.36(1) was in substance carried out, the court:

> "should have regard not so much to the actual facts which preceded the making of the regulations as to the material before the Secretary of State when he made the regulations, that material including facts or information as it appeared or must have appeared to him acting in good faith, and any judgments made or opinions expressed to him before the making of the regulations about those facts which appeared to could have appeared to him to be reasonable".

The effect of this approach was:

> "to give a certain flexibility to the notions of sufficiency, sufficient information, sufficient time and sufficiently informed and consider information and advice in my homespun attempt to define proper consultation. Thus, it can have the effect that what would be sufficient information or time in one case might be more or less than sufficient in another, depending on the relative degrees of urgency and the nature of the proposed regulation. There is no degree of urgency, however, which absolves the Secretary of State from the obligation to consult at all".

His Lordship concluded that while the department was entitled to expect a quick response, the urgency of the situation was not such as to justify requiring views within such a short period that they might be insufficiently informed or considered.

However, the regulations were not quashed. Only one of six local authority associations had challenged the regulations; authorities would by then have adapted to the difficulties created by the regulations; revocation would mean that applicants refused benefit under the amended regulations would be entitled to make fresh claims, but this advantage would only last for six months as the challenged regulations had subsequently been consolidated in the Housing Benefits Regulations 1985, and the consolidation was not challenged.

The principles set out in *AMA* and *Gunning* have been applied in a variety of contexts, including the making of delegated legislation and (commonly) the closure of schools, residential homes and hospitals. Common defects include allowing too short a period for proper consultation (see, e.g. *R. v Secretary of State for Education and Employment Ex p. NUT* [2000] Ed.C.R. 603 (four days allowed for consultation on order modifying teachers' contracts)); a failure to consult when proposals were at a formative stage where there would have been time to do so (*R. v Secretary of State for Social Security Ex p. Association of Metropolitan Authorities* (1993) 25 H.L.R. 131 (a declaration was granted that the minister had not complied with the duty of consultation, but the regulations were not quashed)); and the inclusion of misleading information in the consultation document (*Gunning*).

See also *Howker v Secretary of State for Work and Pensions* [2002] EWCA Civ 1623, where the Social Security Advisory Committee agreed that proposed amending regulations need not be referred to it, but only on the basis of seriously inaccurate information from the DWP as to the nature and effect of the proposed change; this was a material irregularity that invalidated the amending regulations.

(B) Natural Justice: The Duty to Act Fairly[1]

In administrative law the "rules of natural justice" have traditionally been regarded as comprising the rules *audi alteram partem* and *nemo judex in causa sua*. Respectively, these apply to require the maker of a decision to give prior notice of the decision to

---

[1] See generally P. Jackson, *Natural Justice* (2nd ed., 1979); G.A. Flick, *Natural Justice* (2nd ed., 1984); *de Smith, Woolf and Jowell*, Ch. 8; *Craig*, Ch. 8; *Wade and Forsyth*, Pt V.

persons affected by it, and an opportunity for those persons to make representations; and also to disqualify the decision-maker from acting if he or she has a direct pecuniary or proprietary interest, or where there is a real danger that he or she might otherwise be biased. The rules were historically closely tied to judicial decision-making in the courts, but they have been extended to apply to administrative authorities and to administrative decision-making, and it is here that the main difficulties have arisen. It has not been wholly clear how far the rules of natural justice apply to decisions which do not have a significant judicial element. Here, the courts have increasingly prescribed a basic duty to act fairly, which may include some aspects of "natural justice", but which may on occasion, simply amount to a duty to refrain from any abuse of discretion. It is certainly the case that the difficulties have for the most part disappeared with a move to an approach whereby procedural standards are imposed that are appropriate in the particular context.

In the case of each of the twin rules of natural justice two basic issues are involved:

    (a) Does the rule apply to the particular situation; and
    (b) if so, what is the precise content of the rule in that situation?

Finally, of course, if it applies, has the rule been observed?

The common law principles of natural justice are reflected in and thereby further entrenched by Art.6, ECHR (see pp.374–384).

(i) The Right to a Fair Hearing

In the twentieth century, the application of this rule (historically termed *audi alteram partem*) has been considered by the House of Lords in a series of cases including *Board of Education v Rice* [1911] A.C. 179; *Local Government Board v Arlidge* [1915] A.C. 120; *Ridge v Baldwin* (1963) (below, p.658); *Bushell v Secretary of State for the Environment* (1980) (below, p.731); *Lloyd v McMahon* (1987) (below, p.722); *R. v Board of Visitors of H.M. Prison, The Maze Ex p. Hone* (1988) (below, p.726); *Al-Mehdawi v Secretary of State for the Home Department* (1990) (below, p.715) and *R. v Secretary of State for the Home Department Ex p. Doody* (below, p.743). The pivotal decision is that of *Ridge v Baldwin*. This removed some restrictions on the rule's application that had developed since 1914 in lower courts, and led to an "explosion" of natural justice cases.

Briefly stated, the traditional basic principle was that the *audi alteram partem* rule had to be observed by anyone who was making a judicial or quasi-judicial, as distinct from an administrative, decision. Following *Ridge v Baldwin*, a wider variety of decisions were regarded as "judicial" or "quasi-judicial" for this purpose (note the discussion of these categories in Ch.1 of the second edition of this work). In turn this led some judges to argue that it was no longer necessary to distinguish between the "judicial" or "quasi-judicial" and the "administrative" (*e.g.* Lord Denning in *Schmidt v Secretary of State for Home Affairs* [1969] 2 Ch. 149). This has become the accepted position in practice. If a decision seriously affects individual interests, natural justice or fairness must be observed irrespective of the label applicable to that decision, all the legal argument being about the appropriate content of the rule in the particular situation. Another approach that has been taken is to require observation of "natural justice" in the making of judicial or quasi-judicial decisions, and of a "duty to act fairly" in the making of administrative decisions (*e.g.* Lord Parker C.J. in *H.K. (An Infant), Re* (1967) (below, p.676). This will usually lead to the same result as the previous approach, but it preserves the need to label decisions, a task that properly should be redundant.

Each of these approaches may be contrasted with the previous situation where judges adopted an "analytical" approach, denying the relevance of natural justice to non-judicial decisions. This led either to injustice, where natural justice was held not to apply to decisions that substantially prejudiced individual interests (as in *Nakkuda Ali v*

Jayaratne [1951] A.C. 66 (below, p.666) (discussed in *Ridge v Baldwin*), where a decision to revoke a trader's licence and thereby to deprive him of his livelihood was held to be non-judicial), or strained analysis, where clearly administrative decisions were classified as "judicial" (as in *Cooper v Wandsworth Board of Works*, below p.653).

de Smith, Woolf and Jowell comment that:

"The term 'natural justice' is being increasingly replaced by a general duty to act fairly, which is a key element of procedural propriety.

Whichever term is used, the time has come to make a break with the artificial constraints surrounding the situations in which natural justice or the duty to act fairly are required. The previous distinctions were already comatose and should be formally declared moribund. . . . The law has moved on; not to the state where the entitlement to procedural protection can be extracted with certainty from a computer, but to where the courts are able to insist upon some degree of participation in reaching most official decisions by those whom the decisions will affect in widely different situations, subject only to well-established exceptions" (p.401).

Two broad purposes have been identified as justifying the imposition of procedural standards. The first is instrumentalism. Requirements may be imposed to maximise the chances that the decision-making process produces the "right answer". The second is that procedural standards may be "designed to protect values which are independent of the direct outcome of the decision, such as participation, fairness and the protection of human dignity" (G. Richardson in, *Administrative Law & Government Action* (*Richardson and Genn* ed. 1994), p.113. A further point, which draws on both of these considerations, is that "disadvantageous decisions are more likely to be accepted and observed if they are arrived at by means of a fair procedure" (C. Rennig in *Procedural Justice* (Röhl and Machura, 1997), p.207). Most judicial reasoning tends to emphasise the first purpose, although there are references to the second (see, e.g. Lord Mustill in *Doody*, below, pp.746, 747; Laws L.J. in *R. (on the application of Khatun) v Newham LBC* [2004] EWCA Civ 55; [2004] 3 W.L.R. 417 at [27], below, p.675).

In the following subsections we consider (1) the types of decision-making which have been subject to some form of fair hearing obligations, (2) factors which have induced the judiciary to limit the application of the right to a fair hearing, and (3) the content of the right to a fair hearing in particular decision-making contexts.

(a) *When does the "right to a fair hearing" apply?*

COOPER v THE BOARD OF WORKS FOR THE WANDSWORTH DISTRICT

(1863) 14 C.B.(N.S.) 180; 32 L.J.C.P. 185; 8 L.T. 278; 2 NEW REP. 31; 9 JUR.(N.S.) 1155; 11 W.R. 646; 143 E.R. 414 (COURT OF COMMON PLEAS)

The Metropolis Local Management Act 1855, s.76, provided that: "before beginning to lay or dig out the foundation of any new house or building . . . seven days notice in writing shall be given to the . . . board by the person intending to build . . . such house or building . . .". This ensured that the board had opportunity to give directions under the Act as to the drains. section 76 also provided that "in default of such notice . . . it shall be lawful for . . . the board to cause such house or building to be demolished or altered . . . and to recover the expenses thereof from the owner . . .". The plaintiff, a builder, was employed to build a house in Wandsworth. He claimed that he sent a notice under s.76 to the board, but this was denied. He admitted, however, that he had commenced digging out the foundations within five days of the day on which he claimed to have sent the notice. The house had reached the second storey when the board, without giving any notice, sent round their surveyor and a number of workmen at a late hour in the evening. The men razed the house to the ground.

The plaintiff sued for damages for trespass. Willes J. found for the plaintiff. The defendants obtained a rule nisi for a nonsuit. They argued (*inter alia*) (1) that "the great safeguard against abuses . . . is that the members of which these boards are composed are elected by the rate-payers of the district". (2) "What necessity can there be for giving the party notice, when he well knows that he is doing an illegal act, and that the board have power to prostrate his house?" (3) "It is not like the case where a judicial discretion is to be exercised. An arbitrary power is conferred upon the board, which is necessarily to be exercised without any control."

ERLE C.J.: . . . The contention on the part of the plaintiff has been, that, although the words of the statute, taken in their literal sense, without any qualification at all, would create a justification for the act which the district board has done, the powers granted by that statute are subject to a qualification which has been repeatedly recognised, that no man is to be deprived of his property without his having an opportunity of being heard. . . . I think that the power which is granted by the 76th section is subject to the qualification suggested. It is a power carrying with it enormous consequences. The house in question was built only to a certain extent. But the power claimed would apply to a complete house. It would apply to a house of any value, and completed to any extent; and it seems to me to be a power which may be exercised most perniciously, and that the limitation which we are going to put upon it is one which ought, according to the decided cases, to be put upon it, and one which is required by a due consideration for the public interest. I think the board ought to have given notice to the plaintiff, and to have allowed him to be heard. The default in sending notice to the board of the intention to build, is a default which may be explained. There may be a great many excuses for the apparent default. The party may have intended to conform to the law. He may have actually conformed to all the regulations which they would wish to impose, though by accident his notice may have miscarried; and, under those circumstances, if he explained how it stood, the proceeding to demolish, merely because they had ill-will against the party, is a power that the legislature never intended to confer. I cannot conceive any harm that could happen to the district board from hearing the party before they subjected him to a loss so serious as the demolition of his house; but I can conceive a great many advantages which might arise in the way of public order, in the way of doing substantial justice, and in the way of fulfilling the purposes of the statute, by the restriction which we put upon them, that they should hear the party before they inflict upon him such a heavy loss. I fully agree that the legislature intended to give the district board very large powers indeed: but the qualification I speak of is one which has been recognised to the full extent. It has been said that the principle that no man shall be deprived of his property without an opportunity of being heard, is limited to a judicial proceeding, and that a district board ordering a house to be pulled down cannot be said to be doing a judicial act. I do not quite agree with that; neither do I undertake to rest my judgment solely upon the ground that the district board is a court exercising judicial discretion upon the point: but the law, I think, has been applied to many exercises of power which in common understanding would not be at all more a judicial proceeding than would be the act of the district board in ordering a house to be pulled down. The case of the corporation of the University of Cambridge, who turned out Dr Bentley, in the exercise of their assumed power of depriving a member of the University of his rights, and a number of other cases which are collected in the *Hammersmith Rent-Charge* Case, 4 Exch. 96, in the judgment of Parke B., show that the principle has been very widely applied. The district board must do the thing legally; there must be a resolution; and, if there be a board, and a resolution of that board, I have not heard a word to show that it would not be salutary that they should hear the man who is to suffer from their judgment before they proceed to make the order under which they attempt to justify their act. It is said that an appeal from the district board to the metropolitan board (under s.211) would be the mode of redress. But, if the district board have the power to do what is here stated, I am not at all clear that there would be a right of redress in that way. The metropolitan board may not have a right to give redress for that which was done under the provisions of the statute. I think the appeal clause would evidently indicate that many exercises of the power of a district board would be in the nature of judicial proceedings; because, certainly when they are appealed from, the appellant and the respondent are to be heard as parties, and the matter is to be decided at least according to judicial forms. I take that to be a principle of very wide application, and applicable to the present case; and I think this board was not justified under the statute, because they have not qualified themselves for the exercise of their power by hearing the party to be affected by their decision.

WILLES J.: I am of the same opinion. I apprehend that a tribunal which is by law invested with power to affect the property of one of Her Majesty's subjects, is bound to give such subject an opportunity of being heard before it proceeds: and that that rule is of universal application, and founded upon the plainest principles of justice. Now, is the board in the present case such a tribunal? I apprehend it clearly is, whether we consider it with reference to the discretion which is vested in it, or whether we look at the analogy which exists between it and other recognised tribunals (and no one ever doubted that such tribunals are bound by the rules which a court of justice is bound by), or whether you look at it with reference to the estimation in which it is held by the legislature, as appears from the language used in the statute. . . .

. . . With respect to nuisances, the board exercises the power of a criminal court of high jurisdiction, because it has a discretion as to whether it will abate that which is a nuisance altogether, or whether it will simply direct that there shall be a modification of the works which in its opinion are necessary for the health of the neighbourhood. I apprehend it is clear that the powers thus exercised by the board under the Act are powers which have always been considered judicial, and which could not be exercised without giving notice to the party who is to be proceeded against. In this very section, 76, the legislature speaks of coming "under the jurisdiction of the vestry or board"; and it is clear that these boards do exercise judicial powers. The power here is one that, probably more than any, requires that the party to be affected by it should be heard, because of its extent, and because the board may be satisfied with a modification of that which has been done. . . .

[His Lordship summarised s.76.]

The matter to be considered by the board before they make that order [*i.e.* an order giving directions] is, first of all, has any notice been given? And then the party clearly ought to be allowed to show, either that he has given a notice which may have been overlooked, or, if the notice has not been received by the board, to show that he did his best towards doing so, in order to induce them to look on the case favourably—not to demolish the house, but to seen whether any and what qualification is necessary for the purpose of bringing it within what should be done if the notice had been regularly served. In either of those cases, I apprehend, it is clear that it would be the right of the party to be heard. But there is a third case; and that is where, by wilfully disregarding the order, or by the act of some third person, whom he did his best to control, the owner of the house may have subjected his house to demolition by the board, or to be dealt with severely by reason of its defects. That is a case in which judicial power is to be exercised, and in which clearly the party sought to be affected should be heard. Then, as to the appeal section, 211, what light does that throw upon the matter? There is an appeal from the district board, not to any judicial tribunal in the sense of any tribunal more judicial in its form than the local board of works, but to the metropolitan board of works, which is just as much and just as little judicial in its acts as the board whose conduct we are now considering. What is to take place upon such appeal? "And all such appeals shall stand referred to the committee appointed by such board for hearing appeals, as herein provided; and such committee shall *hear and determine* all such appeals." Nothing can be more clear than that the legislature thought that the matters which might come before the board upon appeal, that is, the same matters which came before the local board of works in the first instance, were proper, not only to be determined, but also to be heard; and, if fit to be heard upon an appeal, a *fortiori* fit to be heard in the first instance, before a wrongful decision can make an appeal lie. . . .

. . . There is another remark to be made with reference to these parties' proceedings. The board are not only to do the work of demolishing the house, if they think proper, or modifying it, but they are to charge the expenses on the person who has erred against the Act. His property is affected and his purse is further affected. What happens upon that? and how is the money to be got? That is a proceeding under the 225th section, which is a section giving jurisdiction to the justices before whom the costs are to be ascertained and recovered; and it is clear that under that section the justices could not proceed without having before them the person against whom the expenses are to be adjudged. And it does seem an absurdity to say, that, in determining the amount of expenses, the party shall be heard, but that, in determining whether proceedings should be taken, his mouth should be closed. I cannot help thinking that a board exercising this large power should follow the ordinary rule, that the party sought to be affected should be heard; and I think that the verdict for the plaintiff ought to stand.

BYLES J.: I am of the same opinion. This is a case in which the Wandsworth district board have taken upon themselves to pull down a house, and to saddle the owner with the expenses of demolition, without notice of any sort. There are two sorts of notice which may possibly be required, and neither of them has been given: one, a notice of a hearing, that the party may be heard if he has anything to say against the demolition; the other is a notice of the order, that he may consider whether he can mitigate the wrath of the board, or in any way modify the execution of the order. Here they have given him neither opportunity. It seems to me that the board are wrong whether they acted judicially or ministerially. I conceive they acted judicially, because they had to determine the offence, and they had to apportion the punishment as well as the remedy. That being so, a long course of decisions, beginning with Dr Bentley's case,[2] and ending with some very recent cases, establish, that, although there are no positive words in a statute requiring that the party shall be heard, yet the justice of the common law will supply the omission of the legislature. The judgment of Mr Justice Fortescue, in Dr Bentley's case, is somewhat quaint, but it is very applicable, and has been the law from that time to the present. He says, "The objection for want of notice can never be got over. The laws of God and man both give the party an opportunity to make his defence, if he has any. I remember to have heard it observed by a very learned man, upon such an occasion, that even God himself did not pass sentence upon Adam before he was called upon to make his defence. 'Adam' (says God), 'where art thou? Hast thou not eaten of the tree whereof I commanded thee that thou shouldest not eat?' And the same question was put to Eve also." If, therefore, the board acted judicially, although there are no words in the statute to that effect, it is plain they acted wrongly. But suppose they acted ministerially—then it may be they were not bound to give the first sort of notice, *viz.* the notice of the hearing; but they were clearly bound, as it seems to me, by the words of the statute, to give notice of their order before they proceeded to execute it. Section 76 contains these words: "The vestry or district board shall make their order in relation to the matters aforesaid, and cause the same to be notified" (observe what follows) "to the person from whom such notice was received, within seven days after the receipt of the notice." The plain construction of those words, as it seems to me, is this: the order is to be notified, and, in the case of a person who has given a notice, that notification is to be conveyed to him within seven days from the date of his notice. That has not been done. There has been neither notice of the one sort nor of the other; and it seems to me, therefore, that, whether the board acted judicially or ministerially, they have acted against the whole current of authorities, and have omitted to do that which justice requires, and contravened the words of the statute. I entirely agree with what my Brother Willes has said about section 211, which clearly shows, that, if the board acted ministerially, they ought to give notice of the latter character. I cannot entertain any doubt that in this case the board have exercised their power wrongfully.

KEATING J.: delivered a concurring judgment.

Rule discharged.

Notes

1. A wide variety of arguments are advanced by the judges; note in particular their avowed aim of promoting good administration. They do not simply incant "no man shall be deprived of his property without a hearing".

2. Note the willingness of Byles J. to read words requiring a hearing into the statute. Compare the views of the Privy Council in *Furnell v Whangarei School Board* [1973] 1 All E.R. 400, PC. The majority (Lords Morris of Borth-y-Gest, Simon of Glaisdale and Kilbrandon) were of the opinion that where a detailed and elaborate disciplinary code was prescribed by statutory regulations, as it was for the investigation of complaints against teachers in New Zealand, it was "not lightly to be affirmed" that it was

---

[2] *The King v The Chancellor, of Cambridge*, 1 Stra. 557; 2 Ld.Raym. 1334; 8 Mod. 148; Fortescue 202.

unfair "when it has been made on the advice of the responsible Minister and on the joint recommendation of organisations representing teachers employed and those employing. Nor is it the function of the court to redraft the code" (at 411). The approach of the minority (Viscount Dilhorne and Lord Reid) was to ask first whether the nature of the powers exercised gave rise to a presumption that they were to be exercised only after the person affected had been given a fair hearing. If a fair hearing was necessary but had not been given, the burden shifted to the authority to establish that the regulations "clearly show an intention to exclude that which natural justice would otherwise require" (at 417). Which approach is preferable? See case note by J.M. Evans, (1973) 36 M.L.R. 439 and article by J.F. Northey, [1972] N.Z.L.J. 307. For the contemporary view of the House of Lords, see Lord Bridge's speech in *Lloyd v McMahon* (below, p.722), following the latter.

RIDGE v BALDWIN

[1964] A.C. 40; [1963] 2 W.L.R. 935; 127 J.P. 295; 107 S.J. 313; [1963] 2 All E.R. 66; 61 L.G.R. 369 (HOUSE OF LORDS)

The Municipal Corporations Act 1882 provided by s.191: "(4) The Watch Committee, . . . may at any time dismiss, any borough constable whom they think negligent in the discharge of his duty, or otherwise unfit for the same". The Police Act 1919 provided by s.4(1): "It shall be lawful for the Secretary of State to make regulations as to the . . . conditions of service of the members of all police forces within England and Wales, and every police authority shall comply with the regulations so made". It was accepted that the 1919 Act did not impliedly repeal the relevant provisions of the 1882 Act. The relevant regulations contained detailed provisions as to the procedure to be followed where a report or allegation was received by the police authority from which it appeared that a chief constable might have committed an offence against the "Discipline Code" (set out in the regulations).

According to the regulations, the detailed procedure, which involved a formal hearing before a specially constituted tribunal, could only be dispensed with if the chief constable admitted that he had committed an offence against the code.

Charles Ridge was appointed chief constable of the County Borough of Brighton in 1956. The appointment was "subject to the Police Act and Regulations". In 1957, Ridge, two police officers and two others were indicted for conspiracy to obstruct the course of justice between 1949 and 1957. Ridge was acquitted, but the other two police officers were convicted. On February 28, in passing sentence, the trial judge, Donovan J., made certain observations as to the chief constable's conduct. In the words of Lord Evershed:

"As I understand the language of Donovan J. . . . the appellant had been shown not to possess a sense of probity or of responsibility sufficient for the office which he held, and so had been unable to provide the essential leadership and example to the police force under his control which his office properly required".

On March 6, no evidence was offered against R on a further charge of corruption. Here Donovan J. referred to the police force's need for a leader "who will be a new influence and who will set a different example from that which has lately obtained." The following day, the Watch Committee, purporting to act under s.191(4) of the 1882 Act summarily dismissed R on the ground that in their opinion he had been negligent in the discharge of his duty, and was unfit for the same. He was given neither any notice of the meeting, nor any opportunity to make representations. The regulations were in no way operated. On March 18, the committee heard representations from R's solicitor, but gave no further particulars of the case against him. On July 5, the Home Secretary dismissed R's appeal under the Police (Appeals) Act 1927 (as amended), holding "that there was sufficient material on which the Watch Committee could properly exercise their power of dismissal under section 191(4)". The appeal had been made expressly without prejudice to any rights to contend that the purported dismissal was bad in law as being contrary to natural justice and not in accordance with the regulations.

R then brought an action in the High Court for a declaration that the dismissal was illegal, *ultra vires* and void, and for damages. His main purpose was to obtain the opportunity to resign voluntarily, his pension rights thus being preserved.

Eight significant issues arose:

1. Did the regulations apply? If they did, there had been a clear non-compliance.
2. If they did not, did the *audi alteram partem* rule of natural justice nevertheless apply?
3. If it applied, was it complied with?
4. If the decision to dismiss was bad under either of the foregoing heads, was it void or voidable?
5. If the initial dismissal was bad, was it cured by the second meeting of the committee on March 18?
6. Did the exercise of the right of appeal cure any invalidity?
7. Was the invalidity cured by the Police (Appeals) Act 1927, s.2(3), which stated that the Secretary of State's decision should be final and binding on all parties?
8. Should the invalidity be ignored, on the ground that the case was "as plain as a pikestaff?".

Streatfeild J. at first instance ([1961] 2 W.L.R. 1054), held that natural justice had to be observed, and that the Watch Committee had done so. The Court of Appeal ([1963] 1 Q.B. 539) held that natural justice did not have to be observed as the action of the committee was "administrative" or "executive". They were not deciding a question between two contending parties. Ridge's appeal to the House of Lords was allowed. The leading speeches were those of Lord Reid, who dealt mainly with natural justice at common law, and Lord Morris of Borth-y-Gest, who dealt mainly with the regulations. Lord Hodson came to the same conclusions as both Lord Reid and Lord Morris. Lord Devlin's speech was based solely on the regulations. Lord Evershed dissented.

LORD REID: . . . The appellant's case is that in proceeding under the Act of 1882 the watch committee were bound to observe what are commonly called the principles of natural justice. Before attempting to reach any decision they were bound to inform him of the grounds on which they proposed to act and give him a fair opportunity of being heard in his own defence. The authorities on the applicability of the principles of natural justice are in some confusion, and so I find it necessary to examine this matter in some detail. The principle *audi alteram partem* goes back many centuries in our law and appears in a multitude of judgments of judges of the highest authority. In modern time opinions have sometimes been expressed to the effect that natural justice is so vague as to be practically meaningless. But I would regard these as tainted by the perennial fallacy that because something cannot be cut and dried or nicely weighed or measured therefore it does not exist. The idea of negligence is equally insusceptible to exact definition, but what a reasonable man would regard as fair procedure in particular circumstances and what he would regard as negligence in particular circumstances are equally capable of serving as tests in law, and natural justice as it has been interpreted in the courts is much more definite than that. It appears to me that one reason why the authorities on natural justice have been found difficult to reconcile is that insufficient attention has been paid to the great difference between various kinds of cases in which it has been sought to apply the principle. What a minister ought to do in considering objections to a scheme may be very different from what a watch committee ought to do in considering whether to dismiss a chief constable. So I shall deal first with cases of dismissal. These appear to fall into three classes: dismissal of a servant by his master, dismissal from an office held during pleasure, and dismissal from an office where there must be something against a man to warrant his dismissal.

The law regarding master and servant is not in doubt. There cannot be specific performance of a contract of service, and the master can terminate the contract with his servant at any time and for any reason or for none. But if he does so in a manner not warranted by the contract he must pay damages for breach of contract. So the question in a pure case of master and servant does not at all depend on whether the master has heard the servant in his own defence: it depends on whether the facts emerging at the trial prove breach of contract. But this kind of case can resemble dismissal from an office where the body employing the man is under some statutory or other restriction as to the kind of contract which it can make with its servants, or the grounds on which it can dismiss them. The present case does not fall within this class because a chief constable is not the servant of the watch committee or indeed of anyone else.

Then there are many cases where a man holds an office at pleasure. Apart from judges and others whose tenure of office is governed by statute, all servants and officers of the Crown hold office at pleasure, and this has been held even to apply to a colonial judge (*Terrell v Secretary of State for the Colonies* [1953] 2 Q.B. 482). It has always been held, I think rightly, that such an officer has no right to be heard before he is dismissed, and the reason is clear. As a person having the power of dismissal need not have anything against the officer, he need not give any reason. That was stated as long ago as 1670 in *R. v Stratford-on-Avon Corporation* (1809) 11 East 176 where the corporation dismissed a town clerk who held office *durante bene placito*. The leading case on this matter appears to be *R. v Darlington School Governors* (1844) 6 Q.B. 682 although that decision was doubted by Lord Hatherley L.C. in *Dean v Bennett* (1870) L.R. 6 Ch. 489 and distinguished on narrow grounds in *Willis v Childe* (1851) 13 Beav 117. I fully accept that where an office is simply held at pleasure the person having power of dismissal cannot be bound to disclose his reasons. No doubt he would in many cases tell the officer and hear his explanation before deciding to dismiss him. But if he is not bound to disclose his reason and does not do so, then, if the court cannot require him to do so, it cannot determine whether it would be fair to hear the officer's case before taking action. But again that is not this case. In this case the Act of 1882 only permits the watch committee to take action on the grounds of negligence or unfitness. Let me illustrate the difference by supposing that a watch committee who had no complaint against their present chief constable heard of a man with quite outstanding qualifications who would like to be appointed. They might think it in the public interest to make the change, but they would have no right to do it. But there could be no legal objection to dismissal of an officer holding office at pleasure in order to put a better man in his place.

So I come to the third class, which includes the present case. There I find an unbroken line of authority to the effect that an officer cannot lawfully be dismissed without first telling him what is alleged against him and hearing his defence or explanation. An early example is *Bagg's Case* (1615) 11 Co.Rep.

93b though it is more properly deprivation of the privilege of being a burgess of Plymouth. *R. v Gaskin* (1799) 8 Term Rep. 209 arose out of the dismissal of a parish clerk, and Lord Kenyon C.J. referred to *audi alteram partem* as one of the first principles of justice. *R. v Smith* (1844) 5 Q.B. 614 was another case of dismissal of a parish clerk, and Lord Denman C.J. held that even personal knowledge of the offence was no substitute for hearing the officer: his explanation might disprove criminal motive or intent and bring forward other facts in mitigation, and in any event delaying to hear him would prevent yielding too hastily to first impressions. *Ex parte Ramshay* (1852) 18 Q.B. 173 is important. It dealt with the removal from office of a county court judge, and the form of the legislation which authorised the Lord Chancellor to act is hardly distinguishable from the form of section 191, which confers powers on the watch committee. The Lord Chancellor was empowered if he should think fit to remove on the ground of inability or misbehaviour, but Lord Campbell C.J. said (*ibid.*, 190) that this was "only on the implied condition prescribed by the principles of eternal justice". In *Osgood v Nelson* (1872) L.R. 5 H.L. 636 at 649, H.L., objection was taken to the way in which the Corporation of the City of London had removed the clerk to the Sheriff's Court, and Lord Hatherley L.C. said: "I apprehend, my Lords, that, as has been stated by the learned Baron who has delivered, in the name of the judges, their unanimous opinion, the Court of Queen's Bench has always considered that it has been open to that court, as in this case it appears to have considered, to correct any court, or tribunal, or body of men who may have a power of this description, a power of removing from office, if it should be found that such persons have disregarded any of the essentials of justice in the course of their inquiry, before making that removal, or if it should be found that in the place of reasonable cause those persons have acted obviously upon mere individual caprice."

That citation of authority might seem sufficient, but I had better proceed further. In *Fisher v Jackson* [1891] 2 Ch. 84 three vicars had power to remove the master of an endowed school. But, unlike the *Darlington* case, 6 Q.B. 682 the trust deed set out the grounds on which he could be removed—briefly, inefficiency or failing to set a good example. So it was held that they could not remove him without affording him an opportunity of being heard in his own defence. Only two other cases of this class were cited in argument, *Cooper v Wilson* [1937] 2 K.B. 309 and *Hogg v Scott* [1947] K.B. 759. Both dealt with the dismissal of police officers and both were complicated by consideration of regulations made under the Police Acts. In the former the majority at least recognised that the principles of natural justice applied, and in deciding the latter Cassels J. in deciding that a chief constable could dismiss without hearing him an officer who had been convicted of felony, appears to have proceeded on a construction of the regulations. Of course, if the regulations authorised him to do that and were *intra vires* in doing so, there would be no more to be said. I do not think it necessary to consider whether the learned judge rightly construed the regulations, for he did not expressly or, I think, by implication question the general principle that a man is not to be dismissed for misconduct without being heard.

Stopping there, I would think that authority was wholly in favour of the appellant, but the respondent's argument was mainly based on what has been said in a number of fairly recent cases dealing with different subject-matter. Those cases deal with decisions by ministers, officials and bodies of various kinds which adversely affected property rights or privileges of persons who had had no opportunity or no proper opportunity of presenting their cases before the decisions were given. And it is necessary to examine those cases for another reason. The question which was or ought to have been considered by the watch committee on March 7, 1958, was not a simple question whether or not the appellant should be dismissed. There were three possible courses open to the watch committee—reinstating the appellant as chief constable, dismissing him, or requiring him to resign. The difference between the latter two is that dismissal involved forfeiture of pension rights, whereas requiring him to resign did not. Indeed, it is now clear that the appellant's real interest in this appeal is to try to save his pension rights.

It may be convenient at this point to deal with an argument that, even if as a general rule a watch committee must hear a constable in his own defence before dismissing him, that case was so clear that nothing that the appellant could have said could have made any difference. It is at least very doubtful whether that could be accepted as an excuse. But, even if it could, the respondents would, in my view, fail on the facts. It may well be that no reasonable body of men could have reinstated the appellant. But as between the other two courses open to the watch committee the case is not so clear. Certainly on the facts, as we know them, the watch committee could reasonably have decided to forfeit the appellant's pension rights, but I could not hold that they would have acted wrongly or wholly unreasonably if they had in the exercise of their discretion decided to take a more lenient course.

I would start an examination of the authorities dealing with property rights and privileges with *Cooper v Wandsworth Board of Works* (1863) 14 C.B.(N.S.) 180.

[His Lordship summarised this case, and *Hopkins v Smethwick Local Board of Health* (1890) 24 Q.B.D. 712; *Smith v The Queen* (1878) L.R. 3 App.Cas. 614, P. C.; and *De Verteuil v Knaggs* [1918] A.C. 557.]

I shall now turn to a different class of case—deprivation of membership of a professional or social body. In *Wood v Woad* (1874) L.R. 9 Ex. 190 the committee purported to expel a member of a mutual insurance society without hearing him, and it was held that their action was void, and so he was still a member. Kelly C.B. said of *audi alteram partem* (*ibid.* 196): "This rule is not confined to the conduct of strictly legal tribunals, but is applicable to every tribunal or body of persons invested with authority to adjudicate upon matters involving civil consequences to individuals." This was expressly approved by Lord Macnaghten giving the judgment of the Board in *Lapointe v L'Association de Bienfaisance et de Retraite de la Police de Montréal* [1906] A.C. 535, P.C. In that case the board of directors of the association had to decide whether to give a pension to a dismissed constable—the very point the watch committee had to decide in this case—and it was held (*ibid.* p.539) that they had to observe "the elementary principles of justice".

Then there are the club cases, *Fisher v Keane* (1878) 11 Ch.D. 353 and *Dawkins v Antrobus* (1879) 17 Ch.D. 615, C.A. In the former, Jessel M.R. said of the committee, 11 Ch.D. 353 at 362–363: "They ought not, as I understand it, according to the ordinary rules by which justice should be administered by committees of clubs, or by any other body of persons who decide upon the conduct of others, to blast a man's reputation for ever—perhaps to ruin his prospects for life, without giving him an opportunity of either defending or palliating his conduct." In the latter case it was held that nothing had been done contrary to natural justice. In *Weinberger v Inglis* [1919] A.C. 606,

H.L., a member of enemy birth was excluded from the Stock Exchange, and it was held that the committee had heard him before acting. Lord Birkenhead L.C. said (*ibid.* at 616): ". . . if I took the view that the appellant was condemmed upon grounds never brought to his notice, I should not assent to the legality of this course, unless compelled by authority". He said this although the rule under which the committee acted was in the widest possible terms—that the committee should each year re-elect such members as they should deem eligible as members of the Stock Exchange.

I shall not at present advert to the various trade union cases because I am deliberately considering the state of the law before difficulties were introduced by statements in various fairly recent cases. It appears to me that if the present case had arisen 30 or 40 years ago the courts would have had no difficulty in deciding this issue in favour of the appellant on the authorities which I have cited. So far as I am aware none of these authorities has ever been disapproved or even doubted. Yet the Court of Appeal have decided this issue against the appellant on more recent authorities which apparently justify that result. How has this come about?

At least three things appear to me to have contributed. In the first place there have been many cases where it has been sought to apply the principles of natural justice to the wider duties imposed on Ministers and other organs of government by modern legislation. For reasons which I shall attempt to state in a moment, it has been held that those principles have a limited application in such cases and those limitations have tended to be reflected in other decisions on matters to which in principle they do not appear to me to apply. Secondly, again for reasons which I shall attempt to state, those principles have been held to have a limited application in cases arising out of war-time legislation; and again such limitations have tended to be reflected in other cases. And, thirdly, there has, I think, been a misunderstanding of the judgment of Atkin L.J. in *R. v Electricity Commissioners, Ex p. London Electricity Joint Committee Co.* [1924] 1 K.B. 171.

In cases of the kind I have been dealing with the Board of Works or the Governor or the club committee was dealing with a single isolated case. It was not deciding, like a judge in a lawsuit, what were the rights of the person before it. But it was deciding how he should be treated—something analogous to a judge's duty in imposing a penalty. No doubt policy would play some part in the decision—but so it might when a judge is imposing a sentence. So it was easy to say that such a body is performing a quasi-judicial task in considering and deciding such a matter, and to require it to observe the essentials of all proceedings of a judicial character—the principles of natural justice.

Sometimes the functions of a minister or department may also be of that character, and then the rules of natural justice can apply in much the same way. But more often their functions are of a very different character. If a minister is considering whether to make a scheme for, say, an important new road, his primary concern will not be with the damage which its construction will do to the rights of individual owners of land. He will have to consider all manner of questions of public interest and, it may be, a number of alternative schemes. He cannot be prevented from attaching more importance to the fulfilment of his policy than to the fate of individual objectors, and it would be quite wrong for the courts to say that the minister should or could act in the same kind of way as a board of works deciding whether a house should be pulled down. And there is another important difference. As explained in

Local Government Board v Arlidge [1915] A.C. 120 a minister cannot do everything himself. His officers will have to gather and sift all the facts, including objections by individuals, and no individual can complain if the ordinary accepted methods of carrying on public business do not give him as good protection as would be given by the principles of natural justice in a different kind of case.

We do not have a developed system of administrative law—perhaps because until fairly recently we did not need it. So it is not surprising that in dealing with new types of cases the courts have had to grope for solutions, and have found that old powers, rules and procedure are largely inapplicable to cases which they were never designed or intended to deal with. But I see nothing in that to justify our thinking that our old methods are any less applicable today than ever they were to the older types of case. And if there are any dicta in modern authorities which point in that direction, then, in my judgment, they should not be followed.

And now I must say something regarding war-time legislation. The older authorities clearly show how the courts engrafted the principles of natural justice on to a host of provisions authorising administrative interference with private rights. Parliament knew quite well that the courts had an inveterate habit of doing that and must therefore be held to have authorised them to do it unless a particular Act showed a contrary intention. And such an intention could appear as a reasonable inference as well as from express words. It seems to me to be a reasonable and almost an inevitable inference from the circumstances in which Defence Regulations were made and from their subject-matter that, at least in many cases, the intention must have been to exclude the principles of natural justice. War-time secrecy alone would often require that, and the need for speed and general pressure of work were other factors. But it was not to be expected that anyone would state in so many words that a temporary abandonment of the rules of natural justice was one of the sacrifices which war conditions required—that would have been almost calculated to create the alarm and despondency against which one of the regulations was specifically directed. And I would draw the same conclusion from another fact. In many regulations there was set out an alternative safeguard more practicable in war time—the objective test that the officer must have reasonable cause to believe whatever was the crucial matter. (I leave out of account the very peculiar decision of this House in *Liversidge v Anderson* [1942] A.C. 206.) So I would not think that any decision that the rules of natural justice were excluded from war-time legislation should be regarded as of any great weight in dealing with a case such as this case, which is of the older type, and which involves the interpretation of an Act passed long before modern modifications of the principles of natural justice became necessary, and at a time when, as Parliament was well aware, the courts habitually applied the principles of natural justice to provisions like section 191(4) of the Act of 1882.

The matter has been further complicated by what I believe to be a misunderstanding of a much-quoted passage in the judgment of Atkin L.J. in *R. v Electricity Commissioners, Ex p. London Electricity Joint Committee Co.* [1924] 1 K.B. 171 at 205. He said: ". . . the operation of the writs [of prohibition and certiorari] has extended to control the proceedings of bodies which do not claim to be, and would not be recognised as, courts of justice. Wherever any body of persons having legal authority to determine questions affecting the rights of subjects, and having the duty to act judicially, act in excess of their legal authority, they are subject to the controlling jurisdiction of the King's Bench Division exercised in these writs."

A gloss was put on this by Lord Hewart C.J. in *R. v Legislative Committee of the Church Assembly, Ex p. Haynes-Smith* [1928] 1 K.B. 411. There it was sought to prohibit the Assembly from proceeding further with the Prayer Book Measure 1927. That seems to me to have no resemblance to a question whether a person should be deprived of his rights or privileges, and the case was decided on the ground that this was a deliberative or legislative body and not a judicial body. Salter J. put it in a few lines (*ibid.* at 419): "The person or body to whom these writs are to go must be a judicial body in this sense, that it has power to determine and to decide; and the power carries with it, of necessity, the duty to act judicially. I think that the Church Assembly has no such power, and therefore no such duty." But Lord Hewart said (*ibid.* at 415) having quoted the passage from Atkin L.J.'s judgment: "The question, therefore, which we have to ask ourselves in this case is whether it is true to say in this matter, either of the Church Assembly as a whole, or of the Legislative Committee of the Church Assembly, that it is a body of persons having legal authority to determine questions affecting the rights of subjects, and having the duty to act judicially. It is to be observed that in the last sentence which I have quoted from the judgment of Atkin L.J. the word is not 'or', but 'and'. In order that a body may satisfy the required test it is not enough that it should have legal authority to determine questions affecting the rights of subjects; there must be superadded to that characteristic the further characteristic that the body has the duty to act judicially. The duty to act judicially is an ingredient which, if the test is to be satisfied, must be present. As these writs in the earlier days were issued only to bodies which without any harshness of construction could be called, and naturally would be called, courts, so also today these writs do not issue except to bodies which act or are under the duty to act in a judicial capacity."

I have quoted the whole of this passage because it is typical of what has been said in several subsequent cases. If Lord Hewart meant that it is never enough that a body simply has a duty to determine what the rights of an individual should be, but that there must always be something more to impose on it a duty to act judicially before it can be found to observe the principles of natural justice, then that appears to me impossible to reconcile with the earlier authorities . . . . And, as I shall try to show, it cannot be what Atkin L.J. meant.

In *R. v Electricity Commissioners, Ex p. London Electricity Joint Committee Co.* [1924] 1 K.B. 171, the commissioners had a statutory duty to make schemes with regard to electricity districts and to hold local inquiries before making them. They made a draft scheme which in effect allocated duties to one body which the Act required should be allocated to a different kind of body. This was held to be *ultra vires*, and the question was whether prohibition would lie. It was argued that the proceedings of the commissioners were purely executive and controllable by Parliament alone. Bankes L.J. said (*ibid.* at 198): "On principle and on authority it is in my opinion open to this court to hold, and I consider that it should hold, that powers so far-reaching, affecting as they do individuals as well as property, are powers to be exercised judicially, and not ministerially or merely, to use the language of Palles C.B., as proceedings towards legislation." So he inferred the judicial element from the nature of the power. And I think that Atkin L.J. did the same. Immediately after the passage which I said has been misunderstood, he cited a variety of cases and in most of them I can see nothing "superadded" (to use Lord Hewart's word) to the duty itself. Certainly Atkin L.J. did not say that anything was superadded. And a later passage in his judgment convinces me that he, like Bankes L.J., inferred the judicial character of the duty from the nature of the duty itself. Although it is long I am afraid I must quote it [1924] 1 K.B. 171 at 206–207: "In the present case the Electricity Commissioners have to decide whether they will constitute a joint authority in a district in accordance with law, and with what powers they will invest that body. The question necessarily involves the withdrawal from existing bodies of undertakers of some of their existing rights, and imposing upon them of new duties, including their subjection to the control of the new body, and new financial obligations. It also provides in the new body a person to whom may be transferred rights of purchase which at present are vested in another authority. The commissioners are proposing to create such a new body in violation of the Act of Parliament, and are proposing to hold a possibly long and expensive inquiry into the expediency of such a scheme, in respect of which they have the power to compel representatives of the prosecutors at attend and produce papers. I think that in deciding upon the scheme, and in holding the inquiry, they are acting judicially in the sense of the authorities I have cited."

There is not a word in Atkin L.J.'s judgment to suggest disapproval of the earlier line of authority which I have cited. On the contrary, he goes further than those authorities. I have already stated my view that it is more difficult for the courts to control an exercise of power on a large scale where the treatment to be meted out to a particular individual is only one of many matters to be considered. This was a case of that kind, and, if Atkin L.J. was prepared to infer a judicial element from the nature of the power in this case, he could hardly disapprove such an inference when the power relates solely to the treatment of a particular individual.

The authority chiefly relied on by the Court of Appeal in holding that the watch committee were not bound to observe the principles of natural justice was *Nakkuda Ali v Jayaratne* [1951] A.C. 66. In that case the Controller of Textiles in Ceylon made an order cancelling the appellant's licence to act as a dealer, and the appellant sought to have that order quashed. The controller acted under a Defence Regulation which empowered him to cancel a licence "where the controller has reasonable grounds to believe that any dealer is unfit to be allowed to continue as a dealer".

The Privy Council regarded that (*ibid.* at 77) as "imposing a condition that there must in fact exist such reasonable grounds, known to the controller, before he can validly exercise the power of cancellation." But according to their judgment certiorari did not lie, and no other means was suggested whereby the appellant or anyone else in his position could obtain redress even if the controller acted without a shred of evidence. It is quite true that the judgment went on, admittedly unnecessarily, to find that the controller had reasonable grounds and did observe the principles of natural justice, but the result would have been just the same if he had not. This House is not bound by decisions of the Privy Council, and for my own part nothing short of a decision of this House directly in point would induce me to accept the position that, although an enactment expressly requires an official to have reasonable grounds for his decision, our law is so defective that a subject cannot bring up such a decision for review however seriously he may be affected and however obvious it may be that the official acted in breach of his statutory obligation.

The judgment proceeds: "But it does not seem to follow necessarily from this that the controller must be acting judicially in exercising the power.

Can one not act reasonably without acting judicially? It is not difficult to think of circumstances in which the controller might, in any ordinary sense of the words, have reasonable grounds of belief without having ever confronted the licence holder with the information which is the source of his belief. It is a long step in the argument to say that because a man is enjoined that he must not take action unless he has reasonable ground for believing something he can only arrive at that belief by a course of conduct analogous to the judicial process. And yet, unless that proposition is valid, there is really no ground for holding that the controller is acting judicially or quasi-judicially when he acts under this regulation. If he is not under a duty so to act then it would not be according to law that his decision should be amenable to review and, if necessary, to avoidance by the procedure of certiorari."

I would agree that in this and other Defence Regulation cases the legislature has submitted an obligation not to act without reasonable grounds for the ordinary obligation to afford to the person affected an opportunity to submit his defence. It is not necessary in this case to consider whether by so doing he has deprived the courts of the power to intervene if the officer acts contrary to his duty. The question in the present case is not whether Parliament substituted a different safeguard for that afforded by natural justice, but whether in the Act of 1882 it excluded the safeguard of natural justice and put nothing in its place.

So far there is nothing in the judgment of the Privy Council directly relevant to the present case. It is the next paragraph which causes the difficulty and I must quote the crucial passage (*ibid.* at 78): "But the basis of the jurisdiction of the courts by way of certiorari has been so exhaustively analysed in recent years that individual instances are now only of importance as illustrating a general principle that is beyond dispute. That principle is most precisely stated in the words of Atkin L.J. in *R. v Electricity Commissioners, Ex p. London Electricity Joint Committee Co.* [1924] 1 K.B. 171 at 205"—and then follows the passage with which I have already dealt at length. And then there follows the quotation from Lord Hewart, which I have already commented on, ending with the words— "there must be superadded to that characteristic the further characteristic that the body has the duty to act judicially". And then it is pointed out: "It is that characteristic that the controller lacks in acting under regulation 62."

Of course, if it were right to say that Lord Hewart's gloss of Atkin L.J. stated "a general principle that is beyond dispute", the rest would follow. But I have given my reasons for holding that it does no such thing, and in my judgment the older cases certainly do not "illustrate" any such general principle— they contradict it. No case older than 1911 was cited in *Nakkuda's* case on this question, and this question was only one of several difficult questions which were argued and decided. So I am forced to the conclusion that this part of the judgment in *Nakkuda's* case was given under a serious misapprehension of the effect of the older authorities and therefore cannot be regarded as authoritative.

I would sum up my opinion in this way. Between 1882 and the making of police regulations in 1920 section 191(4) had to be applied to every kind of case. The respondents' contention is that, even where there was a doubtful question whether a constable was guilty of a particular act of misconduct, the watch committee were under no obligation to hear his defence before dismissing him. In my judgment it is abundantly clear from the authorities I have quoted that at that time the courts would have rejected any such contention. In later cases dealing with different subject-matter, opinions have been expressed in wide terms so as to appear to conflict with those earlier authorities. But learned judges who expressed those opinions generally had no power to overrule those authorities, and in any event it is a salutary rule that a judge is not to be assumed to have intended to overrule or disapprove of an authority which has not been cited to him and which he does not even mention. So I would hold that the power of dismissal in the Act of 1882 could not then have been exercised and cannot now be exercised until the watch committee have informed the constable of the grounds on which they propose to proceed and have given him a proper opportunity to present his case in defence.

Next comes the question whether the respondents' failure to follow the rules of natural justice on March 7 was made good by the meeting on March 18. I do not doubt that if an officer or body realises that it has acted hastily and reconsiders the whole matter afresh, after affording to the person affected a proper opportunity to present his case, then its later decision will be valid. An example is *De Verteuil's* case. But here the appellant's solicitor was not fully informed of the charges against the appellant and the watch committee did not annul the decision which they had already published and proceed to make a new decision. In my judgment, what was done on that day was a very inadequate substitute for a full rehearing. Even so, three members of the committee changed their minds, and it is impossible to say what the decision of the committee would have been if there had been a full hearing after disclosure to the appellant of the whole case against him. I agree with those of your Lordships who hold that this meeting of March 18 cannot affect the result of this appeal.

The other ground on which some of your Lordships prefer to proceed is the respondents' failure to act in accordance with the Police Regulations. I have had an opportunity of reading the speech about to be delivered by my noble and learned friend, Lord Morris of Borth-y-Gest, and I agree with his view about this.

Then there was considerable argument whether in the result the watch committee's decision is void or merely voidable. Time and again in the cases I have cited it has been stated that a decision given without regard to the principles of natural justice is void, and that was expressly decided in *Wood v Woad*. I see no reason to doubt these authorities. The body with the power to decide cannot lawfully proceed to make a decision until it has afforded to the person affected a proper opportunity to state his case.

Finally, there is the question whether by appealing to the Secretary of State the appellant is in some way prevented from now asserting the nullity of the respondents' decision. A person may be prevented from asserting the truth by estoppel, but it is not seriously argued that that doctrine applies here. Then it is said that the appellant elected to go to the Secretary of State and thereby waived his right to come to the court. That appears to me to be an attempt to set up what is in effect estoppel where the essential elements for estoppel are not present. There are many cases where two remedies are open to an aggrieved person, but there is no general rule that by going to some other tribunal he puts it out of his power thereafter to assert his right in court; and there was no express waiver because in appealing to the Secretary of State the appellant reserved his right to maintain that the decision was a nullity.

But then it was argued that this case is special because by statute the decision of the Secretary of State is made final and binding. I need not consider what the result would have been if the Secretary of State had heard the case for the appellant and then given his own independent decision that the appellant should be dismissed. But the Secretary of State did not do that. He merely decided "that there was sufficient material on which the watch committee could properly exercise their power of dismissal under section 191(4)". So the only operative decision is that of the watch committee, and, if it was a nullity, I do not see how this statement by the Secretary of State can make it valid.

Accordingly, in my judgment, this appeal must be allowed. There appears to have been no discussion in the courts below as to remedies which may now be open to the appellant, and I do not think that this House should do more than declare that the dismissal of the appellant is null and void and remit the case to the Queen's Bench Division for further procedure. But it is right to put on record that the appellant does not seek to be reinstated as chief constable: his whole concern is to avoid the serious financial consequences involved in dismissal as against being required or allowed to resign.

[LORD EVERSHED (dissenting) held that:

(1) "the shortcomings of the appellant as chief constable" did not fall within the Discipline Code;
(2) therefore, the Watch Committee were entitled to exercise their residual powers under s.191(4) of the 1882 Act without observing the regulations;
(3) there was no "report or allegation" before the Watch Committee. Those words suggested "something in the nature of an accusation as distinct from a conclusion reached after proper inquiry" (i.e. Donovan J.'s conclusion);
(4) that "this was a special and entirely exceptional case outside the scope of the regulations, and, as a matter of public notoriety, requiring instant action by the Watch Committee";
(5) that if natural justice ought to have been observed, a decision in breach of natural justice would normally be voidable, not void, in that the body would be "acting within its jurisdiction." A decision would only be void if based on "frivolous or futile" grounds or if there had been "a real substantial miscarriage of justice";
(6) that apart from the prejudice to pension rights, the Watch Committee need not have given the plaintiff any opportunity to state points he had already made before Donovan J. The committee also had to act urgently. However, his Lordship was prepared to assume that the plaintiff should have had an opportunity to state his case for being allowed to resign;
(7) that justice had been done as representations had been made to the Watch Committee on March 18;
(8) that if he (his Lordship) was wrong on the last point, any defect was cured by the appeal to the Secretary of State, whose decision was rendered "final and binding" by s.2(3) of the Police (Appeals) Act 1927.

Therefore his Lordship would have dismissed the appeal.

LORD MORRIS OF BORTH-Y-GEST held that:

(1) there was a "report or allegation" before the Watch Committee. There were, for example, a transcript of the judge's remarks, and "certain statements made . . . by members of the committee and the town clerk";

(2) the regulations should have been applied. As there was no admission of the commission of an offence, the regulations required a hearing;

(3) as the regulations had been ignored, the dismissal was void. (*Andrews v Mitchell* [1905] A.C. 78, *Lapointe v L'Association de Bienfaisance et de Retraite de la Police de Montreal* [1906] A.C. 535; and *Annamunthodo v Oilfield Workers' Trade Union* [1961] A.C. 945 applied);

(4) the defect was not cured by the second hearing on March 18, as the plaintiff was never given notice of the allegations against him;

(5) the defect was not cured by the appeal to the Secretary of State as the original decision was a nullity, and the plaintiff so maintained during the appeal;

(6) apart from the regulations, natural justice should have been observed. The dismissal was not an "executive or administrative act" as it was based on a "suggestion of neglect of duty";

(7) a decision in breach of natural justice was void not voidable.

LORD HODSON delivered a speech concurring substantially with LORD REID and LORD MORRIS.

LORD DEVLIN held that the regulations applied and should have been observed. Any decision in breach of the regulations would be voidable unless any regulation laid down a "condition precedent to the conferment of authority on the committee which had not been fulfilled". Article 11(1) of the 1882 regulations allowed the police authority to act only on receipt of a report from the tribunal set up under the regulations to hear the evidence and make recommendations. The committee's decision was therefore void *ab initio*.

His Lordship held that a decision in breach of natural justice was voidable only.]

Appeal allowed.

Notes

1. There are many points of interest, including the scope of natural justice, the ways in which defective decisions may or may not be cured, whether such decisions are void or voidable, the application of statutory procedural requirements, and the proper approach that should be taken to cases decided in wartime. The case has been followed and cited in many subsequent cases. See case notes and articles by A.W. Bradley, [1964] C.L.J. 83; G.H.L. Fridman (1963) 113 L.J. 716; A. L. Goodhart, (1964) 80 L.Q.R. 105 and (1963) 26 M.L.R. 543; D.G. Benjafield and H. Whitmore, (1963) 37 A.L.J. 140; D. Paterson, [1966] N.Z.L.J. 107; P. Brett 16 Malaya L.R. 100; K.J. Keith, "*Ridge v Baldwin*—Twenty Years On' (1983) 13 V.U.W.L.R. 239.

2. The dismissal of police officers is now regulated by the Police Act 1996, and regulations made thereunder. See *Cross on Local Government Law*, paras 24–43 to 24–51. See also *Chief Constable of North Wales v Evans* [1982] 1 W.L.R. 1115, where the House of Lords held that a chief constable is subject to the rules of natural justice when exercising his or her power to discharge a probationary constable. Here, the chief constable had acted unfairly in threatening to dismiss E unless he resigned (which E did), on the basis of (inaccurate) rumours concerning E's private life that were never put to him for comment. The House granted a declaration that this was unlawful but did not order reinstatement as this would have "usurped" the power of the chief constable. Sir William Wade suggested ((1983) 99 L.Q.R. 171 at p.172) that E's correct remedy would have been an action for damages for the tort of intimidation, having

been forced to act to his detriment under threat of unlawful injury. See also J. McMullen, (1984) 47 M.L.R. 234.

3. In *Durayappah v Fernando* [1967] 2 A.C. 337, a minister had power to order the dissolution of a municipal council if it appeared to him that it "is not competent to perform, or persistently makes default in the performance of, any duty or duties imposed upon it, or persistently refuse or neglects to comply with any provision of law . . .". Such an order was made in respect of Jaffna Municipal Council, and challenged by the mayor on the ground that no hearing had been given. The Privy Council rejected the view of the Supreme Court of Ceylon, that the subjective wording automatically excluded a duty to act judicially. They pointed out that words could be implied into a statute, as in *Cooper v Wandsworth Board of Works*, and that if the law were otherwise, *Capel v Child* (1832) 2 Cromp. & Jer. 558 would have been decided differently. It would be wrong to attempt to give an exhaustive classification of the cases where the *audi alteram partem* principle should be applied. *Per* Lord Upjohn at 349:

"Outside the well-known classes of cases, no general rule can be laid down as to the application of the general principle in addition to the language of the provision. In their Lordships' opinion there are three matters which must always be borne in mind when considering whether the principle should be applied or not. These three matters are: first, what is the nature of the property, the office held, status enjoyed or services to be performed by the complainant of injustice. Secondly, in what circum-stances or upon what occasions is the person claiming to be entitled to exercise the measure of control entitled to intervene. Thirdly, when a right to intervene is proved, what sanctions in fact is the latter entitled to impose upon the other. It is only upon a consideration of all these matters that the question of the application of the principle can properly be determined".

These matters were considered in turn. First, the Council was by statute a public corporation entrusted with the administration of a large area and the discharge of important duties. It enjoyed a considerable measure of independence from the central government. The responsibility of the Minister to the legislature did not exclude the possibility of "responsibility to the courts under the principle *audi alteram partem*". Secondly, it was a most serious charge to allege persistent default or refusal or neglect to comply with a provision of law. It was not possible to distinguish these from the ground actually alleged here, namely incompetence. It would not be right to hold that whether or not natural justice had to be observed depended on the ground on which the order was eventually made. Thirdly, the sanction was "as complete as could be imagined", the dissolution of the Council and the confiscation of all its properties. The Council owned large areas of land, had a municipal fund, and levied rates. So, on the principle of *Cooper v Wandsworth Board of Works* "that no man is to be deprived of his property without a hearing", in addition to the other grounds, the Minister should have observed natural justice.

Nevertheless, the Mayor of Jaffna was refused a remedy, on the (doubtful) ground that he had insufficient *locus standi*.

See J.M. Eekelaar, (1967) 30 M.L.R. 701; G. Nettheim, (1967) 2 Federal L.R. 215.

4. The cases dealt with in this chapter illustrate a wide range of interests that the courts have found to be worthy of at least a measure of procedural protection. These include personal liberty (*Ex p. Hone*, below, p.726; *Doody*, below, p.743); property (*Cooper v Wandsworth Board of Works*, above, p.653); employment (see *Ridge v Baldwin* and the following note); livelihood (licensing cases, below, p.688); the right of a Commonwealth citizen to enter the United Kingdom (*HK (An Infant), Re*, below, p.676); the handling of the applicant's complaint of race discrimination (*Anderson*, below, p.681); the imposition of a financial penalty (*Lloyd v McMahon*, below, p.722). The list is not closed; indeed protection may be extended to cover any legitimate expectation (see the *CCSU* case, below, p.690).

5. The tripartite classification of employment relationships articulated by Lord Reid in *Ridge* was further refined by his Lordship in *Malloch v Aberdeen Corp.* [1971] 1 W.L.R. 1578. In that case, Mr Malloch was a teacher employed by the corporation. Regulations made under the Education (Scotland) Act 1946, required all teachers employed by education authorities to register with a new statutory body—the General Teaching Council for Scotland. Malloch was entitled to be registered with the Teaching Council, but he refused on a point of principle. Aberdeen Corporation were advised that they could no longer employ Malloch and they informed him (as they were obliged to do under the Education (Scotland) Act 1962) that the education committee would be meeting to pass a resolution for his dismissal. Malloch was permitted to attend the committee's meeting, but he was not allowed to address the meeting. The committee resolved to dismiss him. Malloch then sought judicial review of that decision arguing that it had been made in breach of the rules of natural justice. In the House of Lords, Lord Reid stated (at 1582):

"An elected public body is in a very different position from a private employer. Many of its servants in the lower grades are in the same position as servants of a private employer. But many in higher grades or "offices" are given special statutory status or protection. The right of a man to be heard in his own defence is the most elementary protection of all and, where a statutory form of protection would be less effective if it did not carry with it a right to be heard, I would not find it difficult to imply this right".

His Lordship then went on to find that despite Malloch's employment status, as an office holder dismissable at pleasure, legislation had impliedly given him a right to be heard before being dismissed. Therefore, the Corporation had acted unlawfully (Lords Guest and Morris of Borth-y-Gest dissented).

In *Malloch*, Lord Reid also stated (at 1586), echoing observations by him in *Ridge v Baldwin*:

"At common law a master is not bound to hear his servant before he dismisses him. He can act unreasonably or capriciously if he so chooses but the dismissal is valid. The servant has no remedy unless the dismissal is in breach of contract and then the servant's only remedy is damages for breach of contract".

M. Freedland (*The Personal Employment Contract* (2003), pp.352–353) notes that this statement is unclear as to whether it supports an unrestricted right or power of dismissal or only that a dismissal without a hearing may be contractually wrongful but nevertheless effective in that the remedies available are extremely limited. In any event, there have been three important developments since *Malloch*. First, employees may now be able to take proceedings against their employer (before an Employment Tribunal) for *unfair dismissal* if, *inter alia*, they have not been accorded a fair procedure before being dismissed (see now the Employment Rights Act 1996). A tribunal may not, however, award more than £55,000 by way of compensation. Secondly, the courts have held that individual employment disputes in the public service cannot normally be litigated through the judicial review procedure (see *R. v East Berkshire HA Ex p. Walsh* [1985] Q.B. 152, below, p.957), the relationship being characterised as purely contractual. This has, however, been to an extent balanced by the third development which has seen a greater willingness on the part of the courts to hold that an obligation to observe natural justice is to be implied into the contract of employment, and to grant the remedies of declaration and injunction. See *Stevenson v United Road Transport Union* [1977] I.C.R. 893 (trade union official); *R. v British Broadcasting Corporation Ex p. Lavelle* [1983] 1 W.L.R. 23 (BBC employee); *Irani v Southampton and South-West Hampshire HA* [1985] I.C.R. 590 (injunction granted to prevent implementation of dismissal of ophthalmologist without going through the applicable Whitley Council procedure). The employee's position has been further strengthened by the recognition by the House of Lords in *Mahmud v Bank of Credit and Commerce International SA* [1998] A.C. 20 that there is "a mutual obligation implied in every contract of employment, not, without reasonable and proper cause, to conduct oneself in a manner likely to destroy or seriously damage the relationship of trust and confidence between an employer and employee"

(*per* Auld L.J. in *McCabe v Cornwall CC* [2002] EWCA Civ 1887; [2002] I.C.R. 501 at [8]). The adoption of an unfair disciplinary procedure may give rise to a contractual claim for breach of this implied term, for example loss, including financial loss, suffered in consequence of psychiatric illness caused by the unfair procedure. A major limitation is that an employee has no right of action at common law, either in contract or negligence, to recover damages *arising from the unfair manner of his or her dismissal* as such a right would be inconsistent with the statutory code relating to unfair dismissal, which includes the limit on the total compensation that may be awarded (*Johnson v Unisys Ltd* [2001] UKHL 13; [2003] 1 A.C. 518). This does not, however, prevent a claim in respect of pre-dismissal unfair treatment (*Eastwood v Magnox Electrics Plc*; *McCabe v Cornwall CC* [2004] UKHL 35; [2004] 3 W.L.R. 322). (The *Johnson v Unisys* limitation is itself controversial given the clarification that an employment tribunal may not award compensation in respect of non-pecuniary loss (*Dunnachie v Kingston-upon-Hull City Council* [2004] UKHL 36; [2004] 3 W.L.R. 310), and the point that it can become cheaper for an employer to dismiss than to take action short of dismissal. See further Lord Steyn's dissent in *Johnson* and concurring speech in *Eastwood*.)

6. Note Lord Reid's dismissal of the argument that nothing the chief constable could have said would have made any difference. The same point arose in *Malloch v Aberdeen Corp* (above, n.5). The Corporation argued that a hearing was unnecessary as they were bound by the regulations to dismiss Mr Malloch. Lord Wilberforce said (at 1595):

"The appellant has first to show that his position was such that he had, in principle, a right to make representations before a decision against him was taken. But to show this is not necessarily enough, unless he can also show that if admitted to state his case he had a case of substance to make. A breach of procedure, whether called a failure of natural justice, or an essential administrative fault, cannot give him a remedy in the courts, unless behind it there is something of substance which has been lost by the failure. The court does not act in vain".

His Lordship accepted Lord Reid's view that something of substance was at stake. Lord Reid said (at 1582–1583):

"Then it was argued that to have afforded a hearing to the appellant before dismissing him would have been a useless formality because whatever he might have said could have made no difference. If that could be clearly demonstrated it might be a good answer. But I need not decide that because there was here, I think, a substantial possibility that a sufficient number of the committee might have been persuaded not to vote for the appellant's dismissal. The motion for dismissal had to be carried by a two-thirds majority of those present, and at the previous meeting of the committee there was not a sufficient majority to carry a similar motion. Between these meetings the committee had received a strong letter from the Secretary of State urging them to dismiss the teachers who refused to register. And it appears that they had received some advice which might have been taken by them to mean that those who failed to vote for dismissal might incur personal liability. The appellant might have been able to persuade them that they need not have any such fear.

Then the appellant might have argued that on their true construction the regulations did not require the committee to dismiss him and that, if they did require that, they were *ultra vires*. The question of *ultra vires* was not argued before us and on that I shall say no more than that it is not obvious that the Secretary of State had power under any statute to make regulations requiring the dismissal of teachers who failed to acquire and pay for a new qualification such as registration. But the question of the proper construction of the regulations was argued and there I think that the appellant had at least an arguable case . . .".

These speeches accordingly both recognised the possibility that the court might not have intervened if a hearing would have made no difference, and rejected the argument on the facts.

Two possibilities should be noted. The law could be that as a matter of substance there is no *breach* of natural justice unless something of substance has been lost (D.H. Clark, [1975] PL. 27 at p.48, argues that this is what Lord Wilberforce meant in *Malloch*). Alternatively, this factor could simply be considered by the court in deciding, in the exercise of its discretion, whether to grant a remedy. This approach is illustrated by the following case. In *Glynn v Keele University* [1971] 1 W.L.R. 487, Pennycuick V.C. held that the university vice-chancellor was "acting in a quasi-judicial capacity" in exercising his disciplinary power to suspend a student who had "appeared naked" on the campus. This could not be regarded as a matter merely of "internal discipline" (which would not "lie within the purview of the court in its control over quasi-judicial acts") because it was "so fundamental to the position of the student in the university" (at 495). The student had been given no prior notice of the decision, and no opportun-i-ty to make representations, and his Lordship held this to be a clear breach of natural justice. Nevertheless, an injunction was refused in the exercise of the court's discretion:

"I recognise that this particular discretion should be very sparingly exercised in that sense where there has been some failure in natural justice. On the other hand, it certainly should be exercised in that sense in an appropriate case, and I think this is such a case. There is no question of fact involved, as I have already said. I must plainly proceed on the footing that the plaintiff was one of the individuals concerned. There is no doubt that the offence was one of a kind which merited a severe penalty according to any standards current even today. I have no doubt that the sentence of exclusion of residence in the campus was a proper penalty in respect of that offence. Nor has the plaintiff in his evidence put forward any specific justification for what he did. So the position would have been that if the vice-chancellor had accorded him a hearing before making his decision, all that he, or anyone on his behalf, could have done would have been to put forward some plea by way of mitigation. I do not disregard the importance of such a plea in an appropriate case, but I do not think the mere fact he was deprived of throwing himself on the mercy of the vice-chancellor in that way is sufficient to justify setting aside a decision which was intrinsically a perfectly proper one.

In all the circumstances, I have come to the conclusion that the plaintiff has suffered no injustice . . .".

(See case notes by M.H. Matthews, [1971] C.L.J. 181; H.W.R. W[ade], (1971) 37 L.Q.R. 320.)

In either form, the argument needs to be viewed with caution. Where, *ex hypothesi*, the adjudicating body has failed to observe natural justice, *its* protestations that a hearing would have made no difference must be in principle viewed with scepticism (see further D.H. Clark, [1975] P.L. 27 at pp.43–60). In *John v Rees* [1970] Ch. 345, Megarry J. said (at 402):

"As everybody who has anything to do with the law well knows, the path of the law is strewn with examples of open and shut cases which, somehow, were not; of unanswerable charges which, in the event, were completely answered; of inexplicable conduct which was fully explained; of fixed and unalterable determinations that, by discussion suffered a change".

For further examples of cases where the argument has been rejected on the facts, see *R. v Secretary of State for the Environment Ex p. Brent LBC* [1982] Q.B. 593 at

645–646 (in respect of the discretion to refuse a remedy) and *Lloyd v McMahon* [1987] A.C. 625 at 669, where Woolf L.J. (in the Court of Appeal) said in respect of the submission that the result would have inevitably been the same even if there had not been such a defect in procedure:

"I recognise that there can be cases where such a submission will have to be considered by the court. However, I regard the authorities on which [counsel] relies, including *George v Secretary of State for the Environment* [see below] and *Malloch v Aberdeen Corporation* . . . as having application in very limited circumstances, and certainly I would not regard them as applying here".

(On the House of Lords' decision, see below, p.722.)

See also *R. v Secretary of State for Education Ex p. Prior* [1994] I.C.R. 877 at 896; *R. v Broxtowe BC Ex p. Bradford* [2000] B.L.G.R. 386. But *cf. R (on the application of Wainwright) v Richmond upon Thames LBC* [2001] EWCA Civ 2062.

Lord Denning has also doubted the validity of this kind of argument. In *Annamunthodo v Oilfield Workers Trade Union* [1961] A.C. 945, he said (at 956):

"Mr Lazarus did suggest that a man could not complain of a failure of natural justice unless he could show that he had been prejudiced by it. Their Lordships cannot accept this suggestion. . . . It is a prejudice to any man to be denied justice. . . . [H]e can always ask for the decision to be set aside".

Then, in *Kanda v Government of Malaya* [1962] A.C. 322, he said (at 337): "The court will not go into the likelihood of prejudice. The risk of it is enough." However, in *George v Secretary of State for the Environment* (1979) 77 L.G.R. 689, 695 Lord Denning M.R. stated, equally firmly, in the context of a statutory application to quash (see below, pp.805–816), that:

". . . there is no such thing as a technical breach of natural justice . . . the position under the first limb is almost indistinguishable from that under the second limb. You should not find a breach of natural justice unless there has been substantial prejudice to the applicant as a result of the mistake or error which has been made."

[Under the second limb, the ground of challenge was that the applicant had been substantially prejudiced by a failure to comply with a (procedural) requirement.] On the facts, the court seemed justified in holding that Mrs George was not prejudiced where the council failed to serve her with notice of a compulsory purchase order: the council mistakenly thought that Mr George was the sole owner (whereas they were joint owners); Mr George had been served, had appeared at the local public inquiry, and "took every objection that was open to either of them. . . . She was not prejudiced, either substantially or at all" (*per* Lord Denning M.R. at 694). (*cf. Cheall v A.P.E.X.* [1983] 2 A.C. 180 and Brandon L.J. in *Cinnamond v British Airports Authority*, below, p.700.) A preference for the approach in *George* as opposed to the dicta in *Kanda* was expressed by Henriques J. in *R. (on the application of George Harrison (Whitby) Ltd) v Secretary of State for the Environment, Transport and the Regions*, unreported, October 24, 2000, QBD, at [83]–[85].

The question cannot, accordingly, be regarded as wholly settled.

7. In *R. (on the application of Khatun) v Newham LBC* [2004] EWHC Civ 55; [2004] 3 W.L.R. 417, Laws L.J. identified three possible sources for a right to be heard (here, the opportunity for a homeless person to view accommodation offered by the housing authority and make representations before being required to accept it):

"23. . . . I think there are three potential sources. The first is the most obvious: it is where the right is conferred by statute . . . . The second potential source of such a right consists in the demands of procedural fairness or, in the older language, natural justice. Thus it would be said that it is unfair if the applicant is not given such an opportunity to view and comment. The third consists in the council's duty to perform its functions reasonably according to the *Wednesbury* principle (see *Associated Provincial Picture Houses Ltd v Wednesbury Corpn* [1948] 1 KB 223), or at any rate one aspect of it, namely its duty to apprise itself of all factors relevant to its decision as to the suitability of a property to the needs of the applicant. Thus it would be said that unless the applicant is given such an opportunity, the council will have failed to take the necessary reasonable steps to inform itself of these relevant factors. But this last case is not a true instance of a conferment of a right. Rather, the need (if it arises) to have regard to the applicant's views about the offered accommodation is an aspect of the council's general duty to perform its statutory function properly. The practical consequence of this duty's proper execution, however, may be to entitle the applicant to view the property and have his say. . . .

27. . . . I recognise that it is not always useful to assess the merits of public law claims by making distinctions such as that between rights of procedural fairness and the discipline of sound reasoning. These two goods often run into one another, and austere legalisms may stunt rather than prosper the principled development of the law. But there is an important difference of substance between a statutory scheme within which an affected party enjoys a right to be heard truly so called, and one within which he enjoys only the right to take the benefit of an executive decision in his favour if the relevant public body so concludes, albeit the decision-maker's duty to have regard to relevant considerations may require him to take into account the affected person's views about the subject matter. In the second class of case, consulting the affected person is only a means to an end: the end of accurate decision-making. But in the first class of case the right to be heard (while it may no doubt promote accurate decision-making) is an end in itself: it is simply the doing of justice, which requires no utilitarian justification".

The Court of Appeal held that no such rights arose under any of the heads.

Compare *R. v National Lottery Commission Ex p. Camelot Group Plc* [2001] E.M.L.R. 3, where Richards J. held that the Commission's decision to negotiate exclusively with The People's Lottery, one of two applicants for the new licence to run the National Lottery to run from October 1, 2001, was so conspicuously unfair to the other applicant (the existing licence holder, Camelot) as to amount to an abuse of power; the decision was also *Wednesbury* unreasonable. The court here did not address the question whether the procedure was simply unfair.

H.K. (AN INFANT), Re

[1967] 2 Q.B. 617; [1967] 2 W.L.R. 962; 111 S.J. 296; *SUB NOM. RE K. (H.) (AN INFANT)* [1967] 1 All E.R. 226 D.C.
(QUEEN'S BENCH DIVISION)

Until the Commonwealth Immigrants Act 1962 came into force, Commonwealth subjects were entitled as of right to come to the United Kingdom. Thereafter, under s.2(1) of that Act, an immigration officer had a discretion to refuse admission to Commonwealth citizens, or to admit them subject to conditions. However, under s.2(2), that discretion could not be exercised in respect of

"any person who satisfies an immigration officer that he . . . (a) is ordinarily resident in the United Kingdom or was so resident at any time within the past two years; or (b) is the . . . child under 16 years of age, of a Commonwealth citizen who is resident in the United Kingdom . . .".

Paragraph 2(4) of Sch.1 to that Act gave an immigration officer power to cancel a notice refusing a person admission.

Abdul Rehman Khan, a native of Pakistan, settled in Bradford in 1961. He claimed that he had left in Pakistan a wife and five children. In 1966, he went to Pakistan and returned with H.K., whom he said was his son aged 15½. On arrival at London Airport they were interviewed by an immigration officer. Abdul Rehman appeared to be within s.2(2)(a). However, the officer's suspicions were aroused because H.K. appeared to be well over 15. The officer sent H.K. to the port medical officer, who estimated the boy's age at "17 years". The officer then interviewed A.R. and H.K. separately, with the aid of interpreters. His suspicions were increased, and he referred the matter to the chief immigration officer, Mr Collison. As a result of further interviews Mr Collison made up his mind that he was not satisfied that H.K. was under 16, and a notice refusing admission was served on November 21. H.K. was to be removed at noon on the following day. The following morning, further inquiries were made concerning a school certificate which gave as a date of birth February 29, 1951 (a non-existent date). Abdul Rehman applied for a writ of habeas corpus, and H.K.'s departure was delayed. During the course of the hearing by the Divisional Court he was given leave to move also for an order of certiorari to quash the decision to refuse H.K. admission.

LORD PARKER C.J.: . . . Mr Gratiaen [counsel] submits that in deciding whether or not he is satisfied as to the matter set out in the subsection—in this case whether he is satisfied that the boy is under 16—an immigration officer is acting in a judicial or quasi-judicial capacity and must conform to the rules of natural justice. Subject to there being due compliance with those rules, Mr Gratiaen admits that the decision of the immigration officer cannot be chal-lenged and that this court could not interfere. He does, however, maintain that the rules of natural justice require that before reaching his decision the immigration officer must give the immigrant an opportunity to satisfy him and if, as in this case, he has formed an impression that the immigrant is 16 or more, he must give the immigrant an opportunity to remove that impression. He claims that if that opportunity had been given, evidence would have been provided such as has been produced before us in these proceedings and that such evidence would have satisfied the officer. Having regard to the course which these proceedings have taken, it is unnecessary and, I think, indeed inadvisable to comment on that further evidence. . . . One thing I myself am quite clear on and that is that even if an immigration officer is required to act judicially or quasi-judicially, even if that is so, he is not under any duty to hold a full-scale inquiry or to adopt judicial process and procedure. The burden here under the Act is on the immigrant to satisfy the immigration officer and the provisions of the Schedule to which I have referred quite clearly show that it is impossible and therefore not contemplated that an immigration officer should hold any inquiry of that sort. . . . I doubt whether it can be said that the immigration authorities are acting in a judicial or quasi-judicial capacity as those terms are generally understood. But at the same time, I myself think that even if an immigration officer is not in a judicial or quasi-judicial capacity, he must at any rate give the immigrant an opportunity of satisfying him of the matters in the subsection, and for that purpose let the immigrant know what his immediate impression is so that the immigrant can disabuse him. That is not, as I see it, a question of acting or being required to act judicially, but of being required to act fairly. Good administration and an honest or bona fide decision must, as it seems to me, require not merely impartiality, nor merely bringing one's mind to bear on the problem, but acting fairly; and to the limited extent that the circumstances of any particular case allow, and within the legislative framework under which the administrator is working, only to that limited extent do the so-called rules of natural justice apply, which in a case such as this is merely a duty to act fairly. I appreciate that in saying that it may be said that one is going further than is permitted on the decided cases because heretofore at any rate the decisions of the courts do seem to have drawn a strict line in these matters according to whether there is or is not a duty to act judicially or quasi-judicially. It has sometimes been said that if there is no duty to act judicially or quasi-judicially there is no power in the court whatever to interfere. I observe that in the well-known case of *Nakkuda Ali v M.F. de S. Jayaratne* [1951] A.C. 66 again a decision of the Privy Council, the court were considering this kind of case. There the Controller of Textiles in Ceylon was empowered to revoke licences where the controller had reasonable grounds to believe that any dealer was unfit to be allowed to continue as a dealer. Those were the words to be considered in that case which are of course different in the present case. But Lord Radcliffe, when giving the advice of the Judicial Committee, began by distinguishing that case from the well-known case of *Liversidge* [1942] A.C. 206 and went on to consider the position of the controller in law. He said [1951] A.C. 66 at 78:

> "In truth, when he cancels a licence he is not determining a question: he is taking executive action to withdraw a privilege because he believes, and has reasonable grounds to believe, that the holder is unfit to retain it."

He goes on to say that:

> "the power conferred on the controller . . . stands by itself on the bare words of the regulation and, if the mere requirement that the controller must have reasonable grounds of belief is insufficient to oblige him to act judicially, there is nothing else in the context or conditions of his jurisdiction that suggests that he must regulate his action by analogy to judicial rules."

Having come to that decision, Lord Radcliffe then went on in effect to deal with the position if that was wrong, and if the controller was acting in a judicial capacity. He said (*ibid.* at 81):

> "It is impossible to see in this any departure from natural justice. The respondent had before him ample material that would warrant a belief that the appellant had been instrumental in getting the interpolations made and securing for himself a larger credit at the bank than he was entitled to. Nor did the procedure adopted fail to give the appellant the essentials that justice would require, assuming the respondent to have been under a duty to act judicially."

That might be understood as saying that if there was no duty to act judicially, then it would be impossible to interfere, even if the applicant had not been given the essentials that justice requires. I very much doubt, however, whether it was intended to say any more than that there is no duty to invoke judicial process unless there is a duty to act judicially. I do not understand him to be saying that if there is no duty to act judicially, then there is no duty even to be fair.

When, however, that has been said, it seems to me impossible in the present case to say that the decision made on the evening of November 21, 1966, was not arrived at, as I put it, fairly. It is impossible to believe other than that both father and son knew full well of what they had to satisfy the authorities. They were, as it seems to me, given ample opportunity to do so, and the fact that the officer was not satisfied is not, as is admitted, a matter for this court.

[His Lordship then held that any question as to whether the authorities should have taken any further steps in the light of evidence adduced after the decision had been taken was not a matter for certiorari or habeas corpus. Furthermore the matter was now having the personal attention of the Home Secretary. "Accordingly, it seems to me that Mr Gratiaen has had even more that he hoped for, and that there is no reason why this court should retain any further control over it. . . . I would dismiss both the application for habeas corpus and the application for certiorari."]

SALMON L.J.: . . . I have no doubt at all that . . . the immigration officer is obliged to act in accordance with the principles of natural justice. That does not of course mean that he has to adopt judicial procedures or hold a formal inquiry, still less than he has to hold anything in the nature of a trial, but he must act, as Lord Parker C.J. has said, fairly in accordance with the ordinary principles of natural justice. If, for example, and this I am sure would never arise, it could be shown that when he made an order refusing admission he was biased or had acted capriciously or dishonestly, this court would have power to intervene by the prerogative writ. There are, as my Lord has said, a good many cases in which the view has been expressed that unless a person exercising a power is acting in a judicial or quasi-judicial capacity the courts cannot intervene. Of course, an immigration officer is acting in an administrative rather than in a judicial capacity. What, however, is a quasi-judicial capacity has, so far as I know, never been exhaustively defined. It seems to me to cover at any rate a case where the circumstances in which a person who is called upon to exercise a statutory power and make a decision affecting basic rights of others are such that the law impliedly imposes upon him a duty to act fairly. When Parliament passed the Commonwealth Immigrants Act 1962, it deprived Commonwealth citizens of their right of unrestricted entry into the United Kingdom. It laid down conditions under which they might enter and left it to the immigration officers to decide whether such conditions existed. Their decision is of vital importance to the immigrants since their whole future may depend upon it. In my judgment it is implicit in the statute that the authorities in exercising these powers and making decisions must act in accordance with the principles of natural justice.

Mr Gratiaen has not suggested, nor would it be possible to suggest on the evidence before this court, that when on November 21, 1966, the immigration officer refused admission to H.K. to enter the United Kingdom, he acted otherwise than in accordance with the rules of natural justice. It is quite plain that no one could say that on the material then before him as a fair man he must have been satisfied that this boy was under 16 years of age. The material before him did not satisfy him and I for one am not at all surprised. Therefore the refusal made and the notice served on November 21, 1966, are unimpeachable. It follows that the boy's detention pending his removal abroad was lawful.

Accordingly, the application in this case is quite hopeless.

BLAIN J.: . . . I would only say that an immigration officer having assumed the jurisdiction granted by those provisions [*i.e.* to cancel a notice refusing admission, under Sched. 1, para.2(4)] is in a position where it is his duty to exercise that assumed jurisdiction, whether it be administrative, executive or quasi-judicial, fairly, by which I mean applying his mind dispassionately to a fair analysis of the particular problem and the information available to him in analysing it. If in any hypothetical case, and in any real case, this court was satisfied that an immigration officer was not so doing, then in my view mandamus would lie. That is not the position in this case, nor indeed is the court in this case moved for leave to issue a writ of mandamus.

I need say no more other than that I agree with what has fallen from my Lords.

Applications refused.

Notes

1. The modern "duty to act fairly" is sometimes said to originate in this case. There are no authorities cited to support such a duty. There are dicta in earlier cases which indicate that certain decisions by administrative authorities must be taken "fairly". In *L.G.B. v Arlidge* [1915] A.C. 120, Viscount Haldane L.C. said (at 133) that the board should act "judicially and fairly" although they need not observe the procedures of a court. Lord Shaw said that they must "do their best to act justly, and to reach just ends by just means". In *Board of Education v Rice* [1911] A.C. 179, Lord Loreburn L.C. indicated that the Board was "under a duty to act in good faith, and to listen fairly to both sides". Many other judgments stress that natural justice does not require the scrupulous procedures of courts to be imposed on administrative authorities. The concepts of "fairness", "just means", "substantial justice" are indistinguishable, and require elaboration in decided cases to be properly understood.

2. The "duty to act fairly" has subsequently been held to be applicable to decisions on asylum claims. See *R. v Secretary of State for the Home Department Ex p. Gaima* [1989] Imm. A.R. 205 (apply in *Re H.K.*); *R. v Secretary of State for the Home Department Ex p. Thirukumar* [1989] Imm. A.R. 270; *R. v Secretary of State for the Home Department Ex p. Ramarajah* [1994] Imm. A.R. 472 (legitimate expectation that asylum seekers will be interviewed and given reasons for rejection). (See further N. Blake and R. Husain, *Immigration, Asylum and Human Rights* (2003), pp.222–229). In *R. (on the application of Q) v Secretary of State for the Home Department* [2003] EWCA Civ 364; [2004] Q.B. 36, the Court of Appeal held that the system adopted for interviewing asylum seekers following the enactment of s.55 of the Nationality, Immigration and Asylum Act 2002 (which provided that where the Secretary of State was not satisfied that an asylum claim was made as soon as reasonably practicable after arrival in the United Kingdom he could not provide support except to the extent necessary to avoid a breach of Convention rights) was neither fair nor operated fairly. *Inter alia*, the purpose of the interviews was not explained in clear terms; the interviewers had not been properly directed as to the relevant test and should have tried to ascertain the precise reason asylum had not been claimed on arrival; and the claimant should have been given the opportunity of rebuttery any suggestion that he or she was not credible. Followed in *R. (on the application of B) v Merton LBC* [2003] EWHC 1689; [2003] 4 All E.R. 280 (unfair not to put inconsistencies in claimant's account of her history to her before deciding that she was aged at least 18).

Compare *R. (on the application of L) v Secretary of State for the Home Department* [2003] EWCA Civ 25; [2003] 1 W.L.R. 1230 (fast-track procedure for certain human rights or asylum claims certified by the Secretary of State as clearly unfounded held not to be inherently unfair); *R. (on the application of Refugee Legal Centre) v Secretary of*

State for the Home Department [2004] EWHC 684 (separate fast-track pilot scheme for asylum seekers considered to have straightforward claims also held not to be unfair).

A duty to act fairly has also been implied by the courts in many cases outside immigration law. See, for example, *R. v Birmingham City Justice Ex p. Chris Foreign Foods (Wholesalers) Ltd* [1970] 1 W.L.R. 1428 (proceedings for the condemnation of unfit food); *Cinnamond v British Airports Authority* [1980] 1 W.L.R. 582 (exercise of the power to ban specific persons from Heathrow airport; see below, p.700); and *Bushell v Secretary of State for the Environment* (below, p.731) (public inquiry proceedings). For further discussions of "fairness", see D.J. Mullan, "Fairness: The New Natural Justice?" (1975) 25 U.T.L.J. 281, the response by M. Loughlin at (1978) 28 U.T.L.J. 215 and D.J. Mullan, "Natural Justice and Fairness—Substantive as well as Procedural Standards for the Review of Administrative Decision-Making?" (1982) 27 McGill L.J. 250.

3. The modern approach was summarised as follows by Taylor L.J. in *R. v Army Board of the Defence Council, Ex p. Anderson* [1992] 1 Q.B. 169. A, the only black soldier in his platoon, went absent without leave after various incidents of racial harassment and abuse. He was subsequently arrested and returned to his unit. His commanding officer called in the Special Investigation Branch of the Royal Military Police to inquire into his allegations of racial discrimination. A copy of the SIB's report was not made available to A despite his request. A pleaded guilty at his court-martial to going AWOL, and was sentenced to detention. After the court-martial, the Ministry of Defence gave him a summary of the SIB report, which stated that his complaints of verbal abuse, but not assault, had been borne out by the admissions of other soldiers, but also alleged that A had sought to exploit the racial issue. A made a formal complaint of racial discrimination, which under the Race Relations Act 1976 was referred to his C.O. rather than an industrial tribunal. The C.O. rejected the complaint and informed him that disciplinary action had been taken against two soldiers who had admitted racial abuse. A then complained to the Army Board. His requests for disclosure of the SIB report and other documents and for an oral hearing were rejected. The complaint was dealt with by two members of the board, who considered the papers separately and reached their individual conclusions without meeting to discuss the matter. The board stated that appropriate action had been taken against those responsible for the abuse, but refused compensation or apology and gave no reasons for that refusal.

The Court of Appeal quashed the board's decision. On the question of what procedural requirements were necessary, Taylor L.J. said (at 185–186):

"What procedural requirements are necessary to achieve fairness when the Army Board considers a complaint of this kind? In addressing this issue, counsel made much of the distinction between judicial and administrative functions. Were it necessary to decide in those terms the functions of the Army Board when considering a race discrimination complaint, I would characterise it as judicial rather than administrative. The board is required to adjudicate on an alleged breach of a soldier's rights under the 1976 Act and, if it be proved, to take any necessary steps by way of redress. It is accepted that the board has the power, inter alia, to award compensation. A body required to consider and adjudicate upon an alleged breach of statutory rights and to grant redress when necessary seems to me to be exercising an essentially judicial function. It matters not that the body has other functions which are non-judicial: see *R. v Secretary of State for the Home Dept, Ex p. Tarrant* [1985] Q.B. 251, 268.

However, to label the board's function either 'judicial' or 'administrative' for the purpose of determining the appropriate procedural regime is to adopt too inflexible an approach. We were referred to many decided cases, but the principles laid down in *Ridge v Baldwin* [1964] A.C. 40 are well summarised by Sir William Wade in his *Administrative Law* (6th ed., 1988), pp.518–519, as follows:

'[Lord Reid] attacked the problem at its root by demonstrating how the term "judicial" had been misinterpreted as requiring some superadded characteristic over and above the characteristic that the power affected some person's rights. The mere fact that the power affects rights or interests is what makes it 'judicial', and so subject to the procedures required by natural justice. In other words, a power which affects rights must be exercised "judicially", *i.e.* fairly, and the fact that the power is administrative does not make it any the less "judicial" for this purpose. Lord Hodson put his point very clearly ([1964] A.C. 40 at 130): ". . . the answer in a given case is not provided by the statement that the giver of the decision is acting in an executive or administrative capacity as if that were the antithesis of a judicial capacity. The cases seem to me to show that persons acting in a capacity which is not on the face of it judicial but rather executive or administrative have been held by the Courts to be subject to the principles of natural justice" '.

This approach was echoed by Lord Lane C.J. in *R. v Commission for Racial Equality, Ex p. Cottrell & Rothon* [1980] 1 W.L.R. 1580, 1587. He said:

'It seems to me that there are degrees of judicial hearing, and those degrees run from the borders of pure administration to the borders of the full hearing of a criminal cause or matter in the Crown Court. It does not profit one to try to pigeon-hole the particular set of circumstances either into the administrative pigeon-hole or into the judicial pigeon-hole. Each case will inevitably differ, and one must ask oneself what is the basic nature of the proceeding which was going on here' ".

Taylor L. J. also referred to *Lloyd v McMahon*, below, p.722. He accepted the arguments of counsel for the board that by deliberately excluding soldiers' complaints from industrial tribunals, it could not be axiomatic that all the tribunal's procedures had to be made available by the board. On the other hand, he rejected the argument that the board's duty of fairness required no more than that it should act *bona fide*, not capriciously or in a biased manner, and that it should afford the complainant a chance to respond to the basic points put against him. This did not go far enough:

"The Army Board as the forum of last resort, dealing with an individual's fundamental statutory rights, must by its procedures achieve a high standard of fairness".

The requirements were:

(1) There must be a proper hearing "in the sense that the board must consider, as a single adjudicating body, all the relevant evidence and contentions before reaching its conclusions": accordingly, the board should meet.
(2) The hearing did not necessarily have to be an oral hearing in all cases:

"Whether an oral hearing is necessary will depend upon the subject matter and circumstances of the particular case and upon the nature of the decision to be made. It will also depend upon whether there are substantial issues of fact which cannot be satisfactorily resolved on the available written evidence. This does not mean that, whenever there is a conflict of evidence in the statements taken, an oral hearing must be held to resolve it. Sometimes such a conflict can be resolved merely by the inherent unlikelihood of one version or the other. Sometimes the conflict is not central to the issue for determination and would not justify an oral hearing. Even when such a hearing is necessary, it may only require one or two witnesses to be called and cross-examined".

There did not have to be oral hearings in all discrimination cases. On the other hand the board here had fettered its discretion by having an inflexible policy never to hold oral hearings.

(3) The board had a discretion whether to have the evidence tested by cross-examination.

(4) "Whether oral or not, there must be what amounts to a hearing of any complaint under the 1976 Act. This means that the Army Board must have such a complaint investigated, consider all the material gathered in the investigation, give the complainant an opportunity to respond to it and consider his response.

But what is the board obliged to disclose to the complainant to obtain his response? Is it sufficient to indicate the gist of any material adverse to his case or should he be shown all the material seen by the board? Mr Pannick submits that there is no obligation to show all to the complainant. He relies upon three authorities, *R. v Secretary of State for the Home Department, Ex p. Mughal* [1974] Q.B. 313; *R. v Secretary of State for the Home Department, Ex p. Santillo* [1981] Q.B. 778 and *R. v Monopolies and Mergers Commission, Ex p. Matthew Brown plc* [1987] 1 W.L.R. 1235. However, in each of those cases, the function of the decision-making body was towards the administrative end of the spectrum. Because of the nature of the Army Board's function pursuant to the Race Relations Act 1976, already analysed above, I consider that a soldier complainant under that Act should be shown all the material seen by the board, apart from any documents for which public interest immunity can properly be claimed. The board is not simply making an administrative decision requiring it to consult interested parties and hear their representations. It has a duty to adjudicate on a specific complaint of breach of a statutory right. Except where public interest immunity is established, I see no reason why on such an adjudication the board should consider material withheld from the complainant."

Here, A's response had been hampered by the lack of full information.

On point (2), see also *R. v Department of Health, Ex p. Gandhi* [1991] 1 W.L.R. 105, (Secretary of State not obliged to hold an oral hearing when dealing with an appeal against a decision of a Medical Practices Committee raising a complaint of racial discrimination).

McINNES v ONSLOW-FANE

[1978] 1 W.L.R. 1520; [1978] 3 All E.R. 211 (CHANCERY DIVISION, MEGARRY V.C.)

The plaintiff had held a promoter's licence for boxing matches issued in the 1950s by the British Boxing Board of Control (a voluntary self-regulatory organisation). In 1971 the board granted him a trainer's licence and in 1973 a master of ceremonies' licence. After an incident at a boxing match in 1973, the Board withdrew all the plaintiff's licences. Subsequently, he applied to the Board for a manager's licence on five occasions, but his applications were rejected. The plaintiff sought a declaration against the Board (represented by two of its members) that it had acted contrary to the rules of natural justice/or unfairly by (1) failing to inform the plaintiff of the case against him so that he could answer those concerns and (2) by not granting him an oral hearing prior to rejecting his last licence application.

MEGARRY V.C.: . . . It was common ground between Mr Beloff [counsel for the plaintiff] and Mr Moses [counsel for the defendants] that the point before me was the subject of no direct authority: although expulsion from clubs and other bodies is the subject of an ample range of authorities, the refusal of applications for membership is much less richly endowed. It was also accepted that the point is of considerable general importance. There are many bodies which, though not established or operating under the authority of statute, exercise control, often on a national scale, over many activities which are important to many people, both as providing a means of livelihood and for other reasons. Sometimes that control is exercised, as by the board, by means of a system of granting or refusing licences, and sometimes it is operated by means of accepting or rejecting applications for membership. One particular aspect of this is membership of a trade union, without which it is impossible to obtain many important forms of work. In such cases it is plainly important, both to the body and the applicant, for them to know whether, before the application is rejected, the applicant is entitled to prior notice of any case against granting him a licence or admitting him to membership, and whether he is entitled to an oral hearing.

I think that I should take the matter by stages. First, there is the question of whether the grant or refusal of a licence by the board is subject to any requirements of natural justice or fairness which will be enforced by the courts. The question is not one that is governed by statute or contract, with questions of their true construction or the implication of terms; for there is no statute, and there is no contract between the plaintiff and the board. Nevertheless, in recent years there has been a marked expansion of the ambit of the requirements of natural justice and fairness reaching beyond statute and contract. A striking example is *Nagle v Feilden* [1966] 2 Q.B. 633. There, a woman sought a declaration and injunctions against the Jockey Club to enforce her claim that she ought not to be refused a trainer's licence for horse-racing merely because she was a woman. At first instance her claim had been struck out, but the Court of Appeal reversed this decision. Lord Denning M.R. accepted that social clubs could refuse to admit an applicant for membership as they wished; but the Jockey Club exercised "a virtual monopoly in an important field of human activity", and what gave the courts jurisdiction was "a man's right to work": see pp.644, 646. In reaching his conclusion, Lord Denning M.R. observed that being a jockey could be regarded as being an unsuitable occupation for a woman, whereas being a trainer could not: see p.647.

. . . [W]here the court is entitled to intervene, I think it must be considered what type of decision is in question. I do not suggest that there is any clear or exhaustive classification; but I think that at least three categories may be discerned. First, there are what may be called the forfeiture cases. In these, there is a decision which takes away some existing right or position, as where a member of an organisation is expelled or a licence is revoked. Second, at the other extreme there are what may be called the application cases. These are cases where the decision merely refuses to grant the applicant the right or position that he seeks, such as membership of the organisation, or a licence to do certain acts. Third, there is an intermediate category, which may be called the expectation cases, which differ from the application cases only in that the applicant has some legitimate expectation from what has already happened that his application will be granted. This head includes cases where an existing licence-holder applies for a renewal of his licence, or a person already elected or appointed to some position seeks confirmation from some confirming authority: see, for instance, *Weinberger v Inglis* [1919] A.C. 606; *Breen v Amalgamated Engineering Union* [1971] 2 Q.B. 175; and see *Schmidt v Secretary of State for Home Affairs* [1969] 2 Ch. 149, 170, 173 and *R. v Barnsley Metropolitan Borough Council, Ex p. Hook* [1976] 1 W.L.R. 1052, 1058.

It seems plain that there is a substantial distinction between the forfeiture cases and the application cases. In the forfeiture cases, there is a threat to take something away for some reason: and in such cases, the right to an unbiased tribunal, the right to notice of the charges and the right to be heard in answer to the charges (which in *Ridge v Baldwin* [1964] A.C. 40, 132, Lord Hodson said were three features of natural justice which stood out) are plainly apt. In the application cases, on the other hand, nothing is being taken away, and in all normal circumstances there are no charges, and so no requirement of an opportunity of being heard in answer to the charges. Instead, there is the far wider and less defined question of the general suitability of the applicant for membership or a licence. The distinction is well-recognised, for in general it is clear that the courts will require natural justice to be observed for expulsion from a social club, but not on an application for admission to it. The intermediate category, that of the expectation cases, may at least in some respects be regarded as being more akin to the forefeiture cases than the application cases; for although in form there is no forfeiture but merely an attempt at acquisition that fails, the legitimate expectation of a renewal of the licence or confirmation of the membership is one which raises the question of what it is that has happened to make the applicant unsuitable for the membership or licence for which he was previously thought suitable.

I pause there. I do not think that I need pursue the expectation cases, for in the present case I can see nothing that would bring the plaintiff within them. . . .

. . . In my judgment, the case is plainly an application case in which the plaintiff is seeking to obtain a licence that he has never held and had no legitimate expectation of holding; he had only the hope (which may be confident or faint or anything between) which any applicant for anything may always have.

. . . [T]here is the question of the requirements of natural justice or fairness that have to be applied in an application case such as this. What are the requirements where there are no provisions of any statute or contract either conferring a right to the licence in certain circumstances, or laying down the procedure to be observed, and the applicant is seeking from an unofficial body the grant of a type of licence that he has never held before, and, though hoping to obtain it, has no legitimate expectation of receiving?

I do not think that much help is to be obtained from discussing whether "natural justice" or "fairness" is the more appropriate term. It one accepts that "natural justice" is a flexible term which imposes different requirements in different cases, it is capable of applying appropriately to the whole range of situations indicated by terms such as "judicial", "quasi-judicial" and "administrative". Nevertheless, the further the situation is away from anything that resembles a judicial or quasi-judicial situation, and the further the question is removed from what may reasonably be called a justiciable question, the more appropriate it is to reject an expression which includes the word "justice" and to use instead terms such as "fairness", or "the duty to act fairly": see *Re H.K. (An Infant)* [1967] 2 Q.B. 617, 630, *per* Lord Parker C.J.; *Re Pergamon Press Ltd* [1971] Ch. 388, 399, *per* Lord Denning M.R.; *Breen's* case [1971] 2 Q.B. 175, 195, *per* Edmund Davies L.J. ("fairly exercised"); *Pearlberg v Varty* [1972] 1 W.L.R. 534, 545, *per* Viscount Dilhorne, and at 547, *per* Lord Pearson. The suitability of the term "fairness" in such cases is increased by the curiosities of the expression "natural justice". Justice is far from being a "natural" concept. The closer one goes to a state of nature, the less justice does one find. Justice, and with it "natural justice", is in truth an elaborate and artificial product of civilisation which varies with different civilisations: see *Maclean v Workers' Union* [1929] 1 Ch.602, 624, *per* Maugham J. To Black J., "natural justice" understandably meant no more than "justice" without the adjective: see *Green v Blake* [1948] I.R. 242, 268. However, be that as it may, the question before me is that of the content of "the duty to act fairly" (or of "natural justice") in this particular case. What does it entail? In particular, does it require the board to afford the plaintiff not only information of the "case against him" but also an oral hearing?. . .

I think it is clear that there is no general obligation to give reasons for a decision. Certainly in an application case, where there are no statutory or contractual requirements but a simple discretion in the licensing body, there is no obligation on that body to give their reasons. . . .

As I have said, Mr Moses accepted that the board were under a duty to reach an honest conclusion without bias and not in pursuance of any capricious policy. That, I think, is right: and if the plaintiff showed that any of these requirements had not been complied with, I think the court would intervene. Mr Beloff accepted that the burden of proof would have been on him if any such questions had arisen. But assume a board acting honestly and without bias or caprice: why should a duty to act fairly require them to tell an applicant the gist of the reasons (which may vary from member to member) why they think he ought not to be given a licence? Is a college or university, when selecting candidates for admission or awarding scholarships, or a charity when making grants to the needy, acting "unfairly" when it gives no reason to the unsuccessful? Are editors and publishers "unfair" when they send out unreasoned rejection slips? Assume that they are under no enforceable duty to act fairly, and it may still be a matter of concern to them if they are to be told that they are acting "unfairly" in not giving the gist of their reasons to the rejected. Again, do judges act unfairly when, without any indication of their reasons, they refuse leave to appeal, or decide questions of costs?. . .

Looking at the case as whole, in my judgment there is no obligation on the board to give the plaintiff even the gist of the reasons why they refused his application, or proposed to do so. This is not a case in which there has been any suggestion of the board considering any alleged dishonesty or morally culpable conduct of the plaintiff. A man free from any moral blemish may nevertheless be wholly unsuitable for a particular type of work. The refusal of the plaintiff's application by no means necessarily puts any slur on his character, nor does it deprive him of any statutory right. There is no mere narrow issue as to his character, but the wide and general issue whether it is right to grant this licence to this applicant. In such circumstances, in the absence of anything to suggest that the board have been affected by dishonesty or bias or caprice, or that there is any other impropriety, I think that the board are fully entitled to give no reasons for their decision, and to decide the application without any preliminary indication to the plaintiff of those reasons. The board are the best judges of the desirability of granting the licence, and in the absence of any impropriety the court ought not to interfere.

There is a more general consideration. I think that the courts must be slow to allow any implied obligation to be fair to be used as a means of bringing before the courts for review honest decisions of bodies exercising jurisdiction over sporting and other activities which those bodies are far better fitted to judge than the courts. This is so even where those bodies are concerned with the means of livelihood of those who take part in those activities. The concepts of natural justice and the duty to be fair must not be allowed to discredit themselves by making unreasonable requirements and imposing undue burdens. Bodies such as the board which promote a public interest by seeking to maintain high standards in a field of activity which otherwise might easily become degraded and corrupt ought not to be hampered in their work without good cause. Such bodies should not be tempted or coerced into granting licences that otherwise they would refuse by reason of the courts having imposed on them a procedure for refusal which facilitates litigation against them. As Lord Denning M.R. said in *Re Pergamon Press Ltd* [1971] Ch. 388, 400, "No one likes to have an action brought against him, however unfounded." The individual must indeed be protected against impropriety; but any claim of his for anything more must be balanced against what the public interest requires.

That brings me to the fifth point, the contention that the board are obliged to afford the plaintiff a hearing. This, I think, has in large part been disposed of by what I have said in rejecting the contention that the plaintiff has a right to be told the gist of the reasons for proposing to reject his application. The contention that the plaintiff ought to be given a hearing seems to have been put forward mainly as an ancillary to the alleged obligation to inform him of the gist of the reasons for provisionally deciding not to grant him the licence, and so as to enable him to meet what is said. However, if one treats the right to a hearing as an independent requirement, I would say that I cannot see how the obligation to be fair can be said in a case of this type to require a hearing. I do not see why the board should not be fully capable of dealing fairly with the plaintiff's application without any hearing. The case is not an expulsion case where natural justice confers the right to know the charge and to have an opportunity of meeting it at a hearing. I cannot think that there is or should be any rule that an application for a licence of this sort cannot properly be refused without giving the applicant the opportunity of a hearing, however hopeless the application, and whether it is the first or the fifth or the fiftieth application that he has made. Certainly Mr Beloff has not referred me to any authority which appears to me to give any real support to such a proposition in a case such as this. I therefore reject the contention that the board should be required to give the plaintiff a hearing or interview.

In my judgment, therefore, the plaintiff's claim fails. It is easy to understand a very natural curiosity and, doubtless, anxiety on his part to know what it is that stands between him and the grant of the licence that he seeks. He may wonder whether it is something that endeavour on his part may put right, or whether it is something beyond cure. It may be that it would be considerate of the board if they were to give him at least some indication of what stands in his way. I for one would not be surprised if his previous career as a licence-holder had played a substantial part in this, although no details of the various episodes have been put before me. At the same time, I can well see that the board would be reluctant to adopt a more elaborate and time-consuming procedure for determining applications for licences, and even more reluctant to be required to give reasons (whether in full or in outline) which might provide ammunition for litigation against the board. The board's regulations seem to me to make fair and reasonable provisions for disciplinary cases which may lead to the suspension or withdrawal of a licence and so on, and the distinction under the regulations between such cases and applications for the grant of licences seems to me to be proper and generally in accordance with the law. Furthermore, the offer of a hearing made by the board's solicitors after the originating summons had been issued seems to me to have been reasonable and benign; I regret that the plaintiff's solicitors should have been insistent upon the board paying the plaintiff's costs. My duty, however, is simply to apply the law as I understand it; and for the reasons that I have given, I hold that on the questions that are before me the plaintiff's claims fail and will be dismissed.

Summons dismissed.

Notes

1. Eleven years after the above decision, Michael Beloff Q.C. (who had been counsel for Mr McInnes) expressed the following view regarding the judicial attitude towards legal actions brought against the governing bodies of different sports:

> "no less than three Vice-Chancellors of different generations and jurisdictions have taken the view that the courts should abstain where possible from interfering with the decisions of bodies controlling sporting spheres. . . . It is, I suspect, the flood-gates argument that is the unspoken premise of the Vice-Chancellarial observations, the fear that limited court time will be absorbed by a new and elastic category of case with much scope for abusive or captious litigation. It is an argument which intellectually has little to commend it, and pragmatically is usually shown to be ill-founded. For it is often the case that, once the courts have shown the willingness to intervene, the standards of the bodies at risk of their intervention tend to improve. The threat of litigation averts its actuality" ("Pitch, Pool, Rink, . . . Court? Judicial Review in the Sporting World" [1989] P.L. 95 at pp.109–110).

See also E. Grayson, *Sport and the Law* (2nd ed., 1994).

In *Jones v Welsh Rugby Football Union, The Times,* March 6, 1997, Ebsworth J. granted the plaintiff, a player with Ebbw Vale RFC, an interinjunction lifting a four-week suspension imposed on him by the defendants for allegedly fighting during a match. Her Ladyship considered that the plaintiff had an arguable case that the defendants had not followed a fair disciplinary procedure by, *inter alia*, preventing the plaintiff effectively challenging the allegations against him. Her Ladyship observed that:

> "sport was now big business; many people earned their living from it in one way or another. It would be naïve to pretend that the modern world of sport could be conducted as it used to be not very many years ago".

The Court of Appeal dismissed an appeal (*The Times,* January 6, 1998). The WRFU changed its rules in the light of the judge's comments, permitting a player's representative to question the referee and to call and cross-examine witnesses, video evidence to be viewed in the parties' presence and requests for legal representation to be considered on their merits.

The view that there should be self-restraint in the review of decisions of sporting bodies is not appropriate where serious questions of reputation or livelihood are at stake. The courts are very reluctant to hold that sporting bodies are amenable to judicial review (see below, pp.952–955), but requirements of procedural fairness are applied, normally as a matter of express or implied contractual terms (see, *e.g. Modahl v British Athletic Federation (No.2)* [2001] EWCA Civ 1447; [2002] 1 W.L.R. 1192 (procedure whereby M's suspension for failing a doping test was overturned on appeal held to be fair overall); *Bradley v Jockey Club* [2004] EWHC 2164, QBD).

2. Where licensing decisions under statutory powers do have an effect on livelihood, the court have generally been willing to imply procedural standards in application cases as well as cases of non-renewal or revocation. In *R. v Huntingdon DC Ex p. Cowan* [1984] 1 W.L.R. 501, Glidewell J. held that when dealing with an application for an entertainment licence under Part I of the Local Government (Miscellaneous

Provisions) Act 1982 a local authority must inform the applicant of the substance of any objection or representation in the nature of an objection (not necessarily the whole of it, nor to say necessarily who has made it); and give the applicant an opportunity to make representations in reply. (See also *R. v Preston BC Ex p. Quietlynn Ltd* and other cases (1984) 83 L.G.R. 308, C.A.). In *R. v Bristol City Council Ex p. Pearce* (1984) 83 L.G.R. 711, the same judge held that when considering an application for a street trading consent under para.7 of Sch.4 to the Local Government (Miscellaneous Provisions) Act 1982, a local authority was obliged to tell the applicants of the content of any objection (other than from its own officers or the police) and to give them some opportunity to comment. However, an oral hearing need not be held, and reasons need not be given. (His Lordship held that the applicant here did not have a legitimate expectation, but that nevertheless some procedural standards were applicable.) In *R. v Wear Valley DC Ex p. Binks* [1985] 2 All E.R. 699, the council decided to terminate the applicant's contractual licence to station a caravan on the council's land (in a market place). The applicant used the caravan to earn her living by selling take-away food. Taylor J. held that the council was obliged to give notice of and the reasons for the proposed termination, and an opportunity to be heard, notwithstanding that the licence was contractual and not statutory. See also the *Quark* case, above, p.535 and below, p.707.

3. Megarry J.'s analysis was regarded as helpful by the Court of Appeal in *R. (on the application of Khatun) v Newham LBC* [2004] EWCA Civ 55; [2004] 3 W.L.R. 417 in holding that a homeless person had no right to view accommodation offered by the housing authority before being required to accept it. The distinction between "forfeiture" and "application" cases was, however,

31. . . . "not hard and fast. There may be cases where refusal of the application (for example, the refusal of a passport) will carry adverse implications for other rights or interests which the applicant may expect to enjoy. But in general the distinction possesses much force. In an application case there is likely to be legal space for the decision-maker to exercise a discretion whether or not to accord a right to be heard. In doing so, he will of course have regard to the practicalities of the statutory scheme's operation. A perceived need in the general interest to process applications speedily, against a background of many applicants and scarce resources, may be a legitimate and important factor.
32. In light of all these considerations I conclude that the common law's standards of procedural fairness do not require the court to confer a right to be heard, properly so called, upon applicants for Part VII accommodation. This is-and I do not for a moment undervalue the acute importance of the matter to the homeless person seeking a roof over his head-a paradigm of an application case. In my judgment it belongs to the second kind of scheme which I have described, that is one in which there is no right to be heard as such and the applicant enjoys only the right to take the benefit of an executive decision in his favour if the relevant public body so concludes".

Furthermore, it could not be said that no reasonable council would fail to accord such an opportunity.

4. Where a decision does adversely affect a person's reputation, unlike the position in *McInnes v Onslow Fane*, there are strong grounds at common law (and under Art.8 ECHR) for the imposition of procedural standards. See, *eg. R. (on the application of X) v Chief Constable of the West Midlands Police* [2004] EWHC 61; [2004] 2 All E.R. 1, where Wall J. held that the chief constable was obliged to give X an opportunity to make representations before releasing to a prospective employer (a social work agency) information about his arrest for indecent exposure, the charge having subsequently been dropped. This was reversed by the Court of Appeal ([2004] EWCA Civ 1068; [2005] 1 All E.R. 610) on the ground that X had a statutory opportunity to correct a certificate (given by the Secretary of State on the advice of the Chief Constable).

COUNCIL OF CIVIL SERVICE UNIONS v MINISTER FOR THE CIVIL SERVICE

[1985] A.C. 374; [1985] I.C.R. 14; [1984] 3 W.L.R. 1174; [1984] 3 All E.R. 935 (HOUSE OF LORDS)

The main functions of Government Communications Headquarters ("GCHQ") were to ensure the security of military and official communications and to provide the Government with signals intelligence; they involved the handling of secret information vital to national security. Since 1947, staff employed at GCHQ had been permitted to belong to national trade unions, and most had done so. There was a well-established practice of consultation between the official and trade union sides about important alterations in the terms and conditions of service of the staff. On December 22, 1983, the Minister for the Civil Service gave an instruction, purportedly under art. 4 of the Civil Service Order in Council 1982, for the immediate variation of the terms and conditions of service of the staff with the effect that they would no longer be permitted to belong to national trade unions. There had been no consultation with the trade unions or with the staff at GCHQ prior to the issuing of that instruction. The applicants, a trade union and six individuals, sought judicial review of the Minister's instruction on the ground that she had been under a duty to act fairly by consulting those concerned before issuing it. In an affidavit, the Secretary to the Cabinet deposed to disruptive industrial action in support of national trade unions that had taken place at GCHQ as part of a national campaign by the unions designed to damage government agencies and that it had been considered that prior consultation about the minister's instruction would have involved a risk of precipitating further disruption and would moreover have indicated vulnerable areas of GCHQ's operations. Glidewell J. granted the applicants a declaration that the instruction was invalid and of no effect. The Court of Appeal allowed an appeal by the minister, and a further appeal was dismissed.

The House of Lords held (1) that the Government's action was not immune from judicial review merely because it was in pursuance of a common law or a prerogative power; (2) that the applicants would apart from national security considerations have had a legitimate expectation that unions and employees would have been consulted before the instruction was issued; but (3) that the Minister had shown that her decision had in fact been based on considerations of national security that outweighed the applicant's legitimate expectation.

LORD FRASER OF TULLYBELTON: . . .

The duty to consult

Mr Blom-Cooper submitted that the Minister had a duty to consult the CCSU, on behalf of employees at GCHQ, before giving the instruction on December 22, 1983, for making an important change in their conditions of service. His main reason for so submitting was that the employees had a legitimate, or reasonable, expectation that there would be such prior consultation before any important change was made in their conditions.

It is clear that the employees did not have legal right to prior consultation. The Order in Council confers no such right, and article 4 makes no reference at all to consultation. The Civil Service handbook (*Handbook for the New Civil Servant*, 1973 ed. as amended 1983) which explains the normal method of consultation through the departmental Whitley Council, does not suggest that there is any legal right to consultation; indeed it is careful to recognise that, in the operational field, considerations of urgency may make prior consultation impracticable. The Civil Service Pay and Conditions of Service Code expressly states:

"The following terms and conditions also apply to your appointment in the Civil Service. It should be understood, however, that in consequence of the constitutional position of the Crown, the Crown has the right to change its employees' conditions of service at any time, and that they hold their appointments at the pleasure of the Crown."

But even where a person claiming some benefit or privilege has no legal right to it, as a matter of private law, he may have a legitimate expectation of receiving the benefit or privilege, and, if so, the courts will protect his expectation of judicial review as a matter of public law. This subject has been fully explained by my noble and learned friend, Lord Diplock, in *O'Reilly v Mackman* [1983] 2 A.C. 237 and I need not repeat what he has so recently said. Legitimate, or reasonable, expectation may arise either from an express promise given on behalf of a public authority or from the existence of a regular practice which the claimant can reasonably expect to continue. Examples of the former type of expectation are *R. v Liverpool Corporation, Ex p. Liverpool Taxi Fleet Operators' Association* [1972] 2 Q.B. 299 and *Attorney-General of Hong Kong v Ng Yuen Shiu* [1983] 2 A.C. 629. (I agree with Lord Diplock's view, expressed in the speech in this appeal, that "legitimate" is to be pre-ferred to "reasonable" in this context. I was responsible for using the word "reasonable" for the reason explained in *Ng Yuen Shiu*, but it was intended only to be exegetical of "legitimate.") An example of the latter is *R. v Board of Visitors of Hull Prison, Ex p. St Germain* [1979] Q.B. 425 approved by this House in *O'Reilly*, at 274D. The submission on behalf of the appellants is that the present case is of the latter type. The test of that is whether the practice of prior consultation of the staff on significant changes in their conditions of service was so well established by 1983 that it would be unfair or inconsistent with good administration for the Government to depart from the practice in this case. Legitimate expectations such as are now under consideration will always relate to a benefit or privilege to which the claimant has no right in private law, and it may even be to one which conflicts with his private law rights. In the present case the evidence shows that, ever since GCHQ began in 1947, prior consultation has been the invariable rule when conditions of ser-vice were to be significantly altered. Accordingly in my opinion if there had been no question of national security involved, the appellants would have had a legitimate expectation that the minister would consult them before issuing the instruction of December 22, 1983.

National security

The issue here is not whether the minister's instruction was proper or fair or justifiable on its merits. These matters are not for the courts to determine. The sole issue is whether the decision on which the instruction was based was reached by a process that was fair to the staff at GCHQ. As my noble and learned friend Lord Brightman said in *Chief Constable of the North Wales Police v Evans* [1982] 1 W.L.R. 1155, 1173: "Judicial review is concerned, not with the decision, but with the decision-making process."

I have already explained my reasons for holding that, if no question of national security arose, the decision-making process in this case would have been unfair. The respondent's case is that she deliberately made the decision without prior consultation because prior consultation "would involve a real risk that it would occasion the very kind of disruption [at GCHQ] which was a threat to national security and which it was intended to avoid." I have quoted from paragraph 27(i) of the respondent's printed case Mr Blom-Cooper conceded that a reasonable minister could reasonably have taken that view, but he argued strongly that the respondent had failed to show that, that was in fact the reason for her decision. He supported his argument by saying, as I think was conceded by Mr Alexander, that the reason given in paragraph 27(i) had not been mentioned to Glidewell J. and that it had only emerged before the Court of Appeal. He described it as an "afterthought" and invited the house to hold that it had not been shown to have been the true reason.

The question is one of evidence. The decision on whether the requirements of national security outweigh the duty of fairness in any particular case is for the Government and not for the courts; the Government alone has access to the necessary information, and in any event the judicial process is unsuitable for reaching decisions on national security. But if the decision is successfully challenged, on the ground that it has been reached by a process which is unfair, then the Government is under an obligation to produce evidence that the decision was in fact based on grounds of national security. Authority for both these points is found in *The Zamora* [1916] 2 A.C. 77. The former point is dealt with in the well known passage from the advice of the Judicial Committee delivered by Lord Parker of Waddington, at p.107:

"Those who are responsible for the national security must be the sole judges of what the national security requires. It would be obviously undesirable that such matters should be made the subject of evidence in a court of law or otherwise discussed in public."

The second point, less often referred to, appears at p.106 and more particularly at p.108 where this passage occurs:

"In their Lordships' opinion the order appealed from was wrong not because, as contended by the appellants, there is by international law no right at all to requisition ships or goods in the custody of the court, but because the judge had before him *no satisfactory evidence* that such a right was exercisable." (Emphasis added.)

What was required was evidence that a cargo of copper in the custody of the Prize Court was urgently required for national purposes, but no evidence had been directed to the point. The claim on behalf of the Crown that it was entitled to requisition the copper therefore failed; considering that the decision was made in 1916 at a critical stage of the 1914–1918 war, it was a strong one. In *Chandler v Director of Public Prosecutions* [1964] A.C. 763, which was an appeal by persons who had been convicted of a breach of the peace under section. I of the Official Secrets Act 1911 by arranging a demonstration by the Campaign for Nuclear Disarmament on an operational airfield at Wethersfield, Lord Reid said, at p.790:

"The question more frequently arises as to what is or is not in the public interest. I do not subscribe to the view that the Government or a minister must always or even as a general rule have the last word about that. But here we are dealing with a very special matte—interfering with a prohibited place which Wethersfield was."

But the court had had before it evidence from an Air Commodore that the airfield was of importance for national security. Both Lord Reid and Viscount Radcliffe, at p.796, referred to the evidence as being relevant to their refusal of the appeal.

The evidence in support of this part of the respondent's case came from Sir Robert Armstrong in his first affidavit, especially at paragraph 16. Mr Blom-Cooper rightly pointed out that the affidavit does not in terms directly support paragraph 27(i), ante pp.401H–402A. But it does set out the respondent's view that to have entered into prior consultation would have served to bring out the vulnerability of areas of operation to those who had shown themselves ready to organize disruption. That must be read along with the earlier parts of the affidavit in which Sir Robert had dealt in some detail with the attitude of the trade unions which I have referred to earlier in this speech. The affidavit, read as a whole, does in my opinion undoubtedly constitute evidence that the Minister did indeed consider that prior consultation would have involved a risk of precipitating disruption at GCHQ. I am accordingly of opinion that the respondent has shown that her decision was one which not only could reasonably have been based, but was in fact based, on considerations of national security, which outweighed what would otherwise have been the reasonable expectation on the part of the appellants for prior consultation. In deciding that matter I must with respect differ from the decision of Gidewell J. but, as I have mentioned, I do so on a point that was not argued to him. . . .

LORD DIPLOCK: . . . Judicial review, now regulated by R.S.C., Ord. 53, provides the means by which judicial control of administrative action is exercised. The subject-matter of every judicial review is a decision made by some person (or body of persons) whom I will call the "decision-maker" or else a refusal by him to make a decision.

To qualify as a subject for judicial review the decision must have consequences which affect some person (or body of persons) other than the decision-maker, although it may affect him too. It must affect such other person either:

(a) by altering rights or obligations of that person which are enforceable by or against him in private law; or

(b) by depriving him of some benefit or advantage which either (i) he had in the past been permitted by the decision-maker to enjoy and which he can legitimately expect to be permitted to continue to do until there has been communicated to him some rational grounds for withdrawing it on which he has been given an opportunity to comment; or (ii) he has received assurance from the decision-maker will not be withdrawn without giving him first an opportunity of advancing reasons for contending that they should not be withdrawn. (I prefer to continue to call the kind of expectation that qualifies a decision for inclusion in class (b) a "legitimate expectation" rather than a "reasonable expectation," in order thereby to indicate that it has consequences to which effect will be given in public law, whereas an expectation or hope that some benefit or advantage would continue to be enjoyed, although it might well be entertained by a "reasonable" man, would not necessarily have such consequences. The recent decision of this House in *Re Findlay* [1985] A.C. 318 presents an example of the latter kind of expectation. "Reasonable" furthermore bears different meanings according to whether the context in which it is being used is that of private law or of public law. To eliminate confusion it is best avoided in the latter.)

For a decision to be susceptible to judicial review the decision-maker must be empowered by public law (and not merely, as in arbitration, by agreement between private parties) to make decisions that, if validly made, will lead to administrative action or abstention from action by an authority endowed by law with executive powers, which have one or other of the consequences mentioned in the preceding paragraph. The ultimate source of the decision-making power is nearly always nowadays a statute or subordinate legislation made under the statute; but in the absence of any statute regulating the subjectmatter of the decision the source of the decision-making power may still be the common law itself, *i.e.* that part of the common law that is given by lawyers the label of "the prerogative". Where this is the source of decision-making power, the power is confined to executive officers of central as distinct from local government and in constitutional practice is generally exercised by those holding ministerial rank.

It was the prerogative that was relied on as the source of the power of the Minister for the Civil Service in reaching her decision of December 22, 1983, that membership of national trade unions should in future be barred to all members of the home civil service employed at GCHQ. . . .

. . . whatever label may be attached to them there have unquestionably survived into the present day a residue of miscellaneous field s of law in which the executive government retains decisions making powers that are not dependent upon any statutory authority but nevertheless have consequences on the private rights or legitimate expectations of other persons which would render the decision subject to judicial review if the power of the decision-maker to make them were statutory in origin. From matters so relatively minor as the grant of pardons to condemned criminals, of honours to the good and great, of corporate personality to deserving bodies of persons, and of bounty from moneys made available to the executive government by parliment, they extent to matters so vital to the survival and welfare of the nation as the conduct of relations with foreign states and—what lies at the heart of the present case— the defence of the realm against potential enemies. Adopting the phraseology used in the European Convention on Human Rights 1953 (Convention for the Protection) of Human Rights and Fundamental Freedoms (1953) (Cmd. 8969) to which the United Kingdom is a party it has now become usual in statutes to refer to the latter as "national security."

My Lords, I see no reason why simply because a decision-making power is derived from a common law and not a statutory source, it should *for that reason only* be immune from judicial review. Judicial review has I think developed to a stage today when without reiterating any analysis of the steps by which the development has come about, one can conveniently classify under three heads the grounds upon which administrative action is subject to control by judicial review. The first ground I would call "illegality", the second "irration ality" and the third "procedural impropriety". That is not to say that further development on a case by case basis may not in course of time add further grounds. I have in mind particularly the possible adoption in the future of the principle of "proportionality" which is recognised in the administrative law of several of our fellow members of the European Economic Community;

but to dispose of the instant case the three already well-established heads that I have mentioned will suffice.

By "illegality" as a ground for judicial review I mean that the decision-maker must understand correctly the law that regulates his decision-making power and must give effect to it. Whether he has or not is par excellence a justiciable question to be decided, in the event of dispute, by those persons, the judges, by whom the judicial power of the state is exercisable.

By "irrationality" I mean what can by now be succinctly referred to as "*Wednesbury* unreasonableness" (*Associated Provincial Picture Houses Ltd v Wednesbury Corporation* [1948] 1 K.B. 223). It applies to a decision which is so outrageous in its defiance of logic or of accepted moral standards that no sensible person who had applied his mind to the question to be decided could have arrived at it. Whether a decision falls within this category is a question that judges by their training and experience should be well equipped to answer, or else there would be something badly wrong with our judicial system. To justify the court's exercise of this role, resort I think is today no longer needed to Viscount Radcliffe's ingenious explanation in *Edwards vBairstow* [1956] A.C. 14 of irrationality as a ground for a court's reversal of a decision by ascribing it to an inferred though unidentifiable mistake of law by the decision-maker. "Irrationality" by now can stand upon its own feet as an accepted ground on which a decision may be attacked by judicial review.

I have described the third head as "procedural impropriety" rather than failure to observe basic rules of natural justice or failure to act with procedural fairness towards the person who will be affected by the decision. This is because susceptibility to judicial review under this head covers also failure by an administrative tribunal to observe procedural rules that are expressly laid down in the legislative instrument by which its jurisdiction is conferred, even where such failure does not involve any denial of natural justice. But the instant case is not concered with the proceedings of an administrative tribunal at all.

My Lords, that a decision of which the ultimate source of power to make it is not a statute but the common law (whether or not the common law is for this purpose given the label of "the prerogative") may be the subject of judicial review on the ground of illegality is, I think, established by the cases cited by my noble and learned friend, Lord Roskill, and this extends to cases where the field of law to which the decision relates is national security, as the decision of this House itself in *Burmah Oil Co. Ltd. v Lord Advocate*, 1964 S.C. (H.L.) 117 shows. While I see no a priori reason to rule out "irrationality" as a ground for judicial review of a ministerial decision taken in the exercise of "prerogative" powers, I find it difficult to envisage in any of the various fields in which the prerogative remains the only source of the relevant decision-making power a decision of a kind that would be open to attack through the judicial process upon this ground. Such decisions will generally involve the application of government policy. The reasons for the decision-maker taking one course rather than another do not normally involve questions to which, if disputed, the judicial process is adapted to provide the right answer, by which I mean that the kind of evidence that is admissible under judicial procedures and the way in which it has to be adduced tend to exclude from the attention of the court competing policy considerations which, if the executive which judges by their upbringing and experience are ill-qualified to perform. So I leave this as an open question to be dealt with on a case to case basis if, indeed, the case should ever arise.

As respects "procedural propriety" I see no reason why it should not be a ground for judicial review of a decision made under powers of which the ultimate source is the prerogative. Such indeed was one of the grounds that formed the subject matter of judicial review in *Reg. v Criminal Injuries Compensation Board, Ex parte Lain* [1967] 2 Q.B. 864. Indeed, where the decision is one which does not alter rights or obligations enforceable in private law but only deprives a person of legitimate expectations, "procedural impropriety" will normally provide the only ground on which the decision is open to judicial review. But in any event what procedure will satisfy the public law requirement of procedural propriety depends upon the subject matter of the decision, the executive functions of the decision-maker (if the decision is not that of an administrative tribunal) and the particular circumstances in which the decision came to be made.

My Lords, in the instant case the immediate subject matter of the decision was a change in one of the terms of employment of civil servants employed at GCHQ. That the executive functions of the Minister for the Civil Service, in her capacity as such, include making a decision to change any of those terms, except in so far as they related to remuneration, expenses and allowances, is not disputed. It does not seem to me to be of any practical significance whether or not as a matter of strict legal analysis this power is based upon the rule of constitutional law to which I have already alluded that the employment of any civil servant may be terminated at any time without notice and that upon such termination the same civil servant may be re-engaged on different terms. The rule of terminability of employment in the civil service without notice, of which the existence is beyond doubt, must in any event have the consequence that the continued enjoyment by a civil servant in the *future* of a right under a particular term of his employment cannot be the subject of any right enforceable by him in private law; at most it can only be a legitimate expectation.

Prima facie, therefore, civil servants employed at GCHQ who were members of national trade unions had, at best, in December 1983, a legitimate expectation that they would continue to enjoy the benefits of such membership and of representation by those trade unions in any consultations and negotiations with representatives of the management of that government department as to changes in any term of their employment. So, but again *prima facie* only, they were entitled, as a matter of public law under the head of "procedural propriety", before administrative action was taken on a decision to withdraw that benefit, to have communicated to the national trade unions by which they had theretofore been represented the reason for such withdrawal, and for such unions to be given an opportunity to comment on it. . . .

[His Lordship held that there was ample evidence that there was a real risk that advance notice would attract the very disruptive action prejudicial to the national security the recurrence of which the decision to bar trade union membership was designed to prevent. Accordingly, procedural propriety had to give way to national security.]

LORDS ROSKILL, SCARMAN and BRIGHTMAN delivered concurring speeches.

Notes

1. This case is of importance on a number of points including: (1) Lord Diplock's overview of the grounds for judicial review (see above, p.242); (2) the extent to which prerogative decisions are subject to judicial review; (3) the doctrine of legitimate

expectation; and (4) the circumstance in which procedural propriety must give way to national security (see further below, p.702). On the prerogative point, Lords Diplock, Scarman and Roskill agreed that exercises of prerogative powers were reviewable proved the subject matter was justiciable. Lords Fraser of Tullybelton and Brightman were content simply to hold that powers *delegated* under the royal prerogative were not immune from review. One of the first actions of the new labour government elected in May 1997 was to undertake to restore trade union membership rights for GCHQ staff.

2. The approach to legitimate expectations adopted in *CCSU* was based on two earlier cases. First was the decision of the Court of Appeal in *R. v Liverpool Corporation Ex p. Liverpool Taxi Fleet Operation Association* [1972] 2 Q.B. 299. Here the council's committee responsible for taxi licensing agreed in 1971 that the limit on the number of licences should be raised in stages from the existing number of 300, and removed altogether from 1974. However, the committee's chairman gave a public undertaking, confirmed by letter, that the number would not be increased until a private Bill controlling private hire vehicles was in force. The two associations that represented the holders of existing taxi licences had been promised that they would be consulted about any increase and had indeed made representations to the sub-committee that made the recommendation approved by the committee. Having been advised that the chairman's undertaking had been unlawful, the sub-committee later in 1971 made fresh recommendations, including removal of the limit from January 1, 1973. The associations were not told officially, but found out and asked for a further hearing. On December 7 they were told there were no new important material facts and asked to provide details of any of which they were aware by return. The following day, the committee approved the new recommendations, and the council confirmed them on December 22. The Court of Appeal granted an order of prohibition prohibiting the corporation from issuing more than 300 licences without hearing any representations which might be made by interested persons, including the applicants. Roskill L.J. said that whether or not the council was originally under a duty to hear representations from the applicants (the point was left open),

> "now to allow the council to resile from [its] undertaking without notice to and representations from the applicants is to condone unfairness in a case where the duty was to act fairly".

The relief claimed would ultimately assist the council to perform rather than inhibit the performance of its statutory duties (p.311). Sir Gordon Willmer adopted a similar approach (pp.312–313). Lord Denning M.R. articulated broader principles. First, the council in considering applications for taxi licences was under a duty to act fairly.

> "This means that they should be ready to hear, not only the particular applicant, but also any other persons or bodies whose interests are affected"(p.307.)

The council was accordingly under a duty to hear the applicants, because their members could be greatly affected. Secondly, the council was bound by its undertaking so long as it was not in conflict with its statutory duty.

> "So long as the performance of the undertaking is compatible with their public duty, they must honour it. And I should have thought that this undertaking was so compatible. At any rate they ought not to depart from it except after the most serious consideration and hearing what the other party has to say: and then only if they are satisfied that the overriding public interest requires it. The public interest may be better served by honouring their undertaking than by breaking it. This is just such a case. It is better to hold the corporation to their undertaking than to allow them to break it." (p.308).

The council had acted wrongly, first, by taking decisions without hearing from the applicants and, secondly, by breaking their undertaking without any sufficient cause or excuse. (Lord Denning's dicta form part of the development of the doctrine of substantive legitimate expectations, above, pp.591–621).

The *Liverpool* case was approved by the Privy Council in *Att-Gen of Hong Kong v Ng Yuen Shiu* [1983] 2 A.C. 629, PC. N entered Hong Kong illegally in 1976, from Macau, and remained undetected, becoming part-owner of a factory which employed several workers. On October 28, 1980, the Hong Kong Government announced a change in immigration policy to the effect that illegal immigrants from Macau would be interviewed in due course and that, although no guarantees could be given, they would not subsequently be removed, each case would be treated on its merits. The following day, N reported to an immigration officer and after being interviewed he was detained until a removal order was made against him. On an application for judicial review, the Privy Council quashed the removal order. The Privy Council assumed, without deciding, that the Court of Appeal of Hong Kong rightly decided that there was no general right in an alien illegal entrant to have a hearing in accordance with the rules of natural justice before a removal order was made against him. However, N had a legitimate expectation of being accorded a fair hearing.
Lord Fraser of Tullybelton said (at 636–638):

> "The narrower proposition for which the applicant contended was that a person is entitled to a fair hearing before a decision adversely affecting his interests is made by a public official or body, if he has 'a legitimate expectation' of being accorded such a hearing. . . .
> The expectations may be based upon some statement or undertaking by, or on behalf of, the public authority which has the duty of making the decision, if the authority has, through its officers, acted in a way that would make it unfair or inconsistent with good administration for him to be denied such an inquiry.
> One such case was *Reg. v Liverpool Corporation, Ex parte Liverpool Taxi Fleet Operators' Association* [1972] 2 Q.B. 299. . . .
> Their Lordships see no reason why the principle should not be applicable when the person who will be affected by the decision is an alien, just as much as when he is a British subject. The justification for it is primarily that, when a public authority has promised to follow a certain procedure, it is in the interest of good administration that it should act fairly and should implement its promise, so long as implementation does not interfere with its statutory duty. The principle is also justified by the further consideration that, when the promise was made, the authority must have considered that it would be assisted in discharging its duty fairly by any representations from interested parties and as a general rule that is correct".

In the interview, N had not been able to explain the humanitarian grounds for the discretion not to remove him to be exercised.
3. The literature on legitimate expectations is listed above at p.620, n.12. The argument that a legitimate expectation gives rise to procedural rights has been less controversial than the notion it can also place substantive restrictions on the powers of the decision-maker (see above, pp.591–621).
4. Simon Brown L.J. has distinguished four broad categories in the use of the phrase "legitimate expectation" (*R. v Devon CC Ex p. Baker; R. v Durham CC Ex p. Curtis* [1995] 1 All E.R. 73 at 88–89):

> "(1) Sometimes the phrase is used to denote a substantive right: an entitlement that the claimant asserts cannot be denied him. It was used in this sense and the assertion upheld in cases such as *R. v Secretary of State for the Home Dept, Ex p. Khan* [1985] 1 All E.R. 40; [1984] 1 W.L.R. 1337 and *R. v Secretary of State for the Home Dept, Ex p. Ruddock* [1987] 2 All E.R. 518; [1987] 1 W.L.R. 1482. It was used in the same sense but unsuccessfully in, for instance, *R. v Board of Inland Revenue, Ex p. MFK Underwriting Agencies Ltd* [1990] 1 All E.R. 91; [1990] 1 W.L.R. 1545 and *R. v Jockey Club, Ex p. RAM Racecourses Ltd* (1990) [1993] 2 All ER 225.

These various authorities show that the claimant's right will only be found established when there is a clear and unambiguous representation upon which it was reasonable for him to rely. Then the administrator or other public body will be held bound in fairness by the representation made unless only its promise or undertaking as to how its power would be exercised is inconsistent with the statutory duties imposed upon it. The doctrine employed in this sense is akin to an estoppel. In so far as the public body's representation is communicated by way of a stated policy. This type of legitimate expectation falls into two distinct sub-categories: cases in which the authority are held entitled to change their policy even so as to affect the claimant, and those in which they are not. An illustration of the former is *R. v Torbay B.C., ex p. Cleasby* [1991] C.O.D. 142; of the latter, *Ex p. Khan*.

(2) Perhaps more conventionally the concept of legitimate expectation is used to refer to the claimant's interest in some ultimate benefit which he hopes to retain (or, some would argue, attain). Here, therefore, it is the interest itself rather than the benefit that is the substance of the expectation. In other words the expectation arises not because the claimant asserts any specific right to a benefit but rather because his interest in it is one that the law holds protected by the requirements of procedural fairness; the law recognises that the interest cannot properly be withdrawn (or denied) without the claimant being given an opportunity to comment and without the authority communicating rational grounds for any adverse decision. Of the various authorities drawn to our attention, *Schmidt v Secretary of State for Home Affairs* [1969] 1 All E.R. 904; [1969] 2 Ch. 149, *O'Reilly v Mackman* [1982] 3 All E.R. 1124; [1983] 2 A.C. 237 and the recent decision of Roch J. in *R. v Rochdale Metropolitan B.C., Ex p. Schemet* [1993] 1 F.C.R. 306 are clear examples of this head of legitimate expectation.

(3) Frequently, however, the concept of legitimate expectation is used to refer to the fair procedure itself. In other words it is contended that the claimant has a legitimate expectation that the public body will act fairly towards him. As was pointed out by Dawson J. in *Att-Gen for New South Wales v Quin* (1990) 93 A.L.R. 1 at 39 this use of the term is superfluous and unhelpful: it confuses the interest which is the basis of the requirement of procedural fairness with the requirement itself:

> 'No doubt people expect fairness in their dealings with those who make decisions affecting their interests, but it is to my mind quite artificial to say that this is the reason why, if the expectation is legitimate in the sense of well founded, the law imposes a duty to observe procedural fairness. Such a duty arises, if at all, because the circumstances call for a fair procedure and it adds nothing to say that they also are such as to lead to a legitimate expectation that a fair procedure will be adopted.'

(4) The final category of legitimate expectation encompasses those cases in which it is held that a particular procedure, not otherwise required by law in the protection of an interest, must be followed consequent upon some specific promise or practice. Fairness requires that the public authority be held to it. The authority is bound by its assurance, whether expressly given by way of a promise or implied by way of established practice. *Re Liverpool Tax Owners' Association* [1972] 2 All E.R. 589; [1972] 2 Q.B. 299 and *Att-Gen of Hong Kong v Ng Yuen Shiu* [1983] 2 All E.R. 346; [1983] 2 A.C. 629 are illustrations of the court giving effect to legitimate expectations based upon express promises; *Council of Civil Service Unions v Minister for the Civil Service* an illustration of a legitimate expectation founded upon practice albeit one denied on the facts by virtue of the national security implications".

5. A legitimate expectation of being consulted may arise simply from the nature of the applicant's interests, as distinct from past practice or an express undertaking. In *R. v Brent LBC Ex p. Gunning* (1985) 84 L.G.R. 168, Hodgson J. held that while there was no statutory duty placed upon local education authorities to consult parents of pupils before making proposals for the closure or amalgamation of schools, parents nevertheless had a legitimate expectation that they would be consulted.

"The interest of parents in the educational arrangements in the area in which they lived is self-evident. It is explicitly recognised in the legislation (see, e.g. section 6 of the Education Act 1980). The legislation places clear duties upon parents, backed by draconian criminal sanctions."

Local authorities (including Brent) habitually consulted on these matters, and were exhorted to do so by the Secretary of State. On the facts here, the consultative document was wholly inadequate and misleading as to the cost of the proposals and the period allowed for consultation was unreasonably short. Furthermore, as the proposals ultimately adopted were materially different from those on which consultation had taken place, the parents of schoolchildren in the area should have been given a further opportunity to be consulted. The authority's decision to make the proposals was quashed.

(Hodgson J. stated (at 187) that their legitimate expectation gave them the same right as if it had been specifically given by statute. In *R. v Gwent CC Ex p. Bryant*, *The Independent*, April 19, 1988, his Lordship stated that he had gone too far in equating a legitimate expectation with a statutory right. In the former case, a defect in consultation could be rectified by the Secretary of State, in the latter, it could not; *R. v Northampton CC Ex p. Tebbutt*, unreported, June 26, 1986, applied. See also *R. v Haberdashers' Aske's Hatcham School Governors, Ex p. Inner London Education Authority, The Times*, March 7, 1989.) See P. Meredith [1988] P.L. 4. The Court of Appeal has expressed the view that the duty of public authorities to consult affected persons is an aspect of the general duty of fairness. In the context of local authorities' decisions to close residential homes for the elderly that are owned and operated by the councils, the Court held that the duty of consultation required:

"(1) that the residents should have known that closure of the homes was under consider-ation well before the final decision to close them was made, (2) that the residents should have had a reasonable time to put to the council their objections to the closure of the homes and (3) that the residents' objections should have been considered by the council"

(*per* Dillon L.J. at 83 in *Devon* CC above, n.4). See further above, p.607.

An authority is not required to consult on all possible options, being entitled to consult on its preferred option (*R. (on the application of Kidderminster and District Community Health Council) v Worcestershire Health Council*, unreported, May 28, 1999, CA), although a consultation may be flawed if a major option is not set out, without explanation (*R. (on the application of National Association of Health Stores) v Secretary of State for Health* [2003] EWHC 3133, appeal allowed on other grounds, [2005] EWCA Civ 154)).

6. There is some authority than a person's misconduct may deprive him or her of a *legitimate* expectation. In *Cinnamond v British Airports Authority* [1980] 1 W.L.R. 582, the authority exercised its power under byelaws to prohibit six car-hire drivers from entering Heathrow airport (save as a *bona fide* passenger), until further notice. Each of the six had many convictions under the byelaws for loitering and offering services to passengers, and all had unpaid fines outstanding. The authority had received many complaints that car-hire drivers charged exorbitant fares in comparison with the licensed taxis. The drivers sought a declaration that the notices were invalid. One ground was that they had not been given an opportunity to make representations. Lord Denning M.R. said (at 590–591) that the drivers had no legitimate expectation:

". . . suppose that these car-hire drivers were of good character and had for years been coming into the airport under an implied licence to do so. If in that case there was suddenly a prohibition order preventing them from entering, then it would seem only fair that they should be given a hearing and a chance to put their case. But that is not this case. These men have a long record of convictions. They have large fines outstanding. They are continuing to engage in conduct which they must know is unlawful and contrary to the byelaws. When they were summonsed for past offences, they put their case, no doubt, to the justices and to the Crown Court. Now when the patience of the authority is exhausted, it seems to me that the authority can properly suspend them until further notice—just like the police officer I mentioned. In the circumstances they had no legitimate expectation of being heard. It is not a necessary preliminary that they should have a hearing or be given a further chance to explain. Remembering always this: that it must have been apparent to them why the prohibition was ordered: and equally apparent that, if they had a change of heart and were ready to comply with the rules, no doubt the prohibition would be withdrawn. They could have made representations immediately, if they wished, in answer to the prohibition order. That they did not do".

Shaw L.J. said (at 592):

"As to the suggestion of unfairness in that the drivers were not given an opportunity of making representations, it is clear on the history of this matter that the drivers put themselves so far outside the limits of tolerable conduct as to disentitle themselves to expect that any further representations on their part could have any influence or relevance. The long history of contraventions, of flouting the regulations, and of totally disregarding the penalties demonstrate that in this particular case there was no effective deterrent. The only way of dealing with the situation was by excluding them altogether.

It does not follow that the attitude of the authority may not change if they can be persuaded by representations on behalf of the drivers that they are minded in future to comply with the regulations".

Brandon L.J. agreed with Lord Denning and Shaw L.J. on the natural justice point, and then said (at 593):

"If I am wrong in thinking that some opportunity should have been given, then it seems to me that no prejudice was suffered by the minicab drivers as a result of not being given that opportunity. It is quite evident that they were not prepared then, and are not even prepared now, to give any satisfactory undertakings about their future conduct. Only if they were would representations be of any use. I would rely on what was said in *Malloch v Aberdeen Corporation* [1971] 1 W.L.R. 1578, first *per* Lord Reid at 1582 and secondly *per* Lord Wilberforce at 1595. [See above, p.438.] The effect of what Lord Wilberforce said is that no one can complain of not being given an opportunity to make representations if such an opportunity would have availed him nothing".

de Smith, Woolf and Jowell disagree with Lord Denning's approach:

". . . it is wrong to suggest that a legitimate expectation can be forfeited, for example by unmeritorious conduct on the part of the applicant. Unless the expectation were expressly made conditional upon the applicant's 'good behaviour', the decision whether to rely on the expectation or to waive it lies with the applicant alone. It would also seem wrong to prejudge the merits of the applicant's present case on his previous wrongdoing" (at pp.429–430).

An expectation may properly be held not to be legitimate where it arises out of an activity that is itself unlawful, even though there is a practice of non-enforcement (*R. (on the application of Dinev) v Westminster City Council*, unreported, October 24, 2000, QBD) (street traders (portrait artists) had no legitimate expectation to be consulted about the introduction of a temporary licensing scheme notwithstanding the effect on their livelihood).

(b) *Limitations on the right to a fair hearing*

(1) *National security*

R. v SECRETARY OF STATE FOR HOME AFFAIRS Ex p. HOSENBALL

[1977] 1 W.L.R. 766; [1977] 3 All E.R. 452. (COURT OF APPEAL)

The appellant was a US citizen who worked as a journalist in the United Kingdom. At first he worked for the weekly journal *Time Out* and was responsible for an article entitled "The Eavesdroppers" about communications monitoring by the Government, which appeared in May 1976. During July 1976, Hosenball moved to the *Evening Standard* as a general news reporter. In November 1976, he was informed that the Home Secretary had decided to deport him on the grounds that Hosenball's "departure from the United Kingdom would be conducive to the public good as being in the interests of national security". The Home Secretary considered that Hosenball had sought and obtained for publication information harmful to the security of the United Kingdom and prejudicial to the safety of Crown servants. Hosenball had no right of appeal against the decision under the terms of the Immigration Act 1971. However, he was given a non-statutory hearing before "three advisers" (appointed by the Home Secretary) who reported back in confidence to the Secretary of State. The Home Secretary later made a deportation against Hosenball. Hosenball then applied for an order of certiorari to quash the deportation order on the ground, *inter alia*, that the principle of *audi alteram partem* had been breached by the failure to supply him with details of the case against him prior to his appearance before the "three advisers". The High Court dismissed Hosenball's application and he then appealed to the Court of Appeal.

LORD DENNING M.R.: . . . Now I would like to say at once that if this were a case in which the ordinary rules of natural justice were to be observed, some criticism could be directed upon it. For one thing, the Home Secretary himself, and I expect the advisory panel also, had a good deal of confidential information before them of which Mr Hosenball knew nothing and was told nothing: and which he had no opportunity of correcting or contradicting; or of testing by cross-examination. In addition, he was not given sufficient information of the charges against him so as to be able effectively to deal with them or answer them. All this could be urged as a ground for upsetting any ordinary decision of a court of law or of any tribunal, statutory or domestic: see *Kanda v Government of Malaya* [1962] A.C. 322, 337.

But this is no ordinary case. It is a case in which national security is involved: and our history shows that, when the state itself is endangered, our cherished freedoms may have to take second place. Even natural justice itself may suffer a set-back. Time after time Parliament has so enacted and the courts have loyalty followed. In the first world war in *R. v Halliday* [1917] A.C. 260, 270 Lord Finlay L.C. said: "The danger of espionage and of damage by secret agents . . . had to be guarded against." In the second world war in *Liversidge v Sir John Anderson* [1942] A.C. 206, 219 Lord Maugham said:

". . . there may be certain persons against whom no offence is proved nor any charge formulated, but as regards whom it may be expedient to authorise the Secretary of State to make an order for detention."

That was said in time of war. But times of peace hold their dangers too. Spies, subverters and saboteurs may be mingling amongst us, putting on a most innocent exterior. They may be endangering the lives of the men in our secret service, as Mr Hosenball is said to do.

If they are British subjects, we must deal with them here. If they are foreigners, they can be deported. The rules of natural justice have to be modified in regard to foreigners here who prove themselves unwelcome and ought to be deported. . . .

So it seems to me that when the national security is at stake even the rules of natural justice may have to be modified to meet the position. I would refer in this regard to the speech of Lord Reid in *R. v Lewes JJ., Ex p. Secretary of State for the Home Department* [1973] A.C. 388, 402. . . .

The information supplied to the Home Secretary by the Security Service is, and must be, highly confidential. The public interest in the security of the realm is so great that the sources of the information must not be disclosed— nor should the nature of the information itself be disclosed—if there is any risk that it would lead to the sources being discovered. The reason is because, in this very secretive field, our enemies might try to eliminate the sources of information. So the sources must not be disclosed. Not even to the House of Commons. Nor to any tribunal or court of inquiry or body of advisers, statutory or non-statutory. Save to the extent that the Home Secretary thinks safe. Great as is the public interest in the freedom of the individual and the doing of justice to him, nevertheless in the last resort it must take second place to the security of the country itself. . . .

There is a conflict here between the interests of national security on the one hand and the freedom of the individual on the other. The balance between these two is not for a court of law. It is for the Home Secretary. He is the person entrusted by Parliament with the task. In some parts of the world national security has on occasions been used as an excuse for all sorts of infringements of individual liberty. But not in England. Both during the wars and after them, successive ministers have discharged their duties to the complete satisfaction of the people at large. They have set up advisory committees to help them, usually with a chairman who has done everything he can to ensure that justice is done. They have never interfered with the liberty or the freedom of movement of any individual except where it is absolutely necessary for the safety of the state. In this case we are assured that the Home Secretary himself gave it his personal consideration, and I have no reason whatever to doubt the care with which he considered the whole matter. He is answerable to Parliament as to the way in which he did it and not to the courts here.

I would dismiss the appeal.

GEOFFREY LANE L.J.: There are occasions, though they are rare, when what are more generally the rights of an individual must be subordinated to the protection of the realm. When an alien visitor to this country is believed to have used the hospitality extended to him so as to present a danger to security, the Secretary of State has the right and, in many cases, has the duty of ensuring that the alien no longer remains here to threaten our security. It may be that the alien has been in the country for many years. It may be that he has built a career here in this country, and that consequently a deportation order made against him may result in great hardship to him. It may be that he protests that he has done nothing wrong so far as this country's security is concerned. It may be that he protests that he cannot understand why any action of this sort is being taken against him. In ordinary circumstances common fairness—you can call it natural justice if you wish—would demand that he be given particulars of the charges made against him; that he be given the names of the witnesses who are prepared to testify against him and, indeed, probably the nature of the evidence which those witnesses are prepared to give should also be delivered to him. But there are counter balancing factors. . . .

It may well be that if an alien is told with particularity what it is said he has done it will become quite obvious to him from whence that information has been received. The only person who can judge whether such a result is likely is the person who has in his possession all the information available. That, in this case, is the Secretary of State himself. If he comes to the conclusion that for reasons such as those which I have just endeavoured to outline he cannot afford to give the alien more than the general charge against him, there one has the dilemma. The alien certainly has inadequate information upon which to prepare or direct his defence to the various charges which are made against him, and the only way that could be remedied would be to disclose information to him which might probably have an adverse effect on the national security. The choice is regrettably clear: the alien must suffer, if suffering there be, and this is so on whichever basis of argument one chooses. . . .

Different principles and strict principles apply where matters of the safety of the realm are at stake. What is fair cannot be decided in a vacuum: it has to be determined against the whole background of any particular case. The advisory panel system is an effort to ensure fairness as far as possible in these difficult circumstances, but in the end it is the Secretary of State who must in those circumstances be trusted to speak the last word. . . .

I would dismiss the appeal.

CUMMING-BRUCE L.J. I agree with all that has fallen from Lord Denning M.R. and Geoffrey Lane L.J. . . .

Appeal dismissed.

Notes

1. After the above legal action Hosenball returned to the United States from where he contributed to the *Sunday Times*.

2. Lord Denning's contented view of the relationship between the legitimate needs of national security and individual liberty has not been endorsed by either the European Commission of Human Rights or the Committee of Ministers of the Council of Europe. In the case of *Hewitt and Harman and N. v UK* (1989) 67 D.R. 88, the Commission reached the opinion that the Security Service had violated the applicants' right to privacy (under Art.8 ECHR) by means of secret surveillance and information gathering directed at the applicants. As a consequence of this case the Government secured the passage of the Security Service Act 1989, which placed the Service on a statutory basis and created a Tribunal to deal with complaints against the organisation. Further institutional reforms, including the creation of an oversight committee composed of Parliamentarians, were introduced by the Intelligence Services Act 1994. See further S.H. Bailey, D.J. Harris and D.C. Ormerod, *Civil Liberties: Cases and Materials* (5th ed, 2001), pp.877–893.

3. During the Gulf War of early 1991, the Home Secretary decided to deport a number of Iraqis and other Arab persons living in the United Kingdom, on the grounds that their continued presence was not conducive to national security. In one instance a Lebanese citizen, who had lived in the United Kingdom for 15 years, sought judicial

review of the Home Secretary's decision arguing, *inter alia*, that the denial of legal representation before the three advisers and the provision of less than full particulars of the allegations against him violated natural justice. Lord Donaldson M.R. emphasised the limited role of the courts in reviewing matters of national security:

"... the responsibility is exclusively that of the government of the day, but its powers are limited by statute and the courts will intervene if it is shown that the minister responsible has acted otherwise than in good faith or has in any way overstepped the limitations upon his authority which are imposed by the law" (at 334).

His Lordship rejected the appellant's contentions by noting that, "... natural justice has to take account of realities and something which would otherwise constitute a breach is not to be so considered if it is unavoidable" (at 335): *R. v Secretary of State for the Home Department Ex p. Cheblak* [1991] 2 All E.R. 319. See I. Leigh, [1991] P.L. 331.

In *Chahal v UK* (1997) 23 E.H.R.R. 413, the European Court of Human Rights, unanimously, found the limited processes of review offered by the High Court and the "three advisers" to a potential national security deportee did not meet the requirements of Art. 5(4) ECHR (right to review by a court of the lawfulness of detention).

C was released; the Secretary of State's subsequent decision to refuse *ex gratia* compensation was upheld (*R. v Secretary of State for the Home Department Ex p. Chahal* (1999) 1 H.R.L.R. 261). In consequence of the decision in *Chahal v UK*, a special appeal procedure was established by the Special Immigration Appeal Commission Act 1997 to replace (*inter alia*) the Three Advisers procedure. The Commission as constituted for any particular case must comprise three members; at least one must hold or have held high judicial office and at least one must be or have been a chief immigration adjudicator or a legally qualified member of the Immigration Appeal Tribunal (s.1, Sch.1). The Commission may hear appeals where a right to appeal against an immigration decision (including removal and deportation) or rejection of an asylum claim (where leave to enter or remain in the United Kingdom for more than a year (in aggregate) has been granted) (National Immigration and Asylum Act 2002, ss.82(1), 83(2)), is barred by a certificate of the Secretary of State (in person) under s.97 of the 2002 Act. This applies to decisions taken wholly or partly on the ground that a person's exclusion or removal from the United Kingdom is in the interests of national security or of the relationship between the United Kingdom and another country; or where the decision was taken wholly or partly in reliance on information which in the opinion of the Secretary of State should not be made public in either of those interests or otherwise in the public interest.

Appellants are entitled to legal representation but the rules may provide for proceedings to take place without the appellant being given full particulars of the reasons for the decision, and in the absence of any person, including the appellant and any legal representative appointed by him or her. In the latter event, a special advocate must be appointed by the Attorney-General to represent the appellant's interests (1997 Act, ss.5,6; Special Immigration Appeals Commission (Procedure) Rules 2003 (SI 2003/1034)). Evidence disclosed to the special advocate in the absence of the appellant and his representative must not be disclosed by him or her; there is no lawyer-client relationship between the two. This arrangement, commended by the ECtHR in *Chahal*, was based on a model developed in Canada, and has been extended to other contexts (see, *e.g.* the Northern Ireland Act 1998, s.90; Fair Employment and Treatment (NI) Order 1998 (SI 1998/3162 (NI 21)), concerning the vetting of contractors; Employment Tribunals Act 1996, ss.10(1) and 16(2)–(9), substituted by the Employment Relations Act 1999, Sch.8, para.3, concerning the dismissal of Crown employees on national security grounds). The special advocate procedure has also been held to be both implied authorised by statute in respect of proceedings before the Parole Board (*Roberts v Parole Board* [2005] UKHL 45). This kind of arrangement is undoubtedly an improvement on the Three Advisers' procedure, which did not include provision for a special advocate. Depending on the circumstances of the particular case, it would seem that it can be both ECHR compliant and not open to challenge on common law natural justice grounds. An appeal lies to the Court of Appeal (s.7). SIAC has subsequently been established as a superior court of record, which both excludes it from the High Court's judicial review jurisdiction and allows it to exercise that jurisdiction itself in respect of other decision-makers (Anti-terrorism, Crime and Security Act 2001, s.35, amending s.1 of the 1997 Act).

In *Secretary of State for the Home Department v Rehman* [2001] UKHL 47; [2003] 1 A.C. 153, the House of Lords held that a deportation in the interests of national security could only be justified by the existence of some possibility of risk or danger to the well-being of the nation, that risk did not have to be the result of a "direct threat" to the United Kingdom and the interests of national security were not limited to action by an individual which could be said to be "targeted at" the United Kingdom, its system of government or its people. (See Lord Slynn at [15]). SIAC's narrower view was wrong in law. Furthermore, it was not necessary for the Secretary of State to satisfy SIAC "to a high civil balance of probabilities" that the grounds for deportation were made out because the applicant had engaged in conduct that endangered national security. SIAC had to give "due weight to the assessment and conclusions of the Secretary of State . . . He is undoubtedly in the best position to judge what national security requires even if his decision is open to review. The assessment of what is needed in the light of changing circumstances is primarily for him" (*per* Lord Slynn at [26]). See also Lord Hoffmann at [57], noting that where, as here, the question was one of the evaluation of risk, an appellate body "traditionally allows a considerable margin to the primary decision-maker"; it should not ordinarily interfere where it considers that the Home Secretary's view is one which could reasonably be entertained. SIAC's jurisdiction was extended by the 2001 Act to include appeals by a person certified by the Secretary of State on the ground that he reasonably (a) believed the person's presence in the United Kingdom was a risk to national security, and (b) suspected that the person was a terrorist (2001 Act, s.21). Such a person could be the subject of administrative steps towards removal (s.22) or detained (s.23). On an appeal, SIAC was required to cancel the certificate if it considered that there were no reasonable grounds for a belief or suspicion of the kind referred to in s.21(1)(a) or (b) or it considered that for some other reason the certificate should not have been issued (s.25). SIAC was also required to conduct periodic reviews (s.26).

On an appeal under s.25, it was for SIAC to come to its own judgment in respect of the issue in question, not merely to review the Secretary of State's decision (*Secretary of State for the Home Department v M* [2004] EWCA Civ 324; [2004] H.R.L.R. 22, *per* Lord Woolf C.J. at [15]; here the Court of Appeal held that while there was evidence of suspicious circumstances, SIAC had been entitled to conclude in all the circumstances that there was not *reasonable* suspicion), cf. *A v Secretary of State for the Home Department* [2004] EWCA 1123, [2004] H.R.L.R. 38 where the Court of Appeal held that SIAC had been entitled on the facts not to cancel certificates.

The power of detention under s.23 has, however, been declared by the House of Lords to be incompatible with Arts 5 and 14 ECHR, insofar as it is disproportionate and permits detention of suspected international terrorists in a way that discriminates on the ground of nationality or immigration status (*A v Secretary of State for the Home Department* [2004] UKHL 56). See further above, p.351.

4. An Irish national, Gallagher, who had been imprisoned in Ireland for possession of firearms for an unlawful purpose, came to work in the United Kingdom. The Home Secretary made an exclusion order against Gallagher, under the Prevention of Terrorism (Temporary Provisions) Act 1989, because he was satisfied that Gallagher was or had been involved in acts of terrorism concerned with Northern Ireland. Gallagher consented to his removal to Ireland where he was granted an interview, at the British Embassy in Dublin, before an unnamed person appointed by the Home Secretary, who listened to Gallagher's contentions but was unable to give

further particulars regarding the reasons for the exclusion order. The Home Secretary reconsidered his decision in the light of the person's report and determined not to revoke the order. Gallagher challenged his actions in the British courts alleging, *inter alia*, a breach of his European Community law rights. The majority of the Court of Appeal held that the procedure followed had infringed Gallagher's rights under Art. 9 of Council Directive 64/221 and that the interpretation of those provisions should be referred to the European Court of Justice: *R. v Secretary of State for the Home Department Ex p. Gallagher, The Times*, February 16, 1994. Subsequently, the ECJ ruled that Art. 9 did not prevent the person (called "the competent authority") hearing the representations of the EU Member State national from being appointed by the Home Secretary, provided that the competent authority was able to perform his/her duties in absolute independence. Except in cases of urgency, the competent authority should be able to give an opinion on the proposed expulsion before such an order is made by the Home Secretary. However, the Directive did not require the competent authority to identify its members to those making representations: move up *R. v Secretary of State for the Home Department Ex p. Gallagher*, Case C–175/94, [1995] E.C.R. I–4253. For a related case see also *R. v Secretary of State for the Home Department Ex p. McQuillan* [1995] 4 All E.R. 400.

5. In the *CCSU* case, the House of Lords unanimously agreed that on the facts the normal requirements or procedural propriety were overridden by considerations of national security, notwithstanding the suspicion that the reason ultimately advanced was a retrospective rationalisation. The European Commission of Human Rights subsequently found that the banning order was justifiable under the national security exception to Art. 11 ECHR.

6. Outside the context of national security,

"foreign policy issues are an area of government decision-making as regards which our public law principles of fairness will not impose a requirement upon the Secretary of State to invite representations from parties who may be affected by the decision"

per Laws L.J. in *R. (on the application of Quark Fishing Ltd) v Secretary of State for Foreign and Commonwealth Affairs* [2002] EWCA Civ 1409 at [57], holding that the applicants had no right to be heard on the decision to reduce the number of licences to fish for Patagonian toothfish to be allocated to UK vessels (see further above, pp.535, 689), There was, however, a right to be heard on the application of the criteria for the allocation of the reduced number of licences (at [58]).

(2) *Withholding of confidential information*

R. v GAMING BOARD FOR GREAT BRITAIN Ex p. BENAIM AND KHAIDA

[1970] 2 Q.B. 417; [1970] 2 W.L.R. 1009; 114 S.J. 266; [1970] 2 All E.R. 528 (COURT OF APPEAL)

The Gaming Act 1968 prohibited gaming except in premises licensed for this purpose by the justices. Before any person could apply for a licence he had to obtain a "certificate of consent" from the Gaming Board, a body set up by the 1968 Act. The present applicants, the joint managing directors of Crockford's gaming club, applied unsuccessfully for a certificate. The board declined to give reasons for the refusal. In particular they refused to specify the matters which troubled them. The applicants sought certiorari to quash the refusal, and mandamus to compel the board to give sufficient information to enable them to answer the case against them.

LORD DENNING M.R.: . . . To what extent are the board bound by the rules of natural justice? That is the root question before us. Their jurisdiction is country wide. They have to keep under review the extent and character of gaming in Great Britain: see s.10(3). Their particular task in regard to Crockford's is to see if the applicants are fit to run a gaming club: and if so, to give a certificate of consent.

Their duty is set out in Schedule 2, para.4(5) and (6):

". . . (5) . . . the board shall have regard only to the question whether, in their opinion, the applicant is likely to be capable of, and diligent in, securing that the provisions of this Act and of any regulations made under it will be complied with, that gaming on those premises will be fairly and properly conducted, and that the premises will be conducted without disorder or disturbance.

(6) For the purposes of sub-paragraph (5) . . . the board shall in particular take into consideration the character, reputation and financial standing—(a) of the applicant, and (b) of any person (other than the applicant) by whom . . . the club . . . would be managed, or for whose benefit . . . that club would be carried on, but may also take into consideration any other circumstances appearing to them to be relevant in determining whether the applicant is likely to be capable of, and diligent in, securing the matters mentioned in that sub-paragraph."

Note also that Schedule 1, paragraph 7, gives the board power to regulate their own procedure. Accordingly the board have laid down an outline procedure which they put before us. It is too long to read in full. So I will just summarise it. It says that the board will give the applicant an opportunity of making representations to the board, and will give him the best indications possible of the matters that are troubling them. Then there are these two important sentences:

"In cases where the *source* or *content* of this *information* is *confidential*, the board accept that they are obliged to withhold particulars of the disclosure of which would be a breach of confidence inconsistent with their statutory duty and the public interest. . . .

In the course of the interview the applicant will be made aware, to the greatest extent to which this is consistent with the board's statutory duty and the public interest, of the matters that are troubling the board."

Mr Quintin Hogg criticised that outline procedure severely. He spoke as if Crockford's were being deprived of a right of property or of a right to make a living. He read his client's affidavit saying that "Crockford's has been established for over a century and is a gaming club with a worldwide reputation for integrity and respectability", with assets and goodwill valued at £185,000. He said that they ought not to be deprived of this business without knowing the case they had to meet. He criticised especially the way in which the board proposed to keep that confidential information. He relied on some words of mine in *Kanda v Government of Malaya* [1962] A.C. 322, 337, when I said "that the judge or whoever has to adjudicate must not hear evidence or receive representations from one side behind the back of the other".

Mr Hogg put his case, I think, too high. It is an error to regard Crockford's as having any right of which they are being deprived. They have not had in the past, and they have not now, any right to play these games of chance—roulette, chemin-de-fer, baccarat and the like—for their own profit. What they are really seeking is a privilege—almost, I might say, a franchise—to carry on gaming for profit, a thing never hitherto allowed in this country. It is for them to show that they are fit to be trusted with it.

If Mr Hogg went too far on his side, I think Mr Kidwell went too far on the other. He submitted that the Gaming Board are free to grant or refuse a certificate as they please. They are not bound, he says, to obey the rules of natural justice any more than any other executive body, such as, I suppose, the Board of Trade, which grant industrial development certificates, or the Television Authority, which awards television programme contracts. I cannot accept this view. I think the Gaming Board are bound to observe the rules of natural justice. The question is: What are those rules?

It is not possible to lay down rigid rules as to when the principles of natural justice are to apply: nor as to their scope and extent. Everything depends on the subject-matter: see what Tucker L.J. said in *Russell v Norfolk (Duke of)* [1949] 1 All E.R. 109, 118 and Lord Upjohn in *Durayappah v Fernando* [1967] 2 A.C. 337, 349. At one time it was said that the principles only apply to judicial proceedings and not to administrative proceedings. That heresy was scotched in *Ridge v Baldwin* [1964] A.C. 40. At another time it was said that the principles do not apply to the grant or revocation of licences. That too is wrong. *R. v Metropolitan Police Commissioner, Ex p. Parker* [1953] 1 W.L.R. 1150 and *Nakkuda Ali v Jayaratne* [1951] A.C. 66 are no longer authority for any such proposition. See what Lord Reid and Lord Hodson said about them in *Ridge v Baldwin* [1964] A.C. 40, 77–79, 133.

So let us sheer away from those distinctions and consider the task of this Gaming Board and what they should do. The best guidance is, I think, to be found by reference to the cases of immigrants. They have no right to come in, but they have a right to be heard. The principle in that regard was well laid down by Lord Parker C.J. in *Re H.K. (An Infant)* [1967] 2 Q.B. 617. He said, at 630:

"... even if an immigration officer is not in a judicial or quasi-judicial capacity, he must at any rate give the immigrant an opportunity of satisfying him of the matters in the subsection, and for that purpose let the immigrant know what his immediate impression is so that the immigrant can disabuse him. That is not, as I see it, a question of acting or being required to act judicially, but of being required to act fairly."

Those words seem to me to apply to the Gaming Board. The statute says in terms that in determining whether to grant a certificate, the board "shall have regard only" to the matters specified. It follows, I think, that the board have a duty to act fairly. They must give the applicant an opportunity of satisfying them of the matters specified in the subsection. They must let him know what their impressions are so that he can disabuse them. But I do not think that they need quote chapter and verse against him as if they were dismissing him from an office, as in *Ridge v Baldwin* [1964] A.C. 40; or depriving him of his property, as in *Cooper v Wandsworth Board of Works* (1863) 14 C.B.N.S. 180. After all, they are not charging him with doing anything wrong. They are simply inquiring as to his capability and diligence and are having regard to his character, reputation and financial standing. They are there to protect the public interest, to see that persons running the gaming clubs are fit to be trusted.

Seeing the evils that have led to this legislation, the board can and should investigate the credentials of those who make application to them. They can and should receive information from the police in this country or abroad who know something of them. They can, and should, receive information from any other reliable source. Much of it will be confidential. But that does not mean that the applicants are not to be given a chance of answering it. They must be given the chance, subject to this qualification: I do not think they need tell the applicant the source of their information, if that would put their informant in peril or otherwise be contrary to the public interest. Even in a criminal trial, a witness cannot be asked who is his informer. The reason was well given by Lord Eyre C.J. in *Hardy's* case [*R. v Hardy*] 24 *State Trials* 199, 808:

"... there is a rule which has universally obtained on account of its importance to the public for the detection of crimes, that those persons who are
the channel by means of which that detection is made, should not be unnecessarily disclosed."

And Buller J. added, at 818: "... if you call for the name of the informer in such cases, no man will make a discovery, and public justice will be defeated." That rule was emphatically reaffirmed in *Attorney-General v Briant* (1846) 15 M. & W. 169 and *Marks v Beyfus* (1890) 25 Q.B.D. 494. That reasoning applies with equal force to the inquiries made by the Gaming Board. That board was set up by Parliament to cope with disreputable gaming clubs and to bring them under control. By bitter experience it was learned that these clubs had a close connection with organised crime, often violent crime, with protection rackets and with strong-arm methods. If the Gaming Board were bound to disclose their sources of information, no one would "tell" on those clubs, for fear of reprisals. Likewise with the details of the information. If the board were bound to disclose every detail, that might itself give the informer away and put him in peril. But, without dis-closing every detail, I should have thought that the board ought in every case to be able to give to the applicant sufficient indication of the objections raised against him such as to enable him to answer them. That is only fair. And the board must at all costs be fair. If they are not, these courts will not hesitate to interfere.

Accepting that the board ought to do all this when they come to give their decision, the question arises, are they bound to give their reasons? I think not. Magistrates are not bound to give reasons for their decisions: see *R. v Northumberland Compensation Appeal Tribunal, Ex p. Shaw* [1952] 1 K.B. 338, at 352. Nor should the Gaming Board be bound. After all, the only thing that they have to give is their *opinion* as to the capability and diligence of the applicant. If they were asked by the applicant to give their reasons, they could answer quite sufficiently: "In our opinion, you are not likely to be capable of or diligent in the respects required of you." Their opinion would be an end of the matter.

Tested by those rules, applying them to this case, I think that the Gaming Board acted with complete fairness. They put before the applicants all the information which led them to doubt their suitability. They kept the sources secret, but disclosed all the information. Sir Stanley Raymond said so in his affi-davit: and it was not challenged to any effect. The board gave the applicants full opportunity to deal with the information. And they came to their decision. There was nothing whatever at fault with their decision of January 9, 1970. They did not give their reasons. But they were not bound to do so.

But then complaint is made as to what happened afterwards. It was said that the board did not pin-point the matters on which they thought the explanations were not satisfactory. They did not say which of the matters (a) to (e) they were not satisfied about. But I do not see anything unfair in that respect. It is not as if they were making any charges against the applicants. They were only saying they were not satisfied. They were not bound to give any reasons for their misgivings. And when they did give some reasons, they were not bound to submit to cross-examination on them.

Finally, complaint was made that the board refused to consider a new or amended application in respect of these premises of Crockford's in the current round. They refused to consider applications in other names or in new names. But here again I see nothing unfair. Crockford's had full opportunity of putting their application in the first instance. If there had been a technical defect in it, I feel sure that the board would have allowed an amendment. But if the application fails in matters of substance, that should be the end of it. There must be an end to the claim to "cut and come again."

In all the circumstances I think that all the criticisms of the board's conduct fail, and in my opinion the application should be dismissed.

LORD WILBERFORCE and PHILLIMORE L.J. agreed.

Application dismissed.

Notes

1. See comments by H.W.R. Wade, (1970) 86 L.Q.R. 309 and S.A. de Smith, [1970] C.L.J. 177. The decision was applied by Glidewell J. in *R. v Bristol City Council Ex p. Pearce*, above, p.689. For developments in obligations to give reasons, see *Doody*, p.743.

2. The doctrine of Public Interest Immunity may also be invoked by bodies performing some public function, to justify the withholding of confidential information during the course of legal proceedings. For an account of this doctrine, see A.W. Bradley and K.D. Ewing, *Constitutional and Administrative Law* (13th ed., 2003), pp.778–783; and for the application of this doctrine to the work of the Gaming Board, see *R. v Lewes JJ. Ex p. Secretary of State for Home Department* [1973] A.C. 388. The doctrine has been applied in the context of national security matters in *Balfour v Foreign and Commonwealth Office* [1994] 2 All E.R. 588, and the House of Lords has considered its relevance to the police complaints system in *R. v Chief Constable of the West Midlands Ex p. Wiley* [1995] A.C.274.

3. It is not normally fair for a decision-maker in a disciplinary case to act on the evidence of an informant, while refusing to disclose that evidence to the accused in order to protect the informant's identity. (*R. v Governing Body of Dunraven School Ex p. B* [2000] Ed. L.R. 156). The choice will normally be either to proceed without that evidence or to reveal the informer's identity. Similarly, the injustice of using anonymised witness statements may be even greater than the injustice of not using them (Schiemann L.J. in *R. (on the application of S) v Brent LBC* [2002] EWCA Civ 693, [2002] E.L.R. 556, at [29]); it will be unfair to rely on anonymised statements which are damaging in specific respects which, in the tribunal's judgment, the respondent could not be expected to deal with without knowing the identity of the author (*R. (on the application of T) v Head Teacher of Elliott School* [2002] EWCA Civ 1349; [2003] E.L.R. 160, per Sedley, L.J. at [50]). Schiemann L.J. noted (at [24]):

"In principle, in proceedings of this kind, the discipline committee and the appeal panel are entitled to look at statements without their makers being called to give evidence. They should bear in mind when deciding what weight to give to those statements the fact that no cross-examination has been possible. They are entitled to look at those statements, even if they are anonymous. However, doing so can give rise, not merely to the problems associated with an inability to cross-examine but also to problems arising from the fact of anonymity. The statement may have been made by a well-known liar, or by someone who has a particular reason to entertain a bias against, or indeed a bias in favour of, the pupil concerned. The fact that the maker of the statement is not known to the other side may prevent that other side from calling evidence which would have cast doubt on the reliability of that statement. Thus singular care is required from tribunals which pay regard to such statements".

On the facts, the anonymised statements in question contained general rather than specific allegations (there were "no specific allegations of a kind which are incapable of challenge if one does not know who the author is" (*per* Sedley L.J. at [53])), and they were not by any means the only evidence (*ibid*); overall it was not unfair to rely on them.

(3) *Emergency action*

R. v SECRETARY OF STATE FOR TRANSPORT Ex p. PEGASUS HOLDINGS (LONDON) LTD

[1988] 1 W.L.R. 990; [1989] 2 All E.R. 481 (SCHIEMANN J.)

The applicant companies provided foreign holidays from the United Kingdom and used aircraft chartered from a Romanian organisation and flown by a Romanian crew. In order for the Romanian aircraft and crew to be allowed to operate such holiday flights from the United Kingdom, they had received a permit from the Secretary of State granted under the authority of the Air Navigation Order 1985, Art.83. Article 62 of the Order empowered the Transport Secretary to provisionally suspend permits if he thought fit, pending a full investigation of the matter. During the middle of July 1987, five Romanian pilots voluntarily undertook flying tests conducted by the British Civil Aviation Authority; all these pilots failed the test (four displayed an inability to manoeuvre the aircraft). On July 29 at midday, the Department of Transport received a letter from the CAA, informing them of these test results. During the ensuing afternoon the Department alerted the applicants to the concerns of the CAA. On July 30 the Secretary of State signed provisional suspension orders (made under Art.62) regarding the Romanians' permit to operate the holiday charter flights from the United Kingdom. This decision caused the applicant package holiday company great difficulties in transporting its customers. The applicants sought a judicial review of the decision of the Transport Secretary, claiming, *inter alia*, that the suspension orders had been made in breach of the requirements of natural justice.

SCHIEMANN J.: . . . So far as the law is concerned, I do not think that there is anything between the parties as to the principles to be applied. These are conveniently set out in the leading case of *Wiseman v Borneman* [1971] A.C. 297, where Lord Guest, at 311, cites an earlier judgment by Tucker L.J. in *Russell v Duke of Norfolk* [1949] 1 All E.R. 109, 118 in which Tucker L.J. opined:

"There are, in my view, no words which are of universal application to every kind of inquiry and every kind of domestic tribunal. The requirements of natural justice must depend on the circumstances of the case, the nature of the inquiry, the rules under which the tribunal is acting, the subject-matter that is being dealt with, and so forth. Accordingly, I do not derive much assistance from the definitions of natural justice which have been from time to time used, but, whatever standard is adopted, one essential is that the person concerned should have a reasonable opportunity of presenting his case."

Mr Flint accepts that the opportunity to state a case can in certain circumstances be excluded in relation to such provisional matters as those with which I am concerned but says that they should not be excluded unless the situation genuinely demands it.

Mr Pannick referred me to a Court of Appeal case, *Lewis v Heffer* [1978] 1 W.L.R. 1061, where there are discussions in the various unreserved judgments delivered by the court that are not precisely to the same effect in what they say. In particular, he drew my attention to the following comments of Lord Denning M.R., at 1073. After having quoted Megarry J. in *John v Rees* [1970] Ch. 345 where he had said, at 397:

"suspension is merely expulsion *pro tanto*. Each is penal, and each deprives the member concerned of the enjoyment of his rights of membership or office. Accordingly, in my judgment the rules of natural justice *prima facie* apply to any such process of suspension in the same way that they apply to expulsion."

Lord Denning M.R. went on to say:

"Those words apply, no doubt, to suspensions which are inflicted by way of punishment: as for instance when a member of the Bar is suspended from practice for six months, or when a solicitor is suspended from practice. But they do not apply to suspensions which are made, as a holding operation, pending inquiries. Very often irregularities are disclosed in a government department or in a business house: and a man may be suspended on full pay pending inquiries. Suspicion may rest on him: and so he is suspended until he is cleared of it. No one, so far as I know, has ever questioned such a suspension on the ground that it could not be done unless he is given notice of the charge and an opportunity of defending himself and so forth. The suspension in such a case is merely done by way of good administration. A situation has arisen in which something must be done at once. The work of the department or the office is being affected by rumours and suspicions. The others will not trust the man. In order to get back to proper work, the man is suspended. At that stage the rules of natural justice do not apply: . . ."

It is right to point out that the other Lords Justices tend not to go quite as far as Lord Denning M.R. in that formulation.

In the present case, I am content to proceed on the basis that the rules of natural justice do apply but that, in the words chosen by Mr Pannick, in such an emergency as the present, with a provisional suspension being all that one is concerned with, one is at the low end of the duties of fairness. Mr Pannick referred me in the course of his submissions on this point to *R. v Civil Aviation Authority, Ex p. Northern Air Taxis Ltd* [1976] 1 Lloyd's Rep. 344. That case, which was a Divisional Court case, was concerned with matters not dissimilar in some ways to the present. Natural justice as such was not argued; the matters were dealt with on the basis of the statutory requirements, but undoubtedly the result does lend some support to the view that, when one is dealing with this type of situation, not much is required of the Secretary of State in order to act fairly.

The way the case is put by Mr Flint is this. He says that in the present case the Secretary of State could not reasonably decline to afford Tarom[3] a short period to put its case as to why the permit should not be suspended, having regard to a number of matters that Mr Flint identified. One of these is the lack of action on the letter of July 14, which I have read. As I have indicated, I regard that letter as irrelevant. A second matter to which Mr Flint drew my attention in this context was the time that the CAA took to refer the matter, which he said was some indication as to its view of the urgency. I have set out the relevant dates. It is clear that the failing of the tests took place on July 17, and the Secretary of State was not informed until July 29. That may or may not be a legitimate criticism of the CAA, but in my judgment, so far as the action of the Secretary of State is concerned, it cannot be regarded as unfair in the circumstances of this case that he acted in the speedy way in which he did act. One has in the context of unfairness to bear in mind, on the one hand, the no doubt substantial economic damage to the applicants and perhaps the irritation and inconvenience that I do not doubt the passengers suffered. On the other hand, one has to bear in mind the magnitude of the risk, by which I mean not so much the high percentage chance of it happening but the disastrous consequences of what would happen if something did happen. It is the old problem that one has with installations of nuclear power, or vehicles such as aeroplanes carrying a large number of people, that, if something goes wrong, then very many lives will be lost. While I do not doubt that different people, and maybe different Secretaries of State, would react differently to the same basic material, I am not prepared to say that the failure of the Secretary of State to permit more by way of representations than I have indicated took place was a breach of the rules of natural justice. . . .

Application dismissed.

Notes

1. Apart from the need to take emergency action, another factor present in the above case was the nature of the decision being taken—*i.e.* to suspend *provisionally* the Romanians' permit. Other cases indicate that where the challenged decision is a preliminary determination, which will be subject to a more detailed later consideration, then the full rigour of the *audi alteram partem* principle may not be invoked against the procedures leading up to the preliminary decision. For example in *Pearlberg v Varty* [1972] 1 W.L.R. 534, a taxpayer asserted that the Inland Revenue were obliged to give him a fair hearing prior to seeking to make tax assessments on him. The House of Lords rejected his claims and Lord Hailsham L.C. stated:

"the third factor which affects my mind is the consideration that the decision, once made, does not make any final determination of the rights of the taxpayer. It simply enables the inspector to raise an assessment, by satisfying the commissioner that there are reasonable grounds for suspecting loss of tax resulting from neglect, fraud, or wilful default, that is that there is a *prima facie* probability that there has been

---

[3] The Romanian organisation which owned and operated the aircraft.

neglect, etc., and that the Crown may have lost by it. When the assessment is made, the taxpayer can appeal against it, and, on the appeal, may raise any question, (*inter alia*) which would have been relevant on the application for leave, except that the leave given should be discharged".

2. The Court of Appeal has held that local authority trading standards officers are not under a general duty to consult businesses prior to issuing them with a suspension notice prohibiting the supply of unsafe products for up to six months under the terms of the Consumer Protection Act 1987. The Court believed that to impose such a duty would frustrate the statutory purpose of protecting consumer safety. Also, affected business have a right of appeal to the magistrates' court and to compensation where an order has been wrongly issued: *R. v Birmingham City Council Ex p. Ferrero Ltd* [1993] 1 All E.R. 530.

3. In the field of financial services the Court of Appeal has determined that a self-regulatory body, exercising statutory powers, is not under a duty to hear the representations of affected businesses prior to urgent intervention action carried out with the objective of safeguarding the interests of investors. But Glidewell L.J. considered that

"if a decision-making body is to exercise powers such as those of serving an intervention notice without giving anybody the opportunity to make representations beforehand, its procedures should provide that those who might otherwise expect to have been allowed to make representations should at least be allowed to make immediate application to set the decision aside and to appeal against it" (at 560).

See *R. v Life Assurance and Unit Trust Regulatory Organisation Ltd Ex p. Ross* [1993] 1 All E.R. 545.

(4) *Failings of the individual's legal advisers*

AL-MEHDAWI v SECRETARY OF STATE FOR THE HOME DEPARTMENT

[1990] 1 A.C. 876; [1989] 3 All E.R. 843 (HOUSE OF LORDS)

The respondent was an Iraqi citizen who was refused a further extension of his leave to remain in the United Kingdom during May 1984. In March 1985, the respondent was notified that the Home Secretary had decided to make a deportation order against him. The respondent instructed solicitors to appeal against the deportation decision. The solicitors were notified of the hearing date for the appeal before an immigration adjudicator; however, neither they nor the respondent attended the appeal. Consequently, the adjudicator determined the appeal on the basis of the documents before him and dismissed the appeal. There was no appeal lodged against the adjudicator's decision within the statutory time-limits. Subsequently, it emerged that the respondent's solicitors had sent notice of the hearing date and the adjudicator's decision to a previous address of the respondent (even though they knew his current one) with the result that he had received no information regarding the appellate proceedings. The respondent sought judicial review of the adjudicator's decision on the ground that there had been a breach of the rules of natural justice in that he had been denied a hearing. The High Court granted his application and the Court of Appeal affirmed that decision. The Home Secretary appealed to the House of Lords.

LORD BRIDGE OF HARWICH: . . . The appeal raises a question of great importance with respect to the scope of the remedy by order of certiorari to quash the decision of an inferior tribunal. Does certiorari lie to quash a decision given without hearing the applicant for certiorari when the tribunal giving the decision has acted correctly in the procedure adopted but the applicant was deprived of the opportunity to put his case by the negligence of his own legal advisers or otherwise without personal fault on the part of the applicant. This question had been considered once before by the Court of Appeal in *R. v Diggines, Ex p. Rahmani* [1985] 1 Q.B. 1109. That was another case relating to the decision of an adjudicator under the Act of 1971 who was mistakenly informed by the United Kingdom Immigrants Advisory Service ("U.K.I.A.S."), acting for the appellant, that they had no instructions. The Court of Appeal quashed the decision on the ground of a denial of natural justice to the appellant arising from the fault of the U.K.I.A.S. The Court of Appeal proceeded on the assumption that there had been no error of procedure by the adjudicator. However, when *Ex p. Rahmani* came before your Lordships' House on appeal the House held that the question decided by the Court of Appeal did not arise and dismissed the appeal on the ground that the adjudicator had erred in determining the appeal without a hearing in reliance on rule 12(c) of the Immigration Appeals (Procedure) Rules 1972 (S.I. 1972 No. 1684), the rules then in force, since there was no material before the adjudicator which justified him in finding under that sub-rule that no person was authorised to represent the appellant at the hearing. In the instant case, by contrast, no criticism is, nor could be, made of the procedure adopted by the adjudicator in hearing and determining the appeal in the absence of the appellant in the exercise of the express discretion conferred on him by rule 34(2) of the Rules of 1984. . . .

The central submission made by Mr Laws, for the Secretary of State, is that the so-called rules of natural justice are concerned solely with the propriety of the procedure adopted by the decision maker. In particular, the rule expressed in the Latin maxim *audi alteram partem* requires no more than that the decision maker should afford to any party to a dispute an opportunity to present his case. This view certainly receives support from many classic statements of the doctrine. The duty "fairly to hear both sides" is described by Lord Loreburn L.C. in *Board of Education v Rice* [1911] A.C. 179, 182 as "a duty lying upon every one who decides anything". In *Ridge v Baldwin* [1964] A.C. 41, 64, Lord Reid said of the watch committee who had dismissed the chief constable without a hearing:

> "Before attempting to reach any decision they were bound to inform him of the grounds on which they proposed to act and give him a fair opportunity of being heard in his own defence."

. . . Mr Laws submits that the very concept of impropriety in the procedure by which a decision is reached necessarily connotes an irregularity in the conduct of the proceedings by the decision maker. Conversely, a failure by the legal adviser or any other agent to whom a party to any proceedings has entrusted the conduct of his case, being beyond the knowledge and control of the decision maker, cannot involve either any procedural impropriety or the breach of any duty which the decision maker owes to that party.

However, the authority on which Sir Charles Fletcher-Cooke [counsel for the respondent] relies, and which persuaded the Court of Appeal that the procedural impropriety involved in a breach of the rules of natural justice could not be confined to errors on the part of the decision-making body, is

R. v Leyland Justices, Ex p. Hawthorn [1979] Q.B. 283. In that case the driver of one of two cars involved in a collision had been prosecuted and convicted for driving without due care and attention. The police had taken statements from two witnesses of the accident, but these witnesses were not called by the prosecution and their existence was not disclosed to the defence. The driver successfully applied for an order of certiorari to quash the conviction. Delivering the first judgment Lord Widgery C.J. said, at 286:

"There is no doubt that an application can be made by certiorari to set aside an order on the basis that the tribunal failed to observe the rules of natural justice. Certainly if it were the fault of the justices that this additional evidentiary information was not passed on, no difficulty would arise. But the problem—and one can put it in a sentence—is that certiorari in respect of breach of the rules of natural justice is primarily a remedy sought on account of an error of the tribunal, and here, of course, we are not concerned with an error of the tribunal; we are concerned with an error of the police prosecutors. Consequently, amongst the arguments to which we have listened an argument has been that this is not a certiorari case at all on any of the accepted grounds.

"We have given this careful thought over the short adjournment because it is a difficult case in that the consequences of the decision either way have their unattractive features. However, if fraud, collusion, perjury and suchlike matters not affecting the tribunal themselves justify an application for certiorari to quash the conviction, if all those matters are to have that effect, then we cannot say that the failure of the prosecution which in this case has prevented the tribunal from giving the defendant a fair trial should not rank in the same category.

"We have come to the conclusion that there was here a clear denial of natural justice. Fully recognising the fact that the blame falls on the prosecutor and not on the tribunal, we think that it is a matter which should result in the conviction being quashed. In my judgment, that is the result to which we should adhere."

This decision was followed in *R. v Blundeston Prison Board of Visitors, Ex p. Fox-Taylor* [1982] 1 All E.R. 646.

Though I do not question the correctness of the decision in *Ex p. Hawthorn* [1979] Q.B. 283, I do question whether it is correctly classified as a case depending on either procedural impropriety or a breach of the rules of natural justice. Certainly there was unfairness in the conduct of the proceedings, but this was because of a failure by the prosecutor, in breach of a duty owed to the court and to the defence, to disclose the existence of witnesses who could have given evidence favourable to the defence. Although no dishonesty was suggested, it was this *suppressio veri* which had the same effect as a *suggestio falsi* in distorting and vitiating the process leading to conviction, and it was, in my opinion, the analogy which Lord Widgery C.J. drew between the case before him and the cases of fraud, collusion and perjury which had been relied on in counsel's argument, which identified the true principle on which the decision could be justified.

In any event, *Ex p. Hawthorn*, if it is relied on as an authority to support the conclusion of the Court of Appeal in *Ex p. Rahmani* [1985] Q.B. 1109 and the instant case, proves too much. If unfairness resulting from a failure by the prosecutor to disclose the names of witnesses, so that the defence is deprived of their evidence, is taken as a precedent for allowing certiorari on the ground of a failure in the conduct of proceedings by the defendant's own legal advisers, the logic of the argument would lead to the conclusion that a negligent failure by the defendant's own legal advisers to secure the attendance of necessary defence witnesses would entitle the defendant to have his conviction quashed if he was personally free of blame for the failure. But this was a conclusion which Sir Charles Fletcher-Cooke rightly declined to support. . . .

But there are many familiar situations where one party to litigation will effectively lose the opportunity to have his case heard through the failure of his own legal advisers, but will be left with no remedy at all except against those legal advisers. I need only instance judgments signed in default, actions dismissed for want of a prosecution and claims which are not made within a fixed time limit which the tribunal has no power to extend. In each of these situations a litigant who wishes his case to be heard and who has fully instructed his solicitor to take the necessary steps may never in fact be heard because of his solicitor's neglect and through no fault of his own. But in any of these cases it would surely be fanciful to say that there had been a breach of the *audi alteram partem* rule. Again, take the case of a county court action where a litigant fails to appear at the hearing because his solicitor has neglected to inform him of the date and consequently judgment is given against him. He can at best invite the court in its discretion to set aside the judgment and it is likely to do so only on the terms that he should pay the costs thrown away. Yet, if it can be said that he has been denied natural justice, he ought in principle to be able to apply for certiorari to quash the judgment which, if he is personally blameless, should be granted as a matter of course.

These considerations lead me to the conclusion that a party to a dispute who has lost the opportunity to have his case heard through the default of his own advisers to whom he has entrusted the conduct of the dispute on his behalf cannot complain that he has been the victim of a procedural impropriety or that natural justice has been denied to him, at all events when the subject-matter of the dispute raises issues of private law between citizens. Is there any principle which can be invoked to lead to a different conclusion where the issue is one of public law and where the decision taken is of an administrative character rather than the resolution of a *lis inter partes*? I cannot discover any such principle and none has been suggested in the course of argument. . . .

But I would add that, if once unfairness suffered by one party to a dispute in consequence of some failure by his own advisers in relation to the conduct of the relevant proceedings was admitted as a ground on which the High Court in the exercise of its supervisory jurisdiction over inferior tribunals could quash the relevant decision, I can discern no principle which could be invoked to distinguish between a "fundamental unfairness", which would justify the exercise of the jurisdiction, and a less than fundamental unfairness, which would not. Indeed, Sir Charles Fletcher-Cooke was constrained to rest on the proposition that, in the last analysis, it was all a matter of discretion and the court could be trusted only to exercise its discretion in extreme cases where justice demanded a remedy. I am of the opinion that the decision of the Court of Appeal can only be supported at the cost of opening such a wide door which would indeed seriously undermine the principle of finality in decision-making.

The effect of this conclusion in a deportation case may appear harsh, though no harsher than the perhaps more common case when an immigrant's solicitor fails to give notice of appeal under section 15 within the time limited by rule 4 of the Rules of 1984. But it is perhaps worth pointing out that in neither case is the immigrant left wholly without a remedy. In the case of a notice of appeal served out of time, the Secretary of State has a discretion under rule 5 to extend the time "if he is of the opinion that, by reason of special circumstances, it is just and right so to do". In the case where the immigrant has failed to attend the hearing of his appeal to the adjudicator and the appeal has been heard and dismissed in his absence, the Secretary of State has the discretion conferred on him by section 21 of the Act whereby he "may at any time refer for consideration under this section any matter relating to the case which was not before the adjudicator". If such a reference is made, the adjudicator is required by section 21(2) to "consider the matter which is the subject of the reference and report to the Secretary of State the opinion of the adjudicator . . . thereon". It would, as it seems to me, certainly be open to the Secretary of State, if persuaded that the merits of a case required it, to invite an adjudicator to hear the oral evidence of an appellant whose appeal had, through no fault of his own, been dismissed in his absence, and to report his opinion whether this evidence would have affected the outcome of the appeal.

I would allow the appeal, set aside the orders of MacPherson J. and the Court of Appeal and restore the determination of the adjudicator.

LORDS ROSKILL, BRANDON OF OAKBROOK, OLIVER OF AYLMERTON and GOFF OF CHIEVELEY agreed with the speech given by LORD BRIDGE.

Appeal allowed.

Notes

1. The above decision has been criticised for unduly circumscribing the application of the *audi alteram partem* principle. One critic has suggested the following approach:

> "By drawing on the theory that natural justice—and judicial review as a whole—is vitally concerned with setting standards for public authorities and structuring the exercise of public power, it is suggested that the House of Lords should have held that certiorari for breach of natural justice could lie although a tribunal was not responsible for the defect, but only where responsibility for the procedural impropriety can be attributed to a body exercising public authority: either the prosecutor (in a criminal case) or a party to an adversarial process with a public law function (for example, the Home Office in proceedings before the immigration adjudicator). Such a view recognises the strong argument in favour of finality of litigation, but holds that finality should not override the importance of natural justice in 'policing' public power . . .".

(J. Herberg, "The Right to a Hearing: Breach Without Fault?" [1990] P.L.467 at pp.474–475).

2. *Ex p. Hawthorn* was applied, and *Al-Mehdawi* distinguished, in *R. v Bolton JJ. Ex p. Scally* [1991] 2 All E.R. 619, where the Divisional Court quashed convictions for driving with excess alcohol based on scientific evidence subsequently shown to be flawed. There had been no dishonesty, but the prosecutor had "corrupted the process leading to conviction in a manner which was unfair". A later Divisional Court held that only where a prosecutor's conduct was "analogous to fraud" would it quash a conviction in the magistrates' court. The notification, by the Crown Prosecution Service, after the completion of a trial of defects in the procedure by which a blood

sample had been obtained from a suspected drink driver did not fall into this category of conduct: *R. v Burton Upon Trent JJ. Ex p. Woolley* [1995] R.T.R. 139. This approach was endorsed in *R. v Dolgellau JJ. Ex p. Cartledge, The Times*, August 4, 1995, where the High Court dismissed an application for judicial view because there was no evidence that the prosecution had falsified or suppressed evidence that might have led to an acquittal.

(5) *The making of legislation*

BATES v LORD HAILSHAM OF ST MARYLEBONE

[1972] 1 W.L.R. 1373; 116 S.J. 584; [1972] 2 All E.R. 1019 (MEGARRY J.)

Mr Bates was a solicitor and a leading member of the British Legal Association, to which about 2,900 of the 26,000 solicitors with practising certificates belonged. On May 1, 1972, the Lord Chancellor announced at a press conference that the scale fees for conveyancing work prescribed under Sch.1 to the Solicitors' Remuneration Order 1883, would be replaced by a *quantum meruit* system. The British Legal Association sent a circular to all solicitors opposing the changes. The Law Society received a draft order for the implementation of the changes from the Lord Chancellor's department as required by the Solicitors' Act 1957, s.58(3). A period of one month was prescribed by s.56 for observations to be submitted to the statutory committee which would make the new order. The date of the meeting of the committee was fixed for July 19, at 4.30pm. On June 21, the draft order was published in the Law Society's Gazette. The British Legal Association sent submissions and letters to the committee on July 11 and 14, requesting postponement of the changes "for perhaps two months", and further consultations. On July 18, the Lord Chancellor wrote to the British Legal Association refusing their requests. The plaintiff the same day served a writ against the members of the committee. He contended that the draft order had been prepared by the Lord Chancellor's department and had not been considered by the committee. He claimed: (i) a declaration that any order made by the committee under s.56 would be *ultra vires* and void unless the draft had been considered by the committee and an opportunity had been given for representations on the order to be made by the British Legal Association and others; (ii) an injunction restraining the committee from making an order until these steps had been taken. At 2.00pm on July 19, the plaintiff moved *ex parte* for an injunction to stop the committee making an order at its 4.30pm meeting.

MEGARRY J.: . . . His [*i.e.* Counsel for the plaintiff's] two main points were, first, that if the order was made at the meeting of the committee, the committee would not be complying with its duty to act fairly. The committee, he said, would be exercising not judicial or quasi-judicial functions, but administrative functions; and where, as here, so vast a change was going to be made as the overturn of the entire basis of charging in conveyancing transactions, a basis that had lasted for nearly 90 years and affected a profession of some 26,000 spread throughout the country, it was not fair to make it without a substantially longer period for consultation and representations. His second point was one which he accepted as being technical; but in effect he said that it was advanced in a good cause. It was that it was implicit in section 56(3) that the draft of the order which was to be sent to the council of the Law Society must be a draft prepared or approved by the committee, and not, as appeared to be the case here, a draft prepared by or on behalf of the Lord Chancellor's department, without previous consultation with the committee.

On the first point, Mr Nicholls relied on *R. v Liverpool Corporation, Ex p. Liverpool Taxi Fleet Operators' Association* [1972] 2 Q.B. 299 [above, p.697]; and he read me some passages from the judgments of Lord Denning M.R. and Roskill L.J. It cannot often happen that words uttered by a judge in his judicial capacity will, within six months, be cited against him in his personal capacity as defendant; yet that is the position here. The case was far removed from the present case. It concerned the exercise by a city council of its powers to license hackney carriages, and a public undertaking given by the chairman of the relevant committee which the council soon proceeded to ignore. The case supports propositions relating to the duty of a body to act fairly when exercising administrative functions under a statutory power: see at 307,308 and 310. Accordingly, in deciding the policy to be applied as to the number of licences to grant, there was a duty to hear those who would be likely to be affected. It is plain that no legislation was involved: the question was one of the policy to be adopted in the exercise of a statutory power to grant licences.

In the present case, the committee in question has an entirely different function: it is legislative rather than administrative or executive. The function of the committee is to make or refuse to make a legislative instrument under delegated powers. The order, when made, will lay down the remuneration for solicitors generally; and the terms of the order will have to be considered and construed and applied in numberless cases in the future. Let me accept that in the sphere of the so-called quasi-judicial the rules of natural justice run, and that in the administrative or executive field there is a general duty of fairness. Nevertheless, these considerations do not seem to me to affect the process of legislation, whether primary or delegated. Many of those affected by delegated legislation, and affected very substantially, are never consulted in the process of enacting that legislation; and yet they have no remedy. Of course, the informal consultation of representative bodies by the legislative authority is a commonplace; but although a few statutes have specifically provided for a general process of publishing draft delegated legislation and considering objections (see, for example, the Factories Act 1961, Schedule 4), I do not know of any implied right to be consulted or make objections, or any principle upon which the courts may enjoin the legislative process at the suit of those who contend that insufficient time for consultation and consideration has been given. I accept that the fact that the order will take the form of a statutory instrument does not *per se* make it immune from attack, whether by injunction or otherwise; but what is important is not its form but its nature, which is plainly legislative.

There is a further point. The power in question in the *Liverpool Corporation* case [1972] 2 Q.B. 299 was a general power to "license . . . such number of hackney coaches or carriages . . . as they think fit" under section 37 of the Town Police Clauses Act 1847, with no special procedure laid down for the process of licensing. Here, Parliament has laid down the procedure to be followed. *Expressum facit cessare tacitum.* It is easier to imply procedural safeguards when Parliament has provided none than where Parliament has laid down a procedure, however inadequate its critics may consider it to be. Parliament has here provided that the committee must, before making any order, consider any observations in writing submitted to it by the council of the Law Society within one month of the draft having been sent to the council. What in effect the plaintiff is seeking to do is to add by implication a further requirement that if the draft will make momentous changes, more than a month must be allowed, and opportunities must be given for representations to be made by bodies other than the council of the Law Society. Mr Nicholls understandably shrank from asserting that the process of consultation need go beyond any substantial organised body of solicitors, or that the committee need accede to a request for further time from any other body or persons. My difficulty is to see how even the organised bodies that he postulated can be implied into the subsection or imposed upon it. If the procedure laid down by Parliament is fairly and substantially followed, I cannot see that the committee need do more; and I see nothing in the evidence to suggest that the committee has not fully and fairly complied with the statutory requirements. . . .

[His Lordship then rejected the plaintiff's second point.]

Notes

1. The unwillingness of the judiciary to place common law procedural obligations upon legislative processes has been alluded to by the House of Lords. In a case involving the disciplinary powers of prison governors, Lord Oliver stated:

> "it is a public function which affects the liberty and, to a degree, the status of the persons affected by it. As such it must, as it seems to me, be subject to the general common law principle which imposes a duty of procedural fairness when a public authority makes a decision not of a *legislative nature* affecting the rights, privileges and interests of individuals" (emphasis added): *Leech v Parkhurst Prison Deputy Governor* [1988] 1 All E.R. 485 at 509.

2. Duties to consult in respect of the making of delegated legislation are commonly imposed by statute. See J.F. Garner, [1976] P.L. 307 and A. Jergesen, [1978] P.L. 290. More generally see the chapter on delegated legislation above, Ch.4, and pp.41 *et seq.* on the Code of Practice on Consultation.

3. Similarly, a local authority need not give an opportunity for persons to be heard before making a decision that is universal in its application such as the fixing by the authority of the rates for the year (now the level of council tax) or the scale on which fees are to be charged (*R. v Greater London Council Ex p. The Rank Organisation Ltd, The Times*, February 19, 1982). However, where a decision to set fees or charges affects a discrete class, those persons may have a legitimate expectation that they will have the opportunity to make representations (*R. v Birmingham City Council Ex p. Dredger* (1993) 91 L.G.R. 532). The distinction seems to be one of degree.

Where a decision is legislative in form but affects only one person or company, it should not be treated as legislative for the purpose of excluding obligations of procedural fairness (*cf R. v Secretary of State for Health Ex p. US Tobacco International Inc.* [1992] 1 Q.B. 353).

(c) *Specific aspects of the right to a fair hearing in particular decision-making contexts*

(1) *Oral or written representations?*

LLOYD v McMAHON

[1987] 1 A.C. 625; [1987] 2 W.L.R. 821; [1987] 1 All E.R. 1118
(HOUSE OF LORDS)

During 1984, Liverpool Council had delayed making a rate until July of that year. In April of 1985, the district auditor sent a report to the council expressing concern that a rate had not yet been made for 1985. On May 21 the district auditor sent a further report to the council in which he stated that unless a rate was made by the end of May he would commence action under the Local Government Act 1982, s.20, to recover any financial losses occasioned by the failure to make a rate from the members responsible for incurring them. On June 6, the Audit Commission ordered that an extraordinary audit of the council be carried out. The council made a rate on June 14. On June 26, the district auditor sent a notice to 42 councillors (who by their voting or absence might have failed to discharge their duties as councillors) stating that he had to consider whether to certify the sum of £106,103 as lost by their wilful misconduct. The individual councillors were informed that they could make written representations to the district auditor before he reached a decision. The councillors (assisted by the chief executive of the council) made a collective written response to the district auditor. They did not seek an oral hearing before the district auditor. In September 1985 the district auditor certified that the named councillors were jointly and severally liable for the above sum. The councillors appealed to the High Court (under s.20(3) of the Act) against the district auditor's decision. The High Court dismissed their appeal and that decision was confirmed by the Court of Appeal. The councillors then appealed to the House of Lords.

LORD KEITH OF KINKEL: . . . The argument by counsel for the appellants did not invite your Lordships to enter deeply into the merits of the question whether or not they had been guilty of wilful misconduct, nor was attention drawn to any details of the affidavits and other material placed before the Divisional Court. The substance of the argument was that the district auditor's decision had been vitiated by his failure to offer the appellants an oral hearing before reaching it, and should therefore have been quashed. The argument was supported by an examination of earlier legislation in regard to local government audits, starting with the Poor Law Amendment Act 1844 (7 & 8 Vict. c. 101), where oral hearings were the order of the day, and by reference to the Code of Local Government Audit Practice for England and Wales, made under section 14 of the Act of 1982 and approved by resolution of both Houses of Parliament. The code, by paragraphs 16 to 20, contemplates that an oral hearing will be held where the auditor is dealing with a notice of objection given under section 17(3) of the Act of 1982, which itself refers to the objector attending before the auditor. The code does not deal with the procedure to be followed where the auditor takes action under section 20(1). Counsel produced a list of all instances since 1972 where a district auditor had occasion to consider an issue of wilful misconduct, indicating that in all but one of them an oral hearing had been offered. This had the effect, so it was maintained, of creating a legitimate expectation on the part of the appellants that they would be offered an oral hearing before the district auditor arrived at his decision.

My Lords, if the district auditor had reached a decision adverse to the appellants without giving them any opportunity at all of making representations to him, there can be no doubt that his procedure would have been contrary to the rules of natural justice and that, subject to the question whether the defect was capable of being cured on appeal to the Divisional Court, the decision would fall to be quashed. In the event, written representations alone were asked for. These were duly furnished, in very considerable detail, and an oral hearing was not requested, though that could very easily have been done, and there is no reason to suppose that the request would not have been granted. None of the appellants stated, in his or her affidavit before the Divisional Court, that they had an expectation that an oral hearing, though not asked for, would be offered. The true question is whether the district auditor acted fairly in all the circumstances. It is easy to envisage cases where an oral hearing would clearly be essential in the interests of fairness, for example where an objector states that he has personal knowledge of some facts indicative of wilful misconduct on the part of a councillor. In that situation justice would demand that the councillor be given an opportunity to depone to his own version of the facts. In the present case the district auditor had arrived at his provisional view upon the basis of the contents of documents, minutes of meetings and reports submitted to the council from the auditor's department and their own officers. All these documents were appended to or referred to in the notice of June 26 sent by the district auditor to the appellants. Their response referred to other documents, which were duly considered by the district auditor, as is shown by his statement of reasons dated September 6, 1985. No facts contradictory of or supplementary to the contents of the documents were or are relied on by either side. If the appellants had attended an oral hearing they would no doubt have reiterated the sincerity of their motives from the point of view of advancing the interests of the inhabitants of Liverpool. It seems unlikely, having regard to the position adopted by their counsel on this matter before the Divisional Court, that they would have been willing to reveal or answer questions about the proceedings of their political caucus. The sincerity of the appellants' motives is not something capable of justifying or excusing failure to carry out a statutory duty, or of making reasonable what is otherwise an unreasonable delay in carrying out such a duty. In all the circumstances I am of opinion that the district auditor did not act unfairly, and that the procedure which he followed did not involve any prejudice to the appellants. . . .

Upon the view which I take, that the district auditor's decision was not vitiated by procedural unfairness, the question whether such unfairness, had it existed, was capable of being cured by the appeal to the High Court does not arise directly for decision. It is, however, my opinion that the particular appeal mechanism provided for by section 20(3) of the Act of 1982, considered in its context, is apt to enable the court, notwithstanding that it finds some procedural defect in the conduct of an audit which has resulted in a certificate based on wilful misconduct, to inquire into the merits of the case and arrive at its own decision thereon. Section 20(3)(b) empowers the court to "confirm the decision or quash it and give any certificate which the auditor could have given". The relevant rules of court enable a rehearing of the broadest possible scope to take place. Evidence may be given on oath, which is not possible before the auditor, and there is no limit to the further material which may be introduced so as to enable the whole merits to be fully examined. There is no question of the court being confined to a review of the evidence which was available to the auditor. . . .

I may add that I agree entirely with all that is said upon this aspect of the appeal in the speech of my noble and learned friend Lord Bridge of Harwich.

LORD BRIDGE OF HARWICH: My Lords, the so-called rules of natural justice are not engraved on tablets of stone. To use the phrase which better expresses the underlying concept, what the requirements of fairness demand when any body, domestic, administrative or judicial, has to make a decision which will affect the rights of individuals depends on the character of the decision-making body, the kind of decision it has to make and the statutory or other frame-work in which it operates. In particular, it is well-established that when a statute has conferred on any body the power to make decisions affecting individuals, the courts will not only require the procedure prescribed by the statute to be followed, but will readily imply so much and no more to be introduced by way of additional procedural safeguards as will ensure the attainment of fairness. . . .

I followed with interest Mr Blom-Cooper's [counsel for the appellants] carefully researched review of the history of local government audit legislation, but I did not find that it threw any light on what, in particular, is required to provide such an opportunity in the circumstances of any particular case under the statute presently in force. Still less do I attach any significance to the fact that since 1972, when provisions substantially to the like effect as those which we find in the Act of 1982 first reached the Statute Book, auditors have, as a matter of practice, always invited oral representations from members of local authorities before certifying the amount of any loss or deficiency as due from them. When a single individual is thought to have failed to bring a sum into account or by his wilful misconduct to have caused a loss or deficiency, it is no doubt a very appropriate practice to invite his explanation orally. But I fail to understand how that practice can constrain the courts to construe the statute as requiring an auditor proposing to act under section 20 to invite oral representations as a matter of law in every case. . . .

The proposition that it was, *per se*, in breach of the rules of natural justice not to invite oral representations in this case is quite untenable. . . .

These conclusions would be sufficient to dispose of the appeals. But I return to the question of more general importance whether, if there had been any unfairness in the procedure followed by the auditor, this would necessarily have led, as the Divisional Court thought, to the quashing of the certificate or whether, as the Court of Appeal concluded, the full hearing of the appeal to the court on the merits was in law able to make good any deficiency in the auditor's procedure. It was in order to set this question in its proper context that I thought it necessary, earlier in this opinion, to set out the relevant statutory provisions *in extenso*. The question how far in domestic and administrative two-tier adjudicatory systems a procedural failure at the level of the first tier can be remedied at the level of the second tier was considered by the Privy Council in *Calvin v Carr* [1980] A.C. 574 in which all the relevant previous authorities on the subject are reviewed. I do not find it necessary in this case to examine the general principles there discussed, nor would I think it appropriate in this case to seek to lay down any principles of general application. This is because the question arising in the instant case must be answered by considering the particular statutory provisions here applicable which establish an adjudicatory system in many respects quite unlike any that has come under examination in any of the decided cases to which we were referred. We are concerned with a point of statutory construction and nothing else. . . .

In every case it must be for the court, as a matter of discretion, to decide how in all the circumstances its jurisdiction under section 20(3) can best be exercised to meet the justice of the case. But I am clearly of opinion that when the court has, as here, in fact conducted a full hearing on the merits and reached a conclusion that the issue of a certificate was justified, it would be an erroneous exercise of discretion nevertheless to quash the certificate on the ground that, before the matter reached the court, there had been some defect in the procedure followed.

Lords Brandon and Griffiths agreed. Lord Templeman delivered a concurring speech.

Appeal dismissed.

Notes

1. A local fund was established to raise the moneys needed to discharge the councillors' legal liabilities. By 1990 the fund had collected such an amount. As to the role of the auditor, see *Cross*, Ch.13. The auditor's powers to recover unlawful expenditure from the local councillors who authorised it were repealed by the Local Government Act 2000, s.90.

2. The second limb of their Lordships' decision concerned the issue of "curative appeals" which is examined below (p.740) in the case of *Calvin v Carr*.

3. On the oral hearing point see also *R. v Army Board of the Defence Council Ex p. Anderson*, above, p.446, applied in *R. v Secretary of State for Health Ex p. Gandhi* [1991] 4 All E.R. 547 at 556–577. The High Court decided, following *Anderson*, that a committee of the Legal Aid Board acted unlawfully by circulating documents to each of the members individually; rather than reconvening a meeting with all the members attending in person for group deliberation: see *R. v Legal Aid Board Ex p. Donn & Co.* [1996] 3 All E.R. 1. The House of Lords had held that the Parole Board had acted unfairly through being insufficiently willing to offer an oral hearing to prisoners who sought to challenge the revocation of their release on licence (*R. (on the application of West) v Parole Board* [2005] UKHL 1).

4. The Court of Appeal has held that a convicted prisoner does not have a right in all circumstances to be present in court to argue every civil case he or she may initiate. It was, therefore, lawful for the Home Secretary to require prisoners to make a formal application for permission to be allowed to attend such proceedings and for the Secretary of State to require the prisoners to pay the costs incurred in producing them in court: *R. v Secretary of State for the Home Department Ex p. Wynne* [1992] 1 Q.B. 406. Staughton L.J. said at 428):

> "Finally, I turn to considerations of natural justice. There are two aspects of this which cause me concern. The first is that, if a prisoner is not allowed to be present in court when his case is heard, he will not be able to answer new arguments put forward by the other side or to rebut new evidence which is produced against him. The importance of this point depends on the nature of the case. When, as here, it is a prisoner's application for judicial review, the judge at the hearing should be careful to allow no new evidence and no new arguments, beyond those which the prisoner has already had the opportunity to answer in writing. Then no injustice can arise. In other types of case it may be an important factor for the Home Office to have in mind when deciding whether to allow production and if so on what terms".

(2) *A right to legal representation?*

R. v BOARD OF VISITORS OF H.M. PRISON, THE MAZE, Ex p. HONE

[1988] 1 A.C. 379; [1988] 2 W.L.R. 177; [1988] 1 All E.R. 321
(HOUSE OF LORDS)

The appellant was a prisoner serving a life sentence in Northern Ireland. He was charged with an offence against discipline of assaulting a prison officer contrary to r. 31(5) of the Prison Rules (Northern Ireland) 1982. Because of the seriousness of the charge it was referred to the board of visitors for determination. The board found the charge proved (the appellant had pleaded not guilty) and sentenced him to 30 days' cellular confinement and a concurrent loss of privileges for 60 days. The appellant sought judicial review of the board's decision arguing, *inter alia*, that it was unlawful as he had been denied the right to legal representation before the board. The High Court dismissed the application and this decision was confirmed by the Court of Appeal. The appellant then appealed to the House of Lords.

This case was dealt with as a consolidated appeal together with a similar action brought by another prisoner, McCartan.

LORD GOFF OF CHIEVELEY: . . . Before your Lordships' House, the submissions on behalf of the appellants were as follows. The basic submission was that a convicted prisoner retains all his civil rights, except those which are taken away from him expressly or by necessary implication; and that an ordinary citizen charged with a criminal offence is entitled to legal representation before the tribunal which hears the charge against him. It was, however, accepted that, on an inquiry by the governor of a prison, a prisoner has no right to legal representation; such a right, it was submitted, applied only to hearings before boards of visitors, when the prisoner is charged with a criminal offence or the equivalent of a criminal offence.

. . . The first of the authorities is the decision of the Court of Appeal in *R. v Assessment Committee of St Mary Abbotts, Kensington* [1891] 1 Q.B. 378. In that case it was held that a householder who objected to a valuation list and wished his objection to be advanced before the assessment committee need not appear in person before the committee but could depute another person to do so on his behalf. This decision has been invoked on subsequent occasions in support of the proposition that any person appearing before a disciplinary tribunal is entitled to legal representation. The decision of the Court of Appeal in *Pett v Greyhound Racing Association Ltd* [1969] 1 Q.B. 125 appeared, at first sight, to give some credence to that proposition. In that case the plaintiff claimed the right to legal representation at an inquiry by the association into a disciplinary matter, concerned with a serious charge against the plaintiff relating to the circumstances in which a greyhound of his was withdrawn from a race, it being alleged that traces of barbiturates were found in the dog's urine. On an interlocutory appeal Lord Denning M.R., in holding that natural justice required that in matters affecting a man's reputation or livelihood or any matters of serious purport he should, if he wished, be legally represented, relied upon the *St Mary Abbotts* case; and Russell L.J., at 135, referred to his "common law right" to be so represented. However, on the substantive hearing (*Pett v Greyhound Racing Association Ltd (No. 2)* [1970] 1 Q.B. 46), Lyell J. concluded that the only duty on the association was to observe the rules of natural justice, and distinguished the *St Mary Abbotts* case as being concerned not with legal representation before a tribunal but with a man employing an agent to communicate with a body performing an administrative act. He said, at 63:

"It appears to me that the Court of Appeal regarded the overseers as performing an administrative act in preparing the valuation lists . . . It has, so far as I am aware, never been suggested that the valuation officer in considering such objections is acting otherwise than in an administrative capacity. In view of the many authorities that domestic tribunals are subject only to the duty of observing what are called the rules of natural justice and any procedure laid down or necessarily to be implied from the instrument that confers their power, I am unable to follow the views expressed by the Court of Appeal, that the plaintiff is entitled to appear by an agent unless such right was expressly negatived by the rules of the club."

Subsequent cases have proceeded on the same basis. Thus in *Enderby Town Football Club Ltd v Football Association Ltd* [1971] Ch.591, Lord Denning M.R. rejected the suggestion that a man who is charged before a domestic tribunal is entitled as of right to be legally represented; on the contrary, he regarded that matter as being within the discretion of the tribunal. A similar suggestion was rejected by the Court of Appeal in *Fraser v Mudge* [1975] 1 W.L.R. 1132, which is very much in point in the present case. There a prisoner asked for an injunction to restrain a board of visitors from inquiring into a charge against him of assaulting a prison officer unless he was represented by a solicitor and counsel of his choice. The case therefore raised the question whether, in such circumstances, the prisoner was entitled to legal representation as of right. Chapman J. refused to grant the injunction, and his decision was affirmed by the Court of Appeal. Roskill L.J. said, at 1134:

"The argument of Mr Sedley, as I follow it, really involves that justice cannot be done or cannot at least be seen to be done by the defendants, the visitors, in this case unless there is legal representation of the plaintiff. I wish to make it plain that I do not subscribe to the view that in every type of case, irrespective of the nature or jurisdiction of the body in question, justice can neither be done nor be seen to be done without legal representation of the party or parties appearing before that body. Such a proposition to my mind is untenable. There are many bodies before which a party or parties can be required to appear but who can do justice and can be seen to do justice without the party against whom complaint is made being legally represented. Further, as Lord Denning M.R. has said, if the argument in relation to rule 49(2) of the Prison Rules 1964 were well founded, it would equally apply to complaints heard by the governor to which the same language applies, a proposition which I think is also untenable. One looks to see what are the broad principles underlying these rules. They are to maintain discipline in prison by proper, swift and speedy decisions, whether by the governor or the visitors; and it seems to me that the requirements of natural justice do not make it necessary that a person against whom disciplinary proceedings are pending should as of right be entitled to be represented by solicitors or counsel or both."

Subsequently, in *R. v Secretary of State for the Home Department, Ex p. Tarrant* [1985] Q.B. 251, a Divisional Court (consisting of Kerr L.J. and Webster J.) accepted *Fraser v Mudge* as binding authority that, before a board of visitors, a prisoner charged with a disciplinary offence has no right to legal representation, though it was held that a board of visitors has a discretion to grant representation; and, in his full and careful judgment, Webster J. referred to considerations which he considered that every board of visitors should take into account when exercising its discretion whether to allow legal representation, or indeed the assistance of a friend or adviser, to a prisoner appearing before it on a disciplinary charge. . . .

In advancing his submissions for the appellants in the present case before your Lordships' House, Mr Hill had of necessity to submit that the decision of the Court of Appeal in *Fraser v Mudge* was wrong. In support of his sub-missions, which I have already summarised, he relied upon rule 30(2) of the Rules of 1982, which provides that at an inquiry into a charge against a prisoner he shall be given a full opportunity of presenting his own case. He stressed that a hearing before a board of visitors is a sophisticated hearing. In particular, he submitted, there is an oral hearing; a formal plea is entered; cross-examination is allowed and witnesses are called; the onus and standard of proof are the same as in a criminal trial; free legal aid is available; punishments are imposed; a plea in mitigation can be entered; and the board has greater powers of punishment than those exercised by magistrates' courts. He also, like others before him, invoked the *St Mary Abbotts* case [1891] 1 Q.B. 378 as authority for the proposition that each appellant had a common law right to appoint a lawyer as his agent to appear before the board of visitors on his behalf.

I am unable to accept these submissions. I would first of all reject the argument founded upon the *St Mary Abbotts* case as misconceived, for the very reasons given by Lyell J. in *Pett v Greyhound Racing Association Ltd (No. 2)* [1970] 1 Q.B. 46, 63, quoted above, that the case is not in point since it was concerned only with the making of a communication to an administrative body. But, so far as Mr Hill's wider submissions are concerned, I am unable to accept his second proposition that any person charged with a crime (or the equivalent thereof) and liable to punishment is entitled as a matter of natural justice to legal representation. No doubt it is true that a man charged with a crime before a criminal court is entitled to legal representation—both before the Crown Court and (as a matter of statute) before a magistrates' court: see section 122 of the Magistrates' Courts Act 1980 . . . . Nodoubt it is also correct that a board of visitors is bound to give effect to the rules of natural justice. But it does not follow that, simply because a charge before a disciplinary tribunal such as a board of visitors relates to facts which in law constitute a crime, the rules of natural justice require the tribunal to grant legal representation. Indeed, if this were the case, then, as Roskill L.J. pointed out in *Fraser v Mudge* [1975] 1 W.L.R. 1132, exactly the same submission could be made in respect of disciplinary proceedings before the governor of a prison. Mr Hill was at pains to escape from this conclusion by attempting to distinguish between a governor and a board of visitors, on the basis that there was no right of legal representation before the governor but an absolute right to legal representation before the board of visitors. I for my part am unable to accept this distinction. Each, both governor and board of visitors, is exercising a disciplinary jurisdiction; and, as the Rules of 1982 clearly demonstrate, each may do so in respect of offences against discipline which could in law constitute criminal offences. Each must also be bound by the rules of natural justice. The difference between them is not so much a legal as a practical difference. The jurisdiction exercised by the governor is of a more summary nature, and should properly be exercised with great expedition; furthermore the punishments which he can award are limited to those set out in rule 32 of the Rules of 1982, though he can refer the matter to the Secretary of State (and, through him, to a board of visitors) under rule 33(1)(e) if he considers that it may be desirable that a more severe punishment should be awarded. In the nature of things, it is difficult to imagine that the rules of natural justice would ever require legal representation before the governor. But though the rules of natural justice may require legal representation before a board of visitors, I can see no basis for Mr Hill's submission that they should do so in every case as of right. Everything must depend on the circumstances of the particular case, as is amply demonstrated by the circumstances so carefully listed by Webster J. in *R. v Secretary of State for the Home Department, Ex p. Tarrant* [1985] Q.B. 251 as matters which boards of visitors should take into account. But it is easy to envisage circumstances in which the rules of natural justice do not call for representation, even though the disciplinary charge relates to a matter which constitutes in law a crime, as may well happen in the case of a simple assault where no question of law arises, and where the prisoner charged is capable of presenting his own case. To hold otherwise would result in wholly unnecessary delays in many cases, to the detriment of all concerned including the prisoner charged, and to wholly unnecessary waste of time and money, contrary to the public interest. Indeed, to hold otherwise would not only cause injustice to prisoners; it would also lead to an adventitious distinction being drawn between disciplinary offences which happen also to be crimes and those which happen not to be so, for the punishments liable to be imposed do not depend upon any such distinction. . . .

Lord Mackay of Clashfern L.C., Lord Bridge of Harwich, Lord Ackner and Lord Oliver of Aylmerton agreed with the above speech.

Appeals dismissed.

Notes

1. The criteria articulated by Webster J. in *R. v Secretary of State for the Home Department Ex p. Tarrant* [1985] Q.B. 251, were the following:

    (a) The seriousness of the charge and of the potential penalty;
    (b) Whether any points of law are likely to arise in the proceedings;
    (c) The capacity of the prisoner to present his/her own case (i.e. their intellectual and educational abilities);
    (d) Procedural difficulties (*e.g.* whether the prisoner has been able to interview relevant witnesses prior to the hearing);
    (e) The need for reasonable speed in making an adjudication;
    (f) The need for fairness between prisoners and between prisoners/prison officers.

2. In *Tarrant*, it was reported that, nationally, boards of visitors reached approximately 3,000 adjudications per year. Woolf L.J. (as he then was) recommended the abolition of the disciplinary powers of boards of visitors, because of the difficulty of combining that role with the boards' responsibility for protecting the interests of prisoners, in his report *Prison Disturbances* (Cm.1456) (examining the Strangeways and other subsequent prison riots). He favoured increasing the role of the ordinary criminal courts in dealing with serious misbehaviour inside prisons. The Government accepted this recommendation and from April 1992 boards of visitors ceased to have a role in disciplinary adjudication.

3. M.J. Dixon is critical of Lord Goff's speech in *Hone* because:

"It is unfortunate that the House of Lords in *Hone* did not seize the opportunity to examine the whole matter in closer detail. As it is, they were content to rely on general propositions about the flexible nature of natural justice and on previous decisions which are not altogether satisfactory. The jurisdiction of a board of visitors is non-voluntary, and it is not enough to rely on cases that deny the right of legal representation before tribunals whose jurisdiction depends wholly on the consent of the parties . . . However, not only has the decision in *Hone* extinguished any possibility of a prisoner being entitled to legal representation as of right, Lord Goff's emphasis on administrative efficiency may encourage visitors to exercise that discretion against a prisoner in all but the most extreme cases" ((1989) 40 N.I.L.Q. 71 at 77).

4. Parties to proceedings in the ordinary courts have a right to be advised, in court, by a lay person who is not a qualified lawyer. The court can only exclude such an adviser:

". . . if it becomes apparent that the 'assistance' is unreasonable in nature or degree or if it becomes apparent that the 'assistance' is not being provided bona fide, but for an improper purpose or is being provided in a way which is inimical to the proper and efficient administration of justice, by for example, causing the party to waste time, advising the introduction of irrelevant issues or the asking of irrelevant or repetitious questions" (at 946).

The Court of Appeal, therefore, held that justices had acted unlawfully in denying a defendant the right to be assisted by an adviser during proceedings for a liability order in respect of failure to pay the community charge ("poll tax"), when there was no reason to exclude the adviser: see *R. v Leicester City JJ. Ex p. Barrow* [1991] 3 All E.R. 935.

5. The European Court of Human Rights has held that Art.6(3)(c) ECHR obliges the United Kingdom to provide legal assistance at a magistrates' court hearing (at no cost to the defendant if he/she cannot afford to pay) for a defendant facing a sentence of imprisonment for failing to pay the community charge: see *Benham v UK* (1996) 22 E.H.R.R. 293.

6. *Ex p. Hone* is one in a series of cases that hold that prisoners must be given an effective opportunity to make representations before decisions are made that may affect their release date. See, *e.g. Doody* (below, p.743); *R. (on the application of Hirst) v Secretary of State for the Home Department (Category Status)* [2001] EWCA Civ 378, *The Times*, March 22, 2001 (recategorisation of category status from C to B that significantly affected prospects for release on licence).

The same applies to decisions that have a significant impact on the conditions of detention, such as a decision to move a prisoner into a segregation unit (*R. (on the application of SP) v Secretary of State for the Home Department* [2004] EWHC 1418).

(3) A right to cross-examine opponents?

BUSHELL v SECRETARY OF STATE FOR THE ENVIRONMENT

[1981] A.C. 75; [1980] 3 W.L.R. 22; [1980] 2 All E.R. 608; (1980) 78 L.G.R. 269 (HOUSE OF LORDS)

The Department had proposed the construction of two adjoining stretches of motorway in the West Midlands. Local residents, and other amenity groups, objected to the proposals. Under the terms of the Highways Act 1959, the Secretary of State was obliged to hold a local public inquiry in such objections. One local inquiry was convened to hear the above objections (100 different parties were present at the inquiry which lasted for 100 working days). The respondents were objectors who sought to challenge the statistical methods used by the department to predict future traffic needs. The inspector allowed the respondents to criticise the department's methodology (contained in the "Red Book") and to call expert witnesses to support their criticisms, but he would not permit them to cross-examine the department's representatives upon this matter. The inspector noted the respondents' criticisms in his report which was generally favourable to the department's proposals. The Secretary of State accepted the inspector's recommendations and made schemes for the construction of these sections of motorway. The respondents applied, under Sch.2 to the 1959 Act, to the High Court to quash the schemes on the ground, *inter alia*, that the inspector had been wrong in law to disallow them from cross-examining departmental representatives on the "Red Book". The High Court dismissed their application, but the Court of Appeal (Templeman L.J. dissenting) allowed their appeal. The Secretary of State appealed to the House of Lords.

LORD DIPLOCK: The provision and improvement of a national system of routes for through traffic for which a government department and not a local authority should be the highway authority has formed a part of national transport policy since the passing of the Trunk Roads Act in 1936. As part of this national network, or superimposed upon it, there have been constructed by stages during the course of the last 30 years special roads familiarly known as motorways which were first authorised by the Special Roads Act 1949. The construction of motorways is a lengthy and expensive process and it has been the policy of successive governments, which would in any event have been dictated by necessity, to construct the network by stages. The order in which the various portions of the network are to be constructed thus becomes as much a matter of government transport policy as the total extent and configuration of the motorway network itself. It also has the consequence that schemes for the provision of special roads which the Minister proposes to make under section 11 of the Highways Act 1959 deal with comparatively short stretches in a particular locality of what, when the other stretches are completed, will be integral parts of the national network. It follows, therefore, that there will be a whole series of schemes relating to successive stretches of the national network of motorways each of which may be the subject of separate local inquiries under Schedule 1, paragraph 9, to the Act.

. . . So from the publication of the draft scheme to the actual construction of the stretch of motorway which is authorised the process is necessarily a long one in the course of which circumstances may alter and even government policy may change.

Where it is proposed that land should be acquired by a government department or local authority and works constructed on it for the benefit of the public either as a whole or in a particular locality, the holding of a public inquiry before the acquisition of the land and the construction of the works are authorised has formed a familiar part of the administrative process ever since authorisation by ministerial order of compulsory acquisition of land for public purposes began to be used to replace parliamentary authorisation by Private Bill procedure in the nineteenth century. The essential characteristics of a "local inquiry", an expression which when appearing in a statute has by now acquired a special meaning as a term of legal art, are that it is held in public in the locality in which the works that are the subject of the proposed scheme are situated by a person appointed by the Minister upon whom the statute has conferred the power in his administrative discretion to decide whether to confirm the scheme. The subject-matter of the inquiry is the objections to the proposed scheme that have been received by the Minister from local authorities and from private persons in the vicinity of the proposed stretch of motorway whose interests may be adversely affected, and in consequence of which he is required by Schedule 1, paragraph 9, to hold the inquiry. The purpose of the inquiry is to provide the Minister with as much information about those objections as will ensure that in reaching his decision he will have weighed the harm to local interests and private persons who may be adversely affected by the scheme against the public benefit which the scheme is likely to achieve and will not have failed to take into consideration any matters which he ought to have taken into consideration.

. . . The Highways Act 1959 being itself silent as to the procedure to be followed at the inquiry, that procedure, within such limits as are necessarily imposed by its qualifying for the description "local inquiry", must necessarily be left to the discretion of the Minister or the inspector appointed by him to hold the inquiry on his behalf, or partly to one and partly to the other. In exercising that discretion, as in exercising any other administrative function, they owe a constitutional duty to perform it fairly and honestly and to the best of their ability, as Lord Greene M.R. pointed out in his neglected but luminous analysis of the quasi-judicial and administrative functions of a Minister as confirming authority of a compulsory purchase order made by a local authority, which is to be found in *B. Johnson & Co. (Builders) Ltd v Minister of Health* [1947] 2 All E.R. 395, 399–400. That judgment contains a salutary warning against applying to procedures involved in the making of administrative decisions concepts that are appropriate to the conduct of ordinary civil litigation between private parties. So rather than use such phrases as "natural justice" which may suggest that the prototype is only to be found in procedures followed by English courts of law, I prefer to put it that in the absence of any rules made under the Tribunals and Inquiries Act 1971, the only requirement of the Highways Act 1959, as to the procedure to be followed at a local inquiry held pursuant to Schedule 1, paragraph 9, is that it must be fair to all those who have an interest in the decision that will follow it whether they have been represented at the inquiry or not. What is a fair procedure to be adopted at a particular inquiry will depend upon the nature of its subject-matter.

What is fair procedure is to be judged not in the light of constitutional fictions as to the relationship between the Minister and the other servants of the Crown who serve in the government department of which he is the head, but in the light of the practical realities as to the way in which administrative decisions involving forming judgments based on technical considerations are reached. To treat the Minister in his decision-making capacity as someone separate and distinct from the department of government of which he is the political head and for whose actions he alone in constitutional theory is accountable to Parliament is to ignore not only practical realities but also Parliament's intention. Ministers come and go; departments, though their names may change from time to time, remain. Discretion in making administrative decisions is conferred upon a Minister not as an individual but as the holder of an office in which he will have available to him in arriving at his decision the collective knowledge, experience and expertise of all those who serve the Crown in the department of which, for the time being, he is the political head. The collective knowledge, technical as well as factual, of the civil servants in the department and their collective expertise is to be treated as the Minister's own knowledge, his own expertise. It is they who in reality will have prepared the draft scheme for his approval; it is they who will in the first instance consider the objections to the scheme and the report of the inspector by whom any local inquiry has been held and it is they who will give to the Minister the benefit of their combined experience, technical knowledge and expert opinion on all matters raised in the objections and the report. This is an integral part of the decision-making process itself; it is not to be equiparated with the Minister receiving evidence, expert opinion or advice from sources outside the department after the local inquiry has been closed. . . .

It is evident that an inquiry of this kind and magnitude is quite unlike any civil litigation and that the inspector conducting it must have a wide discretion as to the procedure to be followed in order to achieve its objectives. These are to enable him to ascertain the facts that are relevant to each of the objections, to understand the arguments for and against them and, if he feels qualified to do so, to weigh their respective merits, so that he may provide the Minister with a fair, accurate and adequate report on these matters.

Proceedings at a local inquiry at which many parties wish to make representations without incurring the expense of legal representation and cannot attend the inquiry throughout its length ought to be as informal as is consistent with achieving those objectives. To "over-judicialise" the inquiry by insisting on observance of the procedures of a court of justice which professional lawyers alone are competent to operate effectively in the interests of their clients would not be fair. It would, in my view, be quite fallacious to suppose that at an inquiry of this kind the only fair way of ascertaining matters of fact and expert opinion is by the oral testimony of witnesses who are subjected to cross-examination on behalf of parties who disagree with what they have said. Such procedure is peculiar to litigation conducted in courts that follow the common law system of procedure; it plays no part in the procedure of courts of justice under legal systems based upon the civil law, including the majority of our fellow Member States of the European Community; even in our own Admiralty Court it is not availed of for the purpose of ascertaining expert opinion on questions of navigation—the judge acquires information about this by private inquiry from assessors who are not subject to cross-examination by the parties. So refusal by an inspector to allow a party to cross-examine orally at a local inquiry a person who has made statements of facts or has expressed expert opinions is not unfair *per se*.

Whether fairness requires an inspector to permit a person who has made statements on matters of fact or opinion, whether expert or otherwise, to be cross-examined by a party to the inquiry who wishes to dispute a particular statement must depend on all the circumstances. In the instant case, the question arises in connection with expert opinion upon a technical matter. Here the relevant circumstances in considering whether fairness requires that cross-examination should be allowed include the nature of the topic upon which the opinion is expressed, the qualifications of the maker of the statement to deal with that topic, the forensic competence of the proposed cross-examiner, and, most important, the inspector's own views as to whether the likelihood that cross-examination will enable him to make a report which will be more useful to the Minister in reaching his decision than it otherwise would be is sufficient to justify any expense and inconvenience to other parties to the inquiry which would be caused by any resulting prolongation of it.

The circumstances in which the question of cross-examination arose in the instant case were the following. Before the inquiry opened each objector had received a document containing a statement of the Minister's reasons for proposing the draft scheme. It was itself a long and detailed document, and was accompanied by an even longer and more detailed one called "Strategic Studies Information", which gave an account of various traffic studies that had been undertaken between 1964 and 1973 in the area to be served by M42 Bromsgrove and M40 Warwick, the methodology used for those studies and the conclusions reached. The second paragraph of the Minister's statement of reasons said: "The Government's policy to build these new motorways" (*sc.* for which the two schemes provided) "will not be open to debate at the forthcoming inquiries [*sic*]: the Secretary of State is answerable to Parliament for this policy."

"Policy" as descriptive of departmental decisions to pursue a particular course of conduct is a protean word and much confusion in the instant case has, in my view, been caused by a failure to define the sense in which it can properly be used to describe a topic which is unsuitable to be the subject of an investigation as to its merits at an inquiry at which only persons with local interests affected by the scheme are entitled to be represented. A decision to construct a nationwide network of motorways is clearly one of government policy in the widest sense of the term. Any proposal to alter it is appropriate to be the subject of debate in Parliament, not of separate investigations in each of scores of local inquiries before individual inspectors up and down the country upon whatever material happens to be presented to them at the particular inquiry over which they preside. So much the respondents readily concede.

At the other extreme the selection of the exact line to be followed through a particular locality by a motorway designed to carry traffic between the destinations that it is intended to serve would not be described as involving government policy in the ordinary sense of that term. It affects particular local interests only and normally does not affect the interests of any wider section of the public, unless a suggested variation of the line would involve exorbitant expenditure of money raised by taxation. It is an appropriate subject for full investigation at a local inquiry and is one on which the inspector by whom the investigation is to be conducted can form a judgment on which to base a recommendation which deserves to carry weight with the Minister in reaching a final decision as to the line the motorway should follow.

Between the black and white of these two extremes, however, there is what my noble and learned friend, Lord Lane, in the course of the hearing described as a "grey area". Because of the time that must elapse between the preparation of any scheme and the completion of the stretch of motorway that it authorises, the department, in deciding in what order new stretches of the national network ought to be constructed, has adopted a uniform practice throughout the country of making a major factor in its decision the likelihood that there will be a traffic need for that particular stretch of motorway in 15 years from the date when the scheme was prepared. This is known as the "design year" of the scheme. Priorities as between one stretch of motorway and another have got to be determined somehow. Semasiologists may argue whether the adoption by the department of a uniform practice for doing this is most appropriately described as government policy or as something else. But the propriety of adopting it is clearly a matter fit to be debated in a wider forum and with the assistance of a wider range of relevant material than any investigation at an individual local inquiry is likely to provide; and in that sense at least, which is the relevant sense for present purposes, its adoption forms part of government policy.

The "need" for a new road to carry traffic between given destinations is an imprecise concept. If it is to be used as an important factor in comparing one situation with another for the purpose of determining priorities, there must be uniform criteria by which that need in each locality is to be measured. The test of future needs in the design year which the department has adopted is: whether, if the new stretch of motorway is not constructed, there will be undue congestion of traffic on existing roads, either in the locality or forming other parts of the national network of motorways, for which the new stretch of motorway would provide an alternative route. To apply this test of need to a design year 15 years ahead involves, among other things, estimating (1) the amount of traffic that the existing roads in the locality are capable of bearing without becoming so congested as to involve unacceptable delays; and (2) the amount of traffic that in the absence of the new stretch of motorway would in the design year be using those existing roads which the motorway is intended to relieve.

The methods used by the department for arriving at these estimates are very complicated. So far as I am capable of understanding them as one who is by now (I hope) a reasonably well-informed layman, it is obvious to me that no one who is not an expert in this esoteric subject could form a useful judgment as to their merits. The methods used are kept under periodical review by the department's own experts as a result of which they are revised from time to time. They are described in published documents. One which it will be necessary to mention dealt with the capacity of rural roads; but that which is most relevant to the respondents' complaint about refusal to permit cross-examination in the instant case has been referred to as the "Red Book". It was published in 1968 under the title *Traffic Prediction for Rural Roads (Advisory Manual on)* and described the method that had been used for predicting the growth of traffic up to the design year on the roads which the M42 Bromsgrove and M40 Warwick were intended to relieve. Important features of the method set out in the Red Book for predicting traffic that will be using the roads in a particular locality are the assumptions (1) that in general, traffic on rural roads throughout the country will grow at the same rate in all areas, except where exceptional changes can be foreseen as likely to take place in a particular locality; and (2) that the annual rate of growth will fall off as vehicle ownership in the country approaches saturation point; and that the best way of predicting what the growth will have been up to a particular design year is by assuming that it can be graphically represented by a curve that is asymptotic (*i.e.* broadly "S"-shaped) and whose shape where it represents future years can be extrapolated (*i.e.* predicted) from the shape of the curve which represents the observed annual increase in vehicle registrations over past years. It was recognised that predictions as applied to individual roads could only be very approximate and were subject to margins of error as high as 10 per cent to 20 per cent.

The decisions to make these two assumptions for the purpose of calculating and comparing what traffic needs will be in all localities throughout the country in which it is proposed to construct future stretches of the national network of motorway might not, in a general context, be most naturally described as being government policy; but if a decision to determine priorities in the construction of future stretches of the national network of motorways by reference to their respective traffic needs in a design year 15 years ahead can properly be described as government policy, as I think it can, the definition of "traffic needs" to be used for the purposes of applying the policy, *viz.* traffic needs as assessed by methods described in the Red Book and the departmental publication on the capacity of rural roads, may well be regarded as an essential element in the policy. But whether the uniform adoption of particular methods of assessment is described as policy or methodology, the merits of the methods adopted are, in my view, clearly not appropriate for investigation at individual local inquiries by an inspector whose consideration of the matter is necessarily limited by the material which happens to be presented to him at the particular inquiry which he is holding. It would be a rash inspector who based on that kind of material a positive recommendation to the Minister that the method of predicting traffic needs throughout the country should be changed and it would be an unwise Minister who acted in reliance on it.

At the local inquiry into the M42 Bromsgrove and the M40 Warwick, objectors including the respondents, whose property would be affected by the scheme, and the M42 Action Committee, a "pressure group" which supported them primarily upon environmental grounds, had studied in advance the Minister's reasons for the schemes, the "Strategic Studies Information" and the Red Book. They came to the inquiry prepared to criticise the methods used to predict the traffic needs in the design year on local roads in the localities of the M42 Bromsgrove and M40 Warwick and to call evidence of witnesses with professional qualifications to testify to their unreliability. The circumstances in which the inspector was induced to give an early ruling as to what evidence he would admit and what cross-examination he would allow are recounted in the speeches of my noble and learned friends. In the result— and when one is considering natural justice it is the result that matters—the objectors were allowed to voice their criticisms of the methods used to predict traffic needs for the purposes of the two schemes and to call such expert evidence as they wanted to in support of their criticisms. What they were not allowed to do was to cross-examine the department's representatives upon the reliability and statistical validity of the methods of traffic prediction described in the Red Book and applied by the department for the purpose of calculating and comparing traffic needs in all localities throughout the country. This is the only matter in relation to the conduct of the inquiry by the inspector of which complaint is made.

Was this unfair to the objectors? For the reasons I have already given and in full agreement with the minority judgment of Templeman L.J. in the Court of Appeal, I do not think it was. I think that the inspector was right in saying that the use of the concept of traffic needs in the design year *assessed by a particular method* as the yardstick by which to determine the order in which particular stretches of the national network of motorways should be constructed was government policy in the relevant sense of being a topic unsuitable for investigation by individual inspectors upon whatever material happens to be presented to them at local inquiries held throughout the country . . . .

LORD EDMUND-DAVIES (dissenting): . . . My Lords, for the present I defer considering whether the outcome of the inquiry would, or might have been, different had cross-examination been allowed. The topic now under consideration relates solely to the propriety of its refusal. I have natural diffidence in differing from your Lordships in regarding that refusal as clearly wrong, but such is my considered view. It is beyond doubt that the inspector could—and should—disallow questions relating to the merits of government policy. But matters of policy are matters which involve the exercise of political judgment, and matters of fact and expertise do not become "policy" merely because a department of government relies on them. And, as the Franks committee had put it in 1957: "We see no reason why the factual basis for a departmental

view should not be explained and its validity tested in cross-examination."
(*Report of the Committee on Administrative Tribunals and Inquiries* (Cmnd.
218), para.316.)

Then, if the Red Book is not "government policy," on what basis can the
cross-examination of departmental witnesses relying on its methodology be
properly refused? Sir Douglas Frank Q.C. surprisingly asserted, 76 L.G.R.
460, 472–473 (a) that its *authors* "were the only persons competent to
answer questions on it", and (b) that "it seems to me necessarily to follow
that the inspector was entitled to disallow cross-examination on it of a person
who had had nothing to do with its preparation". But expert witnesses frequently quote and rely upon the publications of others and are regularly
cross-examined upon the works so relied upon even though they played no
part in their preparation. Nor, my Lords, is it right to assume, as was suggested in the course of the inquiry and as some of your Lordships appear to
accept, that Mr Brooks, the highly qualified and experienced traffic engineer,
would have been incompetent to deal in cross-examination with questions
directed to establishing the unreliability of the Red Book methodology upon
which he himself heavily relied, albeit not without some emendations. Indeed,
in paragraph 567 of this report the inspector described the witness as "thoroughly competent".

Pausing there, I conclude that the grounds hitherto considered for refusing cross-examination are unacceptable. But is it the case that, in an inquiry
such as that with which this House is presently concerned, some special rule
prevails which renders regular a procedure which in other circumstances
would undoubtedly have been condemned as irregular? The general law
may, I think, be summarised in this way: (a) In holding an administrative
inquiry (such as that presently being considered), the inspector was performing quasi-judicial duties. (b) He must therefore discharge them in
accordance with the rules of natural justice. (c) Natural justice requires that
objectors (no less than departmental representatives) be allowed to cross-
examine witnesses called for the other side on all relevant matters, be
they matters of fact or matters of expert opinion. (d) In the exercise of jurisdiction outside the field of criminal law, the only restrictions on cross-
examination are those general and well-defined exclusionary rules which
govern the admissibility of relevant evidence (as to which reference may
conveniently be had to *Cross on Evidence*, (5th ed., 1979), p.17); beyond
those restrictions there is *no* discretion on the civil side to exclude cross-
examination on relevant matters.

There is ample authority for the view that, as Professor H.W.R. Wade Q.C.
puts it (*Administrative Law* (4th ed., 1977), p.418): ". . . it is once again quite
clear that the principles of natural justice apply to administrative acts generally." And there is a massive body of accepted decisions establishing that
natural justice requires that a party be given an opportunity of challenging by
cross-examination witnesses called by another party on relevant issues; see, for
example, *Marriott v Minister of Health* (1935) 52 T.L.R. 63, *per* Swift J.,
at 67—compulsory purchase orders inquiry; *Errington v Minister of Health*
[1935] 1 K.B. 249, *per* Maugham L.J., at 272—clearance order; *R. v Deputy
Industrial Injuries Commissioner, Ex p. Moore* [1965] 1 Q.B. 465, *per*
Diplock L.J., at 488A, 490E–G; and *Wednesbury Corporation v Ministry of
Housing and Local Government (No. 2)* [1966] 2 Q.B. 275, *per* Diplock L.J.,
at 302G–303A—local government inquiry.

Then is there any reason why those general rules should have been departed from in the present case? We have already seen that the parameters of the inquiry, as agreed to by the department representatives, embraced *need* as a topic relevant to be canvassed and reported upon. We have already considered the unacceptable submission that the Red Book was "government policy". And, while I am alive to the inconvenience of different inspectors arriving at different conclusions regarding different sections of a proposed trunk road, the risk of that happening cannot, in my judgment, have any bearing upon the question whether justice was done at this particular inquiry, which I have already explained was, in an important respect, unique of its kind.

There remains to be considered the wholly novel suggestion, which has found favour with your Lordships, that there is a "grey area"—existing, as I understand, somewhere between government policy (which admittedly may not be subjected to cross-examination) and the exact "line" of a section of a motorway (which may be)—and that in relation to topics falling within the "grey area" cross-examination is a matter of discretion. I find that suggestion to be too nebulous to be grasped. Furthermore, *why* such an area should exist has not been demonstrated—certainly not to my satisfaction—nor have its boundaries been defined, unlike those existing restrictions on cross-examination to which I have already referred. And I confess to abhorrence of the notion that any such area exists. For the present case demonstrates that its adoption is capable of resulting in an individual citizen denied justice nevertheless finding himself with no remedy to right the wrong done to him.

My Lords, it is for the foregoing reasons that I find myself driven to the conclusion that the refusal in the instant case to permit cross-examination on what, by common agreement, was evidence of cardinal importance was indefensible and unfair and, as such, a denial of natural justice. . . .

VISCOUNT DILHORNE and LORD LANE delivered concurring speeches.
LORD FRASER OF TULLYBELTON agreed with them and LORD DIPLOCK.

Appeal allowed.

Questions
How does Lord Diplock's elaboration of the concept of "policy" differ from that articulated by Lord Edmund-Davies? Is it significant that Lord Diplock subjects local inquiries to the requirements of "fairness", whereas Lord Edmund-Davies applies the rules of natural justice to the holding of such inquiries?

Notes
1. For a fuller consideration of inquiries see above, pp.111–145.
2. The statutory provisions regulating highway inquiries are now contained in the Highways Act 1980 and the Highways (Inquiries Procedure) Rules 1994, SI 1994/3263.
3. Professor Jackson concludes:

"Dicta abound for, and against the view that natural justice (or fairness) requires a right to cross-examine. To take them out of context as authority for an absolute rule is misleading. *Bushell* demonstrates, in an unusually full discussion of the problem, that the answer depends on a number of factors including the purpose of the hearing, the issue involved, the nature of the evidence" ((1980) 96 L.Q.R. 497).

4. Giving the opinion of the Privy Council, Lord Diplock stated that in the context of a New Zealand Royal Commission (a body analogous to a Tribunal of Inquiry in the United Kingdom):

"The technical rules of evidence applicable to civil or criminal litigation form no part of the rules of natural justice. What is required . . . is that the decision to make the finding must be based upon some material that tends logically to show the existence of facts consistent with the finding and that the reasoning supportive of the finding, if it be disclosed, is not logically self-contradictory"

(*Mahon v Air New Zealand Ltd* [1984] A.C. 808 at 821).

(4) *Can a breach of the right to a fair hearing be cured by a later rehearing or appeal?*

CALVIN v CARR

[1980] A.C. 574; [1979] 2 W.L.R. 755; [1979] 2 All E.R. 440 (PRIVY COUNCIL)

The appellant was the part-owner of a racehorse which competed in a race organised under the auspices of the Australian Jockey Club. The horse did not run as well as expected and his performance was subject to a stewards' inquiry. The stewards interviewed, *inter alios*, the jockey, the trainer and the appellant. They also saw film of the horse running in other races. Thirteen days after the race, the stewards determined that the jockey was guilty of an offence under the Club's Rules of Racing (namely not running a horse on its merits) and that the appellant was a party to that breach. They disqualified the appellant from membership of the Club for one year, which prevented him from entering any horse in a race organised by the Club for that period. The appellant exercised his right, under the Rules, to appeal against the stewards' decision to a committee of the Club. Before the committee he was represented by counsel and had full opportunity to call witnesses and subject others to cross-examination. The committee dismissed his appeal. The appellant then brought an action in the Supreme Court of New South Wales for a declaration that his disqualification from the Club was unlawful and an injunction to restrain the Club from acting on the purported disqualification. The major argument advanced by the appellant was that the stewards had acted in breach of the right to a fair hearing, consequently their decision was invalid, and this defect could not be cured by a lawful hearing before the appellate committee. The action was dismissed by the Australian court, so the appellant brought this appeal before the Privy Council.

LORD WILBERFORCE: . . . The plaintiff's second argument can be stated, for purposes of description, as being that such defects of natural justice as may have existed as regards the proceedings before the stewards were not capable of being cured by the appeal proceedings before the committee, even though, as was not contested before this Board, these were correctly and fairly conducted. The defendants contend the contrary. . . . [T]heir Lordships recognise and indeed assert that no clear and absolute rule can be laid down on the question whether defects in natural justice appearing at an original hearing, whether administrative or quasi-judicial, can be "cured" through appeal proceedings. The situations in which this issue arises are too diverse, and the rules by which they are governed so various, that this must be so. There are, however, a number of typical situations as to which some general principle can be stated. First there are cases where the rules provide for a rehearing by the original body, or some fuller or enlarged form of it. This situation may be found in relation to social clubs. It is not difficult in such cases to reach the conclusion that the first hearing is superseded by the second, or, putting it in contractual terms, the parties are taken to have agreed to accept the decision of the hearing body, whether original or adjourned. Examples of this are *De Verteuil v Knaggs* [1918] A.C. 557, 563; *Posluns v Toronto Stock Exchange and Gardiner* (1965) 53 D.L.R. (2d) 193; *Re Clark and Ontario Securities Commission* (1966) 56 D.L.R. (2d) 585; *Re Chromex Nickel Mines Ltd* (1970) 16 D.L.R. (3d) 273; and see also *Ridge v Baldwin* [1964] A.C. 40, 79, *per* Lord Reid.

At the other extreme are cases, where, after examination of the whole hearing structure, in the context of the particular activity to which it relates (trade union membership, planning, employment, etc.) the conclusion is reached that a complainant has the right to nothing less than a fair hearing both at the original and at the appeal stage. This was the result reached by Megarry J. in *Leary v National Union of Vehicle Builders* [1971] Ch.34. In his judgment in that case the judge seems to have elevated the conclusion thought proper in that case into a rule of general application. In an eloquent passage he said, at 49:

> "If the rules and the law combine to give the member the right to a fair trial and the right of appeal, why should he be told that he ought to be satisfied with an unjust trial and a fair appeal? . . . As a general rule . . . I hold that a failure of natural justice in the trial body cannot be cured by a sufficiency of natural justice in an appellate body."

In their Lordships' opinion this is too broadly stated. It affirms a principle which may be found correct in a category of cases: these may very well include trade union cases, where movement solidarity and dislike of the rebel, or renegade, may make it difficult for appeals to be conducted in an atmosphere of detached impartiality and so make a fair trial at the first—probably branch—level an essential condition of justice. But to seek to apply it generally overlooks, in their Lordships' respectful opinion, both the existence of the first category, and the possibility that, intermediately, the conclusion to be reached, on the rules and on the contractual context, is that those who have joined in an organisation, or contract, should be taken to have agreed to accept what in the end is a fair decision, notwithstanding some initial defect.

In their Lordship's judgment such intermediate cases exist. In them it is for the court, in the light of the agreements made, and in addition having regard to the course of proceedings, to decide whether, at the end of the day, there has been a fair result, reached by fair methods, such as the parties should fairly be taken to have accepted when they joined the association. Naturally there may be instances when the defect is so flagrant, the consequences so severe, that the most perfect of appeals or rehearings will not be sufficient to produce a just result. Many rules (including those now in question) anticipate that such a situation may arise by giving power to remit for a new hearing. There may also be cases when the appeal process is itself less than perfect: it may be vitiated by the same defect as the original proceedings: or short of that there may be doubts whether the appeal body embarked on its task without predisposition or whether it had the means to make a fair and full inquiry, for example where it has no material but a transcript of what was before the original body. In such cases it would no doubt be right to quash the original decision. These are all matters (and no doubt there are others) which the court must consider.

Whether these intermediate cases are to be regarded as exceptions from a general rule, as stated by Megarry J., or as a parallel category covered by a rule of equal status, is not in their Lordships' judgment necessary to state, or indeed a matter of great importance. What is important is the recognition that such cases exist, and that it is undesirable in many cases of domestic disputes, particularly in which an inquiry and appeal process has been established, to introduce too great a measure of formal judicialisation. While flagrant cases of injustice, including corruption or bias, must always be firmly dealt with by the courts, the tendency in their Lordships' opinion in matters of domestic disputes should be to leave these to be settled by the agreed methods without requiring the formalities of judicial processes to be introduced. . . .

It remains to apply the principles above stated to the facts of the present case. In the first place, their Lordships are clearly of the view that the proceedings before the committee were in the nature of an appeal, not by way of an invocation, or use, of whatever original jurisdiction the committee may have had . . . .

In addition to these formal requirements, a reviewing court must take account of the reality behind them. Races are run at short intervals; bets must be disposed of according to the result. Stewards are there in order to take rapid decisions as to such matters as the running of horses, being entitled to use the evidence of their eyes and their experience. As well as acting inquisitorially at the stage of deciding the result of a race, they may have to consider disciplinary action: at this point rules of natural justice become relevant. These require, at the least, that persons should be formally charged, heard in their own defence, and know the evidence against them. These essentials must always be observed but it is inevitable, and must be taken to be accepted, that there may not be time for procedural refinements. It is in order to enable decisions reached in this way to be reviewed at leisure that the appeal procedure exists. Those concerned know that they are entitled to a full hearing with opportunities to bring evidence and have it heard. But they know also that this appeal hearing is governed by the Rules of Racing, and that it remains an essentially domestic proceeding, in which experience and opinions as to what is in the interest of racing as a whole play a large part, and in which the standards are those which have come to be accepted over the history of this sporting activity. All those who partake in it have accepted the Rules of Racing, and the standards which lie behind them: they must also have accepted to be bound by the decisions of the bodies set up under those rules so long as when the process of reaching these decisions has been terminated, they can be said, by an objective observer, to have had fair treatment and consideration of their case on its merits.

In their Lordships' opinion precisely this can, indeed must, be said of the present case. The plaintiff's case has received, overall, full and fair consideration, and a decision, possibly a hard one, reached against him. There is no basis on which the court ought to interfere, and his appeal must fail. . . .

Appeal dismissed.

Notes

1. Elliott considers that the most significant aspect of this judgment was "the way it eschews statements of abstract principle". Instead, he approves of Lord Wilberforce's pragmatic attitude towards the tailoring of procedural obligations to different decision-making contexts. But, Elliott wonders whether "an administrative law adversarial

action before judges with necessarily limited knowledge may not be the best place to assess the procedures that particular situations require . . .": M. Elliott, "Appeals, Principles and Pragmatism in Natural Justice" (1980) 43 M.L.R. 66.

Do the views of Elliott represent a fundamental attack upon the process of procedural review undertaken by the courts? What other institutions might be better suited to this task?

2. Although *Calvin v Carr* concerns the decision of a sporting body, it is clear that the principles stated by Lord Wilberforce may apply to administrative bodies exercising statutory powers. See *R. v Oxfordshire Local Valuation Panel Ex p. Oxford City Council* (1981) 79 L.G.R. 432; the Court of Appeal decision in *Lloyd v McMahon* [1987] A.C. at 655, 669 (see above, p.722); and *R (on the application of AM) v Governing Body of Kingsmead School* [2002] EWCA Civ 1822, [2003] L.G.R. 371 (apparent bias of governing body in deciding on permanent exclusion can be cured by a fair appeal before the Independent Appeal Panel). *cf. R. v Brent LBC Ex p. Gunning* (1985) 84 L.G.R. 168 (above, p.699). In *Ex p. Gunning* it was argued that any defects in the local council's consultation process could be cured by the procedure in the Education Act 1980, s.12(3), (4) and (6), under which objections could be made to the Secretary of State. Hodgson J. doubted whether the principles of fairness "developed in the quasi-judicial field of domestic disciplinary proceedings", could apply to "purely administrative procedures of the sort with which we are concerned". If he was wrong on that, he expressed a preference for the approach of Megarry J. in *Leary v National Union of Vehicle Builders* [1971] Ch.34 at 49 (cited by Lord Wilberforce in *Calvin v Carr*, above, p.741), and the approach of the Privy Council in *Calvin v Carr* itself (see at 192–193). Here:

"in any event, in the circumstances of this case, the statutory procedures are themselves fatally flawed by the inadequacies of the previous consultation" (at 193).

3. In the context of criminal cases determined by magistrates' courts a procedurally unfair conviction can be cured by a fair appeal, involving a complete rehearing, before the Crown Court. Turner L.J. held that; "in the field of criminal law, their Lordships knew of no principle, let alone authority, to suggest that a person was entitled to more than one fair trial". However, following *Calvin v Carr*, other considerations might apply when examining the effect of appeals within domestic or specialist tribunal systems. See *R. v Peterborough JJ. Ex p. Dowler* [1997] Q.B. 911. In the subsequent High Court case of *R. v Hereford Magistrates' Court Ex p. Rowlands* [1998] Q.B. 110, Lord Bingham C.J. emphasised that a defendant's right to fairness was stronger in criminal proceedings before magistrates than in administrative or domestic tribunals. It was not doubted that *Dowler* was correctly decided but the decision was not to be treated as authority that a party complaining of procedural unfairness or bias in the magistrates' court should be denied leave to move for judicial review and left to whatever rights he might have in the Crown Court.

(5) *Does fairness require the decision-maker to give reasons?*

R. v SECRETARY OF STATE FOR THE HOME DEPARTMENT Ex p. DOODY

[1994] 1 A.C. 531; [1993] 3 W.L.R. 154; [1993] 3 All E.R. 92 (HOUSE OF LORDS)

The respondents, Doody and three others, were prisoners who had been convicted of murder and sentenced to a mandatory term of life imprisonment. After consulting the trial judge and the Lord Chief Justice, the Home Secretary (or another Minister at the

Home Office) determined the period of imprisonment (the tariff or penal element) that the respondents should serve before the Parole Board would consider whether to recommend, to the Home Secretary, that the prisoner could be released on life licence. The respondents sought judicial review of the Home Secretary's decisions regarding the penal elements of their sentences on the ground that he had followed an unfair procedure. One significant element in the respondents' challenge was their argument that fairness required the Home Secretary to give reasons where he decided to impose a different penal element from that recommended by the judiciary. The High Court dismissed the application, but on appeal the Court of Appeal decided in part in favour of the respondents. The Home Secretary appealed to the House of Lords.

LORD MUSTILL: My Lords, the sentencing of a convicted murderer according to English law is a unique formality. Although it is a very grave occasion it is a formality in this sense, that the task of the judge is entirely mechanical. Once a verdict of guilty is returned the outcome is preordained. No matter what the opinion of the judge on the moral quality of the act, no matter what circumstances there may be of mitigation or aggravation, there is only one course for him to take, namely to pass a sentence of life imprisonment.

This purely formal character of the sentencing process is unique in more than one respect. Thus, whilst it is true that there are other, comparatively unimportant, offences where a particular sentence, or component of a sentence, is prescribed by law, there is in practice no other offence besides murder for which a custodial sentence is mandatory. This singularity is not to be accounted for by the fact that the crime has resulted in the death of the victim, since although the offence of manslaughter carries a maximum penalty of life imprisonment the sentence is discretionary and the maximum is rarely imposed; and other offences in which the death of the victim is an element are subject to maximum fixed terms. Nor can the uniqueness of the mandatory sentence of murder be ascribed to the uniquely wicked quality of the intent which accompanies the fatal act, since as every law student knows, although many who speak in public on the subject appear to overlook, it is possible to commit murder without intending to kill, and many of those convicted of murder have intended to do no more than commit grievous bodily harm. In truth the mandatory life sentence for murder is symbolic.

The sentence of life imprisonment is also unique in that the words which the judge is required to pronounce do not mean what they say. Whilst in a very small minority of cases the prisoner is in the event confined for the rest of his natural life, this is not the usual or the intended effect of a sentence of life imprisonment, as a judge faced with a hard case will take pains to explain to the offender before sentence is passed. But although everyone knows what the words do not mean, nobody knows what they do mean, since the duration of the prisoner's detention depends on a series of recommendations to, and executive decisions by, the Home Secretary, some made at an early stage and others much later, none of which can be accurately forecast at the time when the offender is sent to prison. There is, however, another form of life sentence, of which the philosophy, statutory framework and executive practice are quite different even though the words pronounced by the judge are the same. This is the discretionary life sentence. . . .

The discretionary life sentence may thus be regarded as the sum of two sentences, to be served consecutively. First, a determinate number of years appropriate to the nature and gravity of the offence. This is often called the "tariff" element of the sentence. For my part, although I recognise that this is not inappropriate in the context of a discretionary life sentence, I consider that for reasons which I will later develop it is illogical and misleading when the usage is transferred to a mandatory sentence. I therefore prefer to avoid this terminology and will instead call the first component of the life sentence the "penal element". The second component is an undeterminate period, which the offender begins to serve when the penal element is exhausted. I will call this the "risk element". . . .

The respondents to the appeal . . . were each convicted of murder and sentenced to life imprisonment on various occasions between 1985 and 1987. It is possible to deduce from the dates fixed by the Secretary of State for the Home Department for the first review of their cases by the Parole Board (and in the case of Pierson from correspondence with the Home Office) that the penal elements of these life sentences fixed by Secretary of State were respectively 15 years, not more than 20 years; 12 years; and 11 years. So much each prisoner knows, but what he does not know is why the particular term was selected, and he is now trying to find out: partly from an obvious human desire to be told the reason for a decision so gravely affecting his future, and partly because he hopes that once the information is obtained he may be able to point out errors of fact or reasoning and thereby persuade the Secretary of State to change his mind, or if he fails in this to challenge the decision in the Courts. Since the Secretary of State has declined to furnish the information the respondents have set out to obtain it by applications for judicial review.

[His Lordship summarised the history of life sentences.]

My Lords, I believe that this summary has shown how, in contrast with the position as regards discretionary life sentences, the theory and the practice for convicted murderers are out of tune. The theory—and it is the only theory which can justify the retention of the mandatory life sentence—was restated by Mrs Rumbold[4] less than two years ago. It posits that murder is an offence so grave that the proper "tariff" sentence is invariably detention for life, although as a measure of leniency it may be mitigated by release on licence. Yet the practice established by Mr Brittan[5] in 1983 and still in force founds on the proposition that there is concealed within the life term a fixed period of years, apt to reflect not only the requirements of deterrence, but also the moral quality of the individual act (retribution). These two philosophies of sentencing are inconsistent. Either may be defensible, but they cannot both be applied at the same time.

I make this point, not to argue for one regime rather than another, nor to suggest that each of them is unsatisfactory. This is a question for Parliament and we must take the law as it stands. The importance of the inconsistency for present purposes is that the choice of the theory goes a long way towards determining the requirements of fairness with which the practice should conform . . . .

For this reason I believe it impossible to proceed any distance towards determining the present appeal without deciding which of the two competing philosophies is to form the starting point. As it seems to me, the only possible choice is the regime installed by Mr Brittan, as later modified. This is the regime by which successive Home Secretaries have chosen to exercise the wide powers conferred by Parliament, and the arguments have throughout assumed

---

[4] Minister of State at the Home Office in 1991 (ed.).
[5] Home Secretary in 1983 (ed.).

that the regime is firmly in place, and that the task of the courts is to decide what the elements of fairness demand as to the working out of that regime, in the light of the sentencing philosophy which is expressed to underlie it. This being so, I think it essential not to cloud the discussion by introducing the inconsistent theory enunciated by the Minister of State, and I shall leave this entirely out of account. . . .

What does fairness require in the present case? My Lords, I think it unnecessary to refer by name or to quote from, any of the often-cited authorities in which the courts have explained what is essentially an intuitive judgment. They are far too well known. From them, I derive the following. (1) Where an Act of Parliament confers an administrative power there is a presumption that it will be exercised in a manner which is fair in all the circumstances. (2) The standards of fairness are not immutable. They may change with the passage of time, both in the general and in their application to decisions of a particular type. (3) The principles of fairness are not to be applied by rote identically in every situation. What fairness demands is dependent on the context of the decision, and this is to be taken into account in all its aspects. (4) An essential feature of the context is the statute which creates the discretion, as regards both its language and the shape of the legal and administrative system within which the decision is taken. (5) Fairness will very often require that a person who may be adversely affected by the decision will have an opportunity to make representations on his own behalf either before the decision is taken with a view to producing a favourable result, or after it is taken, with a view to procuring its modification, or both. (6) Since the person affected usually cannot make worthwhile representations without knowing what factors may weigh against his interests fairness will very often require that he is informed of the gist of the case which he has to answer.

My Lords, the Secretary of State properly accepts that whatever the position may have been in the past these principles apply in their generality to prisoners, including persons serving life sentences for murder, although their particular situation and the particular statutory regime under which they are detained may require the principles to be applied in a special way. Convesely, the respondents acknowledge that it is not enough for them to persuade the court that some procedure other than the one adopted by the decision-maker would be better or more fair. Rather, they must show that the procedure is actually unfair. The court must constantly bear in mind that it is to the decision-maker, not the court, that Parliament has entrusted not only the making of the decision but also the choice as to how the decision is made. . . .

I accept without hesitation, and mention it only to avoid misunderstanding, that the law does not at present recognise a general duty to give reasons for an administrative decision. Nevertheless, it is equally beyond question that such a duty may in appropriate circumstances be implied, and I agree with the analyses by the Court of Appeal in *R. v Civil Service Appeal Board, Ex p. Cunningham* [1991] 4 All E.R. 310 of the factors which will often be material to such an implication.

Turning to the present dispute I doubt the wisdom of discussing the problem in the contempoary vocabulary of "prisoner's rights", given that as a result of his own act the position of the prisoner is so forcibly distanced from that of the ordinary citizen, nor is it very helpful to say that the Home Secretary should out of simple humanity provide reasons for the prisoner, since any society which operates a penal system is bound to treat some of its citizens in a way which would, in the general, be thought inhumane. I prefer simply to assert that within the inevitable constraints imposed by the statutory framework, the general shape of the administrative regime which ministers have lawfully built around it, and the imperatives of the public interest, the Secretary of State ought to implement the scheme as fairly as he can. The giving of reasons may be inconvenient, but I can see no ground at all why it should be against the public interest: indeed, rather the reverse. This being so, I would ask simply: is a refusal to give reasons fair? I would answer without hesitation that it is not. As soon as the jury returns its verdict the offender knows that he will be locked up for a very long time. For just how long immediately becomes the most important thing in the prisoner's life. When looking at statistics it is easy to fall into the way of thinking that there is not really very much difference between one extremely long sentence and another: and there may not be, in percentage terms. But the percentage reflects a difference of a year or years: a long time for anybody, and longer still for a prisoner. Where a defendant is convicted of, say, several armed robberies he knows that he faces a stiff sentence: he can be advised by reference to a public tariff of the range of sentences he must expect; he hears counsel address the judge on the relationship between his offences and the tariff; he will often hear the judge give an indication during exchanges with counsel of how his mind is working; and when sentence is pronounced he will always be told the reasons for it. So also when a discretionary life sentence is imposed, coupled with an order under s.34. Contrast this with the position of the prisoner sentenced for murder. He never sees the Home Secretary; he has no dialogue with him: he cannot fathom how his mind is working. There is no true tariff, or at least no tariff exposed to public view which might give the prisoner an idea of what to expect. The announcement of his first review date arrives out of thin air, wholly without explanation. The distant oracle has spoken, and that is that.

My Lords, I am not aware that there still exists anywhere else in the penal system a procedure remotely resembling this. The beginnings of an explanation for its unique character might perhaps be found if the Executive had still been putting into practice the theory that the tariff sentence for murder is confinement for life, subject only to a wholly discretionary release on licence: although even in such a case I doubt whether in the modern climate of administrative law such an entirely secret process could be justified. As I hope to have shown, however, this is no longer the practice, and can hardly be sustained any longer as the theory. I therefore simply ask, is it fair that the mandatory life prisoner should be wholly deprived of the information which all other prisoners receive as a matter of course. I am clearly of the opinion that it is not.

My Lords, I can moreover arrive at the same conclusion by a different and more familiar route, of which *Ex p. Cunningham* [1991] 4 All E.R. 310 provides a recent example. It is not, as I understand it, questioned that the decision of the Home Secretary on the penal element is susceptible to judicial review. To mount an effective attack on the decision, given no more material than the facts of the offence and the length of the penal element, the prisoner has virtually no means of ascertaining whether this is an instance where the decision-making process has gone astray. I think it important that there should be an effective means of detecting the kind of error which would entitle the court to intervene, and in practice I regard it as necessary for this purpose that the reasoning of the Home Secretary should be disclosed. If there is any difference between the penal element recommended by the judges and actually imposed by the Home Secretary, this reasoning is bound to include, either explicitly or implicitly, a reason why the Home Secretary has taken a different view. Accordingly, I consider that the respondents are entitled to an affirmative answer on the third issue. . . .

"It is declared that: (1) The Secretary of State is required to afford to a prisoner serving a mandatory life sentence the opportunity to submit in writing representations as to the period he should serve for the purposes of retribution and deterrence before the Secretary of State sets the date of the first review of the prisoner's sentence. (2) Before giving the prisoner the opportunity to make such representations, the Secretary of State is required to inform him of the period recommended by the judiciary as the period he should serve for the purposes of retribution and deterrence, and of any other opinion expressed by the judiciary which is relevant to the Secretary of State's decision as to the appropriate period to be served for these purposes. (3) Secretary of State is obliged to give reasons for departing from the period recommended by the judiciary as the period which he should serve for the purposes of retribution and deterrence."

LORDS KEITH, LANE, TEMPLEMAN AND BROWNE-WILKINSON agreed with the speech given by LORD MUSTILL.

Appeal dismissed. Cross-appeal allowed in part and further declaration granted.

Notes
1. Whilst the House of Lords was not willing in *Doody* to recognise or impose a general duty on all administrative decision-makers to give reasons for their decisions (presumably because such a requirement might be seen as a judicial usurpation of Parliament's legislative function; and the public administration costs could outweigh the benefits to the public), the judgment represents a watershed in the judicial attitude towards the giving of reasons by public persons and bodies. As Lord Mustill noted in the above case

"I find in the more recent cases on judicial review a perceptible trend towards an insistence on greater openness, or if one prefers the contemporary jargon 'transparency', in the making of administrative decisions" (at 561).

By recognising that in certain decision-making contexts fairness necessitated the giving of reasons, their Lordships have opened up the possibility for the lower courts to apply the *Doody* principle in other areas of administration. For commentaries see A.R. Mowbray, (1994) *Journal of Forensic Psychiatry* 137 and N.R. Campbell, [1994] P.L. 184.

The High Court elaborated upon the extent of the duty to give reasons in *R. v Higher Education Funding Council Ex p. Institute of Dental Surgery* [1994] 1 All E.R. 651. There the applicant Institute had its research output assessed by the Funding Council. The Council awarded a lower grade to the Institute's work, compared with the previous grade allocated. As a consequence of this lower grade, the Institute received £270,000 less in research funds from the Council. The Council refused to give any reasons for the lower grade as it considered that the assessment had been made by a peer group of experts using their collective professional judgment. The applicant sought judicial review of the assessment decision, claiming that it violated the concept of fairness in that reasons had not been given for the decision. The judgment of the Divisional Court (Mann L.J. and Sedley J.) was delivered by Sedley J.:

". . . each case will come to rest between two poles, or possibly at one of them: the decision which cries out for reasons, and the decision for which reasons are entirely inapposite. Somewhere between the two poles comes the dividing line separating those cases in which the balance of factors calls for reasons from those where it does not. At present there is no sure indication of where the division comes. . . . No doubt the common law will develop, as the common law does, case by case. It is not entirely satisfactory that this should be so, not least because experience suggests that in the absence of a prior principle irreconcilable or inconsistent decisions will emerge. But from the tenor of the decisions principles will come, and if the common law's pragmatism has a virtue it is that these principles are likely to be robust. At present, however, this court cannot go beyond the proposition that, there being no general obligation to give reasons, there will be decisions for which fairness does not demand reasons" (at 666).

Following on from *Doody* his Lordship concluded that:

"(1) There is no general duty to give reasons for a decision, but there are classes of case where there is such a duty. (2) One such class is where the subject matter is an interest so highly regarded by the law—for example personal liberty—that fairness requires that reasons, at least for particular decisions, be given as of right. (3)(a) Another such class is where the decision appears aberrant. Here fairness may require reasons so that the recipient may know whether the aberration is in the legal sense real (and so challengeable) or apparent. (b) It follows that this class does not include decisions which are themselves challengeable by reference only to the reasons for them. A pure exercise of academic judgment is such a decision" (at 672–673).

Consequently, the application was dismissed. From this judgment we can see the court beginning the refinement of *Doody* by starting to explain the different situations where fairness does require the provision of reasons for decisions.

See further P. Craig, [1994] C.L.J. 282 and Sir Patrick Neill Q.C., "The Duty to Give Reasons: the Openness of Decision-making" in *The Golden Metwand and the Crooked Cord* (Forsyth and Hare, 1999), pp.161–184. Subsequent to the *HEFC* case, Sedley L.J. stated that the law should be regarded as developing, that it was arguable that the categories derived from that case were incomplete, and that even within them there may be exercises of academic judgment which, though never patently aberrant, are nevertheless of sufficient importance to the individual to require that reasons be given for them (*R. v Cambridge University Ex p. Evans* [1998] E.L.R. 515). Sedley L.J. is not sure that the *HEFC* case would necessarily be decided the same way today (*R. (on the application of Wooder) v Feggetter* [2002] EWCA Civ 554 at [41]).

3. Fairness has been held to require reasons to be given for the decision of the Court of Alderman of the City of London to refuse to accept the applicant's election as an Alderman of the City (*R. v City of London Corp. Ex p. Matson* [1997] 1 W.L.R. 765; the court noting that this was an elected office and the effect of rejection on M's reputation); and for the decision of a doctor that a detained patient should be given medical treatment against her will (*Wooder*, above).

4. Fairness did not require a local authority to provide reasons for its decision to refuse an application for a housing renovation grant: *R. v Bristol City Council Ex p. Bailey* (1994) 27 H.L.R. 307. This was not a case where a duty to give reasons arose because the subject-matter was an interest so highly regarded by the law or because the decision appeared aberrant.

Even in a case where a stronger interest is at stake, a duty to give reasons may be held not to arise where that would involve disclosure of sensitive intelligence information (*cf.* the *Gaming Board* case, above p.707; *Hosenball*, above, p.702; *R. (on the application of Tucker) v Director General of the National Crime Squad* [2003] EWCA Civ 03; [2003] I.C.R. 599 (no need to give reasons for termination of officer's secondment to NCS).

5. In borderline cases, it may be difficult to make a distinction between (1) the question whether any reasons are required as a matter of law and (2) the content of the reasons to be given if there is an obligation to do so. This point was made by Lord Woolf L.J. at [27] in *R. (on the application of the Asha Foundation) v The Millennium Commission* [2003] EWCA Civ 88; *The Times*, January 24, 2003. Here, it was held that while the Commission was obliged to explain why an application did not fulfil the eligibility criteria for a capital grant, and to give a particular ground if that was the reason for refusal, if the refusal was simply on the basis that there were other eligible applications that were preferred, there was no need to say more than that. To say more would require an explanation of the full nature and details of the other applications and the Commissioners' views on them, and that would be an "undue burden" and "impracticable as a matter of good administration" (at [29]). See A. Denny, [2003] J.R. 228. *Asha* was followed in *R. (on the application of Agnello) v Hounslow LBC* [2003] EWHC 3112, in respect of decisions as to the allocation of a reduced number of tenancies in a new market (held to be unfair on other grounds).

6. The Home Secretary is obliged to give reasons, because of fairness, where he refuses entry clearance for an alien to enter the United Kingdom on the ground that entry would not be conducive to the public good. Sedley J. considered that this requirement was especially relevant in the context of an application for leave to enter the United Kingdom made by an unpopular person. The judgment was given in the case of the "Rev" Sun Myung Moon, the Korean leader of "the Unification Church" (frequently called the "Moonies" by the media): *R. v Secretary of State for the Home Department Ex p. Moon, The Times*, December 8, 1995. This decision would appear to fall within Sedley J.'s class of cases involving highly regarded interests; see the *HEFC* case (above). In *R. v Secretary of State for the Home Department Ex p. Fayed* [1998] 1 W.L.R.763, Lord Woolf M.R. similarly concluded that, in principle, the decision to refuse an application for naturalisation (as a British citizen) was subject to a duty to give reasons. However, that common law requirement was overridden by s.44(2) of the British Nationality Act 1981, which expressly stated that the Home Secretary was not obliged to supply reasons for such decisions. For subsequent developments, see below, p.778.

7. There is no general duty on local planning authorities to give reasons for granting planning permission neither is there such a duty when an authority changes its mind and grants permission after an earlier refusal: *R. v Aylesbury Vale DC Ex p. Chaplin* (1997) 76 P. & C.R. 207 (the court left open the possibility that fairness might in an appropriate case require reasons to be given).

8. Where fairness requires the provision of reasons the courts will also examine the adequacy of any reasons given by the decision-maker. The Court of Appeal has stated that: "the question the court has to decide, therefore, is whether the reasons in fact given by the minister enable the reader to know what conclusions he has reached on the principal important controversial issues" (*per* Brooke L.J. in *R. v Secretary of State for Transport Ex p. Richmond upon Thames LBC (No.4)* [1996] 4 All E.R. 903 at 919). In that case it was held that the brief reasons given by the Secretary, for his promulgation of a statutory order imposing new night flight restrictions at London's major airports, were acceptable as they had been preceded by a detailed consultation paper. But *cf.* the *Astra Foundation* case, n.5 above. More generally on the adequacy of reasons see *Save Britain's Heritage*, below, pp.851–853.

9. A duty to give reasons that would otherwise arise may be excluded where there is a compelling public interest, the strength of the public interest being balanced against the interest of the complainant (see the *Gaming Board* case, above, p.707; *R. (on the application of Tucker) v Director-General of the National Crime Squad* [2003] EWCA Civ 57; [2003] I.C.R. 599 (no need to give detailed reasons for the termination of a police officer's secondment to the NCS even though reasons were

normally given in such cases; NCS work was highly sensitive work dealing with confidential information)).

(ii) The Rule Against Interest or Bias

This rule (historically termed *nemo judex in causa sua potest*) has the objective of ensuring that decision-makers do not participate in decisions where they have a prohibited financial interest in the matter or where there is a real possibility of bias on their part because of some other pre-existing connection with the issue (*e.g.* a friendship with one party to a legal dispute). As *de Smith, Woolf and Jowell* state:

> "the decision-maker should not be biased or prejudiced in a way that precludes fair and genuine consideration being given to the arguments advanced by the parties. Although perfect objectivity may be an unrealisable objective, the rule against bias thus aims at preventing a hearing from being a sham or a ritual or a mere exercise in 'symbolic reassurance', due to the fact that the decision-maker was not in practice persuadable" (p.521).

The rule is primarily concerned with the appearance of regulated public decision-making. Thus, the courts take no account of the fact that a decision-maker with a direct pecuniary interest did not allow him- or herself to be influenced by it in any way; such an interest disqualifies automatically. Also, it is generally easier to establish an improper appearance than actual impropriety. Confusion in the case law regarding the correct test to be applied by the courts when determining if apparent bias has been established (*i.e.* the existence of "a reasonable suspicion of bias" or "a real likelihood of bias": see the second edition of this book at pp.576–585) was resolved by the House of Lords in *R. v Gough* (below, p.760) in favour (essentially) of the latter. The test was further modified to bring it into line with the requirement of Art.6 ECHR, in *Re Medicaments* (below, p.755).

Traditionally, the rule against bias or interest applied only to decision-making processes which the courts classified as "judicial" or "quasi-judicial" (see *Franklin v Minister of Town and Country Planning* below, p.774. However, as we have seen above, the development of the principle of procedural fairness has resulted in the extension of a right to a fair hearing being applied to a much broader range of decision-making. The judgment of the Sedley J. in *R. v Secretary of State for the Environment Ex p. Kirkstall Valley Campaign Ltd* (below, p.778) endorses a similar extension in the ambit of the rule against bias or interest.

For general readings see: *de Smith, Woolf and Jowell*, Ch.12, *Craig*, Ch.9, *Wade and Forsyth*, Ch.14.

(a) *The rule against interest*

DIMES v GRAND JUNCTION CANAL PROPRIETORS

(1852) 3 H.L.CAS. 759; 8 STATE TR. N.S. 85; 19 L.T.O.S. 317; 17 JUR. 73; 10 E.R. 301 (HOUSE OF LORDS)

In 1796, the canal proprietors, a company incorporated under statute, purchased some land, part of which was used for the canal and towpath. This land was the subject of litigation between the proprietors and Dimes, an attorney who was the Lord of the Manor, which dragged on from 1831 to 1852. In 1838, 1848 and 1850, Lord Chancellor Cottenham affirmed decrees made by the Vice-Chancellor in favour of the proprietors, including an injunction to restrain Dimes from obstructing the canal (for example, by throwing bricks into it), and an order subsequently committing him to prison for contempt in disobeying the injunction. In 1849, Dimes discovered that the Lord Chancellor had for over 10 years held several thousand pounds' worth of shares in the canal company, some in his own right and the others as trustee. The Lord Chancellor continued to hear matters concerned with the litigation, relying on the advice of the Master of the Rolls with whom he sat. Dimes appealed to the House of Lords against all the decrees and orders made in the litigation. He was represented by the Solicitor-General and other counsel, who argued that the whole proceedings were void in that the Lord Chancellor was disqualified by interest, and that his incompetency affected his deputy, the Vice-Chancellor. On the other hand, it was accepted that the formal act of enrolling the order to enable an appeal to be brought to the House of Lords had to be performed by the Lord Chancellor:

> "The enrolment of this order is a matter of necessity, but it is also a matter of form, and is not an act which decides the case, but only enables the party to make the decision the subject of an appeal. The House cannot say to an appealing party who complains of the wrongful exercise of an unwarranted jurisdiction, that he cannot come here to make the complaint without getting the Lord Chancellor's signature, and yet, when he gets it, that he thereby admits the jurisdiction. That would be to make the wrong itself a reason for refusing the remedy".

This was not to say that it was necessary for the Lord Chancellor to hear the main issues. "There might have been a bill of complaint addressed to the Sovereign in the High Court of Chancery, and it would have been referred to the Master of the Rolls. . . ." (3 H.L. Cas. at 770).

The House of Lords took the advice of the Judges:

MR BARON PARKE: In answer to the first question proposed by your Lordships, I have to state the unanimous opinion of the Judges, that, in the case suggested, the order or decree of the Lord Chancellor was not absolutely *void*, on account of his interest, but *voidable* only.

If this had been a proceeding in an inferior court, one to which a prohibition might go from a court in Westminster Hall, such a prohibition would be granted, pending the proceedings, upon an allegation that the presiding Judge of the court was interested in the suit: whether a prohibition could go to the Court of Chancery, it is unnecessary to consider.

If no prohibition should be applied for, and in cases where it could not be granted, the proper mode of taking the objection to the interest of the Judge would be, in courts of common law, by bringing a writ of error. . . .

The former course was stated to be proper in the case of *Brooks v Earl of Rivers* (Hardr. 503), it being suggested that the Earl of Derby, who was Chamberlain of Chester, had an interest in the suit; and the Court held that, where the Judge had an interest, neither he nor *his deputy* can determine a cause or sit in court; and if he does, a prohibition lies.

The latter course was adopted in the case of *The Company of Mercers and Ironmongers of Chester v Bowker* (1 Stra. 639), where it was assigned for error in fact, on the record of a judgment for the Company of Mercers in the Mayor's Court at Chester, that after verdict, and before judgment, one of the Company of Mercers became mayor; and for that reason the judgment was reversed in the Court of Quarter Sessions, and that judgment of reversal affirmed in the King's Bench.

In neither of these cases was the judgment held to be absolutely void. Till prohibition had been granted in one case, or judgment reversed in the other, we think that the proceedings were valid, and the persons acting under the authority of the Court would not be liable to be treated as trespassers.

The many cases in which the Court of King's Bench has interfered (and may have gone to a great length), where interested parties have acted as magistrates, and quashed the orders made by the Court of which they formed part, afford an analogy.

None of these orders is absolutely void; it would create great confusion and inconsequence if it was. The objection might be one of which the parties acting under these orders might be totally ignorant till the moment of the trial of an action of trespass for the act done (see, with relation to this point, the observations of the Lord Chancellor in the case of *Scadding v Lorant, ante,* at 447); but these orders may be quashed after being removed by *certiorari,* and the Court shall do complete justice in that respect.

We think that the order of the Chancellor is not void; but we are of opinion, that as he had an interest which would have disqualified a witness under the old law, he was disqualified as a Judge; that it was a voidable order, and might be questioned and set aside by appeal or some application to the Court of Chancery, if a prohibition would not lie.

[The Judges also advised that the Vice-Chancellor was not the mere deputy of the Lord Chancellor, but exercised an independent jurisdiction; that his decrees took effect unaffected by the Lord Chancellor's disqualification; and that as the latter's signature was required by statute for the enrolment of the decrees the disqualification did not affect that act.]

For this is a case of necessity, and where that occurs the objection of interest cannot prevail. Of this the case in the Year Book (Year Book, 8 Hen. 6, 19; 2 Roll. Abr. 93) is an instance, where it was held that it was no objection to the jurisdiction of the Common Pleas that an action was brought against all the Judges of the Common Pleas, in a case in doubt which could only be brought in that court. . . .

[Their Lordships then heard arguments on the merits, in form acting as if on an appeal directly from the Vice-Chancellor. At its conclusion, their Lordships expressed their views on the disqualification issue.]

LORD ST LEONARDS L.C. and LORD BROUGHAM concurred in the opinion of the Judges, and said that it was proper to reverse the orders of Lord Cottenham L.C.

LORD CAMPBELL: I take exactly the same view of this case as do my noble and learned friends, and I have very little to add to their observations. With respect to the point upon which the learned Judges were consulted, I must say that I entirely concur in the advice which they have given to your Lordships. No one can suppose that Lord Cottenham could be, in the remotest degree, influenced by the interest that he had in this concern; but, my Lords, it is of the last importance that the maxim that no man is to be a judge in his own cause should be held sacred. And that is not to be confined to a cause in which he is a party, but applies to a cause in which he has an interest. Since I have had the honour to be Chief Justice of the Court of Queen's Bench, we have again and again set aside proceedings in inferior tribunals because an individual, who had an interest in a cause, took a part in the decision. And it will have a most salutary influence on these tribunals when it is known that this high Court of last resort, in a case in which the Lord Chancellor of England had an interest, considered that his decree was on that account a decree not according to law, and was set aside. This will be a lesson to all inferior tribunals to take care not only that in their decrees they are not influenced by their personal interest, but to avoid the appearance of labouring under such an influence. . . .

[The Vice-Chancellor's decrees and orders were upheld on the merits.]

Notes

1. A pecuniary interest in order to disqualify must not be "too remote". In *R. v Rand* (1866) L.R. 1 Q.B. 230, Bradford Corporation were empowered by statute to take water flowing into Harden Beck. They could do so without the consent of the millowners on that beck, if they obtained first a justices' certificate that a certain reservoir was completed, of a given capacity, and filled with water. Two of the justices who granted this certificate were trustees of institutions which held Bradford corporation bonds. The Court of Queen's Bench held that these justices were not disqualified by interest, even though "the security of their *cestui que trusts* would be improved by anything improving the borough fund, and anything improving the waterworks . . . would produce that effect". The two justices might have been disqualified by interest had they been "liable to costs, or to other pecuniary loss or gain" in consequence of being trustees (*per* Blackburn J. at 232).

2. A direct pecuniary interest will disqualify even if it is small (*Serjeant v Dale* (1877) 2 Q.B.D 558, 566–567). This is subject to a *de minimis* exception where the potential effect of any decision on the judge's personal interest is so small as to be incapable of affecting his decision one way or another, although any doubt should be resolved in favour of disqualification (dictum in *Locabail (UK) Ltd v Bayfield Properties Ltd* [2000] Q.B. 451 at [10]; applied in *Weatherill v Lloyds TSB Bank Plc* [2000] C.P.L.R. 584 (in respect of the judge's shareholding of 570 out of a total of 5.5 billion shares in issue).

3. Where there is an indirect pecuniary interest, disqualification is not automatic but may still follow if there is a real possibility of bias, *cf. R v Mulvihill* [1990] 1 W.L.R. 438 (no automatic disqualification and no reasonable suspicion of bias (the test then applicable) where the Crown Court judge presiding over a trial for robberies at various banks and building societies held shares in one of the banks).

4. As Lord Campbell says in *Dimes*, a decision-maker is automatically disqualified where he or she is a party. This principle has been applied where a person is both prosecutor and judge. See *Taylor v NUS* [1967] 1 W.L.R. 532; *R. v London CC Ex p. Akkersdyk* (below, p.778); *R. v Barnsley MBC Ex p. Hook* [1976] 1 W.L.R. 1052. In *Hook*, a complaint was made about the behaviour of H, a stallholder, to the manager of Barnsley market. At a subsequent hearing before a council sub-committee, the manager was present throughout, gave evidence in the absence of H and his representatives, and acted as "prosecutor". The decision to revoke H's licence to hold a stall in the market was quashed.

5. Note that *Dimes* concerned a superior court. In the case of inferior courts, and tribunals and other decision-makers, the better view is that breach of the *nemo judex* principle renders a decision void not voidable. See *cf. Cooper v Wilson* [1937] K.B. 309 (below, p.778).

6. There seems no good reason why the list of interests that disqualify automatically should be extended beyond those recognised in *Dimes*. This position was nevertheless taken by the House of Lords in *R. v Bow Street Metropolitan Stipendiary Magistrate Ex p. Pinochet Ugarte (No.2)* [2000] 1 A.C. 119. The House in *R. v Bow Street Stipendiary Magistrate Ex p. Pinochet Ugarte (No.1)* [2000] 1 A.C. 61 held by three to two that a warrant for the extradition of P to Chile was valid. Amnesty International (AI) had been given leave to intervene in the proceedings and had supported the validity of the warrant. It subsequently emerged that one of the majority, Lord Hoffmann, was a director and chairman of Amnesty International Charity Ltd (AICL). This, together with Amnesty International Ltd, had been incorporated to

carry out, respectively, charitable and other work of AI's international headquarters in the United Kingdom. Both were controlled by AI. The House in *Pinochet (No.2)* unanimously set aside its earlier decision. It did not reach the question whether there was a real possibility of bias, but held instead that automatic disqualification followed where the judge's decision would lead to the promotion of a cause in which the judge was involved together with one of the parties. Lord Hoffmann's links with AICL were sufficient for disqualification. It was clear that Lord Hoffmann had no pecuniary interest, direct or indirect. Lord Browne-Wilkinson said (at 135) that:

> "there must be a rule that automatically disqualifies a judge who is involved, whether personally or as a director of a company, in promoting the same causes in the same organisation as is a party to the suit".

This enabled the House to avoid the more delicate question whether there was a real possibility that one of their judicial colleagues was biased. However, given the cases subsequent to *Pinochet (No.2)* (see below, pp.755–774) that emphasised that this has to be judged by reference to the appearance of the matter to the fair-minded observer rather than a calculation of the actual risk of bias, it is submitted that this would have been the preferential approach, given the definitional uncertainties of the *Pinochet (No.2)* rule.

It has been stated that this principle is confined to judicial bodies (*per* Ouseley J. in *Bovis Homes Ltd v New Forest DC* [2002] EWHC 483 at [87]). The Court of Appeal has stated that any further extension of the present rule on automatic disqualification would be undesirable unless that could be "plainly required to give effect to the important underlying principles on which the rule is based" (*Locabail (UK) Ltd v Bayfield Properties Ltd* [2000] Q.B. 451 at [14]).

There was no breach of the *Pinochet (No.2)* principle (and no apparent bias) where a judge of the Court of Appeal of Jamaica sat on an appeal in 1998 concerning the constitutionality of an Act of 1992 he had certified as constitutional in his previous capacity of Attorney-General (*Panton v Minister of Finance* [2001] UKPC 33); or where a tribunal chairman heard a case where her barrister husband had appeared occasionally for one of the parties (*Jones v DAD Legal Expenses Insurance Co.* [2003] EWCA Civ 1071; [2004] I.R.L.R. 218). In neither case could the judge be said to be anywhere near being a party.

For an argument that a rule requiring automatic disqualification is "Draconian, disproportionate and unnecessary" see A.A. Olowofoyeku, [2001] P.L. 456. For a comment on *Pinochet (No.2)* see T.H. Jones, [1999] P.L. 391.

(b) *The rule against bias*

MEDICAMENTS AND RELATED CLASSES OF GOODS (NO.2), Re

[2001] 1 W.L.R. 700 (COURT OF APPEAL)

On October 2, 2000, the Restrictive Practices Court began the trial of a contested application by the Director-General of Fair Trading under the Resale Prices Act 1976 to discharge a 1970 order of the Court exempting branded medicaments from the general statutory ban on resale price maintenance. The Director contended that this restrictive practice could no longer be justified. His application was contested by two trade associations representing many of the manufacturers and retailers of branded over-the-counter medicaments. One of three members of the Court, Dr Penelope Rowlatt, was an economist. On November 3, she telephoned Frontier Economics, an economic consultancy, to ask if they would consider her for a part-time post. Although she had known earlier that a co-founder and director of that firm, Mr Zoltan Biro, was an expert witness on behalf of the Director in the *Medicaments* case, she did not recall this fact at the time. She spoke to the Managing Director's PA, who mentioned Mr Biro's name. After she rang off, she realised that this might be of some significance and she informed the court's presiding judge, Lightman J., and the parties on November 7. She had received no reply from Frontier Economics, and now told them that her application could not be pursued until after the conclusion of the trial. The trade associations invited Dr Rowlatt to recuse herself. On November 13, Dr Rowlatt made a further personal statement, recording a further telephone conversation with the PA in which Dr Rowlatt said she could not speak to her, and the PA replied that Frontier Economics had come to the same conclusion. She also received a letter from Frontier Economics declining her request to meet and stating that they were unlikely to have vacancies for the foreseeable future for a person of her experience. She also stated that as soon as she appreciated that Frontier Economics was instructed by the Director in this case, she realised that it would be inappropriate to join that firm, and it was now clear that they had no interest in her joining them. She would be happy to give an undertaking not to join that firm for two years after the final order in these proceedings or indeed for any lengthier period the parties might request. She was confident that she retained the essential independence of mind required of a court member and declined to recuse herself. On November 17, the court decided that there was no objective justification for fears of lack of impartiality, there was no real danger or reasonable apprehension of bias and there was no need for Dr Rowlatt to recuse herself. The trade associations appealed on a point of law to the Court of Appeal, which allowed the appeal.

The judgment of the court (Lord Phillips of Worth Matravers M.R., Brooke and Robert Walker L.JJ.) was delivered by LORD PHILLIPS OF WORTH MATRAVERS M.R.: . . .

The law in relation to bias

34. Article 6 of the Convention for the Protection of Human Rights and Fundamental Freedoms (1953) provides:

"Right to a fair trial

1. In the determination of his civil rights and obligations or of any criminal charge against him, everyone is entitled to a fair and public hearing within a reasonable time by an independent and impartial tribunal established by law."

Since 2 October 2000 English courts have been obliged under the Human Rights Act 1998 to give effect to the right to a fair trial as embodied in article 6.

35. The requirement that the tribunal should be independent and impartial is one that has long been recognised by English common law. An appellate or reviewing court will set aside a decision affected by bias. The precise test to be applied when determining whether a decision should be set aside on account of bias has, however, given rise to difficulty, reflected in judicial formulations that have appeared in conflict. The House of Lords in *R. v Gough* [1993] AC 646 attempted to resolve that conflict. In *Locabail (UK) Ltd v Bay field Properties Ltd* [2000] QB 451, 476 this court observed that the test in *R. v Gough* had not commanded universal approval outside this jurisdiction and that Scotland and some Commonwealth countries preferred an alternative test which might be "more closely in harmony with the jurisprudence of the

European Court of Human Rights". Since 2 October the English courts have been required to take that jurisprudence into account. This then is an occasion to review *R. v Gough* to see whether the test it lays down is, indeed, in conflict with Strasbourg jurisprudence.

36. Judicial tribunals come in many forms. We shall refer to "the judge" to embrace all forms of judicial tribunal, including juror, lay magistrate and judge of a superior court. For convenience we shall refer to the judge as "he" rather than "he or she".

37. Bias is an attitude of mind which prevents the judge from making an objective determination of the issues that he has to resolve. A judge may be biased because he has reason to prefer one outcome of the case to another. He may be biased because he has reason to favour one party rather than another. He may be biased not in favour of one outcome of the dispute but because of prejudice in favour of or against a particular witness which prevents an impartial assessment of the evidence of that witness. Bias can come in many forms. It may consist of irational prejudice or it may arise from particular circumstances which, for logical reasons, predispose a judge towards a particular view of the evidence or issues before him.

38. The decided cases draw a distinction between "actual bias" and "apparent bias". The phrase "actual bias" has not been used with great precision and has been applied to the situation (1) where a judge has been influenced by partiality or prejudice in reaching his decision and (2) where it has been demonstrated that a judge is actually prejudiced in favour of or against a party. "Apparent bias" describes the situation where circumstances exist which give rise to a reasonable apprehension that the judge may have been, or may be, biased.

39. Findings of actual bias on the part of a judge are rare. The more usual issue is whether, having regard to all the material circumstances, a case of apparent bias is made out. We do not propose to refer to more than a few of the many cases that were reviewed in *R. v Gough* and the *Locabail* case. We believe that two critical and interrelated questions are raised by the authorities, and we propose to focus on the cases which exemplify those questions. The questions are: (1) must the reasonable apprehension of bias be that of the reviewing court itself, or that which the reviewing court would attribute to an informed onlooker? (2) What are the circumstances that fall to be taken into account when applying the test of bias and how are those circumstances to be determined?

40. It has long been held that, where a judge has a pecuniary interest in the outcome of a case, he is automatically disqualified, whether or not that interest gives rise to a reasonable apprehension of bias: see *Dimes v Proprietors of Grand Junction Canal* (1852) 3 HL Cas 759. That principle and its extension in *R. v Bow Street Stipendiary Magistrate, Ex p. Pinochet Ugarte (No. 2)* [2000] 1 AC 119 have been subjected to a powerful critical analysis by Professor Olowofoyeku in "The Nemo Judex Rule: The Case Against Automatic Disqualification" [2000] PL 456. We are not concerned with this category of case and do not propose to pick up the gauntlet thrown down in that article.

41. We start our analysis of the authorities with the decision of the Divisional Court in *R. v Sussex Justices, Ex p. McCarthy* [1924] 1 KB 256. That decision concerned a prosecution before the lay justices for dangerous driving. Unknown to the defendant and his solicitors, the clerk to the justices was a member of the firm of solicitors acting in a civil claim against the defendant arising out of the accident that had given rise to the prosecution.

The clerk retired with the justices, who returned to convict the defendant. On learning of the clerk's provenance, the defendant applied to have the conviction quashed. The justices swore affidavits stating that they had reached their decision to convict the defendant without consulting their clerk. In giving the leading judgment Lord Hewart CJ said, at pp.258–259:

> "It is said, and, no doubt, truly, that when that gentlemen retired in the usual way with the justices, taking with him the notes of the evidence in case the justices might desire to consult him, the justices came to a conclusion without consulting him, and that he scrupulously abstained from referring to the case in any way. But while that is so, a long line of cases shows that it is not merely of some importance but is fundamental importance but is of fundamental importance that justice should not only be done, but should manifestly and undoubtedly be seen to be done. The question therefore is not whether in this case the deputy clerk made any observation or offered any criticism which he might not properly have made or offered; the question is whether he was so related to the case in its civil aspect as to be unfit to act as clerk to the justices in the criminal mater. The answer to that question depends not upon what actually was done but upon what might appear to be done. Nothing is to be done which creates even a suspicion that there has been an improper interference with the course of justice. Speaking for myself, I accept the statements contained in the justices' affidavit, but they show very clearly that the deputy clerk was connected with the case in a capacity which made it right that he should scrupulously abstain from referring to the matter in any way, although he retired, with the justices; in other wards, his one position was such that he could not, if he had been required to do so, discharge the duties which his other position involved. His twofold position was a manifest contradiction. In those circumstances I am satisfied that this conviction must be quashed, unless it can be shown that the applicant or his solicitor was aware of the point that might be taken, refrained from taking it, and took his chance of an acquittal on the facts, and then, on a conviction being recorded, decided to take the point. On the facts I am satisfied that there has been no waiver of the irregularity, and, that being so, the rule must be made absolute and the conviction quashed."

42. Had Lord Hewart CJ asked the question "Was there any likelihood that the clerk's connection with the case influenced the verdict?" he would have answered in the negative on the basis that he accepted the evidence that the clerk had not intervened in the justices' discussion. Had he asked the question "Would a reasonable onlooker aware of all the material facts, including the fact that the clerk did not speak to the justices after retiring, have concluded that the clerk's connection with the case might have influenced the verdict?" he would equally have answered in the negative. His decision was reached on the premise that what actually transpired between the clerk and the justices behind closed doors was not relevant. The fact that the clerk had retired with the justices gave an appearance of the possibility of injustice, and that was enough to lead to the quashing of the verdict.

43. Lord Hewart CJ's decision apparently led to a number of cases in which verdicts were quashed on the ground that the circumstances gave rise to a suspicion of bias, even where the suspicion was fanciful. In *R. v Camborne Justices, Ex p. Pearce* [1955] 1 QB 41 the cases were reviewed in a reserved judgment of

the Divisional Court, presided over by Lord Goddard CJ. That case also involved an allegation of bias on the part of a justices' clerk. The applicant had been convicted by the justices on charges of offences under the Food and Drugs Act 1938 which had been brought under the authority of the health committee of the Cornwall County Council. The clerk to the justices was a councillor member of the council, but he did not serve on the health committee. The court found on the evidence before it that the clerk was summoned by the justices to advise on a point of law, that he did not discuss the facts of the case with them at all during the short time that he was with them and that the justices returned and gave their decision some appreciable time after the clerk had returned to court.

44. The court had the assistance of the Solicitor General, Sir Reginald Manningham-Buller QC, as amicus. He submitted, at pp.46–47, that the correct test was whether or not there was a "real likelihood" of bias, that is "something to which a person in possession of such facts as are readily available to him would take exception to". This submission was reflected in the judgment of the court, which reviewed the authorities, and concluded, at p.51:

> "In the judgment of this court the right test is that prescribed by Blackburn J [in *R. v Rand* (1866) LR 1 QB 230], namely, that to disqualify a person from acting in a judicial or quasi-judicial capacity upon the ground of interest (other than pecuniary or proprietary) in the subject matter of the proceeding, a real likelihood of bias must be shown. This court is further of opinion that a real likelihood of bias must be made to appear not only from the materials in fact ascertained by the party complaining, but from such further facts as he might readily have ascertained and easily verified in the course of his inquiries."

45. The court held that on the full facts of the case, most of which would have been available to the applicant, there was no real likelihood of bias. It added this observation, at pp.51–52:

> "The frequency with which allegations of bias have come before the courts in recent times seems to indicate that Lord Hewart's reminder in the *Sussex Justices* case [1924] 1 KB 256, 259 that it 'is of fundamental importance that justice should not only be done, but should manifestly and undoubtedly be seen to be done' is being urged as a warrant for quashing convictions or invalidating orders upon quite unsubstantial grounds and, indeed, in some cases upon the flimsiest pretexts of bias. Whilst indorsing and fully maintaining the integrity of the principle reasserted by Lord Hewart, this court feels that the continued citation of it in cases to which it is not applicable may lead to the erroneous impression that it is more important that justice should appear to be done than that it should in fact be done."

It is noteworthy that leading counsel for the applicant did not contend that the clerk had improperly influenced the bench, but relied upon the contention that the circumstances gave rise to a reasonable apprehension of bias.

46. Over the next four decades it was possible to identify two alternative tests applied by the courts, usually in criminal proceedings, when considering whether a decision was vitiated on account of bias. (1) Did it appear to the court that there was a real danger that the judge had been biased? (2) Would an objective onlooker with knowledge of the material facts have a reasonable suspicion that the judge might have been biased?

47. It seems to us that the two tests should produce the same result *unless*, when applying the first test, the court has regard to matters which do not form part of the "material facts" that fall to be taken into account when applying the second test. This was precisely the position in *R. v Gough* [1993] AC 646, at least on the approach of the Court of Appeal.

48. In *R v Gough* the issue was whether a guilty verdict was unsafe by reason of apparent bias on the part of a juror. The juror had, for two years, lived next door to the brother of the defendant. This was of particular significance as the defendant was charged with conspiracy with that brother to commit burglaries. After the guilty verdict had been entered, the brother started shouting in court. The juror then informed the judge of the fact that she lived next door to the brother. A photograph of the brother had been placed before the jury in the course of the trial, and his address had been read out. The juror, however, subsequently stated on affidavit that she had only become aware that her next door neighbour was the defendant's brother after the verdict had been delivered.

49. On appeal counsel for the appellant accepted that the juror was telling the truth when she stated that she only became aware after the verdict that she lived next door to the brother. At the same time, however, he submitted that this claim of ignorance would not be acceptable to a fair-minded observer. While accepting that there was no actual danger that the verdict had been affected by bias, counsel submitted that the verdict could not stand because an objective observer would have a reasonable suspicion that a fair trial was not possible.

50. The Court of Appeal accepted, at p.652, that, if the correct test was the impression that would be made on a fair-minded observer, it would not be right to include in the material facts known to the observer the fact that the juror was unaware that she lived next to the defendant's brother:

"Mr Hytner submits, applying that test, that the fair-minded observer would suspect in the present case that a fair trial was not possible. In this case Mrs Smith in her affidavit evidence has stated that she was unaware of the relevant facts connecting her to the appellant until after the jury had delivered its verdict. This evidence was unchallenged. Accordingly this can be distinguished from the various authorities which have been cited to us in that in these latter cases the relevant 'connecting' facts giving rise to the alleged bias have already been known to the particular member of the tribunal, against whom bias has been raised, throughout the trial in question. This did not apply in the present case. If the fact that Mrs Smith was not aware of the relevant facts connecting her to the appellant had been known to the fair-minded observer, then surely the observer would, in those circumstances, have regarded the trial as having been a fair one. Should we impute knowledge of Mrs Smith's particular state of mind to the fair-minded observer? Mr Hytner submits that such an observer would be bound to conclude that Mrs Smith must have realised who the case concerned when she heard the address referred to in the statement and also when she saw David Gough's photograph. Her claim of ignorance would be unacceptable to a fair-minded observer. We think there is force in this contention. Accordingly we do not seek to distinguish the instant case by imputing to the fair-minded observer *actual* knowledge of Mrs Smith's unawareness of the relevant facts until after the verdict had been delivered."

51. The court held, however, that the authorities showed that, at least in the case of jury trials, the "real danger" of bias rather than the "reasonable suspicion" of bias was the correct test. On that basis it was common ground that the appeal could not succeed.

52. In the House of Lords the appeal proceeded on the basis that there was no likelihood, or even possibility, that the verdict had in fact been affected by bias. The issue was whether the Court of Appeal had been correct to apply the test of "real danger" rather than the test of whether the objective onlooker would have a reasonable apprehension or suspicion of bias.

53. Lord Goff of Chieveley gave the leading speech. At the outset he explained, at pp.659–660, the difficulty confronting the court when bias was alleged:

"A layman might well wonder why the function of a court in cases such as these should not simply be to conduct an inquiry into the question whether the tribunal was in fact biased. After all it is alleged that, for example, a justice or a juryman was biased, *i.e.* that he was motivated by a desire unfairly to favour one side or to disfavour the other. Why does the court not simply decide whether that was in fact the case? The answer, as always, is that it is more complicated than that. First of all, there are difficulties about exploring the actual state of mind of a justice or juryman. In the case of both, such an inquiry has been thought to be undesirable; and in the case of the juryman in particular, there has long been an inhibition against, so to speak, entering the jury room and finding out what any particular juryman actually thought at the time of decision. But there is also the simple fact that bias is such an insidious thing that, even though a person may in good faith believe that he was acting impartially, his mind may unconsciously be affected by bias—a point stressed by Devlin LJ in R. *v Barns ley Licensing Justices, Ex p Barnsley and District Licensed Victuallers'* Association [1960] 2 QB 167, 187. In any event, there is an overriding public interest that there should be confidence in the integrity of the administration of justice, which is always associated with the statement of Lord Hewart CJ in R. *v Sussex Justices*, Ex p McCarthy [1924] 1 KB 256, 259, that it is 'of fundamental importance that justice should not only be done, but should manifestly and undoubtedly be seen to be done'. I shall return to that case in a moment, for one of my tasks is to place the actual decision in that case in its proper context. At all events, the approach of the law has been (save on the very rare occasion where actual bias is proved) to look at the relevant circumstances and to consider whether there is such a degree of possibility of bias that the decision in question should not be allowed to stand."

54. Later in his speech Lord Goff considered the decisions both in the *Sussex Justices* case [1924] 1 KB 256 and the *Camborne Justices* case [1955] 1 QB 41, concluding that the test in the latter was to be preferred. He went on, in the course of reviewing the authorities, to quote with approval the approach commended by Devlin L.J in R. *v Barnsley Licensing Justices, Ex p. Barnsley and District Licensed Victuallers' Association* [1960] 2 QB 167, 187:

"We have not to inquire what impression might be left on the minds of the present applicants or on the minds of the public generally. We have to satisfy ourselves that there was a real likelihood of bias—not merely satisfy ourselves that that was the sort of impression that might reasonably get abroad.

The term 'real likelihood of bias' is not used, in my opinion, to import the principle in *R v. Sussex Justices* to which Salmon J referred. It is used to show that it is not necessary that actual bias should be proved. It is unnecessary, and, indeed, might be most undesirable, to investigate the state of mind of each individual justice. 'Real likelihood' depends on the impression which the court gets from the circumstances in which the justices were sitting. Do they give rise to a real likelihood that the justices might be biased? The court might come to the conclusion that there was such a likelihood, without impugning the affidavit of a justice that he was not in fact biased. Bias is or may be an unconscious thing and a man may honestly say that he was not actually biased and did not allow his interest to affect his mind, although, nevertheless, he may have allowed it unconsciously to do so. The matter must be determined upon the probabilities to be inferred from the circumstances in which the justices sit."

55. Lord Goff went on in *R v Gough* [1993] AC 646, 666 to observe the apparent dissent of Lord Denning M.R. in *Metropolitan Properties Co (FGC) Ltd v Lannon* [1969] 1 QB 577, 599, from Devlin L.J.'s approach:

"in considering whether there was a real likelihood of bias, the court does not look at the mind of the justice himself or at the mind of the chairman of the tribunal, or whoever it may be, who sits in a judicial capacity. It does not look to see if there was a real likelihood that he would, or did, in fact favour one side at the expense of the other. The court looks at the impression which would be given to other people. Even if he was as impartial as could be, nevertheless if right-minded persons would think that, in the circumstances, there was a real likelihood of bias on his part, then he should not sit . . . There must be circumstances from which a reasonable man would think it likely or probable that the justice, or chairman, as the case may be, would, or did, favour one side unfairly at the expense of the other. The court will not inquire whether he did, in fact, favour one side unfairly. Suffice it that reasonable people might think he did. The reason is plain enough. Justice must be rooted in confidence: and confidence is destroyed when right-minded people go away thinking: 'The judge was biased.'"

56. Lord Goff concluded, at pp.667–668, that the difference between the two approaches was more apparent than real:

"both considered that it was not necessary that actual bias should be proved, the court having therefore to proceed upon an impression derived from the circumstances; and that the question is whether such an impression reveals a real likelihood of bias. The only difference between them seems to have been that, whereas Devlin LJ spoke of the impression which the court gets from the circumstances, Lord Denning M.R. looked at the circumstances from the point of view of a reasonable man, stating that there must be circumstances from which a reasonable man would think it likely or probable that the justice, or chairman, was biased. Since however the court investigates the actual circumstances, knowledge of such circumstances as are found by the court must be imputed to the reasonable man; and in the result it is difficult to see what difference there is between the impression derived by a reasonable man to whom such knowledge has been imputed, and the impression derived by the court, here personifying the reasonable man. It is true that Lord Denning M.R. expressed the test as being whether a reasonable man would think it 'likely or probable' that the justice or chairman was biased. If it is a correct reading of his judgment (and it is by no means clear on the point) that it is necessary to establish bias on a balance of probabilities, I for my part would regard him as having laid down too rigorous a test. In my opinion, if, in the circumstances of the case (as ascertained by the court), it appears that there was a real likelihood, in the sense of a real possibility, of bias on the part of a justice or other member of an inferior tribunal, justice requires that the decision should not be allowed to stand. I am by no means persuaded that, in its original form, the real likelihood test required that any more rigorous criterion should be applied. Furthermore the test as so stated gives sufficient effect, in cases of apparent bias, to the principle that justice must manifestly be seen to be done, and it is unnecessary, in my opinion, to have recourse to a test based on mere suspicion, or even reasonable suspicion, for that purpose. Finally there is, so far as I can see, no practical distinction between the test as I have stated it, and a test which requires a real danger of bias, as stated in *R. v Spencer* [1987] AC 128. In this way, therefore, it may be possible to achieve a reconciliation between the test to be applied in cases concerned with justices and other members of inferior tribunals, and cases concerned with jurors."

57. At the end of his speech Lord Goff summarised his understanding of the law, at p.670:

"In conclusion, I wish to express my understanding of the law as follows. I think it possible, and desirable, that the same test should be applicable in all cases of apparent bias, whether concerned with justices or members of other inferior tribunals, or with jurors, or with arbitrators. Likewise I consider that, in cases concerned with jurors, the same test should be applied by a judge to whose attention the possibility of bias on the part of a juror has been drawn in the course of a trial, and by the Court of Appeal when it considers such a question on appeal. Furthermore, I think it unnecessary, in formulating the appropriate test, to require that the court should look at the matter through the eyes of a reasonable man, because the court in cases such as these personifies the reasonable man; and in any event the court has first to ascertain the relevant circumstances from the available evidence, knowledge of which would not necessarily be available to an observer in court at the relevant time. Finally, for the avoidance of doubt, I prefer to state the test in terms of real danger rather than real likelihood, to ensure that the court is thinking in terms of possibility rather than probability of bias. Accordingly, having ascertained the relevant circumstances, the court should ask itself whether, having regard lo those circumstances, there was a real danger of bias on the part of the relevant member of the tribunal in question, in the sense that he might unfairly regard (or have unfairly regarded) with favour, or disfavour, the case of a party to the issue under consideration by him; though, in a case concerned with bias on the part of a justices' clerk, the court should go on to consider whether the clerk has been invited to give the justices advice and, if so, whether it should infer that there was a real danger of the clerk's bias having infected the views of the justices adversely to the applicant."

58. In a concurring speech, Lord Woolf summarised his view of the law in the following passage, at pp.672–673.

"It must be remembered that except in the rare case where actual bias is alleged, the court is not concerned to investigate whether or not bias has been established. Whether it is a judge, a member of the jury, justices or their clerk, who is alleged to be biased, the courts do not regard it as being desirable or useful to inquire into the individual's state of mind. It is not desirable because of the confidential nature of the judicial decision making process. It is not useful because the courts have long recognised that bias operates in such an insidious manner that the person alleged to be biased may be quite unconscious of its effect. It is because the court in the majority of cases does not inquire whether actual bias exists that the maxim that justice must not only be done but seen to be done applies. When considering whether there is a real danger of injustice, the court gives effect to the maxim, but does so by examining all the material available and giving its conclusion on that material. If the court having done so is satisfied there is no danger of the alleged bias having created injustice, then the application to quash the decision should be dismissed. This, therefore, should have been the result in the *Sussex Justices* case if Lord Hewart CJ's remarks are to be taken at face value and are to be treated as a finding, and not merely an assumption, that there was no danger of the justices' decision being contaminated by the possible bias of the clerk."

59. It appears to us that the House of Lords in *R. v Gough* laid down the following approach to be adopted by a court reviewing whether a decision of an inferior tribunal should be set aside on the ground of bias: (1) the reviewing court should first identify all the circumstances that are relevant to the issue of bias; (2) the reviewing court should not then consider the effect that those circumstances would have upon a reasonable observer; rather (3) the reviewing court should itself decide whether, in the light of the relevant circumstances, there was a real danger that the inferior tribunal was biased.

60. The House of Lords indicated that, had this approach been adopted in the *Sussex Justices* case [1924] 1 KB 256, the decision of the justices should have been upheld. The Divisional Court should have found as a fact that the clerk had not intervened in the discussion of the justices and, in the light of that finding, should have ruled that there was no danger that the justices' decision had been affected by bias. In *R v Gough* [1993] AC 646 itself, it was common ground that the juror was telling the truth when she said that she had not been aware, until after the verdict, that her next door neighbour was the brother of the defendant. Hence, applying the "real danger" test, the validity of the verdict was not in doubt. The House of Lords did not have to consider the question of how the reviewing court should approach evidence given by the inferior tribunal where that evidence was challenged by the application for review.

61. In *R. v Inner West London Coroner, Ex p. Dallaglio* [1994] 4 All ER 139, 162 this court applied the test in *R. v Gough*, when holding that injudicious remarks made by a coroner gave rise to a real possibility that the coroner had unconsciously allowed his decision to be influenced by a feeling of hostility towards the applicant and other members of an action group, with the result that his decision to refuse to continue an inquest should be quashed.

In the leading judgment Simon Brown LJ set out, at pp 151–152, the following propositions which he derived from *R. v Gough:*

"From *R v Gough* I derive the following propositions: (1) Any court seised of a challenge on the ground of apparent bias must ascertain the relevant circumstances and consider all the evidence for itself so as to reach its own conclusion on the facts. (2) It necessarily follows that the factual position may appear quite differently as between the time when the challenge is launched and the time when it comes to be decided by the court. What may appear at the leave stage to be a strong case of 'justice [not] manifestly and undoubtedly be[ing] seen to be done', may, following the court's investigation, nevertheless fail. Or, of course, although perhaps less probably, the case may have become stronger. (3) In reaching its conclusion the court 'personifies the reasonable man'. (4) The question upon which the court must reach its own factual conclusion is this: is there a real danger of injustice having occurred as a result of bias? By 'real' is meant not without substance. A real danger clearly involves more than a minimal risk, less than a probability. One could, I think, as well speak of a real risk or a real possibility. (5) Injustice will have occurred as a result of bias if 'the decision-maker unfairly regarded with disfavour the case of a party to the issue under consideration by him'. I take 'unfairly regarded with disfavour' to mean 'was predisposed or prejudiced against one party's case for reasons unconnected with the merits of the issue'. (6) A decision-maker may have unfairly regarded with disfavour one party's case either consciously or unconsciously. Where, as here, the applicants expressly disavow any suggestion of actual bias, it seems to me that the court must necessarily be asking itself whether there is a real danger that the decision-maker was unconsciously biased. (7) It will be seen, therefore, that by the time the legal challenge comes to be resolved, the court is no longer concerned strictly with the appearance of bias but rather with establishing the possibility that there was actual although unconscious bias."

62. Sir Thomas Bingham MR, remarked, at p 162, that the effect of the decision in *R. v Gough* was that:

"The famous aphorism of Lord Hewart CJ in *R. v Sussex Justices, Ex p. McCarthy* [1924] 1 KB 256, 259 that 'justice . . . should manifestly and undoubtedly be seen to be done' is no longer, it seems, good law, save of course in the case where the appearance of bias is such as to show a real danger of bias."

63. The decision in *R. v Gough* received critical analysis by the High Court of Australia in *Webb v The Queen* (1994) 181 CLR 41. In the leading judgment, Mason CJ and McHugh J commented, at pp 50–52:

"In considering the merits of the test to be applied in a case where a juror is alleged to be biased, it is important to keep in mind that the appearance as well as the fact of impartiality is necessary to retain confidence in the administration of justice. Both the parties to the case and the general public must be satisfied that justice has not only been done but that it has been seen to be done. Of the various tests used to determine an allegation of bias, the reasonable apprehension test of bias is by far the most appropriate for protecting the appearance of impartiality. The test of 'reasonable likelihood' or 'real danger' of bias tends to emphasise the court's view of the facts. In that context, the trial judge's acceptance of explanations becomes of primary importance. Those two tests tend to place inadequate emphasis on the public perception of the irregular incident. We do not think that it is possible to reconcile the decision in *Gough* with the decisions of this court. In *Gough*, the House of Lords specifically rejected the reasonable suspicion test and the cases and judgments which had applied it in favour of a modified version of the reasonable likelihood test. In *R. v Watson, Exp Armstrong* (1976) 136 CLR 248 faced with the same conflict in the cases between the two tests, this court preferred the reasonable suspicion or apprehension test. That test has been applied in this court on no less than eight subsequent occasions. In the light of the decisions of this court which hold that the reasonable apprehension or suspicion test is the correct test for determining a case of alleged bias against a judge, it is not possible to use the 'real danger' test as the general test for bias without rejecting the authority of those decisions. Moreover, nothing in the two speeches in the House of Lords in *Gough* contains any new insight that makes us think that we should re-examine a principle and a line of cases to which this court has consistently adhered for the last 18 years. On the contrary, there is a strong reason why we should continue to prefer the reasoning in our own cases to that of the House of Lords. In *Gough*, the House of Lords rejected the need to take account of the public perception of an incident which raises an issue of bias except in the case of a pecuniary interest. Behind this reasoning is the assumption that public confidence in the administration of justice will be maintained because the public will accept the conclusions of the judge. But the premise on which the decisions in this court are based is that public confidence in the administration of justice is more likely to be maintained if the court adopts a test that reflects the reaction of the ordinary reasonable member of the public to the irregularity in question. References to the reasonable apprehension of the 'lay observer', the 'fair-minded observer', the 'fair-minded, informed lay observer', 'fair-minded people', the 'reasonable or fair-minded observer', the 'parties or the public', and the 'reasonable person' abound in the decisions of this court and other courts in this country. They indicate that it is the court's view of the public's view, not the court's own view, which is determinative. If public confidence in the administration of justice is to be maintained, the approach that is taken by fair-minded and informed members of the public cannot be ignored. Indeed, as Toohey J pointed out in *Vakauta v Kelly* (1989) 167 CLR 568, 585 in considering whether an allegation of bias on the part of a judge has been made out, the public perception of the judiciary is not advanced by attributing to a fair-minded member of the public a knowledge of the law and the judicial process which ordinary experience suggests is not the case. That does not mean that the trial judge's opinions and findings are irrelevant. The fair-minded and informed observer would place great weight on the judge's view of the facts. Indeed, in many cases the fair-minded observer would be bound to evaluate the incident in terms of the judge's findings."

64. These comments presuppose that the "real danger" test may lead the court to reach a conclusion as to the likelihood of bias which does not reflect the view that the informed observer would form on the same facts—and this because the viewpoint of the judge may not be the same as that of members of the public. This objection was addressed by this court in *Locabail (UK) Ltd v Bayfield Properties Ltd* [2000] QB 451, 477:

"In the overwhelming majority of cases we judge that application of the two tests would anyway lead to the same outcome. Provided that the court, personifying the reasonable man, takes an approach which is based on broad common sense, without inappropriate reliance on special knowledge, the minutiae of court procedure or other matters outside the ken of the ordinary, reasonably well informed member of the public, there should be no risk that the courts will not ensure both that justice is done and that it is perceived by the public to be done."

65. We do not find it easy to reconcile this passage with an approach that requires the court to decide whether there was in fact a real danger that a particular judge was biased. Once the reviewing court excludes from consideration matters known to it which would be outside the ken of ordinary, reasonably well informed members of the public, it seems to us that a hypothetical rather than an actual test of the likelihood of bias is being applied.

66. A similar conclusion flows from a subsequent passage in the judgment in the *Locabail* case, at pp.477–478:

"While a reviewing court may receive a written statement from any judge, lay justice or juror specifying what he or she knew at any relevant time, the court is not necessarily bound to accept such statement at its face value. Much will depend on the nature of the fact of which ignorance is asserted, the source of the statement, the effect of any corroborative or contradictory statement, the inherent probabilities and all the circumstances of the case in question. Often the court will have no hesitation in accepting the reliability of such a statement; occasionally, if rarely, it may doubt the reliability of the statement; sometimes, although inclined to accept the statement, it may recognise the possibility of doubt and the likelihood of public scepticism. All will turn on the facts of the particular case. There can, however, be no question of cross-examining or seeking disclosure from the judge. Nor will the reviewing court pay attention to any statement by the judge concerning the impact of any knowledge on his mind or his decision: the insidious nature of bias makes such a statement of little value, and it is for the reviewing court and not the judge whose impartiality is challenged to assess the risk that some illegitimate extraneous consideration may have influenced the decision."

67. What is the court to do where, although inclined to accept a statement about what the judge under review knew at any material time, it recognises the possibility of doubt and the likelihood of public scepticism? It is invidious for the reviewing court to question the word of the judge in such circumstances, but less so to say that the objective onlooker might have difficulty in accepting it.

68. Such a situation highlights a wider consideration. Jurors are warned by the judge to put all extraneous considerations and prejudices from their minds and to try the case on the evidence, and are normally expected to achieve this.

A professional judge is adept, by training and experience, at reaching decisions by objective appraisal of the facts. A finding that in a particular case there is a real danger that a particular judge was biased inevitably carries with it a slur on the judge in question, albeit that the reviewing court may take pains to emphasise that the bias may have been unconscious. As Deane J put it in *Webb v The Queen* 181 CLR 41, 71–72:

"One advantage of the test of reasonable apprehension on the part of a fair-minded and informed observer is that it makes plain that an appellate court is not making an adverse finding on the question whether it is possible or likely that the particular judge or juror was in fact affected by disqualifying bias. In contrast, the real danger test is focused upon that very question. Regardless of an appellate court's care to make plain that its finding is only one of possibility of danger, such a finding is likely to be unfairly damaging to the reputation of the person concerned who will commonly not have been a party to the proceedings before the appellate court and whose subjective thought processes will not have been investigated in the appellate court."

69. The problem with the "real danger" test is particularly acute where a judge is invited to recuse himself. In such a situation it is invidious to expect a judge to rule on the danger that he may actually be influenced by partiality. The test of whether the objective onlooker might have a reasonable apprehension of bias is manifestly more satisfactory in such circumstances.

70. Mr Sumption submitted that the test in *R v Gough* [1993] AC 646 was no different in reality from the "reasonable apprehension of bias" test favored in Scotland and most other common law jurisdictions. He added that, if it was different, it had to be discarded in favor of the reasonable apprehension test in the light of the Human Rights Act 1998 as this was unequivocally the test applied by the Strasbourg court. This submission received support from Mr Philipson for the Director General. We turn to consider the Strasbourg jurisprudence.

[[71]–[82] His Lordship considered *Delcourt v Belgium* (1970) 1 E.H.R.R. 355; *Piersack v Belgium* (1982) 5 E.H.R.R. 169; *De Cubber v Belgium* (1984) 7 E.H.R.R. 236; *Hauschildt v Denmark* (1989) 12 E.H.R.R. 266; *Borgers v Belgium* (1991) 15 E.H.R.R. 92; and *Gregory v UK* (1997) 25 E.H.R.R. 577.]

83. We would summarise the principles to be derived from this line of cases as follows: (1) If a judge is shown to have been influenced by actual bias, his decision must be set aside. (2) Where actual bias has not been established the personal impartiality of the judge is to be presumed. (3) The court then has to decide whether, on an objective appraisal, the material facts give rise to a legitimate fear that the judge might not have been impartial. If they do the decision of the judge must be set aside. (4) The material facts are not limited to those which were apparent to the applicant. They are those which were ascertained upon investigation by the court. (5) An important consideration in making an objective appraisal of the facts is the desirability that the public should remain confident in the administration of justice.

84. This approach comes close to that in *R. v Gough* [1993] AC 646. The difference is that, when the Strasbourg court considers whether the material circumstances give rise to a reasonable apprehension of bias, it makes it plain that it is applying an objective test to the circumstances, not passing judgment on the likelihood that the particular tribunal under review was in fact biased.

85. When the Strasbourgh jurisprudence is taken into account, we believe that a modest adjustment of the test in *R. v Gough* is called for, which makes it plain that it is, in effect, no different from the test applied in most of the Commonwealth and in Scotland. The court must first ascertain all the circumstances which have a bearing on the suggestion that the judge was biased. It must then ask whether those circumstances would lead a fair-minded and informed observer to conclude that there was a real possibility, or a real danger, the two being the same, that the tribunal was biased.

86. The material circumstances will include any explanation given by the judge under review as to his knowledge or appreciation of those circumstances. Where that explanation is accepted by the applicant for review it can be treated as accurate. Where it is not accepted, it becomes one further matter to be considered from the viewpoint of the fair-minded observer. The court does not the fair-minded observer would consider that there was a real danger of bias notwithstanding the explanation advanced. Thus in *R. v Gough*, had the truth of the juror's explanation not been accepted by the defendant, the Court of Appeal would correctly have approached the question of bias on the premise that the fair-minded onlooker would not necessarily find the juror's explanation credible.

The material circumstances in the present case

[[87]–[91] His Lordship rejected the appellants' claim that the Frontier letter was a contrivance, although the fair-minded observer might well conclude that it was a reaction to embarrassment felt by Frontier at Dr Rowlatt's application rather than a reflection of the fact that her qualifications were not ones they were likely to need in the foreseeable future. The appellants also challenged the credibility of Dr Rowlatt's statement that, when she applied for a position with Frontier, she did not recall that Mr Biro of that firm was an expert witness in the case. The main report for the Director, prominent in the reading lists for the reading-in period before the hearing contained abundant references to Frontier, sometimes in conjunction with Mr Biro's name; Frontier had a high profile and it was not understood how a professional economist sitting in the court could have failed to recall the name of this one of the two firms in her own field (out of a possible field of only about eight) engaged by the parties to the litigation.]

92. The court below, of which Dr Rowlatt was a member, found itself in the unenviable position of having to address this challenge to Dr Rowlatt's credibility. It did so on an objective basis, concluding that it was more credible that she did not have Frontier's position in mind when she applied for a post with them, rather than that she had it in mind and, having made her application to them, then felt impelled to bring the matter to the attention of the judge.

93. We do not think that it was appropriate that the court below should have set out to answer the question of whether or not Dr Rowlatt's statement was truthful. The court should have considered what impression her conduct, including her explanation for it, would have had on a fair-minded observer.

94. We do not consider that the reasoning of the court would have left the fair-minded observer confident that Dr Rowlatt had forgotten frontier's role as experts in the case when she applied for a post with them. It is indeed, hard to credit that, had she had this fact in mind, she would have made the

application, only to appreciate no sooner had she done so that it was inappropriate. But it is equally hard to credit, for the reasons given by Ms Bendall, that Dr Rowlatt could have lost sight of the fact that Frontier were providing critical expert evidence in the case. Thus any concerns that Dr Rowlatt's initial application would have raised in the mind of the observer would have been augmented rather than allayed by the fact that she proffered an explanation which it was not easy to accept.

95. What concerns would the remarkable facts that we have set out above raise in the mind of a fair-minded observer? The Restrictive Practices Court is, in this case, going to have to resolve a fundamental conflict of economic analysis between rival economic consultants. Ms Bendall stated that her clients consider that Dr Rowlatt had, by making her application for employment to one of these consultants, indicated a partiality to them which could not be undone. We consider that the fair-minded observer would be concerned that, if Dr Rowlatt esteemed Frontier sufficiently to wish to be employed by them, she might consciously or unconsciously be inclined to consider them a more reliable source of expert opinion than their rivals.

96. Mr Sumption advanced a more basic contention: that an objective bystander would conclude that Dr Rowlatt might still habour hopes that, sooner or later, she might find employment with Frontier and that this might induce in her, whether consciously or unconsciously, a reluctance to reject as unsound evidence advanced by Frontier's experts.

97. We agree with Mr Sumption that the fair-minded observer would not be convinced that all prospects of Dr Rowlatt working for Frontier at some time in the future had been destroyed, nor that she might not still hope, in due course, to work for Frontier. He would not be reassured by the fact that initially, albeit on the advice of the judge, she wrote to Frontier asking that her application should not be pursued until "after the conclusion of the trial" and that she later offered an undertaking not to join Frontier "for two years after the final order in these proceedings or indeed for any lengthier period which either party may request". The observer's concern at the possibility that Dr Rowlatt's wish to work for Frontier demonstrated partiality would be augmented by a concern that she might still have hopes of doing so.

98. It is for these reasons that we concluded that a fair-minded observer would apprehend that there was a real danger that Dr Rowlatt would be unable to make an objective and impartial appraisal of the expert evidence placed before the court by Frontier and that, on objection being taken, she should have recused herself.

99. Having reached this decision, we then had to consider the position of the other two members of the court. The trial had reached this decision, we then had to consider the position of the other two members of the court. The trial had reached an advance stage by the time that it was interrupted by the appellants' application. Dr Rowlatt must have discussed the economic issues with the other members of the court. We concluded that it was inevitable that the decision that Dr Rowlatt should be disqualified carried with it the consequence that the other two members of the court should stand down.

100. We reached our decision with great regret. Its consequence is that an immense amount of industry will have gone for nothing, and very substantial costs will be thrown away. But Mr Philipson for the Director General made it plain that he did not advance the argument that these considerations ought to influence our decision.

Postscript

101. While we were preparing this judgment it came to the attention of Lord Phillips of Worth Matravers MR that Dr Rowlatt was known to him, although only by sight, because she is a near neighbour. While that is not a fact which could cast doubt on the objectivity with which we have addressed the issues in this case, it is right that it should be recorded.

Appeal allowed.

Notes

1. Following this decision, proceedings began again before a reconstituted RPC. The trade associations withdrew their objections following an indication by the court that it was unsympathetic to their points. They sought to recover from the Lord Chancellor £1 million costs wasted because the proceedings had to begin again. They claimed there had been an infringement of their right to a trial by an impartial tribunal under Art.6(1) ECHR. The Court of Appeal (*Medicaments and Related Classes of Goods (No.4), Re* [2001] EWCA Civ 1217; [2002] 1 W.L.R. 269) held (1) that one of the trade associations did not qualify as a "victim" for the purpose of Art.34, ECHR and s.7(7) of the Human Rights Act 1998; (2) that there had been no breach of Art.6(1) as the defect had been remedied on appeal by the Court of Appeal.

2. The question of the appropriate test for apparent bias was subsequently considered by the House of Lords in *Porter v Magill* [2001] UKHL 67; [2002] 2 A.C. 357. For the background and other points in this case, see above, pp.536–543. One question was whether the conduct of the auditor when on January 13, 1994 he announced his provisional views gave rise to an appearance of bias. In the words of the Divisional Court (96 L.G.R. 157, 173):

> "a televised announcement was arranged at which the auditor himself appeared and, although he said that his views were provisional, he expressed them in florid language and supported them by reference to the thoroughness of the investigation which he claimed to have carried out. There was a further feature of the event which should have had no place in the middle of a quasi-judicial inquiry. A stack of ring binders on the desk at which the auditor sat bearing the name of his firm for the benefit of the cameras was, ostensibly, under the protection of a security guard: unless it was being implied that the persons under investigation might wish to steal the documents, it is not clear what was the purpose of this posturing".

The auditor subsequently decided not to disqualify himself stating that he was not biased and that there was no real danger of bias applying the *Gough* test. In the House of Lords, Lord Hope of Craighead (with whom the other members of the House agreed) said:

> "103. I respectfully suggest that your Lordships should now approve the modest adjustment of the test in *R. v Gough* set out in [para.[85], above p.769]. It expresses in clear and simple language a test which is in harmony with the objective test which the Strasbourg court applies when it is considering whether the circumstances give rise lo a reasonable apprehension of bias. It removes any possible conflict with the test which is now applied in most Commonwealth countries and in Scotland. I would however delete from it the reference to a 'real danger'. Those words no longer serve a useful purpose here, and they are not used in the jurisprudence of the Strasbourg court. The question is whether the fair-minded and informed observer, having considered the facts, would conclude that there was a real possibility that the tribunal was biased.

104. Turning to the facts, there are two points that need to be made at the outset. The first relates to the auditor's own assertion that he was not biased. The Divisional Court said, at p.174$_{\text{A-B}}$, that it had had particular regard to his reasons for declining to recuse himself in reaching its conclusion that he had an open mind and was justified in continuing with the subsequent hearings. I would agree that the reasons that he gave were relevant, but an examination of them shows that they consisted largely of assertions that he was unbiased. Looking at the matter from the standpoint of the fair-minded and informed observer, protestations of that kind are unlikely to be helpfu. I think that Schiemann L.J. adopted the right approach in the Court of Appeal when he said that he would give no weight to the auditor's reasons, ante, p.4000. The second point relates to the emphasis which the respondents place on how the auditor's conduct appeared from the standpoint of the complainer. There is, as I have said, some support in the jurisprudence of the Strasbourgh court for the proposition that the standpoint of the complainer is improtant. But in *Hanschildt v Denmark* 12 EHRR 266, 279, para.48 the court emphasised that what is desicive is whether any fears expressed by the complainer are objectively justified. The complainer's fears are clearly relevant at the initial stage when the court has to decide whether the complaint is one that should be investigated. But they lose their importance once the stage is reached of looking at the matter objectively.

105. I think that it is plain, as the Divisional Court observed, at p.174$_{\text{B}}$, that the auditor made an error of judgment when he decided to make his statement in public at a press conference. The main impression which this would have conveyed to the fair-minded observer was that the purpose of this exercise was to attract publicity to himself, and perhaps also to his firm. It was an exercise in self-promotion in which he should not have indulged. But it is quite another matter to conclude from this that there was a real possibility that he was biased. Schiemann L.J. said, at p.1457D-E, that there was room for a casual observer to form the view after the press conference that the auditor might be biased. Nevertheless he concluded, at p.1457H, having examined the facts more closely, that there was no real danger that this was so, I would take the same view. The question is what the fair-minded and informed observer would have thought, and whether his conclusion would have been that there was real possibility of bias. The auditor's conduct must be seen in the context of the investigation which he was carrying out, which had generated a great deal of public interest. A statement as to his progress would not have been inappropriate. His error was to make it at a press conference. This created the risk of unfair reporting, but there was nothing in the words he used to indicate that there was a real possibility that he was biased. He was at pains to point out to the press that his findings were provisional. There is no reason to doubt his word on this point, as his subsequent conduct demonstrates. I would hold, looking at the matter objectively, that a real possibility that he was biased has not been demonstrated".

The authoritative settlement of what is the test to be applied is welcome. Attention can now be focused on the application of that test to the facts of different cases. Cases decided before *Medicaments, Re* must be viewed with some caution, although it is also recognised that the various changes in the formulation of the test are likely to affect the outcome in only a small proportion of cases.

3. Before the decision in *Pinochet (No.2)* (above, p.754) allegations of bias in the courts were rare; since then they have become increasingly prevalent (see Lord Woolf C.J. in *Taylor v Lawrence* [2003] Q.B. 528 at [60]). There have been a large number of cases arising in respect of proceedings of courts and tribunals, the courts being concerned to ensure that allegations of bias with little foundation are not employed by those disappointed with the outcome as a means of keeping litigation going.

Circumstances that may give rise to a real possibility of bias include personal hostility, friendship, family relationship or (particularly where an issue of credibility arises), close acquaintance with a party or a witness; or where a judge has previously expressed views on a question at issue in such extreme and unbalanced terms as to throw doubt on his or her ability to try the issue with an objective judicial mind. On the other hand, objections cannot be soundly based on the religion, ethnic or national origin, gender, age, class, means or sexual orientation of the judge. Nor, at least ordinarily, can an objection be soundly based on his or her social or educational, or service on employment, background or history, nor those of any member of his or her family, or previous political associations, or membership of social, or sporting or charitable bodies; or extra-curricular utterances; or previous receipt of instructions to act for or against any party, solicitor or advocate engaged in a case before him or her (*Locabail* [2000] Q.B. 451 at [18]–[26]). Accordingly, there was no real danger (now possibility) of bias where a solicitor sitting as a deputy High Court judge had heard a case in circumstances that, unknown to him, his firm had acted for parties to other proceedings against the applicant's husband (*Locabail*); or where the barrister husband of a tribunal chairman occasionally appeared for one of the parties (*Jones v DAS Legal Expenses Insurance Co. Ltd* [2003] EWCA Civ 1071; [2004] I.R.L.R. 218).

Conversely, there was a real danger where a personal injuries case in which insurers were the real defendants was heard by a recorder who had published articles that had expressly pronounced pro-claimant anti-insurer views (*Timmins v Gormley*, heard with *Locabail*).

Other cases where a real possibility of bias have been found include *R. (on the application of Chief Constable of Lancashire) v Preston Crown Court* [2001] EWHC Admin 928; [2002] 1 W.L.R. 1332 (where licensing justices sat in the Crown Court on an appeal from the licensing committee of which they were members, although they had not been party to the decision in question; *Lawal v Northern Spirit Ltd* [2003] UKHL 35; [2004] 1 All E.R. 187 (where a part-time EAT judge appeared as advocate before an EAT that included a lay member who had previously sat with him).

Cases the other way include *Taylor v Lawrence* [2002] EWCA Civ 90, [2003] Q.B. 528 (no real possibility of bias where judge at boundary dispute trial and his wife used services of claimants' solicitors, without charge, to amend their wills the night before he delivered judgment; the fair-minded observer could be expected to be aware of the legal traditions and culture of the English jurisdiction and that in the ordinary way contacts between the judiciary and the legal profession should not be regarded as giving rise to a possibility of bias).

4. The courts have generally not accepted arguments that where a decision-maker has come to a decision on a particular question, the allocation to the same decision-maker of responsibility to make a redetermination of the same (or essentially the same) question will itself give rise to a real possibility of bias. See *Feld v Barnet LBC; Pour v Westminster City Council* [2004] EWCA Civ 1307 (decision of review officer as to suitability of particular accommodation for a homeless person); *Amec Capital Projects Ltd v Whitefriars City Estates Ltd* [2004] EWCA Civ 1418 (adjudicator's determination of building dispute held to be without jurisdiction; matter subsequently referred (validly) to the same adjudicator). In these cases, the courts looked to see whether there was evidence that the reappointed decision-maker had prejudged the matter. Compare *R. v Kent Police Authority Ex p. Godden* [1971] 2 Q.B. 662, where prohibition was granted to prevent a medical practitioner from determining whether a police officer was "permanently disabled" for the purposes of the Police Pensions Regulations on the ground that he had previously expressed a view on the matter when certifying he was unfit for duty. Lord Denning M.R. said that it must inevitably appear that he could not bring an impartial judgment to bear on this matter. This was not cited to the Court of Appeal in *Feld* and *Amec*, and seems difficult to reconcile on the facts.

5. The *Locabail* test does not apply to objections to the participation of particular counsel, as an advocate has no duty not to be partisan. Instead the question is whether there was a real risk that his or her continued participation would lead to a situation where an order made at trial would have to be set aside on appeal (*Geveran Trading Co. Ltd v Skjevesland* [2002] EWCA Civ 1567; [2003] 1 W.L.R. 912 (prior acquaintance between the wife or a party and the opponent's counsel insufficient to justify a retrial)). Similarly, where there is an issue as to the effects of prejudicial publicity, it is

better to consider whether the proceedings were, and appeared to be, fair, rather than to use the terminology of apparent bias (per Carnwath L.J. in R. *(on the application of Mahfouz) v Professional Conduct Committee of the General Medical Council* [2004] EWCA Civ 233 at [32]).

6. *Independence.* The equation of the principles of the common law of natural justice with those under Art.6(1) ECHR, involves recognises that in appropriate circumstances there is a right to an *independent* and not only an *impartial* tribunal. These rights are distinct but closely related (see above, p.384). In terms of domestic law, however, both matters are addressed through asking whether there is a real possibility of bias and whether a fair-minded and informed observer would conclude that the safeguards in place were inadequate to guarantee the independent and impartiality of the members of the tribunal. See *R. v Spear; R. v Boyd* [2002] UKHL 31; [2003] 1 A.C. 734, *per* Lord Rodger of Earlsferry at [56], in the course of holding that revised arrangements for RAF and army courts-martial were not in breach of Art.6(1).

The requirement that exclusion appeal panels (under the School Standards and Framework Act 1998) have regard to the guidance issued by the Secretary of State does not undermine their independence for the purposes of Art.6(1) provided that it is treated as guidance and not as rules or directions. Neither does the role of the representative of the local education authority before the tribunal, provided that person is there to present relevant factual evidence rather than to press for a conclusion one way or another as to whether the pupil should remain excluded (R. *(on the application of S) v Brent LBC* [2002] EWCA Civ 693; [2002] E.L.R. 556). (The court assumed that the right not to be permanently excluded from school without good reason was a civil right for the purposes of Art.6(1)).

(c) *The types of decision-making processes subject to the rule against bias or interest*

FRANKLIN v MINISTER OF TOWN AND COUNTRY PLANNING

[1948] A.C. 87; [1947] L.J.R. 1440; 63 T.L.R. 446; 111 J.P. 497;
[1947] 2 All E.R. 289; 45 L.G.R. 581 (HOUSE OF LORDS)

In January 1946, a committee appointed in 1945 by the Minister and the Secretary of State for Scotland (the "Reith Committee") made an interim report (Cmd.6759) which pointed out that Stevenage was suggested in the Greater London Plan 1944 as one of the new towns in the outer ring round London. The committee had been informed that this development was urgently needed, and they recommended that a government-sponsored corporation should be established in advance of legislation. The Minister, Lewis Silkin, introduced the New Towns Bill in the House of Commons in April.

On May 6, 1946, Mr Silkin spoke at a public meeting in Stevenage Town Hall, called to consider a proposal for the designation of land near Stevenage as the site of a new town. The meeting was lively. Mr Silkin explained the plans for the development of new towns to relieve London's population density. His speech included the following passages:

"In anticipation of the passage of the Bill—and I have no doubt that it will go through—certain preliminary steps have been taken regarding Stevenage by way of discussion with some of the local authorities concerned—(*Voice:* There has been no discussion with the Stevenage Local Authority)—and the preparation of a plan, and the giving of notices for the acquisition of land under powers which I already have in pursuance of the Town and Country Planning Act, 1932 . . . I think you will agree that if we are to carry out our policy of creating a number of new towns to relieve congestion in London we could hardly have chosen for the site of one of them a better place than Stevenage. Now I know that many objections have been raised by the inhabitants of Stevenage, perhaps not unnaturally. . . . The project will go forward. It will do so more smoothly and more successfully with your help and co-operation. Stevenage will in a short time become world famous—(*Laughter*). . . In answer to a question as to whether the rates would be increased by the development, the respondent said: No, in due course Stevenage will gain. Local authorities will be consulted all the way through. But we have a duty to perform, and I am not going to be deterred from that duty. While I will consult as far as possible all the local author-ities, at the end, if people are fractious and unreasonable, I shall have to carry out my duty—(*Voice*: Gestapo!)".

The New Towns Bill received the Royal Assent on August 1, 1946. On August 3, the Minister prepared the draft Stevenage New Town (Designation) Order 1946 under para.1 of Sch.1 to the Act. The draft order was publicised as required by the Act. Objections to the designation were received from the appellants and others. A public local inquiry was held on behalf of the Minister in October. The inspector's report to the Minister summarised the objector's submissions and evidence.

In November, the Minister wrote to the objectors that he had decided to make the order, "after giving careful consideration to the various submissions made to him . . .". He dealt with the main objections raised. The order was made on November 11. The following month, the present appellants who owned houses and land in the area, applied to the High Court to have the order quashed on the grounds that: (1) The order was not within the powers of the Act, or alternatively that the Act's requirements had not been complied with to the substantial prejudice of the appellants' interests, in that—(a) before considering the objections the Minister stated that he would make the order and was thereby biased in any consideration of the order; and (b) the Minister did not before making the order cause a public local inquiry to be held with respect thereto; and (2) That the Act impliedly required that the appellants' objections should be fairly and properly considered by the Minister and that the Minister should give fair and proper effect to the result of such consideration in deciding whether the order should be made, and that such implied requirements were not complied with.

The Minister swore an affidavit which was not challenged, stating (*inter alia*):

"Before causing the said order to be made, I personally carefully considered all the objections made by the objectors including the present [appellants] together with the submissions made and evidence given on their behalf as appearing in the said transcript" (of the inquiry proceedings).

He also stated that he carefully considered the inspector's report.

Henn Collins J. (63 T.L.R. 143) held that the Minister had not fulfilled his duty to act judicially in considering the objections.

The Court of Appeal (63 T.L.R. 187) reversed this decision, holding that the appellants had not discharged the onus of proving that the Minister was biased when he made the order.

The appellants appealed to the House of Lords.

LORD THANKERTON: [stated the facts, expressed agreement with the Court of Appeal's views that the appellant had not proved that the Minister was biased, and continued:] My Lords, I agree with the decision of the Court of Appeal, but I am of opinion that an incorrect view of the law applicable in this case was taken by the learned judge, and I feel bound, despite the assumption of its correctness by the Court of Appeal, to examine the correctness of the learned judge's view as to the proper inference from the respondent's speech of May 6, 1946. While the fact that the speech was made just before the second reading

of the Bill, and some months before the statutory duties as to designation of
new towns was imposed on the respondent has some bearing on the fair construction of the speech, I am prepared to assume in favour of the appellants
that, under the Bill as introduced, it was proposed to impose these duties on the
respondent, as Minister of Town and Country Planning, and that these duties
presented no material difference from those contained in the Bill when passed
into law. It could hardly be suggested that, prior to its enactment, he was subject
to any higher duty than is to be found in the statute. In my opinion, no judicial,
or quasi-judicial, duty was imposed on the respondent, and any reference to
judicial duty, or bias, is irrelevant in the present case. The respondent's duties
under section 1 of the Act and Sched. I thereto are, in my opinion, purely administrative, but the Act prescribes certain methods of or steps in, discharge of that
duty. It is obvious that, before making the draft order, which must contain a
definite proposal to designate the area concerned as the site of a new town, the
respondent must have made elaborate inquiry into the matter and have consulted any local authorities who appear to him to be concerned, and obviously
other departments of the Government, such as the Minister of Health, would
naturally require to be consulted. It would seem, accordingly, that the respondent was required to satisfy himself that it was a sound scheme before he took
the serious step of issuing a draft order. It seems clear also, that the purpose of
inviting objections, and, where they are not withdrawn, of having a public
inquiry, to be held by someone other than the respondent, to whom that person
reports, was for the further information of the respondent, in order to the final
consideration of the soundness of the scheme of the designation; and it is important to note that the development of the site, after the order is made, is primarily
the duty of the development corporation established under section 2 of the Act.
I am of opinion that no judicial duty is laid on the respondent in discharge of
these statutory duties, and that the only question is whether he has complied
with the statutory directions to appoint a person to hold the public inquiry, and
to consider that person's report. On this contention of the appellants no suggestion is made that the public inquiry was not properly conducted, nor is there
any criticism of the report by Mr. Morris. In such a case the only ground of
challenge must be either that the respondent did not in fact consider the report
and the objections, of which there is here no evidence, or that his mind was so
foreclosed that he gave no genuine consideration to them, which is the case
made by the appellants. Although I am unable to agree exactly with the view
of the respondent's duty expressed by the learned judge, or with some of the
expressions used by the Court of Appeal in regard to that matter, it does appear
to me that the issue was treated in both courts as being whether the respondent
had genuinely considered the objections and the report, as directed by the Act.
    My Lords, I could wish that the use of the word "bias" should be confined
to its proper sphere. Its proper significance, in my opinion, is to denote a
departure from the standard of even-handed justice which the law requires
from those who occupy judicial office, or those who are commonly regarded
as holding a quasi-judicial office, such as an arbitrator. The reason for this
clearly is that, having to adjudicate as between two or more parties, he must
come to his adjudication with an independent mind, without any inclination
or bias towards one side or other in the dispute. . . . But, in the present
case, the respondent having no judicial duty, the only question is what the
respondent actually did, that is, whether in fact he did genuinely consider the
report and the objections.

Coming now to the inference of the learned judge from the respondent's speech on May 6, that he had not then a mind open to conviction, the learned judge states it thus (1947) 176 L.T. 200 at 203: "If I am to judge by what he said at the public meeting which was held very shortly before the Bill, then published, became an Act of Parliament, I could have no doubt but that any issue raised by objectors was forejudged. The Minister's language leaves no doubt about that. He was not only saying there must and shall be satellite towns, but he was saying that Stevenage was to be the first of them." It seems probable that the learned judge's mind was influenced by his having already held that the respondent's function was quasi-judicial, which would raise the question of bias, but, in my view, I am clearly of opinion that nothing said by the respondent was inconsistent with the discharge of his statutory duty, when subsequently objections were lodged, and the local public inquiry took place, followed by the report of that inquiry, genuinely to consider the report and the objections. . . .

[His Lordship referred to the contentious passages from the Minister's speech.]

My Lords, these passages in a speech, which was of a political nature, and of the kind familiar in a speech on second reading, demonstrate (1) the speaker's view that the Bill would become law, that Stevenage was a most suitable site and should be the first scheme in the operation, and that the Stevenage project would go forward, and (2) the speaker's reaction to the hostile interruptions of a section of the audience. In my opinion, these passages are not inconsistent with an intention to carry out any statutory duty imposed on him by Parliament, although he intended to press for the enactment of the Bill, and thereafter to carry out the duties thereby involved, including the consideration of objections which were neither fractious nor unreasonable. I am, therefore of opinion that the first contention of the appellants fails, in that they have not established either that in the respondent's speech he had forejudged any genuine consideration of the objections or that he had not genuinely considered the objections at the later stage when they were submitted to him. . . .

[His Lordship went on to hold that the Act did not require evidence to be led at the public inquiry in support of the order. Paragraph 3 of Sch.1 to the 1946 Act required that, if objections were made, "the Minister shall, before making the order, cause a public local inquiry to be held with respect thereto. . . . The last three words were held to mean "with respect to the objections". Thus the inquiry was properly held.]

LORDS PORTER, UTHWATT, DU PARCQ and NORMAND concurred.

Appeal dismissed.

Notes and Questions

1. This case was decided at a time when the courts tied the label "judicial" only to *lis inter partes* situations. In the context of planning, a minister was held to be acting in a judicial capacity only after objections had been received and an inquiry was necessary. See *Errington v Minister of Health* [1935] 1 K.B. 249.

2. How would this case be decided today in the light of the principles applied in the *Kirkstall* case (below, p.778) (assuming that those principles were themselves to be approved by the House of Lords)? Woolf J.'s comment in *R. v City of London Corporation Ex p. Allan*, unreported, July 31, 1980 that counsel in that case had described *Franklin* "with some degree of accuracy as being the low-water mark of administrative law". *Franklin* has been only rarely cited in the courts since the 1960s.

3. What should the position have been if the deciding minister had had a direct or indirect pecuniary interest in land affected by the new town order? How do you think the House of Lords would have decided the case?

4. The *Franklin* case did not expressly cast any doubt on earlier cases in which the *nemo judex* principle had been applied to the decisions of administration authorities. These included the decision of London County Council to refuse renewal of a music and dancing licence (*R. v London CC Ex p. Akkersdyk* [1892] 1 Q.B. 190 (three councillors who voted against renewal in committee instructed counsel to oppose renewal before the full council, and were present at the council meeting although they did not vote; they were held to have acted both as accusers and judges at the same time); the rejection by a Watch Committee of an appeal against dismissal brought by a police sergeant (*Cooper v Wilson* [1937] 2 K.B. 309 (chief constable both dismissed the sergeant and was present during the Watch Committee deliberations; decision void); and the *Chorley* case (below, p.785).

5. Another allegation of ministerial prejudgement was made in *R. v Secretary of State for the Home Department Ex p. Al Fayed* [2001] Imm. A.R. 134. Mr Mohammed Al Fayed applied for naturalisation as a British citizen. He successfully challenged the Home Secretary's refusal of the application without giving reasons (above, p.750). Following the change of government in 1997, the new Home Secretary, Jack Straw M.P., announced a change of policy on the giving of reasons and that the Government's appeal to the House of Lords was to be withdrawn. Mr Al Fayed's application was accordingly to be redetermined by Mr Straw.

In September 1998, the *Sunday Express* published an article (based on an "absolutely impeccable" but unnamed source), stating that Mr Straw had said to friends "I just don't see how he can have citizenship if he paid MPs", although the report of officials on the matter "has yet to arrive on Mr Straw's desk". Mr Al Fayed was subsequently told that the Home Secretary was minded to refuse his application by reference to two matters of concern (a High Court judgment against Mr Al Fayed arising out of the alleged theft from a safe deposit box held by Mr "Tiny" Rowland at Harrods and payments to MPs) and he was given the opportunity to comment. The application was subsequently refused on those grounds, and Mr Al Fayed sought judicial review.

Mr Straw's position, as stated in the witness statement of civil servant, was that he had no recollection of making, and did not believe that he ever made such comments; he had not denied making the comments in response to the *Sunday Express* article as the quotations were hearsay. The Court of Appeal held that the evidence was not sufficient to establish that the words were spoken, and that, even if they had been, they were no more than "the expression of a preliminary view" which did not amount to either prejudgement or the appearance of prejudgment (see Nourse L.J. at [60]) or, in the words of Rix L.J., actual bias or apparent bias (at [106]).

Furthermore, subsequent communications between the two sides demonstrated that Mr Al Fayed and his solicitors:

"Through knowing that the Home Secretary had not denied that he had spoken the words attributed to him, were nevertheless content that he should continue to deal with the application personally".

The conditions of waiver were therefore established (see further below, p.786).

R. v SECRETARY OF STATE FOR THE ENVIRONMENT Ex p. KIRKSTALL VALLEY CAMPAIGN LTD

[1996] 3 All E.R. 304 (QUEEN'S BENCH DIVISION)

The applicant amenity organisation sought an order of certiorari to quash decisions made in 1995 by Leeds Development Corporation, an urban development corporation created under the Local Government Planning and Land Act 1980 and dissolved later in 1995, granting outline planning permission for the construction of a superstore in the Kirkstall Valley near the centre of Leeds. The applicants contended that the decisions were unlawful because of alleged bias on the part of the chairman of the Corporation and two fellow board members together with the commercial director of the Corporation. The alleged bias resulted from a number of different interests including: property interests, membership of a political party and membership of a rugby club whose playing fields were subject to the disputed planning permissions. The application was contested by the Secretary of State, in his capacity as the residual authority for the dissolved Corporation, and by a grocery company which had paid over £2 million to purchase the relevant land and planning permissions from the rugby club.

SEDLEY J.: . . . Although Mr Drabble [counsel for the Secretary of State] in his submissions for the Secretary of State was content to accept Mr Hobson's [counsel for the applicant company] governing proposition that the law on apparent bias is now to be found in unitary form in the decision of the House of Lords in *R. v Gough* [1993] 2 All E.R. 724; [1993] A.C. 646, as developed in *R. v Inner West London Coroner, Ex p. Dallaglio* [1994] 4 All E.R. 139, Mr Ryan [counsel for the superstore developers/owners] has advanced a radical alternative: that non-judicial bodies such as an urban development corporation are governed by a different set of principles, to be found in a succession of cases beginning with the decision of Glidewell J. in *R. v Sevenoaks D.C., Ex p. Terry* [1985] 3 All E.R. 226. If Mr Ryan is right, the question to be asked in relation to an impugned decision of a body such as the Leeds Development Corporation, is not whether on the facts now known to the court there was a real danger of bias in one or more members of the decision-making body, but whether the body as a whole can be shown to have gone beyond mere predisposition in favour of a particular course and to have pre-determined it. . . .

[His Lordship considered the decision in *R. v Gough* [1993] A.C. 646 and *R. v Inner West London Coroner Ex p Dallaglio* [1994] 4 All E.R. 139].

The different principle for which Mr Ryan contends is exemplified in the decision of Glidewell J. in *R. v Sevenoaks DC, Ex. p Terry* [1985] 2 All ER 226. In that case a local authority's grant of planning permission to a developer was attacked on the ground that the local authority, which owned the land and had leased it at a substantial premium to the applicant developers, had fettered its own discretion. Glidewell J distinguished both Lannon's case and *R v Hendon R.D.C., ex p Chorley* [1933] 2 KB 696, [1933] All ER Rep 20 (to which I shall come later) in this way:

"Both Lannon and Chorley were cases in which the circumstances differed from those of the present case. In Chorley it was an individual councilor who took part in the voting, although he had a financial interest and was thus biased. In Lannon the proceedings were judicial in nature, and thus the maxim that justice most not only be done but be seen to be done applied. The present case is an illustration of an administrative, as opposed to a judicial, decision, where it is the council itself, not only individual councilor, which has an interest in [the premises]". (See [1985] 3 All ER 226 at 232–233.)

Answering the question posed to him, which was whether the council in the circumstances was able to exercise a proper discretion, Glidewell J. held that it was. In coming to this conclusion he had considered the decision of the

New Zealand Court of Appeal in *Lower Hutt City Council v Bank* [1974] 1 NZLR 545, where McCarthy P. had accepted that a council could impartially decide a planning question relating to land in which it had on interest, but that the Lower Hutt Council has so compromised itself that its decision could not stand. In arriving at a contrary conclusion on the facts of the case before him, Glidewell J cited with evident approval the following parts of McCarthy P's judgment (at 548–549):

". . . We believe that the clear-cut distinction, once favoured by the Courts, between administration functions, on the one hand, and judicial functions on the other, as a result of which it was proper to require the observance of the rules of natural justice in the latter but not in the former, is not in these days to be accepted as supplying the answer in a case such as we have before us . . . So, in our opinion, whether the principles of natural justice should be applied to the function of a council in considering objections . . . does not turn on any fine classification of that function as judicial or administrative, but that instead whether they apply is to be decided upon a realistic examination of the legislation, the circumstances of the case and the subject matter under consideration." [See [1985] 3 All E.R. 226 at 229–230.)

In my view, when in the passage quoted earlier Glidewell J. characterized the decision before him as 'an administrative, as opposed to a judicial decision', he was doing so not in order to erect differential standards of adjudication but, as the passage shows, in order to point out that it was not bias on the part of an individual councilor, but the interest of the council itself, which was the foundation of the challenge. If the applicant had made it his case that the council was acting as judge in its own cause, the submission would have met with the plain answer that Parliament had authorised it to do so. Hence the different line of attack based on the fettering of discretion. The case is not, in my judgment, a case on the disqualification through personal interest of a member of a decision-making body; nor does it support the proposition that such a ground of challenge is unavailable in local government law.

It is true that in *Anderton v Auckland City Council* [1978] 1 NZLR 657 Mahon J. decided an issue concerning long-term collaboration between the planning authority and a developer in the light of the law of (as he called it) presumptive bias, sub-dividing this into the bias which is irrebutably presumed on proof of a pecuniary interest and bias which is inferred from proof of a real likelihood that the issue has been predetermined. But this case is relied upon by Mr Hobson for a different proposition, namely that the effect of bias can be cumulative. If one goes from the discussion of presumptive bias (at 686–687) to the final reasoning of Mahon J. (at 696–698) his conclusion that actual predetermination had been established was based upon his find that—

"the council had become so closely associated with the company in attempts to secure planning permission for the company's project that . . . it had completely surrendered its powers of independent judgment as a judicial tribunal."

The surrender by a decision-making body of its judgment, which would have been another way of putting the ground of challenge in *Ex p. Terry*, while it can legitimately be described as a form of bias, is jurisprudentially a different thing from a disqualifying interest held by a participant in the process. There may well be facets of the statutory set-up which contemplate dealings at less than arm's length between a planning authority and a developer, and these may in turn qualify the questions upon which independent judgment must be brought to bear, and so preserve a decision in which the planning authority has a pecuniary or other interest. But there is a difference of kind and not merely of degree between this situation and the situation of a participant member of a decision-making body who has something personally to gain or lose by the outcome.

. . . there is, in my judgment, nothing in the jurisprudence of *R. v Gough* which necessarily limits to judicial or quasi-judicial tribunals the rule against the participation of a person with a personal interest in the outcome. The line of authority relied upon by Mr Ryan represents, in my view, a different although equally important principle: that the decision of a body, albeit composed of disinterested individuals, will be struck down if its outcome has been predetermined whether by the adoption of an inflexible policy or by the effective surrender of the body's independent judgment. The decision of the House of Lords in *Franklin v Minister of Town and Country Planning* [1947] 2 All E.R. 289; [1948] A.C. 87 cannot now be regarded as diluting this principle. . . .

If, conformably with Mr Ryan's submission, there are not two separate principles in play, but only the one for which he contends, remarkable results follow. Suppose that I want to erect in my garden a building which the neighbours consider any eyesore and which will materially diminish the value of their properties; and that I find later that one of my objecting neighbours was a member of the committee which turned down my planning application. Mr Ryan, standing by the logic of his argument, submits that the neighbour's participation is unobjectionable in law unless it can be shown that not only he, but the committee had predetermined, not merely was predisposed, to refuse my application; and that although the neighbour can now be prosecuted under s.94 of the local Government Act 1972 for taking part in a decision on a matter in which he had a pecuniary interest, and although I can appeal to the Secretary of State and expect to recover my costs on the ground of my neighbour's unreasonable behaviour, nevertheless this court is powerless to strike down a decision in which an individual with a disqualifying personal and pecuniary interest has participated. It would be strange if it were so.

Not only is there, therefore, no authority which limits the *Gough* principle to judicial or quasi-judicial proceedings; there are sound grounds of principle in modern public law for declining so to limit it. The concrete reason, which is not always given the attention it deserves, is that in the modern state the interests of individuals or of the public may be more radically affected by administrative decisions than by the decisions of courts of law and judicial tribunals. The individual who has just been tried for a minor road traffic infraction will not be much comforted by the fact that he was tried with the full safeguards of the criminal law if on returning home he finds that an administrative decision in which he had no say is going to take away his home or his job. Nothing in the years since the publication of Robson's *Justice and Administrative Law* (2nd ed., 1947) has diminished the accuracy of what Robson wrote (pp.4–5):

". . . it is probably the fact that some functions of government are not capable of classification into legislative, executive and judicial powers. It is very difficult to discover any adequate method by which, in a highly developed country like England, judicial functions can be clearly distinguished from administrative functions. Mere names are of no avail, for, as we shall see, judges often administer, and administrators often judge. It is easy enough to take a typical example of each kind of function, and to identify it as belonging to a particular category. But that does not get us out of the difficulty, unless we can extract from it some characteristics essential to its nature. A further difficulty arises from the fact that many of the features which once belonged almost exclusively to activities that were carried on only in courts of law, are now to be observed as attaching also, to a greater or less extent, to activities carried on by other departments of government. Furthermore, what we may call the judicial attitude of mind has spread from the courts of law, wherein it originated, to many other fields, with the result that an increasingly large number of governmental activities bear the marks of both the administrative process *and* the judicial process, and cannot be distinguished by any simple test. 'The changing combinations of events will beat upon the walls of ancient categories', a distinguished American judge has observed; and that is precisely what has occurred in the classification of governmental functions in England."

This is why modern public law, since the landmark decision in *Ridge v Baldwin* [1963] 2 All E.R. 66; [1964] A.C. 40, has set its face against the partitioning of proceedings into judicial, administrative and something in between. The distinctions are not only increasingly hard to make in the variety of adjudicative processes in the modern state; they were historically mistaken. The celebrated chapter of Professor Wade's *Administrative Law* on the right to a fair hearing (currently Chap. 15 in *Wade and Forsyth's Administrative Law* (7th ed., 1994)) shows how the centuries-old jurisdiction of this court over both administrative and judicial acts was mistakenly collapsed into a notion of control over judicial acts only, followed by an artificial expansion of the concept of the judicial to include much that was in truth administrative. Since *Ridge v Baldwin*, although not without occasional deviations, public law has returned to the broad highway of due process across the full range of justiciable decision-making. . . .

I hold, therefore, that the principle that a person is disqualified from participation in a decision if there is a real danger that he or she will be influenced by a pecuniary or personal interest in the outcome, is of general application in public law and is not limited to judicial or quasi-judicial bodies or proceedings.

How then will the principle apply to a body exercising town and country planning powers? In the case of an elected body the law recognises that members will take up office with publicly stated views on a variety of policy issues. In the case of an urban development corporation the Secretary of State will have had regard, in making his appointments, to "the desirability of securing the services of people having special knowledge of the locality" (para.2(2) of Sched. 26 to the 1980 Act), as well as to the proactive purpose of the corporation set out in s.136(1) "to secure the regeneration of its area". In both cases, where predetermination of issues or forfeiture of judgment is alleged, the court will be concerned to distinguish, within the statutory framework, legitimate prior stances or experience from illegitimate ones. But such issues will be governed by the separate line of authority on predetermination. So far as concerns apparent bias, there can be little if any difference between an elected and an appointed planning authority. In both cases there is a constant risk that the body will have to decide matters in which a member happens to have pecuniary or personal interest. In such cases, as the Secretary of State's successive codes for urban development corporations and for local government recognise, unless it is too remote or insignificant to matter, the interest must be declared and the member concerned must not participate in the decision. The likelihood that some such conflict of interest will sooner or later arise for a member appointed to an urban development corporation pursuant to the provisions of the 1980 Act, is no more an excuse for non-observance of the principle of disqualification than it would be for a member elected to a planning authority on a platform of planning issues. The *Gough* test of bias will be uniformly applied: what will differ from case to case is the significance of the interest and its degree of proximity or remoteness to the issue to be decided and whether, if it is not so insignificant or remote as to be discounted, the disqualified member has violated his disqualification by participating in the decision.

. . . the next issue which the present case raises: what should a member of a body do or refrain from doing when a conflict of interest arises?. . . Where the issue arises in a lis inter partes, the course described by Lord Widgery in *R. v Altrincham JJ Ex p. Pennington* [1975] 2 All ER 78 at 83, [1975] Q.B. 549 at 554 can readily be adopted: If either party objects to the continued participation of the person declaring an interest, the objection is ordinarily conclusive; and even in the absence of objection it may be wise in some cases for the decision-maker to stand down, bearing in mind what Shaw J. added in the *Altrincham Justices'* case [1975] 2 All ER 78 at 84, [1975] QB 549 at 556: ". . .wherever a question of this kind does arise it would be prudent for the magistrate concerned to apply a meticulous rather than a casual test to the situation." Where, however, the body is taking a decision in which all those interested are not before it and able to waive the object on, which is the general case in local government and equally in urban development corporations' proceedings, then the disqualification operates without the possibility of waiver. Indeed, with some force, the need to be rigorous about non-participation is even greater in a body such as an urban development corporation which does not necessarily or ordinarily meet in public or publish its proceedings, as compared with an elected local authority which is required by law to sit in public and to publish its proceedings, save only in relation to confidential items.

It is accordingly Mr Hobson's submission, and one which is important in relation to the facts of this case, that any member of a decision-making body who has an interest requiring to be declared must not only refrain from voting on the issue but must absent himself or herself from the meeting while the issue is discussed. Mr Drabble submits that there is no such rule. For the reasons explained by the House of Lords in *R v Gough*, I accept that there is no such rule—but this is a long way from concluding that a member with an interest to declare has no need to do more than refrain from voting. The applicable principle is not a matter of form but of substance: it is that an individual with a personal, pecuniary or proprietary interest in the subject matter of the decision is disqualified from participating in it. Mr Drabble has accepted, subject to possible questions of discretion, that the participation of a single member who is disqualified by bias vitiates the decision.

Participation can manifestly be more than voting or discussion. A justice who, on retirement, tells his colleagues that it is his car which the defendant is charge with taking and wrecking, and who then sits with arms folded while the other justices reach a conclusion, might not be regarded by this court as having abstained from participation simply by having declared his or her interest and neither spoken nor voted. The silent presence on the appeal committee of the chief constable, who as the instigator of the charges had no right to be there, was one of the factors which moved the Court of Appeal to interfere in *Cooper v Wilson* [1937] 2 All ER 726 at 742, [1937] 2 KB 309 at 344:

> "But even if the presence of the respondent sitting to all appearances among the members of the tribunal could be said not to vitiate the proceedings, the fact that he remained with them when the court was cleared for the committee to consider its decision is fatal to the validity of the proceedings. It makes no difference whether he then discussed the case with them or not . . . as there was, from the appellant's point of view, secrecy, and the risk of bias through the tribunal seeing one party without the other being present." (Per Scott L.J.)

Similarly, it is not necessary for a disqualified member to cast a vote which is counted in order to be guilty of participation. In *R. v Hendon RDC, Ex p. Chorley* [1933] 2 KB 696, [1933] All ER Rep 20 the Divisional Court treated a disqualified councilor as having voted on a decision which had been taken by general assent.

It is thus distinctly possible that the mere declaration of a disqualifying interest, followed by abstention from discussion or voting, will not be enough to negate participation in the decision. This is why the courts, like the Secretary of State, have repeatedly counselled caution, not only for the sake of appearances, but because the line between participation and abstention is in many cases a fine one. . . .

Application dismissed.

Notes

1. His Lordship found: (1) that the chairman of the Corporation had either a prohibited direct pecuniary interest or interests which created a real danger of bias in the early years of the Corporation's activities concerning the redevelopment of the Kirkstall Valley. But, those interests did not "contaminate" the later decisions granting planning permission. (2) One board member's only interest with the land was as an honorary vice-president of the rugby club and that this did not create a real danger of bias. (3) Another board member, who was a surveyor, had a professional relationship with the rugby club and Sedley J. concluded that this person's presence (although he had declared his interests and did not vote) at early meetings of the Corporation created a real danger of bias. However, this person did not attend any of the later meetings where the impugned decision were taken. (4) The commercial director's vice-presidency of the rugby club and his membership of the same ward association of the Conservative party as the chairman did not amount to a real danger of bias in the advice that he provided to the Corporation.

2. It is submitted that Sedley J'.s analysis is not affected by the modification of the *Gough* approach by subsequent case law (above, pp.755–774). It has not as yet been considered in any detail by the Court of Appeal or the House of Lords, but is, with report, highly persuasive.

3. Sedley J.'s judgment helpfully illuminates the relationship between two distinct lines of authority. The personal interests of the decision-maker (or one or more members of a collective body that is the decision-maker) may give rise to a real possibility of bias (to use the terminology subsequently approved by the House of Lords in *Porter v Magill*) and this may render a decision open to challenge whether judicial or administrative. However, a wish to further a policy (assuming it to have been adopted

lawfully) cannot in the case of decisions towards the administrative end of the spectrum itself gives rise to a real possibility of bias, but will render the ultimate decision open to challenge if the matter has effectively been predetermined. In such a case the discretion will have been fettered (*cf.* above, pp.482–495). In a further development on the second point, it has subsequently been held that it is sufficient to make out a challenge that:

> "from the point of view of the fair-minded and informed observer, there was a real possibility that the planning committee or some of its members were biased in the sense of approaching the decision with a closed mind and without impartial consideration of all relevant planning issues"

(*per* Richards J. in *Georgiou v Enfield LBC* [2004] EWHC 799; [2004] L.L.R. 453; applied by his Lordship in *Ghadami v Harlow DC* [2004] EWHC 1883).

Illustrations of the first of these propositions include cases where a councillor has had an indirect financial interest in the project in question (*R. v Hendon RDC Ex p. Chorley* [1933] 2 K.B. 696, where planning permission under pre-1947 planning legislation was granted to the potential purchaser of a site and safeguarded a right to compensation in the event of the site being affected by a town planning scheme; one of the councillors who voted for the grant was an estate agent acting for the site owner); close association with a body particularly affected by a decision (see, *e.g.* the *Kirkstall* case; *R. v Kirklees MBC Ex p. Beaumont* (2000) 3 L.G.L.R. 177 (real danger of bias where councillors who were school governors voted on a proposal to close a rival school)); and close involvement with an external special interest group (*Bovis Homes Ltd v New Forest DC* [2002] EWHC 483 (involvement of chairman of planning committee as member of external committee influential in developing policy for the New Forest Heritage Area held to give rise to real possibility of bias in respect of approval by the council of the local plan)).

In the case of collective bodies, the disqualifying personal interest of one member will be sufficient to validate the decision (*Bovis Homes, per* Ouseley J. at [103]–[106]).

Conversely, the more remote the involvement a person with a disqualifying interest in the decision-making, the less likely the decision will be open to challenge (*Kirkstall*; *R. v Newport CBC Ex p. Avery* (1998) 1 L.G.L.R. 205 (no real danger of bias where councillor assisted applicant for planning permission but took no part in the decision-making); *R. v Holderness BC Ex p. James Robert Developments Ltd* (1992) 66 P. &. C.R. 46 (not necessarily improper for a builder to sit on a local authority planning committee considering applications for detailed planning permission submitted by a rival builder); *R.(on the application of the Council for National Parks Ltd) v Pembrokeshire Coast National Park Authority* [2004] EWHC 2907 (no apparent bias where planning permission for a holiday village in a national part was granted by the NPA, whose membership included county councillors, that council having already agreed to make a loan to the developers).

The second proposition is illustrated by a series of cases where a local authority determines an application for planning permission in respect of a project in which it is involved; a grant of permission will be struck down only if the application has effectively been, or there is a real possibility that it has been, predetermined (see *R. v Amber Valley DC Ex p. Jackson* [1985] 1 W.L.R. 298; *R. v Sevenoaks DC Ex p. Terry* [1985] 3 All E.R. 226; *Bovis Homes* (above) and *R. (on the application of Partingdale Lane Residents Association) v Brent LBC* [2003] EWHC 947 (predetermination found on the facts)); *Georgiou* (above); *Ghadani* (above) (close personal involvement of councillor in major town centre redevelopment gave rise to real possibility of predetermination).

4. By virtue of Pt 3 of the Local Government Act 2000, local authorities must adopt codes of conduct that conform to principles prescribed by the Secretary of State. Breaches of the code are dealt with by case tribunals or local standards committees which have a range of sanctions available. These arrangements replaced provisions of

the Local Government Act 1972 that required members to disclose specified interests in matters being considered by the council and non participation in voting; breach of these rules was a criminal offence. They operate more broadly and in parallel to the common law rules against interest and bias; only breach of the latter can render the decision in question unlawful.

See further *Cross*, paras 4–73 to 4–106.

(d) *Exemptions*

Notes

Where the facts are otherwise sufficient to justify a finding that the rules against interest and bias have been infringed, the ground of challenge will nevertheless not be made out where (1) it was necessary for the decision-maker to act; or (2) the person affected, with full knowledge of the decision-maker's interest in the circumstances said to disqualify automatically or give rise to an appearance of bias unequivocally waives any such objection.

Necessity will for example, arise where all those with statutory authority to make a particular decision are affected by the same interest that would otherwise disqualify (*The Judges v Att-Gen for Saskatchewan* (1937) 53 T.L.R. 464; the *Dimes* case above, p.751; R.R.S. Tracey, [1982] P.L. 628.

Where necessity is established, but the case falls within the scope of Art.6(1) ECHR, the position is likely to be incompatible with Convention rights under the Human Rights Act 1998 (see the discussion of *Kingsley v UK* (2001) 33 E.H.R.R. 288 by I Leigh, [2002] P.L. 407). But note that the Court of Appeal in *R. (on the application of PD) v West Midlands and North West Mental Health Review Tribunal* [2004] EWCA Civ 311 said at [11]:

> "In *Piersack v Belgium* (1982) 5 E.H.R.R. 169 the Court appears to have contemplated that the practical problems of finding properly qualified members of a Tribunal may be relevant when considering whether a member is disqualified on account of bias. We would not exclude the possibility that such considerations might be relevant in an extreme case where it was impossible, or virtually impossible, to assemble a Tribunal free of connections that might give rise to apprehension of apparent bias".

The court did not consider this was such case, but held that in any event there was no breach of Art.6(1) or real possibility of bias in the presence on a MHRT of a consultant psychiatrist employed by (but not an officer of) the NHS Trust responsible for the patient's detention. Other Trust employees were barred by the MHRT Conflict of Interest Guidelines, but medical members were only barred if, *inter alia*, they worked at the particular hospital where the patient was detained.

Waiver needs to be established by clear evidence that the person concerned acted freely and in full knowledge of the facts (*per* Lord Browne-Wilkinson) in *Pinochet (No.2)* (above, p.754) [2000] 1 A.C. 119 at 137; *Al Fayed* (above, pp.778); *Miller v Dickson (Procurator Fiscal, Elgin)* [2001] UKPL 74; [2002] 1 W.L.R. 1615 (no voluntary, informed and unequivocal election by defendants in trials before temporary sheriffs to waive objections based on the arguments that a temporary sheriff was not an independent and impartial tribunal for the purposes of Art.6(1), ECHR; temporary sheriffs were appointed by the Lord Advocate, a member of the Scottish Executive and were held by the High Court of Justiciary not to be "independent" for these purposes (*Starrs v Procurator Fiscal Linlithgow* 2000 J.C. 648)); *Jones v DAS Legal Expenses Insurance Co. Ltd* [2003] EWCA Civ 1071; [2004] I.R.L.R. 218 (waiver by litigant in person).

There is authority for the proposition that "displays of blatant bias, likely to undermine public confidence in the justice system, should not necessarily be capable of private waiver" (*per* Cooke P. in the New Zealand Court of Appeal in *Auckland Casino Ltd v Casino Control Authority* [1995] 1 N.Z.L.R. 142, 152; "tentatively" accepted as accurately representing English law by Kennedy L.J. in *R. v Secretary of State for the Home Department Ex p. Al Fayed* [2001] Imm. A.R. 134 at [87]. Rix L.J. agreed (at [110]–[113]) that waiver might not be possible in cases of "established an obvious bias". Nourse L.J. (at [62] agreed with both judgments. The argument against waiver by the individual litigant is that:

> "the existence and appearance of impartiality on the part of the judiciary belongs not to the litigant alone but to the public at large and the legal system of which the judge is a member"

(*per* Kirby P. in *Gotkas v Government Insurance Office of NSW* [1992] 31 N.S.W.L.R. 684 at 687), cited by Cooke P. in *Auckland Casino* and in *Al Fayed*. Kirby P's view is that waiver should not ordinarily be available in cases of apparent bias either, but this view is against the weight of authority (*cf. Pinochet (No.2)* and the High Court of Australia in *Vakauta v Kelly* (1989) 167 C.L.R. 568 at 586ff).

CHAPTER 11

APPEALS

In law, an appeal against a decision is possible only if it has been established by statute. In the context of administrative law, Parliament has not been consistent in the creation of rights of appeal. There are considerable variations in the type of decision appealable, the possible grounds of appeal and the body to which an appeal may be made. Appeals in the context of tribunals and inquiries were considered by the Franks Committee (below) and appeals to the High Court by the Law Commission (*Administrative Law: Judicial Review and Statutory Appeals*, Consultation Paper No.126 (1993) and Report, Law Com. No.226 (1994)). Suggestions have been made for rationalisation of appeal rights and procedures, the Law Commission ultimately proposed limited changes (below, p.791).

Because appeals depend on a statutory, as distinct from a common law, origin, the grounds of appeal will be confined to those specified in, or to be deduced from, the statute. Appeals to the High Court are governed by CPR r.52, and may, in accordance with that rule, take the form of a rehearing or a review. These appeals must be distinguished from review by the courts under their common law powers. A key difference is that on an appeal to the High Court, as distinct from an application for judicial review, the Court may commonly substitute a different decision for that originally reached.

See *Lewis*, Ch.13.

(A) When Should an Appeal be Available?

Notes

1. The Franks Committee on Administrative Tribunals and Enquiries (Cmd.218, 1957), stated (at para.104) that:

"The existence of a right of appeal is salutary and makes for right adjudication. Provision for appeal is also important if decisions are to show reasonable consistency. Finally, the system of adjudication can hardly fail to appear fair to the applicant if he knows that he will normally be allowed two attempts to convince independent bodies of the soundness of his case".

In the absence of special considerations, the ideal appeal structure should take the form of an appeal on fact, law or merits to an appellate tribunal, not necessarily always to be heard orally. As a matter of principle an appeal should not lie to a minister. No second appeal was necessary where the tribunal was exceptionally strong, such as the Pensions Appeal Tribunal (para.105). All decisions of tribunals should be subject to review by the courts on points of law, generally by an appeal, but by certiorari in the case of National Assistance Appeal Tribunals. Appeals might be to the county court, a nominated judge of the High Court, a Divisional Court of the Queen's Bench Division; it would be wrong to lay down a hard and fast rule. There should then be one further appeal in law, by leave, and no more.

The recommendation that there always be a right of appeal on the merits from a tribunal of first instance to an appellate tribunal has not been implemented, no doubt at least in part for reasons of cost. However, the Tribunals and Inquiries Act 1958 provided for appeals on points of law; see now the 1992 Act, s.11, above, p.108

2. The task of National Assistance Appeal Tribunals was said by the Franks Committee much to resemble:

"that of an assessment or case committee, taking a further look at the facts and in some cases arriving at a fresh decision on the case of need" (para.182).

Questions of assistance needed to be determined as quickly as possible. No further appeal was recommended. Following considerable criticism of the quality of their decision making (see, *e.g.* M. Adler and A.W. Bradley, *Justice, Discretion and Poverty* (1975), pp.213–216, a right of an appeal on a point of law to the High Court was established in 1978 (SI 1977/1735) and replaced by an appeal on a point of law to the Social Security Commissioners (Supplementary Benefits Act 1976, s.15A, inserted by the Social Security Act 1979, s.6), with a further appeal on a point of law to the Court of Appeal (Social Security Act 1980, s.14).

Controversially, on the replacement of supplementary benefit by income support and payments from the social fund, under Pt III of the Social Security Act 1986, appeals were only established in respect of income support. Payments from the cashlimited social fund (replacing single payments and urgent needs payment under the supplementary benefit legislation), mostly in the form of loans, are made by social fund officers appointed by the Secretary of State. These are, in theory, discretionary payments, but the detailed directions given to the officers by the Secretary of State operate very much in the manner of regulations. Instead of an appeal, there is provision for internal review by social fund inspectors, who are DWP officials appointed as inspectors by the Social Fund Commissioner. The Commissioner is appointed by the Secretary of State. The lack of a proper appeal to an independent tribunal was criticised (to no avail) by the Council on Tribunals: Special Report, *Social Security—Abolition of Independent Appeals under the Proposed Social Fund*, Cmnd.9722 (1986), above, pp.110–111. See H. Bolderson (1988) 15 J.L.S. 279; R. Drabble and T. Lynes [1989] P.L. 297. The arrangements have been defended by a former Commissioner as appropriate in the specific context of the Social Fund, the inspectors being both expert decision-makers and accountable for the quality of their work (J. Sumption in *Administrative Justice in the 21st Century* (Harris and Partington ed., 1999), pp.157–160).

3. The Council for many years pressed for the introduction of a right of appeal from the Immigration Appeal Tribunal to the courts, on a point of law, replacing applications for judicial review (Annual Report, 1990–91 (1991–92 HC 97), pp.8–9). The Asylum and Immigration Appeals Act 1993, s.9, provided for such an appeal. Prior to the 1993 Act, there was no right for a person whose claim for asylum had been rejected to appeal against the consequent immigration decision, *e.g.* to refuse leave to enter. The only recourse was to apply for judicial review (*e.g. R. v Secretary of State for the Home Department Ex p. Sivakumaran* [1998] A.C. 958, where "most anxious scrutiny" was applied under *Wednesbury* to the underlying decision to refuse asylum). In *Vilvarajah v UK* (1991) 14 E.H.R.R. 248, the European Commission of Human Rights held that judicial review was an inadequate remedy for the purposes of Art.13 ECHR, to prevent a breach of Art.3 ECHR, following removal. Accordingly, s.8 of the 1993 Act introduced for the first time a general right of appeal to a special adjudicator against the underlying immigration decision on the ground that removal would be contrary to the United Kingdom's obligations under the Refugee Convention 1951. However, provisions were also introduced enabling the Secretary of State to certify that particular claims were without foundation in which case, if the special adjudicator agreed, there was no right to appeal to the IAT (1993 Act, Sch.2, para.5).

The appeal structure did not, however, remain settled, because of the caseload and consequent delays affecting those whose claims would ultimately succeed, and enabling the rest to delay their removal. New or modified arrangements were introduced in turn by the Asylum and Immigration Act 1996, Pt IV of the Immigration and

Asylum Act 1999, Pt 5 of the Nationality, Immigration and Asylum Act 2002 and ss.26–32 of the Asylum and Immigration (Treatment of Claimants, etc.) Act 2004. Features of the various changes worthy of particular note include:

(1) the extension of grounds on which particular claims could be certified, preventing a further appeal to the IAT (Asylum and Immigration Act 1996, ss.1–3, substituting a new Sch.2 para.5 in the 1993 Act; re-enacted in the 1999 Act, Sch.4, para.9); replaced by provision for human rights or asylum claims to be certified as "clearly unfounded" with the consequence that appeals can only be brought from outside the United Kingdom (2002 Act, s.94);

(2) the introduction of the Special Immigration Appeals Commission to deal with sensitive national security and other cases (Special Immigration Appeals Commission Act 1997; see above, p.705);

(3) the introduction of a one-stop appeals procedure under which the applicant must raise all the grounds for wishing to enter or remain in the United Kingdom in one appeal (1999 Act, s.74–77, replaced by the 2002 Act, s.85);

(4) the abolition of appeals on the merits from adjudicators to the IAT, leaving only an appeal on a point of law (2002 Act, s.101);

(5) the introduction and extension of fast track procedures for particular classes of appeal (Immigration and Asylum Appeals (Fast Track Procedure) Rules 2003 (SI 2003/801));

(6) the introduction of an attenuated procedure for statutory review of IAT decisions to grant or refuse permission to appeal; the review, for error of law, is conducted by a High Court judge by reference only to written submissions; the judge's decision is final (2002 Act, s.101(2)-(4), replacing judicial review);

(7) the replacement of the IAT and adjudicator as separate tiers by a single Asylum and Immigration Tribunal (2004 Act, s.26); and

(8) an attempt ultimately unsuccessful to exclude appeals from or (with very limited exceptions) judicial review of IAT decisions (see below, pp.918–920).

On the other hand, the grounds of appeal have been extended to include the ground that the decision-maker has acted or failed to act in relation to the appellant in a way made unlawful by the Human Rights Act 1998, s.6(1) (1999 Act, s.65, re-enacted in the 2002 Act, s.84).

The area of immigration and asylum appeals illustrates a difficult tension between considerable political pressure to reduce delays and significant concerns over the quality of Home Office decision-making (see the criticisms of the Home Affairs Select Committee Report on the Asylum and Immigration (Treatment of Claimants, etc.) Bill (First Report, 2003–04 HC 109) and the Constitutional Affairs Select Committee's Report on Asylum and Immigration Appeals (Second Report, 2003–04 HC 211); the Government claimed that decision-making was not "poor" and was improving: Response to the latter report (Cm.6236, 2004).

The Council on Tribunals expressed concern in consultation on the 2004 Bill that "abolition of the second tier would jeopardise the consistency and quality of decision-making." As much as possible should be done in single-tier system to reduce the risks by training monitoring and appraisal (Annual Report 2003–04, (2003–04 HC 750), p.18). These reservations were echoed by the Court of Appeal in *Subesh* (below, p.800).

It is likely that the model of statutory review on the papers of permission to appeal decisions enshrined in s.101 of the 2002 Act will prove attractive to the Government in other contexts where it wishes to streamline processes, and as requirements for permission to appeal are extended (see below, p.793). The effectiveness of the approach in limiting judicial review was confirmed in *R. (on the application of M) v Immigration Appeal Tribunal* [2004] EWCA Civ 1731. Here, the Court of Appeal noted that the Secretary of State now accepted that s.101 did not exclude the judicial review *jurisdiction* of the High Court (as held by Collins J. at first instance), but that it was a proper exercise of the court's discretion to decline to entertain an application for judicial review of issues which had been, or could have been, the subject of statutory review. The statutory review procedure provided an adequate and proportionate protection of an asylum seeker's rights, even though there was no oral hearing, and to permit judicial review as well would make the resolution of a claim for asylum more rather than less protracted. A similar procedure has been included as part of the structure for review of decisions of the new Asylum and Immigration Tribunal (1999 Act, ss.103A-103E, inserted by the 2004 Act, s.26).

For further discussion, see R. Thomas, [2003] P.L. 260 and 479 and [2004] P.L.612.

4. Rather more unusually, an appeal on a point of law to the *county court* in respect of decisions made under the remodelled homelessness legislation (Pt VII of the Housing Act 1996) has been created by s.204 of the 1996 Act. This was designed to curtail the stream of applications for judicial review to the High Court in homelessness cases. See annotations in A. Arden (ed.), *Encyclopedia of Housing Law and Practice*.

5. Sir Harry Woolf argued cogently that order needs to be introduced into the chaos of appeals to the High Court and Court of Appeal from inferior tribunals and other judicial and quasi-judicial bodies ("A Hotchpotch of Appeals—The Need for a Blender" (1988) 7 C.J.Q. 44). Appeals from a court should go to the Court of Appeal direct, normally with a requirement of leave, and with the same time limits applying to all appeals. Appeals from other bodies should only lie to the Court of Appeal if the sole issue turns on the construction of a statute or document or involves a conflict between previous decisions of the court; or the appeal is from an appellate body such as the EAT. Otherwise, the sole method of application should be by way of an application for judicial review.

The Law Commission's Report on *Administrative Law: Judicial Review and Statutory Appeals* (Law Com. No.226, 1994), contained modest reform proposals in respect of appeals (Pt XII, pp.102–115). These included recommendations that all public law procedures should be consolidated into one set of Crown Office Rules; that no new case stated provisions should be created in the future (although abolition of existing procedures was not proposed); that a model application to quash (App. E) be used in future (although it was not suggested that existing provisions should be altered); that the test for standing under statutory appeals ("person aggrieved") should not be widened; that intervention by third parties should be permitted; and that the orders available on statutory appeals (apart from applications to quash) be harmonised. There was no proposal to standardise time-limits, to establish a general judicial discretion to extend time or to introduce a general leave requirement. The cautious nature of the proposals perhaps reflects scepticism as to whether the benefits of rationalisation would justify the cost. In 2004, the DCA consulted on proposals to introduce (1) a permission stage for all appeals and statutory applications to quash (termed "statutory reviews"; (2) common time-limits (with a few exceptions) of 28 days for statutory appeals and six weeks for statutory reviews; (3) provision for third-party interventions on a similar basis to judicial review: DCA, *Statutory Appeals and Statutory Review. Proposals for Rationalising Procedures* (February 2004).

A much more radical change to the structure of appeals from tribunals is to be introduced following the Leggatt Review (above, p.88), as set out in the Government's White Paper, below.

6. As regards procedures relating to land, the Franks Committee (paras 355–359) was satisfied with the regime generally applicable of statutory *ultra vires* clauses (see below, pp.805–816). There was no need to add a ground of appeal that the inspector's report or minister's letter contained errors of fact or that the decision was not "reasonably" based on the evidence at the inquiry and the facts found by the inspector, as this would have the effect of introducing an appeal on the merits.

WHITE PAPER, TRANSFORMING PUBLIC SERVICES: COMPLAINTS, REDRESS AND TRIBUNALS (Cm. 6243, 2004)

A more coherent system of appeals and reviews

7.14 The current approach to second-tier appeals has been described by both Lord Woolf and Sir Andrew Leggatt as a "hotchpotch". It has developed alongside the unstructured growth of the tribunals themselves. Some tribunals have an appeal route to another tribunal; some do not. Relationships with the higher courts also vary.

7.15 We propose to establish a simple and coherent appellate system, based upon the principle that tribunal cases should only go to the courts when issues of the weight and importance normally decided by an appeal court need to be resolved.

7.16 In most cases we would expect that the decision of the first instance tribunal will be accepted. With the exception of immigration and asylum cases, this is what happens now. Where there is need for an appeal we believe that the appropriate forum for decision is (with some exceptions detailed below) an appellate tier within the new tribunal structure. This will become the new default position. This will mean changes for some tribunals, particularly the tax tribunals and our proposals for them are discussed in Chapter 9.

7.17 Within the new appellate tier, the Employment Appeal Tribunal will maintain its distinctive identity. Appeals from first instance tribunals in the administrative justice area will go to a new appeals tribunal. This will bring together the jurisdictions of the Social Security and Child Support Commissioners, the Lands Tribunal, the Transport Tribunal and the new upper tier of the reformed tax tribunals. Within the new appeals tribunal the same assignment principle as set out earlier in respect of the tribunal and judiciary will apply - that is, an individual tribunal appellate judge will only sit in jurisdictions to which he or she has been appointed or assigned. However, we would expect over time that some parts of the appeals tribunal will draw closer together. For instance, even now, the Social Security Commissioners would welcome the assistance of the kind of expertise held by the Special Commissioners of Income Tax, and Special Commissioners would welcome the expertise of Surveyor Members of the Lands Tribunal. The administrative appeals tribunal will also be available to take on appeals from tribunals in England and Wales where the appeal would otherwise lie to the High Court either by way of statutory appeal or judicial review. Its composition, including the use of non-legal members, would vary according to need and type of case. We would welcome views on what the new appeals tribunal should be called. At present we favour the Administrative Appeals Tribunal.

7.18 There will be exceptions to the two tier structure described above.

- where the first appeal to a tribunal is from an independent body rather than a government department we do not think it is necessary to provide a second tier of appeal. This would apply to the Financial Services and Market Appeals Tribunal and the Criminal Injuries Compensation Appeal Panel;
- The Special Immigration Appeals Commission and the Proscribed Organisations Appeals Commission deal with a small caseload of complex and sensitive cases. They are presided over by a High Court

Judge and have a direct line of appeal to the Court of Appeal. Because of the unusual nature of their jurisdictions we do not intend that these two bodies should be brought within the new judicial organisation although their administrative backup will be supplied by staff from the new service; and

• The Asylum and Immigration Tribunal (AIT) is a new body being created by the Asylum and Immigration (Treatment of Claimants etc) Bill. It has been created as a single tier organisation in part to reduce the impact of the abuse of the present two tier appeal system in asylum cases. It would be contrary to the underlying principles for the creation of the AIT if an appeal were to lie from it to another tribunal;

7.19 To discourage unmeritorious appeals we will also introduce a permission requirement. This requirement will be similar to Section 54 of the Access to Justice Act 1999. We will also introduce a power for jurisdictional Presidents to establish ways of reviewing tribunal decisions, to avoid mistakes having to go to the appeals tribunal. An appeal from a first instance tribunal should generally be limited to a point of law, although for some jurisdictions this may in practice be interpreted widely, for instance to allow for guidance on valuation principles in rating cases. The general principle is that an appeal hearing is not an opportunity to litigate again the factual issues that were decided at the first tier. The role is to correct errors and to impose consistency of approach.

7.20 To enable the appellate tier to properly fulfil its role in achieving consistency in the application of the law and so as to encourage the development of precedent across tribunals, a series of common principles with regard to precedent will be developed in partnership with the jurisdictional Presidents. This will promote a common view of how these issues should be tackled across jurisdictions, but leave scope for a flexible approach in particular jurisdictions. To prevent uncertainty, it will have to be clear whether and how existing precedents are affected by any change.

7.21 For tribunal users, this will provide a system that is quicker and simpler to navigate. For those tribunals where there is currently no right of appeal or review, we will introduce one. For the taxpayer the system will be more efficient, with more cases remaining within the tribunal system.

Membership of the appellate tier

7.22 The appellate tier will initially be constituted from the jurisdictional Presidents, and the panel members who currently sit in appellate tribunals, supplemented where appropriate by a mixture of High Court and Circuit Judges (and possibly their Scottish and Northern Irish equivalents) seconded to the tribunal for a period of time. We anticipate that in time there will be some direct appointments to this tier and some tribunal judges promoted to it. But we also think it is important that the more senior members of the tribunal judiciary should bring their expertise to bear on selected first instance appeals as well so we anticipate that tribunal appellate judges will also sit at first instance.

7.23 The decision as to which cases merit this kind of treatment will be partly determined by the tribunals procedure committee and partly by case by case decisions by jurisdictional Presidents. If the reason for assigning a case to a tribunal appellate judge is to provide authoritative guidance or because it is likely that the case will be taken on to the Court of Appeal the usual procedure will be to bring the case into the administrative appeals tribunal. The existing first instance jurisdictions of the component parts of the administrative appeals tribunal will remain as they are now.

Clarifying the relationship between tribunals & the courts . . .

7.26 In his report, Sir Andrew Leggatt drew attention to the unsatisfactory nature of the inconsistent rights of appeal from tribunals that then existed. He said that "if only for reasons of the greater complexity of procedure, [judicial review] cannot be regarded as a real alternative to an effective right of appeal."[1] He added that the current arrangements lacked cohesion and he proposed in their place a divisional system of tribunals, each with a corresponding appellate tribunal.

7.27 For the reasons set out earlier we are not proposing to establish a divisional structure but instead propose to create an administrative appeals tribunal from the existing higher-tier appellate tribunals. Our intention is that the new upper tier would be strengthened by the secondment of circuit judges and, for cases of sufficient weight. High Court Judges with the relevant expertise. The courts' traditional supervisory or appellate role would then, in most cases, be exercised by the Court of Appeal, which would be concerned only with appeals that raised an important point of principle or practice, or where some other compelling reason existed that warranted the attention of that court. Our intention is that appeals from tribunals should for the most part remain within the tribunals system and that where novel or difficult points of law are raised appeals should be to the Court of Appeal rather than the High Court.

7.28 Permission to appeal will be necessary both for an appeal from the first tier to the second tier and from an appeal from the second tier to the Court of Appeal. With this structure the only possible role for judicial review in the High Court would be on a refusal by the first and second tier to grant permission to appeal. It is this possible route to redress which has caused so much difficulty for both the Immigration Appellate Authorities and the Courts. When permission to appeal has been refused by both tiers, and provided that the tribunal appellate judiciary are of appropriate quality, as we intend that they should be, there ought not to be a need for further scrutiny of a case by the courts. However, complete exclusion of the courts from their historic supervisory role is a highly contentious constitutional proposition and so we see merit in providing as a final form of recourse a statutory review on paper by a judge of the Court of Appeal.

Notes

1. Chapter 9 of the White Paper set out proposals for a two-tier structure for tax appeals. This would include a unified structure for the first tier covering the jurisdiction of the General and Special Commissioners of Income Tax, the VAT and Duties Tribunal and the tribunal established by s.703 of the Income and Corporation Taxes Act 1988; with appeals to the new Administrative Appeals Tribunal. Complex cases could be assigned direct to the appellate tier.

---

[1] Paragraph 6.8, p.69.

2. The identification of clear principles for the structure of tribunals generally makes the exemption of the Asylum and Immigration Tribunal from them all the more remarkable. A change of policy on this matter so soon after enactment of the Asylum and Immigration (Treatment of Claimants, etc.) Act 2004 was not, however, to be expected.

3. A separate report by the Law Commission (*Land, Valuation and Housing Tribunals: The Future* (Law Com. No.281, 2003)) proposed a unified structure for a number of tribunals in related areas. These were the Adjudicator to HM Land Registry, the Agricultural Land Tribunal, the Commons Commissioners, the Lands Tribunal, the Leasehold Valuation Tribunal, the Rent Assessment Committee, the Rent Tribunal and the Valuation Tribunal. The proposed model was a generic Property and Valuation Tribunal (PVT) to hear the majority of first instance cases and a reformed Lands Tribunal to hear at first instance cases within its current first instance jurisdictions, and those of the Commons Commissioner and the Adjudicator, and all appeals from the PVT. Such appeals should not be restricted to points of law as if they were "the Lands Tribunal would not be able to exercise its key roles in deciding and developing valuation principles". Appeals from the Lands Tribunal would lie, as now, to the Court of Appeal, on a point of law only. The Law Commission is, however, to undertake a further "full and wide ranging review" of the whole field of housing adjudication, of which these specialist tribunals form part (White Paper, Annex D).

(B) Appeals on Questions of Fact or Merits

SAGNATA INVESTMENTS LTD v NORWICH CORP.

[1971] 2 Q.B. 614; [1971] 3 W.L.R. 133; [1971] 2 All E.R. 1441; 69 L.G.R. 471 (COURT OF APPEAL)

The Betting, Gaming and Lotteries Act 1963, Sch.6, para.2 provided that the grant of a permit for amusements with prizes should be "at the discretion of the local authority". Schedule 6, para.6, provided that where a local authority refused an application for a permit, the applicant could "appeal in accordance with the provisions of the Quarter Sessions Act 1849" to quarter sessions. Section 1 of the 1849 Act provided that

"In every case of appeal . . . to any court of quarter sessions 14 clear days' notice of appeal . . . shall be given . . . and such notice of appeal shall be in writing, . . . and the grounds of appeal shall be specified in every such notice: Provided always, that it shall not be lawful for the appellant or appellants, on the trial of any such appeal, to go into or give evidence of any other ground of appeal besides those set forth in such notice".

Sagnata applied for a permit for amusements with prizes at an amusement arcade to be built at Old Post Office Court in Norwich. This was refused by the Corporation's Fire Service and Licensing Committee, applying the corporation's policy decision not to grant such permits for any such amusement places in Norwich. Sagnata appealed to Norwich City Quarter Sessions, their stated ground of appeal being "that the decision . . . was unreasonable, having regard to the information available to the committee and contrary to natural justice." The recorder, Michael Havers Q.C., allowed the appeal and his decision was ultimately upheld by the Court of Appeal (Edmund Davies and Phillimore L.J.J., Lord Denning M.R. dissenting). One issue was the nature of the appeal to quarter sessions.

EDMUND DAVIES L.J.: . . . This litigation is said to raise in an acute form the question as to the nature of appeals to quarter sessions in such cases as the present. At one stage, Lord Denning M.R. summarised the issue in this way:

"Is the hearing to be treated as a new trial to be determined on evidence de novo, without being influenced by what the local authority has done? Or is the hearing to be treated as an appeal proper, in which the local authority's decision is to be regarded as of considerable weight, and is not to be reversed unless their decision is shown to be wrong?"

With profound respect, however, I do not think that this is the proper antithesis, and I shall seek to show that there is a half-way house between these two approaches.

It is well established that no right of appeal exists apart from statute. As already observed, the only statutory provision relevant to the present case is that "the applicant may appeal in accordance with the provisions of the Quarter Sessions Act 1849". In *Drover v Rugman* [1951] 1 K.B. 380, dealing with a case stated by quarter sessions on an appeal from the juvenile court, Lord Goddard C.J. said, at 382:

"When a case goes to a quarter sessions it is reheard; the person seeking an order proves his case over again. That only means that quarter sessions are taking the place, as it may be expressed, of petty sessions; but the proceedings are none the less an appeal."

This, he explained, was due to the fact that there was no formal record of proceedings before justices, an observation equally true of proceedings before the licensing committee of this local authority, which (as Lord Denning M.R. has observed) are wholly dissimilar to those conducted by a body exercising judicial functions.

For my part, I cannot see how it is practicable in cases such as the present for an appeal to quarter sessions to be other than by way of a complete rehearing. Having no record before him of what transpired before the local authority, how could the recorder otherwise begin to judge the cogency of the written reasons placed before him? . . .

As it appears to me, Mr Tapp [counsel for the corporation] has attached excessive weight to the fact that the granting or renewal of a permit under the Act of 1963 is expressed to be "at the discretion of the local authority" when he concludes therefrom that quarter sessions are bound by the decision of the local authority and its stated reasons unless it can be demonstrated that they were wrong. A similar contention was raised—and rejected—in *Stepney Borough Council v Joffe* [1949] 1 K.B. 599, where street traders' licences to trade were revoked by the borough council. This they had done pursuant to a statutory provision where "the applicant or licensee is on account of misconduct or for any other sufficient reason in their opinion unsuitable to hold such licence . . .". Section 25(1) of the London County Council (General Powers) Act 1947 provided that persons aggrieved by such refusal "may appeal to a petty sessional court and on any such appeal the court may confirm, reverse or vary the decision of the borough council . . .". The traders accordingly appealed to a magistrate, whereupon the council contended (1) that the magistrate was not entitled to substitute his own opinion as to the suitability of the traders to hold licences for that of the council; (2) that he was not empowered to review the merits; and (3) that his jurisdiction was limited to considering whether or not there was any material on which the council could reasonably have arrived at their decisions to revoke the licences. (One may note, in parenthesis, the close similarity of those submissions to that advanced by the present appellant.) But the magistrate would have none of this. He held that he was bound to consider the whole matter de novo, and he allowed the appeals. Upholding that decision in the Divisional Court, and referring to the submission that the magistrate had not been entitled to substitute his opinion for that of the borough council and that all he could decide was whether there was evidence upon which the council could arrive at their conclusion, Lord Goddard C.J. said, at 602:

"If that argument be right, the right of appeal, ... would be purely illusory. Such an appeal would . . . really be only an appeal on the question of law whether there was any evidence upon which the borough council could have formed an opinion. If their decision were a mere matter of opinion and that opinion were to be conclusive, I do not know that the borough council would be obliged to have any evidence. They could simply say: 'In our opinion this person is unsuitable to hold a licence.' It is true that they must give a sufficient reason, but they could give any reason they liked and say: 'That is sufficient in our opinion.' I do not know how a court could then say on appeal that that was not a sufficient reason. If the reason need only be one which is sufficient in the opinion of the borough council, it is difficult to see how any court of appeal could set aside their decision. It seems to me that [section 25(1)] gives an unrestricted right of appeal, and if there is an unrestricted right of appeal, it is for the court of appeal to substitute its opinion for the opinion of the borough council."

I would apply those words in full measure to the present case. The provision for an appeal to quarter sessions seems to me largely, if not entirely, "illusory" if the contention of the appellant council is right. If it is, I am at a loss to follow how the recorder would set about discharging his appellate function. Lacking all information as to what had happened before the local authority, save the bare knowledge that they had refused the application and their written grounds for refusal, he would be powerless, as I think, to make any effective examination of the validity of those reasons. Furthermore, unless he is free to embark on a complete consideration of all the relevant material presented to him, how can he in due course proceed to state a case for the Divisional Court if called upon to do so? The customary (and preferable) way of doing this is *inter alia* to set out in separate paragraphs those facts found by the lower court to have been "proved or admitted", and indeed we were shown a copy of the draft case prepared (but ultimately not used) by the local authority in the present case which was in that form. But how could the recorder proceed to state what *his* findings of fact were if he was not free to receive evidence and assess it? No satisfactory answer to this question has, in my judgment, been advanced, and for this reason, among others, I am forced to the conclusion that the appellants are wrong in their main contention. I hold that the proceedings before this recorder were by way of a complete rehearing.

But, contrary to what has been contended, this conclusion does *not* involve that the views earlier formed by the local authority have to be entirely disregarded by quarter sessions. . . . Here again, *Stepney Borough Council v Joffe* [1949] 1 K.B. 599 establishes what I regard as the proper approach, for, having made the point that there was in that case an unrestricted appeal, Lord Goddard C.J. continued, at 602, 603:

> "That does not mean to say that the court of appeal, in this case the metropolitan magistrate, ought not to pay great attention to the fact that the duly constituted and elected local authority have come to an opinion on the matter, and ought not lightly, of course, to reverse their opinion. It is constantly said (although I am not sure that it is always sufficiently remembered) that the function of a court of appeal is to exercise its powers when it is satisfied that the judgment below is wrong, not merely because it is not satisfied that the judgment was right."

I find no reason for thinking that the recorder in the present case failed in any degree to pay proper regard to the decision arrived at by an overwhelming majority of the local authority. On the contrary, he manifestly entertained considerable sympathy with their attitude. But, as he said, he was ultimately obliged to act on the totality of the material placed before him, balancing that called for the appellants against that presented by the local authority and paying due regard to the existing decision being appealed from. Having done so, he concluded that the appellants had made out their case, the Divisional Court in its turn have upheld him, and for my part I have to say that it was not established to my satisfaction that either erred in law. I therefore find myself compelled to hold that this appeal should be dismissed and that the order of the recorder granting the permit be upheld.

PHILLIMORE L.J.: . . . [agreed with EDMUND DAVIES L.J. that the appeal to Quarter Sessions was by way of rehearing.]

Appeal dismissed.

Notes

1. On the policy fetter dimension of this case, see above, p.491. See case note by J. Prophet, [1971] P.L. 162.

2. Appeals which formerly lay to quarter sessions now lie to the Crown Court: the Courts Act 1971, ss.8, 9, Schs 1, 9; I.R. Scott, *The Crown Court* (1972), paras 204–233.

3. The grant of permits in respect of the provision of amusements with prizes is now governed by Pt III of the Gaming Act 1968 (gaming by means of machines) and the Lotteries and Amusements Act 1976 (see C. Milner Smith and S.P. Monkcom, *The Law of Betting, Gaming and Lotteries* (1987), Chs 10 and 11; *R. v Chichester Crown Court Ex p. Forte* (1995) 160 J.P. 285.

The *Sagnata* approach applies also to appeals to the Crown Court concerning general gaming club licences (*i.e.* casino and bingo club licences) (*R. v Crown Court at Knightsbridge Ex p. Aspinall Curzon Ltd*, *The Times*, December 16, 1982; Smith and Monkcom, *op.cit.*, pp.218–220). See also *Sutton LBC v Davis* [1994] Fam. 241, where Wilson J. held that the justices on an appeal under the Children Act 1989, s.77, against the local authority's refusal to register the applicant as a childminder, had to look at the matter *de novo* and decide for themselves whether she was a fit person. The justices were not obliged to accept the local authority's policy that any person who declined to give an undertaking not to smack the children was unfit; and *Brent LBC v Reynolds* [2001] EWCA Civ 1843, where the decision of a county court judge allowing an appeal (by way of rehearing) against the refusal of registration of a House in Multiple Occupation was held to be erroneous in law on the ground (*inter alia*) that the judge had not referred to, and gave no weight to, the council's policy and objectives in respect of the registration of HMOs.

In *Darlington BC v Kaye* [2004] EWHC 2836, it was "common ground" that on an appeal by way of rehearing to the magistrates' court, the magistrates

> "ought to have regard to the fact that the local authority has a policy and should not lightly reverse the local authority's decision or, to put it another way, the magistrates must accept the policy and apply it as if it was standing in the shoes of the council considering the application"

(assuming the policy to be lawful) (*per* Wilkie J. at [28]). It is submitted that the second of these propositions (1) is distinct from and not a different way of putting the first; and (2) overstates the position, in comparison with *Sagnata* and *Davies*. However, it was accepted that the magistrates were on the appeal entitled to make an exception to the general policy, and obliged to be prepared to do so, in accordance with ordinary principles (as indeed was the council itself).

4. The fact that an appeal is by way of rehearing enables the court to consider evidence of matters arising between the original decision appealed against and the appeal: *Rushmoor BC v Richards* [1996] C.O.D. 313 (appeal against refusal to extend licensing hours of a nightclub under the Local Government (Miscellaneous Provisions) Act 1982, Sch.1; court entitled to hear evidence that the nightclub was badly run.

5. The proper interpretation of the grounds for what was in effect an appeal was considered in *R. (on the application of Dart Harbour and Navigation Authority) v Secretary of State for Transport, Local Government and the Regions* [2003] EWHC 1494. Here, a local Act provided that the authority had power to grant licences for the use of land adjacent to a tidal harbour, that the authority "shall not unreasonably refuse to grant a licence", and that "any question whether the grant of a licence has been unreasonably refused shall be determined by the Secretary of State". Lightman J. held that the Secretary of State was not confined to applying the *Wednesbury* test for unreasonableness. He was not free to substitute his own view for that of the authority, but "he can and should decide on the basis of the material before him as a matter of common-sense and common justice whether the previous decision was just, fair and reasonable" (per Lightman J. at [29]).

6. In other contexts, a narrow interpretation has been given to the scope of an appeal notwithstanding that no grounds have been specified in the statute. Thus, in *John Dee Ltd v Customs and Excise Commissioners* [1995] S.T.C. 941, the Court of Appeal held that a Value Added Tax Tribunal on an appeal under the Value Added Tax Act 1983, s.40(1)(n), against a decision of the Commissioners where it appeared requisite for the protection of the revenue to provide security for the payment of VAT, could not exercise a fresh discretion in the matter. The protection of the revenue was not a matter for a tribunal or a court. The tribunal merely had to consider whether the commissioners had acted in a way in which no reasonable panel of commissioners could have acted or whether they had taken into account some irrelevant matter or had disregarded something to which they should have given weight. Rather confusingly, the court was also at pains to emphasise that the jurisdiction was appellate and not supervisory and that "references in this context to *Wednesbury* principles are capable of being a source of confusion" (*per* Neill L.J. at 952)(!).

SUBESH v SECRETARY OF STATE FOR THE HOME DEPARTMENT

[2004] EWCA Civ 56; [2004] Imm. A.R. 112 (COURT OF APPEAL)

Conjoined appeals were brought in four cases concerning Tamil asylum-seekers from Sri Lanka. In each of them, the Secretary of State had rejected the appellant's asylum and/or human rights claims and consequently refused leave to enter or remain in the United Kingdom; the adjudicator had allowed an appeal; and the Immigration Appeal Tribunal had in turn allowed an appeal brought by the Secretary of State. One of the questions for the Court of Appeal concerned the nature of the appeal from the adjudicator to the IAT. Schedule 4, para.22 to the Immigration and Asylum Act 1999 (as it then stood) provided:

"1. Any party to an appeal . . . to an Adjudicator may, if dissatisfied with his determination, appeal to the Immigration Appeal Tribunal.
    2. The Tribunal may affirm the determination or make any other determination which the Adjudicator would have made".

The appellants argued that the IAT was only entitled to allow an appeal if the adjudicator's conclusions were "plainly wrong or unsustainable," (*Oleed v Secretary of State for the Home Department* [2002] EWCA Civ 1906; [2003] Imm. A.R. 499) or "exceeded the generous ambit within which a reasonable disagreement is possible" (*Tanfern Ltd v Cameron-Macdonald* [2000] 1 W.L.R. 1311).

In *Indrakumar v Secretary of State for the Home Department* [2003] EWCA Civ 1677, Hale L.J. summarised the position as follows:

"13. There is . . . room for some debate about nuances of meaning between terms such as 'wrong', 'plainly wrong', 'clearly wrong', or 'unsustainable'. But consideration of all of those cases and the principles which they adopt leads me to the following propositions:
    (1) The [IAT] is not different from this court or any other court with jurisdiction to hear appeals on fact as well as law . . .
    (2) The [IAT], like this court or any other court, can only interfere if there has been an error: that is, if, on analysis, the adjudicator's decision was wrong . . . It is not enough that the [IAT] might have reached a different conclusion itself.
    (3) I . . . do not find adverbs such as 'plainly' or 'clearly' wrong helpful in the context of a fact-finding exercise. They have sometimes proved useful for appellate courts when reviewing the exercise of a discretion.
    (4) The test is the same, whatever the nature of the error alleged, but its application will often depend on the type of evidence on which the finding of fact is based. One can distinguish at least four different types:
        (i)   There are findings of fact based on oral evidence and the assessment of credibility. These can only very rarely be overturned by an appellate Tribunal.
        (ii) There are findings based on documentary evidence specific to the individual case. These can be more readily overturned because the appellate tribunal is in just as good a position to assess it. But even there theremay be an important relationship between the assessment of the person involved and the assessment of those documents. If so, great caution once again will be required.
        (iii) There are findings as to the general conditions or the backdrop in the country concerned which will be based on the objective country evidence. The [IAT] will be at least as well placed to assess this as is the adjudicator. Although in our law the notion of a factual precedent is,

as Laws LJ termed it in *S and Others v Secretary of State for the Home Department* [2002] INLR 416 at paragraph 28, 'exotic', in this context he considered it to be 'benign and practical'. There will be no public interest and no legitimate individual interest in multiple examinations of this backdrop at any particular time once that had been considered in detail and guidance is given by the [IAT].

(iv) There are findings as to the application of those general country conditions to the facts of the particular case. These will be an inference to be drawn by the adjudicator and then, if appropriate, by the [IAT]. The [IAT] will be entitled to draw its own inferences, just as is the appellate court under the CPR, once it has detected an error in the adjudicator's approach.

14. How should those principles be applied to this case? The question, as I have already indicated, is whether the [IAT] was simply taking a different view from the adjudicator. If that were the case that would be an error of law on the part of the [IAT], with which this court could interfere. On the other hand, was the [IAT], having found an error in the adjudicator's approach, simply substituting its own inferences for those drawn by the adjudicator? This is something that the [IAT] is entitled to do and this court cannot interfere".

The Court of Appeal held in the present case that these formulations were too narrow. (The Court noted that in respect of appeals determined after June 8, 2003, (and all decisions made after March 31, 2003) appeals from an Adjudicator to the IAT had been limited to points of law, but regarded its analysis as being of more general application.)

The judgment of the court (JUDGE, LAWS AND KAY L.JJ.) was delivered by LAWS L.J.: . . .

The Primary Issue Confronted—Conclusions

[40] There are two straightforward points that can be got out of the way. First, an appeal from the Adjudicator to the IAT under para.22 to Sch 4 of the 1999 Act is available on fact as well as law. So much is uncontentious. But it means that the IAT's appreciation of factual issues is not limited to what might be called the *Wednesbury* ([1948] 1 KB 223, [1947] 2 All ER 680.) question, that is, whether the Adjudicator's conclusion on the material factual issue is perverse or flawed for breach of the requirement that only (but all) relevant considerations have to be taken into account. In fairness Miss Jegarajah [counsel for the first appellant] did not suggest that this was the test for the IAT; although her reliance on *Tanfern* was not far distant from such a stance. And we are clear that Schiemann LJ in *Oleed* cannot be taken as indicating that anything like a Wednesbury approach is required to be adopted by the IAT in confronting an Adjudicator's prior determination.

[41] The second straightforward point concerns the difference between a finding which depends upon the Adjudicator's assessment of oral testimony upon a disputed issue (for example: was the appellant detained and ill-treated as he claims?) and a finding which consists in an inference from proved or admitted primary facts. It is accepted on all hands, from *Montgomerie* [[1904] A.C. 73] onwards and perhaps before, that in the former class of case an appellate court which has not heard the material oral testimony must be slow to impose its own view. So much is commonplace. But this has nothing to with the reach of the appeal court's jurisdiction. It merely recognises the pragmatic limitations to which the appeal court, not having heard the evidence, must be subject.

[42] Those two points are the foothills. Now, it may also readily be accepted as a matter of principle (and we would certainly hold) that the appeal process is not merely a re-run second time around of the first instance trial. This is just as true where the appeal is open-ended (as it is under para.22 of Sch.4 to the 1999 Act), as when it is for example limited to points of law only or subject to other limitations or qualifications. But what is the nature of the constraint upon the appeal process which this proposition implies? It is not merely attributable to the circumstance that the first instance court has heard the witnesses, since its application is not confined to appeals on disputed issues of fact which the judge below has resolved by reference to oral testimony. Thus Lord Halsbury's opening paragraph in Montgomerie is with respect of little assistance.

[43] The constraint has been expressed, not least by Hale LJ in *Indrakumar v Secretary of State for the Home Department* [2003] EWCA Civ 677, as a requirement that the appeal court must identify an error on the part of the lower tribunal before it can interfere. However this notion of an error is more elusive than it appears. In the case of what we have called an open-ended appeal, it is plainly not confined to an error of law. Nor is it confined to an error of fact so gross as to engage the *Wednesbury* principle. How then does the finding by the appeal court of an error on the part of the lower tribunal differ from a "mere disagreement"? What in truth is meant here by "error"? These questions are, with respect, not answered in *Indrakumar*.

[44] The answer is, we think, ultimately to be found in the reason why (as we have put it) the appeal process is not merely a re-run second time around of the first instance trial. It is because of the law's acknowledgement of an important public interest, namely that of finality in litigation. The would-be appellant does not approach the appeal court as if there had been no first decision, as if, so to speak, he and his opponent were to meet on virgin territory. The first instance decision is taken to be correct until the contrary is shown. As Lord Davey put it in *Montgomerie* [[1904] A.C. 73, 82–83,] "[i]n every case the appellant assumes the burden of shewing that the judgment appealed from is wrong" (our emphasis). The burden so assumed is not the burden of proof normally carried by a claimant in first instance proceedings where there are factual disputes. An appellant, if he is to succeed, must persuade the appeal court or tribunal not merely that a different view of the facts from that taken below is reasonable and possible, but that there are objective grounds upon which the court ought to conclude that a different view is the right one. The divide between these positions is not caught by the supposed difference between a perceived error and a disagreement. In either case the appeal court disagrees with the court below, and, indeed, may express itself in such terms. The true distinction is between the case where the appeal court might prefer a different view (perhaps on marginal grounds) and one where it concludes that the process of reasoning, and the application of the relevant law, require it to adopt a different view. The burden which an appellant assumes is to show that the case falls within this latter category.

[45] There are some ancillary points to be made. First, to categorise what we have described as the true distinction as merely being one between perceived error and disagreement not only offers no elucidation of the difference between these two ideas, but may be misleading in practice. Hale LJ's statement (*Indrakumar* para.[13(4)(iv)]) that "[t]he [IAT] will be entitled to draw its own inferences, just as is the appellate court under the CPR, once it has detected an error in the adjudicator's approach" suggests a two-stage process

for the IAT: first identify an error, then proceed to its own inferences. But, with respect, the "error" may consist precisely in the IAT's conclusion that the inferences which it would draw are the right ones. There is no such two-stage process. Neither as a matter of jurisdiction given the terms of para.22 of Sch.4 to the 1999 Act, nor by reference to the general law, is the IAT required to look for an error by the Adjudicator as if that were an exercise hermetically sealed from its own appreciation of the merits of the case. Such an exercise, or something like it, is apt when an appeal court is asked to overturn a pure exercise of discretion by a lower court, as is shown by *G v G* [1985] 1 W.L.R. 647, where it was stated that the appellate courts should only interfere "when they consider that the judge of first instance ... has exceeded the generous ambit within which a reasonable disagreement is possible" and many cases which have followed it. But different considerations are there in play.

[46] Next, we should make it clear that nothing in this judgment is intended to undermine the utility of Hale LJ's categorisation of four different types of evidential issue, set out in para.[13(4)] of her judgment in *Indrakumar*. On the contrary, they shed light on the practical application in the asylum field of what we have ventured to formulate as the true question on appeals, namely whether there are objective grounds which persuade the court that it ought to conclude that a different view from that taken below is the right one. We would draw attention in particular to the third type of issue identified by Hale LJ at para.[13(4)(iii)], dealing with findings made as to the general conditions or the backdrop in the country concerned. In this area the IAT may have particular reason to differ from the Adjudicator, if he has departed without solid justification from an earlier IAT ruling intended to be authoritative as to the situation for the time being in the country in question. Here, this court's judgment in *S and Others* [2002] I.N.L.R. 416; is in point, as is Latham LJ's reference in *Vujnovic* [[2003] EWCA Civ 16 (paragraph [19])] to the IAT's function of review of Adjudicators in order to secure a consistency of approach. We single out this category of case because it is, we think, special to the immigration jurisdiction, and in order to emphasise that the nature of the appeal process, as we have tried to describe it, can be seen to accommodate this "exotic" instance just as readily as more everyday instances of appeal issues.

[47] More generally, in our opinion, once it is recognised that the true question is always whether the process of reasoning, and the application of the relevant law, tell the appeal court that it ought to adopt a different view from that taken below, three benefits flow. First, the principle of finality, the appellant's burden (as Lord Davey put it) "of shewing that the judgment appealed from is wrong", is uniformly preserved. Secondly, all proper scope is given to different kinds of case. Thus what it takes to overturn (say) an Adjudicator's view of an appellant's oral testimony is one thing. What it takes to overturn his view of in-country conditions where the IAT has recently given an authoritative ruling after an exhaustive review of the material may be quite another. Thirdly, the elusive, and in the end unhelpful, distinction between error and disagreement is given its quietus.

[48] Lastly, we hope it is clear that what we have said is not put forward merely as an exercise in the construction of para.22 of Sch.4 to the 1999 Act. It owes such force as it possesses not to any statute, but to the general need to conform the nature of the appeal process with the principle of finality; this is a goal of the common law. It is what might nowadays be called a default position, defeasible in any particular case by statutory provision inconsistent

with it. Thus an appeal to the Crown Court against a conviction in criminal proceedings in the magistrates' court is treated in effect as a new first instance hearing. Evidence is called all over again; it may or may not be the same evidence as was called before the magistrates. There may be other such instances. That process is at variance with the nature of appeals as we have described it. But neither of these approaches undermines the other; the Crown Court instance merely shows the working of a particular statutory regime as it has been interpreted. Cases where statute prescribes a specially restricted right of appeal will equally involve a departure from the default position.

[49] We hope also that the way we have put the matter will not itself be read like a statute so as to constitute a source of further litigation. The approach is a general one, having neither need nor scope for sophisticated refinement. It allows for an infinity of situations in particular appeals and of course is always subject (as we have just made clear) to the bite of any applicable statutory provision.

[50] In our judgment appeals brought under para.22 of Sch.4 to the 1999 Act fall to be conducted consistently with the approach we have set out. We have every reason to suppose that in general they are so conducted. Nothing we have said is intended to assault the general practice of the IAT, including their practice of receiving oral evidence for themselves only exceptionally.

[51] These are our conclusions on the primary issue.

[The court concluded, applying these principles, that the IAT had been entitled in each case to determine, on objective grounds, that a different view from that taken by the Adjudicator was the right one.]

[69] For all the reasons we have given, we would dismiss these appeals. In so doing, we add the following observations.

[70] First, the IAT is a specialist appellate tribunal. An important part of its work has been to identify current trends and problems and, where appropriate, to give general guidance on in-country conditions on the basis of its expert consideration of the latest material. In that way, it has been able to facilitate a consistent approach on the part of adjudicators. Jeyachandran was a case in which such guidance was given. Having provided the guidance it would be absurd if the IAT, in a subsequent case, was unable to make good a decision of an adjudicator made in ignorance, misunderstanding or disregard of that guidance. Fortunately, para.22 of Sch.4 to the 1999 Act has enabled the IAT to substitute a decision, which it considers to be right.

[71] Secondly, as we have indicated, this case will soon be of no more than historic interest. Section 101 of the Nationality Immigration and Asylum Act 2002 has been brought into operation and appeals from determinations of adjudicators promulgated since June 2003 are now confined to points of law. In a case such as the present ones, this will no doubt raise the familiar argument about the ambit of that concept. It would be a matter for regret if the IAT were to be inhibited in the giving of guidance so as to encourage consistency. It should not be forgotten that adjudicators work under great pressure. There are hundreds of them, many of whom are part time. They have been dealing with tens of thousands of appeals each year. We mean no discourtesy to anyone when we say that, inevitably, it is an imperfect system. It is remarkable that it works as well as it does. It is certainly not assisted by the fact that in a significant proportion of appeals, the Secretary of State is unrepresented before the adjudicator, no doubt because of scarcity of resources. The appeal of Suthan was just such a case. We suspect that if the Secretary of State had been repre-

sented, his representative would have been able to have drawn Jeyachandran (which had been notified by the IAT sixteen days earlier) to the attention of the adjudicator. This Court has drawn attention to this problem in another recent case: see Kelangin 28 Janaury 2004 (neutral citation to be added). Be that as it may, it has at least been possible for the IAT to remedy the omission. In this way, consistency - an important aspect of justice - has been achieved.

[72] Thirdly, we permit ourselves a final historical observation. If the Asylum and Immigration (Treatment of Claimants etc) Bill which is now before Parliament is enacted in its present form and the appeal system is "unified", the present ability of the IAT to provide guidance will be lost. A first instance determination would only be reviewable within the proposed Asylum and Immigration Tribunal on paper and then only on the basis that the decision "depended upon an erroneous construction or application of a provision of an Act". It seems to us that this would be a recipe for more and irremediable inconsistencies.

Appeal dismissed.

Note
Under the revised arrangements limiting appeals to the IAT to points of law,

"the general relationship of the IAT to a decision of an adjudicator is similar to that of the Court of Appeal in relation to a decision of a judge at first instance. The Court of Appeal will accept the facts found by the lower court, unless it is shown that the evidence does not support the findings made, or the findings are clearly wrong"

(*per* Lord Woolf C.J. for the court in *P v Secretary of State for the Home Department; M v Secretary of State for the Home Department* [2004] EWCA Civ 1640, at [30]).

(C) STATUTORY *ULTRA VIRES*

ACQUISITION OF LAND ACT 1981

PART IV: VALIDITY AND DATE OF OPERATION OF ORDERS AND CERTIFICATES

Grounds for application to High Court

23.—(1) If any person aggrieved by a compulsory purchase order desires to question the validity thereof, or of any provision contained therein, on the ground that the authorisation of a compulsory purchase thereby granted is not empowered to be granted under this Act or any such enactment as is mentioned in section 1(1) of this Act, he may make an application to the High Court.

(2) If any person aggrieved by—

(a) a compulsory purchase order, or
(b) a certificate under Part III of, or Schedule 3 to, this Act.

desires to question the validity thereof on the ground that any relevant requirement has not been complied with in relation to the order or certificate he may make an application to the High Court.

(3) In subsection (2) above, "relevant requirement" means—

(a) any requirement of this Act, or of any regulation under section 7(2) above, or

(b) any requirement of the Tribunals and Inquiries Act [1992] or of any rules made, or having effect as if made; under that Act.

(4) An application to the High Court under this section shall be made within six weeks.

(a) in the case of a compulsory purchase order to which the Statutory Orders (Special Procedure) Act 1945 applies (and which is not excluded by section 27 below), from the date on which the order becomes operative under that Act,

(b) in the case of a compulsory purchase order to which the said Act of 1945 does not apply, from the date on which notice of the confirmation or making of the order is first published in accordance with this Act,

(c) in the case of a certificate, the date on which notice of the giving of the certificate is first published in accordance with this Act.

Powers of the court

24.—(1) On an application under section 23 above the court may by interim order suspend the operation of the compulsory purchase order or any provision contained therein, or of the certificate, either generally or in so far as it effects any property of the applicant, until the final determination of the proceedings.

(2) If on the application the court is satisfied that—

(a) the authorisation granted by the compulsory purchase order is not empowered to be granted under this Act or any such enactment as is mentioned in section 1(1) of this Act, or

(b) the interests of the applicant have been substantially prejudiced by any relevant requirement (as defined in section 23(3) above) not having been complied with,

the court may quash the compulsory purchase order or any provision contained therein, or the certificate, either generally or in so far as it affects any property of the applicant.

Restriction on other court proceedings

25. Subject to the preceding provisions of this Part of this Act, a compulsory purchase order, or a certificate under Part III of, or Schedule 3 to, this Act, shall not, either before or after it has been confirmed, made or given, be questioned in any legal proceedings whatsoever.

Date of operation

26.—(1) Subject to section 24 above, a compulsory purchase order, other than one to which the Statutory Orders (Special Procedure) Act 1945 applies, shall become operative on the date on which notice of the confirmation or making of the order is first published in accordance with this Act.

(2) Subject to section 24 above, a certificate under Part III of, or Schedule 3 to, this Act shall become operative on the date on which notice of the giving of the certificate is first published in accordance with this Act.

Exclusion of orders confirmed by Act of Parliament

27. This Part of this Act shall not apply to an order which is confirmed by Act of Parliament under section 6 of the Statutory Orders (Special Procedure) Act 1945.

Notes

1. An appeal provision in this form was first introduced in s.11 of the Housing Act 1930, which Act gave greater slum clearance powers to local authorities. The limitations both as to the grounds and the period allowed for appeals were thought necessary in view of the chaos that had been caused by the availability of the prerogative writs to challenge improvement schemes under earlier legislation. In *R. v Minister of Health Ex p. Davis*,[2] the Divisional Court had granted a writ of prohibition to restrain the Minister from confirming a scheme for a site in the centre of Derby. The scheme was held to be *ultra vires* on the ground that some of the land was to be purchased compulsorily for the purpose of resale, and not for any purpose of rearrangement or reconstruction as authorised by the Act. It was alleged that no scheme confirmed by the Minister up to 1929 was valid.[3] Counsel for the property owners in the *Davis* case said that he had examined about 100 schemes, all of which were invalid.[4] As a result new schemes and schemes in progress were held up[5]; "and . . . it was decided that the whole purpose of the Act had been frustrated by the slum landlords and the Court, and that nothing substantial could be done until new legislation was passed".[6]

From 1930, provisions similar to s.11 of the Housing Act 1930 were included in many statutes, perhaps too often as a matter of course.[7] The need for finality is rarely as compelling as it is for large-scale slum clearance schemes, compulsory purchase orders and the like. The main examples of "statutory *ultra vires*" clauses are: the Acquisition of Land Act 1981, Pt IV (compulsory purchase orders: see *Smith v East Elloe RDC*, below, p.907); the New Towns Act 1981, Sch.1 (orders designating the site of a new town: see *Franklin v Minister of Town and Country Planning*, above, p.774); the Highways Act 1980, Sch.2 (orders designating a highway as a trunk road, motorway schemes, etc.); *ibid.*, Sch.7 (public path creation extinguishment and diversion orders); the Town and Country Planning Act 1990, s.287 (structure or local plans, etc.); *ibid.*, s.288 (a large variety of planning matters including decisions of the Secretary of State on appeals against a refusal of planning permission; *cf.* s.289 of the 1990 Act which give rights of appeal on a point of law to the High Court, against decisions of the Secretary of State (*inter alia*) to uphold an enforcement notice.

The attitude the courts should take to statutory *ultra vires* clauses has been restated by Lord Denning M.R. (in the *Ashbridge* and *Coleen* cases, below, pp.808 and 812). Other examples of challenges under these procedures given in this book are *Lavender v MHLG* (p.482); *Stringer v MHLG* (p.488); *Hanks v MHLG* (p.566) and *Franklin v Minister of Town and Country Planning* (p.774). The question of the exclusion of judicial review by procedures other than that laid down in the relevant clause are considered in *Smith v East Elloe RDC* (p.907) and *Ex p. Ostler* (p.911).

---

[2] [1929] 1 K.B. 619.

[3] Sir John Lorden, *Minutes of Evidence of the Donoughmore Committee* (1932), p.68, para.1010.

[4] Mr H.A. Hill, *ibid.*, p.72, para.1027.

[5] The Minister of Health (Mr Arthur Greenwood): oral answer, HC Deb., Vol. 234, col.1164 (January 30, 1930); Second Reading of the Housing Bill, HC Deb., Vol.237, cols 1805–1807 (April 7, 1930).

[6] W.I. Jennings, "Local Government Law" (1935) 51 L.Q.R. 180 at 193.

[7] B. Schwartz lists 18 examples from 1930 to 1948 in *Law and the Executive in Britain* (1949), p.209, n.138.

2. The line between decisions and orders that are protected by a statutory *ultra vires* clause, and decisions that remain subject to judicial review can be complex, and depends on the exact wording of the clause in question. For example, the special appeal provisions apply to a decision by the Secretary of State to confirm a compulsory purchase order, but not a refusal to confirm an order, or a decision to exclude land from an order (*Islington LBC v Secretary of State for the Environment*; *Stockport MBC v Secretary of State for the Environment* (1980) 43 P. & C.R. 300; *R. v Secretary of State for the Environment Ex p. Melton BC* [1986] J.P.L. 190); or a question whether implementation of an order would be unconscionable (*R. v Carmarthenshire DC Ex p. Blewin Trust* (1989) 59 P. & C.R. 379). On the position under the Town and Country Planning Act 1990, see annotations to s.284 in the *Encyclopedia of Planning Law and Practice*.

3. Section 120 of the Enterprise Act 2002 provides for applications to the Competition Appeal Tribunal for the review of certain OFT decisions, the CAT applying judicial review principles: see *OFT v IBA Healthcare Ltd.* [2004] I.C.R. 1364, above, p.52.

ASHBRIDGE INVESTMENTS LTD v MINISTER OF HOUSING AND LOCAL GOVERNMENT

(RE STALYBRIDGE (CASTLE HALL NO.7) AND (ACRES LANE AND LAWTON STREET) COMPULSORY PURCHASE ORDER 1963)

[1965] 1 W.L.R. 1320; 129 J.P. 580; 109 S.J. 595; [1965] 3 All E.R. 371; 63 L.G.R. 400 (COURT OF APPEAL)

Stalybridge Borough Council declared an area to be a clearance area for the purposes of s.42(1) of the Housing Act 1957, on the ground that the houses therein were unfit for human habitation. This area included two adjoining terrace houses of similar appearance, nos 17 and 19 Grosvenor Street, owned by the respondents. Subsequently the local authority made a compulsory purchase order in respect of the clearance area, which was coloured pink on the map of the order, and of certain adjoining land which was coloured grey on the map. The compensation payable in respect of the pink area (unfit houses) was less than that payable in the grey area. Following objections by the owners, a local inquiry was held. The Minister confirmed the order with modifications. One modification was the transfer of No.19 from the pink area to the grey area on the ground that it had lost its identity as a dwelling, and so was not a "house". The owners applied under Sch.4, para.2, to the Housing Act 1957, for an order quashing the compulsory purchase order in so far as it affected No.17, on the ground that it was not a "house", or alternatively was not unfit for human habitation.

Mocatta J. ((1965) 109 S.J. 474) held that the question whether No.17 was a "house" was a question going to the jurisdiction of the Minister and that the court should receive evidence of the facts and reach its own conclusion thereon, and was not confined to the question whether the Minister, on the evidence before him could properly conclude that No.17 was a house. The Minister appealed.

LORD DENNING M.R.: [outlined the facts and continued:] Now the owners make application to the High Court asking for the order to be quashed in regard to No. 17. They say that the Minister has gone outside his jurisdiction because No. 17 is not a house. It is no more a house than No. 19. The owners say that the court should receive evidence afresh on this point and should come to its own conclusion as to whether or no No. 17 is a house or not.

The Minister objects. He says: "This is not a matter on which the court should receive fresh evidence at all, or go into the matter afresh. It is simply a case for the court to ask: Did the Minister have reasonable grounds or no for determining No.17 to be a house?" The Minister concedes that, if he had no evidence before him such as to justify that finding, or if the materials before him were such that he could not reasonably come to the conclusion that it was a house then, of course, the court could interfere. The Minister also concedes that if he has erred in point of law the court can inquire into and quash his decision. But he says that this should be determined on the materials which he had before him, and not on fresh evidence. Mocatta J. has held that the court can look into the matter afresh and receive fresh evidence.

Section 42 of the Housing Act 1957, says: "(1) Where a local authority, upon consideration of an official representation or other information in their possession, are satisfied as respects any area in their district—(a) that the houses in that area are unfit for human habitation ... the authority shall cause that area to be defined on a map", and so on. It is apparent that the question "fit or unfit?" is essentially one for the inspector and the Minister, and the courts would not ordinarily admit fresh evidence on it. But the owners say that, on the question of "house or not a house", the court can and should look into the whole matter itself afresh.

In order to decide this question it is helpful to look at Schedule 3, para.4(3). It says that "If the Minister is of opinion that any land included by the local authority in a clearance area should not have been so included, he shall . . . modify it so as to exclude that land for all purposes from the clearance area." It is clear, therefore, that the Minister can move the land from the pink into the grey if he thinks that it should not have been originally included in the pink area. It seems to me that, in order to determine this matter, the Minister must himself decide the question of "house or not a house", just as he must decide "fit or unfit". The legislature has entrusted it to the Minister for decision. If it is not unfit, he can remove it from the pink to the grey. If it is not a house, he can likewise remove it from the pink to the grey.

Seeing that that decision is entrusted to the Minister, we have to consider the power of the court to interfere with his decision. It is given in Schedule 4, para.2. The court can only interfere on the ground that the Minister has gone outside the powers of the Act or that any requirement of the Act has not been complied with. Under this section it seems to me that the court can interfere with the Minister's decision if he has acted on no evidence; or if he has come to a conclusion to which on the evidence he could not reasonably come; or if he has given a wrong interpretation to the words of the statute; or if he has taken into consideration matters which he ought not to have taken into account, or vice versa; or has otherwise gone wrong in law. It is identical with the position when the court has power to interfere with the decision of a lower tribunal which has erred in point of law.

We have to apply this to the modern procedure whereby the inspector makes his report and the Minister gives his letter of decision, and they are made available to the parties. It seems to me that the court should look at the material which the inspector and the Minister had before them just as it looks at the material before an inferior court, and see whether on that material the Minister has gone wrong in law. We were referred to two cases: *Re Butler, Camberwell (Wingfield Mews) No.2 Clearance Order, 1936* [1939] 1 K.B. 570 and *Re Ripon (Highfield) Housing Confirmation Order, 1938, White and Collins v Minister of Health* [1939] 2 K.B. 838 [above, p.422]. They were decided at a time when the report of the inspector was not open to the parties. There was no letter of decision. There was nothing but the formal order of the Minister.

It was necessary, therefore, for affidavits to be received showing what was the material available before the Minister. They were received in those cases for that purpose. Nowadays, when the material is available, it seems to me that the court should limit itself to that material. Fresh evidence should not be admitted save in exceptional circumstances. It is not correct for the court to approach the case absolutely do novo as though the court was sitting to decide the matter in the first instance. The court can receive evidence to show what material was before the Minister; but it cannot receive evidence of the kind which was indicated in the present case so as to decide the whole matter afresh.

I think that the preliminary point taken on behalf of the Minister, namely, that this is not a matter for fresh evidence, ought to be upheld, and I would allow the appeal accordingly.

HARMAN and WINN L.JJ. delivered concurring judgments.

Appeal allowed.

Notes

1. Clearance area compulsory purchase orders made under the Housing Act 1985, s.290, on or after April 1, 1990, are regulated by the Acquisition of Land Act 1981 (see above, p.805, for the applicable appeal provisions).

2. Differing views had previously been expressed *obiter* in *Smith v East Elloe RDC* [1956] A.C. 736, (below, p.907) on the permissible scope of challenges under a statutory *ultra vires* clause. A majority (Lords Morton (at 754–755), Reid (at 763) and Somervell (at 772)) held that it only covered claims that an order was *ultra vires* in the narrow sense of non-compliance with some requirement (substantive or procedural) to be found in the relevant statute, and not allegations of bad faith or improper motives or (in Lord Reid's formulation, at 762–763) the *Wednesbury* grounds of challenge. Lord Radcliffe disagreed, stating that they covered "any case in which the complainant sought to say that the order in question did not carry the statutory authority which it purported to" (at 768). Viscount Simonds inclined to the same view as Lord Radcliffe but preferred to leave the point open (at 752). These observations were *obiter* given that the issue was whether any form of challenge could be made *after* the six week period. Subsequently, in *Webb v Minister of Housing and Local Government* [1965] 1 W.L.R. 755, Lord Denning M.R. stated *obiter* (in the course of a dissenting judgment) that the "differing voices" in the House of Lords on the scope of the paragraph were "so differing that they give no clear guidance or, at any rate, no guidance that binds us" (at 770). He preferred Lord Radcliffe's approach. Danckwerts and Davies L.JJ. did not mention the point in the course of quashing a compulsory purchase order held not to be made for the purposes set out in the enabling statute. In a discussion of the *Ashbridge* case in *The Discipline of Law* (1979), pp.106–108, Lord Denning described the rejection of the narrow approach of the *Smith v. East Elloe RDC* majority as a "remarkable turn of events. . . . The one who did it— strange to relate—was the Minister himself; through his mouthpiece—the Treasury Devil" (at 106). What makes the matter rather less "strange" is the fact that in argument in *Smith v East Elloe RDC* the Attorney-General, counsel for the respondents, who included the Ministry of Housing and Local Government, accepted the broader interpretation that the ground of challenge extended to "fraud, or bad faith, or on any other ground showing that [the order] was not within the powers conferred by the Act" (at 743).

3. Lord Denning M.R.'s proposition that any error of law will take the order or decision in question outside the powers of the Act can now be seen (in effect) as confirmed by the *Anisminic* principle as explained in *Ex p. Page* (above, p.450). Note also the Court of Appeal's conclusion in *E v Secretary of State for the Home Department* (below,

p.828) that the scope of review on an appeal on a point of law, a statutory application to quash and judicial review is identical; this can be seen as the culmination of the developments enshrined in *Ashbridge* and *Anisminic*. The outcome seems a convenient rationalisation, but is also a little odd given the different formulations deliberately adopted by Parliament as between statutory applications to quash and appeals on a point of law.

4. Four further points may be noted. First, where a "requirement" of the Act is not fulfilled, and there is "substantial prejudice", then a decision may be quashed whether the error is jurisdictional or non jurisdictional (*per* Fisher J., *obiter*, in *Brookdene Investments v Minister of Housing and Local Government* (1970) 21 P. & C.R. 545 at 553).

Secondly, a literal interpretation of the statutory formula would limit the need to show "substantial prejudice" to cases of noncompliance with procedural requirements under the second limb of the statutory formula. Moreover, in some cases, such noncompliance would be so serious as to render the decision *ultra vires* and so open to attack under the first limb (see *Wade and Forsyth*, pp.733–735, where it is suggested that the second limb may well be intended to cover cases of non-compliance with directory procedural requirements: see pp.635–651). It has been suggested, however, that it is necessary to establish "substantial prejudice" under both limbs of the statutory formula (*Manchester (Ringway Airport) Compulsory Purchase Order, Re* (1935) 153 L.T. 219, Branson J.) although this view is difficult to reconcile with the terms of the relevant provisions (*cf.* Forbes J. in *Seddon Properties v Secretary of State for the Environment* (1978) 248 E.G. 950; (1978) 42 P. & C.R. 26 (Note) and in *Bell and Colvill Ltd v Secretary of State for the Environment* [1980] J.P.L. 823 at 828). Establishing that there has been a breach of the rules does not *per se* discharge the onus of showing substantial prejudice (*Bell and Colvill*, above.)

Thirdly, the view has been taken that the provision under the statutory formula that the court "may" quash an order on one or other of the stated grounds gives the court a discretion whether to intervene even where one of the grounds is clearly established (*Errington v Minister of Health* [1935] 1 K.B. 249 at 279 *per* Maugham L.J.; *Miller v Weymouth and Melcombe Regis Corporation* (1974) 27 P. & C.R. 468 at 478–480, Kerr J., criticised by J.E. Alder (1975) 91 L.Q.R. 10; *Preston BC v Secretary of State for the Environment* [1978] J.P.L. 548; *Peak Park Joint Planning Board v Secretary of State for the Environment* (1979) 39 P. & C.R. 361; *London Borough of Richmond upon Thames v Secretary of State for the Environment* [1984] J.P.L. 24); *R.v Tandrige DC Ex p. Al Fayed* (2000) 80 P. & C.R. 90.

In the *Peak Park* case, Sir Douglas Frank said (at 385) that the discretion not to quash should in general only be exercised if the point is technical and there is no possible detriment to the applicant. In the *Richmond* case, Glidewell J. declined to quash a grant of planning permission by an inspector, where the inspector was wrong to hold that a policy in the development plan had been overridden, but where there had been other considerable advantages in the proposed development, and where it would be a waste of time to send the matter back to the Secretary of State.

Fourthly, affidavit evidence may be received if designed to establish "no evidence" on a point in issue (*H. Sabey & Co. v Secretary of State for the Environment* [1978] 1 All E.R. 586); or to establish that proper procedures have not been complied with or that a particular matter of real importance had been left out of the inspector's report (*East Hampshire DC v Secretary of State for the Environment* [1978] J.P.L. 182).

5. The six-week time-limit is applied strictly, see below, pp.907–917. The time-limit is not inconsistent with Art.6(1) ECHR (*Matthews v Secretary of State for the Environment, Transport and the Regions* [2001] EWHC Admin 815, applying *Perez de Rada Cavanilles v Spain* (1998) 20 E.H.R.R. 109, paras 44 and 45). The fixed time-limit pursued the legitimate aim of ensuring legal certainty and finality (which is particularly important in the planning context); and the six-week limit was not so short "as to raise any serious doubt as to whether it is a disproportionate response" to the balancing of the various interests at stake. It was not inconsistent with s.7 to the HRA. See Sullivan J. at paras [30]–[42].

6. "Statutory *ultra vires*" clauses are discussed by J. Alder, (1975) 38 M.L.R. 274; Sir Frederick Corfield and R.J.A. Carnwath, *Compulsory Acquisition and Compensation* (1978), pp.52–66; M. Grant, *Urban Planning Law* (1982), pp.633–644, and annotations to the Town and Country Planning Act 1990, ss.284–288, in the *Encyclopedia of Planning Law and Practice*; *Wade and Forsyth*, pp.727–739; M. Purdue, E. Young and J. Rowan-Robinson, *Planning Law and Procedure* (1989), pp.564–581.

COLEEN PROPERTIES LTD v MINISTER OF HOUSING AND LOCAL GOVERNMENT

[1971] 1 W.L.R. 433; 115 S.J. 112; [1971] 1 All E.R. 1049; 69 L.G.R. 175; 22 P. & C.R. 417 (COURT OF APPEAL)

Tower Hamlets London Borough Council declared two rows of houses, on Clark Street and Sidney Street, to be clearance areas under the Housing Act 1957. By s.43(2) of that Act they had power to purchase compulsorily "any adjoining land the acquisition of which is reasonably necessary for the satisfactory development or use of the cleared area". They wished to exercise this power in respect of Clark House, a good property owned by Coleen Properties Ltd and situated on the corner of the two streets. The owners objected, and an inspector held a public local inquiry and inspected the properties. The council called witnesses (the Medical Officer of Health, Housing Officer and Public Health Housing Inspector) to show that the old houses in the clearance areas were in a bad condition. They did not call any witnesses as to the planning merits, in particular to show that it was necessary to acquire Clark House. They merely asserted, through the mouth of their advocate, the Deputy Town Clerk, that:

"the acquisition of such properties (*i.e.* the added lands including Clark House) is reasonably necessary for the purpose of the satisfactory development or use of the clearance areas (*i.e.* the old houses)".

The objectors called a qualified surveyor and architect to give evidence on the planning merits.

The inspector reported to the Minister as to Clark House:

"This is a first class property and I am of the opinion that its acquisition by the council is not reasonably necessary for the satisfactory development or use of the cleared area".

However, his recommendation that Clark House be excluded from the compulsory purchase order was rejected by the Minister:

"The Minister disagrees with the inspector's recommendation with regard to Reference No.13 (*i.e.* Clark House). It appears to him that by the very nature of its position, the exclusion of this property must seriously inhibit the future redevelopment of the rectangular block of land between Sidney Street and Damien Street in which it stands. He has decided, therefore, that the acquisition of Reference 13 (Clark House) is reasonably necessary for the satisfactory development or use of the cleared area. . .".

The owners applied to the High Court for the order to be quashed in so far as it affected Clark House under Sch.4, para.2 to the Housing Act 1957.

LORD DENNING M.R.: . . . [referred to his statement in the *Ashbridge* case (above, p.809) "the court can interfere . . . lower tribunal which has erred in point of law".] . . .

In my opinion the Minister was in error in reversing the inspector's recommendation. The Minister had before him only the report of the inspector. He did not see the premises himself. To my mind there was no material on which the Minister could properly overrule the inspector's recommendation. Clark House is a first class new property. It has shops with flats over. In order to acquire it compulsorily, the local authority must show that the acquisition "is reasonably necessary for the satisfactory development or use of the cleared area". In order to show it, they ought to have produced some evidence to the inspector as to what kind of development would be a "satisfactory development" of the area, and to show how the acquisition of Clark House is "reasonably necessary". I do not say that they ought to have produced a detailed plan of the proposed development. I realise well enough that in many cases that may not be practicable. For instance, when an area is to be developed for industrial purposes, you cannot go into details until you have the businessmen wanting the factories. But, when an area is to be developed for residential purposes—for the council's own housing plans—it ought to be possible to give an outline plan of the proposed development. I cannot myself see that the council could get any more dwellings on to the site of Clark House than the six flats which are already there. The council may desire to make a neat and tidy development of these two streets, including Clark House, but this may well be possible whilst leaving Clark House standing. At any rate, I am quite clear that the mere *ipse dixit* of the local council is not sufficient. There must be some evidence to support their assertion. And here there was none.

Then there is the report of the inspector. He was clearly of opinion that the acquisition of Clark House was not reasonably necessary. I can see no possible justification for the Minister in overruling the inspector. There was no material whatever on which he could so do. I know that on matters of planning policy the Minister can overrule the inspector, and need not send it back to him, as happened in *Luke v Minister of Housing and Local Government* [1968] 1 Q.B. 172. But the question of what is "reasonably necessary" is not planning policy. It is an inference of fact on which the Minister should not overrule the inspector's recommendation unless there is material sufficient for the purpose. There was none here. In my judgment the Minister was wrong and this court should intervene and overrule him. . . .

SACHS L.J.: . . . [Counsel's] submission raised the question as to whether there was any evidence before the Minister upon which he could properly come to a conclusion which would enable him to exercise the powers that stem from the provisions of Part III of the Act of 1957—clearance and redevelopment: was he entitled to reverse the finding contained in paragraph 37 of the inspector's report to the effect that it was not reasonably necessary for the satisfactory development or use of the cleared area to acquire the property at the corner known as Clark House? The need for evidence to be available to a Minister before he can act has been the subject of earlier decisions. The question before him was not, to my mind, one of policy: it was in essence a question of fact that had to be established as a condition precedent to the exercise of the powers to take away the subject's property. It was no less a question of fact because it involved forming a judgment on matters on which expert opinion can and indeed ought to be given. As long ago as the *Sheffield* case (*Sheffield Burgesses v Minister of Health* (1935) 52 T.L.R. 171 at 173) Swift J. said:

". . . it is for the court, if the matter is brought before it, to say whether there is any material on which the Minister could have come to the conclusion that it was reasonably necessary. If the court comes to the conclusion that there is no such material, then it will not hesitate to quash the Minister's order."

That passage coincides with those passages in the judgment of Lord Denning M.R. in the *Ashbridge* case [1965] 1 W.L.R. 320 to which he has referred.

The Minister, therefore, cannot come to a conclusion of fact contrary to that which the inspector found in this case unless there was evidence before the latter on which he (the Minister) could form that contrary conclusion. Upon the inquiry, an inspector is, of course, entitled to use the evidence of his own eyes, evidence which he as an expert, in this case he was an architect, can accept. The Minister, on the other hand, can only look at what is on the record. He cannot, as against the subject, avail himself of other expert evidence from within the Ministry—at any rate, without informing the subject and giving him an opportunity to deal with that evidence on the lines which are set out in regard to a parallel matter in the Compulsory Purchase by Local Authorities (Inquiries Procedure) Rules 1962.[8] Whilst the inspector, even if not an architect, may well be looked on as an expert for the purpose of forming an opinion of fact, the Minister is in a different position. It is by no means intended as a criticism to say with all respect that no Minister can personally be an expert on all matters of professional opinion with which his officers deal from day to day.

Before turning to the report and examining the evidence, there is a further observation to be made. When seeking to deprive a subject of his property and cause him to move himself, his belongings and perhaps his business to another area, the onus lies squarely on the local authority to show by clear and unambiguous evidence that the order sought for should be granted. What then is the state of the evidence here? Mr Slynn has properly pressed us to look at plan B. . . . From that plan it is quite plain that when developing the rectangle it may well be convenient to have the corner site included in the development, so as perhaps to make it more homogeneous. It is plain that to get possession of it and include it in the development may well be "a tidy idea" according to the canons of Whitehall. It may be that it is better from the point of view of looks. But all that is not enough. It must be reasonably *necessary* for the satisfactory development or use under consideration.

The nature of the development or use under consideration in this case is to be found in paragraph 20 of the report, which refers to "the area zoned in the development plan for residential use" and again in the Minister's own phraseology in his letter of October 25: "The council proposed to redevelop the two clearance areas for housing purposes." That then is the object of the proposed development and use: but what materially serious obstacle to that objective is constituted by the existence of Clark House, a first class property reconstructed in 1956 at public expense and described in paragraphs 29 and 36 as containing, *inter alia*, six self-contained flats with four shops?

On the evidence, there is nothing on which to suggest that there was any material, far less a materially serious obstacle. There is no evidence that the demolition of Clark House would result in even a single extra family being housed. There is no evidence that any addition to the costs of the

---

[8] [ed.] SI 1962/1424: see now SI 1990/512.

redevelopment scheme because Clark House was not acquired would approach or exceed the value of the buildings. There was no evidence that some amenity to the community to be housed on the redeveloped site would be lost: thus there was no question of any gardens of Clark House being needed to such purpose— so far as I can see, it had none. There is no suggestion that Clark House or any portion of the area it occupied was needed for road widening: indeed the contrary was established. Thus there was no evidence whatsoever establishing that Clark House fell within the ambit of section 43(2).

The architect inspector came to his conclusion after an inspection. His conclusions are certainly no help to the submission on behalf of the Minister that this site did fall within the subsection: on the contrary, on the facts of this particular case, one would have thought that his opinion—the only expert opinion—was almost conclusive the other way. Having already made plain that the Minister was not entitled in this case to find as a fact that the premises were reasonably necessary for the purpose mentioned except on evidence before the inspector, and it being clear that there was no such evidence, he had no power to make the order, and in my judgment the appeal should be allowed.

BUCKLEY L.J.: . . . The crucial consideration here I think is whether there was material before the Minister in this case which justified him in the course which he took . . . Mr Slynn, appearing before us on behalf of the Minister, has submitted that that decision is a matter of planning judgment; but he concedes that the judgment must be based upon some evidence. That evidence must be, I take it, evidence of a kind which would justify a reasonable man in reaching the conclusion which the Minister reached. . . . As I think that the Minister had no sufficient material upon which to reach the decision which he did reach, it follows that he acted *ultra vires* the section and that his decision is one which should not be permitted to stand. I therefore agree that this appeal should be allowed.

Appeal allowed.

Notes

1. See case notes by J.M. Evans, (1971) 34 M.L.R. 561 and H.W.R. W[ade], (1971) 87 L.Q.R. 318.

2. In *Migdal Investments Ltd v Secretary of State for the Environment* [1976] J.P.L. 365, Bristow J. distinguished *Coleen* on the ground that evidence of fact and opinion given by a qualified expert (a Senior Planning Officer of the City of Manchester) was not the "mere *ipse dixit*" of the local authority. The statute did not require the authority to place before the Minister a plan of some degree of precision showing why the acquisition of neighbouring land was reasonably necessary for the satisfactory development or use of the relevant clearance areas. In *Banks Horticultural Products Ltd v Secretary of State for the Environment* (1979) 252 E.G. 811, Banks appealed against a refusal of permission to extract peat from certain land. At the inquiry, it became clear that the question turned on whether there were other reasonable sources of supply. By agreement, it was left to the Ministry of Agriculture's witness to supply written evidence on the point after the inquiry. This was done, and the appeal was rejected. Phillips J. held that this evidence provided a wholly insufficient basis for the inspector to reach a conclusion on this point, as it dealt only with the physical characteristics of the alternative supply of peat and not with such questions as availability, suitability and cost. There was either no evidence, or no evidence upon which the inspector could have properly have reached his conclusion.

3. In *R. v Secretary of State for the Environment Ex p. Powis* [1981] 1 W.L.R. 584, the applicant challenged the decision of the Secretary of State to certify under s.57(1) of the Landlord and Tenant Act 1954 that land held by a county council as landlord was requisite for the purposes of the authority, and that its use or occupation be changed. One ground was that the only evidence before the Minister was the bald assertion of the council that no alternative sites were available for its purposes, and that therefore there was no evidence upon which the Secretary of State was entitled to rely, under the *Coleen* principle. The Court of Appeal rejected this argument. Unlike the situation in *Coleen*, s.57 did not envisage a hearing or inquiry. As there was no public hearing, it was for the Minister to weigh the statements submitted to him, and reach a conclusion based on that material.

(D) APPEALS ON QUESTIONS OF LAW

This is the typical ground upon which Parliament has granted rights of appeal to the High Court. See, for example, s.289 of the Town and Country Planning Act 1990, and note the extension of rights of appeal from the decisions of tribunals by s.9 of the Tribunals and Inquiries Act 1958 (now s.11 of the 1992 Act, above, p.108), following recommendations of the Franks Committee (above, p.788).

(E) THE DISTINCTION BETWEEN QUESTIONS OF LAW AND QUESTIONS OF FACT[9]

It is necessary to draw this distinction where an appeal is limited to a question of law. The distinction was formerly important where there was an application for certiorari to quash for error of law on the face of the record, and is of course crucial now that, in most contexts, all errors of law go to jurisdiction (see *Anisminic* and *Page*, above pp.436, 450).

The line between law and fact has been drawn differently in different contexts. The distinction has generated much case law, but the courts have generally been unwilling to adopt a consistent approach. Areas of administrative law which have been particularly fertile include revenue law,[10] workmen's compensation,[11] national insurance,[12] town and country planning[13] and rating.[14] In the wider context, the distinction has been before the courts in connection with magisterial law (particularly appeals by way of case stated to the Divisional Court from decisions of the justices[15]).

It is clear that an issue is one of fact where its resolution depends on the reliability or credibility (but not the admissibility in law) of direct evidence such as a witness's testimony. A finding based on an admission is equivalent to a fact proved by direct

---

[9] See W.A. Wilson, "A Note on Fact and Law" (1963) 26 M.L.R. 609; W.A. Wilson, "Questions of Degree" (1969) 32 M.L.R. 361; C. Morris, "Law and Fact" (1941–1942) 55 Harv.L.R. 1303; L.B. Jaffe, "Judicial Review—Questions of Law" (1955–1956) 69 Harv.L.R. 239; H.W.R. W[ade], (1969) 85 L.Q.R. 18–20; H. Whitmore, [1967] 2 *Federal Law Review* 159; *de Smith, Woolf and Jowell*, pp.277–286; E. Mureinik, "The Application of Rules: Law or Fact" (1982) 98 L.Q.R. 587; J. Beatson, "The Scope of Judicial Review for Error of Law" (1984) 4 O.J.L.S. 22; *Emery and Smythe*, Ch.3 (based on (1984) 100 L.Q.R. 612); G.J. Pitt, "Law, Fact and Casual Workers" (1985) 101 L.Q.R. 217; T. Endicott, (1998) 114 L.Q.R. 292.

[10] "The issue, upon cases stated by the Commissioners . . . has been *directly* before the courts in well over two hundred cases." A. Farnsworth, (1946) 62 L.Q.R. at 248. See *Simon's Direct Tax Service*, para.A3.703.

[11] See *Willis's Workmen's Compensation* (notes to s.1(1)–(3) of the Workmen's Compensation Act 1925).

[12] See, *e.g. R. v National Insurance Commissioner Ex p. Secretary of State* (below, p.824).

[13] See, *e.g. Bendles Ltd v Bristol Corp.* (below, p.818); *Encyclopedia of Planning Law and Practice*, notes to s.289 of the Town and Country Planning Act 1990.

[14] See *Ryde on Rating and the Community Charge* (1991), paras F410–F415.

[15] See the Magistrates' Courts Act 1980, s.111.

evidence. An issue whose resolution depends on probabilities, for example on an inference from circumstantial evidence, is also one of fact. An issue which depends on whether the facts found fall within a statutory description does not fall clearly into either category of fact or law. In different contexts such an issue has been characterised as one of "law", "fact", "mixed law and fact", "fact and degree", "degree", or as *sui generis*.[16] Which view is taken seems to depend on how much control an appellate court wishes to exercise over an inferior court or tribunal, rather than by reference to principle (*cf. Moyna* below, p.821). There may occasionally be a tendency for an appellate court to classify an issue as one of law merely because it thinks the decision below wrong or unjust. Other factors which may be influential include whether the word or phrase in the statute can be said to be an "ordinary English expression" (see *Cozens v Brutus*, discussed in *Moyna* below, p.822), or a "question of fact and degree" (see the *Bendles* case, below, p.818).

BRITISH LAUNDERERS' ASSOCIATION v BOROUGH OF HENDON RATING AUTHORITY

[1949] 1 K.B 462; [1949] L.J.R. 416; 65 T.L.R. 103; 93 S.J. 58; *SUB NOM. BRITISH LAUNDERERS' RESEARCH ASSOCIATION v CENTRAL MIDDLESEX ASSESSMENT COMMITTEE AND HENDON RATING AUTHORITY*, 113 J.P. 72; [1949] 1 All E.R. 21; 47 L.G.R. 113; 41 R. & I.T. 564 (COURT OF APPEAL)

The Association was established to promote research and other scientific work in connection with the laundry and cleaning trades. It owned a site in Hendon with a laboratory block, an experimental laundry, a boiler house and other buildings. The rating authority demanded rates in respect of the site in 1946 for the first time in 20 years. The Association claimed they were exempt from rates by reason of s.1 of the Scientific Societies Act 1843. They appealed successfully on this point to quarter sessions. The Divisional Court reversed the decision of quarter sessions, on an appeal by case stated on a point of law, holding that the Association was not instituted "for the purposes of science . . . exclusively", as required by section 1, but also for commercial purposes which were not merely incidental to the purposes of science. The Association argued that this was a question of fact from which there was no appeal to the Divisional Court.

DENNING L.J.: . . . Mr Rowe says, however, that quarter sessions came to a conclusion of fact in his favour with which the Divisional Court should not have interfered. On this point it is important to distinguish between primary facts and the conclusions from them. Primary facts are facts which are observed by witnesses and proved by oral testimony or facts proved by the production of a thing itself, such as original documents. Their determination is essentially a question of fact for the tribunal of fact, and the only question of law that can arise on them is whether there was any evidence to support the finding. The conclusions from primary facts are, however, inferences deduced by a process of reasoning from them. If, and in so far as, those conclusions can as well be drawn by a layman (properly instructed on the law) as by a lawyer, they are conclusions of fact for the tribunal of fact: and the only questions of law which can arise on them are whether there was a proper direction in point of law; and whether the conclusion is one which could reasonably be drawn

---

[16] See Whitmore, *op. cit*, pp.170–177. As a matter of *theory* it is difficult to resist the conclusion that this is really a question of law: Mureinik, *op. cit.*; *Wade and Forsyth*, pp.943–948.

from the primary facts: see *Bracegirdle v Oxley* [1947] K.B. 349 at 358. If, and in so far, however, as the correct conclusion to be drawn from primary facts requires, for its correctness, determination by a trained lawyer—as, for instance, because it involves the interpretation of documents or because the law and the facts cannot be separated, or because the law on the point cannot properly be understood or applied except by a trained lawyer—the conclusion is a conclusion of law on which an appellate tribunal is as competent to form an opinion as the tribunal of first instance.

. . . The question is whether the association was instituted for the purposes of science exclusively. That is, a conclusion of law to be drawn from the primary facts, particularly, but not exclusively, from the memorandum and articles of association, and involves questions of interpretation of those documents and of the Act. The Divisional Court were able, and indeed bound, to form their own opinion as to the proper conclusion to be drawn from those primary facts, and I find myself in entire agreement with them. . . .

BUCKNILL L.J. and JENKINS J. agreed.

Appeal dismissed.

Notes

1. Compare the principle of planning law that the question whether a change in the use of land is a "material change" and thus development (Town and Country Planning Act 1990, s.55(1)) for which planning permission is required is a "question of fact and degree" (*per* Lord Parker C.J. in *East Barnet UDC v British Transport Commission* [1962] 2 Q.B. 484 at 492; *Bendles Motors Ltd v Bristol Corp.* [1963] 1 W.L.R. 247). The court "can only interfere if satisfied that it is a conclusion that [the minister, on appeal] could not, properly directing himself as to the law, have reached". The test was whether the minister's judgment "was perverse in the sense that the evidence could not support it. That is going a very long way when one is dealing with planning considerations" (*ibid.*). The Minister in *Bendles* was held to be entitled to conclude that the installation of an egg-vending machine on the forecourt of a garage and filling station was a material change in use, and not *de minimis* (the view to which Lord Parker inclined personally). "With this type of machine coming on to the market it may well be that premises like garages premises may become used as shopping centres." Note that the definition of development lies at the heart of planning control. Although not articulated in the *Bendles* case itself, a number of considerations justify the classification of this issue as one of fact and degree. These include the points that the forming of judgment on what land use changes are material is much better to be done by the authorities with responsibility for and expertise in the operation of the whole planning system (local authorities and the Minister) rather than by the courts; that the test of "materiality" is itself opaque, gaining meaning only from a thorough understanding of the context; and that classifying the matter as one of law would overwhelm the courts on appeals on a point of law.

Bendles may be compared with *Birmingham Corp. v MHLG and Habib Ullah* [1964] 1 Q.B. 178 where the Divisional Court held that the Minister had erred in law in holding that the intensification of a use of land could not constitute a material change of use, and remitted the case to him to determine whether on the facts there had been such a change.

See further on the meaning of "development": R.M.C. Duxbury, *Telling and Duxbury's Planning Law and Procedure* (12th ed., 2002), Ch.5; M. Purdue, E. Young and J. Rowan-Robinson, *Planning Law and Procedure* (1989), Ch.5.

2. Note the equation by Lord Parker C.J. of "perversity" with "no evidence". Compare the approach in *Edwards v Bairstow*, below.

EDWARDS (INSPECTOR OF TAXES) v BAIRSTOW

[1956] A.C. 14; [1955] 3 W.L.R. 410; [1955] 3 All E.R. 48
(HOUSE OF LORDS)

In 1946, Harold Bairstow and Fred Harrison, neither of whom had previously undertaken any transactions in machinery, purchased for £12,000 a complete spinning plant, agreeing not to hold it but to make a quick resale. Between then and February 1948, and after various negotiations, the plant was sold in separate lots at a profit of over £18,000. The General Commissioners of Income Tax found that this was not "an adventure . . . in the nature of trade" so as to justify an assessment to income tax under Case I of Sch.D of the Income Tax Act 1918. The Inspector of Taxes appealed by case stated on a point of law to the High Court. The High Court and Court of Appeal (1954) 33 A.T.C. 131 rejected the appeal, treating the matter as a "pure question of fact", but a further appeal was allowed by the House of Lords.

VISCOUNT SIMONDS: . . . [I]n my opinion, whatever test is adopted, that is, whether the finding that the transaction was not an adventure in the nature of trade is to be regarded as a pure finding of fact or as the determination of a question of law or of mixed law and fact, the same result is reached in this case. The determination cannot stand: this appeal must be allowed and the assessments must be confirmed. For it is universally conceded that, though it is a pure finding of fact, it may be set aside on grounds which have been stated in various ways but are, I think, fairly summarized by saying that the court should take that course if it appears that the commissioners have acted without any evidence or upon a view of the facts which could not reasonably be entertained.

. . . [H]aving read and re-read [the facts found by the commissioners] with every desire to support the determination if it can reasonably be supported, I find myself quite unable to do so. The primary facts, as they are sometimes called, do not, in my opinion, justify the inference or conclusion which the commissioners have drawn: not only do they justify it but they lead irresistibly to the opposite inference or conclusion. It is therefore a case in which, whether it be said of the commissioners that their finding is perverse or that they have misdirected themselves in law by a misunderstanding of the statutory language or otherwise, their determination cannot stand. I venture to put the matter thus strongly because I do not find in the careful and, indeed, exhaustive statement of facts any item which points to the transaction not being an adventure in the nature of trade. Everything pointed the other way. . . .

LORD RADCLIFFE: . . . My Lords, I think that it is a question of law what meaning is to be given to the words of the Income Tax Act "trade, manufacture, adventure or concern in the nature of trade" and for that matter what constitute "profits or gains" arising from it. Here we have a statutory phrase involving a charge of tax, and it is for the courts to interpret its meaning, having regard to the context in which it occurs and to the principles which they bring to bear upon the meaning of income. But, that being said, the law does not supply a precise definition of the word "trade": much less does it prescribe as detailed or exhaustive set of rules for application to any particular set of circumstances. In effect it lays down the limits within which it would be permissible to say that a "trade" as interpreted by section 237 of the Act does or does not exist.

But the field so marked out is a wide one and there are many combinations of circumstances in which it could not be said to be wrong to arrive at a conclusion one way or the other. If the facts of any particular case are fairly capable of being so described, it seems to me that it necessarily follows that the determination of the Commissioners, Special or General, to the effect that a trade does or does not exist is not "erroneous in point of law"; and, if a determination cannot be shown to be erroneous in point of law, the statute does not admit of its being upset by the court on appeal. I except the occasions when the commissioners, although dealing with a set of facts which would warrant a decision either way, show by some reason they give or statement they make in the body of the case that they have misunderstood the law in some relevant particular.

All these cases in which the facts warrant a determination either way can be described as questions of degree and therefore as questions of fact. . . .

. . . If a party to a hearing before commissioners expresses dissatisfaction with their determination as being erroneous in point of law, it is for them to state a case and in the body of it to set out the facts that they have found as well as their determination. I do not think that inferences drawn from other facts are incapable of being themselves findings of fact, although there is value in the distinction between primary facts and inferences drawn from them. When the case comes before the court it is its duty to examine the determination having regard to its knowledge of the relevant law. If the case contains anything ex facie which is bad law and which bears upon the determination, it is, obviously, erroneous in point of law. But, without any such misconception appearing ex facie, it may be that the facts found are such that no person acting judicially and properly instructed as to the relevant law could have come to the determination under appeal. In those circumstances, too, the court must intervene. It has no option but to assume that there has been some misconception of the law and that this has been responsible for the determination. So there, too, there has been error in point of law. I do not think that it much matters whether this state of affairs is described as one in which there is no evidence to support the determination or as one in which the evidence is inconsistent with and contradictory of the determination, or as one in which the true and only reasonable conclusion contradicts the determination. Rightly understood, each phrase propounds the same test. For my part, I prefer the last of the three, since I think that it is rather misleading to speak of there being no evidence to support a conclusion when in cases such as these many of the facts are likely to be neutral in themselves, and only to take their colour from the combination of circumstances in which they are found to occur.

If I apply what I regard as the accepted test to the facts found in the present case, I am bound to say, with all respect to the judgments under appeal, that I can see only one true and reasonable conclusion. The profit from the set of operations that comprised the purchase and sales of the spinning plant was the profit of an adventure in the nature of trade. . . .

LORD TUCKER agreed with both speeches.

LORD SOMERVELL agreed with LORD RADCLIFFE.

Appeal allowed.

Notes

1. The *Edwards v Bairstow* approach has been adopted in many other cases in administrative law. See *Emery and Smythe*, pp.114–121, citing, *inter alia*, *R. v Industrial Injuries Commissioner Ex p. A.E.U. (No.2)* [1966] 2 Q.B. 31, where the Court of

Appeal, including Lord Denning M.R., considered the question whether an employee was injured "in the course of employment" (note Lord Denning's comments on this case in *R. v Preston S.B.A.T. Ex p. Moore* [1975] 1 W.L.R. 624, 631–632); *Global Plant Ltd v Secretary of State for Social Services* [1972] 1 Q.B. 139; *O'Kelly v Trust-house Forte Plc* [1984] Q.B. 90 (question whether a contract was "for services" or "of service" held not to be a pure question of law); *IRC v Scottish and Newcastle Breweries Ltd* [1982] 1 W.L.R. 322 (application of the term "plant" for income tax purposes); and *A.C.T. Construction Ltd v Customs and Excise Commissioners* [1982] 1 All E.R. 84 (below, n 4). For a defence of the approach against charges of uncertainty (J. Beatson (1984) 4 O.J.L.S. 22) and that it "smacks of abdication of responsibility" and fails to take rights seriously (G. Pitt, (1985) 101 L.Q.R. 217, 233), see *Emery and Smythe*, pp.121–127.

2. Note Carnwath L.J.'s comment in *OFT v IBA Healthcare* [2004] EWCA Civ 142; [2004] ICR 1364 at [95] that *Edwards v Bairstow* "is sometimes misrepresented as a mere application of *Wednesbury* unreasonableness". This might owe something to Lord Diplock's reference to it in the *CCSU* case (above, p.695); however, "his reference to *Edwards v Bairstow* was simply in relation to his view that 'irrationality' could now 'stand on its own feet', without resort to the inference of a mistake of law". The actual decision of the commissioners in *Edwards v Bairstow* was overturned, yet "could certainly not be described as 'outrageous' in any sense (at least without gross unfairness to the tax commissioners who made it". How does this square with his Lordship's view in *E v Secretary of State for the Home Department* (below, p.828) that the scope of review on appeals on a point of law and on judicial review is identical? Is a possible explanation that the concept of "irrationality" is not limited to the truly "outrageous" *pace* Lord Diplock? Or that the principle of *Wednesbury* unreasonableness or irrationality applies differently as between determination of fact and decisions of policy, greater deference to the decision-maker being appropriate in the case of the latter than the former?

MOYNA v SECRETARY OF STATE FOR WORK AND PENSIONS

[2003] UKHL 44; [2003] 1 W.L.R. 1929; [2003] 4 All E.R. 162
(HOUSE OF LORDS)

M claimed the care component of the disability living allowance on the ground that she was "so severely disabled" that she could not "prepare a cooked meal for [herself] if [she] has the ingredients" (Social Security Contributions and Benefits Act 1992, s.72(1)(a)(ii)). Her claim was rejected by the adjudication officer, the disability appeal tribunal and the Social Security Commissioner on the basis that she could prepare a cooked meal for herself "on most days". The Court of Appeal ([2002] EWCA Civ 408) held that the provision of a cooked main meal was required on a regular basis to enjoy a reasonable quality of life and whenever a claimant had to forgo such a meal on a regular basis by reason of disability the claim would fall within s.72(1)(a)(ii). The "cooking test" was intended to be "straightforward" and produce the same answer on the same facts. The House of Lords unanimously allowed an appeal by the Secretary of State. The "cooking test" was a notional test based on the motor abilities required to prepare a cooked main meal, and was not directed at whether the claimant was regularly able to cook. The decision of the tribunal disclosed no error of law. The following extract deals with the latter point.

LORD HOFFMANN: . . .

20. In any case in which a tribunal has to apply a standard with a greater or lesser degree of imprecision and to take a number of factors into account, there are bound to be cases in which it will be impossible for a reviewing court to say that the tribunal must have erred in law in deciding the case either way: see *George Mitchell (Chesterhall) Ltd v Finney Lock Seeds Ltd* [1983] 2 AC 803,

815–816. I respectfully think that it was unrealistic of Kay LJ to think that he was able to sharpen the test to produce only one right answer. In my opinion the commissioner was right to say that whether or not he would have arrived at the same conclusion, the decision of the tribunal disclosed no error of law.

21. That is sufficient to dispose of the appeal, but I must say something about an alternative submission by Mr Paines, who appeared for the Secretary of State. He said the words "period throughout which . . . he is so severely disabled physically or mentally that . . . he cannot prepare a cooked main meal for himself" were ordinary English words and that their meaning was not a question of law. Consequently the short answer to the appeal was that the decision of the tribunal raised no point of law.

22. This submission was based upon some well known remarks of Lord Reid in *Cozens v Brutus* [1973] AC 854, 861, in which the question was whether the appellant had been guilty of "insulting behaviour":

"The meaning of an ordinary word of the English language is not a question of law. The proper construction of a statute is a question of law. If the context shows that a word is used in an unusual sense the court will determine in other words what that unusual sense is. But here there is in my opinion no question of the word 'insulting' being used in any unusual sense. It appears to me, for reasons which I shall give later, to be intended to have its ordinary meaning. It is for the tribunal which decides the case to consider, not as law but as fact, whether in the whole circumstances the words of the statute do or do not as a matter of ordinary usage of the English language cover or apply to the facts which have been proved."

23. I think that these observations have been given a much wider meaning than the author intended. Lord Reid was in my opinion making two very pertinent points. First, he was drawing attention to a feature of language, namely, that many words or phrases are linguistically irreducible in the sense that any attempt to elucidate a sentence by replacing them with synonyms will change rather than explain its meaning. Lord Kilbrandon made the same point in his reference to Dr Johnson, at p.867. On the other hand, Lord Reid insisted that, whether the statute used simple words or difficult ones, its construction was a question of law.

24. Lord Reid was here making the well-known distinction between the meaning of a word, which depends upon conventions known to the ordinary speaker of English or ascertainable from a dictionary, and the meaning which the author of an utterance appears to have intended to convey by using that word in a sentence. The latter depends not only upon the conventional meanings of the words used but also upon syntax, context and background. The meaning of an English word is not a question of law because it does not in itself have any legal significance. It is the meaning to be ascribed to the intention of the notional legislator in using that word which is a statement of law. It is because of the nature of language that, in trying to ascertain the legislator's meaning, it is seldom helpful to make additions or substitutions in the actual language he has used.

25. Lord Reid's second point is made in the last sentence of the passage I have quoted, when he says that the question of whether the facts found by the tribunal count as "insulting" for the purposes of the statute is a question of fact. There is a good deal of high authority for saying that the question of whether the facts as found or admitted fall one side or the other of some conceptual line drawn by the law is a question of fact: see, for example, *Edwards v Bairstow* [1956] AC 14 and *O'Kelly v Trusthouse Forte plc* [1984] QB 90. What this means in practice is that an appellate court with jurisdiction to entertain appeals only on questions of law will not hear an appeal against such a decision unless it falls outside the bounds of reasonable judgment.

26. It may seem rather odd to say that something is a question of fact when there is no dispute whatever over the facts and the question is whether they fall within some legal category. In his classic work on *Trial by Jury* (1956) Lord Devlin said, at p.61:

"The questions of law which are for the judge fall into two categories: first, there are questions which cannot be correctly answered except by someone who is skilled in the law; secondly, there are questions of fact which lawyers have decided that judges can answer better than juries."

27. Likewise it may be said that there are two kinds of questions of fact: there are questions of fact; and there are questions of law as to which lawyers have decided that it would be inexpedient for an appellate tribunal to have to form an independent judgment. But the usage is well established and causes no difficulty as long as it is understood that the degree to which an appellate court will be willing to substitute its own judgment for that of the tribunal will vary with the nature of the question: see *In re Grayan Building Services Ltd* [1995] Ch 241, 254–255.

28. Applying the first of these two points to the facts of the present case, I think that it was unhelpful for the Court of Appeal to construe the statutory language as if it included words like "daily" or "regularly". Applying the second, I think that the decision of the tribunal was within the bounds of reasonable judgment. I therefore think that, properly understood, Lord Reid's remarks in *Cozens v Brutus* [1973] AC 854, 861 do not lay down some heterodox principle which provides a short cut to dismissing an appeal ("the last resort of counsel appearing on behalf of respondents" as Lord Woolf MR said in *R v Radio Authority, Ex p. Bull* [1998] QB 294, 304) but are in accordance with established principles and common sense.

29. I would therefore allow the appeal and restore the decision of the tribunal.

Lords Nicholls of Birkenhead, Steyn, Rodger of Earlsferry and Lord Walker of Gestingthorpe agreed with Lord Hoffmann

Appeal dismissed

Notes
1. Lord Reid's opinion in *Cozens v Brutus* continued:

"If it is alleged that the tribunal have reached a wrong decision then there can be a question of law but only of a limited character. The question would normally be whether their decision was unreasonable in the sense that no tribunal acquainted with the ordinary use of language could reasonably reach that decision.
   Were it otherwise we should reach an impossible position".

The "ordinary English word" argument has been criticised in the context of criminal law as resulting in the classification of too many matters as question of fact (*cf.* G.

Williams, [1976] Crim. L.R. 472 and 532), and has in that context been ignored more often in practice than applied (D.W. Elliott, "*Brutus v Cozens*: Decline and Fall" [1989] Crim. L.R. 323).

Lord Hoffmann's re-analysis of Lord Reid's comments is helpful and is likely to be frequently cited. His observation that the distinction between law and fact is pragmatic rather than a matter of principle is both right and unusually candid.

2. Lord Reid's comments were not applied in *R. v National Insurance Commissioner Ex p. Secretary of State for Social Services* [1974] 1 W.L.R. 1290 in respect of the meaning of the word "night" for the purposes of the entitlement of a disabled person to attendance allowance if he required, *inter alia*, "prolonged or repeated attention during the night." Lord Widgery C.J. cited Lord Reid's words and continued:

> "However, though 'night' is one of the commonest English words in its ordinary usage, it does have different shades of meaning and the decision of the correct shade of meaning to give to the word in a particular context requires consideration of the context, and thus becomes a matter of construction and therefore a matter of law" (at 1296).

His Lordship thought that in this context "night" meant "the coming of night according to the domestic routine of the household". On the other hand, the question whether particular activities of the disabled person for which he required attention, such as going to bed and getting up, took place in the day or night was a question of fact to be determined in the light of the circumstances of each case.

3. Lord Denning was not always consistent on this question and sometimes suggested that the drawing of inferences from primary facts was always a question of law. *A.C.T. Construction Ltd v Customs and Excise Commissioners* [1981] 1 All E.R. 324, the question was whether work done in underpinning a house with inadequate foundations constituted "maintenance". If it did, the work was positive-rated for VAT; if not, the work was zero-rated. Lord Denning said (at 327–328):

> "The great contest in the case is whether it is 'maintenance' or not. Counsel for the Crown said that the question whether a particular work is 'maintenance' or not is a matter on which two opinions can easily be held without either being unreasonable at all. Quite reasonably one person might say that underpinning is 'maintenance'. Another person might equally reasonably say that it is not 'maintenance'. So he said there is a band in which either view is reasonable. He said that in such a case the courts should not interfere with the decision of a tribunal, whichever way it decided. He said the courts should not interfere with the decision of a tribunal unless it was right outside the band of reasonableness, so unreasonable that no reasonable man could come to that conclusion. He sought to find some support for this argument in some observations of Lord Diplock in the recent case of *Re Racal Communications Ltd* [1980] 2 All E.R. 634 at 639, [1980] 3 W.L.R. 181 at 187–188. But I cannot accept that submission. Once you have the primary facts established, as you have here, about the underpinning, then the question whether the work comes within the word 'maintenance' or not is a question of law for the judges to decide. . . .
>
> I would add that this is especially important in work which is repetitive, and frequently arising, as in this case of underpinning. Throughout the industry it is essential that the contractors and their employers should know whether the work is to be positive-rated or zero-rated. It would be intolerable if one tribunal were to give one view and another tribunal were to give another view, and that no one could decide between them. You would have different rulings in relation to similar work in different parts of the country, according to which tribunal happened to be hearing the case. That cannot be right. I would ask: if there are two tribunals giving different decisions, what are the commissioners to do? Are they to be the arbitrators between the differing views? I hope not. Tax gatherers should not be judges in their own cases. Surely not. When a definite ruling is needed for the guidance of

builders and customers everywhere, it must be for the courts of law to give a definite and final ruling as to the meaning of a word such as 'maintenance' ".

Brandon L.J. stated (at 329) that the question of law was whether the work was "capable of coming within the expression 'maintenance' ". Ackner L.J. said that:

"To my mind this appeal raises a short question of law, *viz.* whether on the true construction of the relevant section of and schedule to the Finance Act 1972, as applied to the undisputed facts in this case, there was a zero-rated supply of service" (at 330).

(To what extent are these formulations different ways of saying the same thing?)

All three members of the Court of Appeal were agreed that the underpinning was a work of alteration and not maintenance. The decision was affirmed by the House of Lords ([1982] 1 All E.R. 84). The sole speech was delivered by Lord Roskill, who regarded the case as raising "a single short point of construction" (at 87), and endorsed Brandon L.J.'s approach (at 88). He concluded:

"My Lords, I decline to attempt to define 'repair or maintenance' when the 1972 Act and the 1972 order do not do so, but leave those ordinary words which are in common use to be given their ordinary meaning. In some cases, there may be room for dispute which side of the line particular work falls. If so, that would be a question of fact or degree for the tribunal of fact concerned to determine. The problem should not prove difficult of solution if their task is approached by applying the facts as that tribunal finds them to the relevant statutory provisions interpreted as I have endeavoured to state" (at 88).

This seems to endorse the *Edwards v Bairstow* approach rather than Lord Denning's (see *Emery and Smythe*, pp.120–121).

4. An illustration of the difficulties in drawing the line between law and fact is provided by the decision of the House of Lords in *Fitzpatrick v IRC; Smith (Inspector of Taxes) v Abbott* [1994] 1 W.L.R. 306. Here, a majority of the House of Lords, led by Lord Templeman, held that the question whether expenditure by journalists on the purchase of newspapers and periodicals was incurred "in the performance of the duties" of the employment so as to qualify as deductible expenses was a question of law. This enabled the House to reconcile different decisions made by Income Tax Commissioners in separate cases in Scotland and England by overturning the English Commissioners' decision in favour of the taxpayers. Lord Browne-Wilkinson dissented, arguing that the issue was essentially one of fact which could only be overturned on *Edwards v Bairstow* principles, which were not established. See A.A. Olowofoyeku, [1996] B.T.R. 28, who argues persuasively that Lord Browne-Wilkinson's approach is to be preferred.

5. The approach adopted in distinguishing questions of law from questions of fact becomes crucial if it is accepted that all errors *of law* go to jurisdiction (above, pp.450–458). The adoption of Lord Denning's approach in the *A.C.T.* case would give the courts a wide power to intervene; the adoption of the *Edwards v Bairstow* approach (or that of Lord Denning himself in *Ex p. A.E.U. (No.2)*), a narrower power. This point is made forcefully by J. Beatson at (1984) 4 O.J.L.S. 22 at pp.39–45, noting that Lord Diplock in *Racal Communications, Re* seemed to prefer the *Edwards v Bairstow* approach (see [1981] A.C. 374, pp.383–384).

(F) Error Of Law

The courts have used many different phrases to describe errors of law, and it is usually possible to describe a particular error in more than one of these ways. Examples include "misinterpreting a statute" (*e.g. R. v Northumberland Compensation Appeal Tribunal Ex p. Shaw* [1952] 1 K.B. 338 (the leading case on the doctrine of error of law on the face of the record)); "taking irrelevant considerations into account" (*e.g. R. v Southampton JJ. Ex p. Green* [1976] Q.B. 11, *cf.* pp.545–569 on abuse of discretion); "applying the wrong legal test" (*e.g.* in determining the "planning unit" relevant to the question whether there has been a material change of use under s.55 of the Town and Country Planning Act 1990: see *Burdle v Secretary of State for the Environment* [1972] 1 W.L.R. 1207; M. Purdue, E. Young and J. Rowan-Robinson, *Planning Law and Procedure* (1989), pp.94–101). Note that Lord Denning equates the grounds for statutory applications to quash with error of law in the *Ashbridge* case (above, p.808). See also the discussion in *E v Secretary of State for the Home Department*, below, p.828.

Four particularly important issues are (i) whether lack of evidence for a decision renders it erroneous in point of law (below), (ii) whether a mistake of fact can constitute error of law (below, p.828); (iii) whether failure to give reasons constitutes error of law (below, p.841) and (iv) whether a point as to *vires* may be raised on an appeal on a point of law (below, p.853).

(i) Lack of Evidence[17]

Notes and questions

1. A number of cases already considered show, in a range of contexts, that a decision based on "no evidence" is erroneous in law: *Bendles Ltd v Bristol Corp.* (above, p.818); *Edwards v Bairstow* (above, p.819); *Ashbridge Investments Ltd v MHLG* (above, p.808); *Coleen Properties Ltd v MHLG* (above, p.812). Note that in *Bendles* "no evidence" was equated with "perversity" and that in *Edwards v Bairstow*, Lord Radcliffe preferred as a test whether "the true and only reasonable conclusion contradicts the determination". Compare these with the formulations in *Bracegirdle v Oxley* set out in the following note.

2. The powers of the Divisional Court in dealing with appeals by way of case stated on a point of law from decisions of magistrates' courts were summarised as follows by Lord Goddard C.J. in *Bracegirdle v Oxley* [1947] 1 K.B. 349 at 353:

". . . [Counsel] concedes that if magistrates come to a decision to which no reasonable bench of magistrates, applying their minds to proper considerations and giving themselves proper directions, could come, then this court can interfere, because the position is exactly the same as if the magistrates had come to a decision of fact without evidence to support it. Sometimes it has been said of the verdict of a jury given in those circumstances, that it is perverse, and I should have no hesitation in applying that term to the decisions of magistrates which are arrived at without evidence to support them".

Humphreys J. stated at 357:

". . . [F]or a very great number of years, whenever justices have found facts from which only one conclusion can be drawn by reasonable persons honestly applying their minds to the question, and have refused to draw that only conclusion, this court has invariably upset the decision of the justices in the appropriate manner".

Denning J. (as he then was) stated at 358:

"In a case under s.11 of the Road Traffic Act 1930, the question whether a speed is dangerous is a question of degree and a conclusion on a question of degree is a

---

[17] See *de Smith, Woolf and Jowell*, pp.282–283, 286, 561; J.M. Evans, (1971) 34 M.L.R. 561 (case note on *Coleen Properties Ltd v M.H.L.G.*); R.R.S. Tracey, (1976) 50 A.L.J. 568.

conclusion of fact. The court will only interfere if the conclusion cannot reasonably be drawn from the primary facts, but that is the case here. In my opinion, the conclusion drawn by these justices from the primary facts was not one that could reasonably be drawn from them".

Will these formulations invariably lead to the same result? Which of them are used in the cases cited in n.1? Do they differ materially from *Wednesbury* unreasonableness of irrationality?

3. In considering the application of the "no evidence" principle the distinction between a (1) jurisdictional or precedent fact and (2) other facts relevant to the ultimate decision must be kept in mind (see above, pp.422–435). In the case of the former, it is for the *court* to determine whether the fact exists, not merely to review the decision on the point reached by the decision-maker. If there is indeed no evidence to support the decision-maker's view that the jurisdictional or precedent fact exists, the court is of course entitled to intervene (consider *White and Collins v Minister of Health* (above, p.422) and *Ashbridge v MHLG* (above, p.808) in the light of this). However, it is important to remember that the role of the court is not limited to applying the "no evidence" rule; even if there is some evidence to support the decision-maker's view on the point, the court is entitled to substitute its own. The important real role of the "no evidence" principle as summarised in the case mentioned in 1 and 2, is as a ground to review factual decisions that are essentially for the decision-maker to reach.

4. In *R. v Nat Bell Liquors Ltd* [1922] 2 A.C. 128, the Privy Council held that where a court had jurisdiction to hear a particular charge it could not lose that jurisdiction by convicting without evidence (see Lord Sumner at 143–144, 151–152). This view is based on a narrow view of the theory of jurisdiction under which if a tribunal has jurisdiction at the commencement of proceedings, it cannot lose that jurisdiction by coming to a wrong decision. This is inconsistent with the broader approach to jurisdictional control subsequently adopted in *Anisminic* and the proposition that in most contexts all errors of law go to jurisdiction (*Ex p. Page*, above, p.450). Accordingly, the *Nat Bell* case does not bar a conclusion that a decision based on no evidence is both erroneous in law and *ultra vires*. See further *Craig*, pp.503–505.

5. The point that there is no evidence to support a particular finding of fact will only form the basis of a successful challenge to a decision where the fact is in some way material to that decision. In criminal cases, what facts are material depends on the definition in law of the offence in question; the prosecution must establish all the factual elements of the offence as thus defined, and the failure to establish any one of them will be fatal. It will be for the trier of fact to determine whether the fact exists, and, as we have seen (above, p.816) there is a grey area where the boundary between law and fact is blurred. In administrative law, the position may be similar, as where decision-makers may only lawfully exercise a power where they are satisfied that specified facts exist. But there is a spectrum of other possibilities according to how broadly or narrowly the power is drawn. There are situations where the law specifies, not that the existence (or non-existence) of a fact is itself determinative, but that it is something which the decision-maker must, or may, take into account. There are yet other situations where it is for the decision-maker to determine (subject to control for *Wednesbury* unreasonableness or irrationality) which facts are relevant. All this is a reflection of the general position as to what *considerations* (a broader concept that includes facts) a decision maker must (or can) take into account (above, pp.545–569), and it is those principles that govern the question whether an error as to the existence of a particular fact renders the decision unlawful.

The case dealt with in the following section comes at all this from a different angle, holding that a mistake of fact causing unfairness constitutes an error of law. The relationship between the two principles is not wholly clear.

6. The equivalent rule in the United States allows a "reviewing court to determine whether an administrative determination made after a formal hearing is supported by

substantial evidence on the record taken as a whole" (*Schwartz and Wade*, p.228, referring to s.10(e)(B)5 of the Federal Administrative Procedure Act 1946, and art.78 of the New York Civil Practice Law and Rules, which are based on case law).

The rule is useful in relation to formal decision-making processes where there is a full record of the proceedings, including the evidence, and it enables the courts to exercise a greater measure of control than the British "no evidence" rule. While a much smaller proportion of decisions in this country are supported by a full record than in the United States, that does not mean that the "substantial evidence" rule should not be applied where a full record is available, for example, in planning appeals with the inspector's report, and Minister's letter.

(ii) Mistake of Fact

E v SECRETARY OF STATE FOR THE HOME DEPARTMENT: R. v SECRETARY OF STATE FOR THE HOME DEPARTMENT

[2004] EWCA Civ 49; [2004] Q.B. 1044; [2004] 2 W.L.R. 1351 (COURT OF APPEAL)

E and R were foreign nationals who applied for asylum on arrival in the United Kingdom in 2001. Their claims were refused by the Secretary of State and adjudicators. They appealed to the IAT. Between the dates of the IAT's hearings and the promulgation of its decisions in the two cases, further relevant evidence became available concerning the risks if they were returned, respectively, to Egypt and Afghanistan. Permission to appeal to the Court of Appeal was refused in each case by the IAT but granted by the Court of Appeal. Issues arose as to (1) whether the IAT could take account of fresh evidence becoming available between the hearing and the decision date; (2) whether the IAT had power under the rules to reopen its decision in order to take it into account if it was first drawn to its attention on an application for permission to appeal; (3) what was the relevance of such evidence to an appeal limited to questions of law; and (4) if it was relevant, what principles should the Court of Appeal exercise in exercising it discretion to admit it. The Court of Appeal held (1) that the IAT (under the legislation then applicable which did not limit appeals to the IAT to points of law) was entitled to admit new evidence up to the date of promulgation; and (2) to direct a rehearing; (3) that mistake of facts giving rise to unfairness was a separate head of challenge on an appeal on a point of law, at least in statutory contexts (including asylum claims) where the parties shared an interest in co-operating to achieve the correct result; and (4) that the admission of new evidence on such an appeal was subject to *Ladd v Marshall* principles, which may be departed from in exceptional circumstances where the interests of justice require. The extracts here deal with points (3) and (4).

The judgment of the court (LORD PHILLIPS OF WORTH MATRAVERS, MANTELL and CARNWATH L.JJ.) was given by CARNWATH L.J.: . . .

Error of fact in administrative law

36. So far as concerns the powers of this court, we have identified two issues: (iii) (relevance) and (iv) (admissibility). In some of the cases they seem to have been conflated. However, it is important in our view to maintain the distinction. The first, and most difficult, question is as to the relevance of new evidence of *fact* on an appeal confined to issues of *law*. Even if that question is answered in E's and R's favour, there is a separate question whether the evidence should be admitted, as an exception to the ordinary rule that the court proceeds on the basis of the material before the tribunal; or whether consideration of any new evidence should be a matter for the Secretary of State on a fresh claim.

37. We will consider first the question of error of fact as a ground for review in administrative law. E's and R's case is that the new evidence shows that the basis of the IAT's decision in each case was mistaken, and that such a mistake can provide grounds for an appeal even where it is limited to questions of law.

38. It is convenient to start from a summary in a recent case in this court of the principles applicable to an appeal on a point of law from a specialist tribunal, in that case the Lands Tribunal: *Railtrack plc v Guinness Ltd* [2003] RVR 280. Having referred to another Lands Tribunal case, in which an appeal had been allowed because the tribunal had failed to take account of the "whole of the evidence" on a particular point (*Aslam v South Bedfordshire District Council* [2001] RVR 65), Carnwath LJ (with whom the other members of the court agreed) said [2003] RVR 280, 287, para.51:

> "This case is no more than illustration of the point that issues of 'law' in this context are not narrowly understood. The court can correct 'all kinds of error of law, including errors which might otherwise be the subject of judicial review proceedings' (*R v Inland Revenue Comrs, Ex p. Preston* [1985] AC 835, 862 per Lord Templeman; see also *de Smith, Woolf & Jowell, Judicial Review of Administrative Action*, 5th ed (1995), p.686, para.15-076). Thus, for example, a material breach of the rules of natural justice will be treated as an error of law. Furthermore, judicial review (and therefore an appeal on law) may in appropriate cases be available where the decision is reached 'upon an incorrect basis of fact', due to misunderstanding or ignorance (see R (*Alconbury Developments Ltd) v Secretary of State for the Environment, Transport and the Regions* [2003] 2 AC 295, 321, para.53, per Lord Slynn of Hadley). A failure of reasoning may not in itself establish an error of law, but it may 'indicate that the tribunal had never properly considered the matter . . . and that the proper thought processes have not been gone through' (*Crake v Supplementary Benefits Commission* [1982] 1 All ER 498, 508)."

In the *Guinness* case the issue was whether the tribunal had misunderstood some of the complicated expert evidence in front of it, resulting in a "double counting" in the valuation. The court accepted that that was a proper ground of challenge on an appeal limited to questions of law, but held that it was not made out on the facts.

39. Two aspects of that summary require elaboration in the context of the present case: first, the relationship of this form of appeal with judicial review; and secondly the availability of appeal "upon an incorrect basis of fact".

Appeal on law, and judicial review

40. There was some discussion in the present case as to whether the grounds upon which the court may question a decision of the IAT differ materially, depending on whether the case comes before the court as an application for judicial review, or as an appeal on a point of law. It would certainly be surprising if the grounds for judicial review were more generous than those for an appeal. In practice, such cases only come by way of judicial review because

the IAT has refused leave to appeal, and its refusal can only be challenged in that way. There is certainly no logical reason why the grounds of challenge should be wider in such cases.

41. More generally, the history of remedies in administrative law has seen the gradual assimilation of the various forms of review, common law and statutory. The history was discussed by the Law Commission in its Consultation Paper Administrative Law: Judicial Review and Statutory Appeals (1994) (No 126), Parts 17-18. The appeal "on a point of law" became a standard model (supplanting in many contexts the appeal by "case stated") following the Franks Committee Report on Administrative Tribunals and Inquiries (1957) (Cmnd 218), which was given effect in the Tribunals and Inquiries Act 1958 (now Tribunals and Inquiries Act 1992, section 11). In other statutory contexts (notably, planning, housing and the like), a typical model was the statutory application to quash on the grounds that the decision was "not within the powers of the Act": see e g *Ashbridge Investments Ltd v Minister of Housing and Local Government* [1965] 1 WLR 1320. Meanwhile the prerogative writ procedures were remodelled into the modern judicial review procedure. In *R v Hull University Visitor, Ex p. Page* [1993] AC 682, the House of Lords acknowledged the evolution of a common set of principles "to ensure that the powers of public decision-making bodies are exercised lawfully": p.701, per Lord Browne-Wilkinson.

42. Thus, in spite of the differences in history and wording, the various procedures have evolved to the point where it has become a generally safe working rule that the substantive grounds for intervention are identical. (The conceptual justifications are another matter; see, for example, the illuminating discussion in *Craig, Administrative Law*, 5th ed (2003), pp 476ff.) The main practical dividing line is between appeals (or review procedures) on both fact and law, and those confined to law. The latter are treated as encompassing the traditional judicial review grounds of excess of power, irrationality, and procedural irregularity. This position was confirmed in *R v Inland Revenue Comrs, Ex p. Preston* [1985] AC 835, 862 (a tax case), where Lord Templeman said:

> "Appeals from the general commissioners or the special commissioners lie, but only on questions of law, to the High Court by means of a case stated and the High Court can then correct all kinds of errors of law including errors which might otherwise be the subject of judicial review proceedings . . ."

43. Of course the application of these principles will vary according to the power or duty under review; and, in particular, according to whether it is a duty to decide a finite dispute (such as that of a tribunal), or a continuing responsibility (such as that of a minister or local authority). As will be seen, this distinction is important in analysing some of the cases cited in this appeal. Furthermore, some decisions reflect the relative procedural flexibility of judicial review. While a statutory appeal is normally confined by the terms of the statute to consideration of the decision appealed against, judicial review is not so confined. An application for judicial review of a particular decision may, subject to the court's discretion, be expanded by amendment to include review of subsequent decisions of the same agency (see e g *R v Secretary of State for the Home Department, Ex p. Turgut* [2001] 1 All ER 719), or even related decisions of other agencies.

Incorrect basis of fact

44. Can a decision reached on an incorrect basis of fact be challenged on an appeal limited to points of law? This apparently paradoxical question has a long history in academic discussion, but has never received a decisive answer from the courts. The answer is not made easier by the notorious difficulty of drawing a clear distinction between issues of law and fact: see *Craig, Administrative Law*, 5th ed, p.488 and *Moyna v Secretary of State for Work and Pensions* [2003] 1 WLR 1929, 1935, para.22ff, per Lord Hoffmann.

45. The debate received new life following the affirmative answer given by Lord Slynn in *R v Criminal Injuries Compensation Board, Ex p. A* [1999] 2 AC 330. In that case the claimant had claimed compensation on the basis that in the course of a burglary she had been the victim of rape and buggery. She was examined five days after the burglary by a police doctor who reported that her findings were consistent with the allegation of buggery. However, at the hearing of her claim that report was not included in the evidence, and the board was given the impression by the police witnesses that there was nothing in the medical evidence to support her case. The claimant did not ask for the report, but, in Lord Slynn's words, at p.343:

"having been told that she should not ask for police statements as they would be produced at the hearing, it would not be surprising that she assumed that if there was a report from the police doctor, it would be made available with the police report."

46. One of the issues discussed in detail in argument was whether the decision could be quashed on the basis of a mistake, in relation to material which was or ought to have been within the knowledge of the decision maker: see pp.333–336. Lord Slynn thought it could. He said, at pp 344–345:

"Your Lordships have been asked to say that there is jurisdiction to quash the board's decision because that decision was reached on a material error of fact. Reference has been made to *Wade & Forsyth, Administrative Law*, 7th ed (1994), pp.316–318 in which it is said: 'Mere factual mistake has become a ground of judicial review, described as "misunderstanding or ignorance of an established and relevant fact", [*Secretary of State for Education and Science v Tameside Metropolitan Borough Council* [1977] AC 1014, 1030], or acting "upon an incorrect basis of fact" . . . This ground of review has long been familiar in French law and it has been adopted by statute in Australia. It is no less needed in this country, since decisions based upon wrong facts are a cause of injustice which the courts should be able to remedy. If a "wrong factual basis" doctrine should become established, it would apparently be a new branch of the ultra vires doctrine, analogous to finding facts based upon no evidence or acting upon a misapprehension of law.' *De Smith, Woolf & Jowell, Judicial Review of Administrative Action*, 5th ed (1995), p.288: 'The taking into account of a mistaken fact can just as easily be absorbed into a traditional legal ground of review by referring to the taking into account of an irrelevant consideration, or the failure to provide reasons that are adequate or intelligible, or the failure to base the decision on any evidence. In this limited context material error of fact has always been a recognised ground for judicial intervention.' For my part, I would accept that there is jurisdiction to quash on that ground in this case . . ."

47. However, Lord Slynn "preferred" to decide the instant case on the alternative basis that there had been a breach of the rules of natural justice amounting to "unfairness". As to that he said, at p.345:

"It does not seem to me to be necessary to find that anyone was at fault in order to arrive at this result. It is sufficient if objectively there is unfairness. Thus I would accept that it is in the ordinary way for the applicant to produce the necessary evidence. There is no onus on the board to go out to look for evidence, nor does the board have a duty to adjourn the case for further inquiries if the applicant does not ask for one . . . Nor is it necessarily the duty of the police to go out to look for evidence on particular matters."

None the less, he considered that the police "do have a special position in these cases", and he noted the evidence that the board is "very dependent on the assistance of and the co-operation of the police who have investigated these alleged crimes of violence". He said, at p.346:

"In the present case, the police and the board knew that [A] had been taken by the police to see a police doctor. It was not sufficient for the police officer simply to give her oral statement without further inquiry when it was obvious that the doctor was likely to have made notes and probably a written report."

He concluded, at p.347:

"I consider therefore, on the special facts of this case and in the light of the importance of the role of the police in co-operating with the board in the obtaining of evidence, that there was unfairness in the failure to put the doctor's evidence before the board and if necessary to grant an adjournment for that purpose. I do not think it possible to say here that justice was done or seen to be done."

48. The other members of the House agreed with Lord Slynn's reasoning, thereby (as I read the speeches) endorsing his "preferred" basis of unfairness. Only Lord Hobhouse of Woodborough made any direct reference to the question of review for "error of fact", specifically reserving that issue for consideration in the future: p.348E.

49. The same statement on that question was repeated by Lord Slynn, in another context, in *R (Alconbury Developments Ltd) v Secretary of State for the Environment, Transport and the Regions* [2003] 2 AC 295, 321, para.53. He referred to the jurisdiction to quash for "misunderstanding or ignorance of an established and relevant fact", as part of his reasons for holding that the court's powers of review (under a statutory procedure to quash for excess of power) met the requirements of the European Convention for the Protection of Human Rights and Fundamental Freedoms. This part of his reasoning was not in terms adopted by the other members of the House of Lords.

The point was mentioned by Lord Nolan and Lord Clyde. Lord Nolan put it in somewhat narrower terms; he said, at p.323, para.61:

> "But a review of the merits of the *decision-making process* is fundamental to the courts' jurisdiction. The power of review may even extend to a decision on a question of fact. As long ago as 1955 your Lordships' House, in *Edwards v Bairstow* [1956] AC 14, a case in which an appeal (from general commissioners of income tax) could only be brought on a question of law, upheld the right and duty of the appellate court to reverse a finding of fact which had no justifiable basis."

He saw *Edwards v Bairstow* as an illustration of "the generosity" with which the courts have interpreted the power to review questions of law, corresponding to a "similarly broad and generous approach" in the development of judicial review [2003] 2 AC 295, 323, para.62. Lord Clyde referred to Lord Slynn's statement on this issue in the *Criminal Injuries Compensation Board* case [1999] 2 AC 330, commenting [2003] 2 AC 295, 355, para.169, that it was: "sufficient to note . . . the extent to which the factual areas of a decision may be penetrated by a review of the account taken by a decision maker of facts which are irrelevant or even mistaken . . ."

50. In the present case E and R rely on Lord Slynn's statement as representing the law. Mr Kovats, for the Secretary of State, contents himself with the observation that the *Criminal Injuries Compensation Board* case is "not in point" because it was a judicial review case, and Lord Slynn's statement was obiter. For the reasons already given, we do not think the fact that the *Criminal Injuries Compensation Board* case was a judicial review case is an adequate ground of distinction. Indeed, Lord Slynn himself (and Lord Clyde) treated it as no less relevant to a statutory review procedure in the *Alconbury* case [2003] 2 AC 295. The fact that the statement was obiter means of course that it is not binding on us, but does not detract from its persuasive force, bearing in mind also the authority of the textbooks cited by him.

51. Although none of the parties found it necessary to examine in any detail the authorities referred to in argument in the *Criminal Injuries Compensation Board* case [1999] 2 AC 330 or in the textbooks, it seems to us difficult to avoid such examination, if we are to address properly the issue in these appeals. Fortunately the ground is very well covered, not only in the textbooks, but also in two excellent articles: by Timothy H Jones, "Mistake of Fact in Administrative Law" [1990] PL 507; and by Michael Kent QC (no doubt stimulated by his unsuccessful advocacy in the *Criminal Injuries Compensation Board* case itself) "Widening the Scope of Review for Error of Fact" [1999] JR 239. The authorities are helpfully summarised in Michael Fordham's invaluable *Judicial Review Handbook*, 3rd ed (2001), pp 730–732: see also Demetriou & Houseman "Review for Error of Fact—A Brief Guide" [1997] JR 27. Michael Kent includes a useful comparison with the concept of "manifest error" as applied by the Court of Justice of the European Communities. He concludes [1999] JR 239, 243:

> "A cautious extension of the power of the court on judicial review to reopen the facts might now be appropriate. This would need to be limited to cases where the error is manifest (not requiring a prolonged or heavily contested

inquiry), is decisive (on which the decision turned) and not susceptible of correction by alternative means . . ."

52. That is not dissimilar to the formulation approved by Lord Slynn, although he required that the error should be "material", rather than "decisive". Before reaching a conclusion that mistake of fact is now a ground for judicial review in its own right, it is necessary to review briefly the authorities mentioned in those articles. Two main points emerge: first, that widely differing views have been expressed as to the existence or scope of this ground of review; but, secondly, that, in practice, this uncertainty has not deterred administrative court judges from setting aside decisions on the grounds of mistake of fact, when justice required it.

Differing views

53. First, there have been several judicial statements by eminent judges on both sides of the debate. The narrower view is exemplified by a recent statement of Buxton LJ, under the heading "Error of fact as a ground for judicial review?" in *Wandsworth London Borough Council v A* [2000] 1 WLR 1246, 1255–1256:

> "The heading of this section of this judgment is, deliberately, the same as that of an important section in *de Smith, Woolf & Jowell, Judicial Review of Administrative Action*, 5th ed (1995), p.286, paras 5–091 and following. That section shows the difficult and elusive nature of this question, viewed as a general issue. However, if our present case is properly analysed the dilemma does not arise. While there may, possibly, be special considerations that apply in the more formalised area of planning inquiries, as suggested by *de Smith, Woolf & Jowell*, p.287, para.5–092, n75; and while the duty of 'anxious scrutiny' imposed in asylum cases by *R v Secretary of State for the Home Department, Ex p. Bugdaycay* [1987] AC 514 renders those cases an uncertain guide for other areas of public law; none the less *de Smith, Woolf & Jowell's* analysis shows that there is still no general right to challenge the decision of a public body on an issue of fact alone. The law in this connection continues, in our respectful view, to be as stated for a unanimous House of Lords by Lord Brightman in *R v Hillingdon London Borough Council, Ex p. Puhlhofer* [1986] AC 484, 518: 'it is the duty of the court to leave the decision [as to the existence of a fact] to the public body to whom Parliament has entrusted the decision-making power save in a case where it is obvious that the public body, consciously or unconsciously, are acting perversely.'"

He adopted the observations of Watkins LJ (sitting with Mann LJ) in *R v London Residuary Body, Ex p. Inner London Education Authority* The Times, 24 July 1987, quoted in the *Judicial Review Handbook*, p.730:

> "Of course, a mistake as to fact can vitiate a decision as where the fact is a condition precedent to an exercise of jurisdiction, or where the fact is the only evidential basis for a decision or where the fact was as to a matter which expressly or impliedly had to be taken into account. Outside those categories we do not accept that a decision can be flawed in this court, which is not an appellate tribunal, upon the ground of mistake of fact."

54. The clearest articulation of the alternative view (before the *Criminal Injuries Compensation Board* case [1999] 2 AC 330) was that of Scarman LJ in the Court of Appeal, in *Secretary of State for Education and Science, Tameside Metropolitan Borough Council* [1977] AC 1014, 1030. (This can be taken as having been implicitly endorsed by Lord Slynn, since it was cited by *Wade & Forsyth, Administrative Law* in the extract quoted by him: see above para.46.) The question in the *Tameside* case was whether the Secretary of State was entitled to hold that the council reacted "unreasonably" in reversing plans of the previous administration to make all the schools in their area "comprehensive". One issue was the practicability of carrying out the necessary selection process within the available time. On the material available to the Court of Appeal, it appeared that the Secretary of State had "either misunderstood or was not informed" as to the professional advice available to the authority on this issue; and that he had wrongly "jumped to the conclusion" that the proposals were unworkable: see pp 1031C, 1032H. Scarman LJ, at p.1030, did not accept that the scope of judicial review was as limited as suggested by counsel for the Secretary of State:

> "I would add a further situation to those specified by him: misunderstanding or ignorance of an established and relevant fact. Let me give two examples. The fact may be either physical, something which existed or occurred or did not, or it may be mental, an opinion. Suppose that, contrary to the minister's belief, it was the fact that there was in the area of the local education authority adequate school accommodation for the pupils to be educated, and the minister acted under the section believing that there was not. If it were plainly established that the minister was mistaken, I do not think that he could substantiate the lawfulness of his direction under this section. Now, more closely to the facts of this case, take a matter of expert professional opinion. Suppose that, contrary to the understanding of the minister, there does in fact exist a respectable body of professional or expert opinion to the effect that the selection procedures for school entry proposed are adequate and acceptable. If that body of opinion be proved to exist, and if that body of opinion proves to be available both to the local education authority and to the minister, then again I would have thought it quite impossible for the minister to invoke his powers under section 68."

55. In the House of Lords, Lord Wilberforce [1977] AC 1014, 1047D–E referred to the need for "proper self-direction" as to the facts. But he made no direct reference to the observations of Scarman LJ, and it may be (as was the view of Buxton LJ: see the *Wandsworth* case [2000] 1 WLR 1246, 1256D) that he was thinking only of the limited forms of factual review later summarised by Watkins LJ in *R v London Residuary Body, Ex p. Inner London Education Authority* The Times, 24 July 1987. The House of Lords held that the Secretary of State had acted unlawfully, principally on the ground that the Secretary of State had set the criterion of unreasonableness too low.

56. More recently, in *R v Independent Television Commission, Ex p. Virgin Television Ltd* The Times, 17 February 1996 cited in Demetriou & Houseman, "Review for Error of Fac—A Brief Guide" [1997] JR 27, 31, para.28,

Henry LJ distinguished between mistakes of fact "not grave enough to undermine the basis of a multi-faceted decision", and "misapprehension of the facts which form the foundation of the commission's decision"; only the latter would justify intervention by the court on judicial review.

57. Timothy H Jones in "Mistake of Fact in Administrative Law" [1990] PL 507 notes that another leading proponent of the wider approach, Sir Robin Cooke, in the New Zealand Court of Appeal, adopted Scarman LJ's formulation, saying:

"To jeopardise validity on the ground of mistake of fact the fact must be an established one or an established and recognised opinion; and . . . it cannot be said to be a mistake to adopt one of two differing points of view of the facts, each of which may be reasonably held." (*New Zealand Fishing Industry Association Inc v Minister of Agriculture and Fisheries* [1988] 1 NZLR 544, 552.)

There was however no majority on this issue in the New Zealand Court of Appeal: see Jones [1990] PL 507, 514–515.

Mistake of law in practice

58. Timothy H Jones in "Mistake of Fact in Administrative Law" [1990] PL 507 cites a number of cases, particularly in the context of town and country planning, where decisions have been set aside because of errors of fact (albeit without detailed discussion of the principle). Examples are: (i) an inspector's mistaken understanding that land had never been part of the Green Belt: *Hollis v Secretary of State for the Environment* (1982) 47 P & CR 351 (Glidewell J); (ii) an inspector's mistaken view that a building extension would not obstruct a particular aspect: *Jagendorf v Secretary of State for the Environment* [1987] JPL 771 (David Widdicombe QC); (iii) the minister's misinterpretation of the inspector's conclusions on evidence relating to viability of restoration of a building: *The Trustees of the Bristol Meeting Room Trust v Secretary of State of the Environment* [1991] JPL 152.

59. More significant, because it was a fully reasoned decision of the Court of Appeal, was another planning case, *Simplex GE (Holdings) v Secretary of State for the Environment* (1988) 57 P & CR 306. The Secretary of State in rejecting the planning appeal had mistakenly thought that the council had carried out a study relevant to the inclusion of the site in the Green Belt, whereas the study related only to what uses should be made within the Green Belt designation. The decision was challenged on the basis that "as a result of the error of fact" the minister had "taken into consideration matters which he was not entitled to consider": p.322. The Court of Appeal accepted that formulation, holding that the error was "undeniably a significant factor in the decision-making process" (p.327, per Purchas LJ), or was one which "was or may have been material": p.329, per Staughton LJ. The decision was therefore quashed.

60. As will be seen, the *Haile* case [2002] INLR 283 (mistake as to the name of a political party) and the *Khan* case [2003] EWCA Civ 530 (ignorance of a conviction in Bangladesh) are best explained as further examples in this court of the same approach to plain errors of fact, as applied in the field of asylum law.

Underlying principle

61. As the passage cited by Lord Slynn shows, the editors of the current edition of *de Smith, Woolf & Jowell, Judicial Review of Administrative Action* (unlike *Wade & Forsyth, Administrative Law*) are somewhat tentative as to whether this is a separate ground of review, at para.5–094:

> "The taking into account of a mistaken fact can just as easily be absorbed into a traditional legal ground of review by referring to the taking into account of an irrelevant consideration, or the failure to provide reasons that are adequate or intelligible, or the failure to base the decision upon any evidence."

62. We are doubtful, however, whether those traditional grounds provide an adequate explanation of the cases. We take them in turn. (i) Failure to take account of a material consideration is only a ground for setting aside a decision, if the statute expressly or impliedly requires it to be taken into account: *In re Findlay* [1985] AC 318, 333–334, per Lord Scarman. That may be an accurate way of characterising some mistakes; for example, a mistake about the development plan allocation, where there is a specific statutory requirement to take the development plan into account (as in the *Hollis* case 47 P & CR 351). But it is difficult to give such status to other mistakes which cause unfairness; for example whether a building can be seen (*Jagendorf's* case [1987] JPL 771), or whether the authority has carried out a particular form of study (the *Simplex* case 57 P & CR 306). (ii) Reasons are no less "adequate and intelligible", because they reveal that the decision-maker fell into error; indeed that is one of the purposes of requiring reasons. (iii) Finally, it may be impossible, or at least artificial, to say that there was a failure to base the decision on "*any* evidence", or even that it had "no justifiable basis" (in the words of Lord Nolan: see above). In most of these cases there is *some* evidential basis for the decision, even if part of the reasoning is flawed by mistake or misunderstanding.

63. In our view, the *Criminal Injuries Compensation Board* case [1999] 2 AC 330 points the way to a separate ground of review, based on the principle of fairness. It is true that Lord Slynn distinguished between "ignorance of fact" and "unfairness" as grounds of review. However, we doubt if there is a real distinction. The decision turned, not on issues of fault or lack of fault on either side; it was sufficient that "objectively" there was unfairness. On analysis, the "unfairness" arose from the combination of five factors: (i) an erroneous impression created by a mistake as to, or ignorance of, a relevant fact (the availability of reliable evidence to support her case); (ii) the fact was "established", in the sense that, if attention had been drawn to the point, the correct position could have been shown by objective and uncontentious evidence; (iii) the claimant could not fairly be held responsible for the error; (iv) although there was no duty on the Board itself, or the police, to do the claimant's work of proving her case, all the participants had a shared interest in co-operating to achieve the correct result; (v) the mistaken impression played a material part in the reasoning.

64. If that is the correct analysis, then it provides a convincing explanation of the cases where decisions have been set aside on grounds of mistake of fact. Although planning inquiries are also adversarial, the planning authority has a public interest, shared with the Secretary of State through his inspector, in ensuring that development control is carried out on the correct factual basis. Similarly, in *Tameside* [1977] AC 1014, the council and the Secretary of State, notwithstanding their policy differences, had a shared interest in decisions being made on correct information as to practicalities. The same thinking can be applied to asylum cases. Although the Secretary of State has no general duty to assist the appellant by providing information about conditions in other countries (see *R. v Secretary of State for the Home Department, Ex p. Abdi* [1996] 1 WLR 298), he has a shared interest with the appellant and the tribunal in ensuring that decisions are reached on the best information. It is in the interest of all parties that decisions should be made on the best available information: see the comments of Sedley LJ in *Batayav's* case [2003] EWCA Civ 1489 at [40]. (We have also taken account of the judgment of Maurice Kay J in *R (Cindo) v Immigration Appeal Tribunal* [2002] EWHC 246 (Admin) at [8]–[11], drawn to our attention since the hearing by Mr Gill, in which some of these issues were discussed.)

65. The apparent unfairness in the *Criminal Injuries Compensation Board* case [1999] 2 AC 330 was accentuated because the police had in their possession the relevant information and failed to produce it. But, as we read the speeches, "fault" on their part was not essential to the reasoning of the House. What mattered was that, because of their failure, and through no fault of her own, the claimant had not had "a fair crack of the whip": see *Fairmount Investments v Secretary of State for the Environment* [1976] 1 WLR 1255, 1266A, per Lord Russell of Killowen. If it is said that this is taking "fairness" beyond its traditional role as an aspect of procedural irregularity, it is no further than its use in cases such as *HTV Ltd v Price Commission* [1976] ICR 170, approved by the House of Lords in *R v Inland Revenue Comrs, Ex p. Preston* [1985] AC 835, 865–866.

66. In our view, the time has now come to accept that a mistake of fact giving rise to unfairness is a separate head of challenge in an appeal on a point of law, at least in those statutory contexts where the parties share an interest in co-operating to achieve the correct result. Asylum law is undoubtedly such an area. Without seeking to lay down a precise code, the ordinary requirements for a finding of unfairness are apparent from the above analysis of the *Criminal Injuries Compensation Board* case. First, there must have been a mistake as to an existing fact, including a mistake as to the availability of evidence on a particular matter. Secondly, the fact or evidence must have been "established", in the sense that it was uncontentious and objectively verifiable. Thirdly, the appellant (or his advisers) must not been have been responsible for the mistake. Fourthly, the mistake must have played a material (not necessarily decisive) part in the tribunal's reasoning.

67. Accordingly, we would accept the submissions of each of E and R, that, if the new evidence is admitted, the court will be entitled to consider whether it gives rise to an error of law in the sense outlined above. As we have said, however, whether the evidence should be admitted raises a separate question to which we now turn.

New evidence

68. Assuming the relevance of showing a mistake of fact in the tribunal's decision, there may need to be evidence to prove it. As has been seen, the court

has a discretion to admit new evidence (CPR r 52.11(2)), but it is normally exercised subject to *Ladd v Marshall* principles, raising in particular the issue whether the material could and should have been made available before the decision.[18]

69. Whether this is a material issue, of course, depends on the nature of the mistake. It may not be relevant if the mistake arises purely from the tribunal's consideration of the evidence (for example, the misinterpretation of the planning study in the case of *Simplex*). However, it may be material, where (as in the present cases) the complaint is of ignorance of evidence which was available before the decision was made. In such cases, it inevitably overlaps with the question of "unfairness". A claimant who had the opportunity to produce evidence and failed to take it may not be able to say that he has not had "a fair crack of the whip".

[In *Kibiti v Secretary of State for the Home Department* [2000] Imm. A.R. 594, the Court of Appeal held that a report written after the hearing of an asylum case by the IAT could not be relied upon in seeking permission to appeal to the Court of Appeal. Peter Gibson L.J. said, at[44], that "it is inappropriate for new material to be presented to this court which could not in any way have affected the decision of the tribunal below". Counsel for the Secretary of State accepted that there are established exceptions to this principle. He adopted the summary in *R. v Secretary of State for the Environment Ex p. Powis* [1981] 1 W.L.R. 584, which, although given in a judicial review case, he accepts as equally applicable to an appeal on law. Dunn L.J., at 595, referred to three permissible categories of new evidence: (1) evidence to show what material was before the tribunal; (2) where the jurisdiction of the tribunal depended "on a question of fact or where the question is whether essential procedural requirements were observed", evidence to establish the "jurisdictional fact or procedural error"; (3) evidence to show misconduct (such as bias or fraud) by the tribunal or parties to it" (at [71]). The Court of Appeal in the present case held the *Ladd v Marshall* principles were applicable, but fresh evidence could also be received where there is "some other exceptional circumstance which justifies its admission and consideration by this court" (*per* Sir John Donaldson M.R. in *R. v Secretary of State for the Home Department Ex p. Momin Ali* [1984] 1 W.L.R. 663 at 670), approved in the present case at [82] in respect of both appeals to the Court of Appeal and judicial review of the IAT's refusal of leave to appeal. The *Ladd v Marshall* principles "remain the starting-point, but there is discretion to depart from them in exceptional circumstances" (*ibid.*). An example of such exceptional circumstances was *R. (on the application of Haile) v Immigration Appeal*

---

[18] [ed.] The general position in respect of appeals to the Court of Appeal was summarised at [23]: "(i) The discretion is subject to any statutory limitations in the scope of the appeal: see CPR r 52.1(4). Thus, where the appeal is limited to questions of law, the power to admit new evidence cannot be used to turn it into an appeal on issues of pure fact (cf *Green v Minster of Housing and Local Government* [1967] 2 QB 606, 615, under the old rules). (ii) New evidence will normally be admitted only in accordance with "*Ladd v Marshall* principles" (see *Ladd v Marshall* [1954] 1 WLR 1489), applied with some additional flexibility under the CPR: see *Hertfordshire Investments Ltd v Bubb* [2000] 1 WLR 2318, 2325 and CPR r 52.11(2). The *Ladd v Marshall* principles are, in summary: first, that the fresh evidence could not have been obtained with reasonable diligence for use at the trial; secondly, that if given, it probably would have had an important influence on the result; and, thirdly, that it is apparently credible although not necessarily incontrovertible. As a general rule, the fact that the failure to adduce the evidence was that of the party's legal advisers provides no excuse: see *R v Secretary of State for the Home Department, Ex p. Al-Mehdawi* [1990] 1 AC 876".

Tribunal [2001] EWCA Civ 663; [2002] I.N.L.R. 283, where fresh evidence was accepted in the Court of Appeal to correct a "crucial mistake" about the identity of the political party in Ethiopia, with which the claimant was connected. The mistake was not spotted by the claimant's advisers earlier. *Haile* was not to be regarded as establishing any general proposition as to how the discretion to admit new evidence should be exercised or supporting any general departure, even in asylum cases, from the decision in *Al-Mehdawi* (above, p.715). This was "a straightforward case of unfairness caused by a mistake of fact, on a point which was uncontroversial and material to the decision" (at [83]).]

93. Applying those principles to the present cases, the actual reasons given by the IAT for refusing to consider the new evidence were erroneous in law. We understand its desire on practical grounds to confine the evidence to that produced at the hearing. However, where, as in these cases, there is substantial delay before the decision is issued, new evidence may emerge which undermines the basis of the conclusions reached at the hearing. If so, it cannot automatically be excluded, where justice requires it to be taken into account.

94. In the present case, the new evidence was not produced until after the decision was promulgated. Mr Kovats submits that in such circumstances, the IAT would have been entitled to reject it, applying *Ladd v Marshall* principles, because it could have been made available earlier. We see the theoretical force of that submission. However, it ignores the practical realities. Assuming some legal assistance is available to the asylum seeker, it is likely to be concentrated at the critical points in the process: that is, for present purposes, the hearings before the adjudicator and IAT, and the consideration of possible appeal following receipt of their decisions. It seems unrealistic to expect continuous monitoring of potential new evidence in the intervening periods. Even if it were possible, it would be very difficult for the IAT (as their stated reasons made clear) to handle such new evidence administratively. The obvious point to review the matter, where necessary, is as part of any application for leave to appeal. If the discretion of the tribunal is limited in the way we have suggested, the extra burden should not be unmanageable.

95. Accordingly, on the view we have taken of its powers under rule 30(2)(c), the IAT should in principle have considered whether the new evidence justified exercising its discretion to direct a rehearing. . . .

98. Accordingly, we think it right for the appeals to be allowed on the narrow ground, that in each case the IAT wrongly failed to consider the new evidence in the context of its discretion to direct a rehearing. The matters will be remitted to the IAT to reconsider in the light of the principles set out in this judgment.

Appeals allowed.
Matters remitted to tribunal.

Notes and questions

1. This case is to be taken as establishing both for appeals on a point of law and for judicial review that a mistake of fact resulting in unfairness constitutes an error of law. Note the narrow tests set out as to what constitutes such an error. These will no doubt be the subject of further analysis (when, for example, will a mistake be "established"?) and possible relaxation (what if the point is objectively verifiable but not wholly uncontentious?) Compare the use of substantive unfairness as a ground for holding an

interference with a legitimate expectation to be unlawful (above, pp.591–621). In the present context does "unfairness" amount to anything different from a mistake of fact that probably (?possibly) affected the outcome? If so, what? Compare cases on the effect of taking account of legally irrelevant considerations (above, pp.545–569). Are you convinced that the application of existing principles are not sufficient to deal with mistakes of fact?

2. Consider the relationship between this principle and the no evidence principle, said by Lord Slynn (cited at [46]) to be "analogous"? If a fact is found by the decision-maker to exist, material to the outcome, and can be shown in a way that is objectively verifiable and uncontentious not to exist will there not normally (if not invariably) be "no evidence" for it? Or is the new principle needed to cover cases where evidence is given on the point but turns out to be wrong?

3. See P. Craig, [2004] P.L. 788.

(iii) Failure to Give Adequate Reasons

R. v WESTMINSTER CITY COUNCIL Ex p. ERMAKOV

[1996] 2 All E.R. 302; (1995) 95 L.G.R. 119 (COURT OF APPEAL)

E, a Uzbekistan national, and his family came to the United Kingdom from Greece. He applied to the council as the local housing authority to be housed as a homeless person. He subsequently made a statement claiming that his father-in-law's relations had persecuted and threatened the lives of him and his family. The council decided that E had become homeless intentionally (and so not entitled to accommodation), and notified him accordingly. Section 64(4) of the Housing Act 1985 provided that when a local housing authority did this "they shall at the same time notify him of their reasons". It wrote to him saying that the council was not satisfied that E and his family experienced harassment and, therefore, it was reasonable for them to remain in occupation at their former address in Greece. E sought judicial review. The principal homelessness officer, Mr Lodge, swore an affidavit explaining that the true reasons for the decision he took were different, namely that even if E's claims were true it was reasonable for him and his family to continue to occupy the accommodation in Greece. The deputy judge, Sir Louis Blom-Cooper Q.C., ruled that the affidavit was admissible and ought to be admitted, and dismissed the application. The Court of Appeal allowed an appeal.

HUTCHISON L.J.: . . .
Characterising the dispute as one of admissibility is perhaps inappropriate. The respondents' case was that they had wrongly stated a reason which was not their true reason. Plainly it was incumbent on them to disclose this fact, by one means or another: it is unthinkable that they should have sought to defend their decision on a false basis. Some authorities might, perhaps, have simply written indicating that they conceded that the claim for judicial review must succeed on the ground that there had been a fundamental failure to comply with the requirements of s.64 as to the provision of reasons.

However, since the authority chose to disclose the true reasons—and the fact that the reasons given in the letter were not the true reasons—on affidavit and wished to continue to contest the proceedings, it was in one sense inevitable that the judge should admit the affidavits. The real question was not whether they should be admitted, but whether the respondents should be permitted to rely on them and justify the legality of their decision on the basis of them.

There is a good deal of authority which touches on this question. Before considering the cases to which we have been referred, I propose to state briefly what appear to me to be some of the factors of special importance to its resolution in this particular case. They are the following factors.

(1) This is a case in which the obligation to give reasons and to give them at the time the decision is communicated is a statutory one. Section 64(4) of the 1985 Act, as material to the present context, provides:

> "If the local housing authority notify the applicant . . . (c) that they are satisfied that he became homeless . . . intentionally . . . they shall at the same time notify him of their reasons."

(2) Nowhere in Pt III of the 1985 Act is there any express requirement that the authority shall take a decision on the questions into which s.62 obliges them to inquire. However, that section and s.64 plainly imply such a requirement. The terms of s.64, the marginal note to which reads 'Notification of decision and reasons', to my mind suggest that decision and notification of it are regarded as going very much hand in hand. Of course, it has to be accepted that a decision must always precede notification, for reasons which are obvious. For practical purposes, however, there is much to be said for the view that the decision and its communication to the applicant are contemporaneous.

(3) The affidavits of Mr Lodge and Mr Humphreys [the officer who wrote to E and now accepted old reason given was wrong] did not merely correct, amplify or explain the reasons given in the decision letter—they put forward entirely new reasons, completely at odds with those given in the letter. Moreover, they put forward those new reasons five or six months after the decision letter had been sent and, of course, only after judicial review proceedings had been launched.

It is well established that an obligation, whether statutory or otherwise, to give reasons for a decision is imposed so that the persons affected by the decision may know why they have won or lost and, in particular, may be able to judge whether the decision is valid and therefore unchallengeable, or invalid and therefore open to challenge. There are numerous authoritative statements to this effect: see eg *Thornton v Kirklees Metropolitan BC* [1979] 2 All ER 349 at 354, [1979] QB 626 at 638 *per Megaw* LJ and *R. v Croydon London Borough, Ex p. Graham* (1993) 26 HLR 286 at 291-292 (a case to which further reference will be made), where Sir Thomas Bingham MR said—

> "I readily accept that these difficult decisions are decisions for the housing authority and certainly a pedantic exegesis of letters of this kind would be inappropriate. There is, nonetheless, an obligation under the [Housing Act 1985] to give reasons and that must impose on the council a duty to give reasons which are intelligible and which convey to the applicant the reasons why the application has been rejected in such a way that if they disclose an error of reasoning the applicant may take such steps as may be indicated."

I should also refer, though Mr Samuels drew our attention to it in a slightly different context, to the classic statement of Lord Scarman in *Great Portland Estates plc v Westminster City Council* [1984] 3 All ER 744 at 752, [1985] AC 661 at 673:

> "Failure to give reasons. When a statute requires a public body to give reasons for a decision, the reasons given must be proper, adequate and

intelligible. In *Re Poyser and Mills's Arbitration* [1963] 1 All ER 612, [1964] 2 Q.B. 467 Megaw J had to consider s.12 of the Tribunals and Inquiries Act 1958 which imposes a duty on a tribunal to which the Act applies or any minister who makes a decision after the holding of a statutory inquiry to give reasons for their decision, if requested. Megaw J commented ([1963] 1 All ER 612 at 616, [1964] 2 Q.B. 467 at 478): . . . Parliament having provided that reasons shall be given, in my view that must clearly be read as meaning that proper, adequate, reasons must be given; the reasons that are set out . . . must be reasons which not only will be intelligible, but also can reasonably be said to deal with the substantial points that have been raised . . ."

Starting from this point of principle, Mr Samuels' argument, expressed in its simplest form, is that it cannot be right to admit, for the purposes of its being relied on in justification of the decision, such evidence as was admitted in this case, since to do so nullifies the very objects and advantages underlying the requirement to provide reasons. He concedes that there are authorities which support the proposition that evidence may be admitted to amplify the reasons given in the decision letter, but he seeks to distinguish them from the present case, and argues that the weight of authority is against allowing wholly deficient statutory reasons to be made good by affidavit evidence in the course of proceedings.

[His Lordship considered a number of authorities at first instance relied upon by Mr. Samuels.]

For the respondents, Mr Jones seeks to support the judge's decision essentially on the grounds relied on by the judge. I begin by referring to para.7 of his concise and helpful skeleton argument. Here he argues that, since the council were bound to state their true reasons, there was no point in the matter being reconsidered simply so that a correct s.64 notice could be served. The requirements of s.64, he argues, are procedural—the decision is one thing, the notification and reasons another. While the reasons should be intelligible, there is no reason why they should not be corrected or supplemented. That this can be done is apparent from the consistent practice of the courts, exemplified by the cases on which the judge relied, of permitting the reasons to be supplemented—he relies in particular on [*R. v Swansea City Council Ex p. John* (1982) 9 H.L.R. 55] Any prejudice can be remedied by adjournments, orders for cross-examination and costs. . . .

In the end, as I understood it, Mr Jones was disposed to concede that, while there might be cases in which the court could and should treat inadequacy of reasons or incorrect reasons as being a ground for quashing the decision, it should, where the true reasons were tendered, allow them to be given and decide the substantial point in the light of the correction.

These submissions seem to me to disregard the authorities to which we have been referred. Moreover, underlying Mr Jones's approach was the notion that the quashing of the decision for lack of proper reasons was a mere formality, in that it left the authority, in a case such as the present, with no more than a sort of mechanical or formal function to perform: they would simply, tomorrow as it were, send a further letter in effect incorporating the reasoning contained in Mr Lodge's affidavit. I do not for a moment accept that that is the correct approach. What was sought by the applicant was not an order of mandamus requiring the authority to give reasons, but an order of certiorari quashing the decision coupled with mandamus directing them to reconsider the application. If such orders are granted, they necessarily involve proper reconsideration. Of course the authority are entitled, on that reconsideration, to take account of the information obtained by them in the course of their earlier inquiries; but reconsideration of the decision is not and cannot be a mere formality. In such a case the authority should invite the applicant to make any further representations that he wishes, and should take account of any made by or on his behalf and of any further information obtained by them or coming into their possession from some other source. The frequent practice of the courts when orders of this sort are quashed is not to make orders of mandamus directing reconsideration, because it is thought unnecessary to make such orders against responsible local authorities, who can be trusted to do without compulsion what an order would direct them to do. It does not need to be said that that practice in no way lessens the obligation that reconsideration entails.

In my judgment the weight of authority to which we have been referred favours the applicant, and I accept the general thrust of Mr Samuels' submissions. My conclusions in relation to this first and main ground of appeal are as follows.

(1) It is unrealistic to seek to draw any significant distinction, in the context of s.64, between the decision and the communication of the decision with reasons, or to treat the giving of reasons as purely procedural. In reaching this conclusion I am influenced by the fact that the section in terms requires reasons to be given at the same time as the decision is communicated; by Schiemann J's observations in [*R. v Tynedale DC Ex p. Shield* (1987) 22 H.L.R. 144]; and by the many cases in which such decisions have been quashed for inadequacy of reasons.

(2) The court can and, in appropriate cases, should admit evidence to elucidate or, exceptionally, correct or add to the reasons; but should, consistently with Steyn LJ's observations in [*R. v Croydon LBC Ex p. Graham* (1993) 26 H.L.R. 286, at 292], be very cautious about doing so. I have in mind cases where, for example, an error has been made in transcription or expression, or a word or words inadvertently omitted, or where the language used may be in some way lacking in clarity. These examples are not intended to be exhaustive, but rather to reflect my view that the function of such evidence should generally be elucidation not fundamental alteration, confirmation not contradiction. Certainly there seems to me to be no warrant for receiving and relying on as validating the decision evidence—as in this case—which indicates that the real reasons were wholly different from the stated reasons. It is not in my view permissible to say, merely because the applicant does not feel able to challenge the bona fides of the decision-maker's explanation as to the real reasons, that the applicant is therefore not prejudiced and the evidence as to the real reasons can be relied upon. This is because, first, I do not accept that it is necessarily the case that in that situation he is not prejudiced; and, secondly, because, in this class of case, I do not consider that it is necessary for the applicant to show prejudice before he can obtain relief. Section 64 requires a decision and at the same time reasons; and if no reasons (which is the reality of a case such as the present) or wholly deficient reasons are given, he is prima facie entitled to have the decision quashed as unlawful.

(3) There are, I consider, good policy reasons why this should be so. The cases emphasise that the purpose of reasons is to inform the parties why they

have won or lost and enable them to assess whether they have any ground for challenging an adverse decision. To permit wholesale amendment or reversal of the stated reasons is inimical to this purpose. Moreover, not only does it encourage a sloppy approach by the decision-maker, but it gives rise to potential practical difficulties. In the present case it was not, but in many cases it might be, suggested that the alleged true reasons were in fact second thoughts designed to remedy an otherwise fatal error exposed by the judicial review proceedings. That would lead to applications to cross-examine and possibly for further discovery, both of which are, while permissible in judicial review proceedings, generally regarded as inappropriate. Hearings would be made longer and more expensive.

(4) While it is true, as Schiemann J recognised in *Ex p. Shield*, that judicial review is a discretionary remedy and that relief may be refused in cases where, even though the ground of challenge is made good, it is clear that on reconsideration the decision would be the same, I agree with Rose J's comments in [*R. v Northampton BC Ex p. Carpenter* (1992) 25 H.C.R. 349 at 356] that, in cases where the reasons stated in the decision letter have been shown to be manifestly flawed, it should only be in very exceptional cases that relief should be refused on the strength of reasons adduced in evidence after the commencement of proceedings. Accordingly, efforts to secure a discretionary refusal of relief by introducing evidence of true reasons significantly different from the stated reasons are unlikely to succeed.

(5) Nothing I have said is intended to call in question the propriety of the kind of exchanges, sometimes leading to further exposition of the authority's reasons or even to an agreement on their part to reconsider the application, which frequently follow the initial notification of rejection. These are in no way to be discouraged, occurring, as they do, before, not after, the commencement of proceedings. They will often make proceedings unnecessary. They are in my judgment very different from what happened in this case.

I also wish to emphasise that all that I have said is with reference only to the provisions of s.64 of the 1985 Act.

(6) The judge did not in my view approach the decision, which in the exercise of his judgment he had to make, with the principles that I consider the authorities establish in mind. Whereas he should have adopted an approach consistent with that indicated in the judgment of Steyn LJ in *Ex p. Graham*, what he did was to treat the application as one which he could not even consider rejecting. This is apparent from the passage in his judgment which I have already cited. I have little doubt that had the judge approached the matter with the correct principles in mind he would have concluded that this was not a case in which the respondents should be permitted to substitute wholly different reasons and, in reliance on those reasons, seek to justify their decision.

(7) On the first ground I consider that this appeal should succeed, the judge's decision should be set aside, the decision of the authority quashed, and the case remitted for reconsideration on the simple ground that, as the affidavit evidence of the respondents concedes, the only reasons given for the decision are defective, in that they are not the true reasons and are not relied on. . . .

THORPE L.J. agreed and NOURSE L.J. delivered a concurring judgment agreeing with HUTCHISON L.J.

Appeal allowed

R. (ON THE APPLICATION OF RICHARDSON AND ANOTHER) v NORTH YORKSHIRE CC

[2003] EWCA Civ 1860; [2004] 1 W.L.R. 1920; [2004] 2 All E.R. 31
(COURT OF APPEAL)

The claimant objected to the grant by the council in June 2002 of planning permission for a quarry extension. The council was required by the Town and Country Planning (Environmental Impact Assessment) (England and Wales) Regulations 1999 (SI 1999/ 293), implementing Council Directive 85/337, to take specified environmental information into consideration, and, by reg.21(1) of the regulations, to make available for public inspection a statement containing the main reasons and considerations on which the decision was based. A notice of decision was issued which included a note that the council had taken into consideration accompanying environmental information, but not the reasons.

The claimants sought judicial review, *inter alia*, on the ground of non-compliance with reg.21(1). Richards J. ([2004] 1 P. & C.R. 23) granted a mandatory order requiring the publication of a statement with the required information. This was upheld by the Court of Appeal. It was accepted that there had not been compliance with reg.21(1).

SIMON BROWN L.J.:. . .

32. The critical question then arising was what the consequences of that failure should be the claimants were contending that the council's attempt at retrospective validation was too late and should in any event be rejected . . .

33. The judgment below contains the most detailed and illuminating review of the many cases down the years which have considered what consequences should attend failures on the part of decision making bodies to comply with the requirement to give reasons imposed upon them in varying contexts. I shall not repeat that review but rather proceed to the judge's cogently expressed conclusions reached in the light of it.

"47. The consequences of a failure to comply with a requirement to give reasons depend very much on statutory context and the particular circumstances of the case. The authorities cited by counsel cover a range of different situations. In evaluating them it is also important to bear in mind that there has been, as it seems to me, a tendency in recent years to adopt a stricter approach to the requirement to give reasons and to be readier to quash a decision for failure to give reasons and less ready to allow a deficiency of reasons to be cured by the provision of reasons or supplemental reasons at a later stage.

48. The closest decision in point of subject matter, though furthest away in point of time (and divorced from the context of an EC directive), is *Brayhead (Ascot) Ltd. v Berkshire County Council* [1964] 2 Q.B. 303, where it was held that a failure to comply with the duty to give reasons for the imposition of a planning condition did not invalidate the condition (let alone the planning permission) and the duty could be enforced by mandamus. At the other end of the spectrum, *R. v Westminster City Council, Ex p. Ermakov* [1996] 2 All FR 302 provides an example of a case, more recent and in a different statutory context, in which a decision was quashed for a failure to comply with the duty to give adequate reasons at the same time as the decision, and the court adopted a restrictive approach to the admissibility of later reasons. *Flannery v Halifax Estate Agencies Ltd*

(trading as Colleys Professional Services) [2000] 1 WLR 377 was concerned with a different context again, namely the duty of a trial judge to give reasons for his decision. In that area a more up to date and detailed analysis is to be found in *English v Emery Reimhold & Strick Ltd (Practice Note)* [2002] 1 WLR 2409, which was not cited by counsel but which makes it clear that it may be appropriate in certain circumstances to remit the case to the trial judge for the provision of additional reasons pp.2418–2419, paras.22–25. Although these and the other cases to which I have been referred provide general guidance, they do not lay down a principle that is determinative of the present case. There is no substitute for a careful examination of the particular statutory context and the precise nature of the requirement to state reasons in each case.

49. As to that, the first and most important point in the present case is that regulation 21(1) looks to the position *after* the grant of planning permission. It is concerned with making information available to the public as to what has been decided and why it has been decided, rather than laying down requirements for the decision-making process itself. It implements the obligation in article 9(1) of the Directive to make information available to the public 'When a decision to grant development consent *has been taken*' (emphasis added). That is to be contrasted with article 2(1) of the Directive, which lays down requirements as to what must be done *before* the grant of planning permission (which may be granted only after a prior assessment of significant environmental effects).

50. The fact that the requirement focuses on the availability of information for public inspection after the decision has been made, rather than on the decision-making process, leads me to the view that a breach of regulation 21(1) ought not to lead necessarily to the quashing of the decision itself. A breach should be capable in principle of being remedied, and the legislative purpose achieved, by a mandatory order requiring the authority to make available a statement at the place, and containing the information, specified in the regulation.

51. Thus, to take a straightforward example, if the members of the committee had agreed in terms at their meeting on a specific statement of the main reasons for the grant of planning permission but the officers had failed to include that statement on the register, a mandatory order requiring the statement to be placed on the register (or, perhaps more accurately, requiring it to be made available for public inspection at the place where the register is kept) would plainly be the appropriate remedy.

52. The difficulties in this case arise out of the fact that there was no such agreement. The need to make a statement of main reasons available for public inspection appears to have been overlooked by the officers, so that members were not advised about it. That was a most unfortunate oversight. It meant that members did not have imposed upon them the same disciplined and structured approach as might have been thought appropriate had they been aware of the duty to make a statement of main reasons available. It also meant that they missed the opportunity to agree in terms on a specific set of reasons. The most obvious way in which that might have been done was by expressing agreement with the reasoning in the director's report, subject to any agreed departures from or additions to that reasoning.

53. The resulting situation is very unsatisfactory. I have reached the conclusion, however, that it is still capable of being remedied by a mandatory

order and that what has happened does not justify the quashing of the grant of planning permission. My reasons are as follows. (i) Although it is necessary to view with caution any subsequent statement of reasons for a decision, especially where the reasons have not been articulated until many months after the decision, I do not think that the exercise of obtaining reasons ex post from the individual members who voted for the resolution is inherently flawed or of such doubtful reliability that the evidence should be rejected. All that the individual members have been asked to do is to cast their minds back to the reasons that actually motivated them to vote for the grant of planning permission. There is no suggestion that they have had any difficulties of recollection. In my view there is nothing in the nature of the exercise or in the evidence obtained to cause concern that the answers might have been distorted by the existence of these proceedings or other extraneous considerations. The process does not involve changing a decision or reconsidering it or anything of that kind. This is a very different exercise from that found unacceptable in *R (Carlton-Conway) v Harrow London Borough Council* [2002] EWCA Civ 927; The Times, 11 July 2002 or in *R (Goodman) v Lewisham London Borough Council* [2003] 2 P. & CR. 262. In both those cases the councils had engaged in a later decision-making process and there was an understandable concern that that might be vitiated by a wish to sustain a former invalid decision. In this case it is simply a matter of being satisfied that the reasons now put forward were the actual reasons that motivated the decision-makers at the time.

[Furthermore, the different sets of "particular reasons" given by the members of the committee could properly be read as meaning that they had all accepted the reasoning and conclusion in the director's report but each attached particular significance to the "particular reasons" they had identified.]

[Simon Brown L.J. fully concurred in Richards J.'s judgment and held that the decision of the House of Lords in *Berkeley v Secretary of State for the Environment* [2001] 2 A.C. 603, that where there was a failure to comply with EIA requirements the ensuing planning permission should normally be quashed, did not require that result here.]

KEENE and SCOTT BAKER L.JJ. agreed.

Appeal dismissed

Notes

1. Earlier authorities on the giving of reasons are discussed by M.B. Akehurst, (1970) 33 M.L.R. 154 and G. Richardson, [1986] P.L. 437, and see A.P. Le Sueur, "Legal duties to give reasons" (1999) 52 C.L.P. 150.

2. There are many authorities on the consequences of a failure to comply with a duty to give reasons on an appeal on a point of law. These are not always easy (or possible) to reconcile, and, as Richards J. says in *Richardson* at [47] of his judgment, echoing a comment by Woolf J. in *Crake v Supplementary Benefits Commission* [1982] 1 All E.R. 498 at 507, the emphasis has changed over time. The possible consequences can be ranged on a spectrum, and include the following:

(1) The decision is quashed on the ground that no, or no adequate reasons have been given (*e.g. Ermakov*). This approach has been adapted in respect of decisions of the National Industrial Relations Court and the Employment Appeal

Tribunal *(Alexander Machinery (Dudley) Ltd. v Crabtree* [1974] I.C.R. 120; *Levy v Marrable & Co.* [1984] I.C.R. 583); and decisions of mental health review tribunals (*R. v Mental Health Review Tribunal Ex p. Pickering* [1986] 1 All E.R. 99). The fact that the legislation that applied in *Ermakov* required the reasons to be given at the same time as the decision has been regarded as an important element of the court's decision (see *Nash*, below, n.4; *cf. Richardson*; *R. (on the application of Ashworth HA) v H*, unreported, November 9, 2001, QBD). *Ermakov* has been held applicable in respect of a reasoned decision produced by a mental health review tribunal after a contested hearing (Stanley Burnton J. in *Ashworth* at [57]); but not to the duty of a medical practitioner under s.3 of the Mental Health Act 1983 to give reasons for a recommendation that a person should be admitted to a hospital for treatment (Sullivan J. in *R. (on the application of H) v Oxfordshire Mental Healthcare NHS Trust* [2002] EWHC Admin 465).

(2) The decision is quashed on the ground that it can be inferred from the insufficiency of reasons that there has been an error of law in arriving at the decision (a possibility recognised by Lord Parker C.J. and Bridge J. in *Mountview Court Properties Ltd v Devlin* (1970) 21 P. & C.R. 689 at 695, 695–696; their Lordships stated that a failure to give adequate reasons could not itself be an error of law, by Woolf J. in *Crake*; Carnwath J. in *South Glamorgan CC v L and M* [1996] E.L.R. 400 at 413; Sedley J. in *R. v Northamptonshire CC Ex p. Marshall* [1998] Ed. C.R. 262; and by the Court of Appeal in *Curtis v London Rent Assessment Committee* [1997] 4 All E.R. 842. Cases where decisions have been quashed on this basis include: *Poyser and Mills' Arbitration, Re* [1964] 2 Q.B. 467, interpreted in *Mountview* as a case where the insufficiency of reasons for an arbitration award gave rise to a proper inference that the arbitrator had misdirected himself in law; *Curtis* (above); followed by Richards J. in *Queensway Housing Association Ltd v Chiltern, Thames and Eastern Rent Assessment Committee* (1998) 31 H.L.R. 945.

(3) The decision is not quashed, but a mandatory order lies to require proper reasons to be given (*Brayhead (Ascot) Ltd v Berkshire CC* [1964] 2 Q.B. 303; *Richardson*).

(4) The decision is not quashed, the decision-maker having been permitted to provide additional contemporary evidence of the reasons for the decision (*Crake* (notes of the tribunal chairman taken at the hearing); *R. (on the application of Jackson) v Parole Board* [2003] EWHC 2437 (the written report that predated the written statement or reasons, which was drafted on a mistaken basis by an inexperienced member of staff); *R. (on the application of B) v Merton LBC* [2003] 4 All E.R. 280; or subsequent evidence of the true reasons (*Richardson*). However, the latter step is normally not permitted (*Ermakov*).

(5) The matter is remitted to the decision-maker for further reasons to be provided (a possibility recognised by Richards J. in *Richardson*; but held not applicable to decisions of Special Education Needs and Disability Tribunals in *VK v Norfolk CC* [2004] EWHC 2921. This can be done on an adjournment, without quashing the original decision (*Mountview*; *R. v London Rent Assessment Committee Ex p. St George's Court* (1982) 265 E.G. 984; when the matter returned with additional reasons, the decision was quashed ((1983) 267 E.G. 523; appeal dismissed (1984) 48 P. & C.R. 230). Such a power is presumably available under the general powers of case management under CPR r.3. There is an express power to remit a decision for redetermination where it is quashed on judicial review (CPR r.54.19), and a similar power on appeals to the High Court (CPR r.52.10).

It would be helpful for the inconsistency of approach between cases where decisions are quashed directly because of the inadequacy of reasons and cases where it is denied that this is possible (categories (1) and (2)) to be resolved by the House of Lords. A sensible solution would be to accept that a failure to comply with a statutory duty to give adequate reasons is an error of law but that the quashing of a decision and remittal for a full rehearing can be avoided where appropriate by the adoption of the approaches in categories (3)–(5).

3. It is frequently affirmed that while reasons must be proper, intelligible and adequate, tribunals "are not required to articulate their reasons to the exacting standards and with the precision required of a court" (*per* Auld L.J. in *Curtis v London Rent Assessment Committee* [1997] 4 All E.R. 842 at 867; in the course of holding that where a rent assessment committee's assessment of a fair rent differs significantly from the market rent indicated by market rent comparables, it must have good reasons, and explain them, including a brief indication of its arithmetic). *cf.* the planning cases in n.6 below.

4. The extent to which the courts are prepared to receive subsequent evidence of reasons has been considered in a series of cases following *Ermakov*.

In *R. (on the application of Nash) v Chelsea College of Art and Design* [2001] EWHC Admin 538, Stanley Burnton J, having reviewed *Ermakov* and other authorities, summarised the relevant principles as follows:

"34. In my judgment, the following propositions appear from the above authorities:
  i. Where there is a statutory duty to give reasons as part of the notification of the decision, so that (as Laws J put it in *R. v Northamptonshire CC Ex p. D* [1998] Ed. C.R. 14) "the adequacy of the reasons is itself made a condition of the legality of the decision", only in exceptional circumstances if at all will the Court accept subsequent evidence of the reasons.
  ii. In other cases, the Court will be cautious about accepting late reasons. The relevant considerations include the following, which to a significant degree overlap:
     a. Whether the new reasons are consistent with the original reasons.
     b. Whether it is clear that the new reasons are indeed the original reasons of the whole committee.
     c. Whether there is a real risk that the later reasons have been composed subsequently in order to support the tribunal's decision, or are a retrospective justification of the original decision. This consideration is really an aspect of (b).
     d. The delay before the later reasons were put forward.
     e. The circumstances in which the later reasons were put forward. In particular, reasons put forward after the commencement of proceedings must be treated especially carefully. Conversely, reasons put forward during correspondence in which the parties are seeking to elucidate the decision should be approached more tolerantly.
35. To these I add two further considerations. The first is based on general principles of administrative law. The degree of scrutiny and caution to be applied by the Court to subsequent reasons should depend on the subject matter of the administrative decision in question. Where important human rights are concerned, as in asylum cases, anxious scrutiny is required; where the subject matter is less important, the Court may be less demanding, and readier to accept subsequent reasons. . .".

His Lordship subsequently accepted that para.[34](i) was too widely expressed in that reasons that merely elucidate reasons given contemporaneously with a decision will normally be considered by the court (*Ashworth*, n.2 above at [56]). Furthermore, in *R. (on the application of Leung) v Imperial College of Science, Technology and Medicine* [2002] E.L.R. 653, Silber J. added two further factors:

"29. . . The first is whether the decision maker would have been expected to state in the decision document the reason that he or she is seeking to adduce later. The reason for considering that factor is that the court will not accept a reason stated after the initial decision was given if, for example, it considers that it is unlikely to be true and that exercise entails considering whether the omission of that reason from the original reasons was excusable. If it is, then the court should be less reluctant to exclude it than if there is no excuse for the decision maker failing to mention the new factor in the original reasons. In addition, the policy reasons for not permitting later reasons to be adduced as described by Hutchison LJ include the need for parties to know at the time of a decision why they have won or lost and to discourage sloppy decision making, but those arguments are less potent when there was no need for reasons to be given when the original decision was made.

30. The second additional and perhaps over-arching factor is whether it would be just in all the circumstances to refuse to admit the subsequent reasons of the decision maker. So if there was no need for a decision to contain reasons, it might be strange if on the facts of a particular case, later reasons could not be adduced to meet a challenge on grounds of, say, a misdirection, unfairness or inconsistency. If this were not so, there might in some cases be unfairness between the parties as the decision maker could not defend himself. Obviously the application of principles of fairness would also enable the court to reach a decision on the cogency of and weight to be given to the new reasons".

5. The duties of courts and other bodies that determine criminal charges or civil rights and obligations to give reasons have been strengthened through both the application of Art.6 ECHR (see p.384) and the common law (*e.g.* the Crown Court in disposing of an appeal from the magistrates' court: *R. v Harrow Crown Court Ex p. Dave* [1994] 1 W.L.R. 98, *R. v Kingston Crown Court Ex p. Ball* (2000) 164 J.P. 633). *Ex p. Ermakov* has been applied to decisions of a housing benefit review board (*R. v Lambeth LBC Housing Benefit Review Board Ex p. Harrington, The Times*, December 10, 1996) and the Parole Board (*R. v Secretary of State for the Home Department Ex p. Lillycrop, The Times*, December 13, 1996).

6. In planning cases, by the Town and Country Planning (Inquiries Procedure) Rules 2000, r.18(1), the Secretary of State is required to give reasons for his decisions in determining appeals. The same duty applies where an appeal is determined by an inspector. A failure to give adequate and intelligible reasons may lead to the decision being quashed under s.288 of the Town and Country Planning Act 1990 on the ground that the applicant's interests have been substantially prejudiced by a failure to comply with a relevant requirement. The reasons must be proper, adequate and intelligible and deal with the substantial points raised (*Poyser and Mills' Arbitration, Re* [1964] 2 Q.B. 467 at 478, approved by the House of Lords in *Westminster City Council v Great Portland Estates Plc* [1985] A.C. 661 at 673) and enable:

"the appellant to understand on what grounds the appeal has been decided and be in sufficient detail to enable him to know what conclusions the inspector has reached on the principal important controversial issues"

(*per* Phillips J. in *Hope v Secretary of State for the Environment* (1975) 31 P. & C.R. 120 at 123, approved by Lord Bridge for the House of Lords in *Save Britain's Heritage v Number 1 Poultry Ltd* [1991] 1 W.L.R. 153 at 165). Decision letters should not be construed as statutes and should be read as a whole (*ibid.*). However, Lord Bridge in the *Save Britain's Heritage* case emphasised that the courts could not set a general standard as to the adequacy of reasons. Commenting on a passage from Woolf L.J.'s judgment in the Court of Appeal ((1990) 60 P. & C.R. 539 at 545), he said (at 166–167):

"I certainly accept that the reasons should enable a person who is entitled to contest the decision to make a proper assessment as to whether the decision should be challenged. But I emphatically reject the proposition that in planning decisions the 'standard', 'threshold' or 'quality' of the reasons required to satisfy the statutory requirement varies according to who is making the decision, how much time he has to reflect upon it, and whether or not he had legal assistance, or depends upon the degree of importance which attaches to the matter falling to be decided. The obligation, being imposed on the Secretary of State and his inspectors in identical terms, must be construed in the same sense.

The three criteria suggested in the dictum of Megaw J. in *Re Poyser and Mills' Arbitration* [1964] 2 Q.B. 467, 478 are that the reasons should be proper, intelligible and adequate. The application of the first two of these presents no problem. If the reasons given are improper they will reveal some flaw in the decision-making process which will be open to challenge on some ground other than the failure to give reasons. If the reasons given are unintelligible, this will be equivalent to giving no reasons at all. The difficulty arises in determining whether the reasons given are adequate, whether, in the words of Megaw J., they deal with the substantial points that have been raised or, in the words of Phillips J. in *Hope v Secretary of State for the Environment* 31 P. & C.R. 120, 123, enable the reader to know what conclusion the decision-maker has reached on the principal controversial issues. What degree of particularity is required? It is tempting to think that the Court of Appeal or your Lordships' House would be giving helpful guidance by offering a general answer to this question and thereby "setting the standard" but I feel no doubt that the temptation should be resisted, precisely because the court has no authority to put a gloss on the words of the statute, only to construe them. I do not think one can safely say more in general terms than that the degree of particularity required will depend entirely on the nature of the issues falling for decision.

Whatever may be the position in any other legislative context, under the planning legislation, when it comes to deciding in any particular case whether the reasons given are deficient, the question is not to be answered *in vacuo*. The alleged deficiency will only afford a ground for quashing the decision if the court is satisfied that the interests of the applicant have been substantially prejudiced by it. This reinforces the view I have already expressed that the adequacy of reasons is not to be judged by reference to some abstract standard. There are in truth not two separate questions: (1) were the reasons adequate? (2) if not, were the interests of the applicant substantially prejudiced thereby? The single indivisible question, in my opinion, which the court must ask itself whenever a planning decision is challenged on the ground of a failure to give reasons is whether the interests of the applicant have been substantially prejudiced by the deficiency of the reasons given. Here again, I disclaim any intention to put a gloss on the statutory provisions by attempting to define or delimit the circumstances in which deficiency of reasons will be capable of causing substantial prejudice, but I should expect that normally such prejudice will arise from one of three causes. First, there will be substantial prejudice to a developer whose application for permission has been refused or to an opponent of development when permission has been granted where the reasons for the decision are so inadequately or obscurely expressed as to raise a substantial doubt whether the decision was taken within the powers of the Act. Secondly, a developer whose application for permission is refused may be substantially prejudiced where the planning considerations on which the decision is based are not explained sufficiently clearly to enable him reasonably to assess the prospects of succeeding in an application for some alternative form of development. Thirdly, an opponent of development, whether the local planning authority or some unofficial body like Save, may be substantially prejudiced by a decision to grant permission in which the planning considerations on which the decision is based, particularly if they relate to planning policy, are not explained sufficiently clearly to indicate what, if any, impact they may have in relation to the decision of future applications".

(The House held, reversing the Court of Appeal, that the reasons given by the Secretary of State in granting planning permission for the demolition of listed buildings and their replacement by a modern building were adequate. See Sir Desmond Heap and

M. Thomas, [1991] J.P.L. 207). Subsequently, in *Bolton MDC v Secretary of State for the Environment* (1995) 71 P. & C.R. 309, the House of Lords made it clear that while the Secretary of State had to have regard to all material considerations, it was not necessary for every such consideration to be dealt with specifically in the reasons for the ultimate decision to grant or withhold planning consent.

(iv) Questions of *Vires*

Notes
There are a number of authorities that suggest or hold that a question of *vires* cannot be raised on an appeal on a point of law. In some, this has been on the doubtful basis that if a decision is *ultra vires* and void there is nothing to appeal against (*Metropolitan Properties Co. (F.G.C.) Ltd. v Lannon* [1968] 1 W.L.R. 815, DC, and *Chapman v Earl* [1968] 1 W.L.R. 1315, DC, below, p.862). In *Henry Moss Ltd. v Customs and Excise Commissioners* [1981] 2 All E.R. 86, Lord Denning M.R. stated (at 90) that the proper way to challenge the validity of regulations and administrative directions made under the authority of a statute was by way of an application for judicial review under Ord.53, and not by an appeal on a point of law. The other members of the Court of Appeal did not mention the point expressly. Counsel for the Commissioners invited the court to deal with the case as if there had been an application for judicial review, and the court acceded to that invitation. This approach was criticised as unduly restrictive by A.W. Bradley, [1981] P.L. 476, as apparently regarding the introduction of Ord.53 as outlawing collateral review.

There are certainly other authorities which accept that a question of *vires can* be raised on an appeal. See, *e.g.* *Elliott v Brighton BC* (1980) 79 L.G.R. 506: a general right to "appeal"; *Nolan v Leeds City Council* (1990) 23 H.L.R. 135 (Housing Act 1985, ss.353 and 367, 362 and 371, which, respectively, provided for an appeal on the ground of an "informality, defect or error in or in connection with the notice", no specified ground, and that "the making of the order was unnecessary"). In *R. v Inland Revenue Commissioners Ex p. Preston* [1985] A.C. 835, Lord Templeman stated (at 862) that on an appeal by case stated on a point of law from the General or Special Commissioners to the High Court, the court:

"can . . . correct all kinds of errors of law including errors which might otherwise be the subject of judicial review proceedings: see *Edwards (Inspector of Taxes) v Bairstow* [1956] A.C. 14".

In *Chief Adjudication Officer v Foster* [1993] A.C. 754, the House of Lords (reversing the Court of Appeal on this point) held that a question of the validity of the income support regulations could be raised through the statutory appellate structure, including the appeal from a social security appeal tribunal to the Social Security Commissioner on the ground that the tribunal's decision was "erroneous in point of law" (Social Security Act 1975, s.101, now the Social Security Administration Act 1992, s.23). See D. Feldman, (1992) 108 L.Q.R 5 and A.W. Bradley, [1992] P.L. 185 on the decision of the Court of Appeal and D. Feldman and N.J. Wikeley, (1993) 109 L.Q.R. 544 and N. Harris, (1993) 56 M.L.R. 710 on the decision of the House of Lords. It is certainly arguable that this broader approach is convenient as it enables cases which raise points of *vires* as well as legality or (if appropriate) merits to be fully disposed of on appeal: *Wade and Forsyth*, p.950.

These cases strictly concern the *jurisdiction* of the appellate court to consider questions of *vires*. The relationship between appeals and judicial review is further complicated by the separate principles (1) that it may be held to be an abuse of process for a point as to *vires* to be raised other than on an application for judicial review (*O'Reilly v Mackman*, below, pp.976–991); and (2) that judicial review will not lie, as a matter of discretion, if there is another more appropriate remedy, such as an appeal (below, pp.1019–1021). It will be noted that these principles pull in different directions. The former was considered in *R. v Oxford Crown Court Ex p. Smith, The Independent*, January 19, 1990, where Simon Brown J. held that it was not an abuse of process for a point as to *vires* to be raised on an appeal to the Crown Court against a clearance notice served under s.65 of the Town and Country Planning Act 1971 (now s.215 of the 1990 Act); his Lordship dealt with the matter as raising the *O'Reilly v Mackman* principle rather than as a question of the proper interpretation of the statutory grounds of appeal. Similarly, in *Nolan v Leeds City Council* (1990) 23 H.L.R. 135, the Court of Appeal held that it was not an abuse of process to raise a matter of *vires* on appeals under the Housing Act 1985. The latter principle was emphasised by Lord Templeman in *Preston* (above), although in that case the allegation was that the conduct of the commissioners in initiating proceedings was unlawful, in which case the relevant appeal procedure could not begin to operate.

Finally, it may be noted that Parliament may expressly provide that certain matters shall not be challenged *except* by judicial review: see, *e.g.* the Local Government Finance Act 1992, s.66, in respect of the setting of the council tax and related matters.

(G) "Persons Aggrieved"

Many appeals established by statute may only be brought by a "person aggrieved". This term has been considered by the courts on many occasions. The view most commonly relied on as to its meaning is that expressed by James L.J. in *Ex p. Sidebotham* (1880) 14 Ch.D. 458 at 465:

> ". . . [T]he words 'person aggrieved' do not really mean a man who is disappointed of a benefit which he might have received if some other order had been made. A 'person aggrieved' must be a man who has suffered a legal grievance, a man against whom a decision has been pronounced which has wrongfully deprived him of something, or wrongfully refused him something, or wrongfully affected his title to something".

The attitude of the court has, however, varied according to the context.

In many areas of local government law, a local authority is empowered to serve a notice requiring a private person to have works done on his property, and a person aggrieved by the notice may appeal to a court. That private person is a "person aggrieved" by the notice, and by a decision of a court upholding a notice. Is the local authority a "person aggrieved" by a decision of the justices against them? A series of decisions of the Divisional Court established that it was not, unless a legal burden was placed upon them as a result of the decision. This was clear where the justices' decision threw a financial burden on the authority (beyond the costs of the magistrates' court proceedings), as in *Phillips v Berkshire CC* [1967] 2 Q.B. 991, where justices decided that a street was not a private street, and thus was maintainable at the public expense. Where the authority was seeking to enforce a restriction on activities, it was unlikely that they would be placed under a burden if the private person appealed successfully to the court. The cases where it was held that a local authority was not a "person aggrieved" by the quashing of an enforcement notice served by the authority had to be overruled by statute (see now s.289 of the Town and Country Planning Act 1990, and *cf.* s.288(2) (*ibid.*)). The obligation to pay costs was in some cases held to be sufficient to render the authority a "person aggrieved" (*e.g.* under s.301 of the Public Health Act 1936: *R. v Surrey Quarter Sessions Ex p. Lilley* [1951] 2 K.B. 749, applied in *Cook v Southend BC* (1987) 151 J.P. 641, DC), but not in others (*e.g. R. v Dorset Quarter Sessions Appeals Committee Ex p. Weymouth Corp.* [1960] 2 Q.B. 230, in relation to the Town and Country Planning Act 1947, s.23).

Another common situation was where the local authority could grant a licence for an activity. A person refused a licence was a "person aggrieved" for the purposes of an appeal (*e.g. Stepney BC v Joffe* [1949] 1 K.B. 599); but it was held that the local authority might not be a "person aggrieved" by the reversal of their decision (*e.g. R. v London Q.S. Ex p. Westminster Corp.* [1951] 2 K.B. 508, applied in *R. v Southwark LBC Ex p. Watts* (1989) 88 L.G.R. 86; but *cf. Penwith DC v McCartan-Mooney, The Times*, October 20, 1984).

The courts showed a less rigid attitude where the question concerned persons affected by the decisions of public authorities (*Morbaine and Turner*, below). The cases concerning public authorities as "persons aggrieved" were reconsidered by the Court of Appeal in *Cook v Southend BC*, below, p.860, and a broader view was adopted.

MORBAINE LTD v FIRST SECRETARY OF STATE

[2004] EWHC 1708; Westlaw Transcript 2004 WL 1640322
(BLACKBURNE J.)

Morbaine Ltd and Ms Abigail Roberts separately sought an order under s.288 of the Town and Country Planning Act 1990 quashing the grant to Lear Management Ltd by the First Secretary of State (on an application called in from the local authority) of planning permission for a substantial development project in Stoke-on-Trent. The grounds were that the Secretary of State had failed to have regard to or apply properly particular planning policies. M Ltd was a commercial property development company based in Widnes. It was involved in negotiations to acquire another development site in Stoke-on-Trent for similar uses, and got to know of Lear's proposals on February 11, 2004, between the issue by the First Secretary of an Interim Decision Letter on December 23, 2003, and the Decision Letter on March 8, 2004. M Ltd feared that the grant of permission for L's project might affect the commercial viability of its own project. R lived very near the site. She objected on the grounds of traffic, pollution and noise. However, she also entered a "collaboration agreement" with M Ltd under which she undertook to take proceedings to challenge the permission, in return for indemnification by M Ltd against all costs and liabilities, and a payment of £1,000.

On an application by L for the claims to be struck out, Blackburn J. held that the claims had no real prospects of success. One issue was whether M Ltd. and B were persons aggrieved.

BLACKBURNE J.: . . . **Are Morbaine and Ms Roberts persons "aggrieved" by the decision to grant planning permission?**

9. It is by no means easy to state exactly what is meant by 'aggrieved' as it appears in s.288. Mr Steel QC, appearing with Mr Tabachnik for Lear, drew my attention to *Times Investments Ltd v Secretary of State for the Environment* (1990) 61 P & CR (a challenge brought under the predecessor section to s.288), in which the Court of Appeal cited a dictum of Ackner J in *Turner v Secretary of State* for the Environment (1974) 28 P & CR 123, referring to 'any person who, in the ordinary sense of the word, is aggrieved by the decision . . .'. I did not, with respect, find that of much assistance. That said, the expression clearly extends at one end of the spectrum to a person who owns or has an interest in a property affected by the decision in question. It was also common ground that it can include the so-called 'public interest litigant'. At the other end of the spectrum it does not extend to someone who is no more that an interfering busybody. In *Attorney-General of Gambia v N'Jie* [1961] AC 617 at 634 Lord Denning said (albeit in a very different context):

"The words 'person aggrieved' are of wide import and should not be subject to a restrictive interpretation. They do not include, of course, a mere busybody who is interfering in things which do not concern him: but they do include a person who has a genuine grievance because an order has been made which prejudicially affects his interests."

In *Lardner v Renfrewshire Council* [1997] SLT 1027 (a decision of the first division of the Court of Session), in which the question arose whether the appellant was a person "aggrieved", in that case, by a determination of a local planning authority to adopt a replacement local plan, the Lord President, Lord Rodger, (delivering the opinion of the court) cited the above passage from *N'Jie* and said (at 1029) this:

"The appellant is not a person whose own property is directly affected by the adoption of the local plan. On the other hand we readily accept that, as someone who lives near the site and uses it, he is not 'a mere busybody'. It may be that, had the appellant lodged an objection to the plan and appeared at the inquiry, he would have fallen into the category of an 'aggrieved person' if he could have averred a genuine grievance of the kind contemplated by the section [section 232 of the Town and Country Planning (Scotland) Act 1972]. The difficulty for the appellant in this case, however, is precisely that he did not object at the proper time and did not take part in the public inquiry at which issues relating to the draft plan were explored. Counsel accepted that the appellant's failure to use the prescribed statutory procedures caused serious difficulties for the appellant in now arguing that he is aggrieved . . .

The appellant in this case . . . is a member of the public who has an interest in what happens to the site because it is near him and he uses it, but on the other hand he did not avail himself of the opportunities which Parliament has afforded for participating in the process for adopting the local plan. We do not suggest, of course, that someone who has not objected to a draft plan or taken part in an inquiry can never be 'a person aggrieved'. On the other hand, there is a difference between feeling aggrieved and being aggrieved: for the latter expression to be appropriate, some external basis for feeling 'upset' is required—some denial of or affront to his expectations or rights. . . . The particular circumstances of any case require to be considered and the question must always be whether the appellant can properly be said to be aggrieved by what has happened. In deciding that question it would usually be a relevant factor that, though no fault of counsel, the appellant has failed to state his objection at the appropriate stage of the procedure laid down by Parliament since that procedure is designed to allow objections and problems to be aired and a decision then to be reached by the Council. The nature of the grounds on which the appellant claims to be aggrieved may also be relevant."

In *R (Kides) v South Cambridgeshire DC* [2003] JPL 431 (an application for judicial review of the defendant council's decision to grant planning permission where, although there is no requirement to show that he is an 'aggrieved' person, the applicant for relief must demonstrate a sufficient interest) Jonathan Parker LJ, with whom Laws and Aldous LJJ agreed, said at paras 132 to 134:

"132. That leaves the issue of standing. As to that, it seems to me that there is an important distinction to be drawn between, on the one hand, a person who brings proceedings having no real or genuine interest in obtaining the relief sought, and on the other hand a person who, whilst legitimately and perhaps passionately interested in obtaining the relief sought, relies as grounds for seeking that relief on matters in which he has no personal interest.

133. I cannot see how it can be just to debar a litigant who has a real and genuine interest in obtaining the relief which he seeks from relying, in support of his claim for that relief, on grounds (which may be good grounds) in which he has no personal interest.

134. It seems to me that a litigant who has a real and genuine interest in challenging an administrative decision must be entitled to present his challenge on all available grounds."

Against that background I consider the particular circumstances of the two claimants.

Morbaine Ltd.
[His lordship summarised the facts]

13. Mr Corner QC, appearing with Mr Walton for Morbaine and Ms Roberts, submitted that there is nothing improper in Morbaine bringing a claim under s.288 to further its own commercial interests. He referred me to *R. (on the application of Springimage Ltd) v Canterbury City Council* and others (1993) 68 P & CR 171. In that case, in which the applicant sought judicial review of the defendant council's grant of planning permission for a retail development, Mr David Keene QC (sitting as a deputy judge of the High Court) stated that 'if the commercial interest of a person may realistically be affected by a decision in a way not common to the general run of the public, then that provides not only a particular interest on the part of the person concerned, but also a sufficient one for the purposes of judicial review'. Mr Corner pointed out that, in that case, the applicant's interest was pursuant to an option to purchase nearby land the prospects of obtaining planning permission for the development of which (and therefore the prospects of the development itself) were affected by the planning permission under challenge. So also here he said: Morbaine is pursuing its commercial interest and that interest is realistically affected by the grant of permission for the application site.

14. But that case, in my view, is very different from the present. In that case the applicant for relief had objected to the planning application and had lodged representations to that effect with the local planning authority. Its interest in the nearby land already subsisted at the time that the planning application was made to which it objected.

15. Here by contrast Morbaine, a complete stranger to the application site and to the area affected by Lear's development proposals, happened by chance upon the Helical site at about the time or shortly after the IDL was published, which, of necessity, was long after the planning inquiry into Lear's development proposals had ended and the inspector had produced her report. Without any commitment to, let alone any proprietary or other enforceable interest in, any land affected by a grant of permission for the application site, Morbaine sees an opportunity to further its own commercial interests through the acquisition of another site if, by means of a successful challenge under s.288, it can upset the grant of planning permission for the application site. In my judgment, commercial opportunism of that nature falls short of

the interest (the 'real or genuine interest in obtaining relief' which the Court of Appeal had in mind in *Kides*) which must be shown to give it standing to complain. It is remote from any denial of or affront to a person's expectations or rights to which Lord Rodger referred in the *Lardner* decision. It follows that Morbaine does not qualify as a person 'aggrieved' by the decision of the Secretary of State to grant planning permission for Lear's proposals for the application site.

Ms Roberts:
[His lordship set out the facts]

19. It is plain that by that agreement Morbaine has purchased (for that is what the £1000 payment to her and the indemnity involve) Ms Roberts' willingness to mount a claim under s.288 in case there should be a challenge, as there has been, to its own standing to bring proceedings under the section. It is seeking indirectly to achieve through Ms Roberts what it fears the court might find that it is not entitled to do directly in its own name. For her part, in entering into the compact, Ms Roberts has surrendered entirely to Morbaine the right to decide whether and for how long any challenge is to be made, the basis upon which the challenge is to proceed and all other matters concerned with the prosecution of the challenge. Moreover, it is plain that, but for Morbaine's approach to her and the indemnity provided by the collaboration agreement, Ms Roberts would not herself have mounted her challenge.

20. In my judgment there is much to be said for the view, advanced by Mr Steel, that, given these circumstances, Ms Roberts' claim amounts to an abuse of the court's process and, accordingly, falls to be struck out on that ground alone. (It is true that Lear's application does not identify abuse of process as a ground for dismissing Ms Robert's claim but Mr Steel's skeleton argument raises the argument and I see no reason why, despite Mr Corner's objection, the point may not be taken, if necessary of the court's own motion). Over and above the suggestion of an abuse of process, I see much force in Mr Steel's further submission that, given the circumstances, it is difficult to regard Ms Roberts as a person 'aggrieved' by the decision of the Secretary of State to grant planning permission for Lear's proposed development of the application site. I should add that, in view of the terms by which she has bound herself to do Morbaine's bidding, it would be irrelevant to this view of Ms Roberts' standing that, as she asserts in her third witness statement, she is aware of Morbaine's wish to purchase the application site and develop it itself (her stance having hitherto been that any substantial retail development is objectionable on grounds of noise, traffic and pollution) or that she entered into the collaboration agreement because it would allow her to challenge the Secretary of State's decision. Nor would it be relevant that, if she were to repudiate the collaboration agreement and pursue her own separate grounds of objection, Morbaine might have difficulty in enforcing its terms. The fact is that she has entered into that agreement and, thus far at any rate, seems happy to abide by and take advantage of its terms.

21. But I do not need to come to any conclusions on Ms Roberts' standing, which I find to be a difficult point, since I have come to a firm view that there is no substance in any event in the grounds of challenge on which Morbaine and Ms Roberts each rely. . ..

Notes

1. Notwithstanding Blackburne J.'s lack of enthusiasm, *Turner* was an important decision in holding that a more liberal view of the term "person aggrieved" should be adopted than that previously applied. Ackner J. declined to follow the decision of Salmon J. in *Buxton v M.H.L.G.* [1961] 1 Q.B. 278. Here, the local planning authority refused permission for the owners of land to develop it by digging chalk and the owners appealed to the minister. An inquiry was held and among those heard were the applicants, four substantial landowners whose land was adjacent to the appeal site. The inspector recommended that the appeal should be dismissed, but the minister allowed it. Salmon J. held that the applicants were not "persons aggrieved" able to challenge the minister's decision, as the term was confined to those with a "legal grievance" (following *Sidebotham, Re* (1880) 14 Ch.D. 458) The decision "infringed none of their common law rights."

A similarly narrow approach was adopted in *Gregory v Camden LBC* [1966] 1 W.L.R. 899 where Paull J. held that third parties in a planning case did not have *locus standi* to be awarded a declaration. Ackner J. noted that two cases in which a broader approach had been adopted had not been cited to Paull J. These were *Att-Gen of Gambia v N'Jie* [1961] A.C. 617, where the Attorney-General was held to have *locus standi* to appeal to the Privy Council as a person aggrieved against a decision of the West African Court of Appeal in a case in which he was not a party; and *Maurice v London CC* [1964] 2 Q.B. 362 where a neighbour's loss of amenity was held to be sufficient to make her a person "aggrieved" for the purposed of a right of appeal against a consent given under the London Building Act 1930 for a proposed block of flats within 100 yards of her premises. Lord Denning in *N'Jie* said expressly (at 634) that the *Sidebotham, Re* definition "is not to be regarded as exhaustive". Ackner J. also noted that while at the time of the *Buxton* decision there were no procedural rules governing such inquiries, such rules had been introduced in 1962.

The current version specified a number of persons entitled to appear at the inquiry, including any persons whom the minister has required notice to be served (Town and Country Planning (Inquiries Procedure) Rules 1969, r.7(1)) and provided that "any other person may appear at the inquiry at the discretion of the appointed person" (r.7(2)). Salmon J. in *Buxton* stated (at 285) that anyone given a statutory right to have his representations considered by the minister impliedly had the right that the minister in doing so act within his powers and comply with the relevant requirements. Counsel for the minister accepted that this covered persons under r.7(1) but denied that it applied to those under r.7(2). Ackner J. held this was an unsustainable distinction.

> ". . .[A]ny person who, in the ordinary sense of the word, is aggrieved by the decision, and certainly any person who has attended and made representations at the inquiry, should have the right to establish in the courts that the decision is bad in law . . .".

This question did not arise in *Buxton* as the Inquiry Procedure rules had not been passed. Furthermore, the approach in *Maurice* gave his Lordship "just sufficient fortitude for not following the decision in the *Buxton* case so reluctantly reached by the judge".

The decision in *Buxton* was obvious unsatisfactory and the decision in *Turner* much more in conformity with the modern more liberal approach to questions standing (see below, pp.994–1010). On "persons aggrieved", see H.M. Purdue and J.E. Trice, [1974] J.P.L. 20; W. Parkes, [1978] J.P.L. 739; B. Hough, [1992] J.P.L. 319.

2. *Turner* has been followed in *Bizony v Secretary of State for the Environment* [1976] J.P.L. 306; *Hollis v Secretary of State for the Environment* (1982) 47 P. & C.R. 351; *Morbaine Ltd. v Secretary of State for the Environment* (1993) 68 P. & C.R. 525 (company chosen to develop appeal site and with an option to purchase it was a "person aggrieved" notwithstanding that it had not appeared at the inquiry); *Bannister v Secretary of State for the Environment* [1994] 2 E.G.L.R. 197 (owner of

land adjoining appeal site across which the site had access, and who attended the inquiry and made written representations was a "person aggrieved") and approved by the Court of Appeal in *Times Investment Ltd. v Secretary of State for the Environment* (1990) 61 P. & C.R. 98, where it was held that a successor in title to land subject to a planning appeal can be a person aggrieved.

3. In *Cook v Southend BC* [1990] 2 Q.B. 1, the council revoked C's hackney carriage vehicle and driver's licence and C appealed successfully to the magistrates' court. The council was held to be a "person aggrieved" for the purposes of a further appeal to the Crown Court. There was no need for the decision appealed against to have placed some legal burden on the council, such as a costs order.

CHAPTER 12

VALIDITY OF UNLAWFUL ADMINISTRATIVE ACTION[1]

(A) PRINCIPLES

What is the exact status and effect of an *ultra vires* act? This question has caused considerable academic controversy and some difficulty in the case law. Attempts to find answers to it have been side-tracked by a debate as to whether all (or some) *ultra vires* acts are to be regarded as "void" or "voidable", concepts or labels borrowed from private law. Employing these labels, it could be argued that an *ultra vires* act should be regarded as null and void for all purposes ("void", a "nullity"). On the other hand, an act which may be set aside only on an appeal, or on an application to quash for non-jurisdictional error of law on the face of the record, could be said to be "voidable"; it is valid until set aside. See *Wade and Forsyth*, pp.305–306. This formulation is, however, deceptively simple and increasingly unhelpful. First, now that all errors of law are normally regarded as jurisdictional errors and the concept of error of law on the face of the record as a dead letter (see *Page* above, pp.452–453) this line now merely marks the divide between decisions challengable on an application for judicial review and those challengable on appeal. Secondly, and more importantly, it is now firmly established that "voidness" in administrative law is a *relative* and not an *absolute* concept. An *ultra vires* act is not totally devoid of legal effect:

(i) In some situations it can simply be ignored (see point (a) below). However, it will often be advisable, or even necessary, for the person affected to obtain a court ruling that the act is *ultra vires*. At this point, it must be remembered that the courts will not always be prepared to intervene. A direct challenge may only be brought by a person with the appropriate *locus standi* and within the relevant time-limit. Even if the applicant makes out a good case as a matter of substance, the court may decline to grant a remedy in the exercise of its discretion. These matters are considered in Ch.14. In consequence, if an act is not challenged by the only persons with *locus standi* to do so then the courts will treat it as valid. For example, only the Chief Constable in *Ridge v Baldwin* would be regarded as having standing to challenge the lawfulness of his own dismissal (*cf.* the discussion of this point in *Durayappah v Fernando* [1967] 2 A.C. 337). This point is also illustrated by the *Rose Theatre Trust case* (below, p.1004), on the assumption that English Heritage would have had standing to challenge the Secretary of State's decision (unlike the applicants in that case), but chose not to do so. Similarly, once a statutory time-limit for challenging an act has expired, it may be regarded as valid (see *Smith v East Elloe RDC*, below p.907; *cf.* the cases on undue delay on an application for judicial review (above, pp.1010–1019)).

(ii) If an act is not invalid on its face, the courts for the purpose of considering whether and, if so, on what basis to grant interim relief, will act on the

---

[1] See: H.W.R. Wade (1967) 83 L.Q.R. 499 and (1968) 84 L.Q.R. 95; M.B. Akehurst (1968) 31 M.L.R. 2, 138; *de Smith, Woolf and Jowell*, pp.256–265, 355–357; A. Rubinstein, *Jurisdiction and Illegality* (1965); P. Cane, "A Fresh Look at Punton's Case" (1980) 43 M.L.R. 266; D. Oliver (1981) C.L.P. 43; G.L. Peiris [1983] P.L. 634; M. Taggart, "Rival Theories of Invalidity in Administrative Law" in Taggart (ed.), *Judicial Review of Administrative Action in the 1980s* (1986), pp.70–103; *Craig*, Ch.20; *Wade and Forsyth*, Ch.9.

assumption that it is valid, unless and until it is set aside (see *F. Hoffmann-La Roche v Secretary of State for Trade and Industry*, below, p.892).

(iii) In exceptional circumstances, an act may be regarded as partially invalid only (see below, pp.894–902).

(iv) An *ultra vires* act may itself constitute a relevant consideration that has to be taken into account in exercising some other power (see *Foster v Eastbourne BC* [2004] EWCA Civ 36, below, p.876).

In some cases, judges have taken the view that the fact that an *ultra vires* act is not totally devoid of legal effects in the senses already discussed means that "voidable" is the only appropriate label. See the speech of Lord Evershed in *Ridge v Baldwin* [1964] A.C. 40, at 86–94; the Privy Council in *Durayappah v Fernando* [1967] 2 A.C. 337; and the views of Lord Denning M.R. in *D.P.P. v Head* [1959] A.C. 83, 111–112; *R. v Paddington Valuation Officer Ex p. Peachey Property Corporation Ltd (No.2)* [1966] 1 Q.B. 380 and *Lovelock v Minister of Transport* (1980) 40 P. & C.R. 336. More recently, the judges have preferred to label *ultra vires* acts as void, given that once a court rules that an act is *ultra vires* and grants a remedy, the act is regarded as void *ab initio*. At the same time, they have accepted that both before and after there has been such a ruling, a challenged act may have substantive legal effects. They have sought to analyse those effects directly without worrying too much about conceptual labels that might be attached.

Where an act is *void*, in the relative sense in which the term is properly understood, several consequences follow:

(a) It may, if appropriate, be ignored by the person affected. If the public authority takes enforcement proceedings, the voidness of the act can be raised as a defence. See, for example, *Maltglade Ltd v St Albans RDC* [1972] 1 WLR. 1230; *Allingham v Minister of Agriculture* [1948] 1 All E.R. 780 (where a notice requiring farmers to grow sugar beet on certain fields was held to be invalid because the task of specifying the fields had been delegated unlawfully by a county agricultural committee to an officer). A person with the appropriate standing is normally permitted to raise a question as to *vires* as a collateral question (pp.877–894): Furthermore, in many situations collateral challenge will be of no use to the person affected. For example, where a decision refuses an applicant some licence or other benefit, he or she will normally have to take direct action to have the decision set aside.

(b) A statutory provision purporting to prohibit recourse to the courts to challenge the validity of an act will normally be interpreted as effective to prevent challenges to voidable acts only. A void act is not an "act", "order", or "decision" protected by the privative clause at all. See below, pp.907 *et seq.* and *Anisminic Ltd v Foreign Compensation Commission* (above, p.436).

(c) The courts may refuse to hear an appeal against a void decision, on the basis that there is nothing to appeal against. See *Metropolitan Properties Co. (F.G.C.) Ltd v Lannon* [1969] 1 Q.B. 577, and *Chapman v Earl* [1968] 1 W.L.R. 1315. In the latter case the Divisional Court, on an appeal on a point of law against the decision of a rent assessment committee, gave leave for the plaintiff to apply for certiorari on the ground that a mandatory procedural step had not been observed by the committee. Certiorari was granted, and the appeal dismissed.

Statute may expressly provide for an appeal on the ground that the act impugned is *ultra vires*: see above, pp.805 *et seq.*; and the Magistrates' Courts Act 1980, s.111 (appeals by way of case stated).

(d) The exercise of a right of appeal to a higher administrative body will not necessarily cure the defect of a void act (*Ridge v Baldwin*, above, p.658). If the proceedings on appeal are by way of a complete rehearing, then the invalidity of the original decision may be irrelevant. The appellate body makes its own, independent, valid decision. (See *Stringer v Minister of Housing and Local Government*, above, pp.488 and 504; *Calvin v Carr*, above, p.740.)

(e) There is a general rule that a void act cannot be validated by the consent, waiver or acquiescence of the person affected by it. In *Mayes v Mayes* [1971] 1 W.L.R. 679, justices dismissed a wife's complaint of desertion after hearing her evidence, without giving her solicitor the opportunity of addressing them on her behalf. This was held to be a breach of natural justice, which was not cured by the fact that the right to address was not asserted at the time. Sir Jocelyn Simon P. stated at 684:

> "I am inclined to think that the general principle is that a rule of natural justice which goes to the very basis of judicature (as I think this does) cannot be waived. You cannot by waiver convert a nullity into a validity."

(f) The general principle that a decision that has been quashed as unlawful is void will apply even where the consequence is that an individual who otherwise would have been released is kept in detention: *R. (on the application of Wirral HA) v Mental Health Review Tribunal* [2001] EWCA Civ 1901. The Court of Appeal rejected an argument that, by analogy with the supposed rule that certiorari will not lie to quash an acquittal (*R. v Simpson* [1914] 1 K.B. 66, *per* Scrutton L.J. at 75), an order by a Mental Health Review Tribunal that a person should be discharged from detention under the Mental Health Act 1983 could not be overturned, even if unlawful. The Court of Appeal held that there was no reason to recognise such qualification to the normal principle that an unlawful decision is a nullity. The Tribunal's decision to discharge was conceded to be unlawful on the ground that inadequate reasons had been given for rejecting a strong body of evidence that advised against discharge. The court also noted that the principle that certiorari does not lie to quash an acquittal itself does not apply where the purported "acquittal" is a nullity (*R. v Hendon JJ. Ex p. DPP* [1994] Q.B. 167).

The general principle that an *ultra vires* act is void, and that a breach of natural justice renders an act void, was stated unequivocally in *Anisminic Ltd v Foreign Compensation Commission* [1969] 2 A.C. 147 (above, p.436), by Lord Reid at 171 (p.439), Lord Pearce at 195 (p.445) and Lord Wilberforce at 207–208. The speeches of Lord Morris and Lord Pearson contained nothing against that principle. The majority in *Ridge v Baldwin* [1964] A.C. 40 similarly had held that breach of the *audi alteram partem* rule of natural justice rendered the decision void. See Lord Reid at 80 (above, p.668), Lord Morris at 125 and Lord Hodson at 136. Lord Morris at 117, Lord Hodson at 135 and Lord Devlin at 139, expressly held that the decision was also void for breach of mandatory procedural requirements. Similarly, in *O'Reilly v Mackman* (below, p.978), Lord Diplock confirmed that breach of natural justice renders the decision void. The Court of Appeal in *Cooper v Wilson* [1937] 2 K.B. 309 held that a decision tainted by bias or interest under the *nemo judex* principle of natural justice (see pp.751–787) was void (dicta to the contrary by Baron Parke in *Dimes v Grand Junction Canal Proprietors* (1852) 3 H.L.C. 759 at 786, were not cited, but were cogently criticised by H.W.R. Wade (1968) 84 L.Q.R. 95, 107–108). Decisions quashed as *Wednesbury* unreasonable have also been characterised as void: *R. v Hendon JJ. Ex p. DPP* [1994] Q.B. 167.

An analogous, but distinct, situation arises where a public official acts in accordance with a view of the law based on a court decision subsequently overruled by a higher court. Under the declaratory theory of the common law, the law is changed with retrospective effect by the later decision, the courts other than under statute having no power to overrule with prospective effect only. In *R. v Governor of Brockhill Prison Ex p. Evans (No.2)* [2001] 2 A.C. 19, the application of this principle in conjunction with the rule that the tort of false imprisonment is one of strict liability meant that a prison governor was liable in damages (£5,000) where a prisoner was held in prison for 59 days longer than she should have been. It was for the governor to calculate the release date, incorporating a discount in respect of time spent in custody before sentence. In making this calculation, the governor acted in accordance with Home Office guidance and a clear line of Divisional Court decisions. However, these decisions were subsequently disapproved by the Divisional Court in the present case ([1997] Q.B. 443). The House of Lords held that it was no defence that the governor had acted reasonably and in good faith in accordance with court decisions; no new special defence of this kind should be established. Whether or not a power to overrule prospectively was desirable, it would not be right to apply such a doctrine where the liberty of the subject was concerned.

This can be contrasted with the position where a criminal conviction is quashed on appeal; detention by virtue of the original sentence passed by the court remains valid up to the time the conviction is quashed (Lord Woolf M.R. in the Court of Appeal in *Evans*, [1999] Q.B. 1043, 1056–1057); and there will, for example, be no cause of action for damages under Art.5 ECHR (*Benham v UK* (1996) 22 E.H.R.R. 293): see the discussion by Lord Hobhouse in *Evans* [2001] 2 A.C. 19 at 46–47.

The cases in the remainder of the chapter concentrate on the issues of the consequences of invalidity, the permissible extent of collateral challenge and partial invalidity, but also contain discressions of the general principles.

(B) The Consequences of Invalidity

CREDIT SUISSE v ALLERDALE BC

[1997] Q.B. 306; [1996] 3 W.L.R. 894; [1996] 4 All E.R. 129 (COURT OF APPEAL, CIVIL DIVISION)

The bank claimed payment under a guarantee given by the council for sums borrowed by a company established by the council to carry out recreational development (the provision of a leisure pool to be paid for by a time share development) which the council itself was unable to carry out because of government limits on spending and borrowing. The company was now in liquidation. Colman J. ([1995] 1 Lloyd's L.R. 315) held that guarantee was *ultra vires* and void. An appeal to the Court of Appeal was dismissed. It was held that the development was not authorised by either (1) s.19 of the Local Government (Miscellaneous Provisions) Act 1976 (power to provide recreational facilities, including power to provide buildings, equipment, supplies and assistance of any kind), or (2) by s.111 of the Local Government Act 1972. As to (1), providing time share accommodation was not the provision of a recreational activity, and the provision of "assistance of any kind" covered assistance to users of the facilities and not to those who provided them. As to s.111, as well as identifying the underlying statutory functions (here, s.19(1) of the 1976 Act and s.2(1) of the Local Authorities (Land) Act 1963) it was necessary to examine the context in which supposed implied powers were to be exercised. This included the basic principle that local authority finances were to be conducted on an annual basis; that the scheme involved incurring substantial financial obligations which could not be met out of the council's ordinary income; that powers to spend and borrow were subject to statutory control, Sch.13 to the 1972 Act containing a comprehensive code defining and limiting borrowing powers. The implied powers in s.111 did not provide an escape route from statutory controls. Hobhouse L.J. also emphasised the point that s.111(1) conferred powers in conjunction with the discharge of functions by the council. Here the functions were discharged by the company, which was not a contractor with or agent of the authority. Furthermore, even if setting up the company was authorised by s.111(1), giving a guarantee would merely be "incidental to the incidental" and barred by the decision of the House of Lords in *McCarthy & Stone* (above, p.397).

The following extracts deal with the consequences of these findings. The bank argued that if the council had no statutory capacity to implement the scheme by the creation of the company and the giving of the guarantee, the guarantee was void and unenforceable. However, if the scheme was *ultra vires* because it had been adopted for improper purposes, or involved some improper delegation, or was *Wednesbury* unreasonable, the court had a discretion whether to give relief. Given that the court held that establishing the company and giving the guarantee was *ultra vires*, the court did not need to deal with this. Nevertheless the following opinions were expressed.

Neill L.J.: . . .

V. THE EFFECT OF THE INVALIDITY OF THE SCHEME
AND THE GUARANTEE . . .

(1) The development of the doctrine of *ultra vires* . . .

In the last hundred years, and particularly in the last fifty, the doctrine of *ultra vires* has become a potent force in many areas of the law. In public law it has been used as the foundation for the intervention by the courts in judicial review proceedings. In private law it has been used as a method of confining the lawful activities of limited companies to those which are authorized by the memorandum of association.

But despite the great importance which the doctrine of *ultra vires* has assumed in the field of public law and, until recently, in relation to the activities of limited companies, the doctrine still gives rise to conceptual and practical difficulties. It is easy to state that if a body with limited powers make a decision which it has no power to make, the decision is void and of no legal effect. But such a statement may not accord with the reality of the situation.

The problem is illustrated by the well-known dictum of Lord Radcliffe in *Smith v East Elloe RDC* [1956] AC 736 at 769, where he said:

"An order, even if not make in good faith, is still an act capable of legal consequences. It bears no brand of invalidity upon its forehead. Unless the necessary proceedings are taken at law to establish the cause of invalidity and to get it quashed or otherwise upset, it will remain as effective for its ostensible purposes as the most impeccable of orders."

Moreover, even an order which is manifestly bad can be effective until its invalidity has been exposed in court. The counterfeit is as good as the genuine article until it has been weighed.

It is no doubt because it has been difficult to find an appropriate epithet to describe the quality of an *ultra vires* decision in the period before it has been pronounced ineffective *ab initio* that judges have depreciated the use of the word "void". By way of example one can take a passage in the speech of Lord Diplock in *F Hoffmann-La Roche & Co AG v Secretary of State for Trade and Industry* [1975] AC 295 at 366, where he said:

"I think it leads to confusion to use such terms as 'voidable', 'voidable ab initio', 'void' or 'a nullity' as descriptive of the legal status of subordinate legislation alleged to be *ultra vires* for patent or for latent defects, before its validity has been pronounced on by a court of competent jurisdiction."

The problem, however, is not merely one of terminology. Even after an order or decision has been declared to be void or a nullity or has been quashed, it may return as a ghost to show that it was once very much alive. The law has not yet found a way to deal satisfactorily with the simulacrum of a decision. . . .

(2) The doctrine of *ultra vires* in relation to limited companies

[His Lordship referred to the distinction drawn between the effect of acts which are *ultra vires* a company and acts beyond the powers of the directors, discussed by Browne-Wilkinson L.J. in *Rolled Steel Products (Holdings) Ltd v British Steel Corp* [1986] Ch. 246 at 302. A transaction outside the objects of the company was beyond its capacity, *ultra vires* and wholly void. However, a transaction falling within the objects of the company was capable of conferring rights on third parties even though the transaction was an abuse or in excess of the powers of the company. In the case of the former, whether or not the third party had notice of the invalidity, property transferred or money paid under such a transaction would be recoverable from the third party. In the case of the latter, the position of the third party would depend on whether or not he had notice that the transaction was in excess or abuse of the powers of the company. This position had, however, been changed by statute (Companies Act 1985, s.35, as substituted by the Companies Act 1989, s.108(1)), providing that a company's capacity is not limited by its memorandum.]

No comparable changes have been introduced by legislation in relation to local authorities. Nevertheless, it is for consideration whether in a private law claim by a third party a distinction can be drawn, similar to that drawn in *Rolled Steel*, between decisions and acts which are beyond the capacity of a public authority and decisions and acts which involve a misuse of power by those controlling the authority.

(3) The doctrine of *ultra vires* in public law

At one time a distinction was drawn between cases where the public authority lacked capacity and the impugned decision was said to be void or a nullity, and cases of wrong decisions 'within jurisdiction', in which the decisions were said to be voidable. But in the recent authorities the term 'void' has been generally adopted, though, as I have already observed, some concern has been expressed as to the confusion to which the use of the term may lead.

A useful starting point is the speech of Lord Reid in *Anisminic Ltd v Foreign Compensation Commission* [1969] 2 AC 147, where in a landmark decision the House of Lords held that an error by the commission within jurisdiction rendered their determination a nullity. Lord Reid said ([1969] 2 AC 147 at 171) [His Lordship quoted the passage "It has sometimes been said that it is only where a tribunal acts without jurisdiction that its decision is a nullity. . . . I do not intend this list to be exhaustive" (see above; pp.438–439)]

It follows therefore that where in judicial review proceedings an order or decision is declared to be *ultra vires* on any of the grounds which are now available, the order or decision is as a matter of law void and a nullity. In legal theory this result is comprehensible and indeed the all-embracing doctrine of *ultra vires* accords with the jurisdictional basis on which the court acts. The court can only intervene where the body which made the original decision made an error which undermined its capacity to act. As Lord Reid explained, in the absence of such error, the body to whom the question was remitted was as much entitled to decide the question wrongly as to decide it rightly (see [1969] 2 AC 147 at 171.)

The public law cases, however, demonstrate some of the conceptual and practical problems to which, as I mentioned earlier, the doctrine of *ultra vires* gives rise.

In the first place, an *ultra vires* decision will in the ordinary way take effect unless and until it is challenged, and challenged promptly, by someone who has the right to do so. Applications for judicial review, which include applications to quash *ultra vires* decisions of public authorities, are subject to the provisions of s 31 of the Supreme Court Act 1981 and of RSC Ord 53. [His Lordship cited s.31 (3) and (6), below, pp.924–925]

It will be seen, therefore, that in the context of judicial review a decision of a public authority, which as a matter of law is *ultra vires*, may survive and remain effective if the applicant for a remedy is adjudged to have no sufficient interest or there has been undue delay and the case falls within the concluding words of s 31 (6) of the 1981 Act.

An illustration of the continuing existence of a void decision is provided by the fact that an appeal can be brought against such a decision. In *Calvin v Carr* [1980] AC 574 the plaintiff, who was the part-owner of a horse, was disqualified for a year by the stewards of the Australian Jockey Club. The plaintiff appealed from the decision of the stewards to the committee of the Jockey Club but his appeal was dismissed. In subsequent proceedings he claimed, inter alia, that because the proceedings before the stewards had been in breach of the rules of natural justice they were void, so that the committee of the Jockey Club had no jurisdiction to hear or determine an appeal. The Privy Council rejected this argument. Lord Wilberforce said ([1980] AC 574 at 590):

"The decision of the stewards resulted in disqualification, an effect with immediate and serious consequences for the appellant . . . These consequences remained in effect unless and until the stewards decision was challenged and, if so, had sufficient existence in law to justify an appeal."

Lord Wilberforce drew attention to the analogy provided by appeals in criminal proceedings where irregularities at the trial may have rendered the trial a nullity (see *Crane v DPP* [1921] 2 AC 299.)

I have already referred to the fact that in a case where the court considers that there has been undue delay in making an application for judicial review, it has a discretion under s 31(6) of the 1981 Act to refuse to grant relief if, for example, it considers that the granting of relief would be, for example, "detrimental to good administration". But it seems clear that in public law cases the court, as a court of review, has some general as opposed to a merely statutory discretion as to the relief which it will grant. It is true that in *Grunwick Processing Laboratories Ltd v Advisory Conciliation and Arbitration Service* [1978] AC 655 at 695 Lord Diplock said that—

"where a statutory authority had acted *ultra vires* any person who would be affected by its act if it were valid is normally entitled *ex debito justiciae* to have it set aside, if he has proceeded by way of certiorari, or to have it declared void . . .".

More recently, however, in *Chief Constable of the North Wales Police v Evans* [1982] 1 WLR 1155 the House of Lords, though it held that the chief constable had failed in the performance of his duty to act fairly in dealing with a probationary constable, granted only a limited declaration. Lord Brightman said ([1982] 1 WLR 1155 at 1176):

"I feel that the choice of remedy is a difficult one. It is a matter of discretion. From the point of view of the respondent who has been wronged in a matter so vital to his life, an order of mandamus is the only satisfactory remedy . . . But it is unusual, in a case such as the present, for the court to make an order of mandamus, and I think that in practice it might border on usurpation of the powers of the chief constable, which is to be avoided. With some reluctance and hesitation, I feel that the respondent will have to content himself with the less satisfactory declaration that I have outlined [affirming that, by reason of such unlawfully induced resignation, the respondent thereby became entitled to the same rights and remedies, not including re-instatement, as he would have had if the appellant had unlawfully dispensed with his services under reg 16(1) of the Police Regulations 1971]."

The existence of this general discretion was also affirmed by Donaldson MR in *R v Panel on Take-overs and Mergers, ex p Datafin plc (Norton Opax plc intervening)* [1987] QB 815 at 840, where he said:

"I think that it is important that all who are concerned with take-over bids should have well in mind a very special feature of public law decisions, such as those of the panel, namely that however wrong they may be, however lacking in jurisdiction they may be, they subsist and remain fully effective unless and until they are set aside by a court of competent jurisdiction. Furthermore, the court has an ultimate discretion whether to set them aside and may refuse to do so in the public interest, notwithstanding that it holds and declares the decision to have been made *ultra vires* (see eg *R v Monopolies and Mergers Commission, ex p Argyll Group plc* [1986] 1 WLR 763). That case . . . further illustrates an awareness that such decisions affect a very wide public which will not be parties to the dispute and that their interests have to be taken into account as much as those of the immediate disputants."

I come now to the present case.

(4) The present case

It is important to remember the nature of the present claim. It is not a claim against a limited company. Nor is it a claim in public law where the court is being asked to exercise a supervisory jurisdiction. It is a private law claim, albeit against a public authority.

I have made some reference to proceedings for judicial review where the court, in the exercise of its supervisory jurisdiction, can grant remedies which, to an extent which I need not further examine, are discretionary. Part of this discretion is conferred by statute. Part of the discretion seems to arise from the nature of the jurisdiction itself.

It was argued on behalf of the bank that in private law proceedings against a public authority the court should exercise a similar discretion where the decision was *ultra vires* not for lack of statutory capacity, but because of some procedural impropriety. In private law too, it was said, there were gradations of *ultra vires*. It was also submitted that it is profoundly unsatisfactory if a decision which is procedurally *ultra vires* can survive a challenge in judicial review proceedings but can nevertheless be treated as a nullity in a claim in private law.

I feel bound to reject these submissions. I know of no authority for the proposition that the *ultra vires* decisions of local authorities can be classified into categories of invalidity. I do not think that it is open to this court to introduce such a classification. Where a public authority acts outside its jurisdiction in any of the ways indicated by Lord Reid in *Anisminic*, the decision is void. In the case of a decision to enter into a contract of guarantee, the consequences in private law are those which flow where one of the parties to a contract lacks capacity. I see no escape from this conclusion.

Furthermore, this conclusion seems to me to accord with the decision of the House of Lords in *Wandsworth London BC v Winder* [1985] AC 461. [See below, p.990]

I do not consider the present law to be satisfactory. I say nothing about the merits of this case which have not been investigated. But there may be cases where it is beyond argument that a third party has entered into a contract with a public body in ignorance of any procedural defect which may later entitle the public body to claim that the contract was made *ultra vires* and so reject liability under it. But if, as I believe there to be, there is only one category of *ultra vires* decisions where a local authority is concerned, I see no room for a judicial discretion. Furthermore, in view of the fact that by s 2(2) of the 1972 Act it is provided that the council is to consist of a chairman and councillors, there is no scope for an argument that a distinction can be drawn between the powers of the council and the powers of the councillors.

PETER GIBSON L.J. [held that the council lacked the capacity to give the guarantee, which was accordingly unenforceable. He preferred not to express any *obiter* views on the question of the effect of invalidity on other grounds of the guarantee.]

HOBHOUSE L.J.: . . .

The relationship of public, private and administrative law

Where a statutory corporation purports to enter into a contract which it is not empowered by the relevant statute to enter into, the corporation lacks the capacity to make the supposed contract. This lack of capacity means that the document and the agreement it contains does not have effect as a legal contract. It exists in fact but not in law. It is legal nullity. The purported contract which is in truth not a contract does not confer any legal rights on either party. Neither party can sue upon it. This conclusion gives rise to no conflict between public law and private law principles. The role of public law is to answer the question: what is the capacity of the local authority to contract? The role of private law is to answer the question: when one of the parties to a supposed contract lacks contractual capacity, does the supposed contract give rise to legal obligations? When a plaintiff is asserting a private law right—a private law cause of action, typically a claim for damages for breach of contract or tort—the plaintiff must establish his cause of action. Any defence raised by the defendant must be one which is recognised by private law. Lack of capacity to contract is a defence recognised by private law.

When one gets beyond situations which can be described as lack of capacity, the private law position becomes more complicated, as was recognised in *Rolled Steel Products (Holdings) Ltd v British Steel Corp* [1986] Ch 246.

The decision of the Court of Appeal was that if the relevant transaction was not *ultra vires* in the sense in which Slade and Browne-Wilkinson LJJ were using it, the defence has to be based on the principles applicable to agents and fiduciaries.

Thus, the question of capacity and *ultra vires* properly so-called does not involve any consideration of questions of fault or notice. On the other hand questions of abuse of power may involve such considerations.

If local authorities were companies incorporated under the Companies Acts, the *Rolled Steel* case would provide the necessary guidance on the treatment of lack of capacity and excess or abuse of power. But local authorities are public law bodies and fall within the purview of administrative law. This means that their decisions are amenable to judicial review and the remedies which that procedure provides. The essence of the modern law of judicial review is that decisions which involve illegality, irrationality or procedural impropriety are treated as *ultra vires* (see *Council of Civil Service Unions v Minister for the Civil Service* [1985] AC 374 at 410 per Lord Diplock). That *ultra vires* was the basis of the jurisdiction of the courts in judicial review proceedings was emphatically reaffirmed by Lord Browne-Wilkinson, with the agreement of the other members of the House, in *Page v Hull University Visitor* [1993] AC 682 at 701, where he adopted what Lord Diplock had said in *O'Reilly v Mackman* [1983] 2 AC 237 at 278 (again with the agreement of the other members of the House) . . . [see above, p.453].

It is an inescapable conclusion that the same words and phrases have a breadth of meaning which differs in administrative law and other parts of the law. In some contexts the terms are clearly used in an equivalent sense. If a tribunal of limited jurisdiction acts in excess of its jurisdiction, its purported decision is a nullity (though such nullity will not prevent an appellate court from deciding that there has been an excess of jurisdiction). A minister who purports to exercise a delegated power to legislate must act within that power and, if he does not, the purported delegated legislation is void and of no legal effect. But in other areas, such as procedural impropriety, difficulties arise. For example, breach of the rules of natural justice has long been held to render invalid and void a decision so reached. In *Ridge v Baldwin* [1964] AC 40 at 80 Lord Reid (representing the view of the majority of their Lordships) said:

"Then there was considerable argument whether in the result the watch committee's decision is void or merely voidable. Time and again in the cases I have cited it has been stated that a decision given without regard to the principles of natural justice is void and that was expressly decided in *Wood v Woad* ((1874) LR 9 Exch 190). I see no reason to doubt these authorities. The body with the power to decide cannot lawfully proceed to make a decision until it has afforded to the person affected a proper opportunity to state his case."

Lord Devlin expressed a different view, agreeing with Lord Evershed on this point: "the miscarriage rendered the watch committee's decision voidable and not null and void *ab initio*" (see [1964] AC 40 at 142).

Lord Hailsham addressed these problems in *London and Clydeside Estates Ltd v Aberdeen DC* [1980] 1 WLR 182 at 189–190:

"In this appeal we are in the field of the rapidly developing jurisprudence of administrative law, and we are considering the effect of non compliance by a statutory authority with the statutory requirements affecting the discharge of one of its functions. In the reported decisions there is much language presupposing the existence of stark categories such as mandatory and directory, void and voidable, a nullity, and purely regulatory. Such language is useful; indeed, in the course of this opinion I have used some of it myself. But I wish to say that I am not at all clear that the language itself may not be misleading in so far as it may be supposed to present a court with the necessity of fitting a particular case into one or other of mutually exclusive and starkly contrasted compartments, compartments which in some cases (eg void and voidable) are borrowed from the language of contract or status, and are not easily fitted to the requirements of administrative law. When Parliament lays down a statutory requirement for the exercise of legal authority it expects its authority to be obeyed down to the minutest detail. But what the courts have to decide in a particular case is the legal consequence of non compliance on the rights of the subject viewed in the light of a concrete state of facts and a continuing chain of events. It may be that what the courts are faced with is not so much a stark choice of alternatives but a spectrum of possibilities in which one compartment or description fades gradually into another. At one end of this spectrum there may be cases in which a fundamental obligation may have been so outrageously and flagrantly ignored or defied that the subject may safely ignore what has been done and treat it as having no legal consequences on himself. In such a case if the defaulting authority seeks to rely on its action it may be that the subject is entitled to use the defect in procedures, simply as a shield or defence without having taken any positive action of his own. At the other end of the spectrum the defect in procedure may be so nugatory or trivial that the authority can safely proceed without remedial action, confident that, if the subject is so misguided as to rely on the fault, the courts will decline to listen to his complaint. But in a very great number of cases, it may be in a majority of them, it may be necessary for a subject, in order to safeguard himself, to go to the court for declaration of his rights, the grant of which may well be discretionary, and by the like token it may be wise for an authority (as it certainly would have been here) to do everything in its power to remedy the fault in its procedures so as not to deprive the subject of his due or themselves of their power to act. In such cases, though language like mandatory, directory, void, voidable, nullity and so forth may be helpful in argument, it may be misleading in effect if relied on to show that the courts, in deciding the consequences of a defect in the exercise of power, are necessarily bound to fit the facts of a particular case and a developing chains of events into rigid legal categories or to stretch or cramp them on a bed of Procrustes invented by lawyers for the purposes of convenient exposition. As I have said, the case does not really arise here, since we are in the presence of a total non compliance with a requirement which I have held to be mandatory. Nevertheless, I do not wish to be understood in the field of administrative law and in the domain where the courts apply a supervisory jurisdiction over the acts of subordinate authority purporting to exercise statutory powers, to encourage the use of rigid legal classifications. The jurisdiction is inherently discretionary and the court is frequently in the presence of differences of degree which merge almost imperceptibly into differences of kind."

In *F Hoffmann-La Roche & Co AG v Secretary of State for Trade and Industry* [1975] AC 295 at 366 Lord Diplock said:

"I think it leads to confusion to use such terms as voidable, voidable ab initio, void or a nullity as descriptive of the legal status of subordinate legislation alleged to be *ultra vires* for patent or latent defects, before its validity has been pronounced on by a court of competent jurisdiction."

In the same vein, it can be added that the use of the term "illegal" or "unlawful" in administrative law is to be contrasted with the use of the term "illegal" in private law.

Chief Constable of the North Wales Police v Evans [1982] 1 WLR 1155 illustrates such considerations. Like *Ridge v Baldwin*, it was a case of wrongful dismissal (Evans having been constructively dismissed) and the House of Lords discussed what remedies were appropriate. The fact that the decision of the relevant authority had been arrived at unlawfully and was therefore to be treated for the purposes of administrative law as *ultra vires* did not carry with it the conclusion that the decision and subsequent actions should be treated as if they never had occurred.

The use of terminology for the purposes of administrative law in a different way to that which would be recognised in private law can be found in very many authorities, as can examples of the use by the court of the discretion to grant or withhold remedies of proceedings for judicial review. One further example will suffice to illustrate the point. In *R v Broadcasting Complaints Commission, ex p Owen* [1985] QB 1153 the Divisional Court held that the commission had acted unlawfully in refusing to consider a certain complaint. But the court refused to grant further relief notwithstanding the invalidity of the decision. May LJ said ([1985] QB 1153 at 1177):

". . . the grant of what may be the appropriate remedies in an application for judicial review is a matter for the discretion of this court. Where one is satisfied that although a reason relied on by a statutory body may not properly be described as insubstantial, nevertheless without it the statutory body would have been bound to come to precisely the same conclusion on valid grounds, then it would be wrong for this court to exercise its discretion to strike down, in one way or another, that body's conclusion."

The discretion of the court in deciding whether to grant any remedy is a wide one. It can take into account many considerations, including the needs of good administration, delay, the effect on third parties, the utility of granting the relevant remedy. The discretion can be exercised so as partially to uphold and partially quash the relevant administrative decision or act (see eg *Agricultural Horticultural and Forestry Industry Training Board v Aylesbury Mushrooms Ltd* [1972] 1 WLR 190).

These factors have in their turn given rise to fundamental difficulties for the theoretical basis of administrative law as discussed by a number of authors— Wade *Administrative Law* (7th edn, 1994), Lord Woolf's Hamlyn Lecture (41st series, 1990), Sir John Laws 'Illegality: The Problem of Jurisdiction' in Supperstone and Goudie, *Judicial Review* (1992) and de Smith Woolf and Jowell *Judicial Review of Administrative Action* (5th edn 1995). What is the status of an *ultra vires* decision which the courts have declined to quash on proceedings for judicial review? In principle any such decision is to be regarded as "void" and a "nullity". Yet the effect of the exercise of the court's discretion is to allow it to stand. Similar questions of theory and terminology exist in relation to the status of an unlawful decision or administrative act before it has been challenged and held to be *"ultra vires"* (see *Smith v East Elloe RDC* [1956] AC 736 and *Hoffmann-La Roche*).

In my judgment, the answer lies in what has been said by Lord Hailsham and Lord Diplock in the passages which I have quoted and the recognition that terms are used differently in administrative law and other branches of the law. Before using the phrase *"ultra vires"* or the words "void" and "nullity", it is necessary to pause and consider the breadth of the meaning which one is giving them. It is not correct to take terminology from administrative law and apply it without the necessary adjustment and refinement of meaning to private law. Where private law rights are concerned, as in the present case, the terminology must be used in the sense which is appropriate to private law.

There is a further dimension which is also fundamental. In judicial review all that an applicant need show in order to have a locus standi is "a sufficient interest in the matter to which the application relates" (see RSC Ord 53, r 3(7)). This need not be any recognisable legal interest and need not involve any assertion of any infringement of the rights of the applicant. On the other hand, in civil proceedings the rights and liabilities of the parties before the court are of the essence of the subject matter of the proceedings. Therefore, whereas in judicial review proceedings it may be appropriate for a court to consider whether an abuse of power should be publicly exposed, in civil proceedings the court is only concerned with whether that abuse of power has affected the private law rights of the parties.

Thus, in *Wandsworth London BC v Winder* [1985] AC 461 the local authority was seeking to evict and obtain a possession order against one of its tenants. It was asserting a private law right. The ground upon which it relied was the tenant's refusal to pay an increased rent. The tenant said that the resolutions of the council and the notices of the increases in rent were *ultra vires* and void in that they did not comply with s 111 of the Housing Act 1957. Accordingly, although the tenant was raising an issue which could have been the subject of judicial review proceedings (had he brought them in time), he was actually raising a narrower point: whether or not he was civilly liable to pay the increased rent. The Court of Appeal by a majority and the House of Lords held that it was not an abuse of process for him to raise this defence in the possession proceedings. The existence of private law rights has to be determined as a private law issue.

In resolving a private law issue it is always necessary to have regard to who are the actual parties to the issue. This may affect the analysis of the issue and the answer which private law gives to it. Some improper conduct of the decision-making body may be material within the broader spectrum of administrative law, but it will not necessarily be material as between the parties to a private law dispute. A want of natural justice is specifically material to the respective private law rights of the aggrieved party and the decision-maker or a person who asserts rights based upon the decision. The private law rights of a third party who himself has not been a victim of any want of natural justice will not be affected.

Similarly, if the abuse of power by one party can properly be categorised as a "fault" of that party, it cannot on private law principles be used as a basis for conferring rights which would not otherwise exist upon the party at fault against another party, who would otherwise have rights against the party at fault or would not be liable to the party at fault. Again, similarly, considerations of the knowledge of, or degree of notice to, a party who is asserting a private law right may be relevant to the question whether the right is enforceable against another where there has been some irregularity in the transaction which is alleged to have given rise to the right.

Private law issues must be decided in accordance with the rules of private law. The broader and less rigorous rules of administrative law should not without adjustment be applied to the resolution of private law disputes in civil proceedings. Public law, that is to say, the law governing public law entities and their activities, is a primary source of the principles applied in administrative law proceedings. The decisions of such entities are the normal subject matter of applications for judicial review. When the activities of a public law body (or individual) are relevant to a private law dispute in civil proceedings, public law may in a similar way provide answers which are relevant to the resolution of the private law issue. But after taking into account the applicable public law, the civil proceedings have to be decided as a matter of private law. The issue does not become an administrative law issue; administrative law remedies are irrelevant.

In the present case, counsel have advanced arguments which have called into question the relationship between private law and administrative law. Mr Sher QC, for the council, has argued that an element of irrationality ("*Wednesbury* unreasonableness": see *Associated Provincial Picture Houses Ltd v Wednesbury Corp* [1948] 1 KB 223) or improper motive would provide the council with a defence to the bank's claim. Mr Clarke QC, for the bank, has argued that any defence should be regarded as discretionary and should be approached in the same way as the decision whether to grant a remedy in judicial review proceedings. These arguments were considered by Colman J in his judgment (see [1995] 1 Lloyd's Rep 315 at 342–358). In my judgment, both these arguments make the error which I have identified of using administrative law language and concepts without making the necessary adjustments. It remains necessary to ask what amounts to a defence to a private law cause of action. Want of capacity is a defence to a contractual claim; breach of duty, fiduciary or otherwise, may be a defence depending upon the circumstances. To say that administrative law categorises all grounds for judicial review as *ultra vires* does not assist. In civil proceedings the question is whether, after taking into account the relevant public law, there is on the facts a private law defence. By a parity of reasoning, how a divisional court would have decided an application for judicial review and what remedy (if any) it would have granted in the exercise of its discretion is not material.

[His Lordship proceeded to hold that the district council did not have the capacity to give the guarantee.]

Appeal dismissed

Notes

1. Is there any significant difference between the approaches of Neill and Hobhouse L.JJ.? In so far as there is a difference, a preference for the former was expressed by Dyson J. in *Bedfordshire CC v Fitzpatrick Contractors Ltd* [2001] L.G.R. 397.

Note Craig's criticism of Neill L.J.'s approach, that "the bank was not seeking to argue that there should be different categories of invalidity, but whether *assuming that the act was invalid*, there could be any discretion as to the granting of the remedy". He argues that in cases such as this the courts should possess a residual discretion, akin to judicial review actions, and take into account the desirability of both protecting citizens against illegal government action and protecting the public purse from the effects of illegal government conduct (*Craig*, p.153). On the other hand, it must also be of significance that Parliament had at that time modified the effect of the *ultra vires* for companies incorporated under the Companies Acts but not local authorities. A measure of protection has now been provided for those contracting with local authorities by the Local Government (Contracts) Act 1997. Under this Act, specially certified contracts are protected from challenge in private law proceedings but not judicial review or proceedings before the auditor. This Act assumes that either of the two kinds of defect discussed in *Allerdale* have the same consequence.

2. The views expressed by Lord Hailsham in the *London of Clydeside* case, cited by Hobhouse L.J., have been criticised as overemphasising the role of the court's discretion.

See also Sedley J. in *R. v London Borough of Tower Hamlets Ex p. Tower Hamlets Combined Traders Association* [1994] C.O.D. 325 (above, p.645). His Lordship held that the *ratio decidendi* of the *London & Clydeside* case was to be found in the speech of Lord Keith, and included the proposition that the question whether non-compliance with a procedural requirement rendered a decision invalid was a question of judgment according to legal criteria and not discretion, and depended on the general significance of the requirement and not the effect of its omission on the particular applicant. It was also clear that the court retained a discretion to refuse to grant a remedy even in respect of a breach of a requirement of fundamental importance. His Lordship had difficulty with Lord Hailsham's speech in so far as it could be interpreted as conflating these separate points:

"This passage, which contains general reflections on a developing area of jurisprudence in public law, is manifestly not intended . . . to qualify the uniform reasoning of the whole House on the issue before it. This reasoning ran to a conclusion that the nature of the breach was such that no question of discretionary refusal on relief arose, so that the 'legal consequence of a non-compliance on the rights of the subject' did not in the event have to be 'viewed in the light of a concrete state of facts and continuing chain of events'. Their Lordships unanimously held the legal consequence of non-compliance in the case before them to be determined by an appraisal of the importance of the statutory purpose without regard to consequent facts or subsequent events. Correspondingly, the "spectrum of possibilities" which Lord Hailsham describes is a range of situations dependent upon the intrinsic importance of the provision and not its extrinsic effect on the complainant. Where, in the final sentence of the passage, Lord Hailsham returns to the question of discretion, I confess that I find his formulation problematical. The differences of degree, meaning presumably the degree of significance of the provision and of the breach of it, can readily be said to merge into differences of kind because their effect has ultimately to be judged to be either fatal or non-fatal to the measure concerned. This is unproblematical. But the prefatory remark ('The jurisdiction is inherently discretionary . . . ') has no obvious link with the proposition that follows and is moreover puzzling in itself; for while the exercise of the jurisdiction may ultimately bring a court to discretionary considerations, the entire exercise which the House was carrying out, including the gauging of differences of degree which Lord Hailsham was here describing, was visibly a matter of judgment according to the legal principles and not to discretion".

Furthermore, the adoption of Lord Hailsham's remarks by the Court of Appeal in *Main v Swansea City Council* (1985) 49 P. & C.R. 26 and *R. v Lambeth LBC Ex p. Sharp* (1986) 55 P. & C.R. 232, was to be regarded as relating to the exercise of discretion whether to grant a remedy and not to the prior question of the legal effect of the failure to comply with a procedural requirement.

3. Where a public authority performs an *ultra vires* act, the fact that it has done so and its circumstances may nevertheless constitute a matter to be taken into account when exercising another statutory power, in particular to ensure that the illegality is not repeated. This is illustrated by *Foster v Eastbourne BC* [2004] EWCA Civ 36. F, the council's Director of Environmental Services, entered a Compromise Agreement with the council on August 25, 1998 under which he would leave his employment on August 31, 1999 by reason of redundancy. He would by then be 50 and thus eligible for the discretionary award by the council of the maximum "added years" (10). The council agreed to make that award, which would lead to an enhanced pension under the then applicable regulations. In the meantime, his directorate was abolished on September 28, 1998 and its functions distributed to other directorates. F continued to deal with one of the matters that had fallen within the responsibility of his directorate (the Coast Protection Scheme). Subsequently, the District Auditor formed the view, and the council agreed, that the Compromise Agreement was *ultra vires*. The council refused to make the redundancy payments and took proceedings against F to recover the salary payments made under the Agreement. The Court of Appeal (*Eastbourne BC v Foster* (2001) 3 L.G.L.R. 1112) held that F's original contract of employment had ended when his post disappeared (through repudiation by the council and acceptance of that repudiation by F). However, he continued in the council's employment in a different role up to August 31, 1999. That was the date for which the council gave him notice, even if that was done pursuant to the void agreement. In respect of this period F was entitled to reasonable remuneration on a *quantum meruit*. However, this was covered by the fact that, although prima facie liable in restitution to repay the sum paid under the void agreement, F was entitled to the defence of change of position. A further point was whether F should be given a discretionary added years award under the regulations now applicable (the Local Government (Early Termination of Employment) (Discretionary Compensation) (England and Wales) Regulation 2000 (SI 2000/1410)). This time, the council decided to award enhanced redundancy payments under the regulations, but, on the stated ground that to do so would be "irrationally generous," not any added years. F's claim for judicial review of the latter decision was dismissed by Moses J. and the Court of Appeal. The Court of Appeal rejected F's argument that the void Compromise Agreement should be totally ignored in considering whether F should be awarded added years:

> "In the phrase used by Mr Mackay QC in his judgment, the law does not require one 'to airbrush it out of existence as if it had never been.' Nor in my view does it require the council or the courts to ignore the fact that the appellant was under 50 when he became redundant and that his employment to the age of 50 in fact occurred as a result of the Compromise Agreement. All this is part of the history of this matter" (*per* Keene L.J. at [32]).

If this were not the case, F would achieve the very result agreed by the parties to the *ultra vires* purpose of the Compromise Agreement. In the court's view, the Agreement was *ultra vires* because it had as an improper purpose that of extending his employment beyond the date his original post became redundant in order to enable him to qualify for an added years award.

Keene L.J. said (at [35]):

> "The purpose of the 2000 Regulations was not to enable an award to be made to someone in the appellant's position. It follows that I agree with Moses J. that it would have been irrational and unlawful to have made any award of added years to the appellant".

A separate ground was that to have awarded the full amount of added years would have been irrationally generous, although a lesser amount might not have been (at [36]).

Baker L.J. and Lord Brown agreed with Keene L.J.

Is the outcome entirely fair to F? Had he not entered the Compromise Agreement with the council, for which the council was as responsible as he (see Lord Brown at [39]) he would probably have stayed in a lower level post on a protected salary; if he had then been made redundant when over 50 he would certainly been eligible for an added years award. Keene L.J. (at [29]) regarded this as irrelevant to the point that to grant added years now would not be within the scope and purpose of the 2000 regulations, although it might be relevant to the issue of irrational generosity. Furthermore, what would have happened absent the Agreement was "speculative" (*ibid.*).

It is submitted that the court's reasoning is unclear in that it confuses the principles of illegality and irrationality, and unconvincing in its view that to award any added years now would give effect to the unlawful Agreement. The fact that F's extended employment had been agreed originally for the "improper purpose" enshrined in the Compromise Agreement of securing eligibility for added years was rightly held to render the Agreement *ultra vires* and unenforceable. However, F did in fact work for the Council until past 50 and it is difficult to see how as a matter of illegality he was not eligible to be considered for an added years award. It would therefore be a matter for the council's discretion whether to make an added years award. In exercising that discretion the fairness considerations mentioned above would be relevant. To grant some added years (although not all those contemplated in the Agreement) could not properly be condemned as using the power for the improper purpose of giving effect to the Agreement. This is not a matter of disregarding the Agreement because it is void (a bad argument). The Agreement is taken into account but is no bar to eligibility now for an added years award. It is not "absurd" (*pace* Keene L.J. at [33]) for the Agreement to be unlawful and unenforceable as such by F and for the council subsequently to reach a similar outcome by a fresh exercise of discretion. The council had taken the view that it would have been unlawful to credit any added years; it is submitted that the matter should have been remitted to the council for reconsideration.

(C) Collateral Challenge

The extent to which an act or decision may be challenged collaterally in civil or criminal proceedings, as distinct from directly on an application for judicial review, raises a number of difficult issues. The following case shows that the extent to which collateral challenge is available depends on the context, and in particular the construction of the relevant legislation.

BODDINGTON v BRITISH TRANSPORT POLICE

[1999] 2 A.C. 143; [1998] 2 W.L.R. 639; [1998] 2 All E.R. 203 (HOUSE OF LORDS)

Section 67(1) of the Transport Act 1962 provided that the British Railways Board could make byelaws "regulating the use and working of, and travel on, their railways, the maintenance of order on their railways and railway premises . . . and the conduct of all persons, including their officers and servants, while on those premises" and in particular byelaws with respect to a number of matters including "the smoking of tobacco in railway carriages and elsewhere and the prevention of nuisances . . .". Byelaw 20 of the British Railways Board's Byelaws provided that no person shall smoke upon the railway "where smoking is expressly prohibited by the Board by notice exhibited in a conspicuous position".

Network South Central decided to introduce a complete smoking ban on all their trains, from January 1, 1993, for commercial reasons and after conducting research. Mr Boddington was convicted of an offence of smoking contrary to byelaw 20 on a train between Falmer and Brighton. This was in an area of the train where prohibition notices were conspicuously displayed. The stipendiary magistrate rejected B's challenges to the validity of the byelaw and to the administrative decision to implement the ban by displaying notices. The Divisional Court ([1997] C.O.D. 3), applying and extending the decision in *Bugg v D.P.P* [1993] Q.B. 473, dismissed an appeal by case stated, holding that issues of the procedural and substantive invalidity of byelaws, and the validity of the administrative decisions, did not fall within the jurisdiction of a criminal court. The court certified as a point of law of general importance, (1) whether a defendant might raise as a defence to a criminal charge a contention that a byelaw or administrative decision made under it was *ultra vires*; and (2) if so (i) whether the answer to the question depended on whether the byelaw or decision was "bad on its face;" and (ii) whether the criminal court might consider whether the byelaw or decision was reasonable, and if so by reference to *Kruse v Johnson* [1898] 2 Q.B. 91, *Wednesbury* principles, or some other criteria. B claimed that the decision to impose a total ban on smoking was *ultra vires* in that the power to "regulate" smoking did not authorise a complete prohibition. The House of Lords dismissed an appeal, but held that collateral challenge was in general permissible.

LORD IRVINE OF LAIRG L.C.:

Raising public law defences to criminal charges

These arguments are regularly raised in the courts in cases in the public law field, concerned with applications for judicial review. The issue is whether the same arguments may be deployed in a criminal court as a defence to a criminal charge.

Challenge to the lawfulness of subordinate legislation or administrative decisions and acts may take many forms, compendiously grouped by Lord Diplock in *Council of Civil Service Unions v Minister for the Civil Service* [1985] A.C. 374 under the headings of illegality, procedural impropriety and irrationality. Categorisation of types of challenge assists in an orderly exposition of the principles underlying our developing public law. But these are not watertight compartments because the various grounds for judicial review run together. The exercise of a power for an improper purpose may involve taking irrelevant considerations into account, or ignoring relevant considerations; and either may lead to an irrational result. The failure to grant a person affected by a decision a hearing, in breach of principles of procedural fairness, may result in a failure to take into account relevant considerations.

The question of the extent to which public law defences may be deployed in criminal proceedings requires consideration of fundamental principle concerning the promotion of the rule of law and fairness to defendants to criminal charges in having a reasonable opportunity to defend themselves. However, sometimes the public interest in orderly administration means that the scope for challenging unlawful conduct by public bodies may have to be circumscribed.

Where there is a tension between these competing interests and principles, the balance between them is ordinarily to be struck by Parliament. Thus whether a public law defence may be mounted to a criminal charge requires scrutiny of the particular statutory context in which the criminal offence is defined and of any other relevant statutory provisions. That approach is supported by authority of this House.

In *Director of Public Prosecutions v Head* [1959] A.C. 83 a defendant was convicted of an offence under section 56(1)(*a*) of the Mental Deficiency Act 1913, of carnal knowledge of "a woman . . . under care or treatment in an institution or certified house or approved home, or whilst placed out on licence therefrom." She had been sent to an institution for defectives as a "moral defective," under an order made by the Secretary of State in purported exercise of his powers under the Act and subsequent orders had been made to transfer her to other institutions. At the time of the alleged offences, she was out on licence from one of these institutions. At the trial, the prosecution conceded that the original order had been made without proper evidence that the woman was a "moral defective" and that it could be successfully challenged on an application for certiorari or a writ of habeas corpus. The Court of Criminal Appeal quashed the conviction, on the ground that the woman was not lawfully detained in the institution. This House, by a majority, upheld that decision.

The majority and Viscount Simonds treated the issue as turning on the proper construction of section 56 of the Act. As a matter of construction did it require the prosecution to prove that the woman was lawfully detained in the institution? The majority (Lord Reid, Lord Tucker and Lord Somervell of Harrow) held that, whilst proof of detention in an institution established a prima facie case that a woman was a defective lawfully under care, that presumption could be rebutted if the defendant showed that the detention was in fact unlawful: see especially p.103, *per* Lord Tucker. The defendant in the case was assisted by the fact that the prosecution had itself adduced the evidence from which the invalidity of the order appeared. But the language of Lord Tucker, delivering the leading speech for the majority, is consistent with an entitlement in the defendant to adduce such evidence himself. If the defendant had adduced other evidence, for instance to show that the Secretary of State had made his order for some improper purpose, so that it could be quashed, I think the majority's view would have entailed the criminal court reviewing this evidence to determine whether the defendant had made out a defence on the basis of it.

Lord Denning, who was in the minority, was of the view that the order was valid as at the date of the alleged offence, so that the alleged offence was made out (p.113), even although the order was voidable and therefore liable to be quashed on certiorari. The majority, however, did not accept that the order was voidable rather than void, but in any event doubted that, even if it was to be characterised as voidable rather than void, a defendant could not raise the matter by way of defence. As Lord Somervell of Harrow put it, at p.104: "Is a man to be sent to prison on the basis that an order is a good order when the court knows it would be set aside if proper proceedings were taken? I doubt it." Viscount Simonds, at p.98, Lord Reid, at p.98 and Lord Tucker, at pp.103–104, agreed with these views. In my judgment the answer to Lord Somervell's question must be "No." It would be a fundamental departure from the rule of law if an individual were liable to conviction for contravention of some rule which is itself liable to be set aside by a court as unlawful. Suppose an individual is charged before one court with breach of a byelaw and the next day another court quashes that byelaw—for example, because it was promulgated by a public body which did not take account of a relevant consideration.

Any system of law under which the individual was convicted and made subject to a criminal penalty for breach of an unlawful byelaw would be inconsistent with the rule of law.

In my judgment the views of the majority in *Director of Public Prosecutions v Head* [1959] A.C. 83 have acquired still greater force in the light of the development of the basic principles of public law since that case was decided. Lord Denning had dissented on the basis of the historic distinction between acts which were *ultra vires* ("outside the jurisdiction of the Secretary of State"), which he accepted were nullities and void, and errors of law on the face of the relevant record, which rendered the relevant instrument voidable rather than void. He felt able to assign the order in question to the latter category. But in 1969, the decision of your Lordships' House in *Anisminic Ltd. v Foreign Compensation Commission* [1969] 2 A.C. 147 made obsolete the historic distinction between errors of law on the face of the record and other errors of law. It did so by extending the doctrine of *ultra vires*, so that any misdirection in law would render the relevant decision *ultra vires* and a nullity: see *Reg. v Hull University Visitor, Ex parte Page* [1993] A.C. 682, 701–702, *per* Lord Browne-Wilkinson (with whom Lord Keith of Kinkel and Lord Griffiths agreed, at p.692), citing the speech of Lord Diplock in *O'Reilly v Mackman* [1983] 2 A.C. [1983] 2 A.C. 237, 278. Thus, today, the old distinction between void and voidable acts on which Lord Denning relied in *Director of Public Prosecutions v Head* [1959] A.C. 83 no longer applies. This much is clear from the *Anisminic* case [1969] 2 A.C. 147 and these later authorities.

What was in issue in the *Anisminic* case was a decision of the Foreign Compensation Commission. The plaintiffs brought an action for a declaration that the decision was a nullity. The Commission replied that the courts were precluded from considering the question by section 4(4) of the Foreign Compensation Act 1950. It provided: "The determination by the Commission of any application made to them under this Act shall not be called in question in any court of law." Lord Reid summarised the case for the Commission in this way, at p.169:

> "The respondent maintains that these are plain words only capable of having one meaning. Here is a determination which is apparently valid: there is nothing on the face of the document to cast any doubt on its validity. If it is a nullity, that could only be established by raising some kind of proceedings in court. But that would be calling the determination in question, and that is expressly prohibited by the statute."

This submission was rejected in Lord Reid's speech. He made it clear that all forms of public law challenge to a decision have the same effect, to render it a nullity: see especially p.171B–F. (Also see pp.195–196, *per* Lord Pearce and p.207D–H, *per* Lord Wilberforce.) The decision of the Commission was wrong in law, and therefore a nullity, rather than a "determination" within the protection of the ouster clause: see pp.170–171.

Thus the reservation of Lord Somervell in *Director of Public Prosecutions v Head* [1959] A.C. 83, 104 (with which the majority allied themselves) whether the order of the Secretary of State could be described as voidable has been vindicated by subsequent developments. It is clear, in the light of *Anisminic* and the later authorities, that the Secretary of State's order in *Director of Public Prosecutions v Head* would now certainly be regarded as a nullity (i.e. as void ab initio), even if it were to be analysed as an error of law on the face of the record. Equally, the order would be regarded as void ab initio if it had been made in bad faith, or as a result of the Secretary of State taking into account an irrelevant, or ignoring a relevant, consideration—that is, matters not appearing on the face of the record, but having to be established by evidence.

Subordinate legislation, or an administrative act, is sometimes said to be presumed lawful until it has been pronounced to be unlawful. This does not, however, entail that such legislation or act is valid until quashed prospectively. That would be a conclusion inconsistent with the authorities to which I have referred. In my judgment, the true effect of the presumption is that the legislation or act which is impugned is presumed to be good until pronounced to be unlawful, but is then recognised as never having had any legal effect at all. The burden in such a case is on the defendant to establish on a balance of probabilities that the subordinate legislation or the administrative act is invalid: see also *Reg. v Inland Revenue Commissioners, Ex parte T. C. Coombs & Co.* [1991] 2 A.C. 283.

This is the principle to which Lord Diplock referred in *F. Hoffmann-La Roche & Co. A.G. v Secretary of State for Trade and Industry* [1975] A.C. 295. There the Secretary of State sought an interlocutory injunction under section 11(2) of the Monopolies and Restrictive Practices (Inquiry Control) Act 1948, to restrain the appellant from charging prices in excess of those fixed by a statutory instrument the Secretary of State had made. The appellant argued that the statutory instrument was *ultra vires*, because it had been based upon a report by the Monopolies Commission, which the appellant maintained had been produced without due regard to principles of natural justice. The Secretary of State objected to giving a cross undertaking in damages and this House ruled that he was not required to give such an undertaking. The ratio of the decision, as subsequently explained in *Kirklees Metropolitan Borough Council v Wickes Building Supplies Ltd.* [1993] A.C. 227, *per* Lord Goff of Chieveley, at pp.271–273 and 274, was that a public authority is not required as a rule to give such an undertaking in a law enforcement action. However, in his speech, Lord Diplock expressed views about the legal status of the statutory instrument in question. He made it clear [1975] A.C. 295, 365 that the courts could "declare it to be invalid" if satisfied that the minister acted outwith his powers conferred by the primary legislation, whether the order was "*ultra vires* by reason of its contents (patent defects) or by reason of defects in the procedure followed prior to its being made (latent defects)." He then said:

"Under our legal system, however, the courts as the judicial arm of Government do not act on their own initiative. Their jurisdiction to determine that a statutory instrument is *ultra vires* does not arise until its validity is challenged in proceedings inter partes either brought by one party to enforce the law declared by the instrument against another party or brought by a party whose interests are affected by the law so declared sufficiently directly to give him locus standi to initiate proceedings to challenge the validity of the instrument. Unless there is such challenge and, if there is, until it has been upheld by a judgment of the court, the validity of the statutory instrument and the legality of acts done pursuant to the law declared by it are presumed. It would, however, be inconsistent with the doctrine of *ultra vires* as it has been developed in English law as a means of controlling abuse of power by the executive arm of Government if the judgment of a court in proceedings properly constituted that a statutory instrument was *ultra vires* were to have any lesser consequence in law than to render the instrument incapable of ever having had any legal effect upon the rights or duties of the parties to the proceedings (cf. Ridge v Baldwin [1964] A.C. 40). Although such a decision is directly binding only as between the parties to the proceedings in which it was made, the application of the doctrine of precedent has the consequence of enabling the benefit of it to accrue to all other persons whose legal rights have been interfered with in reliance on the law which the statutory instrument purported to declare."

Thus, Lord Diplock confirmed that once it was established that a statutory instrument was *ultra vires*, it would be treated as never having had any legal effect. That consequence follows from application of the *ultra vires* principle, as a control on abuse of power; or, equally acceptably in my judgment, it may be held that maintenance of the rule of law compels this conclusion.

This view of the law is supported by the decision of this House in *Wandsworth London Borough Council v Winder* [1985] A.C. 461. That case concerned rent demands made by a local authority landlord on one of its tenants. The local authority, pursuant to its powers under the Housing Act 1957, resolved to increase rents generally. The tenant refused to pay the increased element of the rent. When sued by the local authority for that element, he sought to defend himself by pleading that the resolutions and notices of increase were *ultra vires* and void, on the grounds that they were unreasonable in the *Wednesbury* sense (i.e. irrational: see *Associated Provincial Picture Houses Ltd. v Wednesbury Corporation* [1948] 1 K.B. 223), and counterclaiming for a declaration to that effect. It seems clear from the particulars given in the defence (set out at pp.466–467) that the tenant proposed adducing some evidence to support his case of unreasonableness. The local authority sought to strike out the defence and counterclaim as an abuse of process, on the grounds that the tenant should be debarred from challenging the conduct of the local authority other than by application for judicial review under R.S.C., Ord. 53. This House ruled that Mr. Winder was entitled as of right to challenge the local authority's decision by way of defence in the proceedings which it had brought against him. The decision was based squarely on "the ordinary rights of private citizens to defend themselves against unfounded claims:" *per* Lord Fraser of Tullybelton, delivering the leading speech, at p.509. As a matter of construction of the relevant legislation, those rights had not been swept away by the procedural reforms introducing the new R.S.C., Ord. 53: pp.509–510.

In my judgment, precisely similar reasoning applies, a fortiori, where a private citizen is taxed not with private law claims which are unfounded because based upon some *ultra vires* decision, but with a criminal charge which is unfounded, because based upon an *ultra vires* byelaw or administrative decision. The decision of the Divisional Court in *Reg. v Reading Crown Court, Ex parte Hutchinson* [1988] Q.B. 384 (and the principal authorities referred to in it, including the classic decision in *Kruse v Johnson* [1898] 2 Q.B. 91) is in accord with this view. There it was held that a defendant to a charge brought under a byelaw is entitled to raise the question of the validity of that byelaw in criminal proceedings before magistrates or the Crown Court, by way of defence. There was nothing in the statutory basis of the jurisdiction of the justices which precluded their considering a challenge to the validity of a byelaw: pp.391–393, *per* Lloyd L.J.

In *Bugg v Director of Public Prosecutions* [1993] Q.B. 473 the Divisional Court departed from this trend of authority. They expressed the view, at p.493, that "except in the 'flagrant' and 'outrageous' case a statutory order, such as a byelaw, remains effective until it is quashed." Three authorities were cited which were said to support this approach: *London & Clydeside Estates Ltd. v Aberdeen District Council* [1980] 1 W.L.R. 182, 189–190 in the speech of Lord Hailsham of St. Marylebone L.C.; *Smith v East Elloe Rural District Council* [1956] A.C. 736, 769–770, in the speech of Lord Radcliffe and *F. Hoffmann-La Roche & Co. A.G. v Secretary of State for Trade and Industry* [1975] A.C. 295, 366, in the speech of Lord Diplock. This approach was then elevated by the Divisional Court into a rule that byelaws which are on their face invalid or are patently unreasonable (termed "substantive" invalidity) may be called in question by way of defence in criminal proceedings, whereas byelaws which are invalid because of some defect in the procedure by which they came to be made (termed "procedural" invalidity) may not be called in question in such proceedings, so that a person might be convicted of an offence under them even if the byelaws were later quashed in other proceedings.

Strong reservations about the decision of the Divisional Court in *Bugg v Director of Public Prosecutions* [1993] Q.B. 473 have recently been expressed by this House in *Reg. v Wicks* [1998] A.C. 92. I have reached the conclusion that the time has come to hold that it was wrongly decided.

I am bound to say that I do not think that the three authorities to which I have referred support the position as stated in *Bugg's* case [1993] Q.B. 473. In my judgment Lord Diplock's speech in the *F. Hoffmann-La Roche* case [1995] A.C. 295, when read as a whole, makes it clear that subordinate legislation which is quashed is deprived of any legal effect at all, and that is so whether the invalidity arises from defects appearing on its face or in the procedure adopted in its promulgation. Lord Diplock himself cited, at p.366, the speech of Lord Radcliffe in *Smith v East Elloe Rural District Council* [1956] A.C. 736, 769–770 and regarded him as saying no more about the presumption of validity than he (Lord Diplock) was saying. I agree with that view.

In my judgment, Lord Hailsham L.C., in the passage of his speech relied upon by the Divisional Court in *Bugg's* case, was simply making the observation that in a flagrant case of invalidity a private citizen might feel sure enough of his ground to proceed and rely on his rights to assert the "defect in procedure" (as Lord Hailsham L.C. describes it) as a defence in proceedings brought against him; that, on the other hand, where a defect in procedure is trivial (i.e. one which would not render the public body's act *ultra vires*), the public body may feel safe to proceed without taking further steps to shore up the validity in law of what it had done by reconsideration of the matter; and that in cases in the grey area between these clear examples, it might be necessary for the private citizen to safeguard his position by taking the prudent course of seeking a declaration of his rights, or for the public body to reconsider the matter. But that would be for the citizen or the public body, as the case might be, to decide. Subject to any statutory qualifications upon his right to do so, the citizen could, in my judgment, choose to accept the risk of uncertainty, take no action at all, wait to be sued or prosecuted by the public body and then put forward his arguments on validity and have them determined by the court hearing the case against him. That is a matter of right in a case of *ultra vires* action by the public authority, and would not be subject to the discretion of the court: see *Wandsworth London Borough Council v Winder* [1985] A.C. 461. In my judgment any other interpretation of Lord Hailsham L.C.'s speech could not be reconciled with the decision of this House in the *Anisminic* case [1969] 2 A.C. 147.

In my judgment the reasoning of the Divisional Court in *Bugg's* case, suggesting two classes of legal invalidity of subordinate legislation, is contrary both to the *Anisminic* case and the subsequent decisions of this House to which I have referred. The *Anisminic* decision established, contrary to previous thinking that there might be error of law within jurisdiction, that there was a single category of errors of law, all of which rendered a decision *ultra vires*. No distinction is to be drawn between a patent (or substantive) error of law or a latent (or procedural) error of law. An *ultra vires* act or subordinate legislation is unlawful simpliciter and, if the presumption in favour of its legality is overcome by a litigant before a court of competent jurisdiction, is of no legal effect whatsoever.

The Divisional Court in *Bugg's* case [1993] Q.B. 473 themselves drew attention to Lord Denning's dissenting speech in *Director of Public Prosecutions v Head* and, whilst avowing that "The distinction between orders which are void and voidable is now clearly not part of our law" identified his approach as interesting, because Lord Denning "was drawing a distinction, as we are seeking to do, between different types of invalidity:" see p.496G. However, the distinction which Lord Denning drew is one which was made redundant by the decision in the *Anisminic* case, in which all categories of unlawfulness were treated as equivalent and as having the same effect.

Further, the Divisional Court thought that there was no authority where it had been held that it is proper for a criminal court to inquire into questions of procedural irregularity. With respect to the court, I think it overlooked that that was one basis for the decision of the majority of this House in *Director of Public Prosecutions v Head* [1959] A.C. 83. Lord Tucker, at p.103, envisaged that documents upon which the administrative order were based might be adduced in evidence to rebut the presumption of invalidity. Lord Reid and Lord Somervell agreed with his speech. Lord Somervell, at p.104, thought that the facts of the case itself could also be analysed not as a case of patent error, but as a case where it was shown by evidence that the minister had made his order without having any evidence available to him to justify it, that is, a case of latent procedural, rather than patent, error. Viscount Simonds, Lord Reid and Lord Tucker all agreed. Indeed, on the facts of the case, and this, in my view, was Lord Somervell's point, it was simply fortuitous that the minister's order had made reference on its face to the medical certificates. The result of the case could not have been any different if it had not done so, but appeared on its face to be normal and valid.

Also, in my judgment the distinction between orders which are "substantively" invalid and orders which are "procedurally" invalid is not a practical distinction which is capable of being maintained in a principled way across the broad range of administrative action. This emerges from the discussion of *Wandsworth London Borough Council v Winder* [1985] A.C. 461 by the Divisional Court in *Bugg v Director of Public Prosecutions* [1993] Q.B. 473, 495–496. The court regarded it as a case of "substantive invalidity," i.e. in which either the decision to increase rents or the rent demands themselves were on their face invalid. I disagree. The rent demands appeared perfectly valid on their face. The decision was said by the tenant to be *Wednesbury* unreasonable, because irrelevant matters had, or relevant matters had not, been taken into account, as set out in his pleading. At trial, he would have had to adduce evidence to make out that case. It was not an error on the face of the decision. In *Reg. v Wicks* [1998] A.C. 92, 114, Lord Hoffmann made the same point and at pp.113–114, referred to another problem of the application of the categories proposed by the Divisional Court. Many different types of challenge, which shade into each other, may be made to the legality of byelaws or administrative acts. The decision in *Anisminic* freed the law from a dependency on technical distinctions between different types of illegality. The law should not now be developed to create a new, and unstable, technical distinction between "substantive" and "procedural" invalidity.

In this case, the judgment of Auld L.J. in the Divisional Court justifies such distinctions on pragmatic grounds: the difficulties for magistrates in having to deal with complicated points of administrative law and the dangers of inconsistent decisions, both between different benches of magistrates and between magistrates and the Divisional Court. There is certainly weight in these arguments, although I do not think that magistrates should be underestimated and the practical risks of inconsistency are probably exaggerated. But the remedy proposed, which is in effect to have two systems of challenge to subordinate legislation or administrative action: one in magistrates' courts which is frozen in the pre -*Anisminic* mould and a modern version operated in the Divisional Court, is in my view both illogical and unfair.

Finally, in relation to *Bugg's* case [1993] Q.B. 473, the consequences of the proposed distinction is that, in a case of "procedural" invalidity, a court (whether in civil or criminal proceedings) is to regard byelaws and other subordinate legislation as valid until set aside in judicial review proceedings; and that an individual who contravenes a byelaw commits an offence and can be punished, even if the byelaw is later set aside as unlawful: p.500C–D. I can think of no rational ground for holding that a magistrates' court has jurisdiction to rule on the patent or substantive invalidity of subordinate legislation or an administrative act under it, but has no jurisdiction to rule on its latent or procedural invalidity, unless a statutory provision has that effect. In my judgment, this conclusion in substance revives the distinction between voidable and void administrative acts and is contrary to the decisions of this House to which I have already referred. If subordinate legislation is *ultra vires* on any basis, it is unlawful and of no effect in law. It follows that no citizen should be convicted and punished on the basis of it. For these reasons I would overrule *Bugg v Director of Public Prosecutions*.

However, in every case it will be necessary to examine the particular statutory context to determine whether a court hearing a criminal or civil case has jurisdiction to rule on a defence based upon arguments of invalidity of subordinate legislation or an administrative act under it. There are situations in which Parliament may legislate to preclude such challenges being made, in the interest, for example, of promoting certainty about the legitimacy of administrative acts on which the public may have to rely.

The recent decision of this House in *Reg. v Wicks* [1998] A.C. 92 is an example of a particular context in which an administrative act triggering consequences for the purposes of the criminal law was held not to be capable of challenge in criminal proceedings, but only by other proceedings. The case concerned an enforcement notice issued by a local planning authority and served on the defendant under the then current version of section 87 of the Town and Country Planning Act 1971. The notice alleged a breach of planning control by the erection of a building and required its removal above a certain height. One month was allowed for compliance. The appellant appealed against the notice to the Secretary of State, under section 174 of the Town and Country Planning Act 1990, but the appeal was dismissed. The appellant still failed to comply with the notice and the local authority issued a summons alleging a breach of section 179(1) of the Act of 1990. In the criminal proceedings which ensued, the appellant sought to defend himself on the ground that the enforcement notice had been issued *ultra vires*, maintaining that the local planning authority had acted in bad faith and had been motivated by irrelevant considerations. The judge ruled that these contentions should have been made in proceedings for judicial review and that they could not be gone into in the criminal proceedings. The appellant then pleaded guilty and was convicted. This House upheld his conviction. Lord Hoffmann, in the leading speech, emphasised that the ability of a defendant to criminal proceedings to challenge the validity of an act done under statutory authority depended on the construction of the statute in question. This House held that the Town and Country Planning Act 1990 contained an elaborate code including provision for appeals against notices, and that on the proper construction of section 179(1) of the Act all that was required to be proved in the criminal proceedings was that the notice issued by the local planning authority was formally valid.

The decision of the Divisional Court in *Quietlynn Ltd. v Plymouth City Council* [1988] 1 Q.B. 114 is justified on similar grounds: see *Reg. v Wicks* [1998] A.C. 92, 117–118, *per* Lord Hoffmann. There, a company was operating sex shops in Plymouth under transitional provisions which allowed them to do so until their application for a licence under the scheme introduced by the Local Government (Miscellaneous Provisions) Act 1982 had been "determined." The local authority refused the application. The company was then prosecuted for trading without a licence. It sought to allege that the local authority had failed to comply with certain procedural provisions and that its application had therefore not yet been determined within the meaning of the Act. The Divisional Court held as a matter of construction that the local authority's decision was a determination, whether or not it could be challenged by judicial review. In the particular statutory context, therefore, an act which might turn out for a different purpose to be a nullity (e.g. so as to require the local authority to hear the application again) was nevertheless a determination for the purpose of bringing the transitional period to an end.

However, in approaching the issue of statutory construction the courts proceed from a strong appreciation that ours is a country subject to the rule of law. This means that it is well recognised to be important for the maintenance of the rule of law and the preservation of liberty that individuals affected by legal measures promulgated by executive public bodies should have a fair opportunity to challenge these measures and to vindicate their rights in court proceedings. There is a strong presumption that Parliament will not legislate to prevent individuals from doing so: "It is a principle not by any means to be whittled down that the subject's recourse to Her Majesty's courts for the determination of his rights is not to be excluded except by clear words:" *Pyx Granite Co. Ltd. v Ministry of Housing and Local Government* [1960]

A.C. 260, 286, *per* Viscount Simonds; cited by Lord Fraser of Tullybelton in *Wandsworth London Borough Council v Winder* [1969] A.C. 461, 510.

As Lord Diplock put it in *F. Hoffmann-La Roche & Co. Ltd. v Secretary of State for Trade and Industry* [1975] A.C. 295, 366C: "the courts lean very heavily against a construction of an Act which would have this effect (cf. *Anisminic Ltd. v Foreign Compensation Commission* [1969] 2 A.C. 147)."

The particular statutory schemes in question in *Reg. v Wicks* [1998] A.C. 92 and in the *Quietlynn* case [1988] 1 Q.B. 114 did justify a construction which limited the rights of the defendant to call the legality of an administrative act into question. But in my judgment it was an important feature of both cases that they were concerned with administrative acts specifically directed at the defendants, where there had been clear and ample opportunity provided by the scheme of the relevant legislation for those defendants to challenge the legality of those acts, before being charged with an offence.

By contrast, where subordinate legislation (e.g. statutory instruments or byelaws) is promulgated which is of a general character in the sense that it is directed to the world at large, the first time an individual may be affected by that legislation is when he is charged with an offence under it: so also where a general provision is brought into effect by an administrative act, as in this case. A smoker might have made his first journey on the line on the same train as Mr. Boddington; have found that there was no carriage free of no smoking signs and have chosen to exercise what he believed to be his right to smoke on the train. Such an individual would have had no sensible opportunity to challenge the validity of the posting of the no smoking signs throughout the train until he was charged, as Mr. Boddington was, under byelaw 20. In my judgment in such a case the strong presumption must be that Parliament did not intend to deprive the smoker of an opportunity to defend himself in the criminal proceedings by asserting the alleged unlawfulness of the decision to post no smoking notices throughout the train. I can see nothing in section 67 of the Transport Act 1962 or the byelaws which could displace that presumption. It is clear from *Wandsworth London Borough Council v Winder* [1985] A.C. 461 and *Reg. v Wicks* [1998] A.C. 92, 116, *per* Lord Hoffmann that the development of a statutorily based procedure for judicial review proceedings does not of itself displace the presumption.

Accordingly, I consider that the Divisional Court was wrong in the present case in ruling that Mr. Boddington was not entitled to raise the legality of the decision to post no smoking notices throughout the train, as a possible defence to the charge against him.

Lord Nicholls of Birkenhead noted in *Reg. v Wicks*, at pp.106–107, that there may be cases where proceedings in the Divisional Court are more suitable and convenient for challenging a byelaw or administrative decision made under it than by way of defence in criminal proceedings in the magistrates' court or the Crown Court. None the less Lord Nicholls held that "the proper starting point" must be a presumption that "an accused should be able to challenge, on any ground, the lawfulness of an order the breach of which constitutes his alleged criminal offence:" see p.106. No doubt the factors listed by Lord Nicholls may, where the statutory context permits, be taken into account when construing any particular statute to determine Parliament's intention, but they will not usually be sufficient in themselves to support a construction of a statute which would preclude the right of a defendant to raise the legality of a byelaw or administrative action taken under it as a defence in other proceedings. This is because of the strength of the presumption against a construction which would prevent an individual being able to vindicate his rights in court proceedings in which he is involved. Nor do I think it right to belittle magistrates' courts: they sometimes have to decide very difficult legal questions and generally have the assistance of a legally qualified clerk to give them guidance on the law. For example when the Human Rights Bill now before Parliament passes into law the magistrates' courts will have to determine difficult questions of law arising from the European Convention on Human Rights. In my judgment only the clear language of a statute could take away the right of a defendant in criminal proceedings to challenge the lawfulness of a byelaw or administrative decision where his prosecution is premised on its validity.

[His Lordship proceeded to hold that B's defence was not made out. While the power to "regulate" the use of and working of and travel on the railway could not prohibit the use of or travel on the railway, the total prohibition on smoking was not *ultra vires*.]

LORD BROWNE-WILKINSON [agreed with LORD STEYN, and with LORD IRVINE of LAIRG L.C, except that he preferred to express no view on the consideration that an invalid byelaw is and always has been a nullity.]

LORD SLYNN OF HADLEY [delivered a concurring speech, that included the following passage:]

I consider that the result of allowing a collateral challenge in proceedings before courts of criminal jurisdiction can be reached without it being necessary in this case to say that if an act or byelaw is invalid it must be held to have been invalid from the outset for all purposes and that no lawful consequences can flow from it. This may be the logical result and will no doubt sometimes be the position but courts have had to grapple with the problem of reconciling the logical result with the reality that much may have been done on the basis that an administrative act or a byelaw was valid. The unscrambling may produce more serious difficulties than the invalidity. The European Court of Justice has dealt with the problem by ruling that its declaration of invalidity should only operate for the benefit of the parties to the actual case or of those who had began proceedings for a declaration of invalidity before the courts' judgment. In our jurisdiction the effect of invalidity may not be relied on if limitation periods have expired or if the court in its discretion refuses relief, albeit considering that the act is invalid. These situations are of course different from those where a court has pronounced subordinate legislation or an administrative act to be unlawful or where the presumption in favour of their legality has been overruled by a court of competent jurisdiction. But even in these cases I consider that the question whether the acts or byelaws are to be treated as having at no time had any effect in law is not one which has been fully explored and is not one on which it is necessary to rule in this appeal and I prefer to express no view upon it. The cases referred to in *Wade and Forsyth, Administrative Law* 7th ed. (1997), pp.323–324, 342–344 lead the authors to the view that nullity is relative rather than an absolute concept (p.343) and that "void" is meaningless in any absolute sense. Its meaning is "relative." This may all be rather imprecise but the law in this area has developed in a pragmatic way on a case by case basis. The result, however, in the present case is clear that the validity of the administrative act may be challenged by way of defence. . . .

LORD STEYN [delivered a concurring speech. Having held that the pragmatic case in favour of a rule that magistrates may not decide issues of procedural validity was questionable, his Lordship continued]:

There is also a formidable difficulty of categorisation created by *Bugg's* case [1993] Q.B.D. 473. A distinction between substantive and procedural invalidity will often be impossible or difficult to draw. Woolf L.J. recognised that there may be cases in a grey area, e.g. cases of bad faith: p.500F. I fear that in reality the grey area covers a far greater terrain. In *Associated Provincial Picture Houses Ltd. v Wednesbury Corporation* [1948] 1 K.B. 223, 229, Lord Greene M.R. pointed out that different grounds of review "run into one another." A modern commentator has demonstrated the correctness of the proposition that grounds of judicial review have blurred edges and tend to overlap with comprehensive reference to leading cases: see *Fordham, Judicial Review Handbook*, 2nd ed, pp.514–521. Thus the taking into account by a decision maker of extraneous considerations is variously treated as substantive or procedural. Moreover, even Woolf L.J. categorisation of procedural invalidity is controversial. Wade and Forsyth rightly point out that contrary to normal terminology Woolf L.J. treated procedural invalidity as being not a matter of excess or abuse of power: *Wade and Forsyth, Administrative Law*, 7th ed., p.323. Categorisation is an indispensable tool in the search for rationality and coherence in law. But the process of categorisation in accordance with *Bugg's* case which serves to carve out of the jurisdiction of criminal courts the power to decide on some issues pertinent to the guilt of a defendant, leads to a labyrinth of paths. It is nevertheless an inevitable consequence of *Bugg's* case that magistrates may have to rule on the satellite issue whether a particular challenge is substantive or procedural. That may involve hearing wide-ranging arguments. Even then there may be no clear cut answer. This is a factor militating against the pragmatic case on which Woolf L.J. relied in *Bugg's* case.

The problems of categorisation pose not only practical difficulties. As Lord Nicholls of Birkenhead explained in *Reg. v Wicks* [1998] A.C. 92 they expose a fundamental problem. About the concluding passage in *Bugg's* case [1993] Q.B. 473, 500, which I have quoted, he said, at p.108:

"On this reasoning there is not only a boundary between the two different types of invalidity. There is also an imperative need for the boundary line to be fixed and crystal clear. There can be no room for an ambiguous grey area. On this reasoning the boundary is not merely concerned with identifying the proceedings in which, as a matter of procedure, the unlawfulness issue can best be raised. Rather, the boundary can represent the difference between committing a criminal offence and not committing a criminal offence. According to this reasoning, a decision on invalidity has sharply different consequences, so far as criminality is concerned, in the two types of case. Setting aside an impugned order for procedural invalidity, as distinct from substantive invalidity, has no effect on the criminality of earliest conduct. Despite a court decision that the order was not lawfully made, the defendant is still guilty of an offence, by reason of his prior conduct. Further, it would seem to follow that in the case of procedural invalidity, the defendant could be convicted even after the order is set aside as having been made unlawfully, so long as the non-compliance occurred before the order was set aside. In cases of substantive invalidity the citizen can take the risk and disobey the order. If he does so, and the order is later held to be invalid, he will be innocent of any offence. In case of procedural invalidity, the citizen is not permitted to take this risk, however clear the irregularity may be."

I regard this reasoning as unanswerable. The rule of law requires a clear distinction to be made between what is lawful and what is unlawful. The distinction put forward in *Bugg's* case undermines this axiom of constitutional principle.

Now I turn to modern developments in judicial review which were the principled grounds upon which Woolf L.J. relied. The first and major factor for Woolf L.J. was the proposition that except in "flagrant" and "outrageous" cases a statutory order, such as a byelaw, remains effective until it is quashed. This is a large topic on which there are confusing and contradictory dicta. It is not possible to review the subject in detail in the context of the present case. But I cannot accept the absolute proposition in *Bugg* without substantial qualification. Leaving to one side the separate topic of judicial review of non-legal powers exercised by non statutory bodies, I see no reason to depart from the orthodox view that *ultra vires* is "the central principle of administrative law" as *Wade and Forsyth, Administrative Law*, 7th ed., p.41 described it. Lord Browne-Wilkinson observed in *Reg. v Hull University Visitor, Ex parte Page* [1993] A.C. 682, 701:

> "The fundamental principle [of judicial review] is that the courts will intervene to ensure that the powers of public decision-making bodies are exercised lawfully. In all cases . . . this intervention . . . is based on the proposition that such powers have been conferred on the decision maker on the underlying assumption that the powers are to be exercised only within the jurisdiction conferred, in accordance with fair procedures and, in a Wednesbury sense . . . reasonably. If the decision maker exercises his powers outside the jurisdiction conferred, in a manner which is procedurally irregular or is *Wednesbury* unreasonable, he is acting *ultra vires* his powers and therefore unlawfully. . . ."

This is the essential constitutional underpinning of the statute based part of our administrative law. Nevertheless, I accept the reality that an unlawful byelaw is a fact and that it may in certain circumstances have legal consequences. The best explanation that I have seen is by Dr. Forsyth who summarised the position as follows in "'The Metaphysic of Nullity'—Invalidity, Conceptual Reasoning and the Rule of Law," at p.159:

> "it has been argued that unlawful administrative acts are void in law. But they clearly exist in fact and they often appear to be valid; and those unaware of their invalidity may take decisions and act on the assumption that these acts are valid. When this happens the validity of these later acts depends upon the legal powers of the second actor. *The crucial issue to be determined is whether that second actor has legal power to act validly notwithstanding the invalidity of the first act*. And it is determined by an analysis of the law against the background of the familiar proposition that an unlawful act is void." (Emphasis supplied.)

That seems to me a more accurate summary of the law as it has developed than the sweeping proposition in *Bugg's* case. And Dr. Forsyth's explanation

is entirely in keeping with the analysis of the formal validity of the enforcement notice in *Reg. v Wicks* which was sufficient to determine the guilt of the
defendant.

That brings me to a matter of principle and precedent. In my view the
holding in *Bugg* is contrary to established judicial review principles established
by decisions of high authority. The *general* rule of procedural exclusivity judicially created in *O'Reilly v Mackman* [1983] 2 A.C. 237 was at its birth recognised to be subject to exceptions, notably (but not restricted to the case) where
the invalidity of the decision arises as a collateral matter in a claim for infringement of private rights. The purpose of the rule was stated to be prevention
of an abuse of the process of the court, and that purpose is of prime importance in determining the reach of the general rule: compare *Mercury
Communications Ltd. v Director General of Telecommunications* [1996] 1
W.L.R. 48, 57E, *per* Lord Slynn of Hadley. Since *O'Reilly v Mackman* decisions of the House of Lords have made clear that the primary focus of the
rule of procedural exclusivity is situations in which an individual's sole aim
was to challenge a public law act or decision. It does not apply in a civil case
when an individual seeks to establish private law rights which cannot be determined without an examination of the validity of a public law decision. Nor
does it apply where a defendant in a civil case simply seeks to defend himself
by questioning the validity of a public law decision. These propositions are
established in the context of civil cases by four decisions of the House of
Lords: *Roy v Kensington Family Practitioner Committee* [1992] 1 A.C. 624;
Chief Adjudication Officer v Foster [1993] A.C. 754; *Wandsworth London
Borough Council v Winder* [1985] A.C. 461 and in particular at pp.509–510,
per Lord Fraser of Tullybelton; *Mercury Communications Ltd. v Director
General of Telecommunications* [1996] 1 W.L.R. 48 and in particular at
p.57B–E, *per* Lord Slynn of Hadley. One would expect a defendant in a criminal case, where the liberty of the subject is at stake, to have no lesser rights.
Provided that the invalidity of the byelaw is or maybe a defence to the charge
a criminal case must be the paradigm of collateral or defensive challenge. And
in *Director of Public Prosecutions v Hutchinson* [1990] 2 A.C. 783, a criminal case, the House of Lords allowed a collateral challenge to delegated legislation. The judgment in *Bugg v Director of Public Prosecutions* [1993] Q.B.
473 in effect denies the right of defensive challenge in a criminal case. In my
view the observations in *Bugg's* case are contrary to authority and principle.

There is, above all, another matter which strikes at the root of the decision
in *Bugg's* case. That decision contemplates that, despite the invalidity of
a byelaw and the fact that consistently with *Reg. v Wicks* such invalidity may
in a given case afford a defence to a charge, a magistrate court may not rule
on the defence. Instead the magistrates may convict a defendant under the
byelaw and punish him. That is an unacceptable consequence in a democracy
based on the rule of law. It is true that *Bugg's* case allows the defendant to
challenge the byelaw in judicial review proceedings. The defendant may,
however, be out of time before he becomes aware of the existence of the
byelaw. He may lack the resources to defend his interests in two courts.
He may not be able to obtain legal aid for an application for leave to apply
for judicial review. Leave to apply for judicial review may be refused. At a
substantive hearing his scope for demanding examination of witnesses in
the Divisional Court may be restricted. He may be denied a remedy on a discretionary basis. The possibility of judicial review will, therefore, in no way

compensate him for the loss of *the right* to defend himself by a defensive challenge to the byelaw in cases where the invalidity of the byelaw might afford him with a defence to the charge. My Lords, with the utmost deference to eminent judges sitting in the Divisional Court I have to say the consequences of *Bugg's* case are too austere and indeed too authoritarian to be compatible with the traditions of the common law. In *Eshugbayi Eleko v Government of Nigeria* [1931] A.C. 662, a habeas corpus case, Lord Atkin observed, at p.670, that "no member of the executive can interfere with the liberty or property of a British subject except on condition that he can support the legality of his action before a court of justice." There is no reason why a defendant in a criminal trial should be in a worse position. And that seems to me to reflect the true spirit of the common law.

There is no good reason why a defendant in a criminal case should be precluded from arguing that a byelaw is invalid where that could afford him with a defence. Sometimes his challenge may be defeated by special statutory provisions on analogy with the decision in *Reg. v Wicks* [1998] A.C. 92. The defence may fail because the relevant statutory provisions are held to be directory rather than mandatory. It may be held that substantial compliance is sufficient. But, if an issue as to the procedural validity of a byelaw is raised, the trial court must rule on it.

V. *Subsidiary points arising from Bugg's case*

For the sake of completeness I need to direct attention briefly to three subsidiary matters mentioned in *Bugg's* case. First, Woolf L.J. quoted a passage from Lord Diplock's speech in *Hoffmann-La Roche & Co. A.G. v Secretary of State for Trade and Industry* [1975] A.C. 295, 366, about the presumption that subordinate legislation is valid: see Woolf L.J. [1993] Q.B. 473, 493D–F. As Lord Hoffmann explained in *Reg. v Wicks* [1998] A.C. 92, 116 the context of the *Hoffmann-La Roche* case shows that the presumption of validity is not more than an evidential matter at the interlocutory stage. There is no *rule* that lends validity to invalid acts. In a practical world, however, a court will usually assume that subordinate legislation, and administrative acts, are valid unless it is persuaded otherwise. Secondly, Woolf L.J. [1993] Q.B. 473, 494 said that in the case of substantive invalidity an applicant need only show the invalidity whereas "in the case of procedural invalidity there is also the need for the applicant to show that he has suffered substantial prejudice." As formulated I am unable to accept this proposition. Let me pose two cases: one a breach of a duty to consult before the making of a byelaw and the other a breach of a duty to give a hearing before making an administrative decision. In both cases that establishes the ground of review. It is true that cases could occur where it might be right in regard to an established ground of judicial review to refuse a discretionary remedy and in that respect absence of prejudice may be a relevant factor: see, for example, *Ridge v Baldwin* [1964] A.C. 40 and compare Bingham L.J.'s reasons in *Reg. v Chief Constable of the Thames Valley Police, Ex parte Cotton* [1990] I.R.L.R. 344, as to why denial of a remedy as a matter of discretion in such a case should be a rarity. But that is altogether different from saying that prejudice is an element that an applicant must prove to establish a ground of review. Thirdly, Woolf L.J. [1993] Q.B. 473, 493 commented on the expansion of the circumstances in which courts will intervene to quash decisions. This cannot, however, be a principled ground for carving away by judicial decision part of the jurisdiction of magistrates courts. Nor can the powers of magistrates to rule on the lawfulness of byelaws be deemed to have been frozen at some date in the past. . . .

LORD HOFFMANN agreed with LORD IRVINE and LORD STEYN.

Appeal dismissed.

Notes

1. On collateral challenge generally, see C.T. Emery, "The Vires Defence—'Ultra Vires' as a Defence to Criminal or Civil Proceedings" [1992] C.L.J. 308 (predating *Bugg*), and "Collateral Attack—Attacking Ultra Vires Action Indirectly in Courts and Tribunals" (1993) 56 M.L.R. 643. Emery proposed that any court or tribunal in which a collateral *vires* issue is raised should have jurisdiction to entertain the *vires* argument and should have discretion to pronounce on the point or refer it to the High Court for a ruling.

Lord Steyn in *Boddington* cited a number of academic discussions of *Bugg* that he found of great assistance, including D. Feldman, "Collateral challenge and Judicial Review; The Boundary Dispute Continues" [1993] P.L. 37; C. Emery, "Public or Private Law: The Limits of Procedural Reform" [1995] P.L. 450 at pp.455–461; C. Forsyth, "The Metaphysic of Nullity—Invalidity, Conceptual Reasoning and the Rule of Law"; C. Forsyth and I. Hare (ed.), *The Golden Metwand and the Crooked Cord* (1998), pp.152–153; *Wade and Forsyth, Administrative Law* (7th ed., 1997), pp.321–324; and *Craig, Administrative Law*, (3rd ed., 1994), pp.447–466. Sir Harry Woolf's Hamlyn lecture "Protection of the Public—A New Challenge" (1987) had foreshadowed the reasoning in *Bugg's* case. That reasoning was criticised by J. Beatson, "Public and Private in English Administrative Law" (1987) 103 L.Q.R. 34 at pp.59–61.

The decision in *Boddington* was welcomed by Forsyth ([1999] J.R. 165) not merely for its vindication of the rule of law, but also for vindicating the *ultra vires* doctrine as the foundation of judicial review (see further above, pp.263–264).

2. The foundations for the decision in *Boddington* were laid by the decision of the House of Lords in *Wandsworth LBC v Winder*, which considered the extent to which the procedural exclusivity principle that Lord Diplock in *O'Reilly v Mackman* sought to establish applied to preclude collateral challenge. That principle has itself been significantly eroded by subsequent developments. See below, pp.976 *et seq.*

3. Collateral challenges commonly take the form of a defence to enforcement proceedings. It can operate in other contexts. For example, in *Howker v Secretary of State for Work and Pensions* [2002] EWCA Civ 1623, the Court of Appeal held that the failure of the department properly to consult the Social Security Advisory Committee on amendments to regulations that reduced a particular entitlement to incapacity benefit meant that H was entitled to claim the benefits on the broader basis of the previous regulation that was to be treated as continuing in force in its unamended state.

4. Collateral challenge is clearly available in respect of breaches of the Human Rights Act 1998 given the rule that any court as a public authority may not itself act in breach of the Act unless compelled to do so by or by virtue of primary legislation (1998 Act, ss.6,7). Furthermore, any court may according to the circumstances come under the interpretative duty under s.3 of the 1998 Act. See further Ch.6. Similarly, a challenge to subordinate legislation on Community law grounds may be raised collaterally; to require such a challenge to be made in the Administrative Court would have the effect of removing the immediacy of effect of Community law which would itself be contrary to Community law: *R. v Searby* [2003] EWCA Crim 1910; [2003] L.L.R. 744.

5. In *Caradon DC v Cheeseman* [2000] Crim. L.R. 190, the Divisional Court indicated, without deciding the point, that the street-trading regime fell into the *Wicks*

category for the purpose of limits to collateral challenge. Furthermore, the relevant legislation may be interpreted as precluding collateral challenge even where the order challenged is of general application and not, as in *Wicks*, only of application to the respondent. Thus in *DPP v Memery* [2002] EWHC 1720, it was held that it could not have been intended by Parliament that defendants charged with a drink-driving offence on the basis of intoximeter evidence should be able to challenge the approval by the Secretary of State of the device in question. Relevant factors included the point that the reliability of the particular device could be challenged. See to the same effect: *DPP v Brown (Andrew Earle)* [2001] EWHC Admin 931; *Grant v DPP* [2003] EWHC 130; (2003) 167 J.P. 459.

In *R. v Wicks* [1998] A.C. 92, the House of Lords held that in a prosecution for breach of an enforcement notice, the term enforcement notice is to be read as referring to such a notice issued by the planning authority which is formally valid and has not been quashed on appeal or judicial review (see Lord Hoffmann at 119). In *Palace Properties Ltd v Camden LBC* (2001) 82 P. & C.R. 17, the Divisional Court rejected an argument that the term meant a notice immune from judicial review except on the grounds of bad faith, consideration by the local planning authority of irrelevant matters or procedural impropriety and that arguments based on other judicial review grounds could be raised either on a claim for judicial review or collaterally by way of defence to prosecution for breach. (This would be subject to the statutory qualification in s.285(1) of the Town and Country Planning Act 1990 that the particular grounds specified in s.174 of the 1990 Act may only be taken by way of an appeal to the minister.) The Court of Appeal confirmed that the consequence of the *Wicks* decision was that the only *ultra vires* issues that could be raised by way of defence to enforcement proceedings, were those directed to whether the notice was formally valid, as whether the notice had been issued pursuant to a resolution of the council, or whether a necessary consent to the issuance of a notice had been given. Whether the resolution or consent were lawfully given would, however, be a point for judicial review and would be legally irrelevant to the criminal prosecution.

(D) PARTIAL INVALIDITY

DPP v HUTCHINSON

[1990] 2 A.C. 783; [1990] 3 W.L.R. 196; [1990] 2 All E.R. 836; (1990) 89 L.G.R. 281 (HOUSE OF LORDS)

Section 14(1) of the Military Lands Act 1892 provides:

"Where any land belonging to a Secretary of State . . . is for the time being appropriated by . . . a Secretary of State for any military purpose, a Secretary of State may make byelaws for regulating the use of the land for the purposes for which it is appropriated, and for securing the public against dangers arising from that use, with power to prohibit all intrusion on the land and all obstruction of the use thereof. Provided that no byelaws promulgated under the section shall authorise the Secretary of State to take away or prejudicially affect any right of common".

The Secretary of State for Defence, acting under s.14 of the Act of 1892, made the R.A.F. Greenham Common Byelaws 1985 in respect of common land appropriated for military purposes. Byelaw (2)(b) provided that no person should, *inter alia*, enter or remain in the protected area without the authority or permission of an authorised person. The defendants, who were not commoners, entered the land and were charged with and convicted by the justices of entering it contrary to byelaw 2(b). The Crown Court allowed their appeals, holding that the byelaws were *ultra vires* in that they prejudicially affected rights of common. The Divisional Court of the Queen's Bench Division allowed an appeal by case stated by the Director of Public Prosecutions. The defendants appealed to the House of Lords.

LORD BRIDGE: . . . The Divisional Court (Mann L.J. and Schiemann J.) [1989] Q.B. 583 allowed the Crown's appeal and restored the convictions. They held that the Greenham byelaws, although *ultra vires* on their face, could be severed, so that they might be upheld and enforced as against all except persons entitled to exercise rights of common over the protected area. It mattered not that the severance could only be achieved by reading into the byelaws, where necessary, appropriate exceptions and exemptions, provided that the court was satisfied, as Schiemann J. stated, at 599, that it was, that the Secretary of State, if he had appreciated the limitation on his powers would:

> "nevertheless have gone on to make the byelaws in such a way that the proviso to section 14(1) was given effect but that all the world save commoners would still have been within their ambit . . .".

When a legislative instrument made by a law-maker with limited powers is challenged, the only function of the court is to determine whether there has been a valid exercise of that limited legislative power in relation to the matter which is the subject of disputed enforcement. If a law-maker has validly exercised his power, the court may give effect to the law validly made. But if the court sees only an invalid law made in excess of the law-maker's power, it has no jurisdiction to modify or adapt the law to bring it within the scope of the law-maker's powers. These, I believe, are the basic principles which have always to be borne in mind in deciding whether legislative provisions which on their face exceed the law-maker's power may be severed so as to be upheld and enforced in part.

The application of these principles leads naturally and logically to what has traditionally been regarded as the test of severability. It is often referred to inelegantly as the "blue pencil" test. Taking the simplest case of a single legislative instrument containing a number of separate clauses of which one exceeds the law-maker's power, if the remaining clauses enact free-standing provisions which were intended to operate and are capable of operating independently of the offending clause, there is no reason why those clauses should not be upheld and enforced. The law-maker has validly exercised his power by making the valid clauses. The invalid clause may be disregarded as unrelated to, and having no effect upon, the operation of the valid clauses, which accordingly may be allowed to take effect without the necessity of any modification or adaptation by the court. What is involved is in truth a double test. I shall refer to the two aspects of the test as textual severability and substantial severability. A legislative instrument is textually severable if a clause, a sentence, a phrase or a single word may be disregarded, as exceeding the law-maker's power, and what remains of the text is still grammatical and coherent. A legislative instrument is substantially severable if the substance of what remains after severance is essentially unchanged in its legislative purpose, operation and effect.

The early English authorities take it for granted, I think, that if byelaws are to be upheld as good in part notwithstanding that they are bad in part, they must be both textually and substantially severable. Thus, Lord Kenyon C.J. said in *R. v Company of Fishermen of Faversham* (1799) 8 Durn. & E. 352, 356:

> "With regard to the form of the byelaw indeed, though a byelaw may be good in part and bad in part, yet it can be so only where the two parts are entire and distinct from each other."

[His Lordship also cited *R. v Lundie* (1862) 8 Jur.N.S. 640 and *Strickland v Hayes* [1896] 1 Q.B. 290. He then referred to US and Australian authorities that emphasised the need for both textual and substantial severability.]

Our attention has been drawn to a number of more recent English authorities on the severability of provisions contained in various documents of a public law character. I doubt if these throw much light on the specific problem of severance in legislative instruments. The modern authority most directly in point and that on which the Divisional Court relied is *Dunkley v Evans* [1981] 1 W.L.R. 1522. The West Coast Herring (Prohibition of Fishing) Order 1978 (S.I. 1978 No. 930) prohibited fishing for herring in an area defined in the Schedule to the Order as within a line drawn by reference to co-ordinates and coastlines. The Order was made by the Minister of Agriculture, Fisheries and Food under the Sea Fish (Conservation) Act 1967. The prohibited area included a stretch of sea adjacent to the coast of Northern Ireland, representing 0.8 per cent of the total area covered by the Order, to which the enabling power in the Act of 1967 did not extend. The defendants admitted fishing in part of the prohibited area to which the enabling power did extend but submitted that, by including the area to which the enabling power did not extend, the Minister had acted *ultra vires* and, since textual severance was not possible, the whole Order was invalid. The justices accepted this submission and dismissed the informations. The Divisional Court allowed the prosecutor's appeal. Delivering the judgment of the court, Ormrod L.J. cited, at 1524–1525, the following passage from the judgment of Cussen J. in the Supreme Court of Victoria in *Olsen v City of Camberwell* [1926] V.L.R. 58, 68:

> " 'If the enactment, with the invalid portion omitted, is so radically or substantially different a law as to the subject-matter dealt with by what remains from what it would be with the omitted portions forming part of it as to warrant a belief that the legislative body intended it as a whole only, or, in other words, to warrant a belief that if all could not be carried into effect the legislative body would not have enacted the remainder independently, then the whole must fail.' "

It is to be noted that this quotation is from the judgment in a case where textual severance was possible. Following the quotation the judgment of Ormrod L.J. continued:

> "We respectfully agree with and adopt this statement of the law. It would be difficult to imagine a clearer example than the present case of a law which the legislative body would have enacted independently of the offending portion and which is so little affected by eliminating the invalid portion. This is clearly, therefore, an order which the court should not strive officiously to kill to any greater extent than it is compelled to do. . . . We can see no reason why the powers of the court to sever the invalid portion

of a piece of subordinate legislation from the valid should be restricted to cases where the text of the legislation lends itself to judicial surgery, or textual emendation by excision. It would have been competent for the court in an action for a declaration that the provisions of the Order in this case did not apply to the area of the sea off Northern Ireland reserved by section 23(1) of the Act of 1967, as amended, to make the declaration sought, without in any way affecting the validity of the Order in relation to the remaining 99.2 per cent of the area referred to in the Schedule to the Order. Such an order was made, in effect, by the House of Lords in *Hotel and Catering Industry Training Board v Automobile Proprietary Ltd* [1969] 1 W.L.R. 697, and by Donaldson J. in *Agricultural, Horticultural and Forestry Industry Training Board v Aylesbury Mushrooms Ltd* [1972] 1 W.L.R. 190."

I do not think any light is thrown on the point at issue by the last two cases referred to by Ormrod L.J. In *Hotel and Catering Industry Training Board v Automobile Proprietary Ltd* the subordinate legislation in question was textually severable. In *Agricultural, Horticultural and Forestry Industry Training Board v Aylesbury Mushrooms Ltd* the text was not severable but the issue of severance was never canvassed in argument and I cannot help thinking that the outcome might have been different if it had been. . . .

The modern English authority to which I attach most significance is *Daymond v Plymouth City Council* [1976] A.C. 609, where severability was not in issue, but where it appears to have been taken for granted without question that severance was possible. Section 30(1) of the Water Act 1973 gave power to water authorities:

"to fix, and to demand, take and recover such charges for the services performed, facilities provided or rights made available by them including separate charges for separate services, facilities or rights or combined charges for a number of services, facilities or rights) as they think fit."

The subsection was silent as to who was liable to pay the charges. The Water Authorities (Collection of Charges) Order 1974 (S.I. 1974 No. 448) embodied provisions which required a rating authority to collect on behalf of a water authority a "general services charge" (article 7(2)) referable to sewerage services "from every person who is liable to pay the general rate in respect of a hereditament . . ." (article 10(1)). A householder whose property was not connected to a sewer, the nearest sewer being 400 yards away from his house, refused to pay the charge and brought an action for a declaration that the Order could not properly apply to him. This House held, by a majority of three to two, that on the true construction of the enabling legislation there was no power to impose a charge for sewerage services upon occupiers of property not connected to a sewer. As I have said, the question of severability was not raised, but there is no hint in the speeches that the invalidation of the charging provision in relation to properties not connected to sewers would affect their validity in relation to properties which were so connected.

The test of textual severability has the great merit of simplicity and certainty. When it is satisfied the court can readily see whether the omission from the legislative text of so much as exceeds the law-maker's power leaves in place a valid text which is capable of operating and was evidently intended to operate independently of the invalid text. But I have reached the conclusion, though not without hesitation, that a rigid insistence that the test of textual severability must always be satisfied if a provision is to be upheld and enforced as partially valid will in some cases, of which *Dunkley v Evans* and *Daymond v Plymouth City Council* are good examples, have the unreasonable consequence of defeating subordinate legislation of which the substantial purpose and effect was clearly within the law-maker's power when, by some oversight or misapprehension of the scope of that power, the text, as written, has a range of application which exceeds that scope. It is important, however, that in all cases an appropriate test of substantial severability should be applied. When textual severance is possible, the test of substantial severability will be satisfied when the valid text is unaffected by, and independent of, the invalid. The law which the court may then uphold and enforce is the very law which the legislator has enacted, not a different law. But when the court must modify the text in order to achieve severance, this can only be done when the court is satisfied that it is effecting no change in the substantial purpose and effect of the impugned provision. Thus, in *Dunkley v Evans*, the legislative purpose and effect of the prohibition of fishing in the large area of the sea in relation to which the Minister was authorised to legislate was unaffected by the obviously inadvertent inclusion of the small area of sea to which his power did not extend. In *Daymond v Plymouth City Council* the draftsman of the Order had evidently construed the enabling provision as authorising the imposition of charges for sewerage services upon occupiers of property irrespective of whether or not they were connected to sewers. In this error he was in the good company of two members of your Lordships' House. But this extension of the scope of the charging power, which, as the majority held, exceeded its proper limit, in no way affected the legislative purpose and effect of the charging power as applied to occupiers of properties which were connected to sewers.

To appreciate the full extent of the problem presented by the Greenham byelaws it is necessary to set out the full text of the prohibitions imposed by byelaw (2) which provides:

"No person shall: (a) enter or leave or attempt to enter or leave the protected area except by way of an authorised entrance or exit. (b) enter, pass through or over or remain in or over the protected area without authority or permission given by or on behalf of one of the persons mentioned in byelaw 5(1). (c) cause or permit any vehicle, animal, aircraft or thing to enter into or upon or to pass through or over or to be or remain in or upon or over the protected area without authority or permission given by or on behalf of one of the persons mentioned in byelaw 5(1). (d) remain in the protected area after having been directed to leave by any of the persons mentioned in byelaw 4. (e) make any false statement, either orally or in writing, or employ any other form of misrepresentation in order to obtain entry to any part of the protected area or to any building or premises within the protected area. (f) obstruct any constable (including a constable under the control of the Defence Council) or any other person acting in the proper exercise or execution of his duty within the protected area. (g) enter any part of the protected area which is shown by a notice as being prohibited or restricted. (h) board, attempt to board, or interfere with, or interfere with the movement or passage, of any vehicle, aircraft or other installation in the protected area. (i) distribute or display any handbill, leaflet, sign, advertisement, circular, poster, bill, notice or object within the protected area or affix the same to either side of the perimeter fences without authority of permission given by or on behalf of one of the persons mentioned in byelaw 5(1). (j) interfere or remove from the protected area any property under the control of the Crown or the service authorities of a visiting force or, in either case, their agents or contractors. (k) wilfully damage, destroy, deface or remove any notice board or sign within the protected area. (l) wilfully damage, soil, deface or mark any wall, fence, structure, floor, pavement, or other surface within the protected area."

It is at once apparent that paragraphs (a), (b), (c), (d), (g), (j) and (l) are *ultra vires* as they stand. Paragraphs (e), (f), (i) and (k) appear to be valid and paragraph (h) is probably good in part and bad in part, since the exercise by a commoner of his rights may well interfere with the movement or passage of vehicles. Textual severance can achieve nothing since it is apparent that the valid provisions are merely ancillary to the invalid provisions.

There is exhibited to the case stated by the Crown Court a letter written by an official of the Ministry of Defence to an objector at the time the byelaws were made which concludes with the sentence:

"Finally I can confirm that in accordance with the enabling Act, the Military Lands Act 1892, the byelaws will not affect rights of common."

Mr Laws has invited us to infer from this that the Secretary of State for Defence made the byelaws in the belief that the law would imply the necessary exceptions to prevent the byelaws from prejudicially affecting rights of common. I do not think we are entitled to take account of the letter in considering whether the byelaws may be upheld as valid in part. But in any event it is a matter of pure speculation as to what the writer of the letter had in mind. The draftsman of the byelaws cannot possibly have been in ignorance of the terms and effect of the proviso to section 14(1) of the Act of 1892 and the theory of an inadvertent omission appears the less plausible since five sets of byelaws in relation to common lands used for military purposes which were made by the Secretary of State for Defence under section 14 of the Act of 1892 in the years 1976 to 1980 all contain careful express provisions to safeguard rights of common.

I think the proper test to be applied when textual severance is impossible, following in this respect the Australian authorities, is to abjure speculation as to what the maker of the law might have done if he had applied his mind to the relevant limitation on his powers and to ask whether the legislative instrument

"with the invalid portions omitted would be substantially a different law as to the subject-matter dealt with by what remains from what it would be with the omitted portions forming part of it": *R. v Commonwealth Court of Conciliation and Arbitration, ex p. Whybrow & Co.*, 11 C.L.R. 1, 27.

In applying this test the purpose of the legislation can only be inferred from the text as applied to the factual situation to which its provisions relate. Considering the Greenham byelaws as a whole it is clear that the absolute prohibition which they impose upon all unauthorised access to the protected area is no less than is required to maintain the security of an establishment operated as a military airbase and wholly enclosed by a perimeter fence. Byelaws drawn in such a way as to permit free access to all parts of the base to persons exercising rights of common and their animals would be byelaws of a totally different character. They might serve some different legislative purpose in a different factual situation, as do some other byelaws to which our attention has been drawn relating to areas used as military exercise grounds or as military firing ranges. But they would be quite incapable of serving the legislative purpose which the Greenham byelaws, as drawn, are intended to serve.

For these reasons I conclude that the invalidity of byelaw 2(b) cannot be cured by severance. It follows that the appellants were wrongly convicted and I would allow their appeals, set aside the order of the Divisional Court and restore the order of the Crown Court at Reading.

LORDS GRIFFITH, OLIVER and GOFF agreed with LORD BRIDGE.

LORD LOWRY [agreed with Lord Bridge's conclusion that the byelaw could not survive the test of substantial severability, but also made a reservation in favour of the traditional test of textual severability].

My Lords, the accepted view in the common law jurisdictions has been that, when construing legislation the validity of which is under challenge, the first duty of the court, in obedience to the principle that a law should, whenever possible, be interpreted *ut res magis valeat quam pereat*, is to see whether the impugned provision can reasonably bear a construction which renders it valid. Failing that, the court's duty, subject always to any relevant statutory provision . . . is to decide whether the whole of the challenged legislation or only part of it must be held invalid and ineffective. That problem has traditionally been resolved by applying first the textual, and then the substantial, severability test. If the legislation failed the first test, it was condemned in its entirety. If it passed that test, it had to face the next hurdle. This approach, in my opinion, has a great deal in its favour.

The basic principle is that an *ultra vires* enactment, such as a byelaw, is void *ab initio* and of no effect. The so-called blue pencil test is a concession to practicality and ought not to be extended or weakened. In its traditional form it is acceptable because, once the offending words are ignored, no word or phrase needs to be given a meaning different from, or more restrictive than, its original meaning. Therefore the court has not legislated; it merely continues to apply that part of the existing legislation which is good.

It may be argued that a policy split has developed and that it is time to show common sense and bring our thinking up to date by a further application of the *ut res magis valeat quam pereat* principle. I am, however, chary of yielding to this temptation for a number of reasons. 1. The blue pencil test already represents a concession to the erring law-maker, the justification for which I have tried to explain. 2. When applying the blue pencil test (which actually means ignoring the offending words), the court cannot cause the text of the instrument to be altered. It will remain as the ostensible law of the land unless and until it is replaced by something else. It is too late now to think of abandoning the blue pencil method, which has much to commend it, but the disadvantage inherent in the method ought not to be enlarged. 3. It is up to the law-maker to keep within his powers and it is in the public interest that he should take care, in order that the public may be able to rely on the written word as representing the law. Further enlargement of the court's power to validate what is partially invalid will encourage the law-maker to enact what he pleases, or at least to enact what may or may not be valid, without having to fear any worse result than merely being brought back within bounds. 4. *Dunkley v Evans* [1981] 1 W.L.R. 1522 and *Thames Water Authority v Elmbridge Borough Council* [1983] Q.B. 570 are very special cases. I recall in that regard what McNeill J. said in *R. v Secretary of State for Transport, ex p. Greater London Council* [1986] Q.B. 556, 582D. 5. To liberalise the test would, in my view, be anarchic, not progressive. It would tend in the wrong direction, unlike some developments in the law of negligence, which have promoted justice for physically or economically injured persons, or the sounder aspects of judicial review, which have promoted freedom and have afforded protection from power. 6. The current of decisions and relevant authority has flowed in favour of the traditional doctrine.

[His Lordship concluded by noting that the sole question considered in *Daymond v Plymouth City Council* [1976] A.C. 609 was whether s.30 of the Water Act 1973 empowered the water authority to charge occupiers of property who did not receive the benefit of the authority's services directly.]

I am therefore very reluctant to treat the case as an authority which by implication contradicts the established doctrine of textual severability for the purposes of the present appeal. Accordingly, I would allow this appeal on two grounds, (1) that there is no valid part of byelaw 2(b) which can be severed from the invalid part and stand by itself and (2) that the byelaw would not in any event survive the test of substantial severability.

Appeals allowed.

Notes

1. See comments by A.W. Bradley [1989] P.L.1. (on the decision of the Divisional Court), and [1990] P.L. 293 (on the decision of the House of Lords). Bradley is critical of the fact that it appeared:

"that the Ministry of Defence knew of the limitation upon the Secretary of State's powers and knowingly departed from the previous practice of taking care to comply with the intent of the legislation" (at 295).

He also noted that Lord Lowry's view had "the edge in terms of the previous authorities" (at 300). Lord Bridge's approach, while more generous to the lawmaker, still gave "salutary substance to the spectre of the judge over Whitehall's shoulder" (at 300).

"What previously may have seemed in danger of being entirely at the discretion of the court is now subject to a more structured review" (at 299).

2. In *R. v Secretary of State for Transport Ex p. Greater London Council* [1986] Q.B. 556, McNeill J. quashed a direction by the Secretary of State requiring the GLC to pay a specified sum to London Regional Transport by way of grant. Through a miscalculation, this figure was too high by some £10.2 million. McNeill J. held that the direction was "single and indivisible"; that the deduction of £10.2 million would involve rewriting and changing the character of the direction; and that this could not be justified by reference to the authorities on severance. The direction "stands or falls as one".

3. *D.P.P. v Hutchinson* was applied by the House in *R. v Inland Revenue Commissioners Ex p. Woolwich Equitable Building Society* [1990] 1 W.L.R. 1400. The Revenue conceded that part of a regulation was *ultra vires* in that it purported to

prescribe a rate of income tax for which building societies were accountable different from that of the year of assessment; the House held (reversing the Court of Appeal on this point) that this could not be severed from the rest of the regulation and that this and a linked regulation were wholly *ultra vires*. The fact that the offending part could be deleted without altering the grammatical sense of what was left was insufficient for severance:

> "One has to ask also the question whether the deletion of that which is in excess of the power so alters the substance of what is left that the provision in question is in reality a substantially different provision from that which it was before deletion" (per Lord Oliver at 1413).

Here it was "beyond argument" that the regulation without the offending part:

> "is in substance quite different from the regulation which the draftsman actually produced and intended . . . . What form the regulation might have taken if the invalidity of paragraph (4) had been appreciated is a matter of pure speculation" (per Lord Oliver at 1415–1416).

(*cf*. Lord Goff at 1417–1419.)

4. In *R. (on the application of National Association of Health Stores) v Secretary of State for Health* [2005] EWCA Civ 154, Sedley L.J. suggested *obiter* (at [16]–[20]) that in appropriate cases, the *Hutchinson* reasoning should be applicable to justify making good an improper omission, if this can be done "without disrupting the existing, presumptively lawful, text". *Hutchinson* should not be confined to cases of improper inclusions.

EXCLUSION OF JUDICIAL REVIEW

Parliament may attempt to make a particular act or decision "judge-proof". One general method is to entrust powers in subjective form. Another general method is to use explicit exclusion clauses, purporting for example, to exclude a particular remedy, or to prevent any recourse to the courts at all. Historically these clauses have been controversial both politically and legally. Section 11 of the Tribunals and Inquiries Act 1958 (see now s.12 of the 1992 Act, above, p.109) reduced the effects of such clauses in statutes passed before July 1958. One of the exclusion clauses expressly preserved by the 1958 Act was considered in the *Anisminic* case (above, p.436). Another variety frequently found in legislation is the "finality" clause, which seems to have little effect beyond taking away a right of appeal which would otherwise exist. (See *R. v Medical Appeal Tribunal Ex p. Gilmore*, below.) The other significant modern exclusionary formula is that built into the typical "statutory *ultra vires*" clause (see above, pp.805–816). These protect compulsory purchase orders, etc., from any judicial review apart from on an application to the High Court within six weeks on the stated grounds. The effect of these clauses is discussed in *Smith v East Elloe RDC*, below, p.907, and *Ex p. Ostler*, below, p.911. In the latter case, the Court of Appeal held that the authority of the House of Lords in *Smith v East Elloe* has not been affected by the *Anisminic* case, and that an order cannot be challenged other than in accordance with the statutory procedure.

Another technique is that of empowering a public authority to "define" expressions used in the enabling Act which sets it up. See, for example, the Counter-inflation Act 1973, s.23 and Sch.3, para.1, discussed by V. Korah at (1976) 92 L.Q.R. 42.

One variety of clause to which effect has been given is a "conclusive evidence" clause (see below, p.905). Then the courts may hold that Parliament has entrusted a matter exclusively to another tribunal (below, p.1032). Finally, the courts may refuse a particular remedy in the exercise of their discretion where an alternative remedy is available (see below, pp.1019–1021). Here, it is an increasingly familiar technique for Parliament to create specific new rights of appeal either to the ordinary courts or to a special tribunal whether otherwise there would only be the possibility of recourse to judicial review. This can provide a more suitable procedural route than judicial review (see pp.789–791).

One limiting factor is that statutory ouster clauses of whatever kind cannot be relied on to defeat actions against the state relying on community law: P. Oliver, (1987) 50 M.L.R. 881 at pp.897–898, citing Case 224/84 *Johnston v Chief Constable of the Royal Ulster Constabulary* [1986] E.C.R. 1651; [1986] 3 C.M.L.R. 240; [1987] Q.B. 129, which concerned a "conclusive evidence" certificate under art. 53(2) of the Sex Discrimination (Northern Ireland) Order 1976.

R. v MEDICAL APPEAL TRIBUNAL Ex p. GILMORE

[1957] 1 Q.B. 574; [1957] 2 W.L.R. 498; 101 S.J. 248; *SUB NOM. GILMORE'S APPLICATION, RE* [1957] 1 All E.R. 796 (COURT OF APPEAL)

In 1936, the applicant, a colliery pick sharpener, sustained an injury to both eyes while at work, his right eye being rendered almost blind. In March 1955, he suffered a further injury at work, by which the condition of his left eye was so severely aggravated that in the result he was almost totally blind. On his claim for disablement benefit under the National Insurance (Industrial Injuries) Act 1946, two medical boards provisionally assessed the degree of disablement at 100 per cent; but a third board made no award. The claimant appealed to a medical appeal tribunal which had before it and incorporated in its award an extract from a specialist's report setting out the facts as to the state of both eyes; but in making its award the tribunal assessed the aggravation at only 20 per cent, showing thereby that they had failed to assess in accordance with reg. 2(5) of the National Insurance (Industrial Injuries) (Benefit) Regulations 1948 (relating to industrial injuries to paired organs). If a one-eyed man should lose the sight of his remaining good eye in an industrial accident, this regulation required his disablement to be assessed as if the blindness in the bad eye were itself the result of losing the good eye (*i.e.* as 100 per cent disablement).

Section 36(3) of the National Insurance (Industrial Injuries) Act 1946, provided that ". . . any decision of a claim or question . . . shall be final". The applicant applied for an order of certiorari to quash the decision of the tribunal on the ground that there was a manifest error of law on the face of the record.

The Divisional Court refused leave to apply for certiorari, and so the applicant moved the Court of Appeal ex parte, which granted his request. The court was of opinion that they ought to extend the usual time-limit of six months because he had not been guilty of any delay in seeking redress, and that there was some ground for thinking that there was an error on the face of the record.

On February 12, 1957, the application came on for hearing in the Court of Appeal. After the case had been opened, counsel for the Ministry of Pensions and National Insurance and for the tribunal informed the court that he had carefully considered the matter with the responsible officers of the Ministry and, as a result, he conceded that the decision of the medical appeal tribunal of June 13, 1956, was erroneous in point of law; he added that the Ministry were in some difficulty because the chairman of the tribunal had died.

Despite that concession, the court of its own motion considered that as the application raised points of considerable importance, judgment should be reserved.

DENNING L.J.: [held, first, that the tribunal's decision was vitiated by an error of law on the face of the record.]

The second point is the effect of section 36(3) of the Act of 1946 which provides that "any decision of a claim or question . . . shall be final". Do those words preclude the Court of Queen's Bench from issuing a certiorari to bring up the decision?

This is a question which we did not discuss in *R. v Northumberland Compensation Appeal Tribunal Ex p. Shaw* [1952] 1 K.B. 338, because it did not there arise. It does arise here, and on looking again into the old books I find it very well settled that the remedy by certiorari is never to be taken away by any statute except by the most clear and explicit words. The word "final" is not enough. That only means "without appeal". It does not mean "without recourse to certiorari". It makes the decision final on the facts, but not final on the law. Notwithstanding that the decision is by a statute made "final", certiorari can still issue for excess of jurisdiction or for error of law on the face of the record . . . .

[His Lordship reviewed the authorities.]

In my opinion, therefore, notwithstanding the fact that the statute says that the decision of the medical appeal tribunal is to be final, it is open to this court to issue a certiorari to quash it for error of law on the face of the record. It would seem to follow that a decision of the national insurance and industrial insurance commissioners is also subject to supervision by certiorari (a point left open by the Divisional Court in *R. v National Insurance Commissioner Ex p. Timmis* [1955] 1 Q.B. 139); but they are so well versed in the law and deservedly held in such high regard that it will be rare that they fall into error such as to need correction.

In contrast to the word "final" I would like to say a word about the old statutes which used in express words to take away the remedy by certiorari by saying that the decision of the tribunal "shall not be removed by certiorari". Those statutes were passed chiefly between 1680 and 1848, in the days when the courts used certiorari too freely and quashed decisions for technical defects of form. In stopping this abuse the statutes proved very beneficial, but the court never allowed those statutes to be used as a cover for wrongdoing by tribunals. If tribunals were to be at liberty to exceed their jurisdiction without any check by the courts, the rule of law would be at an end. Despite express words taking away certiorari, therefore, it was held that certiorari would still lie if some of the members of the tribunal were disqualified from acting: see *R. v Cheltenham Commissioners* (1841) 1 Q.B. 467, where Lord Denman C.J. said (*ibid.* at 474): "The statute cannot affect our right and duty to see justice executed." So, also, if the tribunal exceeded its jurisdiction: see *Ex p. Bradlaugh* (1878) 3 Q.B.D. 509; or if its decision was obtained by fraud: see *R. v Gillyard* (1848) 12 Q.B. 527, the courts would still grant certiorari. I do not pause to consider those cases further; for I am glad to notice that modern statutes never take away in express words the right to certiorari without substituting an analogous remedy. This is probably because the courts no longer use it to quash for technical defects but only in case of a substantial miscarriage of justice. Parliament nowadays more often uses the words "final" or "final and conclusive," or some such words which leave intact the control of the Queen's courts by certiorari. . . .

ROMER and PARKER L.JJ. delivered concurring judgments.

Notes

1. *Ex p. Gilmore* considers both "finality" and "no certiorari" clauses. As to the former, it has been held that it would not even prevent an appeal by case stated on a question that might otherwise be resolved by certiorari or a declaration (*Tehrani v Rostron* [1972] 1 Q.B. 182). In *Pearlman v Keepers and Governors of Harrow School* [1979] Q.B. 56, Lord Denning M.R. (at 71) stated *obiter* that a finality clause would only exclude an appeal on the facts and not on a point of law. Eveleigh L.J. was inclined to agree on this point (at 79). Geoffrey Lane L.J. disagreed (at 74) and his view was subsequently endorsed by Lord Diplock and Lord Keith in *Racal Communications Ltd, Re* [1981] A.C. 374, 382. The House of Lords held in that case that a provision that a decision of a High Court judge shall not be appealable meant exactly that. On "no certiorari" clauses see further the *Pearlman* case, above, p.450. Lord Denning M.R. held (at 69) that the "no certiorari" clause (County Courts Act 1959, s.107) only applied to proceedings under the 1959 Act, *Pearlman* arising under the Housing Act 1974. Both Geoffrey Lane L.J. and Eveleigh L.J. treated the clause as applicable.

2. A "finality" clause may help a court decide that no duty of care in negligence is owed: see *Jones v Department of Employment* [1989] Q.B. 1.

3. "Conclusive evidence" clauses were considered by the Court of Appeal in *R. v Registrar of Companies Ex p. Central Bank of India* [1986] Q.B. 1114. The Registrar of Companies registered a charge under s.95(1) of the Companies Act 1948. The Court of Appeal held, on an application for judicial review, that the registrar, in deciding to register the charge in default of delivery of the original documents by which the charge was created or evidenced, had erred in law. However, s.98(2) of the 1948 Act provided

that the registrar's certificate "shall be conclusive evidence that the requirements of this Part of this Act as to registration have been complied with".

The court held that this precluded it from considering evidence adduced to show non-compliance with the requirements for registration and, accordingly, from quashing the registration. This form of clause, although in a pre-1958 statute, was not negatived by s.14 of the Tribunals and Inquiries Act 1971 (now s. 12 of the 1992 Act, above, p.109). Lawton L.J. was of the view that the Registrar had acted in excess of jurisdiction; Slade and Dillon L.JJ. that he had made an error of law within jurisdiction. Slade L.J. at 1175–1176 followed Lord Diplock's approach in *Racal Communications Ltd, Re* (above p.450), concluding that the presumption that administrative authorities, in accordance with *Anisminic*, cannot determine questions of law conclusively was here rebutted in view of s.98(2). His Lordship also noted that counsel for the Registrar accepted that s.98(2) did not bind the Crown, so there was nothing to prevent intervention by the Attorney-General. Moreover, the provisions might not apply where a purported certificate disclosed an error on its face (*per* Slade L.J. at 1177), or was procured by fraud (*per* Lawton L.J. at 1169, Dillon L.J. at 1183).

Ex p. Central Bank of India was followed in *R. v Secretary of State for Foreign Affairs Ex p. Trawnik, The Times,* February 21, 1986. Section 40(3) of the Crown Proceedings Act 1947 provides that:

> "A certificate of a Secretary of State: (*a*) to the effect that any alleged liability of the Crown arises otherwise than in respect of His Majesty's Government in the United Kingdom . . . shall, for the purposes of this Act, be conclusive as to the matter so certified".

The applicant sought a judicial review of two certificates under s.40(3)(a) relating to the possible liability of the Crown in nuisance in respect of the establishment of a machine-gun range in West Berlin. The Court of Appeal held on a preliminary issue that evidence in contradiction of the terms of the certificates was inadmissible. May L.J. said that:

> "As a matter of construction, the words 'shall . . . be conclusive as to the matter so certified' in section 40(3)(a) are equivalent to a provision that the certificate shall be conclusive evidence of the matters certified, whether these be questions of fact or law or of mixed fact and law.
>
> Such words do not preclude an application for judicial review of the certificate but such an application if based on the proposition that that which has been certified is so clearly wrong that the certificate must be a nullity, would be bound to fail because the evidence which counsel would wish to call to prove this very thing could not be adduced".

Emery and Smythe, p.54, argue that this reasoning cannot be reconciled with *Anisminic*.

4. Denning L.J.'s proposition that the remedy of certiorari is never to be taken away by statute except by the most clear and explicit words was held to remain good law in *R. (on the application of Sivasubramaniam) v Wandsworth County Court* [2002] EWCA Civ 1738, [2003] 2 All E.R. 160. Here, the Court of Appeal held that the jurisdiction to hear claims for judicial review of the decision of a county court judge to refuse permission was not taken away by s.54(4) of the Access to Justice Act 1999, which provided that "no appeal shall be made" against such a decision. To give s.54(4) that effect would be to exclude judicial review by implication, which was not possible. However, permission to claim judicial review should not be granted if permission to appeal had not been sought, as a suitable alternative remedy would then be available. If permission to appeal had been refused by the Court of Appeal, permission to apply for judicial review should, as a matter of discretion, only be given in exceptional circumstances:

"where a litigant challenges the jurisdiction of a Circuit judge giving or refusing permission to appeal on the ground of jurisdictional error in the narrow pre-*Anisminic* sense, or procedural irregularity of such a kind as to constitute a denial of the applicant's right to a fair hearing" (*per* Lord Phillips of Worth Matravers M.R. at [56]).

SMITH v EAST ELLOE RDC

[1956] A.C. 736; [1956] 2 W.L.R. 888; 120 J.P. 263; 100 S.J. 282; [1956] 1 All E.R. 855; 54 L.G.R. 233; 6 P. & C.R. 102 (HOUSE OF LORDS)

[For earlier litigation concerning the dispute between S and the authorities, see p.1041.]

By para.15(1) of Pt IV of Sch.1 to the Acquisition of Land (Authorisation Procedure) Act 1946:

"If any person aggrieved by a compulsory purchase order desires to question the validity thereof . . . on the ground that the authorisation of a compulsory purchase thereby granted is not empowered to be granted under this Act . . . he may, within six weeks from the date on which notice of the confirmation or making of the order . . . is first published . . . make an application to the High Court. . . .".

By para.16: "Subject to the provisions of the last foregoing paragraph, a compulsory purchase order . . . shall not . . . be questioned in any legal proceedings whatsoever . . . ".

On November 29, 1948, the Minister of Health confirmed a compulsory purchase order in respect of 8(1/2)acres of land owned by Kathleen Rose Smith, following a public local inquiry. A notice to treat and a notice of entry were duly served on the appellant, and in due course the compulsory purchase price for the said house and land was fixed by the Lands Tribunal at £3,000. The respondent council caused a firm of builders to demolish the house and to erect on its site and on the said land a number of houses.

On July 6, 1954, the appellant issued a writ, claiming:

1. Against the East Elloe Rural District Council: (a) Damages for trespass to the plaintiff's land; (b) An injunction restraining them by their officers, servants and agents and each and every one of them from trespassing upon the aforesaid land and premises; (c) A declaration that the compulsory purchase order was wrongfully made and in bad faith.

2. Against the Ministry of Health: A declaration that the compulsory purchase order was wrongfully confirmed and in bad faith.

3. Against the respondent, J.C. Pywell: A declaration that he knowingly acted wrongfully and in bad faith in procuring the said order and confirmation of the same.

4. Against the Ministry of Housing and Local Government: As having taken over the functions of the [Ministry of Health] a declaration that the said compulsory purchase order and confirmation of the same are in bad faith.

5. Further and other relief.

6. Damages.

7. Costs.

The writ was set aside by Master Clayton on the ground that the court had no jurisdiction to grant the relief sought as the result of para.16 of Pt IV of Sch.1 to the 1946 Act. S appealed unsuccessfully to Havers J., the Court of Appeal. The House of Lords allowed an appeal as regards the claim under para.3 and related matters only.

LORD MORTON OF HENRYTON: My Lords, I think there can be no doubt that the respondents were never entitled to have the writ set aside so far as it claims relief against the respondent Pywell. The relief claimed by paragraph 3 of the writ and the further relief claimed by paragraphs 5, 6 and 7, in so far as that relief affects the respondent Pywell, in no way call in question the validity of the compulsory purchase order of August 26, 1948, or of its confirmation. It is simply alleged, as against Mr Pywell personally, that he knowingly acted wrongfully and in bad faith in procuring the order and the confirmation thereof. It is equally clear that claims 1, 2 and 4 do put in issue the validity of the order. . . .

Mr Roy Wilson, for the appellant, puts forward propositions which I summarize as follows: (1) Paragraph 15 gives no opportunity to a person aggrieved to question the validity of a compulsory purchase order on the ground that it was made or confirmed in bad faith. (2) Although, *prima facie*, paragraph 16 excludes the jurisdiction of the court in all cases, subject only to the provision of paragraph 15, it is inconceivable that the legislature can have intended wholly to exclude all courts from hearing and determining an allegation that such an order was made in bad faith. (3) Therefore, paragraph 16 should be read as applying only to an order or a certificate made in good faith. . . . The Attorney-General, on behalf of the respondents, contends that the opportunity of objection given by paragraph 15 extends to cases where bad faith is alleged, but, whether or not this is so, if the person aggrieved fails to apply to the court within the six weeks' period there mentioned, the jurisdiction of the court is completely ousted by paragraph 16, the terms whereof are unambiguous.

My Lords, I accept Mr Wilson's first proposition. I cannot construe paragraph 15 as covering a case in which all the requirements expressly laid down by statute have been observed, but the person aggrieved has discovered that in carrying out the steps laid down by statute the authority has been actuated by improper motives. It is to be observed that both in the earlier and in the later part of paragraph 15 there is only one ground upon which the validity of the order can be questioned . . . These words seem to me to restrict the complainant to alleging non-compliance with some requirement to be found in the relevant statutes or regulations. If paragraph 15 had been intended to apply to cases of bad faith, surely the restrictive words "on the ground that", etc., would have been left out in both parts. . . .

My Lords, having accepted Mr Wilson's first proposition, . . . I reject his second and third propositions, on the short and simple ground that the words of paragraph 16 are clear, and deprive all courts of any jurisdiction to try the issues raised by paragraphs 1, 2 and 4 of the writ, whereby the appellant undoubtedly seeks to question the validity of the order of August 26, 1948.

Turning first to counsel's second proposition, it does not seem to me inconceivable, though it does seem surprising, that the legislature should have intended to make it impossible for anyone to question in any court the validity of a compulsory purchase order on the ground that it was made in bad faith. It may have been thought that the procedure which has to be followed before such an order is made and confirmed affords sufficient opportunity for allegations of bad faith to be ventilated, and it may have been thought essential, if building schemes were to be carried out, that persons alleging bad faith in the making of an order after the order has been made, should be limited to claims sounding in damages against the persons who, in bad faith, caused or procured the order to be made. The present action started nearly six years after the order now in question was made and confirmed, and illustrates the difficulty which might arise if no such limit were imposed, since houses have already been erected on the land which was the subject of the order. . . .

LORD REID: [held, first, that allegations of misuse of power under the *Wednesbury* principles, whether in good faith or bad faith, fell outside para.15, which only applied to (1) informality of procedure where, for example, some essential step in procedure had been omitted and (2) *ultra vires* in the sense that what was authorised by the order went beyond what was authorised by the enabling Act. . . .]

I turn to paragraph 16. Not only does it prevent recourse to the court after six weeks in cases to which paragraph 15 does apply, but, on the face of it, it prevents any recourse to the court at all in cases to which paragraph 15 does not apply. It uses words which are general and emphatic, and, to my mind, the question is whether this use of general words necessarily leads to the conclusion that the jurisdiction of the court is entirely excluded in all cases of misuse of powers in *mala fide* where those acting in *mala fide* have been careful to see that the procedure was in order and the authority granted by the order was within the scope of the Act under which it was made. A person deliberately acting in bad faith would naturally be careful to do this. In my judgment, paragraph 16 is clearly intended to exclude, and does exclude entirely, all cases of misuse of power in *bona fide*. But does it also exclude the small minority of cases where deliberate dishonesty, corruption or malice is involved? In every class of case that I can think of the courts have always held that general words are not to be read as enabling a deliberate wrongdoer to take advantage of his own dishonesty. Are the principles of statutory construction so rigid that these general words must be so read here? Of course, if there were any other indications in the statute of such an intention beyond the mere generality of the words that would be conclusive: but I can find none.

There are many cases where general words in a statute are given a limited meaning. That is done, not only when there is something in the statute itself which requires it, but also where to give general words their apparent meaning would lead to conflict with some fundamental principle. Where there is ample scope for the words to operate without any such conflict it may very well be that the draftsman did not have in mind and Parliament did not realize that the words were so wide that in some few cases they could operate to subvert a fundamental principle. . . . So, general words by themselves do not bind the Crown, they are limited so as not to conflict with international law, they are commonly read so as to avoid retrospective infringement of rights, and it appears to me that they can equally well be read so as not to deprive the court of jurisdiction where bad faith is involved. . . . I think that there is still room for reason to point out that the general words in this case must be limited so as to accord with the principle, of which Parliament cannot have been ignorant, that a wrongdoer cannot rely on general words to avoid the consequences of his own dishonesty. As I have said, we must take this case on the footing that the appellant might allege deliberate dishonesty of the grossest kind.

It is said that Parliament may have intended that even cases of gross dishonesty should be excluded from redress because otherwise it would be embarrassing to deal with allegations of this kind after a long interval, and, if the case were proved, a local authority and ultimately the ratepayers might be involved in grievous loss. I am not entirely satisfied that the law is powerless to deal justly with such a situation. But, even if that were a possible consequence, I would hesitate to attribute to Parliament the view that considerations of that kind justify hushing up a scandal.

In my judgment this appeal should be allowed.

LORD RADCLIFFE: . . . I should myself read the words of paragraph 15(1), "on the ground that the authorization of a compulsory purchase thereby granted is not empowered to be granted under this Act", as covering any case in which the complainant sought to say that the order in question did not carry the statutory authority which it purported to. In other words, I should regard a challenge to the order on the ground that it had not been made in good faith as within the purview of paragraph 15. After all, the point which concerns the aggrieved person is the same in all cases: an order has been made constituting an ostensible exercise of statutory power and his purpose in resorting to the courts is to show that there is no statutory authority behind the order. I do not see any need to pick and choose among the different reasons which may support the plea that the authorization ostensibly granted does not carry the powers of the Act. But, even if I did not think that an order could be questioned under paragraph 15 on the ground that it had been exercised in bad faith, and I thought, therefore, that the statutory code did not allow for an order being questioned on this ground at all, I should still think that paragraph 16 concluded the matter, and that it did not leave to the courts any surviving jurisdiction.

The appellant's argument for an exception rests on certain general reflections which do not seem to me to make up into any legal principle of construction as applied to an Act of Parliament. It is said that the six weeks which are all the grace that, on any view, paragraph 15 allows an aggrieved person for his taking action, are pitifully inadequate as an allowance of time when bad faith, which may involve concealment or deception, is thought to be present. And indeed they are. Further, it is said that it would be an outrageous thing if a person who by ordinary legal principles would have a right to upset an order affecting him were to be precluded from coming to the courts for his right, either absolutely or after six weeks, when the order is claimed by him to have been tainted by bad faith. And perhaps it is. But these reflections seem to me to be such as must or should have occurred to Parliament when it enacted paragraph 16. They are not reflections which are capable of determining the construction of the Act once it has been passed, unless there is something that one can lay hold of in the context of the Act which justifies the introduction of the exception sought for. Merely to say that Parliament cannot be presumed to have intended to bring about a consequence which many people might think to be unjust is not, in my opinion a principle of construction for this purpose. In point of fact, whatever innocence of view may have been allowable to the lawyers of the eighteenth and nineteenth centuries, the twentieth-century lawyer is entitled to few assumptions in this field. It is not open to him to ignore the fact that the legislature has often shown indifference to the assertion of rights which courts of law have been accustomed to recognize and enforce, and that it has often excluded the authority of courts of law in favour of other preferred tribunals.

At one time the argument as shaped into the form of saying that an order made in bad faith was in law a nullity and that, consequently, all references to compulsory purchase orders in paragraphs 15 and 16 must be treated as references to such orders only as had been made in good faith. But this argument is in reality a play on the meaning of the word nullity. An order, even if not made in good faith, is still an act capable of legal consequences.

It bears no brand of invalidity upon its forehead. Unless the necessary proceedings are taken at law to establish the cause of invalidity and to get it quashed or otherwise upset, it will remain as effective for its ostensible purpose as the most impeccable of orders. And that brings us back to the question that determines this case: Has Parliament allowed the necessary proceedings to be taken?

I am afraid that I have searched in vain for a principle of construction as applied to Acts of Parliament which would enable the appellant to succeed. On the other hand, it is difficult not to recall in the respondents' favour the dictum of Bacon: "*Non est interpretatio, sed divinatio, quae recedit a litera.*"

VISCOUNT SIMONDS and LORD RADCLIFFE were in favour of allowing the appeal to the extent proposed by LORD MORTON. LORD SOMERWELL was in favour of allowing the appeal.

Appeal allowed in part.

Notes

1. Over the two issues as to the scope of para.15 and 16 respectively, the House divided three ways. Lord Morton preferred the narrow interpretation of para.15 and held that para.16 barred all proceedings even in cases of bad faith. Lord Radcliffe held and Viscount Simonds "inclined to the opinion" that para.15 extended to cover cases of misuse of power, but agreed with Lord Morton on the effect of para.16. Lords Reid and Somerwell agreed with Lord Morton as to the effect of para.15 but were prepared to recognise an exception to the effect of para.16 in cases of deliberate dishonesty or fraud. Lord Morton's position that questions of bad faith could be raised *neither* under para.15 *nor* in any other proceedings is difficult to defend. In any event, the courts have subsequently preferred Lord Radcliffe's approach to the interpretation of the grounds of challenge available under a statutory *ultra vires* clause (see above, pp.805–816).

2. See J.S. Hall, (1957) 21 Conv. (N.S.) 455; *Smith v Pywell, The Times*, April 28, 1959.

R. v SECRETARY OF STATE FOR THE ENVIRONMENT
Ex p. OSTLER

[1976] 3 W.L.R. 288; [1977] Q.B. 122; [1976] 3 All E.R. 90; (1976) 75 L.G.R. 45; 120 S.J. 332 (COURT OF APPEAL)

The applicant, a corn merchant with business premises in the market square of Boston, Lincolnshire, applied in December 1975 to the Queen's Bench Divisional Court for leave to apply for an order of certiorari to quash a stopping-up order made under the Highways Act 1959 and a compulsory purchase order made under the Acquisition of Land (Authorisation Procedure) Act 1946. Those orders were made to carry out a road scheme to relieve traffic congestion in the town centre. Both orders had been confirmed by the Secretary of State for the Environment on May 8, 1974. In support of his application he claimed that he had not objected to the original proposals when they were published in 1972 because they appeared not to touch his premises and for that reason had not attended the first public inquiry in September 1973, but that after the orders had been confirmed a supplementary proposed order had been published which would, if carried out, affect his premises; and that he had objected to the supplementary proposals at a further public inquiry in December 1974 but had not been allowed to question the original orders confirmed in May on the ground that they had become final. He alleged that after the supplementary order had been confirmed, it had come to his knowledge that before the 1973 inquiry there had been a secret agreement between an officer of the Department and local wine merchants who were intending to object to the original proposals, guaranteeing that if they were confirmed, the supplementary proposal would be made; that the wine merchants' objections had thereupon been withdrawn; that if he had known of the secret agreement he would have objected before the first proposals were confirmed; and that by reason of his having been deprived of the opportunity to object, the confirmed orders were invalidated by want of natural justice and bad faith verging on fraud.

A preliminary objection was taken on behalf of the Secretary of State that, whatever the facts, any attack on the validity of the confirmed orders was barred in any legal proceedings whatever because the prescribed six-week period under para.2 of Sch.2 to the Act of 1959 and para.15 of Sch.1 to the Act of 1946 had expired; that there was binding House of Lords authority (*Smith v East Elloe RDC*, above, p.907) to that effect on the provisions of the Act of 1946 (which were in terms identical with those of the Act of 1959) and that the application for certiorari should not be permitted to proceed. The Divisional Court, after considering whether speeches in the House of Lords in the *Anisminic* case (above, p.436) had undermined the earlier authority, adjourned the application to go into the merits but later granted the Secretary of State leave to appeal on the preliminary point of law.

LORD DENNING M.R.: . . . Now it is quite clear that if Mr Ostler had come within six weeks, his complaint could and would have been considered by the court . . .

[His Lordship read para.2 of Sch.2 to the 1959 Act.]

That is a familiar clause which appears in many statutes or schedules to them. Although the words appear to restrict the clause to cases of *ultra vires* or non-compliance with regulations, nevertheless the courts have interpreted them so as to cover cases of bad faith. On this point the view of Lord Radcliffe has been accepted (which he expressed in *Smith v East Elloe Rural District Council* [1956] A.C. 736, 769). In addition this court has held that under this clause a person aggrieved—who comes within six weeks—can upset a scheme or order if the Minister has taken into account considerations which he ought not to have done, or has failed to take into account considerations which he ought to have done, or has come to his decision without any evidence to support it, or has made a decision which no reasonable person could make. It was so held in *Ashbridge Investments Ltd. v Minister of Housing and Local Government* [1965] 1 W.L.R. 1320, and the Minister did not dispute it. It has been repeatedly followed in this court ever since and never disputed by any Minister. So it is the accepted interpretation. But the person aggrieved must come within six weeks. That time limit has always been applied . . .

[His Lordship then read para.4.]

So those are the strong words, "shall not . . . be questioned in any legal proceedings whatever . . .".

[His Lordship summarised *Smith v East Elloe RDC*, and the *Anisminic* case.]

Some of their Lordships seem to have thrown doubt on *Smith v East Elloe Rural District Council* [1956] A.C. 736: see what Lord Reid said at [1969] 2 A.C. 147, 170–171. But others thought it could be explained on the ground on which Browne J. explained it. Lord Pearce said, at 201: "I agree with Browne J. that it is not a compelling authority in the present case"; and Lord Wilberforce said, at 208: "After the admirable analysis of the authorities made by Browne J. . . . . no elaborate discussion of authority is needed."

I turn therefore to the judgment of Browne J. His judgment is appended as a note to the case at 223 *et seq*. He put *Smith v East Elloe Rural District Council*, at 224, as one of the "cases in which the inferior tribunal has been guilty of bias, or has acted in bad faith, or has disregarded the principles of natural justice". He said of those cases:

> "It is not necessary to decide it for the purposes of this case, but I am inclined to think that such decisions are not nullities but are good until quashed (*cf.* the decision of the majority of the House of Lords in *Smith v East Elloe Rural District Council* [1956] A.C. 736, that a decision made in bad faith cannot be challenged on the ground that it was made beyond powers and Lord Radcliffe's dissenting speech . . .)."

In these circumstances, I think that *Smith v East Elloe Rural District Council* must still be regarded as good and binding on this court. It is readily to be distinguished from the *Anisminic* case [1969] 2 A.C. 147. The points of difference are these:

First, in the *Anisminic* case the Act ousted the jurisdiction of the court altogether. It precluded the court from entertaining any complaint at any time about the determination. Whereas in the *East Elloe* case the statutory provision has given the court jurisdiction to inquire into complaints so long as the applicant comes within six weeks. The provision is more in the nature of a limitation period than of a complete ouster. That distinction is drawn by Professor Wade, *Administrative Law* (2nd ed., 1967), pp.152–153, and by the late Professor S.A. de Smith in the latest edition of *Halsbury's Laws of England* (4th ed., 1973), vol. 1, para.22, note 14.

Second, in the *Anisminic* case, the House was considering a determination by a truly judicial body, the Foreign Compensation Tribunal, whereas in the *East Elloe* case the House was considering an order which was very much in the nature of an administrative decision. That is a distinction which Lord Reid himself drew in *Ridge v Baldwin* [1964] A.C. 40, 72. There is a great difference between the two. In making a judicial decision, the tribunal considers the rights of the parties without regard to the public interest. But in an administrative decision (such as a compulsory purchase order) the public interest plays an important part. The question is, to what extent are private interests to be subordinated to the public interest.

Third, in the *Anisminic* case, the House had to consider the actual determination of the tribunal, whereas in the *Smith v East Elloe* case the House had to consider the validity of the process by which the decision was reached.

So *Smith v East Elloe Rural District Council* [1956] A.C. 736 must still be regarded as the law in regard to this provision we have to consider here. I would add this: if this order were to be upset for want of good faith or for lack of natural justice, it would not to my mind be a nullity or void from the beginning. It would only be voidable. And as such, if it should be challenged promptly before much has been done under it, as Lord Radcliffe put it forcibly in *Smith v East Elloe Rural District Council* [1956] A.C. 736, 769–770.

[His Lordship read the passage: "But this argument is in reality a play on the meaning of the word nullity . . . Has Parliament allowed the necessary proceedings to be taken?"]

The answer which he gave was "No". That answer binds us in this court today.

Since the *Anisminic* case the court has considered the position in *Routh v Reading Corporation*, December 2, 1970, Bar Library Transcript No. 472 of 1970. Salmon L.J., supported by Karminski and Cairns L.JJ., held that *Smith v East Elloe Rural District Council* was of good authority, even after the *Anisminic* case. In Scotland, too, it has been applied, in *Hamilton v Secretary of State for Scotland*, 1972 S.L.T. 233.

Looking at it broadly, it seems to me that the policy underlying the statute is that when a compulsory purchase order has been made, then if it has been wrongly obtained or made, a person aggrieved should have a remedy. But he must come promptly. He must come within six weeks. If he does so, the court can and will entertain his complaint. But if the six weeks expire without any application being made, the court cannot entertain it afterwards. The reason is because, as soon as that time has elapsed, the authority will take steps to acquire property, demolish it and so forth. The public interest demands that they should be safe in doing so. Take this very case. The inquiry was held in 1973. The orders made early in 1974. Much work has already been done under them. It would be contrary to the public interest that the demolition should be held up or delayed by further evidence or inquiries. I think we are bound by *Smith v East Elloe Rural District Council* [1956] A.C. 736 to hold that Mr Ostler is barred by the statute from now questioning these orders. He ought to be stopped at this moment. I would allow the appeal accordingly.

GOFF L.J.: . . . In my judgment, in *Smith v East Elloe Rural District Council* the majority did definitely decide that those statutory provisions preclude the order from being challenged after the statutory period allowed, then by paragraph 15, and now by paragraph 2, and we are bound by that unless *Anisminic Ltd v Foreign Compensation Commission* [1969] 2 A.C. 147 has to cut across it that we are relieved from the duty of following *Smith v East Elloe Rural District Council* and, indeed, bound not to follow it.

That raises a number of problems. With all respect to Lord Denning M.R. and Professor Wade, I do myself find difficulty in distinguishing *Anisminic* on the ground that in that case there was an absolute prohibition against recourse to the court, whereas in the present case there is a qualified power for a limited period, because the majority in the *Smith* case said either that fraud did not come within paragraph 15, so that, in effect, it was an absolute ouster, or that it made no difference to the construction if it did.

Nevertheless, it seems to me that the *Anisminic* case is distinguishable on two grounds. First, the suggestion made by Lord Pearce [1969] 2 A.C. 147, 201, that *Anisminic* dealt with a judicial decision, and an administrative or executive decision might be different. I think it is. It is true that the Minister has been said to be acting in a quasi judicial capacity, but he is nevertheless conducting an administrative or executive matter, where questions of policy enter into and must influence his decision.

I would refer in support of that to a passage from the speech of Lord Reid in the well-known case of *Ridge v Baldwin* [1964] A.C. 40, 72. I need not read it. It sets out what I have been saying.

Where one is dealing with a matter of that character and where, as Lord Denning M.R. has pointed out, the order is one which must be acted upon promptly, it is, I think, easier for the courts to construe Parliament as meaning exactly what it said—that the matter cannot be questioned in any court, subject to the right given by paragraph 2, where applicable, and where application is made in due time—than where, as in *Anisminic*, one is dealing with a statute setting up a judicial tribunal and defining its powers and the question is whether it has acted within them. I think that is supported by the passage in the speech of Lord Reid in the *Anisminic* case [1969] 2 A.C. 147, 170, where he said:

"But I do not think that it is necessary or even reasonable to construe the word 'determination' as including everything which purports to be a determination but which is in fact no determination at all."

The second ground of distinction is that the ratio in the *Anisminic* case was that the House was dealing simply with a question of jurisdiction, and not a case where the order is made within jurisdiction, but it is attacked on the ground of fraud or *mala fides*. There are, I am fully conscious, difficulties in the way of that distinction, because Lord Somervell of Harrow in *Smith v East Elloe Rural District Council* [1956] A.C. 736, 771, in his dissenting speech, said that fraud does not make the order voidable but a nullity. Lord Reid said the same in the *Anisminic* case [1969] 2 A.C. 147, 170; and at 199 Lord Pearce equated want of natural justice with lack of jurisdiction.

Nevertheless, despite those difficulties, I think there is a real distinction between the case with which the House was dealing in *Anisminic* and the case of *Smith v East Elloe Rural District Council* on that ground, that in the one case the determination was a purported determination only, because the tribunal, however eminent, having misconceived the effect of the statute, acted outside its jurisdiction, and indeed without any jurisdiction at all, whereas here one is dealing with an actual decision made within jurisdiction though sought to be challenged.

It cannot be gain said that some of the speeches in *Anisminic* do appear to cast doubts upon the correctness of the decision in *Smith v East Elloe Rural District Council*, but it certainly was not expressly overruled, nor did any of their lordships, as I see it, say that it was wrong. There are substantial differences, such as Lord Denning M.R. and I have indicated, between the two cases, and it seems to me that *Smith v East Elloe Rural District Council* stands, is binding on this court, and is a decision directly in point. . . .

SHAW L.J. agreed with the reasons given by Lord Denning M.R.

Appeal allowed.

Notes
1. The House of Lords refused leave to appeal: [1977] 1 W.L.R. 258.
2. For discussions of the relationship between *Smith v East Elloe RDC* and the *Anisminic* case written before *Ostler* was decided, see K. Davies, (1971) 35 Conv. (N.S.) 316; J.E. Trice, [1973] J.P.L. 227; E. Young, [1973] J.P.L. 221; J. Alder, (1975) 38 M.L.R. 274.
3. For case notes on *Ostler*, see H.W.R. W[ade], (1977) 93 L.Q.R. 8; C.A. Whomersley, [1977] C.L.J. 4; J. Alder, [1976] J.P.L. 270; C. Harlow, [1976] P.L. 304. For a more extended discussion see the debate between Alder and Gravells: J.E. Alder, (1975) 38 M.L.R. 274 and (1980) 43 M.L.R. 670; N.P. Gravells, (1978) 41 M.L.R. 383 and (1980) 43 M.L.R. 173. Alder argues that *Anisminic* and *Smith v East Elloe RDC* can be reconciled by a process of conceptual reasoning; Gravells that the

Anisminic principle, "formulated in an entirely different factual context," could have no relevance to the treatment of time-limit clauses. See also L.H. Leigh, "Time Limit Clauses and Jurisdictional Error" [1980] P.L. 34.

4. *Anisminic* is the leading example of a case where a "shall not be questioned clause" has been held not to prevent judicial review of an *ultra vires* decision. Others include *Att.-Gen. v Ryan* [1980] A.C. 718, where the Privy Council held that a minister's refusal of an application for citizenship without a fair hearing could be challenged notwithstanding a provision that such a decision "shall not be subject to appeal or review in any court" (followed in *R. v Secretary of State for the Home Department Ex p. Mohammed Al Fayed* [1998] W.L.R. 763, *cf. South East Asia Fire Bricks Sdn Bhd v Non-Metallic Mineral Products Manufacturing Employees Union* [1981] A.C. 363, where the company sought certiorari to quash a decision of the Malaysian Industrial Court that favoured the union for an error of law on the face of the record. The Privy Council held that this remedy was barred by a provision that read:

"Subject to this Act, an award of the Court shall be final and conclusive, and no award shall be challenged, appealed against, reviewed, quashed or called in question in any court of law".

Lord Fraser of Tullybelton stated that this result was achieved not by the finality clause (following *Ex p. Gilmore*, above, p.903), but by the provision that the award should not be "quashed" either alone or in conjunction with the words "shall not be questioned in any court of law". The error alleged here was an error of law within jurisdiction, the Privy Council rejecting the view that all errors of law went to jurisdiction (see further *Page* above, pp.450 *et seq.*). (If that view were to be accepted, little if any effect is left to a "shall not be questioned clause":

". . . [I]f every error is now to be jurisdictional, ouster clauses will have no sphere of operation at all, and the judicial attitude will be exposed as one of naked disobedience to Parliament" (H.W.R. W[ade] (1979) 95 L.Q.R. 163, 166).)

5. *Ex p. Ostler* was applied by Pill J. in *R. v Secretary of State for the Environment Ex p. Kent* (1988) 57 P. & C.R. 431, where the applicant applied on February 11, 1988, for judicial review of the decision of a planning inspector dated November 12, 1987, allowing an appeal against a refusal of planning permission. His Lordship rejected an argument to the effect that the six-week time-limit did not apply as the Secretary of State had not had jurisdiction to entertain the appeal under s.245 of the Town and Country Planning Act 1971 as the local authority's procedure of consultation had been flawed. An appeal to the Court of Appeal was dismissed: [1990] J.P.L. 124. Here, the applicant did not find out until after the six-week period that an application for planning permission had been made in respect of land near his home or had subsequently gone on appeal to the Secretary of State.

Ex p. Ostler was also applied in *Khan v Newport BC* [1991] C.O.D. 157, in respect of a tree preservation order. Staughton L.J. commented that it was not at first sight obvious why any short time limits should be necessary in the case of such an order, as opposed to a compulsory purchase order as in *Ex p. Ostler*. Then, in *R. v Cornwall CC Ex p. Huntingdon* [1992] 3 All E.R. 566, the Divisional Court applied *Ex p. Ostler* in rejecting an application for judicial review of an order under the Wildlife and Countryside Act 1981, s.53(2)(b). The court rejected an argument that the order here was "fundamentally invalid" whereas the orders in *Smith v East Elloe RDC* and *Ex p. Ostler* were not; Mann L.J. expressed the view that there were no "degrees of invalidity". *Ex p. Ostler* was also applied by Pill J. in *R. v Secretary of State for the Environment, Ex p. Upton Brickworks Ltd* [1992] C.O.D. 31 (order under the Wildlife and Countryside Act 1981, s.29); by McCullough J. in *R. v Devon CC Ex p. Isaac* [1992] C.O.D. 371 (modification order relating to a by-way under the 1981 Act, ss.53, 54); by Roch J. in *R. v Camden LBC Ex p. Woolf* [1992] C.O.D. 456 (traffic management order under the Road Traffic Regulation Act 1984, ss.43, 45). The respective decisions of the Divisional Court and McCullough J. were upheld by the Court of Appeal in *R. v Cornwall CC Ex p. Huntingdon; R. v Devon CC Ex p. Isaac* [1994] 1 All E.R. 694 (challenge based on procedural defects barred by ouster clause), followed by Hooper J. in *R. (on the application of Deutsch) v Hackney LBC* [2003] EWHC 2692 (challenge to designation order under Road Traffic Regulation Act 1984, s.45, signed by officer, on the ground that he did not have delegated authority, barred by ouster clause).

6. Lord Denning writing extra-judicially recanted most of his arguments in *Ex p. Ostler*, accepting that a breach of natural justice or bad faith renders a decision a nullity, and expressing the view that the decisions should rest simply on the last paragraph of his judgment (*The Discipline of Law* (1979), pp.108–109).

7. The statutory *ultra vires* clauses of the kind discussed in *Smith v East Elloe RDC* and *Ostler* specify the precise acts, orders or decisions to which they apply. Judicial review remains available in respect of other Acts, etc. that may arise in area in question. For example, where the exclusivity rule applies in respect of the Secretary of State's appeal against a determination by a local authority, it will not prevent the basis for an unappealed determination to be challenged in subsequent proceedings: *Earthline Ltd v Secretary of State for Transport, Local Government and the Regions* [2002] EWCA Civ 1599.

8. Part 4 of the Regulation of Investigatory Powers Act 2000 establishes a number of Commissioners to keep under review the exercise and performance of specified intrusive investigatory powers, including the Interception of Communications Commissioner and the Intelligence Services Commissioner, and conferred additional functions on the Chief Surveillance Commissioner appointed under the Police Act 1997 (see ss.56–64). It also establishes a Tribunal for hearing complaints and other proceedings relating to the 2000 Act which, *inter alia*, replaces specific Tribunals established under the Security Service Act 1989, s.5 (complaints about the Security Service) and the Intelligence Services Act 1994, s.9 (complaints about the Secret Intelligence Service and GCHQ). Section 67(8) of the 2000 Act provides:

"Except to such extent as the Secretary of State may by order otherwise provide, determinations, awards and other decisions of the Tribunal (including decisions as to whether they have jurisdiction) shall not be subject to appeal or be liable to be questioned in any court".

By virtue of s.67(9) (in force from a day to be appointed) there must, however, be an order providing for an appeal to a court against any exercise by the Tribunal of its jurisdiction under s.65(2)(c) and (d) (references by any person that he has suffered detriment as a consequence of any prohibition or restriction, by virtue of s.17, on his relying on any matter in civil proceedings; and other proceedings allocated by order).

A similarly worded exclusion clause in s.5(4) of the 1989 Act was held in *R. v Security Service Tribunal Ex p. Clarke*, unreported, May 20, 1998, to be an "insuperable bar" to C's application for leave to move for judicial review of the Tribunal's decision to reject a complaint by her that the Service had infringed "every single one of her human rights". Tribunal members must hold or have held high judicial office, and the Tribunal applies judicial review principles in deciding whether the required procedures have been followed. Should the clause be construed as an "insuperable bar" even where there is cogent evidence of fraud?

Another similarly worded clause, s.91(10) of the Police Act 1997, which applied to the decisions of a surveillance commissioner to authorise surveillance have been held not to prevent an inquiry at trial pursuant to s.78 of the Police and Criminal Evidence Act 1978 as to whether there had been any unfairness to justify exclusion of evidence obtained thereby (*R. v Templar* [2003] EWCA Crim 3186). Such an issue is clearly distinct from any issue as to the validity of the commissioner's decision as such.

9. Section 29(3) of the Supreme Court Act 1981 provides for judicial review of the Crown Court except "in matters relating to trial on indictment", where there are in fact well-established rights of appeal. The interpretation of the test for exclusion has generated a large body of case law. See *Smalley, Re* [1985] A.C. 622; *Sampson, Re* [1987] 1 W.L.R. 194; *R. v Manchester Crown Court Ex p. DPP* [1993] 1 W.L.R. 1524; *Ashton, Re* [1994] 1 A.C. 9. It has been held that the bar does not apply where an order is made without jurisdiction (*R. v Maidstone Crown Court Ex p. Harrow LBC* [2000] Q.B. 719).

10. Clauses that exclude judicial review either altogether, or where a right of appeal is provided, may need to be justified by reference to Art.6 ECHR (above, p.384). The key question will be whether there has in the determination of civil rights and obligations been a fair and public hearing by an independent and impartial tribunal: this may give rise to a right of effective access to a court (*Golder v UK* (1975) 1 E.H.R.R. 524; *Airey v Ireland* (1979) 2 E.H.R.R. 305). The six-week time-limit on appeals under s.288 of the Town and Country Planning Act 1990 has been held not to constitute a disproportionate restriction on the right of access (*Matthews v Secretary of State for the Environment, Transport and the Regions* [2001] EWHC Admin 815 (*cf. Lam v UK* (App.No. 41671/98), below p.1018)). The Tribunal referred to in n.8 would itself seem to be "independent and impartial" for these purposes.

11. An attempt by the Government to secure the passage in the Asylum and Immigration (Treatment of claimants etc) Bill 2004 of an amendment to the Nationality, Immigration and Asylum Act 2002 that would have severely restricted the role of judicial review in immigration and asylum matters aroused unprecedented opposition. The Bill proposed the replacement of the existing Immigration Adjudicators and Immigration Appeal Tribunal by a single Asylum and Immigration Tribunal. The existing adjudicators and IAT judges would transfer to the new AIT, whose president would be a High Court judge. The President of the AIT could seek guidance on questions of law from the Court of Appeal or the Court of Session, with no further appeal to the House of Lords. The proposed s.108A of the 2002 Act provided:

108A Exclusivity and finality of Tribunal's jurisdiction
   (1) No court shave have any supervisory or other jurisdiction (whether statutory or inherent) in relation to the Tribunal.
   (2) No court may entertain proceeding for questioning (whether by way of appeal or otherwise)—
       (a) any determination, decision or other action of the Tribunal (including a decision about jurisdiction and a decision under section 105 A),
       (b) any action of the President or a Deputy President of the Tribunal that relates one or more specified cases,
       (c) any decision in respect of which a person has or had right of appeal to the Tribunal under—
           (i) section 82, 83 or 109 of this Act, or
           (ii) section 40A of the British Nationality Act 1981 (c.61),
       (d) any matter which the Tribunal—
           (i) was obliged to determine in accordance with section 86 of this Act, or
           (ii) would have been obliged to determine in accordance with that section had right of appeal mentioned in paragraph (c) been exercised, or
       (e) a decision to remove a person from the United Kingdom or to deport a person if –
           (i) the removal or deportation is in consequence of an immigration decision, an
           (ii) the person was notified, in accordance with regulations under section 105, of a right to appeal under section 82(1) against the immigration decisio (whether or not he exercised the right).

(3) Subsections (1) and (2)—
    (a) prevent a court, in particular, from entertaining proceeding to determine whether a purported determination, decision or action of the Tribunal was nullity by reason of—
        (i) lack of jurisdiction,
        (ii) irregularity,
        (iii) error of law,
        (iv) breach of natural justice, or
        (v) any other matter, but
    (b) do not prevent a court from—
        (i) reviewing a decision to issue a certificate under section 94 or 96 of this Act of under Schedule 3 to the Asylum and immigration (Treatment of Claimants etc.) Act 2004 (removal to safe country),
        (ii) entertaining proceeding to determine whether the Tribunal has acted in a way which is incompatible with a person's rights under Article 5 of the Human Rights Convention (liberty and security), or
        (iii) considering whether a member of the Tribunal has acted in bad faith.
(4) court may consider whether a member of the Tribunal has acted in bad faith, in reliance on subsection (3)(b)(iii), only if satisfied that significant evidence has beer adduced of –
    (a) dishonesty,
    (b) corruption, or
    (c) bias.
(5) Section 7(1) of the Human Rights Act 1998 (c. 42) (claim that public authority had infringed Convention right) is subject to subsections (1) to (3) above.
(6) Nothing in this section shall prevent an appeal under section 2, 2B or 7 of the Special Immigration Appeals Commission Act 1997 (c. 68) (appeals to and from Commission).
(7) In this section 'action' includes failure to act.

The purpose of this clause was to limit access to judicial review in view of the large number and proportion of claims for judicial review that arise out of immigration and asylum cases. Very strong criticism was expressed by Lord Woolf C.J. in the Squire Centenary Lecture, [2004] C.L.J. 317, the Bar Council and many others. The clause, although passed by the House of Commons, was withdrawn in the House of Lords. (See A. Le Sueur, [2004] P.L. 225; *Wade and Forsyth*, pp.1002–1003; Lord Lester Q.C., [2004] J.R. 95). There were suggestions that the judges might in defiance of parliamentary sovereignty have denied effectiveness to the clause (Lester, *op.cit.*). It should be noted that, unlike the Tribunal discussed in n.8 which comprises senior judges, most of the judicial members of the AIT are the equivalent of District or Circuit judges.

The arrangements that ultimately emerged in the 2004 Act are as follows. The new s.103A of the 2002 Act (inserted by the 2004 Act, s.26) provides that a party to an appeal under ss.82 (general) or 83 (asylum claims) of the 2002 Act may apply to the High Court, on the grounds that the AIT made an error of law, for an order requiring it to reconsider its decision on the appeal (s.103A(1)). "Decision" here does not include a procedural, ancillary on preliminary decision or a decision following remittal under ss.103B, 103C or 103E (s.103A(7)). The High Court may make such an order "only if it thinks that the Tribunal may have made an error of law" and "only once in relation to an appeal" (s.103A(2)). The application must be brought by the appellant within five days beginning with the day on which he is treated as receiving notice of the AIT's decision if he is in the United Kingdom; 28 days if he is outside the United Kingdom; and an application by another party must be brought within five days (s.103A(3)). Rules of court may provide for days to be disregarded, and the court may permit an application to be made outside the period where it thinks that it could not reasonably practicably have been made within that period (s.103A(4)). An application is to be determined by reference only to written submissions of the applicant and, where rules of court permit, other written submissions (s.103A(5)). A decision of the High Court on an application "shall be final" (s.103A(6)). The section does not apply to a decision of the AIT where its jurisdiction is exercised by three or more legally qualified members (s.103A(8)).

Where an appeal to the AIT has been reconsidered, a party to the appeal may bring a further appeal on a point of law to the Court of Appeal, but only with the permission of the AIT or, if the AIT refuses permission, the Court of Appeal. On such an appeal the court may, *inter alia* affirm the AIT's decision, make any decision the AIT could have made or remit the case to the AIT (s.103B). On an application under s.103A, the High Court, if it thinks the appeal raises a question of law of such importance that it should be decided by the Court of Appeal, may refer that appeal to that court which then may exercise the same powers as on an appeal under s.103B, or restore the application to the High Court (s.103C). Where the AIT comprises three or more legally qualified members an appeal in respect of a decision (other than a procedural, ancillary or procedural decision or one on remittal under ss.103B or 103C) lies on a similar basis as under s.103B to the Court of Appeal (s.103E). These arrangements are described in the Explanatory Note (para.6) as providing for "limited onward review on appeal". Judicial review is not excluded altogether but available within narrower limits as to process and time. In assessing the significance of the change it will be necessary to balance the extent to which injustices are not identified through lack of time and an oral hearing against the time saved in handling claims.

Questions

1. Should *Smith v East Elloe RDC* have been regarded or overruled by *Anisminic* or can it be distinguished as suggested by *Ostler*?

2. Is the distinction made in *Ostler* between "administrative" decisions (*East Elloe*) and "judicial ones" (*Anisminic*) supportable?

3. Why should a decision made on the basis of irrelevant considerations of personal animosity be protected because it may also have been influenced by policy considerations and can be called an "administrative" decision?

4. Is it possible to draft an exclusion clause that effectively excludes the jurisdiction of the courts to review a decision of an administrative agency in *all* circumstances? Consider the provisions summarised and set out in n.11, above

REMEDIES[1]

(A) INTRODUCTION

The position as to remedies in administrative law was materially affected by the introduction of the "application for judicial review", with effect from January 11, 1978, by a revised version of RSC, Ord.53. Prior to that date, the position was as follows.

There was a series of prerogative remedies available against public authorities: *Certiorari* lay to quash a decision that was *ultra vires* or in breach of natural justice, that was affected by an error of law that was apparent on the face of the record or that was procured by fraud. *Prohibition* lay to prevent action or continuing action in excess of jurisdiction or contrary to natural justice. *Mandamus* lay to compel performance of a public duty. Certiorari and prohibition traditionally lay:

"wherever any body of persons having legal authority to determine questions affecting the rights of subjects, and having the duty to act judicially, act in excess of their legal authority . . ." (*per* Atkin L.J. in *R. v Electricity Commissioners Ex p. London Electricity Joint Committee Co.* [1924] 1 K.B. 411 at 415).

Mandamus was never limited to judicial or quasi-judicial functions. The remedies originally took the form of prerogative writs but, by virtue of the Administration of Justice (Miscellaneous Provisions) Act 1938, they had become prerogative orders.

Apart from these public law remedies, from the 1950s in particular, increasing use had been made against public authorities of the private law remedies of *injunction* and *declaration*. A prohibitory injunction might be granted to restrain the performance of *ultra vires* acts. A mandatory injunction might (rarely) be available to compel performance of a public duty. A declaration would simply declare authoritatively the law on a disputed point.

Other remedies that might be available when appropriate included *damages*, where a public authority was held liable in contract or tort, and the prerogative writ of *habeas corpus*, available to test the legality of the actions of the respondent (whether or not a public authority) in holding a person in detention.

Applications for certiorari, prohibition and mandamus were governed by the unreformed RSC, Ord.53 and were heard in the Divisional Court of the Queen's Bench Division, usually by a court presided over by the Lord Chief Justice. Proceedings for a declaration or injunction were ordinary civil proceedings in the High Court, and could be commenced in the Queen's Bench Division or the Chancery Division, in practice according to the preference of counsel for the plaintiff.

The remedies were discretionary, and there were particular rules governing not only the kinds of decisions or acts that could be reached by each remedy, but also such matters as *locus standi*, whether interlocutory relief was available and the grounds on which the remedy could be refused. Some of these rules were by no means settled.

---

[1] See *de Smith, Woolf and Jowell*, Chs 2, 3, 14–20; *Wade and Forsyth*, Chs 16–19; *Craig*, Chs 13–16; *Lewis*, Chs 1–11; M. Supperstone Q.C. and L. Knapman, *Administrative Court Practice: Judicial Review* (2002); J. Manning, *Judicial Review: A Practitioner's Guide* (2nd ed., 2004)

The Law Commission in its Report on Remedies in Administrative Law (Cmnd.6407, 1976, Law Com. No.73) highlighted the defects in the existing arrangements. For example, declarations were available in respect of a wide range of acts and omissions, and proceedings for a declaration could be initiated without leave, with no fixed limit of time and with the advantages of full discovery. However, declarations did not order or prohibit any action and were not available in a provisional form, and there was considerable doubt as to the requirements of standing. Applications for a prerogative order could be made by a wide range of applicants, but leave was necessary, discovery was not in practice available and there was a six-month time-limit for applications for certiorari. A claim for damages or injunction could be joined with an application for a declaration but not an application for a prerogative order. The revised version of RSC, Ord.53 introduced by SI 1977/1958 was largely based on this report, although there was no provision as recommended by the Law Commission for an interim declaration. Express statutory authority for the application for judicial review was subsequently enshrined in the Supreme Court Act 1981, s.31 (see below, p.923).

Under the new Ord.53, any of the remedies summarised above (except *habeas corpus*, which was and continues to be governed by RSC, Ord.52), could be granted on an application for judicial review. This indeed the exclusive procedure by which one of the prerogative orders may be obtained. An injunction or declaration could still be obtained against a public authority in ordinary proceedings, but the House of Lords in *O'Reilly v Mackman* (below, p.976) held that in certain circumstances it will be an abuse of process to attempt to secure an injunction or declaration against a public authority other than on an application for judicial review.

Proposals for further reforms of judicial review procedure were contained in the Law Commission's Report on *Administrative Law: Judicial Review and Statutory Appeals* (Law Com. No.226, 1994), Lord Woolf's Report, *Access to Justice: Final Report* (1996) and the Bowman Report (Sir Jeffery Bowman, *Review of the Crown Office List* (March 2000)). Reforms were introduced as part of the implementation of Lord Woolf's proposals for the fundamental recasting of the whole of civil procedure and the Bowman Report. From the coming into effect of the new Civil Procedure Rules on April 26, 1999, RSC, Ord.53 was included (with some small changes) in Sch.1 to the Rules. From October 2, 2000, Ord.53 was replaced by the new CPR Pt 54, which was extended subsequently to cover Statutory Review under the Nationality, Immigration and Asylum Act 2002. The new Pt 54 introduced some substantial changes. Furthermore, the changes introduced in producing what is now the unified procedure for civil cases in both the County Court and the High Court, have reduced significantly the differences between that and the procedure for public law cases under Pt 54. This has largely addressed the practical difficulties caused by the unfortunate decision of the House of Lords in *O'Reilly v Mackman* (below, p.976).

Among the Bowman Report recommendations was that an Administrative Court should be formally established as a specialist court within the Queen's Bench Division, replacing the Crown Office List, the Crown Office becoming the Administrative Court Office. This was implemented by the *Practice Direction (Admin Ct: Review of the Crown Office List)* [2000] 1 W.L.R. 1654. The Administrative Court is presided over by the Lord Chief Justice, the head of the Queen's Bench Division, but a lead judge is also appointed with overall responsibility for the Court's work. The court produces an Annual Report. A number of High Court and court of Appeal judges (40 as at April 2005) are nominated to hear judicial review applications.

SUPREME COURT ACT 1981

29. [Mandatory, prohibiting and quashing orders]

[(1) The orders of mandamus, prohibition and certiorari shall be known instead as mandatory, prohibiting and quashing orders respectively.

(1A) The High Court shall have jurisdiction to make mandatory, prohibiting and quashing orders in those classes of case in which, immediately before 1st May 2004, it had jurisdiction to make orders of mandamus, prohibition and certiorari respectively.]

(2) Every such order shall be final, subject to any right of appeal therefrom.

(3) In relation to the jurisdiction of the Crown Court, other than its jurisdiction in matters relating to trial on indictment, the High Court shall have all such jurisdiction to make [mandatory, prohibiting or quashing orders] as the High Court possesses in relation to the jurisdiction of an inferior court.

[(3A) The High Court shall have no jurisdiction to make [mandatory, prohibiting or quashing orders] in relation to the jurisdiction of a court-martial in matters relating to—

(a) trial by court-martial for an offence, or
(b) appeals from a Standing Civilian Court;

and in this subsection "court-martial" means a court-martial under the Army Act 1955, the Air Force Act 1955 or the Naval Discipline Act 1957.]

[(4) The power of the High Court under any enactment to require justices of the peace or a judge or officer of a county court to do any act relating to the duties of their respective offices, or to require a magistrates' court to state a case for the opinion of the High Court, in any case where the High Court formerly had by virtue of any enactment jurisdiction to make a rule absolute, or an order, for any of those purposes, shall be exercisable by [mandatory order].

[(5) In any statutory provision—

(a) references to mandamus or to a writ or order of mandamus shall be read as references to a mandatory order;
(b) references to prohibition or to a writ or order of prohibition shall be read as references to a prohibiting order;
(c) references to certiorari or to a writ or order of certiorari shall be read as references to a quashing order; and
(d) references to the issue or award of a writ of mandamus, prohibition or certiorari shall be read as references to the making of the corresponding mandatory, prohibiting or quashing order.]

[(6) In subsection (3) the reference to the Crown Court's jurisdiction in matters relating to trial on indictment does not include its jurisdiction relating to orders under section 17 of the Access to Justice Act 1999.]

30. Injunctions to restrain persons from acting in offices in which they are not entitled to act

(1) Where a person not entitled to do so acts in an office to which this section applies, the High Court may—

(a) grant an injunction restraining him from so acting; and
(b) if the case so requires, declare the office to be vacant.

(2) This section applies to any substantive office of a public nature and permanent character which is held under the Crown or which has been created by any statutory provision or royal charter.

31. Application for judicial review

(1) An application to the High Court for one or more of the following forms of relief, namely—

[(a) a mandatory, prohibiting or quashing order;]
 (b) a declaration or injunction under subsection (2); or
 (c) an injunction under section 30 restraining a person not entitled to do so from acting in an office to which that section applies,

shall be made in accordance with rules of court by a procedure to be known as an application for judicial review.

(2) A declaration may be made or an injunction granted under this subsection in any case where an application for judicial review, seeking that relief, has been made and the High Court considers that, having regard to—

(a) the nature of the matters in respect of which relief may be granted by [mandatory, prohibiting or quashing orders];
(b) the nature of the persons and bodies against whom relief may be granted by such orders; and
(c) all the circumstances of the case,

it would be just and convenient for the declaration to be made or of the injunction to be granted, as the case may be.

(3) No application for judicial review shall be made unless the leave of the High Court has been obtained in accordance with rules of court; and the court shall not grant leave to make such an application unless it considers that the applicant has a sufficient interest in the matter to which the application relates.

[(4) On an application for judicial review the High Court may award to the applicant damages, restitution or the recovery of a sum due if—

(a) the application includes a claim for such an award arising from any matter to which the application relates; and
(b) the court is satisfied that such an award would have been made if the claim had been made in an action begun by the applicant at the time of making the application.]

(5) If, on an application for judicial review seeking [a quashing order], the High Court quashes the decision to which the application relates, the High Court may remit the matter to the court, tribunal or authority concerned, with a direction to reconsider it and reach a decision in accordance with the findings of the High Court.

(6) Where the High Court considers that there has been undue delay in making an application for judicial review, the court may refuse to grant—

(a) leave for the making of the application; or
(b) any relief sought on the application,

if it considers that the granting of the relief sought would be likely to cause substantial hardship to, or substantially prejudice the rights of, any person or would be detrimental to good administration.

(7) Subsection (6) is without prejudice to any enactment or rule of court which has the effect of limiting the time within which an application for judicial review may be made.

Notes

1. The words in square brackets in ss.29 and 31 were substituted by SI 2004/1033, with effect from May 1, 2004, except s.29(3A) (inserted by the Armed Forces Act 2001, s.23(1), (3)) and s.29(6) (inserted by the Access to Justice Act 1999, Sch.4, paras 21, 23). The 2004 amendments formally changed the names of the prerogative orders and introduced the possibility of claiming restitution or recovery of a sum due.

2. Section 31 sets out in primary legislation the main features of the application for judicial review, introduced previously by statutory instrument. It set at rest some concerns that aspects of the instrument in question (Rules of the Supreme Court (Amendment No.3) 1977 (SI 1977/1955) might have been *ultra vires* in so far as they introduced substantive, and not merely procedural changes.

3. The prerogative writ of *habeas corpus ad subjiciendum*, which may be sought to challenge the legality of detention, is governed by a separate procedure (CPR, Sch.1, RSC, Ord.54 and Practice Direction to Ord.54, Sch.1). Such a challenge may also be made through judicial review proceedings. The scope of review on habeas corpus should in principle be the same as for judicial review, although there have been suggestions in the case law that habeas corpus is only available where there is jurisdictional error in the narrow sense (see *Lewis*, pp.447–449). There is no discretion to refuse the remedy if grounds are made out. An attempt to relitigate a matter considered in judicial review proceedings through an application for habeas corpus may be held to be an abuse of process (*R. (on the application of Sheikh) v Secretary of State for the Home Department* [2001] Imm. A.R. 219). The Law Commission did not accept suggestions that habeas corpus should be abolished as it was no longer necessary to retain this ancient procedure (Law Com. No.226, para.11.4). See further R.J. Sharpe, *The Law of Habeas Corpus* (2nd ed., 1989); *Lewis*, Ch.12; Simon Brown L.J., [2000] P.L. 31.

If both habeas corpus and judicial review proceedings are brought, every effort should be made to harmonise how they are dealt with (*per* Lord Woolf M.R. in *R. v Barking, Havering and Brentwood Community Healthcare NHS Trust* [1999] 1 F.L.R. 106 at 117). The Lord Chancellor proposed that habeas corpus should be available as a remedy both by judicial review and in its own right (Consultation Paper, *The Administrative Court: Proposed changes to primary legislation following Sir Jeffery Bowman's Review of the Crown Office List* (July 2001), paras 1–10). This has not, however, been implemented.

CIVIL PROCEDURE RULES

PART 1: OVERRIDING OBJECTIVE

The overriding objective

1.1 (1) These Rules are a new procedural code with the overriding objective of enabling the court to deal with cases justly.
(2) Dealing with a case justly includes, so far as is practicable—

(a) ensuring that the parties are on an equal footing;
(b) saving expense;
(c) dealing with the case in ways which are proportionate—
    (i) to the amount of money involved;
    (ii) to the importance of the case;
    (iii) to the complexity of the issues; and
    (iv) to the financial position of each party;
(d) ensuring that it is dealt with expeditiously and fairly; and
(e) allotting to it an appropriate share of the court's resources, while taking into account the need to allot resources to other cases.

Application by the court of the overriding objective

1.2 The court must seek to give effect to the overriding objective when it—

(a) exercises any power given to it by the Rules; or
(b) interprets any rule.

Duty of the parties

1.3 The parties are required to help the court to further the overriding objective.

Court's duty to manage cases

1.4 (1) The court must further the overriding objective by actively managing cases.
(2) Active case management includes—

(a) encouraging the parties to co-operate with each other in the conduct of the proceedings;
(b) identifying the issues at an early stage;
(c) deciding promptly which issues need full investigation and trial and accordingly disposing summarily of the others;
(d) deciding the order in which issues are to be resolved;
(e) encouraging the parties to use an alternative dispute resolution (GL) procedure if the court considers that appropriate and facilitating the use of such procedure;
(f) helping the parties to settle the whole or part of the case;
(g) fixing timetables or otherwise controlling the progress of the case;

(h) considering whether the likely benefits of taking a particular step justify the cost of taking it;
(i) dealing with as many aspects of the case as it can on the same occasion;
(j) dealing with the case without the parties needing to attend at court;
(k) making use of technology; and
(l) giving directions to ensure that the trial of a case proceeds quickly and efficiently.

PART 54: JUDICIAL REVIEW AND STATUTORY REVIEW

I JUDICIAL REVIEW

Scope and interpretation

54.1 (1) [This Section of this Part][2] contains rules about judicial review.
(2) In this Section—

(a) a 'claim for judicial review' means a claim to review the lawfulness of—
    (i) an enactment; or
    (ii) a decision, action or failure to act in relation to the exercise of a public function.
(b) [revoked]
(c) [revoked]
(d) [revoked][3]
(e) "the judicial review procedure" means the Part 8 procedure as modified by [this Section];
(f) "interested party" means any person (other than the claimant and defendant) who is directly affected by the claim; and
(g) "court" means the High Court, unless otherwise stated.

(Rule 8.1(6)(b) provides that a rule or practice direction may, in relation to a specified type of proceedings, disapply or modify any of the rules set out in Part 8 as they apply to those proceedings)

When this [Section] must be used

54.2 The judicial review procedure must be used in a claim for judicial review where the claimant is seeking—

(a) a mandatory order;
(b) a prohibiting order;
(c) a quashing order; or
(d) an injunction under section 30 of the Supreme Court Act 1981 (restraining a person from acting in any office in which he is not entitled to act).

---

[2] [ed.] substituted by SI 2003/264, r.5.
[3] [ed.] revoked by SI 2003/3361, r.12.

When this [Section] may be used

54.3 (1) The judicial review procedure may be used in a claim for judicial review where the claimant is seeking—

(a) a declaration; or
(b) an injunction[4].

(Section 31(2) of the Supreme Court Act 1981 sets out the circumstances in which the court may grant a declaration or injunction in a claim for judicial review)

(Where the claimant is seeking a declaration or injunction in addition to one of the remedies listed in rule 54.2, the judicial review procedure must be used)

(2) A claim for judicial review may include a claim for damages, [restitution or the recovery of a sum due] but may not seek [such a remedy] alone.

(Section 31(4) of the Supreme Court Act sets out the circumstances in which the court may award damages, [restitution or the recovery of a sum due] on[5] a claim for judicial review)

Permission required

54.4 The court's permission to proceed is required in a claim for judicial review whether started under this [Section] or transferred to the Administrative Court.

Time limit for filing claim form

54.5 (1) The claim form must be filed—

(a) promptly; and
(b) in any event not later than 3 months after the grounds to make the claim first arose.

(2) The time limit in this rule may not be extended by agreement between the parties.

(3) This rule does not apply when any other enactment specifies a shorter time limit for making the claim for judicial review.

Claim form

54.6 (1) In addition to the matters set out in rule 8.2 (contents of the claim form) the claimant must also state—

(a) the name and address of any person he considers to be an interested party;
(b) that he is requesting permission to proceed with a claim for judicial review; and
(c) any remedy (including any interim remedy) he is claiming.

(Part 25 sets out how to apply for an interim remedy)

---

[4] [ed.] "A court order prohibiting a person from doing something or requiring a person to do something" (Glossary).
[5] [ed.] words in square brackets substituted by SI 2003/3361, r.13

(2) The claim form must be accompanied by the documents required by the relevant practice direction.

Service of claim form

54.7 The claim form must be served on—

(a) the defendant; and
(b) unless the court otherwise directs, any person the claimant considers to be an interested party,

within 7 days after the date of issue.

Acknowledgment of service

54.8 (1) Any person served with the claim form who wishes to take part in the judicial review must file an acknowledgment of service in the relevant practice form in accordance with the following provisions of this rule.
(2) Any acknowledgment of service must be—

(a) filed not more than 21 days after service of the claim form; and
(b) served on—
    (i) the claimant; and
    (ii) subject to any direction under rule 54.7(b), any other person named in the claim form,
as soon as practicable and, in any event, not later than 7 days after it is filed.
(3) The time limits under this rule may not be extended by agreement between the parties.
(4) The acknowledgment of service—

(a) must—
    (i) where the person filing it intends to contest the claim, set out a summary of his grounds for doing so; and
    (ii) state the name and address of any person the person filing it considers to be an interested party; and
(b) may include or be accompanied by an application for directions.
(5) Rule 10.3(2) does not apply.

Failure to file acknowledgment of service

54.9 (1) Where a person served with the claim form has failed to file an acknowledgment of service in accordance with rule 54.8, he—

(a) may not take part in a hearing to decide whether permission should be given unless the court allows him to do so; but
(b) provided he complies with rule 54.14 or any other direction of the court regarding the filing and service of—
    (i) detailed grounds for contesting the claim or supporting it on additional grounds; and
    (ii) any written evidence,
may take part in the hearing of the judicial review.

(2) Where that person takes part in the hearing of the judicial review, the court may take his failure to file an acknowledgment of service into account when deciding what order to make about costs.

(3) Rule 8.4 does not apply.

Permission given

54.10 (1) Where permission to proceed is given the court may also give directions.

(2) Directions under paragraph (1) may include a stay[6] of proceedings to which the claim relates.

(Rule 3.7 provides a sanction for the non-payment of the fee payable when permission to proceed has been given)

Service of order giving or refusing permission

54.11 The court will serve—

(a) the order giving or refusing permission; and
(b) any directions,
on—
      (i) the claimant;
      (ii) the defendant; and
      (iii) any other person who filed an acknowledgment of service.

Permission decision without a hearing

54.12 (1) This rule applies where the court, without a hearing—

(a) refuses permission to proceed; or
(b) gives permission to proceed—
      (i) subject to conditions; or
      (ii) on certain grounds only.

(2) The court will serve its reasons for making the decision when it serves the order giving or refusing permission in accordance with rule 54.11.

(3) The claimant may not appeal but may request the decision to be reconsidered at a hearing.

(4) A request under paragraph (3) must be filed within 7 days after service of the reasons under paragraph (2).

(5) The claimant, defendant and any other person who has filed an acknowledgment of service will be given at least 2 days' notice of the hearing date.

Defendant etc. may not apply to set aside[7]

54.13 Neither the defendant nor any other person served with the claim form may apply to set aside an order giving permission to proceed.

---

[6] [ed.] "A stay imposes a halt on proceedings, apart from taking any steps allowed by the Rules or the terms of the stay. Proceedings can be continued if the stay is lifted (Glossary)."
[7] [ed.]"Cancelling a judgement or order on a step taken by a party in the proceedings" (Glossary).

Response

54.14 (1) A defendant and any other person served with the claim form who wishes to contest the claim or support it on additional grounds must file and serve—

(a) detailed grounds for contesting the claim or supporting it on additional grounds; and
(b) any written evidence,

within 35 days after service of the order giving permission.
(2) The following rules do not apply—

(a) rule 8.5 (3) and 8.5 (4)(defendant to file and serve written evidence at the same time as acknowledgment of service); and
(b) rule 8.5 (5) and 8.5(6) (claimant to file and serve any reply within 14 days).

Where claimant seeks to rely on additional grounds

54.15 The court's permission is required if a claimant seeks to rely on grounds other than those for which he has been given permission to proceed.

Evidence

54.16 (1) Rule 8.6 [(1)] does not apply.
(2) No written evidence may be relied on unless—

(a) it has been served in accordance with any—
(i) rule under this [Section] or
(ii) direction of the court; or
(b) the court gives permission.

Court's powers to hear any person

54.17 (1) Any person may apply for permission—

(a) to file evidence; or
(b) make representations at the hearing of the judicial review.

(2) An application under paragraph (1) should be made promptly.

Judicial review may be decided without a hearing

54.18 The court may decide the claim for judicial review without a hearing where all the parties agree.

Court's powers in respect of quashing orders

54.19 (1) This rule applies where the court makes a quashing order in respect of the decision to which the claim relates.

(2) The court may—

(a) remit the matter to the decision-maker; and
(b) direct it to reconsider the matter and reach a decision in accordance with the judgment of the court.

(3) Where the court considers that there is no purpose to be served in remitting the matter to the decision-maker it may, subject to any statutory provision, take the decision itself.

(Where a statutory power is given to a tribunal, person or other body it may be the case that the court cannot take the decision itself)

Transfer

54.20 The court may

(a) order a claim to continue as if it had not been started under this [Section]; and
(b) where it does so, give directions about the future management of the claim.

(Part 30 (transfer) applies to transfers to and from the Administrative Court)

PRACTICE DIRECTION—JUDICIAL REVIEW

THIS PRACTICE DIRECTION SUPPLEMENTS PART 54

1.1 In addition to Part 54 and this practice direction attention is drawn to:

- section 31 of the Supreme Court Act 1981; and
- the Human Rights Act 1998

The court

2.1 Part 54 claims for judicial review are dealt with in the Administrative Court.

2.2 Where the claim is proceeding in the Administrative Court in London, documents must be filed at the Administrative Court Office, the Royal Courts of Justice, Strand, London, WC2A 2LL.

2.3 Where the claim is proceeding in the Administrative Court in Wales (see paragraph 3.1), documents must be filed at the Civil Justice Centre, 2 Park Street, Cardiff, CF10 1ET.

Urgent applications

2.4 Where urgency makes it necessary for the claim for judicial review to be made outside London or Cardiff, the Administrative Court Office in London should be consulted (if necessary, by telephone) prior to filing the claim form.

Judicial review claims in wales

3.1 A claim for judicial review may be brought in the Administrative Court in Wales where the claim or any remedy sought involves:

(1) a devolution issue arising out of the Government of Wales Act 1998; or
(2) an issue concerning the National Assembly for Wales, the Welsh executive, or any Welsh public body (including a Welsh local authority) (whether or not it involves a devolution issue).

3.2 Such claims may also be brought in the Administrative Court at the Royal Courts of Justice.

Rule 54.5—Time limit for filing claim form

4.1 Where the claim is for a quashing order in respect of a judgment, order or conviction, the date when the grounds to make the claim first arose, for the purposes of rule 54.5(1)(b), is the date of that judgment, order or conviction.

Rule 54.6—claim form

Interested parties

5.1 Where the claim for judicial review relates to proceedings in a court or tribunal, any other parties to those proceedings must be named in the claim form as interested parties under rule 54.6(1)(a) (and therefore served with the claim form under rule 54.7(b)).
5.2 For example, in a claim by a defendant in a criminal case in the Magistrates or Crown Court for judicial review of a decision in that case, the prosecution must always be named as an interested party.

Human rights

5.3 Where the claimant is seeking to raise any issue under the Human Rights Act 1998, or seeks a remedy available under that Act, the claim form must include the information required by paragraph 15 of the practice direction supplementing Part 16.

Devolution issues

5.4 Where the claimant intends to raise a devolution issue, the claim form must:

(1) specify that the applicant wishes to raise a devolution issue and identify the relevant provisions of the Government of Wales Act 1998, the Northern Ireland Act 1998 or the Scotland Act 1998; and
(2) contain a summary of the facts, circumstances and points of law on the basis of which it is alleged that a devolution issue arises.

5.5 In this practice direction "devolution issue" has the same meaning as in paragraph 1, schedule 8 to the Government of Wales Act 1998; paragraph 1, schedule 10 to the Northern Ireland Act 1998; and paragraph 1, schedule 6 of the Scotland Act 1998.

Claim form

5.6 The claim form must include or be accompanied by—

(1) a detailed statement of the claimant's grounds for bringing the claim for judicial review;
(2) a statement of the facts relied on;
(3) any application to extend the time limit for filing the claim form;
(4) any application for directions.

5.7 In addition, the claim form must be accompanied by

(1) any written evidence in support of the claim or application to extend time;
(2) a copy of any order that the claimant seeks to have quashed;
(3) where the claim for judicial review relates to a decision of a court or tribunal, an approved copy of the reasons for reaching that decision;
(4) copies of any documents on which the claimant proposes to rely;
(5) copies of any relevant statutory material; and
(6) a list of essential documents for advance reading by the court (with page references to the passages relied on).

5.8 Where it is not possible to file all the above documents, the claimant must indicate which documents have not been filed and the reasons why they are not currently available.

Bundle of documents

5.9 The claimant must file two copies of a paginated and indexed bundle containing all the documents referred to in paragraphs 5.6 and 5.7.
5.10 Attention is drawn to rules 8.5(1) and 8.5(7).

Rule 54.7—service of claim form

6.1 Except as required by rules 54.11 or 54.12(2), the Administrative Court will not serve documents and service must be effected by the parties.

Rule 54.8—acknowledgment of service

7.1 Attention is drawn to rule 8.3(2) and the relevant practice direction and to rule 10.5.

Rule 54.10—permission given

Directions

8.1 Case management directions under rule 54.10(1) may include directions about serving the claim form and any evidence on other persons.

8.2 Where a claim is made under the Human Rights Act 1998, a direction may be made for giving notice to the Crown or joining the Crown as a party. Attention is drawn to rule 19.4A and paragraph 6 of the Practice Direction supplementing Section I of Part 19.

8.3 A direction may be made for the hearing of the claim for judicial review to be held outside London or Cardiff. Before making any such direction the judge will consult the judge in charge of the Administrative Court as to its feasibility.

Permission without a hearing

8.4 The court will generally, in the first instance, consider the question of permission without a hearing.

Permission hearing

8.5 Neither the defendant nor any other interested party need attend a hearing on the question of permission unless the court directs otherwise.

8.6 Where the defendant or any party does attend a hearing, the court will not generally make an order for costs against the claimant.

Rule 54.11—service of order giving or refusing permission

9.1 An order refusing permission or giving it subject to conditions or on certain grounds only must set out or be accompanied by the court's reasons for coming to that decision.

Rule 54.14—response

10.1 Where the party filing the detailed grounds intends to rely on documents not already filed, he must file a paginated bundle of those documents when he files the detailed grounds.

Rule 54.15—where claimant seeks to rely on additional grounds

11.1 Where the claimant intends to apply to rely on additional grounds at the hearing of the claim for judicial review, he must give notice to the court and to any other person served with the claim form no later than 7 clear days before the hearing (or the warned date where appropriate).

Rule 54.16—evidence

12.1 Disclosure is not required unless the court orders otherwise.

Rule 54.17—court's powers to hear any person

13.1 Where all the parties consent, the court may deal with an application under rule 54.17 without a hearing.

13.2 Where the court gives permission for a person to file evidence or make representations at the hearing of the claim for judicial review, it may do so on conditions and may give case management directions.

13.3 An application for permission should be made by letter to the Administrative Court office, identifying the claim, explaining who the applicant is and indicating why and in what form the applicant wants to participate in the hearing.

13.4 If the applicant is seeking a prospective order as to costs, the letter should say what kind of order and on what grounds.

13.5 Applications to intervene must be made at the earliest reasonable opportunity, since it will usually be essential not to delay the hearing.

Rule 54.20—transfer

14.1 Attention is drawn to rule 30.5.

14.2 In deciding whether a claim is suitable for transfer to the Administrative Court, the court will consider whether it raises issues of public law to which Part 54 should apply.

Skeleton arguments

15.1 The claimant must file and serve a skeleton argument not less than 21 working days before the date of the hearing of the judicial review (or the warned date).

15.2 The defendant and any other party wishing to make representations at the hearing of the judicial review must file and serve a skeleton argument not less than 14 working days before the date of the hearing of the judicial review (or the warned date).

15.3 Skeleton arguments must contain:

(1) a time estimate for the complete hearing, including delivery of judgment;
(2) a list of issues;
(3) a list of the legal points to be taken (together with any relevant authorities with page references to the passages relied on);
(4) a chronology of events (with page references to the bundle of documents (see paragraph 16.1);
(5) a list of essential documents for the advance reading of the court (with page references to the passages relied on) (if different from that filed with the claim form) and a time estimate for that reading; and
(6) a list of persons referred to.

Bundle of documents to be filed

16.1 The claimant must file a paginated and indexed bundle of all relevant documents required for the hearing of the judicial review when he files his skeleton argument.

16.2 The bundle must also include those documents required by the defendant and any other party who is to make representations at the hearing.

Agreed final order

17.1 If the parties agree about the final order to be made in a claim for judicial review, the claimant must file at the court a document (with 2 copies) signed by all the parties setting out the terms of the proposed agreed order together with a short statement of the matters relied on as justifying the proposed agreed order and copies of any authorities or statutory provisions relied on.

17.2 The court will consider the documents referred to in paragraph 17.1 and will make the order if satisfied that the order should be made.

17.3 If the court is not satisfied that the order should be made, a hearing date will be set.

17.4 Where the agreement relates to an order for costs only, the parties need only file a document signed by all the parties setting out the terms of the proposed order.

Notes

1. Rules 54.21 to r 54.27 dealt with applications to the High Court under s.101(2) of the 2002 Act for a review of a decision of the Immigration Appeal Tribunal on an application for permission to appeal from an adjudicator. Rules 54.28 to 54–35 (inserted by SI 2005/352) deal with applications for statutory review under s.103A of the 2002 Act. See above, pp.789–791 and 918–920.

2. In most respects, the rules in CPR Pt 54 are similar to those in RSC, Ord.53, and authorities or the earlier rules may still be of value. However, there were some important changes including:

(1) replacement of the titles *mandamus*, prohibition and certiorari;
(2) the additional requirements that the claim form include the name and address of any person considered to be an interested party, and are served on the defendant and any such interested party;
(3) the requirement for acknowledgment of service
(4) abolition of the right to apply for a permission to apply for judicial review to be set aside; and
(5) the provision that all applications for permission are dealt with initially on the papers.

For comments on the changes, see T. Griffiths, [2000] J.R. 209; Collins J., [2002] J.R. 1; M. Fordham, [2001] P.L. 4; T. Cornford and M. Sunkin, [2001] P.L. 11, arguing that the changes seem far more concerned with efficiency than fairness.

3. In cases challenging the withdrawal of support for asylum seekers by virtue of s.55 of the Nationality, Immigration and Asylum Act 2002, it is to be assumed that the time for acknowledgment of service is extended. If an acknowledgment is not provided within two months, the claim is put before a judge within 14 days to consider whether permission should be granted. These arrangements were applied because of the pressure on the Treasury Solicitor's Office. See *Practice Statements (Judicial Review: Asylum Support)* [2004] 1 W.L.R. 644.

4. The Administrative Court Office publishes very helpful *Notes for Guidance on Applying for Judicial Review*. There are also published forms, including N461, *Judicial review claim form*; N462, *Judicial review acknowledgement of service*; N463, *Judicial review application for urgent consideration*. These are available on the Court Service website. Claim forms, acknowledgments of service and witness statements must be verified by a statement of truth under CPR Pt 22. The discontinuance of proceedings is governed by CPR Pt 38.

(C) Scope of the Application for Judicial Review

Traditionally, the key remedy through which the Court of Queen's Bench and subsequently the High Court exercised control over inferior courts and tribunals was the prerogative writ (subsequently order) of certiorari. By the 1960s, the ambit of certiorari had been extended "to cover every case in which a body of persons of a public as opposed to a purely private or domestic character has to determine matters affecting subjects provided always it has a duty to act judicially"

(*per* Lord Parker C.J. in *R. v Criminal Injuries Compensation Board Ex p. Lain* [1967] 2 Q.B. 864 at 862). In *Ex p. Lain*, the Court of Appeal took the step of holding that the Criminal Injuries Compensation Board was amenable to judicial review. This was a body set up not by statute but by an "act of government", the scheme being established by the Crown and announced in Parliament. (Whether this was correctly characterised as an exercise of the royal prerogative is disputed (see above, p.268).) As "a servant of the Crown charged by the Crown, by executive instruction, with the duty of distributing the bounty of the Crown" it was "clearly . . . performing public duties" (*per* Lord Parker C.J., *ibid.*) A further development was the disappearance of the "duty to act judicially" as a required element (see *O'Reilly v Mackman*, below, p.976). On the introduction of the application for judicial review, the same issue arose at to the scope of the judicial review procedure. The next significant steps were decisions of the Court of Appeal that the Panel on Take Overs and Mergers was but the Jockey Club was not amenable to judicial review (*R. v Panel on Takeovers and Mergers Ex p. Datafin* [1987] Q.B. 815; *R. v Disciplinary Committee of the Jockey Club Ex p. Aga Khan* [1993] 1 W.L.R. 909). The application of the detailed reasoning in these cases spawned a considerable case law on the question whether the defendant person or body was performing a "public function", the test now found in r.54.1(2)(a)(ii). The enactment of the Human Rights Act 1998 introduced the comparable issue of which bodies were subject to the requirement of the Act as a "public authority" for all or some purposes. Principles that are very similar, but not in all respects identical are applied to both. The following is a recent case which provides a current overview of the position in the light of these developments.

R. (ON THE APPLICATION OF BEER (TRADING AS HAMMER TROUT FARM)) v HAMPSHIRE FARMERS MARKETS LTD

[2003] EWCA Civ 1056; [2004] 1 W.L.R. 233 (COURT OF APPEAL)

In 1999, Hampshire County Council established farmers markets acting under general powers to promote economic development (Local Government and Housing Act 1989, s.33). B was accepted as a stallholder by Ms Driscoll, who was the farmers' market manager and a council employee. In 2001, the council decided to hand over the running of the markets to the stallholders and set up a company limited by guarantee to take over the markets (Hampshire Farmers' Market Ltd). The company started operating the markets in January 2002. B was refused a licence by the company to participate in 2002. Field J. quashed this decision on the grounds that the decision was (1) both amenable to judicial review and made by a "public authority" under the HRA 1998; and (2) made in breach of natural justice. The council (an interested party) appealed to the Court of Appeal on ground (1), but the appeal was dismissed. It was common ground that the test for identifying a functional public authority within the meaning of the HRA 1998 and for amenability to judicial review were for practical purposes the same.

DYSON L.J.: . . .

The authorities

12. I shall deal with the market cases separately. It is clear from the authorities that there is no simple litmus test of amenability to judicial review. The relevant principles tend to be stated in rather elusive terms.

940

There was a time when courts placed much emphasis on the s‹ than the *nature*, of the power being exercised by the body impugned decision. If the power derived from statute or the ǫ then it was a public body and the decision was amenable to publi lenges. If the source was contractual, then public law had no pa ‿ μiay. The importance of the seminal decision in *R v Panel on Take-overs and Mergers, Ex p. Datafin plc* [1987] Q.B. 815 was its recognition of the fact that the issue of amenability to judicial review often requires an examination of the nature of the power as well as its source. Lloyd LJ said, at p.847, that, where the source of the power did not clearly provide the answer, then the nature of the power fell to be examined:

"If the body in question is exercising public law functions, or if the exercise of its functions have public law consequences, then that may, as Mr Lever submitted, be sufficient to bring the body within the reach of judicial review. It may be said that to refer to 'public law' in this context is to beg the question. But I do not think it does. The essential distinction, which runs through all the cases to which we referred, is between a domestic or private tribunal on the one hand and a body of persons who are under some public duty on the other."

13. Lloyd L.J. did not explain what he meant by "public law functions". But Sir John Donaldson M.R. said, at p.838:

"In all the reports it is possible to find enumerations of factors giving rise to the jurisdiction, but it is a fatal error to regard the presence of all those factors as essential or as being exclusive of other factors. Possibly the only essential elements are what can be described as a public element, which can take many different forms, and the exclusion from the jurisdiction of bodies whose sole source of power is a consensual submission to its jurisdiction."

14. This test of a "public element which can take many forms" is expressed in very general terms, and of itself provides no real guidance. A similar formulation of the general test has been propounded in two recent decisions of this court as to the meaning of "public authority" in section 6 of the Human Rights Act 1998 to which I shall refer in more detail shortly. In *Poplar Housing and Regeneration Community Association Ltd v Donoghue* [2002] Q.B. 48, 69, para.65 Lord Woolf C.J. said that what could make an act, "which would otherwise be private, public is a feature or a combination of features which impose a public character or stamp on the act". In *R (Heather) v Leonard Cheshire Foundation* [2002] 2 All ER 936, 946, para.35 Lord Woolf C.J. referred to the lack of "evidence of there being a public flavour to the functions [of the body]". The issue in the *Donoghue* and *Heather* cases was whether the bodies whose decisions were the subject of challenge were public authorities within the meaning of section 6 of the 1998 Act. As Lord Woolf C.J. pointed out in the judgment of the court in the *Donoghue* case [2002] Q.B. 48, 69, para.65 (i), section 6 "is clearly inspired by the approach developed by the courts in identifying the bodies and activities subject to judicial review". No doubt for this reason it was common ground in oral argument before us that (i) the tests for a functional public authority within the meaning of section 6(3)(b) of the 1998 Act and for amenability to judicial review are, for practical

purposes, the same and (ii) the observations in both the *Donoghue* and *Heather* cases are equally relevant to the application of both tests.

15. Since the completion of the oral argument, however, the House of Lords has decided the appeal in *Aston Cantlow and Wilmcote with Billesley Parochial Church Council v Wallbank* [2003] 3 W.L.R. 283. We have had the benefit of further written submissions from counsel as to the effect of this decision on the appeal in the present case. The issue in the *Aston Cantlow* case was whether the decision of the church council to enforce a lay rector's obligation to meet the cost of chancel repairs was a private act or the discharge of a function of a public nature within the meaning of section 6(3)(b) of the 1998 Act. Certain observations were made as to the relationship between the public functions test in section 6(3)(b) and the test for amenability to judicial review, and I shall come to these later when I consider whether HFML acted as a public authority when it decided to exclude Mr Beer from the farmers' market programme. In my judgment, there is nothing in the speeches in the *Aston Cantlow* case which suggests that what was said in the *Donoghue* and *Heather* cases is not a useful guide to amenability to judicial review. Moreover, and unsurprisingly, their Lordships said nothing about the important market cases to which I refer at paragraphs 20–22 below.

16. It seems to me that the law has now been developed to the point where, unless the source of power clearly provides the answer, the question whether the decision of a body is amenable to judicial review requires a careful consideration of the nature of the power and function that has been exercised to see whether the decision has a sufficient public element, flavour or character to bring it within the purview of public law. It may be said with some justification that this criterion for amenability is very broad, not to say question-begging. But it provides the framework for the investigation that has to be conducted. There is a growing body of case law in which the question of amenability to judicial review has been considered. From these cases it is possible to identify a number of features which point towards the presence or absence of the requisite public law element. I do not propose to examine many of these authorities. Leaving aside the market cases, it seems to me that it is sufficient to refer to the two recent decisions which I have already mentioned.

17. The first is *Poplar Housing and Regeneration Community Association Ltd v Donoghue* [2002] Q.B. 48. The issue in that case was whether a housing association was a public authority performing public functions for the purposes of section 6 of the 1998 Act. The housing association had obtained a possession order evicting the claimant from her home. She contended that the association was a public authority exercising a public function, and that her eviction violated her rights under article 8 of the Convention for the Protection of Human Rights and Fundamental Freedoms Lord Woolf C.J. said, at pp.69–20, para.65 of the judgment of the court:

"In coming to our conclusion as to whether Poplar is a public authority within the Human Rights Act 1998 meaning of that term, we regard it of particular importance in this case that:

(i) While section 6 of the Human Rights Act 1998 requires a generous interpretation of who is a public authority, it is clearly inspired by the approach developed by the courts in identifying the bodies and activities subject to judicial review. The emphasis on public functions reflects the approach adopted in judicial review by the courts and textbooks since the decision of the Court of Appeal (the judgment of Lloyd L.J.) in *R. v Panel on Take-overs and Mergers, Ex p. Datafin plc* [1987] Q.B. 815.

(ii) Tower Hamlets, in transferring its housing stock to Poplar, does not transfer its primary public duties to Poplar. Poplar is no more than the means by which it seeks to perform those duties.

(iii) The act of providing accommodation to rent is not, without more, a public function for the purposes of section 6 of the Human Rights Act 1998. Furthermore, that is true irrespective of the section of society for whom the accommodation is provided.

(iv) The fact that a body is a charity or is conducted not for profit means that it is likely to be motivated in performing its activities by what it perceives to be the public interest. However, this does not point to the body being a public authority. In addition, even if such a body performs functions, that would be considered to be of a public nature if performed by a public body, nevertheless such acts may remain of a private nature for the purpose of sections 6(3)(b) and 6(5).

(v) What can make an act, which would otherwise be private, public is a feature or a combination of features which impose a public character or stamp on the act. Statutory authority for what is done can at least help to mark the act as being public, so can the extent of control over the function exercised by another body which is a public authority. The more closely the acts that could be of a private nature are enmeshed in the activities of a public body, the more likely they are to be public. However, the fact that the acts are supervised by a public regulatory body does not necessarily indicate that they are of a public nature. This is analogous to the position in judicial review, where a regulatory body may be deemed public but the activities of the body which is regulated may be categorised private.

(vi) The closeness of the relationship which exists between Tower Hamlets and Poplar. Poplar was created by Tower Hamlets to take a transfer of local authority housing stock; five of its board members are also members of Tower Hamlets; Poplar is subject to the guidance of Tower Hamlets as to the manner in which it acts towards the defendant.

(vii) The defendant, at the time of the transfer, was a sitting tenant of Poplar and it was intended that she would be treated no better and no worse than if she remained a tenant of Tower Hamlets. While she remained a tenant, Poplar therefore stood in relation to her in very much the position previously occupied by Tower Hamlets."

18. He said, at p.70, para.66 that there is no clear demarcation line between public and private bodies and functions. "In a borderline case, such as this, the decision is very much one of fact and degree." It is necessary to take account of all the circumstances. The conclusion of the court was that "the role of Poplar is so closely assimilated to that of Tower Hamlets that it was performing public and not private functions".

19. The second recent decision is *R. (Heather) v Leonard Cheshire Foundation* [2002] 2 All ER 936. In that case the claimants were persons to whom the local authority owed a statutory duty to provide accommodation. It made arrangements for that accommodation to be provided at public expense by the Leonard Cheshire Foundation ("LCF"), a charitable foundation.

LCF decided to close the home where the claimants had been living for many years. They applied for judicial review of the decision. The first issue was whether, in deciding to close the home, LCF was acting as a public authority exercising functions of a "public nature" within the meaning of section 6(3)(b) of the 1998 Act Giving the judgment of the court Lord Woolf CJ said, at p.946, para.35:

> "The matters already referred to can, however, be put aside. In our judgment the role that LCF was performing manifestly did not involve the performance of public functions. The fact that LCF is a large and flourishing organisation does not change the nature of its activities from private to public. (i) It is not in issue that it is possible for LCF to perform some public functions and some private functions. In this case it is contended that this was what has been happening in regard to those residents who are privately funded and those residents who are publicly funded. But in this case except for the resources needed to fund the residents of the different occupants of Le Court, there is no material distinction between the nature of the services LCF has provided for residents funded by a local authority and those provided to residents funded privately. While the degree of public funding of the activities of an otherwise private body is certainly relevant as to the nature of the functions performed, by itself it is not determinative of whether the functions are public or private. Here we found *R. v HM Treasury. Ex p. University of Cambridge* (Case C–380/98) [2000] 1 W.L.R. 2514, 2523, 2534–2535, relied on by Mr Henderson, an interesting illustration in relation to European Union legislation in different terms to section 6.
>
> (ii) There is no other evidence of there being a public flavour to the functions of LCF or LCF itself. LCF is not standing in the shoes of the local authorities Section 26 of the [National Assistance Act 1948] provides statutory authority for the actions of the local authorities but it provides LCF with no powers. LCF is not exercising statutory powers in performing functions for the appellants (iii) In truth, all that Mr Gordon can rely upon is the fact that if LCF is not performing a public function the appellants would not be able to rely upon article 8 as against LCF. However, this is a circular argument. If LCF was performing a public function, that would mean that the appellants could rely in relation to that function on article 8, but, if the situation is otherwise, article 8 cannot change the appropriate classification of the function. On the approach adopted in *Poplar Housing and Regeneration Community Association Ltd v Donoghue* [2002] Q.B. 48, it can be said that LCF is clearly not performing any public function Stanley Burnton J's conclusion as to this was correct."

The market cases

20. It is sufficient to refer to two of the market cases relied on by Mr Maurici. The first is the well-known case of *R. v Barnslev Metropolitan Borough Council Ex p. Hook* [1976] 1 W.L.R 1052. The applicant applied to have quashed the decision of the council to exclude him from trading in the market and to revoke his right to have a stall His application succeeded on the grounds that the decision had been taken in breach of the rules of natural justice Ms Carrington submitted that this case (and indeed all the market cases relied on by Mr Mauric[8] is distinguishable on the grounds that the decision was made by a local authority. Moreover, she pointed out that the market in the *Hook* case had been the subject of grant by royal charter and later a private Act. But I agree with Mr Maurici that neither of these factors was relied upon by the Court of Appeal as the reason for quashing the decision on the grounds of breach of natural justice Lord Denning M.R. said that the right of a stall-holder to have access to the market was conferred by common law, and could only be taken away for just cause and then only in accordance with the principles of natural justice. He said, at p.1057D. "I do not mind whether the marketholder is exercising a judicial or an administrative function." It is clear that it was irrelevant that the marketholder was a local authority and that the market was authorised by royal charter and statute. What was relevant was that the stallholder had the right at common law to come to a place to which the public had the right of access to sell his goods. The judgment of Scarman L.J. was to similar effect. He emphasised the common law right in the public to go to market to buy and sell, subject to the statutory regulation of the exercise of that right by the local authority. He said, at p.1060.

"Although, therefore there is a contractual element in this case, there is also an element of public law, viz, the enjoyment of rights conferred upon the subject by the common law I think, therefore upon analysis, it is clear that the Barnsley Corporation in its conduct of this market is a body having legal authority to determine questions affecting the rights of subjects."

There is no suggestion here that Scarman L.J. attributed any relevance to the identity of the marketholder (the local authority) or the nature of the market (other than the fact that it was one to which the public had a right of access at common law).

21. The second decision is *R. v Wear Valley District Council, Ex p. Binks* [1985] 2 All ER 699. Here too the marketholder was the local authority. The applicant was a street trader who operated a hot food takeaway caravan from a market place. She had no written licence, and operated under what was described as an informal arrangement with the local authority. Her right to station the caravan in the market place was terminated without notice. Her application to quash the decision on the grounds that it had been made in breach of the rules of natural justice succeeded before Taylor J. He rejected the submission that decisions such as the *Hook* case [1976] 1 W.L.R. 1052 were to be distinguished because the principles enunciated in them were only to be applied where there is a statutory market or something akin to a statutory market. In so doing he relied on a passage in the judgment of Templeman L.J. in *R. v Basildon District Council, Ex p. Brown* (1981) 79 LGR 655, 667 to the effect that the status of the market was not relevant to the crucial question whether the stallholder's licence had been validly terminated. The exercise of the powers (in that case by the local authority) must be governed by the same principles whether in relation to a statutory market or an unofficial market managed by the local authority in the interests of the local community.

---

[8] [ed.] The others were *R. v Basildon DC Ex p. Brown* (1981) 79 L.G.R. 655; *R. v Durham CC Ex p. Robinson, The Times*, January 31, 1992; and *R. v Birmingham CC Ex p. Dredger* (1993) 91 L.G.R. 532.

22. Having rejected this submission Taylor J continued [1985] 2 All ER 699, 703:

> "Moreover, in the present case the market place at Crook is conceded to be a place to which the public has right of resort at all times. It is not a highway, but it is nevertheless a place to which the public has a right of access and on which the council have a discretion whether to allow street traders or not. During the day, the market place is in fact used for a market. When it is not being so used between prescribed hours it is used as a public car park for which no charge is made. It therefore seems to me that the local authority in granting or revoking licences to street traders to operate in the market place are in exactly the same situation as that envisaged in the *Basildon* case by all three members of the Court of Appeal. It seems to me that there is a public law element in the decisions of the council with regard to whom they license and whom they do not license to trade in the market place."

Public authority

Summary of the parties' submissions

23. It was common ground that HFML is not a "core" public authority. It is a "hybrid" authority.[9] It follows that the relevant question is whether the decision to exclude Mr Beer was a private act or the exercise of a public function. Both counsel rely on substantially the same factors in relation to this question as form the basis of their submissions on the amenability issue. In short Ms Carrington submitted that the act of HFML that Mr Beer seeks to challenge was not "governmental" in nature, but was of a private character. The assistance given by the council to HFML and the current use of public land are minor indicia which are insufficient to imbue what would otherwise be a private decision with a public stamp. Mr Maurici submitted that the guidance given by their Lordships in *Asian Cantlow and Wilmcote with Billesley Parochial Church Council v Wallbank* [2003] 3 W.L.R. 283 in relation to hybrid authorities is not significantly different from that given in *Poplar Housing and Regeneration Community Association Ltd v Donoghue* [2002] Q.B. 48 and *R. (Heather) v Leonard Cheshire Foundation* [2002] 2 All ER 936, and that for all the reasons given in relation to the amenability issue the impugned decision was made in the exercise of a public function.

The Aston Cantlow decision

24. Much of the discussion in the speeches in the *Aston Cantlow* case [2003] 3 W.L.R. 283 is on the question whether the parish council was a "core" public authority. The only general guidance on hybrid authorities and what is a public function for the purposes of section 6(3) of the 1998 Act is to be found in the speech of Lord Nicholls of Birkenhead, who said, at p.288:

> "11. Unlike a core public authority, a 'hybrid' public authority, exercising both public functions and non-public functions, is not absolutely disabled from having Convention rights. A hybrid public authority is not a public

---

[9] [ed] See above, pp.316–317.

authority in respect of an act of a private nature. Here again, as with section 6 (1), this feature throws some light on the approach to be adopted when interpreting section 6(3)(b). Giving a generously wide scope to the expression 'public function' in section 6(3)(b) will further the statutory aim of promoting the observance of human rights values without depriving the bodies in question of the ability themselves to rely on Convention rights when necessary.

12. What, then, is the touchstone to be used in deciding whether a function is public for this purpose? Clearly there is no single test of universal application. There cannot be, given the diverse nature of governmental functions and the variety of means by which these functions are discharged today. Factors to be taken into account include the extent to which in carrying out the relevant function the body is publicly funded, or is exercising statutory powers, or is taking the place of central government or local authorities, or is providing a public service."

25. Lord Hope of Craighead considered, at pp.296 and 303, paras 41 and 63 that the question of public function was fact-sensitive and did not admit of an answer in the abstract, an approach with which Lord Scott of Foscote agreed, at p.321, para.130. It is perhaps somewhat surprising that there is no reference to the *Donoghue* case [2002] Q.B. 48 or the *Heather* case [2002] 2 All ER 936 in the *Aston Cantlow* case. Ms Carrington submitted that these decisions have been "superseded" by the *Aston Cantlow* case. If by "superseded" she means that the two earlier decisions are to be taken as having been overruled, then I do not agree. As I have said, apart from what Lord Nicholls said, at p.288, paras 11 and 12, the *Aston Cantlow* case contains no guidance as to what amounts to the exercise by a hybrid public authority of functions of a public nature. Provided that it is bornc in mind that regard should be had to any relevant Strasbourg jurisprudence, then the passages which I have quoted from the judgments in the two earlier cases will continue to be a source of valuable guidance. Indeed, para.12 of Lord Nicholls's speech is redolent of the flavour of that guidance.

Conclusion

26. I can now state my reasons for concluding that Field J. was right to decide that the decision of HFML which is challenged in these proceedings is amenable to judicial review, and that in making that decision HFML was acting as a public authority.

27. I should start by explaining why, in my judgment, if the decision is amenable to judicial review, it was by the same token made by HFML acting as a public authority. I accept that it is possible to conclude that a decision by a public authority is not amenable to judicial review and vice versa. This point was made very clearly by Lord Hope in the *Aston Cantlow* case [2003] 3 W.L.R. 283, 299–200, para.52.

"But, as Professor Oliver has pointed out in her commentary on the decision of the Court of Appeal in this case, 'Chancel repairs and the Human Rights Act' [2001] PL 651, the decided cases on the amenability of bodies to judicial review have been made for purposes which have nothing to do with the liability of the state in international law. They cannot be regarded

as determinative of a body's membership of the class of 'core' public authorities see also *Grosz. Beatson & Duffy. Human Rights: The 1998 Act and
the European Convention* (2000), p.61, para.4–04. Nor can they be
regarded as determinative of the question whether a body falls within the
'hybrid' class. That is not to say that the case law on judicial review may
not provide some assistance as to what does, and what does not, constitute
a 'function of a public nature' within the meaning of section 6(3)(b). It may
well be helpful. But the domestic case law must be examined in the light of
the jurisprudence of the Strasbourg court as to those bodies which engage
the responsibility of the state for the purposes of the Convention."

28. Thus the domestic case law on amenability to judicial review can be
"very helpful". But reliance on domestic cases must be tempered by, and sometimes yield to, relevant Strasbourg jurisprudence. This jurisprudence is especially likely to be helpful in determining whether a body is a core public
authority. It is likely to be less helpful in relation to the fact-sensitive question
of whether in an individual case a hybrid body is exercising a public function.
29. In the present case Ms Carrington has shown us no Strasbourg authority
which points the way. Nor has she advanced any reasons peculiar to the public
authority issue in support of the submission that, even if HFML's decision is
amenable to judicial review, nevertheless it was not made by HFML in the exercise of a public function. In my judgment, she was right not to do so. On the
facts of this case, and I would suggest on the facts of most cases, the two issues
march hand in hand: the answer to one provides the answer to the other.
30. It is important to record the concession by Ms Carrington (in my view
rightly made) that, if the decision to refuse Mr Beer's application had been
made by the council before the incorporation of HFML, it would have been
amenable to judicial review. The reason given by Ms Carrington for her concession was not that the decision would have denied a person access to a public
market; rather it was that the decision would have been made by a public body,
namely a local authority. In my judgment, the correct reason for the concession
is more than the mere fact that the decision would have been made by a public
body. Not all decisions by local authorities are amenable to judicial review or
involve the exercise of public functions. The reason why I consider that the concession was correctly made is that the power being exercised by the council
would have had that public element or flavour to which I have earlier referred.
In this regard the fact that the power was being exercised in order to control
the right of access to a public market is a most important feature.
31. I return to the decision that was actually made by HFML. It is clear from
the market cases that decisions affecting the right of access to certain types of
market may have a sufficient public element to be amenable to judicial review.
There is a distinction between (a) an unofficial market in respect of which there
are no public rights of access and (b) a statutory market in respect of which
public rights do exist. A good example of the former is a car boot sale held on
a person's private land. The paradigm example of the latter is a statutory or
charter market held on land dedicated to public use and to which the public
has a right of access. Where do the markets held by HFML come within the
spectrum of markets? It is true that HFML did not start to operate the markets
until January 2002, a few weeks after the decision of 14 November 2001. But
neither party has suggested that the situation that obtained at the time of the
decision was not likely to continue once HFML took over the running of

the markets, or that it has not done so. The rather exiguous evidence as to the nature of these markets is not directed specifically at the time of the decision. But the brief summary that follows of the present position is the best evidence of the situation that existed at that time.

32. The markets are held on town centre sites. None of the sites is owned by the council but they are all owned by other local authorities. Mrs Stokes says that the markets operated "on town centre sites in close association with the relevant local authorities". She does not explain exactly what she means by "close association with the relevant authorities". But she must mean that HFML and the local authorities who own the sites co-operate in the organising of the markets. The evidence also discloses that at Winchester the market stalls occupy a pedestrianised area and most of the adjacent public car park. The pedestrianised area is used during the week by a conventional market.

33. In my view, it is clear from this evidence that these markets cannot be assimilated to the category of unofficial markets to which the public have no right of access. They are much closer to the second category to which I have referred, even though they are neither statutory nor charter markets. Their essential feature is that they are markets held on publicly owned land to which the public have access.

34. What flows from this? There is much to be said for accepting the submission of Mr Maurici that, for this reason alone, the decision of 14 November 2001 is amenable to judicial review and that in making that decision HFML was exercising public functions and acting as a public authority. The decisions in *R. v Barnsley Metropolitan Borough Council, Ex p. Hook* [1976] 1 W.L.R. 1052 and *R. v Wear Valley District Council, Ex p. Binks* [1985] 2 All ER 699 show that the identity of the marketholder is not decisive, nor is the source of the power to hold the market. What is critical is whether the market is one to which the public has the right of access. It is this feature which led Scarman L.J. in the *Hook* case to speak of the existence of "an element of public law" which opened the door to the remedy of certiorari for breach of natural justice. It was the same feature which led Taylor J. in the *Binks* case to speak of a "public law element". It is significant that "public element" was the phrase used by Sir John Donaldson M.R. in *R. v Panel on Take-overs and Mergers, Ex p. Datafin plc* [1987] QB 815 to describe one of the essential elements of amenability to judicial review.

35. But I do not base my conclusion that there was a sufficient public element in HFML's decision of 14 November 2001 solely on the fact that it involved the denial to Mr Beer of access to a public market. I have already referred to Ms Carrington's concession that, if the decision had been taken by the council before HFML had been incorporated, it would have been amenable to judicial review. This concession brings into sharp focus the need to examine the relationship between the council and HFML I accept the submission of Mr Maurici that there are several features of that relationship which strengthen Mr Beer's case that the decision is amenable to judicial review.

36. First, HFML owes its existence to the council. The company was set up by the council using its statutory powers. It was the council's economic development office which employed and paid for the services of Charles Morrison of Business Link Wessex to assist in the setting up of the company (it was bought "off the shelf"). The council's in-house legal practice undertook the necessary legal work. In the *Donoghue* case [2002] Q.B. 48 it was a relevant feature which pointed towards there being a sufficient public element that the housing

association was *created* by the local authority. By contrast, in *R. v Servite Houses, Ex p. Goldsmith* [2001] LGR 55, Moses J. regarded the fact that Servite was a "private body which does not owe its existence to Wandsworth" as a factor militating against its function being within the scope of public law.

37. Secondly, HFML stepped into the shoes of the council. The phrase "standing in the shoes" of a public body derives from the *Heather* case [2002] 2 All ER 936, 946, para.35(ii). There is also a reflection of it in Lord Nicholls's speech in the *Aston Cantlow* case [2003] 3 W.L.R. 283, 288, para.12 ("or is taking the place of central government or local authorities"). The phrase is not a term of art. But it is clear what it means. It connotes the idea of A performing the same functions as had previously been performed by B, to the same end and in substantially the same way. It was an important feature of the decision in the *Heather* case that LCF was not performing the statutory functions previously performed by the local authority under section 21 of the National Assistance Act 1948. It was merely providing accommodation to the claimants. In the present case the council announced the 2002 programme of farmers' markets in 2001 before HFML started operating. They asked that applications for the 2002 programme be sent to themselves. After 2002 HFML took over the running of the markets, and ran them (as was always envisaged) in the same way as the council had previously run them. It is relevant that the three criteria for admission of farmers to the markets were the same as those promulgated by the council when the scheme was first established. These criteria were devised in what was perceived to be the public interest of promoting the interests of the local farming community Ms Carrington drew attention to the fact that the main objects clause of HFML's memorandum of association was drafted in wide terms, so that it would be open to the company lawfully to change the criteria for admission to the markets, and operate them differently from the way they were previously operated, and indeed not operate markets at all. In theory this is true. Anything might happen in the future. But these proceedings are concerned with the lawfulness of the decision of 14 November 2001. At that time, in so far as HFML was doing anything at all, it had stepped into the shoes of the council in relation to these markets.

38. Thirdly, from the date of incorporation of HFML until the time when the company started operating the markets, and to some extent thereafter, the council assisted the company in a number of respects. For several months after incorporation the company's registered office was in the council's offices. The company has at all times been provided with a desk and computer in one room in the council's main building in Winchester. It has not yet operated from anywhere else. The council agreed to make a discretionary grant to HFML to assist in the development of the markets. Two council personnel have provided important assistance to HFML, and continue to do so. Mrs Stokes is employed by the company as business development manager and is one of its directors. She played an influential role in setting up the company. She chaired the steering group that was established for that purpose. Ms Driscoll, the company's market manager, was employed by the council until April 2002 when her employment was transferred to HFML. In November 2001 she was seconded to the company.

39. In my view, the combined effect of these three features (or groups of features) is sufficient to justify the conclusion that the decision of 14 November is amenable to judicial review I regard the first two features as being of particular significance. To these must be added the fact that the decision was one which affected a person's right of access to a public market.

40. What is Ms Carrington able to put into the scales as a counterweight to these points? She relied strongly on the fact that this is not a case involving the privatisation of the business of government, or the assimilation of HFML's role into a system of statutory control or regulation. It is true that HFML is not performing a function of statutory control or regulation on behalf of the council. The judge agreed that there is no statutory underpinning of the company's role and its functions, and that those functions are not woven into a system of governmental control. In some cases the absence of such features may point decisively against amenability to judicial review. But it is necessary to have regard to all the relevant factors. In this case I do not consider that the absence of statutory underpinning and the lack of interweaving into a system of governmental control is a matter of great weight. HFML was not simply another private company that was established to run markets for profit. It was established by a local authority to take over on a non-profit basis the running of the markets that the authority had previously been running in the exercise of its statutory powers in what it considered to be the public interest.

41. Ms Carrington also relied on the fact that the relationship between Mr Beer and HFML is consensual in character. The answer to this point was provided by Scarman LJ as long ago as 1976 in *R v Barnsley Metropolitan Borough Council, Ex p Hook* [1976] 1 WLR 1052. There is a consensual element in the case. But for the reasons that he gave, and for the additional reasons that I have sought to give in this judgment, there was also a public element too. This is a far cry from the paradigm case discussed in *R v Panel on Take-overs and Mergers, Ex p. Datafin plc* [1987] Q.B. 815 where, as in the case, for example, of a private arbitration, the sole source of power is a consensual submission to jurisdiction.

42. There are some cases which may properly be described as close to the borderline. Lord Woolf C.J. said that the *Donoghue* case [2002] Q.B. 48 was such a case. But, in my view, that is not so here. It seems to me that the factors to which I have referred clearly compel the conclusion that the decision of 14 November 2001 is amenable to judicial review, and that in making that decision HFML was acting as a public authority within the meaning of section 6 of the 1998 Act. For these reasons I would dismiss this appeal.

LONGMORE L.J. agreed that each of the two reasons identified by DYSON L.J. was sufficient in itself to justify his decision. SIR MARTIN NOURSE agreed with DYSON L.J.

Appeal dismissed

Notes

1. Issues as to the scope of judicial review come in two basic forms. First, as in *Datafin*, *Aga Khan* and *Beer*, a question can arise as to whether a body not set up by statute is nevertheless exercising in the particular case a public function. Secondly, there are cases which consider whether a particular act of a statutory body is private rather than an exercise of a public function (see *R. v East Berkshire HA Ex p. Walsh*, below, p.957).

2. *R. v Panel on Takeovers and Mergers Ex p. Datafin* [1987] Q.B. 815 concerned the amenability to judicial review of the Panel, an unincorporated association with members appointed by a range of City institutions. It had no statutory, prerogative or common law powers and it was not in contractual relationships with the financial market or those who dealt with it. Nevertheless, it exercised immense power *de facto* as the vehicle for self-regulation by the financial market of take-overs and mergers. It devised, interpreted

and applied the Takeovers and Mergers Code, and investigated and reported on alleged breaches. In such cases it would hold a hearing; if it found there had been breach it could issue a private reprimand or public censure, or refer certain aspects of the case to the DTi, the Stock Exchange or other appropriate body for the exercise by them of their statutory powers of sanction. According to Sir John Donaldson M.R.:

"As an act of government it was decided that, in relation to take-overs, there should be a central self-regulatory body which would be supported and sustained by a periphery of statutory powers and penalties wherever non-statutory powers and penalties were insufficient or non-existent or where EEC requirements called for statutory provisions.

No one could have been in the least surprised if the panel had been instituted and operated under the direct authority of statute law, since it operates wholly in the public domain. Its jurisdiction extends throughout the United Kingdom. Its code and rulings apply equally to all who wish to make take-over bids or promote mergers, whether or not they are members of bodies represented on the panel. Its lack of a direct statutory base is a complete anomaly, judged by the experience of other comparable markets world wide".

The Panel:

"is without doubt performing a public duty and an important one. This is clear from the willingness of the Secretary of State for Trade and Industry to limit legislation in the field of take-overs and mergers and to use the panel as the centrepiece of his regulation of that market".

A further consideration was that the Panel could not effectively be controlled "by established forms of private law, *e.g.* torts such as actionable combinations in restraint of trade." Lloyd L.J. (at 847) rejected the argument that the source of power was the sole test of whether the body of persons is subject to judicial review.

"Of course, the source of the power will often, perhaps usually, be decisive. If the source of power is a statute, or subordinate legislation under a statute, then clearly the body in question will be subject to judicial review. If, at the other end of the scale, the source of power is contractual, as in the case of private arbitration, then clearly the arbitrator is not subject to judicial review: see *R. v National Joint Council for the Craft of Dental Technicians (Disputes Committee) Ex p. Neate* [1953] 1 Q.B. 704.

But in between these extremes, there is an area in which it is helpful to look not just at the source of the power but at the nature of the power. If the body in question is exercising public law functions, or if the exercise of its functions have public law consequences, then that may, as Mr Lever submitted, be sufficient to bring the body within the reach of judicial review. It may be said that to refer to 'public law' in this context is to beg the question. But I do not think it does. The essential distinction, which runs through all the cases to which we referred, is between a domestic or private tribunal on the one hand and a body of persons who are under some public duty on the other".

Even if the courts, were confined to looking at the source of the power, then the source here "is indeed governmental, at least in part . . . [T]here has been an implied devolution of power. Power exercised behind the scenes is power none the less".

As regards *practical* issues concerning the application of the judicial review jurisdiction to the Panel, counsel for the panel argued that the court having and exercising jurisdiction to review the decisions of the panel would have disastrous consequences. Even unmeritorious applications for judicial review would dislocate the operation of the market during the pendency of proceedings; rulings by the panel were required to have speed and certainty.

In response, Sir John Donaldson noted (1) that a panel decision would remain effective unless set aside; (2) the court retained a discretion whether to grant a remedy; (3) the courts were aware of the need for speed; and (4) an applicant needed leave to make an application. The panel and those affected by its decisions should treat them as valid and binding, unless and until they were set aside.

There would be little scope for complaint that the panel had promulgated rules that were *ultra vires*, save in the unlikely eventuality that they violated the principle, proclaimed by the panel, of being based on the concept of doing equity between one shareholder and another. In interpreting the rules, considerable latitude would be given to the panel, both because they were the legislators, and because the rules laid down principles to be applied in spirit as much as in letter. Moreover, the court might well decline to quash an interpretative decision, instead granting a declaration as to the true meaning of the rule, and leaving it to the panel to promulgate a new rule accurately expressing its intentions (a form of prospective overruling).

As regards the panel's disciplinary function, the internal right of appeal should be exercised before the court could consider intervening. The only circumstances where the use of certiorari would be anticipated would be where there was a breach of natural justice.

Sir John Donaldson concluded (at 842) that the limitations in practice to the scope of intervention by the courts would lead to "a workable and valuable partnership between the courts and the panel in the public interest and would avoid all of the perils to which Mr Alexander alluded".

See also Lord Donaldson M.R.'s comments in *R. v Panel on Takeovers and Mergers Ex p. Guinness Plc* [1990] 1 Q.B. 146 in respect of the grounds of challenge that:

> "It may be that the true view is that in the context of a body whose constitution, functions and powers are sui generis, the court should review the panel's acts and omissions more in the round than might otherwise be the case and, whilst basing its decision on familiar concepts, should eschew any formal categorisation" (at 159–160).

On *Datafin*, see P. Cane, "Self Regulation and Judicial Review" (1987) 6 C.J.Q. 324; L. Hilliard, (1987) 50 M.L.R. 372; H.W.R. Wade, (1987) 103 L.Q.R. 323;C.F. Forsyth, [1987] P.L. 356; C.J. Kinsella, [1987] C.L.J. 200; J. Beatson, "The Courts and the Regulators" (1987) 3 P.N. 121. More generally on the Panel, see Lord Alexander of Weedon, "Judicial Review and City Regulators" (1989) 52 M.L.R. 640, J. Jowell, "The Take-over Panel: Autonomy, Flexibility and Legality" [1991] P.L. 149 and G.K. Morse, "The City Code on Takeovers and Mergers—Self-Regulation or Self Protection" [1991] J.B.L. 509. A statutory framework is to be provided for the panel's powers by virtue of Directive 2004/25 on takeover bids, required to be implemented by May 20, 2006.

3. Prior to the establishment of the application for judicial review, the analogous issue to that considered in *Datafin* was the scope of the prerogative orders of prohibition and certiorari. It was held that these orders lay to bodies performing a public duty, such as inferior courts (*e.g.* an election court: *R. v Cripps, Ex p. Muldoon* [1984] Q.B. 686), statutory tribunals, individuals exercising public functions (*e.g. R. v Kent Police Authority Ex p. Godden*: above, p.773), Ministers of the Crown, Government bodies and bodies established under the royal prerogative (*e.g. R. v Criminal Injuries Compensation Board Ex p. Lain*, above, p.938). They did not lie against the Crown; to a body which had no legal authority (*Re Clifford and O'Sullivan* [1921] 2 A.C. 570: a military court acting under martial law, and not under statute law or the common law, which was to be regarded as a body of military officers advising the military commander); to a non-statutory arbitrator (*R. v Disputes Committee of Dental Technicians* [1953] 1 Q.B. 704); to a legislative assembly (*R. v Church Assembly, Ex p. Haynes-Smith* [1928] 1 K.B. 411) or to a body exercising authority by virtue of a contract (*R. v Post Office, Ex p. Byrne* [1975] I.C.R. 221).

4. Bodies exercising jurisdiction by virtue of a contract have consistently been held not to be subject to judicial review (*cf. R. v British Broadcasting Corporation Ex p. Lavelle* [1983] 1 W.L.R. 23 (where Woolf J. held that the dismissal of a BBC employee could not be challenged by judicial review; with the agreement of the parties Woolf J. proceeded under RSC, Ord.53, r.9(5) to consider the case (and reject it on the merits) on the basis that the action had been begun by writ); Lloyd L.J. in *Datafin*, above, p.950).

Moreover, in *Law v National Greyhound Racing Club Ltd* [1983] 1 W.L.R. 1302, the Court of Appeal refused to strike out claims for declarations against the NGRC, a company limited by guarantee which acted as the judicial body for the discipline and conduct of greyhound racing in Great Britain. The court rejected the NGRC's argument that L should have applied for judicial review, holding that the NGRC was not amenable to the judicial review jurisdiction. The pre-1978 authorities such as *Lain* and *Byrne* were clear that the prerogative orders did not lie to domestic tribunals. The position had not been changed by the new Ord.53, and, in particular, the enactment of s.31 of the Supreme Court Act 1981. Section 31 was not intended to extend the jurisdiction of the court on an application for judicial review to grant an injunction or declaration in respect of a private contractual dispute simply on the basis that it might be considered "just and convenient" so to do (see Lawton L.J. at 1308 and Slade L.J. at 1313–1315).

5. The decision in *Law* has been accepted as good law in post-*Datafin* cases concerning sporting bodies. Decisions of the Jockey Club and the Football Association have been held not to be amenable to judicial review (*R. v Disciplinary Committee of the Jockey Club Ex p. Massingberd-Mundy*, [1993] 2 All E.R. 207, DC; *R. v Jockey Club Ex p. RAM Racecourses Ltd* [1993] 2 All E.R. 225, DC; *R. v Disciplinary Committee of the Jockey Club Ex p. Aga Khan* [1993] 1 W.L.R. 909, CA; *R. v Football Association of Wales Ex p. Flint Town United Football Club* [1991] C.O.D. 44; *R. v Football Association Ltd Ex p. The Football League Ltd* [1993] 2 All E.R. 833. In *Ex p. Massingberd-Mundy*, the Divisional Court stated that if the matter had been free from authority it might (Neill L.J.) or would (Roch J.) have concluded that at least some decisions of the Jockey Club related to quasi-public functions amenable to judicial review; however, the point was concluded by the decision of the Court of Appeal in *Law*.

The decision in *Aga Khan* was particularly controversial. The Aga Khan's filly won the Oaks (a classic race) but was found to have been doped. The Jockey Club's Disciplinary Committee disqualified the filly and fined the trainer. (It was not suggested that either the Aga Khan or the trainer was party to the doping.) The Aga Khan sought judicial review. It was accepted that the Jockey Club, a body established by Royal Charter but with no prerogative or statutory powers, exercised *de facto* control over the racing industry. Nevertheless, the Court of Appeal held unanimously that judicial review did not lie, although the reasoning varied. Sir Thomas Bingham M.R. (at 923–924) accepted that the Jockey Club effectively regulated a significant national activity, exercising powers that affected the public and were exercised in the interest of the public. He was willing to accept that if the Jockey Club did not regulate this activity, the Government would probably do so. But the Jockey Club was not in its origin, history, constitution or membership a public body. It had not been woven into any system of government control of horse-racing:

"perhaps because it has itself controlled horse-racing so successfully that there has been no need for any such government system and such does not therefore exist. This has the result that while the Jockey Club's powers may be described as, in many ways, public they are in no sense governmental".

The facts that those who agreed to abide by the Rules of Racing had no effective alternative to doing so if they wanted to take part in racing in this country, and that any statutory code governing racing would generate similar rights and obligations, did not alter the position that the Jockey Club's powers derived from the agreement of the parties and give rise to private rights. Whether there might be circumstances in which judicial review might be available, as where the applicant had no contract with the Jockey Club, was left open. Farquharson L.J. (at 929–930) held that judicial review was not available as the relationship between the Aga Khan and the Jockey Club was contractual. The decision in *Law* had not been affected by *Datafin*, and there was no relevant distinction between the Jockey Club and the NGRC. Nor could he find

> "any public element in the Jockey Club's position and powers within the meaning of that term as explained in . . . *Datafin* . . . . No doubt . . . many of the decisions of the Jockey Club through its committees will affect members of the public who have no connection with it, but there is a difference between what may affect the public and what amounts to a public duty. . . . The courts have always been reluctant to interfere with the control of sporting bodies over their own sports and I do not detect in the material available to us any grounds for supposing that, if the Jockey Club were dissolved, any governmental body would assume control of racing. Neither in its framework nor its rules nor its function does the Jockey Club fulfil a governmental role".

His Lordship also left open the possibility that judicial review might lie if the applicant had no contractual relationship with the Jockey Club, or the Club failed to fulfil its obligations under its charter by making discriminatory rules. The Aga Khan could always proceed by writ seeking a declaration and injunction. Hoffmann L.J. (at 931–933) held that the Jockey Club operated entirely in the private sector and its activities were governed by private law. While the absence of a formal public source of power was not conclusive the power "needs to be identified as governmental in nature", and neither the Jockey Club nor the NGRC exercised such powers. There was nothing to suggest that if the Jockey Club had not voluntarily assumed the regulation of racing, the government would feel obliged or inclined to set up a statutory body. The mere fact of power, even over a substantial area of economic activity, was not enough. While in some situations, the private law remedies in respect of exercises of private power by domestic bodies were inadequate, the answer was not to patch them up by pretending they were organs of government. Here, however, the private law remedies open to the Aga Khan were entirely adequate. (Contrast the position as it was seen in *Datafin*.)

D. Pannick ([1992] P.L. 1) argues that the courts have taken an unduly restrictive approach to the scope of judicial review. The key question should be whether a body exercises monopolistic powers. If it does, judicial review should not be ruled out on the basis of a consensual submission to jurisdiction, as the individual in question has "no effective choice but to comply with their rules, regulations and decisions in order to operate in that area" (p.3). Moreover, it should not be necessary to speculate as to what Parliament would do but for the existence of the body in question; the fact that powers are monopolistic is sufficient itself to justify the imposition of minimum standards on the substance and procedure of decision-making in that context (p.6).

The Court of Appeal in *Ex p. Aga Khan* clearly took a different view. However, there are difficulties in the reasoning. First, it seems difficult to conclude that powers are not governmental if it is the case that a public body would be established were the private organisation not already in operation; yet this is the position taken by Sir Thomas Bingham M.R. (Farquharson and Hoffmann L.JJ. were agreed that government would not necessarily establish a public regulatory body in the absence of the Jockey Club). Secondly, any argument that because powers are expressed directly or indirectly by contract therefore they cannot be governmental cannot stand with Hoffmann L.J.'s point that a body that exercises governmental powers is "not any the less amenable to public law because it has contractual relations with its members". It is submitted that Hoffmann L.J.'s view is to be preferred. Thirdly, the position of persons significantly affected by Jockey Club decisions (*e.g.* warning them off racecourses) but who are not in a contractual relationship with the Jockey Club could be particularly unfortunate.

On the one hand, there are hints from Sir Thomas Bingham M.R. and Farquharson L.J. that judicial review may be available in such a case (although it is difficult to see how the powers would suddenly become "governmental"). On the other hand, private law might not provide an appropriate remedy, for reasons given by Hoffmann L.J. Fourthly, the extent of the *de facto* monopoly exercised by the Jockey Club provides a good illustration of Pannick's criticism of reliance by the courts on the technicality that jurisdiction is conferred by consent in circumstances where there is "no effective choice".

Much of the comment on *Ex p. Aga Khan* has been critical: see M.J. Beloff Q.C. and T. Kerr, "Judicial Control of Sporting Rules: The Commonwealth Jurisprudence" *Sports and the Law Journal*, Vol.3, issue 1 (Spring 1995), p.5, and "Why *Aga Khan* is Wrong" [1996] J.R. 30. See also N. Bamforth, [1993] P.L. 239. (The Aga Khan responded to the Court of Appeal's decision by withdrawing all his horses from British racing for several years.)

6. The undesirable consequences of *Aga Khan* have been addressed by the firm acceptance in subsequent cases, prompted in part by the unavailability of judicial review, that even in the absence of a contractual relationship between the claimant and a body such as the Jockey Club, the High Court may exercise a supervisory jurisdiction analogous to judicial review in accordance with the principles of *Nagle v Fielden* [1966] 2 Q.B. 633. This enables the court to grant an injunction or declaration to prevent an unreasonable restraint of trade affecting a person's right to work, and is available in "application" as well as "expulsion" or "forfeiture" cases (*cf. McInnes v Onslow Fane*, above, p.683). The existence of this supervisory jurisdiction has been recognised by Carnwath J. in *Stevenage Borough Football Club Ltd v The Football League Ltd, The Times*, August 1, 9, 1996; Latham L.J. in *Modahl v British Athletic Federation Ltd* [2002] 1 W.L.R. 1192 and Richards J. in *Bradley v Jockey Club* [2004] EWHC 2164, QBD.

Indeed Richards J. in *Bradley* stated that essentially the same principles of fairness, rationality and proportionality (in relation to penalties) applied in the exercise of this supervisory jurisdiction, *whether the basis for it was contractual or non-contractual*, as on judicial review. His Lordship cited observations as to the similarity of the principles of fairness applicable on judicial review and where required by contract by Lord Woolf C.J. in *Wilander v Tobin* [1997] 2 LL Rep. 293 at 299–300 and *Modahl v British Athletic Federation*, unreported, July 28, 1997, CA (concerning implied terms requiring procedural fairness in contractual arrangements for the exercise of disciplinary functions by the International Tennis Federation and the BAF) and held that the same should apply where such powers were exercised on a non-contractual basis. Here, a five-year disqualification from involvement in racing was imposed on a jockey who had since retired and, following retirement had carried on business as a bloodstock agent. An eight-year disqualification had been imposed by the Jockey Club's Disciplinary Committee. An independent Appeal Board established by the Rules of Racing dismissed an appeal on liability but reduced the period of disqualification. Richards J. held that this decision was subject to the court's supervisory jurisdiction either (1) on a non-contractual basis; or (2) on the basis of a contract established by a post-retirement exchange of correspondence, into which a term should be implied that the Jockey Club would give effect to the lawful decision of the Appeal Board, or would not implement any penalty or sanction not lawfully decided on by the Appeal Board. The nature of the supervisory jurisdiction was the same on either approach. There could be no implied term that only a proportionate penalty could be imposed and that it was for the court to determine the question of proportionality, making its own assessment. That was not necessary for the efficacy of the contract; one of the grounds of appeal to the Appeal Board was on the ground of lack of proportionality. Instead, the court could only interfere if the decision was unlawful as falling outside the limits of the decision-maker's discretionary area of judgment.

Other points of interest left open by Richards J. were (1) whether *Nagle v Fielden* was in truth itself a restraint of trade case or whether the restraint of trade doctrine is a jurisprudentially distinct basis for supervision by the court in a non-contractual context; and (2) whether in the case of a challenge to the rationality of the Rules it would be for the Jockey Club to justify the rules or for a challenger to show they were unreasonable. (See further Carnwath J. in the *Stevenage* case, where he held that some of the criteria used for promotion of a football club to the (then) Third Division of the Football League were open to objection on the ground of restraint of trade, although it was doubtful whether they were arbitrary or capricious. Nevertheless, the proceedings were dismissed on the ground of delay, and an appeal to the Court of Appeal was dismissed largely for that reason) (1997) 9 Admin. L.R. 109. The Court of Appeal dismissed an appeal, expressly approving Richards J.'s judgment: [2005] EWCA Civ 1056.

This development is to be welcomed. It shows that private law remedies are available on a much stronger basis than assumed by the Court of Appeal in *Datafin*. If that is so, it is submitted that an important part of the *Datafin* analysis is undermined. Is there any reason which a non-contractual private law supervisory jurisdiction should not be applicable to the Take-over Panel?

7. Outside the sporting field, it has been held that a decision of the Chief Rabbi in respect of the dismissal of a Rabbi was not subject to judicial review (*R. v The Chief Rabbi, Ex p. Wachmann* [1992] 1 W.L.R. 1036). To attract the court's supervisory jurisdiction there had to be not merely a public but potentially a governmental interest in the decision-making power in question. It could not be suggested that but for the office of the Chief Rabbi, the Government would impose a statutory regime. By contrast, decisions of the Rabbinical Commission, chaired by the Chief Rabbi, in the exercise of statutory licensing functions under the Slaughterhouses Act 1974, Sch.1, were subject to judicial review (*R. v Rabbinical Commission Ex p. Cohen*, unreported, December 14, 1987, CA). Similarly, in *R. v Imam of Bury Park Jame Masjid, Luton Ex p. Sulaiman Ali* [1994] C.O.D. 142, the Imam's decision that the applicants were not eligible to vote in the election of the executive committee of a mosque was held not to be subject to judicial review. It lacked the requisite public element and involved matters intimate to a religious community.

Other matters and bodies falling outside the scope of judicial review, variously as concerning contractual or non-governmental relationships, include the decision of an independent school to expel a pupil (*R. v Headmaster of Fernhill Manor School Ex p. Brown* [1992] C.O.D. 446); Lloyd's of London (*R. v Lloyd's of London Ex p. Briggs* [1993] 1 Lloyds L.R. 176, DC, followed by Stanley Burnton J. in *Doll-Steinberg v Society of Lloyd's* [2002] EWHC 419 and approved by the Court of Appeal in *R. (on the application of West) v Lloyd's of London* [2004] EWCA Civ 506; [2004] 3 All E.R. 251, the court also holding that Lloyd's, a commercial organisation, was not a public authority within s.6 of the HRA); the Insurance Ombudsman (*R. v Insurance Ombudsman Bureau Ex p. Aegon Life Assurance Ltd*, DC [1994] C.O.D. 426) and the Personal Investment Authority Ombudsman Bureau (*R. (on the application of Mooyer) v Personal Investment Authority Ombudsman Bureau Ltd* [2001] EWHC Admin 247; the actions of a developer not exercising public functions (*R. v Eurotunnel Developments Ltd Ex p. Stephens* (1995) 73 P. & C.R. 1; ABTA in enforcing the Code of Conduct applicable to its members (*R. v Association of British Travel Agents Ex p. Sunspell Ltd* [2001] A.C.D. 16; the Scout Association in respect of its decision not to renew the warrant of a venture scout leader (*Williamson v Hunter* [2001] EWHC Admin 1189); the British Council as regards its accreditation scheme for language schools that teach English to foreign students (*R. (on the application of Oxford Study Centre Ltd) v British Council* [2001] EWHC Admin 207) the actions of a developer not exercising public functions (*R. v Eurotunnel Developments Ltd Ex p. Stephens* (1995) 73 P. & C.R. 1).

8. The position is more difficult where the institution is a statutory body, which is clearly amenable to judicial review in respect of its statutory functions, but which is dealing with what is arguably a contractual matter. This situation was considered in *R. v East Berkshire HA Ex p. Walsh* (below, p.957). Cases near the borderline where a public authority has been held to be performing a public function include *R. v Kidderminster District Valuer Ex p. Powell* (1992) 4 Admin. L.R. 193 where the

Divisional Court held that the valuation by the district valuer of a particular house for the purpose of determining the maximum limit of rent allowance payable to a police officer under the Police Regulations 1987 (SI 1987/851), reg.49(4)(b), was a public function subject to judicial review. It was a function performed within the statutory framework of the regulations and had important public elements.

9. There are, however, cases where the exercise of what appears to be a non-statutory function by a statutory body has been held amenable to judicial review. See *e.g. R v Norfolk County Council Ex p. M* [1989] 1 Q.B. 619, in respect of the council's decision to enter M's name on a register of child abusers even though there was no statutory basis for the register. (But this could be said to be incidental to the council's statutory functions concerning child care, although the case was not argued on that basis.) Other non-statutory bodies which have been held to be amenable to judicial review include the following: a hospital ethics committee (*R. v Ethical Committee of St Mary's Hospital Ex p. Harriott* [1988] 1 F.L.R. 512 (criticised by A. Grubb and D. Pearl, [1988] C.L.J. 167)); the Civil Service Appeal Board, which is a non-statutory body established under the royal prerogative to hear appeals against the dismissal of civil servants (*R. v Civil Service Appeal Board Ex p. Bruce* [1979] I.C.R. 171); the Advertising Standards Authority, a non-statutory body that regulates advertisers (*R. v Advertising Standards Authority Ltd Ex p. The Insurance Service plc* [1990] C.O.D. 42); the Professional Conduct Committee of the General Council of the Bar (*R. v General Council of the Bar Ex p. Percival* [1991] 1 Q.B. 212); the Code of Practice Committee of the Association of the British Pharmaceutical Industry, a voluntary self-regulating body whose Code of Practice had emerged in its present form as a result of consultation with the Department of Health (*R. v Code of Practice Committee of the Association of the British Pharmaceutical Industry Ex p. Professional Counselling Aids Ltd* [1991] C.O.D. 228); LAUTRO (*R. v Life Assurance Trust Regulatory Organisation Ex p. Ross* [1992] 1 All E.R. 422); FIMBRA (*R. v Financial Intermediaries Managers and Brokers Regulatory Association Ex p. Cochrane* [1991] BCLC 106: concession by counsel for FIMBRA); a university visitor (*R. v Visitor of the University of Hull Ex p. Page* [1991] 1 W.L.R. 1277); the judges of the High Court sitting as Visitors to the Inns of Court (*R. v Visitors to the Inns of Court Ex p. Calder* [1993] Q.B. 1); ICSTIS (an independent body set up by agreement between British Telecom and other network operators to supervise premium-rate telephone services, exercising jurisdiction by virtue of contracts between the service providers and the network operators) (*R. v Independent Committee for the Supervision of Telephone Information Services Ex p. Firstcode Ltd* [1993] C.O.D. 325); a company that administers a scheme established by the Securities and Investments Board in the exercise of statutory powers (*R. v Investors Compensation Scheme Ex p. Weyell Ltd* [1994] Q.B. 749; here, the company accepted that it was subject to judicial review); a city technology college (*R. v Governors of Haberdashers' Aske's Hatcham College Trust Ex p. T* [1995] E.L.R. 350, and (possibly) the BBC as regards the allocation of party political broadcasts (*R. v BBC Ex p. Referendum Party* (1997) 9 Admin. L.R. 553); that the BBC was so amenable was assumed by the Court of Appeal and House of Lords in *R. (on the application of Pro Life Alliance) v BBC* [2003] UKHL 23; [2004] 1 A.C. 185; and a private psychiatric hospital registered under the Registered Homes Act 1984 in respect of decisions that affected persons detained under the Mental Health Act 1983, s.3 (*R. (on the application of A) v Partnerships in Care Ltd*) [2002] EWHC Admin 529; [2002] 1 W.L.R. 2610).

10. Where a function falls in general within the scope of judicial review, there must still normally be a *decision* in the exercise of that function if an application is to be entertained. In *R. v London Waste Regulation Authority Ex p. Specialist Waste Management Ltd, The Times*, November 1, 1988, an expression of opinion, to a person using plant to dispose of "controlled waste" within the meaning of the Control of Pollution Act 1974, to the effect that he required a disposal licence, was held not to be amenable to judicial review. It was not a decision to which the applicant had to conform. Similarly, in *R. v Devon CC Ex p. L* [1991] 2 F.L.R. 541, Eastham J. held that

a letter from the council responding to a request that social workers refrained from disseminating the belief that L was a child sex abuser, in the absence of a case conference or other proceedings, was not a "decision" amenable to judicial review: the letter dealt solely with what had occurred in the past and did not deal with the assurance requested. Then, in *R. v Secretary of State for Health Ex p. Imperial Tobacco Ltd*, unreported December 21, 1999, QBD, Hidden J. held that a report of the Scientific Committee on Tobacco and Health that contained damaging criticisms of tobacco companies, including IT Ltd, was not amenable to judicial review; SCOTH was an advisory body and the report was only the first stage of the Secretary of State's assessment of whether the Government's health policy on smoking ought to change; it was "merely a stage in the decision-making process and not the fulfilment of it". (There was also no legitimate expectation of consultation.) *cf. R. v Secretary of State for the Environment Ex p. Greenwich LBC, The Times*, May 17, 1989 (decision to issue leaflet on the community charge potentially open to judicial review for abuse of discretion: see C.R. Munro, [1990] P.L. 1, at pp.7–9); *R. v Secretary of State for Employment Ex p. Equal Opportunities Commission* [1995] 1 A.C. 1 (Secretary of State's letter expressing the view that provisions of the Employment Protection (Consolidation) Act 1978 were compatible with Community law not a "decision" amenable to the supervisory jurisdiction; a declaration stating that the provisions were incompatible was nevertheless available (see further below, p.1031)). See further *Lewis*, Ch.4.

R. v EAST BERKSHIRE HEALTH AUTHORITY Ex p. WALSH

[1985] Q.B. 152; [1985] 3 W.L.R. 818; [1984] I.C.R. 743; [1984] 3 All E.R. 425 (COURT OF APPEAL) (*PET. DIS.*, [1984] 1 W.L.R. 1357, H.L.)

The applicant, a senior nursing officer employed by the health authority under a contract which incorporated the Whitley Council agreement on conditions of service in the health service, was dismissed by a district nursing officer for misconduct. He applied for judicial review under RSC, Ord.53, for an order of certiorari to quash the dismissal on the grounds that the district nursing officer had no power to dismiss him and that there had been a breach of the rules of natural justice in the procedure which led up to his dismissal. The health authority raised the preliminary point whether the subject matter of the application entitled the applicant to apply for judicial review. The judge held that, although the public might have no interest in an ordinary master and servant case, the public was concerned to see that a great public service acted lawfully and fairly to its officers and the remedy of an order of certiorari would be an appropriate remedy. Alternatively, the judge held that it would be appropriate to allow the proceedings to continue under Ord.53, r.9(5), as if they had been begun by writ. The Court of Appeal allowed an appeal by the health authority.

SIR JOHN DONALDSON M.R.:. . . I now return to the main issue, namely whether the applicant's complaints give rise to any right to judicial review. They all relate to his employment by the health authority and the purported termination of his employment and of his contract of employment. Essentially they fall into two distinct categories. The first relates to Miss Cooper's power to act on behalf of the authority in dismissing him. The second relates to the extent to which there was any departure from the rules of natural justice in the procedures which led up to that dismissal. Both fall well within the jurisdiction of an industrial tribunal. The first goes to whether or not the applicant was dismissed at all within the meaning of section 55 of the Employment Protection (Consolidation) Act 1978. The second goes to whether the dismissal, if such there was, was unfair. Furthermore, both are issues which not uncommonly arise when the employer is a company or individual, as contrasted with a statutory authority. However, this only goes to the exercise of the court's discretion, whether or not to give leave to apply for and whether or not to grant judicial review. As the authority seek to have the proceedings dismissed in limine, if they are to succeed they can only do so on the basis that, accepting all the applicant's complaints as valid, the remedy of judicial review is nevertheless wholly inappropriate and the continuance of the application for judicial review would involve a misuse—the term "abuse" has offensive overtones—of the procedure of the court under R.S.C., Ord.53.

The remedy of judicial review is only available where an issue of "public law" is involved, but, as Lord Wilberforce pointed out in *Davy v Spelthorne Borough Council* [1984] A.C. 262, 276, the expressions "public law" and "private law" are recent immigrants and, whilst convenient for descriptive purposes, must be used with caution, since English law traditionally fastens not so much upon principles as upon remedies. On the other hand, to concentrate on remedies would in the present context involve a degree of circularity or levitation by traction applied to shoe-strings, since the remedy of certiorari might well be available if the health authority is in breach of a "public law" obligation, but would not be if it is only in breach of a "private law" obligation.

The judge referred carefully and fully to *Vine v National Dock Labour Board* [1957] A.C. 488; *Ridge v Baldwin* [1964] A.C. 40 and *Malloch v Aberdeen Corporation* [1971] 1 W.L.R. 1578. He seems to have accepted that there was no "public law" element in an "ordinary" relationship of master and servant and that accordingly in such a case judicial review would not be available. However, he held, on the basis of these three cases and, in particular, *Malloch's* case, that the applicant's relationship was not "ordinary". He said:

"The public may have no interest in the relationship between servant and master in an 'ordinary' case, but where the servant holds office in a great public service, the public is properly concerned to see that the authority employing him acts towards him lawfully and fairly. It is not a pure question of contract. The public is concerned that the nurses who serve the public should be treated lawfully and fairly by the public authority employing them. . . . It follows that if in the exercise of my discretion I conclude that the remedy of certiorari is appropriate, it can properly go against the respondent authority."

The judge then said that if he was wrong in this conclusion, it would be appropriate to allow the proceedings to continue as if they had been begun by writ: see R.S.C., Ord.53, r.9(5).

None of the three decisions of the House of Lords to which I have referred was directly concerned with the scope of judicial review under R.S.C., Ord.53. Two, *Ridge v Baldwin* [1964] A.C. 40 and *Malloch v Aberdeen Corporation* [1971] 1 W.L.R. 1578, were concerned with whether or not the plaintiff had a right to be heard before being dismissed and the third, *Vine v National Dock Labour Board* [1957] A.C. 488, with whether the body purporting to dismiss was acting *ultra vires*. *Vine's* case and *Ridge's* case were actions begun by writ. *Malloch's* case was a Scottish proceeding in which the remedy of "production and reduction" was claimed. This is indeed akin to certiorari, but it is available whether or not the claim involves "public" or "administrative" law. There are, however, dicta, particularly in the speech of Lord Wilberforce in *Malloch's* case, which may be thought to point the way in which we should go.

[His Lordship then considered passages by Lord Reid in *Ridge v Baldwin* (above, p.658), and by Lords Reid and Wilberforce in *Malloch* (above, p.672.)]

In all three cases there was a special statutory provision bearing directly upon the right of a public authority to dismiss the plaintiff. In *Vine v National Dock Labour Board* [1957] A.C. 488 the employment was under the statutory dock labour scheme and the issue concerned the statutory power to dismiss given by that scheme. In *Ridge v Baldwin* [1964] A.C. 40 the power of dismissal was conferred by statute: section 191(4) of the Municipal Corporations Act 1882 (45 & 46 Vict. c. 50). In *Malloch v Aberdeen Corporation* [1971] 1 W.L.R. 1578 again it was statutory: section 3 of the Public Schools (Scotland) Teachers Act 1882 (45 & 46 Vict. c.18). As Lord Wilberforce said, at 1595–1596, it is the existence of these statutory provisions which injects the element of public law necessary in this context to attract the remedies of administrative law. Employment by a public authority does not *per se* inject any element of public law. Nor does the fact that the employee is in a "higher grade" or is an "officer". This only makes it more likely that there will be special statutory restrictions upon dismissal, or other underpinning of his employment: see *per* Lord Reid in *Malloch v Aberdeen Corporation*, at 1582. It will be this underpinning and not the seniority which injects the element of public law. Still less can I find any warrant for equating public law with the interest of the public. If the public through Parliament gives effect to that interest by means of statutory provisions, that is quite different, but the interest of the public *per se* is not sufficient.

I have therefore to consider whether and to what extent the applicant's complaints involve an element of public law sufficient to attract public law remedies, whether in the form of certiorari or a declaration. That he had the benefit of the general employment legislation is clear, but it was not contended that this was sufficient to attract administrative law remedies. What is relied upon are statutory restrictions upon the freedom of the authority to employ senior and other nursing officers on what terms it thought fit. This restriction is contained in the National Health Service (Remuneration and Conditions of Service) Regulations 1974 (S.I. 1974 No.296), which provides by regulation 3(2):

"Where conditions of service, other than conditions with respect to remuneration, of any class of officers have been the subject of negotiations by a negotiating body and have been approved by the Secretary of State after considering the result of those negotiations, the conditions of service of any officer belonging to that class shall include the conditions so approved."

The conditions of service of, *inter alios*, senior nursing officers were the subject of negotiations by a negotiating body, namely the Whitley Council for the Health Service (Great Britain) and the resulting agreement was approved by the Secretary of State. It follows, as I think, that if the applicant's conditions of service had differed from those approved conditions, he would have had an administrative law remedy by way of judicial review enabling him to require the authority to amend the terms of service contained in his contract of employment. But that is not the position. His notification of employment dated May 12, 1975, which is a memorandum of his contract of employment, expressly adopted the Whitley Council agreement on conditions of service.

When analysed, the applicant's complaint is different. It is that *under* those conditions of service Miss Cooper had no right to dismiss him and that *under* those conditions he was entitled to a bundle of rights which can be collectively classified as "natural justice". Thus he says, and I have to assume for present purposes that he is correct, that under section XXXIV of the Whitley Council's agreement on conditions of service, his position as a senior nursing officer is such that his employment can only be terminated by a decision of the full employing authority and that this power of dismissal cannot be delegated to any officer or committee of officers. I do not think that he relies upon any express provision of those conditions when claiming the right to natural justice, but if he has such a right, apart from the wider right not to be unfairly dismissed which includes the right to natural justice, it clearly arises out of those conditions and is implicit in them.

The ordinary employer is free to act in breach of his contracts of employment and if he does so his employee will acquire certain private law rights and remedies in damages for wrongful dismissal, compensation for unfair dismissal, an order for reinstatement or re-engagement and so on. Parliament can underpin the position of public authority employees by directly restricting the freedom of the public authority to dismiss, thus giving the employee "public law" rights and at least making him a potential candidate for administrative law remedies. Alternatively it can require the authority to contract with its employees on specified terms with a view to the employee acquiring "private law" rights under the terms of the contract of employment. If the authority fails or refuses to thus create "private law" rights for the employee, the employee will have "public law" rights to compel compliance, the remedy being mandamus requiring the authority so to contract or a declaration that the employee has those rights. If, however, the authority gives the employee the required contractual protection, a breach of that contract is not a matter of "public law" and gives rise to no administrative law remedies. . . .

I therefore conclude that there is no "public law" element in the applicant's complaints which could give rise to any entitlement to administrative law remedies. I confess that I am not sorry to have been led to this conclusion, since a contrary conclusion would have enabled *all* National Health Service employees to whom the Whitley Council agreement on conditions of service apply to seek judicial review. Whilst it is true that the judge seems to have thought that this right would be confined to senior employees, I see no grounds for any such restriction in principle. The most that can be said is that only senior employees could complain of having been dismissed in the exercise of delegated authority, because it is only senior employees who are protected from such dismissal. *All* employees would, however, have other rights based upon the fact that Parliament had intervened to specify and, on this view, protect those conditions of service as a matter of "public law".

In my judgment, this is not therefore a case for judicial review. . . .

[His Lordship declined to allow the matter to proceed under RSC, Ord.53, r.9(5) as if it had been sought in an action begun by writ; this was not designed to allow the applicant to amend and claim different relief and the papers had contained only a brief reference to a possible claim for a declaration and no reference to a claim for damages or in debt for accrued wages.]

MAY and PURCHAS L.JJ. delivered concurring speeches.

Appeal allowed.

Notes

1. See H. Collins, (1984) 13 I.L.J. 174; Y. Cripps, [1984] C.L.J. 214; K.D. Ewing and A. Grubb, (1987) 16 I.L.J. 145 at pp.146–155; B. Walsh, [1989] P.L. 131; S. Fredman and G.S. Morris, [1988] P.L. 58, *The State as Employer* (1989), Chs 3 and 7, (1991) 107 L.Q.R. 298 and [1991] P.L. 485; M.R. Freedland, (1990) 19 I.L.J. 199 and (1991) 20 I.L.J. 72.

2. Note the fine distinction drawn between questions concerning the *incorporation* of Whitley Council conditions and the *application* of the approved conditions. Is this distinction workable? Is it perhaps explained by the variant of the familiar "flood-gates" argument that appears later in Sir John Donaldson's judgment?

3. In *McClaren v Home Office* [1990] I.C.R. 824, a prison officer was suspended without pay for refusing to work a new shift system. The officer brought a private law action claiming, *inter alia*, a declaration that he was still employed on the basis of the previous shift system and the payment of salary withheld. He contended that the new system was in breach of the Fresh Start collective agreement between the Home Office and the Prison Officers' Association and a local agreement, and that these agreements were incorporated into his contract or his conditions of service. The Court of Appeal refused to strike out the claim, rejecting the Home Office's argument that the officer could only apply for judicial review, and holding that it was at least arguable that the officer had a contractual claim. A helpful analysis was provided by Woolf L.J. (at 836–837):

"There are two issues on this appeal. (1) Is the plaintiff required to bring his claim against the Home Office by way of judicial review? (2) If he is not required to bring his proceedings by way of judicial review has he a reasonable cause of action or was his claim correctly struck out as being clearly unsustainable?
The first issue
In resolving this issue the following principles have to be borne in mind.
(1) In relation to his personal claims against an employer, an employee of a public body is normally in exactly the same situation as other employees. If he has a cause of action and he wishes to assert or establish his rights in relation to his employment he can bring proceedings for damages, a declaration or an injunction (except in relation to the Crown) in the High Court or the county court in the ordinary way. The fact that a person is employed by the Crown may limit his rights against the Crown but otherwise his position is very much the same as any other employee. However, he may, instead of having an ordinary master and servant relationship with the Crown, hold office under the Crown and may have been appointed to that office as a result of the Crown exercising a prerogative power or, as in this case, a statutory power. If he holds such an appointment then it will almost invariably be terminable at will and may be subject to other limitations, but whatever rights the employee has will be enforceable normally by an ordinary action. Not only will it not be necessary for him to seek relief by way of judicial review, it will normally be inappropriate for him to do so: see *Kodeeswaran v Attorney-General of Ceylon* [1970] A.C. 1111; *R. v East Berkshire Health Authority, Ex p. Walsh* [1984] I.C.R. 743 and *R. v Derbyshire County Council, Ex p. Noble* [1990] I.C.R. 808.
(2) There can however be situations where an employee of a public body can seek judicial review and obtain a remedy which would not be available to an employee in the private sector. This will arise where there exists some disciplinary or other

body established under the prerogative or by statute to which the employer or the employee is entitled or required to refer disputes affecting their relationship. The procedure of judicial review can then be appropriate because it has always been part of the role of the court in public law proceedings to supervise inferior tribunals and the court in reviewing disciplinary proceedings is performing a similar role. As long as the 'tribunal' or other body has a sufficient public law element, which it almost invariably will have if the employer is the Crown, and it is not domestic or wholly informal, its proceedings and determination can be an appropriate subject for judicial review. An example is provided here by the decision of the Divisional Court in *R. v Civil Service Appeal Board, Ex p. Bruce* [1988] I.C.R. 649. If there had not been available the more effective alternative remedy before an industrial tribunal, the Divisional Court would have regarded the decision of the Civil Service Appeal Board in that case as reviewable upon judicial review. The decision of this court which has just been given in *R. v Secretary of State for the Home Department, Ex p. Attard, The Times*, March 14, 1990 [[1990] C.O.D. 261] is another example of the same situation. There what was being considered by this court were the powers of a prison governor in connection with disciplinary proceedings in respect of prison officers. The prison governor's disciplinary powers in relation to prisoners are reviewable only on judicial review (see *Leech v Deputy Governor of Parkhurst Prison* [1988] A.C. 533) and they can also be reviewed on judicial review where they affect a prison officer on the application of that officer.

(3) In addition if an employee of the Crown or other public body is adversely affected by a decision of general application by his employer, but he contends that that decision is flawed on what I loosely describe as *Wednesbury* grounds (*Associated Provincial Picture Houses Ltd v Wednesbury Corporation* [1948] 1 K.B. 223), he can be entitled to challenge that decision by way of judicial review. Within this category comes *Council of Civil Service Unions v Minister for the Civil Service* [1985] I.C.R. 14. In the House of Lords there was no dispute as to whether the case was appropriately brought by way of judicial review. The House of Lords assumed that it was and I would respectfully suggest that they were right to do so. The decision under challenge was one affecting employees at GCHQ generally. The action which was being challenged was the instruction by the Minister for the Civil Service in the interests of national security to vary the terms and conditions of service of the staff so that they would no longer be permitted to belong to trade unions. Although the decision affected individual members of the staff, it was a decision which was taken as a matter of policy, not in relation to a particular member of staff, but in relation to staff in general and so it could be the subject of judicial review.

(4) There can be situations where although there are disciplinary procedures which are applicable they are of a purely domestic nature and therefore, albeit that their decisions might affect the public, the process of judicial review will not be available. However this does not mean that a particular employee who is adversely affected by those disciplinary proceedings will not have a remedy. The existence of the disciplinary proceedings may be highly material to indicate that the category of employee concerned, unlike an ordinary employee, is not limited to a claim for damages but can in the appropriate circumstances in an ordinary action seek a declaration or an injunction to ensure that the proceedings are conducted fairly. (As to dismissal see *Ridge v Baldwin* [1964] A.C. 40, 65, *per* Lord Reid; *Law v National Greyhound Racing Club Ltd* [1983] 1 W.L.R. 1302 and *R. v British Broadcasting Corporation, Ex p. Lavelle* [1983] I.C.R. 99.)".

Woolf L.J. concluded that the proceedings here fell with the first of these categories, and that concluded the first issue in favour of the plaintiff. (See also his judgment in *R. v Derbyshire CC Ex p. Noble* [1990] I.C.R. 808. For comments on *McClaren* and *Ex p. Noble*, see H. Carty, (1991) 54 M.L.R. 129.)

4. *Ex p. Walsh* has been applied by Macpherson J. in *R. v Trent Regional HA Ex p. Jones, The Times*, June 19, 1986 (refusal to appoint consultant surgeon not subject

to judicial review; no statutory underpinning); by Russell J. in *R. v South Glamorgan HA Ex p. Phillips, The Times*, November 21, 1986 (disciplinary decision of the health authority declared to be of no effect as the disciplinary tribunal had applied the wrong standard of proof; the judge allowed an application for judicial review to be continued as if begun by writ under r. 9(5)); by the Court of Appeal in *R. v Derbyshire CC Ex p. Noble* [1990] I.C.R. 808 (termination of appointment as deputy police surgeon held not to have a sufficient public law element to attract judicial review); by Otton J. in *R. v Secretary of State for the Home Department Ex p. Hebron*, unreported, January 18, 1991 (challenge to dismissal of prison officer held to be a private law matter; leave to apply for judicial review set aside); by the Court of Appeal in *R. v City of London Polytechnic Ex p. Amir Ali Majid*, unreported, November 1, 1993 (failure to appoint lecturer in constitutional and administrative law to principal lectureship, allegedly on racial grounds, held to be a "private matter" although it was "not a question of contract because . . . it was open to anyone to apply"); by the Court of Appeal in *R. v Crown Prosecution Service v Hogg* (1994) 6 Admin. L.R. 778 (dismissal of Crown Prosecutor; however, the Court indicated that had action been based on the exercise of a discretion as prosecutor, there would have been a sufficient public element given the "cardinal importance of maintaining the total independence and impartiality" of the CPS (Hirst L.J.)); and by Scott Baker J. in *Evans v University of Cambridge* [2002] EWHC Admin 1382; [2002] E.L.R. 8 (in respect of the University's promotion procedure for lecturers). These seem to fall into Woolf L.J.'s category (1).

5. Other examples of Woolf L.J.'s category (3) include the following. In *R. v Liverpool City Council Ex p. Ferguson, The Times*, November 20, 1985, the council's decision to dismiss all teachers in order to alleviate the consequences of its failure to set a rate sufficient to balance its budget was declared *ultra vires* as it (1) was the direct consequence of setting an illegal rate; (2) was not made for proper educational purposes; and (3) would lead to a breach of the council's duties under the Education Act 1944, s. 8, to secure the provision of sufficient schools (see G. Morris, (1986) 15 I.L.J. 194). In further proceedings involving most of the same parties, *R. v Liverpool City Council Ex p. Ferguson and Ferguson* [1985] I.R.L.R. 501, the council's decision to refuse to pay teachers who presented themselves for work on a "day of action", but who were unable to work because of the actions of other trade unionists, was quashed on the grounds of unreasonableness. Mann J., applying a statement by Sir John Donaldson M.R. in *R. v Herefordshire CC Ex p. N.U.P.E.* [1985] I.R.L.R. 258 at 260, held that the allegation of *Wednesbury* unreasonableness rendered the matter justiciable by way of judicial review. This broad approach is criticised by Bernadette Walsh at [1989] P.L. 131 at pp.149–152, noting that this:

"puts the cart before the horse. The primary question is surely whether the public authority in the performance of a particular function is subject to judicial review. If it is subject to judicial review, then an applicant may challenge the performance of the particular function on the grounds of unreasonableness. The approach advocated by Donaldson M.R. is rather to ask whether the challenge is based on unreasonableness and, if it is, to conclude that the applicant is entitled to judicial review. . . . It is most unlikely that Donaldson M.R intended that the principles in Walsh should be subverted by the simple expedient of basing a challenge on this ground". (See also M. Stokes, (1985) 14 I.L.J. 117 pp.119–120.)

This comment is perhaps echoed by the Divisional Court in *R. v Hammersmith and Fulham LBC Ex p. NALGO* [1990] I.R.L.R. 249, where Nolan L.J. stated (at 256):

"I do not believe that Woolf L.J. was saying [in his category (3)] that every policy decision of a public authority affecting its employees as a whole is automatically justiciable as a matter of public law".

Nevertheless, he went on to hold that an allegation, as in the present case, that the adoption by a local authority of an employment or redeployment policy that was in breach of the Sex Discrimination Act or the Race Relations Act or was otherwise unlawful on *Wednesbury* grounds, could be challenged by way of judicial review. On the facts, it could not be shown that the policy as a whole was unlawful. The most that could be said was that the implementation of the policy might offend the law in individual cases, depending on how the implementation was carried out. This could only properly be tested on a case-by-case basis in pursuance of the applicants' private law remedies.

A further example is provided by *R. v Walsall MBC Ex p. Yapp* (1993) 92 L.G.R. 110 where the Court of Appeal entertained (but rejected on its merits) an application for judicial review of the council's resolution to seek fresh competitive tenders for building work, brought by employees in the council's Building Works Division. The applicants contended that this resolution interfered with their legitimate expectations arising out of a resolution passed three months earlier by which the work was given to the Building Works Division; the council argued in its defence that acceptance of these claims would fetter its discretion under the relevant statutory powers. Nolan L.J. (at 113) was

> "satisfied . . . that the conduct of the council falls to be judged by public law principles. The statutory element, if nothing else, brings the case within the scope of our public law jurisdiction".

6. The question of the availability (and possible exclusivity) of judicial review has also arisen in cases concerning civil servants. Here, the long-standing view that civil servants are not employed under a contract of employment has come increasingly into question (see S. Fredman and G.S. Morris, *The State as Employer* (1989), pp.61–71 and [1988] P.L. 58). It is no longer thought that there is any constitutional bar to the contractual employment of civil servants (*Kodeeswaren v Att-Gen of Ceylon* [1970] A.C. 1111, PC), and in *R. v Lord Chancellor's Department Ex p. Nangle* [1992] 1 All E.R. 897, the Divisional Court held that there could be, and was, the necessary intention to create legal relations (not following the decision to the contrary of the Divisional Court in *R. v Civil Service Appeal Board Ex p. Bruce* [1988] I.C.R. 649). In *Nangle*, the court concluded that as the applicant was employed by the Crown under a contract of service, then, applying *Ex p. Walsh*, he had no remedy in public law. Furthermore, the court concluded that if it were wrong on that point, and there was no contract between the Crown and the civil servant, there was still not a sufficient public law element to attract judicial review: the case arose out of "internal disciplinary proceedings" which were "of a domestic nature" and "informal". (The court seemed to doubt the decision in *R. v Secretary of State for the Home Department Ex p. Benwell* [1985] Q.B. 554 where the dismissal of a prisoner officer was held to be subject to judicial review; the officer had no private law rights that could be enforced in civil proceedings. (This is alarming. It is one thing to say that a person must pursue contractual remedies rather than judicial review (or vice versa); on this argument the applicant is left without any external remedy.) See S. Fredman and G.S. Morris, [1991] P.L. 485. For further developments, see M.R. Freedland, [1995] P.L. 224. The second point in *Nangle* was, however, echoed by the decision of the Court of Appeal in *R. (on the application of Tucker) v Director General of the National Crime Squad* [2003] EWCA Civ 03; [2003] I.R.L.R. 439, where it held that an operational decision that an officer seconded to the NCS should be returned to his own force on the ground that the NCS had lost confidence in him had an insufficient public law element, not-withstanding that he had no contractual remedy. This was a matter of a "purely domestic nature". A better approach would be to regard the decision as amenable to judicial review and adjust the standard of review to the context: *Lewis*, pp.15–16.

7. The spate of cases in this area in the 1980s is reviewed by S. Fredman and G.S. Morris, "Public or Private? State Employees and Judicial Review" (1991) 107 L.Q.R. 298. They argue that the State as employer:

"has characteristics which mean that the exercise of its employment function cannot simply be regarded as a matter for regulation by private law" (p.315).

These include (pp.309–312) the source of its power to employ from statute or the prerogative; in the case of central government, its power to endow managerial decisions with the force of law; the exclusive power of the executive to decide issues of national security; the weak arrangements for political accountability to which the State is subject; and the fact that the Government derives its revenue to pay employees primarily from taxation, rather than profits. These points require recognition of a public law dimension. However, they argue that current attempts to establish a clear dividing line between the private law and public law dimensions:

"are haphazard, unpredictable and produce illogical results. . . . It is high time that the quest for the ephemeral dividing line was abandoned. Employment decisions relating to public employees should be considered in a single forum which would enable the public interest in good administration to be secured without prejudice to individual rights" (pp.315–316).

8. Outside the field of employment, there are a number of cases where the commercial or business decisions of a public body have been held not to be subject to judicial review. In *R. v National Coal Board Ex p. National Union of Mineworkers* [1986] I.C.R. 791, Macpherson J. held that the Board's decision to close a colliery contrary to a recommendation of an independent review body established by itself and the union, was not the subject of judicial review. This was:

"an executive, or business, or management decision in exactly the same category as a decision in similar circumstances made by a public company" (at 795).

It was not a decision in the exercise of powers or duties under the Coal Industry Nationalisation Act 1946, which would have been subject to judicial review (*cf. R. v British Coal Corp. Ex p. Vardy* [1993] I.C.R. 720, where decisions to close 10 collieries were quashed on the ground of non-compliance with statutory consultation procedures; after consultation, the closures proceeded lawfully: *R. v British Coal Corp. Ex p. Price (No.3), The Times*, May 28, 1993). Similarly, in *R. v Independent Broadcasting Authority Ex p. Rank Organisation Plc, The Times*, March 14, 1986, Mann J. held that the IBA's decision not to permit Rank to exercise voting rights in respect of shares constituting in excess of 5 per cent of the issued voting shares of Granada, was not subject to judicial review. The power arose under Granada's articles of association and not in the exercise of any function under the Broadcasting Act 1981. Then, in *R. (on the application of Hopley) v Liverpool HA* [2002] EWHC Admin 1723; [2002] Lloyd's Rep. Med. 494 the authority's refusal to consent to a structured settlement of a claim against it was held to be a private function. Of particular concern is the decision of the Divisional Court in *R. v Lord Chancellor Ex p. Hibbitt and Sanders (A Firm)* [1993] C.O.D. 326, that the process whereby the Lord Chancellor sought tenders and awarded contracts for the supply of court reporting services was not subject to judicial review. The judges expressly found that the LCD's approach had been, in part at least, unfair. The LCD had advertised for tenders on the basis that bids could be "clarified" in subsequent discussions. In fact it entered discussions with the companies who had submitted the four lowest tenders for services at Chelmsford leading to further reductions in the tenders, and one of these was then accepted. The applicants, who had supplied reporting services at Chelmsford for many years, were not one of the four, and would have responded to the opportunity to submit a lower bid, particularly as there had been some confusion as to the treatment of staff costs. On the jurisdiction point, the court found that there was no evidence to support the applicant's argument that the LCD enjoyed a near-monopoly status as shorthand writers were also needed for arbitrations and professional disciplinary proceedings; although employed pursuant to statutory requirements for shorthand notes to be taken of court proceedings, there was no statutory underpinning to the employment itself; the absence of any alternative remedy was immaterial to the question of the existence of a public law remedy; and it was

> "not appropriate to equate tendering conditions attendant on a common law right to contract with a statement of policy or practice or policy decisions in the spheres of Inland Revenue, immigration and the like, control of which is in the especial province of the State" (Rose L.J.). (See D. Oliver, [1993] P.L. 214.)

In other contexts, the exercise of the contractual powers of public authorities has been held to be subject to judicial review principles. The courts have sometimes, but not always taken the view that this only follows where there is a public law element in the decision (*cf.* the *East Berkshire* case). See the survey by S. Arrowsmith, "Judicial Review and the Contractual Powers of Public Authorities" (1990) 106 L.Q.R. 277. Judicial review has been held to be applicable to the termination of market trader's licences (see the discussion of the market cases in *Beer*, above, p.942; followed *R. (on the application of Agnello v Hounslow LBC* [2003] EWHC 3112 in relation to a market in respect of which the council had statutory powers, including power to make byelaws, held on publicly owned land). Decisions of local authorities as landlords have been held to be subject to judicial review without (in the earlier cases) the courts seeking to identify a public law element: *Cannock Chase DC v Kelly* [1978] 1 W.L.R. 1; *Sevenoaks DC v Emmett* (1979) 79 L.G.R. 346; *Wheeler v Leicester City Council*, above, p.543; as have procurement decisions: *R. v Lewisham LBC Ex p. Shell UK Ltd*, above, p.569; *R. v Enfield LBC Ex p. Unwin* (1989) 46 B.L.R. 1, followed in *R. v Bristol City Council Ex p. D.L. Barnett & Sons* (2001) 3 L.G.R. 163 (where Jackson J. also stated (at [45]) that "as a matter of general principle, a decision by a local authority to strike a contractor of an approved list of tenderers does contain a public law element"). On the other hand, a decision of a local authority to dispose of land under s.123 of Local Government Act 1972 is not normally amenable to judicial review (*R. v Bolsover DC Ex p. Pepper* (2000) 3 L.G.R. 337; *cf. R. (on the application of Ise Lodge Amenity Committee) v Kettering BC* [2002] EWHC Admin 1132 (fact that land had been given to the authority for use as a public open space and it had been so used for a long time sufficient to make it a public law matter)).

Compare Elias J.'s view in *R. (on the application of Molinaro) v Kensington and Chelsea RLBC* [2001] EWHC Admin 896; [2002] B.L.G.R. 336 that the exercise of contractual powers by local authorities is generally amenable to judicial review. The context was the use of the council's contractual powers as landlord to refuse consent to a change of use, to give effect to its planning policy. In these cases, the court often addresses (and rejects) the substantive ground for review as well as deciding that judicial review is not available anyway. Acceptance of Elias J.'s view would simplify litigation without changing outcomes inappropriately.

Arrowsmith (*op.cit.*, p.291) argues that the courts should "adopt the same approach to the judicial review of contractual powers as they do to the review of other activities of government"; review could be negated or limited by special policy factors, but there would be no need to identify a public law element. The *East Berkshire* case is the main (although not the only) obstacle to such a development. Can it be limited to employment cases?

(D) PROCEDURE

Notes

1. *A Pre-action protocol for judicial review* was published in 2001 and came into force on March 4, 2002. It is available on the Administrative Court Office website. It sets out a code of good practice and contains the steps which the parties should generally follow before making a claim (para.5). It is expressly stated that the protocol "will not be appropriate where the defendant does not have the legal power to change the decision being challenged", as in the case of decisions of the Immigration Appeal Authorities, or in urgent cases (para.6). Where the use of the protocol is appropriate the court will normally expect all parties to have complied with it and will take into account compliance or non-compliance when giving directions for case management or awarding costs. Even in emergency cases, it is good practice to fax the draft claim form to the defendant (para.7). The core requirements are that before making a claim, the claimant should send a letter before claim to the defendant, containing: the date and details of the decision, act or omission being challenged; a clear summary of the facts on which the claim is based; details of any relevant information the claimant is seeking and an explanation of why this is considered relevant; and details of any interested parties known to the claimant (paras 8–11). The claim should not normally be made until the proposed reply date given in the letter before claim has passed, unless the circumstances of the case require more immediate action to be taken (para.12). Defendants should normally respond within 14 days with a letter of response to the claimant and all interested parties. Failure to do so will be taken into account by the court and sanctions may be imposed unless there are good reasons (para.13). Whether the claim is being conceded in full, in part or not at all should be stated in clear and unambiguous terms. Where appropriate the letter should contain a new decision identifying the elements of the claim now conceded, or give a clear timescale within which a new decision will be issued. Also where appropriate it should give a fuller explanation, address any points in dispute or explain why they cannot be addressed, endorse any relevant document requested or explain why they are not being enclosed, and confirm whether or not they will oppose any application for an interim remedy. Standard formats for these letters which should normally be used, are set out in Annexes A and B. The protocol cannot vary the time-limits for bringing claims (see below).

The purpose of the Protocol is to facilitate the settlement of case at an early stage.

Parties or possible parties to judicial review proceedings are strongly encouraged to use Alternative Dispute Resolution processes where possible. See the remarks of Lord Woolf C.J. in *Cowl v Plymouth City Council* [2001] EWCA Civ 1935, in the context of a challenge to the closure of a residential care home:

> "1. The importance of this appeal is that it illustrates that, even in disputes between public authorities and the members of the public for whom they are responsible, insufficient attention is paid to the paramount importance of avoiding litigation whenever this is possible. Particularly in the case of these disputes both sides must by now be acutely conscious of the contribution alternative dispute resolution can make to resolving disputes in a manner which both meets the needs of the parties and the public and saves time, expense and stress.
>
> 2. The appeal also demonstrates that courts should scrutinise extremely carefully applications for judicial review in the case of applications of the class with which this appeal is concerned. The courts should then make appropriate use of their ample powers under the CPR to ensure that the parties try to resolve the dispute with the minimum involvement of the courts. The legal aid authorities should co-operate in support of this approach.
>
> 3. To achieve this objective the court may have to hold, on its own initiative, an inter partes hearing at which the parties can explain what steps they have taken to resolve the dispute without the involvement of the courts. In particular the parties

should be asked why a complaints procedure or some other form of ADR has not been used or adapted to resolve or reduce the issues which are in dispute. If litigation is necessary the courts should deter the parties from adopting an unnecessarily confrontational approach to the litigation. If this had happened in this case many thousands of pounds in costs could have been saved and considerable stress to the parties could have been avoided".

2. *The application for permission*. The procedure on a claim for judicial review is a two-stage process, modelled on the pre-1978 practice in relation to the prerogative orders (see CPR Pt 54, above, pp.927–932). The application for permission is determined in the first instance without a hearing. Where the court refuses permission or gives permission subject to conditions or on certain grounds only, it will give reasons and the claimant may within seven days request the decision to be reconsidered at a hearing (r.54.12). The Court may also direct that there should be an oral hearing. As an oral hearing still only determines whether there is an arguable case, it should not ordinarily be lengthy or fully argued (*R. (on the application of Mount Cook Land Ltd) v Westminster City Council* [2003] EWCA Civ 1346, *per* Auld L.J. at para. [73]). The statement can be amended with the court's consent.

The courts require good faith on the part of an applicant. If material facts are suppressed by the applicant, the court may dismiss the application without going into the merits (*R. v Kensington Income Tax Commissioners Ex p. de Polignac* [1917] 1 K.B. 486 (prohibition); *R. v Stevens Ex p. Callender*, [1956] C.L.Y. 2160; *The Times*, October 26, 1956; *O'Reilly v Mackman* [1983] 2 A.C. 237 at 280; *R. v Secretary of State for the Home Department Ex p. Nachatter Singh*, *The Times*, August 2, 1985; *R. v British Coal Corp. and Roo Management Ltd Ex p. G.C. Whittaker (Properties) Ltd* [1989] C.O.D. 528, appropriate to award costs on an indemnity basis *R. v Lloyd's Corp. Ex p. Briggs* [1993] 1 Lloyd's L.R. 176). All matters must be disclosed which are likely to affect the court in exercising its discretion to grant permission. Where an extension of time is granted on the basis of incomplete disclosure of the material facts the court on the *inter partes* application may reconsider the extension and dismiss the application (*R. v British Railways Board Ex p. Great Yarmouth BC*, *The Times*, March 15, 1983).

3. *The grant of permission*. Permission may be refused where the applicant has no reasonable case to put forward: *R. v Hammersmith and Fulham BC Ex p. People Before Profit Ltd* (1981) 80 L.G.R. 322. In *Inland Revenue Commissioners v National Federation of Self-Employed and Small Businesses Ltd* [1982] A.C. 617, Lord Diplock suggested at 644 that it should be sufficient for an applicant to show that he has an "arguable case" for him to be given leave. Lord Scarman stated at 655 that the applicants in that case should have been granted leave had they been able to show reasonable grounds for believing that the board had abused its discretion "or that there was a case to that effect which merited investigation and examination by the court". In *R. v Inspector of Taxes Ex p. Kissane* [1986] 2 All E.R. 37, Nolan J. said (at 39) that on an application for leave "it is not for me to delve too deeply into the arguments. I have to be satisfied, before giving leave, that there is at any rate an arguable case. The threshold, if one excludes obviously hopeless claims, is fairly low". In *R. v Secretary of State for the Home Department Ex p. Swati* [1986] 1 W.L.R. 477, Sir John Donaldson M.R. stated (at 485) that

> "an applicant must show more than that it is not impossible that grounds for judicial review exist. To say that he must show a prima facie case that such grounds do in fact exist may be putting it too high, but he must at least show that it is a real, as opposed to a theoretical, possibility. In other words, he must have an arguable case".

In exceptional circumstances, where the court at a contested permission hearing has all the relevant material before it and has heard full argument, a more demanding test may be applied, the court only granting permission if the case is not merely arguable but likely to succeed (*Mass Energy Ltd v Birmingham City Council* [1994] Env L.R. 289; distinguished in *R. v Northampton BC Ex p. Northampton Rapid Transit System* [2000] N.P.C. 80, where the hearing was not as detailed, and a test between mere arguability and the *Mass Energy* test was applied). It has been suggested that the higher standard should become the norm for contested permission hearings, but that has not been adopted (*Supperstone and Knapman*, para.5.1).

If permission is granted on one ground but refused on others, the court at the substantive hearing is entitled not to permit those other grounds to be reopened (*R. v Staffordshire CC Ex p. Ashworth* (1996) 4 Admin. L.R. 373). This was decided under RSC, Ord.53, but this remains the position under CPR Pt 54, *cf.* r.54.12(1)(b)(ii), (3), which provide expressly that where permission is granted without a hearing on some grounds only, a request may be made for reconsideration at a hearing. If limited permission is granted after a hearing, the court may still in its discretion allow a ground in respect of which permission has been refused to be argued at the substantive hearing if that is in the interests of justice (see, *e.g. R. (on the application of Smith) v Parole Board* [2003] 1 W.L.R. 2548 at [12]–[16]). Amendments raising other additional grounds may be allowed if no injustice would be caused and are allowed fairly freely where the new grounds do not call for further evidence but involve questions of law (CPR r.54.15); *Lewis*, p.348).

The existence of the permission requirement has been controversial. The JUSTICE/All Souls Review of Administrative Law recommended that it should be abolished as a matter of principle:

"The citizen does not require leave to sue a fellow citizen and we do not think that he should have to obtain leave in order to proceed against the state and administrative bodies" (Administrative Justice: *Some Necessary Reforms* (1988), pp.152–155).

However, it was defended by Sir Harry Woolf as a useful filter in respect of vexatious and frivolous applications, as being an inexpensive and simple procedure, and as it "enables a litigant expeditiously and cheaply to obtain the view of a High Court judge on the merits of his application" (*Protection of the Public—A New Challenge* (1990), pp.19–23). A review of the law and practice of the leave requirement by A.P. Le Sueur and M. Sunkin ("Applications for Judicial Review: The Requirement of Leave" [1992] P.L. 102) concluded that the political reality seemed to be that the requirement would remain for the foreseeable future. However, there should be a presumption in favour of the grant of leave; "the exercise of judicial discretion at the leave stage should be more clearly confined, structured and checked"; the "arguability" test should be replaced by a test whether there is a "serious case to be tried"; and consideration should be given to a mechanism to dispense with the leave requirement where both parties agree there is a triable case. See further the proposals of the Law Commission and Lord Woolf, below, pp.1032–1033. The Government generally favours permission requirements for appeals (see above, p.793).

4. *Setting aside a grant of permission.* The court has an inherent jurisdiction to set aside orders (including orders granting permission to apply for judicial review, made without notice to the defendant or other interested party (see *R. v Secretary of State for the Home Department Ex p. Chinoy* (1992) 5 Admin. L.R. 457). Neither the defendant nor any other person served with the claim form (who will accordingly have had notice and the opportunity to make objections in the acknowledgment of service) may apply to set aside an order giving permission (r.54.13). However, such an application is possible if the defendant or an interested party has not been served, or the time to serve the acknowledgment of service has not expired (see, as to the latter, *R. (on the application of Webb) v Bristol City Council* [2001] EWHC Admin 696).

5. *The claim.* Claims for judicial review are entered in the Administrative Court list, along with other public law matters, including proceedings for committal for contempt

of court, applications for *habeas corpus* and a variety of statutory appeals. See *Practice Statement* [2002] 1 All E.R. 633, Annex B (The Procedure for Urgent Applications to the Administrative Court) and Annex C (Listing Policy in the Administrative Court). There are 50 judges nominated to sit in the Administrative Court, including four Chancery Division and four Family Division judges who act as additional judges of the QBD when dealing with Administrative Court cases. Cases are normally heard by a single judge, although a Divisional Court of two or three judges may be used in a case of general importance.

6. *Third parties.* The former Ord.53 r.5(3) required notice of motion to be served on all persons directly affected; r.9(1) provide that apart from this the court may hear any person who desires to be heard and appears to be a proper person to be heard. Only the former made the person a party with a subsequent right of appeal (*per* Lord Keith of Kinkel in *R. v Rent Officer Service Ex p. Muldoon* [1996] 3 All E.R. 498 at 500). The House of Lords in *Ex p. Muldoon* held that the fact that the Secretary of State for Social Security was required to meet up to 95 per cent of the cost of housing benefit did not mean that he was "directly affected" by an application for judicial review of a decision by a local authority to refuse benefit. This test connoted that a person "was affected without the intervention of an intermediate agency" (*per* Lord Keith at 500). Here the Secretary of State would not pay the disputed benefit to the applicants whether directly or through the local authority; instead the amount would be added to the subsidy paid to the local authority at the end of the financial year. See A. Lidbetter, (1997) 113 L.Q.R. 40, who argues that while the decision appears to be correct on its own facts, an unduly restrictive approach will not be appropriate in other contexts (*e.g.* neighbours in environ-mental cases and other unsuccessful bidders in franchising cases). It is submitted, however, that the approach in the case itself is unduly narrow. What if a large sum of money were at stake depending on a disputed question of interpretation of the regulations? (Would the Secretary of State have standing as applicant to challenge a local authority's decision to pay housing benefit in a particular case?)

An interested party (as now defined, in very similar terms, by r.54(2)(f)) is to be served with the Claim Form (r.54.7) and must file an acknowledgment of service if it wishes to take part in the judicial review (r.54.8(1)). If it fails to do so, it may not take part in a permission hearing unless allowed by the court, but may still take part in the hearing if it complies with directions as to the filing and service of detailed grounds for contesting the claim or supporting it on additional grounds (r.54.9).

In *R. (on the application of Williams) v Legal Services Commission* [2004] EWHC 163, McCombe J. held that a drug company was not "directly affected" by the result of proceeding for judicial review of the LSC's decision to end funding for civil proceedings against this (and other) drug companies claiming that the MMR vaccine had caused the claimants serious disabilities. While the drug company might have had standing to seek judicial review of the grant of public funding, the test here was narrower, and the position clearer than it had been in *Muldoon*. (The company was, however, permitted to file written representations under r.54.17.)

In addition, the court has a general discretion to allow any person to be joined as a party, either to file evidence or make (written or oral) representations at the hearing (r.54.17). This implements but in broader terms, recommendations of JUSTICE and the Public Law Project (*A Matter of Public Interest* (1996); see Schiemann L.J., [1996] P.L. 240.

7. *Discovery.* Disclosure is not required in claims for judicial review unless the court otherwise orders (*Practice Direction 54: Judicial Review*, para.12.1). The matter lies in the discretion of the judge. In *Inland Revenue Commissioners v National Federation of Self-Employed and Small Businesses Ltd* [1982] A.C. 617, Lord Scarman said (at 654):

". . . Upon general principles, discovery should not be ordered unless and until the court is satisfied that the evidence reveals reasonable grounds for believing that there has been a breach of public duty; and it should be limited strictly to documents relevant to the issue which emerges from the affidavits".

However, this view may be too restrictive. In *O'Reilly v Mackman* [1983] 2 A.C. 237, Lord Diplock stated simply that discovery should be ordered "whenever, and to the extent that, the justice of the case so requires" (below, p.983).

These views were discussed by Hodgson J. in *R. v Governor of Pentonville Prison Ex p. Herbage (No.2)*, *The Times*, May 29, 1986. Hodgson J. held that in deciding whether to grant discovery in judicial review proceedings the court should apply a standard no higher than that applied when considering whether or not leave to apply for judicial review should be granted (appeal dismissed: [1987] Q.B. 1077, *sub nom. R. v Secretary of State for the Home Department Ex p. Herbage (No.2)*). See also Simon Brown J. in *R. v Inland Revenue Commissioners Ex p. J. Rothschild Holdings* [1986] S.T.C. 410 (appeal dismissed: [1987] S.T.C. 163); *R. v Secretary of State for the Home Department Ex p. Harrison*, *The Independent*, December 21, 1987, considered in *R. v Inland Revenue Commissioners Ex p. Taylor* [1988] S.T.C. 832; *R. v Parole Board Ex p. Bradley* [1990] C.O.D. 375; *R. v Secretary of State for the Environment Ex p. Doncaster BC* [1990] C.O.D. 441. Discovery will only be ordered to go behind the contents of a written statement if there is some material before the court which suggests that the written statement of the party is not accurate: *Ex p. Doncaster BC*; *R. v Secretary of State for the Home Department Ex p. B.H.* [1990] C.O.D. 445; *R. v Secretary of State for the Environment Ex p. Islington LBC*, *The Independent*, September 6, 1991, [1992] C.O.D. 6; *R. v Governors and Appeals Committee of Bishop Challenor R.C. Comprehensive School Ex p. C and P* (1991) 90 L.G.R. 1037. It will not be ordered merely "in the hope that something might turn up" (characterised by Henry J. in *CEMI Ltd, Re*, unreported, February 18, 1987 as "contingent" or "Micawber" discovery): *Ex p. Doncaster BC*, above.

The effect of the restrictive approach to discovery is moderated by the requirement that once permission is granted defendants are expected to explain their actions (*R. v Lancashire CC Ex p. Huddleston* [1986] 2 All E.R. 941; the extension of statutory and common law duties to give reasons; and enhanced statutory rights of access to information under the Freedom of Information Act 2000. On the other hand, disclosure will not be ordered where there is a successful claim to Public Interest Immunity (above, p.711).

8. *Cross-examination on witness statement.* Evidence in judicial review proceedings is normally given by way of written statements. Cross-examination of the person making the statement may be allowed in judicial review proceedings under CPR r.32.1 or under the court's inherent jurisdiction (*R. (on the application of PG) v Ealing LBC* [2002] EWHC 250; [2002] A.C.D. 48). Before the changes introduced in 1978, cross-examination on applications for a prerogative order was possible but permitted only in very exceptional circumstances (*R. v Kent JJ. Ex p. Smith* [1928] W.N. 137; *R. v Stokesley, Yorkshire, JJ. Ex p. Bartram* [1956] 1 W.L.R. 254). Express provision for cross-examination was made by RSC, Ord.53, r.8(1), and it was suggested that practice might properly become more liberal. In *R. v Secretary of State for the Home Department Ex p. Khawaja* [1984] A.C. 74, Lord Bridge stated (at 124–125):

"It may be that the express discretion conferred on the court to permit cross-examination by the new procedure for judicial review under R.S.C. Ord.53 has been too sparingly exercised when deponents could readily attend court. But, however that may be, the discretion to allow cross-examination should only be exercised when justice so demands".

The House of Lords in *O'Reilly v Mackman* [1983] 2 A.C. 237 made it clear that "the grant of leave to cross-examine deponents on applications for judicial review is governed by the same principles as it is in actions begun by originating summons; it should be allowed whenever the justice of the particular case so requires" (*per* Lord Diplock at 282–283). See also *R. v Board of Visitors, Nottingham Prison Ex p. Moseley, The Times*, January 23, 1981 (conflict of affidavit evidence resolved without recourse to cross-examination); *R. v Secretary of State for the Environment Ex p. Manuel, The Times*, March 21, 1984 (cross-examination ordered on the application of the Secretary of State where the applicant, Manuel, had offered himself for cross-examination); *R. v Waltham Forest LBC Ex p. Baxter* [1988] Q.B. 419 (councillors cross-examined as to whether they had fettered their discretion in voting); *R. v Derbyshire CC Ex p. The Times Supplements, The Times*, July 19, 1990 (above, p.554). Even though there is no express provision for cross-examination in CPR Pt 54, the power remains and is to be exercised on a similar basis as before (Munby J in *R. (on the application of PG) v Ealing LBC*, above, citing Lord Diplock's dictum in *O'Reilly v Mackman*). Where in judicial review proceedings there is, exceptionally, full merits review, oral evidence and cross-examination may well be necessary for compliance with the HRA (*R. (on the application of Wilkinson) v Broadmoor Special Hospital Authority* [2002] 1 W.L.R. 419, above, pp.350–351).

On cross-examination and discovery in judicial review, see M. Purdue, "The Scope for Fact Finding in Judicial Review" in; *Droit Sans Frontieres: Essays in Honour of L. Neville Brown* (M. Smith, Hand and McBride (ed.), 1991), pp.193–201 [2001] J.R. The approach of the courts to these matters has been criticised as too restrictive (below, p.138), but the Law Commission and Lord Woolf (below, pp.1033–1034) had no proposals for change.

9. *Interim relief generally.* Provision is made by CPR Pt 25 for the grant of interim relief including interim injunctions and interim declarations (CPR r.25(1)(a) and (b). As the initial step in judicial review is now a written application for permission dealt with without a hearing, a *Practice Statement (Administrative Court: Listing and Urgent Cases)* [2002] 1 W.L.R. 810 sets out the procedure to be followed for urgent applications and interim injunctions (and declarations). The claimant must complete a prescribed form stating (*inter alia*) the need for urgency, and if an interim injunction (or declaration) is sought, the claimant must also provide a draft order and the grounds for the remedy. The claim form and application for urgency (and the additional papers where interim relief is sought) must be served on the defendant and interested party, advising them of the application and that they may make representations. The matter is then considered by a judge, who may make such order as he or she considers appropriate, and may direct an oral hearing.

The normal principles on which an interim injunction may be awarded are set out by the House of Lords in *American Cyanamid Co. v Ethicon Ltd* [1975] A.C. 396. Lord Diplock stated, at 407–408, that the court should consider, first, whether there is "a serious question to be tried", and, if satisfied that there is, proceed to consider the "balance of convenience":

> "As to that, the governing principle is that the court should first consider whether, if the plaintiff were to succeed at the trial in establishing his right to a permanent injunction, he would be adequately compensated by an award of damages for the loss he would have sustained as a result of the defendant's continuing to do what was sought to be enjoined between the time of the application and the time of the trial. If damages in the measure recoverable at common law would be adequate remedy and the defendant would be in a financial position to pay them, no interlocutory injunction should normally be granted, however strong the plaintiff's claim appeared to be at that stage. If, on the other hand, damages would not provide an adequate remedy for the plaintiff in the event of his succeeding at the trial, the court should then consider whether, on the contrary hypothesis that the defendant were to succeed at the trial in establishing his right to do that which was sought to be enjoined, he would be adequately compensated under the plaintiff's undertaking as to damages for the loss he would have sustained by being prevented from doing so between the time of the application and the time of the trial. If damages in the measure recoverable under such an undertaking would be an adequate remedy and

the plaintiff would be in a financial position to pay them, there would be no reason upon this ground to refuse an interlocutory injunction.

It is where there is doubt as to the adequacy of the respective remedies in damages available to either party or to both, that the question of balance of convenience arises. It would be unwise to attempt even to list all the various matters which may need to be taken into consideration in deciding where the balance lies, let alone to suggest the relative weight to be attached to them. These will vary from case to case.

Where other factors appear to be evenly balanced it is a counsel of prudence to take such measures as are calculated to preserve the status quo".

These principles are subject to modification where necessary in public law cases. For example, where the Crown is seeking to enforce the law it may not be right to impose on the Crown the usual undertaking in damages (*per* Lord Goff in *R. v Secretary of State for Transport Ex p. Factortame Ltd (No.2)* [1991] A.C. 603 at 672. Furthermore,

"the court should not restrain a public authority by interim injunction from enforcing an apparently authentic law unless it is satisfied, having regard to all the circumstances, that the challenge the validity of the law is, prima facie, so firmly based as to justify so exceptional a course being taken" (per Lord Goff at 674).

Examples of the application of these principles include the following. In *Smith v Inner London Education Authority* [1978] 1 All E.R. 411, the Court of Appeal discharged interlocutory injunctions restraining the authority from closing a grammar school: the applicants had "no real prospect of . . . succeeding at the trial" (*per* Lord Denning M.R. at 418). In *R. v Westminster City Council Ex p. Sierbien, The Times*, March 30, 1987, the Court of Appeal approved the refusal of Otton J. to grant interlocutory injunctions to restrain the council from enforcing the Local Government (Miscellaneous Provisions) Act 1982. The applicants sought the injunctions pending the outcome of their application for judicial review of the council's refusal to grant them a licence to carry on a sex encounter establishment. The court held that the ordinary financial considerations in *American Cyanamid*, although relevant, had to be qualified by a recognition of the public interest. The grant of an injunction would have the effect of preventing a public body from carrying out its duty and of trespassing on a matter in the domain of the criminal law. In *R. v Servite Houses and Wandsworth LBC Ex p. Goldsmith (Interim Relief)* (2000) 3 C.C.L. Rep. 354, an interim injunction was granted to prevent implementation of a challenged decision to close a residential home; this would be catastrophic for the applicant resident and have irreversible effect although there would be some financial loss to the respondent; interim relief would be over a comparatively short period; *cf. R. v Inspectorate of Pollution Ex p. Greenpeace Ltd (No.1)* [1994] 1 W.L.R. 570 where no interim injunction was granted in respect of G's challenge to a decision where there was no offer of an undertaking as to damages in respect of financial losses to British Nuclear Fuels Plc should the challenge fail. The court has a wide discretion to take the course which seems most likely to produce a just result, not least to minimise the risk of an unjust result (*per* Lord Walker of Gestingthorpe for the Privy Council in *Bellize Alliance of Conservation Non-Governmental Organisations v Department of the Environment* [2003] UKPC 47 (refusing interim injunction to stop work on a controversial claim project in the absence of an undertaking as to damages).

On the availability of a mandatory injunction on an interlocutory application see *De Falco v Crawley BC* [1980] Q.B. 460; *Locabail International Finance Ltd v Agroexport* [1986] 1 W.L.R. 657.

Where permission is giving the court may order a stay of proceedings to which the claim relates (r.54.10(2)). "Proceedings" here is to be construed broadly to cover the process leading up to the making of the decision and the decision itself; a stay can be granted to prevent implementation of the decision or even, in exceptional circumstances, where it has already been implemented (*R. (on the application of H) v Ashworth Hospital Authority* [2002] EWCA Civ 923; [2003] 1 W.L.R. 127. A stay can be granted in respect of administrative decisions (*R. v Secretary of State for Education and Science Ex p. Avon CC (No.2)* [1991] 1 Q.B. 558 (a decision under RSC, Ord.53, r.3(10(a)).

10. *Interim declaratory relief.* Provision has now been made for the award of an interim declaration (see above), implementing a recommendation of the Law Commission (Law Com. No.73, para.51 and Law Com. No.226, para.6.27.) It was previously held that such a remedy could not be granted, although that view had been challenged (see discussion in *M v Home Office* [1994] 1 A.C. 327 and *R. v Secretary of State for the Environment Ex p. Royal Society for the Protection of Birds, The Times,* February 10, 1995).

The general absence of interim declaratory relief caused particular difficulty in respect of proceedings against the Crown. Section 21(2) of the Crown Proceedings Act 1947 provides that "The court shall not in any civil proceedings grant any injunction or make any order against an officer of the Crown if the effect of granting the injunction or making the order would be to give any relief against the Crown which could not have been obtained in proceedings against the Crown". However, the extent of difficulty was moderated by the ruling in the House of Lords in *M. v Home Office* [1994] 1 A.C. 327 that injunctions, including interim injunctions, may be awarded against ministers or other officers of the Crown.

The House of Lords had previously ruled that English courts may be required by European Community law to award interim relief against the Crown, where a point of Community law is involved: Case C-213/89, *R. v Secretary of State for Transport Ex p. Factortame Ltd (No.2)* [1991] 1 A.C. 603, ECJ and H.L. See generally on the *Factortame* litigation, N.P. Gravells, [1989] P.L. 568, [1991] P.L. 180 and [1996] P.L. 567. For other comments on interim relief against the Crown, see J. Alder, (1987) 50 M.L.R. 10; M. Matthews, (1988) 8 O.J.L.S. 154; Sir William Wade, (1991) 107 L.Q.R. 4.

11. *Availability of declarations.* Dicta that a declaration could only be granted under RSC, Ord.53 in circumstances where one of the prerogative orders could lie (*per* Lords Diplock and Scarman in *Inland Revenue Commissioners v National Federation of Self-Employed and Small Businesses* [1982] A.C. 617 at 639, 648) are no longer applicable in view of the enactment of the 1981 Act (see Lord Browne-Wilkinson in *R. v Secretary of State for Employment Ex p. Equal Opportunities Commission* [1995] 1 A.C. 1 at 37; Hodgson J. in *R v Bromley LBC Ex p. Lambeth LBC The Times,* June 16, 1984).

12. *Costs.* The court has jurisdiction to award costs at the permission stage (*R. v IRC Ex p. Mead and Cook (No.2)* [1993] 1 All E.R. 772) and following the substantive hearing. In exceptional circumstances costs may be awarded against a defendant authority where it concedes the validity of the claim before the permission hearing (*R. v Kensington and Chelsea RLBC Ex p. Ghebregiogis* (1994) 27 H.L.R. 602 (there was no doubt the claim was well founded in law, a clear case and a simple point, and clearly set out in the letter before action; the concession was only made following service of notice of proceedings). Where permission is granted, costs at the permission stage are deemed to be costs in the case unless the judge orders otherwise (*Practice Statement (Judicial Review: Costs)* [2004] 1 W.L.R. 1760). A defendant need not attend a permission hearing unless the court directs otherwise, and where the defendant or any party does attend a hearing, the court will not generally make an order for costs against the claimant (PD 54.8.5 and 54.8.6). Accordingly, a successful defendant in an oral permission hearing is not awarded costs against the claimant unless there are exceptional circumstances, although the costs of filing an acknowledgement of service are normally recoverable (*R. (on the application of Leach) v Commissioner for Local Administration* [2001] EWHC Admin 445; *R. (on the application of Mount Cook Land Ltd) v Westminster City Council* [2003] EWCA Civ 1346). Where permission is granted but proceedings are then discontinued, the defendant will normally be awarded costs unless the case against it is clear cut (*R. v Liverpool City Council*

Ex p. Newman [1993] C.O.D. 65; *R. (on the application of Boxall) v Waltham Forest LBC*, unreported, December 21, 2000, QBD, approved by the Court of Appeal in *R. (on the application of Kuzeva) v Southwark LBC (Costs)* [2002] EWCA Civ 781, noting that according to the circumstances it may be appropriate for no order for costs to be made and that care should be taken not to discourage parties from settling judicial review proceedings). Following the substantive hearing, costs normally follow the event (CPR r.44.3(2)), but may be apportioned where the claimant succeeds on some but not all issues. In exceptional circumstances, the court may make a pre-emptive costs order, where the issue is one of general public importance, that the claimant will not be liable for costs if the claim is dismissed (*R. v Lord Chancellor's Department Ex p. Child Poverty Action Group* [1999] 1 W.L.R. 347; distinguished in *R. v Hammersmith and Fulham LBC Ex p. CPRE* [2000] Env. L.R. 544; the principles were restated in *R. (on the application of Corner House Research) v Secretary of State for Trade and Industry* [2005] EWCA Civ 192).

There is, however, no general principle that no order for costs should be made where proceedings are brought in the public interest and not for any motive of personal gain (see Munby J. in *R. (on the application of Smeaton) v Secretary of State for Health* [2002] EWHC Admin 886; [2002] 2 F.L.R. 146, awarding costs against the successful applicant, the Society for the Protection of Unborn Children, after rejecting its contention that the morning-after pill was an abortifacient).

Where a claim is successfully resisted by more than one defendant or interested party, the claimant is only exceptionally to be required to pay more than one set of costs, as where a second defendant or party can demonstrate a separate issue, not covered by the main defendant, on which it was entitled to be heard, or has an interest requiring separate representation (*Bolton MDC v Secretary of State for the Environment* [1995] 1 W.L.R. 1176).

For suggestions that more financial support for litigation in the public interest be provided through legislation, changes in the application of the costs rules and a more consistent public-interest friendly approach to the conduct of proceedings on the part of government departments, see S. Chakrabarti, J. Stephens and C. Gallagher, [2003] P.L. 697.

13. *Appeals in civil cases.* Where permission to apply for judicial review has been refused at a hearing in the High Court, the person seeking that permission may apply to the Court of Appeal for permission to appeal within seven days of the High Court's decision (CPR r.52.15(1)(2). This rule also applies where permission is refused on some but not all grounds (*R. (on the application of Opoku) v Principal of Southwark College* [2002] EWHC Admin 2092; [2003] 1 W.L.R. 234, *per* Lightman J. at [12]). An application for permission to appeal can alternatively be made to the Administrative Court under CPR r.52.3(2)(a); *per* Lord Bingham of Cornhill in *R. v Secretary of State for Trade Ex p. Eastaway* [2000] 1 W.L.R. 2222 at 2225.) On such an application, the Court of Appeal may, instead of giving permission to appeal, give permission to apply for judicial review, in which case the case proceeds in the High Court unless the Court of Appeal orders otherwise (CPR r.52.15(3)(4)). If the Court of Appeal refuses permission to appeal against a refusal of permission to apply for judicial review, there is no further right of appeal (*Poh, Re* [1983] 1 W.L.R. 2; *R. v Secretary of State for Trade and Industry Ex p. Eastaway* [2000] 1 W.L.R. 2222). However, if the Court of Appeal grants permission to appeal but then determines after a full hearing that permission to apply for judicial review should not be granted, an appeal may be taken, with the permission of either the Court of Appeal or the House of Lords, to the House of Lords (*R. (on the application of Burkett) v Hammersmith and Fulham LBC* [2002] UKHL 23, [2002] 1 W.L.R. 1593.)

It appears that there is no right to appeal to the Court of Appeal against the grant of permission. (See Sir John Donaldson M.R. in *R. v Monopolies and Mergers Commission Ex p. Argyll Group Plc* [1986] 1 W.L.R. 763 at 774.)

Following the substantive determination of a claim for judicial review by the Administrative Court, an appeal lies to the Court of Appeal. Permission should be sought from the Administrative Court at the hearing at which the decision to be appealed was made, or from the Court of Appeal by way of an appeal notice; if permission is refused by the lower court, a fresh application may be made to the Court of Appeal. Permission will only be given where the court considers that the appeal would have a real prospect of success or there is some other compelling reason why the appeal should be heard (CPR r.52.3(a), (3), (6)). If the Court of Appeal refuses permission to appeal, no further appeal lies to the House of Lords (see above). If the Court of Appeal proceeds to the substantive determination of the appeal, a further appeal lies to the House of Lords, with the permission of either.

14. *Appeals in criminal cases.* Where the Administrative Court refuses permission to apply for judicial review in a criminal cause or matter, no appeal lies to the Court of Appeal (Supreme Court Act 1981, s.18(1)(a)). The Administrative Court may choose to grant permission, dismiss the substantive application and certify that a question of general public importance arises (*White Book 2004*, para.54.12.4.) Where the Administrative Court proceeds to make a substantive determination on a claim for judicial review in such a matter, an appeal lies direct to the House of Lords provided that the lower court certifies that the case raises a point of law of general public importance and either the lower court or the House grants permission (Administration of Justice Act 1960, ss.1 and 19).

(E) EXCLUSIVITY OF JUDICIAL REVIEW PROCEEDINGS

O'REILLY v MACKMAN

[1983] 2 A.C. 237; [1983] 3 W.L.R. 1096; [1982] 3 All E.R. 1124
(HOUSE OF LORDS)

The four plaintiffs, prisoners in Hull Prison, were charged with disciplinary offences before the board of visitors to the prison, arising out of riots in December 1976 (in the case of three of the plaintiffs) and 1979 (in the case of the fourth). In the case of each plaintiff the board held an inquiry, found the charges proved and imposed penalties. In 1980, three of the plaintiffs brought actions by writ in the Queen's Bench Division of the High Court against the board alleging that it had acted in breach of the Prison Rules and the rules of natural justice and claiming a declaration that the board's findings against them and the penalties awarded were void and of no effect. The fourth plaintiff started proceedings by originating summons in the Chancery Division against the Home Office and the board of visitors alleging bias by a member of the board and claiming a declaration that the board's adjudication was void for want of natural justice. In all four cases the defendants applied to strike out the proceedings. Peter Pain J. dismissed the applications. The Court of Appeal reversed that decision and struck out the proceedings on the ground that they were an abuse of the process of the court and that the plaintiffs' only proper remedy was by way of judicial review under RSC Ord.53. The House of Lords (Lords Diplock, Fraser, Keith, Bridge and Brightman) unanimously dismissed the plaintiffs' appeals. The leading speech was delivered by Lord Diplock.

LORD DIPLOCK:. . . [N]o question arises as to the "jurisdiction" of the High Court to grant to each of the appellants relief by way of a declaration in the terms sought, if they succeeded in establishing the facts alleged in their respective statements of claim or originating summons and the court considered a declaration to be an appropriate remedy. All that is at issue in the instant appeal is the procedure by which such relief ought to be sought. Put in a single sentence the question for your Lordships is: whether in 1980 after R.S.C., Ord. 53 in its new form, adopted in 1977, had come into operation it was an abuse of the process of the court to apply for such declarations by using the procedure laid down in the Rules for proceedings begun by writ or by originating summons instead of using the procedure laid down by Order 53 for an application for judicial review of the awards of forfeiture of remission of sentence made against them by the board which the appellants are seeking to impugn?

In their respective actions, the appellants claim only declaratory relief. It is conceded on their behalf that, for reasons into which the concession makes it unnecessary to enter, no claim for damages would lie against the members of the board of visitors by whom the awards were made. The only claim was for a form of relief which it lies within the discretion of the court to grant or to withhold. So the first thing to be noted is that the relief sought in the action is discretionary only.

It is not, and it could not be, contended that the decision of the board awarding him forfeiture of remission had infringed or threatened to infringe any right of the appellant derived from private law, whether a common law right or one created by a statute. Under the Prison Rules remission of sentence is not a matter of right but of indulgence. So far as private law is concerned all that each appellant had was a legitimate expectation, based upon his knowledge of what is the general practice, that he would be granted the maximum remission, permitted by rule 5(2) of the Prison Rules, of one-third of his sentence if by that time no disciplinary award of forfeiture of remission had been made against him. So the second thing to be noted is that none of the appellants had any remedy in private law.

In public law, as distinguished from private law, however, such legitimate expectation gave to each appellant a sufficient interest to challenge the legality of the adverse disciplinary award made against him by the board on the ground that in one way or another the board in reaching its decision had acted outwith the powers conferred upon it by the legislation under which it was acting; and such grounds would include the board's failure to observe the rules of natural justice: which means no more than to act fairly towards him in carrying out their decision-making process, and I prefer so to put it.

The power of boards of visitors of a prison to make disciplinary awards is conferred upon them by subordinate legislation: the Prison Rules 1964 made by the Secretary of State under sections 6 and 47 of the Prison Act 1952. The charges against the appellants were of grave offences against discipline falling within rule 51. They were referred by the governor of the prison to the board under rule 51(1). It thereupon became the duty of the board under rule 51(3) to inquire into the charge and decide whether it was proved and if so to award what the board considered to be the appropriate punishment. Rule 49(2) is applicable to such inquiry by the board. It lays down expressly that the prisoner "shall be given a full opportunity of hearing what is alleged against him and of presenting his own case". In exercising their functions under rule 51 members of the board are acting as a statutory tribunal, as contrasted with a domestic tribunal upon which powers are conferred by contract between those who agree to submit to its jurisdiction. Where the legislation which confers upon a statutory tribunal its decision-making powers also provides expressly for the procedure it shall follow in the course of reaching its decision, it is a question of construction of the relevant legislation, to be decided by the court in which the decision is challenged, whether a particular procedural provision is mandatory, so that its non-observance in the process of reaching the decision makes the decision itself a nullity, or whether it is merely directory, so that the statutory tribunal has a discretion not to comply with it if, in its opinion, the exceptional circumstances of a particular case justify departing from it. But the requirement that a person who is charged with having done something which, if proved to the satisfaction of a statutory tribunal, has consequences that will, or may, affect him adversely, should be given a fair opportunity of hearing what is alleged against him and of presenting his own case, is so fundamental to any civilised legal system that it is to be presumed that Parliament intended that a failure to observe it should render null and void any decision reached in breach of this requirement. What is alleged by the appellants other than Millbanks would amount to an infringement of the express rule 49; but even if there were no such express provision a requirement to observe it would be a necessary implication from the nature of the disciplinary functions of the board. In the absence of express provision to the contrary Parliament, whenever it provides for the creation of a statutory tribunal, must be presumed not to have intended that the tribunal should be authorised to act in contravention of one of the fundamental rules of natural justice or fairness: *audi alteram partem*.

In Millbanks's case, there is no express provision in the Prison Rules that the members of the board who inquire into a disciplinary offence under rule 51 must be free from personal bias against the prisoner. It is another fundamental rule of natural justice or fairness, too obvious to call for express statement of it, that a tribunal exercising functions such as those exercised by the board in the case of Millbanks should be constituted of persons who enter upon the inquiry without any pre-conceived personal bias against the prisoner. Failure to comply with this implied requirement would likewise render the decision of the tribunal a nullity. So the third thing to be noted is that each of the appellants, if he established the facts alleged in his action, was entitled to a remedy in public law which would have the effect of preventing the decision of the board from having any adverse consequences upon him.

My Lords, the power of the High Court to make declaratory judgments is conferred by what is now R.S.C., Ord.15, r.16. The language of the rule which was first made in 1883 has never been altered, though the numbering of the rule has from time to time been changed. It provides:

> "No action or other proceeding shall be open to objection on the ground that a merely declaratory judgment or order is sought thereby, and the court may make binding declarations of right whether or not any consequential relief is or could be claimed."

This rule, which is in two parts separated by "and", has been very liberally interpreted in the course of its long history, wherever it appeared to the court that the justice of the case required the grant of declaratory relief in the particular action before it. Since "action" is defined so as to have included since 1938 an originating motion applying for prerogative orders, Ord.15, r.16 says nothing as to the appropriate procedure by which declarations of different kinds ought to be sought. Nor does it draw any distinction between declarations that relate to rights and obligations under private law and those that relate to rights and obligations under public law. Indeed the appreciation of the distinction in substantive law between what is private law and what is public law has itself been a latecomer to the English legal system. It is a consequence of the development that has taken place in the last 30 years of the procedures available for judicial control of administrative action. This development started with the expansion of the grounds upon which orders of certiorari could be obtained as a result of the decision of the Court of Appeal in *R. v Northumberland Compensation Appeal Tribunal, Ex p. Shaw* [1952] 1 K.B. 338; it was accelerated by the passing of the Tribunals and Inquiries Act 1958, and culminated in the substitution in 1977 of the new form of R.S.C., Ord. 53 which has since been given statutory confirmation in section 31 of the Supreme Court Act 1981.

[His Lordship referred to the rediscovery in *Ex p. Shaw* of the power to grant certiorari to quash for error of law on the face of the record; and the provisions in the 1958 Act, now replaced by the 1971 Act, requiring most statutory tribunals to give reasons, and repealing most clauses purporting to exclude judicial review.]

[Section 14(1) of the Act (now s.12(1) of the 1992 Act, above, p.109)] it is to be observed, says nothing about any right to bring civil actions for declarations of nullity of orders or determinations of statutory bodies where an earlier Act of Parliament contains a provision that such order or determination "shall not be called into question in any court". Since actions begun by writ seeking such declarations were already coming into common use in the High Court so as to provide an alternative remedy to orders of certiorari, the section suggests a parliamentary preference in favour of making the latter remedy available rather than the former. I will defer consideration of the reasons for this preference until later.

Fortunately for the development of public law in England, section 14(3) contained express provision that the section should not apply to any order or determination of the Foreign Compensation Commission, a statutory body established under the Foreign Compensation Act 1950, which Act provided by section 4(4) an express provision: "The determination by the commission of any application made to them under this Act shall not be called in question in any court of law." It was this provision that provided the occasion for the landmark decision of this House in *Anisminic Ltd v Foreign Compensation Commission* [1969] 2 A.C. 147, and particularly the leading speech of Lord Reid, which has liberated English public law from the fetters that the courts had theretofore imposed upon themselves so far as determinations of inferior courts and statutory tribunals were concerned, by drawing esoteric distinctions between errors of law committed by such tribunals that went to their jurisdiction, and errors of law committed by them within their jurisdiction. The breakthrough that the *Anisminic* case made was the recognition by the majority of this House that if a tribunal whose jurisdiction was limited by statute or subordinate legislation mistook the law applicable to the facts as it had found them, it must have asked itself the wrong question, *i.e.* one into which it was not empowered to inquire and so had no jurisdiction to determine. Its purported "determination", not being a "determination" within the meaning of the empowering legislation, was accordingly a nullity.

Anisminic Ltd v Foreign Compensation Commission was an action commenced by writ for a declaration, in which a minute of the commission's reasons for their determination adverse to the plaintiff company did not appear upon the face of their determination, and had in fact been obtained only upon discovery: but, as appears from the report of my own judgment when the *Anisminic* case was in the Court of Appeal ([1968] 2 Q.B. 862, 893), the case had been argued up to that stage as if it were an application for certiorari in which the minute of the commission's reasons formed part of the "record" upon which an error of law appeared. In the House of Lords the question of the propriety of suing by writ for a declaration instead of applying for certiorari and mandamus played no part in the main argument for the commission. It appears for the first time in the report of the commission's counsel's reply, where an argument that the court had no "jurisdiction" to make the declaration seems to have been put forward upon the narrow ground, special to the limited functions of the commission, alluded to at pp.910–911 of my own judgment in the Court of Appeal that the House overruled; but I did not purport to decide the question because, in the view that I had (erroneously) taken of the effect of section 4(4) of the Act, it appeared to me to be unnecessary to do so.

My Lords, *Anisminic Ltd v Foreign Compensation Commission* [1969] 2 A.C. 147 was decided by this House before the alteration was made to R.S.C., Ord. 53 in 1977. The order of the Supreme Court dealing with applications for the prerogative orders of mandamus, certiorari and prohibition in force at the time of the *Anisminic* case was numbered Order 53 and had been made in 1965. It replaced, but in substance only repeated, the first 12 rules of what had been Order 59 and which had in 1938 itself replaced the former Crown Office Rules of 1906. The pre-1977 Order 53, like its predecessors, placed under considerable procedural disadvantage applicants who wished to challenge the lawfulness of a determination of a statutory tribunal or any other body of persons having legal authority to determine questions affecting the common law or statutory rights or obligations of other persons as individuals. It will be noted that I have broadened the much-cited description by Atkin L.J. in *R. v Electricity Commissioners, Ex p. London Electricity Joint Committee Co. (1920) Ltd* [1924] 1 K.B. 171, 205 of bodies of persons subject to the supervisory jurisdiction of the High Court by prerogative remedies (which in 1924 then took the form of prerogative writs of mandamus, prohibition, certiorari, and quo warranto) by excluding Atkin L.J.'s limitation of the bodies of persons to whom the prerogative writs might issue, to those "having the duty to act judicially". For the next 40 years this phrase gave rise to many attempts, with varying success, to draw subtle distinctions between decisions that were quasi-judicial and those that were administrative only. But the relevance of arguments of this kind was destroyed by the decision of this House in *Ridge v Baldwin* [1964] A.C. 40, where again the leading speech was given by Lord Reid. Wherever any person or body of persons has authority conferred by legislation to make decisions of the kind I have described, it is amenable to the remedy of an order to quash its decision either for error of law in reaching it or for failure to act fairly towards the person who will be adversely affected by the decision by failing to observe either one or other of the two fundamental rights accorded to him by the rules of natural justice or fairness, *viz.* to have afforded to him a reasonable opportunity of learning what is alleged against him and of putting forward his own case in answer to it, and to the absence of personal bias against him on the part of the person by whom the decision falls to be made. In *Ridge v Baldwin* it is interesting to observe that Lord Reid said at 72 "We do not have a developed system of administrative law— perhaps because until fairly recently we did not need it." By 1977 the need had continued to grow apace and this reproach to English law had been removed. We did have by then a developed system of administrative law, to the development of which Lord Reid himself, by his speeches in cases which reached this House, had made an outstanding contribution. To the landmark cases of *Ridge v Baldwin* and *Anisminic Ltd v Foreign Compensation Commission* [1969] 2 A.C. 147 I would add a third, *Padfield v Minister of Agriculture, Fisheries and Food* [1968] A.C. 997, another case in which a too-timid judgment of my own in the Court of Appeal was (fortunately) overruled.

Although the availability of the remedy of orders to quash a decision by certiorari had in theory been widely extended by these developments, the procedural disadvantages under which applicants for this remedy laboured remained substantially unchanged until the alteration of Order 53 in 1977. Foremost among these was the absence of any provision for discovery. In the case of a decision which did not state the reasons for it, it was not possible to challenge its validity for error of law in the reasoning by which the decision had been reached. If it had been an application for certiorari those who were the plaintiffs in the *Anisminic* case would have failed; it was only because by pursuing an action by writ for a declaration of nullity that the plaintiffs were entitled to the discovery by which the minute of the commission's reasons which showed that they had asked themselves the wrong question, was obtained. Again under Order 53 evidence was required to be on affidavit. This in itself is not an unjust disadvantage; it is a common feature of many forms of procedure in the High Court, including originating summonses; but in the absence of any express provision for cross-examination of deponents, as your Lordships who are familiar with the pre-1977 procedure will be aware, even *applications* for leave to cross-examine were virtually unknown—let alone the grant of leave itself—save in very exceptional cases of which I believe none of your Lordships has ever had actual experience. Lord Goddard C.J., whose experience was at that time unrivalled, had so stated in *R. v Stokesley, Yorkshire, JJ., ex p. Bartram* [1956] 1 W.L.R. 254, 257.

On the other hand as compared with an action for a declaration commenced by writ or originating summons, the procedure under Order 53 both before and after 1977 provided for the respondent decision-making statutory tribunal or public authority against which the remedy of certiorari was sought protection against claims which it was not in the public interest for courts of justice to entertain.

First, leave to apply for the order was required. The application for leave which was *ex parte* but could be, and in practice often was, adjourned in order to enable the proposed respondent to be represented, had to be supported by a statement setting out, *inter alia*, the grounds on which the relief was sought and by affidavits verifying the facts relied on: so that a knowingly false statement of fact would amount to the criminal offence of perjury. Such affidavit was also required to satisfy the requirement of *uberrima fides*, with the consequence that failure to make on oath a full and candid disclosure of material facts was of itself a ground for refusing the relief sought in the substantive application for which leave had been obtained on the strength of the affidavit. This was an important safeguard, which is preserved in the new Order 53 of 1977. The public interest in good administration requires that public authorities and third parties should not be kept in suspense as to the legal validity of a decision the authority has reached in purported exercise of decision-making powers for any longer period than is absolutely necessary in fairness to the person affected by the decision. In contrast, allegations made in a statement of claim or an indorsement of an originating summons are not on oath, so the requirement of a prior application for leave to be supported by full and candid affidavits verifying the facts relied on is an important safeguard against groundless or unmeritorious claims that a particular decision is a nullity. There was also power in the court on granting leave to impose terms as to costs or security.

Furthermore, as Order 53 was applied in practice, as soon as the application for leave had been made it provided a very speedy means, available in urgent cases within a matter of days rather than months, for determining whether a disputed decision was valid in law or not. A reduction of the period of suspense was also effected by the requirement that leave to apply for certiorari to quash a decision must be made within a limited period after the impugned decision was made, unless delay beyond that limited period was accounted for to the satisfaction of the judge. The period was six months under the pre-1977 Order 53; under the current Order 53 it is further reduced to three months.

My Lords, the exclusion of all right to discovery in application for certiorari under Order 53, particularly before the passing of the Tribunal and Inquiries Act 1958, was calculated to cause injustice to persons who had no means, if they adopted that procedure, of ascertaining whether a public body, which had made a decision adversely affecting them, had done so for reasons which were wrong in law and rendered their decision invalid. It will be within the knowledge of all of your Lordships that, at any rate from the 1950s onwards, actions for declarations of nullity of decisions affecting the rights of individuals under public law were widely entertained, in parallel to applications for certiorari to quash, as means of obtaining an effective alternative remedy. I will not weary your Lordships by reciting examples of cases where this practice received the express approval of the Court of Appeal, though I should point out that of those cases in this House in which this practice was approved, *Vine v National Dock Labour Board* [1957] A.C. 488 and *Ridge v Baldwin* [1964] A.C. 40 involved, as well as questions of public law, contracts of employment which gave rise to rights under private law. In *Anisminic Ltd v Foreign Compensation Commission* [1969] 2 A.C. 147 the procedural question was not seriously argued, while *Pyx Granite Ltd v Ministry of Housing and Local Government* [1960] A.C. 260, which is referred to in the notes to Order 19 appearing in the *Supreme Court Practice* (1982) as an instance of the approval by this House of the practice of suing for a declaration instead of applying for an order of certiorari, appears on analysis to have been concerned with declaring that the plaintiffs had a legal right to do what they were seeking to do without the need to obtain any decision from the Minister. Nevertheless I accept that having regard to disadvantages, particularly in relation to the absolute bar upon compelling discovery of documents by the respondent public authority to an applicant for an order of certiorari, and the almost invariable practice of refusing leave to allow cross-examination of deponents to affidavits lodged on its behalf, it could not be regarded as an abuse of the process of the court, before the amendments made to Order 53 in 1977, to proceed against the authority by an action for a declaration of nullity of the impugned decision with an injunction to prevent the authority from acting on it, instead of applying for an order of certiorari; and this despite the fact that, by adopting this course, the plaintiff evaded the safe-guards imposed in the public interest against groundless, unmeritorious or tardy attacks upon the validity of decisions made by public authorities in the field of public law.

Those disadvantages, which formerly might have resulted in an applicant's being unable to obtain justice in an application for certiorari under Order 53, have all been removed by the new Order introduced in 1977. There is express provision in the new rule 8 for interlocutory applications for discovery of documents, the administration of interrogatories and the cross-examination of deponents to affidavits. Discovery of documents (which may often be a time-consuming process) is not automatic as in an action begun by writ, but otherwise Order 24 applies to it and discovery is obtainable upon application whenever, and to the extent that, the justice of the case requires; similarly Order 26 applies to applications for interrogatories; and to applications for cross-examination of deponents to affidavits Ord. 28, r. 2(3) applies. This is the rule that deals with evidence in actions begun by originating summons and permits oral cross-examination on affidavit evidence wherever the justice of the case requires. It may well be that for the reasons given by Lord Denning M.R. in *George v Secretary of State for the Environment* (1979) 77 L.G.R. 689, it will only be upon rare occasions that the interests of justice will require that leave be given for cross-examination of deponents on their affidavits in applications for judicial review. This is because of the nature of the issues that normally arise upon judicial review. The facts, except where the claim that a decision was invalid on the ground that the statutory tribunal or public authority that made the decision failed to comply with the procedure prescribed by the legislation under which it was acting or failed to observe the fundamental rules of natural justice or fairness, can seldom be a matter of relevant dispute upon an application for judicial review, since the tribunal or authority's findings of fact, as distinguished from the legal consequences of the facts that they have found, are not open to review by the court in the exercise of its supervisory powers except on the principles laid down in *Edwards v Bairstow* [1956] A.C. 14, 36; and to allow cross-examination presents the court with a temptation, not always easily resisted, to substitute its own view of the facts for that of the decision-making body upon whom the exclusive jurisdiction to determine facts has been conferred by Parliament. Nevertheless having regard to a possible misunderstanding of what was said by Geoffrey Lane L.J. in *R. v Board of Visitors of Hull Prison, ex p. St Germain (No.2)* [1979] 1 W.L.R. 1401, 1410 your Lordships may think this an appropriate occasion on which to emphasise that whatever may have been the position before the rule was altered in 1977 in all proceedings for judicial review that have been started since that date the grant of leave to cross-examine deponents upon applications for judicial review is governed by the same principles as it is in actions begun by originating summons; it should be allowed whenever the justice of the particular case so requires.

Another handicap under which an applicant for a prerogative order under Order 53 formerly laboured (though it would not have affected the appellants in the instant cases even if they had brought their actions before the 1977 alteration to Order 53) was that a claim for damages for breach of a right in private law of the applicant resulting from an invalid decision of a public authority could not be made in an application under Order 53. Damages could only be claimed in a separate action begun by writ; whereas in an action so begun they could be claimed as additional relief as well as a declaration of nullity of the decision from which the damage claimed had flowed. Rule 7 of the new Order 53 permits the applicant for judicial review to include in the statement in support of his application for leave a claim for damages and empowers the court to award damages on the hearing of the application if satisfied that such damages could have been awarded to him in an action begun by him by writ at the time of the making of the application.

Finally rule 1 of the new Order 53 enables an application for a declaration or an injunction to be included in an application for judicial review. This was not previously the case; only prerogative orders could be obtained in proceedings under Order 53. Declarations or injunctions were obtainable only in actions begun by writ or originating summons. So a person seeking to challenge a decision had to make a choice of the remedy that he sought at the outset of the proceedings, although when the matter was examined more closely in the course of the proceedings it might appear that he was not entitled to that remedy but would have been entitled to some other remedy available only in the other kind of proceeding.

This reform may have lost some of its importance since there have come to be realised that the full consequences of the *Anisminic* case, in introducing the concept that if a statutory decision-making authority asks itself the wrong question it acts without jurisdiction, have been virtually to abolish the distinction between errors within jurisdiction that rendered voidable a decision that remained valid until quashed, and errors that went to jurisdiction and rendered a decision void *ab initio* provided that its validity was challenged timeously in the High Court by an appropriate procedure. Failing such challenge within the applicable time limit, public policy, expressed in the maxim *omnia praesumuntur rite esse acta*, requires that after the expiry of the time limit it should be given all the effects in law of a valid decision.

Nevertheless, there may still be cases where it turns out in the course of proceedings to challenge a decision of a statutory authority that a declaration of rights rather than certiorari is the appropriate remedy. *Pyx Granite Co. Ltd v Ministry of Housing and Local Government* [1960] A.C. 260 provides an example of such a case.

So Order 53 since 1977 has provided a procedure by which every type of remedy for infringement of the rights of individuals that are entitled to protection in public law can be obtained in one and the same proceeding by way of an application for judicial review, and whichever remedy is found to be the most appropriate in the light of what has emerged upon the hearing of the application, can be granted to him. If what should emerge is that his complaint is not of an infringement of any of his rights that are entitled to protection in public law, but may be an infringement of his rights in private law and thus not a proper subject for judicial review, the court has power under rule 9(5), instead of refusing the application, to order the proceedings to continue as if they had begun by writ. There is no such converse power under the R.S.C. to permit an action begun by writ to continue as if it were an application for judicial review; and I respectfully disagree with that part of the judgment of Lord Denning M.R. which suggests that such a power may exist; nor do I see the need to amend the rules in order to create one.

My Lords, at the outset of this speech, I drew attention to the fact that the remedy by way of declaration of nullity of the decisions of the board was discretionary—as are all the remedies available upon judicial review. Counsel for the plaintiffs accordingly conceded that the fact that by adopting the procedure of an action begun by writ or by originating summons instead of an application for judicial review under Order 53 (from which there have now been removed all those disadvantages to applicants that had previously led the courts to countenance actions for declarations and injunctions as an alternative procedure for obtaining a remedy for infringement of the rights of the individual that are entitled to protection in public law only) the plaintiffs had thereby been able to evade those protections against groundless, unmeritorious or tardy harassment that were afforded to statutory tribunals or decision-making public authorities by Order 53, and which might have resulted in the summary, and would in any event have resulted in the speedy disposition of the application, is among the matters fit to be taken into consideration by the judge in deciding whether to exercise his discretion by refusing to grant a declaration; but, it was contended, this he may only do at the conclusion of the trial.

So to delay the judge's decision as to how to exercise his discretion would defeat the public policy that underlies the grant of those protections: *viz.*, the need, in the interests of good administration and of third parties who may be indirectly affected by the decision, for speedy certainty as to whether it has the effect of a decision that is valid in public law. An action for a declaration or injunction need not be commenced until the very end of the limitation period; if begun by writ, discovery and interlocutory proceedings may be prolonged and the plaintiffs are not required to support their allegations by evidence on oath until the actual trial. The period of uncertainty as to the validity of a decision that has been challenged upon allegations that may eventually turn out to be baseless and unsupported by evidence on oath, may thus be strung out for a very lengthy period, as the actions of the first three appellants in the instant appeals show. Unless such an action can be struck out summarily at the outset as an abuse of the process of the court the whole purpose of the public policy to which the change in Order 53 was directed would be defeated.

My Lords, Order 53 does not expressly provide that procedure by application for judicial review shall be the exclusive procedure available by which the remedy of a declaration or injunction may be obtained for infringement of rights that are entitled to protection under public law; nor does section 31 of the Supreme Court Act 1981. There is great variation between individual cases that fall within Order 53 and the Rules Committee and subsequently the legislature were, I think, for this reason content to rely upon the express and the inherent power of the High Court, exercised upon a case to case basis, to prevent abuse of its process whatever might be the form taken by that abuse. Accordingly, I do not think that your Lordships would be wise to use this as an occasion to lay down categories of cases in which it would necessarily always be an abuse to seek in an action begun by writ or originating summons a remedy against infringement of rights of the individual that are entitled to protection in public law.

The position of applicants for judicial review has been drastically ameliorated by the new Order 53. It has removed all those disadvantages, particularly in relation to discovery, that were manifestly unfair to them and had, in many cases, made applications for prerogative orders an inadequate remedy if justice was to be done. This it was that justified the courts in not treating as an abuse of their powers resort to an alternative procedure by way of action for a declaration or injunction (not then obtainable on an application under Order 53), despite the fact that this procedure had the effect of depriving the defendants of the protection to statutory tribunals and public authorities for which for public policy reasons Order 53 provided.

Now that those disadvantages to applicants have been removed and all remedies for infringements of rights protected by public law can be obtained upon an application for judicial review, as can also remedies for infringements of rights under private law if such infringements should also be involved, it would in my view as a general rule be contrary to public policy, and as such an abuse of the process of the court, to permit a person seeking to establish that a decision of a public authority infringed rights to which he was entitled to protection under public law to proceed by way of an ordinary action and by this means to evade the provisions of Order 53 for the protection of such authorities.

My Lords, I have described this as a general rule; for though it may normally be appropriate to apply it by the summary process of striking out the action, there may be exceptions, particularly where the invalidity of the decision arises as a collateral issue in a claim for infringement of a right of the plaintiff arising under private law, or where none of the parties objects to the adoption of the procedure by writ or originating summons. Whether there should be other exceptions should, in my view, at this stage in the development of procedural public law, be left to be decided on a case to case basis— a process that your Lordships will be continuing in the next case in which judgment is to be delivered today [*Cocks v Thanet DC* [1983] 2 A.C. 286].

In the instant cases where the only relief sought is a declaration of nullity of the decisions of a statutory tribunal, the Board of Visitors of Hull Prison, as in any other case in which a similar declaration of nullity in public law is the only relief claimed, I have no hesitation, in agreement with the Court of Appeal, in holding that to allow the actions to proceed would be an abuse of the process of the court. They are blatant attempts to avoid the protections for the defendants for which Order 53 provides.

I would dismiss these appeals.

Notes

1. Lord Diplock's speech touches on many aspects of judicial review, including legitimate expectations, review for error of law, the availability of the prerogative orders and the availability of discovery and cross-examination in judicial review proceedings. It continues to be cited regularly on these points, even though, as we shall see, matters have moved on as regards the procedural exclusivity principle he sought to lay down.

Lord Diplock makes it clear that this was not a case where the applicants had any claim to a remedy as a matter of private law. In the 1950s, 1960s and 1970s, the courts had taken a generous view of the availability of private law remedies against public authorities. The orthodox view of the requirement of *locus standi* for an injunction or declaration was that, as private law remedies, they were only available to protect an applicant's private law rights, or where an applicant suffered special damage from interference with a public right. Occasionally, judges adopted this strict approach (*e.g.* *Gregory v Camden LBC* [1966] 1 W.L.R. 899). More commonly, declarations and injunctions were awarded against public authorities in circumstances where it did not seem that the applicant's private law rights were at stake, or that he had suffered special damage, but where no point was taken by the public authority as to the plaintiff's standing on the availability of the remedy (see, *e.g.* *Prescott v Birmingham Corp.* [1955] Ch. 210; *Lee v Department of Education and Science* [1967] 66 L.G.R. 211).

The House of Lords in *Gouriet v Union of Post Office Workers* [1978] A.C. 435, in a case where the plaintiff was seeking an injunction to restrain a threatened breach of the criminal law by the respondent trade union, reaffirmed that the proper test for *locus standi* was whether the plaintiff's legal rights were at stake, or he had suffered special damage. The position where the respondent was a public authority was not tested before the introduction of the new Order 53.

In the light of this, *O'Reilly v Mackman* can be interpreted simply as repudiating the generous, but unsoundly based, approach to standing in injunction and declaration cases that was in any event under a cloud following *Gouriet*. As Laws J. stated in *British Steel Plc v Customs and Excise Commissioners* [1996] 1 W.L.R. 1002 at 1012–1013:

> "Where a complaint sought to be raised in litigation touches only a public law issue, there being no question of a private right involved, the complainant must generally seek his remedy by way of judicial review in the public law court. This is the basic O'Reilly principle. Though it looks like a rule of procedure (and has been castigated as a bad one by Sir William Wade), it is in fact a rule of substance, for reasons explained by Lord Diplock in *O'Reilly* itself and underlined by Lord Slynn in *Mercury* [below, p.989]: namely it would be an abuse of process to litigate such claims by ordinary private law means. The concept of abuse of process is not a function of mere procedural regulation; it is a necessary safeguard against manipulation of court process".

What might have given rise to cause for concern would have been if the new approach had made it more difficult for plaintiffs to vindicate their private law rights where the defendant was a public authority. Subsequent case law has provided some reassurance on the point.

2. The decision of the House of Lords in *Cocks v Thanet DC* [1983] 2 A.C. 286 was delivered on the same day as that in *O'Reilly v Mackman*. Here, C commenced proceedings in the county court claiming a declaration that the local housing authority was in breach of its duties under the Housing (Homeless Persons) Act 1977, consequential mandatory injunctions and damages. The House of Lords held that the functions of housing authorities under the legislation fell into two distinct categories. First, it was for the authority to inquire into and decide whether it was satisfied as to the matters that gave rise to the full housing duty (*i.e.* whether the applicant was (1) homeless and threatened with homelessness; (2) had a priority need; and (3) had not become homeless intentionally). These decisions could only be challenged as a matter of public law, and were subject to the *O'Reilly v Mackman* principle. However, once it was decided that a duty existed under the legislation, that duty was enforceable as a matter of private law. This distinction was applied in subsequent cases (*e.g. Mohram Ali v Tower Hamlets LBC* [1993] Q.B. 407), but was overtaken by the subsequent decision of the House of Lords in *O'Rourke v Camden LBC* [1998] A.C. 188 that the true position was that the homelessness legislation did not at any stage give rise to duties enforceable in private law.

3. *Private law claims. O'Reilly v Mackman* and *Cocks v Thanet DC* spawned a large body of case law (see the previous edition of this book at pp.654–662). The fact that determining the scope of the procedural exclusivity principle generated so much litigation, including a number of further visits to the House of Lords, of itself demonstrates how unclear and unsatisfactory the principle was, particularly as the issues were essentially procedural and not substantive. In subsequent decisions, the House of Lords confirmed that *O'Reilly v Mackman* was not to be interpreted as imposing significant obstacles in the way of the claimants of their rights in private law. There were several landmark cases.

In *Davy v Spelthorne BC* [1984] A.C. 262, D in 1979 entered an agreement with the council under which he undertook not to appeal against an enforcement notice in respect of the use of his land for the production of precast concrete, provided the notice was not enforced for three years. The notice was served in 1980, and D did not appeal. In 1982, D brought proceedings in the Chancery Division claiming (1) an injunction restraining the council from implementing the notice; (2) damages for negligent advice given by the council resulting in a failure to appeal against the notice; and (3) an order that the notice be set aside. The Court of Appeal ((1983) 81 L.G.R. 580) struck out (1) and (3) as an abuse of process as in substance an attack on the validity of the notice designed to have the same effect as would be obtained by an order under RSC, Ord.53. The Court refused to strike out the private law claim for damages, and the council's appeal on this point was dismissed by the House of Lords. Lord Fraser of Tullybelton (at 274) noted that as regards this claim, D did not wish to impugn the notice; his "whole case on negligence depends on the fact that he has lost his chance to impugn it". The House of Lords decision on claim (2) was clearly right. The extent to which the Court of Appeal's decision on claims (1) and (3) placed restrictions on the indication of D's private law rights is debatable. However, there are many situations where public law decisions made in the public interest affect private law rights and the setting of time-limits for claims shorter than the standard limitation period of 6 years has been upheld under the ECHR and HRA as proportionate (see above, p.384) (*cf.* the strict time-limits for challenging compulsory purchase orders). The outcome seems reasonable. D had the right to appeal against the notice but chose not to use it; his claim for compensation could proceed. (Whether a duty of care is owed by the council in such cases is, however, doubtful: see below, p.1063).

The decision of the House of Lords was echoed in *Roy v Kensington and Chelsea and Westminster Family Practitioner Committee* [1992] 1 A.C. 624, where the House of Lords refused to strike out part of an action based on the plaintiff's private law rights to be paid for work done. Lord Lowry (at 653) expressed a preference for a "broad approach" under which *O'Reilly v Mackman* "merely required the aggrieved person to proceed by judicial review only when private law rights were not at stake"; however, the case was decided on a "narrow approach", under which it was to be regarded as an exception to the principle. His Lordship concluded (at 654–655):

"Whichever approach one adopts, the arguments for excluding the present case from the ambit of the rule or, in the alternative, making an exception of it are similar and to my mind convincing.
(1) Dr Roy has either a contractual or a statutory private law right to his remuneration in accordance with his statutory terms of service.
(2) Although he seeks to enforce performance of a public law duty under paragraph 12.1, his private law rights dominate the proceedings.
(3) The type of claim and other claims for remuneration (although not this particular claim) may involve disputed issues of fact.
(4) The order sought (for the payment of money due) could not be granted on judicial review.
(5) The claim is joined with another claim which is fit to be brought in an action (and has already been successfully prosecuted.)
(6) When individual rights are claimed, there should not be a need for leave or a special time limit, nor should the relief be discretionary.
(7) The action should be allowed to proceed unless it is plainly an abuse of process.
(8) The cases . . . show that the rule in *O'Reilly v Mackman* [1983] 2 A.C. 237, assuming it to be a rule of general application, is subject to many exceptions based on the nature of the claim and on the undesirability of erecting procedural barriers. . . .
In conclusion, my Lords, it seems to me that, unless the procedure adopted by the moving party is ill suited to dispose of the question at issue, there is much to be said in favour of the proposition that a court having jurisdiction ought to let a case be heard rather than entertain a debate concerning the form of the proceedings".

See J. Alder, (1993) 13 L.S. 183, arguing that *Roy* renders the *O'Reilly v Mackman* principle "virtually meaningless. Ord. 53 is exclusive only where no private rights are involved at all, that is in cases where no ordinary action would be possible anyway" (p.202); *cf.* A. Tanney, [1994] P.L. 51 (disagreeing with Alder on the basis that Lord Lowry in *Roy* actually adopted the narrow approach to *O'Reilly v Mackman* "leaving the possibility that Ord. 53 is compulsory even in some cases involving a mixture of public and private rights" (p.61)).

There is now a large body of case law that shows that where a claimant enjoys a private right:

> "the claimant may sue at private law even though he must assault an administrative or discretionary decision on the way .. . . If the plaintiff stands in a relationship with the defendant whereby he enjoys a settled and existing private right, it cannot be abusive that he should seek to make it good by ordinary action merely because its value or quantification depends upon the defendant's opinion as to certain aspects given to him to decide"

(*per* Laws J. in *British Steel Plc v Customs and Excise Commissioners* [1996] 1 All E.R. 1002 at 1013; the Court of Appeal reversed Laws J. without criticising this statement: [1997] 1 All E.R. 346. Examples include *An Bord Bainne Co-operative Ltd (Irish Dairy Board) v Milk Marketing Board* [1984] 1 C.M.L.R. 519 (decision in the public law field alleged to constitute infringement of directly effective EEC regulations which created direct rights in private law; these rights could be protected in the same way that an individual could in certain cases sue for breach of statutory duty) affirmed: [1984] 2 C.M.L.R. 584, CA, and referred to with approval by the House of Lords in the *Mercury* case, below; the *British Steel* case, above; *Trustees of Dennis Rye Pension Fund v Sheffield City Council* [1998] 1 W.L.R. 840 (private law right to claim payment of an improvement grant previously approved by the council appropriate for ordinary action even though the dispute was whether the statutory condition for its payment (works being completed to the council's satisfaction) had been fulfilled; the issues were largely ones of fact and did not require the expertise of a Crown Office judge. This line of cases has continued after the decision in *Clark v University of Humberside* (below, p.991). In *Phonographic Performance Ltd v Department of Trade and Industry* [2004] EWHC 1795, ChD; [2004] 1 W.L.R. 2893, a claim for *Francovich* damages for failure to implement an EC directive by ordinary action was held not to be an abuse of process; indeed to subject the individual's rights to a discretion and a time-limit more restrictive than those normally appropriate to a private law claim for breach of statutory duty would itself constitute a breach of EC law.

Then, in *ID v Home Office* [2005] EWCA Civ 38, the Court of Appeal had no doubt at all but that a claim by an asylum seeker for damages for false imprisonment was properly brought as a private action. The Administrative Court could not empanel a jury and in any event could not consider a claim for damages alone. Compensation for unlawfully detained asylum seekers would be hard to come by within the strict time-limits of Pt 54, given severe difficulties over legal representation in detention centres, and to restrict access to justice by insisting on proceedings by Pt 54 would amount to the antithesis of the overriding objective (see Brooke L.J. at paras [105]–[112]).

4. Cases may be dealt with in ordinary proceedings even where it is not obvious that private rights are in issue. In *Mercury Communications Ltd v Director General of Telecommunications* [1996] 1 W.L.R. 48, the House of Lords refused to strike out an originating summons seeking a declaration as to the true construction of phrases in a condition attached to BT's licence to run a telecommunications system granted by the Secretary of State under s.7 of the Telecommunications Act 1984. The dispute in substance and in form was as to the effect of the terms of a contract between Mercury and BT even if it could also be expressed as a dispute as to the terms of the licence. Lord Slynn stated (at 57) that "It is of particular importance . . . to retain some flexiblity as the precise limits of what is called 'public law', and what is called 'private law' are by no means worked out". The procedure by way of originating summons in the Commercial Court was at least as well and might be better suited to the determination of these issues as judicial review. In any event, in dealing with the summons, the trial judge could "have regard to, even if he is not strictly bound by, the procedural protection which would be available to a public authority under the provisions of Order 53" (*per* Lord Slynn at 58). See A. McHarg, [1995] P.L. 539; and P. Craig, (1996) 112 L.Q.R. 531 and *Craig*, pp.798–799, arguing that as it "would have been difficult to

find private rights that M had against DGT" the case stands for the proposition that cases not involving private law rights may still be dealt with in ordinary proceedings provided there is not an abuse of process.

5. *Public law issues raised as a defence.* In O'Reilly v Mackman, Lord Diplock stated (at 285) that an exception might be made "where the invalidity of the decision arises as a collateral issue in a claim for infringement of a right of the plaintiff arising under private law". Subsequent case law has shown that the *O'Reilly v Mackman* principle does not apply to prevent the invalidity of a decision being raised as a defence to enforcement proceedings. The point has arisen in both civil and criminal cases. In *Wandsworth LBC v Winder* [1985] A.C. 461, the House of Lords held that W was entitled to argue in his defence to proceedings in the county court, claiming arrears of rent and possession of the council flat occupied by him, that the council's decisions to increase the rent was *ultra vires* and void as being unreasonable. W was complaining of an infringement of a contractual right in private law to occupy the flat on terms that could only be varied by a notice that was not, *inter alia, Wednesbury* unreasonable. This was furthermore not a "collateral" matter within Lord Diplock's statement; it was "the whole basis of [W]'s defence and it is the central issue which has to be decided" (*per* Lord Fraser of Tullybelton at 508). Notwithstanding the effect of a successful challenge on the council's finances, the *O'Reilly v Mackman* principle was not applicable. It would be a strange use of language to describe W's behaviour in relation to the litigation, that had been stated by the council, as an abuse of process (510–511). (Having been allowed to raise the matter, W's defence was ultimately unsuccessful: *Wandsworth LBC v Winder (No.2)* (1987) 19 H.L.R. 204.) (The decision is perhaps generous to W. While it would be obviously reasonable to allow the person affected the right to argue that a decision that affected him alone was unlawful, it is not so obvious that this was an appropriate vehicle for challenging a general rent increase; *cf.* the *Rhondda* case, below, p.993). Similarly, the *O'Reilly v Mackman* principle does not prevent the defendant in a criminal case relying on the *ultra vires* doctrine in conducting his defence. See *Boddington*, above, p.877.

6. The position where it is the public authority asserting the defence of statutory authority was considered by the Court of Appeal in *The Great House of Sonning Ltd v Berkshire CC* [1996] R.T.R. 407. The Court (Hutchison and Nourse L.J., Saville L.J. dissenting) held that where the council relied on an order temporarily closing a road made under the Road Traffic Regulation Act 1984, as a defence to claims in public nuisance brought by businesses affected by the closure, the matter had to proceed by judicial review. *Per* Hutchison L.J. (at 412):

> "The order prevents that obstruction from being a nuisance, unless and until it is set aside. There is, thus,. . . no private law right that, so long as this order stands, the plaintiffs can assert".

It is submitted that the dissent of Saville L.J. (at 413) is to be preferred:

> "The plaintiffs' claim does not depend on proving that the local authority was unauthorised by statute to obstruct the highway, but merely requires proof that the public authority is threatening to obstruct the highway so as to cause them . . . serious damage".

It was then for the local authority to establish the defence of statutory authority "if it can".

7. *Consent.* In O'Reilly v Mackman, Lord Diplock indicated (above, p.986) that ordinary proceedings might be brought by agreement. In such a case, the public body is presumably content that the protections of judicial review proceedings are not needed (see *Lewis*, pp.119–120). In *Inner London Education Authority v Department of the Environment* (1983) 82 L.G.R. 322, Woolf J. heard proceedings for a declaration commenced by originating summons, in respect of the issue whether the ILEA was

a "local authority" for the purpose of Pt III of the Local Government, Planning and Land Act 1980. No objection was taken to this course and the matter was set down in the Crown Office list. See also *Gillick v West Norfolk and Wisbech Area HA* [1986] A.C. 112, *per* Lord Scarman at 177–178. (Conversely, a private law matter cannot be brought under Ord.53 by agreement: *R. v Durham City Council Ex p. Robinson, The Times*, January 31, 1992.)

8. *The effect of the CPR.* The force of Lord Diplock's analysis in *O'Reilly v Mackman* concerning procedural exclusivity is further undermined by the changes to civil procedure introduced as part of the Woolf reforms, which in various respects increase both flexibility and safeguards against unmeritorious ordinary litigation. This point was made by Lord Woolf C.J. in *Clark v University of Humberside* [2000] 1 W.L.R. 1988. Here, the Court of Appeal held that it was not an abuse of process for a student to bring a claim properly formulated as a contractual action against the University, arising out of claimed breaches of the rules applicable in cases of academic failure, long after the three-month limitation period for judicial review had passed. Lord Woolf C.J. referred to Lord Diplock's speech in *O'Reilly v Mackman*, noting that he had emphasised (at 284) that by proceeding by action, the plaintiff in that case had "been able to evade those protections against groundless unmeritorious or tardy harassment that were afforded to . . . decision-making public authorities by Order 53. . . .". However, the new Civil Procedure Rules now provided that Ord.53 (initially preserved in Sch.1 to the CPR as originally made) was subject to the overriding principle contained in CPR Pt 1.

> "27. In addition, if proceedings involving public law issues are commenced by an ordinary action under Part 7 or Part 8 they are now subject to Part 24. Part 24 is important because it enables the court, either on its own notion or on the application of a party, if it considers that a claimant has no real prospect of succeeding on a claim or an issue, to give summary judgment on the claim or issue. This is a markedly different position from that which existed when *O'Reilly v Mackman* [1983] 2 A.C. 236 was decided. If a defendant public body or an interested person considers that a claim has no real prospect of success an application can now be made under Part 24. This restricts the inconvenience to third parties and the administration of public bodies caused by a hopeless claim to which Lord Diplock referred.
>
> 28. The distinction between proceedings under Order 53 and an ordinary claim are now limited. Under Order 53 the claimant has to obtain permission to bring the proceedings so the onus is upon him to establish he has a real prospect of success. In the case of ordinary proceedings the defendant has to establish that the proceedings do not have a real prospect of success.
>
> A University is a public body. This is not in issue on this appeal. Court proceedings would, therefore, normally be expected to be commenced under Order 53".

His Lordship noted that if a University was subject to the supervision of a visitor there was little scope for judicial review (see *Page*, above, p.450). In the case of a new university created by statute without a visitor, the court would still not involve itself with issues that involve making academic judgment. Summary judgment dismissing such claims should normally be obtainable.

> "32. While the courts will intervene where there is no visitor normally this should happen after the student has made use of the domestic procedures for resolving the dispute. If it is not possible to resolve the dispute internally, and there is no visitor, then the courts may have no alternative but to become involved. If they do so, the preferable procedure would usually be by way of judicial review. If, on the other hand, the proceedings are based on the contract between the student and the university then they do not have to be brought by way of judicial review.
>
> 33. The courts today will be flexible in their approach. Already, prior to the introduction of the C.P.R. the courts were prepared to prevent abuse of their process

where there had been an inordinate delay even if the limitation period had not expired. In such a situation, the court could, in appropriate circumstances, stay subsequent proceedings. This is despite the fact that a litigant normally was regarded as having a legal right to commence proceedings at any time prior to the expiry of the limitation period: see *Birkett v James* [1978] A.C. 297.

34. The court's approach to what is an abuse of process has to be considered today in the light of the changes brought about by the C.P.R. Those changes include a requirement that a party to proceedings should behave reasonably both before and after they have commenced proceedings. Parties are now under an obligation to help the court further the overriding objectives which include ensuring that cases are dealt with expeditiously and fairly: C.P.R., rr. 1.1(2)(*d*) and 1.3. They should not allow the choice of procedure to achieve procedural advantages. The C.P.R. are, as r. 1.1(1) states, a new procedural code. Parliament recognised that the C.P.R. would fundamentally change the approach to the manner in which litigation would be required to be conducted. That is why the Civil Procedure Act 1997 (section 4(1) and (2)) gives the Lord Chancellor a very wide power to amend, repeal or revoke any enactment to the extent he considers necessary or desirable in consequence of the C.P.R.

35. While in the past, it would not be appropriate to look at delay of a party commencing proceedings other than by judicial review within the limitation period in deciding whether the proceedings are abusive this is no longer the position. While to commence proceedings within a limitation period is not in itself an abuse, delay in commencing proceedings is a factor which can be taken into account in deciding whether the proceeding are abusive. If proceedings of a type which would normally be brought by judicial review are instead brought by bringing an ordinary claim, the court in deciding whether the commencement of the proceedings is an abuse of process can take into account whether there has been unjustified delay in initiating the proceedings.

36. When considering whether proceedings can continue the nature of the claim can be relevant. If the court is required to perform a reviewing role or what is being claimed is a discretionary remedy, whether it be a prerogative remedy or an injunction or a declaration the position is different from when the claim is for damages or a sum of money for breach of contract or a tort irrespective of the procedure adopted. Delay in bringing proceedings for a discretionary remedy has always been a factor which a court could take into account in deciding whether it should grant that remedy. Delay can now be taken into account on an application for summary judgment under C.P.R., Part 24 if its effect means that the claim has no real prospect of success.

37. Similarly if what is being claimed could affect the public generally the approach of the court will be stricter than if the proceedings only affect the immediate parties. It must not be forgotten that a court can extend time to bring proceedings under R.S.C., Ord. 53. The intention of the C.P.R. is to harmonise procedures as far as possible and to avoid barren procedural disputes which generate satellite litigation.

38. Where a student has, as here, a claim in contract, the court will not strike out a claim which could more appropriately be made under Order 53 solely because of the procedure which has been adopted. It may however do so, if it comes to the conclusion that in all the circumstances, including the delay in initiating the proceedings, there has been an abuse of the process of the court under the C.P.R. The same approach will be adopted on an application under Part 24.

39. The emphasis can therefore be said to have changed since *O'Reilly v Mackman* [1983] 2 A.C. 237. What is likely to be important when proceedings are not brought by a student against a new university under Order 53, will not be whether the right procedure has been adopted but whether the protection provided by Order 53 has been flouted in circumstances which are inconsistent with the proceedings being able to be conducted justly in accordance with the general principles

contained in Part 1. Those principles are now central to determining what is due process. A visitor is not required to entertain a complaint when there has been undue delay and a court in the absence of a visitor should exercise its jurisdiction in a similar way. The courts are far from being the ideal forum in which to resolve the great majority of disputes between a student and his or her university. The courts should be vigilant to ensure their procedures are not misused. The courts must be equally vigilant to discourage summary applications which have no real prospect of success".

In the light of this, the courts are less willing to strike out proceedings on procedural grounds and litigants seem less willing to risk significant costs on raising such points. "It is greatly to be hoped that complaints . . . about procedural exclusivity may fall away under the CPR regime for the reasons given by Lord Woolf M.R. in *Clark* . . ." (*per* Brooke L.J. in *ID v Home Office* [2005] EWCA Civ 38 at [104]).

Clark is now taken as the starting point for considering abuse of process arguments. Indeed, even the more limited possibility of striking out proceedings as an abuse of process for excessive delay recognized in *Clark*, where a private law claim is based wholly or substantially on "public law issues", does not apply where a public law point is raised as a defence to private law proceedings (*Rhondda Cynon Taff BC v Watkins* [2003] EWCA Civ 129; [2003] 1 W.L.R. 864). Here, the council in 1966 took possession of land under a compulsory purchase order but was immediately wrongfully dispossessed by the owner, W. The council only started possession proceedings in 2000. These would be time-barred unless the council could rely on a deed poll vesting the land in the council executed in 1988. The Court of Appeal held that W was entitled to argue on public law grounds that the deed poll was *ultra vires*. *Wandsworth LBC v Winder* (above, p.990) remained applicable.

The extent to which delay can be used as a basis for the striking out of ordinary proceedings remains uncertain. The mere fact that the claimant waits to the end of the limitation period before commencing proceedings cannot constitute an abuse of process (*Department of Transport v Chris Smaller (Transport) Ltd* [1989] A.C. 1197), but delay may be relevant when considering whether proceedings are abusive for other reasons (Sir Anthony Morritt V.C. in *Phonographic Performance Ltd v Department of Trade and Industry* [2004] EWHC 1795 (Ch); [2004] 1 W.L.R. 2893 at para. [35] citing *Clark* at para. [35]). Here, the Vice-Chancellor held that it was not an abuse of process for the claimant in 2003 to commence proceedings claiming that provisions of the Copyright, Designs and Patents Act 1988 did not comply with an EC Directive that should have been implemented by July 1, 1994. Any breach of duty was a continuing one. Furthermore, his Lordship rejected the Crown's argument that here there was an abuse because the delay was deliberate; had given rise to substantial claims; put the Crown on the horns of a dilemma given that its position was that the provisions did comply but it could do nothing to protect itself if it turned out to be wrong; with the passage of time made it more difficult to obtain evidence as to the question of liability. These were

"neither more nor less than those faced by any defendant facing ordinary civil proceedings based on uncertain legal principles and brought late but within the relevant limitation period".

The Crown should not be put in a privileged position (at para. [52]).

9. Academic reaction to the procedural exclusivity principle as it was worked through in the period before the introduction of the CPR was generally critical. The main themes were (1) the waste of time and money on litigation merely about procedure (J.A. Jolowicz, [1983] C.L.J. 15 at p.18; H.W.R. Wade, (1995) 101 L.Q.R. 180 at p.187) with litigants seeking to use the confusion for tactical advantage (S. Fredman and G. Morris, [1994] P.L. 69 at p.80) (2) the failure of the cases to provide clear and convincing guidance on the difficult distinction between "public law" and "private

law" (J. Beatson, (1987) 103 L.Q.R. 34; C.F. Forsyth, [1985] C.L.J. 415, Fredman and Morris, *op.cit.*).

There have accordingly been arguments that public law and private law procedures should be assimilated. One model would be for the prerogative remedies to be fitted into the mechanism of an ordinary action, with no leave requirement but the possibility for the respondent authority to apply for an expedited procedure incorporating the appropriate Order 53 safeguards (Wade, (1985) 101 L.Q.R 180 at pp.189–190). What has emerged does not, of course, take that form, but the differences between the two forms of proceeding have been reduced. D. Oliver, [2002] P.L. 91, maintains the position that claims for judicial review should be brought by ordinary claim under CPR Pts 7 or 8, with a few modifications. The requirement for permission and the three-month limit would be removed. Sufficient protection would be provided for public authorities by the powers to give summary judgment under P 3 and the discretion to refuse a remedy.

A third line of criticism addresses the twin assumptions: (1) that public authorities need the special safeguards inherent in the judicial review procedure; but (2) that the vindication of private rights ought not to be encumbered by the restrictions that apply in consequence to litigants. If the safeguards are really necessary in the public interest why should they not apply also to private actions against public authorities. Why should interests protected by public law be regarded as less important than private law rights?

". . . [W]hen one considers the subject-matter of some of the public law interests which have generated litigation (*e.g.* remission of sentence, obtaining council housing) this assumption appears absurd" (*Cane*, p.95).

(F) STANDING

R. v INLAND REVENUE COMMISSIONERS Ex p. NATIONAL FEDERATION OF SELF-EMPLOYED AND SMALL BUSINESSES LTD

[1982] A.C. 617; [1981] 2 W.L.R. 722; [1981] 2 All E.R. 93 (HOUSE OF LORDS)

Some 6,000 casual workers in Fleet Street were nominated by their trade unions to work for newspapers on specified occasions. They were given call slips and then collected pay dockets to enable them to draw their pay from their employers but a substantial number of them gave false names and addresses (*e.g.* "Mickey Mouse of Sunset Boulevard" and "Sir Gordon Richards of Tattenham Corner") so that it was impossible for the Inland Revenue to collect the tax which was due from them. The consequent loss to the Revenue was estimated at £1 million a year. In view of the frauds, the Inland Revenue after discussions with the employers and the unions, introduced a special arrangement which would ensure that for the future tax would either be deducted at source or be properly assessed and made it clear that, if the arrangement were generally accepted, and subject to certain other conditions, investigation into tax lost in certain previous years would not be carried out. A federation representing the self-employed and small businesses, who contrasted the attitude taken by the Revenue to the tax evasions of the Fleet Street casuals with that adopted by the Revenue in other cases where tax evasions were suspected, applied for judicial review and claimed a declaration that the Inland Revenue acted unlawfully in granting the amnesty and an order of *mandamus* directed to the revenue to assess and collect income tax from the casual workers.

The Divisional Court granted leave ex parte, but at the hearing *inter partes*, on the Inland Revenue's objection that the federation had no *locus standi*, the Divisional Court held that the federation had not "sufficient interest" within RSC, Ord.53, r. 3(5), to claim the declaration and order sought.

On the federation's appeal, which proceeded on the assumption that the Inland Revenue had no power to grant such a tax "amnesty", the Court of Appeal (by a majority) allowed the appeal ([1980] Q.B. 407) holding that the body of taxpayers represented by the federation could reasonably assert that they had a genuine grievance in the alleged failure of the Inland Revenue to do its duty and the granting of an unlawful tax indulgence to the casual workers, and accordingly they had a "sufficient interest" within the meaning of RSC, Ord.53, r. 3(5) to apply for judicial review under that order.

The Inland Revenue appealed to the House of Lords and the House unanimously allowed their appeal.

LORD WILBERFORCE:. . . [noted that the question of *locus standi* had been taken as a preliminary point of law, and continued:] I think that it is unfortunate that this course has been taken. There may be simple cases in which it can be seen at the earliest stage that the person applying for judicial review has no interest at all, or no sufficient interest to support the application: then it would be quite correct at the threshold to refuse him leave to apply. The right to do so is an important safeguard against the courts being flooded and public bodies harassed by irresponsible applications. But in other cases this will not be so. In these it will be necessary to consider the powers or the duties in law of those against whom the relief is asked, the position of the applicant in relation to those powers or duties, and to the breach of those said to have been committed. In other words, the question of sufficient interest can not, in such cases, be considered in the abstract, or as an isolated point: it must be taken together with the legal and factual context. The rule requires sufficient interest *in the matter to which the application relates*. This, in the present case, necessarily involves the whole question of the duties of the Inland Revenue and the breaches or failure of those duties of which the respondents complain.

Before proceeding to consideration of these matters, something more needs to be said about the threshold requirement of "sufficient interest". The courts in exercising the power to grant prerogative writs, or, since 1938, prerogative orders, have always reserved the right to be satisfied that the applicant had some genuine *locus standi* to appear before it. This they expressed in different ways. Sometimes it was said, usually in relation to certiorari, that the applicant must be a person aggrieved; or having a particular grievance (*R. v Thames Magistrates' Court, ex p. Greenbaum* (1957) 55 L.G.R. 129); usually in relation to mandamus, that he must have a specific legal right (*R. v Lewisham Union Guardians* [1897] 1 Q.B. 498 and *R. v Russell, ex p. Beaver-brook Newspapers Ltd* [1969] 1 Q.B. 342); sometimes that he must have a sufficient interest (*R. v Cotham* [1898] 1 Q.B. 802, 804 (mandamus), *ex p. Stott* [1916] 1 K.B. 7 (certiorari)). By 1977, when R.S.C., Ord. 53 was introduced, the courts, guided by Lord Parker C.J., in cases where mandamus was sought, were moving away from the *Lewisham Union* test of specific legal right, to one of sufficient interest. In *R. v Russell* Lord Parker had tentatively adhered to the test of legal specific right but in *R. v Customs and Excise Com-missioners, ex p. Cook* [1970] 1 W.L.R. 450 he had moved to sufficient interest. Shortly afterward the new rule (R.S.C., Ord. 53, r. 3) was drafted with these words.

R.S.C., Ord. 53 was, it is well known, introduced to simplify the procedure of applying for the relief formerly given by prerogative writ or order—so the old technical rules no longer apply. So far as the substantive law is concerned, this remained unchanged: the Administration of Justice (Miscellaneous Provisions) Act 1938 preserved the jurisdiction existing before the Act, and the same preservation is contemplated by legislation now pending. The Order, furthermore, did not remove the requirement to show *locus standi*. On the contrary, in rule 3, it stated this in the form of a threshold requirement to be found by the court. For all cases the test is expressed as one of sufficient interest in the matter to which the application relates. As to this I would state two negative propositions. First, it does not remove the whole—and vitally important—question of *locus standi* into the realm of pure discretion. The matter is one for decision, a mixed decision of fact and law, which the court must decide on legal principles. Secondly, the fact that the same words are used to cover all the forms of remedy allowed by the rule does not mean that the test is the same in all cases. When Lord Parker C.J. said that in cases of mandamus the test may well be stricter (sc. than in certiorari)—the *Beaverbrook Newspapers* case [1969] 1 Q.B. 342 and in *Cook's* case [1970] 1 W.L.R. 450, 455F, "on a very strict basis", he was not stating a technical rule—which can now be discarded—but a rule of common sense, reflecting the different character of the relief asked for. It would seem obvious enough that the interest of a person seeking to compel an authority to carry out a duty is different from that of a person complaining that a judicial or administrative body has, to his detriment, exceeded its powers. Whether one calls for a stricter rule than the other may be a linguistic point: they are certainly different and we should be unwise in our enthusiasm for liberation from procedural fetters to discard reasoned authorities which illustrate this. It is hardly necessary to add that recognition of the value of guiding authorities does not mean that the process of judicial review must stand still.

In the present case we are in the area of mandamus—an alleged failure to perform a duty. It was submitted by the Lord Advocate that in such cases we should be guided by the definition of the duty, in this case statutory, and inquire whether expressly, or by implication, this definition indicates—or the contrary—that the complaining applicant is within the scope or ambit of the duty. I think that this is at least a good working rule though perhaps not an exhaustive one.

The Inland Revenue Commissioners are a statutory body. Their duties are, relevantly, defined in the Inland Revenue Regulation Act 1890 and the Taxes Management Act 1970.

. . . [I]t is clear that the Inland Revenue Commissioners are not immune from the process of judicial review. They are an administrative body with statutory duties, which the courts, in principle, can supervise. They have indeed done so—see *R. v Income Tax Special Commissioners* (1881) 21 Q.B.D. 313 (mandamus) and *Income Tax Special Commissioners v Linsleys (Established 1894) Ltd* [1958] A.C. 569, where it was not doubted that a mandamus could be issued if the facts had been right. It must follow from these cases and from principle that a taxpayer would not be excluded from seeking judicial review if he could show that the revenue had either failed in its statutory duty toward him or had been guilty of some action which was an abuse of their powers or outside their powers altogether. Such a collateral attack—as contrasted with a direct appeal on law to the courts—would no doubt be rare, but the possibility certainly exists.

The position of other taxpayers—other than the taxpayers whose assessment is in question—and their right to challenge the revenue's assessment or non-assessment of that taxpayer, must be judged according to whether, consistently with the legislation, they can be considered as having sufficient interest to complain of what has been done or omitted. I proceed thereto to examine the revenue's duties in that light.

These duties are expressed in very general terms and it is necessary to take account also of the framework of the income tax legislation. This establishes that the commissioners must assess each individual taxpayer in relation to his circumstances. Such assessments and all information regarding taxpayers' affairs are strictly confidential. There is no list or record of assessments which can be inspected by other taxpayers. Nor is there any common fund of the produce of income tax in which income taxpayers as a whole can be said to have any interest. The produce of income tax, together with that of other inland revenue taxes, is paid into the consolidated fund which is at the disposal of Parliament for any purposes that Parliament thinks fit.

The position of taxpayers is therefore very different from that of ratepayers. As explained in *Arsenal Football Club Ltd v Ende* [1979] A.C. 1, the amount of rates assessed upon ratepayers is ascertainable by the public through the valuation list. The produce of rates goes into a common fund applicable for the benefit of the ratepayers. Thus any ratepayer has an interest, direct and sufficient, in the rates levied upon other ratepayers; for this reason, his right as a "person aggrieved" to challenge assessments upon them has long been recognised and is so now in section 69 of the General Rate Act 1967. This right was given effect to in the *Arsenal* case.

The structure of the legislation relating to income tax, on the other hand, makes clear that no corresponding right is extended to be conferred upon taxpayers. Not only is there no express or implied provision in the legislation upon which such a right could be claimed, but to allow it would be subversive of the whole system, which involves that the commissioners' duties are to the Crown, and that matters relating to income tax are between the commissioners and the taxpayer concerned. No other person is given any right to make proposals about the tax payable by any individual: he cannot even inquire as to such tax. The total confidentiality of assessments and of negotiations between individuals and the revenue is a vital element in the working of the system. As a matter of general principle I would hold that one taxpayer has no sufficient interest in asking the court to investigate the tax affairs of another taxpayer or to complain that the latter has been under-assessed or over-assessed: indeed, there is a strong public interest that he should not. And this principle applies equally to groups of taxpayers: an aggregate of individuals each of whom has no interest cannot of itself have an interest.

That a case can never arise in which the acts or abstentions of the revenue can be brought before the court I am certainly not prepared to assert, nor that, in a case of sufficient gravity, the court might not be able to hold that another taxpayer or other taxpayers could challenge them. Whether this situation has been reached or not must depend upon an examination, upon evidence, of what breach of duty or illegality is alleged. Upon this, and relating it to the position of the complainant, the court has to make its decision.

[His Lordship examined the evidence and concluded that the arrangements in question had been entered by the Inland Revenue, acting genuinely in the care and management of the taxes, under the powers entrusted to them.]

Looking at the matter as a whole, I am of opinion that the Divisional Court, while justified on the *ex parte* application in granting leave, ought, having regard to the nature of "the matter" raised, to have held that the federation had shown no sufficient interest in that matter to justify its application for relief. I would therefore allow the appeal and order that the originating motion be dismissed.

LORD DIPLOCK: . . . The whole purpose of requiring that leave should first be obtained to make the application for judicial review would be defeated if the court were to go into the matter in any depth at that stage. If, on a quick perusal of the material then available, the court thinks that it discloses what might on further consideration turn out to be an arguable case in favour of granting to the applicant the relief claimed, it ought, in the exercise of a judicial discretion, to give him leave to apply for that relief. The discretion that the court is exercising at this stage is not the same as that which it is called upon to exercise when all the evidence is in and the matter has been fully argued at the hearing of the application.

The analysis to which . . . the relevant legislation has been subjected by some of your Lordships, . . . mean that occasions will be very rare on which an individual taxpayer (or pressure group of taxpayers) will be able to show a sufficient interest to justify an application for judicial review of the way in which the revenue has dealt with the tax affairs of any taxpayer other than the applicant himself.

Rare though they may be, however, if, in the instant case, what at the threshold stage was suspicion only had been proved at the hearing of the application for judicial review to have been true in fact (instead of being utterly destroyed), I would have held that this was a matter in which the federation had a sufficient interest in obtaining an appropriate order, whether by way of declaration or mandamus, to require performance by the board of statutory duties which for reasons shown to be *ultra vires* it was failing to perform.

It would, in my view, be a grave lacuna in our system of public law if a pressure group, like the federation, or even a single public-spirited taxpayer, were prevented by outdated technical rules of *locus standi* from bringing the matter to the attention of the court to vindicate the rule of law and get the unlawful conduct stopped. The Attorney-General, although he occasionally applies for prerogative orders against public authorities that do not form part of central government, in practice never does so against government departments. It is not, in my view, a sufficient answer to say that judicial review of the actions of officers or departments of central government is unnecessary because they are accountable to Parliament for the way in which they carry out their functions. They are accountable to Parliament for what they do so far as regards efficiency and policy, and of that Parliament is the only judge; they are responsible to a court of justice for the lawfulness of what they do, and of that the court is the only judge.

I would allow this appeal upon the ground upon which, in my view, the Divisional Court should have dismissed it when the application came to be heard, instead of singling out the lack of a sufficient interest on the part of the federation, *viz.* that the federation completely failed to show any conduct by the board that was *ultra vires* or unlawful.

LORD FRASER:. . . . I agree with the reasoning of Lord Wilberforce and Lord Roskill but I wish to explain my reasons in my own words. . . . The rules of court give no guidance as to what is a sufficient interest for this purpose. I respectfully accept from my noble and learned friends who are so much more familiar than I am with the history of the prerogative orders that little assistance as to the sufficiency of the interest can be derived from the older cases. But while the standard of sufficiency has been relaxed in recent years, the need to have an interest has remained and the fact that R.S.C., Ord.53, r.3 requires a sufficient interest undoubtedly shows that not every applicant is entitled to judicial review as of right.

The new Order 53, introduced in 1977, no doubt had the effect of removing technical and procedural differences between the prerogative orders, and of introducing a remedy by way of declaration or injunction in suitable cases, but I do not think it can have had the effect of throwing over all the older law and of leaving the grant of judicial review in the uncontrolled discretion of the court. On what principle, then, is the sufficiency of interest to be judged? All are agreed that a direct financial or legal interest is not now required, and that the requirement of a legal specific interest laid down in *R. v Lewisham Union Guardians* [1897] 1 Q.B. 488 is no longer applicable. There is also general agreement that a mere busybody does not have a sufficient interest. The difficulty is, in between those extremes, to distinguish between the desire of the busybody to interfere in other people's affairs and the interest of the person affected by or having a reasonable concern with the matter to which the application relates. In the present case that matter is an alleged failure by the appellants to perform the duty imposed upon them by statute.

The correct approach in such a case is, in my opinion, to look at the statute under which the duty arises, and to see whether it gives any express or implied right to persons in the position of the applicant to complain of the alleged unlawful act or omission. On that approach it is easy to see that a ratepayer would have a sufficient interest to complain of unlawfulness by the authorities responsible for collecting the rates. . . . The position of the taxpayer is entirely different . . .

[I]f the class of persons with a sufficient interest is to include all taxpayers it must include practically every individual in the country who has his own income, because there must be few individuals, however frugal their requirements, who do not pay some indirect taxes including value added tax. It would, I think, be extravagant to suggest that every taxpayer who believes that the Inland Revenue or the Commissioners of Customs and Excise are giving unlawful preference to another taxpayer, and who feels aggrieved thereby, has a sufficient interest to obtain judicial review under Order 53. It may be that, if he was relying on some exceptionally grave or widespread illegality, he could succeed in establishing a sufficient interest, but such cases would be very rare indeed and this is not one of them.

LORD SCARMAN:. . . In your Lordships' House the Lord Advocate, who now appears for the appellants, the Inland Revenue Commissioners,. . . has put at the forefront of his argument a reasoned analysis of the statutory duties of the revenue, and has invited the House to hold that the statutory code neither recognises nor imposes upon the revenue a duty such as the federation alleges to the general body, or any group of taxpayers.

Before I consider this submission, it is necessary to deal with a subsidiary point taken by the Lord Advocate. He submitted that, notwithstanding the language of R.S.C., Ord. 53, r.1(2), the court has no jurisdiction to grant to a private citizen a declaration save in respect of a private right or wrong: and he relied on the House's decision in *Gouriet v Union of Post Office Workers* [1978] A.C. 435. Declaration is, of course, a remedy developed by the judges in the field of private law. *Gouriet's* case is authority for the proposition that a citizen may not issue a writ claiming a declaration or other relief against another for the redress of a public wrong unless he can persuade the Attorney-General, on his "relation", to bring the action. The case has nothing to do with the prerogative jurisdiction of the High Court; and it was decided before the introduction of the new Order 53, at a time when a declaration could not be obtained by a private citizen unless he could show (as in a claim for injunction) that a private right of his was threatened or infringed. The new Order has made the remedy available as an alternative, or an addition, to a prerogative order. Its availability has, therefore, been extended, but only in the field of public law where a prerogative order may be granted. I have already given my reasons for the view that this extension is purely a matter of procedural law, and so within the rule-making powers of the Rules Committee. I therefore reject this submission of the Lord Advocate.

I pass now to the two critical issues: (1) the character of the duty upon the revenue and the persons to whom it is owed. Is it legal, political, or merely moral? (2) The nature of the interest which the applicant has to show. It is an integral part of the Lord Advocate's argument that the existence of the duty is a significant factor in determining the sufficiency of an applicant's interest.

The duty

[His Lordship concluded:]
[A] legal duty of fairness is owed by the revenue to the general body of taxpayers. It is, however, subject to the duty of sound management of the tax which the statute places upon the revenue.

The interest

The sufficiency of the interest is, as I understand all your Lordships agree, a mixed question of law and fact. The legal element in the mixture is less than the matters of fact and degree: but it is important, as setting the limits within which, and the principles by which, the discretion is to be exercised. At one time heresy ruled the day. The decision of the Divisional Court in *R. v Lewisham Union Guardians* [1897] 1 Q.B. 498 was accepted as establishing that an applicant must establish "a legal specific right to ask for the interference of the court" by order of mandamus: *per* Wright J. at 500. I agree with Lord Denning M.R. in thinking this was a deplorable decision. It was at total variance with the view of Lord Mansfield C.J. Yet its influence has lingered on, and is evident even in the decision of the Divisional Court in this case. But the tide of the developing law has now swept beyond it, as the Court of Appeal's decision in *R. v Greater London Council, ex p. Blackburn* [1976] 1 W.L.R. 550 illustrates. In the present case the House can put down a marker buoy warning legal navigators of the danger of the decision. As Professor Wade pointed out in *Administrative Law* (4th ed., 1977), p.610, if the *Lewisham* case were correct, mandamus would lose its public law character, being no more than a remedy for a private wrong.

My Lords, I will not weary the House with citation of many authorities. Suffice it to refer to the judgment of Lord Parker C.J. in *R. v Thames Magistrates' Court, ex p. Greenbaum*, 55 L.G.R. 129, a case of certiorari; and to words of Lord Wilberforce in *Gouriet v Union of Post Office Workers*

[1978] A.C. 435, 482, where he stated the modern position in relation to prerogative orders: "These are often applied for by individuals and the courts have allowed them liberal access under a generous conception of *locus standi*." The one legal principle, which is implicit in the case law and accurately reflected in the rule of court, is that in determining the sufficiency of an applicant's interest it is necessary to consider the matter to which the application relates. It is wrong in law, as I understand the cases, for the court to attempt an assessment of the sufficiency of an applicant's interest without regard to the matter of his complaint. If he fails to show, when he applies for leave, a *prima facie* case, or reasonable grounds for believing that there has been a failure of public duty, the court would be in error if it granted leave. The curb represented by the need for an applicant to show, when he seeks leave to apply, that he has such a case is an essential protection against abuse of legal process. It enables the court to prevent abuse by busybodies, cranks, and other mischief-makers. I do not see any further purpose served by the requirement for leave.

But, that being said, the discretion belongs to the court: and, as my noble and learned friend, Lord Diplock, has already made clear, it is the function of the judges to determine the way in which it is to be exercised. Accordingly I think that the Divisional Court was right to grant leave *ex parte*. Mr Payne's affidavit of March 20, 1979, revealed a prima facie case of failure by the Inland Revenue to discharge its duty to act fairly between taxpayer and tax payer. But by the time the application reached the Divisional Court for a hearing, *inter partes*, of the preliminary issue, two very full affidavits had been filed by the revenue explaining the "management" reasons for the decision not to seek to collect the unpaid tax from the Fleet Street casuals. At this stage the matters of fact and degree upon which depends the exercise of the discretion whether to allow the application to proceed or not became clear. It was now possible to form a view as to the existence or otherwise of a case meriting examination by the court. And it was abundantly plain upon the evidence that the applicant could show no such case. But the Court of Appeal, misled into thinking that, at that stage and notwithstanding the evidence available, *locus standi* was to be dealt with as a preliminary issue, assumed illegality (where in my judgment none was shown) and, upon that assumption, held that the applicant had sufficient interest. Were the assumption justified, which on the evidence it was not, I would agree with the reasoning of Lord Denning M.R. and Ackner L.J. I think the majority of the Court of Appeal, in formulating a test of genuine grievance reasonably asserted, were doing no more than giving effect to the general principle which Lord Mansfield C.J. had stated in the early days on the remedy. Any more stringent test would, as Wade, *Administrative Law* (4th ed.), p.612 observes, open up "a serious gap in the system of public law". . . .

LORD ROSKILL:. . . It is clear that the respondents are seeking to intervene in the affairs of individual taxpayers, the Fleet Street casual workers, and to require the appellants to assess and collect tax from them which the appellants have clearly agreed not to do. Theoretically, but one trusts only theoretically, it is possible to envisage a case when because of some grossly improper pressure or motive the appellants have failed to perform their statutory duty as respects a particular taxpayer or class of taxpayer. In such a case, which emphatically is not the present, judicial review might be available to other taxpayers. But it would require to be a most extreme case for I am clearly of the view, having regard to the nature of the appellants' statutory duty and the degree of confidentiality enjoined by statute which attaches to their performance, that in general it is not open to individual taxpayers or to a group of taxpayers to seek to interfere between the appellants and other taxpayers, whether those other taxpayers are honest or dishonest men, and that the court should, by refusing relief by way of judicial review, firmly discourage such attempted interference by other taxpayers. It follows that, in my view, taking all those matters into account, it cannot be said that the respondents had a "sufficient interest" to justify their seeking the relief claimed by way of judicial review. . . .

[His Lordship also expressed agreement with LORD WILBERFORCE and LORD FRASER.]

Notes

1. For comments, see P. Cane, [1981] P.L. 322; D. Feldman, (1982) 45 M.L.R. 92; and *Lewis*, Ch.10. The old law of standing was highly complex, varying according to the remedy sought, and with uncertainty if not conflicting authorities on many points. See generally S.M. Thio, *Locus Standi and Judicial Review* (1971); P. Cane, "The Function of Standing Rules in Administrative Law" [1980] P.L. 303. In theory, the old law was not entirely swept away by the new Ord.53 or the *Fleet Street Casuals* case. Nevertheless, references to the old authorities when points as to standing are considered are now unusual. Points that emerge from the *Fleet Street Casuals* case (also sometimes known as "Mickey Mouse" case) include (1) that the question of *locus standi* cannot be considered in isolation from the legal and factual context of the application; (2) that it is one of mixed law and fact to be decided on legal principles and not simply a matter of discretion; (3) that a decision that an applicant has sufficient interest to be granted leave does not preclude the matter being raised at the full hearing; (4) that the question is inappropriate to be taken on appeal as a preliminary issue; and (5), most significantly, that the courts should not take an unduly restrictive approach to questions of standing. There are a number of difficulties.

On point (1), their Lordships indicate that the court must consider both whether on the facts it is established that the decision is *ultra vires*, and, if so, the nature of the illegality. If this means that no person has standing without a good case on the merits and, conversely, that every person with a good case on the merits has standing, then standing has disappeared as a separate concept. Wade and Forsyth accept that the "House of Lords' new criterion would seem virtually to abolish the requirement of standing" as a distinct concept (*Administrative Law* (9th ed.), p.693). However, this seems to put it too high. Schiemann J., writing extra-judicially, states that:

"wherever someone is . . . excluded by reason of locus standi rules, the law regards it as preferable that an illegality should continue than that the person excluded should have access to the courts" ([1990] P.L. at 342).

(*cf*. his Lordship's comments in the *Rose Theatre* case, below, p.1004).

Too much cannot be read into point (2). While Lords Wilberforce, Scarman and Roskill make this point, it is clear from Lord Scarman's speech that the "legal element is less than the matters of fact and degree" (see above, p.1000). In other words the test of sufficient interest is so broadly expressed as to leave considerable leeways for choice on the part of the judges; whether this is to be labelled "law and fact" or "discretion" is of less significance. Only Lord Diplock was prepared to say that the court has an "unfettered discretion to decide what in its own good judgment it considers to be 'a sufficient interest' on the part of an applicant in the particular circumstances of the case before it" (at 642). Subsequent judges have used the term "discretion" (see, *e.g.* Watkins L.J. in *R. v Felixstowe JJ. Ex p. Leigh* [1987] Q.B.

582 at 597 and Otton J. in *Ex p. Greenpeace (No.2)*, below, p.1005; *cf.* Schiemann J. in the *Rose Theatre* case, below, p.1004 (at 520), where he stated that the matter is "not purely a matter of discretion in the courts").

It is clear from point (3) that the question of standing arises at two stages. One difficulty is that the statutory test in CPR r.54 and the Supreme Court Act 1981, s.31(3) refers expressly to the leave stage; the House of Lords acted on the assumption that this was also the appropriate test on the hearing of the full application. While *formally* the same test applies at both stages, its application differs in that at the leave stage the court is only forming a "provisional" or "*prima facie*" view on the question (see the extracts from Lord Diplock's and Lord Scarman's speeches (above, pp.998 and 999)). A final view can only properly be expressed at the second stage, when the merits of the complaint can be considered. Accordingly, it is only in the clearest of cases that an application will be ruled out at the leave stage on the ground that the applicant lacks *locus*.

2. *Ratepayers and taxpayers*. The House of Lords confirmed, *obiter*, that a ratepayer has *locus standi* to challenge rating decisions concerning other ratepayers in the same area (*cf. Arsenal Football Club Ltd v Ende* [1979] A.C. 1). It is likely that ratepayers and council tax payers will have standing to challenge decisions of local authorities that involve expenditure (and possibly other decisions or acts, though not necessarily all; a council tax is unlikely, for example, automatically to have *locus standi* to challenge a decision in the field of child care).

The general principle that one taxpayer does not have *locus standi* to challenge decisions concerning other taxpayers is not an absolute rule. No member of the House of Lords was willing to say that a taxpayer would *never* have *locus standi* in such a case. Then, in *R. v Att-Gen Ex p. ICI Plc* [1985] 1 CMLR 588, Woolf J. held that ICI had *locus standi* to challenge a valuation of ethane for the purposes of calculating Petroleum Revenue Tax that would be unduly favourable to its rivals, Esso, Shell and BP. ICI's interests were adversely affected by the approach of the Revenue, and was the only body whose interests were likely to be so affected. They were not complaining about a particular assessment in relation to an other taxpayer's affairs but about an approach which, but for the judicial review proceedings, would presumably have continued for a substantial time and was in certain respects wrong in law. Woolf J.'s judgment on this point was endorsed by the Court of Appeal ([1987] 1 C.M.L.R. 72). This case was, however, distinguished in *R. (on the application of Freeserve.com Plc) v Customs and Excise Commissioners* [2003] EWHC 2736; [2003] S.T.C 187, where Freeserve was held not to have standing to challenge a decision that AOL, a telecoms supplier from outside the EU, should not be subject to a charge to VAT; although that the applicant was solely at risk as a result of the decision complained of was not a necessary requirement for there to be an exception to the general rule, it was "not without importance" that Freeserve was merely one of a number of ISPs also affected by AOL's competitive advantage, and a level playing field was now in place.

The position of a taxpayer is stronger when he wishes to challenge unlawful expenditure. In *R. v H.M. Treasury Ex p. Smedley* [1985] 1 Q.B. 657, Slade L.J. said that he did not "feel much doubt" that Mr Smedley, "if only in his capacity as a taxpayer" had sufficient interest to raise a "serious question" as to the *vires* of an Order in Council, which would have led to the expenditure of substantial sums from the Consolidated Fund for the purpose of the European Community budget.

3. *Standing to challenge planning decisions*. There have been many cases considering the standing of individuals, pressure groups and other public bodies to challenge planning decisions. In most of them, a liberal approach has been adopted, according standing at the permission stage to all but "busybodies and troublemakers" (to use Sedley J.'s phrase in *R. v Somerset CC Ex p. Dixon* [1997] C.O.D. 323 at 330). The former, larger, group includes:

(1) an individual who was a local resident, a parish councillor and a member of various bodies concerned with the environment (*Dixon*, in respect of a challenge to the grant of planning permission for the extension of a limestone quarry); *cf. R. (on*

the application of Edwards) v Environment Agency [2004] EWHC 736, where a person affected as a local resident had standing to challenge to the grant of a permit under the Integrated Pollution Prevention and Control regime, notwithstanding that he had not prior to issuing the claim made his opposition known. Furthermore it was not an abuse of process that he had acted because he would be more likely to obtain public funding than a more obvious candidate, given that the Legal Services Commission with knowledge of the facts had decided to provide such funding;

(2) environmental organisations and area amenity societies (*Covent Garden Community Association Ltd v Greater London Council* [1981] J.P.L. 183 (company formed to represent the interests of Covent Garden residents had standing to challenge grant of planning permission in respect of premises in the area)); *R. v Poole BC Ex p. Beebee* [1991] C.O.D. 264 (British Herpetological Society held to have standing to challenge planning permission for part of a heath, long associated with the society in connection with rare species found on it; the society was also named in a condition attached to the permission);

(3) single issue pressure groups (*R. v Hammersmith and Fulham LBC Ex p. People Before Profit Ltd* (1981) 80 L.G.R. 322 (unincorporated association who participated in Local Plan inquiry, the report of which by the inspector was awaited, held to have standing to challenge grant of planning permission in respect of a proposal which was an aspect of the plan to which they had objected; this was so notwithstanding that they had been formed into a company limited by guarantee before applying for judicial review, given that they otherwise had standing, the change of legal entity made no difference); *R. v Leicestershire CC Ex p. Blackfordby and Boothorpe Action Group* [2000] E.W.L.R. 2 (group incorporated for the purpose of proceedings to challenge planning permission for landfill site; individual members had standing as local residents who had made representations against the grant of permission; company held to have standing even if (obiter) one purpose had been to avoid personal liability for costs as this could be covered by requiring the company to give security for costs);

(4) rival developers (*R. v Canterbury City Council Ex p. Springimage* (1994) 68 P. & C.R. 171; but *cf. R. v Tendring DC Ex p. Leonard* (1997) 76 P. & C.R. 567 where a rival developer's interest in a grant of planning permission was held to be too remote on the facts);

(5) public bodies (*R. v Cotswold DC Ex p. Barrington Parish Council* (1997) 75 P. & C.R. 515 (standing accorded to parish council whose area came within three miles of the site, with roads coming from the vicinity of the site through its area).

In *Dixon*, Sedley J. after a full analysis of the authorities confirmed that a liberal approach should be adopted, and that it was not necessary that the claimants have characteristics that "give him an interest greater than that of the general public" ([1997] C.O.D. 323 at 326–331). His Lordship declined to follow one, widely-criticised, case where a narrower approach had been adopted. This was the decision of Scheimann J. in *R. v Secretary of State for the Environment Ex p. Rose Theatre Trust Co* [1990] 1 Q.B. 504. Here, a trust company was set up to secure the preservation of the remains of the Rose Theatre, a theatre of great historical significance recently discovered during the development of a site in central London. Its members included persons of expertise and distinction in archaeology, the theatre and literature, local residents and the local MP. Schiemann J. held that it did not have standing to challenge the Secretary of State's refusal to list the remains in the Schedule of Monuments made under the Ancient Monuments and Archaeological Areas Act 1979, and also that the Secretary of State's decision had been lawful. His Lordship held that to have standing, it was necessary to have an interest greater than that of an "ordinary citizen", that none of the individual members of the company did, and that it was not possible to acquire standing by getting together to form a company. While the third of these propositions is undoubtedly correct, the first is doubtful for the reasons given by Sedley J. in *Dixon* (namely that the purpose of the standing test at the permission stage is to exclude busybodies and troublemakers). (The second is also doubtful on the facts, and was assumed to be the case without discussion.) Having said that, there was no evidence that the remains were under a threat that could have been removed by scheduling, and the interests of local residents and the like were more remotely engaged than in respect of decisions to grant planning permission.

4. *National campaigning bodies.* The courts have consistently accorded standing to well-established national campaigning bodies. For example, in *R. v Inspectorate of Pollution Ex p. Greenpeace Ltd (No.2)* [1994] 4 All E.R. 329, Otton J. held that Greenpeace had *locus standi* to challenge variations of authorisations under the Radioactive Substances Act 1960 to permit testing of British Nuclear Fuels Plc's new thermal oxide processing plant (THORP) at Sellafield, Cumbria, although the application was dismissed on its merits. His Lordship took into account the nature of Greenpeace, the extent of its interest in the issues raised and the nature of the relief sought. Greenpeace International had nearly 5 million supporters worldwide; Greenpeace U.K. had over 400,000 supporters with about 2,500 in the Cumbria region. It was a campaigning organisation with the protection of the natural environment as its prime object. His Lordship continued (at 350–351):

"BNFL rightly acknowledges the national and international standing of Greenpeace and its integrity. So must I. I have not the slightest reservation that Greenpeace is an entirely responsible and respected body with a genuine concern for the environment. That concern naturally leads to a bona fide interest in the activities carried on by BNFL at Sellafield and in particular the discharge and disposal of radioactive waste from its premises and to which the respondents' decision to vary relates. The fact that there are 400,000 supporters in the United Kingdom carries less weight than the fact that 2,500 of them come from the Cumbria region. I would be ignoring the blindingly obvious if I were to disregard the fact that those persons are inevitably concerned about (and have a genuine perception that there is) a danger to their health and safety from any additional discharge of radioactive waste even from testing. I have no doubt that the issues raised by this application are serious and worthy of determination by this court.

It seems to me that if I were to deny standing to Greenpeace, those it represents might not have an effective way to bring the issues before the court. There would have to be an application either by an individual employee of BNFL or a near neighbour. In this case it is unlikely that either would be able to command the expertise which is at the disposal of Greenpeace. Consequently, a less well-informed challenge might be mounted which would stretch unnecessarily the court's resources and which would not afford the court the assistance it requires in order to do justice between the parties. Further, if the unsuccessful applicant had the benefit of legal aid it might leave the respondents and BNFL without an effective remedy in costs. Alternatively, the individual (or Greenpeace) might seek to persuade Her Majesty's Attorney General to commence a relator action which (as a matter of policy or practice) he may be reluctant to undertake against a government department (see the learned commentary by Schiemann J on "Locus Standi" [1990] P.L. 342). Neither of these courses of action would have the advantage of an application by Greenpeace, who, with its particular experience in environmental matters, its access to experts in the relevant realms of science and technology (not to mention the law), is able to mount a carefully selected, focused, relevant and well-argued challenge. It is not without significance that in this case the form 86 contains six grounds of challenge but by the time it came to the substantive hearing before me, the Greenpeace 'team' (if I may call them that) had been able to evaluate the respondents' and BNFL's evidence and were able to jettison four grounds and concentrate on two. This responsible approach undoubtedly had the advantage of sparing scarce court resources, ensuring an expedited substantive hearing and an early result (which it transpires is helpful to the respondents and to BNFL).

I also take into account the nature of the relief sought. In *I.R.C. v National Federation of Self-Employed and Small Businesses Ltd* the House of Lords expressed the view that if mandamus were sought that would be a reason to decline jurisdiction. Here, the primary relief sought is certiorari (less stringent) and, if granted, the question of an injunction to stop the testing pending determination of the main applications would still be in the discretion of the court. I also take into account the fact that Greenpeace has been treated as one of the consultees during the consultation process and that they were invited (albeit with other non-consultees) to comment on the 'minded to vary' letter.

It follows that I reject the argument that Greenpeace is a 'mere' or 'meddlesome busybody'. I regard the applicant as eminently respectable and responsible and its genuine interest in the issues raised is sufficient for it to be granted locus standi. . . .

. . . [I]t must not be assumed that Greenpeace (or any other interest group) will automatically be afforded standing in any subsequent application for judicial review in whatever field it (and its members) may have an interest. This will have to be a matter to be considered on a case by case basis at the leave stage and if the threshold is crossed again at the substantive hearing as a matter of discretion.

I also bear this consideration in mind when I respectfully decline to follow the decision of Schiemann J. in *R. v Secretary of State for the Environment, ex p. Rose Theatre Trust Co.* [1990] 1 All E.R. 754; [1990] 1 Q.B. 504. Suffice it to say that the circumstances were different, the interest group had been formed for the exclusive purpose of saving the Rose Theatre site and no individual member could show any personal interest in the outcome. In any event his decision on the locus standi point (as indeed is mine) was not central to his decision. . . ."

Particularly interesting is the decision of the Divisional Court in *R. v Secretary of State for Foreign and Commonwealth Affairs Ex p. World Development Movement Ltd* [1996] 1 W.L.R. 386 that WDM, an internationally recognised non-partisan pressure group, had standing to challenge (successfully) the legality of the payment of what would have totalled £234 million from the Aid and Trade Provision budget to support the project to build the Pergau Dam in Malaysia. Under s.1 of the Overseas Development and Co-operation Act 1980, the Secretary of State had power to provide such funding "for the purpose of promoting the development" of a country outside the United Kingdom. The grant was unlawful in the light of advice to the Secretary of State that the project was uneconomic; the 1980 Act only authorised grants in respect of economically sound developments. Rose L.J. (at 395–396) found that there was nothing in the *National Federation of Self-Employed* case to deny standing to WDM. The authorities seemed "to indicate an increasingly liberal approach to standing on the part of the courts during the last 12 years". Relevant factors included "the importance of vindicating the rule of law", the likely absence of any other responsible challenger, the nature of the breach of duty and the prominent role of WDM in giving advice, guidance and assistance with regard to aid. Furthermore,

". . . if the Divisional Court in *Ex parte Rees-Mogg* [1994] Q.B. 552, . . . was able to accept that the applicant in that case had standing in the light of his 'sincere concerns for constitutional issues', *a fortiori*, it seems to me that the present applicants, with the national and international expertise and interest in promoting and protecting aid to underdeveloped nations, should have standing in the present application".

The sum at stake would presumably have afforded standing to any taxpayer. (*cf.* above, p.1003). See I. Hare, [1995] C.L.J. 227 and (on the wider background to the case), F. White, I. Harden and K. Donnelly, "Audit, Accounting Officers and Account-ability: The Pergau Dam Affair" [1994] P.L. 526 and I. Harden, F. White and K. Hollingsworth, "Value for Money and Administrative Law" [1996] P.L. 661.

Other examples include the Child Poverty Action Group in respect of the interpretation and administration of social security law (*R. v Secretary of State for Social Services Ex p. Greater London Council, The Times*, August 16, 1984 (Woolf J.) appeal dismissed, *The Times*, August 8, 1985; *R. v Secretary of State for Social Services Ex p.*

Child Poverty Action Group [1990] 2 Q.B. 540); Shelter, in relation to housing law (*R. v Secretary of State for the Environment Ex p. Shelter* [1997] C.O.D. 49) and the Howard League for Penal Reform in respect of prisons (*R. (on the application of Howard League for Penal Reform) v Secretary of State for the Home Department* [2003] 1 F.L.R. 484).

5. *Legitimate expectation.* A person with a "legitimate expectation" protected by public law will have *locus standi* to seek judicial review (see Lord Diplock in *O'Reilly v Mackman* (above, p.997) and pp.690–701).

6. The application of the standing requirement may vary according to the remedy sought, or the actual determination challenged. In *R. v Felixstowe JJ. Ex p. Leigh* [1987] Q.B. 582, a journalist was granted a declaration that the justices had erred in law in deciding as a matter of policy that their identities should not be disclosed. The journalist had not been covering the case in respect of which the decision challenged had been made, but was a "public spirited citizen" acting as "guardian of the public interest in the maintenance and preservation of open justice in magistrates' courts, a matter of vital concern in the administration of justice". This was "a matter of national importance" as a policy of routine non-disclosure was being adopted by a growing number of justices elsewhere: "No one has contended that he has acted as a mere busybody in coming to this court to ask for the relief he seeks. The seriousness of his purpose is apparent. I think he has a sufficient interest . . ." (*per* Watkins L.J. at 598). However, he had insufficient standing to be granted *mandamus* to order disclosure in the case in question, as his aim "was not to report the case; it was to comment on various issues arising out of reports by others of the case" (*per* Watkins L.J. at 597). This reinforces Lord Wilberforce's point that the application of the test may *differ* according to the remedy sought, although Watkins L.J. was "inclined to think" that the test was not *stricter* for *mandamus* (at 597) *cf.* however, Otton J. in *Ex p. Greenpeace (No.2)* (above).

Compare *R. v Manchester City Council Ex p. Baragrove Properties Ltd* (1991) 23 H.L.R. 337, in which the Divisional Court held that a property management company had *locus* to challenge the council's interpretation of a housing benefit regulation, which directly affected the rents receivable by the applicants; the company would not, however, have had *locus* to challenge a determination made in relation to the particular circumstances of a tenant.

7. *Motive.* The claimant's motive may be relevant, in exceptional circumstances.

"Thus, if a claimant seeks to challenge a decision in which he has no private law interest, it is difficult to conceive of circumstances in which the court will accord him standing, even where there is a public interest in testing the lawfulness of the decision, if the claimant is acting out of ill-will or for some improper purpose".

(*per* Dyson L.J. in *R. (on the application of Feakins) v Secretary of State for Environment, Food and Rural Affairs* [2003] EWCA Civ 1546, at [23]–[24]; the courts held that an improper motive (to put pressure on DEFRA to pay compensation) was not established on the facts).

8. In *R. v Secretary of State for Employment Ex p. Equal Opportunities Commission* [1995] 1 A.C. 1, the House of Lords (Lord Jauncey of Tullichettle dissenting) held that the EOC had standing to challenge the compatibility with Community law of legislation concerning the rights of part-time employees, on the grounds of sex discrimination (see further below, p.1031). Under the Sex Discrimination Act 1975, s.53(1), the EOC's duties included those of working towards the elimination of discrimination and promoting equality of opportunity between men and women generally. It would be a

"very retrograde step now to hold that the EOC has no locus standi to agitate in judicial review questions related to sex discrimination which are of public importance and affect a large section of the population" (per Lord Keith of Kinkel at 26).

The EOC had been joined as an applicant by a Mrs Day, a part-time worker made redundant by a public authority in circumstances such that she did not qualify for redundancy pay under the UK legislation. Lord Keith held that hers was a purely private claim against her employer, in which she would be able to raise before an industrial tribunal arguments based on Community law. Indeed, such proceedings had been started and adjourned. She was not properly joined in the present proceedings as "the Divisional Court was not the appropriate forum to adjudicate upon . . . her private law claim". The basis of this is unclear. If all Mrs Day were pursuing was her private law claim, it would fall outside the scope of judicial review under the *East Berkshire* principle (above, p.957). However, she surely had sufficient interest to pursue the general question of the validity of the legislation alongside the EOC (see P. Cane, [1995] P.L. 276 at pp.284–285; C. Harlow and E. Szyszczak, (1995) 32 C.M.L.Rev. 641 pp.644–645). The explanation may be that, as Mrs Day had been employed by a public authority, she could assert her directly effective rights under the directive against her employer. Accordingly, the statute did not "adversely affect" her at all.

9. *Standing outside Part 54.* Prior to the introduction of the application for judicial review, the issue of *locus standi* was considered separately in respect of each administrative law remedy, the courts generally being stricter in respect of the private law remedies of declaration or injunction (see above, pp.999–1000). The orthodox approach in respect of private law remedies was set out in *Boyce v Paddington Corp.* [1903] 1 Ch. 109. The plaintiff, shortly before the action, erected buildings on land abutting on an open space under the control of the borough council. The council resolved to erect a hoarding which would obstruct the access of light to the plaintiff's windows. The plaintiff brought an action to restrain the council from doing this. It was held that as the plaintiff was suing in respect of an alleged private right to the access of light, or in respect of an alleged interference with a public right from which he personally sustained special damage, he could sue without joining the Attorney-General as plaintiff (see below, p.1027). The action failed on grounds unconnected with the right to sue. The House of Lords in *Gouriet v Union of Post Office Workers* [1978] A.C. 435 affirmed that this was the correct approach in respect of a private action for an injunction to restrain a threatened breach of the criminal law by a trade union.

Different views have been expressed on the test for *locus standi* where a private action is brought against a public authority. In *Steeples v Derbyshire CC* [1985] 1 W.L.R. 256, Webster J. held that the plaintiff had the necessary *locus standi* to challenge the grant of planning permission by the council for two interrelated developments, which involved the establishment of a leisure complex at Shipley Park, near Ilkeston, Derbyshire. The plaintiff alleged, *inter alia*, breach of procedural requirements and the breach of the *nemo judex* principle of natural justice. Webster J. held that the plaintiff had the necessary *locus standi* under *Boyce v Paddington BC* [1903] 1 Ch. 109. As regards one of the two interrelated developments ("the ancillary development") the plaintiff's private right was affected as a small part of his land was to be taken for it. The other development ("the leisure development") would take place on land adjacent to his own and would result in his view being impaired, in the ambient noise level being increased, in some interference with his use of a lane which bisected land farmed by him and in a risk of his land being invaded by litter and possibly by vandals or trespassers. This would amount to special damage resulting from interference with a public right:

> "If the Plaintiff can show that a proprietary interest of his, reasonably and probably to be affected by the act in question, will probably be prejudiced by it then, even in the absence of authority, I would hold that he suffers in respect of that act damage under a head recognised by the law".

The judge also held that the plaintiff had *locus standi* in respect of the leisure development by virtue of his undoubted *locus* in respect of the ancillary development, as the two developments were closely connected.

The judge further stated that if it had been necessary to decide the point, he would have held that a person with sufficient interest for the purpose of an application for judicial review, and having thereby *locus standi* to apply for an injunction, would have a similar *locus standi* to seek an injunction in ordinary proceedings. Any difference in substance between the two forms of proceeding could, if necessary, be given effect to when the discretion of the court arose as to the relief to be given. The *Gouriet* case was distinguished on the grounds that the plaintiff here was not attempting to enforce the criminal law but to challenge the decision of a public body which he said was wrongly made, and claimed to be threatened by damage special to himself resulting from that decision.

However, in *Barrs v Bethell* [1982] Ch. 294, three ratepayers of Camden London Borough Council issued a writ and statement of claim in the Chancery Division against the members of the majority group on the council and the council itself claiming certain declarations and other orders. It was alleged that there had been various abuses of discretion, and that the councillors had breached the fiduciary duty owed to the ratepayers, *inter alia*, by failing to make cuts in services and to raise council house rents. Warner J. held that a ratepayer was not entitled to sue a local authority or its members, without the leave of the Attorney-General, unless he could show that he had *locus standi* under the rules laid down in *Boyce v Paddington BC* [1903] 1 Ch. 109. His Lordship disagreed with the view expressed by Webster J. in the *Steeples* case, above, that a person with "sufficient interest" under Ord.53 would have *locus standi* in ordinary proceedings.

10. The precise *purposes* of the requirement of standing in respect of public law remedies are rarely discussed by the judges, including the law lords in the *Fleet Street Casuals* case. The distinctions between standing for remedies in private law and in public law is explained as follows by Cane ([1980] P.L. 303): "In private law entitlement to a remedy and the right to apply for that remedy merge; the two issues are not treated separately—the former entails the latter". For example, the law of tort limits the range of plaintiffs who may sue for economic loss: "By limiting entitlement to the remedy of damages, entitlement to institute proceedings is *ipso facto* also limited" (*ibid.*).

The position in public law is different:

". . . the public law litigant is required to show that the respondent public body has infringed one of the values embodied in the substantive heads of judicial review and *also* that some personal interest of his has been thereby infringed thus giving a reason why *he* should be allowed to complain in court of the abuse of power" (p.304).

The literature generally is clearer on the purposes that are or should *not* be served by standing rules. For example, in discussing these rules in the context of American constitutional law, K.C. Davis wrote, in a passage cited by Cane:

"The law of standing is the wrong tool to accomplish judicial objectives unrelated to the task of deciding whether a particular interest asserted is deserving of judicial protection. The courts should avoid hypothetical or remote questions—through the law of ripeness,[10] not through the law of standing. The courts should decline to enter political areas—through the law of political questions, not through the law of standing. The courts should limit themselves to issues 'appropriate for judicial determination'—through the law of case or controversy, but not through that part of the law of case or controversy pertaining to standing. The courts should avoid taking over functions of government that are committed to executives or administrators—through the law of scope of review, not through the law of standing. The courts should virtually stay away from some governmental activities, such as foreign affairs and military operations—through the law of unreviewability,[11] not through the law of standing. The courts should insist upon competent presentation of cases—through

---

[10] [ed.] *cf.* below, p. 1032.
[11] [ed.] *cf.* above, pp. 265–268.

refusals to respond to inadequate presentations, not through the law of standing".
(37 Univ. of Chicago L.R. 450, 469.)

What is clear is that rules that confined access to judicial review to those whose private
law rights were at stake would not be appropriate. One of the clear purposes of judicial review is to secure the public interest that governmental institutions act within the
law, and this would not be served if standing rules were unduly restrictive. There is
much to be said for Lord Denning's statement in *R. v Greater London Council Ex p.
Blackburn* [1976] 1 W.L.R. 550 at 556:

> "I regard it as a matter of high constitutional principle that if there is good ground
> for supposing that a government department or a public authority is transgressing
> the law, or is about to transgress it, in a way which offends or injures thousands of
> Her Majesty's subjects, then any one of those offended or injured can draw it to the
> attention of the courts of law and seek to have the law enforced, and the courts in
> their discretion can grant whatever remedy is appropriate".

This was endorsed by Lord Diplock in the *Fleet Street Casuals* case (at 641), but
rejected by Lord Roskill (at 661) and by Lord Wilberforce (in the context of relator
actions) in the *Gouriet* case ([1978] A.C. 435 at 483). Note, however, the further
broadening of the requirements for standing proposed by the Law Commission and
Lord Woolf (below, p.1033).

11. Note that a narrower test applies in respect of standing to bring a claim under
the HRA, above, p.319.

12. The issue of standing must be distinguished from that of the capacity of an unincorporated association to apply for judicial review. In *R. v Darlington BC Ex p.
Association of Darlington Taxi Owners*, The Times, January 21, 1994, it was held that
such an association did not have capacity (costs were, however, awarded against the
members of the applicant associations). A different view was taken by Sedley J. in *R.
v London Borough of Tower Hamlets Ex p. Tower Hamlets Combined Traders
Association* [1994] C.O.D. 325 and by Turner J. in *R. v Traffic Commissioners for the
North Western Traffic Area Ex p. "Brake"* [1996] C.O.D. 248. The Law Commission
(Law Com. No.226, p.51) has recommended that express provision should be made
in respect of unincorporated associations: see below, p.1033. See also K. Gledhill,
[1996] J.R. 67.

(G) DISCRETIONARY REFUSAL OF A REMEDY

(i) Delay

Delay was an established ground on which, prior to the introduction of the application for judicial review, the court might, in the exercise of its discretion, refuse one of
the prerogative remedies or an injunction or declaration. The new Ord.53 made
express provision concerning delay, now found in similar terms in CPR r.54.5. This
provides that the claim form must be filed promptly and in any event not later than
three months after the grounds to make the claim first arose. The court has a general
power to extend or shorten the time for compliance with any rule, practice direction
or court order (but not a statutory provision); this power is available even if an application for extension is made after time for compliance has expired (CPR r.3.1(2)(a)).
See also PD 54, para.4.1 and the Supreme Court Act 1981, s.31(6) (above, pp.933,
925). The House of Lords in *R. (on the application of Burkett) v Hammersmith and
Fulham LBC* [2002] UKHL 23; [2002] 1 W.L.R. 1593, accepted that there is "no material difference" between Ord.53 r.4(1) and CPR r.54.5(1) (per Lord Steyn at
para. [36]), and in *R. (on the application of M) v School Organisation Committee*
[2001] EWHC Admin 245 stated (at para. [18]) that the approach to time-limits under

r.54.5 was "certainly no less rigorous" than it used to be under Ord.53. However, as the following case shows, there have been difficulties arising from the defective drafting of the relevant provisions.

R. v DAIRY PRODUCE QUOTA TRIBUNAL Ex p. CASWELL

[1990] 2 A.C. 738; [1990] 2 W.L.R. 1320; [1990] 2 All E.R. 434
(HOUSE OF LORDS)

The applicants, Mr and Mrs Caswell, having failed to qualify for a wholesale quota in respect of milk production, claimed relief under the exceptional hardship provisions set out in the Dairy Produce Quotas Regulations 1984. In February 1985, the Dairy Produce Quota Tribunal, on their construction of the Regulations, dismissed the claim. Initially unaware of a remedy, the applicants took no step to challenge the tribunal's decision until 1987 when they applied for and obtained ex parte leave to move for judicial review. On the hearing of the substantive application the applicants conceded before the judge that there had been "undue delay" within the meaning of s.31(6) of the Supreme Court Act 1981 and RSC, Ord.53, r. 4(1), but they resisted an assertion by the tribunal that since there had been a number of other unsuccessful applications to which the same provisions applied, the grant of relief would be detrimental to good administration. The judge held that the tribunal had erred in their construction of the Regulations but, accepting the tribunal's evidence, he declined to grant relief. The Court of Appeal and the House of Lords dismissed the applicants' appeal. In the House, the sole speech was delivered by Lord Goff.

LORD GOFF: . . . [stated the facts, read Ord.53, r.4 and s.31(6), (7), of the Supreme Court Act 1981 (above p.925). Order 53, r.4 provided:

"(1) [An application for leave to apply for judicial review] shall be made promptly and in any event within three months from the date when grounds for the application first arose unless the Court considers that there is good reason for extending the period within which the application shall be made. . . .
(3) Paragraph (1) is without prejudice to any statutory provision which has the effect of limiting the time within which an application for judicial review may be made".

His Lordship continued:]
When Order 53 was redrawn in 1977, rule 4(1) then provided that, where there had been undue delay in making an application for judicial review, the court might refuse to grant leave for the making of the application, or any relief sought on the application:

"if, in the opinion of the court, the granting of the relief sought would be likely to cause substantial hardship to, or substantially prejudice the rights of, any person or would be detrimental to good administration."

Rule 4(2) then provided that, for an order of certiorari to remove any proceeding for the purpose of quashing it, the relevant period for the purpose of paragraph (1) was three months after the date of the relevant proceeding. In 1980, however, that rule was replaced by the present rule, save only that rule 4(1) referred to "An application for judicial review . . .". Following critical comment by the Court of Appeal in *R. v Stratford-on-Avon District Council, Ex p. Jackson* [1985] 1 W.L.R. 1319, in which it was held that those words must be read as referring to an application for leave to apply for judicial review, the rule was amended to give express effect to that interpretation. Despite the change in Ord.53, r.4, made in 1980, section 31(6) of the Supreme Court Act 1981 mirrored the old rule 4, which had by then been replaced. In 1985, clause 43 of the Administration of Justice Bill of that year contained a provision which would have repealed section 31(6) of the Act of 1981; but the clause was abandoned for other reasons, and the proposed repeal fell with it.

In the result, the courts have been left with the task of giving effect to two provisions relating to delay, which at first sight are not easy to reconcile. First, in Ord.53, r.4(1), undue delay is defined, whereas in section 31(6) it is not. Secondly, rule 4(1) applies only to applications for leave to apply for judicial review, whereas section 31(6) applies both to applications for leave to apply and to applications for substantive relief. Thirdly, rule 4(1) looks to the existence of good reason for extending the specified period, whereas section 31(6) looks to certain effects of delay as grounds for refusing leave, or substantive relief, as the case may be. A further twist is provided by the fact that rule 4(1) and (2) are expressed to be without prejudice to any statutory provision which has the effect of limiting the time within which an application for judicial review may be made; and that section 31(6) is expressed to be without prejudice to any enactment or rule of court which had that effect. These two provisions were said by Lloyd L.J., in the Court of Appeal, to produce a *circulus inextricabilis*: [1989] 1 W.L.R. 1089, 1094F.

The relationship between Ord.53, r.4, and section 31(6) was considered by the Court of Appeal in *R. v Stratford-on-Avon District Council, Ex p. Jackson* [1985] 1 W.L.R. 1319 (to which I have already referred) with particular reference to the meaning of the expression "undue delay". It was there submitted that, where good reason had been held to exist for the failure to act promptly as required by Ord.53, r.4(1), and the time for applying for leave had therefore been extended, the effect of section 31(7) was that in such circumstances there was no power to refuse either leave to apply or substantive relief under section 31(6) on the ground of undue delay, because an extension of time under Ord.53, r.4, itself negatives the existence of undue delay. That submission was rejected by the Court of Appeal. Ackner L.J., who delivered the judgment of the court, said, at 1325:

"This is not an easy point to resolve, but we have concluded that whenever there is a failure to act promptly or within three months there is 'undue delay'. Accordingly, even though the court may be satisfied in the light of all the circumstances, including the particular position of the applicant, that there is good reason for that failure, nevertheless the delay, viewed objectively, remains 'undue delay'. The court therefore still retains a discretion to refuse to grant leave for the making of the application or the relief sought on the substantive application on the grounds of undue delay if it considers that the granting of the relief sought would be likely to cause substantial hardship to, or substantially prejudice the rights of, any person or would be detrimental to good administration."

With this conclusion, I respectfully agree. First, when section 31(6) and (7) refer to "an application for judicial review", those words must be read as referring, where appropriate, to an application for leave to apply for judicial review. Next, as I read rule 4(1), the effect of *the rule* is to limit the time within which an application for leave to apply for judicial review may be made in accordance with its terms, *i.e.* promptly and in any event within three months. The court has, however, power to grant leave to apply despite the fact that an application is late, if it considers that there is good reason to exercise that power; this it does by extending the period. This, as I understand it, is the reasoning upon which the Court of Appeal reached its conclusion in *R. v Stratford-on-Avon District Council, Ex p. Jackson.* Furthermore, the combined effect of section 31(7) and of rule 4(1) is that there is undue delay for the purposes of section 31(6) whenever the application for leave to apply is not made promptly and in any event within three months from the relevant date.

It follows that, when an application for leave to apply is not made promptly and in any event within three months, the court may refuse leave on the ground of delay unless it considers that there is good reason for extending the period; but, even if it considers that there is such good reason, it may still refuse leave (or, where leave has been granted, substantive relief) if in its opinion the granting of the relief sought would be likely to cause hardship or prejudice (as specified in section 31(6)) or would be detrimental to good administration. I imagine that, on an *ex parte* application for leave to apply before a single judge, the question most likely to be considered by him, if there has been such delay, is whether there is good reason for extending the period under rule 4(1). Questions of hardship or prejudice, or detriment, under section 31(6) are, I imagine, unlikely to arise on an *Ex parte* application, when the necessary material would in all probability not be available to the judge. Such questions could arise on a contested application for leave to apply, as indeed they did in *R. v Stratford-on-Avon District Council, Ex p. Jackson*; but even then, as in that case, it may be thought better to grant leave where there is considered to be good reason to extend the period under rule 4(1), leaving questions arising under section 31(6) to be explored in depth on the hearing of the substantive application.

In this way, I believe, sensible effect can be given to these two provisions, without doing violence to the language of either. Unlike the Court of Appeal, I do not consider that rule 4(3) and section 31(7) lead to a *circulus inextricabilis*, because 31(6) does not limit "the time within which an application for judicial review may be made" (the words used in rule 4(3)). Section 31(6) simply contains particular grounds for refusing leave or substantive relief, not referred to in rule 4(1), to which the court is bound to give effect, independently of any rule of court.

Accordingly, in the present case, the fact that the single judge had granted leave to the appellants to apply for judicial review despite the lapse (long before) of three months from the date when the ground for their application first arose, did not preclude the court from subsequently refusing substantive relief on the ground of undue delay in the exercise of its discretion under section 31(6). This was the approach adopted by both courts below, applying (as they were bound to do) the decision of the Court of Appeal in *R. v Stratford-on-Avon District Council, Ex p. Jackson* [1985] 1 W.L.R. 1319. Before your Lordships Mr Gordon for the appellants submitted that the principles stated in *Ex p. Jackson* were erroneous; but, for the reasons I have already given, I am unable to accept that submission.

It follows that there is no doubt that, in the present case, there was undue delay within section 31(6). No suggestion has been made that substantial hardship or substantial prejudice were likely to be caused by the grant of the relief sought. The only questions which remained on the appeal were (1) whether the

Court of Appeal should reject the judge's conclusion that the grant of such relief would be detrimental to good administration; and (2) if not, whether it should interfere with the judge's exercise of his discretion to refuse such relief. The Court of Appeal decided against the appellants on both of these points.

On the question of detriment to good administration, the judge reviewed with care the evidence before him. This consisted of an affidavit sworn by Mr Newton, who was secretary of D.P.Q.T. until September 1988, and two affidavits submitted by the appellants in answer to that affidavit, one sworn by Mr May of the legal department of the National Farmers' Union, and the other by Mr Collinson, a partner in the solicitors acting for the appellants. It appeared from the evidence that the essence of the quota system is that there is a finite amount of milk quota available, so that a quota given to one producer is not available to others. In fact, about 4,000 exceptional hardship appeals were heard by D.P.Q.T. Of these, about 600 were successful, additional quota being granted; so about 3,400 producers failed in their applications for additional quota on this ground. In a large number of these latter cases, the end of the final quota year was stated to be the major consideration. Next, the fact that judicial review was the remedy available to a milk producer aggrieved by a decision of D.P.Q.T. must have become well known at least after September 1985, when the first hearing of an application for judicial review in such a case received wide publicity in the dairy trade.[12] Consideration was given to the possibility of other producers seeking judicial review of adverse decisions of D.P.Q.T. if the appellants' application for substantive relief was successful. It was accepted that sufficient provision had been made to deal with the appellants' claim for extra quota. But, in Mr Newton's opinion, a small but administratively substantial number of milk producers could be encouraged to make applications for judicial review relying on the same point as the appellants, or a variation of it; and that could mean re-opening the quota for the year 1984–85, and for each succeeding year. Further allocations of quota could only be made at the expense of all other producers whose quotas would have to be reduced accordingly. Mr Collinson, in his affidavit, questioned whether other milk producers would be likely to follow the appellants' lead and seek judicial review or whether, if they did so, they would obtain leave to apply after such a long delay.

Having reviewed the evidence, the judge expressed his conclusion on this point in the following passage in his judgment:

> "It is obvious that if there are a number of applications the problem of re-opening these claims, going back now three years, is going to be very great. It arises out of events in 1985. The evidential problems are self-evident, leaving aside the question of being able fairly to deal with claims now in relation to matters in 1985. I think there is likely to be a very real problem in relation to a number of cases. I do not think the number of cases is *de* minimis. I have concluded that the fact that hitherto there have been only these two applications is not a matter which is of very great help in determining what the effect will be of the particular decision in this case. I have come to the clearest view that there will be a detriment to good administration if this application were granted."

---

[12] *R. v Dairy Produce Quota Tribunal for England and Wales Ex p. Atkinson*, unreported, September 25, 1985, Macpherson J.

The judge's conclusion, on the evidence before him, that there was likely to be a very real problem in relation to a number of cases, was a finding of fact with which I can see no reason to interfere. Once that conclusion was reached, it seems to me inevitable that to grant the relief sought in the present case would cause detriment to good administration. As Lloyd L.J. pointed out in his judgment [1989] 1 W.L.R. 1089, 1099, two things emerged from the evidence with sufficient clarity: first that, if the appellants' application for substantive relief were to be successful, there would be a significant number of further applications, and secondly that, if a significant number of applications were granted, then all previous years back to 1984 would have to be re-opened. These facts disclose, in my opinion, precisely the type of situation which Parliament was minded to exclude by the provision in section 31(6) relating to detriment to good administration. Lord Diplock pointed out in *O'Reilly v Mackman* [1983] 2 A.C. 237, 280–281:

> "The public interest in good administration requires that public authorities and third parties should not be kept in suspense as to the legal validity of a decision the authority has reached in purported exercise of decision-making powers for any longer period than is absolutely necessary in fairness to the person affected by the decision."

I do not consider that it would be wise to attempt to formulate any precise definition or description of what constitutes detriment to good administration. This is because applications for judicial review may occur in many different situations, and the need for finality may be greater in one context than in another. But it is of importance to observe that section 31(6) recognises that there is an interest in good administration independently of hardship, or prejudice to the rights of third parties, and that the harm suffered by the applicant by reason of the decision which has been impugned is a matter which can be taken into account by the court when deciding whether or not to exercise its discretion under section 31(6) to refuse the relief sought by the applicant. In asking the question whether the grant of such relief would be detrimental to good administration, the court is at that stage looking at the interest in good administration independently of matters such as these. In the present context, that interest lies essentially in a regular flow of consistent decisions, made and published with reasonable dispatch; in citizens knowing where they stand, and how they can order their affairs in the light of the relevant decision. Matters of particular importance, apart from the length of time itself, will be the extent of the effect of the relevant decision, and the impact which would be felt if it were to be re-opened. In the present case, the court was concerned with a decision to allocate part of a finite amount of quota, and with circumstances in which a re-opening of the decision would lead to other applications to re-open similar decisions which, if successful, would lead to re-opening the allocation of quota over a number of years. To me it is plain, as it was to the judge and to the Court of Appeal, that to grant the appellants the relief they sought in the present case, after such a lapse of time had occurred, would be detrimental to good administration. It is, in my opinion, unnecessary to deal expressly with the detailed arguments advanced by Mr Gordon on behalf of the appellants on this point. They were substantially the same as the arguments canvassed by him before the Court of Appeal, which considered and dismissed each argument seriatim. None of them, in my opinion, made any impact upon the essential matters, which I have identified.

Finally, I can, like the Court of Appeal, see no basis for interfering with the judge's exercise of his discretion. The judge took into account the relevant factors, including in particular the financial hardship suffered by the appellants by reason of the erroneous approach adopted by D.P.Q.T., and in particular the imposition upon them of substantial superlevy in the years 1986–87 and 1987–88. He then balanced the various factors and, as he said, came down firmly against the view of the appellants. I can perceive no error here which would justify interference with the judge's conclusion.

For these reasons, I would dismiss the appeal.

LORDS BRIDGE, GRIFFITHS, ACKNER and LOWRY agreed with LORD GOFF.

Appeal dismissed.

Notes

1. The position as to delay is unduly complex. There are many variables, arising from the interrelationship between the concept of "promptness" and "undue delay", the existence of a three-month time-limit which can be extended, and the point that the matter of delay may need to be considered at the permission stage and at the substantive hearing. The main possibilities are the following:

(i) the judge at the permission stage is satisfied that the claim has been brought promptly (which will be within the three-month period) in which case permission cannot be refused on the ground of delay. It should be noted that:

- The three-month limit is not an *entitlement*; an application for permission must in any event be made promptly. In *Friends of the Earth Ltd, Re,* unreported, July 6, 1987, an application for leave to apply for judicial review of the decision of the Secretary of State for Energy to grant consent for the construction of Sizewell B nuclear power station, made just within the three-month period, was rejected. Kennedy J. held that it had not been made promptly, there were no good reasons for the delay, and there would be considerable prejudice to good administration if leave were granted. The applicants had been aware that time was of the essence. This view was endorsed by the Court of Appeal in respect of two of the grounds: the others were unarguable: [1988] J.P.L. 93. See also *R. v ITC Ex p. TVNI Ltd and TVS Television Ltd, The Times,* December 30, 1991; *R. v Leeds City Council Ex p. N* [1999] E.L.R. 324 (challenge to school reorganisation scheme one week less than the three-month limit); *R. (on the application of I-D Publishing Ltd) v Office of the Deputy Prime Minister* [2003] EWHC 1761 (challenge to regulations which impact on a national level should be brought as soon as reasonably practicable, particularly where the complaint is confined to an alleged breach of duty to the claimant alone).
- A finding on an *inter partes* hearing of an application for leave that the application, brought within three months, has been made promptly, does not prevent the court at the substantive hearing finding that there has been undue delay, and exercising its discretion under section 31(6)(b) of the Supreme Court Act 1981 to refuse to grant any relief: *R. v Swale BC, Ex p. Royal Society for the Protection of Birds* [1991] J.P.L. 39. However, the defendant should be permitted to recanvass, by way of undue delay, an issue of promptness which has been decided at the permission stage in the applicant's favour only: (i) if the judge hearing the initial application has expressly so indicated; (ii) if new and relevant material is introduced on the substantive hearing; (iii) if, exceptionally,

the issues as they have developed at the full hearing put a different aspect on the question of promptness; or (iv) if the first judge has plainly overlooked some relevant matter or otherwise reached a decision *per incuriam* (*R. v Lichfield DC Ex p. Lichfield Securities Ltd* [2001] EWCA Civ 304).

In principle these restrictions should not apply where an issue of promptness has been determined on the papers and not at a contested permission hearing (the equivalent of the *inter partes* leave hearing held in *Lichfield*). While the defendant should have raised any issue of promptness in the acknowledgment of service, it would be undesirable to increase pressure on defendants to appear at an oral permission hearing, where they are not normally awarded costs (see pp.974–975).

The House of Lords in *R. (on the application of Burkett) v Hammersmith and Fulham LBC* [2002] UKHL 23; [2002] 1 W.L.R. 1593 disapproved the suggestion that for proceedings for judicial review of a grant of planning permission to be brought "promptly" they should be brought within six weeks, echoing the time-limit applicable to appeals against refusal of permission. This inference had sometimes been drawn in decisions at first instance from observations of Laws J. in *R. v Ceredigion CC Ex p. McKeown* [1998] 2 P.L.R. 1. Lord Steyn said (at [53]) that "the legislative three month limit cannot be contracted by a judicial policy decision".

(ii) The judge at the permission stage may not be satisfied that the claim (brought within three-months) was brought promptly; or the claim has been brought outside the three-month period. Here, the judge may either refuse permission on the ground of non-compliance with CPR r.54.5(1), or grant permission on the basis that he or she is extending time under CPR r.3.1(2)(a) (which would seem to cover both situations).

The following should be noted:

- time may be extended where there is "good reason" to do so. This test appeared expressly in RSC, Ord.53, r.4(1), and is implicit under the CPR.

  Among the reasons that have been held in the circumstances to justify an extension of time are the following: in the case of a challenge to a resolution to grant planning permission, time taken on the advice of counsel to persuade the Secretary of State to call in the application, and time taken in obtaining legal aid (*R. v Stratford-upon-Avon DC Ex p. Jackson* [1985] 1 W.L.R. 1319); the fact that a test case on the same point is in progress in public law court (*per* Sir John Donaldson M.R. *obiter* in *R. v Hertfordshire CC Ex p. Cheung, The Times*, April 4, 1986); time taken in an internal inquiry into the matter of which complaint was made (*R. v Port Talbot BC Ex p. Jones, The Independent*, January 5, 1988); the council's decision after raising an objection to the jurisdiction of the Local Government Ombudsman to investigate a complaint against it, to wait until his report was received before starting judicial review proceedings (*R. v Commissioner for Local Administration Ex p. Croydon LBC* [1989] 1 All E.R. 1033).

- Where there has been an extension of time, and permission has been given, the question whether permission should be granted is no longer a live issue and cannot be reopened at the substantive hearing (*R. v Criminal Injuries Compensation Board Ex p. A* [1999] 2 A.C. 330, *per* Lord Steyn at 341). It was also Lord Slynn's "provisional view" that permission can now be refused by reference to s.31(6), for the same reason (*ibid*).

- However, where there has been an extension of time (beyond the requirement of promptness or the three-month rule as the case may be) there is "undue delay" and relief may be refused in the exercise of the court's discretion under s.31(6). See *R. v Stratford-upon-Avon DC Ex p. Jackson* (above); *Caswell; R. v Criminal Injuries Board Ex p. A* (above) (where the Board's decision to reject a claim was quashed on the ground that there was unfairness in the failure to put particular evidence before it and the matter remitted to the Board for reconsideration; notwithstanding a ten months' delay, there was no question of any hardship, prejudice or detriment to good administration in doing so).

(iii) A further possibility is that the judge at the permission stage expressly reserves the question of delay to be determined at the substantive hearing. Here the Court at that hearing may both determine the question as to an extension of time under CPR, r.3 and exercise the discretion under s.31(6). This possibility was recognised by the House of Lords in *R. v Criminal Injuries Compensation Board Ex p. A* [1999] 2 A.C. 330, *per* Lord Slynn at 341 (contemplating deferral of the application for permission) and Lord Nolan at 347 (contemplating the grant of permission subject to deferral of the resolution of the issue of the extension of time).

2. Other points:

- The fact that the defendant indicates that no point will be taken on delay is no bar to the court considering the matter of its own motion (*R. v Dairy Produce Quota Tribunal Ex p. Wynn Jones* (1987) 283 E.G. 463).
- The time-limit cannot be extended by agreement between the parties (CPR r.54.5(2) above, p.928).
- Even where an application for leave is brought promptly, a delay before the hearing of the application for leave may give rise to an argument that the discretion to refuse relief under s.31(6) should be exercised (*R. v South Hertfordshire DC Ex p. Felton* [1991] J.P.L. 633, where the argument was rejected on the facts: the hearing of an application for leave to challenge a grant of planning permission was adjourned by agreement, while an alternative site was considered; there was no risk to good administration).
- On the language of s.31(6) there is no requirement for a causal connection between prejudice and undue delay; what is required is a connection between prejudice and the grant of the relief sought: *R. v Secretary of State for Health Ex p. Furneaux* [1994] 2 All E.R. 652, C.A. Here, an application by doctors for judicial review of the Secretary of State's decision to refuse them permission to provide pharmaceutical services was brought after six months. Relief was refused, as to grant it would prejudice a person who had bought a rival pharmacy in reliance on the Secretary of State's decision. The fact that no *additional* prejudice was caused by the delay could be relevant to the exercise of discretion, but on the facts here was an "insignificant point" (*per* Mann L.J. at 658).
- The considerations in s.31(6) may in appropriate circumstances justify the award of a declaration rather than a quashing order. See *R. (on the application of Gavin) v Haringey LBC* [2003] EWHC 2591, where there has been serious procedural errors concerning failure to comply with requirements for publicity and to consider whether an environmental statement was required in respect of an application for planning permission. The claimant, who lived opposite the site, through no fault of his own, only became aware of the grant at a much later date and lodged a claim for judicial review 32 months after the grant. Richards J. refused to quash the permission as this would cause very substantial hardship to the owner, but granted a declaration that there had been non-compliance.

3. The validity of the requirement for promptness under RSC, Ord.53, r.4(1) was upheld by the in *Lam v UK* (App.No.41671/98), noted by Stanley Burnton J. in *R. (on the application of Elliott) v Electoral Commission* [2003] EWHC 395.

4. Establishing the date from which time runs for the purposes of r.54(5) can given rise to much difficulty. In *R. (on the application of Burkett) v Hammersmith and Fulham LBC (No.1)* [2002] UKHL 23; [2002] 1 W.L.R. 1593, the House of Lords held that the time for challenging a grant of planning permission ran from the date of the grant and not the (earlier) date of a resolution conditionally authorising the grant. In *R. (on the application of Elliott) v Electoral Commission* (above), it was held that the

time for challenging an electoral change order ran from the date of the order and not the (earlier) date of a decision by the Commission to accept the recommendation of the Boundary Committee for England on which the order was based. Undue delay and prejudice were nevertheless found.

These cases illustrate the difficulty that frequently arises where decision-making is (quite properly) a staged process. They do not mean that judicial review proceedings cannot be commenced at an earlier stage, seeking to prevent an authority acting unlawfully in the future (see Lord Steyn in *Burkett* at paras [38]–[39]). However, the indication by a decision-maker that he or she is provisionally minded to make a decision adverse to the citizen does not start time running (Lord Steyn at para. [43]). (See discussions of the pre-*Burkett* case law by C.F. Forsyth, [1998], J.R. 8; Jones and Phillpot, [2000] J.P.L. 564; and Roots and Walton, [2001] J.P.L. 136).

In some situations the relevant date is specified in PD 54, para.4.1, above, p.933.

5. The case law on delay is considered by A. Lindsay, "Delay in Judicial Review Cases: A Conundrum Solved?" [1995] P.L. 417; and R. Leiper, [1996] J.R. 201.

(ii) Effect of Alternative Remedies

The *jurisdiction* of the court to entertain judicial review proceedings can only be excluded by the express words (see above, p.904). However, it is well established that the court will not entertain a claim for judicial review where there is some equally convenient and beneficial remedy, such as an appeal to a specialised tribunal, or to the High Court by case stated, or to a more appropriate Division of the High Court. For example, in *R. v Hillingdon LBC Ex p. Royco Homes Ltd* [1974] 1 Q.B. 720, Lord Widgery C.J. held that a planning condition that was invalid in law on its face could be challenged directly by an application for certiorari, notwithstanding the existence of the statutory appeal structure; in such circumstances it might well be "more efficient, cheaper and quicker to proceed by certiorari". In *R. v Paddington Valuation Officer Ex p. Peachey Property Ltd* [1966] 1 Q.B. 380, Lord Denning M.R. stated (at 400) that where it was alleged that a whole valuation list was invalid, the statutory procedure for proposing alterations in a valuation list would be "nowhere near so convenient, beneficial and effectual as certiorari or mandamus". In *R. v Huntingdon DC Ex p. Cowan* [1984] 1 All E.R. 58, Glidewell J. stated that the question was which remedy was "the most effective and convenient in all the circumstances" (at 63). In *Ex p. Waldron* [1986] Q.B. 824 Glidewell L.J. said (at 852):

> "Whether the alternative statutory remedy will resolve the question at issue fully and directly, whether the statutory procedure would be quicker or slower, than procedure by way of judicial review, whether the matter depends on some particular or technical knowledge which is more readily available to the alternative appellate body, these are amongst the matters which a court should take into account when deciding whether to grant relief by way of judicial review when an alternative remedy is available".

More recently, it has been emphasised that where there is a statutory remedy, the mere fact that an application for judicial review might be more convenient and effective may not be sufficient for the court to intervene by way of judicial review: judicial review in such circumstances will only be granted in exceptional cases. In *R. v Chief Constable of the Merseyside Police Ex p. Calveley* [1986] Q.B. 424, complaints were made in 1981 against five police officers in respect of an incident in which the officers had arrested the complainants. An investigating officer was appointed, but the officers were not notified of the complaints until November 1983; the Police (Discipline) Regulations 1977 (SI 1977/580), reg.7, required this to be done "as soon as is practicable". In September 1984, following a disciplinary hearing, the chief constable found the offences proved, required three officers to resign and dismissed the others. The officers gave notice of appeal to an appeal tribunal constituted under the Police (Appeal) Rules 1977 (SI 1977/759), but also sought certiorari to quash the chief constable's decisions, in particular on the ground that the non-compliance with reg. 7 had prejudiced the officers. The Court of Appeal granted certiorari, holding that the officers were not required to exhaust the appeal procedures first. Sir John Donaldson M.R. (with whom Glidewell L.J. agreed) stated that the court would only "very rarely" make judicial review available where there was an alternative remedy by way of appeal. Moreover, the appeal tribunal did possess specialist expertise, which the chief constable had argued rendered it better than a court to assess the prejudice. Nevertheless, here there had been "so serious a departure from the police disciplinary procedure" that judicial review should be granted.

In *R. v Secretary of State for the Home Department Ex p. Swati* [1986] 1 W.L.R. 477, the Master of the Rolls stated that the *Calveley* case decided that "the jurisdiction would not be exercised where there was an alternative remedy by way of appeal, save in exceptional circumstances" (at 485). Note that in this formulation there is no requirement that the alternative remedy be "equally convenient and beneficial". In *Calveley*, May L.J. expressly denied (at 436–437) that the judgment in the *Royco Homes* and *Peachey Properties* cases supported the view that judicial review would be granted merely because it might be more effective and convenient to do so. In *Ex p. Swati* itself, a person refused leave to enter the United Kingdom was refused leave to apply for judicial review, and left to his statutory right of appeal. From the applicant's point of view the latter was certainly less "convenient" as it could only be exercised from outside the United Kingdom, but that consideration did not sway the court, Parker L.J. stating that this did not, even arguably, constitute an "exceptional circumstance". Sir John Donaldson M.R. stated that:

> ". . . where Parliament provides an appeal procedure, judicial review will have no place unless the applicant can distinguish his case from the type of case for which the appeal procedure was provided" (at 485).

These, restrictive dicta are criticised by Wade and Forsyth (*Administrative Law* (9th ed.), pp.703–709) who argue that "if an applicant can show illegality, it is wrong in principle to require him to exercise a right of appeal. Illegal action should be stopped in its tracks as soon as it is shown" (p.708). Factors such as convenience and speed are in principle irrelevant. However, they also note that "In reality the courts are better than their word. When genuine grounds for judicial review are alleged, it is the refusal rather than the grant of review which is the exceptional course" (pp.708–709).

The dicta in *Ex p. Calveley* have been endorsed by the Court of Appeal, notwithstanding Wade's reservations, in *R. v Birmingham City Council Ex p. Ferrero* [1993] 1 All E.R. 530. More reassuringly, in *R. v Devon CC Ex p. Baker* [1995] 1 All E.R. 73, Simon Brown L.J. (at 92) reverted to the formula that which of two available avenues of redress is to be preferred "will depend ultimately upon which is the more convenient, expeditious and effective". On the other hand, Dillon L.J. (at 87) found *Calveley* and *Swati* "particularly helpful". They were agreed that judicial review was more appropriate than a ministerial default power to resolve an issue of law. Farquharson L.J. agreed with both judgments. Also important is Lord Woolf C.J.'s statement in *R. (on the application of Cowl) v Plymouth CC* [2001] EWCA Civ 1935; [2002] 1 W.L.R. 803 at para. [14], that:

> "the parties do not today, under the CPR, have a right to have a resolution of their respective contentions by judicial review in the absence of an alternative procedure which would cover exactly the same ground as judicial review. The courts should not permit, except for good reason, proceedings for judicial review to proceed if a significant part of the issues between the parties would be resolved outside the litigation process. The disadvantages of doing so are limited. If subsequently it becomes apparent that there is a legal issue to be resolved, that can thereafter be

examined by the courts which may be considerably assisted by the findings made by the complaints panel".

This statement was, however, directed to the question whether judicial review proceedings should be stayed, rather than excluded altogether.

For further examples of the many cases where judicial review has been refused on this ground, see *R. v Westminster City Council Ex p. Hilditch* [1991] C.O.D. 434 (complaint already under investigation by the auditor under the Local Government Finance Act 1982); *R. v Blackpool BC Ex p. Red Cab Taxis Ltd* [1994] R.T.R. 402 (unreasonable licence condition not quashed on judicial review as rectification was possible by statutory appeal to magistrates' court); *R. v Royal Borough of Kingston upon Thames Ex p. X* [1993] C.O.D. 470 (complaints procedure under Pt III of the Children Act 1989 more convenient and effective than judicial review); *R. v Secretary of State for the Home Department Ex p. Capti-Mehmet* [1997] C.O.D. 61.

The position is even clearer where Parliament enacts a statutory appeal or review mechanism with the clear intention of replacing judicial review. Even though the statutory words are not clear enough to exclude the court's judicial review *jurisdiction*, it may nevertheless hold as a matter of discretion that judicial review is only available in exceptional circumstances, and that grounds that have been or could be raised through the statutory mechanism can never constitute exceptional circumstances (*R. (on the application of G) v Immigration Appeal Tribunal; R. (on the application of M) v Immigration Appeal Tribunal* [2004] EWHC 588, in respect of statutory review under s.101 of the Nationality, Immigration and Asylum Act 2002 (see further above, pp.789–791)).

Where a party complains of procedural irregularity or bias on the part of a magistrates' court in a criminal case, an application for judicial review may be brought; there is no requirement that an appeal is first taken to the Crown Court: *R. v Hereford Magistrates' Court Ex p. Rowlands* [1998] Q B. 110. Parliament was to be taken to have intended that a defendant is entitled to both a fair trial and a fair retrial on appeal to the Crown Court (*Calvin v Carr*, above, p.740, distinguished).

See generally N. Collar, (1991) 10 C.J.Q. 138; S. Juss, [1986] C.L.J. 372 (on *Swati*); and C. Lewis, [1992] C.L.J. 138 and *Lewis*, pp.408–428. Compare the cases where the courts have held, exceptionally, that the court's supervisory jurisdiction is excluded by the existence of an alternative remedy (below, p.1032); exclusion is normally regarded as a matter of discretion, not jurisdiction: *R. v Deputy Governor of Parkhurst Prison Ex p. Leech* [1988] A.C. 533 at 562 (Lord Bridge).

(iii) Other Grounds

Even where an applicant for judicial review establishes one of the grounds for review, the court retains a discretion whether to grant a remedy. Relevant factors that have already been mentioned include the nature of the applicant's standing, any delay and the existence of alternative remedies. See *R. v Secretary of State for Social Services Ex p. Association of Metropolitan Authorities* [1986] 1 W.L.R. 1, above, p.650.

In *R. v Monopolies and Mergers Commission Ex p. Argyll Group Plc* [1986] 1 W.L.R. 763, Sir John Donaldson M.R. stated (at 774) that in exercising this discretion the court should approach its duties with a proper awareness of the needs of public administration. Among the factors relevant there were that good public administration is concerned with substance rather than form, and with the speed of decision, particularly in the financial field; it requires a proper consideration of the public interest and of the legitimate interest of individual citizens; and requires decisiveness and finality unless there are compelling reasons to the contrary. The court declined to quash a decision of the chairman of the commission to lay aside a reference of a take-over bid to the commission, which decision should have been made by a group of members and not by the chairman alone (see also Dillon L.J. at 778–779 and Neill L.J. at 782–783). In *R. v Secretary of State for Education and Science Ex p. Lewisham LBC* [1990]

C.O.D. 31, the Divisional Court declined to quash a decision of the Secretary of State to give leave to school governors to serve a notice discontinuing two schools as voluntary schools under Pt II of the Education Act 1944, prior to their becoming City Technology Colleges; the Secretary of State's consultation process had been flawed, but the applications were not made with the promptness that the situation demanded, it was virtually certain that the Secretary of State would, after reconsideration, reach the same decision, and granting relief would merely lead to a further year's uncertainty which would be likely to cause substantial hardship to all concerned. (The last two cases were applied in *R. v Warwickshire CC Ex p. Boyden* [1991] C.O.D. 31.) In *Dorot Properties Ltd v Brent LBC* [1990] C.O.D. 378, the Court of Appeal declined to quash a flawed decision to refuse overpaid rates: the ratepayer had wrongfully delayed in paying rates it was obliged to pay, and the sum in question represented no more than fair compensation for the council's loss of interest.

In older cases, certiorari was refused where the applicant had behaved unreasonably. In *Ex p. Fry* [1954] 1 W.L.R. 730, a fireman disobeyed an order (to clean a superior officer's uniform) which he claimed was unlawful. He subsequently sought certiorari to quash the decision to caution him for a disciplinary offence, alleging breach of natural justice. Singleton L.J. thought his disobedience "extraordinarily foolish conduct". He should have obeyed the order and made a complaint later through the procedures laid down by regulations.

See generally, Sir Thomas Bingham, "Should Public Law Remedies be Discretionary?" [1991] P.L. 64; *Lewis*, Ch.11.

(H) Particular Remedies

(i) Quashing and prohibiting orders

(a) *Scope*

A quashing order (formerly an order of certiorari) quashes a decision that had already been made. A prohibiting order (formerly an order of prohibition) restrains a body from acting unlawfully in the future or from completing an act already begun. They were formerly limited to cases where a public authority was under a duty to act judicially (see *Ridge v Baldwin* [1964] A.C. 40 (above, p.658)). They now extend generally to administrative acts and are not limited to cases where there is a duty to act judicially (*R. v Hillingdon LBC Ex p. Royco Homes Ltd* [1974] 1 Q.B. 720 (certiorari granted to quash a grant of planning permission); *O'Reilly v Mackman* [1983] 2 A.C. 237 at 279, *per* Lord Diplock (above, p.980)). Certiorari has been granted, for example, to quash a decision to refuse a mandatory grant to a student (*R. v Barnet LBC Ex p. Nilish Shah* [1983] 2 A.C. 309) and a decision to abolish corporal punishment in schools (*R. v Manchester City Council Ex p. Fulford* (1982) 81 L.G.R. 292). Certiorari has also been granted to quash subordinate legislation, although legislative acts have traditionally been challenged by proceedings for a declaration. See *R. v Secretary of State for Social Security Ex p. Association of Metropolitan Authorities* [1986] 1 W.L.R. 1 (certiorari assumed to be available to quash statutory instrument for lack of consultation but refused in the exercise of discretion); *R. v Secretary of State for Health Ex p. U.S. Tobacco International* [1992] 1 Q.B. 353 (certiorari granted to quash regulations for lack of consultation).

(b) *Grounds*

Certiorari may be granted (i) if a decision is unlawful (as where it is *ultra vires* or contrary to natural justice); (ii) if there is an error of law in the face of the record (above, pp.442–443 (Lord Morris in *Anisminic*)); this doctrine is now obsolete); (iii) if a decision has been procured by assertions shown clearly to be fraudulent or deliberately misleading or (iv) where there is unfairness arising from conduct that can fairly be categorised an analogous to fraud. Ground (iii) is illustrated by *R. v Ashford JJ.* [1956] 1 Q.B. 167; *R. v Wolverhampton Crown Court Ex p. Crofts* [1983] 1 W.L.R. 204 (order quashing conviction procured by perjured evidence); *cf. R. v Knightsbridge Crown Court Ex p. Goonatilleke* [1986] Q.B. 1 (conviction based on evidence of a witness who concealed his previous bad character quashed for breach of natural justice rather than fraud; it was not *certain* that the magistrate would have acquitted but for the fraud or perjury). Ground (iv) is illustrated by *R. v Secretary of State for the Home Department Ex p. Al Mehdawi* [1990] 1 A.C. 876; *R. v Bolton JJ. Ex p. Scally* [1991] 1 Q.B. 537; *R. v Burton upon Trent Magistrates Court Ex p. Woolley* (1995) 159 J.P. 165.

In *R. v West Sussex Quarter Sessions Ex p. Albert and Maud Johnson Trust Ltd* [1973] Q.B. 188, the Court of Appeal (Lord Denning M.R. dissenting) held that certiorari would not lie to quash a decision merely on the ground that fresh evidence, relevant to the issue in the case, had been discovered after the trial. Lord Denning suggested that as evidence was admissible by affidavit to prove fraud or collusion, then it should also be admissible to prove mistake, but the majority (Orr and Lawton L.JJ.) held that the limits of certiorari were well established, and did not extend beyond defects or irregularities at the trial.

A prohibiting order prevents action or continuing action that is unlawful or contrary to natural justice: see, *e.g. Dimes v Grand Junction Canal Co* (above, p.751); *R. v Kent Police Authority Ex p. Godden* (above, p.773).

Disobedience to these orders may lead to proceedings for contempt of court (*cf.* below, p.1024).

(ii) Mandatory orders [13]

(a) *Scope*

Mandatory orders (formerly orders of *mandamus*) lie to compel the performance of a public duty. There has never been any limitation of *mandamus* to judicial or quasi-judicial acts. Alternative methods of enforcing public or statutory duties include an action for damages (below, Ch.15); for a mandatory injunction (below, p.1025); or for a declaration (below, p.1028); criminal prosecution or a statutory default power (above, pp.57–62, 145–148). A mandatory order cannot be granted against the Crown, or a minister of the Crown when acting purely as a servant of the Crown for the purpose of performing a duty owed by the Crown (*R. v Powell* (1841) 1 Q.B. 35), but can be granted against a minister where a duty is imposed on the minister directly (*R. v Commissioners of Customs and Excise Ex p. Cook* [1970] 1 W.L.R. 450). See *Lewis*, pp.234–235.

(b) *Statutory duties*

A statutory duty must be couched in fairly precise terms if it is to be enforceable. See above, pp.406–420. The most straightforward situation is where statute requires a specific act to be done, and it is not done. This may be because the person entrusted with the duty believes that the statute gives him a discretion whether or not to act, and so the main issue before the court is the proper interpretation of the statute.

Where the statute gives a discretion rather than imposes a duty, a mandatory order may still be available to compel the exercise of discretion according to law, for example, where a power is used for an improper purpose (*Padfield v Minister of Agriculture*, above, p.528); where irrelevant considerations are taken into account (see

---

[13] See A.J. Harding, *Public Duties and Public Law* (1989); *Lewis*, pp.228–238.

R. v P.L.A. Ex p. Kynoch Ltd, above, p.484, where *mandamus* was refused on the facts); where a discretion is fettered by reliance on a fixed rule of policy (*R. v Torquay JJ. Ex p. Brockman* [1951] 2 K.B. 784); or where there is an error of law in construing the scope of a discretion (*R. v Vestry of St Pancras*, above, p.523). Indeed, a mandatory order is available wherever an inferior tribunal wrongfully declines to exercise a discretion or jurisdiction that in law it possesses. It would be unusual (although possible) for Parliament to entrust powers to a named body and at the same time to allow them to decline to *consider* whether those powers should be exercised. The courts emphasise in these circumstances that they do not seek to control the merits of an exercise of discretion or jurisdiction, but the circumstances may be such that the inferior tribunal is left with little alternative but to exercise the discretion, or their jurisdiction to determine a dispute, in a particular way (See *R. v Justices of Kingston Ex p. Davey* (1902) 86 L.T. 589; and note the form of the order in *Padfield's* case, above, p.533).

The following cases illustrate situations where a mandatory order lies. *R. v Braintree DC Ex p. Willingham* (1982) 81 L.G.R. 70 concerned s.71 of the Shops Act 1950, which provides that it is the duty of every local authority to enforce the Act. The council decided not to prosecute the operators of a Sunday Market for offences under the Act. The Divisional Court found that they had taken into account the expense of prosecuting and the fact that the market was popular in the locality. The court held that these were irrelevant considerations, and mandamus should go, requiring the council to perform its duty under s.71. The council had no general discretion not to enforce the Act; the only scope for discretion was whether any particular proceedings were necessary to secure observance, and, as an aspect of that, the council could take account of the likelihood of failure. Then, in *R. v Camden LBC Ex p. Gillan* (1988) 21 H.L.R. 114, the council was held to be in breach of its statutory duty to hear and adjudicate upon applications regarding homelessness under Pt III of the Housing Act 1985 where the homeless persons unit was only open between 9.30am and 12.30pm on weekdays. Furthermore, applications had to be made by telephone and not face-to-face. A shortage of money arising from rate capping was not an adequate excuse. Orders of *mandamus* and declarations were granted.

(c) *Effect of disobedience*

If any person or body disobeys a mandatory order, whether derived from the prerogative writ or statute, proceedings for contempt of court may be taken against that person or body. Local councils in Northern Ireland which disobeyed orders of *mandamus* requiring the holding of meetings for the proper dispatch of business were fined: *Cook's Application, Re* [1986] 3 N.I.J.B. 64 (Belfast City Council, £25,000); *Morrow's Application, Re* [1987] 3 N.I.J.B. 16 (Castlereagh BC, £10,000); *Cook's Application, Re* [1987] 4 N.I.J.B. 42 (Belfast City Council, £25,000 fine reimposed). In addition, contempt proceedings may be taken against the individual councillors concerned: *R. v Worcester Corp.* (1903) 68 J.P. 130; (1905) 69 J.P. 269; *R. v Poplar BC (No.2)* [1922] 1 K.B. 95. In the latter case most of the Poplar councillors were imprisoned for a period for contempt: B. Keith-Lucas, "Poplarism" [1962] P.L. 52 at pp.60–62. The same principle applies where a local authority acts in breach of an undertaking given to the court (see *R. (on the application of Bempoa) v Southwark LBC* [2002] EWHC Admin 153, where the judge was highly critical of the conduct of the local authority but imposed no sanction.

(iii) Injunction

"An injunction is an order of a court addressed to a party requiring that party to do or to refrain from doing a particular act" (*de Smith, Woolf and Jowell*, p.705). A prohibitory injunction may be appropriate to restrain the performance of unlawful acts. A mandatory injunction may (rarely) be available to compel performance of a public duty. See generally, *Lewis*, Ch.8. Proceedings for an injunction may include an application for interlocutory relief to maintain the *status quo* pending trial of the main action. (See above, pp.972–974.) An injunction may be granted in one of several different forms, and against private individuals, individuals exercising public functions and both public and private bodies. It may be expressed to last for a fixed period, or for ever, or indefinitely until some condition is fulfilled. It may be suspended to give reasonable time for compliance.

(a) *Examples of the use of injunctions in administrative law*

An example of a case where a mandatory injunction was granted is *Att-Gen. v Bastow* [1957] 1 Q.B. 514 where the Attorney-General at the relation of a local planning authority obtained an order requiring (*inter alia*) the removal of caravans placed on land in breach of planning control. An example of a refusal of an injunction in the exercise of the court's discretion on grounds peculiar to the mandatory form is *Dowty Boulton Paul Ltd v Wolverhampton Corp. (No.1)*, above, p.506; and see *Morris v Redland Bricks* [1970] A.C. 652.

Prohibitory injunctions may lie as follows:

- To restrain breaches of statutory duty (e.g. *Att-Gen Ex rel. McWhirter v I.B.A.* (The "Warhol" case) [1973] 1 Q.B. 629.
- To restrain *ultra vires* acts (e.g. *Att-Gen v Fulham Corp.*, above, p.391; especially where the ultra vires act involves unlawful payments from public funds (*e.g. Att-Gen v De Winton* [1906] 2 Ch.106. See also *Municipal Council of Sydney v Campbell*, above, p.526.
- To restrain repeated breaches of the criminal law, such as breaches of planning control and disobedience to enforcement notices (see *Att.-Gen. v Bastow*, above). Compare *Att.-Gen. v Harris* [1961] 1 Q.B. 74, where Mr and Mrs Harris were restrained by injunction from selling flowers outside Southern Cemetery, Manchester, contrary to the Manchester Police Regulation Act 1844. Mr Harris had been convicted and fined for offences against the Act on 142 occasions, his wife on 95. Further proceedings were taken against them, subsequently, for contempt of court: see *The Times*, September 21, 1960; February 15 and 28, 1961; *cf. Gouriet v Union of Post Office Workers* [1978] A.C. 435, where the House of Lords refused to grant G a declaration that it would be unlawful for the union to seek to interrupt mail between this country and South Africa, on the ground that G lacked *locus standi*. See D. Feldman, "Injunctions and the Criminal Law" (1979) 42 M.L.R. 369. The courts will not grant a declaration that particular conduct does not constitute a criminal offence after a prosecution has been started in respect of that conduct (*Imperial Tobacco Ltd v Att.-Gen.* [1981] A.C. 718) and is generally reluctant to do so as such disputes are best decided in criminal courts (*R. v DPP Ex p. Camelot* (1997) 10 Admin L.R. 93). See further *Zamir and Woolf*, pp.201–216; *Lewis*, pp.264–269 .
- To restrain a public nuisance (*e.g. Pride of Derby Angling Association v British Celanese* [1953] Ch. 149).

(b) Locus standi *in relation to injunctions*

Apart from on a claim for judicial review (see above, pp.994–1010), proceedings for an injunction may be brought:

- by the Attorney-General, on behalf of the Crown as *parens patriae* for "the protection of public rights or public interests as opposed to matters of a private character" (*Thio*, p.134). He may for example seek to restrain a public although not a private nuisance (*Att.-Gen. v P.Y.A. Quarries* [1957] 2 Q.B.

169); to restrain public bodies from exceeding their powers; and to restrain repeated breaches of the criminal law;

- by a private individual "in two cases: first, where the interference with the public right is such that some private right of his is at the same time interfered with . . .; and, secondly, where no private right is interfered with, but the plaintiff, in respect of his public right, suffers special damage peculiar to himself from the interference with the public right" (*per* Buckley J. in *Boyce v Paddington BC* [1903] 1 Ch. 109 at 114). These principles were first established in private actions for public nuisance, but are of wider application, and it is normally a pre-condition for *locus standi* for an injunction for a plaintiff to be in a position to sue for damages for a tort or other wrong. If the execution of an *ultra vires* act would be an actionable tort, then the person affected clearly has *locus standi* to obtain an injunction (*e.g. Westminster Corp. v L.N.W. Ry*, above, p.394). These principles were reaffirmed by the House of Lords in *Gouriet v Union of Post Office Workers* [1978] A.C. 435 (see above, pp.999–1000 and 1025).
- by the Attorney-General in a relator action. See below, p.1027 and *Att.-Gen. v I.B.A.* [1973] Q.B. 629.
- by a public body in support of the discharge of its public responsibilities (see *Broadmoor Special Hospital Authority v R* [2000] Q.B. 775; *Worcestershire CC v Tongue* [2004] EWCA Civ 140; [2004] 2 W.L.R. 1193). This has been characterised as an "innovative" development: see Lord Phillips of Worth Matravers in *Ashworth Hospital Authority v MGN Ltd* [2001] 1 W.L.R. 515 at para. [68].
- by a local authority. Section 222(1) of the Local Government Act 1972 provides that:

"Where a local authority consider it expedient for the promotion or protection of the interests of the inhabitants of their area—
  (a) they may prosecute or defend or appear in any legal proceedings and, in the case of civil proceedings, may institute them in their own name, and
  (b) they may, in their own name, make representations in the interests of the inhabitants at any public inquiry held by or on behalf of any Minister or public body under any enactment".

This has altered the previous rule that local authorities were subject to the same *locus standi* requirements as private individuals (*Thio*, pp.206–215). Now authorities are able to commence *any* civil proceedings in their own name—not just actions for an injunction. Local authorities have frequently relied on s.222 to seek injunctions to restrain breaches of the tree preservation orders (*e.g. Kent CC v Batchelor (No.2)* [1979] 1 W.L.R. 213); enforcement and stop notices (*e.g. Westminster City Council v Jones* (1981) 80 L.G.R. 241; *Runnymede BC v Ball* [1986] 1 W.L.R. 353; see S. Tromans, [1986] C.L.J. 374); unlicensed street trading (*Westminster City Council v Freeman* (1985) 135 N.L.J. 1232); the operation of an unlicensed sex shop (*Portsmouth City Council v Richards* [1989] 1 C.M.L.R. 673); breaches of a noise control notice (*City of London Corp. v Bovis Construction Ltd* (1988) 86 L.G.R. 660); infringement of consumer protection legislation (*Barking and Dagenham LBC v Jones*, unreported, July 30, 1999; or interference with the highway (*Nottingham City Council v Zain* [2001] EWCA Civ 1248; [2002] 1 W.L.R. 607 (to restrain activities of a drug dealer operating on one of their housing estates). Most difficulties arise in respect of injunctions to restrain breaches of the Sunday trading law, particularly on the question of the compatibility of that law with European Community law (see *Stoke-on-Trent City Council v B & Q (Retail) Ltd* [1984] A.C. 754; *Wychavon DC v Midland Enterprises (Special Events) Ltd* (1987) 86 L.G.R. 83; Case 145/88 *Torfaen BC v B & Q Plc* [1989] ECR 3851; [1990] 1 CMLR 337; [1990] 2 Q.B. 19; *W.H. Smith Do-It-All Ltd v Peterborough City Council* [1991] 1 Q.B. 304; *Stoke-on-Trent City Council v B & Q Plc* [1991] Ch. 48). See P. Diamond, "Dishonourable Defences: The Use of Injunctions and the E.E.C. Treaty—Case Study of the Shops Act 1950" (1991)

54 M.L.R. 72. Restrictions on Sunday trading were substantially lifted by the Sunday Trading Act 1994.

The local authority must consider whether the institution of civil proceedings is in the interests of the inhabitants of their area (*Stoke-on-Trent City Council v B & Q (Retail) Ltd*, above. It is for the local authority to make the judgment as to expediency, not the court (*Mole Valley DC v Smith* (1992) 90 L.G.R. 553; *Barking and Dagenham LBC v Jones* (above)). After some uncertainty, the House of Lords has held that a local authority is not necessarily to be required to give an undertaking in damages (*Kirklees MBC v Wickes Building Supplies Ltd* [1993] A.C. 227.

Apart from s.222, local authorities may be given specific powers to seek injunctions. Recent examples include the Environmental Protection Act 1990, s.81(5) (statutory nuisances); the Town and Country Planning Act 1990, s.187B (inserted by the Planning and Compensation Act 1991, s.3) (breaches of planning control): see M. Phillips, [1992] J.P.L. 407.

The enactment of s.222 of the Local Government Act 1972 and the extension of specific powers to seek injunctions means that local authorities are unlikely to have to use relator proceedings. See generally on s.222, B. Hough, "Local Authorities as Guardians of the Public Interest" [1992] P.L. 130; *Cross*, pp.10–87—10–91.

(c) *Relator actions*

Notes

1. Relator actions are proceedings for a declaration or injunction brought by the Attorney-General at the relation of (*i.e.* on the information of) a private individual. In theory, the Attorney has entire control over the proceedings; in practice, once he has given his consent to the proceedings, it is the relator who conducts them and is liable for costs. Where consent is given, no point can be taken as to the relator's standing or motives. The Attorney's approach is to grant consent if a *prima facie* case is shown of an infringement of a public right and there is no countervailing public interest (*de Smith, Woolf and Jowell*, p.153).

2. The House of Lords in *Gouriet v Union of Post Office Workers* [1978] A.C. 435 confirmed that the refusal of the Attorney-General to grant his consent to relator proceedings was not subject to review by the courts; and rejected the dictum by Lord Denning M.R. in *Att-Gen v I.B.A.* [1973] Q.B. 629 at 649 that an individual member of the public can apply for an injunction "if the Attorney-General refuses leave in a proper case, or improperly or unreasonably delays in giving leave, or his machinery works too slowly". On *Gouriet*, see H.W.R. Wade, (1978) 94 L.Q.R. 4; D.G.T. Williams, [1977] C.L.J. 201 and [1977] Crim. L.R. 703; D. Lunny, (1978) 12 U.B.C. Law Rev. 320; D. Feldman, (1979) 42 M.L.R. 369. The same principle applies in respect of the Attorney-General's refusal to prosecute for an offence under the Shops Act 1950 (*R. v Att-Gen Ex p. Edey*, unreported, February 26, 1992, CA); to authorise an application under the Coroners Act 1988, s.13 for the High Court to order an inquest (*R. v Att-Gen Ex p. Ferrante*, unreported, July 1, 1994); or to bring proceedings for contempt of court (*R. v Solicitor-General Ex p. Taylor*, *The Times*, August 14, 1995, DC; see D.J. Feldman and C.J. Miller, (1997) 113 L.Q.R. 36, who note that "it is time to ask whether [the Law Officers'] privileged position can be justified on principled or practical grounds" (at p.40).

3. For an argument that the House of Lords decision in the *CCSU* case extending the scope of judicial review in respect of prerogative powers (above, p.690) should lead to a reconsideration of the Attorney-General's immunity to review, see B. Hough, "Judicial Review Where the Attorney General Refuses to Act: Time for a Change" (1988) 8 L.S. 189.

4. The continued value of the relator action as a mechanism for obtaining a remedy against a public authority is uncertain (see S. Nott, [1984] P.L. 22). The broader the approach to standing under Ord.53 (see above, pp.994–1010), the less the need to seek

the Attorney-General's consent to relator proceedings. One substantial limitation is that the Attorney in practice does not give consent where the proceedings are brought against a minister or a central government department (see *de Smith, Woolf and Jowell,* p.149, who note that if he considered a department was not observing the law, he would presumably advise accordingly and resign if his advice were ignored). Relator proceedings have become something of a rarity (*ibid.,* p.153).

For examples, see *Att-Gen Ex rel. Tilley v Wandsworth LBC* [1981] 1 W.L.R. 854; *Att-Gen Ex rel. Yorkshire Derwent Trust Ltd v Brotherton* [1992] 1 A.C. 270 (assertion of a public right of way). *cf. Att-Gen Ex rel. Scotland v Barratt Manchester Ltd* (1991) 63 P. & CR. 179 (remedy refused as no public right was involved). Relator proceedings presumably constitute an exception to the principle of *O'Reilly v Mackman* (above, pp.976–994). See A. Grubb, [1983] P.L. 190, 200.

5. Lord Woolf has argued the case for the establishment of an office of Director of Civil Proceedings. The DCP would take over from the Attorney-General responsibility for instituting or intervening in proceeding's in the public interest, having the advantage of being outside politics and holding office independently and irrespective of the government of the day. The Attorney-General would retain responsibility for advising, and instituting proceedings on behalf of, the Government. The DCP would also be able to authorise a member of the public to bring proceedings, his decision being subject to the supervision of the courts, and would have general responsibility for the development of the civil law and, in particular, public law. See "Public Law— Private Law: Why the Divide? A Personal View" [1986] P.L. 220 at pp.236–238; *Protection of the Public—A New Challenge* (1990), pp.103–113.

6. See generally on relator actions, *de Smith, Woolf and Jowell,* pp.150–154; *Wade and Forsyth,* pp.579–587; J.Ll.J. Edwards, *The Law Officers of the Crown* (1964), pp.186–195, and *The Attorney-General, Politics and the Public Interest* (1984), pp.129–153; The JUSTICE/All Souls Review of Administrative Law, *Administrative Justice: Some Necessary Reforms* (1988), pp.186–190, 203–204.

(d) *Grounds on which an injunction may be refused*

The injunction is an equitable remedy, and so, like the prerogative remedies, is discretionary. It may be refused in accordance with various recognised principles such as waiver, acquiescence, delay or unmeritorious conduct (see, *e.g. Bates v Lord Hailsham,* above, p.720; but *cf. Islington Vestry v Hornsey UDC,* above, p.513). Similarly, an injunction may be refused if it is unnecessary in view of the availability of an alternative remedy, an undertaking by the defendant, or the triviality of the injury to the plaintiff (*cf. Glynn v Keele University,* above, p.674).

A court cannot grant an injunction or an order for specific performance against the Crown (Crown Proceedings Act 1947, s.21(1)(a)); or against an officer of the Crown "if the effect of granting the injunction or making the order would be to give any relief against the Crown which could not have been obtained in proceedings against the Crown" (*ibid.* s.21(2)). (See above, p.974.)

(iv) Declaration[14]

(a) *General Principles*

CPR r.40.20 provides that the "court may make binding declarations whether or not any other remedy is claimed." Its predecessor, RSC, Ord.15, r.16 provided, possibly more narrowly, that "the court may make binding declarations of right".

In *Dyson v Att-Gen* [1911] 1 K.B. 410, it was established that "in a civil action brought by a competent plaintiff, the court could grant declaratory relief against the

---

[14] See *Zamir and Woolf;* G. Borrie, (1955) 18 M.L.R. 138; P. W. Young, *Declaratory Orders* (2nd ed., 1984); *Lewis,* Ch.7.

Crown as to the legality of actions which the Crown proposed to take" (*per* Lord Browne-Wilkinson in *R. v Secretary of State for Employment Ex p. Equal Opportunities Commission* [1995] 1 A.C. 1, 34).

The declaration is the most useful of the remedies in administrative law in situations where a coercive order, disobedience of which constitutes a contempt, is not required, or where no wrongful act has as yet been committed. In some situations, for example in an action against the Crown, it is the only possible remedy (see above, p.974). Where the defendant is a public authority, there is usually no question but that the law will be obeyed, once the precise legal position has been established authoritatively. Moreover, a declaratory order will be *res judicata* between the parties. For example, a planning condition declared to be *ultra vires* by a court cannot be the subject of enforcement proceedings. There are additional advantages in the considerable flexibility in the form that a declaration may take, and the wide variety of situations in which a declaration may be made. A basic feature is that it is a discretionary remedy.

It is now available on a claim for judicial review or in private law proceedings. In proceedings for a declaration, the court's jurisdiction may be *supervisory* or *original*. The former involves the review by the court of a decision by another person or body; the latter involves a decision by the court itself as to the "contested legal rights, subsisting or future, of the parties represented in the litigation before it" (see Lord Diplock in *Gouriet v Union of Post Office Workers* [1978] A.C. 435 at 501). The role of the court on a claim for judicial review is almost invariably supervisory (*de Smith, Woolf and Jowell*, p.738). The principle of *O'Reilly v Mackman* (above, p.976), taken together with the decision in *Gouriet*, generally prevents applicants whose private law rights are not at stake from seeking declarations under the supervisory jurisdiction in private law proceedings. There are, however, some cases where, perhaps anomalously, this appears to have been permitted (see below).

There is now express power to grant an interim declaration (see above, p.974).

(b) Locus standi *for a declaration*

Outside a claim for judicial review, the principles applicable to injunctions are generally applicable also to declarations (see pp.1025–1027). There have, however, been cases that are difficult to fit within the traditional *locus standi* principles where the courts have given guidance on difficult and contentious issues of law in proceedings for a declaration. In *Royal College of Nursing v Department of Health and Social Security* [1981] A.C. 800, the House of Lords (by 3:2) granted the College a declaration that advice in a DHSS circular that no offence was committed by nurses who terminated a pregnancy by medical induction if a doctor decided on the termination, initiated it, and remained responsible throughout for its overall conduct and control, did not involve the performance of unlawful acts by members of the College. Woolf J. at first instance noted that neither party desired to take any points as to the jurisdiction of the court to grant a declaration; stated that, nevertheless, questions of *locus standi* could not be overcome by consent of the parties; and concluded that he had jurisdiction, accepting the Solicitor General's argument that the case should be regarded as exceptional because of the College's special responsibilities in providing advice and insurance for its members, and the relationship between the department and the nurses, many of whom were employed by bodies acting under the department's supervision. It would, however, have been much better for proceedings to have been brought under Ord.53. This aspect of the case was not mentioned by the Court of Appeal or the House of Lords.

Then, in *Gillick v West Norfolk and Wisbech Area HA* [1986] A.C. 112, the House of Lords held (by 3:2) that a DHSS memorandum of guidance, which stated that in exceptional cases it was a matter for the doctor's clinical judgment to decide whether to prescribe contraception for a child under 16 without the knowledge and consent of the parents, did not contain advice that was an infringement of parents' rights or was unlawful. As in the *RCN* case, it was not suggested that Mrs Gillick was acting inappropriately in instituting proceedings for a declaration. The writ and statement of claim was issued three months before the decision in *O'Reilly v Mackman* (above, p.976) (see Lord Fraser at 163). Lord Scarman stated (at 178) that Mrs Gillick's action was "essentially to protect what she alleges to be her rights as a parent under private law". He did not see her claim "as falling under the embargo imposed by *O'Reilly's* case"; if he was wrong on that he would nevertheless think "that the private law content of her claim was so great as to make her case an exception to the general rule" (at 178). Both the "collateral issue" and "consent" exceptions recognised by Lord Diplock in *O'Reilly* (above, p.986) could be said to apply. Lord Fraser (at 163) agreed with Lord Scarman (at 192). Lord Bridge, in contrast, said (at 192) that Mrs Gillick "had no private right which she is in a position to assert" against the second respondent, the DHSS. Nevertheless, no objection had been or could now be raised on the "procedural technicality that the proceedings were commenced by writ rather than by application for judicial review". Lords Brandon and Templeman did not discuss the procedural question. Lord Bridge expressed concern on another point. He did not agree with Lords Scarman and Fraser that the issue of a memorandum with guidance that would result in unlawful acts would be challengeable as an *ultra vires* abuse of discretion on *Wednesbury* grounds. "Here there is no specific statutory background by reference to which the appropriate *Wednesbury* questions would be formulated" (at 192). Instead, it had to be recognised that the *RCN* case

> "does effect a significant extension of the court's power of judicial review. We must now say that if a government department, in a field of administration in which it exercises responsibility, promulgates in a public document, albeit non-statutory in form, advice which is erroneous in law, then the court, in proceedings in appropriate form commenced by an applicant or plaintiff who possesses the necessary *locus standi*, has jurisdiction to correct the error of law by an appropriate declaration. Such an extended jurisdiction is no doubt a salutary and indeed a necessary one in certain circumstances, as the *Royal College of Nursing* case [1981] A.C. 800 itself well illustrates. But the occasions of a departmental non-statutory publication raising, as in that case, a clearly defined issue of law, unclouded by political, social or moral overtones, will be rare. In cases where any proposition of law implicit in a departmental advisory document is interwoven with questions of social and ethical controversy, the court should, in my opinion, exercise its jurisdiction with the utmost restraint, confine itself to deciding whether the proposition of law is erroneous and avoid either expressing *ex cathedra* opinions in areas of social and ethical controversy in which it has no claim to speak with authority or proferring answers to hypothetical questions of law which do not strictly arise for decision" (at 193–194).

Lord Templeman (at 206) echoed Lord Bridge's warning "against the involvement of the courts in areas of social and ethical controversy or hypothetical questions. Nevertheless the questions raised by this appeal must now be answered".

The willingness of the House of Lords to entertain the case is strongly criticised by C. Harlow (1986) 49 M.L.R. 768, who argues that Mrs Gillick lacked *locus standi* to be granted a private law declaration, and that *O'Reilly v Mackman* should have applied. See also H.W.R. Wade, (1986) 102 L.Q.R. 173; Sir Harry Woolf, *Protection of the Public—A New Challenge* (1990), pp.43–44.

Following these cases, the courts have been prepared to grant declarations as to the lawfulness of proposed medical treatment (see *Re F (Mental Patient: Sterilisation)* [1990] 2 A.C. 1, HL (sterilisation operation on mentally handicapped adult); *Airedale NHS Trust v Bland* [1993] A.C. 789 (artificial discontinuance of life-sustaining treatment and support from patient in a persistent vegetative state); and *St George's Healthcare NHS Trust v S* [1999] Fam. 26 (where the Court of Appeal set aside a declaration, granted on an ex parte application, dispensing with the consent to treatment of S, a pregnant woman with severe pre-eclampsia, and authorising all necessary procedures including a Caesarian section; the court was severely critical of the procedure adopted and set out the appropriate procedure).

As regards the court's *original* jurisdiction, by contrast, the Court of Appeal has confirmed Lord Diplock's statement in *Gouriet* (above) that it is confined to declarations as to the private law rights of the parties (see *Meadows Indemnity Co. v The Insurance Corp. of Ireland Plc and the International Commercial Bank Plc* [1989] 2 Lloyd's Rep. 298; discussed in *Zamir and Woolf*, pp.51–56, which notes that the House of Lords decision in *RCN* and *Gillick* were not cited in *Meadows*, and that in those cases the House was not referred to *Gouriet*). See also Knox J. in *Mid Kent Holdings Plc v General Utilities Plc* [1996] 3 All E.R. 132, holding that a private person had no right to seek a declaration that G was in breach of undertakings given to the Secretary of State under the Fair Trading Act 1973 following a report by the Monopolies and Mergers Commission. On analysis, the breach of statutory duty was not intended to give rise to a civil remedy, whether by damages, injunction or declaration.

Conversely, Lord Browne-Wilkinson in *R. v Secretary of State for Employment Ex p. Equal Opportunities Commission* [1995] 1 A.C. 1 at 34–37, emphasised that it was still possible for a "declaration as to public rights" to be granted on an application for judicial review. Order 53, r.1(2) and s.31 of the Supreme Court Act 1981 (above, pp.924–925) did not limit the grant of declarations to cases where one of the prerogative orders was available. A dictum to the contrary by Lord Scarman in *R. v Inland Revenue Commissioners Ex p. National Federation of Self-Employed and Small Businesses Ltd* [1982] A.C. 617 at 648, was based on the argument that "to do otherwise would be to condemn [r.1(2)] as *ultra vires*" and could not survive the enactment of s.31. Lords Jauncey and Lowry agreed with Lord Browne-Wilkinson's remarks on these points. (See above, p.1007). Thus, the way was open for the House of Lords to grant declarations that the provisions of the Employment Protection (Consolidation) Act 1978 which prescribed less favourable conditions with respect to qualification for redundancy pay and compensation for unfair dismissal for part-time as compared with full-time workers were "incompatible with" European Community law (respectively, Art.119 EEC and the Equal Pay Directive (Dir.75/117) and the Equal Treatment Directive (Dir.76/207)). Lord Keith of Kinkel noted (at 27) that at no stage in the *Factortame* litigation (above, p.974) was it suggested "that judicial review was not available for the purpose of obtaining an adjudication upon the validity of the legislation in so far as it affected the applicants". Whether this is in truth the exercise of the original or the supervisory jurisdiction is, however, uncertain. Perhaps the proper analysis is that this is *sui generis*, a hybrid situation where the court is in reality exercising a supervisory jurisdiction (reviewing the validity of an Act of Parliament in a way similar to that by which it might review the validity of a byelaw) while purporting, out of deference to Parliamentary sensibilities, merely to exercise an original jurisdiction to declare rights.

(c) *Some grounds on which a declaration may be refused*

A declaration may be refused because the matter is non-justiciable, for example, because it is a question of morality rather than law (see *Cox v Green* [1966] 1 Ch. 216: medical ethics); or because it is a question of the Crown's treaty-making power which the courts decline to consider for policy reasons (see *Blackburn v Att-Gen* [1971] 1 W.L.R. 1037 and *McWhirter v Att-Gen* [1972] CMLR 882); or because there is an attempt to challenge the validity of Parliamentary proceedings (see *British Railways Board v Pickin* [1974] A.C. 765; *cf. R. v HM Treasury Ex p. Smedley* [1985] Q.B. 657).

Moreover, there must be a real and not a hypothetical question in dispute between two parties (see Lord Sumner in *Russian Commercial and Industrial Bank v British Bank for Foreign Trade Ltd* [1921] 2 A.C. 438 at 452); J. Jaconelli, (1985) 101 L.Q.R. 587. In *Blackburn v Att-Gen* [1971] 1 W.L.R. 1037, the Court of Appeal declined to make a declaration on the hypothetical question whether by signing the Treaty of Rome, Her Majesty's Government would irreversibly surrender in part the sovereignty of

Parliament. In *R. v Secretary of State for the Environment Ex p. Nottinghamshire CC, The Independent*, November 1, 1986, declarations were refused where they related to determinations subsequently validated by retrospective legislation (*cf. R. v Local Commissioner Ex p. Eastleigh BC* (above, p.188)). Then, in *R. v Secretary of State for Education and Science Ex p. Birmingham City Council*, unreported, May 14, 1991, Brooke J. set aside the grant of leave to the council to seek a declaration that revised arrangements for its secondary schools would enable the council to comply with its obligations under the Sex Discrimination Act 1975. (In *Birmingham City Council v Equal Opportunities Commission* [1989] A.C. 1155, the House of Lords had held the council to be in breach of its obligations under the 1975 Act). The Secretary of State had expressed no view on the question and was not a proper contradictor. It may be noted that, while the courts continue to be reluctant to pronounce on issues that are now academic, they are increasingly prepared to give what are in effect advisory declarations concerning the legality of forthcoming measures (see Sir John Laws, "Judicial Remedies and the Constitution" (1994) 57 M.L.R. 213, citing the *RCN, Gillick* and *Bland* cases and *Ex p. Smedley* (above); Sir John favours the development of this practice). See also D. Kolinsky, "Advisory Declarations Recent Developments [1989] J.R. 225.

The original *jurisdiction* of the court to grant a declaration may be regarded as excluded where Parliament creates new rights and duties and by the same enactment appoints a specific tribunal for their enforcement (*Barraclough v Brown* [1987] A.C. 615, HL, distinguished in *Pyx Granite Co. Ltd v Ministry of Housing and Local Government* [1960] A.C. 260, HL). Where this principle does not apply in respect of the original jurisdiction, and in cases involving the supervisory jurisdiction, the existence of an alternative remedy may instead give rise to a *discretion* to refuse a remedy (above, pp.1019–1021; *Leech v Deputy Governor of Parkhurst Prison* [1988] A.C. 533, HL). See discussion in *Zamir and Woolf*, pp.74–85; *Lewis*, pp.426–427.

(I) Proposals for Reform

A full review of remedies was undertaken by the Law Commission, which reported in 1994 (*Administrative Law: Judicial Review and Statutory Appeals*, Law Com. No.226). Many of its proposals were subsequently endorsed by Lord Woolf in the course of his review of the whole civil justice system (*Access to Justice: Final Report*, HMSO, 1996, Ch.18). There then followed Sir Jeffery Bowman's *Review of the Crown Office List* (2001) (see M. Sunkin, [2001] P.L. 11) which led in turn to Pt 54 of the CPR (above, p.927). Many of Lord Woolf's proposals have been taken forward. Among those yet to be implemented are the following:

1. The possibility of seeking a writ of habeas corpus on a claim for judicial review (para.9);
2. Conferment of an express power to grant advisory declarations (para.10);
3. Incorporation in general terms in the rules of the present generous practice of the courts in interpreting the requirement of "sufficient interest"; a practice guide would indicate relevant factors. An applicant should have standing if he or she "has been or will be adversely affected or if it is in the public interest that the proceedings should be brought" (para.20);
4. Legislation should confer a discretion on the court to order costs to be paid out of public funds where it is in the public interest that proceedings should be brought. If this was not implemented, the court should have a discretion not to order an unsuccessful party to pay the other party's costs, on the grounds that the proceedings have been brought in the public interest. Initially, this discretion should only be exercised where there would otherwise be substantial hardship (para.22).

Notes

1. The Law Commission stated in its 1994 report (Law Com. No.226) that in making their recommendations they had to form a view about the proper balance among "(a) the importance of vindicating the rule of law, so that public law bodies take lawful decisions and are prevented from relying on invalid decisions; (b) the need for speed and certainty in administrative decision-making in cases where the whole community, or large sections of it, will be affected by the decisions of public law bodies; (c) the private interest of individual litigants in obtaining a remedy for their grievances". There was also a public interest in the prompt adjudication of disputes through the courts (p.7). Of particular concern was the increase in case load and delays in recent years (pp.10–16). One measure which would assist would be the creation of a right of appeal to a court or independent tribunal in homelessness cases (p.15) (a recommendation subsequently implemented: see above, p.791).

Many of their specific recommendations were endorsed by Lord Woolf. One advantage for Lord Woolf was that as his remit extended to the whole of the civil justice process he was able to make more radical proposals to address the problems caused by the relationship between public and private law. On the issue of procedural exclusivity, the Law Commission did not favour proposals for a unified procedure for public and private law cases, with provision for striking out rather than a leave requirement. Such a procedure would "prevent the expeditious disposal of public law cases by specialist judges and could increase complexity and costs". It was "essential to filter out hopeless applications" (p.20). Reform should be by a combination of "building on the restrictive approach to the exclusivity principle taken in *Roy v Kensington and Chelsea and Westminster FPC*" (above, p.988), and facilitating the transfer of cases into as well as out of Ord.53 (pp.21–30). Lord Woolf favoured a greater assimilation of procedures, while retaining the three-month time-limit and standing requirement for public law cases.

The Law Commission noted the evidence of the wide disparity in the rates at which different judges granted leave (see above, p.969). Its response was to propose that the Rules should state that "unless the application discloses a serious issue which ought to be determined it should not be allowed to proceed to a substantive hearing" (p.41); and should direct the judge to consider whether the application complies with the requirement as to standing and time-limits and "whether the applicant has, or the reasons why he has not, pursued alternative legal remedies" (pp.40–50). As to standing, the modern liberal approach should be taken further by the express recognition of a judicial discretion to entertain cases where that is considered to be in the public interest. Time-limits should be governed by the Rules rather than the Supreme Court Act 1980. Section 31(6) (above, p.925) should be repealed; the Rules should provide for a three-month limit, a power to refuse an application if it is not "sufficiently prompt" *and* if the grant of ultimate relief "would be likely to cause substantial hardship to, or substantially prejudice the rights of, any person or be detrimental to good administration" and a power to extend time if there is "good reason for the application not having been made" within three months *and* it is not likely to cause hardship, etc. Applicants must either exhaust alternative legal remedies or demonstrate that "despite the existence of such a remedy, judicial review is an appropriate procedure". The court should take account of the pursuit of an alternative remedy as a good reason for extending time.

Other points in Lord Woolf's proposals largely endorsed Law Commission recommendations. However, some were not mentioned, including (a) that the court should be empowered to substitute its own decision for that of an inferior court or tribunal where there was only one lawful decision that could be arrived at and the ground for review arose out of an error of law; and (b) that unincorporated associations should be permitted to apply in their own name through one or more members applying in a representative capacity, where the court is satisfied that the members have been or would be adversely affected or are raising an issue of public interest warranting judicial review, and that the members are appropriate persons to bring that challenge.

Other points (reference to alternative grievance procedures, the possible availability of all private law remedies, directions and case management, the filing of a defence, written disposition of some cases) were based more on the wider work of the *Access to Justice* project than Law Commission proposals. It is notable that neither Lord Woolf nor the Commission had any proposal to widen the use of discovery in judicial review (*cf.* above, p.970).

2. On the Law Commission Report, see R. Gordon, [1995] P.L. 11; N.J. Bamforth, (1995) 58 M.L.R. 722; I. Hare, [1995] C.L.J. 268; C.T. Emery, [1995] P.L. 450 considering the advantages of a unified civil procedure and public law challenge outside the civil justice system.

3. Overall, both sets of proposals involve the further evolution of judicial review procedure rather than radical change, in a number of respects in parallel to developments by the judges. A central feature is that the case for retaining special protection for public authorities has been accepted notwithstanding the views of the sceptics. Indeed, given the recent problems of case load and delay this outcome is wholly unsurprising. Furthermore, the time-limits protection can be seen as all the more necessary with the proposed further relaxation in standing.

Part III

CIVIL LIABILITY

INTRODUCTORY NOTE TO PART III

This Part deals with the application of private law principles of contract, tort and restitution to public authorities. A recurrent theme is the extent to which, if at all, ordinary principles should be modified, by statute or by the judges, to take account of the particular responsibilities of such authorities.

CHAPTER 15

CIVIL LIABILITY OF PUBLIC AUTHORITIES

(A) CONTRACT[1]

Powers to contract may be conferred specifically by statute (see *Cross*, paras 8–101 to 8–106, the Local Government (Contracts) Act 1997, s.1(1), (2) and C. Turpin, *Government Procurement and Contracts* (1989), p.84), generally by such statutory provisions as s.111 of the Local Government Act 1972 and ss.1–3 of the Local Government Act 2000 (above, pp.398–406), and by the common law, such as the general contractual capacity of the Crown apart from statute (Turpin, *op.cit.*, pp.83–84). If an authority enters into a contract when it has no power to do so, the contract is null and void—neither party may sue on it (see *Rhyl UDC v Rhyl Amusements Ltd*, above, p.511; *Credit Suisse v Allerdale BC*, above, p.864) and the authority will not be estopped from denying its validity (*ibid.*). There may, however, be rights conferred by the law of restitution (below, pp.1103–1107). In the case of local authorities, certain contracts self-certified by means of a specified process are presumed to be lawful (as is the certificate). The presumption can be rebutted, but only through judicial review or audit; the contract cannot be challenged in private law. If a contract is declared unlawful and of no effect, compensation is payable to the other party under special terms of the contract (Local Government (Contracts) Act 1997, ss.2–9). The purpose of these provisions is to facilitate the policy of encouraging PFI (Private Finance Initiative) and other partnerships between local authorities and the private sector, following a series of high-profile cases in which contracts entered by local authorities were held to be *ultra vires* (see above, pp.396–397 and pp.804–875). Moreover, a public authority may not disable itself by contract from discharging its primary purposes (see cases given above, at pp.495–509.). This principle is closely related to, if not identical with, the doctrine of *The Amphitrite* (see Turpin, *op.cit.*, pp.85–90, above, p.505). In general, the courts have shown some reluctance to apply judicial review principles to the exercise of contractual powers (see S. Arrowsmith, (1990) 106 L.Q.R. 277; (1990) 10 L.S. 231, arguing that "the contractual nature of a power should in itself generally be irrelevant to the scope of review" (at 239)). See above, pp.957–966 on the scope of the application for judicial review. The exercise of contractual powers is also normally excluded from review by the PCA or the Local Government Ombudsman.

Parliament has imposed express restrictions on the power of local authorities to take account of non-commercial considerations (see above, pp.69–71); *cf.* the use of contracting powers by central government to achieve policy goals (above, pp.68–69). The change in emphasis in the role of local authorities towards being "enablers" of service provision rather than the providers of services was supported by a regime of Compulsory Competitive Tendering under Pt III of the Local Government, Planning and Land Act 1980 and Pt I of the Local Government Act 1988, under which authorities were required to put a wide range of services (including some professional

---

[1] See C. Turpin, *Government Procurement and Contracts* (1989); H. Street, *Governmental Liability* (1953), Ch.3; J.D.B. Mitchell, *The Contracts of Public Authorities* (1954); M. Aronson and H. Whitmore, *Public Torts and Contracts* (1982); S. Arrowsmith, *Government Procurement and Judicial Review* (1988), (1990) 10 L.S. 231; *Civil Liability and Public Authorities* (1992) and *The Law of Public and Utilities Procurement* (1996); P.W. Hogg, *Liability of the Crown* (2nd ed., 1989), Ch.8.

services) through competitive tendering exercises in which private sector organisations could compete against the council's own operation. The Labour Government in office since 1997 has replaced this by a less prescriptive Best Value regime (Local Government Act 1999; *Cross*, Ch.7). A Best Value authority (including all local authorities in England and Wales) must:

> "make arrangements to secure continuous improvement in the way in which its functions are exercised, having regard to a combination of economy, efficiency and effectiveness".

Competition remains an important management tool in achieving Best Value.

Public procurement is now substantially regulated by European Community law. Article 28 (ex 30) of the EC Treaty prohibits quantitative restrictions on the free movement of goods between Member States, which would include decisions that discriminate against goods from other Member States. Public supply and works contracts with an estimated value above the prevailing threshold were made subject to common advertising procedures and award criteria (Directives 77/62, as amended, and 71/305, as amended). Other Directives (70/32 and 71/304) required the abolition of discriminatory practices which might prevent contractors from other Member States from participating in public contracts on equal terms. The enforcement of these obligations was left to the EC Commission to take action in the Court of Justice against a Member State under Art.169 EEC. Directive 89/665 introduced new requirements for the establishment of review procedures in national courts or tribunals in respect of alleged infringement of Community law in the field of public procurement or national rules implementing that law. See S. Weatherill, "National Remedies and Equal Access to Public Procurement" (1990) 10 Y.E.L. 243. The Public Supply Contracts Regulations 1991 (SI 1991/2679) and the Public Works Contracts Regulations 1991 (SI 1991/2680) enacted the relevant EC procurement directives. Directive 92/50 introduced provisions regulating public services contracts and was implemented by the Public Services Contracts Regulations 1993 (SI 1993/3228), as amended. Directive 93/36 consolidated the provisions applicable to supply contracts and was implemented by the Public Supply Contracts Regulations 1995 (SI 1995/201), as amended.

The Supply, Works and Services Regulations, as amended, apply, respectively, to (1) certain contracts for the supply of goods; (2) certain building and engineering works; and (3) certain contracts under which an authority engages a person to provide services, but excluding a contract of employment or other contract of service, and contracts that come under the regime of the other regulations. The current thresholds are 5,000,000 ECU under the works regulations, and 200,000 ECU for the supply (subject to exceptions) and services regulations. The regulations apply to contracts placed by "contracting authorities", a term that includes ministers, government departments, local authorities and many other specified bodies. The regulations make provision in respect of technical specifications in contract documents, procedures leading to the award of contracts, the selection of suppliers or contractors, and the award of contracts. The obligation on a contracting authority to comply with the Regulations and any enforceable Community obligation in relation to the award of a contract is a duty owed to suppliers, contractors and services providers and is actionable by any such person "who, in consequence, suffers, or risks suffering, loss or damage". Proceedings may not be brought unless the supplier, etc. has notified the authority of the breach and of his intention to bring proceedings; and must be brought promptly and in any event within three months from the date when grounds for proceedings first arose unless the court considers there is good reason for extending the period. (*cf.* the position on judicial review, above, pp.1010–1019.) The court may by an interim order (which may include an injunction against the Crown; *cf.* above, p.974) and may set aside a decision or action taken or award damages. If the contract has been entered into, the only remedy is damages. For the enforcement provisions, see SI 1995/201, reg.29,

SI 1991/2680, reg.31 and SI 1993/3228, reg.32. These regulations are fully analysed by S. Arrowsmith, *The Law of Public and Utilities Procurement* (1996), Chs 5–11.

These arrangements are to be replaced by a new Directive 2004/18 of the Parliament and Council on the co-ordination of procedures for the award of public works contracts, public supply contracts and public service contracts. Directive 2004/17 deals with the special sectors of water, energy, transport and postal services. These must be implemented by January 31, 2006.

(B) Tort[2]

Public authorities may both sue and be sued in tort (as for local authorities, see s.222 of the Local Government Act 1972, above, p.1026). The liability of public authorities in tort is of particular interest to administrative lawyers in two respects. First, there can be questions as to the extent to which, if at all, the ordinary principles of liability are modified, or should be modified, to take account of the special position of those authorities in law and society. In many respects a public authority is in no different a position from that of any other plaintiff or defendant. For example, if a local authority van is carelessly driven, and injury is caused, ordinary tort principles apply. (Did the driver fall below the standard of the reasonable driver? Was the driver in the course of his employment, or was he taking the van on a frolic of his own?) It makes no difference that the van was publicly rather than privately owned.

On the other hand, the position of public authorities is complicated by the facts that their powers and duties are usually derived from statute, and that they must act *intra vires*. Statutory authority may be pleaded as a defence to an action in tort. Conversely, the grounds of an action may be failure to perform a statutory power or duty, the negligent performance of a power or duty, or malicious performance of a power. Difficult questions of statutory interpretation may arise. It is a matter of debate how far, if at all, the legitimate interests of public authorities can be sufficiently protected by the application of ordinary tort principles.

On the other hand, there are also questions as to whether the law of tort provides adequately for the compensation for those whose rights are infringed or who suffer loss as the result of unlawful acts or omissions of public authorities. Some causes of action are available most notably:

(1) misfeasance in public office, where powers are misused intentionally or recklessly (below, pp.1090–1101);
(2) the award of damages under ss.7 and 8 of the Human Rights Act 1998 (above, pp.320–339);
(3) the award of damages under the *Francovich* doctrine: where there is a failure to implement a directive or there is national legislation inconsistent with directly effective Community law, individuals suffering loss or injury are entitled to reparation where (i) the Community law rule breached is intended to confer rights upon them (ii) the breach is sufficiently serious; and (iii) there is a direct causal link between the breach and the damages suffered. (Cases C 6 & 9/90, *Francovich v Italy* [1991] E.C.R. I-5357; Cases C 46 & 48/93,

---

[2] See A. Rubinstein, *Jurisdiction and Illegality* (1965), Ch.VI; G.E. Robinson, *Public Authorities and Legal Liability* (1925); H. Street, *Governmental Liability* (1953), Ch.2; B.C. Gould, "Damages as a Remedy in Administrative Law" (1972) 5 N.Z.U.L.R. 105; C. Harlow, "Fault Liability in French and English Public Law" (1976) 39 M.L.R. 516 and *Compensation and Government Torts* (1982); M. Aronson and H. Whitmore, *Public Torts and Contracts* (1982); Lewis, pp.496–545; S. Arrowsmith, *Civil Liability and Public Authorities* (1992); B. Markesinis *et al.*, *Tortious Liability of Statutory Bodies, A Comparitive Analysis of Five English Cases* (1999); J. Wright, *Tort Law and Human Rights* (2001); D. Fairgrieve *et al.* (ed.), *Tort Liability of Public Authorities in Comparative Perspective* (2002); D. Fairgrieve, *State Liability in Tort: A Comparative Law Study* (2003).

Brasserie du Pêcheur SA v Germany; R. v Secretary of State for Transport Ex p. Factortame Ltd [1996] E.C.R. I-1029) (see *Craig*, pp.928–935).

Reparation is to be made in accordance with the national law on liability, on conditions that are not less favourable than those laid down for similar domestic claims or framed in such a way as to make it excessively difficult to obtain reparation. It cannot be made conditional upon fault going beyond the requirement of a sufficiently serious breach; must be commensurate with the loss or damage sustained; and may include an award of exemplary damages if there might be awarded on similar domestic claims (*ibid*).

(4) torts that protect interests in the person or property (*e.g.* trespass to the person (including assault), to land or to goods); false imprisonment and malicious prosecution; nuisance).

Outside these areas, the potential scope of liability is restricted. Breach of statutory duty rarely gives rise to a cause of action outside the context of the protection of health and safety at work. Ordinary principles of negligence do not normally provide a remedy in respect of an omission (a failure to confer a benefit as opposed to the infliction of a loss); or for economic loss or psychiatric injury; and for distress short of psychiatric injury not at all. The general cause of action that covers losses caused by unlawful action (the misfeasance tort) requires proof of intention or recklessness. The field that remains is populated in part by *ex gratia* awards that may be made through complaints schemes or following an ombudsman's report, and it is for consideration whether tort principles should be extended.

It should be noted that the particular officer who commits the tortious act is personally liable, in addition to the vicarious liability of the authority (see *Ministry of Housing and Local Government v Sharp* [1970] 2 Q.B. 223). Moreover, exemplary damages may be awarded in cases of oppressive, arbitrary or unconstitutional action in the exercise of public powers (*Rookes v Barnard* [1964] A.C. 1129 at 1226, *per* Lord Devlin; *Broome v Cassell & Co.* [1972] A.C. 1027). There is no basis for limiting the award of exemplary damages to causes of action in respect of which such an award had been made before 1964, when *Rookes v Barnard* was decided (*Kuddus v Chief Constable of Leicestershire Constabulary* [2001] UKHL 299; [2002] 2 A.C. 122, overruling the decision of the Court of Appeal in *AB v South West Water Services Ltd* [1993] Q.B. 507). The House left open the question whether such an award could be made against a person vicariously liable for acts of the wrongdoer. A case will normally have to involve intentional or reckless wrongdoing to justify an award of exemplary damages (see Lord Nicholls in *A v Bottrill* [2002] UKPC 44; [2003] 1 A.C. 449, PC in relation to the common law position in New Zealand). Awards of exemplary damages have, for example, been made against police officers, in a range of cases, for trespass to the person (assault), false imprisonment and malicious prosecution (see R. Clayton and H. Tomlinson, *Civil Actions Against the Police* (2004), pp.610–613). The maximum appropriate for an award of exemplary damages against the police is £50,000, and then only where officers of at least the rank of superintendent are involved in the unlawful conduct (*Thompson v Commissioner of Police of the Metropolis* [1998] Q.B 498).

A claim for damages may be included in a claim for judicial review or an ordinary claim; if it is the only claim, however, the court has no jurisdiction to consider it by way of judicial review proceedings (see above, p.924; *R. (on the application of Andrews) v Reading BC* [2004] EWHC 970).

(i) The Defence of Statutory Authority[3]

It is a good defence to an action in tort that the act alleged to constitute, for example, nuisance or trespass is expressly or impliedly authorised by statute.

---

[3] See J. Fleming, *The Law of Torts* (8th ed.), pp.439–441; *Cross*, paras 8–15 to 8–21; G. Kodilinye, (1990) 19 Anglo-Am.L.R. 72.

Where the act of a public authority would be a tort if committed by a private person, and it is *ultra vires* the authority, the defence obviously fails. For example, in *Smith v East Elloe RDC and John Champion & Son Ltd* (1952) 160 E.G. 148 ([1952] C.P.L. 738; 103 L.J. 108) Devlin J. (sitting with a jury) gave judgment for the plaintiff for £850, as damages for trespass. The council had continued the requisition of the plaintiff's property although the lawful purposes of the requisition (to house evacuees, and then to help to relieve the consequences of the housing shortage) had ceased because dilapidations (see the sequel, above, p.907). Another example is *Cooper v Wandsworth Board of Works* (above, p.653 (trespass)). A *fortiori*, a public authority may not argue in its *defence* that the act alleged to be tortious was *ultra vires*, and therefore not one which they had a legal power to perform (*Campbell v Paddington Corp* [1911] 1 K.B. 869, where the corporation authorised its employees to erect a stand in the street opposite the plaintiff's house. This was held to be a public nuisance). Rather more difficult are those cases where it it not clear whether the statute authorises the specific act that has been done. There must be a power or duty to perform the specific act in the particular manner complained of (*Metropolitan Asylum District v Hill* (1881) 6 App.Cas. 193: general power to build a smallpox hospital did not confer a defence of statutory authority to a claim in nuisance). Alternatively the infringement of legal rights must be the inevitable or unavoidable result of authorised acts (*Hammersmith Ry v Brand* (1869) L.R. 4 H.L. 171). The key factor is the precision of the statutory authorisation, and not necessarily whether that authorisation is a power or a duty. Thus, on the assumption that the provision of a smallpox hospital can constitute a nuisance to neighbours (*cf. Metropolitan Asylum District v Hill*), a duty to build such a hospital on a particular site negatives liability to the neighbours; a power to build on that site (*i.e.* a choice whether or not to build) presumably also negatives liability *cf. Allen v Gulf Oil Refining Ltd* [1981] A.C. 1001); a power to build with no site specified will not negative liability, unless it is impossible to build without infringing someone's rights. On the defence of statutory authority and the rule in *Rylands v Fletcher*, see *Dunne v N.W. Gas Board* [1964] 2 Q.B. 806, CA. See further *Marriage v E. Norfolk Rivers Catchment Board* [1950] 1 K.B. 284 and *Department of Transport v North West Water Authority* [1984] A.C. 336 at 344, 359–360.

(ii) Negligent Exercise of Powers and Duties[4]; Breach of Statutory Duty[5]

Public authorities may clearly be liable for failures to perform statutory duties and for the negligent exercise of powers and duties. The main difficulties have arisen in respect of some of the specialised activities of public authorities—in particular in determining whether a duty of care is owed. The House of Lords provided a survey of the principles in the following case.

---

[4] There is now an extensive body of literature on the negligence liability of public authorities—see, *e.g.* W. Friedmann (1944) 8 M.L.R. 31; H. Street, *Governmental Liability* (1953), pp.40, 56–80; C.J. Hamson, [1969] C.L.J. 273 (on the Court of Appeal decision in *Home Office v Dorset Yacht Co.*); G. Ganz, "Compensation for Negligent Administrative Action" [1973] P.L. 84; C.S. Phegan, (1976) 22 McGill L.J. 605; C. Harlow, "Fault Liability in French and English Public Law" (1976) 39 M.L.R. 516; (1980) 43 M.L.R. 241, and *Compensation and Government Torts* (1982); P.P. Craig (1978) 94 L.Q.R. 428 and *Craig*, pp.618–632; D. Oliver (1980) 33 C.L.P. 269; M.J. Bowman and S.H. Bailey [1984] P.L. 277; S.H. Bailey and M.J. Bowman [1986] C.L.J. 430 and [2000] C.L.J. 85; S. Todd, "The Negligence Liablity of Public Authorities: Divergence in the Common Law" (1986) 102 L.Q.R. 370 and "Public Authorities' Liability: The New Zealand Dimension" (1987) 103 L.Q.R. 19; P.W. Hogg, *Liability of the Crown* (2nd ed., 1989) Ch.6; S. Arrowsmith, *Civil Liability and Public Authorities* (1992), pp.176–185; *de Smith, Woolf and Jowell*, pp.774–782; K.M. Stanton *et al.*, *Statutory Torts* (2003), Ch.3.
[5] See W.V.H. Rogers, *Winfield & Jolowicz on Tort* (16th ed., 2002), Ch.7; R.A. Buckley (1984) 100 L.Q.R. 204; K.M. Stanton, *Breach of Statutory Duty in Tort* (1986); K.M. Stanton *et al.*, *Statutory Torts* (2003), Ch.2.

X (MINORS) v BEDFORDSHIRE COUNTY COUNCIL

[1995] 2 A.C. 633; [1995] 3 W.L.R. 152; [1995] 3 All E.R. 353
(HOUSE OF LORDS)

The House of Lords heard appeals in five cases on the question whether claims for negligence or for breach of statutory duty should be struck out. Two (*X (Minors) v Bedfordshire CC* and *M (a Minor) v Newham LBC*) concerned powers and duties in relation to the protection of children from abuse; three (*E (a Minor) v Dorset CC; Christmas v Hampshire CC* and *Keating v Bromley LBC*) concerned powers and duties in relation to children with educational needs.

The five plaintiffs in the *Bedfordshire* case claimed damages for personal injury arising out of breach of statutory duty and negligence by the council in failing to protect them from parental abuse. In the *Newham* case, the plaintiff M and her mother claimed damages for personal injuries (psychiatric injury specified as anxiety neurosis) arising out of breach of statutory duty and negligence by the local authority, the area health authority and a consultant psychiatrist employed by the latter. They alleged that the psychiatrist and a social worker employed by the local authority had concluded that M had been sexually abused, but then mistakenly identified the abuser as the mother's cohabitee (who shared the same first name as the cousin whom M intended to identify). This led to the authority's obtaining court orders removing M from her mother, placing her in foster care and restricting the mother's access to her.

In the *Dorset* case, the plaintiff, E claimed damages for breach of statutory duty and negligence by the council, alleging that it had initially wrongly advised his parents and failed to diagnose that he suffered from a special learning disorder, and subsequently, after his difficulties were acknowledged, failed to take the appropriate steps. In the *Hampshire* case, the plaintiff (born in 1973) claimed damages against the council for negligence in the assessment of his educational needs. He alleged that his primary school headmaster had failed to refer him to the council for formal assessment or to an educational psychologist for diagnosis, notwithstanding his exhibiting learning difficulties consistent with dyslexia and behavioural problems. Furthermore, the council's teachers' advisory centre, to which he had been referred, had also failed to ascertain his difficulty. The failure to treat his condition had disadvantaged him in realising his potential and significantly restricted his vocational prospects. In the *Bromley* case, the plaintiff (born in 1971) claimed damages for breach of statutory duty and negligence against the council, alleging failure to place him at a reasonably appropriate school and to identify him as a child with special needs. He claimed damages for the alleged consequent impairment of his development and the disadvantage at which he was placed in seeking employment.

All the claims were struck out at first instance. The Court of Appeal allowed appeals against striking out as regards the claims in the education cases based on negligence. The House of Lords held that all the causes of action should be struck out except those in respect of allegations of professional negligence against one authority directly in respect of its provision of a psychological advice service and against teachers and educational psychologists for whom defendant authorities were vicariously liable.

The leading speech was given by Lord Browne-Wilkinson, with whom Lords Jauncey of Tullichettle, Lane, Ackner and (subject to one point) Nolan agreed.

Lord Browne-Wilkinson: . . .

General approach

Introductory—public law and private law

The question is whether, if Parliament has imposed a statutory duty on an authority to carry out a particular function, a plaintiff who has suffered damage in consequence of the authority's performance or non-performance of that function has a right of action in damages against the authority. It is important to distinguish such actions to recover damages, based on a private law cause of action, from actions in public law to enforce the due performance of statutory duties, now brought by way of judicial review. The breach of a public law right by itself gives rise to no claim for damages. A claim for damages must be based on a private law cause of action . . . .

Private law claims for damages can be classified into four different categories, *viz*: (A) actions for breach of statutory duty simpliciter (*i.e.* irrespective of carelessness); (B) actions based solely on the careless performance of a statutory duty in the absence of any other common law right of action; (C) actions based on a common law duty of care arising either from the imposition of the statutory duty or from the performance of it; (D) misfeasance in public office, *i.e.* the failure to exercise, or the exercise of, statutory powers either with the intention to injure the plaintiff or in the knowledge that the conduct is unlawful.

Category (D) is not in issue in this case. I will consider each of the other categories but I must make it clear that I am not attempting any general statement of the applicable law: rather I am seeking to set out a logical approach to the wide ranging arguments advanced in these appeals.

(A) *Breach of statutory duty simpliciter*

This category comprises those cases where the statement of claim alleges simply (a) the statutory duty, (b) a breach of that duty, causing (c) damage to the plaintiff. The cause of action depends neither on proof of any breach of the plaintiffs' common law rights nor on any allegation of carelessness by the defendant.

The principles applicable in determining whether such statutory cause of action exists are now well established, although the application of those principles in any particular case remains difficult. The basic proposition is that in the ordinary case a breach of statutory duty does not, by itself, give rise to any private law cause of action. However a private law cause of action will arise if it can be shown, as a matter of construction of the statute, that the statutory duty was imposed for the protection of a limited class of the public and that Parliament intended to confer on members of that class a private right of action for breach of the duty. There is no general rule by reference to which it can be decided whether a statute does create such a right of action but there are a number of indicators. If the statute provides no other remedy for its breach and the Parliamentary intention to protect a limited class is shown, that indicates that there may be a private right of action since otherwise there is no method of securing the protection the statute was intended to confer. If the statute does provide some other means of enforcing the duty that will normally indicate that the statutory right was intended to be enforceable by those means and not by private right of action: *Cutler v Wandsworth Stadium Ltd* [1949] A.C. 398; *Lonrho Ltd v Shell Petroleum Co. Ltd (No.2)* [1982] A.C. 173. However, the mere existence of some other statutory remedy is not necessarily decisive. It is still possible to show that on the true construction of the statute the protected class was intended by Parliament to have a private remedy. Thus the specific duties imposed on employers in relation to factory premises are enforceable by an action for damages, notwithstanding the imposition by the statutes of criminal penalties for any breach: see *Groves v Wimborne (Lord)* [1898] 2 Q.B. 402.

Although the question is one of statutory construction and therefore each case turns on the provisions in the relevant statute, it is significant that your Lordships were not referred to any case where it had been held that statutory provisions establishing a regulatory system or a scheme of social welfare for the benefit of the public at large had been held to give rise to a private right of action for damages for breach of statutory duty. Although regulatory or welfare legislation affecting a particular area of activity does in fact provide protection to those individuals particularly affected by that activity, the legislation is not to be treated as being passed for the benefit of those individuals but for the benefit of society in general. Thus legislation regulating the conduct of betting or prisons did not give rise to a statutory right of action vested in those adversely affected by the breach of the statutory provisions, *i.e.* bookmakers and prisoners: see *Cutler's* case [1949] A.C. 398; *R. v Deputy Governor of Parkhurst Prison, Ex p. Hague* [1992] 1 A.C. 58. The cases where a private right of action for breach of statutory duty have been held to arise are all cases in which the statutory duty has been very limited and specific as opposed to general administrative functions imposed on public bodies and involving the exercise of administrative discretions.

(B) *The careless performance of a statutory duty—no common law duty of care*

This category comprises those cases in which the plaintiff alleges (a) the statutory duty and (b) the "negligent" breach of that duty but does not allege that the defendant was under a common law duty of care to the plaintiff. It is the use of the word "negligent" in this context which gives rise to confusion: it is sometimes used to connote mere carelessness (there being no common law duty of care) and sometimes to import the concept of a common law duty of care. In my judgment it is important in considering the authorities to distinguish between the two concepts: as will appear, in my view the careless performance of a statutory duty does not in itself give rise to any cause of action in the absence of either a statutory right of action (Category (A) above) or a common law duty of care (Category (C) below).

Much of the difficulty can be traced back to the confusion between the ability to rely on a statutory provision as a defence and the ability to rely on it as founding a cause of action. The source of the confusion is to be found in the dictum of Lord Blackburn in *Geddis v Proprietors of Bann Reservoir*, 3 App.Cas.430, 455–456:

"For I take it, without citing cases, that it is now thoroughly well established that no action will lie for doing that which the legislature has authorised, if it be done without negligence, although it does occasion damage to anyone; but an action does lie for doing that which the legislature has authorised, if it be done negligently. And I think that if by a reasonable exercise of the powers, either given by statute to the promoters, or which they have at common law, the damage could be prevented it is, within this rule, 'negligence' not to make such reasonable exercise of their powers."

This dictum, divorced from its context, suggests that the careless performance of a statutory duty in itself gives rise to a cause of action for damages. But it has to be read in context.

In *Geddis* the defendants were authorised to construct and maintain a reservoir the water from which was discharged, via a new artificial watercourse, into an old watercourse which the defendants were authorised by the statute to widen and maintain. Water originating from the reservoir flooded from the old watercourse onto the plaintiff's adjoining land, such flooding being due to the "negligent" failure of the defendants to maintain the old watercourse adequately. The cause of action relied upon by the plaintiff is not clear from the report: it could have been either nuisance (including *Rylands v Fletcher* (1868) L.R. 3 H.L. 330) or negligence. If the cause of action founded upon was in nuisance, the question was whether the statutory power to construct and maintain the works provided a defence to what would otherwise constitute an actionable wrong. It is well established that statutory authority only provides a defence to a claim based on a common law cause of action where the loss suffered by the plaintiff is the inevitable consequence of the proper exercise of the statutory power or duty: *Metropolitan Asylum District v Hill*, 6 App.Cas. 193; *Allen v Gulf Oil Refining Ltd* [1981] A.C. 1001. Therefore the careless exercise of a statutory power or duty cannot provide a defence to a claim based on a freestanding common law cause of action, whether in trespass, nuisance or breach of a common law duty of care. If Lord Blackburn's dictum in *Geddis*'s case, 3 App.Cas.430, 455–456, merely refers to the circumstances in which statutory authority can be used as a defence it raises no problems.

In my judgment *Geddis*'s case is best treated as a decision that the careless exercise by the defendant of a statutory duty or power provides no defence to a claim by the plaintiff based on a freestanding common law cause of action. It was so treated by Lord Wilberforce in the *Gulf Oil* case who said [1981] A.C. 1001, 1011:

"It is now well settled that where Parliament by express direction or by necessary implication has authorised the construction and use of an undertaking or works, that carries with it an authority to do what is authorised with immunity from any action based on nuisance. The right of action is taken away: *Hammersmith and City Railway Co. v Brand* (1869) L.R. 4 H.L. 171, 215 *per* Lord Cairns. To this there is made the qualification, or condition, that the statutory powers are exercised without 'negligence'— that word here being used in a special sense so as to require the undertaker, as a condition of obtaining immunity from action, to carry out the work and conduct the operation with all reasonable regard and care for the interests of other persons: *Geddis* . . ."

See also *Sutherland Shire Council v Heyman* (1985) 157 C.L.R. 424, 458 and the article by Sir Gerard Brennan "Liability in Negligence of Public Authorities: The Divergent Views" (1990) 48 *The Advocate* 842, 844–846.

[His Lordship then stated that the same position had been taken by the majority of the House of Lords in *Home Office v Dorset Yacht Co. Ltd* [1970] A.C. 1004 (Lords Morris, Pearson and Reid) although Lord Diplock had adopted a different approach.]

In my judgment the correct view is that in order to found a cause of action flowing from the careless exercise of statutory powers or duties, the plaintiff has to show that the circumstances are such as to raise a duty of care at common law. The mere assertion of the careless exercise of a statutory power or duty is not sufficient.

(C) *The common law duty of care*

In this category, the claim alleges either that a statutory duty gives rise to a common law duty of care owed to the plaintiff by the defendant to do or refrain from doing a particular act or (more often) that in the course of carrying out a statutory duty the defendant has brought about such a relationship between himself and the plaintiff as to give rise to a duty of care at common law. A further variant is a claim by the plaintiff that, whether or not the authority is itself under a duty of care to the plaintiff, its servant in the course of performing the statutory function was under a common law duty of care for breach of which the authority is vicariously liable.

Mr Munby, in his reply in the *Newham* case, invited your Lordships to lay down the general principles applicable in determining the circumstances in which the law would impose a common law duty of care arising from the exercise of statutory powers or duties. I have no doubt that, if possible, this would be most desirable. But I have found it quite impossible either to detect such principle in the wide range of authorities and academic writings to which we were referred or to devise any such principle de novo. The truth of the matter is that statutory duties now exist over such a wide range of diverse activities and take so many different forms that no one principle is capable of being formulated applicable to all cases. However, in my view it is possible in considering the problems raised by these particular appeals to identify certain points which are of significance.

1. Co-existence of statutory duty and common law duty of care

It is clear that a common law duty of care may arise in the performance of statutory functions. But a broad distinction has to be drawn between: (a) cases in which it is alleged that the authority owes a duty of care in the manner in which it exercises a statutory discretion; (b) cases in which a duty of care is alleged to arise from the manner in which the statutory duty has been implemented in practice.

An example of (a) in the educational field would be a decision whether or not to exercise a statutory discretion to close a school, being a decision which necessarily involves the exercise of a discretion. An example of (b) would be the actual running of a school pursuant to the statutory duties. In such latter case a common law duty to take reasonable care for the physical safety of the pupils will arise. The fact that the school is being run pursuant to a statutory duty is not necessarily incompatible with a common law duty of care arising from the proximate relationship between a school and the pupils it has agreed to accept. The distinction is between (a) taking care in exercising a statutory discretion whether or not to do an act and (b) having decided to do that act, taking care in the manner in which you do it.

2. Discretion: justiciability and the policy operational test

(a) Discretion
Most statutes which impose a statutory duty on local authorities confer on the authority a discretion as to the extent to which, and the methods by which, such statutory duty is to be performed. It is clear both in principle and from the decided cases that the local authority cannot be liable in damages for doing

that which Parliament has authorised. Therefore if the decisions complained of fall within the ambit of such statutory discretion they cannot be actionable in common law. However if the decision complained of is so unreasonable that it falls outside the ambit of the discretion conferred upon the local authority, there is no a priori reason for excluding all common law liability.

That this is the law is established by the decision in the *Dorset Yacht* case [1970] A.C. 1004 and by that part of the decision in *Anns v Merton London Borough Council* [1978] A.C. 728 which, so far as I am aware, has largely escaped criticism in later decisions. In the *Dorset Yacht* case Lord Reid said [1970] A.C. 1004, 1031:

"Where Parliament confers a discretion the position is not the same. Then there may, and almost certainly will, be errors of judgment in exercising such a discretion and Parliament cannot have intended that members of the public should be entitled to sue in respect of such errors. But there must come a stage when the discretion is exercised so carelessly or unreasonably that there has been no real exercise of the discretion which Parliament has conferred. The person purporting to exercise his discretion has acted in abuse or excess of his power. Parliament cannot be supposed to have granted immunity to persons who do that."

See also *per* Lord Morris, at 1037F.

Lord Diplock, . . . took a rather different line, making it a condition precedent to any common law duty arising that the decision impugned should be shown to be *ultra vires* in the public law sense. For myself, I do not believe that it is either helpful or necessary to introduce public law concepts as to the validity of a decision into the question of liability at common law for negligence. In public law a decision can be *ultra vires* for reasons other than *Wednesbury* unreasonableness (*Associated Provincial Picture Houses Ltd v Wednesbury Corporation* [1948] 1 K.B. 223) (*e.g.* breach of the rules of natural justice) which have no relevance to the question of negligence. Moreover it leads, in my judgment mistakenly, to the contention that claims for damages for negligence in the exercise of statutory powers should for procedural purposes be classified as public law claims and therefore, under *O'Reilly v Mackman* [1983] 2 A.C. 237 should be brought in judicial review proceedings: see *Lonrho plc v Tebbit* [1992] 4 All E.R. 280. However, although I consider that the public law doctrine of *ultra vires* has, as such, no role to play in the subject under discussion, the remarks of Lord Diplock were plainly directed to the fact that the exercise of a statutory discretion cannot be impugned unless it is so unreasonable that it falls altogether outside the ambit of the statutory discretion. He said [1970] A.C. 1004, 1068:

"These considerations lead me to the conclusion that neither the intentional release of a Borstal trainee under supervision, nor the unintended escape of a Borstal trainee still under detention which was the consequence of the application of a system of relaxed control intentionally adopted by the Home Office as conducive to the reformation of trainees, can have been intended by Parliament to give rise to any cause of action on the part of any private citizen unless the system adopted was so unrelated to any purpose of reformation that no reasonable person could have reached a bona fide conclusion that it was conducive to that purpose. Only then would the decision to adopt it be ultra vires in public law."

Exactly the same approach was adopted by Lord Wilberforce in *Anns v Merton London Borough Council* [1978] A.C. 728 who, speaking of the duty of a local authority which had in fact inspected a building under construction, said, at 755:

> "But this duty, heavily operational though it may be, is still a duty arising under the statute. There may be a discretionary element in its exercise—discretionary as to the time and manner of inspection, and the techniques to be used. A plaintiff complaining of negligence must prove, the burden being on him, that action taken was not within the limits of a discretion bona fide exercised, before he can begin to rely upon a common law duty of care."

It follows that in seeking to establish that a local authority is liable at common law for negligence in the exercise of a discretion conferred by statute, the first requirement is to show that the decision was outside the ambit of the discretion altogether: if it was not, a local authority cannot itself be in breach of any duty of care owed to the plaintiff.

In deciding whether or not this requirement is satisfied, the court has to assess the relevant factors taken into account by the authority in exercising the discretion. Since what are under consideration are discretionary powers conferred on public bodies for public purposes the relevant factors will often include policy matters, for example social policy, the allocation of finite financial resources between the different calls made upon them or (as in *Dorset Yacht*) the balance between pursuing desirable social aims as against the risk to the public inherent in so doing. It is established that the courts cannot enter upon the assessment of such "policy" matters. The difficulty is to identify in any particular case whether or not the decision in question is a "policy" decision.

(b) *Justiciability and the policy operational dichotomy*
In English law the first attempt to lay down the principles applicable in deciding whether or not a decision was one of policy was made by Lord Wilberforce in *Anns v Merton London Borough Council* [1978] A.C. 728, 754:

> "Most, indeed probably all, statutes relating to public authorities or public bodies, contain in them a large area of policy. The courts call this 'discretion' meaning that the decision is one for the authority or body to make, and not for the courts. Many statutes also prescribe or at least presuppose the practical execution of policy decisions: a convenient description of this is to say that in addition to the area of policy or discretion, there is an operational area. Although this distinction between the policy area and the operational area is convenient, and illuminating, it is probably a distinction of degree; many 'operational' powers or duties have in them some element of 'discretion'. It can safely be said that the more 'operational' a power or duty may be, the easier it is to superimpose upon it a common law duty of care."

As Lord Wilberforce appreciated, this approach did not provide a hard and fast test as to those matters which were open to the court's decision. In

Rowling v Takaro Properties Ltd [1988] A.C. 473 the Privy Council reverted to the problem. In that case the trial judge had found difficulty in applying the policy/operational test, but having classified the decision in question as being operational, took the view that as a result there was a common law duty of care. Commenting on the judge's view, Lord Keith of Kinkel said, at 501:

> "Their Lordships feel considerable sympathy with Quilliam J.'s difficulty in solving the problem by reference to this distinction. They are well aware of the references in the literature to this distinction (which appears to have originated in the United States of America), and of the critical analysis to which it has been subjected. They incline to the opinion, expressed in the literature, that this distinction does not provide a touchstone of liability, but rather is expressive of the need to exclude altogether those cases in which the decision under attack is of such a kind that a question whether it has been made negligently is unsuitable for judicial resolution, of which notable examples are discretionary decisions on the allocation of scarce resources or the distribution of risks: see especially the discussion in *Craig on Administrative Law* (1983), pp.534–538. If this is right, classification of the relevant decision as a policy or planning decision in this sense may exclude liability; but a conclusion that it does not fall within that category does not, in their Lordships' opinion, mean that a duty of care will *necessarily* exist." (Emphasis added.)

From these authorities I understand the applicable principles to be as follows. Where Parliament has conferred a statutory discretion on a public authority, it is for that authority, not for the courts, to exercise the discretion: nothing which the authority does within the ambit of the discretion can be actionable at common law. If the decision complained of falls outside the statutory discretion, it *can* (but not necessarily will) give rise to common law liability. However, if the factors relevant to the exercise of the discretion include matters of policy, the court cannot adjudicate on such policy matters and therefore cannot reach the conclusion that the decision was outside the ambit of the statutory discretion. Therefore a common law duty of care in relation to the taking of decisions involving policy matters cannot exist.

3. If justiciable, the ordinary principles of negligence apply

If the plaintiff's complaint alleges carelessness, not in the taking of a discretionary decision to do some act, but in the practical manner in which that act has been performed (*e.g.* the running of a school) the question whether or not there is a common law duty of care falls to be decided by applying the usual principles, *i.e.* those laid down in *Caparo Industries plc v Dickman* [1990] 2 A.C. 605, 617–618. Was the damage to the plaintiff reasonably foreseeable? Was the relationship between the plaintiff and the defendant sufficiently proximate? Is it just and reasonable to impose a duty of care? See *Rowling v Takaro Properties Ltd* [1988] A.C. 473; *Hill v Chief Constable of West Yorkshire* [1989] A.C. 53.

However the question whether there is such a common law duty and if so its ambit, must be profoundly influenced by the statutory framework within which the acts complained of were done. The position is directly analogous to that in which a tortious duty of care owed by A to C can arise out of the performance by A of a contract between A and B. In *Henderson v Merrett Syndicates Ltd* [1994] 3 W.L.R. 761 your Lordships held that A (the managing agent) who had contracted with B (the members' agent) to render certain services for C (the Names) came under a duty of care to C in the performance of those services. It is clear that any tortious duty of care owed to C in those circumstances could not be inconsistent with the duty owed in contract by A to B. Similarly, in my judgment a common law duty of care cannot be imposed on a statutory duty if the observance of such common law duty of care would be inconsistent with, or have a tendency to discourage, the due performance by the local authority of its statutory duties.

4. *Direct liability and vicarious liability*

In certain of the appeals before the House, the local authorities are alleged to be under a direct duty of care to the plaintiff not only in relation to the exercise of a statutory discretion but also in relation to the operational way in which they performed that duty.

This allegation of a direct duty of care owed by the authority to the plaintiff is to be contrasted with those claims which are based on the vicarious liability of the local authority for the negligence of its servants, *i.e.* for the breach of a duty of care owed by the servant to the plaintiff, the authority itself not being under any relevant duty of care to the plaintiff. Thus, in the *Newham* case the plaintiffs' claim is wholly based on allegations that two professionals, a social worker and a psychiatrist, individually owed professional duties of care to the plaintiff for the breach of which the authorities as their employers are vicariously liable. It is not alleged that the authorities were themselves under a duty of care to the plaintiff.

This distinction between direct and vicarious liability can be important since the authority may not be under a direct duty of care at all or the extent of the duty of care owed directly by the authority to the plaintiff may well differ from that owed by a professional to a patient. However, it is important not to lose sight of the fact that, even in the absence of a claim based on vicarious liability, an authority under a direct duty of care to the plaintiff will be liable for the negligent acts or omissions of its servant which constitute a breach of that direct duty. The authority can only act through its servants.

The position can be illustrated by reference to the hospital cases. It is established that those conducting a hospital are under a direct duty of care to those admitted as patients to the hospital (I express no view as to the extent of that duty). They are liable for the negligent acts of a member of the hospital staff which constitute a breach of that duty, whether or not the member of the staff is himself in breach of a separate duty of care owed by him to the plaintiff: *Gold v Essex County Council* [1942] 2 K.B. 293, 301, *per* Lord Green; *Cassidy v Ministry of Health* [1951] 2 K.B. 343, *per* Denning L.J.; *Roe v Minister of Health* [1954] 2 Q.B. 66; see also *Wilsons & Clyde Coal Co. Ltd v English* [1938] A.C. 57; *McDermid v Nash Dredging & Reclamation Co. Ltd* [1987] A.C. 906. Therefore in the cases under appeal, even where there is no allegation of a separate duty of care owed by a servant of the authority to the plaintiff, the negligent acts of that servant are capable of constituting a breach of the duty of care (if any) owed directly by the authority to the plaintiff.

Striking out

In all these cases the defendants are seeking to strike out the claims at an early stage, before discovery has taken place and before the facts are known. It is therefore necessary to proceed on the basis that the facts alleged in the various statements of claim are true. It must be stressed that these allegations are not admitted by the defendants.

Actions can only be struck out under R.S.C., Ord.18, r.19 where it is clear and obvious that in law the claim cannot succeed . . . .

The Abuse Cases

[His Lordship stated the facts of the *Bedfordshire* and *Newham* cases. He then summarised the powers and duties of local authorities to take children into care where, *inter alia*, they are at risk of being harmed (Children and Young Persons Act 1969, ss.1, 2; Child Care Act 1980, ss.1, 2; Children Act 1989, ss.17, 20(1), 47, Sch.2). He noted that from April 1, 1991, there had been a statutory complaints procedure applicable to the Children Act provisions (Local Authority Social Services Act 1970, s.7B; Local Authority Social Services (Complaints Procedure) Order 1990 (SI 1990/2244). His Lordship also referred to the Secretary of State's powers to give guidance and directions under the 1970 Act, ss.7, 7A, which were to be found in the publication *Working Together* (1991).]

The claim for breach of statutory duty: Category (A)

The Court of Appeal were unanimous in striking out these claims in both actions. I agree. My starting point is that the Acts in question are all concerned to establish an administrative system designed to promote the social welfare of the community. The welfare sector involved is one of peculiar sensitivity, involving very difficult decisions how to strike the balance between protecting the child from immediate feared harm and disrupting the relationship between the child and its parents. Decisions often have to be taken on the basis of inadequate and disputed facts. In my judgment in such a context it would require exceptionally clear statutory language to show a parliamentary intention that those responsible for carrying out these difficult functions should be liable in damages if, on subsequent investigation with the benefit of hindsight, it was shown that they had reached an erroneous conclusion and therefore failed to discharge their statutory duties.

It is true that the legislation was introduced primarily for the protection of a limited class, namely children at risk, and that until April 1991 the legislation itself contained only limited machinery for enforcing the statutory duties imposed. But in my view those are the only pointers in favour of imputing to Parliament an intention to create a private law cause of action. When one turns to the actual words used in the primary legislation to create the statutory duties relied upon in my judgment they are inconsistent with any intention to create a private law cause of action.

Thus, the duty imposed by section 2(2) of the Act of 1969 to bring care proceedings is made conditional upon the subjective judgment of the local authority that there are grounds for so doing. Similarly, the duty to receive a child into care under section 2(1) of the Act of 1980 only arises "where it appears to a local authority" that the parents are prevented from providing properly for the child *and* that its intervention is necessary in the interest of the child. So far as the Act of 1989 is concerned, the duty relied on in section 17 is described as "a general duty" which has two parts: (a) to safeguard the children and (b) "so far as is consistent" with (a) to promote the upbringing of the children by their families. Thus not only is the duty not a specific one but the section itself points out the basic tension which lies at the root of so much child protection work: the decision whether to split the family in order to protect the child. I find it impossible to construe such a statutory provision as demonstrating an intention that even where there is no carelessness by the authority it should be liable in damages if a court subsequently decided with hindsight that the removal, or failure to remove, the child from the family either was or was not "consistent with" the duty to safeguard the child.

All the duties imported by Schedule 2 to the Act of 1989 are to "take reasonable steps" to do certain things. The duty to make inquiries under section 47 is limited to "such inquiries as they consider necessary". Thus all the statutory provisions relied upon in the *Bedfordshire* case are, as one would expect, made dependent upon the subjective judgment of the local authority. To treat such duties as being more than public law duties is impossible . . . .

In the *Newham* case, the claim by the plaintiffs for damages for breach of statutory duty (Category (A)) was founded solely on sections 1 and 18 of the Act of 1980: the Act of 1989 was not in force at the relevant time. The claim was only faintly pursued by Mr Munby and, for the reasons given by Peter Gibson L.J. in the Court of Appeal [1994] 2 W.L.R. 554, 590,[6] in my judgment it is ill founded.

For these reasons (which are in substance the same as those of the Court of Appeal), the claims in both abuse cases to the extent that they are based on a claim for damages for breach of statutory duty simpliciter were rightly struck out.

Direct common law duty of care owed by the local authorities

In the *Newham* case it is not alleged that the borough council was under any direct duty of care to the plaintiffs: the case is based solely on the vicarious liability of the council and the health authority for the negligence of their servants.

In the *Bedfordshire* case, Mr Jackson formulated the common law duty of care owed by the county council as being "a duty to children in respect of whom they receive reports of neglect or ill-treatment to take reasonable care to protect such children". The first question is whether the determination by the court of the question whether there has been a breach of that duty will involve unjusticiable policy questions. The alleged breaches of that duty relate for the most part to the failure to take reasonable practical steps, *e.g.* to remove the children, to allocate a suitable social worker or to make proper

---

[6] [ed.] The duties were general duties couched in imprecise terms: a duty to make available such advice, guidance and assistance as would have promoted the welfare of the child by diminishing the need to receive her or keep her in care (s.1) or a duty to give first consideration to the need to promote the welfare of the child (s.18). Peter Gibson L.J. held that neither could have been intended by Parliament to give rise to a private law action.

investigations. The assessment by the court of such allegations would not require the court to consider policy matters which are not justiciable. They do not necessarily involve any question of the allocation of resources or the determination of general policy. There are other allegations the investigation of which by a court might require the weighing of policy factors, *e.g.* allegations that the county council failed to provide a level of service appropriate to the plaintiffs' needs. If the case were to go to trial, the trial judge might have to rule out these issues as not being justiciable. But since some of the allegations are justiciable, it would not be right to strike out the whole claim on this ground.

Next, do the allegations of breach of duty in the operational field all relate to decisions the power to make which Parliament has conferred on the local authority, *i.e.* are they all decisions within the ambit of the local authority's statutory discretion? I strongly suspect that, if the case were to go to trial, it would eventually fail on this ground since, in essence, the complaint is that the local authority failed to take steps to remove the children from the care of their mother, i.e. negligently failed properly to exercise a discretion which Parliament has conferred on the local authority. But again, it would not be right to strike out the claim on this ground because it is possible that the plaintiffs might be able to demonstrate at trial that the decisions of the local authority were so unreasonable that no reasonable local authority could have reached them and therefore, for the reasons given by Lord Reid in the *Dorset Yacht* case [1970] A.C. 1004, 1031 fall outside the ambit of the discretion conferred by Parliament.

I turn then to consider whether, in accordance with the ordinary principles laid down in the *Caparo* case [1990] 2 A.C. 605, the local authority in the *Bedfordshire* case owed a direct duty of care to the plaintiffs. The local authority accepts that they could foresee damage to the plaintiffs if they carried out their statutory duties negligently and that the relationship between the authority and the plaintiffs is sufficiently proximate. The third requirement laid down in *Caparo* is that it must be just and reasonable to impose a common law duty of care in all the circumstances. It was submitted that this third requirement is only applicable in cases where the plaintiffs' claim is for pure economic loss and that it does not apply where, as in the child abuse cases, the claim is for physical damage. I reject this submission: although *Caparo* and many other of the more recent cases were decisions where only pure economic loss was claimed, the same basic principles apply to claims for physical damage and were applied in, for example, *Hill v Chief Constable of West Yorkshire* [1989] A.C. 53.

Is it, then, just and reasonable to superimpose a common law duty of care on the local authority in relation to the performance of its statutory duties to protect children? In my judgment it is not. Sir Thomas Bingham M.R. took the view, with which I agree, that the public policy consideration which has first claim on the loyalty of the law is that wrongs should be remedied and that very potent counter considerations are required to override that policy [1994] 2 W.L.R. 554, 572F. However, in my judgment there are such considerations in this case.

First, in my judgment a common law duty of care would cut across the whole statutory system set up for the protection of children at risk. As a result of the ministerial directions contained in "Working Together" the protection of such children is not the exclusive territory of the local authority's social services. The system is inter-disciplinary, involving the participation of the police, educational bodies, doctors and others. At all stages the system involves joint discussions, joint recommendations and joint decisions. The key organisation is the Child Protection Conference, a multi-disciplinary body which decides whether to place the child on the Child Protection Register. This procedure by way of joint action takes place, not merely because it is good practice, but because it is required by guidance having statutory force binding on the local authority. The guidance is extremely detailed and extensive: the current edition of "Working Together" runs to 126 pages. To introduce into such a system a common law duty of care enforceable against only one of the participant bodies would be manifestly unfair. To impose such liability on all the participant bodies would lead to almost impossible problems of disentangling as between the respective bodies the liability, both primary and by way of contribution, of each for reaching a decision found to be negligent.

Second, the task of the local authority and its servants in dealing with children at risk is extraordinarily delicate. Legislation requires the local authority to have regard not only to the physical wellbeing of the child but also to the advantages of not disrupting the child's family environment: see, for example, section 17 of the Act of 1989. In one of the child abuse cases, the local authority is blamed for removing the child precipitately: in the other, for failing to remove the children from their mother. As the Report of the Inquiry into Child Abuse in Cleveland 1987 (Cm.412) said, at p.244:

> "It is a delicate and difficult line to tread between taking action too soon and not taking it soon enough. Social services whilst putting the needs of the child first must respect the rights of the parents; they also must work if possible with the parents for the benefit of the children. These parents themselves are often in need of help. Inevitably a degree of conflict develops between those objectives."

Next, if a liability in damages were to be imposed, it might well be that local authorities would adopt a more cautious and defensive approach to their duties. For example, as the Cleveland Report makes clear, on occasions the speedy decision to remove the child is sometimes vital. If the authority is to be made liable in damages for a negligent decision to remove a child (such negligence lying in the failure properly first to investigate the allegations) there would be a substantial temptation to postpone making such a decision until further inquiries have been made in the hope of getting more concrete facts. Not only would the child in fact being abused be prejudiced by such delay: the increased workload inherent in making such investigations would reduce the time available to deal with other cases and other children.

The relationship between the social worker and the child's parents is frequently one of conflict, the parent wishing to retain care of the child, the social worker having to consider whether to remove it. This is fertile ground in which to breed ill feeling and litigation, often hopeless, the cost of which both in terms of money and human resources will be diverted from the performance of the social service for which they were provided. The spectre of vexatious and costly litigation is often urged as a reason for not imposing a legal duty. But the circumstances surrounding cases of child abuse make the risk a very high one which cannot be ignored.

If there were no other remedy for maladministration of the statutory system for the protection of children, it would provide substantial argument for imposing a duty of care. But the statutory complaints procedures contained in section 76 of the Act of 1980 and the much fuller procedures now available under the Act of 1989 provide a means to have grievances investigated, though not to recover compensation. Further, it was submitted (and not controverted) that the local authorities Ombudsman would have power to investigate cases such as these.

Finally, your Lordships' decision in the *Caparo* case [1990] 2 A.C. 605 lays down that, in deciding whether to develop novel categories of negligence the court should proceed incrementally and by analogy with decided categories. We were not referred to any category of case in which a duty of care has been held to exist which is in any way analogous to the present cases. Here, for the first time, the plaintiffs are seeking to erect a common law duty of care in relation to the administration of a statutory social welfare scheme. Such a scheme is designed to protect weaker members of society (children) from harm done to them by others. The scheme involves the administrators in exercising discretions and powers which could not exist in the private sector and which in many cases bring them into conflict with those who, under the general law, are responsible for the child's welfare. To my mind, the nearest analogies are the cases where a common law duty of care has been sought to be imposed upon the police (in seeking to protect vulnerable members of society from wrongs done to them by others) or statutory regulators of financial dealings who are seeking to protect investors from dishonesty. In neither of those cases has it been thought appropriate to superimpose on the statutory regime a common law duty of care giving rise to a claim in damages for failure to protect the weak against the wrongdoer: see *Hill v Chief Constable of West Yorkshire* [1989] A.C. 53 and *Yuen Kun Yeu v Attorney-General of Hong Kong* [1988] A.C. 175. In the latter case, the Privy Council whilst not deciding the point said, at 198, that there was much force in the argument that if the regulators had been held liable in that case the principles leading to such liability "would surely be equally applicable to a wide range of regulatory agencies, not only in the financial field, but also, for example, to the factory inspectorate and social workers, to name only a few". In my judgment, the courts should proceed with great care before holding liable in negligence those who have been charged by Parliament with the task of protecting society from the wrongdoings of others.

Vicarious liability

[His Lordship then dealt with arguments that the defendant authorities were vicariously liable for the negligence of their staff.]

The claim based on vicarious liability is attractive and simple. The normal duty of a doctor to exercise reasonable skill and care is well established as a common law duty of care. In my judgement, the same duty applies to any other person possessed of special skills, such as a social worker. It is said, rightly, that in general such professional duty of care is owed irrespective of contract and can arise even where the professional assumes to act for the plaintiff pursuant to a contract with a third party: *Henderson v Merrett Syndicates Ltd* [1994] 3 W.L.R. 761; *White v Jones* [1995] 2 W.L.R. 187. Therefore, it is said, it is nothing to the point that the social workers and psychiatrist only came into contact with the plaintiffs pursuant to contracts or arrangements made between the professionals and the local authority for the purpose of the discharge by the local authority of its statutory duties. Once brought into contact with the plaintiffs, the professionals owed a duty properly to exercise their professional skills in dealing with their "patients", the plaintiffs. This duty involved the exercise of professional skills in investigating the circumstances of the plaintiffs and (in the *Newham* case) conducting the interview with the child. Moreover, since the professionals could foresee that negligent advice would damage the plaintiffs, they are liable to the plaintiffs for tendering such advice to the local authority.

Like the majority in the Court of Appeal, I cannot accept these arguments. The social workers and the psychiatrists were retained by the local authority to advise the local authority, not the plaintiffs. The subject matter of the advice and activities of the professionals is the child. Moreover the tendering of any advice will in many cases involve interviewing and, in the case of doctors, examining the child. But the fact that the carrying out of the retainer involves contact with and relationship with the child cannot alter the extent of the duty owed by the professionals under the retainer from the local authority. The Court of Appeal drew a correct analogy with the doctor instructed by an insurance company to examine an applicant for life insurance. The doctor does not, by examining the applicant, come under any general duty of medical care to the applicant. He is under a duty not to damage the applicant in the course of the examination: but beyond that his duties are owed to the insurance company and not to the applicant.

The position is not the same as in the case of the purchaser of property who is owed a duty of care by a surveyor instructed by the building society which is going to advance the money: see *Smith v Eric S. Bush* [1990] 1 A.C. 831. In such a case the surveyor is only liable to the purchaser in negligence because he is aware that the purchaser will regulate his (the purchaser's) conduct by completing the purchase in reliance on the survey report. In the child abuse cases, even if the advice tendered by the professionals to the local authority comes to the knowledge of the child or his parents, they will not regulate their conduct in reliance on the report. The effect of the report will be reflected in the way in which the local authority acts.

Nor is the position the same as in *Henderson v Merrett Syndicates Ltd* where, pursuant to a contract with the members' agents, the managing agents undertook the management of the insurance business of the indirect Names. The managing agents were held to be under a tortious duty of care to the indirect Names, notwithstanding that the managing agents were operating under the terms of a contract with a third party. But the duty of care to the Names in that case arose from, and fell within the ambit of, the terms of the retainer contained in the contract between the managing agents and the members' agents. The Names were not seeking to impose on the managing agents any obligation beyond that which the retainer itself required to be performed. So also in *White v Jones* [1995] 2 W.L.R. 187.

In my judgment in the present cases, the social workers and the psychiatrist did not, by accepting the instructions of the local authority, assume any general professional duty of care to the plaintiff children. The professionals were employed or retained to advise the local authority in relation to the well being of the plaintiffs but not to advise or treat the plaintiffs . . . .

Even if, contrary to my view, the social workers and psychiatrist would otherwise have come under a duty of care to the plaintiffs, the same considerations which have led me to the view that there is no direct duty of care owed by the local authorities apply with at least equal force to the question whether it would be just and reasonable to impose such a duty of care on the individual social workers and the psychiatrist.

For these reasons, in my judgment the professionals involved were under no separate duty of care to the plaintiffs for breach of which the local authorities could be vicariously liable.

Witness immunity

[His Lordship then held that the psychiatrist in the *Newham* case was entitled to witness immunity from civil liability under *Watson v M'Ewan; Watson v Jones* [1905] A.C. 480 and *Evans v London Hospital Medical College (University of London)* [1981] 1 W.L.R. 184.]

In the present case, the psychiatrist was instructed to carry out the examination of the child for the specific purpose of discovering whether the child had been sexually abused and (if possible) the identity of the abuser. The psychiatrist must have known that, if such abuse was discovered, proceedings by the local authority for the protection of the child would ensue and that her findings would be the evidence on which those proceedings would be based. It follows in my judgment that such investigations having such an immediate link with possible proceedings in pursuance of a statutory duty cannot be made the basis of subsequent claims.

Although anyone would have great sympathy for the plaintiffs in both these cases (if the allegations which they make are true), for these reasons I agree with the Court of Appeal that they have no private law claim in damages. I would dismiss both appeals.

The Education Cases

The legislation

[His Lordship summarised the relevant statutory provisions. The Education Act 1944 as originally enacted imposed duties on local education authorities to provide sufficient schools having regard to the need to secure the provision of special educational treatment for pupils with any disability of mind or body, and to ascertain what children in their area require such treatment (ss.7, 8, 33, 34, 36). The Education Act 1981 introduced new arrangements whereby authorities were to have regard to the need for securing that special educational provision was made for pupils with special educational needs. Such pupils were to be identified and assessed and, if the authority was of the opinion that it should determine the special educational provision that should be made for them, it was to make a statement of educational needs. If the authority decided not to determine such provision, an appeal lay to the Secretary of State. Similarly, there was a right to appeal against the provision specified in a statement to an appeal committee and then to the Secretary of State (see the 1981 Act, ss.2, 4, 5, 7–9).]

The Dorset case

[His Lordship summarised the facts.]

Common law duty of care—direct

. . . As to the claim based on the negligent failure to comply with the statutory requirements of the Act of 1981, it is in essence a claim that the authority was negligent in the exercise of the statutory discretions conferred on the defendant authority by the Act of 1981. The claim cannot be struck out as being not justiciable. Although it is very improbable, it may be that the exercise of the statutory discretions involved in operating the special needs machinery of the Act of 1981 involved policy decisions. The decision as to what should be included in the statement and what provisoin should be made is, by statute, a decision conferred on the defendant authority. Therefore, even if such decisions were made carelessly, the claim will fail unless the plaintiff can show that the decisions were so careless that no reasonable education authority could have reached them. Again, although it seems most improbable that this requirement can be satisfied, it is impossible to be certain until all the facts are known. Therefore the claim cannot be struck out at this stage on the grounds that it is not justiciable or the acts complained of fell within the statutory discretion.

The question, then, is whether it is right to superimpose on the statutory machinery for the investigation and treatment of the plaintiff's special educational needs a duty of care to exercise the statutory discretions carefully? I find this a difficult question on which my views have changed from time to time. In favour of imposing a duty of care is the fact that it was plainly foreseeable that if the powers were exercised carelessly a child with special educational needs might be harmed in the sense that he would not obtain the advantage that the statutory provisions were designed to provide for him. Further, for the reasons that I have given, a common law duty of care in the exercise of statutory discretions can only arise in relation to an authority which has decided an issue so carelessly that no reasonable authority could have reached that decision. Why, it may be asked, should such a grossly delinquent authority escape liability? However, I have reached the conclusion that, powerful though those considerations may be, they are outweighed by other factors.

First, in relation to the special statutory duties imposed by sections 2, 4, 5 and 7 of the Act of 1981, the exercise of the discretions involves the close participation of the parents who are themselves under a duty to cause the child to receive "efficient full-time education suitable to his . . . . ability and aptitude": section 36 of the Education Act 1944. The parents are themselves involved in the process of decision making and can appeal against decisions which they think to be erroneous. Although in the *Dorset* case the parents availed themselves of all the advantages of the statutory machinery, in the generality of cases to allow either the parents (on behalf of the child) or the child when he attains his majority to bring a claim alleging negligence by the authority in the making of the decision would be to duplicate remedies. Although in the present case this factor is not directly in point, if a duty of care is to be held to exist it must apply as much in relation to actions brought by a parent or child who has not used the statutory machinery as in the case of parents or a child who have.

Next, the number of cases which could successfully be brought for breach of such a duty of care would be very small since, as I have said, it would have to be shown that the decision impugned was taken so carelessly that no authority could have reached it. Yet, if a common law duty of care is held to exist, there is a very real risk that many hopeless (and possibly vexatious) cases will be brought, thereby exposing the authority to great expenditure of time and money in their defence. If there were no other remedy open, this is a price which might have to be paid in the interests of justice. But, in almost every case which could give rise to a claim for the negligent exercise of the statutory discretions, it is probable that, as in the present case, there will be an alternative remedy by way of a claim against the authority on the grounds of its vicarious liability for the negligent advice on the basis of which it exercises its discretion: as to which see below.

We were not referred to any category of case by analogy with which, in accordance with the *Caparo* principles [1990] 2 A.C. 605, it would be right to impose a direct duty of care on the authority in the exercise of its statutory discretions. . . .

In my judgment, as in the child abuse cases, the courts should hesitate long before imposing a common law duty of care in the exercise of discretionary powers or duties conferred by Parliament for social welfare purposes. The aim of the Act of 1981 was to provide, for the benefit of society as a whole, an administrative machinery to help one disadvantaged section of society. The statute provides its own detailed machinery for securing that the statutory purpose is performed. If, despite the complex machinery for consultation and appeals contained in the Act, the scheme fails to provide the benefit intended that is a matter more appropriately remedied by way of the Ombudsman looking into the administrative failure than by way of litigation.

For these reasons I reach the conclusion that an education authority owes no common law duty of care in the exercise of the powers and discretions relating to children with special educational needs specifically conferred on them by the Act of 1981.

I turn then to the other duty of care which, it is alleged, the defendant authority owes directly to the plaintiff. There the position is wholly different. The claim is based on the fact that the authority is offering a service (psychological advice) to the public. True it is that, in the absence of a statutory power or duty, the authority could not offer such a service. But once the decision is taken to offer such a service, a statutory body is in general in the same position as any private individual or organisation holding itself out as offering such a service. By opening its doors to others to take advantage of the service offered, it comes under a duty of care to those using the service to exercise care in its conduct. The position is directly analogous with a hospital conducted, formerly by a local authority now by a health authority, in exercise of statutory powers. In such a case the authority running the hospital is under a duty to those whom it admits to exercise reasonable care in the way it runs it: see *Gold v Essex County Council* [1942] 2 K.B. 293.

For these reasons, I can see no ground on which it can be said at this stage that the defendant authority, in providing a psychology service, could not have come under a duty of care to the plaintiff who, through his parents, took advantage of that service. It may well be that when the facts are fully investigated at trial it may emerge that, for example, the alleged psychology service was merely part and parcel of the system established by the defendant authority for the discharge of its statutory duties under the Act of 1981. If so, it may be that the existence and scope of the direct duty owed by the defendant authority will have to be excluded or limited so as not to impede the due performance by the authority of its statutory duties. But at this stage it is impossible to say that the claim under this head must fail.

Common law duty of care—vicarious

The claim is that the educational psychologists and other members of the staff of the defendant authority owed a duty to use reasonable professional skill and care in the assessment and determination of the plaintiff's educational needs. It is further alleged that the plaintiff's parents relied on the advice of such professionals. The defendant authority is vicariously liable for any breach of such duties by their employees.

Again, I can see no ground for striking out this claim at least in relation to the educational psychologists. Psychologists hold themselves out as having special skills and they are, in my judgment, like any other professional bound both to possess such skills and to exercise them carefully. Of course, the test in *Bolam v Friern Hospital Management Committee* [1957] 1 W.L.R. 582 will apply to them, *i.e.* they are only bound to exercise the ordinary skill of a competent psychologist and if they can show that they acted in accordance with the accepted views of some reputable psychologist at the relevant time they will have discharged the duty of care, even if other psychologists would have adopted a different view. In the context of advice on the treatment of dyslexia, a subject on which views have changed over the years, this may be an important factor. But that said, I can see no ground on which, at this stage, the existence of a professional duty of care can be ruled out. The position of other members of the defendant's staff is not as clear, but I would not at this stage strike out the claims relating to them.

The position of the psychologists in the education cases is quite different from that of the doctor and social worker in the child abuse cases. There is no potential conflict of duty between the professional's duties to the plaintiff and his duty to the educational authority. Nor is there any obvious conflict between the professional being under a duty of care to the plaintiff and the discharge by the authority of its statutory duties. If, at trial, it emerges that there are such conflicts, then the trial judge may have to limit or exclude any duty of care owed by the professional to the plaintiff. But at this stage no obvious conflict has been demonstrated.

Finally, the defendant authority submitted that the damage claimed, being the cost of providing alternative fee paying education for the plaintiff, is not recoverable. In my view it is not appropriate to decide this point at the striking out stage: the matter will be better resolved at trial when the true facts are known.

My conclusion therefore in the *Dorset* case is that the defendant authority is under no liability at common law for the negligent exercise of the statutory discretions conferred on them by the Education Acts 1944 to 1981, but could be liable, both directly and vicariously, for negligence in the operation of the psychology service and negligent advice given by its officers.

The Hampshire case

The facts
[His Lordship stated the facts and held that the common law recognised a duty of care owed by a head teacher and an educational advisor to a pupil. There was no incompability between such a duty and the existence of the

statutory special educational needs scheme. The authority would be vicariously liable for the negligence of such teachers in advising on and meeting the educational needs of pupils. The claim would be amended to allege that the failure to treat the plaintiff's dyslexia cause psychological damage sufficiently serious to constitute an identifiable mental illness. The claim should not be struck out.]

The Bromley case

[His Lordship stated the facts and held (1) that breaches of s.8 of the Education Act 1944 (duty to provide sufficient schools) or the 1944 Act provisions concerning special educational treatment and the 1981 Act provisions (summarised above at p.1057) did not give rise to a civil action; (2) as in the *Dorset* case, there was no common law duty of care in relation to the exercise of statutory discretions under the 1944 and 1981 Acts; and (3) possible claims based on vicarious liability for the negligence of one or more professionals employed by the authority should not be struck out.]

Appeals in the Bedfordshire and Newham cases dismissed; appeals in the Dorset and Bromley cases allowed in part; appeal in the Hampshire case and cross-appeal in the Bromley case dismissed.

Notes and questions
   1. This landmark decision on the liability of public authorities for breach of statutory duty and negligence throws much light on the relevant issues. At the same time, some parts of the picture remained clouded or were plunged further into darkness. Particularly helpful are the discussion of breach of statutory duty, the point that liability in negligence must be based on a common law duty of care and the open and full discussion of the policy arguments for and against imposition of a duty of care. More problematic is the failure to consider the point that some of the matters of which complaint were made were omissions and the dicta concerning the approach to be made to discretionary decisions. It is remarkable that a short time later these matters received the full attention of a differently composed House of Lords in *Stovin v Wise, Norfolk CC (Third Party)* (below, pp.1073–1090) (only Lord Jauncey of Tullichettle sat on both appeals). The task of reconciling the two decisions is not straightforward (see below, p.1087). Furthermore, further clarification has been required through yet more decisions of the House of Lords.
   2. *Breach of statutory duty.* Following *X (Minors) v Bedfordshire CC*, the potential scope of civil liability for breaches of statutory duties placed on public authorities is extremely narrow. There are a few situations where a duty is recognised. For example, in *Refell v Surrey CC* [1964] 1 W.L.R. 358, Veale J. held the council liable both at common law and for breach of its duty under the Education Act 1944, s.10, to secure that school premises complied with standards prescribed by regulations, and under the relevant regulation[7] that required the design, construction and properties of materials to be such that the health and safety of the occupants "shall be reasonably assured", where a pupil put her hand through a glass panel in a cloakroom door made of ⅛-inch non-toughened glass. This can be seen to be closely analogous to cases where breach of health and safety regulations made for the protection of factory workers and the like have been held to give rise to civil actions, and the decision is not inconsistent with the principles stated in *X (Minors) v Bedfordshire CC*. Both before and after *X (Minors) v Bedfordshire CC*, the courts have regularly held that breaches of statutory duties placed on public authorities do not give rise to civil claims.

---

[7] Standards for School Premises Regulations 1959 (SI 1959/890), reg.51.

See, *e.g. Wyatt v Hillingdon LBC* (1978) 76 L.G.R. 727 (duty under the Chronically Sick and Disabled Persons Act 1970; remedy for breach provided by ministerial default power); *R. v Deputy Governor of Parkhurst Prison Ex p. Hague* [1992] 1 A.C. 58 (breach of Prison Rules held not to give rise to action for breach of statutory duty *Church of Jesus Christ of Latter Day Saints (Great Britain) v West Yorkshire Fire and Civil Defence Authority* [1997] Q.B. 1004; *O'Rourke v Camden LBC* [1998] A.C. 188 (homelessness legislation; the House overruled *Thornton v Kirklees MBC* [1979] Q.B. 626); *Bowden v South West Water Services* [1998] Env. L.R. 445 (the "regulatory code" established by the Water Industry Act 1991 and the Water Resources Act 1991) The caution of the court in this area is understandable given that liability for breach of statutory duty where it does apply is established simply by demonstrating non-compliance. Such caution is less justifiable where a statutory duty is itself one requiring the exercise of care (*cf. Sephton v Lancashire River Board* [1962] 1 W.L.R. 623).

3. *Negligence: policy.* Lord Browne-Wilkinson advances a series of policy arguments against imposition of a duty of care in both the child abuse and the education cases. Are you convinced? How many of them could apply as arguments justifying an immunity from negligence liability for doctors (whether employed publicly or privately)? Do you agree that these arguments are not valid as regards the teachers and psychologists against whom actions proceeded?

The argument in *Home Office v Dorset Yacht Co. Ltd* [1970] A.C. 1004 in support of an immunity based on policy grounds received short shrift from Lord Reid (at 1032–1033):

"Finally I must deal with public policy. It is argued that it would be contrary to public policy to hold the Home Office or its officers liable to a member of the public for this carelessness— or, indeed, any failure of duty on their part. The basic question is: who shall bear the loss caused by that carelessness—the innocent respondents or the Home Office, who are vicariously liable for the conduct of their careless officers? I do not think that the argument for the Home Office can be put better than it was put by the Court of Appeals of New York in *Williams v State of New York* (1955) 127 N.E. 2d 545, 550:

'. . . . public policy also requires that the State be not held liable. To hold otherwise would impose a heavy responsibility upon the State, or dissuade the wardens and principal keepers of our prison system from continued experimentation with "minimum security" work details—which provide a means for encouraging better-risk prisoners to exercise their senses of responsibility and honor and so prepare themselves for their eventual return to society. Since 1917, the legislature has expressly provided for out-of-prison work, Correction Law, §182, and its intention should be respected without fostering the reluctance of prison officials to assign eligible men to minimum security work, lest they thereby give rise to costly claims against the State, or indeed inducing the State itself to terminate this "salutary procedure" looking toward rehabilitation.'

It may be that public servants of the State of New York are so apprehensive, easily dissuaded from doing their duty and intent on preserving public funds from costly claims that they could be influenced in this way. But my experience leads me to believe that Her Majesty's servants are made of sterner stuff. So I have no hesitation in rejecting this argument. I can see no good ground in public policy for giving this immunity to a government department".

Notwithstanding this, the decision here that there were sufficient policy reasons to exclude a duty of care is echoed in much of the case law. Examples include the following:

(a) regulatory authorities: *Yuen Kun Yeu v Att-Gen of Hong Kong* [1988] A.C. 175 (Commissioner of Deposit-taking Companies in Hong Kong held not to owe a duty of care to potential depositors); *Minories Finance Ltd v Arthur*

Young (a Firm) (Bank of England, Third Party) [1989] 2 All E.R. 105 (Bank of England held not to be under a legal obligation to an individual commercial bank to exercise reasonable care and skill in carrying out its function of supervising the operation of commercial banks); *Davies v Radcliffe* [1990] 1 W.L.R. 821, RC). See H. McLean, "Negligent Regulatory Authorities and the Duty of Care" (1988) 8 O.J.L.S. 442; *cf.* the *Three Rivers* case below, p.1090.

(b) local authorities: *Ephraim v Newham LBC* (1992) 25 H.L.R. 207 (council not liable in respect of injuries suffered by E in a fire at a bed-and-breakfast establishment; E was homeless and had been advised to go there by the council as housing authority, but the essence of the complaint was a failure to inspect the premises and it was not fair, just and reasonable for a duty of care to be owed); *Chung Tak Lam v Brennan and Torbay BC* [1997] 3 P.L.R. 22 (no duty of care owed in the exercise of non-exercise of planning and environmental functions); followed in *Gribler v Harrow LBC* [2000] E.H.L.R. 188.

(c) health authority: *Martine v South East Kent HA, The Times*, March 8, 1993 (authority owed no duty of care in respect of an investigation into a registered nursing home);

(d) police: *Hill v Chief Constable of West Yorkshire* [1989] A.C. 59 (House of Lords held that the police did not owe a duty of care to individual members of the public to identify and apprehend an unknown criminal, even though it was reasonably foreseeable that harm was likely to be caused); *Calveley v Chief Constable of the Merseyside Police* [1989] A.C. 1228 (the House held that police investigating a possible crime did not owe a duty of care to the suspect):

"... it would plainly be contrary to public policy, in my opinion, to prejudice the fearless and efficient discharge by police officers of their vitally important public duty of investigating crime by requiring them to act under the shadow of a potential action for damages for negligence by the suspect" (per Lord Bridge at 1238);

Clough v Bussan [1990] 1 All E.R. 431 (claim in respect of alleged police failure to respond quickly where traffic lights became defective struck out); *Ancell v McDermott* [1993] 4 All E.R. 355 (claim in respect of alleged police failure to deal adequately with traffic hazard resulting from spillage of oil leading to fatal accident struck out); *Alexandrou v Oxford* [1993] 4 All E.R. 328 (claim in respect of allegedly negligent response to burglar alarm dismissed); *Osman v Ferguson* [1993] 4 All E.R. 344 (claim in respect of alleged police failure to prevent a person known to have threatened P from injuring him struck out; see J. Steele and D.S. Cowan, [1994] P.L. 4). But *cf. Swinney v Chief Constable of the Northumbria Police* [1996] 3 All E.R. 449 (arguable that police owe a duty of care to informant to keep the confidential information supplied, including the informant's identity, secure); and see *Osman v UK*, below, p.1069. The core principle of *Hill* was approved by the House of Lords in *Brooks v Commissioner of police of the Metropolis* [2005] 1 W.L.R. 1495.

(e) fire service: *John Munroe (Acrylics) Ltd v London Fire and Civil Defence Authority* [1997] Q. B. 983 (no sufficient proximity between fire brigade and owner of premises which might be ablaze to give rise to a duty to respond to a call for assistance; also contrary to public policy for such a duty to be recognised; once the fire brigade did respond, it would only be liable if it undertook a personal responsibility to some individual during the course of its activity); *Church of Jesus Christ of Latter-Day Saints (Great Britain) v Yorkshire Fire & Civil Defence Authority, The Times*, May 9, 1996 (contrary to public policy for duty of care to be recognised arising out of failure to take reasonable steps to ensure an adequate supply of water at the scene of a fire); *cf. Capital & Counties Plc v Hampshire CC* [1996] 1 W.L.R. 1553 (fire brigade liable where officer negligently ordered sprinkler system in a burning building to be turned off; no public policy immunity). In *Stovin v Wise* (below, p.1073), Lord Hoffmann doubted whether a duty should be owed. The Court of Appeal dismissed appeals in the *London, Yorkshire* and *Hampshire* cases: [1997] Q.B. 1004. But compare the decision in *Kent v Griffiths* [2001] Q.B. 36, where the Court of Appeal held that a duty of care is owed by the ambulance service once a 999 call is accepted. Why the ambulance service should be treated differently from the fire service is not obvious.

(f) others: *Jones v Department of Employment* [1989] Q.B. 1 (adjudication officer owes no duty of care to benefit claimant is deciding whether to allow a claim); *Philcox v Civil Aviation Authority, The Times*, June 8, 1995 (CAA owes no duty of care to owners of aircraft to ensure they maintained them properly); *Skinner v Secretary of State for Transport, The Times*, January 3, 1995 (coastguard owes no duty of care to mariner); *Elguzouli-Daf v Commissioner of Police of the Metropolis* [1995] Q.B. 335 (Crown Prosecution Service owed no duty of care to defendant save where it assumes by conduct responsibility to a particular person); *W v Home Office* [1997] lmm.A.R. 302 (no duty of care owed by immigration officer as regards detention decisions). Cases where a person is released from detention by the defendant's decision (as from prison or from detention under the Immigration Act 1971 or the Mental Health Act 1983) kills or injures a third party normally fail for lack of proximity between defendant and victim (*Palmer v Tees HA* (2000) 2 L.G.L.R. 69; *K v Secretary of State for the Home Department* [2002] EWCA Civ 775; *cf. Home Office v Dorset Yacht Co.* [1970] A.C. 1004 (duty of care owed, by officers in charge of young offenders who allowed them to escape, to owners of property in the immediate vicinity damaged by the offenders during the escape).

It will be noted that many of these cases concern alleged failures to protect the plaintiff from harm caused by third parties or (sometimes) by themselves. As explained by Lord Hoffmann in *Stovin v Wise* (below, p.1073), there are good reasons why it is less appropriate for such omissions to lead to civil liability than positive acts which cause harm.

Recurrent themes in the reasoning to justify the exclusion of a duty include fears that actual litigation would divert officials and resources from more useful tasks and that the fear of litigation would inappropriately inhibit proper decision-making; the existence of alternative remedies; and the fact that if a public authority (with a bottomless purse) is always available as a defendant, it may end up footing the entire bill notwithstanding that the major cause of harm to the plaintiff is another party (now bankrupt).

More recently, decisions of the European Court of Human Rights and domestic courts (in the light of and under the Human Rights Act 1998) have modified the position taken in *X (Minors) v Bedfordshire CC* (see below, pp.1069–1073).

4. *Negligence: discretion.* It is widely accepted that the courts should be particularly cautious before holding that an exercise (or non-exercise) of a statutory discretionary power should lead to liability in negligence for damages. In particular, decisions as to the allocation of limited resources may be made by elected bodies (or by expert agencies accountable to such bodies) with the appropriate mechanism for redress for those injured or disadvantaged by such decisions being through the ballot box rather than through an action for damages. This has given rise to two broad schools of thought. The first sees the need for there to be an immunity in respect of those acts or omissions that can be said to be *policy* decisions; the *operational* implementation of a policy decision then may or may not give rise to liability depending on the circumstances. The second regards this distinction as unworkable and unnecessary, the ordinary principles governing the imposition of the duty of care and, equally importantly, breach of duty are sufficiently sensitive and flexible to ensure that full account is taken of the legitimate interests of public authorities. Curiously, the first of these schools of thought is exemplified by the dicta of Lord Browne-Wilkinson in *X (Minors) v Bedfordshire CC*, and the second by the House of Lords (both majority and minority) in *Stovin v Wise* (below, pp.1073–1090). For further discussion, see below, p.1087.

5. *Negligence: recognised areas of liability.* There are, of course, many situations where the existence of a duty of care is well established and applied to public authorities without more ado. Accidents involving vehicles owned by public authorities are dealt with by the application of ordinary principles (which may admittedly include in the consideration of whether there is a breach of duty reference to the nature of the object to be achieved (*Watt v Hertfordshire CC* [1954] 1 W.L.R. 835)). Local authorities and teachers may owe a duty of care in respect of the physical safety of children in their schools (*Carmarthenshire CC v Lewis* [1955] A.C. 549). Similarly, a local authority may be liable where children in care are physically abused by employees of the authority (*Lister v Hesley Hall Ltd* [2002] 1 A.C. 215 (vicarious liability); *C v Flintshire CC* [2001] EWCA Civ 302; [2001] 2 F.L.R. 33 (breach of direct duty of care). Public authorities as occupiers of land are subject to the Occupiers' Liability Acts 1957 and 1984 (see W.V.H Rogers, *Winfield and Jolowicz on Tort* (16th ed., 2002), Ch.9. Local authorities may be held liable in respect of psychiatric damage to employees caused by stress at work (see *Walker v Northumberland CC; Barber v Somerset CC* [2004] UKHL 13). Public authorities may be liable directly or vicariously for negligence in the performance of professional services, as discussed in *X (Minors) v Bedfordshire CC* itself (above, pp.1055–1057, 1060; n.6 below). They may by their conduct assume responsibility towards individuals, a possibility discussed by Lord Hoffmann in *Stovin v Wise*, below, pp.1074, 1082–1084. More recently, there have been a number of cases outside these established areas of liability where the courts have demonstrated a greater willingness to contemplate a duty of care in the performance of statutory functions, and a concomitant scepticism as to the validity or applicability of the kinds of policy arguments adopted by Lord Browne-Wilkinson in *X (Minors) v Bedfordshire CC*. Among cases where actions have not been struck out are *W v Essex CC* [1999] Fam. 90 and [2001] 2 A.C. 592 (allegation that social worker failed to pass on information to foster parents that foster child was a sexual abuser, the foster child then abusing the foster parents' own children); *Barrett v Enfield LBC* [2001] 2 A.C. 550 (arguable that duty of care was owed by a local authority to a child once it was in the authority's care); *S v Gloucestershire CC; L v Tower Hamlets LBC* [2001] Fam. 313 (action against local authority in respect of alleged child abuse by foster parents); *L (A child) v Reading BC* [2001] EWCA Civ 246, [2001] 1 W.L.R. 1575 (claims by alleged victim of child abuse and the alleged perpetrator (the victim's father) against social worker and police officer alleging use of oppressive interviewing techniques. The first three actions were direct actions against the local authority; the fourth was based on an assumption of responsibility of the officers). Nevertheless, identifying the line between areas where negligence is actionable and those where it is not is problematic. It is not, for example, possible to identify situations where a public authority acts in a private capacity as candidates for the application of ordinary principles. First, all the powers of public authorities other than the Crown must be referable expressly or impliedly to statute. Secondly, legal burdens placed by ordinary law on the supposedly *private* activities of a public authority will have at least an indirect impact on the way it performs its *public* functions (*ex hypothesi*, the authority's *raison d'être*). Thirdly, the case law on the ambit of judicial review and the scope of the HRA (pp.316–317, 938–957) demonstrates the difficulty of drawing a line between "public" and "private" at both the institutional and functional levels, especially given the context where apparently public functions are increasingly discharged by bodies independent of government.

It is also not the case that the distinction between acts and omissions (discussed in *Stovin v Wise*, below, pp.1073–1091 is the touchstone of liability. On the one hand, the public policy arguments against liability may apply in cases where an authority's acts have caused harm as (on the assumed facts) in *X (Minors) v Bedfordshire CC*). Conversely, there are some situations where the common law of negligence recognises positive obligations to act for the benefit of another (see Lord Hoffmann, below, pp.1074, 1082).

6. *Negligent misstatement and the negligent performance of professional services.* Negligent misstatements that give rise to physical damage may lead to liability on

ordinary principles (see the discussion in *X (Minors) v Bedfordshire CC* (above, p.1046). The House of Lords in *Hedley Byrne & Co Ltd v Heller and Partners Ltd* [1964] A.C. 465 recognised that a duty of care could arise in respect of such mis-statements that caused economic loss. However, the defendant will only be liable where he knows that his statement will be communicated to the plaintiff, either as an individual or as a member of an identifiable class, specifically in connection with a particular transaction or kind of transaction, and that the plaintiff would be very likely to rely on it for the purpose of deciding whether to enter that transaction or kind of transaction (Lord Bridge in *Caparo Products Plc v Dickman* [1990] 1 All E.R. 568, 576). In *Henderson v Merrett Syndicates* [1995] 2 A.C. 145, the House stated that the *Hedley Byrne* principle extended beyond the provision of information and advice to cover assumptions of responsibility for the performance of services for the plaintiff (see Lord Goff at 180–181).

Public authorities have been held liable for negligent statements and other acts that cause economic loss to the plaintiff (*Coats Paton (Retail) Ltd v Birmingham Corp.* (1971) 69 L.G.R. 356 (negligent answer to enquiries before purchase of a shop); *Ministry of Housing and Local Government v Sharp* [1970] 2 Q.B. 223 (negligent search of local land charges register); *Harris v Wyre Forest DC* [1990] 1 A.C. 831 (negligent house survey); *Welton v North Cornwall DC* [1997] 1 W.L.R. 570 (environmental health officer negligently required owners of food premises to undertake works which were, in fact, unnecessary); *Lambert v West Devon BC, The Times*, March 27, 1997 (negligent advice by building control officer that L could proceed with building works). By contrast, in *Tidman v Reading BC* [1994] 3 P.L.R. 72, Buxton J. held that a response by council officers to an *informal*, telephoned planning inquiry by a member of the public did not give rise to a duty of care.

An important area where a duty of care had been found to exist, although breach of duty has been difficult to establish, is that of the failure of professionals (teachers, educational psychologists and education officers) to diagnose or act on a school child's dyslexia or other learning difficulties. This was recognised by the House of Lords in *Phelps v Hillingdon LBC; Anderton v Clwyd CC; Re G (a minor); Jarvis v Hampshire CC* [2001] 2 A.C. 619. In *Phelps*, the House restored the order of Garland J., holding that the council was vicariously liable for the negligence of an educational psychologist in failing to diagnose dyslexia, in circumstances where the psychologist was to be taken as having assumed responsibility towards the claimants. While there was no cause of action for breach of statutory duty, there could be liability in negligence. There was no reason to hold that the matter was non-justiciable; the fact that a duty was owed to the council did not exclude the possibility that a duty was also owed to the claimant; the fact that the psychologist was called in pursuant to the council's statutory duties did not mean that a professional *Hedley Byrne* duty of care could not arise; such a duty would prima facie arise where an educational psychologist was specifically called in to advise in relation to the assessment and future provision for a child, and it was clear that the child's parents and teachers would follow that advice (Lord Slynn at 654). Lord Nicholls (at 666) also emphasised the point that "the child was very dependent upon the expert's assessment" and "was in a singularly vulnerable position". Where the psychologist's negligence led to physical or psychological harm, the latter could constitute damage for the purpose of the common law, as could

> "a failure to diagnose a congenital condition and to take appropriate action as a result of which failure a child's level of achievement is reduced (which leads to loss of employment and wages)" (Lord Slynn at 664).

There was no reason of public policy why the council in such a case should not be vicariously liable: recognition of the duty of care would not of itself impose unreasonably high standards; the fact that some claims might be without foundation or exaggerated did not mean that valid claims should necessarily be excluded. The judge had been entitled to find the existence of a duty of care, breach, causation and damage established.

There was on the facts no case based on a direct duty of care owed by the authority, but no reason why such a duty could not arise in a proper case, as where psychologists or other professionals were appointed who at the outset were neither qualified nor competent to carry out duties with respect to children with special educational needs. The decision of the Court of Appeal in *G v Bromley LBC* not to strike out was upheld; the decision in *Jarvis v Hampshire CC* to strike out was overturned, the issues of both vicarious and direct liability being arguable. In *Anderton v Clywd CC*, the House, reversing the decision of the Court of Appeal, held that the damage flowing from a failure to diagnose dyslexia could constitute "personal injury" for the purpose of pre-action discovery under s.33(2) of the Supreme Court Act 1981.

The nature of the damage in cases concerning a negligent failure to diagnose dyslexia has been the subject for further consideration by the Court of Appeal in *Robinson v St Helens MBC* [2002] EWCA Civ 1099; [2002] E.L.R. 681. The court held that the House of Lords in *Phelps* recognised a cause of action where the failure to diagnose foreseeably led to:

"damage in the sense of economic loss (stemming, for instance, from the failure of a child to achieve the level of educational attainment reasonably to be expected) and/or to damage in the sense of emotional or psychological harm which would usually fall short of developing into a recognisable psychiatric injury" (*per* Brooke L.J. at [36]).

Where the latter head of damage was alleged, but not the former, this constituted "personal injury" for the purpose of the application of the law of limitation, the relevant limitation period accordingly being three years from (a) the date of which the cause of action accrued or (b) the date of knowledge of the person concerned (Limitation Act 1980, s.11). The claim was accordingly time-barred, and the court refused to interfere with the judge's refusal to exercise his discretion (under the 1980 Act, s.33) to override the usual limitation rules.

In *Adams v Bracknell Forest BC* [2004] UKHL 29, the House of Lords confirmed the decision in *Robinson* that a claim in respect of a negligent failure to ameliorate the consequences of dyslexia was a claim in respect of personal injury for the purposes of s.11 of the Limitation Act 1980 (s.38(1) of the Act defining "personal injuries" as including ". . . any impairment of a person's physical or mental condition"). Lord Hoffmann cited passages from the judgments of Sir Thomas Bingham M.R, and Evans L.J. in *E (A Minor) v Dorset CC* [1995] 2 A.C. 633 at 703, 706, noting (at [10]) that they:

"were treating the claim as being for a mental disability (not being able to read and write properly) which ought to have been ameliorated but was allowed to persist. Such a claim in a post-Cartesian world is for personal injury and gives rise to a claim for general damages and, by way of special damages, any consequential economic loss such as loss of earnings or the need to pay for remedial treatment".

The award of damages restored by the House of Lords in *Phelps* could in Lord Hoffmann's opinion "be justified only on the basis that the claim was for a personal injury consisting in the lack of ability to read and write" at para.[18]. Furthermore, the reasoning in *Anderton* in respect of s.33(2) of the Supreme Court Act 1981 was equally applicable to s.11 of the 1980 Act. Finally, Lord Hoffmann stated (at para.[20]) that it would be no answer for the authority to argue that the lack of ability to read and write was caused by a congenital brain defect that could not itself be cured; there were steps that could be taken to ameliorate the effects of dyslexia by training other parts of the brain to compensate, and a negligent failure to take such steps could be actionable. Lord Phillips of Worth Matravers, Lord Walker of Gestingthorpe and Baroness Hale of Richmond agreed with Lord Hoffmann. Lord Scott of Foscote, however, held that the deprivation of the benefit of literacy was not in itself an impairment of a physical or mental state, although the consequential panic attacks, social phobia and depression might well be regarded as impairments of the mental state of the sufferer.

With the acceptance of the existence of a duty of care in cases of this kind, usually involving professional defendants for whom the public authority is vicariously liable, more attention has been paid to issues of breach of duty. The courts have confirmed that such a defendant is entitled to the benefit of the test for breach of duty set out in *Bolam v Friern Hospital Management Committee* [1957] 1 W.L.R. 582 under which a professional defendant is not liable if he or she acts in accordance with a practice accepted at the time as proper by a responsible body of professional opinion even though there is a body of competent professional opinion that would take a different view. Furthermore, the Court of Appeal in *Carty v Croydon LBC* [2005] EWCA Civ 19, in the course of holding that an education officer did owe a duty of care in dealing with a child with special educational needs, but had not breached that duty, held that:

> "the nature of the statutory function and the difficulty of decisions such as the assessment of the needs of a child with special educational needs and the determination of the special provision that should be made are such that a court will only hold that it is fair, just and reasonable to impose a duty of care to avoid decisions that are plainly and obviously wrong" (*per* Dyson L.J. at para.[43]).

There is much to be said for this approach, which is broader than *Bolam*. Given the clear difficulties of establishing breach of duty in these cases (the dyslexia cases in particular requiring the investigation of decisions taken many years earlier), it is right that the courts should signal clearly that it will only be worthwhile pursuing the clearest of cases. Whether this is a different test from unreasonableness (*cf.* the concept of gross unreasonableness) or an application of the ordinary, flexible test of unreasonableness in particular contexts is not clear. The disadvantage of introducing a distinct test is that it will involve establishing a hard line around those cases that are subject to it, which will be both difficult to do, and wasteful of costs.

7. Liability in negligence for maladministration. The cases in this section show that the courts have generally taken the position that public authorities do not owe a duty of care when making decisions to exercise or not to exercise a statutory power. What the position is where losses are caused by acknowledged mistakes in implementing decisions is less clear. It is commonly stated that there is no general right of reparation for maladministration. However, Keith J. in *R. (on the application of A) v Secretary of State for the Home Department* [2004] EWHC 1585 held that the Secretary of State did owe a duty of care in the administrative implementation of immigration decisions. The assumed facts of the first of two joined cases concerning asylum seekers were that indefinite leave to remain was given to A, but the terms of the entry clearance granted mistakenly prohibited her from having any recourse to public funds. This was not intended, and prevented her claiming welfare benefits. The mistake was drawn to the Secretary of State's attention but it took over a year for it to be corrected. There was no provision for the retrospective payment of benefits by the DWP, the DWP's scheme for the payment *ex gratia* of compensation for mistakes did not apply where the error was that of the Secretary of State, and the Ombudsman did not have jurisdiction as proceedings for judicial review had been started.

In the other case, the Secretary of State granted K exceptional leave to remain but failed for some eight months to send the "status letter" reflecting this decision that K needed in order to claim benefits. Keith J. rejected the argument that the absence of a general power to backdate benefits showed that Parliament must have intended that liability to pay compensation should not be imposed even if mistakes had resulted in those benefits not being paid. The regulations did provide for the backdating of some payments in defined circumstances without proof of fault; this did not indicate a Parliamentary intention to exclude negligence cases. His Lordship then applied the *Caparo* principles and concluded that a duty of care was owed. The Secretary of State would have been aware of the effect maladministration would certainly have on the claimants; the mistakes were purely administrative in nature; in the absence of the imposition of liability, the claimant would be left without a remedy; there had not merely been an omission, but the carrying out of an action so imperfectly that the officials had not managed to achieve the results they had intended; it was not contended that the matter was not justiciable; the relationship was proximate (distinguishing *Stovin v Wise* (below) where the duty of care contended for and rejected was owed to all members of the public who found themselves at the junction in question); and it was fair, just and reasonable for a duty of care to be owed.

Under this last heading, the judge held that judicial review was not an adequate alternative remedy (it would not provide compensation for lost benefits); imposition of a duty of care would not hamper the effective performance of the system of immigration control (it would indeed enhance public confidence in the system); it was unlikely that the "floodgates" would be significantly opened. His Lordship distinguished *W v Home Office* [1997] Imm. A.R. 302, where the Court of Appeal held that no duty of care was owed by the Home Office where administrative errors led to a decision refusing to release W from detention pending consideration of his claim for asylum being based on the wrong evidence (poor answers to a test of his knowledge of the country of which he claimed to be a citizen) that had been taken by someone else and wrongly put in his file. Keith J. held that this was different as here the errors followed the relevant exercise of judgment rather than causing it.

Notwithstanding Keith J.'s view, this decision does potentially open up a significant new head of liability. As relatively small sums are at stake, the case seems eminently suitable for consideration by the Ombudsman, whose jurisdiction should be made more flexible. Furthermore, the limitation of the DWP's compensation scheme to the correction of its own errors seems to indicate a lack of the "joined-up" government that the Labour Government has committed itself to provide.

In the view of some judges, it is still part of the law that there must be an inquiry "whether even if justiciable, [the matter] involves the exercise of a statutory discretion which only gives rise to liability in tort if it is so unreasonable that it falls outside the ambit of the discretion" separate from the inquiry as to whether it is fair, just and reasonable to impose a duty of care (see Hale L.J. in *A v Essex CC* [2003] EWCA Civ 1848; [2004] 1 W.L.R. 1881 at [33], based on Lord Browne-Wilkinson in *X (Minors) v Bedfordshire CC*). It is submitted that this is based on a misapplication of the defence of statutory authority, which is only available where the authority to commit what would otherwise be a tort is clear and precise (see above, p.1040). Preference for a simpler approach was expressed by Dyson L.J. in *Carty v Croydon LBC* [2005] EWCA Civ 19 at [28], suggesting that there should only be two areas of potential enquiry where the issue arises whether a public authority is liable for negligence in the performance of its statutory functions: (1) whether the decision is justiciable at all; (2) whether a duty arises on the application of the *Caparo* principles.

8. *Decisions of the European Court of Human Rights and their impact.* The European Court of Human Rights in *Osman v UK* (1998) 1 L.G.L.R. 431 found that the United Kingdom was in breach of Art 6 of the Convention (right to a fair trial) in respect of the decision of the Court of Appeal in *Osman v Ferguson* [1993] 4 All E.R. 344. The striking-out of the claimant's claim against the police by reference to a blanket immunity based on public policy was held to infringe the claimant's right of access to the court. Accordingly, as has occurred, for example, in some subsequent cases concerning the police (*e.g. Swinney v Chief Constable of Northumbria Police* [1997] Q.B. 464), the court should consider the public policy arguments for and against imposition of a duty of care in a particular situation rather than recognise a blanket immunity at a high level of generality. It was subsequently accepted that the question whether it is fair, just and reasonable for a duty of care to be owed should not be determined on the basis of hypothetical facts at the striking-out stage (*Barrett v Enfield LBC* [2001] 2 A.C. 550 at 557–560, *per* Lord Browne-Wilkinson).

Subsequently, Lord Woolf M.R. pointed out that where the legal position was clear it would be wrong for courts to be reluctant to strike out on the basis of *Osman*; while this might appear to be a summary remedy, it was in fact indistinguishable from deciding a case on a preliminary point of law: *Kent v Griffiths (No.2)* [2001] 1 Q.B. 36 at para.[38].

The ECtHR decision in *Osman* was criticised on the grounds (1) that Art.6 ECHR, properly interpreted, was concerned with procedural bars on access to a court to vindicate a right recognised by domestic law, and not substantive rules of law that determined the scope of that right; and (2) that the court had misunderstood the striking-out process in English civil procedure which permitted full legal argument by both sides as to whether in law there was a cause of action, upon assumed facts (see Lord Browne-Wilkinson in *Barrett v Enfield LBC* [2001] 2 A.C. 550 at 559–560; Lord Phillips M.R. for the court in *RK v Oldham NHS Trust, D v East Berkshire Community Health NHS Trust, K v Dewsbury Healthcare NHS Trust* [2002] 1 WCA Civ 1151 at [9]–[23]). Lord Browne-Wilkinson stated in *Barrett* that

> "a holding that it is not fair, just and reasonable to hold liable a particular class of defendant whether generally or in relation to a particular type of activity is not to give immunity from a liability to which the rest of the world is subject. It is a prerequisite to there being any liability in negligence at all that as a matter of policy it is fair, just and reasonable in those circumstances to impose liability in negligence".

The view had been taken in cases concerning, for example, some activities of financial regulators, building inspectors, ship surveyors, and social workers dealing with sex abuse cases that the proper performance of their primary functions for the benefit of society as a whole would be inhibited if they were required to look over the shoulder to avoid liability in negligence. This involved weighing the total detriment to the public interest in all cases from holding such a class liable in negligence as against the total loss to all would-be plaintiffs if they were not to have a cause of action. The decision that it was not fair and reasonable to impose liability on a particular class was decided as a question of law not on weighing the balance between the extent of the damage to the claimant and the damage to the public in each particular case.

The *Osman* decision was reconsidered by the ECtHR in *Z v UK* [2001] 2 F.L.R. 612. Here, four of the five unsuccessful claimants in *X (Minors) v Bedfordshire CC* applied to the ECtHR, arguing that the United Kingdom was in breach of Arts 3, 6 and 13 ECHR. The Court held this time that there had been no breach of Art. 6. It said (at para.100) that its reasoning in *Osman* was based on an understanding of the law of negligence "which has to be reviewed in the light of the clarifications subsequently made by the domestic courts and notably the House of Lords". The "fair, just and reasonable" criterion was an intrinsic element of the duty of care, and the ruling of law concerning that element in *X (Minors) v Bedfordshire CC* "does not disclose the operation of an immunity". The inability of the applicants to sue the local authority thus flowed not from an immunity but from the applicable principles governing the substantive right of action in domestic law. There was thus "no restriction or access to court of the kind contemplated in *Ashingdane v UK* (1985) 7 E.H.R.R. 528". The Court went on, however, to hold that applicants were victims of a violation of Art.3 ECHR and that the absence of a domestic remedy for that constituted a violation of Art.13 ECHR. The two claimants in the *Newham* case also made an application to the ECtHR: *TP and KM v UK* [2001] 2 F.L.R. 549, alleging breaches of Arts 6, 8, and 13. The Court held there was no breach of Art.6, for reasons similar to those in *Z v UK*; but found breaches of Arts 8 and 13.

This development does not, however, mean that the creation of a disproportionately overbroad immunity from civil liability will necessarily escape review by the ECtHR. The Court itself in *Fayed v UK* (1994) 18 E.H.R.R. 393 said (at paras 65 and 67):

"Whether a person has an actionable domestic claim may depend not only on the substantive content, properly speaking, of the relevant civil right as defined under national law but also on the existence of procedural bars preventing or limiting the possibilities of bringing potential claims to court. In the latter kind of case Art.6(1) may have a degree of applicability. Certainly the Convention enforcement bodies may not create by way of interpretation of Art.6(1) a substantive civil right which has no legal basis in the State concerned. However, it would not be consistent with the rule of law in a democratic society or with the basic principle underlying Art.6(1)—namely that civil claims must be capable of being submitted to a judge for adjudication if, for example, a State could, without restraint or control by the Convention enforcement bodies, remove from the jurisdiction of the courts a whole range of civil claims or confer immunities from civil liability on large groups or categories of persons. . . . It is not always an easy matter to trace the dividing line between procedural and substantive limitation of a given entitlement under domestic law. It may sometimes be no more than a question of legislative technique whether the limitation is expressed in terms of the right or its remedy".

These paragraphs were repeated by the ECtHR in *Fogarty v UK* (2001) 12 B.H.R.C. 132, six months after *Z v UK*. They were cited by Lord Walker of Geetingthorpe in *Matthews v Ministry of Defence* [2003] 2 W.L.R. 435 at [130] to [140], his Lordship concluding that "the uncertain shadow of *Osman v UK* still lies over this area of the law". (Here the House held that the Crown's immunity from suit in respect of claims in tort by servicemen for personal injury sustained during service, enshrined in s.10 of the Crown Proceedings Act 1947, was a substantive limitation not a procedural bar and was not incompatible with Art.6(1) ECHR.)

It is submitted that the articulation by Lord Keith in *Hill v Chief Constable of West Yorkshire* [1989] A.C. 53 of a broad public-policy based "immunity" (to use Lord Keith's own description) for the police "so far as concerns their function in the investigation and suppression of crime", relied upon as conclusive by the Court of Appeal in *Osman v Ferguson* was indeed such a disproportionately overbroad blanket immunity; and that the ECtHR in *Z v UK* was somewhat generous in distinguishing the situation in *X (Minors) v Bedfordshire CC* from that in *Osman*.

The English courts are now faced with the task of determining the scope of *X (Minors) v Bedfordshire CC* in the light of the ruling of the ECtHR in *Z v UK*. This matter was considered by the Court of Appeal in *RK v Oldham NHS Trust; D v East Berkshire Community Health NHS Trust; K v Dewsbury Healthcare NHS Trust* [2003] EWCA Civ 1151. Here, the three cases involved accusations of abusing a child made against a parent by the professionals concerned for the child's welfare. The accusations proved to be unfounded and in each case a parent claimed damages for psychiatric harm alleged to have been caused by the false accusations or their consequences. In one case (*Dewsbury*), the child also claimed. At first instance in each case, it was held that it was not fair just and reasonable for a duty of care to be owed, applying the decision in *X (Minors) v Bedfordshire CC*.

The Court of Appeal held:

(1) that there was, following Z v UK, no basis for holding that this approach involved a breach of Art. 6(1) ECHR.
(2) that the effect of X (*Minors*) *v Bedfordshire CC* had been "significantly" restricted by the subsequent decisions in *Barnett v Enfield LBC* [2001] 2 A.C. 550 and *Phelps v Hillingdon LBC* [2001] 2 A.C. 619:

"So far as the education authority cases are concerned, doubt was cast in Phelps on the proposition that an education authority owes no duty of care to children when exercising powers and discretions under the 1981 Act. So far as child abuse cases are concerned, much of the reasoning advanced by Lord Browne-Wilkinson to justify holding that there was no duty of care was called into question. Lord Slynn in *Barrett* stated that *Bedfordshire* established that decisions by local authorities whether or not to take a child into care were not reviewable by way of a claim in negligence. We consider that the effect of *Barrett* and the other decisions that we have considered above is to restrict the effect of *Bedfordshire* to that core proposition", (*per* Lord Phillips M.R. at para.[49]).

(3) that the policy arguments against recognising a cause of action in negligence by a child against a local authority in these circumstances, in so far as they had not been discredited by subsequent discussions in the House of Lords, would largely cease to apply as litigation concerning these matters could in any event now be brought under the Human Rights Act 1998 alleging a breach of Art 3. In such an action, the court was likely to have to consider whether the local authority knew, or should have known, that positive action to protect a child was called for. This would necessarily involve consideration of the conduct of the individuals involved. Accordingly, in so far as the position of the child was concerned, the decision in *X (Minors) v Bedfordshire CC* could not survive the Human Rights Act 1998. Given the local authority's obligation to respect a child's Convention rights, the recognition of a duty of care to the child on the part of those involved "should not have a significantly adverse effect on the manner in which they perform their duties" (at [70]–[83]). The fact that the 1998 Act would not apply in respect of acts or omissions occurring before October 2000 was no reason to preserve a limitation of the common law duty of care which was not otherwise justified (at [83]). Accordingly,

> "it will no longer be legitimate to rule that, as a matter of law, no common law duty of care is owed to a child in relation to the investigation of suspected child abuse and the initiation and pursuit of care proceedings. It is possible that there will be factual situations where it is not fair, just or reasonable to impose a duty of care, but each case will fall to be determined on its individual facts" (at para.[84]).

This was not to say, however, that the common law duty of care will replicate the duty not to violate Arts 3 and 8 ECHR, although the area of factual enquiry was to be the same (at [85]).

(4) that there remained cogent reasons why no duty of care should be owed to the parents. The parent's position was very different from that of the child. Where the issue was whether a child should be removed from the parents, the child's Convention rights could be violated by a decision to remove or a decision to do so. However, it would always be in the parents' interest that the child should not be removed. Accordingly, the interests of child and parent were in conflict.

(5) that the appeals should be dismissed, except that the child's claim in Dewsbury should proceed. In coming to these conclusions on the facts, the court rejected the argument in East Berkshire that the duty of care of a medical practitioner was owed to both mother and child; the fact that the mother had referred the child to the practitioner did not mean that she, as well as the child, was a patient. Once the practitioner suspected that the child's injuries might have been exaggerated by the mother, the duty owed to the child was in potential conflict with the interests of his mother. It was essential that the professionals should not be inhibited in acting in the best interests of the child by concern that they might be held to be in breach of a duty owed to the mother (at paras [89]–[99]). A similar point was made in respect of the claim in *Oldham*: see paras [122]–[124].

It is submitted that the decision to permit the child's claim to proceed flows logically from the decision in *Z v UK* for the reasons given. The continuation of the immunity in respect of a claim by a parent is, however, open to criticism. The point that the authority must act in the best interests of the child and that these interests may conflict with those of the parents is right. However, it does not follow that it can only be met by recognising an immunity at the duty stage, it would arguably be sufficient for this to be factored in when considering whether there was a breach of duty. It must be remembered that an incompetent decision by a local authority may breach the Art.8 rights of a parent and so give rise to a damages claim, it is not obvious that there should not be a correlative claim in negligence. Finally, it should be noted that while these cases concerned claims that the defendants had acted negligently it would seem that the same principles would apply where there was a negligent failure to exercise the powers in question, given that liability for breach of Art.3, ECHR, arises where there is culpable inaction.

The House of Lords (*D v East Berkshire Community Health NHS Trust* [2005] UKHL 23, Lord Bingham of Cornhill dissenting) in these cases dismissed appeals by the parents on the ground that as the primary duty of care was owed to the child there would be a conflict of interest were professional defendants held also to owe a duty to a parent under suspicion of causing non-accidental injury to the child. Lord Bingham would not have struck the cases out at this stage. The majority did not accept that breach of duty would provide a sufficient control mechanism. No appeal was taken on the issue concerning the duty owed to the child. However, Lord Bingham said (at [30]) that it could not now be plausibly argued that such a duty could not be owed.

STOVIN v WISE, NORFOLK COUNTY COUNCIL (THIRD PARTY)

[1996] A.C. 923; [1996] 3 W.L.R. 388; [1996] 3 All E.R. 801 (HOUSE OF LORDS)

In December 1988, the plaintiff, Thomas Stovin, was riding a motorcycle along Station Road, Wymondham, Norfolk, when he collided with a motorvehicle which was driven by the defendant, Rita Wise, out of a junction on his left. He was seriously injured. Although the junction was not a busy one, the county council as highway authority knew it to be dangerous because the view of road users turning out of the junction was restricted by a bank of earth on adjoining land. There had been accidents in 1976 and 1982 at the spot. In January 1988, the council wrote to the owner of the land, British Rail, suggesting that part of the bank should be removed and that the council would meet the cost of about £1,000. There was a third accident in March 1988. However, there was no response to the letter and the matter had not been followed up by the council by December.

The trial judge found that Mrs Wise was 70 per cent responsible and the council, brought in as a third party, 30 per cent. The council's appeal to the Court of Appeal was dismissed ([1994] 1 W.L.R 1124). The council's appeal to the House of Lords was allowed by 3:2 (Lords Hoffmann, Goff of Chievely and Jauncey of Tullichettle; Lords Nicholls of Birkenhead and Slynn of Hadley dissenting). The major speeches of the majority and minority were given, respectively, by Lords Hoffmann and Nicholls of Birkenhead.

LORD HOFFMANN: . . .

4. *Acts and omissions*

The judge made no express mention of the fact that the complaint against the council was not about anything which it had done to make the highway dangerous but about its omission to make it safer. Omissions, like economic loss, are notoriously a category of conduct in which Lord Atkin's generalisation in *Donoghue v Stevenson* [1932] A.C. 562 offers limited help. In the High Court of Australia in *Hargrave v Goldman* (1963) 110 C.L.R. 40, 66, Windeyer J.

drew attention to the irony in Lord Atkin's allusion, in formulating his "neighbour" test, to the parable of the Good Samaritan [1932] A.C. 562, 580:

> "The priest and the Levite, when they saw the wounded man by the road, passed by on the other side. He obviously was a person whom they had in contemplation and who was closely and directly affected by their action. Yet the common law does not require a man to act as the Samaritan did."

A similar point was made by Lord Diplock in *Dorset Yacht Co. Ltd v Home Office* [1970] A.C. 1004, 1060. There are sound reasons why omissions require different treatment from positive conduct. It is one thing for the law to say that a person who undertakes some activity shall take reasonable care not to cause damage to others. It is another thing for the law to require that a person who is doing nothing in particular shall take steps to prevent another from suffering harm from the acts of third parties (like Mrs Wise) or natural causes. One can put the matter in political, moral or economic terms. In political terms it is less of an invasion of an individual's freedom for the law to require him to consider the safety of others in his actions than to impose upon him a duty to rescue or protect. A moral version of this point may be called the "why pick on me?" argument. A duty to prevent harm to others or to render assistance to a person in danger or distress may apply to a large and indeterminate class of people who happen to be able to do something. Why should one be held liable rather than another? In economic terms, the efficient allocation of resources usually requires an activity should bear its own costs. If it benefits from being able to impose some of its costs on other people (what economists call "externalities"), the market is distorted because the activity appears cheaper than it really is. So liability to pay compensation for loss caused by negligent conduct acts as a deterrent against increasing the cost of the activity to the community and reduces externalities. But there is no similar justification for requiring a person who is not doing anything to spend money on behalf of someone else. Except in special cases (such as marine salvage) English law does not reward someone who voluntarily confers a benefit on another. So there must be some special reason why he should have to put his hand in his pocket.

In *Hargrave v Goldman*, 110 C.L.R. 40, 66, Windeyer J. said:

> "The trend of judicial development in the law of negligence has been . . . to found a duty to take care either in some task undertaken, or in the ownership, occupation, or use of land or chattels."

There may be a duty to act if one has undertaken to do so or induced a person to rely upon one doing so. Or the ownership or occupation of land may give rise to a duty to take positive steps for the benefit of those who come upon the land and sometimes for the benefit of neighbours. In *Hargrave v Goldman* the High Court of Australia held that the owner and occupier of a 600 acre grazing property in Western Australia had a duty to take reasonable steps to extinguish a fire, which had been started by lightning striking a tree on his land, so as to prevent it from spreading to his neighbour's land. This is a case in which the limited class of persons who owe the duty (neighbours) is easily identified and the political, moral and economic arguments which I have mentioned are countered by the fact that the duties are mutual. One cannot tell where the lightning may strike and it is therefore both fair and efficient to impose upon each landowner a duty to have regard to the interests of his neighbour. In giving the advice of the Privy Council affirming the decision (*Goldman v Hargrave* [1967] 1 A.C. 645) Lord Wilberforce underlined the exceptional nature of the liability when he pointed out that the question of whether the landowner had acted reasonably should be judged by reference to the resources he actually had at his disposal and not by some general or objective standard. This is quite different from the duty owed by a person who undertakes a positive activity which carries the risk of causing damage to others. If he does not have the resources to take such steps as are objectively reasonable to prevent such damage, he should not undertake that activity at all.

5. *Omissions in the Court of Appeal*

[His Lordship rejected views adopted by members of the Court of Appeal (1) that this was an omission in the context of a positive decision to act analogous to the failure of a car driver to apply the brakes (*per* Kennedy L.J. [1994] 1 W.L.R. at 1124 at 1138); and (2) that the highway authority's position was analogous to that of the occupier of premises in relation to visitors (Roch L.J. [1994] 1 W.L.R. 1124 at 1139). As to (1), S's injuries "were not caused by the negotiations between the council and British Rail or anything else which the council did". As to (2), the analogy was insufficient given that an occupier could normally take steps to keep out unwanted entrants; and where he could not, as where a public right of way lay across his land, it was established that there was no duty to take reasonable steps to make the way safe for users (*McGeown v Northern Ireland Housing Executive* [1995] 1 AC. 233, HL).]

6. *Public authorities*

The argument that the council had a positive duty to take action giving rise to a claim for compensation in tort must therefore depend, as the judge and the Court of Appeal recognised, upon the public nature of its powers, duties and funding. The argument is that while it may be unreasonable to expect a private landowner to spend money for the benefit of strangers who have the right to cross his land, the very purpose of the existence of a public authority like the council is to spend its resources on making the roads convenient and safe. For that purpose it has a large battery of powers in the Highways Act 1980. These do not actually include a power which would have enabled the council to go upon the land of British Rail and remove the bank of earth. But there is power under section 79 to serve a notice requiring the bank to be removed. The power is conferred for the purpose of "the prevention of danger arising from obstruction to the view of persons using the highway". Although the allegation is not that the council failed to use this power (it probably would not have been necessary to do so), its existence shows that one of the purposes for which Parliament contemplated that the highway authority would spend its money was the removal of exactly the kind of obstructions which caused the accident in this case.

It is certainly true that some of the arguments against liability for omissions do not apply to public bodies like a highway authority. There is no "why pick on me?" argument: as Kennedy L.J. said, at 1139, the highway authority alone had the financial and physical resources, as well as the legal powers, to eliminate the hazard. But this does not mean that the distinction between acts and omissions is irrelevant to the duties of a public body or that there are not other arguments, peculiar to public bodies, which may negative the existence of a duty of care.

(a) *Negligent conduct in the exercise of statutory powers*
Since *Mersey Docks and Harbour Board Trustees v Gibbs* (1866) L.R. 1 H.L. 93 it has been clear law that in the absence of express statutory authority, a public body is in principle liable for torts in the same way as a private person. But its statutory powers or duties may restrict its liability. For example, it may be authorised to do something which necessarily involves committing what would otherwise be a tort. In such a case it will not be liable: *Allen v Gulf Oil Refining Ltd* [1981] A.C. 1001. Or it may have discretionary powers which enable it to do things to achieve a statutory purpose notwithstanding that they involve a foreseeable risk of damage to others. In such a case, a bona fide exercise of the discretion will not attract liability: *X (Minors) v Bedfordshire County Council* [1995] 2 A.C. 633 and *Dorset Yacht Co. Ltd v Home Office* [1970] A.C. 1004.

In the case of positive acts, therefore, the liability of a public authority in tort is in principle the same as that of a private person but may be *restricted* by its statutory powers and duties. The argument in the present case, however, is that whereas a private person would have owed no duty of care in respect of an omission to remove the hazard at the junction, the duty of the highway authority is *enlarged* by virtue of its statutory powers. The existence of the statutory powers is said to create a "proximity" between the highway authority and the highway user which would not otherwise exist.

(b) *Negligent omission to use statutory powers*
Until the decision of this House in *Anns v Merton London Borough Council* [1978] A.C. 728, there was no authority for treating a statutory power as giving rise to a common law duty of care. Two cases in particular were thought to be against it. In *Sheppard v Glossop Corporation* [1921] 3 K.B. 132 the council had power to light the streets of Glossop. But their policy was to turn off the lamps at 9 p.m. The plaintiff was injured when he fell over a retaining wall in the dark after the lamps had been extinguished. He sued the council for negligence. The Court of Appeal said that the council owed him no duty of care. Atkin L.J. said, at 150:

> "[The local authority] is under no legal duty to act reasonably in deciding whether it shall exercise its statutory powers or not, or in deciding to what extent, over what particular area, or for what particular time, it shall exercise its powers . . . The real complaint of the plaintiff is not that they caused the danger, but that, the danger being there, if they had lighted it he would have seen and avoided it."

In *East Suffolk Rivers Catchment Board v Kent* [1941] A.C. 74, 102 the facts of which are too well known to need repetition,[8] Lord Romer cited *Sheppard v Glossop Corporation* and stated the principle which he said it laid down, at 102:

[8] [ed.] see below, p.1087.

"Where a statutory authority is entrusted with a mere power it cannot be made liable for any damage sustained by a member of the public by reason of a failure to exercise that power."

There are two points to be made about the *East Suffolk* case by way of anticipation of what was said about it in the *Anns* case. First, Lord Wilberforce said [1978] A.C. 728, 757:

"only one of their Lordships [Lord Atkin] considered [the case] in relation to a duty of care at common law ... I believe that the conception of a general duty of care, not limited to particular accepted situations, but extending generally over all relations of sufficient proximity, and even pervading the sphere of statutory functions of public bodies, had not at that time become fully recognised."

I must say with great respect that I do not think that this is a fair description of the reasoning of the majority. As a claim of breach of statutory duty had expressly been abandoned, it is hard to imagine what the majority could have thought was the alleged cause of action unless it was breach of a duty of care at common law. What the majority found impossible was to derive such a duty from the existence of a statutory power: to turn a statutory "may" into a common law "ought".

The second point about the *East Suffolk* case is that Lord Atkin, who dissented, does not appear to have founded a duty of care solely upon the existence of the board's statutory powers. He appears to have held that by going upon the plaintiff's land to do work which the plaintiff himself could have done (see at 91–92) the board accepted a duty to execute the work with due dispatch. On this argument, the only relevance of the board's statutory powers was that it could have done the work. It had no statutory defence which would not have been available to a private contractor who had gone upon the land in similar circumstances. Whether Lord Atkin's reasoning is good or bad, it does not support the proposition that statutory powers can generate a duty of care which would not otherwise have existed.

The equally well known case of *Dorset Yacht Co. Ltd v Home Office* [1970] A.C. 1004 also cast no doubt upon the general principle stated by Lord Romer in *East Suffolk*. The only reference to the case is by Viscount Dilhorne, at 1050G–H, in a dissenting speech. All members of the House plainly did not regard the case as one in which the alleged breach of duty was merely an omission to use a statutory power. The negligence was caused by something which the Borstal officers did, namely to use their statutory powers of custody to bring the trainees onto the island, where they constituted a foreseeable risk to boat owners, and then take no care to prevent them from escaping in the night. The case was therefore prima facie within *Mersey Docks and Harbour Board Trustees v Gibbs*, L.R. 1 H.L. 93, and their Lordships were concerned only with whether the Crown had a defence on the grounds that the alleged breach of duty involved the exercise of a statutory discretion or whether the fact that the damage was caused by the criminal act of the Borstal trainees negatived the causal link with the Crown's breach of duty. Both these defences were rejected.

7. *Anns v Merton London Borough Council*

This brings me to the *Anns* case [1978] A.C. 728. As this case is the mainstay of Mrs Wise's argument, I must examine it in some detail. The plaintiffs were lessees of flats in a new block which had been damaged by subsidence caused by inadequate foundations. They complained that the council had been negligent in the exercise of its statutory powers to inspect the foundations of new buildings. The council said that it owed no duty to inspect and therefore could not be liable for negligent inspection. The House rejected this argument. So far as it held that the council owed a duty of care in respect of purely economic loss, the case has been overruled by *Murphy v Brentwood District Council* [1991] 1 A.C. 398. The House left open the question of whether the council might have owed a duty in respect of physical injury, although I think it is fair to say that the tone of their Lordships' remarks on this question was somewhat sceptical. Nevertheless, it is now necessary to ask whether the reasoning can support the existence of a duty of care owed by a public authority in respect of foreseeable physical injury which is founded upon the existence of statutory powers to safeguard people against that injury.

Lord Wilberforce, who gave the leading speech, first stated the well known two-stage test for the existence of a duty of care. This involves starting with a prima facie assumption that a duty of care exists if it is reasonably foreseeable that carelessness may cause damage and then asking whether there are any considerations which ought to "negative, or to reduce or limit the scope of the duty or the class of person to whom it is owed or the damages to which a breach of it may arise". Subsequent decisions in this House and the Privy Council have preferred to appoach the question the other way round, starting with situations in which a duty has been held to exist and then asking whether there are considerations of analogy, policy, fairness and justice for extending it to cover a new situation: see for example Lord Bridge of Harwich in *Caparo Industries Plc v Dickman* [1990] 2 A.C. 605, 617–618. It can be said that, provided that the considerations of policy etc. are properly analysed, it should not matter whether one starts from one end or the other.

On the other hand the assumption from which one starts makes a great deal of difference if the analysis is wrong. The trend of authorities has been to discourage the assumption that anyone who suffers loss is prima facie entitled to compensation from a person (preferably insured or a public authority) whose act or omission can be said to have caused it. The default position is that he is not.

This does not of course mean that the actual analysis in the *Anns* case was wrong. It has to be considered on its own merits. Lord Wilberforce had to deal with an argument by the council which was based upon two propositions. The first was that if the council owed no duty to inspect in the first place, it could be under no liability for having done so negligently. The second relied upon Lord Romer's principle in the *East Suffolk* case [1941] A.C. 74, 97: a public authority which has a mere statutory powr cannot on that account owe a duty at common law to exercise the power. Lord Wilberforce did not deny the first proposition. This, if I may respectfully say so, seems to me to be right. If the public authority was under no duty to act, either by virtue of its statutory powers or on any other basis, it cannot be liable because it has acted but negligently failed to confer a benefit on the plaintiff or to protect him from loss. The position is of course different if the negligent action of the public authority has left the plaintiff in a worse position than he would have been in if the authority had not acted at all. Lord Wilberforce did however deny the council's second proposition. His reasoning was as follows, at 755:

"I think that this is too crude an argument. It overlooks the fact that local authorities are public bodies operating under statute with a clear responsibility for public health in their area. They must, and in fact do, make their discretionary decision responsibly and for reasons which accord with the statutory purpose; . . . If they do not exercise their discretion in this way they can be challenged in the courts. Thus, to say that councils are under no duty to inspect, is not a sufficient statement of the position. They are under a duty to give proper consideration to the question whether they should inspect or not. Their immunity from attack, in the event of failure to inspect, in other words, though great is not absolute. And because it is not absolute, the necessary premise for the proposition 'if no duty to inspect, then no duty to take care in inspection' vanishes."

The duty of care at common law is therefore derived from the council's duty in public law to "give proper consideration to the question whether they should inspect or not". It is clear, however, that this public law duty cannot in itself give rise to a duty of care. A public body almost always has a duty in public law to consider whether it should exercise its powers, but that does not mean that it necessarily owes a duty of care which may require that the power should actually be exercised. As Mason J. said in *Sutherland Shire Council v Heyman*, 157 C.L.R. 424, 465:

"although a public authority may be under a public duty, enforceable by mandamus, to give proper consideration to the question whether it should exercise a power, this duty cannot be equated with, or regarded as a foundation for imposing, a duty of care on the public authority in relation to the exercise of the power. Mandamus will compel proper consideration of the authority of its discretion, but that is all."

A mandamus can require future consideration of the exercise of a power. But an action for negligence looks back to what the council ought to have done. Upon what principles can one say of a public authority that not only did it have a duty in public law to consider the exercise of the power but that it would thereupon have been under a duty in private law to act, giving rise to a claim in compensation against public funds for its failure to do so? Or as Lord Wilberforce puts it in the *Anns* case [1978] A.C. 728, 754:

"The problem which this kind of action creates, is to define the circumstances in which the law should impose, over and above, or perhaps alongside, these public law powers and duties, a duty in private law towards individuals such that they may sue for damages in a civil court."

The only tool which the *Anns* case provides for defining these circumstances is the distinction between policy and operations. Lord Wilberforce said:

"Most, indeed probably all, statutes relating to public authorities or public bodies, contain in them a large area of policy. The courts call this 'discretion'

meaning that the decision is one for the authority or body to make, and not
for the courts. Many statutes also prescribe or at least presuppose the practical execution of policy decisions: a convenient description of this is to say
that in addition to the area of policy or discretion, there is an operational
area. Although this distinction between the policy area and the operational
area is convenient, and illuminating, it is probably a distinction of degree;
many 'operational' powers or duties have in them some element of 'discretion'. It can safely be said that the more 'operational' a power or duty may
be, the easier it is to superimpose upon it a common law duty of care."

The *East Suffolk* case [1941] A.C. 74 and *Sheppard v Glossop Corporation*
[1921] 3 K.B. 132 were distinguished as involving questions of policy or discretion. The inspection of foundations, on the other hand, was "heavily operational" and the power to inspect could therefore give rise to a duty of care.
Lord Romer's statement of principle in *East Suffolk* was limited to cases in
which the exercise of the power involved a policy decision.

8. *Policy and operations*

Since *Anns v Merton London Borough Council*, there have been differing
views, both in England and the Commonwealth, over whether it was right to
breach the protection which the *East Suffolk* principle gave to public authorities. In *Sutherland Shire Council v Heyman*, 157 C.L.R. 424, 483, Brennan J.
thought that it was wrong: one simply could not derive a common law
"ought" from a statutory "may". But I think that he was the only member of
the court to adhere to such uncompromising orthodoxy. What has become
clear, however, is that the distinction between policy and operations is an inadequate tool with which to discover whether it is appropriate to impose a duty
of care or not. In *Rowling v Takaro Properties Ltd* [1988] A.C. 473, 501 Lord
Keith of Kinkel said:

> "[Their Lordships] incline to the opinion, expressed in the literature, that
> this distinction does not provide a touchstone of liability, but rather is
> expressive of the need to exclude altogether those cases in which the deci-
> sion under attack is of such a kind that a question whether it has been made
> negligently is unsuitable for judicial resolution, of which notable examples
> are discretionary decisions on the allocation of scarce resources or the dis-
> tribution of risks. . . . If this is right, classification of the relevant decision
> as a policy or planning decision in this sense may exclude liability; but a con-
> clusion that it does not fall within that category does not, in their Lordships'
> opinion, mean that a duty of care will necessarily exist."

There are at least two reasons why the distinction is inadequate. The first is
that, as Lord Wilberforce himself pointed out, the distinction is often elusive.
This is particularly true of powers to provide public benefits which involve the
expenditure of money. Practically every decision about the provision of such
benefits, no matter how trivial it may seem, affects the budget of the public
authority in either timing or amount. The *East Suffolk* case, about which Lord
Wilberforce said in the *Anns* case [1978] A.C. 728, 757, that the activities of
the board, though "operational", were "well within a discretionary area, so
that the plaintiff's task in contending for a duty of care was a difficult one" is

a very good example. But another reason is that even if the distinction is clear cut, leaving no element of discretion in the sense that it would be irrational (in the public law meaning of that word) for the public authority not to exercise its power, it does not follow that the law should superimpose a common law duty of care. This can be seen if one looks at cases in which a public authority has been under a statutory or common law *duty* to provide a service or other benefit for the public or a section of the public. In such cases there is no discretion but the courts have nevertheless not been willing to hold that a member of the public who has suffered loss because the service was not provided to him should necessarily have a cause of action, either for breach of statutory duty or for negligence at common law.

There are many instances of this principle being applied to statutory duties, but perhaps the most relevant example of the dissociation between public duty and a liability to pay compensation for breach of that duty was the ancient common law duty to repair the highway. The common law imposed this financial burden upon the inhabitants of the parish. But it saw no need to impose upon them the additional burden of paying compensation to users of the highway who suffered injury because the highway surveyor had failed to repair. The duty could be enforced only by indictment. This rule continued to apply when the duty to maintain was transferred by statute to highway authorities and was only abolished by section 1 of the Highways (Miscellaneous Provisions) Act 1961. Likewise in *Hill v Chief Constable of West Yorkshire* [1989] A.C. 53 it was held that the public duty of the police to catch criminals did not give rise to a duty of care to a member of the public who was injured because the police had negligently failed to catch one. The decision was mainly based upon the large element of discretion which the police necessarily have in conducting their operations, but the judgment excludes liability even in cases in which the alleged breach of duty would constitute public law irrationality.

In terms of public finance, this is a perfectly reasonable attitude. It is one thing to provide a service at the public expense. It is another to require the public to pay compensation when a failure to provide the service has resulted in loss. Apart from cases of reliance, which I shall consider later, the same loss would have been suffered if the service had not been provided in the first place. To require payment of compensation increases the burden on public funds. Before imposing such an additional burden, the courts should be satisfied that this is what Parliament intended.

Whether a statutory duty gives rise to a private cause of action is a question of construction: see *R. v Deputy Governor of Parkhurst Prison, ex p. Hague* [1992] 1 A.C. 58. It requires an examination of the policy of the statute to decide whether it was intended to confer a right to compensation for breach. Whether it can be relied upon to support the existence of a common law duty of care is not exactly a question of construction, because the cause of action does not arise out of the statute itself. But the policy of the statute is nevertheless a crucial factor in the decision. As Lord Browne-Wilkinson said in *X (Minors) v Bedfordshire County Council* [1995] 2 A.C. 633, 739C in relation to the duty of care owed by a public authority performing statutory functions:

"the question whether there is such a common law duty and if so its ambit, must be profoundly influenced by the statutory framework within which the acts complained of were done".

The same is true of omission to perform a statutory duty. If such a duty does not give rise to a private right to sue for breach, it would be unusual if it nevertheless gave rise to a duty of care at common law which made the public authority liable to pay compensation for foreseeable loss caused by the duty not being performed. It will often be foreseeable that loss will result if, for example, a benefit or service is not provided. If the policy of the act is not to create a statutory liability to pay compensation, the same policy should ordinarily exclude the existence of a common law duty of care.

In the case of a mere statutory power, there is the further point that the legislature has chosen to confer a discretion rather than create a duty. Of course there may be cases in which Parliament has chosen to confer a power because the subject matter did not permit a duty to be stated with sufficient precision. It may nevertheless have contemplated that in circumstances in which it would be irrational not to exercise the power, a person who suffered loss because it had not been exercised, or not properly exercised, would be entitled to compensation. I therefore do not say that a statutory "may" can never give rise to a common law duty of care. I prefer to leave open the question of whether the *Anns* case was wrong to create any exception to Lord Romer's statement of principle in the *East Suffolk* case and I shall go on to consider the circumstances (such as "general reliance") in which it has been suggested that such a duty might arise. But the fact that Parliament has conferred a discretion must be some indication that the policy of the act conferring the power was not to create a right to compensation. The need to have regard to the policy of the statute therefore means that exceptions will be rare.

In summary, therefore, I think that the minimum preconditions for basing a duty of care upon the existence of a statutory power, if it can be done at all, are, first, that it would in the circumstances have been irrational not to have exercised the power, so that there was in effect a public law duty to act, and secondly, that there are exceptional grounds for holding that the policy of the statute requires compensation to be paid to persons who suffer loss because the power was not exercised.

9. Particular and general reliance

In *Sutherland Shire Council v Heyman*, 157 C.L.R. 424, 483, Brennan J., as I have mentioned, thought that a statutory power could never generate a common law duty of care unless the public authority had created an expectation that the power would be used and the plaintiff had suffered damage from reliance on that expectation. A common example is the lighthouse authority which, by the exercise of its power to build and maintain a lighthouse, creates in mariners an expectation that the light will warn them of danger. In such circumstances, the authority (unlike the Glossop Corporation in *Sheppard v Glossop Corporation* [1921] 3 K.B. 132) owes a duty of care which requires it not to extinguish the light without giving reasonable notice. This form of liability, based upon representation and reliance, does not depend upon the public nature of the authority's powers and causes no problems.

In the same case, however, Mason J. suggested a different basis upon which public powers might give rise to a duty of care. He said, at 464:

"there will be cases in which the plaintiff's reasonable reliance will arise out of a general dependence on an authority's performance of its function with due care, without the need for contributing conduct on the part of a defendant or action to his detriment on the part of a plaintiff. Reliance or dependence in this sense is in general the product of the grant (and exercise) of powers designed to prevent or minimise a risk of personal injury or disability, recognised by the legislature as being of such magnitude or complexity that individuals cannot, or may not, take adequate steps for their own protection. This situation generates on one side (the individual) a general expectation that the power will be exercised and on the other side (the authority) a realisation that there is a general reliance or dependence on its exercise of the power. . . . The control of air traffic, the safety inspection of aircraft and the fighting of a fire in a building by a fire authority . . . may well be examples of this type of function."

This ground for imposing a duty of care has been called "general reliance". It has little in common with the ordinary doctrine of reliance; the plaintiff does not need to have relied upon the expectation that the power would be used or even known that it existed. It appears rather to refer to general expectations in the community, which the individual plaintiff may or may not have shared. A widespread assumption that a statutory power will be exercised may affect the general pattern of economic and social behaviour. For example, insurance premiums may take into account the expectation that statutory powers of inspection or accident prevention will ordinarily prevent certain kinds of risk from materialising. Thus the doctrine of general reliance requires an inquiry into the role of a given statutory power in the behaviour of members of the general public, of which an outstanding example is the judgment of Richardson J. in *Invercargill City Council v Hamlin* [1994] 3 N.Z.L.R. 513, 526.

It appears to be essential to the doctrine of general reliance that the benefit or service provided under statutory powers should be of a uniform and routine nature, so that one can describe exactly what the public authority was supposed to do. Powers of inspection for defects clearly fall into this category. Another way of looking at the matter is to say that if a particular service is provided as a matter of routine, it would be irrational for a public authority to provide it in one case and arbitrarily withhold it in another. This was obviously the main ground upon which this House in the *Anns* case considered that the power of the local authority to inspect foundations should give rise to a duty of care.

But the fact that it would be irrational not to exercise the power is, as I have said, only one of the conditions which has to be satisfied. It is also necessary to discern a policy which confers a right to financial compensation if the power has not been exercised. Mason J. thought in *Sutherland Shire Council v Heyman*, 157 C.L.R. 424, 464, that such a policy might be inferred if the power was intended to protect members of the public from risks against which they could not guard themselves. In the *Invercargill* case, as I have said, the New Zealand Court of Appeal [1994] 3 N.Z.L.R. 513 and the Privy Council [1996] 2 W.L.R. 367 found it in general patterns of socio-economic behaviour. I do not propose to explore further the doctrine of general reliance because, for reasons which I shall explain, I think that there are no grounds upon which the present case can be brought within it. I will only note in passing that its application may require some very careful analysis of the role which the expected exercise of the statutory power plays in community behaviour.

For example, in one sense it is true that the fire brigade is there to protect people in situations in which they could not be expected to be able to protect themselves. On the other hand they can and do protect themselves by insurance against the risk of fire. It is not obvious that there should be a right to compensation from a negligent fire authority which will ordinarily ensure by right of subrogation to an insurance company. The only reason would be to provide a general deterrent against inefficiency. But there must be better ways of doing this than by compensating insurance companies out of public funds. And while premiums no doubt take into account the existence of the fire brigade and the likelihood that it will arrive swiftly upon the scene, it is not clear that they would be very different merely because no compensation was paid in the rare cases in which the fire authority negligently failed to perform its public duty. . . .

11. *Duties of a highway authority*

I return to consider whether the council owed a duty of care which required it to take steps to improve the junction. Since the only basis for such a duty is the authority's statutory powers, both specifically under section 79 of the Act of 1980 and generally to carry out works of improvement with the consent of British Rail, I will start by asking whether in the light of what the council knew or ought to have known about the junction, it would have had a duty in public law to undertake the work. This requires that it would have been irrational not to exercise its discretion to do so. The trial judge did not address himself to this question. He thought it was sufficient that, as he put it, "a decision had already been taken to deal with the situation" in which "budgetary considerations were not a restraint".

The fact that Mr Longhurst and Mr Deller had agreed to do the work does not show that it would have been unreasonable or irrational for the council not to have done it. That is simply a non sequitur. The Court of Appeal seems to have reasoned that the "decision" to do the work disposed of any question of policy or discretion and left only the operational question of when the work should have been done. But this too seems to me fallacious. The timing of the work and the budgetary year in which the money is spent is surely as much a matter of discretion as the decision in principle to do it. And why should the council be in a worse position than if Mr Longhurst had left Mr Deller's report at the bottom of his in-tray and forgotten about it? In that case, it is said, the council would have been in breach of its duty in public law to give due consideration to the exercise of its powers. Perhaps it would, but that does not advance the case far enough. It would still be necessary to say that if the council had considered the matter, it would have been bound to decide to do the work. One comes back, therefore, to the question of whether it would have been irrational to decide not to do it.

Furthermore, to say that a decision had been taken oversimplifies the situation. Mr Longhurst had not committed himself to any particular time within which the work would be done. There was, as Mr Deller said, a "nil time scale involved"; he did not think it mattered whether the work took one, two or three years. At the time when the letter to British Rail was sent, the March 1988 accident with the police car had not yet happened. Nor was it notified to Mr Longhurst or Mr Deller when it did. The judge found that they would have displayed a greater sense of urgency if they had known about it. But the judge made no finding that the council should have had a system by which Mr Longhurst was notified of every accident on the roads of South Norfolk. Such a system would have been quite impractical. There were 3,500 personal injury accidents in Norfolk every year and their particulars were simply entered on a computer from which the Accident Studies Section in Norwich identified "cluster sites" for special attention. No firm decision had been taken on expenditure either. Mr Deller thought that the work would cost less than £1,000, in which case it would have come within Mr Longhurst's discretionary budget for small works. But he said he could not be sure of the cost until he had consulted a design engineer: "it could be lots and lots more". This caution was justified by events. After Mr Stovin's accident, Mr Brian Meadows, who worked for the Accident Studies Section, inspected the junction and said that the bank could not be regraded within the budget for a low cost remedial scheme.

The judge, as I say, made no finding as to whether it would have been irrational for the council not to have done the work. The unchallenged evidence of Mr Reid, who was head of the Accident Studies Office, would have made it very difficult to do so. In evidence in chief, he was asked about the March 1988 accident:

"Q. So far as you are concerned, what difference, if any, would the signficance of this accident have made in relation to priority given to carrying out work at this site, against the background of what had happened with British Rail? A. In practical terms, it would have made no difference at all to the priority within the accident remedial budget, because our attention and resources would have been directed to those many sites in the county which already had much higher accident records."

There was no suggestion in cross-examination that this was an unreasonable, let alone irrational, attitude to take.

It seems to me therefore that the question of whether anything should be done about the junction was at all times firmly within the area of the council's discretion. As they were therefore not under a public law duty to do the work, the first condition for the imposition of a duty of care was not satisfied.

But even if it were, I do not think that the second condition would be satisfied. Assuming that the highway authority ought, as a matter of public law, to have done the work, I do not think that there are any grounds upon which it can be said that the public law duty should give rise to an obligation to compensate persons who have suffered loss because it was not performed. There is no question here of reliance on the council having improved the junction. Everyone could see that it was still the same. Mr Stovin was not arbitrarily denied a benefit which was routinely provided to others. In respect of the junction, he was treated in exactly the same way as any other road user. The foundation for the doctrine of general reliance is missing in this case, because we are not concerned with provision of a uniform identifiable benefit or service. Every hazardous junction, intersection or stretch of road is different and requires a separate decision as to whether anything should be done to improve it. It is not without significance that the Canadian cases in which a duty of care has been held to exist have all involved routine inspection and maintenance rather than improvements.

I have mentioned earlier that maintenance of the highway was, until 1961, a striking example of a public duty which involved no obligation to compensate a person who had suffered damage because of its breach. The power in section 79 of the Highways Act 1980, upon which the plaintiff principally relies to generate a duty of care, was first enacted as section 4 of the Roads Improvement Act 1925. It seems to me impossible to discern a legislative intent that there should be a duty of care in respect of the use of that power, giving rise to a liability to compensate persons injured by a failure to use it, when there was at the time no such liability even for breach of the statutory duty to maintain the highway.

In my view the creation of a duty of care upon a highway authority, even on grounds of irrationality in failing to exercise a power, would inevitably expose the authority's budgetary decisions to judicial inquiry. This would distort the priorities of local authorities, which would be bound to try to play safe by increasing their spending on road improvements rather than risk enormous liabilities for personal injury accidents. They will spend less on education or social services. I think that it is important, before extending the duty of care owed by public authorities, to consider the cost to the community of the defensive measures which they are likely to take in order to avoid liability. It would not be surprising if one of the consequences of the *Anns* case and the spate of cases which followed was that local council inspectors tended to insist upon stronger foundations than were necessary. In a case like this, I do not think that the duty of care can be used as a deterrent against low standards in improving the road layout. Given the fact that the British road network largely antedates the highway authorities themselves, the court is not in a position to say what an appropriate standard of improvement would be. This must be a matter for the discretion of the authority. On the other hand, denial of liability does not leave the road user unprotected. Drivers of vehicles must take the highway network as they find it. Everyone knows that there are hazardous bends, intersections and junctions. It is primarily the duty of drivers of vehicles to take due care. And if, as in the case of Mrs Wise, they do not, there is compulsory insurance to provide compensation to the victims. There is no reason of policy or justice which requires the highway authority to be an additional defendant. I would therefore allow the appeal.

Appeal allowed.

Notes and questions

1. *The dissent.* In his dissenting speech, Lord Nicholls of Birkenhead's statement of the relevant principles was very similar to Lord Hoffmann's. Thus the distinction between acts and omissions was "fundamentally sound" (at 393); the facts here constituted an omission, the failure to remove a source of danger not created by the council (at 393); and a common law duty "must not be inconsistent with the performance by the authority of its statutory duties and powers in the manner intended by Parliament, or contrary in any other way to the presumed legislative intention" (at 398); there was here no general or particular reliance based on the previous conduct of the council (at 398). However, a concurrent common law duty could be recognised where that did not impose a greater burden than the public law duty not to act irrationally (*i.e.* so unreasonably that no reasonable authority could have so acted), and there was a special circumstance rendering it fair and reasonable for the authority to be under a common law duty (at 399); policy decisions should not be regarded as a "no-go" area, given that the distinction between policy and other areas is artificial and elusive and that no statutory power is inherently immune from judicial review, where no difficulty is found in recognising "that reasonable people can reach widely differing conclusions

when making decisions based on social, political or economic grounds (at 401). The crucial difference was that the minority thought that on the facts the council had behaved irrationally (at 399) and that it was fair and reasonable for a duty to be owed (at 402–403). On the latter point, key elements were that the risk here was of physical injury; that the authority *knew* of the danger; if the council had acted "rationally" the accident would not have happened; the council was made liable by statute for an omission if it failed to take reasonable care to keep the highway itself safe (Highways Act 1980, s.58); the purpose of the relevant statutory powers under the Act was to protect road users; there was some analogy with the liability of an occupier to entrants; it was clearly fair to a "hapless" injured road user unable to sue another insured party to recover from the highway authority and it should not make any difference that (as here) a claim did lie against another insured defendant.

2. *Justiciability and the policy operational dichotomy.* Compare the views of Lord Browne-Wilkinson in *X (Minors) v Bedfordshire CC* and Lord Hoffmann in the present case. Lord Browne-Wilkinson's approach certainly makes it necessary to ask additional complex questions. Perhaps the most telling argument against the identification of a "no-go" area on the basis of "non-justiciability" or "policy" is that this raises questions that are so difficult to resolve that they cannot be employed effectively at the striking-out stage, as amply demonstrated by *X (Minors) v Bedfordshire CC* itself and its associated cases.

Following *Anns*, the lower courts in a number of cases sought to apply the distinction between policy and operational matters expounded by Lord Wilberforce, but encountered difficulties in doing so; see D. Oliver, (1980) 33 C.L.P. 269 and S.H. Bailey and M.J. Bowman, [1986] C.L.J. 430. Commentators were divided on the question whether the concept of "policy" or "discretion" would cover any situation where the authority had an element of choice, or whether it only applied where the issues involved were not suitable for consideration by a court of law (see M. Aronson and H. Whitmore, *Public Torts and Contracts* (1982), pp.69–73; Bailey and Bowman [1986] C.L.J. 430, at pp.437–439).

As time went on, the courts tended simply to rely directly on a variety of public policy arguments in rejecting duties of care (see above, pp.1062–1064) and did not reach or rely on the policy-operational dichotomy (but with some exceptions; see, *e.g.* Sir Nicolas Browne-Wilkinson V.-C. (as he then was) in *Lonrho Plc v Tebbitt* [1991] 4 All E.R. 973; *cf.* Dillon L.J. in the Court of Appeal, [1992] 4 All E.R. 280, 287).

Further consideration to the policy-operational dichotomy was given by the House of Lords in *Barrett v Enfield LBC* [2001] 2 A.C. 550. Lord Slynn stated (at 571–573) that where a statutory power is given to a public authority and damage is caused by what it does pursuant to that power, the ultimate question is whether the particular issue is justiciable or whether the court should accept that it has no role to play. The wider the discretion conferred by the statute and the greater the element of policy involved the more likely it is that the matter is not justiciable. However, it would not be right to say that there is no liability in respect of statutory discretions or "policy" decisions unless the decision in question is *ultra vires*. For one thing,

"[p]olicy and operational acts are closely linked and the decision to do an operational act may easily involve and flow from a policy decision. Conversely, the policy is affected by the result of an operational act . . . ".

For another, his Lordship was reluctant (as was Lord Browne-Wilkinson in *X (Minors) v Bedfordshire CC)* to introduce the concepts of administrative law into the law of negligence (571, 572). See to similar effect Lord Hutton at 577–578.

3. *The status of the East Suffolk and Anns cases.* In *East Suffolk Catchment Board v Kent* [1941] A.C. 74, an exceptionally high spring tide caused the River Deben to overflow its banks and many pastures were flooded. The trial judge found that the Board's staff had so inefficiently carried out repair works that it took them 178 days, whereas with reasonable skill the gap should have been closed in 14 days. The Board has no

statutory *duty* to repair the breach but had a statutory *power* to do this. It was held that the Board could not be made liable in damages. Lord Romer said (at 102):

> "Where a statutory authority is entrusted with a mere power it cannot be made liable for any damage sustained by a member of the public by reason of a failure to exercise that power. If in the exercise of their discretion they embark upon an execution of that power, the only duty they owe to any member of the public is not thereby to add to the damages that he would have suffered had they done nothing. So long as they exercise their discretion honestly, it is for them to determine the method by which and the time within which and the time during which the power shall be exercised; and they cannot be made liable, except to the extent that I have just mentioned, for any damage that would have been avoided had they exercised their discretion in a more reasonable way".

Given that the duty was limited to the avoidance of extra damage there was no causal link between any breach of that duty and the damage of which the plaintiff complained, namely the continuance of the inundation for 164 extra days.

This decision has been the subject of much criticism, not least by Lord Wilberforce in the *Anns* case. However, it has in a large measure been rehabilitated by Lord Hoffmann's speech in *Stovin v Wise* and the decision *Gorringe*. It is submitted that it should be regarded as good law. There seems no good reason why the Board, a body with limited resources, should be liable in negligence to the plaintiffs for inefficiency in rescuing their land from the effects of flooding given that (1) the Board was under no duty to act; (2) that on the facts as found, neither the plaintiffs themselves nor any third party would have been in a position to do the necessary work; and (3) that the plaintiffs had not secured the Board's services under a contract (for which they would have provided consideration). See further, Bowman and Bailey, [1984] P.L. 277. If the Board's employees had through negligence caused additional physical damage to the plaintiff's land, the Board would have been held liable on ordinary principles. In this situation, the Board's *actions* would have caused distinct damage.

The decision in *Anns* was overruled by the House of Lords in *Murphy v Brentwood DC* [1991] 1 A.C. 398, mainly on the ground that the loss suffered by the plaintiff in repairing a house that was inherently defective was properly characterised as pure economic loss. This left open the possibility that an action might lie where a failure to inspect or a faulty inspection of a building led to a collapse that caused property damage or physical injury. Do you think an action could lie here in the light of the principles stated in *X (Minors) v Bedfordshire CC* and *Stovin v Wise*? Can a local authority whose inspector carelessly inspects foundations be said to have assumed responsibility towards the plaintiff? Is there particular or general reliance?

4. The House of Lords returned yet again to a consideration of these matters in *Gorringe v Calderdale MBC* [2004] UKHL 15; [2004] 1 W.L.R. 1057. The claimant was injured in a road accident near a sharp crest in the road, when she braked sharply and skidded into a bus. She was herself found to be blameless and claimed that the council caused the accident by failing to paint the word "SLOW" on the road before the crest. Section 39 of the Road Traffic Act 1988 imposed a duty to carry out measures designed to promote road safety, including studies into accidents arising out of the use of vehicles on roads and appropriate measures to prevent such accidents. It was accepted that this imposed a "target" duty only, that did not give rise to a civil action for breach of statutory duty. The House held, furthermore, that it did not give rise to a common law duty to users of the highway to take reasonable steps to carry out such studies and measures. The Court of Appeal in *Larner v Solihull MBC* [2001] R.T.R. 469 had previously held that a duty of care might arise in exceptional circumstances where the authority had acted wholly unreasonably in respect of a failure to perform its duty under s.39, and thus outside the ambit of the discretion conferred by the section (see Lord Woolf C.J. at 475). No duty had, however, arisen on the facts. In holding that a duty of care could arise, Lord Woolf C.J. appeared to be

adopting the approach set out by Lord Hoffmann, for the majority, in *Stovin v Wise*. Curiously, his Lordship expressly adopted the reasons expressed by Lord Nicholls of Birkenhead for the minority "for the desirability of a duty in the exceptional case" (Lord Woolf C.J. at 475). This approach was firmly disapproved by the House in *Gorringe* ([2004] UKHL 15 at [28]–[31]). Lord Hoffmann noted Lord Woolf C.J. had also cited a passage from Lord Hoffmann's own speech in *Stovin v Wise* ([1996] A.C. 923 at 952–953) in which he had said: "If the policy of an Act is not to create a statutory liability to pay compensation, the same policy should ordinarily exclude the existence of a common law duty of care." Lord Woolf had failed to explain why this did not apply to s.39. When the decision in *Stovin v Wise* was properly analysed:

"The majority rejected the argument that the existence of the statutory power to make improvements to the highway could in itself give rise to a common law duty to take reasonable care to exercise the power or even not to be irrational in failing to do so. It went no further than to leave open the possibility that there might somewhere be a statutory power or public duty which generated a common law duty and indulged in some speculation (which may have been ill-advised) about what that duty might be" (*per* Lord Hoffmann at para.[31]).

Accordingly, no duty of care could be based on s.39 of the Road Traffic Act 1988 (this was the unanimous view of the House: see Lord Steyn at para.[1], Lord Scott of Foscote at paras [72]–[75], Lord Rodger of Earlsferry at paras [89]–[92], Lord Brown of Eaton-under-Heywood at para.[103]). Furthermore, the House was sceptical as to whether a common law duty could ever arise under the test set out by Lord Hoffmann in *Stovin v Wise*. Lord Hoffmann in *Gorringe* himself said:

"Speaking for myself, I find it difficult to imagine a case in which a common law duty can be founded simply upon the failure (however irrational) to provide some benefit which a public authority has power (or a public law duty) to provide" (at [32]).

His Lordship gave as an example the majority reasoning in *Capital & Counties Plc v Hampshire CC* [1997] Q.B. 1004. All the other members of the House agreed with Lord Hoffmann's reasons).

Lord Scott of Foscote agreed, but went further (at para.[71]):

"In my opinion, if a statutory duty does not give rise to a private right to sue for breach, the duty cannot create a duty of care that would not have been owed at common law if the statute were not there . . . I do not accept that a common law duty of care can grow parasitically out of a statutory duty not intended to be owed to individuals".

All the other members of the House expressly agreed with Lord Scott's reasons.

This in terms does not apply to a failure to exercise a statutory power as distinct from failure to perform a target duty, but it is not possible to see any proper basis to distinguish the two situations. This effectively must mean the end of arguments that a common law duty of care can arise solely on an irrational failure to exercise a power or to perform a target duty. As the House recognised in *Gorringe*, that leaves unaffected causes of action based on a duty of care that arises other than out of the mere existence of statutory powers and duties, as where public authorities have "actually done acts or entered relationships or undertaken responsibilities which give rise to a common law duty of care" (*per* Lord Hoffmann at para.[38]). Examples included the duty of care owed by an NHS Trust in providing medical treatment to a patient (*ibid.*); or following the assumption of parental responsibility by a local authority for a child (*Barrett v Enfield LBC* [2001] 2 A.C. 550); the professional duty of care owed by an educational psychologist (*Phelps v Hillingdon BC* [2001] 2 A.C. 619); and the principle:

> "that if a highway authority conducts itself so as to create a reasonable expectation about the state of the highway, it will be under a duty to ensure that it does not thereby create a trap for the careful motorist who drives in reliance upon such an expectation" (*per* Lord Hoffmann at para.[43]).

See also Lord Scott at paras [65], [66]

The highway authority clearly owes a duty of care where it creates the danger: see *Great North Eastern Railway Ltd v Hart* [2003] EWHC 2450, QBD.

(iii) Misfeasance in Public Office

THREE RIVERS DISTRICT COUNCIL v GOVERNOR AND COMPANY OF THE BANK OF ENGLAND (NO.3)

[2003] 2 A.C. 1; [2000] 2 W.L.R. 1220; [2000] 3 All E.R. 1 (HOUSE OF LORDS)

In July 1991, BCCI, a licensed deposit-taker, and its assoc iated companies collapsed, with huge deficiencies, much of which resulted from fraud on a very large scale. An official report (by Bingham L.J.) concluded that until April 1990, the Bank of England, which had principal responsibility for supervising banking activities in the United Kingdom, had been unaware that BCCI was heading for collapse. The plaintiffs, some 6,000 former depositors with BCCI's UK branch, brought an action against the Bank claiming £550 million damages plus interest for misfeasance in public office, in that it had either wrongly granted a licence to BCCI or had failed to revoke it when it knew, believed or suspected that it would probably collapse without being rescued. (The claim was also based on breaches of Community law.) The Bank denied the claim. Clarke J. struck out the claim ([1996] 3 All E.R. 558 at 634). The Court of Appeal (Hirst and Robert Walker L.JJ., Auld L.J. dissenting) upheld this with some differences on the detailed grounds ([2003] 2 A.C. 17). The House of Lords heard an appeal first on the legal issues and secondly on the factual issues, and reversed the Court of Appeal. The extract here concentrates on the ingredients of the misfeasance tort and is taken from the Lord Steyn's speech delivered at the conclusion of the hearing of the legal issues.

LORD STEYN: . . .

Misfeasance in public office

The early history

The history of the development of the tort has been described by Clarke J. and in the judgments in the Court of Appeal: see also Arrowsmith, *Civil Liability and Public Authorities* (1992), pp.226–234. It is traceable to the 17th century: *Turner v Sterling* (1671) 2 Vent 25. But the first solid basis for this new head of tort liability, based on an action on the case, is to be found in *Ashby v White* (1703), best reported in 1 Smith's LC (13th ed) 253. The view ultimately prevailed that an action would lie by an elector who was wilfully denied a right to vote by a returning officer. Despite the recognition of the tort in a number of cases in the 18th and 19th centuries, the Court of Appeal in 1907 denied the existence of the tort in *Davis v Bromley Corpn* [1908] 1 KB 170. But by

1981 the Privy Council described the tort as "well established": *Dunlop v Woollahra Municipal Council* [1982] A.C. 158, 172F. An examination of the ingredients of the tort was still required. The first step towards that goal was the judgments in the Court of Appeal in *Bourgoin SA v Ministry of Agriculture, Fisheries and Food* [1986] Q.B. 716. The present case is the first occasion on which the House has been called on to review the requirements of the tort in a comprehensive manner. Your Lordships are however not asked to prepare an essay on the tort of misfeasance in public office but to state the ingredients of the tort so far as it may be material to the concrete disposal of the issues arising on the pleadings in this case.

The matrix of the tort

The coherent development of the law requires the House to consider the place of the tort of misfeasance in public office against the general scheme of the law of tort. It is well established that individuals in the position of the depositors cannot maintain an action for compensation for losses they suffered as a result of the Bank's breach of statutory duties: *Yuen Kun-Yeu v Attorney General of Hong Kong* [1988] A.C. 175; *Davis v Radcliffe* [1990] 1 W.L.R. 821. Judicial review is regarded as an adequate remedy. Similarly, persons in the position of the depositors cannot sue the Bank for losses resulting from the negligent licensing, supervision or failure to withdraw a licence: *Yuen Kun-Yeu v Attorney General of Hong Kong; Davis v Radcliffe*. The availability of the tort of misfeasance in public office has been said to be one of the reasons justifying the non-actionability of a claim in negligence where there is an act of maladministration: *Calveley v Chief Constable of the Merseyside Police* [1989] A.C. 1228, 1238F. It is also established that an *ultra vires* act will not per se give rise to liability in tort: *X (Minors) v Bedfordshire County Council* [1995] 2 A.C. 633. And there is no overarching principle in English law of liability in tort for "unlawful, intentional and positive acts": see *Lonrho Ltd v Shell Petroleum Co Ltd (No 2)* [1982] A.C. 173, 187G in which the House refused to follow *Beaudesert Shire Council v Smith* (1966) 120 C.L.R. 145, which was subsequently overruled by the Australian High Court in *Northern Territory v Mengel* (1995) 69 ALJR 527. The tort of misfeasance in public office is an exception to "the general rule that, if conduct is presumptively unlawful, a good motive will not exonerate the defendant, and that, if conduct is lawful apart from motive, a bad motive will not make him liable": *Winfield & Jolowicz on Tort*, 15th ed (1998), p.55; *Bradford Corpn v Pickles* [1895] A.C. 587; *Allen v Flood* [1898] A.C. 1. The rationale of the tort is that in a legal system based on the rule of law executive or administrative power "may be exercised only for the public good" and not for ulterior and improper purposes: *Jones v Swansea City Council* [1990] 1 W.L.R. 54, 85F, per Nourse L.J.; a decision reversed on the facts but not on the law by the House of Lords [1990] 1 W.L.R. 1453, 1458.

The tort bears some resemblance to the crime of misconduct in public office: *R. v Bowden* [1996] 1 W.L.R. 98.

The ingredients of the tort

It is now possible to consider the ingredients of the tort. That can conveniently be done by stating the requirements of the tort in a logical sequence of numbered paragraphs.

(1) *The defendant must be a public officer*

It is the office in a relatively wide sense on which everything depends. Thus a local authority exercising private-law functions as a landlord is potentially capable of being sued: *Jones v Swansea City Council* [1990] 1 W.L.R. 54. In the present case it is common ground that the Bank satisfies this requirement.

(2) *The second requirement is the exercise of power as a public officer*

This ingredient is also not in issue. The conduct of the named senior officials of the Banking Supervision Department of the Bank was in the exercise of public functions. Moreover, it is not disputed that the principles of vicarious liability apply as much to misfeasance in public office as to other torts involving malice, knowledge or intention: *Racz v Home Office* [1994] 2 A.C. 45.

(3) *The third requirement concerns the state of mind of the defendant*

The case law reveals two different forms of liability for misfeasance in public office. First there is the case of targeted malice by a public officer, i.e conduct specifically intended to injure a person or persons. This type of case involves bad faith in the sense of the exercise of public power for an improper or ulterior motive. The second form is where a public officer acts knowing that he has no power to do the act complained of and that the act will probably injure the plaintiff. It involves bad faith inasmuch as the public officer does not have an honest belief that his act is lawful.
    The distinction, and the availability of an action of the second type, was inherent in the early development of tort. A group of cases which began with *Ashby v White* (1703) 1 Smith's LC (13th ed) 253, concerned the discretionary refusal of voting rights: see also *Drewe v Coulton* (1787) 1 East 563n; *Tozer v Child* (1857) 7 E & B 377; *Cullen v Morris* (1819) 2 Stark 577. In the second group of cases the defendants were judges of inferior courts, and the cases concerned liability of the judges for malicious acts within their jurisdiction: *Ackerley v Parkinson* (1815) 3 M & S 411; *Harman v Tappenden* (1801) 1 East 555; *Taylor v Nesfield* (1854) 3 E & B 724. These decisions laid the foundation of the modern tort; they established the two different forms of liability; and revealed the unifying element of conduct amounting to an abuse of power accompanied by subjective bad faith. In the most important modern case in England the existence of the two forms of the tort was analysed and affirmed: *Bourgoin SA v Ministry of Agriculture, Fisheries and Food* [1986] Q.B. 716. Clarke J. followed this traditional twofold classification. He expressly held that the two forms are alternative ways in which the tort can be committed. The majority in the Court of Appeal commented on "a rather rigid distinction between the two supposed limbs of the tort" and observed that there was "the need to establish deliberate and dishonest abuse of power in every case": ante, p.58F-G. As a matter of classification it is certainly right to say that there are not two separate torts. On the other hand, the ingredients of the two forms of the tort cannot be exactly the same because if that were so there would be no sense in the twofold classification. Undoubtedly there are unifying features, namely the special nature of the tort, as directed against the conduct of public officers only, and the element of an abuse of public power in bad faith. But there are

differences between the alternative forms of the tort and it is conducive to clarity to recognise this.

The present case is not one of targeted malice. If the action in tort is maintainable it must be in the second form of the tort. It is therefore necessary to consider the distinctive features of this form of the tort. The remainder of my judgment will be directed to this form of the tort.

The basis for the action lies in the defendant taking a decision in the knowledge that it is an excess of the powers granted to him and that it is likely to cause damage to an individual or individuals. It is not every act beyond the powers vesting in a public officer which will ground the tort. The alternative form of liability requires an element of bad faith. This leads to what was a disputed issue. Counsel for the Bank pointed out that there was no precedent in England before the present case which held recklessness to be a sufficient state of mind to ground the tort. Counsel argued that recklessness was insufficient. The Australian High Court and the Court of Appeal of New Zealand have ruled that recklessness is sufficient: *Northern Territory v Mengel*, 69 ALJR 527; *Garrett v Attorney General* [1997] 2 NZLR 332; *Rawlinson v Rice* [1997] 2 NZLR 651. Clarke J. lucidly explained the reason for the inclusion of recklessness [1996] 3 All E.R. 558, 581:

> "The reason why recklessness was regarded as sufficient by all members of the High Court in *Mengel* is perhaps most clearly seen in the judgment of Brennan J. It is that misfeasance consists in the purported exercise of a power otherwise than in an honest attempt to perform the relevant duty. It is that lack of honesty which makes the act an abuse of power."

The Court of Appeal accepted the correctness of this statement of principle, ante, pp.52–53. This is an organic development, which fits into the structure of our law governing intentional torts. The policy underlying it is sound: reckless indifference to consequences is as blameworthy as deliberately seeking such consequences. It can therefore now be regarded as settled law that an act performed in reckless indifference as to the outcome is sufficient to ground the tort in its second form. . . .

Initially, counsel for the plaintiffs argued that in this context recklessness is used in an objective sense. Counsel said that the distinction was between subjective or advertent recklessness in the sense used in *R. v Cunningham* [1957] 2 Q.B. 396 and objective recklessness as explained in *R. v Caldwell* [1982] A.C. 341 and *R. v Lawrence (Stephen)* [1982] A.C. 510. The latter ingredient is present where in a case of an obvious risk the defendant failed to give any thought to the possibility of its existence: see *Smith & Hogan, Criminal Law*, 9th ed (1999), pp.60–69. *Smith & Hogan* trenchantly observed, at p.67:

> "The *Caldwell* test fails to make a distinction which should be made between the person who knowingly takes a risk and the person who gives no thought to whether there is a risk or not. And, on the other hand, it makes a distinction which has no moral basis. The person who, with gross negligence, fails to consider whether there is a risk is liable; but the person who considers whether there is a risk and, with gross negligence, decides there is none, is not liable. The right solution, it is submitted, is to go back to the *Cunningham* test which appears to have been entirely trouble-free in practice."

Counsel argued for the adoption of the *Caldwell* test in the context of the tort of misfeasance in public office. The difficulty with this argument was that it could not be squared with a meaningful requirement of bad faith in the exercise of public powers which is the raison d'être of the tort. But, understandably, the argument became more refined during the oral hearing and counsel for the plaintiffs accepted that only reckless indifference in a subjective sense will be sufficient. This concession was rightly made. The plaintiff must prove that the public officer acted with a state of mind of reckless indifference to the illegality of his act: *Rawlinson v Rice* [1997] 2 NZLR 651. Later in this judgment I will discuss the requirement of reckless indifference in relation to the consequences of the act.

(4) *Duty to the plaintiff*

The question is who can sue in respect of an abuse of power by a public officer. Counsel for the Bank argued that in order to be able to claim in respect of the second form of misfeasance, there must be established "an antecedent legal right or interest" and an element of "proximity". Clarke J. did not enunciate a requirement of proximity. He observed [1996] 3 All E.R. 558, 584:

> "If an officer deliberately does an act which he knows is unlawful and will cause economic loss to the plaintiff, I can see no reason in principle why the plaintiff should identify a legal right which is being infringed or a particular duty owed to him, beyond the right not to be damaged or injured by a deliberate abuse of power by a public officer."

The majority in the Court of Appeal held that "the notion of proximity should have a significant part to play in the tort misfeasance, as it undoubtedly has in the tort of negligence": ante, p.57D. Counsel for the Bank argued that both requirements are essential in order to prevent the tort from becoming an uncontrollable one. It would be unwise to make general statements on a subject which may involve many diverse situations. What can be said is that, of course, any plaintiff must have a sufficient interest to found a legal standing to sue. Subject to this qualification, principle does not require the introduction of proximity as a controlling mechanism in this corner of the law. The state of mind required to establish the tort, as already explained, as well as the special rule of remoteness hereafter discussed, keeps the tort within reasonable bounds. There is no reason why such an action cannot be brought by a particular class of persons, such as depositors at a bank, even if their precise identities were not known to the bank. The observations of Clarke J. are correct.

In agreed issue 4 the question is raised whether the Bank is capable of being liable for the tort of misfeasance in public office to plaintiffs who were potentially depositors at the time of any relevant act or omission of misfeasance by the Bank. The majority in the Court of Appeal and Auld L.J. held that this issue is unsuitable for summary determination. In my view this ruling was correct.

(5) *Causation*

Causation is an essential element of the plaintiffs cause of action. It is a question of fact. The majority in the Court of Appeal and Auld L.J. held that it is unsuitable for summary determination. That is plainly correct. This conclusion disposes of agreed issue 3 so far as it relates to the tort of misfeasance.

(6) Damage and remoteness

The claims by the plaintiffs are in respect of financial losses they suffered. These are, of course, claims for recovery of consequential economic losses. The question is when such losses are recoverable. It would have been possible, as a matter of classification, to discuss this question under paragraph 3 in which the required state of mind for this tort was examined. It is, however, convenient to consider it under the traditional heading of remoteness.

On the assumption that the other requirements can be established, counsel for the plaintiffs argued that the plaintiffs should be able to recover all reasonably foreseeable losses suffered by them. In support of this argument he had the advantage of a powerfully reasoned dissenting judgment by Auld L.J. Counsel for the Bank argued that the rule is more restrictive. He supported the conclusion of the majority in the Court of Appeal. The judge had held that the plaintiffs must prove that the Bank actually foresaw the losses to the plaintiff as a probable consequence. This part of the judgment at first instance provided the reason for the judge refusing to allow the proposed amendments and striking out the claims. The majority observed, ante, p.94F-G:

"[The] formulation, however, may have been too favourable to the plaintiffs. In view of the stringent requirements of the tort of misfeasance in public office, the more appropriate question may be: 'Is it reasonably arguable that the Bank at any stage made an unlawful and dishonest decision knowing at the time that it would cause loss to the plaintiffs?' To that question, in the light of our analysis of the evidence, the answer is plainly 'No.'"

Counsel adopted this formulation as his primary submission. In the alternative he submitted that the test stated by Clarke J. should be adopted. . . .

The issues have been canvassed in great depth in written and oral argument. Taking into account all the matters advanced the choice before the House can be narrowed down. So far as the majority was minded to adopt a stricter test that Clarke J., encapsulated in the words "knowing at the time that [the decision] *would* cause damage to the plaintiffs", they went too far. A test of knowledge or foresight that a decision *would* cause damage does not readily fit into the standard of proof generally required in the law of tort, and specifically in the case of intentional torts. Moreover, this test unnecessarily emasculates the effectiveness of the tort. The real choice is therefore between the test of knowledge that the decision would probably damage the plaintiff (as enunciated by Clarke J.) and the test of reasonable foreseeability (as contended for by counsel for the plaintiffs).

It is now necessary to return to the *Bourgoin* case. While all judges are prone to error and imprecise language from time to time, it is difficult to say that Mann J. and Oliver L.J. used the word "foreseeable" when they meant "foreseen". It is sufficient to point out, as the majority of the Court of Appeal did [2000] 2 W.L.R. 15, 48D, that there was no focus in the *Bourgoin* case on the choice which is now before the House. In these circumstances the observations in the *Bourgoin* case on this particular issue do not greatly assist.

It is true that Clarke J. made new law. He relied on the special nature of the tort. He reasoned from legal principle. It is true that the earlier decision of the majority in the *Mengel* case runs counter to the conclusion of Clarke J.

But apart from the *Mengel* case there has however been no judicial support for a foreseeability test. And there has been no academic criticism of the view of Clarke J. that a test of foreseeability is not enough in this tort. Given that his ground-breaking first instance judgment has been pored over by many judicial and academic eyes, this is a factor of some significance. Nevertheless, it is necessary to consider the merits of the competing solutions from the point of view of principle and legal policy.

Enough has been said to demonstrate the special nature of the tort, and the strict requirements governing it. This is a legally sound justification for adopting as a starting point that in both forms of the tort the intent required must be directed at the harm complained of, or at least to harm of the type suffered by the plaintiffs. This results in the rule that a plaintiff must establish not only that the defendant acted in the knowledge that the act was beyond his powers but also in the knowledge that his act would probably injure the plaintiff or person of a class of which the plaintiff was a member. In presenting a sustained argument for a rule allowing recovery of all foreseeable losses counsel for the plaintiffs argued that such a more liberal rule is necessary in a democracy as a constraint upon abuse of executive and administrative power. The force of this argument is, however, substantially reduced by the recognition that subjective recklessness on the part of a public officer in acting in excess of his powers is sufficient. Recklessness about the consequences of his act, in the sense of not caring whether the consequences happen or not, is therefore sufficient in law. This justifies the conclusion that the test adopted by Clarke J. represents a satisfactory balance between the two competing policy considerations, namely enlisting tort law to combat executive and administrative abuse of power and not allowing public officers, who must always act for the public good, to be assailed by unmeritorious actions.

It is undoubtedly right, as counsel for the plaintiffs pointed out, that the mental element required for the tort of misfeasance in public office means that it is not an effective remedy to deal with state liability for breaches of Community law: *Brasserie du Pêcheur SA v Federal Republic of Germany; R. v Secretary of State for Transport, Ex p. Factortame Ltd (No 4)* (Joined Cases C-46/93 and C-48/93) [1996] Q.B. 404. This consideration cannot, however, affect the decision of the House on the tort. If there is a gap it must be for Community law to fill it. And our courts will loyally apply Community law.

Conclusion on misfeasance in public office

For the reasons given the requirements of the tort are as set out. . . .

[LORD HUTTON's opinion was to similar effect, stating that subjective bad faith was a necessary ingredient of both branches of the tort and that the tort can be constituted by an omission as well as by an act on the part of a public officer. The act or omission must be a deliberate one involving an actual decision and liability will not arise from injury suffered by more inadvertence or oversight. LORD HOBHOUSE OF WOODBOROUGH was in substantial agreement and LORDS HOPE OF CRAIGHEAD and MILLETT in full agreement with LORDS STEYN and HUTTON. The House concluded unanimously there was no liability under Community law.]

Notes

1. The House adjourned the appeal for further argument in respect of the misfeasance claim. The claimants subsequently served new draft particulars. The House proceeded to consider whether the claim should be struck out on the basis that it was bound to fall on the evidence. The trial judge (unreported, July 30, 1997) and Court of Appeal (Hirst and Walker L.JJ., Auld L.J. dissenting) had held that there was no arguable case, relying heavily on the factual findings of a non-statutory private inquiry conducted by Bingham L.J. (as he then was). The House of Lords by 3:2 (Lords Steyn, Hope of Craighead and Hutton, Lords Hobhouse of Woodborough and Millett dissenting) held that the claim should not be struck out. The majority held that no reliance should have been placed on the report (although an "outstanding one produced by an eminent judge": *per* Lord Steyn at para.[5]) as it was not admissible in evidence, and that, overall, fairness required that the case should be examined and tested at a full trial. Lord Hope (at paras [41]–[46]) dealt with the various elements of the misfeasance tort, which he summarised as follows (at para.[42]):

> "First, there must be an unlawful act or omission done or made in the exercise of power by the public officer. Second, as the essence of the tort is an abuse of power, the act or omission must have been done or made with the required mental element. Third, for the same reason, the act or omission must have been done or made in bad faith. Fourth, as to standing, the claimants must demonstrate that they have a sufficient interest to sue the defendant. Fifth, as causation is an essential element of the cause of action, the act or omission must have caused the claimants' loss".

As regards the fourth element, standing, there was no doubt as to the interest of existing depositors and the Bank accepted for the purposes of the present proceedings that it was capable of being liable to claimants who were potential depositors at the time of any relevant act or omission of misfeasance by the bank. The Bank claimed that it was not capable of having caused loss to depositors where the proximate cause was the fraudulent acts of individuals within BCCI. That, however, raised questions of fact which were unsuitable for summary determination. As to the third and fourth requirements, the depositors alleged "untargeted malice". Here:

> "the required mental element is satisfied where the act or omission was done or made intentionally by the public officer; (a) in the knowledge that it was beyond his powers and that it would probably cause the claimant to suffer injury, or (b) recklessly because, although he was aware that there was a serious risk that the claimant would suffer loss due to an act or omission which he knew to be unlawful, he wilfully chose to disregard that risk" (at para.[44]).

The fact that the act or omission is done or made without an honest belief that it is lawful is sufficient to satisfy the requirement of bad faith; as regards (a), bad faith is demonstrated by knowledge of probable loss on the part of the public officer, and as regards (b) it is demonstrated by recklessness on his part in disregarding the risk. The claimant relied on both (a) and (b). Lord Hope (at para.[46]) rejected the Bank's submission that knowledge, belief or suspicion that the act or omission would probably cause loss to depositors or potential depositors, clearly required for (a), was also required for (b), based on recklessness. Overall, sufficient particulars had been given by the depositors for the case to proceed. Lords Hobhouse and Millett held, leaving the Bingham report out of account, that there were still no real prospects of success.

The litigation is proceeding. In *Three Rivers DC v Governor and Company of the Bank of England (No.9)* [2003] EWHC 1269 (Comm), Tomlinson J. held that there had been no concession by the claimants that dishonesty would only be alleged against seven senior officials named in the proceedings before the House of Lords, and that they were entitled to argue that a range of other officials had in bad faith knowingly participated in acts of misfeasance in public office by the Bank. However, it was virtually inconceivable that they could succeed against the Bank without proving that one or more of the seven senior officials committed an act of misfeasance for which the Bank was responsible, as only the senior officials had the power of decision-making. It was not, however, necessary or appropriate to rule on the question whether the claimants would have to establish that at least one natural person had both acted and had the requisite mental element, or whether the Bank's state of mind might properly be looked at "in the round" without necessarily finding the requisite state of mind vested in the ultimate decision-maker.

2. On this tort, see A. Rubinstein, *Jurisdiction and Illegality* (1965), pp.128–133; B. Gould, (1972) 5 N.Z.U.L.R. 105; J. McBride, [1979] C.L.J. 323.

3. So far as the first limb of the tort is concerned (targeted malice), there must be proof of an intent to injure and not merely reclessness: *Benet v Metropolitian Police Commissioner* [1995] 1 W.L.R. 488. Another case on the first limb is *Jones v Swansea CC*, n.5, below. See also *Elliott v Chief Constable of Wiltshire, The Times,* December 5, 1996 (disclosure by police officer of P's previous convictions with intent to injure could amount to the tort, notwithstanding that this did not constitute the exercise of a particular power or authority).

4. The claims in *Three Rivers* are in respect of economic losses allegedly caused by the misfeasance. That the tort is not limited to situations where misfeasance has caused financial loss or physical or mental injury was held by the Court of Appeal in *Watkins v Secretary of State for the Home Department* [2004] EWCA Civ 966; [2004] 4 All E.R. 1158. It was held to be applicable to the interference by prison officers with a prisoner's right of unimpeded access to the court, by, in bad faith, opening legal correspondence (from, respectively, W's solicitor and the county court in which W was pursuing proceedings) in breach of the Prison Rules. The officers in question were found either to know that they were acting unlawfully, or to have been reckless. The Court of Appeal awarded nominal damages and remitted the case to the county court to determine whether there should be an award of exemplary damages. Such an award was not to be constrained by Lord Woolf C.J.'s statement in *Thompson v Commissioner of Police of the Metropolis* [1998] Q.B. 498 that in cases of malicious prosecution or false imprisonment, where exemplary damages were appropriate they were unlikely to be less than £5,000, otherwise the case was probably not one which justified an award of exemplary damages at all. Laws L.J. (with whom Brooke and Clarke L.JJ. agreed) stated (at [67]) that there were two kinds of case:

> "Where a claimant is exposed to economic or material injury by virtue of the public officer's wrongful and malicious act, it will be inherent in his claim that he has suffered quantifiable loss; and he does not have to prove that in causing such loss the public officer has violated some free-standing right which the claimant enjoys. That is one class of case. But the claimant may be adversely affected in a different sense. The wrongful act may have interfered with a right of a kind which the law protects without proof of any loss. In that case, the public officer's interference with the right will complete the tort and no actual damage needs to be shown. This is the second class of case. Its paradigm is the instance where the public officer's unlawful conduct has interfered with a constitutional right".

Three Rivers was an example of the first class. *Ashby v White* and the other election cases were examples of the second, as was the present case.

5. The misfeasance tort is applicable in respect of the abuse of any powers exercisable by a public authority or officer, whether private powers or powers with a statutory or public origin (*Jones v Swansea City Council* [1990] 1 W.L.R. 54: where the Court of Appeal held that the alleged abuse of a contractual power would give rise to the tort; the court left open whether it could in any event properly be regarded as a purely "private" power. This question was left open on appeal to the House of Lords:

[1990] 1 W.L.R. 1453 at 1458). The tort is, indeed, not limited to the exercise of a formal legal power but extends to other acts sufficiently connected with the office (*Elliott v Chief Constable of Wiltshire Constabulary, The Times*, December 5, 1998 (allegation that police officer deliberately and falsely supplied details of convictions to the press); followed in *Cornelius v Hackney LBC* [2002] EWCA Civ 1073 (allegation that council's chief executive make false statement about dismissed employee to councillors and in the press). Both these cases were refusals to strike out.

It is, however, necessary to show that the tort has been committed by a particular authority or individual as distinct from the state (or the Crown). This was confirmed by the Court of Appeal in *Chagos Islanders v Att-Gen* [2004] EWCA Civ 997, in refusing permission to appeal in the case in tort brought by former inhabitants of the Chagos Islands in respect of their removal by virtue of an ordinance subsequently held to be unlawful (in *R. (on the application of Bancoult) v Secretary of State for Foreign and Commonwealth Affairs* [2001] Q.B. 1067, above, p.262). The court held that the rule that no action in tort lies against the Crown (outside the HRA) barred both a claim for the misfeasance tort and for unlawful exile (contrary to Magna Carta). While the Prime Minister and Foreign Secretary of the day were party to the scheme for the depopulation of the islands there was no

> "evidence that they or any of their subordinates (who constitutionally are their alter ego) knew that it was illegal. Such case law as there was (for example *Ibrelebbe v R* [1964] A.C. 900) confirmed that the power to make ordinances for the government of dependencies went extremely wide. It was not until the Divisional Court decided *Bancoult* that a line was drawn".

A case in trespass to the person in respect of individuals forcibly removed was not pleaded. (The claims of a number of the claimants were also barred by their renunciation of such claims effected as part of the settlement in 1982 by the Government of proceedings claiming damages for intimidation, deprivation of liberty and assault.)

6. The application of these principles to the collective decision-making of a local authority was considered in *Jones v Swansea City Council* [1990] 1 W.L.R. 1453, where the House of Lords upheld the decision of the trial judge to dismiss the plaintiff's claim for damages for misfeasance arising out of the council's decision as landlord to refuse consent for the change of use of certain premises leased by the plaintiff. The decision had been taken by 28 to 15, the majority being formed by Labour councillors. The plaintiff's husband was a political opponent of the Labour group. Lord Lowry stated (at 1458–1459) that in such circumstances "generally speaking, if a plaintiff proves that a majority of the councillors present, having voted for a resolution, did so with the object of damaging the plaintiffs, he thereby proves against the council misfeasance in a public office". This apparently would mean 22 out of the 43 councillors present (at 1470). However, the plaintiff's pleadings alleged that all the 28 councillors had been infected by malice, and the judge had rightly found this not to be made out on the evidence.

7. Where loss is an ingredient of the tort (the first case mentioned by Laws L.J. in *Watkins*, above) it will naturally be necessary to show a causal link between the misfeasance and the loss. This is one of the issues in the continuing *Three Rivers* litigation. In *Wood v Blair and the Helmsley RDC, The Times*, July 3, 4, 5, 1957, [1956–57] Admin. L.R. 343, the medical officer of health served notices forbidding the sale of unpasteurised milk from W's farm. The notices were subsequently held to be nullities, but a claim to damages was dismissed as he would have suffered the loss anyway; he would have had to leave the farm because of troubles with the landlord, his registration as a dairy farmer had been cancelled and the T.T. licence revoked. (A claim of £99 for lost milk subsidy was allowed; it did not seem that either defendant knew the notices were invalid, but liability was conceded.)

Where the consequence of misfeasance is alleged to be personal injury or death it is a sufficient pleading that the harm in contemplation was either to a known victim or victims or to one or more victims who would be unknown unless and until the expected harm eventuated (*Akenzua v Secretary of State for the Home Department* [2003] 1 W.L.R. 741).

8. It is possible that the tort may be developed to cover non-feasance. See *Toumia v Evans, The Times*, April 1, 1999, where the Court of Appeal refused to strike out a claim for misfeasance arising out of the refusal of prison officers, in the course of industrial action, to unlock the plaintiff's cell in accordance with the usual routine. This was confirmed by Lord Hutton in the *Three Rivers* case, above, [2003] 2 A.C. 1 at 228, and note Lord Hope's formulation of the ingredients of the tort at the subsequent hearing: see above. See, however, the doubt expressed by Lord Millett at the subsequent hearing, *ibid*. at 236–237:

> "The tort is concerned with the *abuse* of power by public officials who act in excess of their powers to the injury of the subject. It is not concerned with their failure to exercise the powers they do have, particularly when they have a discretion whether to exercise them or not".

9. Exemplary damages can be awarded in respect of the misfeasance tort (*Kuddus v Chief Constable of Leicestershire Constabulary* [2001] UKHL 29; [2002] 2 A.C. 122).

Given the widening in scope of the second limb of the misfeasance tort, in what circumstances will it be profitable or necessary for a plaintiff to seek to establish liability under the first limb?

10. An analogy to the misfeasance tort exists in the form of the common law criminal offence of misconduct in a public office.

This applies to officers of local authorities and not only to officers and agents of the Crown (*R. v Bowden* (1995) 159 J.P. 502). The elements of this offence have been restated by the Court of Appeal in *Att-Gen's Reference (No.3 of 2003)* [2004] EWCA Crim 868; [2004] 3 W.L.R. 451. They are (i) a public officer acting in his capacity as such; (ii) wilfully neglects to perform his duty and/or wilfully misconducts himself; (iii) so far below acceptable standards as to amount to an abuse of the public's trust in the office holder; (iv) without reasonable excuse or justification. To establish wilful neglect or misconduct there has to be awareness of the duty to act or subjective recklessness as to the existence of the duty; there must also be intent or subjective recklessness as to the omission or act of the defendant if the duty does arise. The defendant's motive and the likely consequences of the breach viewed subjectively may be relevant to element (iii). Bad faith is not normally an element of the offence. Prosecutions have for example been brought against police officers (*Crowther's Case* (1599) 2 Hawk P.C. 116 (constable indicted for failure to make a hue and cry after notice of a burglary); *R. v Dytham* [1979] 1 Q.B. 722 (police officer failed to intervene to protect man beaten and kicked to death outside a club); *R. v Ward* [1995] Crim. L.R. 398 (failure to administer a breath test to a fellow police officer after an accident); *Att-Gen's Reference (No.3 of 2003)*, above (defendant acquitted following death of prisoner while in custody)) and a county court registrar (*R. v Llewellyn-Jones* [1968] 1 Q.B. 429 (court orders made with the intention of gaining improper personal advantage)).

11. It is regularly confirmed that there is no cause of action outside the misfeasance tort in respect of breach of a public right or the infliction of loss through unlawful action. For example, in *R. v Knowsley MBC Ex p. Maguire* (1992) 90 L.G.R. 653, Schiemann J. rejected a series of "ingenious arguments, which attempted to remedy the absence of a general right to damages for a breach of administrative law," based on breach of statutory duty, negligence, breach of contract and estoppel by convention in support of a claim for losses caused by refusals of hackney carriage licences that were subsequently quashed. (There had been no negligence in the facts and no need to consider whether there was a duty of care.) See also Lord Goff in *R. v Secretary of State for Transport Ex p. Factortame Ltd (No.2)* [1991] 1 A.C. 603 at 672.

Should a cause of action be recognised? Such a development would significantly add to the costs of and be unwelcome to public authorities. The courts are unlikely to extend the tort of negligence in this way (but *cf. R. (on the application of A) v Secretary of State for the Home Department* (above, p.1068), and the government even less likely to promote legislation to that end (*cf.* turkeys and Christmas). A useful, more modest, development might see some formalisation of the Ombudsman's jurisdiction to recommend compensation for maladministration, and to broadening the jurisdiction to act notwithstanding that legal proceedings have been started.

(iv) Other torts

Notes

1. Most torts may from time to time be committed by or against a public authority. Other torts that give rise to significant litigation against public authorities include trespass and public and private nuisance (the contexts in which the defence of statutory authority (above, pp.1040–1041) most commonly arises). The expansion of general liability in private nuisance (the unreasonable and unjustified interference by the defendant with the use or enjoyment by the claimant of his land) for defendants who do not themselves create a nuisance but who are (or should be) aware that a nuisance is emanating or will emanate from their land and who fail to take reasonable steps to abate it (*Goldman v Hargrave* [1967] 1 A.C. 645) may apply to a public authority (*Page Motors Ltd v Epsom and Ewell BC* (1981) 80 L.G.R. 337 (illegal gypsy encampment on council land)). However, an exception to this principle applies in respect of sewerage undertakers, who benefit from the rule that a complaint that the sewerage system has become inadequate must be raised by way of a complaint to the Director-General of Water Services under the Water Industry Act (*Marcic v Thames Water Utilities Ltd* [2003] UKHL 66; [2004] 2 A.C. 42), mirroring a similar rule under previous legislation that left claimants to pursue a ministerial default power under that legislation (*Glossop v Heston and Isleworth Local Board* (1879) 12 Ch. D. 102).

2. The tort of false imprisonment (the "infliction of bodily restraint which is not expressly or impliedly authorised by the law": *Winfield and Jolowicz*, p.81) features regularly in actions against the police, the prison service and immigration authorities. Once detention is established, it is for the detainor to prove lawful authority. See R. Clayton and H. Tomlinson, *Civil Actions against the Police* (3rd ed., 2004), pp.147–154.

In *ID v Home Office* [2005] EWCA Civ 38, the Court of Appeal held that it was not an abuse of process for civil proceedings for false imprisonment to be brought by asylum seekers claiming that there detention was unlawful. Furthermore immigration officers are not entitled to any immunity from a claim to damages if a detention they order is subsequently found to be unlawful (following the approach of the House of Lords in *R. v Governor of Brockhill Prison Ex p. Evans* in the context of a prisoner detained too long in prison (see above, p.863), and not following *Ullah v Secretary of State for the Home Department* [1995] Imm. A.R. 166). The fact that maladministration by the immigration service does not give rise to a claim in negligence (*W v Home Office* [1997] Imm. A.R. 302) did not mean that there was no cause of action where maladministration leads to unlawful detention.

Compensation for unlawful detention can also be available under Art.5 ECHR: see above, p.333).

Particular difficulties can arise where a person is detained by virtue of subordinate legislation, or an order or decision subsequently held to be *ultra vires*. In principle, such legislation, order or decision is and never has been legally valid, the detention was therefore unlawful and the detainor liable for false imprisonment. That approach was adopted by the House of Lords in *R. v Governor of Brockhill Prison Ex p. Evans (No.2)* [2001] 2 A.C. 19 (above, p.863) where the governor's calculation of the release date proved subsequently to be erroneous in law. The Court of Appeal in *Percy v Hall* [1996] Q.B. 924 had previously held that a police officer would not be liable in false imprisonment in respect of an arrest on reasonable suspicion of an offence contrary to a byelaw, should the byelaw subsequently be held to be *ultra vires.* At the time the events took place, the byelaws were apparently valid and the general doctrine of retro-spectivity with regard to the annulment of invalid instruments did not go so far as to turn the constable's actions into actionably tortious conduct. (This may not be com-patible with *Evans* or with Art.5 ECHR: *Lewis*, p.532) A second reason was that the legislation conferring the power of arrest was to be interpreted as protecting the officer provided he honestly believed on reasonable grounds that he had observed commis-sion of a relevant offence.

In *Evans*, Lord Hope of Craighead regarded *Percy v Hall* as distinguishable. The governor, unlike the constables, could not claim:

> "that he had a lawful justification for doing what he did. His position would have been different if he had been able to show that he was acting throughout within the four corners of an order which had been made by the court for the respondent's detention".

The last point is illustrated by the subsequent decision in *Quinland v Governor of Swaleside Prison* [2003] Q.B. 306, where the prison governors were held not liable for false imprisonment where a prisoner served longer in prison than he should have done as the result of mistakes by the Criminal Appeal Office (see below). They were simply acting in accordance with the sentence passed by the trial judge.

(v) Rules of non-liability

Notes

1. There are a number of areas where the law expressly provides, for reasons of public policy, that there shall be no liability. Such rules, where they are not overbroad and therefore disproportionate (*cf. Osman v UK*, above, p.1069), can be compatible with the ECHR, simply as situations where the law does not recognise a cause of action. Examples include the following.

2. There is an immunity at common law in respect of judicial acts, in different terms as between judges of the High Court and above and judges of inferior courts and tribunals (see *McC, Re* [1985] A.C. 528); the position of justices of the peace, jus-tices clerks and assistant clerks is governed by the Courts Act 2003, ss.31–35). See W.V.H. Rogers, *Winfield and Jolowicz on Tort* (16th ed., 2002), pp.824–826; A. Olowofoyeku, *Suing Judges* (1993). The immunity applies to proceedings before a police disciplinary board and there is no exception in the case of complaints of sex dis-crimination (*Heath v Commissioner of Police for the Metropolis* [2004] EWCA Civ 943). Furthermore, whether or not it operates as a procedural rather than a substan-tive bar, the purpose of the judicial immunity rule is legitimate and is necessary and proportionate in the public interest for the protection of the integrity of the judicial system (*per* Auld L.J. in *Heath* at para.[71]).

Section 2(5) of the Crown Proceedings Act 1947 provides that:

> "No proceedings shall lie against the Crown by virtue of this section in respect of anything done or omitted to be done by a person whilst discharging or purporting to discharge any responsibilities of a judicial nature vested in him, or any responsi-bilities which he has in connection with the execution of judicial process".

This has been held to protect the Lord Chancellor's Department from an action in false imprisonment in where administrative mistakes in the Criminal Appeal Office (the file was put away in error) meant that papers were not put before the Court of Appeal for the correction of a sentence in due time and the plaintiff spent longer in prison than should have been the case (*Quinland v Governor of Swaleside Prison* [2003] Q.B. 306). The officials in question were discharging or purporting to discharge responsibilities in connection with the execution or implementation of the judicial process. The events predated the HRA and the court left open whether the result would be the same post-HRA. On the other hand, s.2(5) does not apply to an adjudication officer determining eligibility for unemployment benefit (*Jones v Department of Employment* [1989] Q.B. 1).

3. Section 10(1) of the Crown Proceedings Act 1947 provided that nothing done or omitted to be done by a member of the armed forces of the Crown while on duty as such shall subject either him or the Crown to liability in tort for causing the death of or personal injury to another member of the armed forces, provided that the other person was on duty or on any land, premises, ship, aircraft or vehicle for the time being used for the purposes of the armed forces, and that the thing suffered would be attributable to service for pensions purposes. The member of the armed forces was not exempted if the court was satisfied that the act or omission was not connected with the execution of his or her duties as a member of the forces. There was also no liability, on the same conditions, in respect of things suffered in consequence of the nature or condition of such land, etc. or equipment or supplies used for the purposes of the forces (s.10(2)). These provisions were repealed by the Crown Proceedings (Armed Forces) Act 1987, in respect of acts or omissions occurring after May 15, 1987. The continuing provision for no liability in respect of earlier acts or omissions has been held to be compatible with Art.6(1) ECHR, on the ground that it defined the scope of the substantive civil law right to claim damages against the Crown, and was not an "immunity" for the purposes of the application of the ECHR (*Matthews v Minister of Defence* [2003] UKHL 4; [2003] 1 A.C. 1163).

It extends to breaches of duty owed to service personnel by the Crown as their employer, (*Post Traumatic Stress Disorder Litigation; Multiple Claimants v Ministry of Defence, Re* [2003] EWHC 1134, in respect of alleged negligent failure to take steps to prevent the development of, or detect, diagnose and treat PTSD in some 2000 members of the armed forces exposed to the stress and trauma of conflict).

(C) RESTITUTION

In recent years the law of restitution has had an increasing impact on public authorities. On the one hand, the House of Lords in *Woolwich Equitable Building Society v Inland Revenue Commissioners* [1993] A.C. 70 expanded the citizen's right to recover money paid to a public authority pursuant to an unlawful demand. On the other, the decision in *Hazell v Hammersmith and Fulham LBC* [1992] 2 A.C. 1, above, p.396, that interest rate swap transactions entered by local authorities were *ultra vires*, has given rise to litigation in which local authorities have recovered money paid to banks in the course of such transactions (and vice versa).

Notes

1. In the *Woolwich Equitable* case, the Building Society paid some £57 million in response to a Revenue demand. The demand was based on regulations subsequently held by the House of Lords to be *ultra vires* (*Woolwich Equitable Building Society v Inland Revenue Commissioners* [1990] 1 W.L.R. 1400 (above, p.901)). The Revenue had repaid the money when the judicial review proceedings had been decided against them at first instance. The Society now claimed the payment of interest on the capital from the date of payment until judgment was given at first instance. The House of Lords (Lords Goff of Chieveley, Browne-Wilkinson and Slynn of Hadley, Lords Keith of Kinkel and Jauncey of Tullichettle dissenting) upheld the Building Society's claim. Prior to this decision, it was established, *inter alia*, that (1) as a general rule, while money paid under a mistake of fact was recoverable, money paid under a mistake of law was not; (2) that money paid under compulsion might be recoverable; and (3) that money is irrecoverable where the

payer has the opportunity to contest liability but instead gives way and pays (see Lord Goff at 164–165).

Depending on the circumstances, a claim to recover money paid to a public authority in response to an unlawful demand might fail on the grounds that there was a mistake of law, an absence of compulsion or, otherwise, a voluntary payment. The House of Lords recognised a separate principle that

"the subject who makes a payment in response to an unlawful demand of tax acquires forthwith a prima facie right in restitution to the repayment of the money" (Lord Goff at 171).

This development was justified by Lord Goff in the following terms:

"The justice underlying Woolwich's submission is, I consider, plain to see. Take the present case. The revenue has made an unlawful demand for tax. The taxpayer is convinced that the demand is unlawful, and has to decide what to do. It is faced with the revenue, armed with the coercive power of the state, including what is in practice a power to charge interest which is penal in its effect. In addition, being a reputable society which alone among building societies is challenging the lawfulness of the demand, it understandably fears damage to its reputation if it does not pay. So it decides to pay first, asserting that it will challenge the lawfulness of the demand in litigation. Now, Woolwich having won that litigation, the revenue asserts that it was never under any obligation to repay the money, and that it in fact repaid it only as a matter of grace. There being no applicable statute to regulate the position, the revenue has to maintain this position at common law.

Stated in this stark form, the revenue's position appears to me, as a matter of common justice, to be unsustainable; and the injustice is rendered worse by the fact that it involves, as Nolan J. pointed out [1989] 1 W.L.R. 137, 140, the revenue having the benefit of a massive interest-free loan as the fruit of its unlawful action. I turn then from the particular to the general. Take any tax or duty paid by the citizen pursuant to an unlawful demand. Common justice seems to require that tax to be repaid, unless special circumstances or some principle of policy require otherwise; prima facie, the taxpayer should be entitled to repayment as of right.

To the simple call of justice, there are a number of possible objections. The first is to be found in the structure of our law of restitution, as it developed during the 19th and early 20th centuries. That law might have developed so as to recognise a *condictio indebiti*—an action for the recovery of money on the ground that it was not due. But it did not do so. Instead, as we have seen, there developed common law actions for the recovery of money paid under a mistake of fact, and under certain forms of compulsion. What is now being sought is, in a sense, a reversal of that development, in a particular type of case; and it is said that it is too late to take that step. To that objection, however, there are two answers. The first is that the retention by the state of taxes unlawfully exacted is particularly obnoxious, because it is one of the most fundamental principles of our law—enshrined in a famous constitutional document, the Bill of Rights 1688—that taxes should not be levied without the authority of Parliament; and full effect can only be given to that principle if the return of taxes exacted under an unlawful demand can be enforced as a matter of right. The second is that, when the revenue makes a demand for tax, that demand is implicitly backed by the coercive powers of the state and may well entail (as in the present case) unpleasant economic and social consequences if the taxpayer does not pay. In any event, it seems strange to penalise the good citizen, whose natural instinct is to trust the revenue and pay taxes when they are demanded of him".

The situation would not appropriately be dealt with by developing the common law concept of compulsion, an approach adopted by the High Court of Australia in *Mason v New South Wales*, 102 C.L.R. 108. Here, Woolwich:

"was in reality suffering from no mistake at all, so much so that it was prepared to back its conviction that the revenue was acting *ultra vires* by risking a very substantial amount of money in legal costs in establishing that fact; and, since the possibility of distraint by the revenue was very remote, the concept of compulsion would have to be stretched to the utmost to embrace the circumstances of such a case as this. It is for this reason that Woolwich's alternative claim founded upon compulsion did not loom large in the argument, and is difficult to sustain. In the end, logic appears to demand that the right of recovery should require neither mistake nor compulsion, and that the simple fact that the tax was exacted unlawfully should prima facie be enough to require its repayment." (Lord Goff at 173).

Furthermore, the recognition of this principle constituted a legitimate development of the law, although the "armoury of common law defences" might have to be extended, for example by imposing short time-limits within which claims had to be advanced (at 173–177). His Lordship concluded:

"I would therefore hold that money paid by a citizen to a public authority in the form of taxes or other levies paid pursuant to an *ultra vires* demand by the authority is prima facie recoverable by the citizen as of right. As at present advised, I incline to the opinion that this principle should extend to embrace cases in which the tax or other levy has been wrongly exacted by the public authority not because the demand was *ultra vires* but for other reasons, for example because the authority has misconstrued a relevant statute or regulation. It is not however necessary to decide the point in the present case, and in any event cases of this kind are generally the subject of statutory regimes which legislate for the circumstances in which money so paid either must or may be repaid. Nor do I think it necessary to consider for the purposes of the present case to what extent the common law may provide the public authority with a defence to a claim for the repayment of money so paid; though for the reasons I have already given, I do not consider that the principle of recovery should be inapplicable simply because the citizen has paid the money under a mistake of law. It will be a matter for consideration whether the fact that the plaintiff has passed on the tax or levy so that the burden has fallen on another should prove a defence to his claim".

The exact scope of the *Woolwich* principle is uncertain. The Law Commission (Law Com. No.227; see below, n.3) has expressed the view that it "may well be held to apply to all taxes, levies, assessments, tolls or charges, whether for the provision of services or not, collected by any person or body under a statutory provision which is the sole source of the authority to charge". It is not:

"limited to payments of tax or to Governmental or quasi-Governmental exactions, or to payments made in accordance with a demand. We believe that the crucial element is that the payment is collected by any person or body which is operating outside its statutory authority, that is, it is acting *ultra vires*. The requirement of *ultra vires* is not in our view confined to the excess of statutory power but also extends to procedural abuses, abuse of power and error of law on the part of the charging authority" (paras 6.32–6.42).

Lord Goff (at 177) and Lord Slynn of Hedley (at 203) were also of the view that the principle applied where tax was not lawfully due for some other reason such as misconstruction of the legislation.

2. There are some statutory provisions which expressly authorise the repayment of overpaid taxes, etc. See *R. v Tower Hamlets LBC Ex p. Chetnik Developments Ltd* [1988] A.C. 858, considering the General Rate Act 1967, s.9. Here, the House of Lords upheld an application for judicial review of the council's refusal to exercise the

discretion under s.9 in favour of the application on the grounds that the council had had regard to irrelevant considerations (the financial circumstances of the overpaying ratepayer or the general body of ratepayers, and the internal finances of the council and the financial constraints to which it was subject). In the *Woolwich* case, it was held that the Building Society's claim fell outside the statutory framework for the repayment of overpaid tax, as it was not the case of an assessment that was erroneously excessive, but of a demand that was *ultra vires* and a nullity (see Lord Goff at 168–169).

3. At the time the *Woolwich* case was decided, the issues of mistakes of law and *ultra vires* receipts and payments were under consideration by the Law Commission (see Law Commission Working Paper No.120, *Restitution of Payments Made Under a Mistake of Law* (1991). The Law Commission's subsequent Report (*Restitution: Mistakes of Law and* Ultra Vires *Public Authority Receipts and Payments*, Law Com. No.227, 1994) proposed (1) that the rule precluding restitution of payments made, services rendered and benefits conferred under a mistake of law be abolished and (2) that there should be a series of specific amendments to the statutory provisions governing recovery of overpaid tax to reflect the *Woolwich* principle. See L. Flynn [1995] B.T.R. 15. One consequence has been the introduction of a statutory right to recover overpaid excise duty (Finance Act 1995, s.20), inserting a new s.137A in the Customs and Excise Management Act 1979; this provision is modelled on section 80 of the Value Added Tax Act 1994.

Then, in *Kleinwort Benson Ltd v Lincoln City Council*, [1999] 2 A.C. 349, the House of Lords held by 3:2 (Lords Goff of Chieveley, Hoffmann and Hope of Craighead, Lords Browne-Wilkinson and Lloyd of Berwick dissenting) that the mistake of law rule should no longer form part of English Law. There is a general right founded on unjust enrichment to recover money paid under a mistake, whether of fact or law, subject to the defences available in the law of restitution such as the defence of change of position. There is no defence that payment was made under a settled understanding of the law or that the defendant honestly believed that he was entitled to retain the money, and no principle that money paid under a void contract is not recoverable because the contract has been fully performed. Lord Browne-Wilkinson and Lord Lloyd agreed that the mistake of law rule should be abolished, but held that should be done by Parliament and not the courts. The courts may develop a defence on the grounds of public policy to protect public bodies from severe budgetary difficulties, as where a mistake of law affects a large number of people (see *Lewis*, pp.552–553, noting that the Courts of Justice of the European Communities in a similar situation has made the right of recovery prospective only in appropriate cases, so that only those who commenced legal proceedings before the date of the judgment establishing the illegality can recover the money paid unlawfully (Case 24/86, *Blaizot v University of Liege* [1988] E.C.R. 379)). It is, however, not currently open to English courts to overrule with prospective effect only.

4. On restitution and public authorities, see P. Birks, (1980) 33 C.L.P. 191 and "Restitution from the Executive" in *Essays on Restitution* (Finn ed., 1990); W. Cornish [1987] J.M.C.L. 41; A. Burrows, "Public Authorities, *Ultra Vires* and Restitution" in *Studies on the Law of Restitution* (Burrows ed., 1991); G. Jones, *Restitution in Public and Private Law* (1991). On the *Woolwich* case, see J. Beatson, (1993) 109 L.Q.R. 1, and "Restitution of Taxes, Levies and other Imposts: Defining the Extent of the *Woolwich* Principle" (1993) 109 L.Q.R. 401; G. Virgo, "The Law of Taxation is not an Island—Overpaid Taxes and the Law of Restitution" [1993] B.T.R. 442; P. Birks, [1992] P.L. 580 and (1993) 46 C.L.P. 157; T. Hill, (1993) 56 M.L.R. 856.

For an argument that a right to recover tax should be based not on restitution but on an action in tort against the Crown for breach of statutory duty under art.4 of the Bill of Rights (1689), see D. Wilde "A 'Revolutionary' Approach to Unlawful Taxation" [1995] B.T.R. 137.

5. Following the decision in the *Hazell* case that interest rate swap agreements were *ultra vires* and void *ab initio*, claims for restitution have been brought variously by

banks and local authorities who were parties to such transactions. Thus, in *Westdeutsche Landesbank Girozentrale v Islington LBC* [1994] 1 W.L.R. 938, the Court of Appeal held that the council receiving payments from a bank under such transactions was obliged at common law to repay the balance of the money on the ground of unjust enrichment at the expense of the bank since there had been no consideration for the bank's payments; in equity it was to be regarded as holding the money on a resulting trust for the bank since the purpose of the payments had wholly failed. There was an appeal to the House of Lords only on the question of the basis of an award for interest ([1996] A.C. 669), the House holding by 3:2 that the bank was entitled only to simple and not compound interest. However, the House held unanimously in the course of deciding this point that there was no basis for the imposition of a resulting trust, the claim properly being based solely on the common law. (See M. Cope, (1996) 112 L.Q.R. 521; G. Jones, [1996] C.L.J. 432.) Suggestions by Hobhouse J. at first instance and the Court of Appeal that the common law claim arose from the *absence* rather than the *total failure* of consideration have been strongly criticised (P. Birks, (1993) 23 U.W.A.L.R. 195; W.J. Swadling, [1994] R.L.R. 73; A. Burrows [1995] R.L.R. 15) and doubted by Lord Goff *obiter* in the House of Lords. (The point was not argued in the House of Lords.)

See also *Kleinwort Benson Ltd v South Tyneside MBC* [1994] 4 All E.R. 972 (Hobhouse J.: bank entitled to recover payments made within the six-year limitation period notwithstanding it had hedged its liabilities under parallel transactions); *Morgan Grenfell & Co. Ltd v Welwyn Hatfield DC Islington LBC (Third Party)* [1995] 1 All E.R. 1 (Hobhouse J.: bank entitled to repayments; swap deals were not wagering contracts); *South Tyneside MBC v Svenska International Plc* [1995] 1 All E.R. 545 (Clarke J.: local authority entitled to recover net payments from bank; no defence of change of position); *Kleinwort Benson Ltd v Birmingham City Council*, [1997] Q.B. 380, CA: (no defence to bank's claim that it had or might have entered independent hedging arrangements so as to suffer no loss).

6. It is established law that any payment made out of the Consolidated Fund without Parliamentary authority is *ultra vires* and may be recovered by the Crown if it can be traced: *Auckland Harbour Board v R* [1924] A.C. 318 at 327, *per* Viscount Haldane. The Law Commission (Law Com. No.227, see above, n.3, paras 17.1–17.21) proposed no change in this rule, on the understanding that the common law defences of change of position and submission or compromise would apply in this context. On the rules applicable to determine when payments can be paid out of public funds, see *R. (on the application of Hooper) v Secretary of State for Work and Pensions* [2003] EWCA Civ 813; [2003] 1 W.L.R. 2623 at [120]–[137].

7. A claim for restitution may now be added to a claim for judicial review (above, p.924).

INDEX